lonely planet

Austria

Mark Honan

LONELY PLANET PUBLICATIONS
Melbourne • Oakland • London • Paris

MAP 1 – AUSTRIA

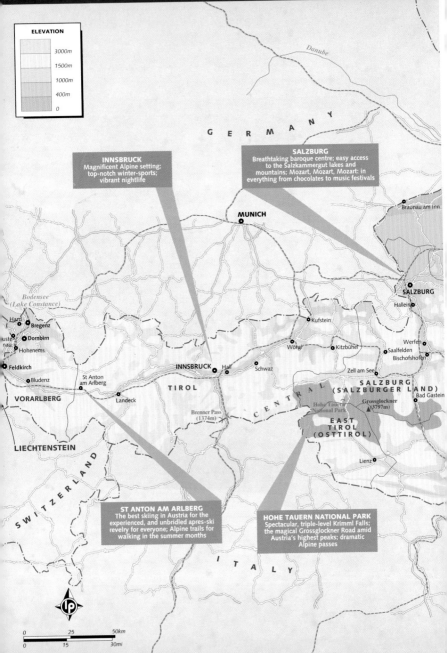

ELEVATION

3000m
1500m
1000m
400m
0

GERMANY

Danube

INNSBRUCK
Magnificent Alpine setting;
top-notch winter-sports;
vibrant nightlife

SALZBURG
Breathtaking baroque centre; easy access
to the Salzkammergut lakes and
mountains; Mozart, Mozart, Mozart: in
everything from chocolates to music festivals

MUNICH

Braunau am Inn

*Bodensee
(Lake Constance)*

Hard
Bregenz
uste
nau
Dornbirn
Hohenems
Feldkirch
Bludenz

St Anton
am Arlberg
Landeck

VORARLBERG

LIECHTENSTEIN

S W I T Z E R L A N D

SALZBURG

Hallein

Kufstein

Wörgl
Kitzbühel
Saalfelden
Bischofshofen

Werfen

INNSBRUCK
Hall
Schwaz

Zell am See

TIROL

Brenner Pass
(1374m)

C E N T R A L

Hohe Tauern
National Park

Grossglockner
(3797m)

Bad Gastein

**SALZBURG
(SALZBURGER LAND)**

**EAST
TIROL
(OSTTIROL)**

Lienz

ST ANTON AM ARLBERG
The best skiing in Austria for the
experienced, and unbridled apres-ski
revelry for everyone; Alpine trails for
walking in the summer months

HOHE TAUERN NATIONAL PARK
Spectacular, triple-level Krimml Falls;
the magical Grossglockner Road amid
Austria's highest peaks; dramatic
Alpine passes

I T A L Y

0   25   50km
0   15   30mi

Berchtesgaden 319
Werfen 319

Southern Salzburg
Province............................320
Tamsweg 321

Mauterndorf 321
Radstadt............................321

THE SALZKAMMERGUT 322

Bad Ischl............................324
Southern Salzkammergut 327
Hallstätter See 327
Hallstatt.............................328
Obertraun 329
Bad Aussee 331

Gosausee 333
Northern Salzkammergut 333
Traunsee 333
Gmunden...........................334
Traunkirchen 336
Ebensee 337

Grünau 337
Attersee.............................337
Wolfgangsee 338
St Wolfgang.......................338
St Gilgen 340
Mondsee 341

UPPER AUSTRIA 343

Linz 343
Around Linz........................350
Mauthausen.......................351
St Florian 351

Steyr 353
Wels 355
Lambach 356
Schmiding Bird Park 356

Kremsmünster 356
Freistadt.............................357
Kefermarkt.........................359
Braunau am Inn 359

LOWER AUSTRIA 361

St Pölten............................361
The Danube Valley 365
West of Melk 366
Melk 366
Schloss Schallaburg 368
Melk to Dürnstein 368
Dürnstein...........................370

Krems an der Donau 371
Around Krems 374
Waldviertel 375
Tulln..................................375
Klosterneuburg 377
Petronell 377
Wienerwald 378

Baden bei Wien 380
Southern Lower Austria 383
Wiener Neustadt 383
Semmering.........................385
Schneeberg 386

LANGUAGE 388

GLOSSARY 392

INDEX 401

Text 401

Boxed Text.........................407

MAP LEGEND back page

METRIC CONVERSION inside back page

Contents – Maps

INTRODUCTION   11

Map 3 – Austria 11

GETTING AROUND   95

Map 4 – Railways 96

VIENNA   105

Map 5 – Greater Vienna ..108   Map 7 – Central Vienna ..112   Map 9 – Vienna
Map 6 – Vienna 110   Map 8 – Vienna – West of   Walking Tour 123
                                     the Ring........................116

BURGENLAND   167

Map 10 – Burgenland 168   Map 11 – Eisenstadt 169

STYRIA   176

Map 12 – Styria   Map 13 – Graz 178   Map 15 – Mariazell..........194
   (Steiermark) 177   Map 14 – Central Graz 180   Map 16 – Bruck an der Mur..197

CARINTHIA   202

Map 17 – Carinthia   Map 20 – Central   Map 22 – Spittal an
   (Kärnten) 203   Carinthia 210   der Drau 222
Map 18 – Klagenfurt 204   Map 21 – Villach 212
Map 19 – Europark Vicinity 206

HOHE TAUERN NATIONAL PARK REGION   226

Map 23 – Hohe Tauern   Map 24 – Zell Am See 229   Map 26 – Lienz 241
   National Park Region 227   Map 25 – Bad Gastein 237

TIROL   245

Map 27 – Tirol 246   Map 29 – Innsbruck   Map 31 – St Anton
Map 28 – Innsbruck 249   Altstadt 251   am Arlberg...................281
                                 Map 30 – Kitzbühel 268

VORARLBERG   284

Map 32 – Vorarlberg 285   Map 33 – Bregenz 286   Map 34 – Bludenz 293

SALZBURG PROVINCE   297

Map 35 – Salzburg   Map 36 – Salzburg   Map 38 – Central
   (Salzburger Land)..........298   & Environs 299   Salzburg 304
                                 Map 37 – Salzburg 302

THE SALZKAMMERGUT   322

Map 39 –   Map 40 – Bad Ischl..........326   Map 42 – Gmunden 334
   The Salzkammergut 323   Map 41 – Bad Aussee 332

UPPER AUSTRIA   343

Map 43 – Upper Austria ..344   Map 44 – Linz 346   Map 45 – Steyr...............354

LOWER AUSTRIA

Map 46 – Lower Austria
  (Niederösterreich) 362
Map 47 – St Pölten..........363

Map 48 – Krems an
  der Donau 372
Map 49 – Baden bei Wien ..380

Map 50 – Wiener
  Neustadt 383

MAP 2 – MAP INDEX

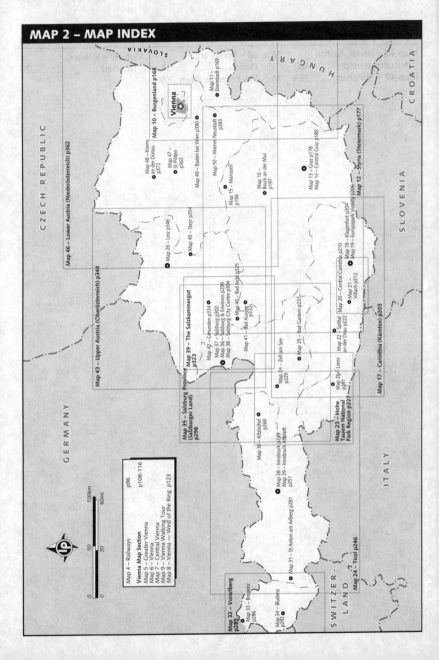

SLOVAKIA

HUNGARY

CROATIA

CZECH REPUBLIC

Map 10 – Burgenland p168

Vienna

Map 11 – Eisenstadt p169

Map 48 – Krems an der Donau p372

Map 47 – St Pölten p363

Map 49 – Baden bei Wien p380

Map 50 – Wiener Neustadt p383

Map 15 – Mariazell p194

Map 16 – Bruck an der Mur p197

Map 13 – Graz p178
Map 14 – Central Graz p180

Map 12 – Styria (Steiermark) p177

Map 46 – Lower Austria (Niederösterreich) p362

Map 26 – Linz p346

Map 45 – Steyr p354

SLOVENIA

Map 43 – Upper Austria (Oberösterreich) p344

Map 40 – Bad Ischl p235

Map 42 – Gmunden p334

Map 37 – Salzburg p302
Map 36 – Salzburg & Environs p299
Map 38 – Salzburg City Centre p304

Map 39 – The Salzkammergut p323

Map 41 – Bad Aussee p352

Map 18 – Klagenfurt p204
Map 19 – Europaplatz Vicinity p206

Map 20 – Central Carinthia p210

Map 21 – Villach p212

Map 25 – Bad Gastein p237

Map 22 – Spittal an der Drau p222

Map 17 – Carinthia (Kärnten) p203

Map 24 – Zell am See p229

Map 35 – Salzburg Province (Salzburger Land) p298

Map 30 – Kitzbühel p268

Map 27 – Lienz p241

Map 23 – Hohe Tauern National Park Region p227

ITALY

Map 28 – Innsbruck p249
Map 29 – Innsbruck Altstadt p251

Map 31 – St Anton am Arlberg p281

Map 24 Tirol p246

SWITZERLAND

Map 32 – Vorarlberg p285

Map 33 – Bregenz p286

Map 34 – Bludenz p292

GERMANY

Map 4 – Railways   p96

Vienna Map Section   p108-116
Map 5 – Greater Vienna
Map 6 – Vienna
Map 7 – Central Vienna
Map 9 – Vienna Walking Tour
Map 8 – Vienna — West of the Ring p123

0   50   100km
0   30   60mi

The Author

Mark Honan

After a university degree in philosophy opened up a glittering career as an office clerk, Mark decided that there was more to life than form-filling and data-entry. He set off on a two-year trip round the world, armed with a backpack and a vague intent to sell travel stories and pictures upon his return to England. Astonishingly, this barely formed plan succeeded and Mark became the travel correspondent to a London-based magazine. Since 1991 he has written Lonely Planet guidebooks to Vienna, Austria and Switzerland, updated Solomon Islands and contributed to guides to Europe, Central America, Mexico and India, as well as to Lonely Planet Unpacked, a book of travel horror stories. Although more than happy not to be a clerk anymore, he finds, curiously, that life as a travel writer still entails a good deal of form-filling and data-entry.

From the Author

Thanks to everyone among the vast cast of characters who helped me organise my research or supplied useful information. The main stars include Marion Telsnig at London's Austrian National Tourist Office, Melanie Grubb at Austrian Airlines, Sabine Gebetsroither in Upper Austria, Martina Skrube in Carinthia, Gabriella Mairinger and Peter Kuhn in Salzburg, and Irmgard and Sandra in Vienna. Thanks also to Neal Bedford, who worked on the latest Vienna guidebook with me. Some of his restaurant and nightlife discoveries made it into this book, as did some of his research in the music special section.

This Book

This 3rd edition of *Austria* was produced in Lonely Planet's Melbourne office. Mark Honan, who also wrote the previous two editions, updated this one. The maps and some of the text for the Vienna chapter were based on Neal Bedford's research for LP's *Vienna 3*.

From the Publisher

A whole crowd of people helped produce this book. The coordinating editor was Erin Corrigan, on loan from LP US. The ever-patient Jacqui Saunders was the coordinating designer and cartographer. Assisting Erin with editing and proofing and a million other things were Darren 'Doc' O'Connell, who also gave much-needed technical assistance, Elizabeth Swan, Kalya Ryan, Shelley Muir, Susannah Farfor, Jennifer Garrett, Justin Flynn, Kerryn Burgess and Tony Davidson. Chris Wyness was the senior editor who oversaw the project. Special thanks to Susannah, who filled in for Chris at the start, just to get things rolling. Jacqui got helping hands from several other map-makers and designers: foremost, Csanad Csutoros, and also Birgit Jordan, who gave us invaluable help by being a native German speaker, Mark Griffiths, Celia Wood, Gus Poo y Balbontin, Huw Fowles, Karen Fry, Adrian Persoglia, Ray Thomson and Paul Edmunds. This crew was gently directed by Kieran Grogan, the senior designer. Emma Koch cast her trained eye over the Language chapter. Janine Eberle helped with style issues and coffee breaks. Yvonnne Byron, with a bit of help from Erin, created the index. Daniel New created the cover. The photographs came from Lonely Planet Images (LPI), and the illustrations were drawn by Mick Weldon (MW), Nicky Castle (NC) and Martin Harris (MH).

Grateful acknowledgment is made to Wienier Linien GmbH&CoKG for permission to reproduce the Vienna U-bahn map; to the Hundertwasser Archive for the use of *Homo humus come va – 10 002 nights;* and to the National Gallery London for the use of Gustav Klimt's *Portrait of Hermine Gallia.*

Contents – Text

THE AUTHOR		6

THIS BOOK & THANKS		7

FOREWORD		10

INTRODUCTION		11

FACTS ABOUT AUSTRIA 12

History	12	Government & Politics	20	Arts	24
Geography & Geology	18	Economy	22	**Austria & Music**	**26**
Climate	18	Population & People	22	Society & Conduct	36
Ecology & Environment	19	Education	22	Religion	37
Flora & Fauna	20	Science & Philosophy	23	Language	37

FACTS FOR THE VISITOR 38

Suggested Itineraries	**38**	Photography & Video	51	Business Hours	59
Planning	38	Time	52	Public Holidays &	
Responsible Tourism	40	Electricity	52	Special Events	59
Tourist Offices	40	Weights & Measures	52	Activities	59
Visas & Documents	41	Laundry	52	Courses	60
Embassies & Consulates	42	Toilets	52	Work	60
Customs	43	Health	52	Accommodation	62
Money	44	Women Travellers	55	**Walking & Skiing in Austria**	**64**
Post & Communications	47	Gay & Lesbian Travellers	56	Food	77
Digital Resources	49	Disabled Travellers	56	Drinks	80
Books	49	Senior Travellers	57	Entertainment	81
Films	51	Travel with Children	57	Spectator Sports	82
Newspapers & Magazines	51	Dangers & Annoyances	57	Shopping	82
Radio & TV	51	Emergencies	58		
Video Systems	51	Legal Matters	58		

GETTING THERE & AWAY 83

Air	83	River	93		
Land	88	Organised Tours	93		

GETTING AROUND 95

Air	95	Bicycle	102	Mountain Transport	103
Bus	95	Hitching	102	Local Transport	103
Train	97	Walking	102	Organised Tours	104
Car & Motorcycle	98	Boat	103		

VIENNA 105

History	105	The West	130	Organised Tours	139
Orientation	106	The South	133	Special Events	139
Information	107	The East	135	Places to Stay	140
Innere Stadt	119	Activities	137	Places to Eat	148
Vienna Walking Tour	**122**	Language Courses	138	Entertainment	154

Spectator Sports..................161
Shopping 161
Getting There & Away 162
Getting Around 164

BURGENLAND 167

Eisenstadt............................167
Around Eisenstadt 171
Neusiedler See.....................171
Neusiedl am See 171
Rust 172
Mörbisch 173
Seewinkel...........................173
Podersdorf 174

STYRIA 176

Graz.....................................177
Around Graz 188
Styrian Wine Routes...........188
Deutschlandsberg...............189
Ehrenhausen 189
Austrian Open-Air
Museum 190
Lurgrotte 190
Piber & Köflach 191
Bärnbach 191
Elsewhere in Styria 193
Mariazell 193
Bruck an der Mur...............196
Leoben................................198
Eisenerz 198
Admont 199
Murau 200
Bad Blumau 200
Riegersburg 200

CARINTHIA 202

Klagenfurt...........................202
Central Carinthia 210
Wörther See 210
Villach 212
Around Villach 214
Eastern Carinthia 215
Friesach 216
Gurk 218
St Veit an der Glan.............218
Burg Hochosterwitz 219
Magdalensberg 220
Maria Saal 220
Western Carinthia 221
Gmünd 221
Spittal an der Drau.............221
Millstatt 224

HOHE TAUERN NATIONAL PARK REGION 226

Zell am See 228
Krimml Falls 232
Gerlos Pass 233
Grossglockner Road 234
Heiligenblut 236
Bad Gastein 237
Around Bad Gastein............240
Lienz 240

TIROL 245

Innsbruck............................248
Around Innsbruck 260
Igls.....................................260
Hall in Tirol 260
Wattens..............................260
Schwaz 261
Stubai Glacier.....................261
Seefeld...............................261
Ehrwald 263
North-Eastern Tirol 263
The Zillertal 263
Zell am Ziller 265
Mayrhofen..........................266
Achensee 267
Kitzbühel 267
Kirchberg 272
St Johann in Tirol 272
Kufstein 273
Söll 275
Western Tirol.....................275
Stams..................................275
The Ötztal 275
Imst....................................277
Landeck 277
The Inn Valley 279
The Paznauntal 279
Arlberg Region 279
St Anton am Arlberg 280

VORARLBERG 284

Bregenz 284
Bregenzerwald 289
Feldkirch 290
Bludenz 291
Brandnertal 294
Kleinwalsertal.....................294
Western Arlberg................295

SALZBURG PROVINCE 297

Salzburg 298
Around Salzburg.................317
Hellbrunn...........................317
Gaisberg 317
Untersberg.........................318
Hallein 318

The Author

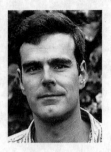

Mark Honan

After a university degree in philosophy opened up a glittering career as an office clerk, Mark decided that there was more to life than form-filling and data-entry. He set off on a two-year trip round the world, armed with a backpack and a vague intent to sell travel stories and pictures upon his return to England. Astonishingly, this barely formed plan succeeded and Mark became the travel correspondent to a London-based magazine. Since 1991 he has written Lonely Planet guidebooks to Vienna, Austria and Switzerland, updated Solomon Islands and contributed to guides to Europe, Central America, Mexico and India, as well as to Lonely Planet Unpacked, a book of travel horror stories. Although more than happy not to be a clerk anymore, he finds, curiously, that life as a travel writer still entails a good deal of form-filling and data-entry.

From the Author

Thanks to everyone among the vast cast of characters who helped me organise my research or supplied useful information. The main stars include Marion Telsnig at London's Austrian National Tourist Office, Melanie Grubb at Austrian Airlines, Sabine Gebetsroither in Upper Austria, Martina Skrube in Carinthia, Gabriella Mairinger and Peter Kuhn in Salzburg, and Irmgard and Sandra in Vienna. Thanks also to Neal Bedford, who worked on the latest Vienna guidebook with me. Some of his restaurant and nightlife discoveries made it into this book, as did some of his research in the music special section.

This Book

This 3rd edition of *Austria* was produced in Lonely Planet's Melbourne office. Mark Honan, who also wrote the previous two editions, updated this one. The maps and some of the text for the Vienna chapter were based on Neal Bedford's research for LP's *Vienna 3*.

From the Publisher

A whole crowd of people helped produce this book. The coordinating editor was Erin Corrigan, on loan from LP US. The ever-patient Jacqui Saunders was the coordinating designer and cartographer. Assisting Erin with editing and proofing and a million other things were Darren 'Doc' O'Connell, who also gave much-needed technical assistance, Elizabeth Swan, Kalya Ryan, Shelley Muir, Susannah Farfor, Jennifer Garrett, Justin Flynn, Kerryn Burgess and Tony Davidson. Chris Wyness was the senior editor who oversaw the project. Special thanks to Susannah, who filled in for Chris at the start, just to get things rolling. Jacqui got helping hands from several other map-makers and designers: foremost, Csanad Csutoros, and also Birgit Jordan, who gave us invaluable help by being a native German speaker, Mark Griffiths, Celia Wood, Gus Poo y Balbontin, Huw Fowles, Karen Fry, Adrian Persoglia, Ray Thomson and Paul Edmunds. This crew was gently directed by Kieran Grogan, the senior designer. Emma Koch cast her trained eye over the Language chapter. Janine Eberle helped with style issues and coffee breaks. Yvonnne Byron, with a bit of help from Erin, created the index. Daniel New created the cover. The photographs came from Lonely Planet Images (LPI), and the illustrations were drawn by Mick Weldon (MW), Nicky Castle (NC) and Martin Harris (MH).

Grateful acknowledgment is made to Wienier Linien GmbH&CoKG for permission to reproduce the Vienna U-bahn map; to the Hundertwasser Archive for the use of *Homo humus come va – 10 002 nights;* and to the National Gallery London for the use of Gustav Klimt's *Portrait of Hermine Gallia.*

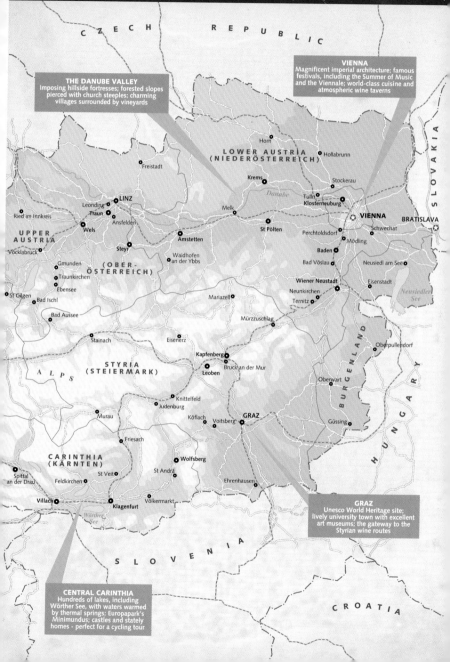

MAP 1 – AUSTRIA

CZECH REPUBLIC

VIENNA
Magnificent imperial architecture; famous festivals, including the Summer of Music and the Viennale; world-class cuisine and atmospheric wine taverns

THE DANUBE VALLEY
Imposing hillside fortresses; forested slopes pierced with church steeples; charming villages surrounded by vineyards

Horn

LOWER AUSTRIA
(NIEDERÖSTERREICH)
Hollabrunn

Freistadt

Krems
Stockerau

LINZ
Tulln
Leonding
Klosterneuburg
Traun
Melk
Ansfelden
St Pölten
VIENNA
BRATISLAVA
Ried im Innkreis
Wels
Perchtoldsdorf
Schwechat
Amstetten
Mödling
SLOVAKIA

UPPER
AUSTRIA
Steyr
Waidhofen
an der Ybbs
Baden
Vöcklabruck
(OBER-
ÖSTERREICH)
Bad Vöslau
Neusiedl am See

Gmunden
Wiener Neustadt
Eisenstadt
Traunkirchen
Mariazell
Neunkirchen
Ebensee
Ternitz
Neusiedler
See
St Gilgen
Bad Ischl
Mürzzuschlag

Bad Aussee
Oberpullendorf

Stainach
Eisenerz
Kapfenberg
A L P S
STYRIA
Bruck an der Mur
(STEIERMARK)
Leoben
BURGENLAND

Murau
Knittelfeld
Oberwart
Judenburg

Friesach
Köflach
Voitsberg
GRAZ
Güssing
HUNGARY

CARINTHIA
Wolfsberg
(KÄRNTEN)

Spittal
an der Drau
St Veit
St Andrä
Ehrenhausen
Feldkirchen

Villach
Klagenfurt
Völkermarkt
GRAZ
Unesco World Heritage site; lively university town with excellent art museums; the gateway to the Styrian wine routes

Wörther
See

S L O V E N I A

CENTRAL CARINTHIA
Hundreds of lakes, including Wörther See, with waters warmed by thermal springs; Europapark's Minimundus; castles and stately homes - perfect for a cycling tour

CROATIA

Austria
3rd edition – March 2002
First published – March 1996

Published by
Lonely Planet Publications Pty Ltd ABN 36 005 607 983
90 Maribyrnong St, Footscray, Victoria 3011, Australia

Lonely Planet offices
Australia Locked Bag 1, Footscray, Victoria 3011
USA 150 Linden St, Oakland, CA 94607
UK 10a Spring Place, London NW5 3BH
France 1 rue du Dahomey, 75011 Paris

Photographs
Many of the images in this guide are available for licensing from
Lonely Planet Images.
Web site: www.lonelyplanetimages.com

Front cover photograph
The Austrian countryside, Innsbruck, with goat (Photographers:
Chris Mellor & Greg Elms; image digitally modified by Lonely Planet).

ISBN 1 86450 344 0

Printed through SNP SPrint Singapore Pte Ltd at
KHL Printing Co Sdn Bhd Malaysia

**Although the authors
and Lonely Planet try
to make the informa-
tion as accurate as
possible, we accept
no responsibility for
any loss, injury or
inconvenience sus-
tained by anyone
using this book.**

Thanks

Kostas Alexopoulos, FR Antony, Claire Antoszewski, John Arwe, Suzi Asmus, Eli Barkay, Barrett Belt, Fletcher Benton, Moshe & Nina Berant, Maxine Beresford, Elaine Boeshe, Aniha Brar, Doris Calhoun, Romelle Castle, Kah Chong, Vivian Choy, Leslie Clark, Brigette Clarke, Adam Coyle, Jolyne Daigle, Nathan Dhillon, Lars Dicht, Tea Die Henrich, J Dober, Terry Dukes, John Dynan, Ben Edmunds, Graham Elliott, Annette English, Martin Fagerer, Teresa Fanning, Kay Fisher, Kathryn Fleming, Miranissa C Florendo, Iain Franklin, Suresh & Axel Fussi, Johanri & Sanet Gerber, Linda Gillespie, Kathryn Godfrey, Bob Greiner, Urich Groaler, Patricia Groom, Ed Gruhl, Reinhard Gruner, Erich Gutsjahr, Werner Hardt Stremayr, Yuko Harmegnies, Jean Harrison, Keith A Havas, Eric Hempsall, Matthew & Lee-Anne Horsfall, Philip Howes, Thng Hui Hong, Loryn Hunter, Rachel Hursthouse, Claire Imrie, Liv Iversen, Rok Jarc, Sue Jeffery, Vera D Jennings, Carl Gustaf Johansson, Jenny Jones, Marius Jones, Chirsten Kasier, Lani Kenworthy, Margit Koestlbauer, A & J Kuoni, Tomaz Lazar, Antonio Lee, Richard Lloyd, Uli Ludikow-ski, Matthew Male, Lia Marcote, Andrea Martin, Antoinette & Gerald Martin, Jo Mason, Olivier Mauron, Ian McAllister, Kylie McCrindle, Margaret McEntegart, Megan McGregor, Paul McIvor, Paul Miller, Basit Mirza, Martin Mischkulnig, Lee Gerard Molloy, Carolina Moreira, Luisella Mori, Jason Mote, Roberta Murray, Caroline Newhouse, D I Niederscheider, Joanne Owen, Casimir Paltinger, Susan Patton, W D Pennycook, Wilco Pruysers, William Reynolds, Peter Richmond, Jason Rodrigues, V M Roffer, Claire Rosenbaum, Joshua Salinger, Matt Salmon, Rachel Samsonowitz, Leo H Sano, Michel Schinz, Paola Sconzo, Michael L Sensor, Jessica Sherwood, Alec Sirken, Joanne Smethurst, Jason Smith, Andy Sparrow, Lisa Spratling, Anthea & David Spurling, Louise Stanley, Gil & Rakefet Stav, Jenny Stewart, Peggy Storniolo, Alex Stovell, E Thomas, Katrin Thomas, Helen Thorne, Dr C Tiligada, Remi Tourtet, Glenn Townend, Brendan Vargas, Paula Vflen, Astrid van der Vlugt, Benedict Wabunoha, A Watson, Scott Wayne, Anton Weber, Diana Webster, Valda White, John Whitten, Per Wickenberg, Kate Wilford, Theo Wilhelm, Fiona Wilson, Rowena Wong, T Wood, Dr Michael L Wyzan, Lea Zore

Foreword

ABOUT LONELY PLANET GUIDEBOOKS

The story begins with a classic travel adventure: Tony and Maureen Wheeler's 1972 journey across Europe and Asia to Australia. There was no useful information about the overland trail then, so Tony and Maureen published the first Lonely Planet guidebook to meet a growing need.

From a kitchen table, Lonely Planet has grown to become the largest independent travel publisher in the world, with offices in Melbourne (Australia), Oakland (USA), London (UK) and Paris (France).

Today Lonely Planet guidebooks cover the globe. There is an ever-growing list of books and information in a variety of media. Some things haven't changed. The main aim is still to make it possible for adventurous travellers to get out there – to explore and better understand the world.

At Lonely Planet we believe travellers can make a positive contribution to the countries they visit – if they respect their host communities and spend their money wisely. Since 1986 a percentage of the income from each book has been donated to aid projects and human rights campaigns, and, more recently, to wildlife conservation.

> Although inclusion in a guidebook usually implies a recommendation we cannot list every good place. Exclusion does not necessarily imply criticism. In fact there are a number of reasons why we might exclude a place – sometimes it is simply inappropriate to encourage an influx of travellers.

UPDATES & READER FEEDBACK

Things change – prices go up, schedules change, good places go bad and bad places go bankrupt. Nothing stays the same. So, if you find things better or worse, recently opened or long-since closed, please tell us and help make the next edition even more accurate and useful.

Lonely Planet thoroughly updates each guidebook as often as possible – usually every two years, although for some destinations the gap can be longer. Between editions, up-to-date information is available in our free, quarterly *Planet Talk* newsletter and monthly email bulletin *Comet*. The *Upgrades* section of our website (**w** www.lonelyplanet.com) is also regularly updated by Lonely Planet authors, and the site's *Scoop* section covers news and current affairs relevant to travellers. Lastly, the *Thorn Tree* bulletin board and *Postcards* section carry unverified, but fascinating, reports from travellers.

Tell us about it! We genuinely value your feedback. A well-travelled team at Lonely Planet reads and acknowledges every email and letter we receive and ensures that every morsel of information finds its way to the relevant authors, editors and cartographers.

Everyone who writes to us will find their name listed in the next edition of the appropriate guidebook, and will receive the latest issue of *Comet* or *Planet Talk*. The very best contributions will be rewarded with a free guidebook.

We may edit, reproduce and incorporate your comments in Lonely Planet products such as guidebooks, websites and digital products, so let us know if you don't want your comments reproduced or your name acknowledged.

How to contact Lonely Planet:
Online: **e** talk2us@lonelyplanet.com.au, **w** www.lonelyplanet.com
Australia: Locked Bag 1, Footscray, Victoria 3011
UK: 10a Spring Place, London NW5 3BH
USA: 150 Linden St, Oakland, CA 94607

Introduction

Austria is terrific as a year-round holiday destination. Much of the country is dominated by the soaring magnificence of the Alps, and this magical mountain landscape has relaxed chalet villages, first-rate winter sport resorts, isolated hiking and walking trails, traditional Alpine festivals and much more.

The cities have plenty to engage visitors, not least their world-class museums and art collections. Vienna is the capital, hub of the country's unrivalled musical tradition and home to some of the most impressive architecture in Europe. Music, art and architecture reached baroque perfection in Salzburg, Mozart's birthplace. Innsbruck is stunningly situated, with snow-capped peaks for a backdrop to its fascinating historic buildings.

Throughout Austria you'll find that the rhythm of normal daily life has a musical beat. Important music festivals, especially those featuring classical music, fill the calendar. There's also an extensive variety of outdoor activities, ranging from lounging on lakeside beaches to paragliding from mountains. It hardly needs adding that you can enjoy a spot of skiing, too. An efficient tourist industry, good transport, charming hotels and atmospheric restaurants make it easy and pleasurable just to be in Austria.

This is a country that has something for everybody, and for all budgets. You can spend plenty if you want, yet it costs nothing to walk amid the stupendous Alpine scenery, to cycle along the castle-strewn, vineyard-rich Wachau stretch of the Danube River, or to admire the exuberant decor of the many baroque churches. It costs nothing to wander around imperial Vienna and enjoy the colourful street artists, or to gaze in awe at the lavish facades of the grandiose public buildings. And it costs nothing to appreciate the wonder of Salzburg's many superb church spires. Sure, it costs something to get there and stay there, but you'll find it's a cost well worth paying.

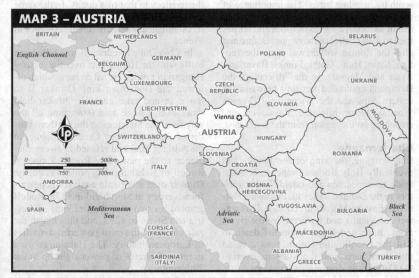

MAP 3 – AUSTRIA

Facts about Austria

HISTORY

The Danube Valley was populated during the Palaeolithic Age, as proved by the discovery there of a 25,000-year-old statuette, the *Venus of Willendorf*. In 1991 the body of a late Stone Age man was discovered in a glacier in the Ötztal Alps (see the boxed text 'Entombed in Ice' in the Tirol chapter). When the Romans arrived in the 1st century BC, there were already Celtic settlements in the Danube Valley, the result of migrations east from Gaul some 500 years earlier. Celts had also long been mining salt in Hallstatt and trading along the north-south alpine trading routes. The Romans established settlements from Brigantium (Bregenz) to Carnuntum (Petronell), 40km east of a military camp known as Vindobona (Vienna). The Danube River, known to the Romans as Danuvius, marked the northern border of the empire and served to discourage advances by Germanic tribes from the north.

By the 5th century AD, the Roman Empire had collapsed and the Romans were forced south by invading tribes. The importance of the Danube Valley as an east-west crossing meant successive waves of tribes and armies tried to gain control of the region. Before and after the Roman withdrawal came the Teutons, Slavs, Huns, Goths, Franks, Bavarians, Avars and Magyars. In the 7th century the Bavarians controlled territory between the eastern Alps and the Wienerwald (Vienna Woods). Meanwhile, the Slavs were encroaching on the region from the south-east.

Charlemagne

Charlemagne, the king of the Franks and eventually Holy Roman Emperor, brushed aside all opposition and established a territory in the Danube Valley known as the Ostmark (Eastern March) in AD 803. This was west of Vienna and bordered by the rivers Enns, Raab and Drau. Upon his death in 814 the Carolingian empire was divided into three parts, and the Magyars overran the Ostmark in determined invasions.

Otto I (the Great), controller of the eastern portion of Charlemagne's old empire, defeated the Hungarians at Augsburg and re-established the Ostmark in 955. Seven years later Pope John XII crowned Otto as Holy Roman Emperor of the German princes. In 996 the Ostmark was first referred to as Ostarrichi, which is a clear forerunner of the modern German word Österreich (Austria), meaning eastern empire.

The Babenbergs

Leopold von Babenberg, a descendant of a noble Bavarian family, became the margrave (German noble ranked above count) of the Ostmark in 976. The Babenbergs gradually extended their sphere of influence and, during the 11th century, Vienna and most of modern-day Lower Austria fell into their hands; in 1192 they also acquired Styria and much of Upper Austria. This was a period of trade and prosperity for the region. In 1156 the Holy Roman Emperor, Friedrich Barbarossa, elevated the territory to that of a duchy. In the same year the Babenbergs, under Duke Heinrich II, established their permanent residence in Vienna.

In 1246 Duke Friedrich II was killed in a battle with the Hungarians over the Austro-Hungarian border. He left no heirs, which allowed the Bohemian king Ottokar II to move in and take control. Ottokar held sway over a huge area (stretching all the way from the Sudeten, on the northern border of the present-day Czech Republic, to the Adriatic Sea) and refused to swear allegiance to the new Holy Roman Emperor, Rudolf of Habsburg. His pride was costly: Ottokar died in a battle against his powerful adversary at Marchfeld in 1278. Rudolf granted his two sons the fiefdoms of Austria and Styria in 1282, and thus began the rule of one of the most powerful dynasties in European history. The Habsburgs were to retain the reins of power right up to the 20th century.

The Habsburg Dynasty

The Habsburgs initially suffered a few reversals (including some humiliating defeats by the Swiss) but managed to consolidate their position: Carinthia and Carniola were annexed in 1335, followed by Tirol in 1363. Rudolf IV (r. 1358 to 1365) went as far as to forge some documents (the *Privilegium maius*) to elevate his status to that of an archduke. He also laid the foundation stone of Stephansdom (St Stephen's Cathedral) in Vienna and founded the University of Vienna. These acts helped to placate the wealthy Viennese families, whose privileges had been reduced in the previous century.

In 1453 Friedrich III managed to genuinely acquire the status that was faked by Rudolf IV and was crowned Holy Roman Emperor. Furthermore, he persuaded Pope Paul II to raise the status of Vienna to that of a bishopric in 1469. Friedrich's ambition knew few bounds. His motto was AEIOU, usually interpreted to mean *Austria Est Imperare Orbi Universo*, though some scholars stake a claim for *Alles Erdreich Ist Österreich Untertan*, or even *Austria Erit In Orbe Ultima*. If the exact wording is in dispute, the meaning isn't, because either way it expressed the view that the whole world was Austria's empire. To try to prove this, Friedrich waged war against King Matthias Corvinus of Hungary, who occupied Vienna (ruled 1485–90). He also made no friend of the Archbishop of Salzburg, who sided with his opponents. Salzburg was a powerful ecclesiastical principality until the 19th century.

Friedrich instigated the famous and extremely successful Habsburg policy of acquiring new territories through politically motivated marriages. The intermarriage policy had a genetic side effect, albeit discreetly played down in official portraits: the distended lower jaw and lip became a family trait. In 1477 Friedrich's son, Maximilian, gained control of Burgundy and the Netherlands by marriage to Maria of Burgundy. Maximilian's eldest son, Philip, was married to the infanta of Spain in 1496. Philip's son Charles eventually gained most from this. He became Charles I of Spain in 1516 (which included control of vast overseas territories) and Charles V of the Holy Roman Empire in 1519.

Charles' acquisitions were too diverse for one person to rule effectively and he handed over the Austrian territories to his younger brother Ferdinand I in 1521. Ferdinand also inherited Hungary and Bohemia through his marriage to Anna Jagiello after her brother, King Lewis II, died in battle in 1526.

The Turkish Threat

Ferdinand became preoccupied with protecting his territories from the incursions of the Turks, who were rampant under the leadership of Süleyman the Magnificent, sultan of the Ottoman Empire; Styria was particularly vulnerable. The Turks overran the Balkans, and killed Lewis II in their conquest of Hungary. In 1529 the Turks reached Vienna, but their 18-day siege of the city foundered with the onset of an early winter. They withdrew but continued to be a powerful force, and it was this threat that prompted Ferdinand to move his court to Vienna in 1533, the first Habsburg to reside in the city permanently. This move increased the city's prestige.

In 1556 Charles abdicated as emperor and Ferdinand was crowned in his place. Charles' remaining territory was inherited by his son, Philip II, finalising the split in the Habsburg line. In 1571 Maximilian II granted religious freedom to his subjects, upon which the vast majority of Austrians turned to Protestantism. In 1576, Maximilian's grandson, Rudolf II, became emperor and embraced the Counter-Reformation; much of the country reverted to Catholicism – not always without coercion. The problem of religious intolerance was the cause of the Thirty Years' War which started in 1618 and had a devastating effect on the whole of Central Europe. In 1645 a Protestant Swedish army marched to within sight of Vienna but did not attack. Peace was finally achieved in 1648 and, through the Treaty of Westphalia, Austria lost some territory to France.

For much of the rest of the century, Austria was preoccupied with halting the advance of the Turks into Europe. Vienna,

The Turks & Vienna

The Ottoman Empire viewed Vienna as 'the city of the golden apple', but it wasn't Apfelstrudel they were after in their two great sieges. The first, in 1529, was undertaken by Süleyman the Magnificent, but the 18-day endeavour was not sufficient to break the resolve of the city. The Turkish sultan subsequently died at the siege of Szigetvár, yet his death was kept secret for several days in an attempt to preserve the morale of the army. The subterfuge worked for a while. Messengers were led into the presence of the embalmed body which was placed in a seated position on the throne. They then unknowingly relayed their news to the corpse. The lack of the slightest acknowledgment of the sultan towards his minions was interpreted as regal impassiveness.

At the head of the Turkish siege of 1683 was the general Kara Mustapha. Amid the 25,000 tents of the Ottoman army that surrounded Vienna he installed his 1500 concubines, guarded by 700 black eunuchs. Their luxurious quarters contained gushing fountains and regal baths, all set up in haste but with great opulence.

Again, it was all to no avail – perhaps the concubines proved too much of a distraction. Whatever the reason, Mustapha failed to put garrisons on Kahlenberg and was surprised by a swift attack from Charles of Lorraine heading a German army and supported by a Polish army led by King Sobieski. Mustapha was pursued from the battlefield and defeated once again, at Gran. At Belgrade he was met by the emissary of the sultan, Mehmed IV. The price of failure was death, and Mustapha meekly accepted his fate. When the Austrian imperial army conquered Belgrade in 1718 the grand vizier's head was dug up and brought back to Vienna in triumph, where it is preserved (but no longer exhibited) in the Historisches Museum der Stadt Wien.

Süleyman the Magnificent

already depleted by a severe epidemic of bubonic plague, found itself in 1683 again under Turkish siege (see the boxed text 'The Turks & Vienna'). The Viennese were close to capitulation when they were rescued by a Christian force of German and Polish soldiers. Combined forces subsequently swept the Turks to the south-eastern edge of Europe. The removal of the Turkish threat saw a proliferation of baroque building in many cities. Under the musical emperor, Leopold I, Vienna became a magnet for musicians and composers.

Years of Reform

The death of Charles II, the last of the Spanish line of the Habsburgs, saw Austria become involved in the War of the Spanish Succession (1701–14). At its conclusion Charles VI, the Austrian emperor, was left with only minor Spanish possessions (such as the Low Countries and parts of Italy). Charles then turned to the problem of ensuring his daughter, Maria Theresa, would succeed him as he had no male heirs. To this end he drew up the Pragmatic Sanction, signed jointly by all the main European powers, and Maria Theresa duly ascended the Habsburg throne in 1740. However, to ensure she stayed there it was necessary to win the War of the Austrian Succession (1740–48).

Maria Theresa, aided by Britain and the Netherlands, had to fight off three rivals to the throne, including the elector of Bavaria. Prussia took advantage of the Europe-wide conflict to wrest control of Silesia from Austria, which it retained in the ensuing peace. In the Seven Years' War (1756–63) the European powers changed alliances. Austria, now opposed by Britain, sought without success to regain Silesia from Prussia.

Mother Theresa

Maria Theresa (1717–80) was a hugely influential figure in Austrian history. Thrust into the limelight when her father died with no male heirs, she held onto power for 40 years, while also managing to give birth to 16 children – among them Marie Antoinette, future wife of Louis XVI, who has gone down in history for her failure to understand why the starving French peasants didn't eat cake. Maria Theresa's fourth child, Joseph II, weighed a daunting 7kg at birth.

Though Maria Theresa pushed through many enlightened reforms, she was also prudish and anti-semitic (Jews had to keep behind a screen when in her presence). One of her less popular measures was the introduction of the short-lived Commission against Immoral Conduct in 1752, which raided private homes, trying to catch men entertaining women of supposed doubtful virtue – the Commission tried to snare Casanova during his visit to Vienna.

Maria Theresa's attitude to philanderers was no doubt coloured by the conduct of her husband, Francis I, who was particularly adept in just that field. Yet despite his questionable conduct, Maria Theresa remained loyal to her spouse, and when he died suddenly in 1765 she stayed in mourning for the rest of her life. She retreated to Schloss Schönbrunn, left the running of the state in the hands of Joseph II, and kept a low-profile, chaste existence while she gradually ballooned in weight. Her achievements weren't fully appreciated during her lifetime; it was only after her death that she began to be acknowledged as the mother of the nation.

Maria Theresa's rule lasted 40 years, and is generally acknowledged as a golden era, in which Austria developed as a modern state. Centralised control was established, along with a civil service. The army and economy were reformed and a public education system was introduced. Vienna's reputation as a centre for music grew apace.

Maria Theresa's son, Joseph II, who ruled from 1780 to 1790 (he was also jointly in charge from 1765), was an even more zealous reformer. He issued an edict of tolerance for all faiths, secularised religious properties and abolished serfdom. Yet Joseph moved too fast for the general population and was ultimately forced to rescind some of his measures.

Crumbling Empire

The rise of Napoleon in France proved to be a major threat to the Habsburg empire: he inflicted major defeats on Austria in 1803, 1805 and 1809. Franz II, the grandson of Maria Theresa, had taken up the Austrian crown in 1804 and was forced by Napoleon in 1806 to relinquish the German crown and the title of Holy Roman Emperor.

In 1809 Klemens von Metternich (1773–1859) was appointed Austrian foreign minister. In an attempt to buy peace he arranged the marriage of Franz II's daughter, Marie Louise, to Napoleon in 1810. But the move came too late – the cost of the war caused state bankruptcy and a currency collapse in 1811.

European conflict dragged on until the Congress of Vienna in 1814–15; the proceedings were dominated by Metternich, who restored some measure of pride to his homeland. Austria was left with control of the German Confederation until it was forced to relinquish it in the Austro-Prussian War in 1866. Thereafter, Austria had no place in the new German empire unified by Otto von Bismarck in 1871.

On the home front, all was not well in post-Congress Vienna. The arts and culture as pursued by the middle class flourished in the Biedermeier period, but the general populace had a harder time. Metternich had established a police state and removed civil rights. Coupled with poor wages and housing, this led to revolution in Vienna in March 1848. The war minister was hanged from a lamppost, Metternich was ousted and Emperor Ferdinand I abdicated. The subsequent liberal interlude was brief, though, and the army helped to reimpose an absolute monarchy. The new emperor, Franz Josef I (1830–1916), a nephew of Ferdinand, was just 18 years old.

Technical innovations led to an improvement in Austria's economic situation. Franz Josef became leader of the dual Austro-Hungarian monarchy, created in 1867 by the *Ausgleich* (compromise), which was Austria's response to defeat by Prussia the previous year. Common defence, foreign and economic policies ensued but unity was not complete, because two parliaments remained. Another period of prosperity began, which particularly benefited Vienna. Universal suffrage was introduced in Austro-Hungarian lands in 1906.

Peace in Europe had been maintained by a complex series of alliances (Austria-Hungary was linked to the German empire and Italy through the secret Triple Alliance), but that peace was wrecked in 1914 when Franz Josef's nephew and heir to the Austrian throne, Franz Ferdinand, was assassinated in Sarajevo on 28 June. A month later Austria-Hungary declared war on Serbia and WWI began.

The Republic

In 1916 Franz Josef died and his successor, Charles I, abdicated at the conclusion of the war in 1918. The Republic of Austria was created on 12 November 1918, marking the end of the centuries-old Habsburg dynasty and the right of the monarchy to participate in government. Under the peace treaty signed by the Allied powers on 10 September 1919, the Republic's planned union with Germany was prohibited, and it was forced to recognise the independent states of Czechoslovakia, Poland, Hungary and Yugoslavia. Previously, these countries, along with Transylvania (now in Romania), had been largely under the control of the

Habsburgs. The loss of so much land caused severe economic difficulties in Austria – the new states declined to supply vital raw materials to their old ruler – and many urban families were soon on the verge of famine. By the mid-1920s, however, the federal government had stabilised the currency and established new trading relations.

The Rise of Fascism

After WWI, Vienna's socialist city government embarked on a program of enlightened social policies. The rest of the country, however, was firmly under the sway of the conservative federal government, causing great tensions between the capital and the state. These tensions were heightened in July 1927, when right-wing extremists were acquitted of an assassination charge (a dubious decision which was widely seen as politically motivated) and the Justizpalast (Palace of Justice) in Vienna was torched by demonstrators. Police fired on the crowd and 86 people were killed.

Political and social tensions, such as the polarisation of political factions and rising unemployment, coupled with a worldwide economic crisis, gave the federal chancellor, Engelbert Dolfuss, an opportunity in 1933 to establish an authoritarian regime. In February 1934 civil war between the left and right-wing factions erupted, with hundreds of people killed over four days. The right wing proved victorious. In July the outlawed Nazis (National Socialists) assassinated Dolfuss. His successor, Kurt von Schuschnigg, couldn't stand up to increased threats from Germany. In 1938 he capitulated and included Nazis in his government.

On 11 March 1938 German troops marched into Austria and encountered little resistance. Adolf Hitler, a native of Austria who had departed Vienna decades before as a failed and disgruntled artist, returned to the city in triumph and held a huge rally at Heldenplatz. Austria was incorporated into the German Reich under the *Anschluss* (joining) on 13 March. A national referendum in April supported this union.

The arrival of the Nazis had a devastating effect on Austrian Jews, though many non-Jewish liberals and intellectuals also fled the Nazi regime. Representing 10% of Vienna's population, the Jews had enjoyed full civil rights. However, after May 1938, Germany's Nuremberg Racial Laws were applicable in Austria, leading to Jews being stripped of many of those rights. They were excluded from some professions and universities, and were forced to wear the yellow Star of David. Vienna's Jewish community was rocked by racial violence on the night of 9 November 1938, when their shops were looted and all but one of the temples burnt down. Many Jews fled the country, but about 60,000 were sent to concentration camps, where all but 2000 perished.

Austria was part of Germany's war machine during WWII. The government was a puppet of the German Nazis, and Austrians were conscripted into the German army. However, there were undercurrents of resistance to Germany: 100,000 Austrians were imprisoned for political reasons and 2700 resistance fighters were executed. Allied bombing was particularly heavy in Vienna in the last two years of the war and most major public buildings were damaged or destroyed, as were about 86,000 homes. As the war neared its end, Allied troops overran Austria from east and west. The Soviets reached Vienna first, entering the city on 11 April 1945.

Post-WWII

Austria was declared independent again on 27 April and a provisional federal government established under Karl Renner. The country was restored to its 1937 frontiers and occupied by the victorious Allies – the USA, the Soviet Union, the UK and France. The country was divided into four zones, one for each occupying power. Vienna, within the Soviet zone, was itself divided into four zones, with control of the city centre alternating between the four powers on a monthly basis. The situation in Austria and Vienna was very similar to that in Germany and Berlin; the Soviet zones in the latter were eventually sealed off, but Austria remained united because

its postwar communists (unlike those in Germany's Soviet sector) failed to gain electoral support.

Delays caused by frosting relations between the superpowers ensured that the Allied occupation dragged on for 10 years. It was a tough time for Austria's people; the black market dominated the flow of goods and the rebuilding of national monuments was slow and expensive. On 15 May 1955 the Austrian State Treaty was ratified, with Austria proclaiming its permanent neutrality. The Allied forces withdrew, and in December 1955 Austria joined the United Nations. As the capital of a neutral country bordering the Warsaw Pact countries, Vienna attracted spies and diplomats in the Cold War years. Kennedy and Khrushchev met there in 1961, as did Carter and Brezhnev in 1979.

Austria's international image suffered when former secretary-general of the United Nations, Kurt Waldheim, was elected as president in 1986, even though it was revealed that he had served as a lieutenant in a German *Wehrmacht* unit implicated in WWII war crimes. There was no specific evidence against Waldheim but several countries barred him from making state visits. Strangely, Waldheim virtually ignored his three years military service in his biography, *In the Eye of the Storm*, published in 1985. A further, if rather belated, recognition of Austria's less than spotless WWII record came with Chancellor Franz Vranitzky's admission in 1993 that Austrians were 'willing servants of Nazism'.

In 1992, Waldheim was succeeded by Thomas Klestil; like Waldheim, he was a candidate of the right-wing Austrian People's Party (ÖVP). Klestil easily won a second term in April 1998.

The EU Years

In the postwar years Austria has worked hard to overcome economic difficulties. In 1972 it established a free trade treaty with the European Economic Community (now known as the European Union, or EU), and full membership was applied for in July 1989. Terms were agreed early in 1994 and the Austrian people endorsed their country's entry into the EU in the referendum of 12 June 1994; a resounding 66.4% were in favour. Austria formally joined the EU on 1 January 1995. Since then, many Austrians have been rather ambivalent about the advantages of EU membership.

Austria suffered international criticism in February 2000, when the far-right Freedom Party (FPÖ) formed a new federal coalition government with the ÖVP under the leadership of Chancellor Schlüssel. This was the first time since the 1970s that the Social Democrats (SPÖ) had not been in sole or joint power. The new administration, though democratically elected, was condemned before it even had the opportunity to put a foot wrong. The EU immediately imposed sanctions against Austria by freezing all high-level diplomatic contacts.

Many Austrians were angered that ÖVP did a deal with the FPÖ, especially as this excluded the highest-polling party, the SPÖ (with 33% of the vote, versus 26.9% each for the ÖVP and the FPÖ). Public demonstrations against the FPÖ were held in several Austrian cities. However, many Austrians, irrespective of their views towards the FPÖ, were also upset at the EU's pre-emptive move, believing that Austria would not have been targeted had it been a more important player in European affairs. Sanctions proved not only futile but counterproductive, and they were withdrawn in September 2000. Nevertheless, the government remains the subject of close international monitoring.

No sooner had the dust settled on Austria's political woes when a new crisis thrust the country into world headlines. The Gletscherbahn underground railway in Kaprun caught fire half way up the mountain in November 2000, killing 155 in the worst ever alpine disaster.

GEOGRAPHY & GEOLOGY

Austria occupies an area of 83,855 sq km, extending for 560km from west to east, and 280km from north to south. The Alps are a dominating feature of the country. Movements of glaciers (beginning about 2½ million years ago) played a major role in shaping the mountains and valleys and creating Austria's lakes – for more on glaciers, see the boxed text 'Glacier Watching' in the Hohe Tauern National Park Region chapter. Two-thirds of Austria is mountainous, with three ranges running west to east and forcing most east-west travel into clearly defined channels.

The Northern Limestone Alps, on the border with Germany, reach nearly 3000m and extend eastwards, almost as far as the Wienerwald (Vienna Woods). The valley of the Inn River separates them from the High or Central Alps, which form the highest peaks in Austria. Many of the ridges in the Central Alps are topped by glaciers and most of the peaks are above 3000m. North-south travel across this natural barrier is limited to a handful of high passes and road tunnels. The Grossglockner is the highest peak at 3797m. The Southern Limestone Alps, which include the Karawanken Range, form a natural barrier along the border with Italy and Slovenia.

Away from the mountains, the mighty Danube (Donau) River is the country's most famous natural feature. The Salzach River joins the Inn River near Braunau, which in turn joins the Danube at Passau, on the German border. The main rivers in the south-east are the Mur and the Drau. Lakes are numerous, particularly in the Salzkammergut region and Carinthia. Neusiedler See (Lake Neusiedl), in the east, is Central Europe's largest steppe lake. In the west, Austria has a small share (along with Germany and Switzerland) of Bodensee (Lake Constance), through which the Rhine River flows.

The most fertile land is in the Danube Valley; cultivation is intensive and 90% of Austria's food is home-grown. North of the Danube the land is mostly flattish and forested. Burgenland is also relatively flat, as is the area south-east of Graz. Lower Austria, Burgenland and Styria are the most important wine-growing regions.

CLIMATE

Austria lies within the Central European climatic zone, though the eastern part of the country has what is called a Continental Pannonian climate, characterised by a mean

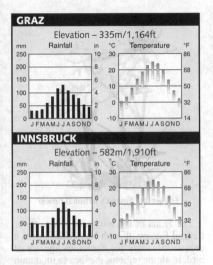

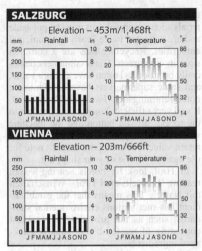

temperature in July above 19°C and annual rainfall usually less than 80cm. Austria's average rainfall is 71cm per year, with the west of the country receiving significantly higher levels. Mountains tend to draw the clouds, though the alpine valleys often escape much of the downfall.

Visitors need to be prepared for a range of temperatures depending on altitude – the higher, the colder – but the sun is also very intense at high elevations, which receive more sunshine in autumn and winter than the alpine valleys. The *Föhn* is a hot, dry wind which sweeps down from the mountains, mainly in early spring and autumn, and can be rather uncomfortable for some people.

Average high temperatures in Vienna are: January 1°C, April 15°C, July 25°C and October 14°C. Average minimum temperatures are lower by about 10°C (summer) to 4°C (winter). Temperatures in Salzburg and Innsbruck are similar to those in Vienna, except that winter is a few degrees cooler.

ECOLOGY & ENVIRONMENT

Austrians are well informed about environmental issues and the country has signed up to various international agreements intended to reduce pollution and preserve natural resources. Austria actually exceeds EU environmental dictates in many regards. Mountains have a fragile ecosystem and environmental measures to protect these areas have been in place in Austria for many years, yet Austria has still experienced some forest degradation caused by air and soil pollution.

Measures introduced to protect the environment range from banning leaded petrol to setting up an 'Eco Fund' to promote natural forms of energy, such as wind and solar power. Vienna's Spittelau incinerator has one of the lowest emission levels of any incinerator worldwide. Environmentally friendly trams are a feature of many cities; bicycles are another popular way to get around. In a 1978 referendum, Austrians voted against developing a nuclear power industry, prompting the federal Nuclear Prohibition Law later that year. The Czech Republic's nuclear reactor at Temelin, just 60km from the Austrian border, was brought online in October 2000 – a move that has angered Austrian environmentalists and politicians alike. The reactor has since suffered a series of technical difficulties.

Recycling is well established. Austrians diligently separate tin cans, paper and plastic from their refuse, for recycling. This isn't dictated by conscience: they are compelled to do so by law. In addition, hazardous materials such as aerosol cans must be put aside and are collected twice-yearly by municipal authorities. Recycling bins are a common sight in city streets. Glass containers (especially beer bottles) often have a return value, and some supermarkets have an automatic bottle-returning area *(Flaschen Rücknahme)*. It's all very efficient. You put your bottle into the recess, press a button and the machine works out what type it is and the appropriate return value. Then out pops a credit note for use against the rest of your shopping.

In Tirol, look for hotels bearing a sign reading 'Umweltsiegel Tirol – Wirtschaften mit Natur'. This means that the establishment has met various environmental standards, such as not providing a breakfast consisting of wasteful, individually packaged ingredients.

Visitors should endeavour to show the landscape and the environment the same respect that the Austrians do. In particular, you must not litter the countryside, and especially the Alpine regions, with nonbiodegradable materials.

FLORA & FAUNA

Nearly half of Austria (46%) is forested. At low altitudes oak and beech are common. At higher elevations conifers such as pine, spruce and larch predominate. At around 2200m trees yield to alpine meadows. Beyond 3000m, only mosses and lichens cling to the stark crags.

Alpine flowers add a palette of colour to the high pastures from about June to September and have adapted to cope with harsh conditions: long roots counter harsh winds, bright colours (a result of strong ultraviolet light) attract the few insects, and hairs and specially developed leaf shapes protect against frost and dehydration. Orchids, edelweiss, dandelions and poppies all survive at higher altitudes. Edelweiss is found on rocks and in crevices, and has white, star-shaped flowers. Although one of Austria's most famous alpine plants, it actually originated in Central Asia. Most alpine flowers are protected species and should not be picked.

Edelweiss, Austria's national flower

The fauna of the lowlands is typical for Central Europe, though Neusiedler See is a unique sanctuary for numerous species of bird. In alpine regions, the ibex (a mountain goat with huge curved horns) was under threat but is now breeding again. The ibex can master the art of leaping around mountains from the day it is born. In July it may migrate to an elevation of 3000m or more. The chamois (a small antelope) doesn't go quite so high, but is equally at home scampering around on mountainsides. It can leap 4m vertically and its hooves have rubbery soles and rigid outer rims – ideal for maintaining a good grip on loose rocks. The chamois is more often seen than the ibex; they have similar habits and tend to rest in the noon heat. The marmot, a chunky rodent related to the squirrel, is also indigenous to the Alps. Butterflies are numerous on the alpine meadows.

GOVERNMENT & POLITICS

The head of state is the president, who is chosen by the electorate for a six year term. The chancellor, appointed by the president, is the head of the federal government and the most influential political figure.

The country is divided into nine federal provinces *(Bundesländer)*, each of which has its own head of government *(Landeshauptmann)* and a provincial assembly *(Landtag)*. As well as being Austria's capital, Vienna has been a federal province in its own right

Marmot Society

The marmot is a type of rodent seen in the mountains, particularly in the Alps of Tirol. It generally lives in colonies comprising about two dozen animals. Members mark out the group's territory using pungent secretions from their cheeks. They all take part in lookout duty, watching not only for predators but also for unfamiliar marmots, which they will attack. Sentries raise themselves on their hind legs to better scan the surrounding area. The warning cry they give upon spotting a predator (such as a fox or golden eagle) is recognised by the chamois, which shares the same enemies.

For living quarters, the marmot builds a complex network of burrows which may have up to 100 exits. The marmot has powerful claws to aid digging and, although it can use its four limbs together, a burrow usually takes several generations to finish. The marmot sleeps on beds of dried grass, which it regularly cleans out and replaces.

Its long hibernation (concluding in April) leaves only five months to complete the breeding cycle and replenish energy for the next hibernation; these monogamous creatures therefore start mating soon after emerging in spring. The young are born blind and stay underground for the first four weeks of life. Once on the surface, they must quickly acquire the family smell (to be recognised as part of the group) and learn the warning cries. The marmot commonly feeds on grass and plants.

since 1922. The term of office for each Landtag is four or five years, depending upon the province. Each has a degree of autonomy over local issues and elects representatives to the Federal Council *(Bundesrat)*, the upper house of the national legislative body. The lower house, the National Council *(Nationalrat)*, is elected every four years in a vote by citizens over the age of 18. In some provinces (eg, Carinthia) the voting age for provincial elections is as low as 16.

In national politics, the 1970s saw the dominance of the Socialist Party, now called the Social Democrats (SPÖ). In the 1990s the SPÖ retained power with aid of coalitions with the Austrian People's Party (ÖVP), but was excluded from power in a contentious deal struck after the 1999 election (see the History section for details).

Despite the fact that the largest political party is left-wing, Austria has been perceived from abroad as retaining a sneaking affection for fascism. Such a view gained ground with the casual acceptance by Austrians of former president Waldheim and his murky past. A more significant factor is the rise of the far-right Freedom Party (FPÖ). The FPÖ made huge gains in the 1990s under the leadership

of the personable but ruthless populist, Jörg Haider, who stands on an anti-immigration, anti-EU, anti-foreigner platform. Haider's personal rise has been marked by a series of inflammatory statements, such as his praising of the employment policy of Hitler's Nazis. He raised the party's support from 4% to around 30%, edging it ahead of the ÖVP as Austria's second-largest party. The FPÖ's support is strongest in Carinthia, the province where Haider is governor.

Since forming part of the federal government in 2000, support for the FPÖ has dwindled – perhaps the reality of the FPÖ gaining power has proved uncomfortable for those who voted FPÖ as a protest against the government. The first warning for the FPÖ came with its poor showing in the Vienna provincial elections in March 2001 (see the Vienna chapter). An opinion poll in June 2001 showed that if a federal election was called, only 21% would vote for the FPÖ, as compared to 36% for the SPÖ and 27% for the VPÖ. Though Haider resigned the leadership of the FPÖ in 2001 in the wake of international condemnation, he remains the party's most influential figure and looks sure to make a comeback at some stage.

ECONOMY

Austria has a strong economy, with unemployment under 5% (one of the lowest rates in Europe) and inflation under 3%. The national economy is bolstered by a large contingent of foreign labour, particularly from Eastern Europe. Guest workers, mostly poorly paid, account for about 8.5% of the workforce.

Industries controlled by government or the big banks have been a feature of life in postwar Austria. However, in common with much of Europe, the federal government embarked on a program of privatisation in the 1990s, which is still ongoing. High profile businesses at least partially privatised by the government include Telekom Austria, Austrian Airlines and Austrian Tabak. In August 2001 the news broke that the impending privatisation of the postal service would entail the closure of 700 post offices – one third of the national total.

Austrian citizens enjoy wide-ranging welfare services including free education and health care, and a benign pensions and housing policy. Nevertheless, some benefits are being cut back – university tuition fees were introduced in September 2001.

Production in labour-intensive manufacturing industries was developed after WWII and now accounts for 75% of Austria's exports. Machinery, metallurgical products and textiles are particularly important. Linz is one of Austria's main iron and steel centres, feeding from iron ore mined at Eisenerz. Austria is relatively poor in natural resources and deposits of oil and natural gas are supplemented by hydroelectric power and imported coal. Forestry and agriculture together employ about 5% of the population. The country's cosseted farmers lost some of their protection with Austria's entry into the EU, but have responded well to the challenge posed by the EU open market.

Austria generally has a trade deficit in visible earnings, which is offset by income from tourism. This industry is hugely important for the whole country, but particularly for Tirol. One-third of Tirol's private farms list providing tourist accommodation as their primary or secondary source of income.

However, earnings from tourism have declined since the early 1990s. The majority of visitors are Germans and Germany is also Austria's largest trading partner.

POPULATION & PEOPLE

Austria has a population of about eight million; Vienna accounts for 1.64 million, followed by Graz (with 245,000), Linz (207,500), Salzburg (145,000) and Innsbruck (120,000). On average, there are 95 inhabitants per sq km. Native Austrians are mostly of Germanic origin. Vienna and the southeast have the most ethnic diversity: industrial expansion in the late 19th century brought an influx of European migrants, particularly from the Czech-speaking parts of the former Habsburg empire.

In 2001 there were 713,000 foreigners living legally in the country, mostly Turks, Poles, Germans, Slovaks and Czechs. Fears of being overrun by immigrants gained momentum in the early 1990s (thanks in part to a cynical anti-foreigner campaign by the Freedom Party), when the figure was 600,000, and the federal government subsequently tightened up immigration controls considerably. Yet Austria still has a problem with illegal immigrants from Eastern Europe, and the forthcoming eastwards expansion of the EU (in which there's freedom of movement between member states) is viewed with trepidation by some Austrians.

National service is compulsory for male Austrians (six months plus two months at a later time), though they may opt out of the military in favour of civil service duties.

EDUCATION

Austrian citizens are among the best educated in the world. The schooling system is uniform throughout the country. Children have nine years of compulsory education, from age six to 15. At age 10 children embark on either a basic secondary education (at a *Hauptschule*) or an extended secondary education (at a *Gymnasium*). The former lasts four years, and leads to a one year technical course or extended vocational training. Gymnasium pupils may also opt for vocational training after four years, or they can graduate at age 18 and try to win a university place. Austria has 13 universities and six fine arts colleges, offering places for over 200,000 students.

SCIENCE & PHILOSOPHY

Salzburg-born Christian Johann Doppler (1803–53), physicist and mathematician, demonstrated that wavelengths of light and sound shorten relative to the observer as objects approach, and lengthen as they move away. This explains why the siren pitch alters as a police car or ambulance speeds past. Known as the Doppler Effect, this principle has been used to demonstrate that other galaxies are moving further away from ours, and that the universe is therefore expanding.

The Vienna Circle (Wiener Kreis) was a group of philosophers centred on the University of Vienna in the 1920s and 1930s. The term logical positivism was coined to describe their views. They owed an initial debt to the work of the Austrian philosopher and scientist Ernst Mach (whose name lives on as a measure of the speed of a body in relation to the speed of sound). The Vienna Circle formulated the verifiability principle as a yardstick for judging whether things are meaningful. Mathematical propositions (eg, $2 + 2 = 4$) are meaningful in that they are tautological and cannot be contradicted. Science is meaningful in that its formulations are answerable and empirically verifiable. However, metaphysical questions (eg, Is there a God?) are meaningless because they cannot be verified. Many members of the Vienna Circle emigrated when the Nazis arrived in 1938. The movement remained influential, though it lost some of its appeal when philosophers couldn't agree whether the verifiability principle itself should be subject to empirical verification.

Sir Karl Popper (1902–94) was loosely connected with the Vienna Circle, but mainly in a critical capacity. He was born in Vienna and lived and worked there until he too emigrated rather than face the Nazis. He had an impact on the way the nature of scientific inquiry was understood. Popper stated that the hallmark of science is based on falsifiability rather than verifiability, which was bad news for the credibility of the logical positivists and their verifiability principle. He pointed out that general scientific laws could never be logically proved to apply all the time, they could only be disproved if and when contrary data became manifest. Scientific laws are therefore accepted until they are seen to require revision (as in the way that Newtonian physics was refined by Einstein), thus leading to the advancement of scientific endeavour. Popper was also known for his work in the field of social and political philosophy.

Ludwig Wittgenstein (1889–1951) made a significant impact with his philosophical writings, not least on the Vienna Circle. He was born in Vienna and died in Cambridge, England, where he spent the latter part of his career as a research fellow at the university. Much of his output was concerned with the scope and limitations of language. His *Tractatus* was an adamant treatise ordered as a series of logical statements. By analysing language using language he ended up in the paradoxical situation of having to say (using language) what he admitted could only be shown using analysis external to language. Nevertheless, Wittgenstein was so convinced that this work had achieved all that it was possible for such a text to do, that he believed it effectively heralded an end to philosophical enquiry. He retreated to the obscurity of a teaching post in rural Austria but later came out of retirement and proceeded to all but contradict his earlier work. His new theories were less rigid and attempted to illuminate the inventiveness of language. Wittgenstein has been hailed as one of the most influential 20th-century philosophers, yet in his personal life he cut a rather lonely figure. One of his great fears was that his writings would be destroyed by fire (only the *Tractatus* was published in his lifetime), and he obsessively stored these in a fireproof safe.

Dr Sigmund Freud (1856–1939), the founder of psychoanalysis, had a love-hate relationship with Vienna, the city where he lived and worked for most of his life (except that in 1938, shortly before he died, he, too,

Sigmund Freud

Sigmund Freud was born in Freiberg, Moravia, on 6 May 1856. Three years later his father, a Jewish wool merchant, relocated the family to the Leopoldstadt district in Vienna. Freud was educated in Vienna and graduated as a Doctor of Medicine in 1881 (his degree took three years longer to complete than was usual, as he spent much of his time engaged in neurological research that wasn't part of the curriculum). In 1886 he set up his first office as a neurologist at 01, Rathausstrasse 7, and later that year married Martha Bernays, who went on to bear him six children. In 1891 he moved his practice to 09, Berggasse 19. He first came up with the term 'psychoanalysis' in 1896.

Although many academics and physicians were hostile towards his published works, Freud was able to gather around him a core of pupils and followers who would meet in his waiting room on Wednesday evenings. Among their number was the Swiss psychologist Carl Jung, who in 1914 severed his links with the group because of personal differences with Freud. In 1923 Freud was diagnosed as having cancer of the palate, an affliction that caused him great pain and forced him to undergo surgery over 30 times. The illness prompted him to largely withdraw from public life; his daughter, Anna (a child psychiatrist), often appeared in his stead at meetings and conventions.

The arrival of the Nazis in 1938 instigated a mass evacuation by many of Vienna's Jews. Freud was allowed to emigrate to London on 4 June, accompanied by Anna. The rest of his children also managed to escape, but other family members weren't so fortunate – four of his elderly sisters were detained in the city, and eventually killed in a concentration camp in 1941. Freud breathed his last breath in London on 23 September 1939.

NC

---

fled the Nazis). Freud's theories were based on his belief that the repression of infantile sexuality was the cause of neurosis in adult life. Central to his treatments was getting the patient to recognise unconscious conflicts. Early on he employed hypnosis to uncover these conflicts, but later abandoned hypnosis in favour of free association and the study of symbolism in dreams. *The Interpretation of Dreams* (1900) was his first major work.

His final psychoanalytical work was *The Ego and the Id* (1923), advancing a new theory in which the tensions between the id (basic urges), the ego (the conscious personality) and the superego (idealised ingrained precepts) were explored. Although Freud's views have always been attacked, his legacy remains enormous. A mental landscape of Oedipus complexes, phallic objects and Freudian slips are a few of these manifestations. Generations of patients supine on couches is another.

ARTS

For a rundown on the country's unrivalled musical heritage, see the 'Austria & Music' special section.

Literature

The outstanding Austrian work produced in the the Middle Ages was the *Nibelungenlied* (Song of the Nibelungs), written around 1200 by an unknown hand. This epic poem told a tale of passion, faithfulness and revenge in the Burgundian court at Worms. Its themes were adapted by Richard Wagner in his *The Ring of the Nibelungen* operatic series.

The first great literary figure in the modern era was the playwright Franz Grillparzer (1791–1872). He even anticipated Freudian themes in his plays, which are still performed at the Burgtheater in Vienna.

[Continued on page 32]

MERRICKVILLE PUBLIC LIBRARY

Austria & Music

JOHANN STRAUSS

AUSTRIA & MUSIC

Above all other artistic pursuits, Austria is known for music, especially classical music. As early as the 12th century, Vienna was known for its troubadours *(Minnesänger)* and strolling musicians. In 1498 Maximilian I relocated the court orchestra from Innsbruck to Vienna.

Composers throughout Europe were drawn to Austria, and especially Vienna, in the 18th and 19th centuries by the willingness of the Habsburgs to patronise this medium. In fact many of the royal family were themselves gifted musicians – Leopold I was a composer, and Charles VI (violin), Maria Theresa (double bass) and Joseph II (harpsichord and cello) were all players. The various forms of classical music – symphony, concerto, sonata, opera and operetta – were explored and developed by the most eminent exponents of the day.

The Austrian love affair with music has by no means waned since then. After WWI and WWII, when people were starving due to a lack of resources, money was still put aside to keep up performances at the Staatsoper (State Opera). In the 21st century, Austria's music festivals are among the most important in the classical music calendar; they include the Salzburg Festival and the Bregenz Festival.

Christoph Willibald von Gluck

Opera originated in Italy around 1600. The genre was reformed by Christoph Willibald von Gluck (1714–87) who settled in Vienna in 1751. He married the operatic music to a more dramatic format (as in *Orpheus & Eurydice* and *Alceste*). His work paved the way for the next generation of composers.

Josef Haydn

Josef Haydn (1732–1809) was the dominant musical figure of the 18th century. He has been credited with ushering in the classicist era – but not without enduring many years of struggle.

Born in Rohrau, Lower Austria, his musical career began at age six, when he left home to live with a cousin, who was a choirmaster, in nearby Hainburg. At age eight he became a chorister at Stephansdom in Vienna, where he remained until age 17 when his voice broke. At this point he was flung out of the choir and was left to eke out a living as a freelance musician. Uneducated in musical theory, he studied intensely (especially works by Bach) in order to develop his own skills as a composer. He finally achieved a degree of financial security in 1761 with his appointment as Kapellmeister (music director) to the Esterházys in Eisenstadt, Burgenland.

Title page: The golden Johann Strauss Memorial statue under the arch in the Stadt Park, Vienna (Photo: John Sharp)

Haydn married Maria Anna Keller in 1760, but the childless union was not a happy one – Haydn's true love was Theresa Keller (Maria's sister), but she went into a convent. Maria had no love of music: her disregard reputedly prompted her to line pastry pans with Haydn's manuscripts. During his lifetime Haydn composed 19 operas and operettas, 107 symphonies, 68 string quartets, 62 piano sonatas and 43 piano trios. Highly acclaimed works include the oratorios *The Creation* (1798) and *The Seasons* (1801) and the *Symphony No 102 in B-flat Major*.

NC

Wolfgang Amadeus Mozart

Mozart (1756–91) is perhaps the best-known classical music virtuoso of all time. Praise for his music came from many quarters – Haydn believed him to be the 'greatest composer' and Schubert effused that the 'magic of Mozart's music lights the darkness of our lives'.

Mozart was only 35 when he died, yet he had composed some 626 pieces: 24 operas, 49 symphonies, over 40 concertos, 26 string quartets, seven string quintets and numerous sonatas for piano and violin. He took opera to new heights, achieving a fusion of Germanic and Italianate styles (his librettos were first in Italian and later, innovatively, in German). Pundits consider Mozart's greatest Italian operas to be *The Marriage of Figaro* (1786), *Don Giovanni* (1787) and *Così fan Tutte* (1790); in each case the librettist was Italian writer Lorenzo da Ponte. Mozart's *The Magic Flute* (1791) was a direct precursor of the German opera of the 19th century.

Mozart was born in Salzburg (one of seven children) and started his career at a young age. His musician father, Leopold, taught him to play the harpsichord at age three. Two years later, Leopold gave his son a small violin, but without musical instruction. A few days afterwards, young Mozart asked a quartet if he could join in. The musicians laughingly agreed, but were amazed when the prodigy played his part perfectly. One went as far as to call it witchcraft. Mozart senior was quick to exploit his son's astounding talent. Along with Wolfgang's sister Nannerl (four years older and also exceptionally gifted), they toured Europe, giving recitals and receiving plaudits wherever they went. Wolfgang spent one-third of his short life on the road.

At the age of six, Wolfgang performed for Empress Maria Theresa at Schönbrunn. By the time he was eight he had toured London, Paris, Rome, Geneva, Frankfurt and The Hague. Four of his sonatas were published before he turned nine, and he could write down complex

Above Right: Josef Haydn

pieces after just one hearing. In 1770, though only 14 years old, Mozart was appointed director of the archbishop of Salzburg's orchestra but departed for Paris in 1777 after an argument with his employer. In 1781 he settled in Vienna. Here Mozart had his most productive years, his music encompassing light-hearted and joyous themes, dramatic emotions and melancholic gloom. He succeeded Gluck as court composer (albeit at less than half of the former's salary!) in 1787.

NC

Although always musically prolific, Mozart was a compulsive gambler and lost large sums of money at billiards, ninepins and cards. He was also something of a ladies' man – at age 24 he proclaimed, 'If I had married everyone I jested with, I would have well over 200 wives'. On 4 August 1782 in Stephansdom he married Constanze Weber, the younger sister of a former girlfriend. He died 5 December 1791, reputedly from typhoid fever.

Mozart was dispatched to the earth on a rainy December day after a meagrely attended and frugal funeral. His body was wrapped in a sack and doused with lime (in accordance with an imperial decree to prevent epidemics) before being buried in a ditch in St Marxer Friedhof (Cemetery of St Mark) in Vienna.

The film *Amadeus* (1985), by Milos Forman and Peter Shaffer, portrayed Mozart as infuriating, enthusiastic, volatile, emotionally immature and effortlessly gifted, an interpretation perhaps not far removed from the truth (though Mozart once announced that nobody had worked harder than himself at studying musical composition).

Ludwig van Beethoven

Beethoven (1770–1827) was born in Bonn, Germany, to a family steeped in musical tradition. However, he was no child prodigy, and it was not until he was in his teens that he began to show signs of genius. Beethoven was sent to Vienna to study with Mozart in 1787, and impressed the maestro with his ability to improvise.

After returning to Bonn following the death of his mother, Beethoven again moved to Vienna, at the age of 21, to study under Haydn. Though he was already a virtuoso pianist, he had much to learn as a composer, and he also studied vocal composition with Antonio Salieri, the imperial Kapellmeister. When Beethoven threatened to leave Vienna after a quarrel with other musicians, several nobles offered him an annuity of 4000 florins, on the condition that he remained in the city to write music. Consequently he stayed in Vienna up to the time of his death, living at as many as 60 addresses.

Above Left: Wolfgang Amadeus Mozart

Beethoven began to lose his hearing at the age of 30, understandably a cause of deep depression to him. In the early stages of the affliction he developed and demonstrated his ability at musical improvisation. As total deafness approached, Beethoven withdrew from the public performances that helped make him so popular. He produced fewer pieces, yet many consider his final 10 years to have been his best period. Dating from this time is the *Ninth Symphony* (concluding with the majestic *Ode to Joy*), one of his greatest and most influential works.

NC

Beethoven was greatly inspired by the Viennese countryside (an influence evident in the *Pastoral Symphony* of 1808, among others). In addition to the numerous symphonies, concertos, string quartets, piano sonatas, masses and overtures created by Beethoven, he wrote just one opera – *Fidelio* (1814).

Beethoven never married, but appears (from letters) to have contemplated it at least three times, and throughout his life he was a great success with the ladies, despite his often dishevelled appearance. He died from cirrhosis of the liver aged 57, and more than 20,000 people attended his funeral.

Franz Schubert

Schubert (1797–1828) was the last in the great line of composers from the Viennese School's Classical period (1740–1825). A native of Vienna, he was responsible for giving the ancient German *Lieder* (lyrical song) tradition a new lease of life, creating a craze for what became known as 'Schubertiade' musical evenings. His musical ability and output is quite staggering: nine symphonies, 11 overtures, seven masses, over 80 smaller choral works, over 30 chamber music works, 450 piano works and over 600 Lieder – more than 960 works in total! All this before he died at the age of just 31 (of syphilis), 18 months after his hero Beethoven.

He was one of 12 children born to an impoverished school master. After a spell in the Vienna Boys' Choir, Schubert had a brief career as a teacher himself before settling on

Above Right: Ludwig van Beethoven

Below Right: Franz Schubert

NC

his true vocation. Unfortunately, his musical genius was not fully recognised during his lifetime – he lived most of his life hand-to-mouth, surviving from the occasional musical tour and the generosity of friends and supporters. Probably Schubert's most famous piece, his *'Unfinished' Symphony*, was written in 1822 when he was only 25. Like almost all of his works, it was first performed after his death. He never married, and lived something of a reclusive existence.

The Strausses & the Waltz

The waltz originated in Vienna at the beginning of the 19th century and went down a storm at the Congress of Vienna. The early masters of this genre were Johann Strauss the Elder (1804–49), who also composed the *Radetzky March*, and Josef Lanner (1801–43). Both toured Europe, bringing the genre to wide prominence.

The man who really made this form his own was Johann Strauss the Younger (1825–99), composer of 400 waltzes. Young Strauss became a musician against the wishes of Strauss senior (who had experienced years of struggle) and set up a rival orchestra to his father's. He composed Austria's unofficial anthem, the *Blue Danube* (1867), and *Tales from the Vienna Woods* (1868).

This joyful if lightweight style became so popular that more 'serious' composers began to feel somewhat disenfranchised. The operetta form became equally fashionable. The younger Strauss proved also to be a master of this style, especially with his eternally popular *Die Fledermaus* (1874) and *The Gipsy Baron* (1885). Strauss was very adept at marketing himself and his music, and was feted both at home and abroad.

Other 19th-Century Composers

Anton Bruckner (1824–96) was raised in Upper Austria and was long associated with the abbey in St Florian. He settled in Vienna on his appointment as organist to the court in 1868. Bruckner is known for dramatically intense symphonies and church music.

In the late 19th century Austria was still attracting musicians and composers from elsewhere in Europe.

Johannes Brahms (1833–97) hailed from Hamburg, and spent 35 years in the Austrian capital. He greatly enjoyed Vienna's village atmosphere and said it had a positive effect on his work, which was of the classical-Romantic tradition.

Hugo Wolf (1860–1903) rivalled Schubert in lieder composition, and had spells of intense creativity. Born in what is now Slovenia, he moved to Vienna when he was 15 and died at the age of 43 in a Viennese lunatic asylum.

Gustav Mahler (1860–1911), also from Germany, is known mainly for his nine symphonies, and was director of the Vienna Court Opera from 1897 to 1907.

Richard Strauss (1864–1949), from Munich, favoured Salzburg above Vienna, though he did have a spell as the conductor and director of the Staatsoper.

Franz Lehár (1870–1948), originally from Hungary, was a notable operetta composer, renowned for *Die lustige Witwe* (The Merry Widow).

The Second Viennese School

Vienna's musical eminence continued in the 20th century with the innovative work of **Arnold Schönberg** (1874–1951), who founded what has been dubbed the 'New School' of Vienna. Schönberg developed theories on 12 tone composition, yet some of his earlier work (such as *Pieces for the Piano op. 11* composed in 1909) went completely beyond the bounds of tonality. Though a key figure for musical theorists, Schönberg's music was never too popular with the public at large, and many Viennese would not thank you to remind them that of all the great composers associated with their city, only Schönberg and Schubert were actually born there. Schönberg was also a competent artist.

The most influential of his pupils were **Alban Berg** (1885–1935) and **Anton von Webern** (1883–1945), who both explored the 12 tone technique, and were also born in Vienna.

Music Today

The wine taverns *(Heurigen)* in Vienna have a musical tradition all their own, with the songs often expressing very maudlin themes. Known as *Schrammelmusik*, it is usually played by musicians wielding a combination of violin, accordion, guitar and clarinet. In the Alpine regions, *Volksmusik* (folk music), based on traditional tunes, is popular.

In the field of rock and pop Austria has made little international impact (unless you count the briefly emergent Falco, who died in a car crash in 1998), though both Vienna and Graz have a thriving jazz scene, and Vienna was home to Joe Zawinul of Weather Report.

Today, Austrian orchestras, such as the Vienna Philharmonic, have a worldwide reputation, and institutions such as the Vienna Boys' Choir, the Staatsoper, the Musikverein and the Konzerthaus are unrivalled. Salzburg and Graz are also major music centres and like Vienna, they host important annual music festivals. Linz has the international Bruckner Festival, Schwarzenberg in Vorarlberg its Schubertiade (Schubert Festival), and Innsbruck its Early Music concerts. The Bregenz Festival is famous for productions performed on a floating stage on Bodensee. A visit to some sort of musical event is an essential part of any trip to Austria.

[Continued from page 24]

Other influential playwrights whose works still regularly get an airing are Johann Nestroy (1801–62), known for his satirical farces, and Ferdinand Raimaund, the 19th-century author of *Der Alpenkönig und der Menschenfeind* (The King of the Alps and the Misanthrope). Adalbert Stifter (1805–68) is credited as being the seminal influence in the development of an Austrian prose style.

Austria's literary tradition really took off around the turn of the century, when the Vienna Secessionists and Sigmund Freud were creating waves. Influential writers who emerged at this time included Arthur Schnitzler, Hugo von Hofmannsthal, Karl Kraus and the poet Georg Trakl. Kraus' apocalyptic drama *Die letzten Tage der Menschheit* (The Last Days of Mankind) employed a combination of reports, interviews and press extracts to tell its tale – a very innovative style for its time. Kraus (1874–1936) had previously founded *Die Fackel* (The Torch), a critical literary periodical. The poet Peter Altenberg produced a body of work depicting the bohemian lifestyle of Vienna.

Robert Musil was a major 20th-century writer, but he only achieved international recognition after his death. He was born in Klagenfurt in 1880 and died in poverty in Geneva in 1942, with his great literary achievement, *Der Mann ohne Eigenschaften* (The Man Without Qualities), still unfinished. Nevertheless, enough of this work was completed for it to fill three volumes (English translation available) and reveal a fascinating portrait of the collapsing Austro-Hungarian monarchy.

Another important figure in the 20th century was Heimito von Doderer (1896–1966). He grew up in Vienna and first achieved recognition with his novel *Die Strudlhofstiege* (The Strudlhof Staircase). His magnum opus was *Die Dämonen* (The Demons), an epic fictional depiction of the end of the monarchy and the first years of the Austrian Republic. It looks at all strata of society and is published in English in three volumes.

The Vienna Group (Wiener Gruppe) was formed in the 1950s by HC Artmann. Its members incorporated surrealism and Dadaism in their sound compositions, textual montages, and Actionist happenings. (See also the boxed text 'Art through Action' in this chapter.) Public outrage and police intervention were a regular accompaniment to their meetings. The group's activities came to an end in 1964 when Konrad Bayer, its most influential member, committed suicide.

Thomas Bernhard (1931–89) was born in Holland but grew up and lived in Austria. He was obsessed with negative themes such as disintegration and death but in later works, such as *Cutting Timber*, he turned to polemic attacks against social conventions and institutions. His novels are seamless (no chapters or paragraphs, few full stops) and seemingly repetitive, but surprisingly readable once you get into them. He also wrote plays and short stories. Bernhard was influenced by Ludwig Wittgenstein's writings, and even wrote an autobiographical novel about his friendship with the philosopher's nephew. Both *Cutting Timber* and *Wittgenstein's Nephew* are published in English translations.

Austria's best-known living writer is perhaps Peter Handke (1942–). His output encompasses innovative and introspective prose works *(The Left-Handed Woman)* and stylistic plays *(The Hour When We Knew Nothing of Each Other)*.

Contemporary female writers include the provocative novelist Elfriede Jelinek (1946–), who dispenses with direct speech and indulges in strange flights of fancy, but is worth persevering with. Translations of her novels *The Piano Teacher; Lust; Wonderful, Wonderful Times* and *Women as Lovers* have been successfully published in paperback. Friederike Mayröcker, a prominent contemporary poet and author of *Phantom Fan* and *Farewells*, has been described as 'the avant-garde's bird of paradise'.

Painting

Examples of Gothic church art in Austria are best seen in the Middle Ages collection at the Orangery in Vienna's Unteres Belvedere. Early Renaissance art is represented in Austria by the Danube School, which combined landscapes and religious motifs; a few of the

Art through Action

Viennese Actionism spanned the years 1957–68 and was one of the most extreme of all modern art movements. It was linked to the Vienna Group (Wiener Gruppe) and had its roots in abstract expressionism. Actionism sought access to the unconscious through the frenzy of an extreme and very direct art: the Actionists quickly moved from pouring paint over the canvas, which was then slashed with knives, to using bodies (live people, dead animals) as 'brushes', and using blood, excrement, eggs, mud and whatever else came to hand as 'paint'. The traditional canvas was soon dispensed with altogether. The artist's body became the canvas, the site of art became a deliberated event (the scripted action, staged both privately and publicly) and even merged with reality.

It was a short step from self-painting to inflicting wounds upon the body, and engaging in physical and psychological endurance tests. For 10 years the Actionists scandalised the press and public and incited violence and panic – and got plenty of publicity. Often poetic, humorous and aggressive, the actions became increasingly politicised, addressing the sexual and social repression that pervaded the Austrian state. Art in Revolution (1968), the last Action to be realised in Vienna, resulted in six months hard labour all round.

Ed Baxter

notable exponents were Rueland Frueauf the Younger, Wolf Huber, Max Reichlich and Lukas Cranach.

Johann Michael Rottmayr and Daniel Gran were baroque artists from the early 18th century, responsible for many baroque church frescoes. Almost as well known as their contemporary, Paul Troger (1698–1762), who was particularly active in Lower Austria. Franz Anton Maulbertsch was an important canvas painter, who combined mastery of colour and light with intensity of expression.

The leading Biedermeier painters were Georg Ferdinand Waldmüller (1793–1865) and Friedrich Gauermann (1807–62), who captured the age in portraits, landscapes and period scenes. Some of Waldmüller's evocative if idealised peasant scenes can be seen in the Historisches Museum der Stadt Wien and the Oberes Belvedere, both in Vienna. Rudolf von Alt was an exponent of watercolour. Another Biedermeier artist was Moritz Michael Daffinger.

Prominent painters of the historicist period included August von Pettenkofen and Hans Makart (1840–84). Artist Anton Romako (1832–89) anticipated the age of expressionism in his work.

Egon Schiele (1890–1918) and Oskar Kokoschka (1886–1980) were important exponents of Viennese expressionism. The work of these Austrian painters is best viewed in the Oberes Belvedere; the Egon Schiele museum in Tulln, Lower Austria, is also worth a visit.

Gustav Klimt is possibly the most famous Austrian painter. For details of his life, see the boxed text 'Gustav Klimt' in the Vienna chapter.

Architecture

Little is known of pre-Romanesque architecture in Austria, although significant Roman ruins (built between the 1st and 5th centuries AD) can be seen at sites such as Petronell and Magdalensberg. The latter site is particularly interesting as features of pre-Roman Celtic culture can be seen in the remains of the Romano-Celtic town.

Romanesque The Romanesque style in Austria was almost entirely religous in nature and flourished along with the Babenberg dynasty between 976 and 1246. This period saw cathedrals and abbeys constructed throughout the country. The exteriors of Romanesque churches are characterised by thick walls, closely spaced columns and heavy, rounded arches, as well as the use of statues and reliefs on the portals and apses. This use of sculpture was continued inside the buildings in representations of the Crucifixion and the lives of saints.

Romanesque buildings have generally been extended and modified using later architectural styles. One of the purest examples of the Romanesque style is the Gurk Dom (cathedral) in Carinthia. It has not only retained its Romanesque shape, but also has fine Romanesque sculptures and frescoes. Schloss Porcia in Spittal an der Drau is also Romanesque in style.

Gothic This style was popular from the 13th to 16th centuries, originating in France and reaching Austria as the Habsburg dynasty came to power. It was made possible by engineering advances that permitted thinner walls and (in churches) taller, more delicate columns and great expanses of stained glass. Distinctive features include pointed arches and ribbed ceiling vaults, external flying buttresses to support the walls, and elaborately carved doorway columns.

In the 15th century, Austria was the site of some of the grandest architectural experimentation, and the use of stained glass windows enhanced some of the finest sacred buildings ever constructed. The most impressive Gothic structure in Austria is Vienna's Stephansdom. Its three naves of equal height are typical of the Gothic style in Austria. Secular Gothic buildings include the Goldenes Dachl in Innsbruck, the Kornmesserhaus in Bruck an der Mur and the Brummerlhaus in Steyr.

Renaissance The 16th century saw a new enthusiasm for classical forms and an obsession with grace and symmetry. As the Habsburg empire emerged as a major power, the nobility and increasingly prosperous middle class had palaces, mansions and

houses built by Italian architects, who combined Italian and Austrian influences. Generally, though, Renaissance architecture had little impact in Austria except in Salzburg.

One of the hallmarks of the era was the arcade courtyard, and a supreme example of this can be seen at Schloss Schallaburg in Lower Austria. Another typically Renaissance device was the creation of sgraffito facades, in which two layers of different colours are applied and a design scratched in the top layer revealing the colour of the layer beneath. Gmünd in Carinthia has houses displaying this technique.

Baroque This resplendent, triumphal style is closely associated with the rebuilding (and the reimposition of Catholicism) in Austria after the Thirty Years' War. The emperor, the nobility and the church were all responsible for the profusion of buildings in this style, which featured marble columns, emotive sculpture and painting, and rich, gilded ornamentation; it added up to extravagant and awe-inspiring interiors.

Learning from the Italian model, Graz-born architect Johann Bernhard Fischer von Erlach (1656–1723) developed a national style called Austrian baroque. This mirrored the exuberant ornamentation of Italian baroque but gave it a specifically Austrian treatment through dynamic combinations of colour coupled with irregular or undulating outlines.

Among the many outstanding examples of baroque in Austria are Fischer von Erlach's Kollegienkirche in Salzburg and his Karlskirche in Vienna, Johann Lukas von Hildebrandt's Schloss Belvedere, also in Vienna, and Stift Melk in Lower Austria by Jakob Prandtauer (1660–1726).

Rococo In Austria, this style was the product of a combination of Italian baroque and French rococo. Although spectacular, it is essentially late, over-the-top baroque; florid, elaborate and 'lightweight'.

Rococo became popular with architects in the late 18th century and was a great favourite of the empress Maria Theresa. She chose this fussy style for most of the rooms of Schloss Schönbrunn when she commissioned Nicolas Pacassi to renovate it in 1744. Austrian rococo is sometimes referred to as late-baroque Theresien style.

Historicism The revival of old architectural styles became popular after the 1848 revolution. Neoclassicism favoured grand colonnades and pediments, and often huge and simple symmetrical buildings. The Technical University in Vienna is a good example of this.

In the second half of the 19th century, historicism took hold. This is seen principally in Vienna's Ringstrasse developments on the site of the old city walls instigated by Franz Josef I's imperial decree of 1857. The Ringstrasse demonstrates a great diversity of retrograde styles, including French Gothic (Votivkirche), Flemish Gothic (Rathaus), Grecian (Parlament), French Renaissance (Staatsoper) and Florentine Renaissance (Museum für angewandte Kunst).

Modern The end of the 19th century saw the emergence of Art Nouveau (Jugendstil), a sensuous and decorative style of art and architecture that spread through much of Europe. In Vienna the style flowered with the founding of the Secession movement in 1897. Otto Wagner (1841–1918), designer of the Postsparkasse (Post Office Savings Bank) and the Kirche am Steinhof, was one of the leading architects in the field. In the early 20th century, Wagner led the movement towards a style in which the more sinuous and decorative features of Art Nouveau became subservient to functional considerations both in design and building materials. Adolf Loos (1870–1933) was even more important in moving towards a new functionalism. He was a bitter critic of the Ringstrasse buildings, yet also became quickly disillusioned with the ornamentation in Secessionist buildings.

The dominance of the Social Democrats in the Vienna city government of the new republic (from 1918) gave rise to a number of municipal building projects, not least the massive Karl-Marx-Hof apartment complex. Postwar architecture was mostly utilitarian. More recently, some multicoloured, haphazard-looking structures that some may see as downright strange have been erected in Vienna; they're the work of the maverick artist and architect Friedensreich Hundertwasser (see the boxed text 'Peace Empire and a Hundred Waters' in the Vienna chapter). Austria's premier postmodern architect is Hans Hollein, designer of the Haas Haus in Vienna.

Sculpture & Design

The development of sculpture has reflected the changes in architectural styles over the years. The *Verdun Altar* in Klosterneuburg abbey in Lower Austria dates from the Romanesque period. Austria has some beautiful Gothic altars carved using limewood: the best known can be seen in St Wolfgang, and was the work of Michael Pacher (1440–98) – see the boxed text 'Pacher's Religious Art' in the Salzkammergut chapter.

The best Renaissance sculpture is the tomb of Maximilian in Innsbruck's Hofkirche. The same church has impressive statues in bronze, including several by that master of all trades, Albrecht Dürer (1471–1528).

The fountain by George Raphael Donner in Vienna's Neuer Markt, and Balthasar Permoser's statue of Prince Eugene in the Unteres Belvedere are fine examples of baroque sculpture. Baroque even extended to funeral caskets, as created by Balthasar Moll for Maria Theresa and Francis I. All of these are in Vienna, but the baroque style is evident throughout the country.

Neoclassical sculpture is typified by the equestrian statue of Emperor Joseph II in Josefsplatz in Vienna's Hofburg. Salzburg has several distinctive equine fountains in its old town centre.

The Biedermeier period was strongly represented in furniture, examples of which can be seen in Vienna's Museum für angewandte Kunst (Museum of Applied Art). After Biedermeier, the technique of bending wood in furniture, particularly in the backs of chairs, became popular. The bentwood chair has since became known as the Viennese chair.

In 1903, the Vienna Workshops (Wiener Werkstätte) were founded. The artisans who were involved created a range of high-quality, if expensive, household products, as well as garments and jewellery. Aesthetic considerations were given priority over practicality, resulting in some highly distinctive styles, such as Josef Hoffmann's silver tea service (displayed in the Museum für angewandte Kunst). Another key figure involved in the Wiener Werkstätte was Hoffman's co-founder, Kolo Moser (1868–1918).

Cinema

Austrian endeavours in the film industry go mostly unnoticed outside the German-speaking world, with a few exceptions. The director Fritz Lang (1890–1976) was responsible for the innovative science fiction silent film *Metropolis* (1926), and *M* (1931) starring Peter Lorre. Fred Zinnemann *(From Here to Eternity* and *High Noon)* was Austrian born, as was Billy Wilder (*Some Like it Hot*, 1959). Klaus Maria Brandauer is a well-known actor (star of the 1980 film *Mephisto*, among others), as are Romy Schneider, Maximilian Schell and Hedy Lamarr. And of course there's former Mr Universe, Arnold Schwarzenegger, whose bulk fills the screen in a range of Hollywood blockbusters, particularly action epics such as *The Terminator* series.

Theatre

Vienna's tradition in the theatre was – and still is – bolstered by the quality of operas and operettas produced in the golden age of music. In addition to these forms, Greek drama, avant-garde, mime, comedy, farce and other theatrical genres are regularly performed. Vienna is home to the four federal theatres and opera houses – the Staatsoper, Volksoper, Akademietheater and Burgtheater. The Burgtheater is one of the premier theatre and opera venues in the German-speaking world. There are major theatres in all of the provincial capital cities.

SOCIETY & CONDUCT
Traditional Culture

The people in alpine areas often live up to the Austrian stereotype. Women can still be seen in the Dirndl, a full, pleated skirt with tight bodice, worn with traditional apron, bonnet, and blouse with short, puffed sleeves. The men, meanwhile, are anything but self-conscious in collarless loden jackets, green hats, wide braces and shorts or knee breeches. Although such clothes are worn on a daily basis in some out-of-the-way places, as a tourist you're more likely to see them during celebrations and processions.

In early summer, hardy herders climb to alpine pastures with their cattle and live in summer huts while tending their herds. They gradually descend to village level as the grassland is grazed. Both the departure and the return is a cause for celebration and processions. The cattle wear heavy bells and decorated headdresses.

Rural ritual retains a foothold in the consciousness of alpine village folk, and finds exuberant expression in the many festivals scattered through the year. These often act out ancient traditions, such as welcoming the spring with painted masks and the ringing of bells. Yodelling and playing the alphorn are also part of the tradition. Alpine wrestling, where the object is to pin both your opponent's shoulders to the ground at the same time, is another festival event.

Dos & Don'ts

It is customary to greet people with the salutation *Grüss Gott* or *Servus* and to say *Auf Wiedersehen* or *Auf Wiederschauen* when departing. This applies to shop assistants, cafe staff and the like. Not greeting someone will be taken as a personal affront. When being introduced to someone it is usual to shake hands, likewise when you take your leave. This applies even in younger, informal company.

At a meal, Austrians dining together normally raise their glasses and say *Prost* before taking their first sip of wine; look people in the eye while you're doing it – some may consider you insincere otherwise. Similarly, there will be a signal before people start to eat, such as the exchange of a *Guten Appetit* or *Mahlzeit*.

Some older Viennese still cling to the language and etiquette of the old empire, known as *Kaiserdeutsch* or *Schönbrunndeutsch*. This can be seen as pompous or charming depending upon your point of view; it may manifest itself at introductions, with men addressing women as *Gnädige Frau* (gracious lady) and formally adding *Küss die Hand* ('I kiss your hand'), perhaps backing this up by actually performing the act or clicking the heels together. People often address each other using full formal titles (*Herr* for men and *Frau* for women).

You'll see conservative behaviour exhibited in various other ways too, such as in the rigid respect for the 'don't walk' red figure on traffic lights; even if there's no traffic anywhere in sight, people will obediently wait for the lights to change (in theory you could be fined around €8 if the police spot you jaywalking).

Men would be advised to wear a jacket and tie when dining in some of the top restaurants mentioned in this book. Austrians tend to dress up when going to the opera or theatre, and they'd probably appreciate it if you made a similar effort.

On the beach, nude bathing is usually limited to restricted areas (look for a sign saying FKK), but topless bathing is common in many parts. Women should be wary of taking their tops off as a matter of course. The rule is, if nobody else seems to be doing it, don't. It is no problem for men to wear shorts away from the beach.

RELIGION

Religion plays an important part in the lives of many Austrians. In the countryside you'll often see small roadside shrines decorated with fresh flowers. Freedom of religion is guaranteed under the constitution. Even the religious rights of children are protected: up to age 10 their religious affiliation is in the hands of parents, yet from age 10 to 12 the child must be consulted about their preferred religion, and from age 12 to 14 a change of religion cannot be imposed upon any child. Upon reaching 14, children have full independence to choose their own faith.

The national census of 1991 revealed that 78% of the population is Roman Catholic, 5% Protestant and 9% non-denominational. Nearly 5% of Austrians belong to other religious groups and the rest of the population declined to reveal their affiliation. The majority of Austria's Protestants live in Burgenland and Carinthia.

LANGUAGE

The national language of Austria is German, though for a small country there are a surprising number of regional accents and dialects. This is due in part to the isolating influence of high mountain ranges, causing language to evolve differently in different communities. Austrians will probably tell you that they have difficulty understanding the accents of compatriots from other regions; indeed, the dialect spoken in Vorarlberg is much closer to Schwyzertütsch (Swiss-German, a language all but incomprehensible to most non-Swiss people) than it is to the standard Hochdeutsch (High German) dialect.

In some areas of the country, a significant minority may have a different first language to German. In Burgenland about 25,000 people speak Croatian, and in Carinthia about 20,000 people speak Slovene.

Fortunately for visitors, Austrians can switch from their own dialect to High German when necessary, and many speak some English. Young people are usually quite fluent in English. As might be expected, English is more widely spoken in cities and tourist areas than in out-of-the-way rural districts. Staff at tourist and train information offices almost invariably speak English; hotel receptionists and restaurant waiters usually do as well, especially in the more up-market establishments. As with any countries you visit, an attempt to communicate with the people in their native tongue will be appreciated, so some knowledge of German will definitely be an asset. (For some helpful phrases and vocabulary, see the Language chapter later in this book.)

Facts for the Visitor

SUGGESTED ITINERARIES

Depending on how long you have in Austria, try one of these trips:

One week
Spend four days in Vienna, two days in Salzburg and one day visiting the Salzkammergut lakes.

Two weeks
Spend five days in Vienna, three days in Salzburg (with a day trip to the Werfen ice caves and fortress), two days at the Salzkammergut lakes, two days in Innsbruck and two days at a Tirolean Alpine resort, say St Anton or Kitzbühel.

One month
Visit the same places as in the two week scenario but at a more leisurely pace; think about including a Danube cruise. After Tirol add a tour of the south, taking in Lienz, Klagenfurt and Graz.

Two months
Expand the one month itinerary by spending time at Bregenz before heading to the south. While in the south, explore Carinthia's lakes and Styria's wine trails.

PLANNING
When to Go

Summer sightseeing and winter sports make Austria a year-round destination. When to go depends on what you want to do or see. See the 'Festivals of Austria' boxed text and the Public Holidays & Special Events section later in this chapter for seasonal events, and study the climate charts in Facts about Austria to determine what the weather will be like at any particular time of year.

The summer high season is in July and August, when crowds will be bigger and prices higher. This isn't necessarily the best time to visit Austria – it can be uncomfortably hot in the cities and many famous institutions close down, among them the opera, the Spanish Riding School (Spanische Reitschule) and the Vienna Boys' Choir (Wiener Sängerknaben). Consequently, June and September are also busy months for tourism. During the winter you'll find things less crowded in the cities and the hotel prices

lower (except over Christmas and Easter), but it can get very cold. Consider visiting in spring or autumn as a good compromise.

Winter sports are in full swing from mid-December to late March, with the high season over Christmas and New Year and in February. The length of the skiing season depends on the altitude of the resort – nearly year-round skiing is possible on glaciers. Alpine resorts are very quiet from late April to mid June, and in November and early December; at these times some bars, restaurants and hotels close down. Spring in the Alps is in June, when the Alpine flowers start coating the mountains with colour.

Maps

Freytag & Berndt of Vienna has the most comprehensive coverage of the country. It publishes good town maps (1:10,000 to 1:25,000 scale) and has a *Wanderkarte* series for walkers, mostly on a 1:50,000 scale. Motorists should consider buying its *Strassen & Städte* road atlas. This covers Europe (1:350,000), Austria (1:250,000) and 29 Austrian towns. Extremely detailed walking maps are produced by the Austrian Alpine Club, on a scale of 1:25,000. Michelin maps are also of a high standard. Bikeline maps cost €5.90 and are recommended for those travelling round the country by bicycle; eight maps (1:200,000 or 1:150,000) cover the whole country.

For getting around cities, maps provided by tourist offices, in conjunction with the maps in this book, are generally adequate. These are usually free, but where there's a charge – in Salzburg, for instance – you can probably make do with the hotel map instead.

What to Bring

Pack as lightly as you can. Anything you forget to bring can be easily bought in Austria. Allow for colder weather in winter and at high altitudes (several layers of thin clothing are better than one thick one). Even if they prefer to dress informally, men

Highlights

Vienna and Salzburg are Austria's most rewarding cities, followed by Innsbruck and Graz. Be sure to spend time at a traditional coffee house and a wine tavern (*Heurigen* or *Buschenschank*). Make sure you pay a visit to the opera or some other musical event. Take in the chaos and clutter of Vienna's flea market at the Naschmarkt. Spend some time in the Alps; perhaps take a Danube River cruise. Visit the ice caves at Werfen or Dachstein. For skiing and glitz, head for Kitzbühel or Lech, or for a less elitist skiing ambience, try St Anton. For other interests, browse through the following.

Churches & Abbeys

Stephansdom, in Vienna, is *the* Gothic church in Austria. The abbeys at Melk and St Florian are perfect examples of baroque architecture. Friedensreich Hundertwasser's unusual and idiosyncratic design for the St Barbara Kirche in Bärnbach is unique. See the winged high altar in St Wolfgang's pilgrimage church, and the statues and mausoleum in Innsbruck's Hofkirche.

Museums & Galleries

The Kunsthistorisches Museum in Vienna is best for art; the Haus der Natur, Salzburg, is best for natural history. For something a little more bizarre, try the Josephinum, the medical history museum in Vienna. For ancient armaments, go to the Landeszeughaus in Graz. Baroque Austrian art can be viewed in Schloss Belvedere, Vienna.

Palaces

In Vienna, enjoy Schloss Schönbrunn for its grounds and baroque rooms, and the Hofburg for its grand scale and many museum collections. In Salzburg, see Schloss Mirabell for its gardens and Schloss Hellbrunn for its water fountains. Also visit Schloss Eggenberg in Graz and Schloss Ambras in Innsbruck.

Picturesque Views

Take in the Nordkette peaks from Innsbruck's Maria Theresien Strasse, Friesach's castles from near the town moat, Steyr at the confluence of its two rivers, Ehrenhausen's Marktplatz, and Burg Hochosterwitz with its spiralling defences. Don't miss Salzburg's domes from the Salzach, and the panorama from Festung Hohensalzburg. Also view Graz from the Schlossberg, and admire the Schlossberg and Landhaus from the Landeszeughaus.

In the Hohe Tauern National Park region, marvel at the unfolding magnificence of the Grossglockner Road and linger over the view back to Krimml from the top of Krimml Falls. Expansive mountain vistas are part of the package at all ski resorts.

The following were granted Unesco World Heritage site status in the year shown:

1996 – Salzburg Historic Centre (Salzburg province)
1996 – Palace and Gardens of Schönbrunn (Vienna)
1997 – Hallstatt-Dachstein region (Salzkammergut)
1998 – Semmering Railway (Lower Austria)
1999 – Graz Historic Centre (Styria)
2000 – Wachau region (Lower Austria)

will need proper shoes (not trainers or running shoes), smart trousers (not jeans) and a tie to get into casinos and maybe some nightclubs; this is also the accepted attire for top restaurants. Dressing smartly helps when dealing with officials such as police or customs officers.

Whether to take a suitcase or a backpack is a matter of personal choice. If you're travelling by car it doesn't really matter what you take, but a backpack is better if you plan to do a lot of walking. Unfortunately, it doesn't offer too much protection for your valuables; the straps tend to get caught on things and some airlines may refuse to be responsible if the pack is damaged or broken into. Travel-packs are a nifty combination of backpack and shoulder bag, where the backpack straps zip away inside the pack. When city sight-seeing, a small daypack is better than a shoulder bag for deterring bag snatchers.

A padlock (and chain) is useful for lock-ing your bag to a train or bus luggage rack, and may also be needed to secure a youth hostel locker. Swiss Army knives are among the most versatile pocket knives available; get one with at least a bottle opener and corkscrew.

Other items that might be useful include a compass, a flashlight (torch), an alarm clock (or watch alarm), an adapter plug for electri-cal appliances, a universal bath/sink plug (sometimes a film canister will do the job), sunglasses, clothes pegs and string (for an emergency clothesline). A few hostels charge extra for sheets so you may save money if you have your own. If you take a water bot-tle you won't have to keep buying expensive drinks when sightseeing. Consider also ac-quiring a cup water heater to make your own hot beverages. A supply of passport photos is useful for visa or travel pass applications. Condoms, tampons and sanitary pads are widely available in Austria.

Compile a packing list before you leave home, and don't forget wet-weather gear. Pack a few plastic carrier bags: they can help keep your clothes separate, clean and dry. Tag your luggage both inside and out with your name and address.

RESPONSIBLE TOURISM

As a visitor, you have a responsibility to the local people and to the environment. For guidelines on how to avoid offending the people you meet, see Society & Conduct in the Facts about Austria chapter. When it comes to the environment, the key rules are to preserve natural resources and avoid de-grading your surroundings. One way to achieve the former is to follow the local habit

of recycling; for more on this, see Ecology & Environment, also in the Facts about Austria chapter. For pointers towards the latter, see the Walking & Skiing special section for ways to do this. Traffic congestion on the roads is a major problem, and visitors will do themselves and residents a favour if they forgo driving and use public transport.

TOURIST OFFICES
Local Tourist Offices

These offices are efficient and helpful. They may be called different things in German, de-pending on the place – *Fremdenverkehrsver-band*, *Kurort*, *Verkehrsamt*, *Kurverein*, *Tourismusbüro* or *Kurverwaltung* – but they can always be identified by a white 'i' on a green background.

Any town or village that tourists are likely to visit will have a centrally situated tourist office, and at least one of the staff will speak English. Staff can answer a range of inquiries, ranging from where and when to attend religious services for different de-nominations, to where to find vegetarian food. Most offices have an accommodation-finding service, often charging no commis-sion. Maps are always available and usually free.

In addition, each province has its own tourist board, though some of these are geared more to handling written or tele-phone inquiries than dealing with personal callers. In this book their addresses are in-cluded at the beginning of each chapter. Sometimes there are regional offices that promote a designated area, such as the Salzkammergut tourist board in Bad Ischl.

Some local tourist offices hold brochures on other localities, allowing you to stock up on information in advance. If you're empty-handed and arrive somewhere too late in the day to get to the tourist office, try ask-ing at the railway ticket office, as staff there often have hotel lists or city maps. The tourist office may have a rack of brochures hung outside the door, or there may be an accommodation board you can access even when the office is closed. Top hotels usually have a supply of useful brochures in the foyer.

Tourist Offices Abroad

The Austrian National Tourist Office (ANTO) has branches in many countries. Elsewhere, its functions may be taken care of by the Austrian Trade Commission, or the commercial counsellor at the Austrian embassy. Make contact by telephone, letter or email in the first instance – some offices are not geared to receive personal callers. ANTO offices abroad include:

Australia (☎ 02-9299 3621, fax 9299 3808, e info@antosyd.org.au) 1st floor, 36 Carrington St, Sydney, NSW 2000

Canada Contact the US office (☎ 416-967 3381 is a cheaper call that forwards to the New York office)

Czech Republic Österreich Werbung (☎ 2-222 12 057, fax 222 10 256, e oewprag@dovolena -v-rakousku.cz) Box c.738, CZ-111 21 Prague 1

Germany Österreich Information (☎ 089-666 70 100, fax 666 70 200, e info@oewmuc.de) Postfach 701580, D-81315, Munich

Hungary Osztrák Nemzeti Idegenforgalmi Képviselet (☎ 1-391 43 11, fax 391 43 20, e info@oewbud.hu) Völgy utca 30, H-1021 Budapest

Ireland (☎/fax 01-2830 488, e dublin@wko.at) Merrion Centre, Nutley Lane, Ballsbridge, Dublin 4

Italy Austria Turismo (☎ 02-439 90 185, fax 439 90 176, e oewmil@austria-turismo.it) Casella Postale 1255, I-20121, Milan

Japan (☎ 03-358 209 31, fax 381 463 79, e antoyo@magical.egg.or.jp) Akasaka-Dori post office, Tokyo 107-0052

South Africa (☎ 11-442 7235, fax 788 2367, e oewjnb@mweb.co.za) Private Bag X18, Parklands, Johannesburg, ZA-2121

Switzerland Österreich Werbung (☎ 01-451 15 51, fax 451 11 80, e info@oewzrh.ch) Postfach, CH-8036, Zürich

UK (☎ 020-7629 0461, fax 7499 6038, e info@anto.co.uk) PO Box 2363, London W1A 2QB

USA (☎ 212-944 6880, fax 730 4568, e info@oewnyc.com) PO Box 1142, New York, NY 10108-1142

There are also tourist offices in Amsterdam, Brussels, Copenhagen, Madrid, Paris and Stockholm. There's a complete list of all addresses on the ANTO Web site w www .austria-tourism.at (under 'contact' then 'source markets'). New Zealanders can get information from the Austrian consulate in Wellington (see the Austrian Embassies & Consulates section later in this chapter).

VISAS & DOCUMENTS
Visas

Visas are not required for citizens from the EU, EEA (European Economic Area), USA, Canada, Australia or New Zealand. Most visitors may stay a maximum of three months (six months for Japanese). If you need to stay longer you should simply leave the country and re-enter. British and other EU nationals, plus the Swiss, may stay as long as they like, though if they are taking up residency they should register with the local police within five days of arrival. Any other nationals seeking residency should apply in advance in their home country.

Nationals of most African and Arab nations (South Africa included) require a visa; see the Ministry of Foreign Affairs Web site at w www.bmaa.gv.at (it also lists Austrian embassy addresses worldwide). The visa has a validity of up to three months and the procedure varies depending upon the nationality – some nationals may be required to show a return ticket. Visa extensions aren't possible – you'll need to leave and reapply.

There are no border controls between EU nations signed up to the Schengen Agreement, which currently includes all member states except the UK and Ireland. Once you've entered one of these countries, you don't need a passport to move between them (though you should carry one anyway for identification purposes). Similarly, a visa valid for any of them ought to be valid for them all, but double-check with the relevant embassy.

Visa and passport requirements are subject to change, so always double-check before travelling. As a precaution against loss or theft, keep a separate record of document numbers or, better still, photocopy key pages. Ensure your passport is valid until well after you plan to end your trip; if it's not, renew it before you depart. Once you start travelling, carry your passport at all times and guard it carefully. Austrians are required to carry personal identification, and you too will need to be able to prove your identify.

Travel Insurance

Good travel insurance is essential. You should inquire about claims procedures, especially in the event that medical treatment is required as a few insurers require notification *before* treatment is received to confirm that they will meet the claim – tricky in an emergency situation. Other things to look for are whether the policy covers sports such as skiing and mountaineering, and whether ambulances, helicopter rescue or emergency repatriation are included.

Driving Licence & Permits

Proof of ownership of a private vehicle (the Vehicle Registration Document for British-registered cars) should always be carried when touring Europe. A British (except for the old green version) or other Western European driving licence is valid for driving throughout Europe. If you have any other type of licence, you should obtain an International Driving Permit (IDP) from an automobile association.

See the Motorway Tax section in the Getting Around chapter for details of that payment.

Student & Youth Cards

An International Student Identity Card (ISIC) can get the holder all sorts of discounts on admission prices, air and international train tickets and even some ski passes. In Austria, student discounts sometimes only apply to those under 25 or 27 years of age. If you're under 26 years old but not a student, you can apply for other youth cards which, while not so useful, may work for reductions in place of an ISIC. Examples are these are IYTC (International Youth Travel Card) and Euro<26.

Both cards are issued by student unions and by most youth-oriented travel agents in your home country. Within Austria, contact the offices of Ökista (**e** info@oekista.at, **w** www.oekista.at). This travel agency specialises in student and budget fares, and issues ISIC cards for a €5.10 fee if you can prove your student status. Ökista has branches in Vienna, Graz, Linz, Innsbruck and Salzburg – see the relevant city sections for details.

Other Documents

Hostelling International (HI) membership is required to stay in youth hostels; it's cheaper to join in your home country, rather than paying for the guest stamp in Austria.

Copies

It's a good idea to photocopy all important document details, leaving one copy with someone at home and keeping the other with you, separate from the originals.

It's also a good idea to store details of your vital travel documents in Lonely Planet's free online Travel Vault, just in case you lose the photocopies or can't be bothered with them. Your password-protected Travel Vault is accessible online anywhere in the world – create it at **w** www.ekno.lonelyplanet.com.

EMBASSIES & CONSULATES
Austrian Embassies & Consulates

The foreign ministry Web site (**w** www.bmaa.gv.at) lists all Austrian embassy addresses as well as other travel information. Austrian embassies include:

Australia (☎ 02-6295 1376, fax 6239 6751, **w** www.austriaemb.org.au) 12 Talbot St, Forrest, Canberra, ACT 2603
Canada (☎ 613-789 1444, fax 789 3431, **e** embassy@austro.org) 445 Wilbrod St, Ottawa, Ontario K1N 6M7
Ireland (☎ 01-269 4577, fax 283 0860, **e** austroam@iol.ie) 15 Ailesbury Court Apartments, 93 Ailesbury Rd, Dublin 4
New Zealand (☎ 04-499 6393, fax 499 6392) Level 2, Willbank House, 57 Willis St, Wellington (consulate only) – does not issue visas or passports; contact the embassy in Australia for these services
UK (☎ 020-7235 3731, fax 7344 0292, **w** www.austria.org.uk) 18 Belgrave Mews - West, London SW1X 8HU
USA (☎ 202-895 6700, fax 895 6750, **e** obwascon@sysnet.net) 3524 International Court NW, Washington, DC 20008

Embassies & Consulates in Austria

It's important to realise what your own embassy – the embassy of the country of which you are a citizen – can and can't do to help you if you get into trouble.

Generally speaking, it won't be much help in emergencies if the trouble you're in is remotely your own fault. Remember that you are bound by the laws of the country you are in. Your embassy will not be sympathetic if you end up in jail as a result of committing a crime locally, even if such actions are legal in your own country.

In genuine emergencies you might get some assistance, but only if other channels have been exhausted. For example, if you need to get home urgently, a free ticket home is exceedingly unlikely – the embassy would expect you to have insurance. If you have all your money and documents stolen, it might assist with getting a new passport, but a loan for onward travel is out of the question.

Some embassies used to keep letters for travellers or have a small reading room with newspapers from home, but these days the mail holding service has usually been stopped, and if newspapers are provided they are often out of date.

For a complete listing of embassies and consulates, look in the telephone book under 'embassies' *(Botschaften)* or 'consulates' *(Konsulate)*. Double-check visa requirements if you plan to make excursions to neighbouring countries such as Hungary, the Czech Republic or Slovakia.

Embassies are located in Vienna only. Consulates in Vienna share the same contact details unless noted; some other towns, such as Salzburg and Innsbruck, have a consulate too. Countries with embassies in Vienna include the following:

Australia (Map 7, #170; ☎ 512 85 80-0) 04, Mattiellistrasse 2–4
Canada (Map 7, #31; ☎ 531 38-3000) 01, Laurenzerberg 2
Czech Republic (☎ 894 31 11) 14, Penzingerstrasse 11–13
Consulate in Salzburg: (☎ 87 96 24) Bergerbräuhofstrasse 27

France (☎ 502 75-0) 04, Technikerstrasse 2
Consulate in Vienna: (☎ 536 12-0) 01, Wipplinger Strasse 24–26
Germany (☎ 711 54-0) 03, Metternichgasse 3
Consulate in Salzburg: (☎ 84 15 91) Bürgerspitalplatz 1/II
Hungary (Map 7, #47; ☎ 537 80-300) 01, Bankgasse 4–6
Consulate in Klagenfurt: (☎ 50 41 41) Pierlstrasse 33/I
Ireland (☎ 715 42 46-0, consulate ☎ 533 83 76) 03, Landstrasser Hauptstrasse 2, Hilton Center
Italy (☎ 712 51 21-0) 03, Rennweg 27
Consulate in Graz: (☎ 81 79 17) Conrad von Hötzendorfstrasse 8
Consulate in Salzburg: (☎ 87 83 01) Bergstrasse 22/IV
Consulate in Vienna: (☎ 713 56 71-0) 03, Ungarngasse 43
Japan (☎ 531 92-0) 01, Hessgasse 6
New Zealand The New Zealand embassy (☎ 030-20 62 10) in Berlin, Germany, has responsibility for Austria.
Consulate in Vienna: (☎ 318 85 05) 19, Springsiedelgasse 28
Slovakia (☎ 318 90 55) 19, Armbrustergasse 24
Slovenia (☎ 586 13 09, consulate ☎ 585 22 40) 01, Nibelungengasse 13
Consulate in Graz: (☎ 82 19 62) Stempfergasse 3
Consulate in Klagenfurt: (☎ 546 05) Radetzky-strasse 26
Switzerland (☎ 795 05-0) 03, Prinz Eugen Strasse 7
Consulate in Innsbruck: (☎ 53 70-1500) Heiliggeiststrasse 16
Consulate in Salzburg: (☎ 62 25 30) Alpenstrasse 85
UK (Map 6, #42; ☎ 716 13-0) 03, Jaurèsgasse 12
Consulate in Graz: (☎ 82 61 05) Schmiedgasse 10
Consulate in Innsbruck: (☎ 58 83 20) Kaiserjägerstrasse I/I
Consulate in Salzburg: (☎ 84 81 33) Alter Markt 4
Consulate in Vienna: (☎ 716 13-5151) 03, Jaurèsgasse 10
USA (Map 8, #10; ☎ 313 39-0) 09, Boltzmanngasse 16
Consulate in Vienna: (Map 7, #97; ☎ 313 39-0) 01, Gartenbaupromenade 2
Consulate in Salzburg: (☎ 84 97 77) Alter Markt 1/3

CUSTOMS

Duty-free shopping within the EU was abolished in July 1999. Theoretically, if you buy duty-paid alcohol and tobacco in shops in other EU countries, there is no restriction on how much you can bring into Austria. However, to ensure these goods remain for personal use, guideline limits are 800 cigarettes, 200 cigars, 1kg tobacco, 10L of spirits, 90L of wine, 110L of beer and 20L of other alcoholic beverages.

For duty-free purchases made outside the EU, anybody aged 17 or over may bring into Austria 200 cigarettes or 50 cigars or 250g tobacco, plus 2L of wine and 1L of spirits. No duty is payable on items brought in for personal use, nor on gifts or souvenirs up to the value of €175 for air passengers, or €100 if arriving by road from the Czech Republic, Hungary, Slovakia or Slovenia.

MONEY
Currency
On 1 January 2002, the euro (€) replaced the Austrian schilling as the national currency (see the boxed text 'Euro Note' for more on this topic). The euro is divided into 100 cents. There are coins are valued at one, two, five, 10, 20 and 50 cents, as well as to one and two euros. Notes are to the value of five, 10, 20, 50, 100, 200 and 500 euros.

Exchange Rates

country	unit		euro
Australia	A$10	=	€0.60
Bulgaria	1 leva	=	€0.52
Canada	C$1	=	€0.71
Czech Republic	Kč10	=	€0.30
Hungary	Ft100	=	€0.39
Japan	¥100	=	€0.92
New Zealand	NZ$1	=	€0.47
Slovakia	Sk10	=	€0.23
Slovenia	SIT100	=	€0.46
UK	UK£1	=	€1.60
USA	US1	=	€1.12

Exchanging Money
Changing foreign currency is not a problem, and if you've arrived via other euro nations such as Germany or Italy you'll already be familiar with the currency that you'll be spending in Austria.

Exchange rates vary a little between banks. It pays to shop around, not only for

the best exchange rates but also for the lowest commission charges. Changing cash usually attracts lower commission rates, but always check first. If you have travellers cheques in euros, you shouldn't be charged any commission for encashing them.

Austrian banks are open 8am or 9am to 3pm Monday to Friday, with late opening on Thursday until 5.30pm; smaller branches close between 12.30pm and 1.30pm. All but the smallest train stations have extended hours for currency exchange at ticket counters or exchange offices. Branch post offices can exchange money up to 5pm on Monday to Friday and on Saturday morning. Some main post offices in cities have longer hours for exchange.

American Express (AmEx) offices have slightly unfavourable exchange rates but low commission charges – starting at €1.85 for cash and €3.65 for travellers cheques; no commission applies on Amex's own travellers cheques. The post office charges 1% (€2.20 minimum) for cash but no longer encashes cheques, and the rates often aren't great. Exchange counters at train stations charge about €2.95 for cash and €4.70 minimum for cheques. Banks typically charge €7.30 or more. Avoid changing a lot of low-value cheques as commission costs will be higher. Big hotels also change money, but rates are invariably poor. Look especially carefully at the commission rates charged by exchange booths *(Wechselstuben)* – we've seen scandalous commission rates of 10% plus a charge per cheque!

Cash
Avoid carrying large amounts of cash, but it's worthwhile having some with you on arrival. Towards the end of your trip, try not to change more than you think you'll need, as you will lose out if you have to reconvert the excess. Banks rarely accept coins in currencies other than their own, so spend your last coins before departure.

Travellers Cheques
All major travellers cheques are equally widely accepted, though you may want to use AmEx, Visa or Thomas Cook because of

Euro Note

This book was researched when Austria's former national currency, the schilling, still reigned supreme. At this time the embryonic euro was merely a bit-part player in paperless transactions.

Though euro notes and coins were not yet in circulation, dual pricing (in schillings and euros) was already the norm. By law, prices had to show the exact conversion to the euro to two decimal places, and with the euro being fixed at an unwieldy rate of €1 to 13.7603 Austrian schillings (AS), strange prices such as €1.03, €26.34 and €193.87 were appearing all over the place.

We've assumed there would be some rationalisation of these weird euro prices once the schilling was consigned to the piggy bank of history. Accordingly, euro prices quoted have been rounded up (to the nearest five or 10 cents for smaller sums, the nearest whole euro for larger amounts). You'll probably therefore come across small differences to the prices we quote, either higher or lower (some vendors may actually decide to round down rather than round up – stranger things have happened!).

Twelve countries have so far adopted the euro as their national currency: Austria, Belgium, Finland, France, Germany, Greece, Ireland, Italy, Luxembourg, Netherlands, Portugal and Spain. The same euro notes and coins are legal tender in all these nations, though each nation has been permitted to use their own designs on one side of coins (the other side is standard). Austria opted to depict flora on the small coins (one cent = Enzian, two cents = Edelweiss, five cents = Alpenprimel), buildings on the middle coins (10 cents = Stephansdom, 20 cents = Schloss Belvedere, 50 cents = Wiener Secession), and people on the larger coins (€1 = Mozart, €2 = Bertha von Suttner, winner of the 1905 Nobel Peace Prize).

their 'instant replacement' policies. A record of the cheque numbers and the initial purchase details is vital when it comes to replacing lost cheques. Without this, you may well find that 'instant' is a very long time indeed. You should also keep a record of which cheques you have cashed. Keep these details separate from the cheques.

ATMs & Credit Cards

Visa, EuroCard and MasterCard are equally welcome, although a surprising number of shops and restaurants refuse to accept credit cards. The same applies to AmEx and Diners Club charge cards. Plush shops, hotels and restaurants will accept credit cards. Train tickets can be bought by credit card in main stations. You can also use a debit (EDC) card.

Credit cards allow you to get cash advances at most banks. In Austria, automated teller machines (ATMs) are known as Bankomats. They are extremely common and are accessible 24 hours a day. Even villages should have at least one machine: look for the sign showing blue and green horizontal stripes. ATMs are linked up internationally and have English instructions.

You'll need to know your personal identification number (PIN) to get instant cash advances, and the withdrawal limit per transaction is usually €365. However, getting cash advances with cards issued in Australia is sometimes a problem, so check with your bank before departure. Also check to make sure your PIN will work in Austria; you may have to shorten it. Fees may work out lower than using travellers cheques, and the currency conversion rate will be better. There's no charge at the ATM end, but your credit card company will usually charge a 1.5% to 4% fee on the total withdrawn. You can avoid the monthly interest charged on your credit card account (due from the day of withdrawal) by leaving your account in credit at the start of your holiday. You may even earn interest on this credit balance.

International Transfers

To get money sent internationally, transferring funds bank to bank is not always straightforward if you don't have a bank account in the receiving country. It's quicker and easier to have money wired via Western Union's Money Transfer system – receiving offices are all around Austria, including in most large train stations. Or there's the MoneyGram service used by American Express (for AmEx card-holders only), Thomas Cook and some post offices; minimum commission is about US$20/UK£14.

Other Methods

Eurocheques are guaranteed personal cheques, but it's an expensive system to use, and not so popular nowadays. You'd need a European bank account to use them.

Another way to organise your money in Europe is to use the giro system, which operates through post office accounts. Contact your post office for details. If you're staying in Austria for several months or making repeat trips, it might be worth opening an Austrian post office account. There are no fees and you will earn a small amount of interest.

Security

A moneybelt worn around your waist beneath your clothes is probably one of the safest ways of carrying important documents such as cash, your passport and travellers cheques on your person. Some people prefer a pouch attached to a string and worn round the neck, concealed beneath a shirt or jumper. Leather belts with secret compartments are also available from travel goods suppliers.

Costs

Vienna is averagely expensive for a European city – cheaper than London, Paris, Zürich or Rome, similar to Munich, more expensive than Prague or Budapest. With the exception of plush ski resorts such as Lech and Kitzbühel, most of the rest of Austria is noticeably cheaper than Vienna, particularly if you're visiting less touristed regions. Overall, Britons and Americans will probably find things pretty affordable, given the long slide of the euro against sterling and the dollar.

Budget travellers will be able to survive on about €36 (US$31) per day – €12 for a hostel bed, €12 for cheap meals or self-catering, €5 for transport and €7 for admissions and incidentals. However, this is a very stringent estimate – you could spend double per day and still feel you're economising. Purchasing 'luxuries' like a beer in a bar (€2.90), a cup of coffee in a coffee house (€2.20), a foreign newspaper (€2.50) or souvenirs can add up to a sizeable sum very quickly. Transport costs will soar if you take cable cars in the mountains, so hike up where possible. Off the beaten track, the main saving will be from lower accommodation prices.

To stay in a room with a private bathroom, and have a moderate lunch, a decent dinner, some money to spend on evening entertainment and not be too concerned about how expensive a cup of coffee is, a daily allowance of above €125 (US$108) would be needed. Of course, you can spend much more than this if you have the funds available!

Note that children pay lower prices; students and senior citizens often do, too.

Tipping & Bargaining

Hotel and restaurant bills usually include a service charge, but hotel porters and cleaning staff usually expect something for their services. How much you leave depends on the type of place and the quality of the service. It is also customary to tip in restaurants and cafes. Round up small bills and add an extra 5 to 10% to larger ones: simply say the total amount you want them to take when you hand over the money (it's not usual to leave the tip on the table). In plush places, there'll be a wallet or folder to leave the money in. Taxi fares do not include tips and the driver will expect around 10% extra. Tour guides, cloakroom attendants and hairdressers are also usually tipped by a similar amount.

Prices are fixed in shops, but it can't hurt to ask for 'a discount for cash' if you're making several purchases. Bargain hard in flea markets. In theory, hotel prices are not negotiable; in practice, you can often haggle for a better rate in the low season or if you're staying more than a few days.

Taxes & Refunds

Value-added tax in Austria (*Mehrwertsteuer* or MWST) is set at 20% for most goods.

Prices are always displayed inclusive of all taxes.

All non-EU tourists are entitled to a refund of the MWST on purchases over €72.70. To claim the tax, a U34 form or tax-free cheque and envelope must be completed by the shop at the time of purchase (show your passport), and then stamped by border officials when you leave the EU. (If you're leaving Austria for another EU country, you can't get this customs stamp in Austria, you have to get it from customs staff where you finally quit the EU.) The airports at Vienna, Salzburg, Innsbruck, Linz and Graz have a counter for payment of instant refunds. There are also counters at two of Vienna's train stations (Westbahnhof and Südbahnhof) and at major border crossings. The refund is best claimed as you leave the EU; otherwise you will have to track down an international refund office or claim by post from your home country.

Before making a purchase, ensure the shop has the required paperwork; some places display a 'Tax Free for Tourists' sticker. Also confirm the value of the refund; it's usually advertised as 13% (which is the refund of the 20% standard rate of VAT after various commissions have been taken), though it may vary for certain categories of goods.

POST & COMMUNICATIONS

Post office hours vary: typical hours are 8am to noon and 2pm to 6pm (currency exchange only until 5pm) Monday to Friday and (perhaps) 8am to 10am or 11am Saturday. Some main post offices (particularly those located by train stations) may stay open longer hours, including for a few hours on Sunday (see the Information sections of the various chapters). Some post offices have photocopiers, though those in copy shops or universities are cheaper. Find postal information on the Web site **w** www.post.at.

Sending Mail

Sending ordinary mail (up to 50g) within Austria costs €0.51. Sending mail outside Austria, you can choose between priority (ie, the faster service) or nonpriority, except with letters up to 20g within Europe, where

there's just one rate (€0.51). Letters up to 50g cost €0.73/1.02 nonpriority/priority to Europe, or €1.02/1.45 to elsewhere (there's no 20g category outside Europe). Stamps are available in tobacconist shops *(Tabak)* as well as post offices. Airmail takes about four days to the UK, seven days to the USA and about 10 days to Australasia.

The normal weight limit for letter post *(Briefsendung)* is 2kg, which costs €10.17/18.17 nonpriority/priority to Europe and €18.17/32.70 to elsewhere. There are various categories and rates for sending larger packages, depending on the size and contents (printed matter, such as books and brochures, can be sent at a reduced rate). EMS (☎ 0810-010101) is a special (and expensive) express service for national or international mail weighing up to 20kg.

Receiving Mail

'Poste restante' is *'Postlagernde Briefe'* in German, though 'poste restante' is widely understood and you can use either term when addressing letters. Mail can be sent care of any post office and is held for a month; a passport must be shown to collect it. Ask people who are sending you letters to write your surname in capitals and underline it. *Postamt* means post office: this, together with the post code, street name and town, will be sufficient to ensure mail ends up at the correct post office. Get in the habit of crossing sevens in the continental style when addressing mail (and get others to do likewise), as it reduces the possibility of mail being misdirected and eventually returned to sender (or despatched to the recycling bin).

American Express (see Money earlier in this chapter) will also hold mail for 30 days for customers who have its charge card.

Telephone

Telecommunications were liberalised in Austria in 1998, and there has since been a shakeup of services. The cost of telephone calls has recently gone down, particularly for national calls. At present, all of Austria comes within the same charge zone, so whether you're calling next door or across the Alps you pay the same rate of €0.15 per minute.

Public telephone boxes are reasonably numerous (particularly inside or outside post offices) and usually in working order. The minimum charge is €0.15. You can save money and avoid messing around with change by buying a phonecard *(Telefon-Wertkarte)* from a post office, tobacconist or train station ticket office. They're also worth getting as most public call boxes are card operated only nowadays. They come in various denominations (€3.65 to €14.55), some of which give you extra calls for your money.

If you make a call and get the rising three-bleep anthem it means you've dialled an invalid number. Check the phone book or call ☎ 118200 for directory assistance. Getting the fast one-tone beeps means the number is engaged; the slow one-tone beeps is the ringing tone.

You should have no trouble using your mobile phone (called a 'Handy' locally) in Austria, but check with your provider before departure. In fact, Austria is one of the most mobile phone friendly places in Europe. Apparently there have been around six million mobile phones purchased in Austria – pretty incredible for a nation of just eight million people.

For Telekom information, call ☎ 0800-100 100. For the online telephone book, visit **w** www.etb.at.

There's a wide range of local and international phonecards. Lonely Planet's eKno global communication service provides low-cost international calls – for local calls you're usually better off with a local phonecard. eKno also offers free messaging services, email, travel information and an online Travel Vault, where you can securely store all your important documents. You can join online at **w** www.ekno.lonelyplanet.com, where you will find the local-access numbers for 24-hour customer service. Once you have joined, always check the eKno Web site for the latest access numbers for each country and updates on new features. To join and use eKno from Austria, call ☎ 0800-291 018.

Special Numbers Any phone number with the prefix code 0800, 0801, 0802 or 0804 is a freephone number; any numbers beginning 0810 or 05 are classified as local rate calls (however, this is an obsolete concept now that all of Austria comes under the same tariff). Mobile phone numbers begin with 0663, 0664, 0676 or 0699, depending on the network, and calling them is usually more expensive. Premium rate numbers, costing from €0.45 to €3.65 per minute, begin 0900 to 0930.

International Calls To hear the directory of international telephone numbers, dial ☎ 118200 (up until 2002 you had to dial ☎ 118202 for calls outside Austria and Germany). To direct-dial abroad, first telephone the overseas access code (00), then the appropriate country code, then the relevant area code (minus the initial 0 if there is one), and finally the subscriber number. For calling to Austria from abroad, the country code is 43.

The tariff for making international calls depends on the zone (though strangely, different zones may have the same rate) and it's currently the same rate round the clock. To call Australia, New Zealand, South Africa, the UK or USA costs the same: €0.67 per minute.

To reverse the charges (ie, call collect), you have to call a freephone number to place the call. Some of the numbers are listed below (ask directory assistance for others):

Australia	☎ 0800-200 202
Canada	☎ 0800-200 224
Ireland	☎ 0800-200 213
New Zealand	☎ 0800-200 222
South Africa	☎ 0800-200 230
UK	☎ 0800-200 209
USA AT&T	☎ 0800-200 288
USA MCI	☎ 0800-200 235
USA Sprint	☎ 0800-200 236

Fax

Luxury hotels offer fax services but it's cheaper to use the post office. To send a fax from the post office costs €1.35 for five pages plus the cost of the telephone time; receiving faxes costs just the €1.35. Some hotels *may* let you receive the odd fax free of charge.

Telephone Numbers Explained

Telephone numbers for the same town may not always have the same number of digits: the reason for this is that some telephone numbers have an individual line, others a party line, and sometimes numbers are listed with an extension that you can dial direct. This is relevant for reading phone numbers listed in the telephone book. If, for example, you see the number 123 45 67 ... -0, the 0 signifies that the number has extensions. Whether you dial the 0 at the end or not, you will (with a few exceptions) get through to that subscriber's main telephone reception. If you know the extension number of the person you want to speak to, simply dial that instead of the 0 and you'll get straight through to them.

Fax numbers are often an extension of the main number, and it's fairly common to see them listed only by their extension, sometimes following the letters DW (an abbreviation for *Durchwahl*, indicating 'extension'). In this book, any telephone extensions are separated from the main number by a hyphen, and fax numbers are also shown in their entirety. Remember, though, when using online booking services and reading tourist brocures, you have to dial the main number first and then the fax extension to reach the fax machine.

Email & Internet Access

Email is a great way to keep in touch with folks back home. Various servers (such as **W** www.hotmail.com, **W** www.lycos.com and **W** www.yahoo.com) can supply you with a free email account.

There is public Internet access in most Austrian towns, with more outlets opening all the time. Prices are generally around €4 to €8 per hour, though some places are free. For details of Internet cafes, see Information in the relevant city sections. Many hotels and hostels also offer email facilities for their guests. If you have your own laptop and modem, you can sometimes plug into the phone system at your hotel, but ask first. Similarly, a few post offices have pay-at-the-counter phones where you can plug in your modem.

DIGITAL RESOURCES

The World Wide Web is a rich resource for travellers. You can research your trip, hunt down bargain air fares, book hotels, check on weather conditions or chat with locals and other travellers about the best places to visit (or avoid!).

There's no better place to start your Internet explorations than the Lonely Planet Web site (**W** www.lonelyplanet.com). Here you'll find succinct summaries on travelling to most places on earth, postcards from other travellers and the Thorn Tree bulletin board, where you can ask questions before you go or dispense advice when you get back. You can also find travel news and updates to many of our most popular guidebooks, and the subWWWay section links you to the most useful travel resources elsewhere on the Web.

Many Austrian organisations now have a Web site – you'll find the most useful of these listed throughout this book. A US-based press and information service is at **W** www.austria.org; it has current news and good links for a range of topics. The online version of the *Austria Today* newspaper (**W** www.austriatoday.at) has a directory of business services. All main tourist sights and locations are covered (in English) at **W** www.tiscover.com. The Austrian Encyclopaedia (**W** www.aeiou.at) has exhaustive information on things Austrian, again in English. A good Austria-specific search engine is **W** www.austrosearch.at.

BOOKS

A great deal has been written about Austria, especially Vienna. Some bookshops in Austrian cities stock English-language titles, though they will probably cost more than at home. Most books are published in different editions by different publishers in different countries. As a result, a book might be a hardcover rarity in one country while it's readily available in paperback in another. Fortunately, bookshops and libraries search by title or author, so they should be best placed to advise you on the availability of the following titles.

Lonely Planet

For more detail on Vienna, turn to the *Vienna* city guide. Austria is also covered in the *Western Europe*, *Central Europe* and *Europe on a Shoestring* guides; each has a companion phrasebook.

Guidebooks

A useful volume for walkers is *Mountain Walking in Austria* by Cecil Davies. It's periodically updated.

For an enthusiastic assessment of a variety of restaurants, turn to *Eating Out in Austria* by Gretel Beer. The detailed glossary of culinary terms is especially useful. The tongue-in-cheek *Xenophobe's Guide to the Austrians* contains some amusing and revealing insights into Austrian people and society.

Once in Vienna, *Falter's Best of Vienna* (€3.60) is worth looking at. It's a locally available seasonal magazine giving hundreds of useful and up-to-date recommendations for eating, drinking, shopping and entertainment. Some categories are typically quirky and playful; past highlights include best wall to lean against, best workers' *Beisl* (pub) with a parrot, best U-Bahn (underground) station clock, and best wild boar farm in the city. The same publisher releases an annual guide solely dedicated to eating, *Wien, wie es isst*. Both of these publications are in German only, which is a pity for monolinguists, as Falter is known for its witty wordplay.

History & Politics

Steven Beller's *Vienna and the Jews* is concerned specifically with the years 1867 to 1938. You could also try *Austria, Empire and Republic* by Barbara Jelavich. *A History of the Habsburg Empire 1526–1918* is a large tome by Robert A Kann. For an up-to-date perspective, see *Guilty Victim* by Hella Pick, which analyses Austria from the Holocaust to Haider.

General

A number of books deal with Austria from the slant of its musical heritage. *Mozart and the Enlightenment* by Nicholas Till is a scholarly work placing Mozart in historical context, with detailed analysis of his operatic works. *Mozart and Vienna* by HC Robbins Landon focuses on the Vienna years, and successfully evokes the city of the time by quoting extensively from a contemporary work, *Sketch of Vienna* by Johann Pezzl. *Mozart – his Character, his Work* by Alfred Einstein has a self-explanatory title, as does *Gustav Mahler – Memories and Letters* by Alma Mahler. *Freud's Women* by Lisa Appignanesi and John Forrester is a large volume that offers an insight into the psychoanalyst. There's also *The Life and Work of Sigmund Freud* by Ernest Jones.

For fiction lovers, *The Third Man* is Graham Greene's famous Viennese spy story. John Irving's *Setting Free the Bears* is a fine tale about a plan to release the animals from Vienna's zoo. The zoo plot takes place in 1967, yet the book is also very evocative of life in Austria before, during and after WWII. Irving's *The Hotel New Hampshire* is also partially set in Vienna, and offers an interesting perspective on the city. *Invisible Architecture* is a collection of three stories by Steven Kelly. The architecture in question is more to do with the make-up of the Viennese soul than the buildings in the city. The highly acclaimed *An Equal Music* by Vikram Seth is partially set in Vienna's Music Academy.

Mozart and the Wolf Gang by Anthony Burgess is a learned and enjoyable celestial fantasy in which the great composers discourse on music and Mozart. *The Strange Case of Mademoiselle P* by Brian O'Doherty is a story about an attempted medical cure in Maria Theresa's Vienna. It's based on a real incident and gives an insight into the petty power struggles in the imperial court, though it does rather peter out at the end.

The Salzburg Tales by Christina Stead is a *Canterbury Tales*-like novel in which gatherers at the Salzburg Festival in the 1930s tell each other stories. It has some good character sketches but, apart from its setting, sheds little light on Austria. For younger readers, many of the stories in Elinor Brent-Dyer's 'Chalet School' series of books are set in Austria.

See the Literature section in the Facts about Austria chapter for examples of fiction by Austrian authors.

FILMS

The most famous film on Vienna is *The Third Man* – see the boxed text in the Vienna chapter for more on this. Equally renowned is *The Sound of Music*, set in and around Salzburg (see the boxed text 'The Sound of Dollars' in the Salzburg chapter).

NEWSPAPERS & MAGAZINES

English-language newspapers are widely available in Austrian cities, usually on the same day they're published (eg, in Vienna) or the following day. Prices are between €2.20 and €3.70. The first to hit the stands each day are the *Financial Times* and the *International Herald Tribune*. *USA Today*, *Time*, *Newsweek* and most British newspapers are easy to find. The News & Books shops in some major stations stock a particularly wide selection of newspapers and magazines from around the world.

Of the several German-language daily newspapers available, the magazine-size *Kronen Zeitung* (€0.75) has the largest circulation; the tabloid-size *Die Presse* adopts a more serious approach. *Austria Today* is a weekly national newspaper in English (€1.85) with several informative sections and a listing of cultural events.

Austrian newspapers are often dispensed from bags attached to pavement posts, and rely on the honesty of readers to pay for the copies they take. Foreign-language titles are only available from newsstands or pavement vendors.

RADIO & TV

Home-grown commercial TV and radio is a recent phenomenon in Austria, and the state-run network still dominates.

State-run national radio channels are Ö1 (87.8 and 92 FM), giving a highbrow diet of music, literature and science, and Ö3 (99.9 FM), offering pop music and topical

information. The above frequencies are for Vienna: they'll be slightly different in other parts of the country.

FM4 (103.8 FM in Vienna) is a music and chat station broadcasting in English and German. Most of the English segments are between 6am and 2pm, including news on the hour, discussions and reports on cultural events. Outside Vienna you can usually pick up FM4 somewhere between 101 and 105 FM, though it's 97.4 FM in Eisenstadt and 98.8 FM in St Pölten.

The two state-run national TV channels are ÖRF1 and ÖRF2. However, many homes (and hotels) have satellite or cable and can pick up a whole host of TV channels from Germany and elsewhere, plus MTV, Eurosport, CNN (the 24-hour news network) and NBC (featuring American chat shows in the evening). ATV, Austria's first domestic cable/satellite station, started up in 2000. The local newspapers and events magazines give full program listings of all channels.

VIDEO SYSTEMS

Videos in Austria use the PAL image registration system, as in the UK and Australia. This is not compatible with the NTSC system used in the USA, Canada and Japan.

PHOTOGRAPHY & VIDEO

There are no special restrictions on what you can or cannot photograph, though as in many other countries, some art galleries and museums insist you leave your camera in the cloakroom. Don't use a camera flash at the opera, theatre or similar events; it's very distracting for the performers, whether they're humans or Lipizzaner stallions.

Photography in snow can be tricky. The bright whiteness of snow can dominate a picture and cause the subject to be underexposed (dark and dull on the photograph). Some cameras will allow you to compensate for this.

Film & Equipment

Film is widely available and reasonably priced. Note that the price of slide film *(Diafilm)* often excludes mounting *(Rahmung)* and sometimes even processing

(Entwicklung) too. Alternatively, there may be a coupon for processing that is valid only in Austria (check before buying).

The Niedermeyer chain store is one of the cheapest places to buy film, especially if you buy multipacks: a three-pack of 36-exposure Kodak 100 film costs €8 and a twin-pack of Ektachrome 200 slide film is €8.75. Niedermeyer also has its own brand of film that is much cheaper. Its main rival in price and range is Hartlauer; Cosmos is also cheap, but it has only a few outlets. These chains have a good range of cameras and lenses, for which prices are comparable to elsewhere in Europe. Digital camcorder cassettes cost around €22 for a three-pack.

Film developing is pricey, so it'd be better to get this done at home. At Niedermeyer, it costs €3.65 plus €0.20 per 9cm-by-13cm print for the two-day service (express service is a shocking €0.60 per print).

TIME

Austrians use the 24-hour clock for anything written down, instead of dividing the day into am and pm. Austrian time is GMT/UTC plus one hour. If it's noon in Vienna it is 6am in New York and Toronto, 3am in San Francisco, 9pm in Sydney and 11pm in Auckland. Clocks go forward one hour on the last Saturday night in March and back again on the last Saturday night in October.

Note that in German *halb* is used to indicate the half-hour before the hour, hence *halb acht* means 7.30, not 8.30.

ELECTRICITY

The current is 220V, 50Hz AC. Sockets are the round two-pin type standard throughout most of Continental Europe. US and Canadian appliances need a transformer if they don't have built-in voltage adjustment.

WEIGHTS & MEASURES

The metric system is used. Like other continental Europeans, Austrians indicate decimals with commas and thousands with points (full stops). You will sometimes see meat and cheese priced per *dag*, which is an abbreviation referring to 10g (to ask for this quantity say 'deca').

LAUNDRY

Look for *Wäscherei* for self-service *(Selbstbedienung)* or service washes (which are only slightly more expensive). The minimum charge is around €4.50 to wash a 5kg load. Many youth hostels have cheaper laundry facilities, and most good hotels have an expensive laundry service, based on a price per item.

TOILETS

Toilet cubicles in some places, including many train stations, are attended or coin-operated; either way, expect to pay around €0.40 (you can avoid the station charge by using the train toilets instead), though men's urinals are usually free. There are many public toilets to be found: *Damen* means women and *Herren* means men. Toilets in restaurants, museums and galleries are generally unattended and free to use.

HEALTH
Medical Services

There is a charge for hospital treatment and doctor consultations, so some form of medical insurance is advised (cover provided by normal travel insurance would be sufficient). A straightforward, non-urgent appointment with a doctor might cost anything from €40 to €75.

EU nationals can get free emergency medical treatment, though payment must still be made for the actual medication used, and also for most non-urgent treatment. Inquire before leaving home about the documentation required. In Austria British citizens who reside in the UK only need to show a British passport to take advantage of reciprocal health agreements. However, in other European countries British people normally need to show an E111 form (available from the DSS), so it's worth getting one if you're travelling through Europe. The regional health insurance office *(Gebietskrankenkasse)* will know which other countries have reciprocal agreements with Austria (the USA, Canada, Australia and New Zealand don't), but it's wise to establish this with your own health department before you leave home.

These regional offices also provide a health insurance scheme voucher for obtaining medical or dental treatment under reciprocal arrangements (in an emergency situation go straight to the hospital). If you go to a private hospital and the treatment is more expensive than it would be in a public hospital, you'll have to pay the difference (even if you're covered under a reciprocal arrangement). The following are contact details for health insurance offices in major cities:

Vienna (☎ 01-601 220) 10, Wienerbergstrasse 15–19
Graz (☎ 0316-80 35-0) Josef Pongratz Platz 1
Innsbruck (☎ 0512-59 16-0) Klara Pölt Weg 2
Salzburg (☎ 0662-88 89-0) Faberstrasse 19–23

Chemist shops *(Apotheken)* are open normal shop hours, though in some places they operate an after-hours service in rotation. Check at your hotel or in the local paper for details.

Predeparture Planning

No immunisations are required for entry to Austria, unless you're coming from an infected area (in which case you'll need to show an International Health Certificate). However, everyone should keep up-to-date with diphtheria, tetanus and polio vaccinations, and you may want to get protection against encephalitis (see Ticks later in this section).

Make sure you have health insurance; see Travel Insurance in the Visas & Documents section earlier in this chapter.

If you wear glasses, take a spare pair and your prescription. If you require a particular medication take an adequate supply, as it may not be available locally. Take part of the packaging showing the generic name rather than the brand, which will make getting replacements easier. It's a good idea to have a legible prescription or letter from your doctor to show that you legally use the medication to avoid any problems.

A small, straightforward medical kit is a wise thing to carry (see the Medical Kit

---

Medical Kit Check List

Following is a list of items you should consider including in your medical kit – consult your pharmacist for brands available in your country.

- ☐ **Aspirin or paracetamol** – for pain or fever
- ☐ **Antihistamine** – for allergies, eg, hay fever; to ease the itch from insect bites or stings; and to prevent motion sickness
- ☐ **Cold and flu tablets, throat lozenges and nasal decongestant**
- ☐ **Multivitamins** – consider for long trips, when your dietary vitamin intake may be inadequate
- ☐ **Loperamide or diphenoxylate** –'blockers' for diarrhoea
- ☐ **Prochlorperazine or metaclopramide** – for nausea and vomiting
- ☐ **Rehydration mixture** – to prevent dehydration, which may occur, for example, during bouts of diarrhoea; particularly important when travelling with children
- ☐ **Insect repellent, sunscreen, lip balm and eye drops**
- ☐ **Calamine lotion, sting relief spray or aloe vera** – to ease irritation from sunburn and insect bites or stings
- ☐ **Antifungal cream or powder** – for fungal skin infections and thrush
- ☐ **Antiseptic (such as povidone-iodine)** – for cuts and grazes
- ☐ **Bandages, Band-Aids (plasters) and other wound dressings**
- ☐ **Water purification tablets or iodine**
- ☐ **Scissors, tweezers and a thermometer** – note that mercury thermometers are prohibited by airlines
- ☐ **Syringes and needles** – in case you need injections in a country with medical hygiene problems; ask your doctor for a note explaining why you have them

---

Check List for suggestions). All the items in the list can be bought in Austria. An effective local product for clearing up blisters is *Hirschtalg* (Stag Fat).

Basic Rules

Austria is a healthy place and if you're healthy when you arrive, there's no reason why you should experience any particular health problems. Even street snack stands have adequate sanitary standards. Try to avoid food that has been cooked and left to go cold at room temperature (which might happen in some self-service places) and keep your diet varied.

Tap water is perfectly drinkable (except in the rare instance when you come across a sign announcing 'Kein Trinkwasser', or 'Not drinking water'). Beware of natural water, even crystal-clear Alpine streams, and take a full water bottle on long walking trips. If you need to resort to natural water, it should be boiled for 10 minutes; remember that at high altitude water boils at a lower temperature, so germs are less likely to be killed. Iodine is very effective in purifying water and is available in tablet form (such as Potable Aqua), but follow the directions carefully and remember that too much iodine can be harmful.

Environmental Hazards

Altitude Sickness The lack of oxygen at high altitudes (over 2500m) affects most people to some extent. The higher you go, the thinner the air and the easier you need to take things (and incidentally, the quicker you get drunk!). Older people and those with high blood pressure have an increased reaction to altitude. Acute Mountain Sickness (AMS) occurs at high altitude and can be fatal. However, AMS is only a risk above 3000m, so in Austria it may affect mountaineers but is unlikely to be a danger for walkers or skiers. Ascending slowly and drinking extra fluids can reduce the risks.

AMS usually develops during the first 24 hours at altitude, but may be delayed up to three weeks. Mild symptoms include headache, lethargy, dizziness, difficulty sleeping and loss of appetite. AMS may become more severe without warning and can be fatal. Severe symptoms include breathlessness, a dry, irritative cough (which may progress to the production of pink, frothy sputum), severe headache, lack of coordination and balance, confusion, irrational behaviour, vomiting, drowsiness and unconsciousness. Mild altitude problems will generally abate after a day or so, but if symptoms persist or become worse, *immediate descent is necessary*; even as little as 500m can help.

Hypothermia If you are trekking at high altitudes or in a cool, wet environment, be prepared: take waterproof clothing, even if the weather looks fine. Hypothermia occurs when the body loses heat faster than it can produce it and the core temperature of the body falls. It is surprisingly easy to progress from very cold to dangerously cold due to a combination of wind, wet clothing, fatigue and hunger, even if the air temperature is above freezing point. It is best to dress in layers, and wear a hat (a lot of heat is lost through the head). A strong, waterproof outer layer is essential, as keeping dry is vital. Carry basic supplies, including food that contains simple sugars to generate heat quickly, and fluid to drink.

Symptoms of hypothermia can include exhaustion, numb skin (particularly on the toes and fingers), shivering, slurred speech, irrational or violent behaviour, lethargy, stumbling, dizzy spells, muscle cramps and violent bursts of energy. Irrationality may take the form of sufferers claiming they are warm and trying to take off their clothes.

To treat mild hypothermia, first get the person out of the wind and/or rain, remove their clothing if it's wet and replace it with dry, warm clothing. Give them hot liquids – not alcohol – and some high-calorie, easily digestible food. Do not rub victims: instead, allow them to slowly warm themselves. This should be enough to treat the early stages of hypothermia. The early recognition and treatment of mild hypothermia is the only way to prevent severe hypothermia, which is a critical condition.

Motion Sickness Eating lightly before and during a trip will reduce the chances of motion sickness. If you are prone to motion sickness try to find a place that minimises movement – near the wing on aircraft, close to midships on boats, near the centre on buses. Fresh air usually helps; reading and cigarette smoke don't. Commercial motion-sickness preparations, which can cause drowsiness, have to be taken before the trip commences. Ginger (available in capsule form) and peppermint (including mint-flavoured sweets) are natural preventatives and may soothe nausea once it's begun.

Sunburn At high altitude you can get sunburnt surprisingly quickly, even through cloud. Use a sunscreen, a hat, and a barrier cream for your nose and lips. Calamine lotion or a commercial after sun preparation are good for mild sunburn. Protect your eyes with good quality sunglasses, particularly if you will be near water, sand or snow.

Infectious Diseases

Diarrhoea Simple things like a change of water, food or climate can all cause a mild bout of diarrhoea, but a few rushed toilet trips with no other symptoms are not indicative of a major problem, though they may-definitely put a damper on your sightseeing.

Dehydration is the main danger with any diarrhoea, particularly in children or the elderly, as dehydration can occur quite quickly. Under all circumstances *fluid replacement* (at least equal to the volume being lost) is the most important thing to remember. Weak black tea with a little sugar, soda water, or soft drinks allowed to go flat and diluted 50% with clean water are all good. Keep drinking small amounts often. Stick to a bland diet as you recover.

HIV & AIDS Infection with the human immunodeficiency virus (HIV) may lead to acquired immune deficiency syndrome (AIDS), which is a fatal disease. Any exposure to blood, blood products or body fluids may put the individual at risk. The disease is often transmitted through sexual contact or dirty needles – vaccinations, acupuncture, tattooing and body piercing can be potentially as dangerous as intravenous drug use. HIV/AIDS can also be spread through infected blood transfusions.

Cuts, Bites & Stings

Ticks Ticks might be a problem in forested areas and occasionally even in urban situations. You'll see warnings about this hazard in many Austrian train stations. They're usually found below 1200m in undergrowth at the forest edge or beside walking tracks. A very small proportion are carriers of bacterial and viral encephalitis, which may become serious if not detected early. Both types of encephalitis initially appear with influenza-like symptoms, and can affect the skin, nervous system, muscles or heart, often causing headaches and sore joints. Treatment is usually with antibiotics, but inoculations are available for those particularly at risk. In rare instances, encephalitis can be fatal.

You should always check all over your body if you have been walking through a potentially tick-infested area. If a tick is found attached, press down around the tick's head with tweezers, grab the head and gently pull upwards. (Chemist shops may be able to sell you a special instrument for this purpose.) Avoid pulling the rear of the body as this may squeeze the tick's gut contents through the attached mouth parts into the skin, increasing the risk of infection and disease. Smearing chemicals on the tick will not make it let go and is not recommended.

Snakes Austria is home to several types of snake, a couple of which can deliver a nasty, although not fatal, bite. Snakes are more prevalent in the mountains. Wear suitable boots when walking through undergrowth, don't put your hands into holes and crevices, and be careful when collecting firewood.

Rabies Rabies is now rare in Europe, but you should still be wary of making contact with stray dogs or other mammals. Any bite, scratch or even lick from a mammal should be cleaned immediately and thoroughly.

WOMEN TRAVELLERS

In cities, Austrian women enjoy equal status and opportunity with men, though in conservative, rural parts of the country some males still consider that a woman's proper place is in the home.

Female travellers should experience no special problems. Fortunately, physical attacks and verbal harassment are less common than in many other countries. However, normal caution should be exercised when alone or in unfamiliar situations (which obviously occur quite often when you're travelling). Some Austrian trains have a special section for women travelling alone – inquire in advance.

Organisations
Cities usually have a women's centre *(Frauenzentrum)* and/or telephone helplines. In Vienna, for example, there is the Frauenotruf (☎ 01-71 719), an emergency, 24-hour hotline for reporting rape and sexual violence, and the Frauentelefon (☎ 01-408 70 66), for non-urgent problems.

GAY & LESBIAN TRAVELLERS
Vienna is reasonably tolerant towards gays and lesbians, more so than the rest of Austria, and the situation is improving all the time. Gay bashing is virtually unknown in Austria (unlike in ostensibly gay-tolerant cities like Amsterdam or Berlin). In the 1990s two of the three federal statutes concerning homosexuality were repealed – these had banned gay meetings and the promotion of homosexuality. The third statute relates to the age of consent: between men this is 18, in contrast to 14 for heterosexuals. The Austrian government is resisting any change on this inequality, despite pressure from the European parliament. There is no set age of consent for lesbian sex. While lesbians welcome the lack of legislation, they see this as a typical (male) denial of female sexuality.

This book lists some contact addresses and gay and lesbian venues – in the Vienna chapter, for instance – and you will be able to get more information from the following Web sites: Vienna Gay Guide (**W** www .gayguide.at), which also produces the free *Gay Map of Vienna*; and Gay Austria (**W** www.gay.at). You can also pick up the gay magazine *Bussi* at gay venues.

The *Spartacus International Gay Guide*, published by Bruno Gmünder (Berlin), is a good international directory of gay entertainment venues worldwide (mainly for men). Lesbians can turn to *Places of Interest for Women* (Ferrari Publications).

Organisations
The Homosexualle Initiative (HOSI; **W** www.hosi.at) is a national organisation with a branch in many towns – see the Gay & Lesbian sections under Information in the Vienna and Salzburg chapters. Cities generally have other gay or lesbian organisations as well.

DISABLED TRAVELLERS
If you have a physical disability, get in touch with your national support organisation at home (preferably the travel officer if there is one). They often have complete libraries devoted to travel, and can put you in touch with travel agencies that specialise in tours for the disabled or provide useful advice on independent travel.

Within Austria, hotels with three stars and above invariably have a lift (elevator) as well as stairs. More basic places often don't have a lift. Wheelchair ramps are reasonably widespread in cities. Disabled people may get reductions in admission prices – look for the word *Behinderte* – and travel tickets; for example, there is a 50% reduction on regional travel passes in Vorarlberg.

Local tourist offices have information on disabled access, parking, toilets, specialised shops and other matters. The tourist office in Vienna has the very detailed booklet *Accessible Vienna*. The Salzburg office also provides good information, as does the one in Tirol province.

In 2000 the EU issued a standardised Blue Badge which gives EU disabled drivers certain parking rights, which in Austria means they can park free in blue zones. (The UK orange badges, which are being replaced with blue ones as they come up for renewal, are also valid for this concession, though there is a risk the local traffic warden may not know this).

Organisations

The British-based Royal Association for Disability and Rehabilitation (RADAR; ☎ 020-7250 3222, **w** www.radar.org.uk) has some information about travel abroad, but perhaps a more useful organisation is the Holiday Care Service (☎ 01293-774535, **w** www.holidaycare.co.uk), 2nd floor, Imperial Buildings, Victoria Rd, Horley, Surrey RH6 7PZ, which has information sheets on Austria and other countries. In the USA, a useful resource is Mobility International (☎ 541-343 1284, **w** www.miusa.org).

There's no national organisation that provides help for the disabled in Austria, but the city of Vienna runs an advice centre for disabled people, the Behindertenberatungsstelle (☎ 01-531 14-85359), 01, Schottenring 24, open 3pm to 6.30pm Monday and Thursday. For travel on Österreichischen Bundesbahnen (ÖBB; Austrian Federal Railways) trains, contact **e** sabine.scherzer@pv.oebb.at or ☎ 01-9300-35800.

SENIOR TRAVELLERS

Senior travellers are entitled to many discounts on the cost of such things as public transport and museum admission, provided they show proof of age. The minimum qualifying age for Austrians is 65 for men, and 60 for women. If the requisite age is lower in your own country, you *may* be able to persuade the Austrian official to give you a discount at that lower age.

In your home country, you may be entitled to all sorts of interesting travel packages and discounts (on car hire, for instance) through organisations and travel agents that cater for senior travellers. Start hunting at your local senior citizens' advice bureau.

Organisations

The Vienna-based Seniorenbeauftragter der Stadt Wien (☎ 01-4000-8580) can give information on reductions for seniors, plus travel, cultural and leisure-time tips; it's staffed 8am to 3.30pm Monday to Friday.

TRAVEL WITH CHILDREN

Successful travel with young children can require some special effort. Don't try to overdo things; even for adults, packing too much into the time available can cause problems. And make sure your activities include the children as well; for instance, in Klagenfurt balance a tour of the museums with a trip to the Minimundus miniature park. Include children in the trip planning: if they have helped to work out where you will be going, they will be much more interested when they get there. For more information, see Lonely Planet's newly updated *Travel with Children*.

There are sometimes special events and festivals for children. Local tourist offices will be able to supply details. Entry prices are usually reduced for children. In Vienna, during school holidays, children travel free on public transport and get free entry to municipal swimming pools.

DANGERS & ANNOYANCES
Theft

Crime rates in Austria are low by international standards but you should always be security-conscious – you're never more vulnerable to theft than when travelling. Be wary of leaving valuables in hotel rooms. Staff will look after expensive items if you ask them, even in hostels. Don't leave valuables in cars, especially overnight. Beware of pickpockets (who thrive in crowds) and snatch-thieves (a daypack is more secure than a shoulder bag). Carry your own padlock for hostel lockers. Use a moneybelt and keep some emergency money hidden away from your main stash.

Generally, keep your wits about you, and be suspicious of anything that seems out of the ordinary, even unlikely offers of help. Sadly, other travellers are sometimes the people you most have to guard against.

In the event of theft or loss, get a police report – this will be necessary for you to claim on your travel insurance. Your consulate should be able to help replace documents if you're left in a desperate situation.

Other Concerns

Austrian train stations can be a haunt of drunks and vagrants. The problem has lessened now that many stations are locked for

Avalanche Warning

Modern safety precautions mean that the days of entire villages being buried by snow have passed, but the dangers of avalanches should not be underestimated. Each year up to 200 people are killed by avalanches in the Alps. Austria made world headlines in February 1999 when an avalanche smashed through Galtür in Tirol, killing 38.

Problems usually originate on slopes high above the prepared ski runs. Accordingly, mountain resorts now have series of crisscross metal barriers built high on the peaks to prevent snow slips. In addition, helicopter teams routinely drop explosive devices in the mountains to cause controlled slides and prevent the dangerous build-up of snow. Resorts also have a system involving flags or flashing lights to warn skiers of the likelihood of avalanches, and up-to-date reports on weather conditions are always available.

Despite these measures, skiers cannot afford to be complacent. Avalanche warnings should be heeded and local advice sought before detouring from prepared runs. If skiers are buried in an avalanche, chances of rescue are improved if they carry an avalanche transceiver, a radio that transmits and receives a 457kHz signal. These cost US$220 or more. A more expensive precaution (but of debatable value) is an ABS air balloon rucksack. Keeping a mobile phone with you is also a good idea. If you are unfortunate enough to end up buried in snow, dribbling a little spit will help you work out which way is up. If you can't dig your way out, some experts recommend that you urinate, as the smell will attract the tracker dogs. Of course, there's the real possibility that you would have deposited something equally pungent in your pants already!

a few hours at night to stop people sleeping there.

Always treat drugs with a great deal of caution. Don't ever think about trying to carry drugs across the border. Dope (cannabis) is illegal but still available if you look hard enough.

There is some anti-foreigner feeling in areas with high immigrant populations, such as Vienna and Carinthia. It's mostly directed towards Eastern Europeans, Turks and black Africans – residents rather than tourists – and rarely erupts into violent incidents.

Take care if you're mountaineering or embarking on a long-distance walk. Make sure somebody knows where you're going and when you can be expected back.

EMERGENCIES

For urgent service you should call the following country-wide numbers:

Alpine Rescue	☎ 140
Ambulance	☎ 144
Doctor (after hours)	☎ 141
Fire	☎ 122
Police	☎ 133

LEGAL MATTERS

Austria offers the level of civil and legal rights you would expect of any industrialised western nation. If you are arrested, the police must inform you of your rights in a language that you understand.

In Austria, legal offences are divided into two categories: criminal *(Gerichtdelikt)* and administrative *(Verwaltungsübertretung)*. If you are suspected of having committed a criminal offence (such as assault or theft) you can be detained for a maximum of 48 hours before you are committed for trial. If you are arrested for a less serious, administrative offence, such as being drunk and disorderly or committing a breach of the peace, you will be released within 24 hours.

Drunken driving is an administrative matter, even if you have an accident. However, if someone is hurt in the accident it becomes a criminal offence. Possession of a controlled drug is usually a criminal offence but if, for example, you have a small amount of dope that is considered to be for personal use only (there's no hard and fast rule on quantity) you may merely be cautioned and released without being charged. Possession of a large amount of dope (around 300g) or dealing (especially to children) could result in a five-year prison term. Prostitution is legal provided prostitutes are registered and have obtained a permit.

If you are arrested, you have the right to make one phone call to 'a person in your confidence' within Austria, and another to inform legal counsel. If you can't afford legal representation, you can apply to the judge in writing for legal aid.

Free advice is given on legal matters in some towns, for example during special sessions at Vienna's district courts *(Bezirksgerichte)*. As a foreigner, your best bet when encountering legal problems is to contact your national consulate (see the listing earlier in this chapter).

BUSINESS HOURS

Most shops are open from 8am or 9am to between 6pm and 7.30pm Monday to Friday, and on Saturday from 8am or 9am to between 1pm and 5pm. Shops that close at 1pm on Saturday might stay open later only on the first Saturday of the month, known as *Langersamstag* (long Saturday) or *Einkaufsamstag* (shopping Saturday). Some shops also close for up to two hours at noon. Business hours for offices and government departments vary, but are usually 8am to 3.30pm, 4pm or 5pm Monday to Friday.

PUBLIC HOLIDAYS & SPECIAL EVENTS

The public holidays in Austria are:

New Year's Day 1 January
Epiphany (Heilige Drei Könige) 6 January
Easter Monday (Ostermontag) March/April
Labour Day 1 May
Ascension Day (Christihimmelfahrt) – 40 days after Easter
Whit Monday (Pfingstmontag) May – eighth Monday after Easter Monday
Corpus Christi (Fronleichnam) June – the Thursday after the eighth Sunday after Easter Monday
Assumption (Maria Himmelfahrt) 15 August
National Day 26 October
All Saints' Day (Allerheiligen) 1 November
Immaculate Conception (Mariä Empfängnis) 8 December

Christmas Day (Weihnachten) 25 December
St Stephen's Day (Stephanitag) 26 December

Some businesses also close on Good Friday. Banks and shops are closed on public holidays; some restaurants may also close, or else adopt Sunday hours. Some museums also close; others stay open and have free admission.

For information on a selection of Austria's many and varied festivals and special events, see the boxed text 'Festivals of Austria'.

ACTIVITIES

Alpine mountains and lakes provide a superb setting for outdoor sports. For more information about these activities, see the Walking & Skiing special section.

In addition to the sports mentioned in this section, golf, tennis and horse-riding are widely pursued; see individual chapter entries for details of regional centres. Cycling is also extremely popular (see the Getting Around chapter).

Aerial Sports

Mountains are great for paragliding and hang-gliding. Both activities are popular, especially paragliding, for which the equipment is more portable. Many resorts have places where you can hire the gear, get a lesson, or simply go as a passenger on

---

WARNING

Although the author and publisher have done their utmost to ensure the accuracy of all information in this guide, they cannot accept any responsibility for any loss, injury or inconvenience sustained by people using this book. They cannot guarantee that the tracks and routes described have not become impassable for any reason in the interval between research and publication.

The fact that a trip, area or resort is described in this guidebook does not mean that it is safe for you and your party. You are ultimately responsible for judging your own capabilities in the light of the conditions you encounter.

a flight. Hot air ballooning is also taking off, despite the high costs.

Water Sports

Austria's lakes offer equally good sporting facilities as its mountains. Water-skiing, sailing and windsurfing are common on most lakes and courses are usually available. The Österreichischer Segel-Verband (Austrian Sailing Federation; ☎ 01-662 44 62, fax 662 15 58) is at Zetschegasse 21, A-1230 Vienna. Carinthia and Salzkammergut are good regions for water sports. Although you can swim for free in some places, many lakeside beaches charge a moderate entry fee (generally around €1.50 to €5 per day). Anglers should contact the local tourist office to obtain a fishing permit valid for lakes and rivers. Rafting is another popular activity on rivers. Paddleboats or pedalos (Tretboote), rowing boats (Ruderboote) and motorboats (Motorboote or Elektroboote) can usually be hired at lakeside resorts.

COURSES

In addition to activity-based holidays and schools for specific sports, Austria offers the chance to learn new practical skills or academic disciplines. A variety of institutions in the cities offer a host of courses, either on an intensive full-time basis or as evening courses. Inquire at tourist offices for details. The most relevant for visitors are likely to be German-language classes. Language schools are included in the sections on Vienna, Salzburg and Innsbruck (in the Tirol chapter).

WORK

Since January 1993 EU nationals have been able to obtain work in Austria without a work permit, though as prospective residents they need to register with the police within five days of arrival. They can also contact the Aufenthaltsbehörde (residence authority) office in towns, or the Gemeindeamt (council office) in smaller places. The Austrian embassy in your home country will have more information, and the Budesministerium für Arbeit und Soziales (☎ 01-711 00), 01, Stubenring 1, Vienna, may also be helpful.

A good Web site for foreign residents is **w** www.wif.wien.at.

Non-EU nationals need both a work permit and a residency permit, and generally find it pretty hard to get either, though if they are undertaking seasonal work for up to six months they do not require a residence permit. Inquire (in German) about job possibilities via the Arbeitsmarktservice für Wien (☎ 01-515 25-0), Weihburggasse 30, A-1010 Vienna. The work permit needs to be applied for by your employer in Austria. Applications for residence permits must be applied for via the Austrian embassy in your home country. In theory a residence permit might be granted without a pre-arranged work permit, but you need sufficient funds, confirmed accommodation in Austria, and perhaps some form of Austrian sponsorship. A Volunteer Work Permit may be fairly easy to get; the drawback is that with this sort of permit you're not supposed to earn anything. Employers face big fines if they're caught employing workers illegally.

In ski resorts there are often vacancies in snow clearing, chalet cleaning, restaurants and ski equipment shops. These will often involve working unsociable hours. Language skills are particularly crucial for any type of work in service industries. Your best chance of finding work is to start writing or asking around early – in summer for winter work and in winter for summer work. Try to get it all organised before places close for the off season. Some people do get lucky by arriving right at the beginning of the season and asking around. Although it is beyond their brief, tourist offices may be able to help you find work.

In October, grape-pickers are usually required in the wine-growing regions. Street theatre and general busking is not uncommon in Austria and may make you a few euros if you have the required skills. Buskers are occasionally moved on by the police – ask about local regulations before you start up. Also inquire about the relevant permits before trying to sell goods at flea markets.

One publication worth looking at is the fortnightly Rolling Pin International (€2.60). It has articles in German and

Festivals of Austria

Most festivals and cultural events are small-scale local affairs, so it's worth checking with local tourist offices. The Austrian National Tourist Office (ANTO) compiles a list of annual and one-off events taking place in Austria; see the Tourist Offices section earlier in this chapter for contact information. The cycle of music festivals throughout the country is almost unceasing. Religious holidays provide an opportunity to stage colourful processions. Corpus Christi (the second Thursday after Whitsun) brings carnivals, including some held on lakes in the Salzkammergut. National Day on 26 October inspires various events, often accompanied by much patriotic flag-waving.

More details of specific events are given in the text, but here's a selection of annual highlights.

January
New Year concerts
Lavish balls in Vienna (continues into
  February)

February
Fasching (Shrovetide Carnival) week in
  early February

March or April
Easter Festival in Salzburg

May
Maypole dances on 1 May
Gauderfest in Zell am Ziller
Vienna Festival of arts and music (continues
  into June)

June
Midsummer night's celebrations on
  21 June
Donauinselfest in Vienna (last weekend in
  June)
Schubertiade (Schubert Festival) in
  Scwarzenberg, Bregenzerwald

July & August
Summer of Music Festival in Vienna
Salzburg Festival

September
Trade Fairs, especially in Vienna, Graz and
  Innsbruck
Bruckner Festival in Linz

October
Viennale Film Festival in Vienna
Steirischer Herbst (Festival of New Art) in
  Styria
Cattle Roundup in Alpine areas
Wine Harvest celebrations in Burgenland
  and Lower Austria

November
St Martin's Day on 11 November (goose
  eating, Heuriger wine)
Modern Vienna Festival

December
St Nicholas Day parades on 5–6 December
Christmas markets (Christkindlmarkt) in
  Vienna, Salzburg, Innsbruck and elsewhere

continued over

English and carries employment advertisements (mostly for jobs in the hotel industry) from around the world, though by far the biggest section is for jobs in Austria. Unfortunately for guys, the principle of equal opportunity doesn't seem to apply: many jobs specify females only. It should be available in most countries, but if you have difficulty finding a copy, just contact the head office (☎ 0316-811 277, e office@rollingpin.at), PO Box 44, A-8016 Graz. You can also subscribe and peruse jobs online at their Web site w www.rollingpin.at.

Useful books for those searching for work abroad include *Working in Ski Resorts – Europe & North America* by Victoria Pybus, *Work Your Way Around the World* by Susan

And Now for Something Completely Different...

Apart from the usual folk or music fests, you might try an unusual offering:

Perchtenlaufen

(Salzburger Land, on or near 6 January)

Cross-dressing, outlandish apparel and heathen rituals accompany one of the most curious festivals in Austria. The Perchtenlaufen Festival heralds the end of the harsh winter, and is supposed to promote good fortune and a prosperous harvest for the forthcoming year. Thousands of people line the streets for one of the most famous events in Pongau, which rotates annually between the towns of Bad Gastein (2002), Altenmarkt (2003), Bischofshofen (2004) and St Johann im Pongau (2005). Menfolk waltz precariously through the streets crowned with elaborate headdresses, which can weigh anything up to 50kg. Adorned in bright, mirrored costumes to scare off evil spirits, they are accompanied by a gaggle of other masked misfits, ranging from birch-wielding goodly spirits,  mischievous devils and young men masquerading as women (females traditionally are not allowed to participate in the parade). Festive revelry prevails throughout.

The Giant Chocolate Festival

(Bludenz, Vorarlberg, first weekend in July)

Indulge in some hedonistic gorging on one of Austria's specialities: chocolate. The emphasis is on kids; children living in or visiting the area are encouraged to participate in the games and competitions on offer at the Milka Chocolate Festival. Thankfully everyone gets to sample the delights, so it's well worth a visit. One thousand kilograms of the stuff is given away in prizes, with the overall winner taking home their weight in chocolate.

Lederhosen Meeting

(Windischgarsten, 50km south of Linz, beginning of August)

Fun and general merriment is to be had at the annual Lederhosen Meeting. Legend has it that the raucous dancing derives from ancient pagan fertility rituals. Apparently all the slapping and smacking mimicked the workers in the ice-fringed Alps who used similar actions to stimulate their circulation. Coats and gloves can have the same effect, but this seems like more fun.

Festival Rauchkuchldumpling

(St Johann in Tirol, end of September)

Sample some of the 20,000 dumplings prepared by one of the 18 chefs who line the streets of St Johann at the waist-expanding Dumpling Festival. Those attempting to discover the recipes for this traditional dish will be hard pressed to persuade the makers to reveal their arcane knowledge – the exact ingredients are often closely guarded secrets. The proof of the dumpling will have to be in the eating.

Griffith and *The Au Pair and Nanny's Guide to Working Abroad* by Susan Griffith and Sharon Legg; all are published in the UK by Vacation Work (**W** www.vacationwork.co.uk).

ACCOMMODATION

All accommodation is classified and graded in an efficient system, according to the type of

[continued on page 74]

Walking & Skiing in Austria

WALKING

INFORMATION

Walking is popular with Austrians and visitors alike, and thousands of kilometres of trails allow you to explore the Alps. En route there are regular direction signs, and paths may also be indicated by red-white-red stripes on a convenient tree trunk. The practice of marking mountain trails according to their difficulty started in Tirol and is becoming more widespread. Paths are colour-coded according to the skiing system: blue for easy, red for moderate (trails are fairly narrow and steep), and black for difficult (these trails are only for the physically fit; some climbing may be required).

Most tourist offices have free or cheap maps of walking routes. The best trails are away from the towns and in the hills. If you can afford it, take a cable car to get you started.

Tirol has more opportunities than anywhere else in Austria for mountain climbing. Be sure to consult local information phone numbers about weather conditions and avalanche warnings before you set out, and prepare yourself adequately. The Kaisergebirge Mountains in northern Tirol are a favourite with mountaineers, although other areas such as the Ziller Valley are also popular.

The *Walking Guide Tirol*, available free from the Austrian National Tourist Office or the Tirol regional office, contains contact addresses for mountain guides and mountaineering schools in the province, as well as details of alpine huts and walking trails.

The Österreichischer Alpenverein (ÖAV; Austrian Alpine Club) caters for both walkers and mountaineers. Adult membership costs an initial €5.10 plus €48 per year, with substantial discounts for students and people aged under 25 or over 60. ÖAV members pay half-price at alpine huts and get other benefits, including insurance. The ÖAV head office (☎ 0512-58 78 28, fax 58 88 42, **w** www.alpenverein.at) is at Wilhelm Greil Strasse 15, A-6010 Innsbruck. At the same address is its mountaineering school, the Bergsteigerschule (☎ 0512-595 47 34, fax 57 55 28), which offers various mountain touring programs for members, mostly in the summer.

Alpine Huts

There are 500 of these in the eastern Alps, and most are maintained by the ÖAV. Huts are at altitudes of between 900m and 2700m and may be used by the general public. Meals or cooking facilities are often available. Bed prices for non-members are around €30 in a double or €8 in a dorm. Members of the ÖAV or an affiliated club pay half-price and have priority. Contact the ÖAV or local tourist office for lists of huts and to make bookings.

Title page: Looking over the Austrian alps from Valluga Mountains, not far from the St Anton ski resort
(Photo: Patrick Syder)

CHRIS MELLOR

MARK HONAN

Top: Wild flowers and snow colour the Innsbruck countryside

Middle: The picturesque town of Hallstatt is built right into the Alpine slopes

Bottom: Austria's hills and valleys

CHRIS MELLOR

CHRISTIAN ASLUND

CHRISTIAN ASLUND

CHRISTIAN ASLUND

CHRISTIAN ASLUND

Top: A snowboarder carves through some powder in the Arlberg

Middle: St Anton Am Arlberg offers the best off-piste skiing in Austria; All geared up and ready to go

Bottom: Ripping down a slope in the Arlberg

MOUNTAIN SAFETY & EMERGENCIES

First, a sobering statistic: During some summers, fatalities involving walkers account for almost 50% of all deaths resulting from 'mountain recreation accidents'. The remainder lose their lives pursuing more obviously dangerous activities – mainly roped mountaineering, rock-climbing and paragliding. Unlike other mountain sports, however, where the objective risks are higher, most walker deaths are directly attributable to tiredness, carelessness and inadequate clothing or footwear. A fall resulting from sliding on grass, autumn leaves, scree or iced-over paths is a common hazard. Watch out for black ice. In high Alpine routes avalanches and rockfall can be a problem. It's hard to get lost in Austria, where all paths are well signposted, but never leave the marked route and if you get lost turn back immediately. Study the weather forecast before you go and remember that in mountain regions weather patterns change dramatically, so take appropriate clothing and good walking shoes. Make sure you have enough carbohydrate-rich food for the day (including emergency rations) and at least 1L of water per person to avoid dehydration. Increase the length and altitude of your walks gradually, until you are acclimatised to the vast Alpine scale.

Where possible don't walk in the mountains alone. Two is considered the minimum number for safe mountain walking, and having at least one additional person in the party will mean someone can stay with an injured walker while the other seeks help. Properly inform a responsible person, such as a family member, hut warden or hotel receptionist, of your plans, and avoid altering your specified route. Under no circumstances should you leave the marked trails in foggy conditions. With some care, most walking routes can be followed in fog, but otherwise wait by the path until visibility is clear enough to proceed.

The standard Alpine distress signal is six whistles, six calls, six smoke puffs – that is, six of whatever sign you can make – followed by a pause equalling the length of time taken by the calls before repeating the signal again. If you have a mobile phone, take it with you. Mountain rescue in the Alps is very efficient but extremely expensive, so make sure you have insurance.

Mountaineering is a potentially dangerous activity, and you should never climb on your own or without proper equipment.

CONSIDERATIONS FOR RESPONSIBLE WALKING

The popularity of walking is placing great pressure on the natural environment. Please consider the following tips when walking and help preserve Austria's ecology and beauty.

Trail Etiquette

Of course, walking can be a very casual affair, but observing a few simple rules of etiquette will keep you in good stead with other walkers.

Except on very busy routes, it's considered impolite not to greet others you pass along the trail – see the Language chapter for a few handy expressions. The custom on narrow paths is that ascending walkers have right of way over those descending.

Always leave farm gates as you find them. In summer low-voltage electric fences are set up to control livestock on the open Alpine pastures; where an electric fence crosses a path, it usually has a hook that can be easily unfastened to allow walkers to pass through without getting zapped.

Don't pick alpine wild flowers – they really do look lovelier on the mountainsides. Animal watchers should approach wildlife with discretion. Moving too close will unnerve wild animals, distracting them from their vital summer activity of putting on fat for the long Alpine winter.

Rubbish

- Carry out all of your rubbish. If you've carried it in you can carry it out. And don't overlook those easily forgotten items, such as silver paper (tin foil), orange peels, cigarette butts and plastic wrappers. Empty packaging weighs very little anyway, and should be stored as you go along in a dedicated rubbish bag. Make an effort to carry out rubbish left by others.
- Never bury your rubbish: digging disturbs soil and ground cover and encourages erosion. Buried rubbish will more than likely be dug up by animals, who may be injured or poisoned by it. It may also take years to decompose, especially at high altitudes.
- Minimise the waste you must carry out by taking minimal packaging and no more food than you will actually need. If you can't buy in bulk, unpack small-portion packages and combine their contents in one container before your trip. Take reusable containers or stuff sacks.
- Don't rely on bought water in plastic bottles. Disposal of these bottles is creating a major problem in the world. Use iodine drops or purification tablets instead.
- Condoms, tampons and sanitary pads should also be carried out, despite the inconvenience. They burn and decompose poorly.

Human Waste Disposal

- Contamination of water sources by human faeces can lead to the transmission of hepatitis, typhoid and intestinal parasites such as giardia, amoebae and roundworms. It can cause severe health risks to members of your party, to local residents and to wildlife.
- Where there is a toilet, please use it.
- Where there is none, bury your waste. Dig a small hole 15cm deep and at least 100m from any watercourse. Consider carrying a lightweight trowel for this purpose. Cover the waste with soil and a rock. Use toilet paper sparingly and bury that too. In snow, dig down beneath the soil; otherwise your waste will be exposed when the snow melts.
- If the area is inhabited, ask locals if they have any concerns about your chosen toilet site.

Washing

- Don't use detergents or toothpaste in or near watercourses, even if they are biodegradable.
- For personal washing, use biodegradable soap and a water container (or even a lightweight basin) at least 50m away from the watercourse. Disperse the waste-water widely to allow the soil to filter it.
- Wash cooking utensils 50m from watercourses using a scourer, sand or snow instead of detergent.

Erosion

- Mountain slopes and hillsides, especially at high altitudes, are prone to erosion. It is important to stick to existing tracks and avoid short cuts that bypass a switchback. If you blaze a new trail straight down a slope, it will turn into a watercourse with the next heavy rainfall and eventually cause soil loss and deep scarring.
- If a well-used track passes through a mud patch, walk through the mud: walking around the edge will increase the size of the patch.
- Avoid removing the plant life that keeps topsoils in place.

WALKING HIGHLIGHTS

The following is a selection of the many recognised walks in Austria. For detailed maps and further information on each of these and other walks, see the brochures available from Austrian National Tourist Offices. Ensure you have full directions, sufficient provisions and an adequate map before you set off on these walks.

NEUSIEDLER SEE (BURGENLAND)

This walk from Illmitz follows cycle paths and minor roads on flat ground and is suitable for everyone. Over the course of 16km (four to five hours) you'll encounter lakes and reed beds that are a haven for wildlife. In Spring, bring your binoculars to observe the antics of the migrating waterfowl. Storks nesting on rooftops are a common sight in Illmitz and the surrounding towns. For more information, see the the Burgenland chapter.

Map: Freytag & Berndt, *Neusiedler See, Rust & Seewinkel*, 1:50,000

GAMLITZ (STYRIA)

Starting at Gamlitz, follow waymarked route 3. This 17km, five-hour walk explores the farm tracks, footpaths and country lanes snaking through this vineyard region. The gentle hills make walking fairly easy going. Gamlitz is south of Graz, 2km from Ehrenhausen (for more deatils, see Styrian Wine Routes in the Styria chapter).

Map: Kompass Wanderkarte 217, *Südsteirisches Weinland*, 1:35,000

HERMAGOR (CARINTHIA)

This 13km route is a good family walk.that explores the water-carved gorge cut deep into the Karnische Alpen. Although the waterfalls and pools make for some stunning scenery, watch out for the gorge path, which can be slippery in places. Allow 5½ hours if you leave from

Hermagor or 4½ hours if you park at the gorge entrance. Hermagor is about 45km west of Villach, in Carinthia.

Map: Kompass Wanderkarte 60, *Gailtaler Alpen-Karnische Alpen*, 1:50,000

ÖTZTALER ALPEN (TIROL)

The mountain scenery of the Ötztaler Alpen is among the best in Austria, making this 18km, two-day walk well worth the effort for fit and experienced hill walkers. Starting at the Gepatschhaus at the southern end of the Gepatsch reservoir in the Kaunertal, well-signed paths mark the route. Some rock hopping is involved and you have to overcome a steep snow slope from the Ölgrupen Joch. One of the best parts of this walk is the great view after an overnight stay in an alpine hut. The Kaunertal can be reached from Landeck (see Western Tirol in the Tirol chapter).

Map: Kompass Wanderkarte 43, *Ötztaler Alpen*, 1:50,000

STUBAIER ALPEN (TIROL)

Starting at Neustift/Neder in the Stubaital, you will need at least seven to nine days and a good level of fitness to tread the well-marked 120km route of the Stubaier Höhenweg. The huts along the way are as varied as the stunning views, although all are warm and comfortable. Every section involves battling at least one pass, and many sections have fixed wire ropes to assist with difficult steps. Snow patches are possible even in late summer. Buses run along the Stubaital from Innsbruck (see Stubai Glacier in the Tirol chapter).

Map: Kompass Wanderkarte 83, *Stubaier Alpen – Serleskamm*, 1:50,000

INNSBRUCK (TIROL)

From Maria Theresien Strasse in Innsbruck, this 9km walk explores the best of the old town before climbing the vast Nordkette Mountains to expose magnificent views of the town below. Footpaths and minor roads make for easy walking, although there are some steep ascents. For fit walkers, the route should take three to four hours. Innsbruck is described fully in the Tirol chapter.

Map: Freytag & Berndt WK333, *Innsbruck und Umgebung*, 1:25,000

MATREI IN OSTTIROL (EAST TIROL)

This 15km walk is good for exploring the region's valleys, especially if low cloud is obscuring the panoramic mountain views. The pathway walking is gentle, although the uphill forest track can be slightly arduous and sometimes overgrown. There is some interesting architecture along the route, including the delicate whitewashed chapel at Hinteregg and the Romanesque church of St Nikolaus. Leaving from Matrei, allow five hours for this stroll. There's a national park office in Matrei (see Information in the Hohe Tauern National Park Region chapter).

Map: Kompass Wanderkarte 48, *Kals am Grossglockner*, 1:50,000

BIELERHÖHE (VORARLBERG)

Starting at the road-pass linking the Montafon and Paznaun Valleys via the Silvretta Hochalpenstrasse, this 13km walk passes lakes, deep pools and mountains. The best time to visit is early summer when carpets of alpine flowers flourish on the hills. The terrain is fairly gentle, although you will need good walking boots for this five- to six-hour walk. The first descent from Radsattel can be tricky and there may be patches of snow on the route, even in early summer. For information about getting to Bielerhöhe, see Getting There & Away in the Vorarlberg chapter's Bludenz section.

Map: Kompass Wanderkarte 41, Silvretta Verwallgruppe, 1:50,000

TENNENGEBIRGE (SALZBURG PROVINCE)

For fit walkers, this 21km walk covers the high pasture of the Tennengebirge, the area used for the famous opening sequence of *The Sound of Music*. The town of Werfen, overlooked by Burg Hohenwerfen (Werfen fortress), is the start of an idyllic seven- to eight-hour walk through beautiful meadows, forest and farmland. The Eisriesenwelt Caves, the largest ice caves in the world, are nearby. Accommodation options for Werfen are given in the Salzburg Province chapter.

Map: Tennengebirge Wanderkarte (available from the Werfen tourist office), *Werfen, Pfarrwerfen, Werfenweng*, 1:35,000

KATRIN (UPPER AUSTRIA)

Take the cable car from the spa town of Bad Ischl to the Katrin upper cable car station to reach the start of this 11.5km route. Some of the more precarious segments of this walk, where the vegetation gives way to bare rocky ridges, have fixed ropes to assist walkers, who will need a good head for heights. The tough descent is made more bearable by the excellent views of lakes and valleys below. Allow 4½ hours. Information about Bad Ischl and Mt Katrin can be found in the Salzkammergut chapter.

Map: Kompass Wanderkarte 20, *Dachstein, Südliches Salzkammergut*, 1:50,000

HALLSTATT (UPPER AUSTRIA)

Starting at the Steeg-Gosau railway station, most of this 16km walk alongside the Hallstätter See is easy going, although the ascent of a long flight of steps on leaving Hallstatt can be taxing. Hallstatt is one of the most beautiful and historic villages in Austria, so make sure you have time to explore the village before setting off on the return leg. If you're more ambitious, you can take on the 40km Soleweg (brine trail) from Hallstatt north to Ebensee, following the course of the world's oldest pipeline (1607). Hallstatt, Hallstätter See and Ebensee are covered in the Salzkammergut chapter.

Map: Kompass Wanderkarte 20, *Dachstein, Südliches Salzkammergut*, 1:50,000

SKIING

There's a whole range of choice here for skiers. Austria has gentle nursery slopes in picturesque surroundings to inspire any first-timer, as well as world-class serious terrain at resorts such as St Anton am Arlberg and Kitzbühel to satisfy the slickest of professionals. Getting to the slopes is easy, with most of the main areas accessible from major towns, including Salzburg and Innsbruck. Many resorts, such as Sportwelt in Salzburg province or Skiwelt in Tirol, offer regional passes that allow free access to hundreds of different pistes in the district.

While this book contains plenty of skiing information, it is not a skiing guide. Austria has hundreds of top-notch ski resorts and no attempt has been made to cover them exhaustively: Don't assume the skiing is not good in a resort if it is not mentioned here. Rather, ski resorts have been selected if good skiing is allied to fame, scenery and general attractions. For a detailed assessment of resorts based primarily on skiing criteria, consult a specialist book or magazine, such as the UK's *The Good Skiing & Snowboarding Guide*. More information on ski resorts can be provided by the Austrian National Tourist Office and the resort tourist offices.

INFORMATION
Costs, Passes & Seasons

Skiing for tourists is reasonable value, and generally cheaper than in neighbouring Switzerland. Ski passes cover the cost of specified mountain transport, including ski buses between the ski areas. Pass prices for little-known places may be as little as half as that charged in the jet-set resorts such as Kitzbühel. Vorarlberg and especially Tirol are the most popular areas, but there is also skiing in Salzburg Province, Upper Austria and Carinthia. Ski passes are available from ski lifts and usually from buses to the lifts, and also occasionally from tourist offices. Equipment can always be hired at resorts. You may initially get some strange looks if you ask to buy ex-rental stock, but great bargains can be picked up this way.

Ski coupons (passes based on usage rather than time) for ski lifts can sometimes be bought, but usually there are general passes available for full or half days. Count on around €20 to €38 for a one-day ski pass, with substantial reductions for longer-term passes. At the beginning and end of the season, and sometimes in January, ski passes may be available at a reduced rate as this is the low season.

The skiing season starts in December and lasts well into April in the higher resorts. The slopes get the biggest crowds at Christmas/ New Year and in February. Mid-April to June and late October to

Inset: The large ski resort of St Anton Am Arlberg offers spectacular ski runs for experts and is the best in Austria for off-piste skiing on powder snow (Photo: Christian Aslund)

mid-December fall between the summer and winter seasons in mountain resorts. Some cable cars will be closed for maintenance and many hotels and restaurants will be shut, but you'll avoid the crowds and find prices at their lowest. Year-round skiing is possible at several glaciers, such as the Stubai Glacier near Innsbruck. However, most alpine glaciers are now retreating in the face of global warming, and snow coverage is less secure at lower elevations in the early and late season. (For more information on glaciers, see the boxed text 'Glacier Watching' in the Hohe Tauern National Park Region chapter.)

Rental prices for skis, stocks and shoes are around €15 to €25 for one day for downhill and €8 to €13 for cross-country, with reduced rates offered over longer periods. Telemark skis can be hired but are not always easy to find.

Ski Schools
There are numerous schools where you can learn to ski – Tirol province alone has 1600 registered ski instructors. All the ski resorts listed in this book have at least one ski school and you can join a group class or pay for individual tuition on a per-lesson basis. It shouldn't be necessary to arrange these in advance. The ski school in Lech (W www.skischule-lech.com), for example, charges €45 for one day's tuition in group lessons (maximum 10 students), or €175 for individual tuition. Six or seven days in group lessons costs €160. You'll find slightly lower prices in the less well-known resorts, which will also have the benefit of being less crowded.

Snowboarding & Cross-Country Skiing
Snowboarding, the alpine equivalent of surfing, is popular in Austria. Boards can be hired from ski shops. Cross-country skiing (Langlauf) is also extremely popular, and is the cheapest form of skiing: it's usually not necessary to buy lift passes in order to reach the trails, and the slender cross-country skis are generally cheaper to hire than the sturdier downhill version.

Dangers & Annoyances
Despite precautions such as expensive anti-avalanche fences and tunnels, avalanches pose a very real danger in snowbound areas. Each year many people die as a result of these disasters, and whole valleys can be cut off for days. All avalanche-warning signs should be strictly obeyed, whether they are along roads or on ski slopes. They are there for a reason. (For further information, see the boxed text 'Avalanche Warning' in the Facts for the Visitor chapter.) Obviously, always be prepared for conditions and check the weather forecast before you set out.

If you go skiing, it is essential that you are covered by a health insurance policy, as medical costs are expensive and accident rates are high. Not all travel insurance policies cover activities such as skiing, so make certain that your policy does.

SOME RESORTS AT A GLANCE

The following is a selection of some of Austria's varied skiing highlights. Six-day ski passes are quoted here at high season rates; check with local tourist offices or turn to the regional chapter for details on possible discounts.

INNSBRUCK (TIROL)

This attractive Olympic centre and capital of Tirol is the gateway to five main ski areas as well as the Stubai Glacier, which offers virtually year-round skiing. All resorts are connected by skibus, and a ski pass gives access to 51 pistes of varying difficulty. A six-day adult pass costs €138 and the season runs from December to April (except for the glacier). Full information on Innsbruck is given in the Tirol chapter.

Altitude range: 575m-2334m

ISCHGL (TIROL)

Ischgl lies in the Paznaun Valley, and 42 lifts will take you into what is hailed as one of Austria's best skiing areas. A six-day adult pass costs €186 and gives access to 66 runs throughout the valley, including Samnaun in Switzerland. The season runs from December to April. For details, see the Paznauntal section in the Tirol chapter.

Altitude range: 1400m-2872m

KIRCHBERG (TIROL)

Kirchberg is close to high-flying Kitzbühel, but requires less queuing and less expense. The village offers 16 lifts to 14 pistes, as well as access to the vast Kitzbühel ski area (see the following section). Some accommodation and transportation options for Kirchberg are given in the the Tirol chapter.

Altitude range: 860m-1934m

KITZBÜHEL (TIROL)

The medieval town of Kitzbühel, one of Austria's most famous resorts, is the gateway to some excellent intermediate and advanced ski slopes. The area offers 60 lifts to reach 160km of pistes. Ski passes giving access to 328 pistes in the region are also available. In high season a six-day pass costs €160; the entire season lasts from December to April. For detailed resort information, see the Kitzbühel section in the Tirol chapter

Altitude range: 800m-2000m

SAALBACH-HINTERGLEMM (SALZBURG PROVINCE)

This lively twin resort just north of the Hohe Tauern mountain chain has excellent skiing for all standards, but particularly for adept intermediates. Fifty-two lifts take you to 200km of prepared runs. Good snow conditions last from December to the end of March and a six-day adult pass costs €155. Nearby are Zell am See and Kaprun, where there's year-round glacier skiing on Kitzsteinhorn. See Zell am See in the Hohe Tauern National Park Region chapter.

Altitude range: 1003m-2100m

SÖLL (TIROL)

Once notorious for its après-ski scene, Söll has been transformed to recapture some of its Tirolean grace. Near the resort are 30 lifts ascending to 91km of pistes, yet the real asset of Söll is its proximity to Skiwelt, one of Austria's largest ski areas: a ski pass allows access to 250km of pistes. The season runs from December to April, and a six-day adult pass costs (138. Söll is described briefly in the Tirol chapter.

Altitude range: 720m-1892m

LECH (VORARLBERG)

The rich, royal and famous who frequent this resort lend to its air of exclusivity. Most of the closest runs are relatively gentle, although there is some trickier off-piste terrain. Lech is linked by lifts to the nearby resort of Zürs, and both have buses to St Anton am Arlberg. The general ski pass covers all three resorts (see the next listing for details). The Western Arlberg section in the Vorarlberg chapter also offers more information.

Altitude range: 1304m-2811m

ST ANTON AM ARLBERG (TIROL)

Resting between Vorarlberg and Tirol, St Anton am Arlberg is as dynamic as other resorts nearby but less elitist. Popular with advanced skiers, the resort offers over 80 lifts to 260km of prepared pistes and 180km of deep-snow descents plus a vibrant après-ski scene. The season runs from November to mid-April, and a six-day pass, which also covers Lech and Zürs, will cost you €176. For detailed resort information, see St Anton am Arlberg at the end of the Tirol chapter.

Altitude range: 1304m-2811m

Right: Look, no skis! There's more than one way of getting down a mountain.

[continued from page 62]

establishment and the level of comfort it provides. Tourist offices invariably have extensive information on nearly all available accommodation, including prices and on-site amenities. Often the office will find and book rooms for little or no commission. They tend not to deal with the very cheapest places, but this service could save you a lot of time and effort, especially in somewhere very crowded such as Vienna.

In Austria there has been a general move towards providing higher quality accommodation at higher prices. Rooms where guests have to use shared showers *(Etagendouche)* are gradually being upgraded and fitted with private showers. This makes life more difficult for budget travellers, who increasingly will have to rely on hostels.

It's wise to book ahead at all times, but reservations are definitely recommended in July and August and at Christmas and Easter. If the need for a flexible itinerary prevents you from making reservations a long way in advance, a telephone call the day before is better than nothing. However, some places will not accept telephone reservations. Confirmed reservations in writing are binding on either side and compensation may be claimed if you do not take a reserved room or if a reserved room is unavailable.

Breakfast is included in hostel, pension and hotel prices listed in this book, unless stated otherwise. In mountain resorts high-season prices can be up to double the prices charged in the low season (May and November, which fall between the summer and winter seasons). In towns, the difference may be as little as 10%, or even nothing in budget places.

Camping

Austria has over 400 camping grounds that offer a range of facilities such as washing machines, electricity connection, on-site shops and occasionally cooking facilities. Camping Gaz canisters are widely available. Camp sites are often scenically situated in an out-of-the-way place by a river or lake – fine if you're exploring the countryside but inconvenient if you want to sightsee in a

town. For this reason, and because of the extra gear required, camping is more viable if you have your own transport. Places charge around €4 to €8 per adult (children are normally half-price), plus the same again for each tent; in some places there's a charge of around €3 for a car. Alternatively, a few camping grounds charge an all-inclusive rate for a site. For budget solo travellers, hostelling doesn't end up being much more expensive.

Some sites are open all year but the majority close in the winter. If demand is low in spring and autumn, some camp sites shut even though their literature says they are open, so telephone ahead to check during these periods. In high season, camp sites may be full unless you reserve, and higher prices may apply.

The Österreichischer Camping Club (Austrian Camping Club; ☎ 01-711 99-1272, **w** www.campingclub.at), Schubertring 1-3, A-1010 Vienna, sells camping guides. Annual membership costs €8.75 and includes a camping carnet (for reduced site fees).

Free camping in camper vans is OK in Autobahn rest areas and alongside other roads, as long as you're not causing an obstruction (in tents, however, it's illegal). Note that it's prohibited in urban and protected rural areas, and you may not set up camping equipment outside the van. However, Tirol is very strict and even people in camper vans have been asked to move on. Collect all your rubbish and dispose of it responsibly. Check with the owners of private land – they may allow you to camp, either for free or for a small charge.

Alpine Huts

There are 500 of these in the eastern Alps, and most are maintained by the Österreichische Alpenverein (ÖAV; Austrian Alpine Club). For more information, see the Walking & Skiing special section.

Hostels

Hostels are no longer specifically aimed at young people, although most people who stay in them are young, and noisy school groups can sometimes disrupt the peace of such places. Facilities in hostels are pretty good nowadays: four- to six-bed dorms with private shower/toilet are common, and some places have double rooms or family rooms. Some hostels, such as the one in Graz, are even aiming for a 'youth hotel' concept: providing cheap dorm beds and also added services such as longer reception opening hours, on-site shops and pre-made beds. In all hostels, having to do chores is a thing of the past, but the annoying habit of locking the doors during the day (usually from 9am to 5pm) still persists in many places. Only rarely can you check in before 5pm. Night-time curfews can often be avoided by getting a key, or there may be an electronic key-code system.

Austria has over 100 hostels affiliated with Hostelling International (HI), plus a smattering of privately owned hostels. Membership cards are always required except in a few private hostels. It's cheaper to become a member in your home country than to wait until you get to Austria. Non-members pay a surcharge of €2.95 per night for a guest card *(Gästekarte)* but after six nights the guest card counts as a full membership card. Most hostels accept reservations by telephone or email, and some are part of the worldwide computer reservations system. Dorm prices range from €10.20 to €17.50 per night.

The word for youth hostel in German is *Jugendherberge*, though *Jugendgästehaus* or other titles may be used instead. Austria has two hostel organisations. Hostels that are affiliated to the worldwide HI network are linked to one or the other; which one they are linked to is something of a historical legacy and makes no difference to how the hostels are run. Either head office in Vienna can give information on all HI hostels. The Österreichischer Jugendherbergsverband (☎ 01-533 53 53, fax 535 08 61, e oejhv@chello.at) is at 01, Schottenring 28. The Österreichischer Jugendherbergswerk (☎ 01-533 18 33, fax 533 18 33-33, e oejhw@oejhw.or.at) is at 01, Helferstorferstrasse 4. Each of these places has a travel service on the premises.

Cheap dorm-style accommodation is sometimes available in ski resorts even if there is no hostel. Look for *Touristenlager* or *Massenlager;* unfortunately, such accommodation might only be offered to pre-booked groups.

Student Residences

Studentenheime are available to tourists from 1 July to 30 September while students are on holiday. During university terms the kitchen and dining room on each floor are open, but when they're used as seasonal hotels these useful facilities generally remain locked. Rooms are perfectly OK but nothing fancy; some have a private bathroom. Expect single beds (though beds may be placed together in double rooms), a work desk and a wardrobe. The widest selection is in Vienna, but look for them also in Graz, Salzburg and Innsbruck. Prices per person are likely to range from €16 to €36; sometimes breakfast is included.

Pensions & Hotels

Pensions and hotels are rated from one to five stars depending on the facilities they offer. However, as the criteria are different you can't assume that a three-star pension is equivalent to a three-star hotel. Pensions tend to be smaller than hotels, and usually provide a more personal service and less standardised fixtures and fittings. Pensions generally offer a better size and quality of room for the price than hotels. Where they can't usually compete is in services such as room service and laundry, and in on-site facilities such as private car parking, bars and restaurants. If none of that matters , stick with the pensions.

With very few exceptions, rooms in hotels and pensions are clean and adequately appointed. In tourist areas, expect to pay a minimum of around €24/40 for a single/double with shared shower or €30/48 with private shower. In less-visited places the cost may be as much as €3.50 per person lower. In this book, prices ranges are given for some hotels; the price you'll actually pay will depend on the size, situation and style of the room, and perhaps also the length of your stay and the time of the year. In ski resorts, where the price difference

Spa Resorts

Indulgence by the rich and famous in Austria's spa towns has made these resorts some of the most famous in Europe. In an attempt to rid himself of deafness, Beethoven was a regular visitor to Baden, while Princess Sophie proclaimed that the waters of Bad Ischl were a boost to her fertility. The popularity of the treatments has led to the rise of over 100 spa resorts scattered across the country.

The validity of the benefits is a topic of heated debate throughout the medical profession. Sufferers from a variety of conditions ranging from eye diseases to poisoning have hailed the curative properties of the spa as miraculous. Different resorts often promote specialised benefits: the water of Bad Deutsch-Altenburg is rich in sulphur, a substance supposedly beneficial for the relief of spine and joint complaints, and Bad Ischl's abundance of salts is said to alleviate rheumatism. For a list of condition-specific resorts, contact the Austrian National Tourist Office.

Of course, you don't need an ailment in order to enjoy the luxury of a spa treatment. Everything seems to be on offer, from traditional massage to high-tech aroma-light therapy. While the debate rages on, there can be no denying that the stress-relieving qualities of a long hot soak can work wonders for the body and soul.

between seasons can be significant, we've often specified separate summer and winter prices.

If business is slow, mid-range and top-end hotels (and to a lesser extent pensions) may be willing to negotiate on prices. It's always worth asking for a special deal as prices can come down quite substantially. Some places will also offer special weekend rates, or two nights for the price of one. Even in budget places, ask for a special price if you're planning to stay for more than a few days. Credit cards are rarely accepted by cheaper places.

In low-budget accommodation, a room advertised as having a private shower may mean that it has a shower cubicle rather than a proper en suite bathroom. Where there is a telephone in the room it's usually direct-dial, but this will still be more expensive than using a public telephone. TVs are almost invariably hooked up to satellite or cable, which is a definite plus over TVs that only get the two national channels. Higher-quality rooms usually have a mini-bar; prices will be comparable to ordinary bar prices in mid-range accommodation, but quite expensive in upmarket places.

Many hotels and pensions have rooms with three or more beds, or can place a fold-up bed in the room for a child; ask at the establishment. Smaller places with two stars or less tend not to have a lift (elevator); most other places do. Some old Viennese apartment blocks have a lift that needs to be operated by a key, which the pension owner will give you.

Usually, meals are available, either for guests only or, more often, in a public restaurant on-site. A pension that supplies breakfast only is known as a *Frühstückspension;* the hotel equivalent is *Hotel-Garni.* Other hotels and pensions will offer the option of paying for half or even full board. In budget places, breakfast is basic, usually consisting of only a drink, bread rolls, butter, cheese spread and jam. As you pay more, breakfast gets better: in two star places it's usually 'extended' *(erweitert),* and in places with three stars or more it's usually a help-yourself buffet. A typical buffet will include cereals, juices and a selection of cold meats and cheeses – maybe even (in top places) hot food such as scrambled egg, sausage and bacon. In five star hotels breakfast generally costs extra, but may be included in special, lower weekend rates.

Other Accommodation

Self-catering holiday apartments *(Ferienwohnungen)* are very common in mountain resorts, though it is often necessary to book these well in advance. In the UK, for competitive rental deals inquire at Interhome (☎ 020-8891 1294, **w** www.interhome.co.uk). You'll sometimes come across hotels that have self-contained apartment rooms.

A cheap and widely available option, particularly in more rural areas, is to take a room in a private house (€10 to €25 per person) or a farmhouse (*Bauernhof*). In either case, look for signs saying *Zimmer frei* or *Privat Zimmer*.

A *Gästehaus* or *Gasthof* is a small-scale country inn. In these places you may not be able to check in on a day that the restaurant is closed for its rest day (*Ruhetag*). You should phone ahead to check; somebody is normally there in the morning to organise breakfast for the guests.

In many resorts (not so often in cities) a guest card (*Gästekarte*) is issued to people who stay overnight. The card may offer useful discounts on things such as cable cars and admission prices. Check with the tourist office if you're not offered one at your resort accommodation – even camp sites and youth hostels should be included in these schemes. The guest card system is often financed by a resort tax (not payable for children), which may be anything from €0.50 to €2 per night, depending upon the place and type of accommodation. Prices quoted in accommodation lists are usually inclusive of such taxes.

FOOD

The main meal is taken at noon, whether in a restaurant, cafe or tavern. Many places have a set dish (*Tagesteller*) or set meal (*Tagesmenü* or *Mittagsmenü*); a set lunch with soup might cost as little as €4.50. Occasionally a Tagesmenü (day's meal) is available in the evening, whereas a Mittagsmenü (midday meal) isn't. *Jause* is a light meal, served between normal eating times. Note: the full menu of all dishes available is not a *Menü;* it's called the *Speisekarte*.

Chinese restaurants are particularly good value for set meals, and the food is generally reliable. There are around 700 Chinese restaurants in Austria, and around 1000 pizzerias. Wine taverns (called *Heurigen* or *Buschenschenken*) are fairly inexpensive places to eat, and are an Austrian institution, particularly in the suburbs of Vienna.

Coffee houses are another Austrian institution. They basically fall into two types, though the distinction is rather blurred

nowadays. A *Kaffeehaus*, traditionally preferred by men, offers games such as chess and billiards, and serves wine, beer, spirits and light meals as well as coffee. The *Cafe Konditorei* attracts more women and typically has a salon look with rococo mouldings and painted glass. A variety of cakes and pastries is usually on offer.

The cheapest deal around for sit-down food is in university restaurants (*Mensas*). Those mentioned in this book are open to everyone, though they usually only serve weekday lunches and may be closed during university holidays. Expect to find two or three different daily specials, including a vegetarian choice. Students may be able to get a discount of €0.30 or so if they show an ISIC card. Mensas are good places to meet students (who usually speak English well) and find out about the 'in' places round town.

The main train stations all have several options for a cheap meal. Branches of Wienerwald offer unremarkable but reasonably priced chicken dishes, either on an eat-in or takeaway basis. Nordsee is its fishy equivalent. Self-service places are usually the cheapest and are often indicated by 'SB' (*Selbstbedienung*).

For expensive dining, five star hotels invariably have a gourmet restaurant. The more expensive restaurants usually add a cover charge (*Gedeck*), typically around €2 at lunch and €3.50 in the evening. In restaurants without a cover charge, the bread (*Gebäck*) that appears on the table usually costs extra – if in doubt, ask.

If you just want to fill up with fast food, there's usually somewhere you can do this. A McDonald's awaits in every town, but sausage stands (*Würstel Stände*) selling various sausages with bread are more authentically Austrian, as are the schnitzel chains Eurosnack and Schnitzelhaus. Deli shops sometimes offer hot food, such as spit-roasted chicken (an Austrian favourite). Occasionally they have tables so you can eat on the premises.

Be wary of public holidays: restaurants that have a rest day (*Ruhetag*) often close on these days as well. Although inns and

Meat Treat

The *Würstel Stand* (sausage stand) is a familiar Austrian institution and may sell up to a dozen types of sausage. Each comes with a chunk of bread and a big dollop of mustard *(Senf)*, which can be sweet *(süss or Kremser Senf)* or hot *(scharf)*. Tomato ketchup and mayonnaise can be requested. The thinner sausages are served two at a time, except in the less expensive 'hot dog' version, when a single sausage is placed in a bread stick.

Types of sausage include the frankfurter, a standard thin, boiled sausage; the bratwurst, a fat, fried sausage; and *Burenwurst*, the boiled equivalent of bratwurst. *Debreziner* is a thin, spicy sausage from Hungary. *Currywurst* is Burenwurst with a curry flavour, *Käsekrainer* is a sausage infused with cheese and *Tiroler Wurst* is a smoked sausage. In Vienna, if you want to surprise and perhaps impress the server, use the following slang to ask for a Burenwurst with sweet mustard and a crust of bread: *'A Hasse mit an Sóassn und an Scherzl, bitte'*. But you probably won't get it – crusts are reserved for regular customers.

restaurants often stay open till 11pm or midnight, the kitchen is rarely open beyond 9pm or 9.30pm (except in pizzerias and Chinese restaurants).

Self-Catering

If you plan on self-catering, there are several national supermarket chains – Billa is the most widespread. With the exception of a few outlets in or around train stations in big cities, food shops are not open after 7.30pm or on Sunday. Those that do open outside these hours are often much more expensive (though the few Billa outlets that are open Sunday have standard prices).

Austrian Cuisine

Traditional Austrian food is generally quite heavy and hearty, with meat strongly emphasised. In some parts of Austria vegetarians will have a fairly tough time finding varied meals. Even so, many places now offer at least one vegetarian dish, and there has been a noticeable move towards providing light, healthy meals, often called a *Fitnessteller* (fitness meal), especially in summer. Kosher restaurants are few and far between.

You may come across regional variations in the German spellings used below.

Soup is the standard starter to a meal, particularly with a Menü of the day. *Markknödelsuppe* is a clear bone marrow soup with dumplings. *Frittatensuppe,* another specialty, is a clear soup with shreds of crepe-like pancake.

Dumplings *(Knödel)* are an element of many meals, and can appear in soups and desserts as well as main courses. They may be made of a variety of ingredients, such as liver *(Leberknödel)* or bread *(Semmelknödel)*.

Nockerln (sometimes called *Spätzle*, especially in the west) is small home-made pasta with a similar taste to Knödel. *Nudeln* is normally flat pasta (like tagliatelle), except when it's the tiny noodles in a soup. In Carinthia, pasta is made into balls and combined with cheese *(Käsnudeln)*. *Käsnocken*, *Kässpätzle* and *Käsnödel* are variations on a similar theme.

Potato will usually appear as French fries *(Pommes,* pronounced '**pom**-es'), boiled *(Kartoffel)*, roasted *(Bratkartoffel)* or as *Geröstete*, sliced small and sauteed. *Erdapfel* is another word for potato.

Meat & Fish *Wiener Schnitzel* is Vienna's best-known culinary concoction, but it's consumed everywhere, not just in Vienna. It's an escalope covered in a coating of egg and breadcrumbs and fried. The meat is either veal *(Kalb)* or, less expensively, pork *(Schwein)*; occasionally there are variations, such as turkey *(Puter)*.

Goulash *(Gulasch)* is also very popular. It's a meat and vegetable stew made with

DIY Wiener Schnitzel

Wiener Schnitzel is the archetypal Austrian dish. A properly cooked schnitzel should have a puckered coating rather than a flat one – you should be able to easily slip your knife in between the coating and the meat. The outside should be crisp, and should not leave a greasy residue on your plate. A traditional 'authentic' schnitzel is made using veal, though pork is a very common substitute.

If you want to cook up your own Wiener Schnitzel, here's how. The following recipe is based on the one appearing in *The New Austrian Cookbook*, and has been reproduced with the kind permission of the authors, Rudolf & Karl Obauer (**e** r.a.obauer@sbg.at) of the Restaurant-Hotel Obauer, Werfen:

Ingredients (to serve four people):
4 veal schnitzel from the back (ideally just under 1cm thick and weighing 160g)
flour
2 eggs
white breadcrumbs
vegetable oil
salt
pepper

Method:
1. Gently pound the schnitzel, season with salt and pepper. Toss it in flour, dip it in beaten eggs and then dip into white breadcrumbs. Press the breadcrumbs on gently and shake off loose ones.
2. Fry the schnitzel in a generous amount of vegetable oil until golden. Important: the fat has to be hot enough to bubble and spit gently when a schnitzel is put in; fat that is too hot prevents the coating from rising.
3. As soon as the schnitzel has browned underneath, turn over and finish frying (altogether about seven minutes). Remove the schnitzel from the fat and allow to drain on paper towels.
Serve with parsley potatoes, salad and possibly cranberries.

a rich paprika sauce. The savoury spice paprika pops up in various other dishes too, though note that *Gefüllte Paprika* will be a bell pepper (capsicum) stuffed with rice and meat.

Chicken may be called variously *Huhn* (hen), *Geflügel* (poultry) or *Hähnchen* (small chicken) and is usually fried *(Backhuhn)* or roasted *(Brathuhn)*. A great variety of sausage *(Wurst)* is available, and not only at the takeaway stands. Beef *(Rindfleisch)*, lamb *(Lammfleisch)* and liver *(Leber)* are mainstays of many menus. *Kümmelfleisch* is pork stew flavoured with caraway seeds. *Krenfleisch* is pork with horseradish. *Tafelspitz* is boiled beef, often served with *Apfelkren* (apple and horseradish sauce).

Austrians are fond of eating bits of beasts that some other nations ignore. *Beuschel* may be translated on menus as 'calf's lights'. It's

thin slices of calf's lungs and heart in a thick sauce, usually served with a bread dumpling. It's quite tasty. Really. *Tiroler Bauernschmaus* is a selection of meats served with sauerkraut, potatoes and dumplings.

Common fish are trout *(Forelle)*, pike *(Hecht)*, pike-perch *(Fogosch)* and carp *(Karpfen)*. *Saibling* is a local freshwater fish, similar to trout.

Desserts & Cakes

Austria, and especially Vienna, is renowned for excellent but not inexpensive pastries and cakes, which are very effective at transferring bulk from your moneybelt to your waistline.

The most famous Austrian dessert is the strudel, baked dough filled with a variety of fruits – usually apple *(Apfel)* with a few raisins and cinnamon. The Salzburg speciality, *Salzburger Nockerl*, is a fluffy baked

Coffee Concoctions

Legend insists that coffee beans were left behind by the fleeing Turks in 1683, and it was this happy accident that resulted in today's plethora of coffee establishments. Vienna's first coffee house opened in 1685, but it could have been emulating successful establishments already opened in Venice (1647 – the first in Europe), Oxford (1650), London (1652), Paris (1660) and Hamburg (1677), rather than having anything to do with the Turks.

Austrian coffee consumption was modest in the ensuing centuries, and it was only after WWII that it really took hold among the population at large. Austrians now drink more coffee than any other beverage, gulping down 221L per person per year (next in line comes beer at 120L, followed by milk at 104L, soft drinks at 84L, mineral water at 76L, black tea at 39L and wine at 33L). Only Finland, Sweden and Denmark consume more coffee per person.

In traditional coffee houses, especially in Vienna, you'll come across various coffee-based drinks:

Mocca (sometimes spelled *Mokka*) or *Schwarzer* – black coffee
Brauner – black but served with a tiny jug of milk
Kapuziner – with a little milk and perhaps a sprinkling of grated chocolate
Melange – served with milk, and maybe whipped cream too
Einspänner – with whipped cream, served in a glass
Masagran (or *Mazagran*) – cold coffee with ice and Maraschino liqueur
Wiener Eiskaffee – cold coffee with vanilla ice cream and whipped cream

Waiters normally speak English and can tell you about any specialities available. In particular, various combinations of alcohol may be added to give such creations as *Mozart* coffee (with Mozart liqueur), *Fiaker* (with rum), *Mocca gespritzt* (with cognac) and *Maria Theresa* (with orange liqueur). Some people find the basic coffee too strong, so there's the option of asking for a *Verlängerter* (lengthened), a Brauner weakened with hot water. Traditional places will serve the coffee on a silver tray and with a glass of water. Some types of coffee are offered in small *(kleine)* or large *(grosse)* portions. According to an old Viennese tradition, if the waiter fails to give you the bill after three requests you can walk out without paying (three requests in rapid succession don't count!).

pudding made from eggs, flour and sugar. Pancakes are another popular dessert and come in various flavours, such as blueberry *(Moosbeernocken)*. *Germknödel* are sourdough dumplings. *Mohr im Hemd* is chocolate pudding with whipped cream and chocolate sauce. *Pofesen* is stuffed fritters. *Guglhupf* is a cake shaped like a volcano.

DRINKS
Nonalcoholic Drinks
Coffee is the preferred hot beverage rather than tea, though both are expensive in cafes and restaurants. Coffee houses (known as *Kaffeehäuse* or *Café Konditoreien*) are an established part of Austrian life, particularly in Vienna. Strong Turkish coffee is popular. Linger over a cup (from €1.70) and read the free newspapers. Mineral or soda water is widely available, though tap water is fine to drink. Apple juice *(Apfelsaft)* is also popular. Almdudler is a soft drink found all over Austria; it's a sort of cross between ginger ale and lemonade.

Alcoholic Drinks
Austrian wine comes in various categories that designate quality and legal requirements in production, starting with the humble *Tafelwein*, through to *Landwein*, *Qualitätswein* and *Prädikatswein*; the last two have subgroups. In restaurants, wine bought by the carafe or glass will be cheapest. In autumn the whole country goes mad for *Sturm – Heuriger*, or new wine, in its semi-fermented state. For more

on wine and wine taverns *(Heurigen)*, see the boxed text 'Winning Ways With Wine' in the Vienna chapter.

Austria is also known for its beer; brands include Gösser, Schwechater, Stiegl and Zipfer. It is usually a light, golden colour *(hell)*, though you can sometimes get a dark *(dunkel)* version too. In places where both types are on draught you can ask for a *Mischbiere*, a palatable mix of the two. *Weizenbier* (wheat beer), also known as *Weissbier* (white beer) has a full bodied, slightly sweet taste. It can be light or dark, clear or cloudy, and is sometimes served with a slice of lemon straddling the glass rim. Draught beer *(vom Fass)* comes in a either a 0.5L or a 0.3L glass. In Vienna and some other parts of eastern Austria these are called respectively a *Krügerl* (sometimes spelled *Krügel*) and a *Seidel*. Elsewhere these will simply be *Grosse* (big) or *Kleine* (small). A small beer may also be called a *Glas* (glass). A *Pfiff* is just 0.125L,

which will probably satisfy you for all of two seconds. *Radler* is a mix of beer and lemonade.

Austria produces several types of rum. *Obstler* (not a rum) is a spirit created from a mixture of fruits. *Schnaps* is also a popular spirit.

ENTERTAINMENT

In the cities, it's common for places to stay open late, and in Vienna you can party all night. It isn't hard to find bars or taverns featuring traditional or rock music. Some are listed under the Entertainment heading in city sections. Also pick up *Winside*, a free magazine available at many venues, which lists concerts, events, parties and exhibitions nationwide. Many ski resorts, such as St Anton, have a lively après-ski environment. Note that throughout Austria, many a cafe or restaurant sheds its dining function as the evening wears on, and gradually transforms into a full-on drinking den.

Sporting Feats

Austria has witnessed some fabulous feats of determination and resilience from some of its top sporting heroes.

One of the most famous Austrian sportsmen of all time is Niki Lauda, who has won the Formula One motor racing championship three times, the first coming in 1975. Lauda suffered horrific burns in a high speed crash during the 1976 season, yet he was back in his car after missing only two races. That year he narrowly failed to retain the world championship, losing out to James Hunt by a single point on the last race of the season. Undeterred, he regained the title the following year, and proceeded to net his third championship win in 1984.

Thomas Muster, Austria's top tennis player during the 1990s, had his kneecap crushed by a drunk driver, just hours after a stunning win at the 1989 Lipton Championship semi-final in Florida. The resulting damage to the joint made it doubtful he would play tennis again. Yet he showed massive courage in undertaking a gruelling rehabilitation program, which entailed on-court training while strapped to an osteopathic bench. He went on to become world-number-one and in the process earned the nickname 'The Iron Man'.

The somewhat bumbling and chaotic side of skier Hermann Maier has led to him being likened to Superman's human alter ego, Clark Kent. However, in the 1998 Nagano Olympics, Maier showed the amazing toughness and resilience he had gained as a bricklayer and which characterises his all-or-nothing skiing style. During the men's downhill competition, he misjudged a difficult curve, got too close to a gate, somersaulted 30m through the air, bounced over a fence and crashed through two safety nets before finally coming to rest. Austria held its breath as the man known as 'The Herminator' got to his feet, dusted himself down and waved at the crowd. He went on to win two gold medals in the next six days.

Some cinemas show films in their original language. When this is the case, it should be stated on the posters: look for 'OF' *(Original Fassung)* or 'OV' *(Original Version)*. 'OmU' indicates 'Original language with Subtitles'.

The main season for opera, theatre and concerts is September to June. Cheap, standing-room tickets are often available shortly before performances begin and they represent excellent value. Once inside, those standing tie a scarf to the rails or balcony to reserve their place when they go to the bar. If you're really on a budget, bear in mind you can often get into these places free after the first interval.

Casinos

Gamblers can indulge at a dozen casinos around the country, including ones in Vienna, Graz, Linz, Innsbruck and Salzburg. Stakes for blackjack, roulette and other games are from €3.65 (€7.30 after 9pm) up to much more than you can probably afford. There's no entry fee and you need to show identification to get in. To get you started on the gambling road, you only need to pay €19 for your first €22-worth of chips (these are a different colour, so you can't just cash them in and walk out!). Smart dress is required for the gaming tables. A collared shirt, a tie (in winter) and jacket are required. Jackets and ties can sometimes be hired for a refundable deposit. Usual opening hours are from 3pm

to 3am. There may be a slot-machine section without a dress code.

SPECTATOR SPORTS

Football is a major spectator sport. The country's top teams are based in Vienna, Innsbruck, Salzburg and Graz, though there are numerous teams competing in professional or semi-professional leagues across the country. Crowd hooliganism is not generally a problem at the big games, and tickets are usually available at the venue on match day. ATP (Association of Tennis Professionals) tennis events are held in Vienna, St Pölten and Kitzbühel.

Skiing is of course a big draw in winter, with World Cup ski races held annually in Kitzbühel, St Anton and Schladming.

SHOPPING

Local crafts such as textiles, pottery, woodcarvings, wrought-iron work and painted glassware make popular souvenirs.

Unfortunately, shopping in Austria is not cheap. *Heimatwerk* is the official retail outlet for goods adhering to certain standards, and there's one in each major city (see the various city sections for details).

For special reductions, look for signs saying *Aktion*. Top Viennese hotels dispense a free booklet called *Shopping in Vienna* that details all sorts of shopping outlets; Graz and Salzburg each have their own version.

Getting There & Away

Travel within most of the European Union (EU), whether by air, rail or car, has been made easier following the Schengen Agreement, first signed in 1997, which abolished border controls between participating states (see Visas & Documents in the Facts for the Visitor chapter). Border controls still exist when travelling to/from the UK.

AIR

If you're visiting Austria from outside Europe, it may be cheaper to fly to a European 'gateway' city and travel on from there: Munich, for example, is only two hours by train from Salzburg. High season varies from airline to airline, but you can expect slightly higher prices from April to October. You may find you have to pay more if you don't stay a Saturday night or if your trip exceeds one month.

Airports & Airlines

The main air transport hub is Vienna's airport (Flughafen Wien Schwechat), which handles over 12 million passengers a year. It has all the facilities expected of a major airport, such as tourist information, money exchange counters (with high commission rates) and car rental. For information on transport from the airport to the city, see the Getting Around section in the Vienna chapter.

Other Austrian airports that handle international flights are at Graz, Innsbruck, Klagenfurt, Linz and Salzburg. From these airports you can get scheduled or charter flights to a few European destinations, and there are transfer flights to and from Vienna for intercontinental passengers.

Austrian Airlines (W www.aua.com) is the national carrier and has the most extensive services to Vienna. It operates several daily nonstop flights to/from all major European transport centres, such as Amsterdam, Berlin, Frankfurt, Paris, London and Zürich, as well as to many other cities worldwide. Its subsidiary Tyrolean Airways (W www.tyrolean.at) operates domestic routes as well as some international services. Lauda Air is another home-grown airline (W www.laudaair.com). Originally set up to compete with Austrian Airlines, the two are now linked and 'code-share' on many flights.

For all three airlines, call the local rate call centre on ☎ 05-1789.

Buying Tickets

World aviation has never been so competitive, making air travel better value than ever. But you have to research the options carefully to make sure you get the best deal. The Internet is an increasingly useful resource for checking air fares.

Full-time students and those under 26 years (under 30 depending on the airline/country) have access to better deals than other travellers. You have to show a document proving your date of birth or a valid International Student Identity Card (ISIC) when buying your ticket.

Generally, there is nothing to be gained by buying a ticket direct from the airline. Discounted tickets are released to selected travel agencies and specialist discount agencies, and these are usually the cheapest deals going.

One exception to this rule is the expanding number of 'no-frills' carriers, which sell direct to travellers. Unlike the 'full-service' airlines, no-frills carriers often make one-way tickets available at around half the return fare, meaning that it is easy to put together an open-jaw ticket when you fly to one place but leave from another.

The other exception is booking on the Internet. Many airlines, full-service and no-frills, offer some excellent fares to Web surfers. They may sell seats by auction or simply cut prices to reflect the reduced cost of electronic selling.

Many travel agencies around the world have Web sites, which can make the Internet a quick and easy way to compare prices. There is also an increasing number of online

Air Travel Glossary

Cancellation Penalties If you have to cancel or change a discounted ticket, there are often heavy penalties involved; insurance can sometimes be taken out against these penalties. Some airlines impose penalties on regular tickets as well, particularly against 'no-show' passengers.

Courier Fares Businesses often need to send urgent documents or freight securely and quickly. Courier companies hire people to accompany the package through customs and, in return, offer a discount ticket which is sometimes a phenomenal bargain. However, you may have to surrender all your baggage allowance and take only carry-on luggage.

Full Fares Airlines traditionally offer 1st class (coded F), business class (coded J) and economy class (coded Y) tickets. These days there are so many promotional and discounted fares available that few passengers pay full economy fare.

Lost Tickets If you lose your airline ticket an airline will usually treat it like a travellers cheque and, after inquiries, issue you with another one. Legally, however, an airline is entitled to treat it like cash and if you lose it then it's gone forever. Take good care of your tickets.

Onward Tickets An entry requirement for many countries is that you have a ticket out of the country. If you're unsure of your next move, the easiest solution is to buy the cheapest onward ticket to a neighbouring country or a ticket from a reliable airline which can later be refunded if you do not use it.

Open-Jaw Tickets These are return tickets where you fly out to one place but return from another. If available, this can save you backtracking to your arrival point.

Overbooking Since every flight has some passengers who fail to show up, airlines often book more passengers than they have seats. Usually excess passengers make up for the no-shows, but occasionally somebody gets 'bumped' onto the next available flight. Guess who it is most likely to be? The passengers who check in late.

Promotional Fares These are officially discounted fares, available from travel agencies or direct from the airline.

Reconfirmation If you don't reconfirm your flight at least 72 hours prior to departure, the airline may delete your name from the passenger list. Ring to find out if your airline requires reconfirmation.

Restrictions Discounted tickets often have various restrictions on them – such as needing to be paid for in advance and incurring a penalty to be altered. Others are restrictions on the minimum and maximum period you must be away.

Round-the-World Tickets RTW tickets give you a limited period (usually a year) in which to circumnavigate the globe. You can go anywhere the carrying airlines go, as long as you don't backtrack. The number of stopovers or total number of separate flights is decided before you set off and they usually cost a bit more than a basic return flight.

Transferred Tickets Airline tickets cannot be transferred from one person to another. Travellers sometimes try to sell the return half of their ticket, but officials can ask you to prove that you are the person named on the ticket. On an international flight tickets are compared with passports.

Travel Periods Ticket prices vary with the time of year. There is a low (off-peak) season and a high (peak) season, and often a low-shoulder season and a high-shoulder season as well. Usually the fare depends on your outward flight – if you depart in the high season and return in the low season, you pay the high-season fare.

agents such as W www.travelocity.co.uk and W www.deckchair.com, which operate only on the Internet. Online ticket sales work well if you are doing a simple one-way or return trip on specified dates. However, online superfast fare generators are no substitute for a travel agent who knows all about special deals, has strategies for avoiding stopovers and can offer advice on everything from which airline has the best vegetarian food to the best travel insurance to bundle with your ticket.

You may find the cheapest flights are advertised by obscure agencies. Most such firms are honest and solvent, but there are some rogue fly-by-night outfits around. Paying by credit card generally offers protection, as most card issuers provide refunds if you can prove you didn't get what you paid for. Similar protection can be obtained by buying a ticket from a bonded agent, such as one covered by the Air Travel Organisers' Licensing (ATOL; W www.atol.org.uk) scheme in the UK.

Agencies that only accept cash should hand over the tickets straight away and not tell you to 'come back tomorrow'. After you've made a booking or paid your deposit, call the airline and confirm that the booking was made. It's generally not advisable to send money (even cheques) through the post unless the agency is very well established – some travellers have reported being ripped off by fly-by-night mail-order ticket agencies.

Many travellers change their routes halfway through their trips, so be sure to plan carefully before you buy a ticket that is not easily refunded.

Travellers with Special Needs

Airlines can often make special arrangements for travellers, such as wheelchair assistance at airports or vegetarian meals on the flight, if they're warned early enough. Children under two years travel for 10% of the standard fare (or free on some airlines) as long as they don't occupy a seat. They don't get a baggage allowance. 'Skycots', baby food and nappies should be provided by the airline if requested in advance. Children

aged between two and 12 can usually occupy a seat for half to two-thirds of the full fare, and do get a baggage allowance.

Departure Tax

There is no departure tax to pay at the airport when leaving the country, as all Austrian taxes are already included in the ticket price. These include two taxes levied by the Austrian government totalling around €16. Your ticket price may also include a departure tax and 'passenger service charge' levied by your departure country/airport.

The UK

London is one of the world's major centres for buying discounted air tickets, and it should cost less to fly to Austria than to go by train. Cheap fares appear in the weekend national papers and, in London, in *Time Out*, the *Evening Standard* and the free magazine *TNT*.

Austrian Airlines (☎ 020-7434 7300) and British Airways (BA; ☎ 0845-77 333 77, W www.britishairways.co.uk) fly several times daily to Vienna from London Heathrow; Lauda Air (☎ 020-7434 7310) does likewise from London Gatwick, and also has flights from Manchester Sunday to Friday. The lowest return fare at most times of year from London to Vienna is around UK£160, although it will be slightly more from Manchester.

No-frills airlines flying to Austria are Buzz (☎ 0870-240 7070, W www.buzzaway .com) and Ryanair (☎ 0870-333 1231, W www.ryanair.com). Buzz goes daily from London Stansted to Vienna and Ryanair flies twice daily from London Stansted to Salzburg. Fares with either airline start around £45 each way (including taxes), though depending on availability you may have to pay significantly more.

For young travellers under 26 years or students, fares on the full-service airlines should be lower and conditions may be less restrictive – for example, the standard 'Saturday night minimum stay' rule may be waived. One of the leading agencies in the UK is STA Travel (☎ 0870-1600 599, W www.statravel.co.uk), which has many

Lauda Air Takes Off, Hits Turbulence

Austria's Niki Lauda, three-time Formula One racing world champion, founded Lauda Air in 1979. It initially operated as a charter airline, with Lauda himself, a trained pilot, often taking the controls. In 1985 a long battle to operate scheduled flights began. Lauda Air's struggle to establish itself was made harder by the attitude of the state-owned Austrian Airlines, which halved prices on certain routes, denigrated the fledgling airline in the press and was often uncooperative in air traffic rights negotiations.

Though partial approval was given in 1987 it took another three years of intensive political and public pressure (greatly aided by Lauda's status as a national hero) before Lauda Air finally received a worldwide concession to operate scheduled flights.

Lauda Air's innovative style saw it introduce quality in-flight meals (supplied by DO & CO), jeans as part of the staff uniform, and in-flight gambling on the Vienna-Australia route. Its aircraft are named after the likes of Johann Strauss, Enzo Ferrari, James Dean and Bob Marley. The company's success soon made allies out of erstwhile foes, as it didn't take Austrian Airlines long to purchase a 36% stake in Lauda Air.

The Lauda story turned sour in 2000. Niki Lauda's management was publicly criticised, and news broke that the airline was on the verge of bankruptcy, with estimated losses of €73 million. The final blow came in October 2000 when an auditing firm denounced the lack of internal financial control in the airline's foreign currency dealings. The report was instrumental in Niki Lauda's decision to re-sign the following month.

Austrian Airlines has since had the last laugh in its chequered relationship with Lauda Air. In November 2000 it purchased a further 11% in Lauda Air from Lufthansa. A further purchase followed, which gave Austrian Airlines a controlling interest. In August 2001 Lauda agreed to sell his personal shareholding to Austrian Airlines; this left his former rival holding a 90% stake in the airline that bears his name

branches across the UK; they sell tickets to all travellers but cater especially to young people and students.

Mondial Travel (☎ 01580-714714), The Four Wents, Goudhurst Rd, Cranbrook, Kent, is a specialist in budget flights to Austria and can arrange fly-drive deals and city breaks. For other tour outlets, see Organised Tours at the end of this chapter. Trailfinders (☎ 020-7937 5400, **W** www.trailfinders.co.uk) has reasonable fares, and branches across the UK.

Continental Europe

Like spokes on a wheel, flights go from Vienna to all parts of Europe. Routes to the east are as well covered as those to the west, with Austrian Airlines flying regularly to (among other destinations) Bucharest, Kiev, Moscow, St Petersburg, Vilnius and Warsaw.

Amsterdam and Athens are the best-known centres on mainland Europe for budget flights; expect to pay around €200 for Amsterdam-Vienna return and € 282 for Athens-Vienna return. In Amsterdam,

try Budget Air (☎ 020-627 12 51), Rokin 34, or the student agency, NBBS (☎ 020-624 09 89), Rokin 66. In Athens, there are many travel agencies in the backstreets between Syntagma and Omonia squares, as well as the STA-linked ISYTS (☎ 21 03 23 37 67), 1st floor, 11 Nikis St, Syntagma Square.

Depending on where you start, taking the train may be just as viable as flying. The following student/youth-oriented travel agencies can let you know the best way to go: OTU Voyages (☎ 01 40 29 12 12, **W** www.otu.fr), in Paris and elsewhere in France; STA Travel (☎ 030-311 0950, **W** www.statravel.de) in Berlin and elsewhere in Germany; and CTS Viaggi (06 462 0431, **W** www.cts.it) in Rome and elsewhere in Italy.

The USA

The North Atlantic is the world's busiest long-haul air corridor, and various newspapers contain ads placed by consolidators (discount travel agencies). San Francisco is the ticket consolidator capital of USA, although some good deals can be found in Los Angeles, New York and other big cities. Ticket Planet (☎ 1-800-799 8888) has a good itinerary search facility on its Web site at **w** www.ticketplanet.com.

An APEX return on a daily Austrian Airlines flight from New York can be as low as US$430 (nine hours). From Los Angeles, Delta flies daily (via Paris), as does Swissair (via Zürich). Readers should note that in October 2001 Swissair was rescued from bankruptcy by the Swiss government, but the longer-term future of the airline was uncertain. Check with your travel agent for the latest situation. Expect to pay at least US$700 return. Lauda Air (☎ 1-800-588 8399) has four flights a week from Miami; promotional return fares can be as low as US$399. Add around US$60 taxes to all the above fares.

Council Travel, America's largest student travel organisation, has around 60 offices in the USA; its head office (☎ 800-226 8624, **w** www.counciltravel.com) is at 205 E 42 St, New York, NY 10017. STA Travel (☎ 1-800-781 4040, **w** www.statravel.com) has offices in Boston, Chicago, Miami, New York, Philadelphia, San Francisco and other major cities.

Canada

Canadian discount air ticket sellers are also known as consolidators and their air fares tend to be about 10% higher than those sold in the USA. Usually you'll have to fly to Austria via the USA (eg, via Chicago with United Airlines, C$1025, 15 hours total) or a European 'gateway' city. The exception is the direct Toronto-Vienna service with Austrian Airlines, in partnership with Air Canada, which departs five times weekly.

Travel CUTS (☎ 800-667-2887) is Canada's national student travel agency and has offices in all major cities. Its Web address is **w** www.travelcuts.com.

Australia & New Zealand

From this side of the globe it's worth investigating round-the-world (RTW) tickets,

as these may not be much more expensive than a straightforward return. Check travel agencies' ads in the Yellow Pages or newspapers.

From Australia, Lauda Air (☎ 1800-642 438, **w** www.laudaair.com.au) operates the only direct flight to Vienna (via Kuala Lumpur), departing from Melbourne twice weekly and from Sydney three times weekly. 'Red hot special' fares on these flights can be as low as A$950/1550 one-way/return. BA (in association with Qantas), Thai Airways and Singapore Airlines all offer good deals travelling via Asia. There are no direct flights from New Zealand, so you could simply get an Auckland-Melbourne return (from NZ$395) and pick up a Lauda flight from there. Alternatively, RTW tickets start at around NZ$2200.

STA (☎ 1300 360 960) and Flight Centre (☎ 13 3133) are major dealers in cheap air fares from Australia and New Zealand, with Web sites at **w** www.statravel.com.au and **w** www.flightcentre.com.au. In New Zealand, call ☎ 0800 874 773 for STA and ☎ 0800 243 544 for Flight Centre.

Africa

Austrian Airlines flies to Vienna from Cairo (three or four times a week) though generally direct flights from Africa are few and far between. You'll have more options if you plan to fly to somewhere like Frankfurt, Paris, London or Zurich, and transfer from there. Several West African countries, such as Burkina Faso, Gambia and especially Morocco, offer cheap charter flights to France and Germany.

Nairobi (Kenya) has some of the best prices thanks to keen competition between bucket shops; check out what's on offer at Flight Centre (☎ 02-210024, **e** fcswwat@ arcc.or.ke) or Let's Go Travel (☎ 02-340331, **w** www.letsgosafari.com). In South Africa, try Rennies Travel (011-833 1441) at 42 Marshall St, Johannesburg. Rennies has outlets throughout South Africa and is the agent for Thomas Cook; addresses are listed on the Web site at **w** www.renniestravel.co.za.

Asia

Singapore, Hong Kong and Bangkok are the best places in Asia to buy discounted air tickets. It's worth shopping around and asking the advice of other travellers before buying a ticket, as some bucket shops are unreliable. STA has branches in Bangkok, Tokyo, Singapore, Hong Kong and Kuala Lumpur. Austrian Airlines has direct flights to Vienna from Beijing and Tokyo; Lauda Air has them from Bangkok, Kuala Lumpur and Singapore.

In India, Delhi is one of the main air transport centre and offers some decent deals. Drop in to STIC Travels (☎ 011-332 0239), an agent for STA Travel, on the 1st floor, West Wing, Chandralok Building, 36 Janpath, Delhi.

LAND
Bus

Buses are generally cheaper but slower and less comfortable than trains. Europe's biggest network of international buses is provided by a group of bus companies operating under the name Eurolines (**W** www.eurolines.com).

Addresses for Eurolines include:

Deutsche-Touring (☎ 069-23 07 35)
Mannheimerstrasse 4, Frankfurt
Eurolines France (☎ 08-36 69 52 52) Gare Routière Internationale, 28 Ave du Général de Gaulle, 75020 Paris
Eurolines Italy (☎ 06 44 04 009) Ciconvallazione Nonentana 574, Lato Stazione Tiburtina, Rome
Eurolines Nederland (☎ 020-560 87 88)
Rokin 10, 1012 KR Amsterdam
Eurolines UK (☎ 0870-514 3219)
52 Grosvenor Gardens, London SW1

Eurolines Austria (Map 7, #58; ☎ 01-712 04 53, **e** info@eurolines.at) is at 03, Invalidenstrasse 5–7, behind Wien Mitte train station in Vienna. It's open 6.30am to 9pm Monday to Friday, 6.30am to 8am and 4pm to 9pm Saturday, and 6.30am to 11am and 4pm to 9pm Sunday, and buses depart from across the road. There's another office in Salzburg (☎ 0662-42 10 89), at Rudolf Biebl Strasse 43.

There are bus connections across Western and Eastern Europe, with reduced prices (of 10% or more, depending on the operator) for people under 26 and over 60 (this is often noted as a 'concession' fare). Some Eurolines seats can be reserved by telephone, but with many services heading east you have to pay in person at the counter in advance.

Eurolines buses to/from London (Victoria coach station) depart five or six days a week (from UK£65/79 one-way/return; UK£69/89 in July, August and Christmas/New Year for an adult ticket purchased at least seven days in advance, 22 hours).

Eurolines buses to Budapest (€28.40/ 39.30 one-way/return, 3½ hours) depart from Wien Mitte several times daily, starting at 7am or 8am. Buses run every two hours or so to Bratislava in Slovakia (€10.90/ 19.65 one-way/return, 90 minutes), via the airport and Hainburg; but note that it works out cheaper to buy the return leg in Bratislava.

Austrobus has buses to Prague (sometimes continuing to Karlsbad in Germany), leaving Vienna from its stop at 01, Rathausplatz 5 (Map 7, #9). Departures are at 7am Monday to Saturday, and 2pm Sunday (€23.65, five hours). From Prague, buses leave at 9am Monday to Thursday and 2pm Friday to Sunday. Buy tickets from the driver, or in advance from Eurolines (Map 7, #58) or Columbus Reisen (Map 7, #10; ☎ 01-534 11-123), 01, Dr Karl Lueger Ring 8.

Bus Passes If you want to visit several countries by bus, Eurolines UK has passes linking 46 cities: a 15/30-day pass in the high season costs UK£149/222 for adult or £120/162 for youth or senior. Another option is the UK-based Busabout (☎ 020-7950 1661, **e** info@busabout.co.uk), which has buses running along set routes around Europe (including Vienna, Salzburg and St Johann in Tirol) from April to October. There are consecutive passes (eg, UK£309/279 for adult/student, valid one month) or flexipasses (UK£659/599, valid for up to 30 days in four months). See the Web site at **W** www.busabout.com.

Train

Trains are a popular, convenient and relatively environment-friendly way to travel. They are also comfortable, reasonably frequent, and can be good places to meet other travellers.

Stories about train passengers being gassed or drugged and then robbed occasionally surface, though bag-snatching is more of a worry. Sensible security measures include not letting your bags out of your sight (or at least chaining them to the luggage rack) and locking compartment doors overnight.

The *Thomas Cook European Timetable* is the trainophile's bible, giving a complete listing of train schedules, supplements and reservations information. It is updated monthly and is available from Thomas Cook outlets. In the USA, call ☎ 800-367 7984.

UK & Continental Europe Austria benefits from its central location within Europe by having excellent rail connections to all important destinations. Vienna is one of the main rail hubs in Central Europe; for details of the main train stations and the routes they serve, see the Getting There & Away section in the Vienna chapter. Elsewhere in Austria, Salzburg has trains at least every hour to/from Munich (€25.30, two hours) with onward connections north. Express services to Italy go via Innsbruck or Villach. From Villach there are trains going south-east. Trains to Slovenia go through Graz or Villach.

Paris, Amsterdam, Munich and Milan are also important cities for rail connections. From the UK, the main route is through the Channel Tunnel from London Waterloo to Brussels or Paris. On the Brussels route you'll change trains there, and possibly also in Cologne, Frankfurt or Munich. The fastest journey time is about 16 hours. Services are run by the Eurostar passenger train service (☎ 08705-186 186) or the Eurotunnel vehicle-carrying service (☎ 08705-353 535). These operators do not sell through-tickets to Vienna. One place that does is Rail Europe (08705-848 848), 179 Piccadilly, London; the three-hour London-Paris leg costs UK£95 return, via Eurostar, then Paris-Vienna takes 15 hours and costs £188 return (about €286).

Travellers aged under 26 can pick up Billet International de Jeunesse (BIJ) tickets, which cut fares by up to 50%. Various agencies in Europe issue BIJ tickets, including Rail Europe (mentioned earlier) and Voyages Wasteels (☎ 1-43 43 46 10) at 2 rue Michel Chasles, Paris.

Express trains can be identified by the symbols EC (EuroCity, serving international routes) or IC (InterCity, serving national routes). The French TGV and the German ICE trains are even faster. Supplements can apply on fast trains and international trains, and it is a good idea (sometimes obligatory) to make seat reservations for peak times and on certain lines. Overnight trips usually offer a choice of couchette (around US$28) or a more expensive sleeper. Long-distance trains have a dining car or snacks available. Reserving IC or EC train seats in 2nd class within Austria costs €3.50; in 1st class, it's free. In Austria you can sometimes pick up cheap fares on international return tickets valid for less than four days.

The *Orient Express* is an old-style private train that serves European routes. It passes through Austria: inquire at travel agencies.

Asia The direct train from Vienna to Moscow departs every two days and takes 32 hours (€111.50 each way, plus from €16.50 for a sleeper). From there you can choose from four different trains for onwards eastern travel. Three of them (the Trans-Siberian, Trans-Mongolian and Trans-Manchurian) follow the same route to/from Moscow across Siberia but have different eastern railheads. The fourth, the Trans-Kazakhstan, runs between Moscow and Ürümqi (northwestern China) across Central Asia. Prices can vary enormously, depending on where you buy the ticket and what is included, but you won't save money compared with flying. If you have time (between six and nine days minimum), train travel is an interesting option, but only really worthwhile if you want to stop off and explore China and Russia on the way through. Possibilities for overland travel to/from Asia, whether by train, bus or private vehicle, should become more widespread as tourism expands in the region.

European Rail Passes

These may not work out much more expensive than a straightforward return ticket, and are worth considering if you want to explore a number of destinations en route to Austria. Always study the terms and conditions attached to passes. For information on a range of rail passes, visit the Web sites at **w** www.raileurope.com and **w** www.raileurope.co.uk.

Eurail Pass

This pass can only be bought by residents of non-European countries. Eurail passes are valid for unlimited travel on national railways and some private lines in Austria, Belgium, Denmark, Finland, France (including Monaco), Germany, Greece, Hungary, Ireland, Italy, Luxembourg, the Netherlands, Norway, Portugal, Spain, Sweden and Switzerland (including Liechtenstein). The pass is also valid for free or discounted travel on various international ferries and national lake/river steamers.

A standard **Youthpass** for travellers under 26 is valid for unlimited 2nd-class travel within the given time period, ranging from 15 days (US$388) up to three months (US$1089). The Youth Flexipass, also for 2nd class, is valid for freely chosen days within a two-month period: 10 days for US$458 or 15 days for US$599.

The corresponding passes for those aged over 26 are available in 1st class only. The standard Eurail pass costs from US$554 for 15 days up to US$1558 for three months. The Flexipass costs US$654 for 10 days or US$862 for 15 days. Two people travelling together can save around 15% each by buying 'saver' versions of these passes. Eurail passes for children are also available.

Europass is basically a cut-down version of the Eurail pass, covering only France, Germany, Italy, Spain and Switzerland. The adult/youth price is US$348/244 for a minimum five travel days, or US$688/482 for a maximum 15 days. Some countries can be added as 'associate' countries to the scheme; eg, Austria and Hungary, which count as one country. The cost to add any one/two countries is US$60/100 for adult or US$42/70 for youth.

The **Selectpass** is a flexible Eurail pass covering just three adjacent countries; for adult/youth it costs US$328/230 for five days within two months, or US$476/334 for 10 days within two months. The Eurail and Europass Aid Office (☎ 5800-335 98) is in Vienna's Westbahnhof station (Map 6), open 9am to 4pm Monday to Saturday.

Car & Motorcycle

Getting to Austria by road is simple as there are fast and well-maintained motorways through all surrounding countries. German autobahns have no tolls or speed limits, whereas those in France (autoroute) and Italy (autostrada) have both. Switzerland levies a one-off charge of Sfr40 (about US$23/€26)for using its motorways. The Czech Republic and Slovakia also impose a motorway charge, as does Austria (see Motorway Tax & Tunnel Tolls in the Getting Around chapter).

Driving is on the right throughout continental Europe, and priority is usually given to traffic approaching from the right. Road signs are generally standard throughout Europe. Be aware that Europeans are particularly strict on drink-driving laws. The blood-alcohol concentration (BAC) limit when driving is between 0.05 and 0.08%, but in some areas (Eastern Europe, Scandinavia) it can be 0%. For more on motoring regulations within Austria, see the Car & Motorcycle section of the Getting Around chapter.

By road into Austria there are numerous entry points from Germany, the Czech Republic, Slovakia, Hungary, Slovenia, Italy and Switzerland. The only other country that borders Austria, Liechtenstein, is so small that it has just one border crossing point, near Feldkirch in Austria. The presence of the Alps limits options for approaching Tirol from the south (Switzerland and Italy). All main border crossing points are open 24 hours. Those served by minor roads are open from around 6am or 8am until 8pm or 10pm.

European Rail Passes

Inter-Rail Pass

Inter-Rail passes are available in Europe to people who have been resident there for at least six months. The standard Inter-Rail pass is for travellers aged under 26, though older people can get the Inter-Rail 26+ version. The pass divides Europe into eight zones (A to H); Austria is in zone C, along with Denmark, Germany and Switzerland. The standard/26+ fare for any one zone is UK£129/185, valid 22 days. To purchase two/three/all zones (valid one month) costs UK£169/199/229, or UK£239/275/319 for the 26+ version.

The all-zone (global) pass would take you everywhere covered by Eurail, and to Bulgaria, Croatia, Czech Republic, Macedonia, Poland, Romania, Slovakia, Slovenia, Turkey and Yugoslavia. As with Eurail, the pass gives discounts or free travel on ferry, ship and steamer routes.

European East Pass

This is sold in North America and Australia and is valid in Austria, Hungary, Poland, the Czech Republic and Slovakia. In the USA, Rail Europe charges US$210 for five days' 1st-class travel within one month; extra rail days (five maximum) cost US$24 each.

National Rail Passes

There is a **Euro-Domino Pass** for each of the countries covered in the Inter-Rail pass. They're sold in Europe to European residents. Adults (travelling 1st or 2nd class) and youth under 26 can opt for three to eight days' free travel within one month. In the UK, the Austrian 2nd-class version for adult/youth costs UK£67/51 for three days, rising by £8/6 per day up to £107/81 for eight days. If purchased in Eurozone countries, the adult/youth cost for Austria is €104.10/80.05 for three days, rising €13.10/10.05 per day. Note you can't buy it inside Austria.

Outside Europe, travellers can buy a similar product under a different name. In the USA, for example, Rail Europe sells an **Austrian Flexipass**, which is valid on Austrian railways for three to eight days over a 15-day period. The price in 2nd class is US$107 for three days, with extra days costing $15 each.

The *Facts and Sights* map, available at Austrian National Tourist Offices, indicates which are major and which are minor border crossings. Remember that there are no border controls to/from Germany and Italy, thanks to the Schengen Agreement.

To avoid a long drive to/from Austria, consider putting your car on a motorail service run by national railways: many head south from Calais and Paris. German Rail has a service between Salzburg and Cologne that costs €131/88 for one-way/return (yes, it's cheaper to go both ways than one way). This price is for one adult travelling in the low season; extra passengers (about €51 each), larger cars and peak-time travel ups the price. It departs from Salzburg each Thursday and takes 10 hours.

Paperwork & Preparations For information on those documents, see Driving Licence & Permits in the Facts for the Visitor chapter.

Third-party motor insurance is a minimum requirement in Europe; get proof of this in the form of a Green Card, issued by your insurers. Also ask for a 'European Accident Statement' form. Taking out a European breakdown assistance policy, such as the AA Five Star Service or the RAC European Motoring Assistance, is a good investment.

Every vehicle travelling across an international border should display a nationality plate of its country of registration. A warning triangle, to be used in the event of breakdown, is compulsory almost everywhere (including Austria). Recommended accessories are a first-aid kit (compulsory in Austria, Slovenia, Croatia, Yugoslavia and Greece), a spare bulb kit and a fire extinguisher. Contact a motoring organisation for more information, such as the UK's RAC (☎ 0800-550055, W www.rac.co.uk), which has useful motoring information on its Web site.

If you're a member of an automobile association, ask about free reciprocal benefits offered by affiliated organisations in Europe.

Camper Van Travelling in a camper van can be a surprisingly economical option for budget travellers, as it can take care of eating, sleeping and travelling in one convenient package. London is a good place to buy: look in *TNT* magazine and *Loot* newspaper, visit the van market on Market Rd, London N7, or inquire at dealers about 'buy back' options. Expect to spend at least UK£2000 (US$2300). Discreet free camping, such as in autobahn rest areas, is rarely a problem.

A drawback with camper vans is that they're expensive to buy in spring and hard to sell in autumn. A car and tent might do just as well instead.

Motorcycle Touring Europe and Austria are ideal for motorcycle touring, with winding roads of good quality, stunning scenery to stimulate the senses, and an active motorcycling scene. The wearing of crash helmets for motorcyclists and passengers is compulsory everywhere in Europe. Austria, Belgium, France, Germany, Luxembourg, Portugal, Spain, Scandinavia and most countries in Eastern Europe require motorcyclists to use headlights during the day; in other countries it is recommended.

Fuel Leaded petrol is no longer available in Austria, but Super Plus has a special additive which allows it to be used for engines taking leaded petrol. Prices per litre are about €1.05 for Super Plus, €1 for unleaded petrol, and €0.90 for diesel. Petrol is cheaper in the Czech Republic, Slovakia, Hungary and Switzerland, so fill up before departing those countries. Prices in Germany and Italy are comparable to those in Austria.

Bicycle

This is one of the best ways to travel in terms of your bank balance, your health, and the environment, but it does require a high level of commitment to see it through.

If starting from the UK, consider joining the Cyclists' Touring Club (CTC; ☎ 01483-417 217, W www.ctc.org.uk), which is able to provide insurance, itineraries and other information.

If coming from farther afield, bikes can be carried by aeroplane, but check with the carrier in advance, preferably before buying your ticket. To take it as a normal piece of luggage you may need to remove the pedals or turn the handlebars sideways, but beware of possible excess baggage costs.

A primary consideration on long cycling trips is to travel light, but you should take a few tools and spare parts, including a puncture repair kit and a spare inner tube. Panniers are essential to balance your possessions on either side of the bike frame. You should wear a bike helmet and have a sturdy bike lock. Seasoned cyclists can average 80km a day but there's no point overdoing it.

Bicycles are not allowed on European motorways – not that you would want to use those tedious bits of concrete anyway. Stick to small roads or dedicated bike tracks where possible. If you get weary of pedalling or simply want to skip a boring section, you can put your feet up on the train. On slower trains, bikes can usually be taken on board, subject to a small supplementary fee. Fast trains (IC, EC etc) can't always accommodate cyclists travelling with their machines: bikes might need to be sent as registered luggage and may end up on a different train from the one you take. (One solution is to semi-dismantle your bike, shove it in a large bag or sack and take it on a train as hand luggage.) British trains are outside the European luggage registration scheme, except for Eurostar. In Austria, it costs €10.20 to send a bike as international luggage, or to accompany it on a cross-border express train.

Hitching

For advice about hitching, see the Getting Around chapter.

Ferry tickets for vehicles sometimes include a full load of passengers, so hitchers may be able to secure a free passage by hitching before cars board the boat. This also applies to Eurotunnel through the Channel Tunnel.

A safer way to hitch is to arrange a lift through an organisation, such as Allostop-Provoya in France and Mitfahrzentralen in Germany. You could also scan university notice boards. Vienna has a Rot-Weiss-Rot Mitfahrzentrale (☎ 408 22 10, e office@mfz.at); see the Vienna chapter for sample rates.

RIVER

Since the early 1990s the Danube has been connected to the Rhine by the River Main tributary and the Main-Danube canal in southern Germany. The full Amsterdam-Vienna cruise along this route takes 13 days, and there are monthly departures in each direction between May and September. In the UK, bookings can be made through Noble Caledonia (☎ 020-7409 0376, w www.noble-caledonia.co.uk); deck prices start at UK£1940. In the USA, you can book through Uniworld (☎ 1-800 360 9550, w www.cruise uniworld.com).

Several companies run services along the Austrian stretch of the Danube. From Vienna, fast hydrofoils travel eastwards to Bratislava and Budapest. The trip to Bratislava costs €17.45/26.90 one-way/return (1½ hours, once daily Wednesday to Sunday between mid-April and late October). The trip to Budapest costs €60.65/83.60 one-way/return and takes at least 5½ hours; there's one daily departure from early April to late October, except from late July to early September when there are two daily. Bookings can be made in Vienna through Mahart Tours (Map 6, #8; ☎ 01-7292 161) or G Glaser (Map 6, #8; ☎ 01-08 201, e g.glaser@xpoint.at, w www.user.xpoint.at/g.glaser/shipping.htm), both at 02, Handelskai 265, or DDSG Blue Danube (Map 7, #168; ☎ 01-588 80-0, fax 588 80-440, e info@ddsg-blue-danube.at, w www.ddsg-blue-danube.at), 01, Friedrichstrasse 7. Hydrofoils are more expensive than the bus or the train, but make a pleasant change if you can afford them.

Various steamers ply the Danube to the west of Vienna. Several operators run boats on the Lower Austria section of the Danube (see the Danube Valley section in the Lower Austria chapter for details). Boats also go between Linz and Passau, on the German border (see the Linz section in the Upper Austria chapter).

ORGANISED TOURS

For tailor-made tours, see your travel agency or look under Special Interests in the small ads in newspaper travel pages. Walking trip specialists in the UK include Ramblers Holidays (☎ 01707-331 133, w www.ramblers holidays.co.uk) and Sherpa Expeditions (☎ 020-8577 2717, w www.sherpaexpeditions.com). Inn Travel (☎ 01653-629 004, w www.inntravel.co.uk) does walking and cycling trips.

Austrian Holidays (☎ 020-7434 7399, w www.austrianholidays.co.uk), the UK tour operator of Austrian Airlines, can do flight-only deals or arrange holidays based around tourist sights, winter sights or the opera. Austria Travel (☎ 01708-222 000, w www.austriatravel.co.uk), 54 Station Rd, Upminster, RM14 2TT, UK, has competitive air fares, and can construct a tailor-made tour for you.

The Danube is a hook on which to hang a range of tours; operators include Danube Travel (☎ 03-9530 0888) in Melbourne, Australia, and Blue Danube Holidays (☎ 416-362 5000 or 1-800-268 4155, w www.bluedanubeholidays.com) in North America.

Young revellers can take bus tours based on hotel or camping accommodation. Contiki, with representatives worldwide, has trips geared towards the 18-35 age group; several of its tours include Austria – check w www.contiki.com. Kumuka (w www.kumuka.com) is similar, but attracts a broader age range.

For people over 50, Saga offers holidays ranging from cheap coach tours to luxury cruises. In the UK, contact Saga Holidays (☎ 0800-300 500), Saga Building, Middelburg Square, Folkestone, Kent CT20 1AZ; in the USA, Saga Holidays (☎ 1-877-265 6862,

W www.sagaholidays.com) is at 222 Berkeley St, Boston, MA 02116.

WARNING

The information in this chapter is particularly vulnerable to change: prices for international travel are volatile, routes are introduced and cancelled, schedules change, special deals come and go, and rules and visa requirements are amended. At press time, the events surrounding the 11 September attacks in the US have made air travel even more uncertain, as many airlines are struggling to stay in business. Airlines and governments seem to take a perverse pleasure in making price structures and regulations as complicated as possible. You should check directly with the airline or a travel agent to make sure you understand how a fare (and any ticket you buy) works. In addition, the travel industry is highly competitive and there are many lurks and perks.

The upshot of this is that you should get opinions, quotes and advice from as many airlines and travel agents as possible before you part with your hard-earned cash. The details given in this chapter should be regarded as pointers and are not a substitute for your own careful, up-to-date research.

Getting Around

Transport systems in Austria are highly developed and generally very efficient, and reliable information is usually available in English. For detailed planning, consider buying an annual bus or train timetable *(Fahrplan)*. Information staff in train stations will look up specific information from these guides for you, or there may be a copy for you to look through. The rail timetable, available from train stations, costs €7.30 and includes details of the more important ferry and cable car services. On the Internet, **w** www.oebb.at has rail and bus timetables. Some Web sites (including many quoted here) are in German only, but even with those it's easy to figure out prices and transport schedules.

Most provinces (such as Carinthia, Styria, Tirol and Vorarlberg) have an integrated transport system offering day passes covering regional zones, and you can choose between bus or train travel on the same ticket. These passes can often save you money compared with buying standard single tickets, so always inquire about this option before you buy. Day passes for city transport often give a one-zone discount on regional travel.

AIR

Domestic flights are operated by Tyrolean Airways, which is partially owned by Austrian Airlines. There are several flights a day from Vienna to Graz, Klagenfurt, Innsbruck and Salzburg, and one or two a day to Linz. Austrian Airlines is a sales agent for Tyrolean Airways. The price of tickets means that getting around by air is not a viable option for most people. The air fare between Vienna and Klagenfurt, for example, is €135 one-way. The flying time is 55 minutes, and on top of this you have check-in time and the hassle of getting to and from each airport. In comparison, the train takes 3½ hours and costs €34.90 for a one-way ticket.

Rheintalflug (☎ 0800-488 00-8, **w** www.rheintalflug.com) flies daily from Vienna to Altenrhein (Switzerland; one hour), with free bus transfers to/from Bregenz in Vorarlberg.

There's a range of one-way fares, from €217 at weekends up to €275 for a full fare. Rheintalflug was purchased by Austrian Airlines in 2001.

BUS

The Bundesbus (federal bus) network is best considered a backup to the rail service, more useful for reaching out-of-the-way places and local destinations than for long-distance travel. Rail routes are sometimes duplicated by bus services, but buses really come into their own in the more inaccessible mountainous regions. Some of the ski resorts in Tirol and Vorarlberg, for example, can only be reached by Bundesbus or by private transport.

Bundesbuses are painted either yellow or orange/red, and are run by the post office (Postbus) or the rail network (Bahnbus). As far as the traveller is concerned, there's no significant difference between the two types: in this book buses are simply called Bundesbus throughout. The buses are clean and punctual, and usually depart from outside train stations. Note that some bus routes are geared to the needs of school children, so if it's not a school day, the frequency of the service greatly diminishes.

Bus fares are comparable in price to train fares; however, unlike with the train, you can't buy a long-distance ticket and make stopoffs en route. It's possible to buy tickets in advance on some routes, but on others you can only buy tickets from the drivers. Austrian citizens can get some excellent deals on buses, with reduced prices for senior citizens and families.

The Vienna-based telephone number for bus information (☎ 01-711 01) handles bus inquiries for the whole country, though there are also local bus depot numbers you could call instead for regional services. Alternatively, log on to **w** www.oebb.at. The local bus station or tourist office can usually give out free timetables for specific bus routes.

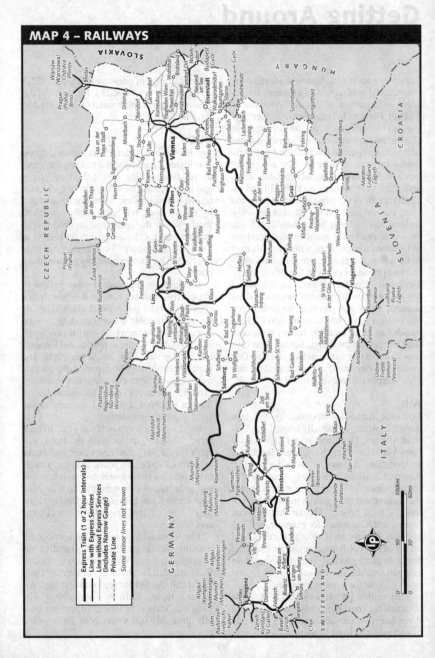

MAP 4 – RAILWAYS

Express Train (1 or 2 hour intervals)
Line with Express Services
Line without Express Services
(includes Narrow Gauge)
Private Line
Some minor lines not shown

Vienna's Burgtheater makes a good backdrop for trick skating

Austria's history shines through its modern style

Kärntner Strasse shop displays tempting treats

Colourful sculpture, Prater amusement park

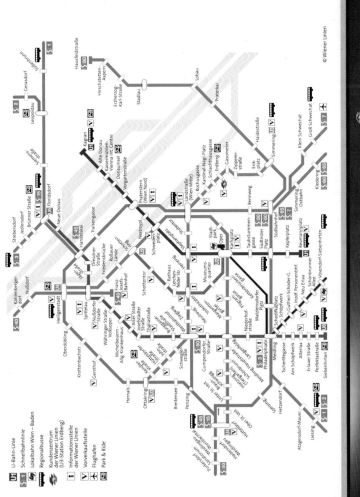

© Wiener Linien

WIENER LINIEN

Die Stadt gehört Dir.

TRAIN

Austrian trains are comfortable, clean and reasonably frequent. The country is well covered by the state network, with only a few private lines. Eurail and Inter-Rail passes (see the boxed text 'European Rail Passes' in the Getting There & Away chapter) are valid on the former; inquire before embarking on the latter. The state network is at least as efficient as most other European national rail systems, especially considering such obstacles as the Alps. However, Österreichischen Bundesbahnen (ÖBB; Austrian Federal Railways) does suffer in comparison with its Swiss neighbour, the Schweizerische Bundesbahnen (SBB), which encounters similar terrain yet manages to run trains as if they were quartz watches on wheels. Austrian trains are often on time, but delays of five to 15 minutes are not uncommon. Think twice before you schedule very tight transport connections.

The German for train station is *Bahnhof* (abbreviated as *Bf*); the main train station is the *Hauptbahnhof* (abbreviated as *Hbf*). Some small rural stations are unstaffed, and at these you should either buy the ticket from a platform dispenser or, more usually, on the train. Such stations are indicated on timetables, either by 'Hu' or a special symbol. All reasonably sized stations have facilities for exchanging foreign currency or travellers cheques. Stations almost always make some provision for luggage storage, either at a staffed counter (usually €2.20 per piece), or in 24-hour luggage lockers. Lockers come in two sizes: the standard size can fit one backpack and costs €1.50 or €2.20; the larger size (two backpacks) costs €2.20 or €2.95. Some stations also have lockers for skis. ÖBB offers a door to door unaccompanied luggage service (up to 25kg per item) within Austria for €12.35/16.75/21.10 for one/two/three items.

Many stations have information centres where the staff speak English. If you can understand some German, pick up the free booklet, *Angebote & Service*, which tells you everything about travelling by rail, including special tickets, reservations and contact numbers.

Platforms at train stations *(Bahnsteig)* are divided into zones A, B and sometimes C: take care as a small rural train may be already waiting at one end while you're waiting in vain for it to arrive at the other. Usually you only realise when the train's pulling out (it's happened to me more than once). Even if you board the correct train, make sure you sit in the correct carriage, as trains occasionally split en route. Diagram boards on the platforms show the carriage order (1st or 2nd class, dining car etc) of IC and EC trains. Separate yellow posters in stations list arrivals *(Ankunft)* and departures *(Abfahrt)*.

Rail Passes

Once upon a time, ÖBB offered several types of rail passes that could be purchased within Austria. Sadly, these were withdrawn a few years ago, and all that's left is the Vorteilscard. Even more annoyingly, this is an annual deal, so it's not worth considering for most tourists. For long stayers, though, or for youths and seniors, it's a good deal. The Vorteilscard (photo required) is valid for a 45% reduction on the ÖBB network and most private lines, and costs €33.75 for one year. The Vorteilscard 26 (for people under the age of 26) costs just €18.20, and the Vorteilscard Senior (men over 65, women over 60) costs €25.50; at these prices you can make savings even during a relatively short stay.

Happily, there are rail passes valid for Austrian trains that can be purchased abroad – see the Getting There & Away chapter.

Types of Train

The type and speed of a train can be identified by its prefix. EC (EuroCity), IC (InterCity) and SC (SuperCity) are all express trains, stopping only at major stations. They usually have a dining car where food and drink are dispensed at quite reasonable prices. EN (EuroNight) is an international night train, with sleeping cars and couchettes. E (*Eilzug*; literally, hurry train) is a fast train which stops at some smaller stations. D Zug trains are medium fast. Slow, local trains have no letter prefix and stop everywhere. On small local trains serving relatively isolated routes, there may be a button to press to request the train to stop (as on buses). Trains have smoking and non-smoking compartments, though Vienna's S-Bahn trains are nonsmoking only.

Long-distance express trains always provide the choice of travelling in 1st or 2nd class, though some local services are 2nd class only. Second class is comfortable enough but 1st class is roomier and less crowded.

Reservations

Reserving train seats in 2nd class within Austria costs €3.50 for most express services; in 1st class, reservations are free. If you haven't reserved a seat, check before you sit whether your intended seat has been reserved by someone else down the line.

Tickets & Costs

Austrian train fares are priced according to distance, eg, €1.55 for 1–10km, €14.85 for 101–110km and €45.10 for 501–520km. These fares are for 2nd class; the equivalent rate in 1st class is €5.85, €25.75 and €71.10. Fares for children aged six to 15 are half-price; younger kids travel free if they don't take up a seat. Small pets (in suitable containers) travel free; larger pets go half-price.

Tickets can be purchased on the train but they cost €2.20 extra (unless you board at an unstaffed station or the ticket machine is out of order). In this book, the fares quoted are always those for 2nd class. Credit cards are accepted at over 130 stations; Eurocheque cards and Eurocheques are accepted at all stations.

One-way tickets for journeys of 100km or under are valid for only one day, and the journey can't be broken up. For trips of 101km or more, the ticket is valid for three days and you can alight en route, but you should tell the conductor so your ticket can be suitably endorsed. This is worth doing, as longer trips cost less per kilometre. Return tickets of up to 100km each way are also valid for one day; tickets for longer journeys are valid one month, though the initial outward journey must still be completed within three days. A return fare is

usually the equivalent price of two one-way tickets.

Reduced rail fares on both national and international routes are sometimes available for those aged under 26: wave your passport and ask. Train information can be obtained from ☎ 05-1717.

CAR & MOTORCYCLE

Rural driving is an enjoyable experience in Austria. Roads are well maintained, well signposted and generally not too congested. Compared with train and bus travel, private transport gives more flexibility (such as the opportunity to stop when you want to admire that alpine view), but it does tend to isolate you to some extent from local people and other travellers. The use of cars is often discouraged in city centres; consider ditching your trusty chariot and relying on public transport.

The fastest roads round the country are Autobahns, identified on maps by national 'A' numbers or pan-European 'E' numbers (both are usually given in this book). These are subject to a general motorway tax (see that section later in this chapter). Their course is often shadowed by alternative fast routes (*Schnellstrassen* or *Bundesstrassen*). These principal routes are as direct as the terrain will allow, sometimes using tunnels to maintain their straight lines. In the mountains, you can opt instead for smaller, slower roads that wind over mountain passes. These can add many minutes and kilometres to your journey but are much more scenic. Some minor passes are blocked by snow from November to May. Carrying snow chains in winter is highly recommended and may be compulsory in some areas.

Cars – in German, *Auto* or *Personenkraftwagen (PKW)* – can be transported by motorail trains *(Autoreisezüge)*. Vienna is linked by a daily motorail service to Feldkirch, Innsbruck, Salzburg and Villach, as is Graz to Feldkirch. Vienna-Feldkirch takes nine hours and costs €76.20/94.40 in low/high season, plus €48.55/72.55 for one person (reducing per person with each additional passenger). Around 200 Austrian train stations offer Park and Ride facilities (free or cheap parking while you continue your journey by train). In rural areas, petrol stations may close on Sunday. See the Car & Motorcycle section of the Getting There & Away chapter for more details on fuel.

Road Rules

The minimum driving age is 18, both for Austrians and foreigners. Like the rest of continental Europe, Austrians drive on the right-hand side of the road. Speed limits are 50km/h in towns, 130km/h on autobahns and 100km/h on other roads. Cars towing a caravan or trailer are limited to 100km/h on autobahns, and may be banned from using some winding Alpine roads. Seat belts must be used, if fitted in the car, and children aged under 12 (or less than 1.5m tall) should have a special seat or restraint.

Motorcyclists and their passengers must wear a helmet, and dipped lights must be used in daytime. Motorcyclists should also carry a first-aid kit, though reportedly the police rarely enforce this regulation. Car drivers must carry a first-aid kit and a warning triangle.

Austrian police have the authority to impose fines for various traffic offences. These can be paid on the spot (ask for a receipt) or within two weeks. The penalty for drink-driving (over 0.05% BAC, or blood-alcohol concentration) is a hefty on-the-spot fine and confiscation of your driving licence.

Give priority to vehicles coming from the right. On mountain roads, buses have priority; otherwise, priority lies with the vehicle which would find it most difficult to stop (generally the one facing downhill). Drive in low gear on steep downhill stretches – as a rule of thumb, use the same gear downhill as you did uphill.

Austrian road signs generally conform to recognised international standards. Triangular signs with a red border indicate dangers, and circular signs with a red border illustrate prohibitions. A sign with a crisscrossed white

Road Distances (km)

	Bad Ischl	Bregenz	Bruck an der Mur	Eisenstadt	Graz	Innsbruck	Kitzbühel	Klagenfurt	Krems	Kufstein	Landeck	Lienz	Linz	Salzburg	St Pölten	Vienna	Villach	Wiener Neustadt
Bad Ischl	---																	
Bregenz	432	---																
Bruck an der Mur	170	577	---															
Eisenstadt	297	704	127	---														
Graz	193	600	54	175	---													
Innsbruck	239	193	384	511	407	---												
Kitzbühel	191	300	275	469	400	113	---											
Klagenfurt	245	510	145	298	133	322	264	---										
Krems	222	626	175	132	229	433	372	320	---									
Kufstein	161	271	331	460	356	78	37	286	355	---								
Landeck	316	117	461	588	484	77	186	394	510	155	---							
Lienz	232	424	266	393	277	178	94	144	432	142	248	---						
Linz	103	507	190	246	237	314	247	253	145	236	391	359	---					
Salzburg	58	374	228	362	264	181	129	223	257	103	258	180	138	---				
St Pölten	206	610	140	123	194	417	356	285	32	339	494	416	129	241	---			
Vienna	266	670	145	50	191	477	420	316	79	399	554	411	189	301	66	---		
Villach	250	486	178	335	170	287	226	37	353	251	370	109	330	188	318	353	---	
Wiener Neustadt	268	675	98	31	146	482	441	267	137	431	559	364	237	339	114	302	53	---

tyre on a blue circular background means that snow chains are compulsory. *Umleitung* is the German for 'diversion', though in Austria you may see the word *Ausweiche* instead. On maps or signs, look for the Austrian word *Maut*, which indicates a toll booth.

Trams are a common feature in Austrian cities; take care if you've never driven among them before. Trams always have priority and no matter how much you might swear at them, they're never going to deviate from their tracks just to suit you. Vehicles should wait behind while trams are slowing down for passenger stops. Be aware that even if you have the green light at road junctions, you may still have to give way to crossing pedestrians before you turn left or right.

Motorway Tax & Tunnel Tolls

There's a general charge for using Austrian motorways, though you don't need to pay if you keep off the motorway system. The fee for the required display disc *(Vignette)*, valid for a calendar year, is €72.70 for cars (below 3.5 tonnes) and €29.10 for motorcycles. Fortunately, unlike in neighbouring Switzerland, there's the option of buying shorter-term passes. The 10-day disc costs €7.65/4.40 for cars/motorcycles, and the two-monthly disc €21.80/10.90. Both are valid from the date of issue, and can be purchased from motoring organisations, border posts, or (in Austria) petrol stations and Tabak shops.

A toll is levied on some mountain roads and tunnels (*not* covered by the motorway tax). Toll roads and Alpine passes are mentioned in this book when relevant, but not all are covered. The useful *Facts and Sights*, a free brochure from the Austrian National Tourist Office (ANTO), has a serviceable country map and lists all toll roads and prices, and all Alpine passes and their altitudes. For more detailed information, consult a motoring organisation.

Urban Parking

Most town centres have a designated *Kurzparkzone* (short-term parking zone), which means that on-street parking is limited to a maximum of 1½ or three hours (depending upon the place) between specified times.

These are known as blue zones because of their blue markings; a parking voucher *(Parkschein)* should be purchased from a Tabak shop or pavement dispenser and displayed on the windscreen. Sometimes blue zone parking is free, but you should get a clock indicator from a Tabak shop or a police station to show the time at which you first parked. Outside the specified hours there are no parking restrictions in blue zones.

On some streets stopping may be prohibited altogether (marked by a circular blue sign with a red border and red cross) or only permitted for 10 minutes (a circular blue sign with a red border and single diagonal line – a *Halten* area). Plaques under the sign will state any exceptions or specific conditions (eg, the Halten sign may also be marked as a Kurzparkzone, allowing 1½ or three hours parking). Motorcycles cannot be parked on the pavement.

Parking tickets incur a fine of €21.90 if you pay within two weeks. Don't assume you can get away with it if you're due to leave the country, as Austria has reciprocal agreements with some countries for the collection of such debts. Don't risk getting towed, as you'll find it expensive (at least €73) and inconvenient to retrieve your vehicle.

Motoring Organisations

The main national motoring organisation is the Österreichischer Automobil, Motorrad und Touring Club (ÖAMTC; Map 7, #122; ☎ 01-711 99-0, W www.oeamtc.at), Schubertring 1–3, A–1010 Vienna. For 24-hour emergency assistance within Austria, dial ☎ 120. The ÖAMTC has many affiliations with motoring clubs worldwide and members of these clubs do not have to pay for assistance (ask your club before leaving home). If you're not entitled to free assistance, call-out charges are €87.25 during the day or €98.15 from 10pm to 6am. The ÖAMTC also offers ordinary travel agency services.

The other national motoring club, the Auto, Motor und Radfahrerbund Österreichs (☎ 01-891 21-0, W www.arboe.at), 15, Mariahilfer Strasse 180, A-1150 Vienna, has fewer international affiliations, but it offers 24-hour emergency assistance on ☎ 123.

Both of these organisations have branches throughout Austria.

Rental

For the lowest rates, organise car rental before departure. Holiday Autos has low rates and offices or representatives in over 20 countries; check W www.holidayautos.com. In the UK call ☎ 08705-300 400; in the USA call Kemwel Holiday Autos (☎ 800-576 1590). In the UK, a competitor with even lower prices is Autos Abroad (☎ 020-7287 6000); the Web site is at W www.autos abroad.co.uk. Autos Abroad charges UK£159 (about €260) for one week for its lowest category car including airport surcharge, unlimited mileage and collision damage waiver (CDW).

Within Austria, shop around to get the best deal; sometimes the same company may have two or more different rates – *Lokal Tarif*, *City Tarif*, *Hotel Tarif* and so on – plus you can pay by the kilometre or go for unlimited rates. Also, there are lower-priced deals for weekend rental, which usually (but not always) runs from noon Friday to 9am Monday. Generally though, local walk-in rates with the multinationals are pretty expensive. You'll be looking at around €50 to €60 per day in the lowest category with unlimited kilometres, though there may be special offers from time to time. Weekend deals work out at around €30 to €40 per day.

All the multinational rental companies are present in Austria. You should be able to make advance reservations online. Central reservation numbers in Austria and international Web sites are:

Avis ☎ 0800-0800 87 57 (toll free)
  W www.avis.com
Budget ☎ 07242-777 74-12
  W www.budget.com
Europcar ☎ 01-740 50-4000
  W www.europcar.com
Hertz ☎ 01-795 32
  W www.hertz.com

All of these companies have branches in main cities and may also have an airport office

(though prices are 12% higher than in city offices). National, known in Austria as ARAC (☎ 01-866 16-33, W www.arac.at), has branches in Vienna and other big cities, and charges from €24 per day including 100km. Another Austrian rental company to try is Sixt (☎ 01-503 66 16, W www.sixt.de), Wiedner Gürtel 1a, Vienna, which is linked to Eurodollar. Local rental agencies can often have very competitive rates; the local tourist office will have details.

Rental charges include a small daily sum to cover the motorway tax, and drivers under 25 or under 21 may have to pay a surcharge. Prices are subject to 20% VAT (known as MWST in Austria).

The minimum age for renting small cars is 19, for prestige models it is 25, and driving licences must have been held for a year or sometimes more. Be sure to inquire about all terms and conditions before commencing a rental. For example, some rental companies will not allow you to drive the car outside Austria or outside the EU (or will add a surcharge even if it's permissible).

You don't only have to note the headline rate when comparing prices, as surcharges can vary wildly between the different companies. For example, Avis charges €26.20 per day for additional drivers and the same again for drivers under 25. With Hertz, the charge in each case is only €4.40. On the other hand, Hertz's daily road fee is €2.45, whereas with Avis it is €0.65.

All companies offer a collision damage waiver for an additional charge, eg, it's €21.40 per day with Avis. Personal accident insurance (PAI; around €6.50 per day) is an optional extra and may not be necessary if you or your passengers hold travel insurance.

Europcar rents motorcycles in the summer season; also see under Car & Motorcycle in the Getting Around section of the Vienna chapter.

Purchase & Leasing

If you're planning a long trip, leasing a car instead of renting might work out cheaper. This can be done through large car sales outlets in your home country; the head offices of car manufacturing companies can supply details.

In Austria, numberplates are issued to the owner, so whether you buy new or second-hand, the vehicle will come without plates. If you sell a vehicle, you remove the plates and return them to the motor registration office (or transfer them to your new car). All Austrian-registered cars must undergo an annual technical inspection.

Importing a vehicle into Austria is a tedious bureaucratic process, and all newly registered cars must be fitted with a catalytic converter.

BICYCLE

Cycling is a popular activity in Austria, and most regional tourist boards have brochures on cycling facilities and routes within their region. In Vienna, Argus is an organisation which provides information for cyclists; for more details, see the Information section in the Vienna chapter.

Separate bike tracks are common (in cities, make sure you're walking on the footpath, not the bike path). The Danube cycling trail is something of a Holy Grail for cyclists, though there are many other excellent bike routes in the country. Most are close to bodies of water, where there are fewer hills to contend with.

A good reference for people wanting to go cycle-touring in Austria is **W** www.Cycle -Europe.com. It offers many tips and inspirations, as well as links to the ANTO tourist office and other useful sites.

Bicycles can be hired between April and October from nearly 40 train stations. You'll need to show a passport or other photo ID to rent a bike. The rate for a normal bike (called a city bike) is €13.10 per day, or €8.75 if you can show either a train ticket valid for that day (or for arrival at that station after 3pm the previous day) or a Vorteilscard. Rental for one week costs €65.45, or €43.60 with a ticket. Rental periods operate per calendar day, not per 24 hours. At the end of the rental you can return the bike to a different station, but you'll face a hefty surcharge – inquire when renting.

Within Austria, you can take your bike with you on slower trains, on special 'Rad Tramper' trains (eg, along the Danube) and

on the Fahrradbus round Neusiedler See. A bicycle ticket (transferable) valid on trains costs €2.95 per day, €6.55 per week and €19.65 per month. There is a fixed fare of €10.20 for transporting a bike as registered luggage on a train (not necessarily the same train as you travel on). This may be the only option on EC and IC trains, though a few do allow you to accompany your machine (€7.30 for a day ticket).

HITCHING

Hitching is never entirely safe in any country in the world, and we don't recommend it. Travellers who do hitch should understand they are taking a small but potentially serious risk. Hitchers will be safer if they travel in pairs and let someone know where they are planning to go.

Throughout Europe, hitching is illegal on motorways – stand on the slip roads, or approach drivers at petrol stations, border posts and truck stops. You can increase your chances of getting a lift by looking presentable and cheerful, and by making a cardboard sign indicating your intended destination in the local language. Showing a flag or some other indication of your country of origin can also help. Don't try to hitch from city centres: take public transport to suburban exit routes and hitch from there. Never hitch where drivers can't stop in good time or without causing an obstruction. Once you find a good spot, stay put and hope for the best, and when it starts getting dark – forget it!

Hitching in Austria is patchy, but not too bad overall (though the route west from Salzburg to Munich was identified in a hitching guide as one of the most difficult spots in Europe to get a lift). It is illegal for minors (people aged under 16 years) to hitch in Burgenland, Upper Austria, Styria and Vorarlberg.

WALKING

Many city centres are compact enough to enable major tourist sights to be seen on a walking tour, but walking really comes into its own in rural areas. See the 'Walking & Skiing' special section in the Facts for the

Top Trips

Best Road Journey
- Wind your way along the Grossglockner Road (Hohe Tauern National Park)
- Shadow the Danube by car or bicycle (Upper & Lower Austria)

Best Train Trips
- Follow the Inn and Rosanna Rivers between Innsbruck and St Anton am Arlberg (Tirol)
- Absorb the scenery of the Gasteiner Tal on the journey between Schwarzach and Spittal (Hohe Tauern National Park & Carinthia)
- Chug along Europe's first Alpine railway between Payerbach and Mürzzuschlag (Lower Austria)
- Climb above the Inn Valley from Innsbruck to Seefeld

Best Cogwheel Train Trips
- Haul up Schafberg (Salzkammergut)
- Ascend Schneeberg to gaze into the stark Breite Ries (Lower Austria)

Best Cable Car Ascents
- Soar up to the Hafelekar belvedere (2334m) above Innsbruck (Tirol)
- Take the short cut to fine hikes on the Kitzbüheler Horn (1996m) above Kitzbühel (Tirol)
- Take in views of German and Swiss peaks from the mighty Zugspitze (2962m) near Erhwald (Tirol)
- Glide over the glacier on the Kitzsteinhorn (3203m) south of Zell am See (Hohe Tauern National Park)

Visitor chapter for further information and a selection of walks.

BOAT

Services along the Danube are slow and expensive scenic excursions rather than functional transport. Nevertheless, a boat ride is definitely worth it if you like lounging on deck and having the scenery come to you rather than the other way round. See the Danube Valley section in the Lower Austria chapter and the Linz section in the Upper Austria chapter for more details on Danube services. There are boat services on the larger lakes throughout the country. On some, such as Bodensee and Wörthersee, special day passes offer good deals.

MOUNTAIN TRANSPORT

Austria has nearly 3500 transport facilities in steep Alpine regions, compared with just 26 in 1945. These fall into five main categories. A funicular *(Standseilbahn)* is a pair of counter-balancing cars drawn by cables

along an inclined track. A cable car *(Luftseilbahn)* is a cabin dramatically suspended from a cable high over a valley, with a twin that goes down when it goes up. A gondola *(Gondelbahn)* is a smaller version of a cable car except that it is hitched onto a continuously running cable once the passengers are inside. Most people use the terms gondola and cable car interchangeably, so we haven't worried about the distinction in this book. A cable chair *(Sesselbahn)* is likewise hitched onto a cable but is unenclosed. A ski lift *(Schlepplift)* is a T-bar hanging from a cable, on which the skiers hold or sit while their ski-clad feet slide along the snow. T-bars aren't as safe as modern cable cars (a careless skier could let go) and are being phased out.

LOCAL TRANSPORT

Buses cover urban areas efficiently and comprehensively, and in many larger cities they are supplemented by convenient and environmentally friendly trams. Vienna also has an underground metro system which is great for getting round the city quickly but you don't get to sightsee as you go. Most towns have an integrated transport system, meaning you can switch between bus and tram routes on the same ticket. You can usually buy excellent-value one-day or 24-hour tickets costing from €2 (Bregenz) to €4.40 (Vienna). Weekly or three-day passes may be available too, as well as multi-trip tickets, which will work out cheaper than buying individual tickets for each journey. Tickets are usually transferable, so you can sell (or even give!) unused portions to other travellers.

Passes and multi-trip tickets are available in advance from Tabak shops, pavement dispensers, and occasionally tourist offices. They usually need to be validated upon first use in the machine on buses or trams. In some towns drivers will sell single tickets, but rarely the better-value passes. Sometimes drivers don't sell any tickets, so even single tickets must be bought in advance (in Linz, for example). Single tickets may be valid for one hour, 30 minutes, or a single journey, depending on the place. If you're a senior, at school in Austria, or travelling as a family, you may be eligible for reduced-price tickets in some towns.

Keep alert when you're about to get off a bus: if you haven't pressed the request button and there's nobody waiting at the bus stop, the driver will go right past.

On-the-spot fines of between €29 and €43 apply to people caught travelling without tickets. Depending on the inspector, you could have real problems if you aren't carrying enough cash to pay the fine at the time you're caught.

Public transport runs from about 5am or 6am to midnight, though in smaller towns evening services may be patchy or finish for the night rather earlier.

Taxi

Taxis are metered and there are two elements to the fare: a flat starting fee plus a charge per kilometre. Owing to the good level of public transport, you're unlikely to need a taxi unless returning to your hotel particularly late at night. Taxis can usually be found waiting outside train stations and large hotels. There's usually a surcharge of approximately €0.75 to €2.20 for calling a radio taxi. Telephone numbers for radio taxis are given under Getting Around in the Graz, Innsbruck, Klagenfurt, Salzburg and Vienna sections.

ORGANISED TOURS

These vary from two-hour walks in a city centre to all-inclusive packages covering regional attractions. Arrangements can usually be made through tourist offices or local travel agents; details are given in the regional chapters. Sometimes you can pick up good deals on excursions via train and boat or bus. Look for brochures at train stations or inquire in train station travel offices. A brochure called *Erlebnis Bahn & Schiff*, available from train stations and some travel agents, details all sorts of trips by ferry and/or steam train.

Vienna

☎ 01 ● pop 1.64 million ● elev 156m

Vienna conjures up countless images: elaborate imperial palaces, coffee houses crammed with rich cakes and baroque mirrors, angelic choirboys, Art Nouveau masterpieces, strutting Lipizzaner stallions and many more. Its musical tradition is all-pervasive: the mighty Danube (Donau) River may slice through 2840km of Europe, from the Black Forest to the Black Sea, but it owes its fame largely to Vienna – thanks to the Strauss waltz, it will be forever pictured 'blue' in numerous minds.

Vienna has gradually cast off its image as a haunt for genteel old ladies. The somewhat staid delights of its historical heritage remain, yet it is also a city where you can party all night, if that's what you want. Mix together the music, the nightlife, the stunning architecture and some of the best museums in Europe and you get a city fully deserving of a leisurely exploration.

HISTORY

Vindobona, the military camp established by the Romans in the 1st century AD, was in the heart of Vienna's current Innere Stadt (1st district). A civilian town sprang up outside the camp and flourished in the 3rd and 4th centuries. During this time a visiting Roman emperor, Probus, introduced vineyards to the hills of the Wienerwald (Vienna Woods).

After the departure of the Romans in the 5th century, 'Wenia' was mentioned in the annals of the archbishopric of Salzburg in 881, and it became an important staging post for armies travelling to and from the Crusades. The city continued to flourish as the seat of the Babenbergs, descendants of a noble Bavarian family who granted Vienna its city charter in 1221.

The Babenbergs were succeeded by the Habsburgs. Although this dynasty was active in Vienna from the 13th century, the first of the Habsburgs to permanently reside in the city was Ferdinand I, who moved his court to Vienna in 1533. The music-loving Habsburgs helped Vienna become the music

Highlights

- Admire Stephansdom's Gothic spire, the picture gallery of the Kunsthistorisches Museum and the baroque splendour in the palaces of Schönbrunn and Belvedere

- Take a tour of the Ringstrasse by foot, tram, bicycle or fiacre

- Pick through the chaos and clutter of the Naschmarkt flea market

- Let street performers along Kärntner Strasse and Graben entertain you

- Enjoy the wine in a Heurigen or an evening of high culture in the Staatsoper

- Marvel at the bizarre waxworks in the Josephinum museum

capital of Europe, especially during the 18th and 19th centuries.

Vienna developed apace under the Austro-Hungarian dual monarchy, created in 1867, and it hosted the World Fair in 1873. At the end of WWI, the Republic of Austria came into being and, in 1919, voting rights were extended to all Viennese adults. The Social Democrats (SPÖ) gained an absolute majority and embarked on an impressive series of social policies, particularly for communal housing and health. Karl-Marx-Hof on Heiligenstädter Strasse, which originally contained 1325 apartments, is the best example of the municipal buildings created in this so-called 'Red Vienna' period. In 1934, after the socialists were defeated in the civil war, Vienna's city council was dissolved and all progressive policies instantly stopped. Democracy was not re-established in the city until after WWII.

Vienna's provincial assembly (which serves for a five-year term) also functions as the city council *(Gemeinderat)*. Likewise, the offices of provincial governor and mayor are united in the same person. The Rathaus (City Hall) is the seat of these offices.

The vote for the provincial assembly in 1996 yielded the first postwar coalition, in which the SPÖ (the largest party) joined forces with the ÖVP, thereby excluding the anti-EU, right-wing Freedom Party (FPÖ) which had won 28% of the vote. In the March 2001 election the SPÖ's vote recovered: it won a 46.8% share, which yielded a majority 52 members, allowing it again to govern the city alone. The FPÖ meantime saw its share of the vote squeezed to 20%.

ORIENTATION

Vienna occupies more than 400 sq km in the Danube Valley, with the hills of the Wienerwald beyond the suburbs to the north and west. The Danube River divides the city diagonally into two unequal parts. The old city centre and nearly all the tourist sights are south of the river, mostly in the Innere Stadt. This is encircled by the Ringstrasse, or Ring, a series of broad roads sporting sturdy public buildings. Circling the Ring at a distance of between 1.75km and 3km is a larger traffic artery, the Gürtel (literally, 'belt'), which is fed by the flow of vehicles from outlying autobahns.

The Danube runs down a long, straight channel, built between 1870 and 1875 to eliminate flooding. This was supplemented 100 years later by the building of a parallel channel, the New Danube (Neue Donau), creating a long, thin island between the two. This is known as Danube Island (Donauinsel), and is now a recreation area. The Old Danube (Alte Donau), the remnant of the original course of the river, forms a loop to the north of the New Danube. This loop encloses the Donaupark, beaches and water-sports centres. North and east of the

Old Danube are relatively poor, residential districts.

In the Donaupark is the Vienna International Center (UNO City), where the international organisations are housed, including the most important base of the United Nations (UN) after New York and Geneva. UNO City has extraterritorial status so take your passport when visiting. The park also contains the Austria Centre Vienna, Austria's largest convention hall. Small trade fairs are held in UNO City, though the main centre for trade fairs is the exhibition centre *(Messegelände)* in the Prater, a large park to the east of the Innere Stadt.

Stephansdom (St Stephen's Cathedral), with its slender spire, is in the heart of the Innere Stadt and is Vienna's principal landmark. Leading south from Stephansplatz station is Kärntner Strasse, an important pedestrian street that terminates at Karlsplatz, a major transport hub for the centre.

The majority of hotels, pensions, restaurants and bars are in the Innere Stadt or west of the centre between the Ringstrasse and the Gürtel.

Addresses

Vienna is divided into 23 districts *(Bezirke)*, fanning out in approximate numerical order clockwise around the Innere Stadt. Take care when reading addresses. The number of a building within a street *follows* the street name. Any number *before* the street name denotes the district. The middle two digits of a postcode correspond to the district. Thus a postcode of 1010 means the place is in district one, and 1230 refers to district 23. Another thing to note is that the same street number may cover several adjoining buildings, so if you find that what you thought was going to be a pizza restaurant at Wienstrasse 4 is really a rubber fetish shop, check the buildings either side before you resign yourself to a radical change of eating habits.

Maps

Freytag & Berndt (see the Bookshops section) produces a variety of clear maps of Vienna, though the excellent free map provided by the tourist office is sufficient for most purposes. This shows public transport routes, but doesn't have a street index.

INFORMATION
Tourist Offices

The main tourist office (Map 7, #126) is at 01, Am Albertinaplatz, and has extensive free literature. *Ten good reasons for Vienna*, clearly aimed at the young with its overly hip style, contains lots of useful information for everyone. There are also free lists of museums, events, hotels and restaurants, as well as a room-finding service (€2.95 commission per reservation). The office is open 9am to 7pm daily.

Vienna From A to Z (€3.65) covers information on over 200 sights, and includes walking tour itineraries of the centre. The Vienna Card (€15.30) includes a 72-hour travel pass (see the Getting Around section later in this chapter) plus numerous benefits, particularly discounts on shopping and admission to attractions. Both are available from the tourist office and elsewhere.

Telephone inquiries, advance requests for brochures and marketing matters are dealt with at the head office of the Vienna Tourist Board (☎ 211 14, fax 216 84 92, e wtv@ info.wien.at, w www.info.wien.at), Obere Augartenstrasse 40, A-1025 Wien. Opening hours are 8am to 4pm Monday to Friday; but the office is not set up to handle visits in person from the public.

The Austria Information Office, or Österreich Werbung (Map 6, #37; ☎ 587 20 00, fax 588 66 48, e oeinfo@oewwien.via.at, w www.austria-tourism.at), 04, Margaretenstrasse 1, is open 9.30am to 5pm Monday to Friday (to 6pm on Thursday), and has information about the whole country.

There is a Lower Austria Information Centre (Map 7, #137) at 01, Kärntner Strasse 38, but as it's part of a travel agency its main intent is to sell you packages. Alternatively, try the Niederösterreich Information head office (☎ 536 10-6200, fax 536 10-6060, e tourismus@noe.co.at, w www.niederoster reich.at).

Information and room reservations (€2.95 commission per reservation) are also avail-

able in offices at various entry points to the city (all are open daily):

Airport Arrivals hall, 8.30am to 9pm
Train stations Westbahnhof, 7am to 10pm; Südbahnhof, 6.30am to 10pm (to 9pm from 1 November to 30 April)
From the west by road A1 autobahn exit Wien-Auhof, 8am to 10pm (10am to 6pm November to March)
From the south by road A2 exit Zentrum, Triester Strasse, 9am to 7pm (Easter to June, and October) and 8am to 10pm (July to September); closed in winter
From the north by road At Floridsdorfer Brücke (bridge) on Danube Island (Donauinsel), 10am to 6pm; closed October to April

Other Information Offices

The city information office (Map 7, #45) in the Rathaus (City Hall) is open 8am to 6pm Monday to Friday. Phone inquiries (☎ 525 50) will also be answered from 8am to 4pm on Saturday and Sunday, as well as during office hours. It provides information on social, cultural and practical matters, geared as much to residents as to tourists. There are two touch-screen computer terminals with useful information; they plug directly into the city government site (w www.wien.gv.at), which has some great features, including maps and an address-searching facility.

Staff at Jugendinfo (Youth Info; Map 7, #133; ☎ 17 79, e jugendinfowien@wienX tra.at), at 01, Babenbergerstrasse 1, can tell you about events around town, as well as provide tickets for such events at reduced rates for those aged between 14 and 26. It also offers cheap Internet access. It's open noon to 7pm Monday to Saturday.

Argus (Map 6, #38; ☎ 505 84 35), 04, Frankenberggasse 11, is an organisation promoting cycling that provides maps and cycling information covering the whole of Austria. It's open 2pm to 6pm Monday to Thursday, 2pm to 8pm Friday.

Money

There are banks and currency exchange offices all over the city, but compare commission rates before changing money.

[continued on page 117]

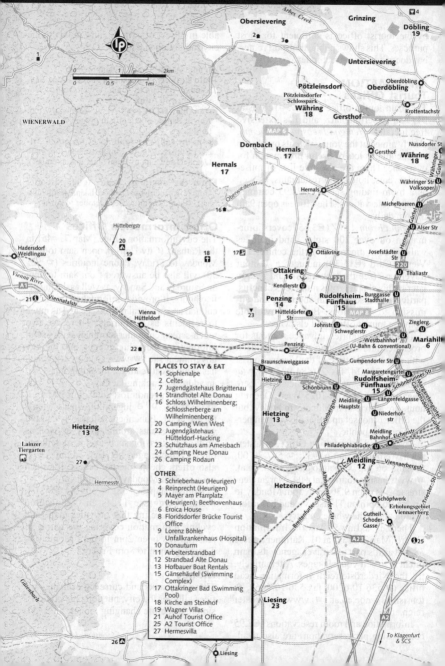

MAP 5 - GREATER VIENNA

WIENERWALD

Obersievering

Grinzing

Döbling
19

Untersievering

Pötzleinsdorf
Pötzleinsdorfer
Schlosspark

Oberdöbling

Oberdöbling

Währing
18

Gersthof

Krottenbachstr

Dornbach

Hernals
17

Gersthof

Nussdorfer St

Währing
18

Hernals
17

Hernals

Währinger Str
Volksoper

Michelbeuern

Hüttelbergstr

Alser Str

Ottakring

Josefstädter
Str

Hadersdorf
Weidlingau

Thaliastr

Vienna River

Ottakring
16

Kendlerstr

Rudolfsheim-
Fünfhaus
15

Burggasse
Stadthalle

Viennatalstr

Penzing
14

Hütteldorfer
Str

Johnstr

Schweglerstr

Ziegierg.

Mariahil
6

Vienna
Hütteldorf

Penzing

Westbahnhof
(U-Bahn & conventional)

Braunschweiggasse

Gumpendorfer Str

Schlossberggasse

Margaretengürtel

Rudolfsheim-
Fünfhaus
15

Hietzing

Schönbrunn

Längenfeldgasse

Meidling-
Hauptstr

Niederhof-
str

Hietzing
13

Hietzing
13

Meidling
Bahnhof Eichenstr

Philadelphiabrücke

Lainzer
Tiergarten

Hermesstr

Meidling
12

Viennaerbergstr

Hetzendorf

Schöpfwerk

Erholungsgebiet
Viennaerberg

Gutheil-
Schoder-
Gasse

Breitenfurter-Str

Altmannsdorfer-Str

Trester-Str

Liesing
23

Liesing

To Klagenfurt
& SCS

Gütenbach

PLACES TO STAY & EAT
1 Sophienalpe
2 Celtes
7 Jugendgästehaus Brigittenau
14 Strandhotel Alte Donau
16 Schloss Wilhelminenberg;
   Schlossherberge am
   Wilhelminenberg
20 Camping Wien West
22 Jugendgästehaus
   Hütteldorf-Hacking
23 Schutzhaus am Ameisbach
24 Camping Neue Donau
26 Camping Rodaun

OTHER
3 Schrieberhaus (Heurigen)
4 Reinprecht (Heurigen)
5 Mayer am Pfarrplatz
   (Heurigen); Beethovenhaus
6 Eroica House
8 Floridsdorfer Brücke Tourist
   Office
9 Lorenz Böhler
   Unfallkrankenhaus (Hospital)
10 Donauturm
11 Arbeiterstrandbad
12 Strandbad Alte Donau
13 Hofbauer Boat Rentals
15 Gänsehäufel (Swimming
   Complex)
17 Ottakringer Bad (Swimming
   Pool)
18 Kirche am Steinhof
19 Wagner Villas
21 Auhof Tourist Office
25 A2 Tourist Office
27 Hermesvilla

MAP 5 - GREATER VIENNA

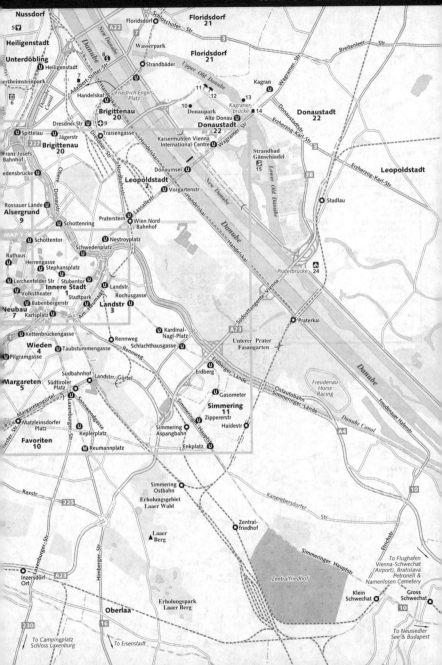

MAP 6 - VIENNA

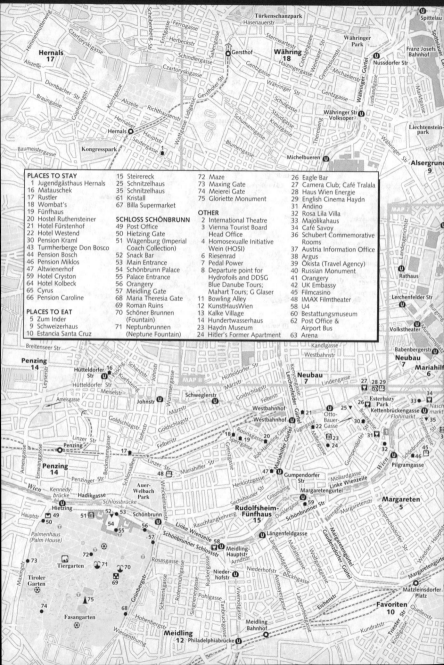

PLACES TO STAY
1 Jugendgästhaus Hernals
16 Matauschek
17 Rustler
18 Wombat's
19 Fünfhaus
20 Hostel Ruthensteiner
21 Hotel Fürstenhof
22 Hotel Westend
30 Pension Kraml
43 Turmherberge Don Bosco
44 Pension Bosch
46 Pension Miklos
47 Altwienerhof
59 Hotel Cryston
64 Hotel Kolbeck
65 Cyrus
66 Pension Caroline

PLACES TO EAT
5 Zum Inder
9 Schweizerhaus
10 Estancia Santa Cruz

15 Steirereck
25 Schnitzelhaus
35 Schnitzelhaus
61 Kristall
67 Billa Supermarket

SCHLOSS SCHÖNBRUNN
49 Post Office
50 Hietzing Gate
51 Wagenburg (Imperial Coach Collection)
52 Snack Bar
53 Main Entrance
54 Schönbrunn Palace
55 Palace Entrance
56 Orangery
57 Meidling Gate
68 Maria Theresia Gate
69 Roman Ruins
70 Schöner Brunnen (Fountain)
71 Neptunbrunnen (Neptune Fountain)

72 Maze
73 Maxing Gate
74 Meierei Gate
75 Gloriette Monument

OTHER
2 International Theatre
3 Vienna Tourist Board Head Office
4 Homosexuelle Initiative Wein (HOSI)
6 Riesenrad
7 Pedal Power
8 Departure point for Hydrofoils and DDSG Blue Danube Tours; Mahart Tours; G Glaser
11 Bowling Alley
12 KunstHausWien
13 Kalke Village
14 Hundertwasserhaus
23 Haydn Museum
24 Hitler's Former Apartment

26 Eagle Bar
27 Camera Club; Café Tralala
28 Haus Wien Energie
29 English Cinema Haydn
31 Andino
32 Rosa Lila Villa
33 Majolikahaus
34 Café Savoy
36 Schubert Commemorative Rooms
37 Austria Information Office
38 Argus
39 Ökista (Travel Agency)
40 Russian Monument
41 Orangery
42 UK Embassy
45 Filmcasino
48 IMAX Filmtheater
58 U4
60 Bestattungsmuseum
62 Post Office & Airport Bus
63 Arena

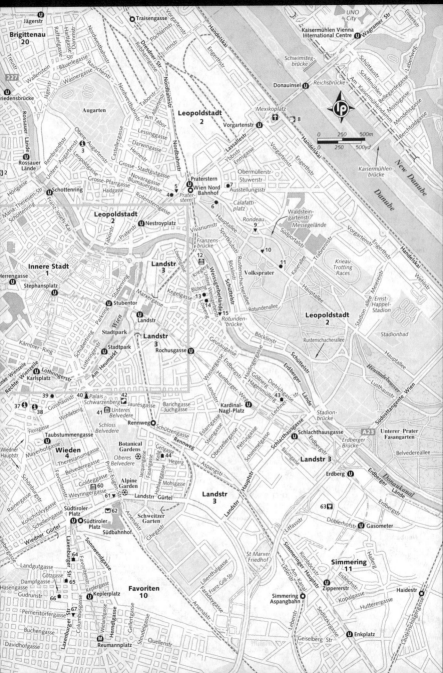

MAP 6 - VIENNA

MAP 7 - CENTRAL VIENNA

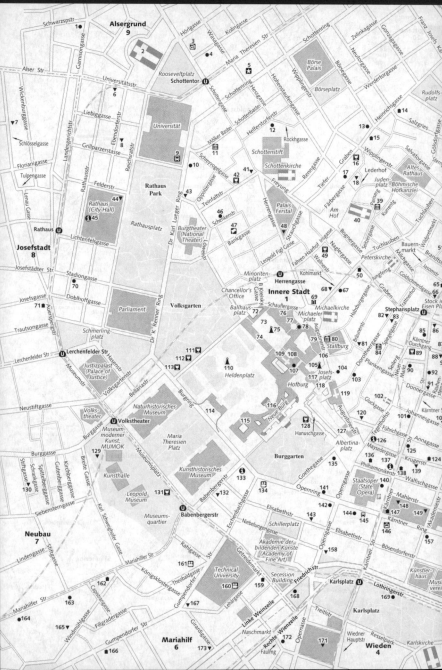

MAP 7 - CENTRAL VIENNA

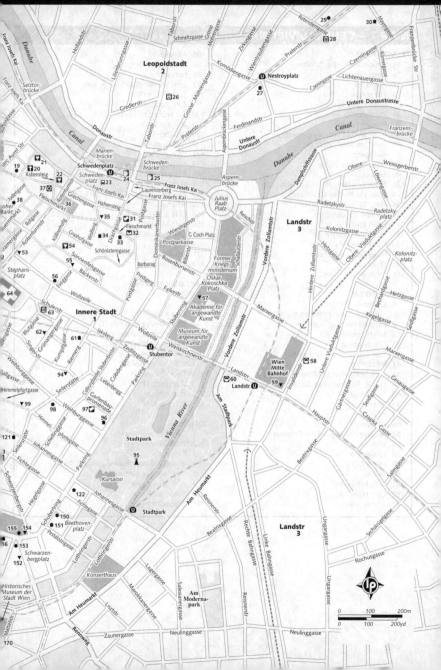

MAP 7 – CENTRAL VIENNA

PLACES TO STAY

14 Schweizer Pension Solderer
15 Hotel Orient
27 Aphrodite
30 Praterstern
33 Hotel Post
34 Hotel Austria
50 Pension Nossek
61 Appartement Pension Riemergasse
65 Hotel am Stephansplatz
71 Auersperg
87 Hotel Kaiserin Elisabeth
96 Marriott Hotel
121 Music Academy Hotel & Mensa
124 Hotel zur Wiener Staatsoper
136 Hotel Sacher; Café Sacher
138 Pension am Operneck
147 Hotel Bristol
151 Hotel am Schubertring
156 Hotel Imperial
159 Hotel-Mecure Secession
162 Quisisana
166 Kolping-Gästehaus

PLACES TO EAT

6 University Mensa
7 Gasthaus Zur Böhmischen Kuchl
8 Katholisches Studenthaus Mensa
18 Brezel Gwölb
35 Griechenbeisl
36 Spar Supermarket; First Floor
41 Naschmarkt
43 Café Restaurant Landtmann
44 Wiener Rathauskeller; Grinzinger Keller
48 Café Central
51 Wrenkh
53 Pizza Bizi
55 Alt Wien
57 Academy of Applied Art Cafeteria
59 Interspar
62 La Crêperie
66 DO & CO
68 Demel
81 Café Bräunerhof
82 Café Hawelka
83 Trzesniewski

86 Akakiko
88 Drei Husaren
91 Nordsee
93 Zum Weissen Rauchfangkehrer
94 Zu den 3 Hacken
99 Zum Kuckuck
100 Zur Fischerin Capua
120 Yugetsu Saryo
129 Glacisbeisl
130 Amerlingbeisl
132 Grotta Azzurra
139 Restaurant Siam
143 Restaurant Smutny
148 Korso
149 Restaurant Marché Mövenpick
152 Naschmarkt
154 Café Schwarzenberg
158 Café Museum
165 K&K Bierkanzlei
167 Café Sperl
171 Technical University Mensa
173 Café Drechsler

BARS & NIGHTCLUBS

16 Why Not?
21 Jazzland
22 Krah Krah
42 Molly Darcy's Irish Pub
49 Esterházykeller (Heurigen)
54 Zwölf Apostelkeller (Heurigen)
89 American Bar
111 Volksgarten Pavillon
112 Tanz Volksgarten
113 Volksgarten Disco
128 Palmenhaus
131 Porgy & Bess

OTHER

1 Ökista (Travel Agency)
2 Votivkirche
3 Café Stein
4 Reisebuchladen (Bookshop & Bus Tours)
5 Vienna Police Headquarters
9 Austrobus Buses
10 Columbus Reisen
11 Pasqualati House

MAP 7 – CENTRAL VIENNA

12 ÖJHW (Youth Hostel Head Office)
13 Cityrama
17 Former Civic Armoury
19 Shakespeare & Co Booksellers
20 Ruprechtskirche
23 Night Bus Departures
24 DDSG Blue Danube Canal Tour Departures
25 Donau Schiffahrt Canal Tour Departures
26 Serapionstheater im Odeon
28 Johann Strauss Residence
29 2 Rad-Börse
31 Canadian Embassy
32 Main Post Office
37 Stadttempel
38 Ankeruhr (Anker Clock)
39 Uhren Museum
40 Kirche Am Hof
45 City Information Office
46 British Council Library
47 Hungarian Embassy
52 Swissair
56 Morawa
58 Eurolines Office
60 City Air Terminal
63 Mozart's Apartment (Figaro House)
64 Stephansdom (St Stephen's Cathedral)
67 Freytag & Berndt
69 Loos Haus
70 KlangBogen Office
72 Amalia Wing
73 In der Burg Courtyard
74 Leopold Wing
75 Monument to Emperor Franz II
76 Imperial Chancery Wing
77 Kaiserappartements & Silberkammer Collection
78 Spanish Riding School Office
79 Spanish Riding School
80 Lipizzaner Museum
84 Jüdisches Museum
85 Österreichische Werkstätten
90 Inlingua Sprachschule
92 American Express
95 Johann Strauss Statue
97 US Consulate
98 British Bookshop
101 J&L Lobmeyr

102 Kapuzinerkirche; Kaisergruft
103 Dorotheum
104 Palais Palffy
105 Monument to Emperor Josef II
106 Entrance to Spanish Riding School
    (Training Session Viewing)
107 Schatzkammer (Imperial Treasury)
108 Schweizerhof (Swiss Courtyard)
109 Burgkapelle (Royal Chapel)
110 Monument to Archduke Charles
114 Palace Gates
115 Museum für Völkerkunde
116 Nationalbibliothek (National Library) &
    Sammlung Alter Musikinstrumente
117 Prunksaal
118 Entrance to Prunksaal
119 Augustinerkirche
122 ÖAMTC
123 Haus der Musik
125 Casino (Esterházy Palace)
126 Main Tourist Office
127 Albertina & Österreichische
    Filmmuseum
133 Jugendinfo
134 Burg Kino
135 Bundestheaterkassen
137 Lower Austria Information Centre
140 Wien Ticket
141 Lauda Air
142 Internationales Kulturinstitut
144 Avis
145 Bus to Baden
146 Lokalbahn Tram to Baden
150 National Car Rental - ARAC
153 Austrian Airlines Office
155 Hertz
157 British Airways Office
160 Audimax der TU
161 Top Center
163 Virgin Megastore
164 Niedermeyer Store
168 Österreichisches Verkehrsbüro; DDSG
    Blue Danube Office
169 Stadt Pavillons
170 Australian Embassy
172 Reisebüro Mondial

MAP 8 - VIENNA - WEST OF THE RING

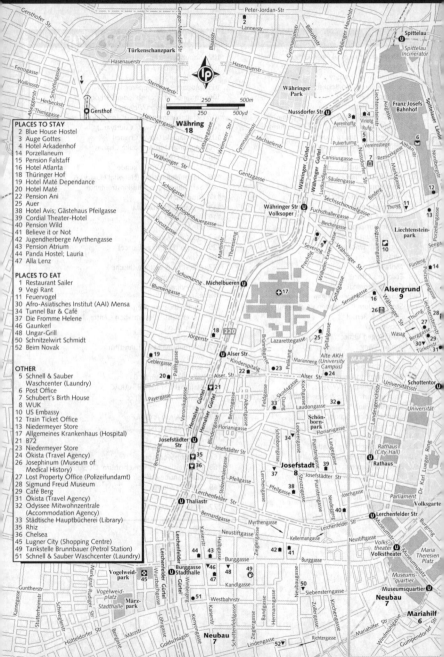

PLACES TO STAY
2 Blue House Hostel
3 Auge Gottes
4 Hotel Arkadenhof
14 Porzellaneum
15 Pension Falstaff
16 Hotel Atlanta
18 Thüringer Hof
19 Hotel Maté Dependance
20 Hotel Maté
22 Pension Ani
25 Auer
38 Hotel Avis; Gästehaus Pfeilgasse
39 Cordial Theater-Hotel
40 Pension Wild
41 Believe it or Not
42 Jugendherberge Myrthengasse
43 Pension Atrium
44 Panda Hostel; Lauria
47 Alla Lenz

PLACES TO EAT
1 Restaurant Sailer
9 Vegi Rant
11 Feuervogel
30 Afro-Asiatisches Institut (AAI) Mensa
34 Tunnel Bar & Café
37 Die Fromme Helene
46 Gaunkerl
48 Ungar-Grill
50 Schnitzelwirt Schmidt
52 Beim Novak

OTHER
5 Schnell & Sauber
    Waschcenter (Laundry)
6 Post Office
7 Schubert's Birth House
8 WUK
10 US Embassy
12 Train Ticket Office
13 Niedermeyer Store
17 Allgemeines Krankenhaus (Hospital)
23 B72
24 Niedermeyer Store
26 Ökista (Travel Agency)
27 Josephinum (Museum of
    Medical History)
28 Sigmund Freud Museum
29 Café Berg
31 Ökista (Travel Agency)
32 Odysse Mitwohnzentrale
    (Accommodation Agency)
33 Städtische Hauptbücherei (Library)
35 Rhiz
36 Chelsea
45 Lugner City (Shopping Centre)
49 Tankstelle Brunnbauer (Petrol Station)
51 Schnell & Sauber Waschcenter (Laundry)

[continued from page 107]

Be particularly vigilant at exchange booths *(Wechselstuben)* – we've seen scandalous rates of 10% plus a charge per cheque. The information offices in Westbahnhof and Südbahnhof exchange money, as do post offices. Moneychangers at the airport tend to charge high commission, though the exchange rates are standard.

American Express (see the Travel Agencies section) charges €3.65 to €5.85 commission for cashing non-Amex travellers cheques; Amex cheques are cashed free of charge. Cash exchanges attract a small commission on a sliding scale.

There are ATM Bankomats at all main train stations, at the airport and at 200 branches of Bank Austria.

Post & Communications

The main post office (Map 7, #32; Hauptpost 1010) is at 01, Fleischmarkt 19. It's open 24 hours a day for collecting and sending mail, changing money, using the telephone and sending faxes. Only a few services (like using a Privatsparbuch, a type of post office savings account) are not available round the clock. There are also post offices open daily at Südbahnhof (Map 6, #62; 7am to 10pm), Franz Josefs Bahnhof (Map 8, #6; 6am to 10pm) and Westbahnhof (Map 6; 6am to 11pm).

Branch post offices are open 8am to noon and 2pm to 6pm Monday to Friday, and 8am to 10am on Saturday. They generally have a counter for changing money, but these close at 5pm on weekdays.

Vienna has numerous places offering public access to online services. Happily, some places are free, such as Haus Wien Energie (Map 6, #28; ☎ 581 200), 06, Mariahilfer Strasse 63, open 9am to 6pm weekdays (to 8pm Thursday, to 3pm Friday) and the Städtische Hauptbücherei (library; Map 8, #33; ☎ 4000-84 551), 08, Skodagasse 20, open 10am to 7.30pm Monday and Thursday and 2pm to 7.30pm Tuesday and Friday.

If you're not prepared to queue, drop into places that charge (typically €4.40 to €8 per hour), such as Café Stein (Map 7, #3; ☎ 319

72 411), 09, Währinger Strasse 6, and the Virgin Megastore (Map 7, #163; ☎ 588 37-0), 06, Mariahilfer Strasse 37-39. Jugendinfo (see Other Information Offices earlier) charges just €0.75 for 30 minutes.

Travel Agencies

American Express (Map 7, #92; ☎ 515 40, fax 515 40-777, e info@amex.co.at), 01, Kärntner Strasse 21-23, is open 9am to 5.30pm Monday to Friday, 9am to noon Saturday.

The Ökista head office (Map 7, #1; ☎ 401 48, fax 401 48-2290, e info@oekista .at), 09, Garnisongasse 7, is open 9am to 5.30pm Monday to Friday. There are other Ökista offices at 09, Türkenstrasse 6-8 (Map 8, #31; ☎ 401 48-7000); 04, Karlsgasse 3 (Map 6, #39; ☎ 502 43); Altes AKH-Campus, 09, Alserstrasse 4/Hof 1 (Map 8, #24; ☎ 902 07); and DZ-Im Libro, Donaustadtstrasse 1/2 (☎ 202 48 08).

Österreichisches Verkehrsbüro (Map 7, #168; ☎ 588 00, fax 586 85 33, e info@ verkehrsbuero.at), 01, Friedrichstrasse 7 and elsewhere, is a major national agency. Cedok (☎ 512 43 72, fax 512 43 72-85), 01, Parkring 10 (entry from Liebenberggasse), is a specialist agency for travel to the Czech Republic.

Bookshops

Many bookshops can be found on Wollzeile, near Stephansdom; Morawa (Map 7, #56; ☎ 515 62-0) at No 11 is the biggest. The British Bookshop (Map 7, #98; ☎ 512 19 45), 01, Weihburggasse 24-6, has the largest selection of English-language books. Shakespeare & Co Booksellers (Map 7, #19; ☎ 535 50 53), 01, Sterngasse 2, is smaller but has some second-hand books. Freytag & Berndt (Map 7, #67; ☎ 533 20 94), 01, Kohlmarkt 9, stocks a vast selection of maps and sells English-language travel guides. Reisebuchladen (Map 7, #4; ☎ 317 33 84), 09, Kolingasse 6, is a travel bookshop with many Lonely Planet guides.

Libraries

Libraries are dotted around Vienna. Anyone can use them but only residents can borrow books. The main branch is the Städtische Hauptbücherei (Map 8, #33; ☎ 4000-84 551), 08, Skodagasse 20, open 10am to 7.30pm Monday and Thursday, and 2pm to 7.30pm Tuesday and Friday. The British Council (Map 7, #46; ☎ 533 26 16-81), 01, Schenkenstrasse 4, has a library with newspapers and magazines in English.

The Nationalbibliothek (Map 8, #116) in the new wing of the Hofburg contains huge reference and lending sections plus collections of CD-ROMs, papyrus and musical scores. The reading room upstairs has the *Times* newspaper and many other publications in English. The main part of the library is open 9am to 7pm (to 3.45pm from 1 July to 31 August) Monday to Friday and 9am to 12.45pm Saturday.

Cultural Centres
The main cultural centre is the Museumsquartier (see the Things to See & Do section); WUK, west of the Ring (see Entertainment), is also an interesting venue.

Gay & Lesbian Travellers
Probably the best organisation to contact is Rosa Lila Villa (Map 6, #32), 06, Linke Wienzeile 102. It provides telephone counselling, literature and advice and has information on what's on offer in the city, including listings of gay-friendly hotels, shops, bars, cafes and clubs. It's open 5pm to 8pm Monday to Friday. The lesbian centre (☎ 586 81 50, **e** lesbenberatung@villa.at) is on the ground floor, and the gay men's centre (☎ 585 43 43, **e** schwulenberatung@villa.at) is on the 1st floor. Also on the premises is Café Willendorf, open 6pm to 2am daily (with good food till midnight).

The Homosexualle Initiative Wien (HOSI; (Map 6, #4; ☎ 216 66 04, **e** office@hosi wien.at), 02, Novaragasse 40, has telephone counselling 6pm to 8pm on Tuesday and 7pm to 9pm Wednesday and Thursday. It's open to visitors on Tuesday from 5pm to 10pm.

Laundry
Schnell & Sauber Waschcenter (Map 8, #51), 07, Urban Loritz Platz, Westbahnstrasse, is open 24 hours daily, and has instructions in English. It costs €4.40 to wash a 6kg load, plus €0.40 for powder, €0.75 to spin and from €0.75 to dry. Another branch is at 09, Nussdorfer Strasse 80 (Map 8, #5), open 6am to 11pm daily.

Medical Services
Medical treatment is available at the Allgemeines Krankenhaus (general hospital; Map 8, #17; ☎ 404 00-0, extension 1964 for emergencies) at 09, Währinger Gürtel 18-20. Other hospitals with emergency departments include Unfallkrankenhaus Lorenz Böhler (☎ 331 10-0), 20, Donaueschingenstrasse 13, and Unfallkrankenhaus Meidling (☎ 601 50-0), 12, Kundratstrasse 37.

The Universitäts-Zahnklinik (University Dental Hospital; ☎ 42 77-670 01) is at 09, Währinger Strasse 25a. For recorded information on out-of-hours dental treatment, call ☎ 512 20 78; the recording is in German only, but you should still be able to figure out the address of the nearest open dentist.

Chemist shops or drugstores *(Apotheken)* are open normal shop hours, though they operate an out-of-hours service in rotation; dial ☎ 1550 for recorded information in German on which are open.

Emergency
The Frauenotruf (☎ 71 719) is a 24-hour emergency hotline for reporting rape and sexual violence. Other emergency telephone numbers in Vienna include:

Ambulance	☎ 144
Doctor	☎ 141
Fire	☎ 122
Police	☎ 133

The police headquarters for the Innere Stadt (Map 7, #5; ☎ 313 47-0) is at 01, Deutschmeisterplatz 3; there are police stations at Stephansplatz and Karlsplatz U-Bahn stations.

Dangers & Annoyances
Vienna is a very safe city, but use common sense: avoid unlit streets and parks after dark. Drug addicts sometimes congregate in

the Karlsplatz U-Bahn station near the Secession exit. The Prater and Mexikoplatz can also be dodgy areas at night.

INNERE STADT
Stephansdom

The latticework spire of this Gothic masterpiece rises high above the city and is a focal point for visitors.

The cathedral *(Map 7, #64; ☎ 515 52-3767; 01, Stephansplatz)* was built on the site of a 12th-century church, of which the surviving Riesentor (Giant's Gate, the main entrance) and the Heidentürme (Towers of the Heathens) are incorporated into the present building. Both are Romanesque in style; however, the church was rebuilt in Gothic style after 1359.

The dominating feature, the skeletal **Südturm** *(south tower; €2.20; open 9am-5.30pm daily)*, is nicknamed 'Steffl'. It stands 136.7m high and was completed in 1433 after 75 years of building work. Negotiating 343 steps will bring you to the cramped viewing platform for an impressive panorama. It was to be matched by a companion tower on the north side *(€2.95; open 8.30am-5pm daily Nov-Mar, 8.30am-5.30pm Apr, May, June, Sept & Oct, 8.30am-6pm July & Aug)*, accessible by lift, but the imperial purse withered and the Gothic style went out of fashion, so the incomplete tower was topped off with a Renaissance cupola in 1579. Austria's largest bell, the **Pummerin** (boomer bell), was installed here in 1952; it weighs 21 tonnes.

Interior walls and pillars are decorated with fine statues and side altars. The **stone pulpit**, fashioned in 1515 by Anton Pilgram, is a magnificent Gothic piece. The expressive faces of the four fathers of the church (the saints Augustine, Ambrose, Gregory and Jerome) are at the centre of the design, and Pilgram himself can be seen peering out from a window below. The baroque **high altar** in the main chancel depicts the stoning of St Stephen. The left chancel contains a winged altarpiece that was moved here from Wiener Neustadt and dates from 1447; the right chancel houses the red marble tomb of Friedrich III, which

is Renaissance in style. Under his guidance the city became a bishopric (and the church a cathedral) in 1469.

Don't ignore the decorations and statues on the outside of the cathedral: at the rear the agony of the Crucifixion is well captured, although some irreverent souls attribute Christ's pained expression to toothache. A striking feature of the exterior is the glorious **tiled roof**, showing dazzling chevrons on one end and the Austrian eagle on the other; a good view can be had from Schulerstrasse.

The **Katakomben** *(catacombs; €2.95; guided tours every 15 or 30 mins 10am-11.30am & 1.30pm-4.30pm Mon-Sat, 1.30pm-4.30pm Sun & holidays)* are in the cathedral. The tours (with English commentary if there's sufficient demand) include sights such as a mass grave of plague victims, a bone house, and rows of urns containing the internal organs of the Habsburgs. One privilege of being a Habsburg was to be dismembered and dispersed after death: their hearts are in the Augustinerkirche in the Hofburg *(☎ 533 70 99; 01, Augustinerstrasse 3; entry €1.10)* and the rest of their bits are in the Kaisergruft (see the entry later in this chapter). This macabre attraction can be viewed by prior appointment only; after Sunday High Mass, about 12.15pm, is usually possible.

Hofburg

The huge Hofburg (Imperial Palace; Map x) in the 1st district is an impressive repository of culture and heritage. The Habsburgs were based here for over six centuries, from the first emperor (Rudolf I in 1279) to the last (Charles I in 1918). During that time new sections were periodically added, including the early baroque Leopold Wing (Map 7, #74), the 18th-century Imperial Chancery Wing (Map 7, #76), the 16th-century Amalia Wing (Map 7, #72) and the Burgkapelle (Royal Chapel; Map 7, #109), which was commissioned by Friedrich III and refitted in baroque style by Empress Maria Theresa. This is where the Vienna Boys' Choir sings Sunday Mass. The palace now houses the offices of the Austrian president.

The oldest part is the 13th-century **Schweizerhof** (Swiss Courtyard; Map 7, #108), named after the Swiss guards who used to protect its precincts. The Renaissance Swiss gate dates from 1553. The courtyard adjoins a much larger courtyard, **In der Burg** (Map 7, #73), with a monument to Emperor Franz II (Map 7, #75) at its centre. The buildings which surround it are from various eras.

Kaiserappartements The former Imperial Apartments *(Map 7, #77; ☎ 533 75 70; St Michael's Gate, admission adult/student under 26/child €6.95/5.45/2.55; open 9am-4.30pm daily)* are as opulent as you might expect, with fine furniture, hanging tapestries and bulbous crystal chandeliers. However, they don't match those in Schloss Schönbrunn (see later in this chapter). Rooms in this part of the palace were occupied by Franz Josef I and Empress Elisabeth. You also get to see the **Silberkammer** (Silver Treasury) of porcelain and tableware. An English audioguide costs €2.95.

Schatzkammer The Imperial Treasury *(Map 7, #107; ☎ 533 79 31; Schweizerhof; adult/ concession €7.20/5; open 10am-6pm Wed-Mon)* contains secular and ecclesiastical treasures of great value and splendour. The sheer wealth exhibited is staggering: Room 7 contains a 2860-carat Colombian emerald, a 416-carat balas ruby and a 492-carat aquamarine. In Room 2, the imperial crown dates from the 10th century; the private crown of Rudolf II (1602) is a more delicate piece. Room 5 contains mementoes of Marie Louise, daughter of Franz II and wife of Napoleon. Room 8 contains two unusual objects formerly owned by Ferdinand I: a 75cm-wide bowl carved from a single piece of agate, and a narwhal tusk, 243cm long and once claimed to have been a unicorn horn.

The religious relics include fragments of the True Cross, one of the nails from the Crucifixion, and one of the thorns from Christ's crown. Ecclesiastical vestments display delicate and skilled work.

Allow anything from 30 minutes to two hours to get around. Entry price includes a personal electronic guide.

Prunksaal The Prunksaal *(literally, Magnificent Hall; Map 7, #117; ☎ 534 100; Josefsplatz 1; adult/concession €4.40/2.95; open 10am-2pm Mon-Sat Nov-Apr, 10am-4pm Mon-Wed, Fri & Sat, 10am-7pm Thurs, 10am-2pm Sun & holidays May-Oct)* is an archetypal baroque structure, created by the Fischer von Erlachs (Johann and his son Josef) between 1723 and 1726. It was commissioned by Charles VI, whose statue stands under the central church-like dome, on which is a Daniel Gran fresco depicting the emperor's apotheosis. Leather-bound, scholarly books line the walls, and rare 15th-century volumes stored in glass cabinets are opened to beautifully illustrated sections of text.

Neue Burg Museums These three museums-in-one in the Neue Hofburg *(Map 7; ☎ 525 240; Heldenplatz; adult/concession €7.30/5.85; open 10am-6pm Wed-Mon)* can be seen for a single admission. The Sammlung Alter Musik Instrumente (Collection of Ancient Musical Instruments) is the best part. The free audio commentary (on headphones) is activated by infrared as you walk round, providing a relaxing and evocative musical accompaniment to the variety of instruments on display. Instruments of all shapes and sizes are to be found, including horns shaped like serpents and violins with carved faces. Different rooms are dedicated to different composers, such as Haydn, Mozart and Beethoven, and contain instruments played by those notables.

The **Ephesus Museum** contains relief statues and a scale model of the famous archaeological site in Turkey. The **Hofjagd und Rüstkammer** (arms and armour) collection dates mostly from the 15th and 16th centuries and houses some fine examples of ancient armour; note the bizarre pumpkin-shaped helmet from the 15th century.

Kaisergruft

The high-peaked Imperial Burial Vault *(Map 7, #102; ☎ 512 68 53 12; 01, Neuer Markt;*

[continued on page 126]

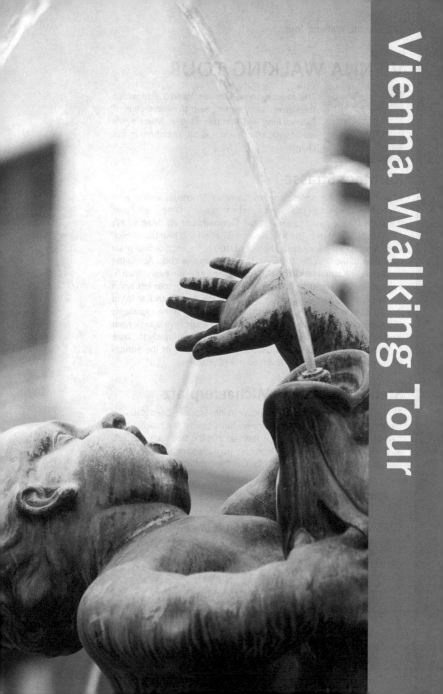

Vienna Walking Tour

VIENNA WALKING TOUR

This orientation walk covers about 2.5km within the Innere Stadt, starting near the intersection of Kärnter Ring and Kärntner Strasse. Major sights are considered in greater detail elsewhere in this chapter.

Kärntner Strasse

Walk north up the pedestrian-only Kärntner Strasse, a walkway of plush shops, trees, cafe tables and street entertainers. Detour left down the short Donnergasse to look at the **Donnerbrunnen** (Map 9, #2; 1739) in Neuer Markt. The four naked figures on this fountain (which were too revealing for Maria Theresa's taste) represent the four main tributaries of the Danube: the Enns, March, Traun and Ybbs. Across the square is the **Kapuzinerkirche** (Church of the Capuchin Friars; Map 9, #3) and the **Kaisergruft.** Back on Kärntner Strasse, detour left again down Kärntner Durchgang. Here you'll find the **American Bar** (Map 9, #4), designed in 1908 by Adolf Loos, one of the prime exponents of a functional Art Nouveau style, though the facade here is somewhat garish. Next door is a strip club, Chez Nous. This was formerly the base for the art club of the Vienna Group; ironically, many of the group's performance art events also involved naked postures.

Stephansplatz To Michaelerplatz

From Kärntner Strasse, the street opens out into Stock im Eisen Platz. On the left-side corner of Kärntner Strasse, flush against the building, is a **nail-studded stump** (Map 9, #5). It is said that this tree trunk acquired its crude metal jacket in the 16th century from blacksmiths banging in a nail for luck when they left the city. On the right across the square is

Title page: Detail of a cherub and fish on the Fountain Donnerbrunnen, in the Neuer Market, Vienna (Photo: Martin Moos)

Left: The strong contrast between the Gothic Stephansdom (St Stephen's Cathedral) and Hans Hollein's 'Haas Haus' has caused much controversy among the Viennese

MAP 9 – VIENNA WALKING TOUR

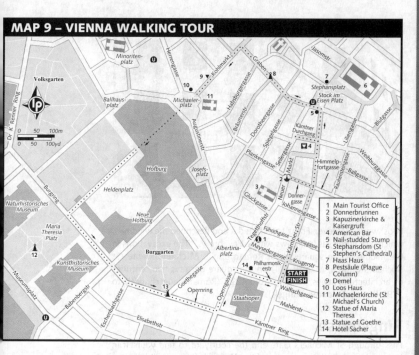

1 Main Tourist Office
2 Donnerbrunnen
3 Kapuzinerkirche & Kaisergruft
4 American Bar
5 Nail-studded Stump
6 Stephansdom (St Stephen's Cathedral)
7 Haas Haus
8 Pestsäule (Plague Column)
9 Demel
10 Loos Haus
11 Michaelerkirche (St Michael's Church)
12 Statue of Maria Theresa
13 Statue of Goethe
14 Hotel Sacher

Stephansplatz and Vienna's prime landmark, **Stephansdom** (St Stephen's Cathedral; (Map 9, #6). Facing it is the unashamedly modern **Haas Haus** (Map 9, #7) built by Hans Hollein and opened in 1990. Many Viennese were rather unhappy about this curving silver structure crowding their beloved cathedral, but tourists seem happy enough to snap the spindly reflections of Stephansdom's spire in its rectangular windows.

Leading north-west from Stock im Eisen Platz is the broad pedestrian thoroughfare of **Graben**, another plush shopping street. Like Kärntner Strasse and Stephansplatz, it's a fine place to linger, soak up the atmosphere and appreciate the musicianship of street artists. Graben is dominated by the knobbly outline of the **Pestsäule** (Plague Column; Map 9, #8), completed in 1693 to commemorate the 75,000 victims of the Black Death who perished in Vienna some 20 years earlier. Adolf Loos was busy in Graben, creating the Schneidersalon Knize at No 10 and, rather appropriately given his surname, the toilets nearby.

Turn left into Kohlmarkt, so named because charcoal was once sold here. At No 14 is one of the most famous of the Konditorei-style cafes in Vienna, **Demel** (Map 9, #9). Just beyond is Michaelerplatz, with the dome of St Michael's, the gateway to the **Hofburg**, towering above.

The so-called **Loos Haus** (the Goldman & Salatsch building; Map 9 #10; 1910) on Michaelerplatz is a typical example of the clean lines of

PATRICK HORTON

Loos' work. However, Franz Josef hated it and described the windows, which lack lintels, as 'windows without eyebrows'. The excavations in the middle of the square are of Roman origin. **Michaelerkirche** (St Michael's Church; Map 9, #11) on the square portrays five centuries of architectural styles, ranging from 1327 (Romanesque chancel) to 1792 (baroque doorway angels).

Ringstrasse

Pass through St Michael's Gate and the courtyard to find yourself in Heldenplatz, with the vast curve of the **Neue Hofburg,** built between 1881 and 1908, on your left. Hitler addressed a rally here during his triumphant return to Vienna in 1938. Walk past the line of fiacres, noting the Gothic spire of the **Rathaus** (1873–83) rising above the trees to the right. Ahead, on the far side of the Ring, stand the rival identical twins, the **Naturhistorisches Museum** (1872–81) and the **Kunsthistorisches Museum** (1872–91). They were the work of Gottfried Semper, who designed the exteriors, and Karl von Hasenauer, who did the interiors. Between the museums is a large statue of Maria Theresa (Map 9, #12), surrounded by key figures of her reign. She sits regally, holding her right hand out, palm upwards, as if in an early version of the 'gimme five' greeting.

Emperor Franz Josef was largely responsible for the monumental architecture round the **Ringstrasse**. In 1857 he decided to tear down the redundant military fortifications and exercise grounds and replace them with grandiose public buildings in a variety of historical styles. Work began the following year and reached a peak in the 1870s. Ironically, the empire the buildings were supposed to glorify was lost after WWI. Plans for a grand walkway connecting the Hofburg and the museums, and for a companion wing to the Neue Hofburg, were shelved due to a lack of money and determination. A full tour of the Ringstrasse is recommended, or at least the section from the university to the Staatsoper (under

Above: The Goldman & Salatsch Building, also known as the Loos Haus (after the 19th-century architect), with its clean lines and lintel-less windows, drew negative comments from Franz Josef, who described it as having 'windows without eyebrows.'

DIANA MAYFIELD

2km). Break up your walk by relaxing en route in the **Volksgarten,** with its many roses, or in the Rathauspark, featuring statues and fountains. The **Burggarten,** formerly reserved for the pleasure of the imperial family and high-ranking officials, contains statues of Mozart (erected 1896) and Franz Josef, as well as the **Schmetterlinghaus** (Butterfly House).

From the Hofburg, walk anticlockwise round the Ring, passing a vast statue of a seated Goethe (Map 9, #13), until you reach the **Staatsoper** *(State Opera; ☎ 51444-2613, 01; Opernring 2; guided tour adult/student/senior €4.40/2.20/3.30, schedules vary),* built between 1861 and 1869. This may appear the equal of any other Ringstrasse edifice, but initial public reaction was so hostile that one of the designers, Eduard van der Müll, committed suicide. The building was all but destroyed in WWII and reopened only in 1955. The opulent interior is best explored during the interval of a performance, or you can also take a guided tour – see the timetable at the window on the Kärntner Strasse side.

At the north-western corner of the Staatsoper is **Albertinaplatz,** adjoining which is the south-eastern extremity of the Hofburg. This wing contains the famous Albertina collection of graphic arts, though it has been closed for long-term renovations (expected to reopen in late 2002). On the square is a troubling work by sculptor and graphic artist Alfred Hrdlicka (1928–), created in 1988. This series of pale block-like sculptures commemorates Jews and other victims of war and fascism. Some of the stone originally came from the Mauthausen concentration camp in Upper Austria.

Turn into Philharmonikerstrasse, passing between the Staatsoper and the **Hotel Sacher** (Map 9, #14) purveyor of a famous cake, the Sacher Torte. Sacher and Demel had a long-running dispute over who was the true creator of the authentic chocolate torte: the former was Metternich's cook, the latter was pastry cook to the Habsburgs.

Another few steps will bring you back to Kärntner Strasse.

Above: The Kunsthistorisches Museum (Museum of Fine Arts), designed by Gottfried Semper and Karl von Hasenauer, is one of the finest museums in Europe.

[continued from page 120]

adult/concession €2.95/2.20; open 9.30am-4pm daily) is beneath the Kapuzinerkirche (Church of the Capuchin Friars). Its construction was instigated by Empress Anna (1557–1619), and her body and that of her husband, Emperor Matthias (1557–1619), were the first to be placed here. Since then, all but three of the Habsburg dynasty found their way here (in bits and pieces), the last being Empress Zita in 1989. The only non-Habsburg is the Countess Fuchs.

The royals' fashion extends even to tombs: those in the vault range from the unadorned to the ostentatious. By far the most elaborate caskets are those portraying 18th-century baroque pomp, such as the huge double sarcophagus containing Maria Theresa and Franz I. The tomb of Charles VI has been expertly restored. Both were the work of Balthasar Moll.

Parlament

The parliament building (1873–83), on Dr Karl Renner Ring, was designed by Theophil Hansen. It displays a Greek revival style, with huge pillars and figures lining the roof. The beautiful **Athena Fountain** at the front was sculpted by Karl Kundmann. Choosing a Grecian style of architecture was not a mere whim. Greece was the home of democracy and Athena was the Greek goddess of wisdom. It was hoped both qualities would be a permanent feature of Austrian politics.

The Parlament *(Map 7; ☎ 401 10-2570; 01, Dr Karl Renner Ring 3; guided tours €2.95 11am & 3pm Mon-Thur, 11am, 1pm, 2pm & 3pm Fri, not during sessions)* is the seat of the two federal assemblies. Call ahead to check whether sessions are in.

Am Hof

The Babenberg rulers of Vienna once had a fortress on Am Hof square before moving to the Hofburg, and there are also Roman ruins here. The **Kirche Am Hof** *(Map 7, #40; ☎ 533 83 94; 01, Schulhof 1; free; open daylight hours)*, on the southern side, is a baroque adaptation of its fire-damaged Gothic predecessor. On the northern side is

the former 16th-century civic armoury *(Map 7, #17; 01, Am Hof 10)*, but you can only view this from the outside. The **Mariensäule** (a column dedicated to the Virgin Mary) in the centre of the square was erected in 1667. **Judenplatz**, the old Jewish quarter, is to the north-east, and features a pale, modern, concrete box of a monument to Holocaust victims.

Ankeruhr

This picturesque Art Nouveau clock, mounted on the Anker insurance company's buildings at Hoher Markt 10-11 (Map 7, #38), was created by Franz von Matsch in 1911. Over a 12-hour period, figures such as Josef Haydn and Maria Theresa slowly pass across the clock face – details of who's who are outlined on a plaque on the wall below. It draws crowds of tourists at noon when all the figures trundle past in turn, and organ music from the appropriate period is piped out. If you walk north under the clock you'll come across **Ruprechtskirche** *(St Rupert's Church; Map 7, #20; ☎ 535 60 03; 01, Ruprechtsplatz; free; open daylight hours)*, the oldest church in Vienna, built in the 11th century.

Postsparkasse

This celebrated building, the Post Office Savings Bank, was the work of Otto Wagner. The design and the choice of materials were both innovative: inside, in the main savings hall *(Map 7; ☎ 514 00-2816; 01, Georg Coch Platz 2; free; open 8am-3pm Mon-Fri, to 5.30pm Thur)*, note the sci-fi aluminium heating ducts and the exposed stanchions – pared-down functionality *par excellence*. Compare the modern appearance of the Postsparkasse with the classical looks of the former **Kriegsministerium** (Imperial War Ministry) opposite on Stubenring; it was built around the same time (1909).

Kunsthistorisches Museum

The Museum of Fine Arts *(Map 7; ☎ 525 240, W www.khm.at; 01, Maria Theresien Platz; adult/concession €8.70/6.50; open 10am-6pm Tues-Sun, picture gallery open to 9pm Thur)* is one of the finest museums in Europe and should not be missed. The Habsburgs were great collectors and the huge extent of land under their control led to many important works of art being funnelled back to Vienna.

Rubens was appointed to the service of a Habsburg governor in Brussels, so it is not surprising that the museum has one of the best collections of his works. The collection of paintings by Pieter Bruegel the Elder is also unrivalled. The building itself has some delightful features. The murals between the arches above the stairs were created by three artists, including a young Klimt (northern wall), painted before he broke with classical tradition.

It's impossible to see the whole museum in one visit, so concentrate on specific areas. Guided tours in English depart at 3pm (€2) and provide an interesting analysis of a handful of main works. Written guides are also available on site. The admission price may vary with special exhibitions.

Ground Floor In the west wing is the Egyptian collection, including the burial chamber of Prince Kaninisut and mummified animal remains. The Greek and Roman collection includes the Gemma Augustea cameo (displayed in Saal XV), made from onyx in AD 10.

The east wing contains sculpture and decorative arts covering a range of styles. There's some exquisite 17th-century glassware and ornaments, and unbelievably lavish clocks from the 16th and 17th centuries (Saal XXXV and Saal XXXVII). The prime item in this wing (in Saal XXVII) is the gold salt cellar by Benvenuto Cellini, made for Francis I of France in 1543. It depicts two naked deities, the goddess of the earth and the god of the sea, and has tiny wheels within so it can be pushed easily around the table.

First Floor The picture gallery (Gemälde-galerie) on this floor is the most important part of the museum. Some rooms provide information cards in English giving a critique of particular works. In a slightly confusing system, this floor has smaller rooms

(1-24) leading off from a series of interconnected halls (Saal I to Saal XV).

East Wing This wing is devoted to German, Dutch and Flemish paintings. Saal X is home to the Bruegel collection, amassed by Rudolf II. A recurrent theme in Bruegel the Elder's work is nature, as in *The Hunters in the Snow* (1565). Bruegel's peasant scenes, such as *The Battle Between Carnival and Lent* (1559), are also excellent.

The next gallery (Saal XI) displays the warm, larger-than-life scenes of Flemish baroque, in vogue some 80 years after Bruegel. The motto in *The King Drinks* by Jacob Jordaens (1593–1678), to which the revellers are raising their glasses, translates as 'None resembles a fool more than the drunkard'.

Works by Albrecht Dürer (1471–1528) are displayed in Rooms 16 and 17. His brilliant mastery of colour is shown in *The Holy Trinity Surrounded by All Saints*, originally an altarpiece. The *Martyrdom of 10,000 Christians* is another fine work.

The paintings by the mannerist Giuseppe Arcimboldo (1527–93) in Room 19 use a device well explored by Salvador Dalí – familiar objects arranged to appear as something else – the difference being that Arcimboldo did it nearly 400 years earlier!

Peter Paul Rubens (1577–1640) synthesised northern European and Italian traditions. His dramatic baroque scenes are displayed in Saal XIII, Saal XIV and Room 20.

There are several self-portraits by Rembrandt in Saal XV. Vermeer's *The Art of Painting* (1665–66) is in Room 24. It's a strangely static scene of an artist in his studio, but one that transcends the mundane by its composition and use of light.

West Wing Saal I has some evocative works by Titian, a member of the Venetian school. In Room 2 hangs The Three Philosophers (1508), which is one of the few properly authenticated works by Giorgione. Room 4 contains Raphael's harmonious and idealised Madonna in the Meadow (1505). The triangular composition and the complementary colours are typical features of the Florentine high Renaissance. Compare this with Caravaggio's Madonna of the Rosary (1606) in Saal V, in which the supplicants' dirty feet are an example of the new realism of early baroque.

Tintoretto's *Susanna at her Bath* (1555) can be found in Saal III. It re-creates the Old Testament tale and successfully portrays both serenity and implicit menace. Tintoretto employs several mannerist devices (contrasting light, extremes of facial features) to achieve his effect.

Saal VII contains paintings by Bernardo Bellotto (1721–80), Canaletto's nephew. He was commissioned by Maria Theresa to paint scenes of Vienna. Several are shown here, though some landscapes, such as the view from the Belvedere, are not faithful representations but have been creatively recomposed.

Room 10 houses portraits of the Habsburgs. Juan Carreño's portrait of Charles II of Spain shows the characteristic Habsburg jaw. Most of the young women in Diego Velázquez's royal portraits are wearing dresses broad enough to fit round a horse, but the artist still manages to make the subjects come to life.

Naturhistorisches Museum

The Museum of Natural History *(Map 7; ☎ 521 770; 01, Maria Theresien Platz; adult/student €3.65/1.85; open 9am-6.30pm Thur-Mon, 9am-9pm Wed)* is the scientific counterpart of the Kunsthistorisches Museum. The building is just as grand but the exhibits aren't quite in the same league. Minerals, meteorites and animal remains are displayed in jars; zoology and anthropology are covered in detail and there's a children's corner. The 25,000-year-old *Venus of Willendorf* statuette is on display (see the boxed text in the Lower Austria chapter) and there are some good dinosaur exhibits. The museum also has occasional special exhibitions, and tours of the roof are possible.

Museum für angewandte Kunst

The Museum of Applied Art *(MAK; Map 7; ☎ 711 360; 01, Stubenring 5; adult/conces-sion/family €6.55/3.30/10.90; open 10am-6pm Wed-Sun, 10am-midnight Tues)* was built in high Renaissance style in 1871. The **exhibition rooms** highlight different styles, such as Renaissance, baroque, Oriental and Wiener Werkstätte. The layout of each room was the responsibility of a specific artist, and their reason for displaying the exhibits as they have done is explained. In the room by Barbara Bloom, Art Nouveau chairs are back-lit and presented behind translucent white screens. There's a Klimt frieze upstairs, and some interesting pieces in the 20th-century Design & Architecture room (eg, the cardboard chair by Frank Gehry).

In the basement is the **Study Collection**, which groups exhibits according to the type of materials used. There are some particularly good porcelain and glassware pieces, with casts showing how they're made.

If there's no special exhibition, admission only costs €2.20/1.10/3.65, and the museum is free 14 April, 26 October and 24 December.

Akademie der bildenden Künste

The Academy of Fine Arts *(Map 7; ☎ 58816-225; 01, Schillerplatz 3; adult/student €3.65/1.50; open 10am-4pm Tues-Sun & holidays)* has a picture gallery. Hieronymus Bosch's *The Last Judgement* altarpiece is the most impressive exhibit, though Flemish painters are well represented. The building itself has an attractive facade (which was constructed between 1872 and 1876) and was designed by Theophil Hansen. It was this academy that turned down would-be artist Adolf Hitler. In front of the Academy is a statue of Schiller.

Secession Building

In 1897 the Vienna Secession movement was formed when 19 progressive artists broke away from the conservative artistic establishment that met in the Künstlerhaus. Their aim was to present current trends in contemporary art and leave behind the historicism then in vogue. Among their number were Gustav Klimt, Josef Hoffman, Kolo Moser and Josef M Olbrich, a former student of Otto Wagner.

Otto Wagner

Along with Adolf Loos, Otto Wagner (1841–1918) was one of the most influential fin de siècle Viennese architects. He was trained in the classical tradition, and became a professor at the Akademie der bildenden Künste (Academy of Fine Arts). His early work was in keeping with his education, and he was responsible for some neo-Renaissance buildings along the Ringstrasse. But as the new century approached he developed an Art Nouveau style, with flowing lines and decorative motifs. Wagner joined the Secession in 1899 and attracted public criticism in the process, one of the reasons why his creative designs for Vienna's Historical Museum were never adopted. In 1905, Wagner, Gustav Klimt and others split from the Secession. Wagner began to discard the more decorative aspects of his designs, concentrating instead on presenting the functional features of buildings in a creative way.

In 1898, Olbrich designed the movement's exhibition centre *(Map 7; ☎ 587 53 07; 01, Friedrichstrasse 12; adult/concession €4.40/ 2.95; open 10am-6pm Tues, Wed & Fri-Sun, 10am-8pm Thur)* Its most striking feature is the enormous golden sphere (prosaically described as a 'golden cabbage' by some Viennese) rising from a turret on the roof. Above the door are highly distinctive mask-like faces with dangling serpents instead of earlobes. The motto above the entrance asserts: 'Der Zeit ihre Kunst, der Kunst ihre Freiheit' (To each time its art, to art its freedom). Could the unspoken implication be: to historicism its dustbin?

The 14th exhibition held in the building, in 1902, featured the famous *Beethoven Frieze* by Klimt. This 34m-long work was only supposed to be a temporary display, but has been painstakingly restored and is on view in the basement. The frieze, combining both dense and sparse images, shows willowy women with bounteous hair jostling for attention with a large gorilla, while slender figures float and a choir sings. Beethoven would no doubt be extremely surprised to learn that it is based on his Ninth Symphony.

The rest of this so-called 'temple of art' holds true to the original ideal of presenting contemporary art, though it may leave you wondering exactly where the altar is. 'Sometimes people just walk past the art, they think they're in empty rooms,' the lady at the desk once told me. You have been warned! The Secession building also has an outside cafe.

Jüdisches Museum

The Jewish Museum *(Map 7, #84; ☎ 535 04 31; 01, Dorotheergasse 11; adult/concession €5.10/2.95; open 10am-6pm daily, to 8pm Thur, closed Sat)* documents the history of the Jews in Vienna, from the first settlements at Judenplatz in the 13th century to the present. Relations between the Jews and Viennese have not always been tranquil: Jews were expelled in 1420 (the 300 who remained were burned to death in 1421) and again in 1670. The darkest chapter came with the arrival of the Nazis in 1938 and the consequent curtailment and eradication of Jewish civil rights. Violence was unleashed on the night of 9 November 1938, known as the *Reichskristallnacht* (night of broken glass). All the synagogues in the city except for the Stadttempel *(Map 7, #37; 01, Seitenstettengasse 4)* were destroyed and more than 7000 of Vienna's Jews were sent to concentration camps. There are now 12,000 Jews in the city, compared with 185,000 before 1938.

Haus der Musik

The imaginatively presented House of Music *(Map 7, #123; ☎ 516 48 51; 01, Seilerstätte 30; adult/concession €8.50/6.50, open 10am to 10pm daily)* opened in June 2000. Floor 2 explains the physics of sound, using fun interactive computer terminals. You can also play around with sampled sounds and record your own CD. Floor 3 has interesting rooms devoted to the great composers (hand-held commentary in English) – Haydn, Mozart, Beethoven, Schubert, Strauss, Mahler and the Viennese School. The 'virtual conductor' room allows you to conduct the Vienna Philharmonic (the recording responds to your movements). Floor 4 has experimental and electronic music, which you can also modify.

On the 1st floor is a separate section devoted to the Vienna Philharmonic *(adult/ concession €5/3, €10/5 combined ticket with main museum)*, though it's rather brief and most visitors' appetite for things musical would have been satiated already.

Lipizzaner Museum
The Lipizzaner Museum *(Map 7; #80; ☎ 533 78 11; 01, Reitschulestrasse 2; adult/concession €5/3.60; open 9am-6pm daily)* by the Hofburg expounds on Lipizzaner stallions, the Spanish Riding School (Spanishe Reitschule) and the stud farm (Bundesgestüt Piber). There's English text, but the content is a little thin. Windows allow a view directly into the stallion stables, albeit obscured by thick glass and fine mesh.

Stadtpark
The city park (Map 7) lies on the eastern side of Parkring. It has a pond, winding walkways and several statues. The **Kursalon** at the south-western corner hosts waltz concerts in the afternoon and evening daily from April to late October. Nearby is the golden statue of **Johann Strauss** (Map 7, #95) under a white arch that will be familiar to many from tourist brochures.

Karlsplatz
This open square (Map 7), really a small park, straddles the 1st and 4th districts. At its northern edge sit Otto Wagner's **Stadt Pavillons** (Map 7, #169), the station buildings for Vienna's first public transport system, built between 1893 and 1902. Wagner was in charge of the design of the metro lines, bridges and buildings. Here he incorporated floral designs and gold trim on a steel and marble structure. His Stadt Pavillon at Hietzing, on the outskirts of Vienna near Schönbrunn, is also worth a look.

Immediately north of Karlsplatz you can see two traditional Viennese buildings, the white **Künstlerhaus** and the rust and white **Musikverein** (1867–9).

JON DAVISON

Stadt Pavillon: Vienna's first metro station

THE WEST
Linke Wienzeile
This road runs south-west of the Secession building and into the 6th district. Passing the Theater an der Wien, you soon reach two Art Nouveau buildings created by Otto Wagner. No 38 features a facade of golden medallions by Kolo Moser, railings created from metal leaves and a brace of jesters on the roof who look like they could be shouting abuse at the traditional buildings nearby. No 40 (Map 6, #33) is known as the **Majolikahaus** (1899) because Wagner used majolica tiles to create the flowing floral motifs on the facade.

Schloss Schönbrunn
This sumptuous baroque palace is one of Vienna's most popular attractions. It's in Schönbrunn Park, Schönbrunner Schlossstrasse, in the 13th district (Map 6), and can be reached on U-Bahn line No 4.

Leopold I commissioned Johann Bernhard Fischer von Erlach to build a luxurious summer palace where a 'beautiful fountain' *(schöner Brunnen; Map 6, #70)* had previously stood. The building was completed in 1700 but was nowhere near as grand as originally envisaged. Maria Theresa chose Nikolaus Pacassi to renovate and extend the palace between 1744 and 1749. The interior was fitted out in rococo style and had 2000 rooms as well as a chapel and a theatre. Like most imperial buildings associated with Maria Theresa, the exterior was painted a rich yellow, her favourite colour. Napoleon lived in the palace in 1805 and 1809. In 1918 the last Habsburg emperor,

Peace Empire & a Hundred Waters

Artist, architect and activist Friedensreich Hundertwasser was born as Friedrich Stowasser on 15 December 1928. Though Hundertwasser achieved little international notice, he was a major national figure.

In 1948, he spent three months at the Akademie der bildenden Künste (Academy of Fine Arts), and the following year adopted his new name, meaning 'peace empire' and 'a hundred waters'. Environmental themes were present even in his early work, eg, *People (Complement to Trees)* from 1950, now displayed in the KunstHausWien. His paintings employ vivid colours, metallic silver and spirals, which are sometimes reminiscent of Klimt's ornamental backgrounds.

Hundertwasser felt that 'the straight line is Godless'. He faithfully adhered to this principle in all his building projects, proclaiming that his uneven floors 'become a symphony, a melody for the feet, and bring back natural vibrations to man'. He believed that cities should be more harmonious with their surrounding (natural) environment: buildings should be semisubmerged under undulating meadows, homes should have 'tree tenants' that pay rent in environmental currency.

Hundertwasser was always something of an oddity to the Viennese establishment, and he complained that his more radical building projects were quashed by the authorities. Nevertheless, he was commissioned to re-create the facade of the Spittelau incinerator. This was opened in 1992; it's the most unindustrial-looking heating plant you'll ever see (it's just north of Franz Josefs Bahnhof: take U3 to Spittelau). Hundertwasser stated that man is shielded from nature by three levels of insulation: cities, houses and clothes. He tried to limit the effect of the first two levels with his building projects. His proposed solution to the third was to go naked, and he did make a couple of public speeches in the nude in the 1960s.

Hundertwasser died of a heart attack in February 2000 on board the *Queen Elizabeth II* ship, but to the end, he was one of Vienna's most idiosyncratic inhabitants. Whether organising a campaign to retain Austria's traditional car numberplates, designing postage stamps, redesigning national flags or simply painting pictures, he was always passionate, sometimes irritating and usually a challenge to established thinking.

Charles I, abdicated in the Blue Chinese Salon.

The Palace Suitably majestic is the interior of Schloss Schönbrunn *(Map 6, #54; ☎ 811 13-239, W www.schoenbrunn.at; 22-room Imperial Tour adult/student under 26/child €7.50/6.90/4, 40-room Grand Tour €9.80/8/5; open 8.30am-7pm daily July & Aug, 8.30am-5pm Apr-June, Sept & Oct, 8.30am-4.30pm Nov-Mar).* It features frescoed ceilings, tapestries, crystal chandeliers and gilded ornaments, though the endless stucco and gold twirls can seem overdone. Franz Josef evidently thought so too, for he ordered the rococo excesses stripped from his personal bedchamber in 1854.

The pinnacle of finery is reached in the **Grosse Galerie** (Great Gallery); numerous lavish balls were held here, including one for the delegates to the Congress of Vienna (1814–15). The **Spiegelsaal** (Mirror Room) is where Mozart, aged six, played his first royal concert in 1762 in the presence of Maria Theresa. Afterwards young Wolfgang leapt onto the lap of the empress and kissed her. The **Rundes Chinesisches Kabinett** (Round Chinese Cabinet) had a table that could be drawn up and down through the floor for serving food so that servants need not enter during secret consultations. The **Millionenzimmer** (Million Gulden Room) has Persian miniatures set in rosewood panels in rocaille frames.

The two self-guided tours include a personal audioguide in English. During the busy summer months you should buy your ticket for the tour straight away and then explore the gardens till your allocated departure time. Neither tour gives access to the exotic **Bergl**

Rooms, painted by Johann Wenzl Bergl (1718–89), though these can be visited from April to October with the VIP pass, which gives free access to the Grand Tour (with no waiting time), the Gloriette, the Maze and the imperial bakery. It costs €14 (€12.50/7 students/children).

Wagenburg The Imperial Coach Collection *(Map 6, #51; ☎ 877 32 44; adult/ concession €4.30/2.90; open 9am-6pm daily Apr-Oct, 9am-4pm Tues-Sun Nov-Mar)* on the western side of the palace displays carriages ranging from tiny children's wagons up to great vehicles of state. The most ornate is the imperial coach of the court, built (of course) for Maria Theresa around 1765. This is an example of extreme baroque on wheels, with fussy gold ornamentation and painted cherubs. Allow 30 minutes to look round.

Gardens The beautifully tended formal gardens *(open 6am-sunset daily)*, arranged in French style, are a symphony of colour in the summer. The extensive grounds contain Roman ruins (now the site of summer concerts), the **Neptune Fountain** (Neptunbrunnen; Map 6, #71), a riotous ensemble from Greek mythology, and the crowning glory on the hill, the **Gloriette monument** (Map 6, #75). The view from the monument towards the palace and Vienna is excellent, virtually as good as that from its roof *(€2.20, Apr-Oct)*. There's also a maze *(Map 6, #72; €2.20)* and the **Palmenhaus** *(Palm House; Map 6; ☎ 877 50 87-406; adult/student €3.30/2.20; open 9.30am-4.30pm daily Oct-Apr, 9.30am-5.30pm May-Sept)*, where butterflies are enticed onto fake flowers sprayed with honey.

The attractively laid-out **Tiergarten** *(zoo; Map 6; ☎ 877 92 94-0; adult/senior/student under 27/child€8.75/5.85/4/2.90; open 9am-6.30pm daily)* is the oldest zoo in the world, established in 1752. The once-cramped animal cages have now mostly been improved. Feeding times are interesting – displayed maps tell you who's dining when. The zoo closes an hour or two earlier in the winter months.

Kirche am Steinhof

This distinctive Art Nouveau church *(1904–07; ☎ 91060-11204; 14, Baumgartner Höhe 1; guided tours in German 3pm Sat, €4)* was the work of Otto Wagner. Kolo Moser chipped in with the mosaic windows. The design illustrates the victory of function over ornamentation prevalent in much of Wagner's work, even down to the sloping floor to drain cleaning water. It's in the grounds of the Psychiatric Hospital of the City of Vienna (Psychiatrische Krankenhaus der Stadt Wien), about 6km west of the Innere Stadt, near the end of bus route No 48A. You can visit on other days with a group by prior arrangement: telephone between 8am and 3pm weekdays.

Less than 2km west of the church is Hüttelbergstrasse, where you'll find two **villas** designed by Wagner at Nos 26 and 28. The more unusual (No 26) was built in 1888 and is now the Ernst Fuchs private museum *(☎ 914 85 75; adult/concession €10.20/ 5.85)*. In the gardens (visible from the road) are some interesting statues and ceramics and the ornate Brunnenhaus created by Fuchs. Take bus No 148 or 152.

Josephinum

The Josephinum, also known as the Geschichte der Medizin *(Museum of Medical History; Map 8, #26; ☎ 4277-63401; 09, Währinger Strasse 25; adult/student €1.50/0.75; open 9am-3pm Mon-Fri, closed public holidays)*, is on the 1st floor of the right-hand wing of the university medical centre. This small museum is fascinating, and a little bizarre. The prime exhibits are the wax specimen models of the human frame, created more than 200 years ago by Felice Fontana and Paolo Mascagni. They were used in the Academy of Medico-Surgery, set up by Joseph II in 1785 to improve the skills of army surgeons who lacked medical qualifications. These models, showing the make-up of the body under the skin, were intended to give the students a three-dimensional understanding of the organs, bones, veins and muscles. Three rooms of this gore will make you feel like you've wandered onto the set of a tacky

Museumsquartier

Vienna's shiny new Museumsquartier on Museumsplatz (Map 7) is one of the 10 largest cultural complexes in the world. Years in the planning, the refurbished former imperial stables officially reopened in June 2001, and now contain a range of museums, arts venues and other attractions. Though much of the original baroque architecture remains, the three principal museums – the Leopold Museum, the Museum of Modern Art and the Kunsthalle – are housed in striking new buildings. Other attractions include the Zoom children's museum, dance performances, restaurants and bars. One of the restaurants is Glacisbeisl *(Map 7, #129; ☎ not available)*, which feels miles away from the city centre: ascend the path to garden tables surrounded by trees, a trellis and vines.

The **Leopold Museum** *(☎ 525 70-0, adult/concession €9/5.50, open 11am-7pm Wed-Mon, to 9pm Fri)* offers the world's largest collection of works by Egon Schiele, though many other famous Austrian artists are represented – among them Klimt, Kokoschka, Loos, Hoffmann, Otto Wagner, Waldmüller and Romako.

The **Museum of Modern Art** *(Museum moderner Kunst; MUMOK; ☎ 317 69 00; adult/concession €6.50/5; open 10am-6pm Tues-Sun, to 9pm Thur)* has the largest exhibition space. The various movements in 20th-century art are shown: expressionism, cubism, futurism, constructivism, surrealism, pop art, photo-realism, conceptual and minimal art, installations and Viennese Actionism. Well-known artists represented include Picasso, Klee, Warhol, Magritte, Ernst and Giacometti. Yoko Ono is represented by an all-white chess set – and you thought she could only sing badly!

The **Kunsthalle** *(☎ 521 89-33; adult/concession €5.85/4.40; open 10am-7pm daily, to 10pm Thur)* is a showcase for international modern and contemporary art, hosting temporary exhibitions.

horror movie. One strange touch is the necklace on the female model lying down in the first room. Why this ornamentation? She's hardly ready for a sophisticated night out, seeing that half her torso is missing.

The rest of the museum contains cases of arcane medical instruments, photos of past practitioners, accounts of unpleasant-looking operations, and some texts (one book is thoughtfully left open on a page dealing with the dissection of eyeballs).

Votivkirche

In 1853, Franz Josef survived an assassination attempt when a knife-wielding Hungarian failed to find the emperor's neck through his collar – reports suggested that a metal button deflected the blade.

This church *(Map 7, #2; ☎ 406 11 92; 09, Rooseveltplatz; open 9am-1pm & 4pm-6.30pm Tues-Sat, 9am-1pm Sun)* was commissioned in thanks for his lucky escape. Heinrich von Ferstel designed this twin-towered Gothic construction, which was completed in 1879.

Sigmund Freud Museum

This museum *(Map 8, #28; ☎ 319 15 96; 09, Berggasse 19; adult/concession €4.40/ 2.95; open 9am-5pm daily)* is in the apartments where Freud lived and worked from 1891 to 1938, when he fled the Nazis. It contains his furniture, possessions, letters, documents and photographs; very detailed notes in English illuminate the exhibits. Students and Freud freaks could spend a while here but most visitors will probably just saunter through the three main rooms and wonder what on earth Freud wanted with a terracotta votive offering of male genitals (exhibit 35). There's also a fairly dull home movie on Freud, narrated by his daughter, Anna. It's open till 6pm in July and August.

THE SOUTH
Karlskirche

St Charles' Church *(Map 7; ☎ 504 61 87; 04, Karlsplatz; open daylight hours)*, southeast of Ressel Park, was built between 1716 and 1739 in fulfilment of a vow made by

Charles VI at the end of the 1713 plague. It was designed by Johann Bernhard Fischer von Erlach, who began the construction, which was completed by his son, Josef. Although predominantly baroque, it combines several architectural styles. The twin columns are modelled on Trajan's Column in Rome, and show scenes from the life of St Charles Borromeo (who succoured plague victims in Italy), to whom the church is dedicated. The huge oval dome is 72m high and its interior is graced by cloud-bound celestial beings painted by Johann Michael Rottmayr.

About 100m east of the church is the Schwarzenbergplatz, site of the **Russian Monument** (Map 6, #40), a reminder that the Russians liberated Vienna at the end of WWII. In front of the monument is the Hochstrahlbrunnen fountain, and behind stands Palais Schwarzenberg, co-created by Johann Bernhard Fischer von Erlach and Johann Lukas von Hildebrandt.

Schloss Belvedere

This splendid baroque palace (Map 6) was built for Prince Eugene of Savoy between 1714 and 1723, and was the work of Johann Lukas von Hildebrandt. The Unteres (Lower) Belvedere was Eugene's summer residence and the Oberes (Upper) Belvedere was used for banquets and other festivities. Running

between the two is a long garden laid out in French style, lined with statues of sphinxes and other mythical beasts. Immediately east of this is the Botanical Gardens *(Map 6; ☎ 4277-54190; 03, Mechelgasse 2; free; open 9am-one hour before dusk, Easter-31 Oct, closed in bad weather)*, which belongs to the university. The Habsburgs were rather irked that Prince Eugene should have a residence to match the Hofburg, and the palace was eventually purchased by Maria Theresa.

The two palaces of Schloss Belvedere are now home to the **Österreichische Galerie** *(Austrian Gallery; ☎ 795 57 261; 03, Prinz Eugen Strasse 27; adult/concession €7.30/ 5.10; open 10am-6pm Tues-Sun)*. The baroque section is in the Unteres Belvedere, and 19th- and 20th-century art is displayed in the Oberes Belvedere. The entry ticket is good for both parts, and you needn't visit them on the same day.

Oberes Belvedere (Map 6; 03, Prinz Eugen Strasse 27; take tram No 71 from Schwarzenbergplatz) This houses the most important collection. Grand baroque fixtures include Herculean figures and a fresco depicting the apotheosis of Prince Eugene. The 19th-century section includes paintings from the Biedermeier period, including many paintings by Georg Waldmüller, and work by Hans Makart and Anton Romako

---

Gustav Klimt

Born in Baumgarten, near Vienna, in 1862 Gustav Klimt was the leader and best-known member of the Secession movement founded in 1897. The movement was born when a group of young artists revolted against the traditional art establishment and established their own journal *(Ver Sacrum)*, exhibition forum (The Secession Hall) and unique modern style. The Secession artists worked in a highly decorative style. Klimt's famous painting *The Kiss* is typical of the rich ornamentation, vivid colour and floral motifs favoured by the Secession artists. His later pictures (such as the two portraits of Adele Bloch-Bauer) employ a harmonious but ostentatious use of background colour with much metallic gold and silver to evoke or symbolise the emotions of the main figures.

Klimt became the most celebrated artist in Vienna at the turn of the century. His works were renowned then, as now, for their sexuality and decadence. However, his *femmes fatales* exuded an eroticism and power too explicit for their time. Klimt was accused of ugliness, pornography and perverted excess. His response was typical: a work entitled *Goldfish* or *To My Critics*, portraying a voluptuous flame-haired maiden baring her bottom to the world.

which had an influence on the Viennese Art Nouveau artists.

The 20th-century section of the gallery contains the best exhibits. One of Gustav Klimt's best-known and most intriguing works, *The Kiss* (1908), is displayed here. Pundits disagree as to whether the kiss in question is proffered willingly or conceded under coercion. Some of Klimt's impressionistic landscapes are also here.

Egon Schiele produced intense, melancholic work, typified by the hypnotic and bulging eyes on the portrait of his friend, *Eduard Kosmack* (1910). Schiele's bold, brooding colours and unforgiving outlines are a contrast to Klimt's golden tapestries and idealised forms. He lived with one of Klimt's models for a while – but Schiele's portraits of her were much more explicit, bordering on the pornographic. *The Family* was Schiele's last work before he died of Egyptian flu in 1918.

Other Austrian artists represented here include Herbert Boeckl, Anton Hanak, Arnulf Rainer and Fritz Wotruba. There are several examples of the work of the influential expressionist, Oskar Kokoschka. The gallery also displays some exhibits from non-Austrian artists such as Munch, Monet, Van Gogh, Renoir and Cézanne.

Unteres Belvedere (Map 6; 03, Rennweg 6a, take tram D from Schwarzenbergplatz) The baroque section offers some good statuary, such as the originals from Donner's Neuer Markt fountain (1738–39), and especially The Apotheosis of Prince Eugene (again!), this time fashioned in marble in 1721 by the baroque sculptor Balthasar Permoser. Eugene was presumably experiencing delusions of grandeur by this time, for he commissioned the latter work himself; the artist, not to be outdone, depicted himself at the prince's feet. Paintings include portraits of Maria Theresa and Franz I. A whole room is devoted to the vibrant work of Franz Anton Maulbertsch (1724–96).

The **Orangery** (Map 6, #41) houses a collection of Austrian medieval art comprising religious scenes, altarpieces and statues.

There are several impressive works by Michael Pacher, who was influenced both by early art from the Low Countries and the early Renaissance of northern Italy.

Cemeteries

The **Zentralfriedhof** *(Central Cemetery; ☎ 760 41; 11, Simmeringer Hauptstrasse 232-244; open 7am-6pm Mar, Apr, Sept & Oct, 7am-7pm May-Aug, 8am-5pm Nov-Feb)* contains the memorial tombs of numerous famous composers including Beethoven, Brahms, Gluck, Schubert and Schönberg. Mozart also has a monument here, but he was actually buried in an unmarked grave in **St Marxer Friedhof** *(Cemetery of St Marx; Map 6; 03, Leberstrasse 6-8; open 7am-5pm Apr & Oct, 7am-6pm May & Sept, 7am-7pm June-Aug, 7am-dusk Nov-Mar)*. Many years after the true location had been forgotten, grave-diggers cobbled together a poignant memorial from a broken pillar and a discarded stone angel. For the Friedhof St Marx, take tram No 71 to Landstrasser Hauptstrasse then follow the signs (a 10-minute walk).

From St Marx, take tram No 71 or 72 to the Zentralfriedhof's Tor (gate) 2 to visit the aforementioned composers' graves and those of postwar Austrian presidents. Behind the memorial church are simple plaques devoted to those who fell in the world wars. These contrast with the ostentatious displays of wealth exhibited in the mausoleums of the rich, who couldn't take it with them but certainly tried. Most graves are neat and well tended, and garlanded with fresh flowers, though the old Jewish section is a tangle of broken and lopsided headstones and unfettered undergrowth, a reminder that few relatives are around to maintain these graves.

THE EAST
KunstHausWien

This art gallery *(Map 6, #12; ☎ 712 04 91-0; 03, Untere Weissgerberstrasse 13; adult/concession €6.90/5.10, €3.45 Mon except public holidays; open 10am-7pm daily)* looks like something out of a toyshop. It was designed by Friedensreich Hundertwasser, whose highly innovative buildings feature uneven floors, coloured ceramics, patchwork decoration, irregular corners and grass and trees on the roof.

The permanent contents of the Kunst-HausWien are something of a tribute to Hundertwasser, presenting his paintings, graphics, tapestry, philosophy, ecology and architecture. Hundertwasser's quotes are everywhere, ranging from the profound to the cringe-worthy ('Each raindrop is a kiss from heaven'). There's a cafe round the back. Entry to temporary exhibits costs a separate admission fee.

While you are in the area, walk down the road to see the **Hundertwasserhaus** (Map 6, #14), a block of residential flats designed by Hundertwasser on the corner of Löwengasse and Kegelgasse. It is now one of Vienna's most prestigious addresses, albeit council-owned rented accommodation. Opposite is the **Kalke Village** (Map 6, #13; ☎ 710 41 16; 03, Kegelgasse 37-39; free; open 9am-5pm, or 7pm in summer, daily), also by Hundertwasser, created in an old Michelin factory. It contains a cafe, and souvenir and art shops.

Prater

East of the Innere Stadt is a large amusement park, often known as the Volksprater or the Wurstelprater (Map 6; 02, Strasse des Ersten Mai; rides €1.10-4). It is dominated by the giant **Riesenrad** (Ferris wheel; Map 6, #6; ☎ 729 54 30; €4; open 10am-6pm daily Nov-Feb, 10am-10pm Mar, Apr, Oct & Nov, 10am-midnight May-Sept), built in 1897. This achieved celluloid fame in The Third Man in the scene where Holly Martins confronts Harry Lime. The wheel is almost 65m high and weighs 430 tonnes. It rotates very slowly, allowing plenty of time to enjoy the view from the top.

The amusement park contains all sorts of funfair rides, but it's a great place simply to wander round and soak up the atmosphere. As you walk, you're liable to come across one of the colourful metal sculptures depicting humans caught up in strange hallucinogenic happenings. Look for them on Rondeau and Calafatti Platz.

Donauturm

The Donauturm (Danube Tower; ☎ 263 35 72; 22, Donauturmstrasse 4; adult/child €5.20/4; open 10am-midnight daily), recently rechristened the Neue (new) Donauturm by the marketing folk, is the tallest structure in Vienna. The only 'new' thing about this 40-year-old tower is that a frightening 150m bungy-jump is now offered. At heights of 170m and 160m, two (expensive) revolving restaurants allow the more sedentary to enjoy a fine panorama; consider ascending (by lift) to watch the sun set behind the Wienerwald. The tower stands in the Donaupark.

ACTIVITIES

The best place to check for information on sporting facilities is the Sportamt (Map 6; ☎ 4000-84111; Ernst Happel Stadion, 02, Meiereistrasse 7; open 7.30am-3.30pm Mon-Fri).

The Prater is an important location for participatory sports (Map 6). It has tennis courts (€16-26 per hour), a bowling alley (Map 6, #11; ☎ 728 07 09; 02, Hauptallee 124; €3.65 per person), horse riding, sports stadia and swimming pools. A more compact sports complex is the Stadthalle (☎ 98 100; 15, Vogelweidplatz 15), which has a swimming pool (€4.40, open 7am-9pm Sat & Sun, 8am-9pm Mon-Fri), and during winter also offers ice skating and a bowling alley.

Walking

To the west of the city, the rolling hills and marked trails of the Wienerwald are perfect for walking. The Prater also has a wood with walking trails. The Wander bares Wien leaflet, available from the Sportamt, shows trails close to the city and explains how to get to them. A good one in the north-west starts in Nussdorf (take tram D from the Ring) and reaches Kahlenberg, at an altitude of 484m, giving a fine view over the city. On your return to Nussdorf you can counteract all that exercise by imbibing a few drinks at a Heurigen (wine tavern). The round trip is an 11km walk; to save your legs try taking the Nussdorf-Kahlenberg 38A bus in one or both directions.

Municipal Museums

There are several municipal museums run by the City of Vienna. Entry to these is free before noon on Friday (except holidays).

The **Historisches Museum der Stadt Wien** *(Vienna Historical Museum; Map 7; ☎ 505 87 47-84021; 04, Karlsplatz 5; adult/senior/student €3.65/1.85/1.50; open 9am-6pm Tues-Sun, closed Mon)*, by Karlskirche, is the best. It gives details on the development of Vienna from prehistory to the present day, and puts the city and its personalities in context. There are three floors of exhibits, including maps and plans, artefacts, paintings (by such artists as Klimt, Schiele and the Biedermeier painters) and reconstructed rooms from the homes of Adolf Loos and Franz Grillparzer. Models show the development of the Ringstrasse, and there are also some good period photographs.

The **Uhren Museum** *(Clock Museum; Map 7, #39; ☎ 533 22 65; 01, Schulhof 2; adult/senior/student €3.65/1.85/1.50; open 9am-4.30pm Tues-Sun)* displays 1200 clocks and watches, ranging from 15th-century pieces to a 1989 computerised clock.

The **Hermesvilla** *(☎ 804 13 24; 13, Hermesstrasse)* in the Lainzer Tiergarten (see Walking in the Activities section of this chapter) is a former hunting lodge. It features the private apartments of Franz Josef and Empress Elisabeth.

Several municipal museums are based in the former residences of the great composers, and generally contain assorted memorabilia and the furniture of their exalted former inhabitants. Admission to each costs adult/student €1.85/0.75, and a visit may take up to 30 minutes:

Eroica-Haus *(☎ 369 14 24; 19, Döblinger Hauptstrasse 92; open 9am-12.15pm & 1pm-4.30pm Tues-Sun)* This house was named after Beethoven's symphony No 3, which was written here.
Haydn Museum *(Map 6, #23; ☎ 596 13 07; 06, Haydngasse 19; open 9am-12.15pm & 1pm-4.30pm Tues-Sun)* Haydn lived here for 12 years, during which he composed most of his oratorios The Creation and The Seasons. He died here in 1809. The museum also has rooms devoted to Brahms.
Johann Strauss Residence *(Map 7, #28; ☎ 214 01 21; 02, Praterstrasse 54; open 9am-12.15pm & 1pm-4.30pm Tues-Sun)* Strauss composed The Blue Danube waltz here.
Mozart's Apartment *(Figaro House; Map 7, #63; ☎ 513 62 94; 01, Domgasse 5; open 9am-6pm Tues-Sun)* Mozart spent 2½ productive years here, including the writing of The Marriage of Figaro.
Pasqualati House *(Map 7, #11; ☎ 535 89 05; 01, Mölker Bastei 8; open 9am-12.15pm & 1pm-4.30pm Tues-Sun)* Beethoven lived on the 4th floor of this house from 1804 to 1814.
Schubert Commemorative Rooms *(Map 6, #36; ☎ 581 67 30; 04, Kettenbrückengasse 6; open 1.30pm-4.30pm Tues-Sun)* Schubert lived here briefly before his death in 1828. You can also see the house where he was born (Map 8, #7; 09, Nussdorfer Strasse 54).

Another place in the Wienerwald to roam around is the Lainzer Tiergarten animal preserve, open between 8am and dusk from February to November. To get there take tram No 62 to Hermesstrasse and then bus No 60B to the terminal.

Swimming

Most swimming pools *(Bäder)* are operated by the city, and you can get information on these by calling ☎ 60112-8044 from 7.30am to 3.30pm on weekdays; the tourist office should also be able to supply a brochure. City-owned pools and bathing complexes all have the same entry fees: €3.65 per adult, or €2.95 after noon and €1.85 after 4pm (all including a locker); kids under six years old get free entry, those aged between six and 15 get free entry during the summer holidays. Pools are open daily, although the open-air complexes are only open from around May to September, depending on the weather.

Several of these outdoor municipal bathing complexes line the Old (Alte)

Corpse Disposal, Viennese Style

It is said that nowhere are people so obsessed with death as in Vienna. Songs performed in wine taverns often deal with the subject, and the city has a unique museum dealing with coffins and the undertakers' craft (the Bestattungsmuseum; Map 6, #60). The country as a whole has one of the highest suicide rates in the world. Being able to afford a lavish funeral at death is a lifetime ambition for many Viennese. Joseph II caused outrage in the 1780s with his scheme to introduce false-bottomed, reusable coffins.

In 1784 the huge Zentralfriedhof (Central Cemetery) was opened, because there was simply no more space in the city cemeteries. To try to persuade the populace that their future dearly departed would rest better in this new location, they shipped the coffins of famous composers to the Zentralfriedhof, where they now rest together in group 32A. An unusual method was contemplated for transporting bodies to the suburban site: engineers drew up plans for a tube, many kilometres long, down which coffins would be fired using compressed air. However, the high cost of this scheme (one million florins) led to its abandonment.

At dawn, before the public are admitted to the Zentralfriedhof, special hunters are employed to shoot male pheasants, hares and wild rabbits. The reason is that these inconsiderate creatures have a tendency to eat or disturb the carefully arranged flowers around the graves. Meanwhile, you won't find any cemeteries for pets in Vienna. It is expressly forbidden to bury animals in the soil, as the high water table might be contaminated by seepage of chemicals used in inoculations and in putting the pets down. Pet cremations are now big business, although they are strictly controlled.

Danube: the biggest is Gänsehäufel (☎ 269 90 16-0; 22, Moissgasse 21, open around 9am-8pm, weather depending), which has a nude section. Some indoor city-owned swimming baths have sauna facilities (for which seniors get discounts). One such place is Ottakringer Bad (☎ 914 81 06; 16, Johann Staud Strasse 11; sauna €10.90; open noon-8pm Mon, 9am-8pm Tues-Fri, 8am-8pm Sat & Sun).

Stadionbad (Map 6; ☎ 720 21 02; 02, Meiereistrasse; €4.40, open 9am-8pm weather depending, late April-mid-Sept) is a large privately owned complex of pools in the Prater. Bus No 80B runs there from the U3 stop Schlachthausgasse.

There are free swimming spots with easy access to the water on both banks of the New Danube. Some of these, mostly near the edge of the city, are for nude bathing and are marked FKK (Freikörperkultur, or 'free body culture') on maps and signs.

Boating

The Old Danube is the favoured area for sailing and other types of boating, and several places rent the required equipment.

Hofbauer (☎ 219 34 30; 22, Obere Alte Donau; open 9am-sunset daily early Apr-26 Oct) charges €11/58 per hour/day for sailing boats and €6/31 for rowing boats.

LANGUAGE COURSES

Many places conduct German courses (the tourist office can supply a full list), and they usually offer the option of accommodation for the duration.

Inlingua Sprachschule (Map 7, #90; ☎/fax 512 94 99; 01, Neuer Markt 1) charges €415 for a minimum two weeks (20 lessons per week), with additional weeks costing around €160 each. There are monthly starts and a limit of eight students per class. It also does individual tuition and evening classes.

The Internationales Kulturinstitut (Map 7, #142; ☎ 586 73 21, fax 586 29 93, e office @ikivienna.at, w www.ikivienna.at, 01, Opernring 7) has intensive courses (15 hours per week, €357 for four weeks; monthly starts) and evening classes (four hours per week, €306 for 10 weeks; starting in January, April and October). There are 10 to 16 students per class.

ORGANISED TOURS

Official tourist guides (☎ 876 71 11, w www.wienguide.at) conduct around 50 different walking tours, covering a range of themes. The monthly *Wiener Spaziergänge* leaflet from the tourist office details all of these (indicating whether the commentaries are in English) and gives the various departure points. Tours last about 1½ hours and cost €10.90 (€5.85 for those under 18 years). The Third Man Tour, conducted in English, departs at 4pm on Monday and Friday. The meeting place is the U4 Stadtpark station, Johannesgasse exit, and you should have a torch and good footwear. The tour takes in all the main locations used in the film, including the underground sewers, home to 2.5 million rats, and Harry Lime's apartment at Josefsplatz.

Vienna Sightseeing Tours (☎ 712 46 83, fax 714 11 41, w www.viennasightseeingtours .com; 03, Stelzhamergasse 4/11) This outfit offers a wide variety of tours in English with free hotel pick-up. Some city tours include performances of the Vienna Boys' Choir (€49.45, three hours) or the Lipizzaner stallions (€43.65, 3½ or five hours). This is one way to see such performances when other tickets have sold out.

Cityrama (Map 7, #13; ☎ 534 13, fax 534 13-22, w www.cityrama.at; 01, Börsegasse 1) Similar choices and prices can be found at Cityrama. Both companies have reductions for children aged 12 or under.

Reisebuchladen (Map 7, #4; ☎ 317 33 84, e robinreisen@vienna.at; 09, Kolingasse 6; €27 per person) This is a critical alternative to the normal sightseeing tour, concentrating on 'Red Vienna' and Art Nouveau sights. English narration may be possible with advance notice.

Boat tours of the Danube canal are provided from early April to late October and depart from Schwedenplatz on the Danube Canal or Reichsbrücke on the Danube River.

DDSG Blue Danube (Map 7, #168; ☎ 588 80-0, fax 588 80-440, w www.ddsg-blue -danube.at; 1½-hour tour €9.45, 3½-hour tour €13.10) Various sightseeing tours are available on two-level ships with sundecks. Kids under 10 years old sail for free.

Donau Schiffahrt Pyringer-Zopper (Map 7, #25; ☎ 715 15 25-20, w www.donauschif fahrtwien.at; 1½-hour tour €6.75, 3½-hour tour €13.10) These ships show you the sights via a round-trip loop.

Pedal Power (Map 6, #7; ☎ 729 72 34, fax 729 72 35, e office@pedalpower.at; 02, Ausstellungsstrasse 3) This group conducts half-day bicycle tours from 1 May to 31 October. Tours cost €23 (€19 for students), or €16 if you have your own bike.

From May to October at weekends, 'old-time tram' tours depart from Karlsplatz (€14.55, children €5.10); for more information call ☎ 7909-440 26.

SPECIAL EVENTS

No matter what time of year you visit Vienna, there will be something special happening – get the monthly booklet of events from the tourist office. Tickets for many events are available to personal callers at Wien Ticket (Map 7, #140; ☎ 588 85) in the hut by the Staatsoper. They charge little or no commission; cash only.

On New Year's Eve various celebrations are arranged in the Innere Stadt, and one of the evening's musical events is relayed onto a giant screen at Stephansplatz. The Opera Ball at the Staatsoper is one of the most lavish of the 300 or so balls held in January and February.

The Vienna Festival (from mid-May to mid-June) has a wide-ranging arts program and is considered the highlight of the year. Contact Wiener Festwochen (☎ 589 22-0, fax 589 22-49, e festwochen@festwochen .at, w www.festwochen.at), 07, Museumsplatz 1, for details after December. At the end of June, look out for three days of free rock, jazz and folk concerts, plus general outdoor fun in the Donauinselfest.

Vienna's Summer of Music (from July to mid-August) fills an otherwise flat spot in the musical calendar. Contact KlangBogen (Map 7, #70; ☎ 427 17, e tickets@klang bogen.at, w www.klangbogen.at), 01, Stadiongasse 9. Reduced-price student tickets go on sale at the various venues 10 minutes before the performance. In the first two weeks of July there's a Jazz Festival at the

The Third Man

'I had paid my last farewell to Harry a week ago, when his coffin was lowered into the frozen February ground, so that it was with incredulity that I saw him pass by, without a sign of recognition, among the host of strangers in the Strand.' Thus wrote Graham Greene on the back of an envelope. There it stayed, for many years, an idea without a context. Then Sir Alexander Korda asked him to write a film about the occupation of postwar Vienna. The film was to be directed by Carol Reed, who had worked with Greene on an earlier film, The Fallen Idol.

So Greene now had an opening scene and a framework. He still needed a plot. He flew to Vienna in 1948 and roamed the bomb-damaged streets, searching with increasing desperation for inspiration. Nothing came to mind until, with his departure imminent, Greene had lunch with a British intelligence officer. The conversation proved more nourishing than the meal. The officer told him about the underground police who patrolled the huge network of sewers beneath the city. He also waxed lyrical on the subject of the black-market trade in penicillin, which the racketeers exploited with no regard for the consequences. Greene put the two ideas together and created his story.

Another chance encounter completed the picture. After filming one night, Carol Reed went drinking in the Heurigen area of Sievering. There he discovered Anton Karas playing a zither and was mesmerised by the hypnotic rhythms the instrument produced. Although Karas could neither read nor write music, Reed flew him to London where he recorded the soundtrack. The bouncing, staggering refrain that became Harry Lime's theme dominated the film, became a hit and earned Karas a fortune.

As a final twist of serendipity, the most memorable lines of dialogue came not from the measured pen of Greene but from the improvising tongue of Orson Welles as Harry Lime. They were delivered in front of the camera in the Prater, under the towering stanchions of the Ferris wheel: 'In Italy for 30 years under the Borgias they had warfare, terror, murder, bloodshed – they produced Michelangelo, Leonardo da Vinci and the Renaissance. In Switzerland they had brotherly love, 500 years of democracy and peace, and what did that produce? The cuckoo clock. So long Holly.'

And in Vienna they had the ideal setting for a classic film.

Staatsoper and elsewhere; check the Web site at **W** www.viennajazz.org.

The free open-air Opera Film Festival on Rathausplatz runs throughout July and August. Films of operas, operettas and concerts are shown on a large screen at dusk. Food stands and bars are erected to take care of bodily needs. Throughout November there's the Wien Modern festival, featuring modern classical and avant-garde music, performed in the Konzerthaus and elsewhere.

Vienna's traditional Christmas market (Christkindlmarkt) takes place in front of the Rathaus from mid-November to 24 December. Trees are decorated in the Rathaus park, and inside the Rathaus there are free concerts of seasonal music.

PLACES TO STAY

Vienna can be a nightmare for budget travellers. Even those who can afford a range of options may find their accommodation choice full, especially in the summer. Reserve in advance or at least inquire by telephone before you trek all over town. Reservations are especially recommended at Christmas and Easter and between June and October.

From July to September student residences are converted to seasonal hotels, giving a much-needed boost to the number of beds at the lower end of the market. A few rooms in private homes are on offer, mostly in the suburbs, but economic affluence over recent years has reduced the supply; expect a three-day minimum stay.

Accommodation Agencies

Several agencies can help you find accommodation. Tourist offices (see the Facts for the Visitor chapter) charge a commission of €2.95 per reservation, irrespective of the number of rooms being booked. They can help to find private rooms but don't have lists to give out. They can also give you the useful *Jugendherbergen* pamphlet detailing youth hostels and camp sites, and a booklet of hotels and pensions, revised annually.

Ökista (Map 7, #1; ☎ 401 48, fax 401 48-2290; 09, Garsonigasse 7) charges €10.90 to find hotel rooms (three-star and above) for a minimum of three nights. For stays of at least two weeks it can find a room in a family house from €14.55 per night B&B (€58.15 commission). The Odyssee Mitwohnzentrale (Map 8, #32; ☎ 402 60 61, fax 402 60 61-11, e mitwohnzentrale@odyssee.vienna.at), 08, Laudongasse 8, finds private rooms from €25.50/47.25 for a single/double, including commission. Monthly rates for furnished apartments start at €475 per month (€365 in summer) and commission is 25% of the rent for one month, reducing proportionately for longer stays. The office is open 10am to 2pm and 3pm to 6pm Monday to Friday.

Another approach for those seeking longer-term accommodation is to check university notice boards or scan the ads in the magazines *Bazar* and *Falter*, available at newsstands. Kolping-Gästehaus (see under Hotels & Pensions – Budget) has cheap monthly rates.

Choosing a Location

Staying within the Innere Stadt is convenient for the sights, although inevitably accommodation here is the most expensive in the city. Most hotels and pensions are between the Ring and the Gürtel; these are better value and still within easy striking distance of the centre. Places in the suburbs have the lowest prices but are less accessible; these are a more viable option if you're not too interested in late-night attractions in the city.

If you have a car, parking costs in the city centre can be high. A better option might be to find somewhere farther out where you can safely leave your car, and then rely on public transport. Even if you stay out late and have to take a taxi home, the taxi fare will still be less than a day's garage fees. Hotels outside the Innere Stadt with private garages charge from around €8 to €18 for 24 hours

parking (about two-thirds of the going rate in the Innere Stadt); the farther from the centre the place is, the cheaper it gets. Street parking is no problem in the suburbs.

Camping

For Vienna's camp sites, visit the Web site w www.wiencamping.at. In Austria, the fees for camping are charged both per adult and per tent; sometimes a fee per car is added.

Camping Wien West (☎ 914 23 14, fax 911 35 94; 14, Hüttelbergstrasse 80) Price per adult/tent €4.95/2.95, four-bed bungalows €29.10. Closed Feb. There are cooking facilities at this convenient camping ground. To get there, take U4 or the S-Bahn to Hütteldorfer, then bus No 148 or 152. Rates are slightly higher in July and August.

Aktiv Camping Neue Donau (☎/fax 202 40 10; 22, Am Kleehäufel) Price per adult/tent €4.95/2.95. Open mid-May-early Sept. This camping ground is the closest to the city centre and the only one east of the Danube. Take U1 to Kaisermühlen, then the No 91A bus. Rates are slightly higher in July and August.

Camping Rodaun (☎/fax 888 41 54; 23, An der Au 2) Price per adult/tent €5.30/4.40. Open late Mar-early Nov. This place promotes itself as bicycle-friendly. Take S1 or S2 to Liesing then bus No 60A.

Campingplatz Schloss Laxenburg (☎ 02 236-713 33, fax 73 966; Münchendorfer Strasse) Price per adult/tent €5.45/2. Open 1 Apr-31 Oct. This camp site, beyond the city to the south, is the largest and has a swimming pool and boat rental. Sadly, there's no convenient public transport into Vienna. Rates are slightly higher in July and August.

Hostels

Near the Centre No hostels invade the imperial elegance of the Innere Stadt, but you can find several west of the Ring.

Turmherberge Don Bosco (Map 6, #43; ☎ 713 14 94, no fax; 03, Lechnerstrasse 12) Beds €5.85. Open 1 Mar-31 Nov. The hostel, situated south-east of the Ring in a church tower, has 50 of the cheapest dorm beds in town. However, the place hasn't been modernised since the 1950s – some

Hot Wine and Cold Snow: Vienna's Christmas Markets

The idea of a Christmas market (*Weihnachtsmarkt* or *Christkindlmarkt*) might strike some as a potential tourist nightmare, but to do so would be far too Scrooge-like. Vienna has an over-400-year-old tradition of Christmas markets, which range in size from the enormous to the minute. They can be found throughout the city during the Advent season (usually from late November) and are wildly popular with locals who stop by these open-air affairs after work for some gossip and *Glühwein* (hot, spiced mulled wine).

Although the streets may be covered with snow, a few minutes surrounded by boisterous crowds sipping hot wine followed by a *Kartoffelpuffer* (potato pancake) or perhaps a *heisse Maroni* (roasted chestnut) or two will surely warm the cockles.

There's usually a few stands selling ornaments and at least one run by a local charity peddling *Punsch*, which ranges from rum-spiked apple juice to appalling concoctions of tooty-fruity fluids and grain alcohol.

Lists of Christmas markets are widely available from hotels and tourist offices during the season. They're usually open every day, at least from noon to 9pm. Here's a few of my favourites from the 30 or more held each year:

Rathausplatz – Vienna's largest, this market occupies a vast area in front of city hall and features a huge Christmas tree, rides, artificial snow machines and more. There are more than 140 booths selling everything from Santas made in China to sausages made in Slovenia. Prices are low, which makes this one popular with day-tripping Austrians and Czechs.
Schönbrunn – This high-end Christmas market forms a circle near the entrance to the palace. Everything has a bit of a regal touch, right down to the prices for the better-than-average Glühwein. The ornaments on offer are often lovely and hand-made. School groups perform carols around a Christmas tree to the delight of their camera-toting parents.
Freyung – At the juncture with Herrengasse, this classic market is mobbed from 6pm weekdays as Viennese meet friends and toss back hot beverages.
Spittelberg – Winding through the Biedermeier lanes, this market verges on the too cute – what with all manner of coy little toys on display – but is saved by the ever-sardonic locals arguing the merits of one punch versus another.

A final note: each of the markets usually has an official mug you pay a deposit for in order to quaff your Glühwein. Unless you really love it, you can hand the mug back for a deposit at any booth and use your change on one last Maroni.

Ryan Ver Berkmoes

rooms are cramped and have few lockers (no locks). There are only basic kitchen facilities and breakfast isn't provided. There's a one-off payment of €1.85 for sheets if required. Reception closes noon-5pm, check-in is from 5pm on, telephone reservations are accepted and there's an 11.45pm curfew.

Hostel Ruthensteiner (Map 6, #20; ☎ 893 42 02, fax 893 27 96, e *info@hostelruthensteiner.com; 15, Robert Hamerling Gasse 24)* Dorms €11.60 (€10 with seasonal deals), beds including sheets in 3- to 5-bed rooms €13, singles/doubles including sheets €19.50/37.60. Open 24 hours. Facilities at

this enjoyable hostel include a kitchen, laundry, a shady rear courtyard and Internet access. Optional breakfast costs €2.15. If you need sheets for the dorm, you pay an extra €1.40. The hostel is near Westbahnhof, one block south of Mariahilfer Strasse.

Believe it or Not (Map 8, #41; ☎ 526 46 58; 07, Apartment 14, Myrthengasse 10) Dorm beds €12/9 summer/Nov-Easter. This small, private hostel opposite the Myrthengasse hostel has no signs outside, except on the doorbell. It has a friendly atmosphere, though one room has triple-level bunks and can get hot in summer. Breakfast isn't provided: use the kitchen facilities instead. You get your own key so there's no curfew.

Panda Hostel *(Map 8, #44; ☎ 522 53 53, no fax,* **e** *panda_vienna@hotmail.com; 07, 3rd floor, Kaiserstrasse 77)* Dorm beds €12/9 summer/Nov-Easter. This sociable hostel in a residential block provides a TV in every room, your own door key, and at least 20 beds. It's linked to Lauria (see Hotels & Pensions – Budget later in this chapter).

Jugendherberge Myrthengasse *(Map 8, #42; ☎ 523 63 16, fax 523 58 49,* **e** *hostel@chello.at; 07, Myrthengasse 7).* Beds in 6- or 4-bed dorms €15, double rooms €17 per person. Based in two buildings, this HI hostel is convenient for the centre, very busy and offers daytime check-in. All rooms have a private shower and bedside lights. Lunch or dinner is €5 and laundry is €3.65 per load.

Wombat's *(Map 6, #18; ☎ 897 23 36, fax 897 25 77,* **e** *wombats@chello.at,* **w** *www.wombats.at; 15, Grangasse 6)* Dorms €14, singles/doubles with shower/toilet €18/36, open 24 hours. This friendly, newly built non-HI hostel has a pub and courtyard garden. Optional breakfast costs €2.55. It's about a 10-minute walk from Westbahnhof and you can book online.

In the Suburbs ***Jugendgästehaus Brigittenau*** *(☎ 332 82 94, fax 330 83 79,* **e** *jgh.1200 wien@chello.at; 20, Friedrich Engels Platz 24)* Bed in 24-bed dorm €11, bed in 2- to 6- bed room €17/15 with/without private shower and toilet. Prices drop by €1 in winter. Reception open 24 hours though rooms closed from 9am to 1pm. This HI hostel has 434 beds in a modern multistorey building a couple of minutes' walk from the Danube (trams N, 31 and 33 stop outside). Dinners cost €5 and there's a cafe, games room and garden.

Jugendgästehaus Hütteldorf-Hacking *(☎ 877 02 63, fax 877 02 63-2,* **e** *jgh@wigast.com; 13, Schlossberggasse 8)* Dorm bed €14 Apr-Oct or €12 Nov-Mar (€10 surcharge for single occupancy). Doors are locked from 9.30am-3pm, & at 11.45pm. This HI hostel is a long way from the centre of town, but only five minutes' walk from both the U4 Hütteldorf station and the N49 nightbus route. There are 285 beds, meals are available and there are laundry facilities and a lounge. You can buy a key card (€2.20) that will give you late entry.

Schlossherberge am Wilhelminenberg *(☎ 485 85 03-700, fax 485 85 03-702,* **e** *shb@wigast.com; 16, Savoyenstrasse 2)* Bed in 4-bed dorm with shower/toilet €18, doubles €56. Reception open 7am-11pm, no curfew. The great view from this HI hostel includes Vienna and some vineyards, but it's a long way from the centre: Bus Nos 46B and 146B link with city-bound trams J, 44 and 46.

Student Residences

These *Studentenheime* become seasonal hotels from 1 July to 30 September – see the Accommodation section in the Facts for the Visitor chapter for details. Most are outside the Innere Stadt.

Auge Gottes *(Map 8, #3; ☎ 319 44 88-10, fax 319 44 88-11; 09, Nussdorfer Strasse 75)* reopened after being fully renovated and upgraded in 2002.

Blue House Hostel *(Map 8, #2; ☎ 369 55 85-0, fax 369 55 85-12; 19, Peter Jordan Strasse 29)* Singles/doubles with shared shower/toilet €16/26.20, breakfast €3.30. This is an excellent choice – small-scale and friendly, with free Internet access, a washing machine, and kitchens that stay open.

Porzellaneum *(Map 8, #14; ☎ 317 72 82, fax 317 72 82-30,* **e** *office@porzellaneum.sth.ac.at; 09, Porzellangasse 30)* Singles/doubles with shared shower €16.50/32. Reception is open 24 hours. Rooms are small and spartan.

Gästehaus Pfeilgasse & Hotel Avis *(Map 8, #38; ☎ 401 74, fax 401 76-20; 08, Pfeilgasse 4-6)* Singles/doubles/triples with shared shower/toilet €21/38/51, with bathroom €46/62/81. Reception open 24 hours. Two places in one – Pfeilgasse has the simpler, showerless rooms.

Auersperg *(Map 7, #71; ☎ 406 25 40, fax 406 25 49-13; 08, Auerspergstrasse 9)* Singles/doubles with bathroom €37.80/62.50, without €27.30/45.10. Reception open 24 hours. This place is conveniently near the Ringstrasse. Unless you're inquiring only a few days ahead, make advance reservations via Albertina Hotels Austria (☎ 512 74 93, fax 512 19 68), 01, Führichgasse 10.

Music Academy Hotel (Map 7, #121; ☎ 514 84-7700, fax 514 84-7799, e jagers berger@mdw.ac.at; 01, Johannesgasse 8) Singles/doubles with private bath/toilet €36/68, without €32/56, triples/quads €63/ 76. This place is central, with 24-hour reception and one apartment available year-round.

Hotels & Pensions – Budget

Kolping-Gästehaus (Map 7, #166; ☎ 587 56 31-0, fax 586 36 30, e reservierung@wien -zentral.kolping.at; 06, Gumpendorfer Strasse 39, entrance Stiegengasse) Singles/ doubles with shower, toilet & TV €51/73, singles without €13.50-20.50. The rooms are reasonable value in this student residence, though even the hotel section has something of an institutionalised aura.

Pension Miklos (Map 6, #46; ☎ 587 51 61, fax 587 27 50; 05, Schönbrunner Strasse 41) Singles with shared shower €19, singles/doubles with private shower and toilet €33/43. The rooms are rather basic conversions from residential flats, but most are large, with a lounge area. For an additional €3.30 per person you can get breakfast. It's near the Naschmarkt and transport routes.

Lauria (Map 8, #44; ☎ 522 25 55, no fax, e lauria_vienna@hotmail.com; 07, 3rd floor, Kaiserstrasse 77) Dorms €12 per person; bunk-bed rooms with shared shower for one/two/three people €35/35/45; doubles /triples/quads with private shower €60/ 70/80, without €40/60/70; fully equipped apartments for four to eight people €105 to €190. This welcoming place has clean, well-decorated rooms, some with large pictorial scenes and homey touches; all have a TV, and there are communal kitchens (no breakfast provided). Credit cards are accepted, and there may be a two-day minimum stay for reservations.

Praterstern (Map 7, #30; ☎ 214 01 23, fax 214 78 80, e hotelpraterstern@aon.at; 02, Mayergasse 6) Singles/doubles €24/43, with shower/toilet €36/54. This place is east

of the Ring. Some readers have complained about the attitude of one or two of the staff, but they've always been fine when we've made our (anonymous) visits.

Quisisana (Map 7, #162; ☎ 587 71 55, fax 587 71 56-33, e office@quisisana-wien .co.at; 06, Windmühlgasse 6) Singles/doubles with shower €30/48, without €25/41. Rooms vary in size and quality but are generally good value. It's close to the centre.

Cyrus (Map 6, #65; ☎/fax 604 42 88; 10, Laxenburger Strasse 14) Singles €22-37, doubles €44-66. Room rates depend on the size, furnishings and whether they have a private toilet. All rooms have a shower and cable TV. This place is down the road from Hotel Kolbeck.

Pension Kraml (Map 6, #30; ☎ 587 85 88, fax 586 75 73; 06, Brauergasse 5) Singles/doubles €25/47, large doubles with shower €54, with shower and toilet €62, triples €62, family apartments €75. This family-run place is small and friendly.

Auer (Map 8, #25; ☎ 406 21 21, fax 406 21 21-4; 09, Lazarettgasse 3) Singles/doubles with shared shower €27/41, doubles with private shower €46. Reception is on the 1st floor and there's no lift in this friendly, pleasant and Viennese-style place.

Hotel Kolbeck (Map 6, #64; ☎ 604 17 73, fax 602 94 86, e hotelkolbeck@chello.at; 10, Laxenburger Strasse 19) Singles/doubles with shared shower €29/51, with bathroom and cable TV €51/84. Reception is open 24 hours. This place is just 10 minutes' walk from Südbahnhof, and some rooms are renovated.

Hotel Westend (Map 6, #22; ☎ 597 67 29, fax 597 67 29-27; 06, Fügergasse 3) Singles/doubles €30.60/50.20, with shower €36.40/ 61.80. Reception is open 24 hours. This place is close to Westbahnhof and has reasonable rooms. The new owner plans to offer dorm-style rooms to backpackers.

Pension Falstaff (Map 8, #15; ☎ 317 91 86, fax 317 91 86-4, e majidi_s@hotmail .com; 09, Müllnergasse 5) Singles/doubles with shower €40/59, without €33/51. Prices are around €7 lower in winter, and there is an irksome fee of €2.20 to use the hall shower. The rooms are long but some are narrow; fittings are ageing but adequate. It's convenient for tram D to the Ring and Nussdorf.

Fünfhaus (Map 6, #19; ☎ *892 35 45, fax 892 04 60; 15, Sperrgasse 12)* Singles/doubles €30/44, with bathroom €38/54. Courtyard parking costs €3.65. Closed mid-November to 1 March. Near Westbahnhof, this pension has a range of clean rooms – some of them are new, fresh and large.

Pension Bosch (Map 6, #44; ☎ *798 61 79, fax 799 17 18; 03, Keilgasse 13)* Singles/doubles with shared shower €33/55, with private shower €43/65, with shower/toilet €44/72. Reception is on the 1st floor (there's a lift). The rooms at this pension have personal touches, satellite TV, and (usually) old-fashioned furnishings.

Pension Wild (Map 8, #40; ☎ *406 51 74, fax 402 21 68; 08, Langegasse 10)* Singles/doubles with shared shower €36/43, singles/doubles/triples with private shower €43/58/77, with shower, toilet and cable TV €51/72/90. This central, gay-friendly, everyone-friendly place has 24-hour reception and kitchens. 'Wild' is the family name, not a description.

Pension Caroline (Map 6, #66; ☎ *604 80 70, fax 602 77 67,* e *fruehstueckspension .caroline@netway.at; 10, Gudrunstrasse 138)* Singles/doubles €38/62. This place has attractive, renovated rooms with shower, toilet and satellite TV, a lift and convenient local transport.

Pension Ani (Map 8, #22; ☎ *408 10 60, fax 408 10 82; 09, Kinderspitalgasse 1)* Singles/doubles €40/55, with private toilet €44/66. This pension offers decent value for its reasonably equipped rooms, yet even so, rates are often negotiable. All rooms have shower, cable TV and phone.

In the Suburbs *Jugendgästehaus Hernals (Map 6, #1;* ☎ *480 79 16; 17, Sautergasse 34)* Singles/doubles/triples €20/32/48. Unless you're inquiring only a few days ahead, make advance reservations via Albertina Hotels Austria (☎ *512 74 93, fax 512 19 68),* 01, Führichgasse 10. This former student residence offers standardised

rooms with two or three single beds. Most have shared showers, and rates are slightly less from November to March. Tram No 43 (stop: Wattgasse) goes to the Ring.

Matauschek (Map 6, #16; ☎/*fax 982 35 32; 14, Breitenseer Strasse 14)* Singles/doubles with shared shower (26/44, doubles with bathroom (37/59. The simple restaurant is closed Wednesday and Thursday, though reception stays open. Matauschek is opposite the new Hütteldorfer Strasse U3 stop; it has 25 variable rooms with TV.

Rustler (Map 6, #17; ☎/*fax 982 01 62; 14, Linzer Strasse 43)* Singles/doubles €30/48, with shower €42/61, with shower/toilet €55/75. Closed Nov-Mar, except over Christmas/New Year. This efficiently run place has a pretty garden (with garden gnomes) and rooms with TV. It is close to the Schönbrunn U4 stop, or you can take tram No 52 from Westbahnhof.

Sophienalpe (☎ *486 24 32, fax 485 16 55 12,* e *sophienalpe@hotels.or.at; 14, Sophienalpe 13)* Singles €40, doubles €59-66. Check-in daily Apr-Oct, Sat & Sun only Nov-Mar. This place, west of the city in the Wienerwald, has an indoor swimming pool and a restaurant. There's no adequate public transport so you really need a car to stay here. All rooms have private bathrooms.

Hotels & Pensions – Mid-Range
Innere Stadt *Hotel Post (Map 7, #33;* ☎ *515 83-0, fax 515 83-808,* e *office@ hotel-post-wien.at; 01, Fleischmarkt 24)* Singles/doubles with shower/toilet €70/110, without shower €41/66. This renovated hotel sports bright colours. The rooms with shared shower are a good deal for the Innere Stadt.

Schweizer Pension Solderer (Map 1, #14; ☎ *533 81 56, fax 535 64 69,* e *schweizer .pension@chello.at; 01, Heinrichsgasse 2)* Singles/doubles with shared shower €36/56, with private shower €52/69, with shower/toilet €60/80. Most rooms have cable TV and ornamental ceramic stoves. This pension is as spick and span as you would expect from somewhere that is operated by Swiss sisters. There are parking places in the street for €5.10.

Pension Am Operneck *(Map 7, #138;* ☎ *512 93 10, fax 512 93 10-20; 01, Kärntner Strasse 47)* Singles/doubles €46/66. Opposite the tourist office, this small-scale popular place has big rooms with bathroom and TV and is usually booked up months ahead.

Pension Nossek *(Map 7, #50;* ☎ *533 70 41, fax 535 36 46; 01, Graben 17)* Singles €48-62, doubles €92-118. Clean, comfortable baroque-style rooms are individually priced depending on the size, view and facilities. It offers good value considering its ideal situation: you have to book weeks ahead during the high season.

Hotel Orient *(Map 7, #15;* ☎ *533 73 07, fax 535 03 40; 01, Tiefer Graben 30)* Singles €52-73, doubles €68-110. This hotel has a *fin-de-siècle* hallway and facade, and rooms, all with private shower, are decked out in a variety of interesting styles. Scenes from *The Third Man* were shot here. Some rooms are rented by the hour for discreet liaisons, but it's by no means a seedy place.

Near the Centre ***Pension Atrium*** *(Map 8, #43;* ☎ *523 31 14, fax 523 31 14-9,* e *pension .atrium@chello.at; 07, Burggasse 118)* Singles €49-70, doubles €51-77, apartment €84. Near Alla Lenz, this pension has clean, renovated rooms with shower, toilet and TV.

Altwienerhof *(Map 6, #47;* ☎ *892 60 00, fax 892 60 00-8,* e *altwienerhof@netway.at; 15, Herklotzgasse 6)* Singles/doubles €51/85. This small, family-run hotel offers good-value, decent-sized stylish rooms with shower, toilet, TV and phone, and a quality restaurant.

Alla Lenz *(Map 8, #47;* ☎ *523 69 89-0, fax 523 69 89-55,* e *alla-lenz@magnet.at; 07, Halbgasse 3-5)* Singles €52-72, doubles €72-125, apartments €165. The lower rates apply during winter and for stays of two nights or more. The rooms have air-con, bathroom, telephone and cable TV. This excellent, top-of-the-range pension has a rooftop swimming pool (free to guests) and a garage next door (€10.90 per day). The single rooms aren't such a good deal.

Hotel Cryston *(Map 6, #59;* ☎ *813 56 82, fax 812 37 01-70,* e *hotel.cryston@netway .at; 12, Gaudenzdorfer Gürtel 63)* Singles €54-72, doubles €86-102. There are pleasant rooms with shower/toilet and satellite TV, and free private parking. It's a busy road outside, though double glazing masks most of the noise.

Hotel Fürstenhof *(Map 6, #21;* ☎ *523 32 67, fax 523 32 67-26,* e *reception@hotel -fuerstenhof.com; 07, Neubaugürtel 4)* Singles with shower/toilet and TV €64-88, doubles €104, singles/doubles with shared shower/toilet €42/60. This typically Viennese family-run hotel is opposite Westbahnhof.

Hotel Maté Dependance *(Map 8, #19;* ☎ *404 66, fax 404 55; 17, Bergsteiggasse 22)* Singles €62-80, doubles €94-137, a bit less Nov-Mar. Rooms with shower, toilet and cable TV are average, but there's free tea and coffee, and guests can also use the good facilities in the main Hotel Maté (see Places to Stay – Top End).

In the Suburbs ***Strandhotel Alte Donau*** *(*☎ *204 40 94, fax 204 40 94-40,* e *strand hotel@alte-donau.at; 22, Wagramer Strasse 51)* Singles/doubles with TV and telephone €33/49, with shower €35/52, with toilet €70/100. This is one of the few places on the east bank of the Alte Donau, and it's a five-minute walk from the U1 line. The hotel has two sections, with the larger, newer rooms situated across the (free) car park. There's also a garden with private swimming access.

Schloss Wilhelminenberg *(*☎ *485 85 03, fax 485 48 76,* e *schloss.wilhelminenberg@ austria-trend.at; 16, Savoyenstrasse 2)* Singles €80-95, doubles €110-130. This grand hotel has a big garden, stately appearance, very high ceilings and fine views. Rooms have a shower, toilet and cable TV Bus Nos 46B and 146B stop outside and link to city-bound trams J, 44 and 46. There's plenty of parking.

Hotels – Top End

All rooms in this category should have, as a minimum, a private shower or bath and toilet, cable TV, direct-dial telephone, radio and minibar. These hotels will have all the facilities business visitors might require. Nearly all of Vienna's five-star hotels, including those listed below, are within the Innere Stadt. Breakfast generally costs extra, but may be included in special, lower weekend rates.

Innere Stadt *Hotel zur Wiener Staatsoper* *(Map 7, #124;* ☎ *513 12 74, fax 513 12 74-15,* e *office@zurwienerstaatsoper.at; 01, Krugerstrasse 11)* Singles €77-88, doubles €102-128. This hotel has an attractive stuccoed facade and quiet, compact rooms. Garage parking is discounted to €16 per day.

Hotel Austria (Map 7, #34; ☎ *515 23, fax 515 23-506,* e *office@hotelaustria-wien .at; 01, Am Fleischmarkt 20)* Singles/doubles €94/137. This hotel is reached via a quiet cul-de-sac; it has pleasantly furnished rooms which are a good deal for the price. Prices are substantially lower from November to March.

Appartement Pension Riemergasse (Map 7, #61; ☎ *512 72 200, fax 513 77 78,* e *otto@otto.co.at; 01, Riemergasse 8)* Apartments €91-306 for 1-7 people. Breakfast €4.80 per person; credit cards are not accepted. There's a range of different-sized apartments, and the facilities (kitchenette, cable TV, telephone and bath/toilet) make this a good option for longer stays (monthly rates available). They can arrange parking for €14.55 a day.

Hotel am Schubertring (Map 7, #151; ☎ *717 02-0, fax 713 99 66,* e *hotel.am schubertring@chello.at; 01, Schubertring 11)* Singles €106-135, doubles €135-205. This hotel is a good choice. Maze-like corridors lead to well-equipped rooms with Biedermeier or Art Nouveau furniture. Prices are lower from November to March.

Hotel am Stephansplatz (Map 7, #65; ☎ *53 405-0, fax 53 405-711,* e *hotel @stephansplatz.co.at; 01, Stephansplatz 9)* Singles €105-117, doubles €144-189. This hotel is the closest you can sleep to Stephansdom without building a nest in the belfry. The rooms are comfortable and sizable.

Hotel Kaiserin Elisabeth (Map 7, #87; ☎ *515 26, fax 515 26-7,* e *info@kaiserin elisabeth.at; 01, Weihburggasse 3)* Singles/doubles €113/193, smaller singles €76. The plain frontage of this hotel belies its pleasant

interior and long history (Mozart stayed here). It has nicely decorated rooms.

Hotel Sacher (Map 7, #136; ☎ *51 456-0, fax 51 456-810,* e *hotel@sacher.com; 01, Philharmonikerstrasse 4)* Singles €205-348, doubles €306-400. Elegance and tradition go hand in hand at this hotel, where rooms have baroque furnishings and genuine 19th-century oil paintings.

Marriott Hotel (Map 7, #96; ☎ *515 18-0, fax 515 18-6736,* e *mhrs.vieat.qm@ marriott.com; 01, Parkring 12a)* Rooms (single or double occupancy) €262. This hotel has harmonious, galleried lobby shelters, shops, cafes and a waterfall tumbling down fake rocks. The rooms are large and the excellent facilities, including a fitness room, sauna and 13m swimming pool, are free to guests.

Hotel Bristol (Map 7, #147; ☎ *515 16-536, fax 515 16-550,* e *Hotel.Bristol@ westin.com; 01, Kärntner Ring 1)* Rooms (single or double occupancy) €298-538. This place is very impressive, an explosion of imperial elegance.

Hotel Imperial (Map 7, #156; ☎ *501 10-333, fax 501 10-410,* e *Hotel_Imperial@ Sheraton.com; 01, Kärntner Ring 16)* Singles €320-393, doubles €400-553. This is a truly palatial period hotel.

Near the Centre In the places listed below, prices are usually lower from November to March.

Hotel Maté (Map 8, #20; ☎ *404 55, fax 404 55-888,* e *mate@xpoint.at; 17, Ottakringer Strasse 34-36)* Singles €72-108, doubles €123-166. This hotel has four-star rooms but five-star facilities, with a swimming pool, solarium, sauna and fitness room (all free for guests).

Thüringer Hof (Map 8, #18; ☎ *401 79-0, fax 401 79-600,* e *thuehof@via.at; 18, Jörgerstrasse 4-8)* Singles/doubles €76/100. Some of the rooms at this hotel are very spacious and have impressive chandeliers. There's parking for €5.85 and a rooftop terrace.

Hotel Mecure Secession (Map 7, #159; ☎ *588 38-0, fax 588 38-212,* e *H3522@ accor-hotels.com; 06, Getreidemarkt 5)*

VIENNA

Singles €72-121, doubles €130-152, self-contained two-person apartments €169. Formerly called Pension Schneider, this extensively renovated hotel is close to the Theater an der Wien, and in the lobby are displayed signed photos of actors and opera stars who have stayed here.

Hotel Atlanta (Map 8, #16; ☎ 405 12 30, fax 405 53 75, e hotel.atlanta@cybertron .at; 09, Währinger Strasse 33) Singles/doubles/triples €80/125/140. This hotel has reasonably spacious, often elegant rooms.

Aphrodite (Map 7, #27; ☎ 211 48, fax 211 48-15; 02, Praterstrasse 28) Singles/doubles €85-120/165, €77-106/131 Nov-Mar. This four-star hotel has a unique extra: beauty treatments for both men and women (a three-day program costs €400). Rooms bedazzle with many mirrors so you can admire your progress, and there's a rooftop terrace, swimming pool, sauna and fitness room, all free for guests.

Hotel Arkadenhof (Map 8, #4; ☎ 310 08 37, fax 310 76 86, e management @arkaden hof.com; 09, Viriotgasse 5) Singles/doubles €115/151. Arkadenhof is comfortable, stylish and small-scale. Rooms have air-con.

Cordial Theater-Hotel (Map 8, #39; ☎ 405 36 48, fax 405 14 06, e chdwien@ cordial.co.at; 08, Josefstädter Strasse 22) Singles/doubles €134/182, €102/151 Nov-Mar. This 54-room hotel has an Art Nouveau aura. Rates are often open to negotiation.

In the Suburbs

Celtes (☎ 440 41 51, fax 440 41 51-116; 19, Schwedenplatz 3-4) Singles/doubles €66/102. This is a small hotel with modern, moderately priced rooms in the Neustift am Walde Heurigen area (take bus No 35 from Spittelau). There's a bar and a garden.

Parkhotel Schönbrunn (☎ 87 804, fax 87 804-3220, e parkhotel.schoenbrunn@ austria-trend.at; 13, Hietzinger Hauptstrasse 10-20) Singles €105-145, doubles €145-203. Franz Josef partially funded the construction of this hotel, and he considered it his guesthouse. The lobby and grand ballroom all have the majesty of a five-star place, and the rooms surround a large garden with sun lounges, trees and grass.

There's also a 12m swimming pool, fitness room and sauna (all free for guests). It is easily accessible from the centre by U4 (get off at the Hietzing stop).

PLACES TO EAT

Vienna has thousands of restaurants covering all budgets and all styles of cuisine. Coffee houses and Heurigen are almost defining elements of the city, and these are places where you can eat well. *Beisl* is a Viennese name for a small tavern or restaurant that dishes up standard Viennese fare. If you haven't the time or money for a sit-down meal, there are many takeaway places, including Würstel stands, another Viennese institution; they provide a quick snack of sausage and bread from about €1.50 to €2.60. Some of these display signs that belie their humble status; for instance, some proclaim *mein Kunde ist König* (my customer is king), while others counter with *mein Kunde ist Kaiser* (my customer is emperor).

Vienna has dozens of Chinese restaurants. These are generally reliable and most have a cheap weekday lunch menu. Branches of *Wienerwald* and *Nordsee* are also reliable and inexpensive stand-bys, as are the many pizzerias. The *Schnitzelhaus* chain is an excellent place for fast food, and prices are low at €3.30 for a schnitzel with fries or potato salad, a schnitzel burger for €1.85, and large cans of beer for €1.85. There are over 30 branches round town open 10am to 10pm daily.

Self-Service & Budget Restaurants

Innere Stadt If you only want a snack, try one of the *Würstel stands*. Alternatively, there's a *Nordsee (Map 7, #91; ☎ 512 73 54; 01, Kärntner Strasse 25)*.

University Mensa (Map 7, #6; ☎ 406 45 94; 01, Universitätsstrasse 7) Dishes €3-5. Open 11am-2pm Mon-Fri, closed Sat & Sun. Take the lift to the 6th floor then walk up one storey. The cafe adjoining the mensa has the same meals and longer hours (8am to 6pm Monday to Friday, also during summer).

Katholisches Studenthaus Mensa (Map 7, #8; ☎ 408 35 85; 01, Ebendorferstrasse 8) Lunches €3-5. Open 11.30am-2pm Mon-Fri, closed Sat & Sun & Aug-mid-Sept. This place is close to the university and has a salad buffet.

Academy of Applied Art Cafeteria (Map 7, #57; ☎ 718 66 95; 01, Oskar Kokoschka Platz 2) Open 9am-6pm Mon-Thur, 9am-3pm Fri, closed Sat & Sun. This mensa has cheap snacks and light meals for around €2 to €4.

AdnB Mensa (☎ 58 81 61 38; 01, Schiller-platz 3) Open 8.30am-6pm Mon-Thur, 8.30am-3pm Fri, closed Sat & Sun & July-Sept. This small mensa is in the Akademie der bildenden Künste (Map 7).

Music Academy Mensa (Map 7, #121; ☎ 512 94 70; 01, Johannesgasse 8) Breakfast €2.10, lunch €3.05-4.50. Open 7.30am-2.30pm Mon-Fri. This is the most central university cafeteria.

Zur Fischerin Capua (Map 7, #100; ☎ 512 62 45; 01, Johannesgasse 3) Meals €4.95-6.55. Open 8am-2am daily. A pleasant bar and restaurant with fishing trophies on the walls and dining tables on the 1st floor above the bar area. Meals are available from around 11am to 4pm Monday to Friday only.

Trzesniewski (Map 7, #83; ☎ 512 32 91; 01, Dorotheergasse 1) Open 8.30am-7.30pm Mon-Fri, 9am-1pm Sat, closed Sun. At this basic deli bar you stand in line to choose your food from the counter. The sandwiches (€0.65), with a variety of toppings, are tiny (two bites and they're gone), but this is a famous Viennese institution and you may want to sample a few, if only to emulate Kafka (he was a regular here). Beer comes in equally tiny *Pfiff* (125mL) measures.

Rosenberger Markt Restaurant (☎ 512 34 58; 01, Maysedergasse 2) Buffet meals €5-10. Open 10.30am-11pm daily. In the same block as the main tourist office, the buffet area is downstairs from the ground-floor cafe, and offers a fine array of meats, drinks and desserts. If you really want to save euros, concentrate on the salad or vegetable buffet: Some people pile a Stephansdom-shaped food tower on a small plate (from €2.35). There are free lockers for bags.

Restaurant Marché Mövenpick (Map 7, #149; ☎ 512 50 06; 01, Kärntner Ring 5-7) Meals €4.50-10. Open 9am-11pm Mon-Sat,

11am-11pm Sun & holidays. Downstairs in the Ringstrassen Galerien shopping complex, this is almost the same as Rosenberger except the small salad or vegetable bowls are only €1.90. Another good feature is the pizza for €4.75, where you can help yourself to a variety of toppings.

Akakiko (Map 7, #86; ☎ 513 79 46; 01, Singerstrasse 4) Sushi €1.80, lunch boxes €6.05. Open 10am-midnight daily. This small restaurant has the same fast-food ethos as the McDonald's next door, but the food has more panache.

Pizza Bizi (Map 7, #53; ☎ 513 37 05; 01, Rotenturmstrasse 4) Open 11am-11.30pm daily. This convenient self-service place has salad and vegetable buffets, and you have a choice of sauces for your pasta (€4.75); pizza slices cost €2.20.

Brezel Gwölb (Map 7, #18; ☎ 533 88 11; 01, Ledererhof 9) Dishes €4.95-12.75. Open 11.30am-1am daily. This cosy restaurant offers Austrian food in a cobbled courtyard or an atmospheric, cellar-like interior.

Restaurant Siam (Map 7, #139; ☎ 533 52 35; 01, Krugerstrasse 6) Meals €4.50-13.95. Open 11.30am-3pm & 5.30pm-midnight daily. Upstairs you can get Chinese food: at weekday lunchtimes there are set menus (around €4.50) or an all-you-can-eat buffet (€5.70). On the ground floor there's a Japanese 'running sushi' buffet where dishes are delivered by conveyor belt; it costs €6.90 at lunch (€10 on weekends/holidays) or €11.05 in the evening.

Naschmarkt (Map 7, #41; ☎ 533 51 86; 01, Schottengasse 1) Open 10.30am-9pm Mon-Fri, 10.30am-3.30pm weekends & holidays. *(Map 7, #152; ☎ 505 31 15; 01, Schwarzenbergplatz 16)* Open 6.30am-10.30pm Mon-Fri, 9am-10.30pm Sat & Sun. Meals €5-11. This chain restaurant offers a good choice of buffet-style meals, including a three-course lunch menu for €5.15 (€5.90 on weekends).

Restaurant Smutny (Map 7, #143; ☎ 587 13 56; 01, Elisabethstrasse 8) Dishes €4-14. Open 10am-midnight daily. Smutny serves typical Viennese food in a room with wall tiles and colourful lightshades. Dishes are filling and reasonably priced.

The North-West There are many cheap places to eat to the north and west of the university.

Afro-Asiatisches Institut (AAI) Mensa (Map 8, #30; ☎ 310 51 45-0; 09, Türkenstrasse 3) Meals €3.60-5. Open 11.30am-4.50pm Mon-Fri, 11.30am-2pm Mon-Fri July & Aug, closed Sat & Sun. This mensa has courtyard eating in the summer. The cafe on the 1st floor is open daily and has copies of *Newsweek*.

Tunnel Bar & Cafe (Map 8, #34; ☎ 405 34 65; 08, Florianigasse 39) Meals €2.50-8.75. Open 9am-2am daily. The food at this student haunt is satisfying and easy on the pocket. You can get a great breakfast for €2.50, lunch specials start at €5, and there's cheap pasta and pizza. Bottled beer costs from €2.10 for 500mL. Tunnel also has a cellar bar with live music (see the Entertainment section later in this chapter).

Vegi Rant (Map 8, #9; ☎ 407 82 876 54; 09, Währinger Strasse 57) Meals €5-10, three-course menu €8. Open 11.30am-2.30pm Mon-Fri, closed Sat & Sun. Vegetarians will probably rave over the meatless cutlets and other veg-only fare on offer here. There is a health food shop next door.

Gasthaus Zur Böhmischen Kuchl (Map 7, #7; ☎ 402 57 31; 08, Schlösselgasse 18) Lunch menus €4, meals €4-9. Open 11am-11pm Mon-Fri, closed Sat & Sun. This quaint restaurant serves up good Czech and Slovak food, and there's occasional live music.

The South-West The nearby Naschmarkt has plenty of places to eat, many on a Turkish theme; filling kebabs for around €2.55 are popular for lunch.

Technical University Mensa (Map 7, #171; ☎ 586 65 02; 04, Resselgasse 7-9) Lunches €3.55-4.30. Open 11am-2.30pm Mon-Fri, closed Sat & Sun. The food is above average for a mensa. Once in the building, find the yellow area and go upstairs to the 1st floor.

There are two *Schnitzelhaus* branches just off Mariahilfer Strasse, one at 06, Otto-Bauer-Gasse 24 *(Map 7, #25; ☎ 587 87 26)*, the other at 05, Kettenbrückengasse 19 *(Map 7, #35; ☎ 586 17 74)*.

Schnitzelwirt Schmidt (Map 8, #50; ☎ 523 37 71; 07, Neubaugasse 52) Meals €5-11. Open 10am-10pm Mon-Fri, 10am-2.30pm & 5pm-10pm Sat, closed Sun. This informal, often hectic place prides itself on its enormous schnitzel portions; you really have to visit to see the size of these things. It offers many variations on the basic schnitzel: one can feed two people (they're used to supplying two plates!) or leftovers can be wrapped to take away. Extra garnishes cost around €1.75 each.

Gaunkerl (Map 8, #46; ☎ 523 95 76; 07, Kaiserstrasse 50) Meals €6-14. Open 11am-midnight Mon-Sat, 11am-2pm Sun (closed Sun Apr-Oct). The decor in the front room of this place creates the illusion that you're sitting outside, complete with glowing stars and witches on broomsticks flying overhead. The fantasy becomes more convincing after a couple of beers.

Amerlingbeisl (Map 7, #130; ☎ 526 16 60; 07, Stiftgasse 8) Meals €4.50-12. Open 9am-2am daily. This place attracts mainly young people, both as an eating and a drinking venue; in summer people flock into the rear courtyard. The beer is €2.75 a *Krügerl* (0.5L glass). It's in the Spittelberg quarter, a historic area with restored Biedermeier houses, various interesting shops and bars and plenty of tempting restaurants to seek out.

K&K Bierkanzlei (Map 7, #165; ☎ 581 79 61; 06, Windmühlgasse 20) Menus €4.30-6.50. Open 11am-10pm Mon-Fri, 11am-6pm Sat, closed Sun. This small, cheap and typically Viennese place serves filling and straightforward menus. There are many images of Franz Josef and Elisabeth – their faces even appear on the salt and pepper pots.

Schutzhaus am Ameisbach (☎ 914 61 55; 14, Braillegasse 1) Meals €5-11. Open 3pm-midnight Tues, 9am-midnight Wed-Sat, 9am-11pm Sun. Kitchen closes 9.30pm Mon-Sat, 9pm Sun. Out in the western suburbs, this is great value and has many tables in a large garden, plus a play area for kids. A popular choice is spare ribs: the full serving for €10.20, including sauces and baked potato, will feed two (a half-portion is €5.80). Take bus No 51A from Hietzing to Braillegasse.

The South *Kristall (Map 6, #61;* ☎ *504 63 27; 10, Wiedner Gürtel 4)* Meals €4.35-9. Open 7am-4am daily. The food is surprisingly good for the price at this simple place opposite Südbahnhof, and there's plenty of it. There's an English menu, too.

The East *Interspar supermarket (Map 7, #59;* ☎ *712 41 83, Wien Mitte Bahnhof)* Meals €4.35-6.55. Open 8am-7.30pm Mon-Fri, 8.30am-5pm Sat, closed Sun. The self-service restaurant is upstairs. This is one of several places ideal for cheap and quick eating in Wien Mitte station.

Zum Inder Kristall (Map 6, #5; ☎ *216 21 96; 02, Praterstrasse 57)* Meals €5.75-10. Open 11am-3pm & 6pm-11pm daily. This small restaurant serves good Indian food; wander by for the enjoyable *mittagsbuffet* at weekday lunchtimes for €5.75.

Middle & Top-End Restaurants

Innere Stadt *La Crêperie (Map 7, #62;* ☎ *512 56 87; 01, Grünangergasse 10)* Meals €7-17.80. Open 4pm-midnight Mon-Fri, 11am-midnight Sat & Sun. This place has various rooms with diverse and creative decor, ranging from arty odds and ends and ancient books to an imitation circus tent complete with clowns' faces. There's also outside seating during summer. If you stick to its speciality, crêpes, a light meal can be inexpensive. These are available with sweet or savoury fillings; the Florentine (€7.15) is a good combination of spinach, ham, cheese and egg with a dollop of sour cream. Otherwise, meat and fish dishes are above €10.55. Beer and wine are available.

Zu den Drei Hacken (Map 7, #94; ☎ *512 58 95; 01, Singerstrasse 28)* Meals €6.25-16. Open 9am-midnight Mon-Sat. This down-to-earth place has outside tables and a small room devoted to Schubert (despite the anachronistic WWII radio). It serves typical Austrian food.

Wrenkh (Map 7, #51; ☎ *533 15 26; 01, Bauernmarkt 10)* Dishes €7-14, Mittagsmenü €7.15. Open 11.30am-3pm & 6pm-midnight daily. This moderately upmarket, exclusively vegetarian place serves meticulously prepared dishes – try the three-course

evening menu for €14.20. It has a bar next door serving the same meals, and a simpler *Gasthaus (*☎ *892 33 56; 15, Hollergasse 9).*

Zum Weissen Rauchfangkehrer (Map 7, #93; ☎ *512 34 71; 01, Weihburggasse 4)* Meat specialities €8.75-16.75, additional €2.20 cover charge. Open 5pm-midnight Tues-Sun. This place provides a complete contrast to Wrenkh's vegetarian sensibilities, with meat-oriented fare and many hunting trophies on the wall. There are partitioned booths, and live piano music nightly from 7pm.

Griechenbeisl (Map 7, #35; ☎ *533 19 41; 01, Fleischmarkt 11)* Main dishes €11.65-17.45. Open 11.30am-11.30pm daily. This famous old tavern was once frequented by the likes of Beethoven, Schubert and Brahms. Choose from the many different vaulted rooms displaying hanging antlers, or sit in the plant-fringed front garden and chow down on quality Viennese fare. There's live piano music from 7.30pm.

Grotta Azzurra (Map 7, #132; ☎ *586 10 44-0; 01, Babenbergerstrasse 5)* Dishes €9-20, additional €2.55 cover charge. Open noon-3pm & 6.30pm-midnight daily. This quality restaurant serves up good Italian food. Try the popular antipasti buffet.

Wiener Rathauskeller (Map 7, #44; ☎ *405 12 10; 01, Rathausplatz 1)* Dishes €10.55-20. Open 11.30am-3pm & 6pm-11.30pm Mon-Sat, closed Sun. This two-in-one place is in the Rathaus (the entrance is in the northeastern corner) and serves Viennese and international dishes. Enjoy the atmosphere in the arcaded Rittersaal (Knights' Hall), where the walls are covered with murals and floral designs; live harp music (after 7pm, extra charge of €1.10) adds to the ambience.

Grinzinger Keller (Map 7, #44; ☎ *405 12 10; 01, Rathausplatz 1)* Set meal €32.70. Open 8pm-11pm Tues-Sat, 1 Apr-31 Oct. Down the corridor from the Wiener Rathauskeller, this place is similar if barer. It puts on a dinner show comprising music, waltzing and a three-course meal.

DO & CO (Map 7, #66; ☎ *535 39 69-0; 01, Stephansplatz 12)* Dishes €13.45-17.80. Open noon-3pm & 6pm-midnight daily. This busy place in Haas Haus serves superb international and oriental food, with a great view of the cathedral to boot. Book well ahead. There's also a cafe-bar (open 9am to 2am).

Zum Kuckuck *(Map 7, #99; ☎ 512 84 70; 01, Himmelpfortgasse 15)* Dishes €12.75-19, multicourse gourmet menus €16-25. Open noon-2.30pm & 6pm-11pm Mon-Sat. This tiny place with a vaulted ceiling serves interesting variations on Viennese food.

Yugetsu Saryo *(Map 7, #120; ☎ 512 27 20; 01, Führichgasse 10)* Meals €15-25, lunch menus €8-12, evening set menus €26-36. Kitchen open noon-2.30pm & 6pm-11pm Mon-Sat, closed Sun. This restaurant serves high-quality Japanese food. On the ground floor is a sushi bar, and upstairs they'll cook the food in front of you on a large hotplate built into the table.

Korso *(Map 7, #148; ☎ 515 16-546; 01, Mahlerstrasse 2)* Dishes €19.65-29. Open noon-3pm & 6pm-12.30am Sun-Fri, 6pm-midnight Sat, closed Sun noon and Sat July-Aug. Wood-panelled elegance crowned by opulent chandeliers creates an excellent ambience for tucking into Viennese and international specialities or dipping into the vast wine cellar. Korso's proximity to the opera prompts it to offer a light three-course meal (€48) for those who are replete with culture but depleted of cuisine.

Drei Husaren *(Map 7, #88; ☎ 512 10 92-0; 01, Weihburggasse 4)* Dishes €21-31. Open noon-3pm & 6pm-1am daily. This traditional Viennese restaurant is formal and refined, with soothing live piano music to aid digestion. There's a huge selection of excellent hors d'oeuvres, which are priced according to season and selection.

The North-West *Die Fromme Helene (Map 8, #37; ☎ 406 91 44; 08, Josefstädter Strasse 53)* Lunch €5.45, dinner €12.20-18.20. Open 11.30am-2.30pm & 6pm-midnight Mon-Fri, 6pm-midnight Sat. This is an elegant small restaurant with a cluttered salon look, and it turns out good Viennese food.

Restaurant Sailer *(Map 8, #1; ☎ 479 21 21-0; 18, Gersthofer Strasse 14)* Meals €12.35-20. Open noon-3pm & 6pm-

midnight daily. Restaurant Sailer serves traditional Viennese dishes with refined touches. The quality and service are exceptional for the price. There's also a garden.

Feuervogel *(Map 8, #11; ☎ 317 53 91; 09, Alserbachstrasse 21)* Meals €10.20-18. Open 6pm-2am Mon-Sat. A Russian restaurant, it has been run by the same family of Ukrainians for around 80 years. The colourful decor matches the conversational gambits (in English) of the surviving generations. The food is hearty rather than refined, but tasty nonetheless, and there's sometimes live music at the weekend.

The South-West *Ungar-Grill (Map 8, #48; ☎ 523 62 09; 07, Burggasse 97)* Meals €7.30-12, cover charge €0.80. Open 6pm-midnight Mon-Sat. This Hungarian restaurant has a patio area and live gypsy music every night. Authentic Hungarian dishes include fish, chicken and grills. Reserve ahead as it's popular with tour groups.

Beim Novak *(Map 8, #52; ☎ 523 32 44; 07, Richtergasse 12)* Meals €7-20. Open 11.30am-3pm & 6pm-midnight Mon-Fri, 5pm-midnight Sat, closed Sun & Aug. This place has traditional Austrian food, a detailed English menu and attentive service. A speciality is *Überbackene Fledermaus* (bat au gratin) – the 'bat wings' are actually cuts of beef.

The Hotel **Altwienerhof** *(Map 6, #47; ☎ 892 60 00; 15, Herklotzgasse 6)* Meals €17.50-22. This elegant restaurant serves quality French and international cuisine. There's a huge wine cellar.

The East *Zum Inder (Map 6, #5; ☎ 216 21 96; 02, Praterstrasse 57)* Meals €5.75-13. Open 11am-3pm & 6pm-11pm daily. This Indian restaurant is especially worth visiting for its *mittagsbuffet* for €5.75.

Schweizerhaus *(Map 6, #9; ☎ 728 01 52; 02, Strasse des Ersten Mai 116)* Meals €6-14. Open 10am-11pm daily, mid-Mar-31 Oct. This large restaurant in the Prater is famous for its roasted pork hocks *(Hintere Schweinsstelze)*. A meal consists of a massive chunk of meat on the bone (about 750g minimum at €13.55 per kilogram – expect to be rolled away from the table afterwards if you tackle one alone), best served with mustard (€1.10) and freshly grated horseradish (€0.75). Chomping your way through vast slabs of pig smacks of medieval banqueting, but it's very tasty when washed down with draught Czech Budweiser. There are many outside tables but it gets incredibly busy.

Estancia Santa Cruz (Map 6, #10; ☎ 728 03 80; 02, Hauptallee 8) Meals €5.95-10.35. Open 4pm-1am Mon-Fri, noon-1am Sat & Sun, Mar-Oct. This colourful place in the Prater has many outside tables in a shady garden. It serves Latin American and Tex-Mex food, including several vegetarian choices.

Steirereck (Map 6, #15; ☎ 713 31 68; 08, Rasumofskygasse 2) Mains €22-35, 3-course lunch €28.70, multicourse dinner €65.05 or €103.95 including wine. Open noon-3pm & 7pm-midnight Mon-Fri. This gourmet place is rated as one of the best restaurants in Austria, so book well ahead. Different parts of the restaurant have a different ambience, but it's pretty formal throughout – even the toilets are stylish! Choose from creative concoctions with ingredients such as lobster, venison or pigeon.

Self-Catering

There are *supermarkets* scattered around the city. Outside normal shopping hours you can stock up with groceries at the main train stations, though prices are usually considerably higher (not in the Billa stores).

Westbahnhof has a large shop (selling alcohol and food) in the main hall, open 6am to 10.50pm daily. Wien Nord station (Map 6) has a Billa supermarket open 7am to 6.30pm Monday to Saturday (to 8pm Friday, to 2pm Saturday), and several small provisions shops open 5.30am to 9pm daily. Franz Josefs Bahnhof (Map 6) has a Billa open 7am to 7.30pm daily, and Südbahnhof (Map 6) has a smallish Okay supermarket open 5.30am to 11pm daily. Wien Mitte has a large Interspar supermarket (Map 7, #59) open 8am to 5.30pm weekdays, 8.30am to 5pm Saturday, and small snack and provisions stores open daily. Near the S-Bahn exit in the airport is a Billa open 7.30am to 10pm daily.

See the Shopping section in this chapter for information on markets.

Coffee Houses

The coffee house is an integral part of Viennese life. The story goes that the tradition started in the 17th century after retreating Turkish invaders left behind their supplies of coffee beans.

Small/large coffees cost about €1.75/2.75. Although that's expensive, the custom is to take your time. Linger as long as you like and enjoy the atmosphere or read the cafe's newspapers – some places stock British and other foreign titles (saving you the €2.20 or so it would cost to buy them). Traditional places will serve a glass of water with your coffee (see also the boxed text 'Coffee Concoctions' in the Facts for the Visitor chapter).

Café Museum (Map 7, #158; ☎ 586 52 02; 01, Friedrichstrasse 6) Open 8am-midnight daily. This Kaffeehaus has chess, newspapers and outside tables. The building was created by Adolf Loos in 1899 but has since been extensively renovated.

Café Bräunerhof (Map 7, #81; ☎ 512 38 93; 01, Stallburggasse 2) Open 7.30am-8.30pm Mon-Fri, 7.30am-6.30pm Sat, 10am-6.30pm Sun. Relax here and enjoy British newspapers and free classical music from 3pm to 6pm on weekends and holidays.

Café Central (Map 7, #48; ☎ 533 37 63-26; 01, Herrengasse 14) Open 8am-8pm Mon-Sat, 10am-6pm Sun. This stylish place has a fine ceiling and pillars, and piano music from 4pm to 7pm. Trotsky came here to play chess. Note the plaster patron near the door with the walrus moustache – a model of the poet Peter Altenberg.

Café Hawelka (Map 7, #82; ☎ 512 82 30; 01, Dorotheergasse 6) Open 8am-2am Mon & Wed-Sat, 4pm-2am Sun & holidays, closed Tues. At first glance it's hard to see what the attraction of this famous coffee house is: scruffy pictures and posters, brown-stained walls, smoky air, cramped tables. At second glance you see why – it's an ideal location for people-watching. The whole gamut of Viennese society comes here, from students to celebrities. It's also a traditional haunt for artists and writers. After 10pm it gets really busy. You're constantly being shunted up to accommodate new arrivals at the table, the elderly organising Frau seizing on any momentarily vacant chair to reallocate it elsewhere – curtail those toilet visits!

Alt Wien (Map 7, #55; ☎ *512 52 22; 01, Bäckerstrasse 9)* Open 10am-2am daily. Students and arty types frequent this rather dark coffee house. At night it becomes a lively drinking venue; beer is €2.50 a Krügerl. It's also known for its goulash (€4/5.80 small/large).

Café Drechsler (Map 7, #173; ☎ *587 85 80; 06, Linke Wienzeile 22)* Meals €4-6.50. Open 3am-8pm Mon-Fri, 3am-6pm Sat, closed Sun. After a hard night drinking or dancing, greet the dawn at this cafe, where you'll rub shoulders with Naschmarkt traders. There are pocketless billiard tables.

Café Sacher (Map 7, #136; ☎ *514 56-0; 01, Philharmonikerstrasse 4)* Open 6.30am-11.30pm daily. Attached to the luxury hotel, this touristy cafe is a picture of opulence with chandeliers, battalions of waiters and rich, red walls and carpets. It is famous for its chocolate apricot cake, *Sacher Torte* (€4 a slice).

Demel (Map 7, #68; ☎ *535 17 17-39; 01, Kohlmarkt 14)* Open 10am-7pm daily. This expensive, elegant, mirrored place is the archetypal Konditorei establishment. It's the main rival of Café Sacher in terms of torte.

Café Schwarzenberg (Map 7, #154; ☎ *512 89 98; 01, Kärntner Ring 17)* Open 7am-midnight Sun-Fri, 10am-midnight Sat. Another traditional coffee house, it has live piano music 8pm-10pm Tues-Fri, 4pm-7pm & 8pm-10pm Sat & Sun. There are outside tables and English newspapers.

Café Restaurant Landtmann (Map 7, #43; ☎ *532 06 21-0; 01, Dr Karl Lueger Ring 4)* Open 8am-midnight daily. An elegant, upmarket cafe with outside tables and English newspapers.

Café Sperl (Map 7, #167; ☎ *586 41 58; 06, Gumpendorfer Strasse 11)* Open 7am-11pm Mon-Sat, 11am-8pm Sun & holidays, closed Sun July & Aug. This was Hitler's former haunt. It has the *Times* newspaper and billiard tables.

ENTERTAINMENT

The tourist office produces a monthly listing of concerts and other events. Publications worth referring to are the weekly magazines *City* (€0.75) and *Falter* (€2.05); the *Kronen Zeitung* newspaper (€0.75) also has listings, particularly on Thursday.

Apart from the more modern sounds swirling from bars and clubs, classical music still dominates Vienna. The program of music events is never-ending, and as a visitor in the centre you'll continually be accosted by people in Mozart-era costume trying to sell you tickets for concerts or ballets (a couple of readers have warned against buying tickets from these persistent people). Even some of the buskers playing along Kärntner Strasse and Graben are classical musicians.

Bars & Clubs

Vienna has plenty of places for a night out and, unlike some other European capital cities, you don't have to spend a lot of money in nightclubs to drink until late. Venues are by no means limited to the Innere Stadt – dozens of small bars and cafes in the 6th, 7th, 8th and 9th districts stay busy until well after midnight, and in summer Danube Island bursts forth with open-air bars and restaurants and a partying atmosphere.

Innere Stadt The best-known area for a night out is around Ruprechtsplatz, Seitenstettengasse, Rabensteig and Salzgries. This compact area has been dubbed the *Bermuda-Dreieck* (Bermuda Triangle), as drinkers can disappear into the numerous pubs and clubs and apparently be lost to the world.

Krah Krah (Map 7, #22; ☎ *533 81 93; 01, Rabensteig 8)* Open 11am-2am Mon-Sat, 11am-1am Sun & holidays. Attracting a range of ages, this bar has over 50 different brands of beer (from about €2.85 for 0.5L).

First Floor (Map 7, #36; ☎ *533 78 66; 01, Seitenstettengasse 5)* Open 7pm-4am Mon-Sat, 7pm-3am Sun. Choose from over 100 cocktails (from €6.55 upwards) and enjoy the 1930s interior, aquarium and eclectic crowd.

Hitler's Vienna

Born in Braunau am Inn, Upper Austria, in 1889, Adolf Hitler moved to Vienna when he was just 17. Six unsettled, unsuccessful, poverty-stricken years later he abandoned the city to make a name for himself in Germany. He later wrote in *Mein Kampf* that his Vienna years were 'a time of the greatest transformation which I have ever been through. From a weak citizen of the world I became a fanatical anti-Semite'. Hitler briefly returned to Vienna in 1938 at the head of the Nazi army, to be greeted by enthusiastic crowds.

Although Vienna would be happy for the world to forget its association with Hitler, an increasing number of tourists are retracing the Vienna footsteps of the infamous fascist. He spent several years living in a small, dimly lit apartment at Stumpergasse 31 (Map 6, #24), in the 6th district. It's a private block, but frequent visits by curious tourists have prompted plans (as yet unrealised) to turn the apartment into a museum.

Hitler was a regular visitor to the opera and, despite his poverty, preferred to pay extra to stand in sections that were barred to women. Café Sperl (see the Coffee Houses section earlier in this chapter) is another address on the Hitler itinerary: Here he would noisily express his views on race and other matters. Among his gripes was probably the fact that the nearby Akademie der bildenden Künste (Academy of Fine Arts) twice rejected an application by the would-be artist, dismissing his work as 'inadequate'. Although convinced that proper training would have made him into a very successful artist, these rejections made Hitler speculate to a friend that perhaps fate may have reserved for him 'some other purpose'.

Jazzland (Map 7, #21; ☎ 533 25 75; 01, Franz-Josefs-Kai 29) Entry €11-30. Open 7pm or 8pm-2am Mon-Sat. Hear cool jazz on hot nights here.

Palmenhaus (Map 7, #128; ☎ 533 10 33; 01, Burgring, entrance off Albertina). Open 10am-2pm daily. This beautifully renovated palmhouse has outside seating during summer, the occasional clubbing night and quality food.

Flex (☎ 533 75 25, W www.flex.at; 01, Donaukanal, Augartenbrücke) Open 8pm-4am. Flex is one of Vienna's best clubs. The crowd is typically black-clad, yet is prepared to party to a different musical theme nightly, including dub, hip-hop, alternative and indie. Live bands or touring DJs sometimes appear (cover €5-10).

The Volksgarten has three adjacent venues at 01, Burgring 01, that appeal to a variety of tastes. See the Web site W www.volksgarten.at.

Volksgarten Disco (Map 7, #113; ☎ 533 05 18) Entry €7.30-9.50. This place plays different music on successive nights starting at about 10pm: check the weekly listings newspapers for details. There's a garden bar

(drinks from €4) and the dance-floor roof can be opened to reveal the night sky.

Tanz Volksgarten (Map 7, #112; ☎ 532 42 41) Entry €5.50, live concerts €10.50. This is where serene and somewhat restrained couples glide waltz-style across the open-air dance floor to 'evergreen' classics. It opens around 7.30pm nightly in summer (it's closed in winter as it's largely open-air).

Volksgarten Pavillon (Map 7, #111; ☎ 532 09 07) Open 11am-2am daily, closed 1 Oct-30 Apr. It has garden tables, a DJ and food – ideal for chilled-out evenings on balmy summer nights. Entry is free except if you're going to one of the occasional 'unplugged' concerts or garden barbecues.

Irish bars have popped up all over town, offering cool Guinness and animated English banter. One of the most authentic is *Molly Darcy's Irish Pub (Map 7, #42; ☎ 533 23 11; 01, Teinfaltstrasse 6)* Open 11am-2am Mon-Thur, 11am-3am Fri & Sat, noon-1am Sun.

Other Districts *Tunnel (Map 8, #34; ☎ 405 34 65, W www.tunnel-vienna-live.at; 08, Florianigasse 39)* Entry €2.20-7.30. Attached to a low-cost restaurant (see the

Places to Eat section), this cellar bar has live music from 9pm nightly, though on Sunday there's generally a free 'Jazzsession'.

Porgy & Bess *(Map 7, #131;* ☎ *503 70 09; 07, Museumsplatz 1)* Entry €7.50-25. Open 8pm-2am Mon-Fri, 8pm-4am Sat & Sun, closed in summer. This jazz club in the Museumsquartier often has a 'jam session' on Wednesday, when entry costs only €3.65.

Chelsea *(Map 8, #36;* ☎ *407 93 09,* W *www.chelsea.co.at; 08, Lechenfelder Gürtel 29-31)* Open 4pm or 6pm-4am daily. This pub has a DJ spinning loud sounds (usually indie, sometimes techno) and live bands playing weekly, when there may be an entry charge. There's also English football via satellite.

Chelsea lodges within the U-Bahn arches of the Gürtel. Other bars within the same arches, heading north, are ***Rhiz*** *(Map 8, #35;* ☎ *409 25 05,* W *www.rhiz.org; 08, Lechenfelder Gürtel 37-38)*, open 6pm to 4am daily and favouring modern electronic music, and ***B72*** *(Map 8, #21;* ☎ *409 21 28,* W *www.b72 .at; 08, Hernalser Gürtel 72)*, open 8pm to 4am daily with varied bands and DJs.

Andino *(Map 6, #31;* ☎ *587 61 25,* W *www.andino.at; 06, Münzwardeingasse 2)* Meals €5-10. Open noon-2am daily. This Latin American bar and restaurant has lively murals and meals. Upstairs it has a venue where there's live music or theme parties, usually on Friday and Saturday; tickets are €4.50 to €10.50 (less if bought in advance).

Camera Club *(Map 6, #27;* ☎ *523 32 18, Neubaugasse 2)* Entry €3.65. Open 9.30pm-4am daily. This mellow bar features DJs and rock videos. The patrons seem to have a relaxed attitude to dope smoking. During the day (from 11am) it goes under the name Cafe Tralala (no entry fee), and is much quieter.

WUK *(Map 8, #8;* ☎ *401 21,* W *www .wuk.at; 09, Währinger Strasse 59)* Entry free to €7.30. This interesting venue offers a variety of events, including alternative bands, classical music, dance, theatre, children's events, political discussions and practical-skills workshops. It is subsidised by the government but pursues an independent course. There's also a Beisl in the cobbled courtyard.

Arena *(Map 6, #63;* ☎ *798 85 95,* W *www .arena.co.at; 03, Baumgasse 80)* This is another good venue, centred in a former slaughterhouse. From May to September, headline rock, soul and reggae bands play on the outdoor stage (€18.50 to €26), though in August this space becomes an outdoor cinema. All year, smaller bands play in one of two indoor halls (entry from €7.50), and there's sometimes theatre, dance and discussions. Keep an ear open for the monthly all-night parties.

U4 *(Map 6, #58;* ☎ *815 83 07,* W *www .u4club.at; 12, Schönbrunner Strasse 222)* Entry €5-8. Open 10pm-4am or 5am daily. This well-established club has two rooms, a slide show and affordable drinks prices. Each night has a different style of music and attracts a different clientele. Friday ('80s and '90s music) is a popular night. The Sunday 'Speak Easy' revives '60s and '70s music; Thursday is gay night. Occasionally there are live bands.

Gay & Lesbian Venues

Some places popular with gays and lesbians are: ***Café Berg*** *(Map 8, #29;* ☎ *319 57 20; 09, Berggasse 8)*, open 10am to 1am daily; ***Café Savoy*** *(Map 6, #34;* ☎ *586 73 48; 06, Linke Wienzeile 36)*, open 5pm to 2am Monday to Friday, 9am to 2am Saturday; and ***Eagle Bar*** *(Map 6, #26;* ☎ *587 26 61; 06, Blümelgasse 1)* open 9pm to 4am daily, a men's bar attracting a leather-clad crowd. There's also ***Why Not?*** *(Map 7, #16;* ☎ *925 30 24; 01, Tiefer Graben 22)*, a bar and disco open from 10pm to 4am or 5am Thursday to Saturday.

Heurigen

Heurigen (wine taverns) can be identified by a green wreath or branch *(Busch'n)* hanging over the door. Many have outside tables in large gardens or courtyards. Inside, they're fairly rustic and have an ambience all their own. Heurigen almost invariably serve food, which you select from hot and cold buffet counters; prices are generally reasonable. You should be able to eat well for €6 to €10, depending on the place and how much food you take. Although it was once the tradition, it's no

Winning Ways With Wine

The *Heurigen* (wine tavern) tradition in Vienna dates back to the Middle Ages, but in 1784 it was Joseph II who first officially granted producers the right to sell their wine directly from their own premises. It proved to be one of his more enduring reforms. These taverns are now one of Vienna's institutions most popular with visitors. The term *Heuriger* refers to the year's new vintage, which officially comes of age on St Martin's Day (11 November). It continues to be Heuriger wine up to its first anniversary, at which time it is promoted (relegated?) to the status of Alte (old) wine. St Martin's Day is a day of much drinking and consumption of goose.

A *Buschenschank* is a type of Heurigen within the Vienna region that may only open for 300 days a year. It can only sell its own wine, either new or old, and must close when supplies have dried up. The term 'Buschenschank' is protected. Not so 'Heurigen': taverns can use the term to describe themselves even if they buy in stocks from outside; in fact some don't even produce their own wine. Similar wine taverns are found in other wine-producing provinces, especially Lower Austria, Burgenland and Styria.

Austrian wine production is 80% white and 20% red. The most common variety (36%) is the dry white Grüner Veltliner; it also tends to be the cheapest on the wine list. Other common varieties are Riesling and Pinot Blanc. Sekt is a sparkling wine. Some of the young wines can be a little sharp, so it is common to mix them with 50% soda water, called a *Gespritzer* or *G'spritzer*. The correct salute when drinking a Heuriger wine is Prost (cheers). But Austrians can't wait for 11 November to drink the new vintage, and are prepared to consume it early, as unfermented must *(Most)*, partially fermented *(Sturm)*, or fully fermented but still cloudy *(Staubiger)*; they taste a little like cider. The correct salute when drinking these versions is *Gesundheit* (health), perhaps in recognition of the risk taken by the palate.

longer really acceptable to bring your own food along.

Heurigen usually have a relaxed atmosphere which gets livelier as the mugs of wine – and customers – get drunk. Many feature traditional live music, perhaps ranging from a solo accordion player to a fully fledged oompah band; these can be a bit touristy but great fun nonetheless. The Viennese tend to prefer a music-free environment. Opening times are approximately 4pm (before lunch on weekends) to 11pm or midnight. In the less touristy regions some may close for several weeks at a time before reopening, and some are only open in the summer or from Thursday to Sunday.

The common measure for *Heuriger*, or new vintage, wine is a *Viertel* (0.25L) in a glass mug, costing around €1.90 to €2.30, but you can also drink by the *Achterl* (0.125L). A Viertel of wine mixed with soda water *(Gespritzer)* costs €1.30 to €1.50.

Heurigen are concentrated in the wine-growing suburbs to the north, south, west and north-west of the city. Once you pick a region to explore, the best approach is to simply go where the spirit moves you (or to whichever places happen to be open at the time); taverns are very close together and it would be easy to visit several on the same evening.

City Heurigen *Esterházykeller (Map 7, #49; ☎ 533 34 82; 01, Haarhof 1)* Open 11am-11pm Mon-Fri, 4pm-11pm Sat, Sun & holidays. This busy wine cellar, off Naglergasse, has cheap wine from €1.75 for 0.25L, as well as meals and snacks.

Zwölf Apostelkeller (Map 7, #54; ☎ 512 67 77; 01, Sonnenfelsgasse 3) Open 4.30pm-midnight daily. This is a vast multilevel cellar, with a lively and rowdy atmosphere fuelled by free-flowing wine.

North The north-west is the most well-known region. The area most favoured by tourists is Grinzing (count the tour buses lined up outside in the evening), and this is probably the best area if you want live music and a lively atmosphere. However, bear in mind that this area is mostly eschewed as a tourist ghetto by Viennese. There are several good Heurigen in a row along Cobenzlgasse and Sandgasse, near the terminal of tram 38 (which starts at Schottentor on the Ring).

Reinprecht (☎ 320 14 71; 19, Cobenzl-gasse 22) Open 3.30pm-midnight 1 Mar-15 Nov. This is a very large, lively, sing-along place, kingpin of the tourist zone.

Mayer am Pfarrplatz (☎ 370 33 61; 19, Pfarrplatz 3) Open 4pm-midnight Mon-Sat, 11am-midnight Sun & holidays, 15 Jan-20 Dec. This is where Beethoven lived in 1817. It's now a Heurigen with a garden, many rooms and live music.

From Grinzing, you can hop on the 38A bus to Heiligenstadt. From Heiligenstadt it's just a few stops on tram D to Nussdorf, where a couple of Heurigen await right by the tram terminal. But don't just settle for these without exploring first; there are several others worth visiting along Kahlenberger Strasse.

Farther west are the areas of Sievering (terminal of bus No 39A) and Neustift am Walde (bus 35A); in the latter awaits (among others) *Shreiberhaus* (☎ 440 38 44; 19, Rathstrasse 54), with its fine garden. Both these buses link up with the No 38 tram route. Ottakring is a small but authentic Heurigen area a short walk west of the tram J terminal.

The Heurigen out in the 21st district are less visited by tourists and are therefore more typically Viennese, catering to a regular clientele. They are also cheaper: a Viertel costs around €1.60. Live music is not the norm. Stammersdorf (terminal of tram No 31) is Vienna's largest wine-growing district, producing about 30% of its wine. From the tram stop, walk north to Stammersdorfer Strasse, the next street running east-west. The western end of this street has many Heurigen, including *Weinhof Wieninger* (☎ 292 41 06; 21, Stammersdorfer Strasse 78) and *Weingut Klager* (☎ 292 41 07; 21, Stammersdorfer Strasse 14).

Strebersdorf is at the terminal of tram No 32, or about a 30-minute walk west of

Stammersdorf. The Heurigen are north of the tram terminal. *Weingut Schilling* (☎ 292 41 89; 21, Langenzersdorferstrasse 54) has a good reputation for wine. Another good place is *Noschiel-Eckert* (☎ 292 25 96; 21, Strebersdorfer Strasse 158).

South As in the north, tourists are less prevalent in the Heurigen in these districts. Mauer is in the south-west, at the edge of the Wienerwald. Take the U4 to Hietzing and then tram No 60 to Mauer Hauptplatz. Oberlaa is farther east. To get there, take the U1 to Reumannplatz, bus 66A or 67A to Wienerfeld, and then transfer to bus 17A. This runs along Oberlaaer Strasse, where there are several Heurigen.

Classical Music

Musikverein (Map 7; ☎ 505 81 90, **e** tickets@musikverein.at, **w** www.musikverein .at; 01, Bösendorferstrasse 12) Seats €22-110. Ticket office open 9am-7.30pm Mon-Fri, 9am-5pm Sat, Sept-June. This is said to have the best acoustics of any concert hall in Austria. The interior is appropriately lavish and can sometimes be visited on a guided tour. Standing room costs €3.65. The Vienna Philharmonic Orchestra performs in the Grosser Saal (large hall). In the smaller Brahms Saal the cheapest tickets (€4.35) have no view.

Konzerthaus (Map 7; ☎ 712 12 11, **e** ticket@konzerthaus.at, **w** www.konzert haus.at; 03, Lothringerstrasse 20) Seats €11.65-60, students under 27 with ISIC half-price. Ticket office open 9am-7.45pm Mon-Fri, 9am-1pm Sat. This is Vienna's other major venue for classical and other music; it has three separate halls.

There are sometimes free concerts at the *Rathaus* (Map 7) or in one of the churches; check with the tourist office.

Opera *Staatsoper* (Map 7; ☎ 514 44-2960; 01, Opernring 2) Seats €5.10-179. Operas performed Sept-June. Productions here are lavish affairs and shouldn't be missed. Standing-room tickets *(Stehparterre)* for €3.65 put you in a good position at the back of the stalls, whereas those costing €2.20

leave you high up at the rear of the gallery. The Viennese take their opera very seriously and dress up accordingly (you'd better leave your clown costume at home). Wander around the foyer and the refreshment rooms in the interval to fully appreciate the gold and crystal interior. There are no opera performances in July and August, but the venue may be used for other events.

Volksoper *(☎ 514 44-3670; 09, Währinger Strasse 78)* Seats €4.40-66. This other main venue for opera is close to the Gürtel and the U6 line. Kitsch operettas and musicals are included in its repertoire.

Vienna Boys' Choir *Burgkapelle (Royal Chapel; Map 7; #109; 533 99 27,* e *hof musikkapelle@asn-wien.ac.at)* Seats €5.10-27.65, standing room free. Ticket office open 11am-1pm & 3pm-5pm Fri, performance at 9.15am Sun Sept-June. Another famous institution, the Vienna Boys' Choir (Wiener Sänger-knaben) is actually four separate choirs; duties are rotated between singing in Vienna, touring the world, resting and perhaps even occasionally going to school. The choir was instigated in 1498 by Maximilian I and at one time numbered Haydn and Schubert in its ranks.

The choir sings in the Burgkapelle in the Hofburg, and tickets must usually be booked weeks in advance, but it might be worth checking for last-minute cancellations at the box office. You should queue by 8.30am to find standing room inside, although you can get the flavour of what's going on from the TV in the foyer. Also interesting is the scrum afterwards when everybody struggles to photograph, and be photographed with, the serenely patient choir members.

The choir also sings a mixed program of music in the Musikverein (see earlier) at 4pm on Friday in May, June, September and October. Tickets (€28-40) are available through Reisebüro Mondial *(Map 7; #172;* ☎ *588 04 141,* e *ticket@mondial.at; 04, Faulmanngasse 4)* and some hotels.

Theatre

There are performances in English at the ***English Theatre*** *(☎ 402 12 60-0,* w *www .englishtheatre.at; 08, Josefsgasse 12)*, tickets €14-36, students (under 27) €11.20-28.80, or €9.10 for last-minute leftovers;

Buying Opera & Theatre Tickets

An hour before performances start, standing-room *(Stehplatz)* tickets go on sale at the **Staatsoper** (€2.20 and €3.65), **Volksoper** (€1.45 and €2.20), **Burgtheater** (€1.45) and **Akademietheater** (€1.45). Queue up at the venue concerned: for major productions you may have to allow two or three hours; for minor works, you can often get tickets with minimal queuing. There is a separate queue for same-day student tickets at these venues. These left-over tickets are released one hour before performances, and sold at the same price as the cheapest seats (from €3.65) to students under age 27 who can show university ID and an ISIC card. Buying cheap, restricted-view seats doesn't involve queuing.

The state ticket office is the **Bundestheaterkassen** *(Map 7; #135;* ☎ *514 44-7880; 01, Goethegasse 1)*, usually closed from 1 July to late August, though it may be open limited hours. It doesn't charge commission and sells tickets for the four venues mentioned above. Tickets are available here in the month prior to the performance and credit cards are accepted (for September performances at the Staatsoper, apply in June); credit card bookings can also be made by telephone (☎ 513 15 13). For postal bookings at least three weeks in advance, apply to the Bundestheaterverband (☎ 514 44-2653, fax 514 44-2969) at the same address. You pay only after your reservations are confirmed.

Agents around town sell tickets for all sorts of venues, but beware of hefty commission rates (20% to 30%!). Wien Ticket (☎ 588 85; 01, Kärntner Strasse; open 10am-7pm daily) in the hut by the Opera charges negligible commission (0% to 6%).

and the smaller *International Theatre (Map 6, #2; ☎ 319 62 72, W www.internationaltheatre.at; 09, Porzellangasse 8)*, adults €18.25-20.35, concession €10.20, closed for around five weeks at the beginning of August, entrance on Müllnergasse. It has a linked venue, *Fundus (09, Müllnergasse 6a)*.

Mime performances (generally avant-garde) are held at the *Serapionstheater im Odeon (Map 7, #26; ☎ 214 55 62-20; 02, Taborstrasse 10)*, tickets €10-30, but only during certain times of the year; check local listings or visit W www.odeon-theater.at.

If you can follow German, the best theatre to visit is the *Burgtheater (Map 7; ☎ 514 44-4440, W www.burgtheater.at; 01, Dr Karl Lueger Ring 2)*, tickets €3.65-44, though there are plenty of other theatres, such as the nearby *Volkstheater (Map 7; ☎ 523 22 20, e ticket@volkstheater.at; 07, Neustiftgasse 1)*, tickets €3.60-38, to the north-west of the Museumsquartier. The *Theater an der Wien (☎ 588 30 265; 06, Linke Wienzeile 6)*, tickets €7.30-179, usually puts on musicals; standing-room and student tickets are available.

Cinemas

Cinema entry prices are typically €5.50 to €10.50, depending on the seat, place or film; Monday is known as *Kinomontag*, when all cinema seats go for the lowest category price (€5.50 to €8). You can find film listings in daily newspapers, plus the magazines previously mentioned (*Falter*, *City*, *Winside*). The following cinemas (among others) show films in the original language:

Audimax der TU (Map 7, #160; ☎ 588 01-41930; 06, Getreidemarkt 9, in the Technical University)

Burg Kino (Map 7, #134; ☎ 587 84 06; 01, Opernring 19)

English Cinema Haydn (Map 6, #29; ☎ 587 22 62; 06, Mariahilfer Strasse 57)

Filmcasino (Map 6, #45; ☎ 587 90 62; 05, Margaretenstrasse 78)

IMAX Filmtheater (Map 6, #48; ☎ 894 01 01; 14, Mariahilfer Strasse 212)

Österreichische Filmmuseum (Map 7, #127; ☎ 533 70 54-0, W www.filmmuseum.at; 01,

Augustinerstrasse 1, annual membership €7.30, then €4.35, open 1 Oct-30 June)

Top Center (Map 7, #161; ☎ 587 55 57; 06, Rahlgasse 1)

Spanish Riding School

(Spanische Reitschule; Map 7, #79; no ☎, fax 535 01 86, e tickets@srs.at) The Lipizzaner stallions that strut their stuff here are famous Viennese performers with a difference. The breed was imported from Spain by Maximilian II in 1562, and in 1580 a stud was established at Lipizza, now in Slovenia. They perform an equine ballet to a program of classical music while the audience cranes to see from pillared balconies, and chandeliers shimmer above. Although they are born dark, the mature stallions are all snow-white and the riders wear traditional clothing. This is a long-established Viennese institution, truly reminiscent of the Habsburg era.

Performances are booked up months in advance: for tickets, write to the Spanische Reitschule, Michaelerplatz 1, A1010 Wien. Contact this office direct, as ticket agents charge at least an extra 22%. Last minute, ask in the office about cancellations; cancelled tickets are sold around two hours before performances. You need to be pretty keen on horses to pay €21.80 to €65.50 for seats or €14.55 for standing room, although a few of the tricks, such as seeing a stallion bounding along on only its hind legs like a demented kangaroo, do tend to stick in the mind.

Tickets to watch the horses train can be bought on the day (€11.65) at gate No 2, Josefsplatz in the Hofburg. Training is from 10am to noon Tuesday to Saturday, mid-February to mid-December, except when they're on tour or in July and August when they go on their summer holidays to Lainzer Tiergarten (even stallions have to let down their hair – er, manes – once in a while). Queues are very long early in the day, but if you try at around 11am most people have gone and you can get in fairly quickly – indicative of the fact that training is relatively dull except for isolated high points. On the half-hour you can sometimes see the stallions crossing between the school and the *Stallburg* (stables).

Hotel Zodiac St Veit in Carinthia

Town mascot, spitting and waving, Carinthia

Lonely winter roads in Hohe Tauern National Park

Friesach, Carinthia's oldest town, has a filled moat around the old centre

655 coats of arms in Klagenfurt's Landhaus

Grossglockner Peak, Hohe Tauern National Park

Tongues of ice lap across the Pasterze Glacier

MARK HONAN

For details of the Lipizzaner stud farm see the Piber & Köflach section in the Styria chapter.

Casino

(Map 7, #125; ☎ *512 48 36-0; 01, Kärntner Strasse 41)* Downstairs slot machines open 11am-midnight, upstairs games 3pm-3am. Vienna's casino is opposite the tourist office. A dress code applies upstairs and jackets and ties can be hired at the counter. There's blackjack, roulette and other games.

SPECTATOR SPORTS

As in any large city, plenty of sports are played. Prices depend on the nature of the event; call if you need to know in advance.

Ernst Happel Stadion *(Map 6;* ☎ *72 71 80; 02, Meiereistrasse 7)* International and domestic soccer games are held here, in the Prater.

Stadthalle *(*☎ *98 100; 15, Vogelweidplatz)* This arena hosts competitions ranging from an ATP tennis tournament (mid-October) to water polo.

Freudenau *(*☎ *728 95 35; 02, Rennbahnstrasse 65)* Admission €3.65. There is horse racing here, usually every second weekend. Also in the Prater, there are trotting races at Krieau.

Vienna's Spring Marathon is run (jogged, walked, abandoned – depending upon the fitness of the participants) in April or May. The route takes in Schönbrunn, the Ringstrasse and the Prater.

SHOPPING

Vienna is not a place for cheap shopping but does offer numerous elegant shops and quality products. Local specialities include porcelain, ceramics, wrought-iron work, handmade dolls and leather goods. *Shopping in Vienna* is a free guide, distributed in upmarket hotels.

Shopping hours vary, though typically they are 9am to 6pm on weekdays and 9am to noon or 1pm on Saturday. Some supermarkets and large stores stay open till 7.30pm on weekdays and 5pm on Saturday. *Bazar* (€1.85), a newspaper available from pavement newsstands, contains privately advertised items.

Where to Shop

The main shopping streets in the Innere Stadt are the pedestrian-only thoroughfares of Kärntner Strasse, Graben and Kohlmarkt. Mainly upmarket and specialist shops are found here. Generally speaking, outside the Ring is where you'll find shops catering for those with shallower pockets. Mariahilfer Strasse is regarded as the best shopping street, particularly the stretch between the Ring and Westbahnhof, and has numerous large department stores. Other prime shopping streets are Landstrasser Hauptstrasse, Favoritenstrasse and Alser Strasse.

Niedermeyer has stores at various locations in the city; they're good places to look for hi-fi, radios, TVs, video and audio tapes, photographic equipment and computer hardware and software.

Ringstrassen Galerien *(*☎ *512 51 81-11; 01, Kärntner Ring 5-7)* Open 10am-7pm Mon-Sat. This is Vienna's most central covered shopping mall.

Lugner City *(Map 8, #45;* ☎ *981 50-0; 15, Gablenzgasse 5-13)* Open 9am-7pm Mon-Fri, 9am-5pm Sat. Not far from the Gürtel, this is another good mall. It has everything from computers to fine clothing.

Shopping City Süd *(SCS;* ☎ *699 39 69-0; Triester Strasse)* Open 9am-6.30pm Mon-Fri, 9am-4.30pm Sat. For major shopping expeditions, the Viennese head to Shopping City Süd. It's said to be the biggest shopping centre in Europe, and is south of the city precincts at Vösendorf, near the junction of the A21 and A2. Take the free shuttle bus (Map 7, #145) departing every 90 minutes during shopping hours from opposite the Staatsoper (near the tram No 2 stop). The return leg costs €1.50. The Lokalbahn tram service (Map 7, #146) to Baden, departing from opposite Hotel Bristol in Opernring, stops at SCS (every 15 minutes; fare €2.95, or €1.55 for those with a city travel card).

What to Buy

There are various souvenir shops in the arcade that connects the old and new Hofburgs. These shops sell artefacts such as mugs, steins, dolls, petit point embroidery, porcelain Lipizzaner stallions and so on.

Pawlata (☎ 512 17 64; 01, Kärntner Strasse 14) Open 9.30am-6.30pm Mon-Fri, 10am-5pm Sat. This place has lower prices than most souvenir shops, and also stocks lots of distinctive tableware from Gmunden.

Augarten Porcelain Factory (☎ 512 14 94-0, ₩ www.augarten.at; 01, Stock im Eisen Platz) Open 9.30am-6pm Mon-Fri. A variety of gifts and ornaments are crafted here, including little Lipizzaners. There's also a branch at 06, Mariahilfer Strasse 99.

Österreichische Werkstätten (Map 7, #85; ☎ 512 24 18, ₩ www.oew.at; 01, Kärntner Strasse 6) Open 9.30am-6pm Mon-Fri, 10am-5pm Sat. This cooperative sells jewellery, handicrafts and ornaments in eye-catching designs. *J&L Lobmeyr (Map 7, #101; ☎ 512 05 08-0; 01, Kärntner Strasse 26)* Open 9am-6pm Mon-Fri, 10am-5pm Sat. This nearby shop is well known for glassware and has a small museum (admission free).

Dorotheum (Map 7, #103; ☎ 515 60-0, ₩ www.dorotheum.com; 01, Dorotheergasse 17) Open 10am-6pm Mon-Fri, 9am-5pm Sat. Selling works of art is big business – just take a look at the auctions here. It was founded in 1707 by Joseph I and it's interesting to watch the proceedings even if you don't intend to buy anything. Lots can be inspected in advance and have the opening prices marked – up for grabs could be anything from expensive antiques to undistinguished household knick-knacks. If you do want to buy but haven't got the confidence to bid you can commission an agent to do it for you. On the 2nd floor is the *'Freier Verkauf'* ('free sale') section, where you can buy on the spot at marked prices. There are many other antique shops and art galleries along Dorotheergasse and the surrounding streets.

Markets

Naschmarkt (Map 7; 06, Linke Wienzeile) Open 6am-6pm Mon-Fri, 6am-5pm Sat. The biggest and best-known market is this 'farmer's market', mainly consisting of meat, fruit and vegetable stalls, but there are some clothes and curios. Prices are said to get lower the farther from the Ring end you

go. The Naschmarkt is also a good place to eat cheaply in snack bars.

Flohmarkt (Map 6) Open 6am-5pm Sat. On Saturday a flea market is tacked onto the south-western end of the Naschmarkt, extending for several blocks. It's very atmospheric and shouldn't be missed, with goods piled up in apparent chaos on the walkway. You can find anything you want (and plenty you don't want): books, clothes, records, ancient electrical goods, old postcards, ornaments, carpets ... you name it. I even saw a blow-up doll (second-hand, of course). Bargain for prices here.

GETTING THERE & AWAY
Air

Vienna is the main centre for international flights – see the Getting There & Away chapter for details on these. There are many airline offices on Opernring and Kärntner Ring, and they can be found in the Gelbe Seiten telephone book under *'Fluggesellschaften'*. Offices include:

Aer Lingus (☎ 585 21 00) 01, Opernring 1/R/8
AirCanada (☎ 503 61 81) 01, Kärntner Ring 18
Air France (☎ 502 22-2400) 01, Kärntner Strasse 49
Austrian Airlines (Map 7, #153; ☎ 05-1789) 01, Kärntner Ring 18
British Airways (Map 7, #157; ☎ 795 67-567) 01, Kärntner Ring 10
Delta Airlines (☎ 795 67-023) 01, Kärntner Ring 17
Lauda Air (Map 7, #141: ☎ 7000-76730) 01, Opernring 6
Lufthansa (☎ 0800-900 800) 06, Mariahilfer Strasse 123
South African Airways (☎ 587 15 85-0) 01, Opernring 1/R/8
Swissair (Map 7, #52; ☎ 960 07-0) 01, Rotenturmstrasse 5-9

Bus

Since the closure of the Wien Mitte Autobusbahnhof (bus station) in 2001, national Bundesbuses arrive and depart from several different locations in Vienna. It depends on the destination – many routes south (eg, Eisenstadt) go from Südtiroler Platz. For information, call ☎ 71101, 7am to 8pm daily.

For information on international buses, see the Getting There & Away chapter.

Train

Vienna has excellent train connections to Europe and the rest of Austria. Check with information centres in train stations or tele-phone the 24-hour information line (☎ 05-1717) for the best way to go: Not all destinations are exclusively served by one station and schedules are subject to change. All of the following stations (except Meid-ling) have lockers, currency exchange, Bankomats and places to eat and buy pro-visions for your journey.

Westbahnhof This is one of the main entry points to Vienna. Trains to Western and northern Europe and western Austria depart from Westbahnhof. Services head to Salzburg city approximately every hour (€33.50, 3½ hours). Some of these services continue to Munich (€60, five daily, five hours) and ter-minate in Paris Gare de l'Est (€157, two daily, 14½ hours). Three daytime trains run to Zürich (€80.30, nine hours), as well as a sleeper service departing at 9.15pm (add charge for a fold-down seat/couchette). Six daily trains go to Budapest (€31.10, three to four hours), from where there are several connections to Bucharest, though there's also one direct train from Westbahnhof at 7.36pm (€89.60, 18 hours). Westbahnhof is on U-Bahn lines U3 and U6, and many trams stop outside.

Südbahnhof This is the other main station, sending trains to Italy, the Czech Republic, Slovakia, Hungary and Poland. To Rome, a direct train leaves at 7.29pm (€108.50, 14 hours via Venice and Florence), or there are two other services requiring a change in Venice. Five trains a day go to Bratislava (€12.35/16 one-way/return, 1½ hours); five go to Prague (€40, five hours), with one continuing to Berlin (€88.40, 10 hours). Trams D (to the Ring and Franz Josefs Bahnhof) and O (to Wien Mitte and Prater-stern) stop outside. Transfer to Westbahnhof in about 20 minutes by taking tram 18, or the S-Bahn to Meidling and then the U6.

Franz Josefs Bahnhof This handles re-gional and local trains, including to Tulln, Krems and the Wachau region (see the Lower Austria chapter). From outside, tram D goes to the Ring, and tram No 5 goes to West-bahnhof (via Kaiserstrasse) in one direction and Praterstern (Wien Nord) in the other.

Other Stations Wien Mitte is used for local trains, and is adjacent to the U3 stop at Land-strasse. Wien Nord handles local and regional trains, including the airport service, which also stops at Wien Mitte. It's at the Praterstern stop on the U1. Praterstern is a hub for many tram routes. Meidling is a stop for most trains to/from Südbahnhof; it is linked to the Philadelphiabrücke stop on the U6.

Car & Motorcycle

Driving into Vienna is straightforward: the A1 from Linz and Salzburg and the A2 from Graz join the Gürtel ring road; the A4 from the airport leads directly to the Ring, and the A22 runs to the centre along the north bank of the Danube.

Rental Offices See the Getting Around chapter earlier in this book for a comparison of rental charges.

Avis (Map 7, #144; ☎ 587 62 41) 01, Opernring 3-5
Budget (☎ 714 65 65) 03, Hilton Air Terminal
Europcar (☎ 799 61 76) 03, Park & Ride U3 Erdberg, Erdbergstrasse 202/1
Hertz (Map 7, #155; ☎ 512 86 77, or ☎ 795 32 central reservations) 01, Kärntner Ring 17
National (Map 7, #154; ARAC Autovermi-etung; ☎ 714 67 17) 01, Schubertring 9

All of these companies have an airport office.

Motorcycles can be rented from 2 Rad-Börse (Map 7, #29; ☎ 214 85 95-0, fax 214 85 95-26), 02, Praterstern 47. Various Hondas are available, ranging from a 50cc scooter (€28.35; €0.15 per kilometre) to a Gold-wing 1500cc (€181; €0.40 per kilometre). These rates are for 24 hours and include 100km free. The weekend rates (from 5pm Friday to 10am Monday) include 200km free and are €57.50 and €363 respectively. Hel-met hire is €7.30/14.55 a day/weekend.

VIENNA

Hitching

Before you start hitching, take public transport to the main traffic routes in the suburbs. Heading west from Vienna, the lay-by across the footbridge from the U4 Unter St Veit stop has been recommended.

Vienna has an agency that links up hitchers and drivers. Rot-Weiss-Rot Mitfahrzentrale (☎ 408 22 10, e office@mfz.at) has set charges for hitchers, and drivers get the balance after the agency takes its cut. Lifts across Austria tend to be limited, but there are usually many cars going to Germany. In Vienna, examples of fares for hitchers are: Salzburg €18.20, Innsbruck €25.45, Klagenfurt €19.65, Vorarlberg €29.10, Brussels €43.65, Cologne €43.65, Frankfurt €36.35 and Munich €25.45. There's no walk-in office but you can telephone 24 hours, seven days a week.

Boat

Steamers head west (mostly from Krems) and fast hydrofoils head east. See the Getting There & Away and Lower Austria chapters for details.

GETTING AROUND
To/From the Airport

Flughafen Wien Schwechat (☎ 7007; 7007-22233 for flight inquiries) is 19km east of the city centre. The cheapest way to get to the airport is by S-Bahn on line S7. The fare is €2.95 (including a bus/tram connection downtown), or €1.55 if you have a city pass. Trains leave from Wien Nord, usually at 24 and 47 minutes past the hour, calling at Wien Mitte three minutes later. The trip takes about 35 minutes and the first/last trains depart at 4.36am/9.24pm. In the opposite direction, trains usually depart at four and 40 minutes past the hour, with the first/last service at 6.05am/10.17pm. (There are earlier trains in both directions on weekdays only.)

Buses run from the City Air Terminal (Map 7, #60) at the Hotel Hilton to the airport every 20 or 30 minutes from 4.30am (5am in the opposite direction) to 12.30am. From 1 April to late October, buses also run through the night, but less frequently. The 20-minute journey costs €5.10/9.50 one-way/return. Buses also run from Westbahnhof between 5.30am and 10pm (to 1.10am in summer), stopping at Südbahnhof after 15 minutes. The fare is also €5.10/9.50 and departures are every 30 or 60 minutes. For more information on airport buses, phone ☎ 930 00-2300.

If taking a taxi is the only option, you're usually quoted around €29 to €33. However, C&K Airport Service (☎ 1731, fax 689 69 69) does the trip for €21.10 fixed fare. Reserve ahead if you can, though in the airport you could approach their drivers holding signs by the passenger exit area and ask them to point out the coordinator.

Public Transport

Vienna has a comprehensive and unified public transport network that is one of the most efficient in Europe. Verkehrverbund Ost-Region (VOR) covers neighbouring provinces too, but all your travel in Vienna will be within the one central zone.

Flat-fare tickets are valid for trams, buses, the U-Bahn (the underground metro system) and the S-Bahn (trains to the suburbs; Inter-Rail and Eurail rail passes are also valid on these). Services are frequent, and you rarely have to wait more than five or 10 minutes for a vehicle to arrive. Public transport begins at around 5am or 6am. Buses and trams usually stop running by midnight, though some S-Bahn and U-Bahn services may continue until 1am.

Buses tend to cover a wider area than trams and always have a number followed by an 'A' or 'B'. These usually link to a tram number. Thus, bus 38A connects with tram 38, and bus 72A continues from the terminal of tram 72.

Night buses to all suburbs run every 30 minutes from 12.30am or 1am to about 5am. Most routes meet the Ringstrasse, generally at Schwedenplatz (Map 7, #23), Schottentor and the Staatsoper; the fares are not covered by daily passes: pay €1.10 for one ticket or €3.30 for a strip of four.

Transport routes are shown on the free tourist office map. The Vienna Line map is reproduced with the Vienna colour maps earlier in this chapter. In addition, there are transport information offices: those at Karlsplatz, Stephansplatz and Westbahnhof are open 6.30am to 6.30pm Monday to Friday, 8.30am to 4pm weekends and holidays, while those at Floridsdorf, Landstrasse, Philadelphiabrücke, Praterstern, Spittelau and Volkstheater are open 6.30am or 7am to 6.30pm Monday to Friday only. For public transport information in German, call ☎ 7909-105.

Tickets & Passes Single tickets, valid for immediate use, cost €1.60 from the VOR ticket machines on trams and buses. They're only €1.40 each from VOR ticket machines in U-Bahn stations, or from ticket offices or Tabak shops; these (and the passes mentioned below) must be validated in the blue boxes (inside buses and trams, beside U-Bahn escalators) at the beginning of the journey. There's a €40.70 fine (plus the fare) for being caught without a valid ticket. Children aged between six and 15 travel half-price, or free on Sunday, public holidays and Vienna school holidays (photo ID necessary); younger children always travel free. Seniors are eligible for special tickets. VOR machines give change for certain bills only, so you need to check the instructions carefully.

Daily city passes *(Stunden-Netzkarte)* are a good deal if you're doing extensive sightseeing. Costs are €4.40 (valid for 24 hours from first use) and €10.90 (valid for 72 hours). Validate the ticket before your first journey only. An eight-day, multiple-user pass *(8-Tage-Karte)* costs €21.80 and is valid for eight freely chosen days; eg, eight days for one person, one day for eight people, and so on. Validate the ticket once per day per person.

There are also two transferable passes which are even better value if the dates fit your visit: weekly (9am Monday to 9am Monday), costing €11.30 and monthly (calendar month) for €40.70. The yearly pass costing €386 is not transferable and a photo is required.

Car & Motorcycle

Taking public transport is an easier option than driving in the city centre. Irrespective of the complications created by one-way streets, you'll find it inconvenient and expensive to park in the centre. The underground parking garage by the Staatsoper on Kärntner Strasse is open 24 hours a day and charges €2.20/26 per hour/day. The one at Museumsplatz is cheaper, charging €1.85/10.90 per hour/day, but it's closed from midnight to 6am (8am on weekends and holidays). Garages outside the centre are generally cheaper.

All of the Innere Stadt is a blue parking zone (except where parking is prohibited altogether), allowing a maximum of 1½ hours parking between 9am and 7pm from Monday to Friday. Vouchers *(Parkschein)* for parking on these streets cost €0.45 per 30 minutes. In the districts bordering the Ring, blue zones apply on weekdays from 9am to 8pm (two hours maximum stop). Farther out you can still find white zones with no time restrictions on parking.

Petrol stations are dotted around the city and some are self-service. Very late at night, you may find that the only stations open are near the autobahn exits. The Austrian Car, Motorcycle and Touring Club (ÖAMTC; Map 7, #122; ☎ 711 99-0, fax 713 18 07) is at 01, Schubertring 1-3.

Taxi

Taxis are metered for city journeys. The flag fall starts at €1.90 (€2 on Sunday, holidays and from 11pm to 6am). The rate is then about €1.10 per kilometre (€1.20 on Sunday etc), plus €0.15 per 22 seconds of being stuck in traffic. The rate for trips outside the city borders is usually double, but try negotiating. Taxis are found by train stations and top hotels, or can simply be flagged down in the street. There is a €1.90 surcharge for phoning a radio taxi; numbers include ☎ 31 300, ☎ 40 100, ☎ 60 160 and ☎ 81 400.

Bicycle

There are 480km of bicycle tracks in and around Vienna, including those along the banks of the Danube. Pick up the *Nützliche Tips für Radfahrer* booklet from the tourist office, showing circular bike tours. This also lists bike rental outfits *(Radverleih)*. Bicycles can be rented at Westbahnhof and

VIENNA

Südbahnhof from 7.15am, and returned up till 9.45pm. Bikes can be carried on the S-Bahn and U-Bahn outside rush-hour times for half the adult fare.

Fiacre

More of a tourist novelty than a practical mode of transport, a fiacre *(Fiaker)* is a traditional-style open carriage drawn by a pair of horses. These charming vehicles can be found at Stephansplatz, Albertinaplatz and Heldenplatz at the Hofburg. Commanding €36.50 for a 20-minute trot, these horses must be among Vienna's richest inhabitants. Drivers all quote the same price (you could try to bargain); they generally have a fairly good command of English and point out places of interest en route.

Burgenland

Burgenland is a province of tree-lined hills, vineyards and orchards. Wine production is particularly important for this agricultural region. Tasting the local wines, either over a meal or on an organised tour, is an extremely popular activity with visitors. The most interesting area for tourists is Neusiedler See and the resorts nearby.

History

Austria and Hungary contested ownership of this region for centuries. Hungary appeared to have won out when Austria's Ferdinand III relinquished it in 1647, yet Hungary itself became wholly or partially subservient to the Habsburgs in the ensuing years. Austria finally lost control of Hungary after WWI, but the German-speaking western region of Hungary went to Austria under the Treaty of St Germain, concluded in 1919.

A further twist was to follow. The people of Sopron, the natural capital of the region, voted in 1921 to stay in Hungary. Some Austrians maintain that the Hungarian government manipulated the vote by importing extra Hungarian citizens on voting day.

The new province was named Burgenland, not for its numerous castles, but for the 'burg' suffix of the old western Hungarian district names. Eisenstadt became the capital. Across the border, Sopron has meanwhile become little more than a shopping centre for Austrians seeking lower Hungarian prices.

Orientation

Burgenland occupies 3965 sq km and is one-third forested. Geschriebenstein, at a mere 884m, is the highest point; at 117m, Illmitz is Austria's lowest town. The province is home to 272,000 people, mostly living in the north. One-fifth of the area is owned by the Esterházys, one of the richest families in the country.

This Austrian province receives far fewer foreign visitors than any other. As a consequence there is less tourist literature avail-

Highlights

- Visit Eisenstadt, the provincial capital and home of Haydn
- Set sail on Neusiedler See, Central Europe's only steppe lake
- Explore the national park at Seewinkel, a haven for birdlife
- Sample the local wine in one of Rust's numerous *Buschenschenken* (wine taverns)

able than one normally finds, and what is produced is sometimes only in German.

Information

The provincial tourist board is Burgenland Tourismus (☎ 02682-633 84-0, fax 02682-633 84-32, **e** info@burgenland-tourism .co.at, **w** www.burgenland.at/tourismus), Schloss Esterházy, A-7000 Eisenstadt. It's not set up for in-person visits, but can send out provincial maps and information on accommodation, cycling routes, wine-tasting and annual events.

Eisenstadt

☎ 02682 ● pop 13,000 ● elev 181m

Eisenstadt received its town charter in 1373, and its status was enhanced in 1622 when it became the residence of the Esterházys, a powerful Hungarian family. In 1648

MAP 10 – BURGENLAND

Eisenstadt was granted the status of *Freistadt* (free city). It has been the provincial capital since 1925.

Eisenstadt really milks its connection with the seminal 18th-century musician and composer Josef Haydn. 'Fascinating, not only for Josef Haydn', the town's tourist literature trumpets. Unfortunately, beyond the traces of Mozart's mentor, the sources of this fascination are somewhat elusive.

Orientation & Information

Eisenstadt lies 50km south of Vienna. To reach the town centre from the train station,

walk straight ahead down Bahnstrasse for about 10 minutes until you get to the pedestrian-only Hauptstrasse, a street with cafes, shops and restaurants. Turn left for Schloss Esterházy, which houses the tourist office, Eisenstadt Tourismus (Map 11, #8; ☎ 673 90, fax 673 91, e tourism@eisenstadt.co.at). It's open 9am to 5pm daily (closes 1pm on Sunday; closed weekends from 1 November to early May). Good free maps are available, as well as a brochure listing hotels, private rooms and details of museum opening times and prices.

The main post office (Map 11, #17; Postamt 7000) is on Pfarrgasse. Nearby at Pfarrgasse 18 is Ricky's Cafe (☎ 661 77), where you can log onto the Internet from 9.30am to 2pm daily.

Things to See & Do

Josef Haydn revealed that Eisenstadt was 'where I wish to live and to die'. He achieved the former, being a resident for 31 years, but it was in Vienna that he finally tinkled his last tune. He also rather carelessly neglected to give any directive about his preferred residence after death. His skull was stolen from a temporary grave shortly after he died in 1809, after which it ended up on display in a Viennese museum. The headless cadaver was subsequently returned to Eisenstadt (in 1932), but it wasn't until 1954 that the skull joined it.

Haydn's white marble tomb can now be seen in the **Bergkirche** *(Map 11, #2; ☎ 628 38, Haydnplatz 1; adult/senior/student €2.20/1.85/1.10; 9am-noon & 1pm-5pm daily 7 Apr-31 Oct).* The church itself is remarkable for the Kalvarienberg, a unique calvary display; access is via a separate entrance to the rear of the church. Life-sized figures depict the Stations of the Cross in a series of suitably austere, dungeon-like rooms.

Schloss Esterházy *(Map 11, #7; ☎ 719-3000, Esterházyplatz; adult/concession €4.40/2.95 for 40-minute guided tour, €6.90/5.45 for longer Grand Tour; open 9am-5pm Mon-Fri Nov-Mar, 9am-6pm daily Apr-Oct)* dates from the 14th century. The castle was restored initially in baroque and later in classical style. The

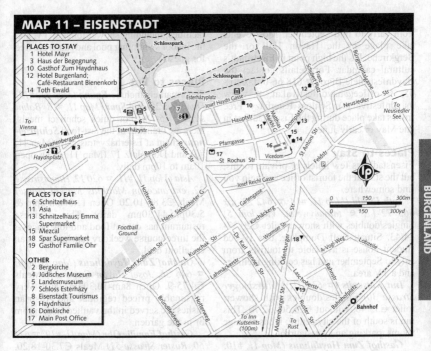

MAP 11 – EISENSTADT

PLACES TO STAY
1 Hotel Mayr
3 Haus der Begegnung
10 Gasthof Zum Haydnhaus
12 Hotel Burgenland;
   Café-Restaurant Bienenkorb
14 Toth Ewald

PLACES TO EAT
6 Schnitzelhaus
11 Asia
13 Schnitzelhaus; Emma
   Supermarket
15 Mezcal
18 Spar Supermarket
19 Gasthof Familie Ohr

OTHER
2 Bergkirche
4 Jüdisches Museum
5 Landesmuseum
7 Schloss Esterházy
8 Eisenstadt Tourismus
9 Haydnhaus
16 Domkirche
17 Main Post Office

BURGENLAND

provincial government now occupies two-thirds of the interior, and the rest can be visited by guided tour. Egotists will enjoy the multiple reflections in the mirrored corridor. The highlight of either the regular tour or the Grand tour is the frescoed **Haydn Hall**; its former marble floor was replaced by an aesthetically inferior but acoustically superior wooden floor (it's rated the second-best concert hall in Austria, after Vienna's Musikverein). The hall is where Haydn conducted the orchestra on a near-nightly basis; he worked for the Esterházys in this capacity from 1761 to 1790. There's also an exhibition on the Esterházy family. The tours are occasionally in English – inquire ahead, or ask for the English notes. They depart at 10am and 2pm; the shorter tour departs hourly from April to October.

Haydn's former residence, **Haydnhaus** (Map 11, #9; ☎ 626 52-29, Josef Haydn Gasse 21; adult/concession/family €2.20/

1.10/4.40; open 9am-noon & 1pm-5pm daily Easter Sunday-31 Oct) is now a small museum containing unexciting Haydn memorabilia. The **Landesmuseum** (Map 11, #5; ☎ 600-3607, Museumgasse 1-5; adult/student €2.20/1.10; open 9am-noon & 1pm-5pm Tues-Sun) collection includes Roman mosaics, ancient artefacts, wine-making equipment and items relating to 20th-century history (with some good period posters). There's also a Franz Liszt room, complete with a warty death mask of the Hungarian composer. The **Jüdisches Museum** (Map 11, #4; ☎ 651 45, Unterbergstrasse 6; adult/student €3.65/2.95; 10am-5pm Tues-Sun 2 May-26 Oct) primarily has exhibitions concerning the Jewish religion. Temporary exhibitions cost the same again.

Special Events

Behind Schloss Esterházy is the large, relaxing Schlosspark, the setting for the Fest der 1000 Weine in late August.

A Haydn festival, the Haydntage, is staged from early to mid-September. Most events take place in the Haydn Hall or the Bergkirche. It's the high point in Eisenstadt's cultural calendar. For details contact the Haydnfestspiele Büro (☎ 618 66-0, fax 618 05, e office@haydnfestival.at, w www .haydnfestival.at), Schloss Esterházy. Free frolics take place during the Eisenstadtfest in late May or early June.

Places to Stay
Eisenstadt has few hotels or private rooms, but the staff at the tourist office can help you find somewhere.

Toth Ewald *(Map 11, #14; ☎ 642 22, fax 665 72-17, e toth@vwe.at, Vicedom 5)* Singles/doubles with shower/toilet €20/37-24/43. Situated off Domplatz, this 10-bed student house is available to tourists from July to September and has cooking facilities and a TV area.

Inn Kutsenits *(☎ 635 11, Mattersburger Strasse 30)* Singles/doubles with shower/toilet €33/40, without €25.50/ 32.70. This inn is south of the city centre; it has average rooms, parking and a restaurant.

Gasthof Zum Haydnhaus *(Map 11, #10; ☎ 646 36, Josef Haydn Gasse 24)* Singles/doubles €29.10/43.60. Closed Christmas-31 Jan. This place is central and offers sizable rooms with private shower/toilet and a strange taste in wallpaper.

Hotel Mayr *(Map 11, #1; ☎ 627 51, fax 627 51-4, e hotel.mayer@burgenland.org, Kalvarienbergplatz 1, entrance on Werner Strasse)* Singles/doubles €33/59. This hotel offers clean, quiet, decent-sized rooms with shower/toilet & TV; ring the small blue bell for reception.

Haus der Begegnung *(Map 11, #3; ☎ 632 90, fax ☎ 632 90-90, e bildungshaus@ hdb-eisenstadt.at, Kalvarienbergplatz 11)* €37.50/62. This church-run place has modern, three-star rooms with shower and toilet. There's parking, and TVs are available for €3.65 per day.

Hotel Burgenland *(Map 11, #12; ☎ 696, fax 655 31, e burgenland@austria-hotels .co.at, Franz Schubert Platz 1)* Singles/doubles €86/120. This is the town's only four-star hotel. The rooms have all requisite facilities, including shower/toilet & TV, and the indoor swimming pool and sauna are free for guests.

Places to Eat
Supermarkets include **Emma** *(Map 11, #13; Domplatz 20)* and **Spar** *(Map 11, #18; Bahnstrasse 16-18)*. For quick schnitzel meals, there are branches of the fast-food **Schnitzelhaus** chain at Esterházystrasse 16 (Map 11, #6) and Domplatz 17 (Map 11, #13); open 10am to 10pm daily.

Asia *(Map 11, #11; ☎ 620 12, Hauptstrasse 32, entrance on Matthias Markhl Gasse)* Meals €3.80-10.20. Open 11.30am-3pm & 5.30pm-11.30pm daily. This Chinese restaurant has decent food and low prices – the three-course weekday lunch menu is an excellent deal.

Gasthof Zum Haydnhaus *(Map 11, #10; ☎ 646 36, Josef Haydn Gasse 24)* Meals €4.75-9. Open 8am-10.30pm daily. Very reasonably priced regional and Austrian dishes are served in the vaulted *Stube* room or in the garden.

Gasthof Familie Ohr *(Map 11, #19; ☎ 624 60, Ruster Strasse 51)* Meals €7.30-18.20. Open 7am-11pm Tues-Sun. This Gasthof is a little more expensive and offers a wide selection of meals, including Pannonian (west Hungarian) cooking.

Mezcal *(Map 11, #15; ☎ 655 19, Vicedom 3)* Meals €5.70-12.50. Open 5pm-11pm Tues-Sun. This Tex-Mex bar and restaurant is a good choice for grills, ribs or chilli in a lively environment.

Café-Restaurant Bienenkorb *(Map 11, #12; ☎ 696, Franz Schubert Platz 1)* Dishes €7.50-15. Open 8am-midnight daily. This restaurant in Hotel Burgenland is comfortable yet affordable, with Austrian and international dishes.

Getting There & Away
Regular trains depart every one or two hours from Vienna's Südbahnhof, calling at Wien Meidling. One train a day is direct, otherwise you will have to change at Neusiedl am See (€6.10, 80 minutes) or Wulkaprodersdorf (€7.65, 70 minutes). If you have a Vienna

city card, it will cost €6.10 by either route. Direct buses take 70 minutes and depart from Südtiroler Platz (€7.65, hourly). Wiener Neustadt is on the Vienna-Graz train route: buses from there take 30 minutes (€4.60, usually hourly). All buses arrive at Domplatz in Eisenstadt (Map 11).

AROUND EISENSTADT
Burg Forchtenstein

About 20km south-west of Eisenstadt and 15km south-east of Wiener Neustadt, this is the best known of Burgenland's many castles *(Map 10; ☎ 02626-812 12, w www.burg -forchtenstein.at, Melinda Esterhazy-Platz 1; guided tour adult/senior/student €5.10/4.75/ 3.30; self-guided tour of treasury €5.10/ 4.75/3.30; open 9am-4pm (last entry) daily Apr-Oct).* It was built in the 14th century and enlarged by the Esterházys in 1635, in whose hands it remains. A large and imposing pile, it's topped by a circular tower and an onion dome, and has an extensive arms and armour collection.

Getting There & Away Forchtenstein is not on a railway line, though Bundesbuses run there at varying frequencies from both Eisenstadt (€4.60, 70 minutes) and Wiener Neustadt.

Neusiedler See

Birdwatchers flock to Neusiedler See (Map 10), the only steppe lake in Central Europe. It's ringed by a wetland area of reed beds, providing an ideal breeding ground for nearly 300 bird species. The Seewinkel area is the favoured site for ornithologists (see that section later in this chapter).

Neusiedler See is only 1m to 2m deep and there is no natural outlet, giving the water a slightly saline quality. The shallowness means the water warms quickly in summer. Water sports are a big draw: boats and windsurfers are for hire at resorts around the lake, and there are many bathing beaches. Typical prices round the lake for boat hire per hour are: *Ruderboot* (rowing boat) €2.20, *Elektroboot* (motorboat) €10, *Tretboot* (pedal

boat) €5.80 and *Segelboot* (sailing boat) €13. Beaches are invariably cordoned off and a modest fee (about €2 to €3) is charged for admission. Swimming is also possible in some of the Seewinkel lakes. Horse riding and fishing are other popular pursuits.

For ambitious cyclists, a cycle track winds all the way round the reed beds; you can make a full circuit of the lake but it'll take more than one day to do it. Remember to take your passport as the southern section is in Hungary (path open April to October). The boat services that cross the lake will carry bikes. In summer (Sunday and holidays only) there's a special Fahrradbus that loops round the lake once a day between Mörbisch and Illmitz, via Neusiedl am See and all resorts in between.

In late August or early September the national triathlon is held at Neusiedler See. Watch 500 people voluntarily put themselves through hell – 42km of running, 180km of cycling and 3.8km of swimming in under nine hours. You could even join the torture: contact the Podersdorf tourist office (see the Podersdorf section later in this chapter).

Neusiedler See is a place to be visited in summer; tourist trade is much reduced in the winter, when many hotels and restaurants close down. If you stay in the area, inquire about the useful Neusiedler See Gästekarte, provided by the local tourist office upon receipt of your accommodation slip.

NEUSIEDL AM SEE
☎ 02167 ● pop 5300 ● elev 133m

Neusiedl (Map 10) is the region's main town and is easily accessible from Vienna. There's no real reason to base yourself here; the smaller places round the lake are preferable – they are closer to the lake, more scenic and more representative of the region.

Neusiedl has a tourist office (☎ 2229, e info@neusiedlamsee.at) in the Rathaus at Hauptplatz 1. The lake (where there's bathing and boating) is a 10-minute walk through the reed beds from the edge of town, or 20 minutes from Hauptplatz. Neusiedl also has a couple of museums, and the Tabor, a tiny ruin (free entry) with a view of the lake.

Staff at the tourist office will help you find somewhere to stay; options include an inconveniently sited HI *Jugendherberge* (*☎/fax 2252,* e *jugend.herberge@utanet .at, Herbergsgasse 1)*, where beds per adult/under 19 are €13/11.50 (open March to November).

Getting There & Away

Hourly trains from Vienna's Südbahnhof take 50 minutes and cost €6.10. Neusiedl train station is a 2km walk from the centre of town, or a €1.10 bus ride. Occasional buses from the train station continue to the beach via Hauptplatz. Bundesbuses leave from outside the train station, though those to Seewinkel also stop at Hauptplatz.

For road access, the A4 from Vienna to Bratislava passes just north of the town.

RUST

☎ 02685 ● pop 1700 ● elev 121m

Rust (Map 10), 14km east of Eisenstadt, is famous for storks and wine. Its name derives from *Rüster*, the German word for elm tree. The town's prosperity has been based on wine for centuries, and you can sample this history in one of the many wine taverns. In 1524 the emperor granted local vintners the right to display the letter 'R' on their wine barrels; corks today still bear this insignia.

Orientation & Information

Bundesbuses unload at the post office, 100m from Conradplatz, which leads to the town hall and Rathausplatz, the bigger square of the two and the focal point of the village.

The tourist office (☎ 502, fax 502-10, e info@rust.or.at) is in the Rathaus, Conradplatz 1; it has lists of hotels and private rooms, and staff can give details of winetasting venues. Opening hours vary depending on the season: maximum hours (July and August) are 9am to noon and 1pm to 6pm Monday to Friday, 9am to noon and 1pm to 4pm Saturday, 9am to noon Sunday; minimum hours (November to March) are 9am to noon and 1pm to 4pm Monday to Thursday, 9am to noon Friday. There's a 24-hour accommodation notice board outside the office.

Things to See & Do

Rust's affluent past has left a legacy of attractive burghers' houses on and around the main squares. **Storks** descend on Rust from the end of March, rear their young, then fly to new pastures in late August. Many homes in the centre (particularly on Rathausplatz and Conradplatz) have a metal platform on the roof to entice storks to build a nest there. A good vantage point is attained from the tower of the **Katholische Kirche** on Kirchengasse at the southern end of Rathausplatz, but that's currently closed for security reasons – check with the tourist office in case it reopens. The **Fischerkirche** *(Rathausplatz 16; adult/child €0.75/0.40; open 10am-noon & 2.30pm-6pm Mon-Sat, 11am-noon & 2pm-6pm Sun, 2 May-30 Sept)* at the other end of Rathausplatz is the oldest church in Rust, built between the 12th and 16th centuries.

Access to the **lake** and bathing facilities is 1km down the reed-fringed Seepromenade. Here you'll find a swimming pool *(☎ 591, Seebad; €3.65 per day; open daily May-Sept)*, schools for windsurfing and sailing, mini-golf and motorboats, pedal boats and sailing boats for hire.

Places to Stay

Storkencamp (☎ *595, fax 595-2,* e *office@ gmeiner.co.at, Ruster Bucht)* Sites per adult/tent/car €5.10/3.20/3.20. Open Apr-Oct. This camp site by the lake has a shop and a cheap restaurant; guests get free entry to the swimming pool.

Ruster Jugendgästehaus (☎ *591, fax 591-4,* e *jgh_rust@yahoo.de, Ruster Bucht 2)* Bed in 2-4 bed room €13.10/15.30 under/ over three nights. Check in 8am-noon, or call mobile ☎ 0664-571 50 91 for later arrival. Open year-round. This lakeside HI hostel was built in 1998 and has pristine modern rooms.

Gästehaus Ruth (☎/*fax 6828, Dr Ratz Gasse 1)* Singles/doubles with shower €20.40/33.50. This friendly guest house is conveniently central, on the corner with Weinberggasse.

Pension Halwax (☎ *520, Oggauer Strasse 21)* Singles/doubles with shower/toilet €21.10/39.30. The rooms are clean and fresh in this small pension.

Magdalenenhof (☎ *373, fax 373-4,* **e** *rema61@yline.com, Feldgasse 40)* Singles/doubles with shower/toilet & TV €36.50/65.50. This three-star pension has good facilities, including a sauna, garden and outdoor swimming pool.

Alexander (☎ *301, fax 301-4,* **e** *pension .alexander@aon.at, Dorfmeistergasse 21)* Singles/doubles with shower/toilet & TV €29/52-37/63. Though this has four stars, prices are very reasonable. Plus points are the sauna, wood balconies and the garden with a swimming pool.

Places to Eat
Create a picnic to eat by the lake at the *ADEG* supermarket *(Oggauer Strasse 3)*. It is open 7am to noon and 3pm to 6pm Monday to Friday, 7am to noon Saturday. Opposite, you can pick up cheap pizzas from *Zum Weinfass'l* (€3.65 to €7.20, closed Wednesday).

For sit-down meals in an enjoyable environment, look no farther than the many *Buschenschenken* (wine taverns) around town. Many have outside tables in attractive courtyards; staff at the tourist office can provide a list.

Peter Schandl (☎ *265, Hauptstrasse 20)* Meals €5.20-9.90, wine from €1.60 a *Viertel* (0.25L). Open 4pm-midnight Mon-Fri, 11am-midnight Sat, Sun & holidays. This Buschenschank has good food and good wine.

Haydn-Keller (☎ *210, Haydngasse 4)* Meals €5.25-11. Open 8am-10pm daily. This place is another possibility; the *Aal* (eel, €8.75) is recommended.

Rathauskeller (☎ *261, Rathausplatz 1)* Meals €5.50-12. Open 11.30am-11pm Thur-Tues, closed Wed. This 300-year-old cellar restaurant serves local specialities and has several vegetarian choices.

Getting There & Away
Buses run approximately hourly to/from Eisenstadt (€3.05, 30 minutes), but services cease in the early evening. Rust receives many bicycle tourists, and several places in the centre rent bikes. Schiffahrt Gmeiner (☎ 5538, **w** www.gmeiner.co.at)

sends boats across the lake to Podersdorf (€6.90, including bicycles; weekends Easter to 28 October, also Wednesdays June to August).

MÖRBISCH
☎ 02685 ● pop 2400
Six kilometres round the lake south of Rust, Mörbisch (Map 10) is just a couple of kilometres short of the Hungarian border. It's worth spending an hour or so here, enjoying the relaxed atmosphere and the quaint whitewashed houses with hanging corn and flower-strewn balconies.

There's a tourist office (☎ 8856, fax 8430-9, **e** tourismus@moerbisch.com) on the main street at Hauptstrasse 23. Staff can fill you in on the Seefestspiele, an important summer operetta festival (☎ 662 10, **w** www.seefestspiele-moerbisch.at, mid-July to late August), and on the lakeside facilities. Plenty of pensions and private rooms await if you decide to stay the night. As in Rust, several Buschenschenken (on Hauptstrasse and elsewhere) will happily fill you with food and wine.

Getting There & Away
By bus, the fare to Rust is €1.55 (10 minutes, every one or two hours) and to Eisenstadt it's €3.05 (strangely, the fare only from Rust to Eisenstadt is also €3.05). South of Mörbisch, cyclists may cross into Hungary (April to October) but there's no road through for cars. To cross the border, car drivers need to return almost to Eisenstadt and then take Hwy 16 to Sopron.

Frequent boats cross the lake to Illmitz – see under Seewinkel below.

SEEWINKEL
☎ 02175
Nature lovers are particularly attracted to this area (Map 10), a national park of grassland and wetland interspersed with myriad small lakes on the eastern shore of Neusiedler See. Tourist offices have information in English on the park and the bird species that visit particular lakes, though for more detail on the nature reserve areas you should contact the Nationalparkhaus (☎ 3442-0, fax 3442-4,

BURGENLAND

e neusiedlersee.np@netway.at), Hauswiese, A-7142 Illmitz.

The protected areas cannot be directly accessed by visitors, so to really get into the **birdwatching** you need a pair of binoculars. There are viewing stands along the way. The vineyards, reed beds, shimmering waters and constant bird calls make this an enchanting region for an excursion. Even if you're not an ornithologist, this is an excellent area to explore on foot (see the Walking & Skiing special section) or by bicycle.

There are no hills in the Seewinkel, so a cheaper, gearless bicycle from the rental places is all you need. Another option is to go by *Pferdewagen*, a carriage pulled by ponies that's large enough to take up to 20 passengers. Tours last one hour to half a day. There are several different operators (inquire in the Illmitz tourist office – see below). Gerhard Gangl (☎ 02175-2382, Ufergasse 34, Illmitz) charges €21.80 for one to three people for one hour, with each additional person paying €3.65.

The town of **Illmitz** (Map 10) is surrounded by the national park area and makes a good base. Staff at its tourist office (☎ 2383, fax 2383-4, **e** illmitz@illmitz.co.at), at Obere Hauptplatz 2-4, can provide information on both the town and Seewinkel. There are lots of pensions and private rooms available in the town. Like Rust, Illmitz has some rooftop platforms to encourage storks to nest. The beach at Illmitz is 3km from the town. From there, Gangl (☎ 2158, Seebad, Illmitz, **w** www.schiffahrt-gangl.at) has all types of boats for hire and runs several **lake tours**. In the summer it also sends hourly ferries across the lake to Mörbisch (€4.40 one way or €7.30 return; bikes carried free; runs Apr-Oct).

Another possible base is nearby **Apetlon** (Map 10; ☎ 2220 for the tourist office); Podersdorf is also convenient.

PODERSDORF
☎ 02177 • pop 2100 • elev 121m
Podersdorf (Map 10), on the eastern shore, is the most popular holiday destination on the lake, receiving more visitors than anywhere else in Burgenland. The town owes

this status to its position directly on the shore, made possible by the absence of reed beds in the immediate area.

Information
Staff at the tourist office (☎ 2227, fax 2170, **e** info@podersdorfamsee.at), Hauptstrasse 2, can help find accommodation. The office is open daily in summer, weekdays only in winter, and there's a computer screen in the entrance displaying room vacancies (this service is accessible daily until late evening).

Things to See & Do
Podersdorf offers the most convenient bathing opportunities on Neusiedler See, with a long grassy **beach** for swimming, boating and windsurfing *(admission €2.95 Apr-Sept, free Oct-Mar; open daily)*. Note that even if you have your own windsurfer, you will have to pay a daily charge of €3.30 to go windsurfing here. Other beachside facilities include mini-golf and volleyball.

The town is also within easy reach of the protected lakes in the Seewinkel area: the nearest, 5km to the south, are the Stinkersee lakes. Cyclists of all ages stream along the lakeside bike trail from the town. **Bikes** can be hired from various places in Podersdorf. Tauber *(☎ 2204, Strandplatz 2; rental €1.45/ 6.55/25.45 per hour/day/week; open 8am-7pm or 8pm daily Easter-Oct)* offers several categories of bikes.

Places to Stay & Eat
It's worth booking ahead in the high season, especially for the limited number of single rooms. In winter, many places close for a few months. Note that many guesthouses in the resort share the same family name (eg, Steiner), so make sure you end up in the right place. Seestrasse, the street leading from the beach to Hauptstrasse, has many small places to stay.

Strandcamping *(☎ 2279, fax 2279-16, Strandplatz 19)* Sites per adult/tent/car €6.40/4.75/4.75. Open 30 March-4 Nov. This camping ground has 800 sites right by the beach.

Steiner *(☎ 2358, Seestrasse 89)* Doubles €29.50, singles with shared shower €15.50.

Closer to the beach, this place is also a *Heurigen* (wine tavern) with cold buffets, wine for €1.50 a Viertel, and a zither player strumming three or four nights a week in July and August – on these nights it can be a bit noisy here till about 11.30pm.

Ettl *(☎ 2366, Seestrasse 46)* Doubles with shower/toilet & TV €32. Rooms are good value, and this place is about 300m from the beach.

Hotel Pannonia *(☎ 2245, fax 2720-4,* **e** *pannonia.florian@nextra.at, Seezeile 20)* Doubles with shower/toilet & TV €31-35, two singles €28. Meals €5.50-17.50. This hotel has standard three-star rooms, but good general facilities such as a garden, sauna and indoor swimming pool. The restaurant is pretty good too, offering a range of meals.

Gasthaus Zum Heiligen Urban *(☎ 2221, Neusiedler Strasse 1)* Meals €5-10.90. Open 9am-10pm daily. This Gasthaus, on the cor-ner with Seestrasse, has a small garden; the *Dorschfilet* (€5.10), fish in batter with a gen-erous portion of potatoes and salad, is cheap and tasty.

Gasthof Kummer *(☎ 2263, An der Prom-enade 5)* Meals €5.25-12. Open 11am-9pm daily Apr-Oct, closed winter. This is just one of several places to eat near the beach, with lots of outside tables. It has good food and low prices.

For self-caterers, there's a ***Spar*** super-market *(Seestrasse 16)*.

Getting There & Away

Bundesbuses between Neusiedl am See and Podersdorf (€3.05, 20 minutes) run approx-imately hourly in both directions on week-days but are infrequent at weekends; they continue to Illmitz and Apetlon. Ferries connect Podersdorf to Rust (see the Rust section for details) and Breitenbrunn on the western shore.

Styria

Occupying 16,387 sq km, Styria (Steiermark) is Austria's second-largest province and has a population of around 1.2 million. It encompasses mountain ranges, forested hills and green pastures. The main river, the Mur, flows through Graz, the provincial capital.

Graz is the major tourist attraction, but other places worth visiting in Styria include the pilgrimage site of Mariazell and the Open-Air Museum at Stübing. The Lipizzaner stud farm at Piber and the St Barbara Kirche at nearby Bärnbach combine to make an excellent day trip. Styria accounts for about 5% of Austria's wine production, and exploring the wine routes south of Graz is a popular excursion for those with their own transport. Styria extends as far as the Salzkammergut to the north-west, and this holiday region is dealt with in the Salzkammergut chapter.

History

When Duke Ottokar IV died without an heir in 1192, Styria passed to the Babenberg duke Leopold V as an inheritance. Control subsequently fell to King Ottokar II of Bohemia and then (in 1276) to the Habsburgs. In the next century the population grew, but there followed two centuries of local conflicts and invasions by the Turks and Hungarians. The year 1480 was particularly dire; it was known as the year of the 'Plagues of God' – the Turks, the Black Death and locusts all paid unwelcome visits. Exactly 200 years later one-quarter of the population of Graz was wiped out in a further epidemic of the Black Death.

The Turkish threat was removed after 1683 and the economy and infrastructure of the region developed. Then, in 1779, 1805 and 1809, it was the turn of the French to invade. After the Nazi occupation of WWII, the first Allied troops to liberate the area were from the Soviet Union, followed by the British, who occupied Graz until 1955.

Highlights

- Check out the medieval metalware in the provincial armoury in Graz
- Gaze over the red rooftops of Graz from the Schlossberg
- Pay your respects at Hundertwasser's church in Bärnbach – as much a work of art as a place of worship
- Take a short-cut through the country's architecture and crafts in the Austrian Open-Air Museum at Stübing
- Relish the Styrian *Kürbiskernöl* (pumpkin-seed oil) in regional dishes

Orientation & Information

Styria is in south-eastern Austria and is bordered by Slovenia. Although Graz is the capital, Bruck an der Mur is the main railhead for the region. Styria is subdivided into various tourist regions, though information on the whole province is available to personal callers at Graz's main tourist office (see Information under Graz, later in this chapter). For information sent by post, contact the provincial tourist board: Steirische Tourismus (☎ 0316-40 03-0, fax 0316-40 03-10, **e** info@steiermark.com), St Peter Hauptstrasse 243, A-8042 Graz.

Landesmuseum Joanneum, founded in 1811, is Austria's oldest museum; exhibits are dispersed among 10 sites in Styria (eight

MAP 12 – STYRIA (STEIERMARK)

of which are in Graz). A seven-day pass for all sections costs €14.55, and is available from any of the individual sites. See the museum's Web site at **W** www.museum -joanneum.at.

Getting Around

As in most other provinces, regional transport (including city transport) is integrated under a zonal ticketing system. Zonal tickets are valid for trains and buses, including on the private GKB rail lines running between Graz and Köflach and Graz and Wies-Eibiswald (via Deutschlandsberg). Single tickets are valid for periods varying from one hour (one zone) to five hours (22 zones). The zonal passes are available for 24 hours, one week, one month or one year. A 24-hour pass is often cheaper than buying two single tickets, so inquire about the various options before purchasing, though experienced ticket officers should offer the cheapest option for your route.

Graz

☎ 0316 ● pop 245,000 ● elev 365m

The green of the parks, the red of the rooftops and the blue of the river combine to make Graz an attractive city in which to linger. It has a number of interesting sights and is a good base for a variety of excursions. The large student population (some 40,000 in three universities) helps to make Graz lively after dark.

Graz was considered a city as early as 1189, and in 1379 it became the seat of the Leopold line of the Habsburgs. Friedrich III, King of Germany, Emperor of Austria and Holy Roman Emperor, resided here and left his famous motto, AEIOU (*Austria Est Imperare Orbi Universo*: Austria rules the world) inscribed in various places around town. In 1564, Graz became the administrative capital of Inner Austria, an area covering present-day Styria and Carinthia, plus the former possessions of Carniola, Gorizia and

STYRIA

Istria. Once strongly fortified against Turkish attack, in 1784 Graz was one of the first European cities to dismantle its city walls.

Today, the second-largest city in Austria hosts prestigious fairs and festivals and has an important opera house and theatre. The old town (historic centre) of Graz was awarded the status of a Unesco World Heritage site in 1999.

Orientation

Graz is dominated by the Schlossberg, which rises over the medieval town centre. The river Mur cuts a north-south path west of the

hill, dividing the old centre from the Hauptbahnhof (main train station). The Ostbahnhof (east train station) is south of the old town centre, close to the Messegelände (exhibition centre), where trade fairs are commonly held.

Tram Nos 3, 6 and 14 run from the Hauptbahnhof to Hauptplatz in the town centre. A number of streets radiate from this square, including Sporgasse, an important shopping street, and Herrengasse, the main pedestrian thoroughfare. South-east of Hauptplatz, Jakominiplatz is a major transport hub for local buses and trams.

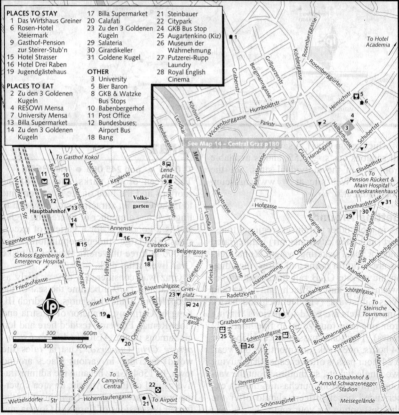

STYRIA

MAP 13 – GRAZ

PLACES TO STAY
1 Das Wirtshaus Greiner
2 Rosen-Hotel Steiermark
9 Gasthof-Pension zur Steirer-Stub'n
15 Hotel Strasser
16 Hotel Drei Raben
19 Jugendgästehaus

PLACES TO EAT
2 Zu den 3 Goldenen Kugeln
4 RESOWI Mensa
7 University Mensa
13 Billa Supermarket
14 Zu den 3 Goldenen Kugeln

17 Billa Supermarket
20 Calafati
23 Zu den 3 Goldenen Kugeln
29 Salateria
30 Girardikeller
31 Goldene Kugel

OTHER
3 University
5 Bier Baron
8 GKB & Watzke Bus Stops
10 Babenbergerhof
11 Post Office
12 Bundesbuses; Airport Bus
18 Bang

21 Steinbauer
22 Citypark
24 GKB Bus Stop
25 Augartenkino (Kiz)
26 Museum der Wahrnehmung
27 Putzerei-Rupp Laundry
28 Royal English Cinema

Information

Tourist Offices The main tourist office (Map 14, #37; ☎ 80 75-0, fax 80 75-15, e info@graztourismus.at) is at Herrengasse 16. It's open 9am to 6pm Monday to Friday, 9am to 3pm Saturday, and 10am to 3pm Sunday. From 1 June to 31 September hours extend to 7pm on weekdays and 6pm on Saturday. Information about both the city and the province is available. Most of it's free, although there is a charge of €1.10 for the *World Heritage Site Graz* booklet, which describes central sites and shows them on a map. Ask about their guided city tours (in English) by foot (€5.45) or bus (€7.30).

The provincial tourist board (see the Orientation & Information section earlier) sends information about Graz by post.

There is another tourist information office (☎ 80 75-21) at the Hauptbahnhof (Map 13). While the station is being rebuilt (scheduled to finish mid-2003) the tourist office can be found alongside the train information counters in the white hut outside the main entrance. Opening hours (subject to change) are 9am to 6pm Monday to Friday.

Money The Hauptbahnhof has a money exchange, Western Union office and a Bankomat. You'll also find Bankomats and banks on Herrengasse. There's no longer an American Express office but Bankhaus Krentschker, Hamerlinggasse 8 (Map 14, #54) and Am Eisernen Tor 3 (Map 14, #52), will exchange American Express travellers cheques without charging commission.

Post & Communications The main post office (Map 14, #48; Hauptpostamt Graz; A-8010), at Neutorgasse 46, is open 6.30am to 8pm weekdays and 8am to noon Saturday. There's another post office (Map 13, #11; Postamt A-8020) next to the Hauptbahnhof at Bahnhofgürtel 48, open 8am to midnight weekdays, 7am to 2pm Saturday, and 3pm to 10pm Sunday and holidays.

Email & Internet Access Surfing rates are €4.40 per hour at Jugendgästehaus (see Places to Stay – Budget) and Café Zentral (Map 14, #46) at Andreas Hofer Platz 9 (open 7am to midnight weekdays, 7am to noon Saturday). Leykam bookshop (Map 14, #36), Stempfergasse 3, has a couple of free terminals.

Travel Agencies Ökista (Map 14, #50; ☎ 82 62 62-0) has an office at Raubergasse 20. It's open 9am to 5.30pm Monday to Friday.

Bookshops The large English Bookshop (Map 14, #31; ☎ 82 62 66), Tummelplatz 7, has English and French books. It's open 9am to 6pm weekdays, 9am to noon Saturday.

Laundry Putzerei-Rupp (Map 13, #27; ☎ 82 11 83), Jakoministrasse 34, has self-service machines and offers service washes. It's open 8am to 5pm Monday to Friday, 8am to noon Saturday.

Medical Services The main hospital is the Landeskrankenhaus (☎ 385-0) at Auenbruggerplatz. It provides emergency treatment, as does the emergency hospital (Unfallkrankenhaus; ☎ 505-0), Göstingersrasse 24, at tram No 1 terminus.

Hauptplatz to Hofgasse

Amid the clamour and bustle of Hauptplatz lies the Renaissance-style **Rathaus** (Map 14, #40), built in 1550. The female figures around the central fountain in the square represent the four main rivers of the region: Mur, Enns, Drau and Sann. On Hofgasse, the 15th-century **Burg** (Map 14, #9) now contains government offices. At the far end of the courtyard, on the left under the arch, is an ingenious double staircase from 1499 (Map 14, #7) – the steps diverge and converge as they spiral. Beyond the passage is a grassy area containing busts of famous people associated with Graz.

The **Domkirche** *(Map 14, #28; ☎ 82 16 83-0, Burggasse 3; free; open approx 7am-8pm daily)* is a late-Gothic building dating from the 15th century, though it only became a cathedral in 1786. The interior combines Gothic and baroque elements, with reticulated vaulting on the ceiling and many side altars. The exterior has a faded fresco showing life during the 1480 plagues.

STYRIA

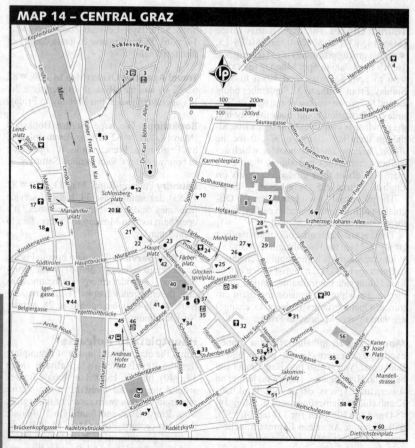

MAP 14 – CENTRAL GRAZ

Next door is a more impressive sight, the mannerist-baroque **mausoleum** of Ferdinand II *(Map 14, #29; ☎ 82 16 83, Burggasse 2; adult/child up to 15 years €0.75/0.40; open 11am-noon & 2pm-3pm daily May-Oct, 11am-noon Nov-Apr; closed holidays)*. Construction was started in 1614 by an Italian architect, Pietro de Pomis, who spent nearly 20 years on the project. After his death, Pietro Valnegro completed the structure. Inside, the exuberant stucco and frescoes were the work of Johann Bernhard Fischer von Erlach. Ferdinand, his wife and his son are interred in the crypt below, their tomb modestly set into the wall. In a clever arrangement, the dome of the crypt has a hole in the centre, allowing you to look up into the larger dome above. Pride of place in the crypt goes to the red marble sarcophagus of Ferdinand's parents, Charles II and Maria. However, only Maria lies within; Charles rests in Seckau Abbey (a former centre of the diocese of Styria) near Knittelfeld.

Heading back towards Hauptplatz, look out for figures emerging from an upper window in Glockenspielplatz. The figures twirl to **Glockenspiel** (Map 14, #26) music at 11am, 3pm and 6pm daily.

MAP 14 – CENTRAL GRAZ

PLACES TO STAY
13 Schlossberg Hotel
18 Hotel Mariahilf
22 Hotel Erzherzog Johann & Wintergarten Restaurant
33 Grazerhof
43 Grand Hotel Wiesler & Schauer

PLACES TO EAT
5 Laufke
6 Promenade Café
10 Zur Goldenen Pastete
15 Food Market
19 Mohrenwirt
21 Feinspitz; Eurospar; Kastner & Öhler Department Store
25 Gamlitzer Weinstube
27 Stainzerbauer
34 Landhaus Keller
42 Fast-Food Stands
44 Mangolds Vollwert Restaurant
49 Restaurant Gösser Bräu

51 Fast-Food Stands
53 Operncafé
57 Food Market
59 Restaurant Athen
60 Alt Wien

OTHER
1 Schlossbergbahn
2 Open-Air Museum
3 Military Museum & Bell Tower
4 Café Harrach
7 Double Staircase
8 Schauspielhaus
9 Burg
11 Uhrturm
12 Schlossberg Cave Railway
14 Club avantgarde
16 Brot & Spiele
17 Mariahilfkirche
20 Palais Attems; Styriarte & Steirischer Herbst Offices
23 Kölz
24 MI Bar

26 Glockenspiel
28 Domkirche
29 Mausoleum of Ferdinand II
30 Kommod & Triangel
31 English Bookshop
32 Stadtpfarrkirche
35 Landeszeughaus
36 Leykam Bookshop
37 Main Tourist Office
38 Landhaus Courtyard
39 Steirisches Heimatwerk
40 Rathaus
41 Casino
45 Hertz
46 Café Zentral
47 Bus Station
48 Main Post Office
50 Ökista
52 Bankhaus Krentschker
54 Bankhaus Krentschker
55 Tageskasse
56 Opernhaus
58 Avis

Landeszeughaus

A sight not to be missed is the Landeszeughaus *(provincial armoury; Map 14, #35; ☎ 80 17-9810, Herrengasse 16; adult/concession €4.40/2.95, or €5.50/4.40 including a tour (in English with several days notice); open 9am-5pm Tues-Sun 1 Mar-31 Oct, 10am-3pm Tues-Sun 3 Nov-6 Jan)*. It houses an incredible array of gleaming armour and weapons, over 30,000 pieces – enough to equip many more soldiers than you would care to meet in a foreign field. Most of it dates from the 17th century when the original armoury was built. Its purpose was to provide a quick distribution point for equipping the local population when invasion was imminent. Some of the armour is beautifully engraved; other exhibits are crude and intimidating. The sheer weight of the metalware (such as the two-handed swords) suggests that battles were conducted in bizarre, staggering slow motion. The view from the 4th floor of the next-door Landhaus (Styrian Parliament building), over the Italian Renaissance courtyard (Map 14, #38) and the Schlossberg beyond, is stunning.

Churches

South-east of the Landeszeughaus is the **Stadtpfarrkirche** *(parish church; Map 14, #32; ☎ 82 96 84-0, Herrengasse 23; admission free; open daylight hours)*. It's worth peeking in at the stained glass: one small panel (left of the high altar, fourth from the bottom on the right) shows Hitler and Mussolini looking on as Christ is scourged.

The **Mariahilferkirche** *(Map 14, #17; ☎ 71 31 69-0, Mariahilferplatz 3; open daylight hours)* has a baroque facade, created between 1742 and 1744 by Josef Hueber. Part of the church was built by Pietro de Pomis, who is buried inside.

Parks

Paths wind up the **Schlossberg** from all sides. The climb takes under 30 minutes and rewards walkers with excellent views. Along the way there are gardens and seating terraces. Alternatively, the **Schlossbergbahn** (castle hill railway; Map 14, #1) runs from Franz Josef Kai up the Schlossberg every 15 minutes till late evening (public transport tickets are valid – see Getting Around, later in this section). At the top is an **open-air**

STYRIA

theatre (Map 14, #2), a small **military museum** and a **bell tower** (Map 14, #3) that dates from 1588 and which formed part of the now-demolished castle. To the south is the emblem of Graz, the **Uhrturm** (clock tower; Map 14, #11). Unusually, the larger hand on the clock face shows the hours; the minute hand was added much later. The townsfolk paid the French a ransom of 2987 florins and 11 farthings not to destroy the clock tower during the 1809 invasion. By the Uhrturm is a lift back down to Schlossbergplatz (public transport tickets valid).

East of Schlossberg is the **Stadtpark** (Map 14). The park's large fountain and flower beds make it a relaxing place to sit or stroll.

Schlossberg Cave Railway

This is a good activity for those with kids. Schlossberg Cave Railway *(Map 14, #12; ☎ 82 40 95, Schlossbergplatz)* is the longest grotto railway in Europe, winding for 2km around scenes from fairy tales. Unfortunately, it's closed till around 2003. Next door is a pedestrian tunnel through the hill, which has viewing windows into WWII air-raid caverns; admission is free.

Schloss Eggenberg

Schloss Eggenberg *(☎ 58 32 64-0, Eggenbergen Allee 90; admission to park, staterooms and museums adult/concession/family €5.85/4.40/8.75; staterooms/museums open 9am-5pm Tues-Sun 8 Apr-31 Oct)* is 4km west of the centre; take tram No 1 to Schloss Eggenberg, backtrack a few metres and take the first street on the right. This was the home of the Eggenberg dynasty in the 15th century; the baroque palace was constructed by de Pomis around the original building. He was commissioned by Johann Ulrich (1568–1634), who was celebrating the power and prestige of being appointed governor of Inner Austria in 1625.

Astronomical themes and symbols dominate: the palace has 365 windows and 24 **Prunkräume** (staterooms). The Planet Hall is a riot of white stucco surrounding baroque frescoes, painted by Hans Adam Weissenkircher. The frescoes portray the seven planets (all that were then discovered), the four elements and the 12 signs of the zodiac. Other rooms show mythological, classical and contemporary scenes. There's also a church, a Chinese room and games rooms. One room shows a portrait of Empress Maria Theresa painted as a slender figure even though by then she already weighed 100kg. Guided tours are included in the entry price and depart at 10am, 11am, noon, 2pm, 3pm and 4pm. The tours are conducted in German, though an English translation is possible (inquire in advance).

The palace houses two museums. The **Münzensammlung** (coin collection) displays coins and notes from the past 2500 years, plus other antiquities. The Archaeology collection covers early history and its prize exhibit is the votive *Chariot of Strettweg* (7th century BC); this piece in bronze is dramatically lit in a dark room.

The palace is set in parkland *(€0.15; open 8am-5pm winter, 8am-7pm summer)* where peacocks and deer roam, and Roman stone reliefs can be seen. A cafe is open in summer.

Like the Landeszeughaus, Schloss Eggenberg forms part of the Landesmuseum Joanneum.

Other Attractions

The **Museum der Wahrnehmung** *(Museum of Perception; Map 13, #26; ☎ 81 15 99, w www.muwa.at, Friedrichgasse 41; adult/concession/family €3.50/2.50/8; open 2pm-6.30pm Wed-Mon)* is a small but unusual collection that explores sensory illusions.

At the southern end of the No 4 tram line is the **Arnold Schwarzenegger Stadion**, renamed in 1997 after the Styrian-born actor. Football (soccer) is played at the Stadion but it also houses the **gym** *(☎ 48 24 82, Stadionplatz 1; admission free; open 5.45am-10pm Mon-Fri, 10am-9pm Sat, Sun & holidays)* where Schwarzenegger worked out in his body-building days. There's not much to see (some equipment, a few old photos) but plenty of tourists make the trip.

Activities

One of several bathing complexes, Bad Eggenberg *(☎ 58 15 51, Janzgasse 21; swimming pool day pass adult/student or child €5.10/3.30; open 8am-10pm daily)* also has a sauna and massages. Take tram No 1 to the complex.

Special Events

The Styriarte is a theme-based music festival (mostly but not exclusively classical) held from late June to late July: for information contact the Styriarte Kartenbüro (Map 14, #20; ☎ 82 50 00, fax 877 38 36, e tickets@ styriate.com, w www.styriate.com), Sackstrasse 17, A-8010.

Steirischer Herbst is an avant-garde festival of new art held during October. Events include music, theatre, films, exhibitions and art installations, and are staged at a dozen different locations around town. Contact Steirischer Herbst Informationsbüro (Map 14, #20; ☎ 82 30 07-0, fax 83 57 88, e info@steirischerbst.at, w www .steirischerbst.at), Sackstrasse 17. Offices for both events are housed in Palais Attems.

The autumn trade fair, Grazer Herbstmesse International, takes place in the Messegelände (Map 13; ☎ 80 88-0), Messeplatz 1, during the first week in October.

The Graz marathon takes place in mid- or late October.

Places to Stay – Budget

Except for the camping ground and the Jugendgästehaus, Graz has few budget places to stay, so try to book ahead. Even most private rooms (listed in the tourist office accommodation booklet) are pricey or a long way from the centre. Staff at the tourist office will book rooms without charging commission.

Camping Central (☎ 28 18 31, fax 69 78 24, e freizeit@netway.at, Martinhofstrasse 3) 1/2 person sites €11.65/17.80. Open 1 Apr-31 Oct. It's about 6km south-west of the city centre. Take bus No 32 from Jakominiplatz (Map 14). The prices are a little high but guests have free use of the swimming pool.

Jugendgästehaus (Map 13, #19; ☎ 71 48 76, fax 71 48 76-88, e jgh.graz@jgh.at, Idlhofgasse 74) Bed in 4-bed dorm with private shower/toilet €18.20, bed in large basement dorm €13.85, singles/doubles with private shower/toilet €25.10/42.20. Add €2.20 first

night's surcharge if staying less than 4 nights. Reception 7am-10pm Mon-Sat, closed Sat in July & Aug, Sun & holidays. Laundry costs €2.95 to wash and dry. This HI hostel casts its net wide, offering a children's play area as well as conference rooms and seminar deals. There are extensive lawns and parking, and self-service lunches are €4.75 (available to non-guests).

Hotel Strasser (Map 13, #15; ☎ 71 39 77, fax 71 68 56, e hotel.strasser@noten.com, Eggenberger Gürtel 11) Singles/doubles with private shower €34.90/50.20, with shared shower €27.65/42.90. A short walk south of the Hauptbahnhof, this hotel has functional but pleasant rooms. There is a reasonably priced restaurant on the premises.

Gasthof Kokol (☎/fax 68 43 20, Thalstrasse 3) Singles/doubles with shower/toilet €28.40/46.60, doubles with shower only €40.70. Reception open 7am-10pm, except 1pm to 6pm Sat & Sun. This place offers simple, compact rooms with pine beds. It's north-west of the centre, easily reached by bus No 40 from Jakominiplatz or No 85 (the final stop) from the train station. Reservations are advised.

Places to Stay – Mid-Range

Hotel Academia (☎ 32 35 58, fax 32 35 58-3520, e graz@academia-hotels.co.at, Untere Schönbrunngasse 7–11) Singles/doubles with shower/toilet €36.50/58.50. This 170-room student residence is used as a hotel from 1 July to 30 September.

Rosen-Hotel Steiermark (Map 13, #6; ☎ 38 15 02-0, fax 38 15 02-62, e graz@ rosenhotel.com, Liebiggasse 4) This is another student residence offering hotel rooms in summer. It was being rebuilt in 2001 – expect prices and standards to be similar to those in Hotel Academia.

Gasthof-Pension zur Steirer-Stub'n (Map 13, #9; ☎/fax 71 68 55, e birgit.sommer@ chello.at, Lendplatz 8) Singles/doubles €33/59. This small pension gives a taste of rural charm in downtown Graz. Window shutters, cut flowers, dried corn and homey knick-knacks create the effect. Rooms have shower, toilet and TV.

STYRIA

Pension Alt Eggenberg (☎/fax 58 66 15, *Baiernstrasse 3)* Singles/ doubles €34/48. Sometimes known as Wagenhofer, this pension has rooms with bathroom, satellite TV, balconies and ageing fittings. There's also an inexpensive restaurant with a garden. The pension is west of the city centre but easily reached by tram No 1 (get off at the stop after Schloss Eggenberg).

Pension Köppel (☎/fax 58 55 47, *Göstinger Strasse 25)* Singles/doubles €35/56. This peaceful place, at the terminal of tram No 1, is welcoming and comfortable. Rooms have bathroom and satellite TV.

Das Wirtshaus Greiner (Map 13, #1; ☎ 68 50 90, fax 68 50 90-4, e das.wirtshaus .greiner@eunet.at, *Grabenstrasse 64)* Singles €32-62, doubles with shower/toilet and TV €43-72. Reception/restaurant open 11am-2.30pm & 6pm-midnight Mon-Fri. Phone ahead for check-in outside these times. North of Schlossberg, this small-scale place has very clean, renovated rooms. Price depends on size and aspect (some of the cheaper ones suffer traffic noise).

Pension Rückert (☎/fax 32 30 31, *Rückertgasse 4)* Singles/doubles €45/ 60. On a quiet residential street east of the town centre, this pension features renovated rooms with shower, toilet, satellite TV and other cheering touches; a lift is to be installed. Take tram No 1 to Tegetthoffplatz, walk 100m in the direction of the tram route then turn right.

Hotel Mariahilf (Map 14, #18; ☎ 71 31 63-0, fax 71 76 52, e office@hotelmariahilf.at, *Mariahilfer Strasse 9)* Singles/doubles with shower/toilet €59/102, with shower €30/51. This old hotel has large rooms – some are quite grand; others look like they've been furnished from a junk shop, though these are gradually being renovated. Phone ahead, as this place may become a residential home in a couple of years.

Grazerhof (Map 14, #33; ☎ 82 43 58, fax 81 96 33-40, w www.grazerhof.at, *Stubenberggasse 10)* Singles/doubles with private facilities €53/85, shared facilities €35/60. Prices are relatively high for a three-star place, but that's because it is the only hotel in the old centre. Rooms are standard though some are on the small side. The hotel adjoins two pedestrian streets, but the receptionist can tell you where to park.

Places to Stay – Top End

Hotel Drei Raben (Map 13, #16; ☎ 71 26 86, fax 71 59 59-6, e dreiraben@vivat.at, *Annenstrasse 43)* Singles €57-62, doubles €89-95, triples €117-120. This comfortable and convenient hotel has stylish rooms with bathroom and satellite TV and a smattering of modern art.

Hotel Erzherzog Johann (Map 14, #22; ☎ 81 16 16, fax 81 15 15, e office@erzher zog-johann.com, *Sackstrasse 3-5)* Singles/ doubles €102/157, €94/142 from Nov-March except over New Year. This hotel is central and housed in a 400-year-old building. Large, well-furnished, baroque-style rooms, with shower, toilet and TV, are built around a pleasant, plant-strewn atrium and guests have free use of the sauna. Nearby parking costs €13.10 per day.

Schlossberg Hotel (Map 14, #13; ☎ 80 70-0, fax 80 70-70, e office@schlossberg -hotel.at, *Kaiser Franz Josef Kai 30)* Singles €128-164, doubles €179-222. This charming four-star hotel is small enough for guests to receive personal service. Rooms (all with shower, toilet and TV) vary in size and style but all have character. There's a sauna and a fitness room, a summer swimming pool and a rooftop terrace.

Grand Hotel Wiesler (Map 14, #43; ☎ 70 66-0, fax 70 66-76, e wiesler@weitzer.com, *Grieskai 4)* Singles/doubles with all facilities €157/175. This is the only five-star hotel in town. Its elegant rooms exhibit subtle art-nouveau touches, though they vary greatly in size. Guests have free use of the sauna.

Places to Eat

Graz is an absolute bargain when it comes to cheap eats – you can get a good feed for lower prices than anywhere else in Austria. See also the bars listed in the Entertainment section for more eating options.

Self-Catering The main *food markets* are at Kaiser Josef Platz *(Map 14, #57)* and Lendplatz *(Map 14, #15)*; they're open from

7am to 1pm Monday to Saturday. There are also *fast-food stands* at Hauptplatz *(Map 14, #42)* and Jakominiplatz *(Map 14, #51)*. There are *Billa* supermarkets at Annenstrasse 23 *(Map 13, #17)* and in the below-ground Annen Passage *(Map 13, #13)*, opposite the Hauptbahnhof. *Laufke (Map 14, #5; ☎ 32 34 70-0, Elisabethstrasse 6)*, also called Elisabethhof, is open each weekday to 11pm; the restaurant and food store are expensive, but if you're stuck with nothing to eat late at night, they're an option.

Self-Service & Budget Aside from what's listed here, there are several cheap places near the university (Map 13, #3) that are popular with students: wander down Halbärthgasse, Zinzendorfgasse and Harrachgasse.

Zu den 3 Goldenen Kugeln (Map 13, #14; ☎ 71 43 00, Bahnhofgürtel 89) Meals €2.40-4.55. Open 9am-midnight daily. Schnitzel-dominated food at unbelievable prices: two course *Menütellers* for €2.40 – how do they do it? There's another branch *(Map 13, #23; ☎ 71 25 00)* at Griesplatz 4, and one *(Map 13, #2; ☎ 36 16 36)* at Heinrichstrasse 18.

Calafati (Map 13, #20; ☎ 71 68 89, Lissagasse 2) Meals €3.30-12. Open 11.30am-3pm & 5.30pm-11pm. Various Chinese restaurants are dotted round Graz, and most offer good value. Though this one is a little out of the way (near the Jugendgästehaus), it has decent food at minimal prices. Three-course lunches Monday to Saturday start at just €3.30.

Mensa (Map 13, #7; ☎ 33 362, Sonnenfelsplatz 1) Meals €3.60-4.10, salad/vegetable buffet €1.40-3.75, discounts for students. Open 8.30am-2.30pm Mon-Fri, closed 5-19 Aug. This university cafe has good food considering the prices.

Salateria (Map 13, #29; ☎ 38 32 39, Leonhardstrasse 18) Meals €2.65-5.55. Open 11am-7pm Mon-Thurs, 11am-3pm Fri, closed holidays. Near Goldene Kugel, this very cheap place concentrates on salads and veggies, though there are some meat choices.

Mangolds Vollwert Restaurant (Map 14, #44; ☎ 71 80 02, Griesgasse 11) Hot and cold buffets €1.15 per 100g. Open 11am-8pm Mon-Fri, 11am-4pm Sat, closed holidays.

This self-service place offers vegetarian delights, including various desserts.

RESOWI Mensa (Map 13, #4; ☎ 34 97 92, Universitätsstrasse 15) Meals €3.60-4.10. Open 8am-7pm Mon-Fri 31 Aug-17 Aug, 8am-2pm Sat Sept-May. This Mensa has less choice than others, but longer hours.

Mohrenwirt (Map 14, #19; ☎ 71 20 08, Mariahilfer Strasse 16) Dishes €1.45-9.45. Open 10am-midnight Sat-Wed. This small, old-fashioned Gasthof greets a local clientele. Ask about daily specials as they're not written down.

Feinspitz (Map 14, #21; ☎ 870-0, 2nd floor Kastner & Öhler Department Store, Sackstrasse 7–11) Meals €4.60-6.55. Open 9am-6.30pm Mon-Fri, 9am-5pm Sat. This buffet-style restaurant serves appealing main dishes and cheap snacks and drinks. Downstairs is a *Eurospar* supermarket.

Goldene Kugel (Map 13, #31; ☎ 32 31 08, Leonhardstrasse 32) 2-course weekday lunches €4.95-5.70; a la carte €5.40-10.40. Open 9am-1am Sun-Fri. This is a good place to try Austrian home cooking, not to mention about 50 different types of beer!

Girardikeller (Map 13, #30; ☎ 38 29 15, Leonhardstrasse 28) Meals €4-5.10. Open 5pm-2am Mon-Fri, 6pm-2am Sat, Sun & holidays. Near Goldene Kugel, this cellar bar has free live music most weekends from September to February. The food is very cheap – the weekday special is just €4, and big pizzas with five toppings cost €5.10.

Alt Wien (Map 14, #60; ☎ 82 95 84, Dietrichsteinplatz 2) Meals €4.60-9.20, salad buffet small/large plate €2.35/4.60. Open 10am-midnight Mon-Fri, closed holidays. This calm restaurant has friendly staff and competently-prepared Austrian food.

Cafes *Operncafé (Map 14, #53; ☎ 82 13 83, Opernring 22)* Cakes/coffee €1.85-5.10. Open 7.30am-midnight Mon-Sat, 9am-midnight Sun. This is a traditional Austrian coffee house. There's free piano music from 7pm on Wednesday.

Promenade (Map 14, #6; ☎ 81 38 40, Erzherzog Johann Allee 1) Open 9am-midnight daily. This cafe in the Stadtpark has decent food and outside seating.

Mid-Range & Top End *Restaurant Gösser Bräu (Map 14, #49; ☎ 82 99 09, Neutorgasse 48)* Dishes €5.70-14.55. Open 10am-midnight Mon-Fri, 9am-midnight Sun & holidays. This large place has many different rooms with a typical beer-hall ambience, and a garden terrace. A wide selection of local Gösser beers await (from €2.55 for 0.5L).

Gamlitzer Weinstube (Map 14, #25; ☎ 82 87 60, Mehlplatz 4) Meals €5.85-11.50. Open 9am-11pm Mon-Fri, closed holidays. This is a good place for Styrian dishes: try the *Steirerpfand'l* (€5.85), which is a tasty and filling combination of home-made spätzle (pasta), cheese, minced meat and mushroom sauce served in a pan. As with every other place nearby, there are outside tables on the square.

Zur Goldenen Pastete (Map 14, #10; ☎ 82 34 16, Sporgasse 28) Meals €7.65-13.85. Open 11am-midnight Mon-Sat, closed holidays. This is Graz's oldest inn, and serves affordable Styrian and vegetarian meals.

Restaurant Athen (Map 14, #59; ☎ 81 61 11, Dietrichsteinplatz 1) Dishes €6.40-17.80. Open 11am-midnight Mon-Sat, 5pm-midnight Sun & holidays. This Greek restaurant has live music on Friday night, when it's prudent to book ahead.

Landhaus Keller (Map 14, #34; ☎ 83 02 76, Schmiedgasse 9) Meals €9.80-19.90. Open 11.30am-midnight Mon-Sat, closed holidays. What started as a spit-and-sawdust pub in the 16th century eventually evolved into an atmospheric and high-quality restaurant. Flowers, coats of arms, medieval-style murals and soft background music contribute to the historical ambience. It serves interesting Styrian specialities as well as international dishes and vegetarian choices. In the summer, outside tables overlook the Landhaus courtyard.

Stainzerbauer (Map 14, #27; ☎ 82 11 06, Bürgergasse 4) 2-course weekday lunch €6.35, meals €6.70-20.70, evening cover charge €2.05. This place cooks up Styrian and Austrian specialities and has a courtyard garden. The set-price lunch is a bargain.

Wintergarten Restaurant (Map 14, #22; ☎ 81 16 16, Sackstrasse 3-5) Meals €12-18.50. Open 11.30am-2pm & 7pm-11pm Tues-Sun. Tucked away in the atrium of the Hotel Erzherzog Johann, this airy restaurant dispenses fine Austrian and international dishes. There's live piano music from 7pm to 1pm Thursday to Sunday.

Schauer (Map 14, #43; ☎ 70 66-83, Grieskai 4) Meals €17.50-22.60, cover charge €2.95. Open noon-2.30pm & 6pm-10pm daily. Located in the Grand Hotel Wiesler, this is a top spot for gourmet meals.

Entertainment

Bars *Grand Hotel Wiesler (Map 14, #43; ☎ 70 66-0, Grieskai 4)* Entry including buffet €31. This hotel is famous for its jazz brunch from 11am to 2pm on Sunday (early October to late June). It attracts well-known performers.

Babenbergerhof (Map 13, #10; ☎ 71 13 18, Babenbergerstrasse 39) Open 3pm-2am Mon-Fri, closed holidays. This smallish bar has live jazz (free) on Wednesday, and occasional impromptu jamming sessions. Anni, the vivacious English-speaking hostess, treats her customers as friends.

Café Harrach (Map 14, #4; ☎ 32 26 71, Harrachgasse 26) Open 9am-midnight weekdays, 7pm-midnight weekends. The area around the university has various places where you can mix with students, such as this cafe.

Bier Baron (Map 13, #5; ☎ 315 10, Heinrichstrasse 56) Open 11am-1am Mon-Sat. This large, busy bar is just north of the university. There are rows of gleaming silver beer pumps, a garden and reasonably priced Austrian meals.

Mehlplatz and Prokopigasse, in the centre of town, are full of relatively inexpensive, lively bars and cafes. They offer snacks or meals until late, and there's an accompanying hubbub of voices from countless outside tables. Like its Viennese parallel, this area has been dubbed the 'Bermuda Triangle'.

MI (Map 14, #24; ☎ 81 12 33, 3rd floor, Färberplatz) Open 10am-2am Mon-Sat, 4pm-midnight Sun. This three-storey bar and cafe offers many cocktails and a good view of the city, especially from the roof terrace.

Kommod (Map 14, #30; ☎ 82 91 39, Burggasse 15) Meals €5.75-7.05. Open

11.30am-2am Mon-Fri, 5pm-2am Sat, Sun & holidays. This bright and busy bar attracts a mostly youngish crowd. For later drinking, adjourn to *Triangel*, its cellar bar (open till 4am, closed Sunday and sometimes Monday).

Brot & Spiele (Map 14, #16; ☎ 71 50 81, Mariahilfer Strasse 17) Meals €4.65-10. Open 10am-2am Mon-Fri, 1pm-2am Sat, Sun & holidays. This games-oriented bar offers beer, Internet, chess, darts and lots of pool tables (€7 per hour). Food is served after 4pm.

Club avantgarde (Map 14, #14; ☎ 0676-615 17 84, Stockergasse 2) Open 5pm-2am Mon-Thur, 6pm-3am Fri & Sat. This mellow bar showcases local artists and has a free disco on Friday and Saturday. There's also a lesbian disco on Wednesday and occasional live alternative bands.

Bang (Map 13, #18; ☎ 71 95 49, Drei-hackengasse 4) Entry Fri & Sat €3.65, free other nights. Open 8pm-2am Wed & Thur, 9pm-4am Fri-Sat, 8pm-midnight Sun. This bar and disco has a mixed gay/straight clientele. There are also occasional cabaret shows – check **W** www.bang-inside.at.

Cinemas & Casino As in other cities, cinemas are cheaper on Monday (€5.50). The *Royal English Cinema (Map 13, #28; ☎ 826 133, Conrad von Hötzendorf Strasse 10)* screens English-language films. *Augarten-kino (Kiz) (Map 13, #25; ☎ 82 11 86, Friedrichgasse 24)* regularly shows films (mostly arthouse) in their original language (€6.20; €5.50 Monday to Wednesday; students €4.75). Graz *casino (Map 14, #41; ☎ 83 25 78)* is at Landhausgasse 10.

Theatre & Opera Graz is an important cultural centre, hosting musical events throughout the year, though the main venues, the *Schauspielhaus (theatre; Map 14, #8; ☎ 80 05, Hofgasse 11)* and *Opernhaus (opera; Map 14, #56; ☎ 80 08, Kaiser Josef Platz 10)*, are closed in August. Seats cost €8-38.90. Students aged under 27 pay half-price at these places. An hour before performances, students can buy leftover tickets for €5.85 at the venue, and anybody can buy standing-room tickets for €2.55 (theatre) or €2.95 (opera). Get performance details and tickets (no commission charged) for both venues at the *Tageskasse (Map 14, #55; ☎ 80 00, **W** www.buehnen-graz.com, Kaiser Josef Platz 10)* Open 8am-6.30pm Mon-Fri, 8am-1pm Sat. Check local listings for free musical and other events in various venues around town.

Shopping

Styria is known for painted pottery and printed linen. Other popular souvenirs include metal and china plates, steins, cow bells, dolls and statuettes. Quality handicrafts are available at *Steirisches Heimatwerk (Map 14, #39; ☎ 82 90 45, Herrengasse 10)*. Another souvenir shop in the town centre is *Kölz (Map 14, #23; ☎ 82 60 74, Hauptplatz 11)*. Opposite is *Niedermeyer (☎ 82 30 97-0, Hauptplatz 7)*, the photography and electrical goods chain. The *Kastner & Öhler* department store *(Map 14, #21; ☎ 870-0, Sackstrasse 7–11)* is north of Hauptplatz.

Citypark (Map 13, #22; ☎ 71 15 80-0, Lazarettgürtel 55) is a shopping centre with 75 shops to choose from (take bus No 35 from Jakominiplatz).

A *flea market* is held at Kelperstrasse 15 from 8am to 1pm every Saturday. Occasional handicrafts markets show up on Färberplatz.

Getting There & Away

Air The airport (☎ 29 02-0, **W** www .flughafen-graz.at) is 10km south of the town centre, just beyond the A2. Several flights a day go to/from Vienna, Frankfurt, Zürich and (not at weekends) Munich and Salzburg.

Bus Bundesbuses depart from outside the Hauptbahnhof (Map 13, # 12) and from the bus station at Andreas Hofer Platz (Map 14, #47), where there's a bus information office (☎ 81 18 18, open 7am to 6pm weekdays). GKB buses (☎ 0316-59 87-0) run to Piber and Bärnbach from Griesplatz (Map 13, #24). Watzke buses (☎ 0316-40 20 03) make the trip to the Austrian Open-Air Museum at Stübing, departing from Lendplatz (Map 13, #8).

STYRIA

Train Call ☎ 05-17 17 for train information. Direct IC trains to Vienna's Südbahnhof depart hourly (€24.75, two hours 40 minutes). Trains depart two-hourly to Salzburg (€33.45, four hours), either direct or requiring a change at Bischofshofen. All trains running north or west go via Bruck an der Mur (€7.70, 40 minutes, every 30 minutes), where it's sometimes necessary to change for onward travel. Even if you want to go south-west to Klagenfurt you still have to go north to Bruck first; the total trip takes about 3½ hours (€26.20, every two hours). Trains to eastern Styria via Graz's Ostbahnhof originate at the Hauptbahnhof.

Two direct trains depart daily for Zagreb (€27.10, 3½ hours). There are no direct services to Budapest. The quickest routing is via Vienna (€48.40, 6¾ hours), though going east via Szentgotthárd is cheaper (€33, 7½ hours, every two hours).

Car & Motorcycle The A2/E59 from Vienna to Klagenfurt passes a few kilometres south of the city. Leading north from the A2, the A9 passes under the city and emerges to take a north-west course to the Salzkammergut, with the S35 branching off to Bruck an der Mur. To the south, the A9 heads to Maribor in Slovenia.

Car Rental City offices include: Avis (Map 14, #58; ☎ 81 29 20), Schlögelgasse 10, and Hertz (Map 14, #45; ☎ 82 50 07), Andreas Hofer Platz 1. See the Getting Around chapter for rates. Steinbauer (Map 13, #21; ☎ 71 50 83), Fabriksgasse 29, near Citypark shopping centre, rents from €37 per day, and also sells and repairs cars.

Getting Around

To/From the Airport Bus No 631 runs from Jakominiplatz hourly between 5am and 10.20pm (€1.45, 18 minutes) – some of these start from the Hauptbahnhof (the bay by Café Steirertreff). From the Hauptbahnhof you can also take a train every one or two hours (€1.45, eight minutes).

Public Transport All of Graz is covered by one zone, zone 101. Single tickets (€1.45) are valid for one hour, and you can switch between buses, trams and the Schlossbergbahn. Ten one-zone tickets cost €11.65. A 24-hour pass costs €3.05, a weekly pass €7.30 and a monthly pass €25.80 (valid from first use in each case). If you buy a city pass, it reduces regional travel fares by one zone.

Hourly and 24-hour tickets can be purchased from the driver; the other passes can be purchased from Tabak shops, pavement ticket machines or the tourist office.

Other Transport You can park in areas marked as blue zones for a maximum of three hours between specified times (approximately shopping hours); buy tickets (*Parkschein*) at Tabak shops or the tourist office (€0.60 per 30 minutes).

To call a taxi, dial ☎ 2801, ☎ 878 or ☎ 889. Taxis cost €2.05 at taxi ranks or €2.65 if you phone for one, plus €0.95 per kilometre (€1.10 per kilometre between 8pm and 6am).

Around Graz

The Graz tourist office has brochures in English giving plenty of ideas for trips near Graz; most are within a 40km radius of the city.

STYRIAN WINE ROUTES

You can explore the Graz region by following different wine routes. The *Steirische Weinführer* booklet (in German), free from the Graz tourist office, has information on these so-called *Weinstrassen* (wine roads) and the various places where you can sample the beverages along the way. To explore these routes you really need your own transport, as the train will take you to only one or two points on a certain route. For example, it will get you to Gleisdorf, the starting point of the East Styria Roman Wine Road (Oststeirische Römerweinstrasse), but then takes a very circuitous diversion before it rejoins the main route at Hartberg. To try to follow a route by bus would be slow and tedious, involving many changes.

An alternative to driving a car is to hire a bicycle in Graz and take it on the train to one of the stations on a wine route. Deutschlandsberg is the main town on the Schilcher Wine Road (Schilcher Weinstrasse) and can be reached by hourly train from Graz (five zones from Graz, €6.55, one hour). The train terminates at Wies-Eibiswald, which is also the end of this wine route. Ehrenhausen is the start of the South Styria Wine Road (Südsteirischen Weinstrasse) and can be reached by hourly trains from Graz (five zones, €6.55, 45 minutes). Leibnitz, a station en route, is the start of the Sausaler Wine Road (Sausaler Weinstrasse).

DEUTSCHLANDSBERG
☎ 03462 • pop 7800 • elev 375m
This town (Map 12) is the centre of the production of Schilcher wine, a light, dry rosé. A good view of Deutschlandsberg can be had from **Burg Landsberg**, about 25 minutes' walk from the town centre: head west from Hauptplatz and take the first right turn after crossing the railway tracks. The castle also contains a museum of early history. On the festival of Corpus Christi (late May or early June), church altars in town are specially decorated with flowers.

The tourist office (☎ 75 20, fax 75 55, e tourismus.deutschlandsberg@netway.at), Hauptplatz 37, will help you sort out somewhere to stay. It's open 9am to noon and 3pm to 6pm Monday to Thursday, 9am to 3pm Friday, 9am to noon Saturday. From November to March hours reduce to 9am to 3pm weekdays, 9am to noon Saturday.

EHRENHAUSEN
☎ 03453 • pop 1200 • elev 258m
Ehrenhausen (Map 12) is smaller and more picturesque than Deutschlandsberg, and a better place to visit if you just want a fleeting glimpse of the wine region.

Orientation & Information
Hauptplatz (sometimes called Marktplatz) is the centre of the village, and has a bank and Bankomat. To walk there from the train station takes four minutes; turn left and cross

the stream, then turn right. The post office is by the station.

Ehrenhausen has no tourist office itself, but it comes under the jurisdiction of the Tourismusregionalverband Südsteirisches Weinland (☎ 03452-767 11, fax 715 60, e suedsteiermark@styria.com), Sparkassenplatz 4a, Leibnitz. Leibnitz is 7km north (one stop by train), and has a wider range of accommodation than Ehrenhausen.

Things to See & Do
Before embarking on the South Styria Wine Road there are a couple of things worth doing in town. The Eggenberg family was associated with Ehrenhausen, and purchased Schloss Ehrenhausen in 1543. A more interesting building, however, is the **mausoleum** of Ruprecht von Eggenberg (1546–1611), who was a hero in battles against the Turks. It rests on a plateau above Hauptplatz, and a path leads up just to the right of the Rathaus (less than 10 minutes' walk). The white and yellow building has two large warriors gazing down from the terrace. The stucco inside is starkly white, with many embellishments clinging to the central dome and vines swirling around supporting pillars. There's a good view from the terrace to Hauptplatz.

Before climbing up, get the key from the manse (*Pfarrhof*; ☎ 2633) next to the **Pfarrkirche** on Hauptplatz. Take the opportunity to explore the church itself: the altars inside are vivid baroque, with lots of gold and painted statues. Don't leave Ehrenhausen without admiring the view from the western end of Hauptplatz: the pastel colours of the houses in the foreground, topped by the church steeple and the mausoleum crowning the hill, form a fine picture.

Near Ehrenhausen is **Gamlitz**, where there's a good walking route (see the Walking & Skiing special section).

Places to Stay & Eat
There are several private rooms available in Ehrenhausen. The tourist office can supply details and phone places to check vacancies. If you're more independent-minded, you can figure out where to go because the places will have a sign outside on the wall.

STYRIA

Zur Goldenen Krone (☎/fax 26 40, *Hauptplatz 24*) Singles/doubles €26/48. This traditional, small-scale place has just eight rooms, so phone ahead. The rooms have private shower and toilet. English is not spoken.

To find somewhere to eat you need look no farther than Hauptplatz. It offers several choices.

Hauptplatz has a *Nah & Frisch* supermarket (through the Raiffeisen Bank arch); open 7.30am to 6pm weekdays, 7.30am to 12.30pm Saturday. There's also a market here on Friday afternoon.

Painer Gasthof & Fleischeri (☎ 24 08, *Hauptplatz 3*) Meals €4.40-11. Open 10am-10pm Wed-Mon. Right by the church, this no-frills place has tables inside and out, and serves inexpensive Austrian food.

AUSTRIAN OPEN-AIR MUSEUM

Seven provinces in Austria have open-air museums showing regional architecture. Styria's Österreichischen Freilichtmuseum (*Austrian Open-Air Museum; Map 12; ☎ 03124-53 700, W www.freilichtmuseum.at, adult/student/child €6.25/3.65/2.95; open 9am-5pm Tues-Sun 1 Apr-31 Oct, 9am-6.30pm Tues-Sun July & Aug*) in Stübing is the best to visit as you get to sample the whole country in one go. The main complex is about 2km from one end to the other and is arranged in order as if the visitor is walking through Austria from east to west. First comes Burgenland, then Styria, Carinthia, the Danube Valley, Salzburg, Tirol and finally Vorarlberg.

Two to three hours is sufficient for a visit. At the entrance, buy the detailed booklet (in English) for €2.20, giving a rundown on the 80-odd buildings in the complex. Smoking is not permitted in the complex, as most buildings are timber. Fresh bread is baked daily on site, or there is a restaurant outside.

Building No 20 is a west Styrian grocery, with old-fashioned goods on display and a few modern items for sale. No 38 is a Styrian schoolhouse with a classroom and an exhibition. Other highlights include the *sgraffito* decorations and unified structure of the farmhouse from Upper Austria (No 58),

the crisscross construction of the barn (No 56), and the Salzburg *Rauchhaus,* or smoke house (No 77), so-called due to the absence of a chimney – smoke was supposed to seep through chinks in the ceiling and dry grain in the loft. One exhibition hall provide the background to this and other European open-air museums (text in German); another traces the development of agriculture.

A notice board by the ticket office announces when country-craft demonstrations take place. As these don't occur on a regular basis, it's worth inquiring (by telephone or Internet) before planning your visit. The buildings tend to look a bit similar after a while, unless there's something happening to liven things up. At the end of September, **Erlebnistag,** a special fair with crafts, music and dancing, is held at the complex.

Getting There & Away

There are hourly trains from Graz to Stübing (two zones, €2.95, 15 minutes). From the train station, walk left for 20 minutes, eventually passing over the rail tracks, then under them just before the entrance. A Watzke bus (☎ 0316-40 20 03) goes to the museum Monday to Saturday, departing from Lendplatz bay 3 in Graz at 9am and 12.30pm (€2.95, 35 minutes), returning at 1.23pm and 4.40pm.

LURGROTTE

These caves, 20km north of Graz, are Austria's largest. They can be combined easily with the open-air museum on a day trip from Graz (do the caves first). The temperature in the caves is about 9°C.

There are two entrances to the Lurgrotte, and you can take a one-hour tour from either entrance. The eastern one is at Semriach (*Map 12; ☎ 03127-83 19, W www.lurgrotte -semriach.at; guided tours €4.75; tours 10am-4pm daily 15 Apr-31 Oct, 11am & 2pm Sat, Sun and holidays 1 Nov-14 Apr, in winter by arrangement*). Buses to Semriach depart Lendplatz in Graz every one or two hours (fewer Sunday; €4.10, 30 minutes). If you also want to visit the open-air museum, it's easier to use the western entrance to the caves at Peggau (*Map 12; ☎ 03127-25 80, W www.lurgrotte-peggau.networld.at; guided tours €5.10; tours 9am-4pm daily 1 Apr-31 Oct; in winter by arrangement).* Peggau is on the same train route as Stübing, and it's one zone farther from Graz (€4.10, 20 minutes, hourly). The caves are 15 minutes' walk from the station.

PIBER & KÖFLACH
☎ 03144

Piber's (Map 12) claim to fame is the world-famous Lipizzaner stallion stud farm, 3km from the small town of Köflach (Map 12).

Orientation & Information
Piber is about 40km west of Graz. Train travellers arrive first in Köflach, which has a tourist office (☎ 25 19-750, fax 25 19-777), Peter Rosegger Gasse 1, near Hauptplatz. Opening hours are 8am to 4.30pm Monday to Thursday, 7.30am to 1pm Friday. Staff can outline eating and sleeping options in town.

Piber Stud Farm
The Bundesgestüt Piber *(Piber Stud Farm;* ☎ 33 23, e piber@netway.at, Piber 1; *guided tour adult/senior/student €7.30/5.85/ 3.65; tours 9am-10.30am & 1.30pm-3.30pm Easter-31 Oct)* has been in operation since 1920 and now comes under the wing of the Ministry of Agriculture. The stud farm was moved here when the original location, Lipizza, became part of Slovenia after WWI. About 40 foals are born at the farm every year; of these only about five stallions are of the right height and aptitude to be sent to the Spanish Riding School *(Spanische Reitschule)* in Vienna for training, which lasts at least five years. Even before training, each stallion is worth about €15,000. Favoured veteran stallions return to the farm to breed the mares – currently, there are six different bloodlines. Foals are born dark and take between five and 12 years to achieve their distinctive white colouring.

Tours depart as soon as enough interested participants are assembled (it doesn't take long). Visitors see a film (with English commentary on the English tour – phone ahead for details) and museum exhibits, then tour the stables to meet some of the equine residents.

Lipizzaner mares resting on the farm

To reach the stud farm from Köflach station, walk up Bahnhofstrasse, turn right along Hauptplatz (300m) and then left for a 3km walk along Piberstrasse (signposted). Walking is a better option than cooling your heels at a bus stop, cursing the nonappearance of infrequent buses.

Gasthof Bardel (☎ *34 22, Fesselweg 1)* Singles/doubles €26/44. This Gasthof, also known as Gasthof Ross-Stuberl, is right next to the stud farm. It offers modern rooms with shower and toilet, and affordable Austrian food.

Getting There & Away
Köflach is the final stop for GKB private trains running approximately hourly from Graz (50 minutes). The fare is €5.25 one-way, or €10.05 for a 24-hour pass. The same tickets are valid for GKB buses from Graz, leaving from Griesplatz and (less frequently) Lendplatz. For information call GKB (☎ 03 16-59 87-281).

BÄRNBACH
☎ 03142 ● pop 5160 ● elev 432m

This small town (Map 12) is worth visiting primarily for the unique St Barbara Kirche, and can easily be combined with a trip to Piber. From the stud farm, return to Piberstrasse and then walk (buses are as rare as non-skiing Austrians) about 2km east (away from Köflach). You can't miss the church on the main road. Continue in the same direction for Hauptplatz and, across the stream, the glass-making centre. A left turn at Hauptplatz will take you into Hauptstrasse and the road to the **Alt Kainach castle** (2km), which contains historical exhibits. Get tourist information from Bärnbach town hall (☎ 615 50, **e** stadtgemeinde.post@gv.baernbach.at).

Things to See & Do

Although built after WWII, **St Barbara Kirche** (☎ 625 81, Piberstrasse; open daylight hours) needed renovating in the late 1980s. About 80% of the town population voted to commission the maverick Viennese artist Friedensreich Hundertwasser to undertake the redesign; work began in 1987 and was completed in 1988. It was a bold move: Hundertwasser was known for his unusual design concepts, particularly in discarding the straight line in building projects (for more on Hundertwasser, turn to the boxed text 'Peace Empire and a Hundred Waters' in the Vienna chapter). The gamble paid off; the church is a visual treat inside and out, yet is still clearly a place of worship rather than a pseudo art gallery. Leave a donation and pick up the explanation card in English, which reveals the symbolic meaning behind the architectural design features.

The church is surrounded by 12 gates, each representing a different faith: Hinduism, Islam and so on, all connected by an uneven pathway. By the west facade is a powerful mosaic war memorial by Franz Weiss. The distinctive church steeple is topped by a gold onion dome. Features you wouldn't see in any other church include the bowed roof with green splodges along its flanks, the irregular windows, and the grass growing on the side porch roofs.

The interior also has striking and thoughtful touches: Hundertwasser's 'spiral of life' window (which reflects the afternoon sun onto the font); the modern-art Stations of the Cross by Rudolf Pointer; the glass altar and podium filled with 12 layers of different types of earth representing the 12 tribes of

Glassblowing in Bärnbach

Glass is made from silica (usually sand), which is fused at high temperatures with borates or phosphates. Glass has been made for nearly 6000 years, though glassblowing with the aid of a pipe began only about 2000 years ago.

Glassblowers have plied their trade in the Bärnbach region for 300 years. In the old days they would establish camps in the forest, to make it easier to collect the 5000kg of wood that was required to produce 2kg of glass. The wood was needed to create potash, as well as to fire the ovens. Other materials required were quartz sand and lime.

The glass-making methods used in the Stölzle Glas Center are not substantially different to ones used all those years ago in the forest camps. The glass is melted in a large tank furnace which always contains about eight tonnes of glass (over one tonne is used per day). The glass is kept molten at a temperature of 1200°C: The furnace is kept at this temperature 24 hours a day. If the furnace is ever shut off, it has to be done gradually, to avoid the risk of an explosion (to go from 1200°C to room temperature would require between five and seven days!).

The glassblower uses a 1.2m-long hollow iron pipe with a mouthpiece at one end. The end of the pipe is used to collect a small amount of molten glass, which the glassblower expands by blowing into the pipe. Several different glassblowers will work in turn on the same piece. It's necessary to periodically reheat the glass while it's being worked, using special ovens called muffels. Any handles or decorative pieces are added when the glass is hot, then it's placed in the cooling oven. It is cooled slowly (a process called annealing, which reduces brittleness) and each piece takes around four or five hours to pass through the 30m-long cooling oven.

The glass object is then ready to be cut, engraved, enamelled or painted to produce the finished product. A range of glassware can be admired and purchased in the factory shop.

CHRIS MELLOR

CHRIS MELLOR

CHRIS MELLOR

CHRIS MELLOR

The various faces of time in Tirol

Gustav Klimt, *Portrait of Hermine Gallia*

Friedensreich Hundertwasser, *10002 Nights – Homo Humus Come Va – How Do You Do*

A floral display with a musical theme at Vienna's Schloss Esterházy

Israel; and the harmonious ceramics surrounding the image of Christ on the Cross in the chancel.

Also worth seeing is the **Mosesbrunnen** (Moses Fountain), in the Stadtpark on Hauptstrasse, created by Ernst Fuchs in Hunderwasseresque style.

Bärnbach has been known for its glassmaking for at least two centuries. The museum at the **Stölzle Glas Center** (☎ 629 50, **w** www.stoelzle.at, Hochtregisterstrasse 1; adult/family €5.45/11.65; open 9am-5pm Mon-Fri, 9am-1pm Sat early Apr-15 Dec, also 9am-1pm Sun & holidays May-Oct) is dedicated to glass. Included in the price is a one hour tour of the factory. Guided tours are conducted in German (although you can phone ahead and request the English version) and commence at 9am, 10am and 11am and noon Monday to Thursday, and at 9am, 10am and 11am on Friday.

Places to Stay & Eat

There's an information board by the church, which lists local facilities, including the limited accommodation options – these are confined to a few small guesthouses.

Gästehaus Lackner Hatzl (☎ 625 85, Hauptstrasse 62) Singles/doubles €22 per person. This 18-bed place is conveniently central.

There's a *Billa* supermarket at Hauptplatz 2, next to the town hall. Rooms have shower, toilet and TV.

Ratskeller Bärnbach (☎ 620 20, Schulstrasse 1) Meals €5.50-12. Open 9am-6pm Sun-Wed, 9am-10pm Thur-Sat. Close to the church, this Gasthaus turns out decent Austrian food and has outside tables.

Gasthaus Alten Lind (☎ 615 00, Hauptstrasse 1) Meals €4.50-10. Open 9am-midnight Tues-Sun. This is another good choice for inexpensive Austrian food.

Getting There & Away

Bärnbach is on the Graz-Köflach train line, one stop (five minutes) before Köflach. The train station is 2km out of the town centre. To get to the train station from St Barbara Kirche, go to Hauptplatz and turn right down Dr Niederdorfer Strasse; continue until the

rail tracks pass under the road, then take the next left. GKB Graz-Köflach buses stop in Bärnbach town centre.

Elsewhere in Styria

If you have time on your hands to explore the province of Styria you'll uncover some unusual and engaging sites.

MARIAZELL
☎ 03882 ● pop 2000 ● elev 868m

Mariazell is the most important pilgrimage site in Austria. It was founded in 1157 and a number of miracles have since been attributed to the Virgin of Mariazell, including Lewis I of Hungary's unlikely victory over the Turks in 1357. The town will be most crowded with pilgrims on 15 August (Assumption) and 8 September (Mary's 'name day').

Orientation

Mariazell is in the extreme north of Styria, close to Lower Austria and within the lower reaches of the eastern Alps. The train station is in St Sebastian, 1.5km north of Hauptplatz, the centre of Mariazell.

Information

Staff at Mariazell's tourist office (Map 15, #6; ☎ 23 66, fax 39 45, **e** tv-mzl@kom.at), Hauptplatz 13, will find rooms without charging. Ask about reductions given with the Gästekarte. Opening hours are 9am to 12.30pm and 2pm to 5.30pm Monday to Friday, 9am to 12.30pm and 2pm to 4pm Saturday, and (not in October) 9am to noon Sunday, May to October. Opening hours for the rest of the year are 9am to noon and 2pm to 5pm Monday to Friday, and 9am to noon Saturday.

The post office (Map 15, #10; Postamt A-8630), Ludwig Leber Strasse, is just west of Hauptplatz. Café Faro (Map 15, #5; ☎ 37 13), Hauptplatz 8, has Internet access (€0.10 per minute, closed Wednesday).

Monday is the quietest day of the week, so many hotels and restaurants take their rest day then.

STYRIA

MAP 15 – MARIAZELL

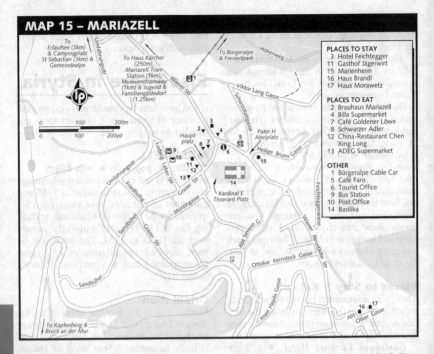

PLACES TO STAY
3 Hotel Feichtegger
11 Gasthof Jägerwirt
15 Marienheim
16 Haus Brandl
17 Haus Morawetz

PLACES TO EAT
2 Brauhaus Mariazell
4 Billa Supermarket
7 Café Goldener Löwe
8 Schwarzer Adler
12 China-Restaurant Chen Xing Long
13 ADEG Supermarket

OTHER
1 Bürgeralpe Cable Car
5 Café Faro
6 Tourist Office
9 Bus Station
10 Post Office
14 Basilika

Basilika

This church *(Map 15, #14;* ☎ *25 95, Kardinal Eugen Tisserant Platz 1; admission free; open 8am-8pm daily)* is Mariazell's *raison d'être* and most visible feature. The original Romanesque church was converted to Gothic in the 14th century, then expanded and refitted as baroque in the 17th century. The result from the outside is a strange clash of styles, with the original Gothic steeple bursting like a wayward skeletal limb from between two baroque onion domes. The interior works better, with Gothic ribs on the ceiling combining well with baroque frescoes and lavish stuccowork. Both Johann Bernhard Fischer von Erlach and his son Josef Emmanuel had a hand in the baroque face-lift; the crucifixion group (1715) on the high altar is by Lorenzo Mattielli.

In the centre of the church is the **Gnaden-kapelle** (Chapel of Miracles), a gold and silver edifice that houses the Romanesque statue of the Madonna. Within the church is

the **Schatzkammer** *(treasury;* ☎ *25 95, Kardinal Eugen Tisserant Platz 1; adult/student/child €2.95/1.50/1.10; open 10am-3pm Tues-Sat, 11am-4pm Sun & holidays 1 May-26 Oct).* The treasury contains votive offerings spanning six centuries, mainly naïve paintings.

Activities

Skiers have the chance to throw themselves downhill from **Bürgeralpe** (1270m); a day pass costs €22.50 (children €12). There are a couple of restaurants at the top. In summer, Bürgeralpe offers many different hiking trails and a **Freizeitpark,** or leisure park (Erlebniswelt Holzknechtland; open 9am to 5pm daily, May to October), with a museum showing different uses of wood. The cable car (Map 15, #1) fare for adults is €5.85/8.40, or €8.75/10.90 including entry to Freizeitpark.

Gemeindealpe (1626m) is 5km northwest of Mariazell overlooking Mitterbach, but its chair lift is closed indefinitely.

From either peak you'll get a good view of **Erlaufsee**. This lake lies a few kilometres north-west of Mariazell and provides good opportunities for water sports such as windsurfing and scuba diving. Contact addresses of bodies running such sports are listed in the booklet *Mariazellerland von A-Z*, which is available free from the tourist office. A novel way of getting to the lake is by the steam **Museumstramway** (€5.85 return), which runs at weekends and on holidays between July and September. It leaves from the Museumstramway Bahnhof.

Places to Stay

Campingplatz St Sebastian (☎ 49 37, fax 21 8-22) Adult/tent/car €3.65/2.95/2.20. Open 1 May-mid Sept. This small camping ground is at the south-eastern end of Erlaufsee.

Jugend & Familiengästedorf (☎ 26 69, fax 26 69-88, e jgh.mariazellerland@jgh.at, Erlaufseestrasse 49) Bed in 2-6 bed dorm €16. This HI hostel is located in a new building at the Freizeitzentrum sports centre in St Sebastian.

There's a smattering of private houses. These are a good option for budget accommodation, but phone ahead as places only have a few rooms.

Haus Brandl (Map 15, #16; ☎ 28 66, Abt Otker Gasse 3) Doubles with shower/toilet €30.60. This pleasant house, south-east of Hauptplatz, has rooms available in the summer only.

Haus Morawetz (Map 15, #17; ☎ 21 94, Abt Otker Gasse 7) Doubles with shower/toilet and TV €30 in summer, €33.50 in winter; add €3.65 for single night stay.

Haus Kärcher (☎ 39 32, Wiener Strasse 70) Singles/doubles with shower/toilet €13.10-32, depending on length of stay. This house offers 10 rooms, and is situated mid-way between the train station and the Basilica. There's a garden, sauna and car parking.

Marienheim (Map 15, #15; ☎ 25 45, fax 49 71, Pater H Abelplatz 3) Reception 8am-1pm and 3pm-8pm. Singles/doubles with private shower/toilet €25/50 in summer, €28/56 in winter; with shared shower €19/38 in summer, €22/44 in winter. This place provides a calm and peaceful setting. Well, it is run by nuns!

There are plenty of elegant three- and four-star hotels on or around Hauptplatz.

Gasthof Jägerwirt (Map 15, #11; ☎ 23 62, fax 43 53, e jaegerwirt@netway.at, Hauptplatz 2) Singles/doubles €34/54. This hotel is in a fine location and offers standard three-star rooms with shower, toilet and TV. It also serves good, traditional Austrian meals for around €10.

Hotel Feichtegger (Map 15, #3; ☎ 24 16-0, fax 24 16-80, e feichtegger@net way.at, Wiener Strasse 6) Singles €34-49, doubles €68-98. This four-star hotel has loads of facilities, including a swimming pool. All rooms have shower, toilet and TV.

Places to Eat

There's an *ADEG* supermarket (Map 15, #13) on Grazer Strasse and a *Billa* (Map 15, #4) just north of the tourist office.

Hauptplatz has many cafes and hotel restaurants, and it's easy to compare menus before deciding.

China-Restaurant Chen Xing Long (Map 15, #12; ☎ 25 91, Hauptplatz 3) Meals €4.40-9. Open 11am-11pm daily. Next door to Gasthof Jägerwirt, this restaurant is particularly worth visiting for its cheap weekday lunches. It also does Austrian food.

Café Goldener Löwe (Map 15, #7; ☎ 24 44, Hauptplatz 1a) Meals €5.25-9.50. Open 9am-7pm Tues-Sun. Meals are served either inside or on the outside terrace overlooking the church. Men should visit the toilet upstairs to meet the Piss-Wand, a metal figure, which will join in while you urinate.

Schwarzer Adler (Map 15, #8; ☎ 28 63-0, Hauptplatz 1) Meals €6.50-14.60. Open 9am-11pm daily. Next door to Café Goldener Löwe, this upmarket hotel restaurant serves affordable set meals or more expensive à la carte dishes. It also has an outside terrace.

Brauhaus Mariazell (Map 15, #2; ☎ 25 23-0, Wiener Strasse 5) Meals €6.60-16. Open 10am-11pm Fri-Wed. This Gasthof brews its own beer and serves mid-price Austrian and Styrian food to help wash it down.

STYRIA

Getting There & Away

A narrow-gauge train departs from St Pölten, 85km to the north, every two to three hours. It's a slow 2½-hour trip (€10.90), though the scenery is good for the last hour. The ÖBB plans to close this line sometime after June 2002, though it is hoped a private buyer will take over the route before then. Unless you have a car, the only way to travel on without returning to St Pölten is to take the bus. There are several routes heading south, departing from the bus station (Map 15, #9) next to the post office. At least four Bundesbuses a day depart for Bruck an der Mur (€7.70, 100 minutes) with two continuing to Graz (€13.85, three hours in total). For bus information call ☎ 23 66 or ☎ 01-711 01.

BRUCK AN DER MUR

☎ 03862 ● pop 15,000 ● elev 491m

Bruck is at the confluence of the Mur and Mürz rivers (the Mürz is actually a significant waterway, but they probably decided 'Bruck an der Mur und der Mürz' was too much of a mouthful). The town is at the junction of routes to all four points of the compass. If you're passing through, it deserves a quick perusal.

Orientation & Information

The train station and a post office (Map 16, #1; Postamt A-8600) are at the eastern end of Bahnhofstrasse, and money can be exchanged at either; there's also a Bankomat here. Walk down Bahnhofstrasse and bear left at the roundabout for the town centre, Koloman Wallisch Platz. On the north side of the square you'll find the tourist office (Map 16, #7; ☎ 890-121, fax 890-102, e stadtmarketing@bruckmur.at) in the Rathaus. Updated computerised information is accessible daily. There's also another post office (Map 16, #15) on the Platz.

Things to See & Do

Several paths wind up to the ruins of Schloss Landskron (Map 16, #4); the walk takes less than 10 minutes. Not much of the castle remains except a clock tower and a few cannons, and you don't quite gain enough height for an enhanced view, but at least it provides a pleasant setting for a picnic. One path leads to Bauernmarkt, where there's a food and flower market (Wednesday and Saturday) beside the 15th-century Gothic Pfarrkirche (parish church; Map 16, #8).

The remaining sights in Bruck are on Koloman Wallisch Platz. The Rathaus (Map 16, #7) has an arcaded courtyard. The Kornmesserhaus (Map 16, #6) has an attractive arcaded frontage with fussy ornamentation that betrays both Gothic and Renaissance influences. This late-15th-century building was erected at the behest of a rich merchant, Pankraz Kornmess, for whom it is named. There are other old historic houses lining the square, though the building at No 10 is more recent and boasts an Art Nouveau facade (Map 16, #12).

On the square itself is a fine Renaissance-style wrought-iron well (Map 16, #10) created by Hans Prasser in 1626. Also here is the Mariensäule (Map 16, #13), a column dedicated to the Virgin Mary erected in 1710 after the town survived fire, plague and flooding.

Bruck is filled with street performers on the first Friday in August for the Murenschalk free festival. North-west of Bruck are some Alpine lakes such as the tiny but scenic Grünersee (Map 12), about 25km from the town, near the source of the Laming River.

Places to Stay & Eat

There are only a few hotels in Bruck.

Jugend und Familiengästedorf (☎ 584 58, fax 584 58-88, e jgh.bruck@oejhv.or.at, Stadtwaldstrasse 1) Bed in 2-5 bed room with shower/toilet €16.75, singles €20.35. This family-friendly HI hostel is in the woods 10 minutes' walk south of the centre.

Gasthof Koppelhuber (Map 16, #2; ☎ 516 38, Pischerstrasse 11) Singles/doubles with shared shower €24.50/34.60, breakfast €4.40. Elderly hostess, elderly large rooms – this is very much a time warp experience. Take the stairs down to the left immediately after leaving the train station.

Gasthof Pension Malissa (Map 16, #11; ☎ 511 58, fax 518 08, Koloman Wallisch Platz 9) Singles/doubles €29.10/47.25. Reception and restaurant open 8am-midnight

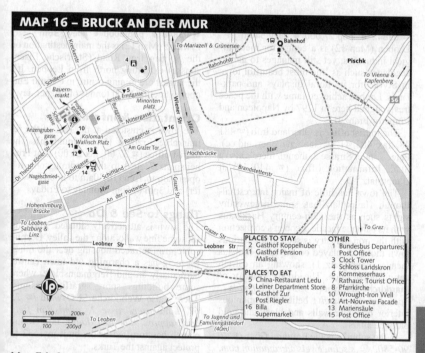

MAP 16 – BRUCK AN DER MUR

PLACES TO STAY	OTHER
2 Gasthof Koppelhuber	1 Bundesbus Departures;
11 Gasthof Pension	Post Office
Malissa	3 Clock Tower
	4 Schloss Landskron
PLACES TO EAT	6 Kornmesserhaus
5 China-Restaurant Ledu	7 Rathaus; Tourist Office
9 Leiner Department Store	8 Pfarrkirche
14 Gasthof Zur	10 Wrought-Iron Well
Post Riegler	12 Art-Nouveau Facade
16 Billa	13 Mariensäule
Supermarket	15 Post Office

Mon-Fri, 8am-noon Sat, closed holidays. This Gasthof has just three rooms, each with shower and toilet. Soft colours, newish decor and homey touches add up to a decent deal. The restaurant has a pleasant ambience but a limited range of Austrian snacks and meals for €1.75 to €9.20.

Provisions can be purchased at the **Billa** supermarket (Map 16, #16), Am Grazerhof 1.

Leiner Department Store (Map 16, #9; ☎ 535 58-0, 4th floor, Dr Theodore Körner Strasse 8–10) Open 8.30am-6pm Mon-Fri, 8.30am-5pm Sat. The self-service restaurant has a hot and cold buffet that costs €5.75 from 11am to 2.30pm and just €3.60 from 2.30pm to 3pm. Before 11am it's breakfast time (€2.85).

China-Restaurant Ledu (Map 16, #5; ☎ 521 59, Herzog Ernstgasse 15) Meals €6-10. Open 11.30am-2.30pm & 5.30pm-11.30pm daily. A good deal here is the three-course lunch buffet (not available Sunday) for €5.70.

Gasthof Zur Post Riegler (Map 16, #14; ☎ 549 04, Koloman Wallisch Platz 11) Meals €5.40-15.70. Open 9am-midnight Mon-Sat. This Gasthof has a varied menu, including traditional Styrian and vegetarian meals, as well as interesting daily specials. There are several dining rooms of varying formality and some outside tables for more relaxed meals.

Getting There & Away

Bruck is the main rail hub for the region; all fast trains to Graz (€7.70, 40 minutes, every 30 minutes) go via Bruck. Other major destinations include Vienna's Süd-bahnhof (€19.65, two hours, hourly), Klagenfurt (€21.10, 2½ hours, every two hours) and Linz (€23.30, three hours, every two hours).

By road, the main autobahns intersect to the south-east of the town. If you're planning to cycle in the region, the tourist office can supply some useful maps.

STYRIA

LEOBEN

☎ 03842 ● pop 27,000 ● elev 540m

Leoben (Map 12) is a centre for metallurgical industries, yet still manages to garner accolades such as 'the most beautiful town in Styria' for its floral displays and parklands. Leoben achieved fame with the peace treaty signed here in 1797 by Napoleon and Emperor Franz II.

The tourist office is Oberland Info (☎ 481 48, fax 483 41, **e** leoben@oberland.cc), Peter Tunner Strasse 2, though there's also a Stadt Information office (☎ 440 18) at Hauptplatz 12.

The town has little of major interest, although Hauptplatz has some noteworthy sights such as the 17th-century **Hacklhaus** with its baroque facade. Leoben's connection with the iron industry is seen in the curious town motif (displayed on the Altes Rathaus facade, Hauptplatz 1), showing an ostrich eating horseshoes. The dreary exterior of **Pfarrkirche St Xaver** (☎ 432 36, Kirchplatz 1; open 8am-7pm daily) belies a harmonious interior of white walls and black-and-gold baroque altars.

In the suburbs is the **Brauerei Göss** (☎ 20 90-5802, **e** s.schneeweis@brauunion.com, Gösser Platz 1; adult/student €4.40/2.20; open 9am-6pm Sat & Sun), which makes Gösser beer. Entry includes a tour (at 11am, 1pm and 3pm), the museum and a sample.

Leoben town centre has no budget accommodation, although you can eat cheaply in and around Hauptplatz. Ask at the tourist office if you need to find a place to stay.

Mensa (☎ 451 07, Franz Josef Strasse 18) Lunches €3.60-4.90. Open 7.30am-2pm Mon-Fri, hot food 11am-1.30pm. This self-service cafeteria is open to all. It's near the train station, en route to Hauptplatz.

Getting There & Away

Leoben is 16km west of Bruck and is on the main rail route from there to Klagenfurt or Linz. The town centre is 10 minutes' walk from Leoben Hauptbahnhof: cross the Mur and bear right. The brewery is 1.5km south of Leoben-Göss Bahnhof (only two-hourly regional trains stop), or city buses go there from Leoben centre (€1.50).

EISENERZ

☎ 03848 ● pop 6000 ● elev 736m

Eisenerz (Map 12) is the main destination on the Styrian Iron Road (Steirische Eisenstrasse) extending north from Leoben. It's the largest ore mining centre in Central Europe, extracting 8000 tonnes of ore per day.

Orientation & Information

The town is clustered at the foot of the remarkable Erzberg (Iron Mountain). The tourist office (☎ 37 00, fax 21 00) is at Freiheitsplatz 7, next to the Stadtmuseum. It's open 9am to 1pm (10.30am to noon in winter) and 3pm to 5pm Monday to Friday.

Things to See & Do

The town is attractively situated, allowing for some fine walks along the valley. Despite some grim terraced housing near the mine, Eisenerz has a charming old town centre, particularly around Bergmannsplatz, where some buildings sport sgraffito designs. There's also **Wehrkirche St Oswald** (☎ 22 67, Lindmoserstrasse 2; admission free; open approx 9am-5pm daily); this Gothic church has fortified walls, built in 1532 to protect against the Turks.

The **Stadtmuseum** (☎ 36 15, Schulstrasse 1; adult/senior/student €3.30/2.20/1.35; open 9am-5pm Mon-Fri, 10am-noon & 2pm-5pm Sat May-Oct, 9am-noon Mon-Fri Nov-Apr) covers history, folklore and mining.

The main reason to come to Eisenerz is the **Erzberg**. This peak has been completely denuded by opencast stope mining to such an extent that it resembles a step pyramid. The outcome is surprisingly beautiful, with its orange and purple shades contrasting with the lush greenery and grey crags of surrounding mountains.

The **Erzberg ironworks** (☎ 32 00, fax 32 00-22, **e** erzberg@steirer-oberland.co.at, **w** www.abenteuer-erzberg.at, Erzberg 1; tours adult/student €12.75/5.85, combined ticket €21.50/10.55; tours 10am-3pm 1 May-31 Oct) can be visited in two ways. Firstly, a 90-minute 'Schaubergwerk' tour burrows into the mountain to the underground mines, abandoned in 1986 (guaranteed tours at 10am, 12.30pm and 3pm). Secondly, the

'Hauly Abenteuerfahrt' is a one-hour tour of the surface works aboard a huge truck, with fine views along the way (reserve ahead). Both tours are usually in German, with English-language notes available. The departure point is a 10-minute walk from the centre, following the course of the river.

Places to Stay & Eat

Staff at the tourist office will help you find somewhere to stay. There are few private rooms.

Bräustüberl *(☎ 23 35, Flutergasse 5)* Singles/doubles €22/37. Snacks/meals €3.50-12.75. Reception/restaurant open 9am-midnight Tues-Sat, 9am-2pm Sun. This central place has a few new-looking rooms with shower and toilet, and excellent food in its wood-lined restaurant (closed on Monday).

Zur Post *(☎ 22 32, Lindmoserstrasse 10)* Singles/doubles €23/38. Meals €4-7.70. Reception/restaurant open 9am-midnight Tues-Sun. This place has indifferent staff, darkish rooms with shower, toilet and (usually) TV, but it's inexpensive and convenient.

Gästehaus Weninger *(☎ 22 58-0, fax 22 58-5, e weninger@eisenerz.com, Krumpentalerstrasse 8)* Singles €28-36, doubles €41-49, apartments sleeping 2-4 €37. This central place has bright, comfortable rooms with shower, toilet, cable TV and telephone, and a garden.

There are a couple of supermarkets in town, as well as a few snack places.

Imbiss Moser *(☎ 30 95, Dr Karl Renner Strasse 9)* Snacks/meals €1.35-6.90. Open 7.30am-noon & 3pm-10pm Mon-Fri, 7.30am -noon Sat. Simple meals are available either in the deli shop or the sit-down bar area.

Getting There & Away

From Leoben, Bundesbus services run north to Eisenerz every one or two hours (€5.25, one hour). They're about the same frequency from Eisenerz to Hieflau (€2.95, 25 minutes), where there are train connections to Selzthal.

Trains no longer operate to Eisenerz, except for the special Vordernberg-Eisenerz *Nostalgie* (nostalgic) train (☎ 03849-832, w www.erzbergbahn.at), which only runs on Sunday in the summer.

ADMONT

☎ 03613 ● pop 2900 ● elev 641m

This small town (Map 12) at the entrance to the Gesäuse Valley is known for its **Benedictine abbey** *(☎ 23 12-601, Admont 1; entry €4.40; open 10am-1pm & 2pm-5pm daily 1 Apr-31 Oct)*. The most important part of the abbey for visitors is the *Stiftsbibliothek* (abbey library), survivor of a fire in 1865 that severely damaged the rest of the abbey. It displays 150,000 volumes, and has ceiling frescoes by Bartolomeo Altomonte. The best features are the statues (in wood, but painted to look like bronze) by Josef Stammel (1695–1765), especially the *Four Last Things* series. To understand the symbolism inherent in these works, buy the leaflet in English (€0.40). The abbey museum collections are closed until 2003; when they re-open they'll be much expanded, covering history, modern art, and religious relics. The abbey is 10 minutes' walk from the train station – turn left on leaving the station, then take the second right-hand turn.

The tourist office (☎ 21 64, fax 36 48, e tourismus@admont.at) is near the abbey church at Hauptplatz 36; it's open weekdays and, from July to September, on Saturday morning.

There are also a couple of pensions and places to eat near the abbey.

Jugendherberge *(☎ 24 32, fax 279 583)* Bed in 6-bed dorm/double with private bathroom €13.50/24.80 per person; some with TV. Check-in 7am-10pm, closed 1 Nov-27 Dec. Phone ahead as it fills up with school groups. This HI hostel has luxurious rooms, and is sited in splendour in Schloss Röthelstein. The castle is clearly visible above the trees, but the only way up is by a looping 3km road (no buses).

Getting There & Away

Admont is 15km to the east of Selzthal, on the route to Hieflau; trains run every two hours.

MURAU

☎ 03532 ● pop 2500 ● elev 830m

The Liechtenstein family was once dominant in the Murau (Map 12) region and built **Schloss Obermurau** *(☎ 27 20, Schlossberg 1; interior tours €2.20, 3pm Wed & Fri 13 June-14 Sept)* in 1250. This was taken over by the Schwarzenberg family and converted to a Renaissance building in the 17th century.

Dating from the 13th century, **Stadtpfarrkirche St Matthäus** *(St Matthew's Church; ☎ 24 89, Schlossberg 8; open daylight hours)* is yet another Gothic church that was remodelled in baroque style. Both elements work well together, as in the combination of the Gothic crucifixion group (1500) and the baroque high altar (1655). The frescoes date from the 14th to 16th century. Enjoy the view of the church, castle and scenic centre from across the river, near the train station.

The local Murau Brewery has a **brewery museum** *(☎ 326 60, Raffaltplatz 19–23; entry €2.95; open 3pm-5.30pm Wed & Fri July-Sept)*.

Skiing and walking are enjoyed on the nearby 2000m peaks, Kreischberg (Map 12) and Frauenalpe.

Places to Stay & Eat

If you decide to linger overnight, staff at the tourist office (☎/fax 27 20, ℮ tourismus@ murau.at) by the train station will sort out a pension or private room.

Jugend & Familiengästehaus (☎ 23 95, fax 23 95-88, ℮ jgh.murau@jgh.at, St Leonhard Platz 4) Bed in 2-7 bed room with shower/toilet €14.70-22.60. This HI hostel has modern facilities.

Gasthof Bärenwirt (☎ 20 79, fax 20 79-4, Schwarzenbergstrasse 4) Doubles with/ without private shower and toilet €51/32. Meals €5.90-12. Reception/restaurant open 7am-midnight Sun-Fri, 7am-2pm Sat. This central place has convenient rooms and serves inexpensive regional food (till 9pm).

The *Murau Brauerei (☎ 326 60, Raffaltplatz 19–23)* has a restaurant and beer cellar.

Getting There & Away

Murau is on Hwy 96 between Tamsweg and Judenburg. Murau is also on a narrow-gauge private line connecting Unzmarkt and Tamsweg (€5.25, 40 minutes); Inter-Rail and Eurail passes aren't valid. Departures are only every two or four hours, and there are even fewer on weekends. More of a tourist excursion than a mode of transport is the steam train that chugs between Murau and Tamsweg up to three times a week in the summer. For information, visit **w** www.stlb .co.at or call ☎ 03532-2231-0.

BAD BLUMAU

☎ 03383

Fans of the architectural style of Friedensreich Hundertwasser won't want to miss this unusual place (Map 12). It's a whole health resort designed by him and featuring his characteristic trademarks – uneven floors, grass on the roof, colourful ceramics and golden spires; it opened in May 1997.

Rogner-Bad Blumau Hotel (☎ 5100-0, fax 5100-808, ℮ spa.blumau@rogner.com) Singles €99-113, doubles €146-175. If you want to stay, this is the only option. Rates include use of swimming pools and sauna but not the various health treatments, such as massages, on offer. The hotel organises guided tours of the resort for non-guests.

Getting There & Away

Bad Blumau is a short detour south of the A2/E59, the highway connecting Graz and Vienna. Blumau (the main village, about 300m from the resort) is on the rail line between Hartberg and Fürstenfeld.

RIEGERSBURG

☎ 03153

Riegersburg is about 50km east of Graz. The main attraction here is the hill-top **Schloss Riegersburg** *(Map 12; ☎ 821 31, combined ticket adult/student/family €9.45/6.55/23.25; 10am-5pm Mon-Fri 1 Apr-31 Oct)*, a hugely impressive 13th-century castle that offers fine views of the Grazbach Valley. Formerly a crucial bastion against invading Hungarians and Turks, it now has a couple of museums among its numerous rooms; the Hexenmuseum features witchcraft and the Burgmuseum expounds the history of the owners, the Liechtenstein family. A war memorial is a reminder of fierce fighting in 1945, when Germans occupying the castle were attacked by Russian troops. The castle is the setting for a daily **bird-of-prey show** *(Greifvogel-Flugschau;* ☎ *73 90, adult/child €4.40/2.95).* There's an HI hostel (☎ 82 17, fax 82 17-88, Im Cillitor 3) built into the castle walls, but it's closed till 2003.

For more information about the Schloss or activities, contact the tourist office (☎ 86 70, fax 200 70, **e** tourismus@riegersburg.com) in the village.

Getting There & Away

Public transport connections are not ideal. Buses run from Graz only once daily (€7.70, 1½ hours). The nearest train station is Feldbach (€6.55 from Graz, one hour); from there, the bus takes 20 minutes (seven daily, €1.50).

Carinthia

Carinthia (Kärnten) is known primarily for its many lakes: there are 1270 within the province, of which about 200 have bathing facilities. The most famous of these is Wörther See (Lake Wörth); its waters are warmed by thermal springs. Many lakes provide ideal opportunities for angling; tourist offices have information on permits (these can be expensive) and regulations about official fishing seasons and the size of fish you can keep. The attraction of water sports means that summer is the main season in Carinthia (it proclaims itself Austria's sunniest province), though it also offers winter sports.

Carinthia shares an area of outstanding natural beauty, the Hohe Tauern National Park, with neighbouring Salzburg province and Tirol. This mountainous area is covered in the Hohe Tauern National Park Region chapter.

Carinthia doesn't seem too embarrassed that its provincial governor is the much-vilified Jörg Haider (see Government & Politics in the Facts About Austria chapter) – he's highly visible in streetside posters around the region.

Orientation & Information

Carinthia is the fifth-largest Austrian province, with an area of 9533 sq km and a population of 548,000, 3% of whom speak Slovene. The terrain ranges from gentle hills to precipitous Alpine peaks. The main river is the Drau.

The administrative capital is Klagenfurt, but the provincial tourist board is in nearby Velden: Kärntner Tourismus (☎ 04274-52 100, fax 04274-52 100-50, e info@kaernten.at, w www.kaernten.at), Casinoplatz 1, A-9220 Velden. You can book rooms and obtain information via the 24-hour Carinthia 'hotline' (☎ 0463-30 00).

The Kärnten Card, which is available from mid-May to mid-October from tourist offices and hotels, gives free access to 106 attractions – museums, cable cars,

---

Highlights

- Take a summertime stroll around Klagenfurt's Europapark
- Bathe in warm Wörther See, heated by thermal springs
- Explore historic Friesach surrounded by its moat and hillside castles
- Visit Burg Hochosterwitz, with its impressive girdle of gate towers
- Enjoy a range of excursions from Villach, particularly to Burgruine Landskron

---

swimming pools and much else, as well as free use of local public transport. It's valid for three weeks and costs €28.75 (€11.65 for children aged six to 15).

Getting Around

As in other provinces, Carinthia is divided into regional zones for public transport, with the option of buying single tickets or passes valid for 24 hours, seven days, 30 days or one year. Ticket clerks will advise you, or you could call the Verkehrsverbund Kärnten hotline (☎ 0463-500 830).

Klagenfurt

☎ 0463 ● pop 87,000 ● elev 446m

Klagenfurt is an enjoyable city with a pleasant climate. The town centre itself is worthy of exploration, but the big draw for tourists

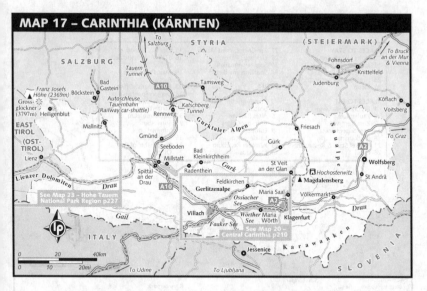

MAP 17 – CARINTHIA (KÄRNTEN)

is Europapark, in particular the world-in-miniature Minimundus. Wörther See, which extends west from Klagenfurt, is another well-known attraction.

After twice being destroyed by fire, Klagenfurt became the capital of Carinthia in 1518, courtesy of Maximilian I. The symmetrical town plan was conceived by Domenico de Lalio, but he was only one of several architects who contributed to the Italianate flavour of the centre. The old city walls were razed in 1809 following the occupation of the town by French forces.

Orientation

Klagenfurt lies 30km from Slovenia and 60km from Italy. The town centre is enclosed by a square of ring roads, with Neuer Platz (New Square) at its heart. North of Neuer Platz is Alter Platz (Old Square), which is surrounded by narrow streets and arcaded courtyards. One block west of Neuer Platz is Heiligengeistplatz, the hub for local buses.

The Hauptbahnhof (main train station; Map 18) is just over 1km south of Neuer Platz. Wörther See is about 4km west of the city centre, with Europapark on its eastern shore.

Information

Tourist Offices The main tourist office (Map 18, #22; ☎ 53 72 23, fax 53 72 95, e tourismus@klagenfurt.at) is in the Rathaus at Neuer Platz 1. Opening hours are 8am to 8pm Monday to Friday, 10am to 5pm weekends and holidays; from 1 October to 30 April, hours reduce to 8am to 6.30pm Monday to Friday, 10am to 1pm weekends. Staff will find rooms (no commission) and bike rental is available (€3.65/6.55/8.75 for three/12/24 hours).

Post & Communications The main post office (Map 18, #19; Postamt 9010) is at Pernhartgasse 4, one block to the west of Neuer Platz. Opening times are 7.30am to 6pm Monday to Friday, 8am to 11am Saturday. There's another post office (Map 18, #37; Postamt 9020) by the Hauptbahnhof at Südbahngürtel 7, open 7.30am to 10.30pm Monday to Friday, 8am to 9pm weekends and holidays.

Email & Internet Access Café-bar G@tes (Map 18, #8; ☎ 50 97 77, e gates@gates .at), Waagplatz 7, is open 9am to 1am Monday to Friday and 7pm to 1am weekends and

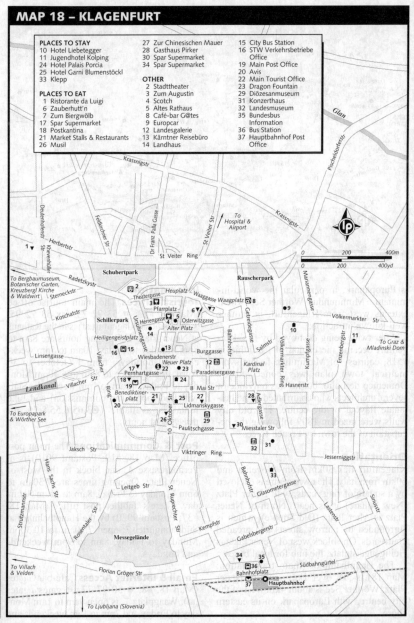

MAP 18 – KLAGENFURT

PLACES TO STAY
10 Hotel Liebetegger
11 Jugendhotel Kolping
24 Hotel Palais Porcia
25 Hotel Garni Blumenstöckl
33 Klepp

PLACES TO EAT
1 Ristorante da Luigi
6 Zauberhutt'n
7 Zum Biergwölb
17 Spar Supermarket
18 Postkantina
21 Market Stalls & Restaurants
26 Musil

27 Zur Chinesischen Mauer
28 Gasthaus Pirker
30 Spar Supermarket
34 Spar Supermarket

OTHER
2 Stadttheater
3 Zum Augustin
4 Scotch
5 Altes Rathaus
8 Café-bar G@tes
9 Europcar
12 Landesgalerie
13 Kärntner Reisebüro
14 Landhaus

15 City Bus Station
16 STW Verkehrsbetriebe
   Office
19 Main Post Office
20 Avis
22 Main Tourist Office
23 Dragon Fountain
29 Diözesanmuseum
31 Konzerthaus
32 Landesmuseum
35 Bundesbus
   Information
36 Bus Station
37 Hauptbahnhof Post
   Office

CARINTHIA

holidays. Surfing the net costs €0.75 for 10 minutes.

Travel Agencies Kärntner Reisebüro (Map 18, #13; ☎ 56 4 00-0, fax 56 4 00-78, e travel@krb.at), Neuer Platz 2, is a helpful and central travel agency. Student fares are available and ISIC cards are issued (€5.10). It's open 8.30am to 6pm Monday to Friday and 9am to noon Saturday.

Medical Services The hospital (☎ 538-0) is at St Veiter Strasse 47.

Central Attractions
To take a walking tour, pick up the relevant brochure in English from the tourist office. It has a map and detailed descriptions of monuments, historic buildings and hidden courtyards. Free guided tours depart from the tourist office at 10am daily during July and August.

Neuer Platz is dominated by the Dragon Fountain (Map 18, #23), the emblem of the city. This winged beast is modelled on the *Lindwurm* (dragon) of legend, said to have resided in a swamp here long ago, devouring cattle and virgins. Markets and festivals are held in the square, which also has a statue of Empress Maria Theresa dating from 1873.

Alter Platz is the oldest part of the city and contains a number of historic buildings. On the corner with Wiener Gasse you'll find the 17th-century Altes Rathaus (Map 18, #5), which has an arcaded courtyard.

The 16th-century **Landhaus** *(Map 18, #14; ☎ 577 57-0, Landhaushof 1; entry Wappensaal adult/concession €1.10/0.40; open 9am-1pm & 2pm-5pm Mon-Sat 1 Apr-30 Sept)* stands just to the west of Alter Platz. Now housing government offices, it's favoured with a two-storey courtyard and two steeples. The interior walls of its Wappensaal (Hall of Arms) are painted with 655 coats of arms belonging to the estates of Carinthia. Perhaps more impressive than the walls of the Landhaus is its ceiling, which has a gallery painted on it to give the illusion it is vaulted; it is actually perfectly flat. The scene, which was rendered by the Carinthian artist Josef Ferdinand Fromiller (1693–1760), depicts the

Carinthian estate owners paying homage to Charles VI. Stand in the centre of the room for the best effect.

Museums The **Landesmuseum** *(Map 18, #32; ☎ 305 52, Museumgasse 2; adult/student €2.95/1.45; open 9am-4pm Tues-Sat, 10am-1pm Sun & holidays)* contains exhibits illuminating Carinthia's history and culture since Roman times, including a fine mosaic floor. One oddity is the *Lindwurmschädel*, a fossilised rhinoceros head which was the not-so-comely artist's model for the head of the Dragon Fountain.

The **Diözesanmuseum** *(Diocesan Museum; Map 18, #29; ☎ 577 70-84, Lidmanskygasse 10/3; admission €2.20; open 10am-2pm Mon-Sat 1 June–mid-Oct, 10am-2pm & 3pm-5pm 15 June-14 Sept)* near the 16th-century Domkirche (cathedral), contains religious art.

The **Landesgalerie** *(Map 18, #12; ☎ 305 42, Burggasse 8; adult/concession €1.45/0.40; open 9am-6pm Mon-Fri, 10am-noon Sat & holidays)* features temporary exhibitions of recent art.

The **Bergbaumuseum** *(Mining Museum; ☎ 51 12 52, Prof-Dr Kahler Platz 1; adult/concession €3.65/1.85; open 9am-6pm daily 1 Apr-31 Oct)* covers, would you believe it, mining. Exhibits are housed in tunnels in the hill which lead from the **Botanischer Garten** *(Botanical Gardens; admission free; open 9am-6pm daily May-Sept)* at the far end of Radetzkystrasse. Adjoining the gardens is the **Kreuzbergl Kirche**, with mosaic stations of the cross on the approaching path, and walking trails up the hill behind.

Europapark Vicinity
Europapark and Wörther See are centres for summer activities, generally available from May to September, although balmy weather can extend the season. Bus Nos 10, 11, 12, 20, 21 and 22 from Heiligengeistplatz run to Minimundus, though usually only Nos 10, 11 and 12 continue the short distance to Strandbad.

Minimundus *(Map 19, #5; ☎ 211 94-0, Villacher Strasse 241; adult/child/concession/family €9.45/7.35/3.65/20.75; open 9am-*

MAP 19 – EUROPAPARK VICINITY

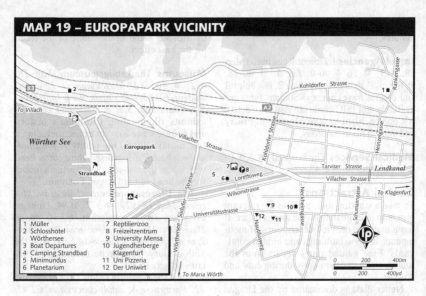

1 Müller
2 Schlosshotel
   Wörthersee
3 Boat Departures
4 Camping Strandbad
5 Minimundus
6 Planetarium
7 Reptilienzoo
8 Freizeitzentrum
9 University Mensa
10 Jugendherberge
   Klagenfurt
11 Uni Pizzeria
12 Der Uniwirt

5pm daily early Apr-late Oct, 9am-6pm daily May, June & Sept, 9am-7pm Sun-Fri, 9am-9pm Sat July & Aug) is the most touristy offering in the park, but it's quite fun, especially for children. Detailed 1:25 scale models of about 170 famous international buildings are displayed. The models are numbered, not labelled (you can pick up a catalogue for €2.60) but some buildings are instantly recognisable: the miniature of St Peter's Basilica in Rome is one of the most impressive. The Eiffel Tower, the Statue of Liberty and the Taj Mahal are also featured, along with many Austrian buildings. A cafe and restaurant (normal-sized) are on site.

Reptilienzoo *(Map 19, #7; ☎ 235 25, Villacher Strasse 237; adult/concession/child €8/6.55/3.65; open 8am-5pm daily winter, 8am-6pm daily summer)* offers a chance to shudder at a variety of snakes, spiders and similar creatures. Brief but informative signs in English provide details on the various species: spiders hear, taste and smell through their legs, and the blue poison arrow frog from Suriname, despite being less than 4cm long, can produce enough poison to kill 10 humans or 20,000 mice. Outside are crocodiles, model dinosaurs and giant turtles.

Strandbad *(Map 19, ☎ 26 25 00, Metnitzstrand 2; day card adult/child €2.55/1.10; open 8am-8pm daily approx early May-late Sept)* is a private beach on the lake with cabins (€2.20 per day), wooden piers, shady grassy areas, a nude sunbathing terrace (for men on Tuesday, Thursday and Saturday; for women on other days) and a restaurant. After 3pm tickets cost €1.45/0.75.

Next to the Strandbad (on the north side) are places where you can hire rowing boats (€1.85), pedal boats (€3.05) and motorboats (€5.25); rates are for 30 minutes.

Other Attractions Europapark is a fine place for a stroll, with winding pathways, fountains, statues and colourful flowerbeds. There's a skateboarding course and tennis courts nearby. Next to the Reptilienzoo is a **planetarium** *(Sternen theatre; Map 19, #6; ☎ 217 00, Villacher Strasse 239; adult/child/concession €6.20/4.75/3.30)* where the 45-minute shows have German commentary.

Opposite the zoo and planetarium is **Freizeitzentrum Europark** *(Map 19, #8; ☎ 236 59, Villacher Strasse 235; open 9am-7pm daily, Easter–31 Oct)* This place has a crazy golf course (€2.50 per person per round), table tennis (€2.20 per hour) and pool (€0.75 per game), and you can rent bicycles for the same prices as at the tourist office.

The departure point (Map 19, #3) for cruises on the lake is only a few hundred metres north of Strandbad. See the Wörther See section in this chapter for information on timetables and lakeside resorts.

Castles

Klagenfurt is ringed by castles and stately homes. The tourist office has a free map detailing routes, which is ideal if you have your own transport. These are close enough to be visited on a cycling tour (see the Getting Around section for more details).

Special Events

There are several free festivals, including the Klagenfurter Stadtfest, a two-day festival in early July, and a New Orleans jazz festival in late June. Sports events include the Kärnten Ironman Triathlon in mid-July and beach volleyball at the beginning of August. The tourist office will willingly supply details of all festivals and events.

Places to Stay – Budget

Staying in Klagenfurt entitles visitors to a *Gästekarte* (guest card), which gives various discounts and is available from hotels, hostels and camp sites.

Camping Strandbad (Map 19, #4; ☎ 211 69, fax 211 69-93, e camping@stw.at, Metnitzstrand 5) Price per adult €3.65, 20 June-20 Aug €5.80; large site (including car) €7.30, small site (under 20 sq metres) €1.45. Registration fee €0.95. Open 1 May-30 Sept. This camping ground enjoys a good location by the lake in Europapark. There is a shop with a buffet on site and campers have free use of the Strandbad swimming complex.

Jugendherberge Klagenfurt (Map 19, #10; ☎ 23 00 20, fax 23 00 20-20, e oejhv-kaernten@oejhv.or.at, Neckheimgasse 6) Bed in 4-bed dorm €15.55, singles/doubles €22.85/38.40. Reception is closed from noon to 5pm, though you can leave your bags during the day. Front door keys are available. This HI hostel near Europapark has modern facilities; rooms have shower and toilet. To get there from the centre, take bus No 10, 12 or 22 and get off at Jugendgästehaus or (depending on the bus route) Neckheimgasse.

Jugendhotel Kolping (Map 18, #11; ☎ 569 65, fax 569 65-632, Enzenbergstrasse 26) Singles/doubles/triples €24.75/37.10/56.60. Open 10 July-10 Sept. This student home becomes a HI hotel during summer, and it's about 800m east of Neuer Platz. Rooms have shower and toilet. Add €2.95 per person for a single-night stay.

Mladinski Dom (☎ 356 51, fax 356 51-11, e mladinski.dom@chello.at, Mikschalle 4) Singles/doubles/triples €20.40/33.50/37.10. Open early Jul-beginning Sept. Built in the 1980s, this is also a student home for most of the year. It's 1km east of Völkermarkter Ring, and there's parking. Rooms have shower and toilet.

There are about a dozen homes that offer private rooms for between €13.50 and €23.50 per person, but these are mostly in the suburbs. An exception is *Klepp* (Map 18, #33; ☎ 322 78, Platzgasse 4), charging €21.90/36.40 for old-fashioned rooms with shared shower and no breakfast.

Hotel Liebetegger (Map 18, #10; ☎ 569 35, fax 569 35-6, Völkermarkter Strasse 8) Singles/doubles with shower, toilet & TV €29.10/50.90, without €21.80/43.60. This is a three-star hotel but it can serve as a budget choice if you skip breakfast. Breakfast costs €5.85 per person. Scattered amid the modern fixtures and fittings are some striking art-deco features.

The other economical choices are a bit out of the way.

Müller (Map 19, #1; ☎/fax 212 54, e VM 18514@i-one.at, Rankengasse 21) Singles €20.35-25.45, doubles €39.25-55.25. This place is not too badly placed between the centre and Europapark, within a small community that has a surprisingly rural feel. Rooms vary in size and furnishings, but all are comfortable and have shower and toilet.

The restaurant (open daily) has inexpensive Austrian food and is a haunt for chess players.

CARINTHIA

Places to Stay – Mid-Range & Top End

Waldwirt (☎ 426 42, fax 466 80, Josefiwaldweg 2) Singles/doubles €32.75/65.50. This small place, on the Kreuzbergl hill northwest of the city, is worth considering if you have your own transport. It has a swimming pool. Rooms have a shower and usually a toilet.

Schlosshotel Wörthersee (Map 19, #2; ☎ 211 58-0, fax 211 58-8, e office@schloss-hotel.at, Villacher Strasse 338). Singles €39.25-45.10, doubles €50.20-65.20. Prices vary depending on size, season and situation. This lakeside hotel has a stately appearance, though the rooms are not overly ornate. There's a stretch of private beach, a restaurant and parking, but no lift. Rooms have a bathroom and cable TV and most have a balcony.

Hotel Garni Blumenstöckl (Map 18, #25; ☎ 577 93, fax 577 93-5, 10 Oktober Strasse 11) Singles €42.15-54.50, doubles €72.70-80. This small, central, family-run place is in a 400-year-old building, with rooms ranged around a flora-filled courtyard. Rooms have bath, toilet and cable TV.

Hotel Palais Porcia (Map 18, #24; ☎ 51 15 90, fax 51 15 90-30, e schlosshotel@mail.palais-porcia.co.at, Neuer Platz 13) Singles €77-182, doubles €99-197. This central place has a sumptuous lounge on the third floor, with portraits, period furniture and ornate mirrors. Most of the rooms match this opulence.

Places to Eat

Eating cheaply in the town centre isn't too hard. Several snack stands dot the area, or you can stock up at the **Spar** supermarkets on Dr Hermann Gasse (Map 18, #17) or Bahnhofstrasse (Map 18, #30) – the latter has a snack stand outside. The **Spar** supermarket at the Hauptbahnhof (Map 18, #34) is also open Sunday (9am to noon and 5pm to 7pm).

A fruit and vegetable **market** (Map 18, #21) occupies Benediktinerplatz from Monday to Saturday, bolstered by a flower market on Thursday and Saturday morning. There are several tiny restaurants in the market arcade, where meals only cost about €3.60 to €4.80.

Musil (Map 18, #26; ☎ 51 16 60, 10 Oktober Strasse 14). Open 8.30am-7pm Mon-Sat 9am-9pm Sun. This is a bakery with an attached coffee shop. Fancy guzzling a Lindwurm-shaped confection? You have the opportunity here.

Postkantina (Map 18, #18; ☎ 51 30 33, Pernhartgasse 7) Lunch specials Mon-Fri €3.80. Open 7am-3pm Mon-Fri. Though this very cheap canteen is on the 1st floor of the post office administration (in the building immediately to the west of the actual post office), it's open to the public. Pick up a bargain meal or snack for the price of a postage stamp.

University Mensa (Map 19, #9; ☎ 27 00, Universitätsstrasse 90) Meals €3-6. Open 11.30am-2.30pm Mon-Fri. This cut-price student cafeteria is open to all, including over the summer. It's west of town and convenient for the Jugendherberge and Europapark.

Zur Chinesischen Mauer (Map 18, #27; ☎ 59 17 08, Lidmanskygasse 19) Lunch menu Mon-Fri €4.95-7.65. Open 11am-3pm & 5pm-11.30pm daily. This Chinese restaurant offers the usual oriental fare.

Der Uniwirt (Map 19, #12; ☎ 21 89 05, Nautilusweg 11) Meals €5.50-7.30. Open 9am-midnight Mon-Fri, 10am-6pm weekends & holidays. Opposite the university building, this is also student territory. Food is inexpensive and unremarkable, but there's a free Internet terminal for customers.

Uni Pizzeria (Map 19, #11; ☎ 250 88, Universitätsstrasse 33) Meals €4.55-19.30. Open 11am-midnight daily. This Italian restaurant, also close to the university, has pavement tables, a warm ambience and a wide range of tasty Italian food.

Zauberhutt'n (Map 18, #6; ☎ 547 95, Osterwitzgasse 6) Meals €4.75-16.35. Open 11.30am-2pm & 5.30pm-midnight Mon-Fri, 5.30pm-midnight Sat. This restaurant offers good-value Italian food. It has outside tables, though inside there are rustic motifs offset by modern art.

Gasthaus Pirker (Map 18, #28; ☎ 571 35, Adlergasse 16) Meals €4.90-16. Open 8am-midnight Mon-Fri. This family-orientated restaurant is a good place for Austrian food.

It has a comfortable interior, a bar area, and a diverse choice of meals and *Menüs*.

Zum Biergwölb (Map 18, #7; ☎ 50 26 54, Osterwitzgasse 7) Meals €6.70-14.20. Open 11am-2pm & 5pm-11pm Mon-Sat. This place serves local cuisine, including vegetarian choices. Eat inside amid real tree trunks and shiny plastic leaves, or outside on the square.

Ristorante da Luigi (Map 18, #1; ☎ 51 66 51, Khevenhüller Strasse 2) Meals €12-20. Open 11.30am-3pm & 6pm-midnight Tues-Sat, 6pm-midnight Mon. This top-notch but informal Italian restaurant has an engaging host. Don't expect pizza – crustaceans are more their speciality.

Entertainment

I once overheard a disgruntled young traveller describe Klagenfurt as 'the city of the dead'. She must have been trying to get her kicks in the war cemetery, because it's really not that bad.

For example, the eastern end of Klagenfurt's Herrengasse is wall-to-wall bars. Pfarrplatz and Pfarrhofgasse (which leads west from Pfarrplatz) also have a couple of decent bars worth visiting.

Scotch (Map 18, #4; ☎ 540 97-2, Pfarrplatz 20) Admission free. Open 11pm-4am, closed Sun. This lively disco-bar is a local favourite; it'll scotch any rumours that Klagenfurt people can't party.

Zum Augustin (Map 18, #3; ☎ 51 39 92, Pfarrhofgasse 2) Open 11am-midnight Mon-Sat, closed Sun & holidays. This popular place brews its own beer and has seven ales on tap (from €2.50 for 0.5L). Food costs €6 to €18 and there's a courtyard.

You can see plays, operettas and operas at the *Stadttheater (Map 18, #2; ☎ 540 64, W www.stadttheater-klagenfurt.at, Theaterplatz 4)* Tickets €20-70. Open mid-Sept–mid-June. Ticket office open 9am-noon & 4pm-6pm Tues-Sat. Standing-room tickets are sometimes available.

The *Konzerthaus (Map 18, #31; ☎ 542 72, Miesstaler Strasse 8)* puts on other musical events. There's a yearly or monthly booklet with a timetable of events available from the tourist office.

Getting There & Away

Air The airport (☎ 415 00-0) is 3km north of the city centre. Tyrolean Airways sends six flights a day to Vienna and three daily to Frankfurt; Crossair goes once daily to Zürich. The only other options are chartered flights.

Bus Bundesbuses depart from outside the Hauptbahnhof (Map 18, #36), where there's a Bundesbus information office (Map 18, #35; ☎ 543 40) open 7.30am to 11am and 11.30am to 3.30pm Monday to Friday; a timetable board is outside. See the Wörther See Getting Around section for information on buses to resorts at the lake.

Train Trains to Graz depart every one to two hours (€26.20, three hours); these go via Bruck an der Mur (€21.10, 2¼ hours), 170km to the north-east. IC trains run to Vienna (€34.90, four hours) every two hours. Trains to western Austria, Italy, Slovenia and Germany go via Villach (€5.70; 30 to 40 minutes, two to four per hour). Heading to Ljubljana, Slovenia, you can avoid the trip to Villach by taking the local line from Klagenfurt to Rosenbach (€5.70, 30 minutes), and continuing from there. However, these non-express trains are much less frequent, so saving time depends on getting a good connection. Call ☎ 05-1717 for train information between 7am and 10pm daily.

Car & Motorcycle Since the opening of a bypass, the A2/E66 between Villach and Graz skirts the north of Klagenfurt.

Car rental offices include:

Avis (Map 18, #20; ☎ 559 38) Villacher Strasse 1c
Europcar (Map 18, #9; ☎ 51 45 38) Völkermarkter Ring 9
Hertz (☎ 561 47) St Ruprechter Strasse 12

Getting Around

To get to the airport, take bus No 40 or 42 from the Hauptbahnhof (Map 18, #36); these go via Heiligengeistplatz (Map 18, #15) in the town centre, where you can also pick up bus No 45 or 46.

Single bus tickets (which you buy from the driver) cost €0.80 for two or three stops or €1.60 for one hour's validity. Drivers also sell 24-hour passes for €4.05, but these cost only €3.35 when purchased in advance from ticket machines or the STW Verkehrsbetriebe office (Map 18, #16) on Heiligengeistplatz (open from 6.30am to 2.30pm Monday to Friday). A strip of 10 tickets costs €11.95 when bought in advance. The advance purchase tickets and passes must be validated in the machine after boarding the bus.

Bus services are sparse in the evening; free timetables are available from the tourist office or STW office. Bus Nos 40, 41 and 42 run from the Hauptbahnhof to the town centre.

As well as renting bikes, the tourist office provides a *Radwandern* cycle map, listing sights and distances. Tours (the longest being 34km) are arranged by themes. You can rent bikes from the Hauptbahnhof for the standard rate; the counter is open daily from 6.30am (7am on Sunday and holidays) to 10.30pm.

For taxi services in Klagenfurt, call ☎ 311 11 or ☎ 27 11.

Central Carinthia

WÖRTHER SEE

Wörther See (Map 20) is one of the warmer lakes in the region owing to thermal springs: the average water temperature between June and September is 21°C. Summers in this part of Carinthia are very hot in any case, so it's an ideal location for frolicking amid the lapping waves, or for the serious pursuit of water sports. The lake stretches from west to east between Velden and Klagenfurt and the long, thin shoreline provides unfolding vistas on a boat trip.

The northern shore has the best transport access and is the busiest section. On this side, the first main resort west of Klagenfurt is **Krumpendorf** (Map 20). This place has plenty of parkland and facilities for tennis, golf and water sports. The tourist office, the Kurverwaltung (☎ 04229-23 13, fax 04229-2343-99, e heidi.messner@ktn.gde.at), is in the Rathaus at Hauptstrasse 145.

The next resort to the west is **Pörtschach** (Map 20), which has a distinctive tree-lined peninsula with a curving bay on either side. Along the lake shore is a pleasant promenade

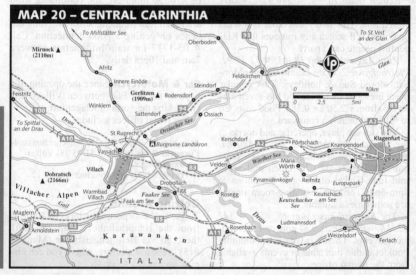

MAP 20 – CENTRAL CARINTHIA

lined with flowers. The resort has a golf course and the usual water sports. Contact the tourist office (☎ 04272-23 54, fax 37 70, e poetschach@carinthia.com), Hauptstrasse 153, for details.

On the southern shore lies **Maria Wörth** (Map 20), a small resort dominated by two churches. The largest combines Gothic, baroque and Romanesque elements; the smaller 12th-century Winterkirche features Romanesque frescoes of the apostles. On the hill south-west of Maria Wörth is **Pyramidenkogel** *(Map 20; ☎ 04273-2443; adult/ child €4.75/1.85; open 10am-6pm daily Apr & Oct, 9am-7pm May & Sept, 9am-8pm June, 9am-9pm July & Aug)*, a rather ugly tower that nevertheless provides fine views of Wörther See and the surrounding mountain ranges. It reaches 905m, 435m higher than the lake. Further details of these attractions are available from the tourist office (☎ 04273-44 88 33, fax 37 03, e maria-woerth@carinthia.com), Süduferstrasse 110.

Velden (Map 20) exudes an aura of affluence and is one of the most popular holiday destinations on the lake. Apart from strolling around enjoying the relaxed atmosphere, the main attractions are water activities; you can take a dip at one of the lakeside swimming complexes (for an entrance fee), hire a boat, windsurf or water-ski. Velden tourist office, the Kurverwaltung (☎ 21 03-0, fax 21 03-50, e velden@carinthia.com) is at Villacher Strasse 19.

The hills north of Velden provide good views of the Karawanken mountain range to the south. Five kilometres south of Velden is **Rosegg** (Map 20), with a **Wildpark** (animal park; ☎ 04274-523 57) and a **Schloss** (palace; ☎ 04274-30 09); both are closed in winter.

For accommodation details, contact the tourist offices in the individual resorts. *Cap Wörth (☎ 0463-23 00 19, fax 0463-23 00 19-13, e jgh.capwoerth@oejhv.or.at, Seecorso 37–39)* Dorms €20, singles/doubles €27.30/47.30. This brand new HI hostel in Velden is a good budget option.

Getting Around

Bus & Train Bundesbuses travel along both shores of the lake, stopping at all the main resorts; for information call ☎ 0463-543 40. Buses run between Villach and Klagenfurt four to seven times a day each way, travelling along the northern shore; they take 45 minutes to cover the 23km of the Velden-Klagenfurt leg (€4.40). Buses also run along the southern side of the lake between Klagenfurt and Velden via Maria Wörth, but there are only a few departures each day and none on Sunday.

The railway line between Klagenfurt and Villach runs along the northern shore of the lake, with trains chugging by every 30 to 60 minutes. Regional trains stop at Krumpendorf, Pörtschach and Velden; express trains stop at only one or two of those stations. Fares from Velden are €2.95 to Villach (10 to 15 minutes) and €4.40 to Klagenfurt (15 to 20 minutes).

Car & Motorcycle The A2/E66 and Hwy 83, which runs closer to the shore, are on the northern side of the lake. On the southern side, the route is classified as a main road, but it's much smaller.

Bicycle A circuit of the lake is about 50km, well within the limits of most casual cyclists, especially with an overnight stop somewhere. There is a *Rent a Radl* (Rent a Bike) scheme in the summer, by which you can rent a bicycle at one of several outlets round the lake, and return it at any other outlet. Rental rates are €3.65/6.55/8.75 for three/ 12/24 hours and €21.80 for one week. One outlet is Freizeitzentrum (Map 19, #8; ☎ 0463-236 59) in Europapark (see the Klagenfurt section). Bikes can also be hired at the Klagenfurt, Pörtschach and Velden train stations but there's a surcharge if you don't return it to the same station.

Boat STW (☎ 0463-211 55, fax 0463-211 55-15, e schiffahrt@stw.at), St Veiter Strasse 31, Klagenfurt, runs steamers on the lake from early May to early October. Boats call at both sides, stopping at Klagenfurt, Krumpendorf, Sekirn, Reifnitz, Maria Wörth, Pörtschach, Dellach, Weisses Rössl, Auen and Velden, and return by the same route, departing from Klagenfurt at least every two hours. A stopoff is allowed en route. The longest trip (Klagenfurt-Velden) takes 1¾ hours and costs €8.40 one-way. The *Rundfahrtkarte* (round-trip) ticket allows unlimited trips in one day; it costs €12.35 for adults and €27.65 for families. A four-week pass costs €29.10 for adults (photo required), €14.55 for children. STW also runs evening cruises with music and dancing.

VILLACH
☎ 04242 ● pop 55,000 ● elev 500m

This is an important transport hub for routes into Italy and Slovenia, and the influence of both countries can be discerned in the town's ambience and inhabitants. Villach has several sights and serves as a base for exploring nearby lakes and other attractions. See the Around Villach section for details.

Orientation & Information

The old town centre is south of the Drau River. North of the river is the Hauptbahnhof (Map 21), containing a train information office, shops, restaurants and snack bars. Close by is the bus station (Map 21, #2) and a post office (Map 21, #1; open 7am to 7pm Monday to Friday, 8am to noon Saturday).

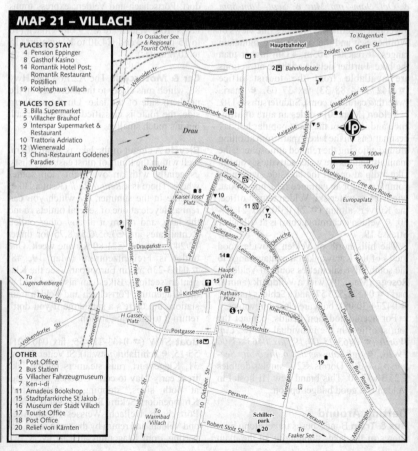

MAP 21 – VILLACH

PLACES TO STAY
4 Pension Eppinger
8 Gasthof Kasino
14 Romantik Hotel Post;
   Romantik Restaurant
   Postillion
19 Kolpinghaus Villach

PLACES TO EAT
3 Billa Supermarket
5 Villacher Brauhof
9 Interspar Supermarket &
   Restaurant
10 Trattoria Adriatico
12 Wienerwald
13 China-Restaurant Goldenes
   Paradies

OTHER
1 Post Office
2 Bus Station
6 Villacher Fahrzeugmuseum
7 Ken-i-di
11 Amadeus Bookshop
15 Stadtpfarrkirche St Jakob
16 Museum der Stadt Villach
17 Tourist Office
18 Post Office
20 Relief von Kärnten

To Ossiacher See & Regional Tourist Office
To Klagenfurt
Hauptbahnhof
Zeidler von Goerz Str
Willroiderstr
Kassinstr
Bahnhofplatz
Klagenfurter Str
Brauhausgasse
Draupromenade
Drau
Kaigasse
Bahnhofstrasse
Draulande
Burgplatz
Lederergasse
Nikolaigasse
Free Bus Route
Europaplatz
Bamberggasse
Kaiser Josef Platz
Widmanngasse
Karlgasse
Rathausgasse
Ankershofengasse
Ringmauergasse
Parceréusgasse
Seilergasse
Leiningengasse
Ankershofen Dietrich
Drauparkstr
Freihausgasse
Drau
Fabrikgasse
Haupt-platz
Steinwenderstr
Free Bus Route
Kirchenplatz
Rathaus Platz
Khevenhüllergasse
Gerbergasse
Draulande
Free Bus Route
To Jugendherberge
Tiroler Str
H Gasser Platz
Postgasse
Moritschstr
Volkendorfer Str
Italiener Str
10 Oktober Str
Hausergasse
Peraustr
Peraustr
Schiller-park
To Warmbad Villach
Robert Stolz Str
To Faaker See
Mitterlingstr
0 50 100m
0 50 100yd

The town centre is south of the river, as is the tourist office (Map 21, #17; ☎ 205-2900, fax 205-2900-2999, **e** villach.tourismus@ villach.at), Rathausplatz 1. It's open 8am to 12.30pm and 1.30pm to 6pm Monday to Friday, 9am to noon Saturday.

Internet access is in the Amadeus Bookshop (Map 21, #11; Hauptplatz 4), or the noisy Ken-i-di bar (Map 21, #7; open 11am to 2pm daily) at Lederergasse 16.

Things to See & Do

The small city bus that completes a circuit of the centre every 20 minutes during shopping hours is free. The tourist office provides a map with English text guiding visitors through a walk of the old town; alas, there's nothing spectacular to see. The pedestrian-only hub of the town is the long, slender Hauptplatz, at the southern end of which stands **Stadtpfarrkirche St Jakob** (parish church of St Jakob; Map 21, #15; ☎ 240 66, Kirchenplatz 8; admission €1.80; open 10am-4pm Mon-Sat May & October; 10am-6pm Mon-Thurs & Sat, 10am-9pm Fri June-Sept). This Gothic church has a tower, a rococo altar, carved gravestones and an unusual pulpit.

A large **relief map** (Relief von Kärnten; Map 21, #20; ☎ 20 53 550, Peraustrasse; adult/child €1.80/1; open 10am-4.30pm Mon-Sat 2 May-31 Oct) is housed in Schillerpark, south of the old town. This huge relief map of Carinthia covers 182 sq metres and depicts the province at a scale of 1:10,000 (1:5000 vertically, to exaggerate the mountains). It can help you plan your trip (or track your progress) through the region, and there are some interesting photos on the walls.

Museum der Stadt Villach (Map 21, #16; ☎ 20 53 500, Widmanngasse 38; adult/student €2.50/1.80; open 10am-4.30pm Mon-Sat 2 May-31 Oct) covers local history, archaeology and medieval art.

The **Villacher Fahrzeugmuseum** (Map 21, #6; ☎ 25 530, Draupromenade 12; admission €5.45; open 9am-5pm daily mid-July–mid-Sept, 10am-noon & 2pm-4pm Mon-Sat other months), displays motorcycles and cars, mostly from the 1950s and '60s. Many are crammed together without

any apparent regard for their condition or curiosity value. The bicycles with tiny motors are quite fun.

Special Events

On the first Saturday in August the pedestrian centre is taken over by a folklore festival, the Kirchtag, which is held from noon to midnight. Entry is €4.40. Some events begin during the preceding week.

Places to Stay

Jugendherberge (☎ 563 68, fax 563 68-20, **e** jgh.villach@oejhv.or.at, Dinzlweg 34) Dorm bed €14.20, €3.65 extra for single/ double occupancy. Reception 7am-10am and 5pm-10pm, doors open during the day. This HI hostel is about 1km west of the pedestrian centre. From H Gasser Platz, head west along Tiroler Strasse over the railway tracks and then bear right on St Martiner Strasse. Dinzlweg is the first on the left, but car drivers need to stay on Tiroler Strasse, which eventually loops round. Rooms have shower and toilet. Don't abuse their hospitality in the serve-yourself breakfast. Dinner is served for €5.85. You can rent bikes for only €5.85 per day.

Pension Eppinger (Map 21, #4; ☎ 243 89, Klagenfurter Strasse 6) Singles/doubles with shared shower €16/23.30, private shower €20.35/27.65, shower/toilet €23.30/30.55. This pension is set back from the street, through a green gate. It has simple, good-value rooms, courtyard parking and a friendly hostess who doesn't speak English (and may go out occasionally, so phone ahead). Breakfast isn't available.

Kolpinghaus Villach (Map 21, #19; ☎ 270 71-0, fax 270 71-4, Hausergasse 5) Singles/ doubles €23.65/36. Reception 8am-10am & 4pm-9pm. This student house with 94 beds offers functional rooms to tourists from the end of July to the beginning of August. Rooms have shower and toilet.

Gasthof Kasino (Map 21, #8; ☎ 244 49, fax 244 49-4, **e** office@hotel-kasino.at, Kaiser Josef Platz 4) Singles/doubles €43.60/83.60. This three-star hotel, with fresh, new-looking rooms, is two blocks west of Hauptplatz. It has a garage (free for guests) and an inexpensive restaurant (closed on Sunday), but lacks a lift. Rooms have shower, toilet and TV.

Romantik Hotel Post *(Map 21, #14;* ☎ *261 01-0, fax 261 01-420,* **e** *romantik-hotel@ magnet.at, Hauptplatz 26)* Singles €32.70-87.30, doubles €69-112.70. This atmospheric hotel occupies a historic building with a garden and a sauna (free for guests). Rooms vary greatly in size and style; those overlooking the square can be noisy thanks to the old, ill-fitting windows. The rooms have a bathroom or shower, toilet and satellite TV.

It's also possible to stay in Warmbad Villach (see the Around Villach section) – there are actually more hotels and pensions there than in Villach itself. Staff at the Warmbad Villach tourist office (☎ 04242-372 44, **e** therme.warmbad@villach.at) find rooms commission-free.

Places to Eat

A **Billa** supermarket (Map 21, #3) sits opposite the train station, with various snack places close by. At the northern end of Hauptplatz there's a **Wienerwald** (Map 21, #12) with a takeaway section. There are cafes in the pedestrian centre that give a taste of Slovenia or, particularly, Italy (ie, pizzerias are ubiquitous); many have outside tables.

Interspar *(Map 21, #9;* ☎ *292 02, Ringmauergasse 9)* Meals €4.65-6.50, salad buffet €0.95 per 100g. Open 8.30am-7.30pm Mon-Fri, 8am-5pm Sat. This shopping centre and supermarket near the pedestrian area has a self-service restaurant. Meals are cheap anyway but look out for half-price deals after 6pm.

China-Restaurant Goldenes Paradies *(Map 21, #13;* ☎ *25 01 49, Hauptplatz 14)* Mains €5.85-13, lunch menus Mon-Fri €4.05-5.10. Open 11.30am-3pm & 5.30pm-11.30pm daily. Located above the Billa supermarket, this place has great lunches.

Villacher Brauhof *(Map 21, #5;* ☎ *232 22, Bahnhofstrasse 8)* Meals €6.30-14.70. Open 9am-midnight daily. Enjoy a beerhall atmosphere (or the garden), Austrian food and a choice of nine draught beers brewed in the adjacent brewery.

Trattoria Adriatico *(Map 21, #10;* ☎ *263 74, Bambergergasse 5)* Meals €6.70-18.20, cover charge €2.55. Open 6pm-midnight Mon-Sat. This quality Italian restaurant has good, reasonably priced pasta and seafood specialities.

The **Romantik Restaurant Postillion** *(Map 21, #14;* ☎ *261 01-0, Hauptplatz 26)* Meals €7.65-19.30. Kitchen open noon-2.30pm & 6pm-9.30pm daily. This restaurant is attached to the Romantik Hotel Post has an ambience that tries to live up to its name. It serves acclaimed regional specialities. Midday *Menüs* (meat or veg) are good value.

Getting There & Away

Villach is on three Austrian IC express rail routes, serving Salzburg (€21.80, 2½ hours, every two hours), Lienz (€10.20, 70 minutes, hourly) and Klagenfurt (€5.70, 30 minutes, hourly). It is also the junction at which two international EC routes diverge and head south. Direct services go to many destinations, for example, Venice, Italy (€13.40, 3½ hours, three per day), Ljubljana, Slovenia (€17.30, 1¾ hours, four daily), and Zagreb, Croatia (€36.20, 4½ hours, three daily).

Villach is equally well-served by roads. The autobahns cross in a confusion of slip roads 4km east of the centre. Various bus routes radiate from Villach; call ☎ 2020-1510 for Bundesbus information.

AROUND VILLACH

Three kilometres south of the town centre is **Warmbad Villach** (Map 20), a complex of thermal pools (33°C) and rejuvenating radioactive mineral waters, reputed to hinder the ageing process rather than cause unpleasant mutations. Nearly 40 million litres of water gush daily from six springs.

Kinetotherapy, mud baths, massages, saunas and other treatments are on offer in plush hotels and at Kurzentrum Heilbad Thermalbad Warmbad *(*☎ *370 00, Kadischenallee 24-26; day pass for pool €8.75; open 9am-8pm daily).* In the latter you can also enjoy the indoor thermal pool with water slide, whirlpools and so on. Erlebnistherme Warmbad *(*☎ *378 89, Kadischenallee 25-27; €9.45; open 9am-8pm* *daily)* has an 'adventure pool' with a water slide and indoor and outdoor swimming areas. City bus No 1 goes to Warmbad (€1.60).

East of Villach many lakes, big and small, provide plenty of swimming and boating opportunities. The largest are **Faaker See** (Map 20), close to the Karawanken range, and **Ossiacher See** (Map 20), a long, narrow lake only 4km north-east of Villach. Boats on Ossiacher See complete a crisscross tour of the lake in 2½ hours (€9.85) from around May to October. Departures are from Steindorf and, in high season, St Andrä. They're every 75 minutes or so in the high season (from late June to early September). Boats also navigate the Drau River between Villach Kongresshaus and Wernberg Bad (€9.10) up to four times a day between late April and early October. Both of these services are operated by Drau und Ossiacher See Schiffahrt (☎ 04242-580 71, e drau@schiffahrt.at, w www.schiffahrt.at/drau). A combined ticket for both tours is €14.55.

If you have young kids you might want to check out one of several **puppet museums** in the region, such as the Puppenmuseum (☎ 04242-228 55, open April to December) at Vassacher Strasse 65, Vassach (Map 20), or Elli Riehl's Puppenwelt (☎ 04248-23 95, open mid-April to mid-October) at Winklern 14, Innere Einöde (Map 20).

Between Villach and Ossiacher See is **Burgruine Landskron** (Map 20) on Schlossweg. The castle, partially in ruins, is famous for its 40-minute eagle show *(Adler-Flugschau; ☎ 04242-428 88; adult/child €6/3; shows at 11am & 3pm daily May-Sept, 11am, 3pm & 6pm July-Aug)* in which captive predators are released to soar and swoop above the crowds. Also here is the Affenberg *(monkey mountain; ☎ 04242-31 97 02; adult/child €6/3; open 9.30am-5.30pm daily 1 Apr-31 Oct)*, a monkey reserve where simians roam free. There's a great view of the castle from the nearby village of St Andrä, with the Karawanken peaks as a backdrop.

The backdrop to the north of Ossiacher See is Gerlitzen (Map 20; 1909m), one of the main areas for winter **skiing**; a day pass costs €25.50.

Another nearby ski area is Dobratsch (Map 20; 2166m; day pass €20.75), in the Villacher Alpen about 12km west of Villach. In summer this area is ideal for walking and mountain cycling, and at 1500m there's an **Alpine garden** *(☎ 570 47-0; admission €1.50; open 9am-6pm daily mid-June–31 Aug)* containing flora from the southern Alps. To reach the garden, follow the Villacher Alpenstrasse from the town. This is a toll road (€12.35 for cars, €6.55 for motorcycles, bicycles €4.40), though from about November to mid-March it's free. It's closed to caravans.

Places to Stay
You could quite happily base yourself in Villach to explore the whole region, though there are also numerous accommodation options around Ossiacher See and Faaker See, including camp sites, hotels, pensions, private rooms and holiday apartments. Refer to the region-wide accommodation brochure obtainable from the Villach tourist office, or contact the regional tourist office (☎ 04242-420 00, fax 04242-420 00-42, e office@vi-fa-os.at), Töbringer Strasse 1, Villach. The local tourist offices at the specific lake resorts can also help out.

Getting There & Around
From Villach Hauptbahnhof (Map 21) hourly trains run to Warmbad Villach (€1.55) and along the northern shore of Ossiacher See; trains to Faaker See are less frequent. Bundesbuses run to both lakes from Villach bus station (Map 21, #2), but distances are so short that it's easy and more pleasant to explore the region by bicycle. You can hire bikes at Villach and Bodensdorf train stations, and from many other places.

Eastern Carinthia

The best sights in Eastern Carinthia are north of Klagenfurt, on or close to Hwy 83 and the rail route between Klagenfurt and Bruck an der Mur. There are mountain ranges on either side: the Seetaler Alpen and Saualpe to the east and the Gurktaler Alpen to the west.

FRIESACH

☎ 04268 ● pop 5700 ● elev 636m

Friesach (Map 17) has a peaceful, unhurried air that belies the bristling fortifications on every hill top. It is Carinthia's oldest town, once important for its key location on the Vienna-Venice trade route. Friesach became part of the diocese of Salzburg in 860. Ensuing centuries saw invasions by the Bohemians, Hungarians, Turks and French, until the town came under the wing of the Habsburgs in 1803.

Orientation & Information

Friesach lies in the Metnitz Valley. At the centre of town, the picturesque Hauptplatz is a few minutes' walk from the train station along Bahnhofstrasse: turn left on leaving the station and follow the road as it branches right. The city's tourist office (☎ 43 00, fax 42 80, e tourismusinformation@friesach.at), Hauptplatz 1, is open 9am to noon and 2pm to 4pm Monday to Friday, and there may also be staff there on weekends. In July and August hours are 9am to 6pm daily.

Things to See & Do

Friesach is unique in Austria in retaining a filled moat around its ancient city walls. Flower borders seduce strollers who meander along the bank. North of the moat is a **Dominican monastery** *(Stadtgrabengasse 5; no entry)*; its 13th-century Gothic church, which is open to the public from dawn til dusk daily, is noted for its wooden crucifix and a sandstone statue of the Virgin.

Linger in Hauptplatz, an enchanting square with a Renaissance fountain. Just to the north is the **Stadtpfarrkirche**, on Wienerstrasse, which has a fine 12th-century font and a distinctive tiled roof. To see the interior of the slender 14th-century **Heiligblutkirche** *(Church of the Holy Blood, Seminarpark; open by arrangement)*, visible on the hill to the south-west of Hauptplatz, you need to join one of the tourist office's guided tours (€2.20 per person).

Ranged along the hills rising above Hauptplatz to the west stand four ancient fortifications, all providing excellent views of the town and valley. The northernmost is

Burg Geyersberg; the farthest south is the Virgilienberg Ruins. The middle two are the most easily visited from the town. A path winds up by the Heiligblutkirche to the **Rotturm**, a 13th-century tower of which little remains. A better view is from **Peterskirche**, accessible by paths ascending from in front of the Stadtpfarrkirche. To see the Gothic interior of Peterskirche, ask for the key at the house next door (☎ 23 19).

Behind Peterskirche, **Petersberg** houses the town museum *(☎ 26 00; adult/child/ concession €2.95/0.75/1.50; open 1pm-5pm Tues-Sun 1 May-30 June & 1 Sept-10 Oct, 10am-6pm Tues-Sun July-Aug),* which covers history and religious art. The Petersberg castle is also the site for open-air theatre performing anything from Shakespeare to Brecht in summer. Obtain details and tickets (prices ranging from €10.20 to €18.50) from the tourist office.

Friesach really plays on its long history (it hosted a summer-long medieval festival in 2001) – the tourist office can tell you about 'knight-style' dinners and other events. The **Spectaculum** is one evening in early August where the Middle Ages lives again: electric lights are extinguished, the townsfolk don ancient costumes, stage duels and other events, and meals must be paid for in medieval currency (which you have to buy in town – at 21st-century rates, naturally).

Places to Stay & Eat

You'll find a place to eat or sleep at a handful of hotels and guesthouses in town.

Zum Goldenen Anker (☎ 23 13, fax 23 13-4, Bahnhofstrasse 3) Singles/doubles €27/46.60. Reception is in the attached restaurant, open 8am-10pm Mon-Fri, 8am-2pm Sat-Sun. This small Gasthof, by Hauptplatz, is the best budget deal in the centre. Rooms are variable but generally good value – many have new bathrooms, but all have shower, toilet and cable TV. The food is also favourably priced: Austrian meals, as well as good pizzas, are €5 to €9.

Weisser Wolf (☎ 22 63, fax 22 63-4, Hauptplatz 8) Singles/doubles €30.60/49.50, with shower/toilet €32.80/53.80. This Gasthof has comfortable rooms with TV, and

Maypole Madness

Anybody travelling in Austria during May is certain to see many maypoles, as nearly every village and town raises one. The maypole (Maibaum) is traditionally erected on the night of 30 April.

The 'pole' is actually a sturdy tree trunk, 30 or even 40m long, usually topped off by a small Christmas tree from which hang circles of pine branches. The maypole is dedicated to someone, either a local celebrity, the village girls, innkeepers or, in these more egalitarian times, simply 'everybody'. The raising of the maypole by the traditional method is quite a performance, and is well worth stopping to watch. (Sadly, nowadays many villages 'cheat' and use hydraulic lifts instead.)

It can take 25 men three hours to raise the pole from horizontal to vertical, using a combination of hurdle-like supports, elongated pitchforks and brute strength. They force it upwards inch by exhausting inch, each upward movement accompanied by cheers of encouragement from other villagers. An alternative to pitchforks is a series of long, supporting poles, each attached to the maypole by a noose. Each noose is gradually manoeuvred down towards the base of the maypole while the other poles and nooses take the strain.

Once vertical, the maypole rests in a small pit, and is fixed in place by hammering large wood splints around the base. The night I witnessed the raising of a maypole the local villagers indulged in an all-night party, which comprised music from a rather amateurish local brass band, accompanied by synchronised clapping from the onlookers, and much guzzling of frothy beer and fried sausages.

'It's a tradition that the party goes on all night,' a villager told me. 'We have to make sure nobody steals the maypole.' An unlikely occurrence, but as an excuse for an all-night party, it's not a bad one.

Yet it's not only an excuse: in some parts of the country the attempted theft of a maypole is all part of the ritual. If marauding villagers manage the task, they can demand a king's ransom in beer for its return. In May 2000 villagers from Alkoven (in Upper Austria) successfully carted off the 26m-high maypole from neighbouring Eferding. Armed with a tractor, a crane and a trailer, they effected the deed in just 7½ minutes!

Sometime during the summer (traditionally at the end of May, on the last Sunday in the month), the maypole is pulled down and chopped up – another good excuse for a party.

---

a restaurant. Meals in vaulted rooms (or on the terrace) cost €6.55 to €12; in winter it's closed on Monday after 2pm.

Metnitztalerhof (☎ 25 10-0, fax 25 10-54, **e** metnitztalerhof@burgenstadt.at, Hauptplatz 11) Singles €48-51, doubles €80-86. This is the only four-star hotel in Friesach; the higher-priced rooms have a big balcony with good views; all rooms have shower and toilet. The restaurant (closed Friday in winter) is reasonably priced and serves Austrian

and Carinthian fare for €6.20 to €18. There's a fine view of the square from the raised terrace tables.

For self-caterers, supermarkets include a *Spar* on Hauptplatz.

Getting There & Away

Friesach is on the railway line between Vienna's Südbahnhof (€30.50, 3¾ hours, every two hours) and Villach (€10.20, 70 minutes, hourly). Bruck an der Mur (€16.60,

110 minutes) and Klagenfurt (€8.70, 40 to 55 minutes) are on this route. Travel between Friesach, Klagenfurt and Villach is covered by a regional travel pass (€10.20 for 24 hours), which also covers Bundesbuses – these run to Friesach from Klagenfurt via St Veit approximately hourly.

GURK
☎ 04266 ● pop 1340 ● elev 662m
This small town (Map 17), some 18km west of the Friesach-Klagenfurt road, is notable for its **Dom** *(☎ 82 36-12, Domplatz 11; open daily except during services)*. It was built between 1140 and 1200 and is one of the finest examples of Romanesque architecture in Austria. The relatively plain exterior of the cathedral is dominated by two huge onion domes capping square-sided twin towers. The interior has Gothic reticulated vaulting on the ceiling, and most of the church fittings are baroque or rococo. The early-baroque high altar is particularly impressive: it's laden with 72 statues and 82 angels' heads.

The frescoes in the Bischofskapelle *(Episcopal Chapel; guided tour at 1.20pm, 2.20pm & 3.50pm daily, adult/concession €3.65/2.95)*, dating from around 1200, are made all the more affecting by their primitive colours. This chapel can be viewed by guided tour only.

Those with children might be interested in visiting the nearby **Zwergenpark** *(Dwarfs Park; ☎ 80 77, Fliegenpilz 1; adult/child €4.75/3.30; open 10am-noon & 2pm-6pm daily early May–mid-Sept, 10am-6pm daily late June–early Sept)*, which is populated by garden gnomes. It has a mini-railway.

Getting There & Away
Gurk cannot be reached by rail, and Bundesbuses go there from Klagenfurt (via St Veit an der Glan) only three times a day (twice on Sunday). Private transport makes a visit much easier: the town is on Hwy 93.

ST VEIT AN DER GLAN
☎ 04212 ● pop 13,000 ● elev 476m
St Veit (Map 17) was historically important as the seat of the dukes of Carinthia from 1170 until 1518, when the dukes skipped

down the road to Klagenfurt and the town diminished in status.

Orientation & Information
St Veit is near the junction of primary road routes to Villach (Hwy 94) and Klagenfurt (Hwy 83). To get to the pedestrian-only town centre from the Hauptbahnhof (where you can usually pick up a free map), walk left down Bahnhofstrasse for 600m and then go one block right.

The tourist office (☎ 55 55-13, fax 55 55-112) is in the Rathaus at Hauptplatz 1, in the heart of the pedestrian area. It's open Monday to Friday, but only from around June to September. The rest of the year tourists have to fend for themselves.

Things to See & Do
The town centre can keep visitors occupied for a couple of hours. Places of interest line the long **Hauptplatz**, with a fountain at either end and a central column erected in 1715 as a memorial to plague victims. The northeastern fountain, the **Schüsselbrunnen,** is surmounted by a bronze statue, created in 1566. This figure is the town mascot: its hand is raised as if in greeting, yet at the same time a jet of water spits forth from its mouth. The south-western fountain bears a statue of local medieval poet, Walther von der Vogelweide.

The most impressive facade on Hauptplatz belongs to the **Rathaus.** Its baroque stuccowork was applied in 1754 and features a double-headed eagle on the pediment. St Veit (the saint, not the town) stands between the eagle's wings. Walk through the Gothic vaulted passage to admire the arcaded courtyard, bedecked with sgraffito designs.

Close to the town hall is the **Verkehrsmuseum** *(Transport Museum; ☎ 55 55-64, Hauptplatz 29; adult/student €2.55/1.50; open 9am-noon & 2pm-6pm daily 1 May-15 Oct, noon-2pm Mon-Fri early July-early Sept)*. It does a reasonable job of making the development of transport in the region seem interesting, and displays old travel documents, motorcycles, model trains and mannequins wearing uniforms; there are no English labels. The WWII display includes photos of bomb-damaged Villach and Klagenfurt train stations; appropriately, the guard dummy in this section sports a ludicrous Hitler moustache. There's also a city museum (in the former ducal castle on Burggasse, one block north of Hauptplatz) and a Romanesque Stadtpfarrkirche, adjoining Hauptplatz.

The colourful, almost mosque-like Hotel Zodiac St Veit (see Places to Stay) is worth a look; it was built in 1998 and has astrological symbols by Ernst Fuchs.

Places to Stay

There is a range of places to stay in St Veit, including private rooms, though as ever, the cheaper choices are less convenient.

Gasthof Steirerhof (☎ 24 42, *Klagenfurter Strasse 38*) Rooms with shared showers €19 per person. This is one of the more accessible budget places, about 300m south of the centre. There are ageing but adequate rooms; however, it's for sale, and the new owner may upgrade facilities.

Gasthof Sonnhof (☎ 24 47, *fax 24 47-10, Völkermarkter Strasse 37*) Singles/doubles €28/51. South of the rail tracks, Sonnhof has clean, fresh, though slightly impersonal rooms, some with a balcony. Rooms have shower, toilet and TV. There's also a good-value restaurant with a terrace (closed Monday). Though it's 15 minutes by foot from the centre, it's only eight minutes from the train station. From the station, leave by the south-eastern exit, take the path to the right (which soon joins a road); at the main road junction, turn left.

Weisses Lamm (☎ 23 62, *fax 23 62-62, e office@weisseslamm.at, Unterer Platz 4-5*) Singles €40-45, doubles €73-85. This place has four stars, and the accommodation is only just adequate for that category, although rooms do have a shower, toilet and TV. The rooms are arranged round a quiet, arcaded courtyard, and the hotel itself is ideally central.

Hotel Zodiac St Veit (☎ 46 60-0, *fax 46 60-660, e hotel.st.veit@rogner.com, Friesacher Strasse 1*) Singles €83-94, doubles €123-144. This place is modern architecture treat, incorporating bold colours, striking pillars

and creative mosaics. Though this creativity continues into the public areas, the corporate-style rooms are disappointingly normal.

Places to Eat

Opposite the Hauptbahnhof there's a *Billa* supermarket.

Pizza Max (☎ 728 73, *Bahnhofstrasse 30*) Meals €3.60-6.90. Open 11am-2pm & 5pm-midnight daily, closed Tues in winter. This cheap takeaway and eat-in restaurant is near the Hauptbahnhof, opposite the *Spar* supermarket.

Interspar (☎ 726 55, *Völkermarkter Strasse 38*) Hot meals €3.60-7.50. Open 8.30am-7.30pm Mon-Fri, 8am-5pm Sat. This large supermarket has a self-service restaurant, with the usual cheap deals, including half-price food after 6pm.

There are lots of comfortable places to eat in the compact pedestrian area, many with outside tables.

Gasthof Traube (☎ 23 29, *Oktober Platz 2*) Meals €6.50-10. Kitchen 9am-7.30pm Tues-Sun, 9am-2pm Mon. This place, just west of Hauptplatz, has a garden and inexpensive regional food. There are various options available, such as meals with a drink included.

Pukelsheim (☎ 24 73, *Erlgasse 11*) Meals €9.10-19.50. Kitchen open noon-2pm & 6pm-9.30pm Tues-Sat. This place serves Austrian and regional meals, and the high prices reflect the quality; they use herbs and vegetables from their own garden plot next door.

Getting There & Away

St Veit is 33km south of Friesach and 20km north of Klagenfurt. Hourly express trains on the Vienna-Villach route stop at St Veit; the journey to Villach (€8.15) takes 45 minutes. Fares are €5.70 to Friesach (30 minutes) and €2.95 to Klagenfurt (20 minutes).

Bundesbuses run to Klagenfurt, Maria Saal and Friesach about every hour.

BURG HOCHOSTERWITZ

This fortress (Map 17) drapes itself around the slopes of a hill and is a stunning sight, especially when viewed from the north-west.

The visual impact is due mainly to the 14 gate towers and their connecting walls that circle the hill to the summit. These were built between 1570 and 1586 by Georg Khevenhüller, the then owner, to protect against Turkish invasion. It certainly looks impregnable, and the information booklet (in English; €2.50) outlines the different challenges presented to attackers by each gate – they're something of a medieval forerunner to the multiple levels in modern computer adventure games!

The castle itself was first mentioned in documents in 860. A small **museum** *(☎ 20 20; adult/child €7.30/3.65; open 9am-5pm daily, Palm Sunday-31 Oct, 8am-6pm May-Sept)* features family portraits and arms and armour (one suit would fit a 2m-tall giant). There's a cheap restaurant in the grounds.

Getting There & Away
Regional trains on the St Veit-Friesach route stop at Launsdorf Hochosterwitz station, 3km north-east of the car park and the first gate, where a lift will take you directly to the castle for €3. Infrequent buses from either Klagenfurt or St Veit will get you 1km closer (to the Brückl crossroads). If you don't have time to visit, you can at least absorb the sight of the castle to the east of the train.

MAGDALENSBERG
Four kilometres south of Burg Hochosterwitz, this 1058m peak (Map 17) provides an excellent 360°-panorama. There's also a Roman archaeological open-air museum here *(☎ 22 55, Pischeldorf; admission €2.95; open 9am-7pm daily, 1 May–mid-Oct)* and a Gothic chapel. The road up approaches from the south. Buses from Klagenfurt arrive once a day on schooldays (at 2.35pm), and depart five minutes later. This means taking the bus is not viable, unless you're prepared to walk down the hill to one of the nearby villages to pick up another bus or a train.

MARIA SAAL
☎ 04223 • pop 3200
On a fortified hill stands the pilgrimage church of Maria Saal (Map 17). Its twin spires are visible from afar. This small town is 10km north of Klagenfurt.

The road from the train station splits in two and encloses the church hill. Behind the church is Hauptplatz, with a bank and several restaurants. The tourist office (☎ 22 14-25, fax 22 14-23, **e** gemeinde@maria .saal.at), Am Platzl 1, is in the centre of Hauptplatz.

Things to See & Do
The **church** *(☎ 22 14-12, Domplatz 1; open 8am-4.30pm daily)*, sometimes known as the Wallfahrtskirche, was built in the early 15th century from volcanic stone. Originally Gothic, it later received Romanesque and baroque modifications. The exterior south wall is embedded with relief panels and ancient gravestones: look for the Keutschach family tombstone in red marble, and the Roman mail wagon carved into one of the stones used in the building of the church. There are unusual outbuildings within the walled enclosure. The interior of the church is nicely proportioned when looking down the nave. Overhead, the ceiling is fan-vaulted and there are frescoes of people growing out of bulbous flowers (that's not as hallucinatory as it sounds – it represents the genealogy of Christ). The image of the Virgin on the high altar dates from 1425; on either side of the main altar are Gothic winged altars. There's an explanatory pamphlet, in English, available in the church.

About 500m north is the **Carinthian Open-Air Museum** *(Kärntner Freilichtmuseum; ☎ 31 66, **e** freilichtmuseum-mariasaal@ aon.at, Domplatz 3; adult/child/family €5.10/2.95/ 13.10; open 10am-6pm Tues-Sun 1 May– mid-Oct weather permitting)*. It contains over 30 typical or historical Carinthian rural dwellings and features demonstrations of country crafts.

Getting There & Away
There are no official left-luggage facilities in the small train station, but the ticket clerk may look after your bags if you ask nicely. Maria Saal is on the same Vienna-Klagenfurt rail route as Friesach and St Veit, but only the

slower hourly regional trains stop here. Fares are €2.95 to St Veit and €1.55 to Klagenfurt; each journey only takes about 10 minutes. Buses run to both places from below the church.

Western Carinthia

Excluding Hohe Tauern National Park (see the Hohe Tauern National Park chapter), the main points of interest in Western Carinthia are close to the primary road route north from Villach, the A10/E55 which ultimately leads to Salzburg. It has a toll section between Rennweg and a point north of the Tauern Tunnel (€10.20, €7.30 for motorcycles); to avoid the toll, take Hwy 99.

The rail route from Villach takes a more westerly course after Spittal an der Drau, before also turning north. It is shadowed by Hwy 106 (later 105), the road to Bad Gastein. However, driving this way necessitates using the railway car-shuttle service *(Autoschleuse Tauernbahn)* through the tunnel from Mallnitz-Obervellach in Carinthia to Böckstein in Salzburg. The fare for cars is €14.55 one-way (€10.20 if purchased in advance from Austrian motoring clubs, some banks and garages) or €23.30 return (valid for two months). The price is €8/13.10 for motorcycles and €4.40 for bicycles. For information on services through this tunnel, telephone ☎ 04784-600 390 in Mallnitz-Obervellach or ☎ 06434-26 36 32 in Böckstein. Departures are every 30/60 minutes (summer/winter), except at night.

GMÜND
☎ 04732 • pop 2700 • elev 749m
Gmünd's (Map 17) ancient city walls, still partially intact, are a reminder of its former strategic importance – it was owned by a succession of powerful rulers, not least being the Archbishops of Salzburg. Gmünd was founded in the 11th century.

The walled centre is attractive, with small streets leading off Hauptplatz and running beneath various arches. The most impressive old building is the 13th-century **Alte**

Burg on the hill. Although the Burg is partially in ruins, cultural events are still held inside.

Also a mere stone's throw from Hauptplatz, but of an entirely different era, is the privately owned **Porsche Museum** *(☎ 24 71, Riesertratte 4a; admission €5.10; open 9am-6pm daily 15 May-15 Oct, 10am-4pm daily 16 Oct-14 May)*. A Porsche factory was sited in Gmünd from 1944 to 1950, and the first car to bear that famous name (a 356) was handmade here. One of these models is on display (only 52 were built), together with about 15 other models and a couple of the wooden frames used in their construction. There's a film (in German) on Dr Porsche's life and work. It's rather pricey for a small museum.

Places to Stay & Eat
Gmünd has a range of inexpensive accommodation, including hotels specifically geared towards families with young children. Staff at the tourist office (☎ 22 22, fax 39 78, **e** info@familiental.com), in the Rathaus on Hauptplatz, can outline accommodation options. There are a couple of places on Hauptplatz, and these have affordable restaurants.

Burggasthof Alte Burg *(☎ 36 39, Schlossbichl 1)* Meals 6-13. Open 11am-11pm Tues-Sun May-Oct, 11am-11pm daily July-Aug. Located in the castle, this is an ideal setting for a romantic meal. The restaurant is open limited hours in winter so phone ahead.

Getting There & Away
Gmünd is not on a rail route, though buses do go there from Spittal an der Drau (€3.15, 30 minutes); departures are usually every two hours, though there are only two buses on Sunday.

SPITTAL AN DER DRAU
☎ 04762 • pop 16,200 • elev 556m
Spittal is an important economic and administrative centre in upper Carinthia. Its name comes from a 12th-century hospital and refuge that once succoured travellers on this site.

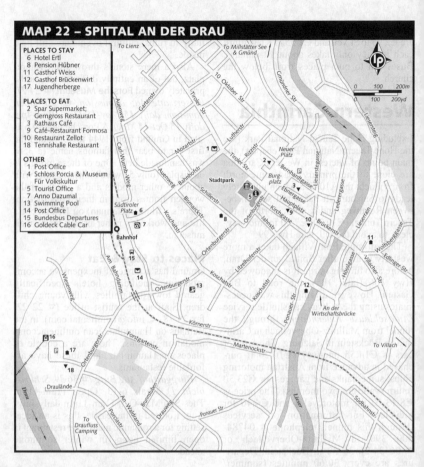

MAP 22 – SPITTAL AN DER DRAU

PLACES TO STAY
- 6 Hotel Ertl
- 8 Pension Hübner
- 11 Gasthof Weiss
- 12 Gasthof Brückenwirt
- 17 Jugendherberge

PLACES TO EAT
- 2 Spar Supermarket; Gerngross Restaurant
- 3 Rathaus Café
- 9 Café-Restaurant Formosa
- 10 Restaurant Zellot
- 18 Tennishalle Restaurant

OTHER
- 1 Post Office
- 4 Schloss Porcia & Museum Für Volkskultur
- 5 Tourist Office
- 7 Anno Dazumal
- 13 Swimming Pool
- 14 Post Office
- 15 Bundesbus Departures
- 16 Goldeck Cable Car

Orientation & Information

The tourist office (Map 22, #5; ☎ 56 20 220, fax 32 37, ⓔ tourismusbuero@spittal-drau .at) is at Burgplatz 1, at the side of the main tourist attraction, Schloss Porcia. Opening hours are 9am to 6pm (8pm in July and August) Monday to Friday, 9am to noon Saturday. Getting there from the train station you can cut across Stadtpark, a 10-minute walk.

The post office (Map 22, #14; Postamt 9800) near the train station opens 7.30am to 7pm Monday to Friday, 9am to noon Saturday. Free Internet access (for customers) is at Anno Dazumal (Map 22, #7; ☎ 339 99), a bar-cafe at Bahnhofstrasse 19, open 1pm to midnight or later (closed Tuesday).

Things to See & Do

Schloss Porcia (Map 22, #4) is an excellent Renaissance edifice, built between 1533 and 1597. The Italianate arcaded courtyard is particularly eye-catching. The top floors contain the Museum für Volkskultur *(Map 22, #4; ☎ 28 90; adult/child €4.50/2.25; open 9am-6pm daily 15 May-31 Oct, 1pm-4pm Mon-Thur 1 Nov-14 May)*. This regional museum gives an effective evocation of life in the locality, covering art, artefacts, rustic crafts and culture. Of interest are the primitive wooden skis and the crudely carved school desks. Many signs are in English. Cultural events are also held in the Schloss.

Spittal's nearest mountain, offering inspiring views, is the **Goldeck** (2142m), to the south-west. In summer, the peak can be reached by cable car (Map 22, #16; €10/15 one-way/return) or by the Goldeckstrasse toll road (cars/motorbikes €12/6; reductions with Gästekarte). The road stops 260m short of the summit. In winter, the peak is the domain of skiers: day passes cost €24.75/21.10 for adults/seniors. The cable car doesn't run from mid-April to mid-June or from mid-September to mid-December.

Special Events
On a weekend in late June every odd-numbered year (2003, etc), the historical legend of Katharina von Salamanca (said to haunt Schloss Porcia in retribution for the violent death of her son) is re-enacted in the Salamanca Festival, held in the town centre. Admission is free.

Places to Stay
Staff at the tourist office will track down accommodation free of charge.

Draufluss Camping (☎ 24 66, fax 362 99, Schwaig 10) Sites €14.60. Open Apr-Oct. This camping ground is about 3.5km from the town centre on the southern bank of the Drau River.

Jugendherberge (Map 22, #17; ☎ 32 52, fax 32 52-4, Zur Seilbahn 2) Dorm beds €6.55, single occupancy surcharge €3.65. Check-in 5pm-9pm. This HI hostel is near the base of the Goldeck cable car. From the train station, turn right and cross under the rail tracks. There are basic cooking facilities and a good-value restaurant. Breakfast costs €2.20. This hostel may close in off-season (phone ahead). Non-HI members pay €0.75 extra but don't get the guest stamp. Another HI *Jugendherberge* (☎ 27 01, **e** goldeck@ gmx.at) is at the Goldeck mid-station (1650m), accessible only by cable car.

There are few convenient pensions, so budget travellers may have to resort to private rooms.

Gasthof Brückenwirt (Map 22, #12; ☎/fax 27 72, An der Wirtschaftsbrücke 2) Singles/doubles with sink, shower/toilet €23.30/46.55, with shared facilities €19.65/ 39.30. This chalet is a few minutes' walk east of the town centre, by the Lieser River. The old-fashioned rooms have a balcony and usually a TV; there's a garden, cheap restaurant and friendly staff.

Gasthof Weiss (Map 22, #11; ☎ 23 41, Edlingerstrasse 1a) Singles/doubles €25.50/ 43.60. This place, just over the Lieser, has a few budget rooms, but phone ahead as it's probably being sold.

*Pension Hübner (Map 22, #8; ☎ 21 12, fax 352 59, **e** huebner@carinthia.com, Schillerstrasse 20)* Singles €26-33, doubles €47-57. This pleasing pension, near Schloss Porcia, is run by the owners of the shop of the same name. Most rooms have shower, toilet and satellite TV. Prices depend on the season and length of stay. There are also apartments with kitchens (minimum stay five days).

*Hotel Ertl (Map 22, #6; ☎ 204 80, fax 204 85, **e** hotel.ertl@carinthia.com, Bahnhofstrasse 26)* Singles/doubles €51/88. Rooms are variable – some bathrooms are on the small side. Ask for a room overlooking the hotel's peaceful garden and swimming pool. Most rooms have a shower, toilet and satellite TV.

Places to Eat
On Neuer Platz there's a Gerngross store (Map 22, #2) with a *Spar* supermarket and a cheap *Gerngross* self-service restaurant (open normal shop hours). *Café-Restaurant Formosa (Map 22, #9; ☎ 350 02, Hauptplatz 20; open daily)* is one of several cheap Chinese restaurants.

Tennishalle Restaurant (Map 22, #18; ☎ 40 49, Zur Seilbahn 5) Meals €4.90-12. Open 9am-midnight daily. Though attached to a tennis centre, this place serves surprisingly good (and inexpensive) food; the *Forelle* (trout) for €9.80 is excellent.

Rathaus Café (Map 22, #3; ☎ 49 18, Ebnergasse 5) Meals €5.85-14.50. Open 7am-midnight or later Mon-Sat. This place has a first-floor terrace, a pub ambience and not bad nosh.

Gasthof Brückenwirt *(Map 22, #12;* ☎ *27 72, An der Wirtschaftsbrücke 2)* Meals €4.95-10. Kitchen open 11.30am-1.30pm & 5.30pm-8pm daily, closed 3pm Sun in winter. An unpretentious local hangout with low prices, it serves Austrian food and pizzas.

Restaurant Zellot *(Map 22, #10;* ☎ *21 13, Am Torbogen)* Meals €6.60-18. Open 10am-2.30pm & 5pm-midnight Tues-Sat, kitchen closes 9.30pm. The cuisine served in this stylish place changes according to monthly festivals. The walls provide exhibition space for up-and-coming local artists.

Getting There & Away

Spittal-Millstättersee train station (Map 22) is at an important rail junction: two-hourly IC services run north to Bad Gastein (€8.15, 52km, 45 minutes) and west to Lienz (€9.30, 67km, one hour). Villach (€5.70, 30 minutes), 37km to the southeast, gets hourly trains. The route north via Mallnitz-Obervellach yields some excellent views as the railway track clings high to the side of the valley (sit on the left).

Bundesbuses leave from outside the train station (Map 22, #15), including about 12 a day to Gmünd (€3.15, 30 minutes); there are fewer on Sunday. Call ☎ 39 16 for schedule information.

MILLSTATT

☎ 04766 ● pop 3300 ● elev 588m

Millstatt (Map 17) lies 10km east of Spittal an der Drau on the northern shore of Millstätter See. The lake is attractively situated, bordered by tree-lined hills on its southern side and a sprinkling of small resorts on its northern shore.

Orientation & Information

Millstatt is roughly in the middle of the 12km-long northern shore of Millstätter See. The Millstatt tourist office, the Kurverwaltung (☎ 20 22-0, fax 34 79, **e** tourismus buero-millstatt@aon.at), is housed in the Rathaus, in the town centre at Marktplatz 8. The comprehensive booklet *Informationen-Veranstaltungen* covers the whole lake and provides information on festivals and events, sports facilities and prices, transport timetables and much else. Across the square at No 14 is the Millstätter See tourist office (☎ 37 00, fax 37 00-8, **e** info@millstatt-see.co.at), with touch-screen computer information outside.

Things to See & Do

The resort is dominated by a **Benedictine abbey**, founded in 1070. The abbey's Romanesque church has a distinctive inner doorway, complete with grotesque faces peering from the columns. The heavy Gothic ceiling vaulting vies for attention with the gold statues and baroque altars. The fresco of the Last Judgement (1513–16), to the right of the high altar, is by Urban Görtschacher. In the arcaded courtyard stands an old linden tree; there's an even more ancient tree (about 1000 years old) outside. The **Stiftsmuseum** *(abbey museum;* ☎ *0676-46 06 413, Stiftgasse 1; adult/child €2.20/1.10; open 9am-noon & 2pm-6pm daily 1 June-30 Sept)* deals with the history of the town, as well as the geology of the region.

The lake is up to 141m deep and teems with possibilities for **water sports** such as sailing, scuba diving, swimming, waterskiing, windsurfing and fishing. Several types of boat are available for hire. Simply strolling along the Seepromenade, lined with statues and flowers, is pleasant. **Boat cruises** *(☎ 20 75, Seemühlgasse 83; full circuit of lake adult/child/family €10.20/5.10/23.30; 30 Apr–mid-Oct)* take two hours.

East of Millstatt is **Bad Kleinkirchheim**, a spa resort and winter skiing centre. Its tourist office (☎ 04240-82 12, **e** office@BKK.at) can provide details.

Places to Stay & Eat

The summer season is from Easter to mid-October, with the highest prices (those quoted here) applicable from June to September. Many quiet, mid-priced B&Bs line Alexanderhofstrasse and Tangernerweg, to the west of the resort centre. Millstatt has some winter tourism, but most hotels, pensions and private rooms close at this time. The winter hibernators don't open until sometime in May, including the places

CARINTHIA

mentioned below – check availability with the tourist office in the non-winter months.

Gasthof Zum Brunnen *(☎ 20 80, Markt-platz 30)* Doubles €21.10, with shared facilities €16.75. This small place is cheap and central with basic rooms.

Pension Pleikner *(☎ 20 36, fax 20 36-2,* e *pension-pleikner@newsclub.at, Seemühl gasse 57)* Doubles €21.50-28.75 per person. Come here for pleasant rooms with shower and toilet, parking facilities and private lake access. Single occupancy is possible outside peak season. It's above and part of ***Pizzeria Peppino***, serving pizza, schnitzel and spaghetti (€4.75 to €11). Rooms are available in summer only, but the restaurant is open 4pm to midnight daily, year-round. Seemühlgasse is between Kaiser Franz Josef Strasse and the boat station.

Hotel See-Villa *(☎ 21 02, fax 22 21,* e *see-villa@hotel.at, Seestrasse 68)* Singles/ doubles €48/75.20. Overlooking the lake, rooms have all you would expect for the price, including a bathroom, telephone and balcony. There's also a good restaurant where main dishes, including fish specialities, are €9.50 to €20.50 (open daily). Menu prices are reduced by 20% if you stay here.

Several other mid-price restaurants overlook the lake; alternatively, compile a picnic at the ***ADEG*** supermarket, Kaiser Franz Josef Strasse 24, near Schwarzstrasse.

For pub entertainment, try ***Full House*** *(☎ 20 73, Kaiser Franz Josef Strasse)*, near Seemühlgasse. This small American bar has live music and opens 2pm to 2am daily in summer, 7pm to 2am Wednesday to Sunday in winter.

Getting There & Away

Bundesbuses to Millstatt depart from outside Spittal train station (€2.50, 20 minutes, two hourly), with some continuing to Bad Kleinkirchheim (from Spittal €4.95, one hour). The road from Spittal stays close to the lake shore.

Hohe Tauern National Park Region

Austria's highest peak and its tallest waterfall, the longest glacier in the eastern Alps, snow-capped crags, lush valleys, soaring bearded vultures, skipping ibex, burrowing marmots – all this and more awaits the visitor to the Hohe Tauern National Park (Nationalpark Hohe Tauern), accessible by roads twisting past some of the finest views in the country.

Orientation

In 1971 the provinces of Carinthia, Salzburg and Tirol agreed to the creation of a national park; regions were added in stages until it became Europe's largest national park, comprising 1787 sq km. Salzburg has contributed 805 sq km, Tirol 610 sq km, and Carinthia 372 sq km. The most famous route in Austria, the Grossglockner Road, starts in Salzburg province and ends in Carinthia. The park's highest point is the mighty Grossglockner (3797m), which straddles the border between East Tirol and Carinthia. On the western side of the park stands the second-highest peak in the region, Grossvenediger (3674m), the high point of the border between East Tirol and Salzburg.

The boundaries of the park are extremely irregular, but it can be thought of as having three sections: west of the Felber Tauern Road (containing Grossvenediger), the vicinity of Grossglockner, and the eastern portion between Mallnitz and Bad Gastein. Zell am See, Bad Gastein and Lienz each border the park and are covered in this chapter.

Information

The Hohe Tauern National Park is open year-round and there's no admission charge; however, most of the roads to and through the park have toll sections, and some are impassable or closed in winter (see the Getting Around section later in this chapter). This is a protected nature area but not a wilderness

area: 60,000 people live within its borders in 29 communities.

All tourist offices in places bordering the park have information on Hohe Tauern, including the offices in Zell am See, Krimml, Bad Gastein and Lienz; they should also be able to provide free maps of the park. The *Experience in Nature* map (in English) shows information offices and overnight accommodation spots. It also highlights many tour suggestions, with descriptions on the reverse side.

The office that has jurisdiction over the whole park is known as the Nationalparkrat (☎ 04875-51 12, fax 04875-51 12-21, e nprht@netway.at), Rauterplatz 1, A-9971

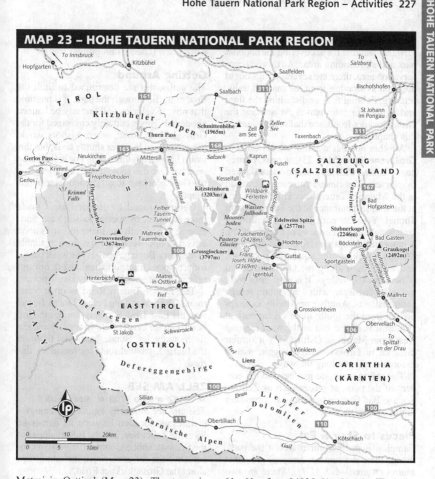

MAP 23 – HOHE TAUERN NATIONAL PARK REGION

Matrei in Osttirol (Map 23). The town is south of the tunnel on the Felber Tauern Road (Felbertauernstrasse). In addition, there is a Nationalparkverwaltung office run by each province and covering its own portion of the park. The one for Tirol (☎ 04875-51 61, fax 04875-51 61-20, **e** npht@tirol.gv.at) shares the same address as the Nationalparkrat. The one for Salzburg (☎ 06565-65 58, fax 06565-65 58-18, **e** nationalpark@salzburg.at), A-5741 Neukirchen am Grossvenediger 306, is at Neukirchen (Map 23) in the north-west of the national park region, near Krimml. The Carinthia office (☎ 04825-

61 61, fax 04825-61 61-16, **e** hohe.tauern@nationalpark-kaerten.or.at) is at Döllach 14, A-9843 Grosskirchheim (Map 23). You could also investigate the national park's Web site at **w** www.hohetauern.org. Information on accommodation options is available from these offices.

Activities

The park has more than 300 mountains above 3000m, and 246 glaciers. There are also numerous rivers, lakes, waterfalls and ravines. **Walking** while enjoying this unspoiled environment is the main activity in the park. Freytag & Berndt produces nine 1:50,000 walking maps covering the national park and surrounding areas. As this is a conservation area, there are several things *not* to do, such as straying from the marked trails, littering, lighting fires or disturbing the flora and fauna. For information on walking the Grossglockner Road, see that section later in this chapter.

Another popular walking excursion is to **Grossvenediger** (Map 23), a peak permanently coated with ice and snow and flanked by glaciers. The closest you can get by road is the Matreier Tauernhaus Hotel (1512m) at the southern entrance to the Felber Tauern Tunnel. You can park here and within an hour's walk gain fine views of the mountain. A more athletic option is to park at the Hopffeldboden parking area, south of Neukirchen, and walk south along the Obersulzbachtal (Obersulzbach Valley). It is a 10-hour walk to Grossvenediger, with a mountain refuge about halfway. Another possibility is to approach from the south; there's a car park at Hinterbichl, at the end of the road running west from Matrei in Osttirol. It's a similar distance to Grossvenediger, again with a mountain refuge along the way.

The **skiing** areas are just beyond the borders of the park, at places such as Zell am See and Bad Gastein (see those sections later in this chapter).

Places to Stay & Eat

Camping is not permitted within the park, though there is a summer camping ground at Matrei (☎/fax 04875-51 11). There are two other camping grounds on the road leading west (one is open in winter too).

For short excursions into the park, it's easy to base yourself somewhere like Zell am See or Lienz. Within Hohe Tauern itself, some small-scale guesthouses provide food and accommodation, but they are widely scattered. Contact the regional or local tourist offices for accommodation lists. If you plan to undertake major walking expeditions you should schedule your overnight stops in advance.

On the food front, regional specialities include *Erdapfelnidei* (potato noodles),

Fleischkrapfen (meat-filled dumplings) and *Kasnocken* (cheese dumplings).

Getting Around

The authorities are determined to limit the flow of traffic through the park. It is possible that private vehicles will one day be banned altogether. This is certainly envisaged for the Grossglockner Road, where visitors would have to rely on buses or shuttle taxis, but this won't happen anytime soon. For information on travelling this route in the meantime, see the Grossglockner Road section later in this chapter.

Getting around by Bundesbus is made more attractive by special passes; such deals change periodically, so make inquiries upon arrival (a one-week pass has been available in the past). Buying zonal day or week passes for provincial transport should work out significantly cheaper than buying single tickets.

The Felber Tauern Road is open year-round. The 5.5km-long Felber Tauern Tunnel is at the East Tirol–Salzburg border: the toll is €10.20 for cars (€9.45 in winter) and €8 for motorcycles. Bundesbuses and those on the Lienz-Kitzbühel route operate along this road.

ZELL AM SEE

☎ 06542 • pop 9700 • elev 758m

Zell am See is ideally situated. It enjoys a picturesque location between its namesake lake, the Zeller See, and the ridged slopes of the Schmittenhöhe mountain. It's also a convenient base for excursions, including trips along the Grossglockner Road.

Zell am See has teamed up with **Kaprun** (Map 23) to create the Europa Sports Region. Sports brochures, available from the tourist office in either place, will usually cover the whole region. Kaprun can be lively and it has good access to ski slopes, but isn't so convenient for water sports.

Orientation & Information

Compact Zell am See lies on the western bank of the Zeller See. Almost adjacent to the main resort is residential Schüttdorf, barely clinging to the southern side of the lake; it is generally cheaper for accommodation.

The tourist office, or Kurverwaltung (Map 24, #18; ☎ 770-0, fax 720 32, e zell@gold .at), is at Brucker Bundesstrasse 1. It's open 8am to noon and 2pm to 6pm Monday to Friday, 9am to noon Saturday; in the high season it's also open Saturday afternoon and Sunday morning. There's an accommodation board in the foyer with a free telephone (8am to midnight daily).

The post office (Map 24, #13; Postamt 5700) is on Postplatz, and is open standard hours. Get online at Stadtcafé Estl (Map 24, #19; ☎ 726 10), Bahnhofstrasse 1, open daily 7.30am (9am or 10am Saturday and Sunday) to 10pm.

If you want to stay in Kaprun, contact its tourist office (☎ 06547-86 43-0, fax 06547-81 92, e kaprun@kaprun.net), Salzburger Platz, for advice on accommodation. You should ask to be given the *Gästekarte* (guest card) wherever you stay.

Skiing

This region has a long history of skiing. In 1927 the first cable car in Salzburg province (the fifth in Austria) was opened on Schmittenhöhe, and the first glacial ski run was opened on Kitzsteinhorn in 1965. The Europa Sports Region operates 55 cable cars and lifts, giving access to over 130km of runs for people of all abilities. Ski passes for the region cost €59 for a two-day minimum (cheaper in the low season; reductions for senior citizens, young people and children). Ski buses are free for ski pass holders. Ski rental prices are about €15.10 for one day.

The **Schmittenhöhe** (Map 23) cable car reaches 1965m. Other cable cars from Zell am See ascend to the ridge on either side of this point. These operate from mid-December to mid-April. There are several black (difficult) runs that twist between the tree-lined flanks of the mountain.

Kaprun is the closest resort to **Kitzsteinhorn** (Map 23; 3203m), offering year-round glacier skiing. Start early in the day during the high season to avoid long queues. Cable cars soar over the glacier and up to 3029m, within 200m of the summit. The Gletscherbahn underground railway which caught fire in 2000 (see History in the Facts about

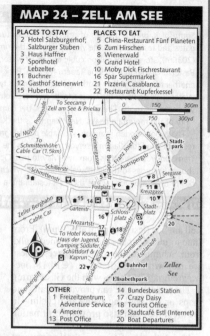

MAP 24 – ZELL AM SEE

PLACES TO STAY	PLACES TO EAT
2 Hotel Salzburgerhof; Salzburger Stuben	5 China-Restaurant Fünf Planeten
3 Haus Haffner	6 Zum Hirschen
7 Sporthotel Lebzelter	8 Wienerwald
11 Buchner	10 Grand Hotel
12 Gasthof Steinerwirt	10 Moby Dick Fischrestaurant
15 Hubertus	16 Spar Supermarket
	21 Pizzeria Casablanca
	22 Restaurant Kupferkessel

OTHER	
1 Freizeitzentrum; Adventure Service	14 Bundesbus Station
4 Ampere	18 Tourist Office
13 Post Office	19 Stadtcafé Estl (Internet)
	20 Boat Departures

Austria chapter) is no longer used to carry people; a memorial to the victims is planned. A day pass for Kitzsteinhorn or Schmittenhöhe costs €32.50, with reductions in the low season and for non-skiers. First-timers can try a cheap taste of winter skiing on the Maiskogel lift, costing €10.50 after 2pm. The short Lechnerberg-lift costs just €1.60 for one ride (medium difficulty).

Other Activities

From Schmittenhöhe you can gaze at 30 peaks over 3000m. The **Pinzgauer Spaziergang walk** from Schmittenhohe peak takes less than seven hours and exploits to the full the magnificent views; the path is marked, and a map is available from the tourist office. There is very little change in altitude along the way. You descend via the Schattbergbahn cable car to Saalbach (which, along with Hinterglemm, is an excellent skiing area – see the Walking & Skiing special section), and take the Bundesbus back from there to

Alpine Reservoirs

South of Kaprun is a series of reservoirs in a picturesque setting of Alpine peaks. There are walking paths and restaurants in the vicinity. The southernmost of the accessible reservoirs, the Mooserboden (2036m), stores 89.9 million cubic metres of water; two-thirds of this quantity is meltwater from the Pasterze Glacier in the Hohe Tauern National Park, which is transported through a 12km tunnel from another reservoir further south. Mooserboden has two dams at its northern end and an electricity plant. Water spills down to the Wasserfallboden reservoir (1672m), and is then pumped up again to create yet more electricity. The smooth arches of the dams provide a striking contrast to the rugged irregularity of the mountain peaks. Near Kaprun is the Klamm reservoir and the main stage power plant.

The Mooserboden reservoir is a viable day trip from Zell am See in summer. Bundesbuses run year-round beyond the Klamm reservoir and as far as the Kesselfall Alpenhaus, which is the limit of car travel. Transport from here runs from mid-May to mid-October and costs €15.30 (seniors €12.35) return: a shuttle bus goes to the Lärchwand funicular, which ascends 431m and connects with another shuttle bus to Mooserboden, where there's a restaurant, a tourist office and a museum with free admission.

Zell am See (last departure at 6.30pm). From June to mid-October there are guided walks from Schmittenhöhe to other places. These are free with the lift ticket (€14/18 one-way/return; €12.40/16 with the Gästekarte).

The tourist office can provide details and maps on all walking paths and **cycling** in the area; they can also provide information on where to play **golf** and **tennis**.

In the centre of town is the Freizeitzentrum *(Map 24, #1; ☎ 785-0, Steinergasse 3-5; open 10am-10pm daily)*, with an adventure **swimming** pool (€6.90), saunas, steam room and massage, as well as tenpin bowling and an ice stadium.

Adventure Service *(Map 24, #1; ☎ 735 25, fax 742 89, W www.zellamsee.at/adventure, Steinergasse 9)*, near Freizeitzentrum, is one of several places peddling high adrenalin activities, such as **rafting** on the Salzach River for €36.50.

The lake Zeller See offers opportunities for boat trips and water sports. **Boat trips** *(☎ 789-0; €6.55/3.65 adult/child; open early May-early Oct)* on the lake depart from Zell am See Esplanade (Map 24, #20), and complete a 40-minute circuit. Boats also shuttle passengers across the lake, occasionally stopping at Seecamp Zell am See *(€2.20/3.65 one-way/return)*. Rowing boats, pedal boats and motor boats can be hired from various places by the shore between April and October. Anglers need a fishing permit. Of the **water sports** available at other resorts around the lake, Thumersbach has a water-skiing school and Prielau has a windsurfing and sailing school.

Special Events

Zell am See celebrates a full calendar of seasonal events, including two lake festivals. The first, in mid-July, features sporting events, and the second, in early August, has music and costume parades.

Places to Stay

Budget As in other ski resorts, many hotels close between seasons, so be sure to phone ahead at these times.

Seecamp Zell am See (☎ 721 15, fax 721 15-15, Thumersbacher Strasse 34, Prielau) Price per adult/tent €6.90/3.65. Open year-round. This huge complex with a shop and restaurant is on the northern shoreline (head clockwise from the town).

Camping Südufer (☎ 562 28, fax 562 28-4, Seeuferstrasse 196) Price per adult/tent €4.75/1.90. Though cheaper, this camping ground to the south-east of town is not by the lake.

Haus der Jugend (☎ 571 85, fax 571 85-4, e hostel.zell-see@salzburg.co.at, Seespitzstrasse 13, Schüttdorf) Dorm beds €14.55/13.85/12.75 in 2/4/6-bed rooms. Single night surcharge €1.45. Overnight tax €0.85 for over 15s. Reception open 7.30am-9.30pm

& 4pm-10pm, closed Nov. This HI hostel is a 15-minute walk around the lake. Exit the train station on the lakeside (Zum See), take the footpath along the shore and turn left at the end. Rooms include bathroom and lockers. The food is good and you should pre-order dinner (€4.75).

Nearby Kaprun also has an HI *Jugendherberge* (☎ 06547-85 07, fax 06547-85 07-3, **e** jgh.kaprun@jgh.at, *Nikolaus Gassner Strasse 448*) Dorm beds €15.10-20. Open year-round. This 114-bed hostel is 1km east of the centre.

Private rooms are another cheap option in Zell am See. *Haus Haffner* (*Map 24, #3;* ☎ 723 96, fax 723 96-20, **e** haffner@netway .at, *Schmittenstrasse 29*) Singles/doubles with shared shower €19/35, with private bathroom €23.30/39.60, apartments €51-69 for 2-4 people. This place, just west of the Zeller Bergbahn cable car, has 12 rooms with balcony and TV, as well as a few apartments.

Mid-Range & Top End The price difference between the low and high seasons (the latter is quoted here) is more marked in this category of accommodation. Because the busy period is during winter, some prices drop in summer.

Gasthof Steinerwirt (*Map 24, #12;* ☎ 725 02, fax 725 02-47, **e** stw@netway.at, *Schlossplatz 1*) Singles €22-35, doubles €44-70. This central hotel is by the pedestrian zone and has convenient parking and wood-lined rooms, with private bathroom and TV.

Buchner (*Map24, #11;* ☎/fax 726 36, *Seegasse 12*) Doubles with/without private bathroom €56.70/50.90. This place is right in the centre on a pedestrian street, yet there's parking around the back. Rooms are average-sized with wood furnishings, and some have a balcony.

Hubertus (*Map 24, #15;* ☎ 724 27, fax 724 27-27, **e** 3sterne@hubertuspension.at, *Gartenstrasse 4*) Singles/doubles €37/57. This chalet-style place, near the Zeller Bergbahn cable car station, offers rooms in different styles, each with private bathroom, and parking.

Hotel Krone (☎ 574 21, fax 574 21-7, **e** krone@aon.at, *Kitzsteinhornstrasse 16*) Singles/doubles €46/91. Better value but less convenient, this chalet-style place, south of the lake in Schüttdorf, has a sauna, steam bath, fitness room and a small swimming pool. All rooms have private bathroom; apartments are also available.

Sporthotel Lebzelter (*Map 24, #7;* ☎ 776-0, fax 724 11, **e** zell@hotel-lebzelter.at, *Dreifaltigkeitsgasse 7*) Singles €54-62, doubles €100-117. Centrally located, this hotel has better rooms than the Steinerwirt and more facilities: there's a sauna and cellar bar.

Hotel Salzburgerhof (*Map 24, #2;* ☎ 765-0, fax 765-66, **e** 5sterne@salzburgerhof.at, *Auerspergstrasse 11*) Singles €124-138, doubles €218-247 half-board. This central, big chalet has a rustic-style interior, complemented by the traditional dress worn by staff, yet all modern luxuries are provided. The indoor swimming pool, sauna and fitness room are free for guests, and there's ample parking and an attractive garden.

Places to Eat

For self-caterers, there are several central supermarkets, including a *Spar* (*Map 24, #16; Brucker Bundesstrasse 4*). There's also a branch of the chicken fast-food chain *Wienerwald* (*Map 24, #8; Seegasse 5*).

Pizzeria Casablanca (*Map 24, #21;* ☎ 473 57, *Brucker Bundesstrasse 9*) Pizza/pasta €5.45-9.85. Open 11am-midnight daily, closed Monday in low season. This is a reasonably good place for eat-in or takeaway pizzas, and there are also more expensive meat and fish dishes available.

Moby Dick Fischrestaurant (*Map 24, #10;* ☎ 733 20, *Kreuzgasse 16*) Meals €6.55-13.50. Open 9am-6pm Mon-Fri, 9am-1pm Sat. It's pretty much fish or fish here. Prices are reasonable, but it's a shame about that cloying smell of cooking oil.

China-Restaurant Fünf Planeten (*Map 24, #5;* ☎ 701 34, *Loferer Bundesstrasse 3*) Meals €7-14.50, lunch menu €4-5.90 Mon-Fri. Open 11.30am-3pm & 5.30pm-midnight daily. Weekday lunches are the best deal: they include a starter of soup or a huge crispy spring roll.

Gasthof Steinerwirt (Map 24, #12; ☎ 725 02, Schlossplatz 1) Meals €5.85-14.60. Open 11am-11pm daily, closed between seasons. This hotel-restaurant serves inexpensive Austrian fare.

Restaurant Kupferkessel (Map 24, #22; ☎ 727 68, Brucker Bundesstrasse 18) Meals €5.50-18.75. Open 11am-2am Mon-Sat, 5pm-1am Sun. This is a former petrol station and retains the old forecourt. It has seating areas arranged around a central bar and a youthful ambience (but not exclusively so). The menu is varied and reasonably priced, including pizza, pasta, fish and steaks, as well as vegetarian and Austrian food; there's also a salad bar.

Zum Hirschen (Map 24, #6; ☎ 774, Dreifaltigkeitsgasse 1) Meals €7.70-23. Open 11am-11pm daily, closed between seasons. This hotel-restaurant serves quality Austrian and international fare in a room with wood-panelled interior.

Salzburger Stuben (Map 24, #2; ☎ 765-0, Auerspergstrasse 11) Mains €16.70-19, cover charge €2.20. Kitchen open 11.30am-1.30pm & 6.30pm-10pm daily, closed Nov. This gourmet restaurant is in the Hotel Salzburgerhof and offers top food in plush surroundings.

Grand Hotel (Map 24, #9; ☎ 788, Esplanade 4) Meals €16.70-19.60. Kitchen open noon-2.30pm & 6pm-9pm daily. The main restaurant is a culinary temple, though there's also the option of cheaper, all-day dining (from €9.50) on the lakeside terrace.

Entertainment

Zell am See has a reasonable choice of bars and discos.

Crazy Daisy (Map 24, #17; ☎ 725 16 57, Brucker Bundesstrasse 10-12) Open 4pm-1am daily winter, 8pm-1am daily summer. This is considered the best bar for après-ski activities; it's a fun place in summer too. Sometimes there are live bands, especially in winter, and there's usually no cover charge.

Ampere (Map 24, #4; ☎ 723 63, Schmittenstrasse 12) Open early afternoon-late daily winter, 4pm-late daily summer. This bar, with a classy restaurant upstairs, is another possible après-ski spot.

Getting There & Away

Train destinations from Zell am See include Salzburg (€10.90, 1½ hours, hourly), Kitzbühel (€8.15, 45 minutes, every two hours) and Innsbruck (€11.65, two hours, hourly). The town is also at the head of the narrow-gauge railway line to Krimml Falls (see the Krimml Falls Getting There & Away section later in this chapter). You can hire bikes at the train station.

Bundesbuses leave from outside the train station and the bus station (Map 24, #14), behind the post office. They run to various destinations, including hourly to Kaprun (€2.30, 17 minutes) and to Krimml Falls (€7.30, 1½ hours). For details of buses to Lienz via Franz Josefs Höhe, see the Grossglockner Road Getting There & Away section.

Zell am See is on Hwy 311 running north to Lofer, where it joins Hwy 312 connecting St Johann in Tirol with Salzburg (passing through Germany). It's also just a few kilometres north of the east-west highway linking St Johann im Pongau with Tirol (via the Gerlos Pass).

KRIMML FALLS

About 55km west of Zell am See, these triple-level falls (Map 23) are an inspiring sight and attract hordes of visitors in summer. In winter, the slopes above the village of Krimml become a ski area, and the falls just one more static lump of ice.

Orientation & Information

The Krimml Falls (Krimmler Wasserfälle) are on the north-western edge of the national park, within the protected area.

Krimml Ort (that is, Krimml village), at an elevation of 1076m, is about 500m north of the path to the falls, on a side turning from Hwy 165, which goes towards the falls. There are parking spaces (€3.65 per day) near the path to the falls, which branches to the right just before the toll booths for the Gerlos Pass road (see the Gerlos Pass section later in this chapter).

The tourist office (☎ 06564-72 39, fax 06564-75 50, e krimml.info@aon.at) is in the village centre next to the white church. Opening hours are 8am to noon and 2.30pm to 5.30pm Monday to Friday, 8.30am to 10.30am Saturday. In the low season, hours are much reduced. The post office is next door.

Viewing the Falls

The Krimml Falls path (Wasserfallweg) is 4km long. The combined height of the falls is 380m, over three main sections connected by a fast-flowing, twisting river and rapids. This lessens the immediate impact, but also means you can ascend for 1½ hours or more and enjoy ever-unfolding vistas. The highest free fall of water is 65m, in the lower falls. The middle section is mostly dissipated into a series of mini-falls, the highest being 30m, and the upper section has a free fall of 60m. The trail is steep in certain sections, but many elderly people manage the incline.

The Austrian Alpine Club (ÖAV) ticket and information offices (☎ 06564-72 12; admission €1.50/0.40 adult/child 8am-6pm daily May-Nov, admission free Dec-Apr) are a few minutes' walk along the path. A short distance past the offices is the first view-point of the lower falls, where a curtain of spray beats down onto a plinth of rock. Every few hundred metres, small paths deviate from the main trail and offer alternative viewpoints of the falls; each gives a worthwhile perspective. The excellent view back towards Krimml can often be seen through the treetops.

After about an hour's walk you'll reach the Gasthof Schönangerl (1300m), where you can take refreshments and buy souvenirs. This point is just above the middle level of the falls. After another five to 10 minutes the terrain opens out and you can see the final, upper section of the falls. A steep, further 20 minutes' walk will bring you to the top of that level (known as the Bergerblick viewpoint) for a truly memorable view over the lip of the falls and back down to the valley.

If you stop off at all or most of the view-points on the way up, it'll take about two hours to reach Bergerblick – more if you stop for food. A fast, straight descent can take as little as 40 minutes. If you're unable or un-willing to walk up to the falls, a national park taxi can take you to the upper levels; ask

the village's tourist office to make a reserva-tion. Private cars are not allowed on this route.

Places to Stay & Eat

Unless you want to continue walking past the third level of the falls and along the Krimml River (Krimmler Ache), Krimml is easily visited as a day trip from Zell am See. There are places to stay either in the village or on the way up to the falls; staff at the Krimml Ort tourist office can advise on ac-commodation options, or use its 24-hour accommodation board.

Near the church in Krimml is an *ADEG* supermarket, useful for creating a picnic. There are snack stands and restaurants (with reasonable prices) on the walk to the falls. *Gasthof Schönangerl* (☎ 06564-72 28), above the middle section of the falls, is open daily year-round except for a few weeks in November and December.

Getting There & Away

Krimml can be reached from either the west or the east. The only rail route is the narrow-gauge Pinzgauer Lokalbahn from Zell am See (€7.30, 1½ hours). It calls at many places (including Schüttdorf, near the Zell am See Haus der Jugend) on its pleasant trip through small villages and cow pastures. Departures are approximately hourly with the last train back to Zell am See at 5.35pm. In summer, Bundesbuses run from Krimml train station to the falls, but only as far as Krimml Ort at other times; the bus fare is covered by your train ticket. Alternatively, you can do the whole trip by Bundesbus from Zell am See in 1½ hours (€7.30; last return bus at 6.05pm). Krimml Ort is only about 500m short of the path to the falls. The Krimml Falls path starts near the beginning of the Tauernradweg (cycle path) to Salzburg (175km) and Passau (325km).

GERLOS PASS

This pass (Map 23; 1507m) is north-west of Krimml and is a scenic route to the Zillertal (Ziller Valley). Just south-west of Krimml there are fine views of the whole of the Krimml Falls; further on, peaks and Alpine lakes abound. There is a toll on this route: €6.55 for cars or €3.65 for motorcycles.

Bundesbuses make the trip from Krimml to/from the Zillertal (in Tirol) twice daily from mid-June to early October (€10 each way including toll, 80 minutes); phone ☎ 05285-62352-10 for details. By car, you can avoid using the toll road; take the old route, signposted 'Alte Gerlosstrasse'. This 11km stretch of road branches off from Hwy 165 at Wald im Pingau, 9km east of Krimml (on the road to Zell am See) and joins the new Gerlos road just west of the toll section.

GROSSGLOCKNER ROAD

You won't want to miss this – it's easily the most spectacular road trip in Austria. The Grossglockner Hochalpenstrasse (High Alpine Road; Map 23) was built between 1930 and 1935, following the course of an important trading route between Italy and Germany since the Middle Ages. The present road takes visitors on a magical 50km journey between 800m and 2500m above sea level, traversing a range of geographical features and climatic conditions. You'll find a dozen restaurants along the route, some of which offer accommodation.

Even before reaching the park, the trip south from Zell am See is picturesque. Cows graze in green fields and white peaks appear over the steep sides of the valley. **Wildpark Ferleiten** *(Map 23; ☎ 06456-220; admission €4.40/2.55 adult/child; open 8am-dusk daily May-Nov)*, south-west of Fusch, is home to more than 200 Alpine animals, including chamois, marmots, wolves and bears.

Once through the toll gate near the Wildpark, the road rises steeply. At 2260m there's an Alpine **Natur Schau** *(nature show; admission free; open 9am-5pm daily)*, a small museum of flora, fauna and ecology. A little further on is **Fuschertörl** (Map 23; 2428m), where there's a restaurant and excellent views on both sides of the ridge. From here a 2km side road (no coaches allowed) goes up to **Edelweiss Spitze** (Map 23; 2577m), where there's an even better panorama.

Continuing south, the road descends, then rises. At **Knappenstube** (2450m), which is

midway between Fuschertörl and Hochtor, directly on the road, there are traces of medieval gold mining. The peak of activity was in 1557 when 900kg of gold was found here; much of it went to swell the already bulky coffers of the archbishopric of Salzburg. Hochtor (Map 23; 2503m) is the highest point on the road, after which there is a steady descent to Guttal (Map 23; 1950m). Here the road splits: to the east is Heiligenblut and the route to Lienz, to the west is the Gletscherstrasse (Glacier Road). This 9km road ascends to **Franz Josefs Höhe** (Map 23; 2369m), the viewing area for Grossglockner.

Taking the Gletscherstrasse, the initial views south to the Heiligenblut Valley are fantastic, yet you soon concentrate on the approaching massif of Grossglockner itself (sit on the left for the best views). At Franz Josefs Höhe there are places to park, eat, sleep and buy souvenirs. The Grossglockner looms from across a vast tongue of ice, the **Pasterze Glacier** (Map 23). The cracks and ridges in this 10km-long mass of ice create a marvellous pattern of light and dark. Steps lead down to the edge of the glacier, or, for ease, you can take the Gletscherbahn (€4.40/7.20 one-way/return; departures every 10 minutes). There are several walks that start from Franz Josefs Höhe. The most popular is the Gamsgrubenweg, winding above the glacier and leading to a waterfall; allow up to 1½ hours return.

Getting There & Away

The Grossglockner Road (Hwy 107) is open from May to November, daily between 5am and 10pm. There's a toll section between Wildpark Ferleiten and a point just north of Heiligenblut (€25.50 for cars, €16.80 for motorcycles). An eight-day pass (consecutive days) is €33.50/22.60. You can walk or cycle the road free of charge; the hills are steep (up to 12% gradient), but hardy mountain cyclists manage the trip. For recorded information on road conditions, call ☎ 04824-22 12.

Franz Josefs Höhe is accessible from north and south by Bundesbus, but as the buses don't run every day you should inquire locally before making firm plans. The toll charges are included in the ticket price.

Glacier Watching

With fears of global warming growing, glaciers are increasingly under scrutiny. Of the world's supply of fresh water, 80% is stored in ice and snow, and 97% of this is in Antarctica and Greenland. Glaciers are also important in the rest of the world – without glacier meltwater, many areas at the foot of high mountain ranges would be desert or steppes. Most Austrian glaciers are in Tirol and Vorarlberg. The Pasterze Glacier is the largest in the eastern Alps.

There's much more to glaciers than lumps of ice. They begin as snow which, over the course of years, is compressed to firn (sometimes called névé). A depth of about 10m of fresh snow reduces to a depth of 1m of firn, which eventually evolves into ice. Surprisingly, ice takes longer to form in 'cold' glaciers (those below 0°C) than in 'temperate' glaciers. Glaciers are filled with air bubbles, created during the transformation of snow to ice, and the gas content of these bubbles may be modified by water flows in a temperate glacier.

The ice at the bottom of glaciers (in the ablation zone) may be centuries old, making it possible to measure past environmental pollution. The eruption of Krakatoa volcano in Indonesia in 1883 can be measured in glacial ice, and there are traces of the 1977 Sahara dust storms in Alpine glaciers. The peak of nuclear testing and fallout, 1963, is a benchmark year in dating glacial ice.

Glaciers are always moving; whether retreating (shrinking) or advancing (growing), the ice always moves down the valley. You might think the movement so slow as to be insignificant. Not so. The pylon feet of glacier ski lifts are set in the ice and may have to be repositioned several times each year, as is the case on the Kitzsteinhorn Glacier. Over summer, huge crevasses open in the ice and must be filled before skiing starts in winter. Even filled, they can still be hazardous – never leave the marked trails when skiing on glaciers. Ice avalanches from glaciers are another significant hazard.

MH

From Zell am See, buses to Franz Josefs Höhe run between mid-June and early October, taking two hours and 10 minutes. The one-way fare is €7, plus €1.40 toll. Depending on the season, up to three morning buses depart from Zell am See, with the same number returning in the afternoon; you could have up to five hours at the site in the high season (early July to early September) without staying overnight.

Buses from Lienz to Franz Josefs Höhe (1¾ hours) only run between late June and late September, with additional buses from mid-July to mid-September. It's possible to spend up to six hours at the site on a same-day trip. The return trip is covered under Carinthia's zonal transport tickets; a 24-hour pass costs €10.20, plus the toll of €2.80.

In the high season, you can get from Zell am See to Lienz (or vice versa) and still have plenty of time at Franz Josefs Höhe. Outside the high season this same-day trip is only possible travelling north (Lienz to Zell am See).

HEILIGENBLUT
☎ 04824 ● pop 1250 ● elev 1300m
The beautifully situated village of Heiligenblut (Map 23), 39km north of Lienz, is both a summer and winter resort, close to the boundaries of the national park.

Information
The local tourist office (☎ 20 01-21, fax 20 01-21-43, e glockner@netway.at) is on the main street, close to the 'Hotel Post' bus stop. It's open 8.30am to noon and 2.30pm to 6pm Monday to Friday and (from June to September) 9am to noon and 4pm to 6pm Saturday.

Close by, in the Gästehaus Schober, is a national park information office (☎ 27 00, e hohe.tauern@nationalpark-kaernten.or), which is open 9am to 6pm daily from 30 June to 30 September. There are some museum exhibits, and from 4pm to 6pm Monday to Friday in the same office there's someone from the Bergführerinformationsbüro (mountain guides office) available to give advice on climbing and walking.

Things to See & Do
Heiligenblut's **church** was built between 1430 and 1483; its slender pale steeple is clearly visible from far away on the Gletscherstrasse. The church contains many statues of saints, and its ceiling and altar are both Late Gothic in style. The high altar is winged, with intricate figures carved in relief. The tabernacle is purported to contain a tiny phial of Christ's blood, hence the name of the village (*Heiligenblut* means holy blood).

Most of the **skiing** above the resort is done from the Schareck (2604m) and Gjaidtroghöhe (2969m) peaks. A one-day local lift pass costs €25.50; passes of 1½ days or more will also get you into other resorts in Carinthia and East Tirol. In the summer, **mountaineering** is another popular local pursuit.

Places to Stay & Eat
Staff at the tourist office can provide information about a wide variety of accommodation, including hotels, pensions, private rooms, apartments and farmhouses. At the budget end, prices start at about €17 per person in winter, €15 in summer.

Grossglocknercamping (☎/fax 20 48, Hadergasse 11) Sites €14. This camping ground is open year-round.

Jugendherberge (☎/fax 22 59, fax 22 59-19, e jgh.heiligenblut@oejhv.or.at, Hof 36) Dorm beds €14.20, dinner €4.80. Reception open 7am-10am & 5pm-10pm daily. Open 18 Dec-15 Oct. This HI hostel is located near the church and below the *ADEG* supermarket.

Restaurants and cafes in town aren't too expensive.

Café Dorfstüberl (☎ 20 19, Hof 5) Meals €6-14. This place, near the tourist office, serves pizza and Austrian food.

Getting There & Away
In addition to the Bundesbuses to the Franz Josefs Höhe viewing area, buses run year-round to/from Lienz (€6/10.10 one-way/return, 70 minutes). They depart every one or two hours Monday through Friday, though there's only one on Sunday.

BAD GASTEIN

☎ 06434 ● pop 5600 ● elev 1100m

Bad Gastein is the chief resort in the scenic north-south Gasteiner Tal (Gastein Valley). Bad Gastein's fame rests on its radon-rich hot springs, which have attracted cure-seekers since the Middle Ages. It used to be called Badgastein until, in 1997, the local authorities decided that two names were better than one.

Orientation & Information

Bad Gastein clings to the valley slopes – this means there are lots of hills and plenty of scenic vantage points. Tumbling through the centre in a series of waterfalls is the valley river, the Gasteiner Ache. The roar of its waters can be heard throughout the centre.

The train station (Map 25) is on the western side of town. The town centre, Kongressplatz, is down the hill to the east: make your way down near the Hotel Salzburger Hof. You can save some legwork by going to the Apcoa car park at the top of Haus Austria and taking the lift down.

To reach the tourist office (Map 25, #3; ☎ 25 31-0, fax 25 31-37, e fvv.badgastein@ aon.at), Kaiser Franz Josef Strasse 27, go left from the train station exit and walk down the hill. It's open 8am to 6pm Monday to Friday; in high season additional hours are 10am to 4pm Saturday and 10am to 2pm Sunday. Staff will find you accommodation free of charge, and a Gästekarte is available. There's computer information on the national park in the foyer.

The post office (Map 25, #17; Postamt 5640) is next to the train station, and is open 8am to noon and 2pm to 6pm Monday to Friday, 8am to 10am Saturday.

Get online at Kir Royal Music Pub (Map 25, #14; ☎ 61 08), Grillparzerstrasse 2, open 11am to 5am in winter, 3pm to 5am in summer (€0.75 for six minutes).

Things to See

Bad Gastein became popular in the 19th century and many of the building facades reflect the grandeur of that era. It's worth taking a stroll around town to soak up the ambience.

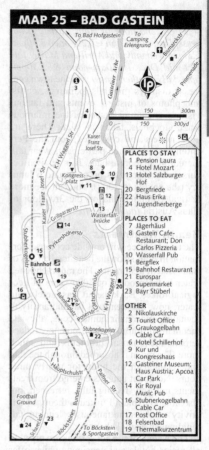

MAP 25 – BAD GASTEIN

PLACES TO STAY
1 Pension Laura
4 Hotel Mozart
13 Hotel Salzburger Hof
20 Bergfriede
22 Haus Erika
24 Jugendherberge

PLACES TO EAT
7 Jägerhäusl
8 Gastein Cafe-Restaurant; Don Carlos Pizzeria
10 Wasserfall Pub
11 Bergflex
15 Bahnhof Restaurant
21 Eurospar Supermarket
23 Bayr Stüberl

OTHER
2 Nikolauskirche
3 Tourist Office
5 Graukogelbahn Cable Car
6 Hotel Schillerhof
9 Kur und Kongresshaus
12 Gasteiner Museum; Haus Austria; Apcoa Car Park
14 Kir Royal Music Pub
16 Stubnerkogelbahn Cable Car
17 Post Office
18 Felsenbad
19 Thermalkurzentrum

From the eastern bank by the Wasserfallbrücke (waterfall bridge; Map 25), a path runs south up the hill. At the upper bridge, take Kötschachtaler Strasse and follow it eastwards up to the Hotel Schillerhof (Map 25, #6): from here you have one of the best views of the town and the valley. Work your way down via paths and roads to the small church with the dark tiled roof. This is **Nikolauskirche** (Map 25, #2), built in the 14th and 15th centuries round a central pillar. It is Gothic in style and charmingly simple inside, with an uneven flagstone floor and faded, child-like murals.

The **Gasteiner Museum** *(Map 25, #12;* ☎ *34 88, 2nd floor of Haus Austria, Kongressplatz; admission €2.20; open 3.30pm-5.30pm Wed only mid April-end May & late Oct-mid Dec, 10.30am-noon & 3.30pm-6pm daily at other times)* is in the town centre. It displays minerals, paintings, crafts, and photos of historic events and famous visitors, including a shot of the infamous Nazi, Goebbels, taken in 1938. There are also models and costumes from the **Perchten Festival**, when participants wear tall, incredibly elaborate hats. This festival occurs every four years on or around 6 January (the next is in 2002). You can see more festival paraphernalia on the 3rd floor of Haus Austria *(admission free)*.

Health Treatments

The tourist office will provide copious information in English on the beneficial effects of Bad Gastein treatments. The radon-enriched water is the product of 3000 years of geological forces. Back then it was merely rain water; now, apparently, it has the ability to revitalise and repair human cells, alleviate rheumatism, improve male potency, reduce female menopausal problems and much more. The radon is absorbed through the skin and retained in the body for nearly three hours. No doubt patients emerge from treatments not only feeling fully refreshed, but also able to explain Einstein's theory of relativity while simultaneously leaping tall buildings in a single bound.

The waters of the hot springs are piped to all major hotels and pensions, which offer their own health treatments. **Felsenbad** *(Map 25, #18;* ☎ *22 23, Bahnhofplatz 5; €11.30/5.85 adult/child; open 9.30am-8pm, 9pm or 10pm daily)*, opposite the train station, has an indoor swimming pool (dug into sheer rock) and several steaming outdoor pools. Admission includes saunas and lockers. Curative massages next door in the **Thermalkurzentrum** *(Map 25, #19;* ☎ *27 11-0, Bahnhofplatz 7; open 8am-noon & 2pm-5pm Mon-Fri, 7am-noon Sat)* cost €16.10/20.20 partial/full massage. The Gastein water can also be drunk to beneficial effect here.

Activities

Winter is the main season thanks to the extensive **skiing**. Ski passes cost about €31.50/169 for one day/week. With single-day passes you're limited to lifts in and around Bad Gastein and Bad Hofgastein (see the Around Bad Gastein section in this chapter) – that's plenty for one day, though. Passes of 1½ days or more give access to a huge area (260 lifts and 800km of ski runs), including the Sportwelt Amadé region. Bad Gastein's main peaks are Stubnerkogel (Map 23; 2246m) and Graukogel (Map 23; 2492m). Cross-country skiing is also possible here.

In summer, both peaks are excellent for **walking**. The two-section Stubnerkogelbahn cable car (Map 25; #16), near the town's train station, costs €11.65 up or €13.85 return. The Graukogelbahn (Map 25; #5), near Hotel Schillerhof, is the same price.

Places to Stay

Phone ahead in the low season as many places close during that time.

Camping Erlengrund *(☎/fax 27 90)* Price per adult/site €5.10/5.10. Open year-round. This camping ground is 2km north of Bad Gastein in Kötschachdorf, accessible by Bundesbuses, which depart from outside the Bahnhof (train station).

Jugendherberge *(Map 25, #24;* ☎ *20 80, fax 506 88,* e *hostel@badgastein.salzburg.co.at, Ederplatz 2)* Dorm beds €13.85/15.50 summer/winter, doubles €15.30/17.30. Reception open 8am-10pm, closes around 2pm-4pm winter, 1.30pm-6pm summer. This HI hostel is about 1km south of the train station and even has a sauna.

There are many private rooms, some of which the tourist office leaflet lists.

Haus Erika *(Map 25, #22;* ☎ *22 16, Stubnerkogelstrasse 40)* Rooms with private bathroom €19 per person. This 12-room house is not far from the Stubnerkogelbahn cable car station. The owner is friendly and the walls decked with interesting pictures.

Pension Laura *(Map 25, #1;* ☎ *27 04, fax 27 04-20, Bismarckstrasse 20)* Singles/doubles/triples (B&B) €32.30/41.50/56 summer high season, €36 per person half-board winter. Open year-round, but usually pre-booked in winter. This small place near Nikolauskirche has cheerful rooms with private bathroom and TV, a restaurant, a sauna and radon baths. It represents good value.

Bergfriede (Map 25, #20; ☎/fax 20 11, K H Waggerl Strasse 23) Doubles €53. Furnishings at this pension-restaurant are almost museum pieces – rustic and old-fashioned, with painted designs – although the private bathrooms are new. The writer Karl Heinrich Waggerl was born in this house in 1897.

Hotel Mozart (Map 25, #4; ☎ 26 86-0, fax 26 86-62, e hotelmozart@s-online.at, Kaiser Franz Josef Strasse 25) Singles/doubles €51/98. This three-star hotel offers pleasant rooms with high ceilings, private bathroom and cable TV. There's a radon bath on site.

Hotel Salzburger Hof (Map 25, #13; ☎ 20 37-0, fax 38 67, e salzburger-hof@ gasteinertal.com, Grillparzerstrasse 1) Singles €85-128, doubles €140-226, depending on the month. This hotel is convenient to the train station. Rooms are standard for four-star class, though the singles are a little too compact for comfort. There is live music almost every night in the bar. The hotel has a health centre, within which the thermal pool and sauna are free for guests.

Places to Eat

Supermarkets in town include the *Eurospar* (Map 25, #21), south of the train station.

Finding cheap prepared food will be a struggle, though there are a few places around, such as the snack kiosk outside Eurospar.

Bayr Stüberl (Map 25, #23; ☎ 20 71, Böcksteinerstrasse 146) 2-course lunch menu €5.45 & €6.90. Open 8am-7pm Mon-Fri, 8am-2pm Sat. This cafe near the Jugendherberge serves inexpensive Austrian meals and snacks, and has a food shop next door.

Wasserfall Pub (Map 25, #10; ☎ 54 70, Kaiser Franz Josef Strasse 2) Meals €5.40-11. Open 11am-1.30am daily, closed Mon in summer. This bar by the Wasserfallbrücke offers various meals, including pizza, pasta and schnitzels, and beer costs €2.80 for 0.5L. The slightly higher prices are worth it for the view of the waterfall from the pavement tables.

Gastein Cafe-Restaurant (Map 25, #8; ☎ 50 97, Kaiser Franz Josef Strasse 4) Meals €5-15. Open 9am-10pm or later daily. This place is more cafe than restaurant yet offers a good range of food. There's lots of outdoor seating, albeit within the brutal concrete surrounds of Kongressplatz. The cafe works with the adjoining *Don Carlos Pizzeria* (Map 25, #8), which in summer merely supplies the cafe with pizzas, yet in the winter has its own entrance and cosy dining space.

Hotel Mozart (Map 25, #4; ☎ 26 86-0, Kaiser Franz Josef Strasse 25) Meals €6-14. Open 11am-10pm daily. A competent and reasonably-priced hotel restaurant, this place turns out all the usual Austrian standards.

Bahnhof Restaurant (Map 25, #15; ☎ 21 66, Bahnhofplatz 10) Meals €5.50-13, 3-course set menu €10. Open 8am-10pm Fri-Wed summer, 8am-11pm daily winter. Despite its relatively humble location in the train station, this is a high-quality, comfortable and popular place. The set menu is available for lunch and dinner, and is affordable and filling.

Bergflex (Map 25, #11; ☎ 25 51-0, Kaiser Franz Josef Strasse 5) Meals €6.20-14.50. Open 5pm-midnight daily summer, 5pm-4am daily winter. Though there's a bar ambience and loudish music, this informal place in Arcotel Elisabethpark turns out decent grub. It's particularly lively in winter.

Jägerhäusl (Map 25, #7; ☎ 301 62, Kaiser Franz Josef Strasse 9) Austrian meals €10.90-16. Open noon-1.30pm and 5.30pm-10pm daily summer, 5pm-11pm daily winter. This two-storey restaurant with a terrace produces fine fare. Pizzas (from €5.40) are among the best in town, but sadly it only does them in winter.

Getting There & Away

Express trains trundle through Bad Gastein every two hours, connecting the resort to points both north and south, including Spittal-Millstättersee (€8.15, 50 minutes), Salzburg (€10.90, 1¼ hours) and Innsbruck (€24.75, three hours). There are good views to the right of the train when travelling north from Bad Gastein to Bad Hofgastein. Travelling south, also sit on the right, as the view is good after the second tunnel.

To take your car south, you need to use the railway car-shuttle service *(Autoschleuse Tauernbahn)* through the tunnel that starts at Böckstein (€14.55 one way). For more details, see the Western Carinthia section in the Carinthia chapter.

AROUND BAD GASTEIN

Three kilometres south of Bad Gastein, at the head of the Gasteiner Tal, is **Böckstein** (Map 23; 1131m), a village with a museum and a baroque church. It also has a medieval gold mine, which has been converted into a health treatment centre, the **Gasteiner Heilstollen** *(☎ 37 53-0, W www.gasteiner-heilstollen .com; open mid Jan-late Oct)*. Patients are delivered by a small tunnel train 2.5km into the mountain, where they take their cure. The initial 'test' trip/admission is €23.30, then the full three-week cure costs €466 for 10 trips (book well in advance).

Leading west from Böckstein is a toll road (€3.65, included in the ski pass) to **Sportgastein** (Map 23; 1588m), a centre for skiing and other sports. Seven kilometres north of Bad Gastein is **Bad Hofgastein** (Map 23; 858m), another spa centre, with good winter sports facilities. Bad Gastein, Bad Hofgastein and Böckstein are linked by bus and rail; Sportgastein has infrequent buses.

There are two access roads to the national park (with parking spaces at the terminus): the road to Sportgastein is one; the other turns east just south of Bad Gastein and follows the Kötschachtal.

LIENZ
☎ 04852 ● pop 13,000 ● elev 686m

The administrative capital of East Tirol, Lienz combines winter sports and summer walking with a relaxed, small-town ambience. The jagged Dolomites crowd the southern skyline. Lienz has been inhabited since Roman times, and was granted a town charter in 1252.

Orientation

The Italian influence is evident in Lienz (it's only 40km from the border): restaurants usually offer Italian menu translations ahead of English, and various shopkeepers proclaim their facility in that language.

The town centre is within a 'v' formed by the junction of the rivers Isel and Drau. The pivotal Hauptplatz is directly in front of the train station (Map 26); three other squares lead from it. Hauptplatz has lots of parking – it's a Kurzparkzone, with a 90-minute limit during indicated hours.

Information

The local tourist office (Map 26, #19; ☎ 652 65, fax 652 65-2, e tvblienz@aon.at) is just off Hauptplatz, at Europaplatz 1. It's open 8am to 6pm Monday to Friday, 9am to noon Saturday. In the high seasons (30 June to mid-September and mid-December to Easter) it's also open until 7pm Monday to Friday, 5pm to 7pm Saturday and 10am to noon Sunday. Staff will find accommodation (even private rooms) free of charge; if the office is shut, there's an accommodation board outside with a free telephone. Wherever you stay, ask your host for the Gästekarte, and get it stamped at the tourist office.

The East Tirol tourist office, the Osttirol Werbung (☎ 653 33, fax 653 33-2, e osttirol@netway.at), is at Albin Egger Strasse 17 in Lienz. Staff will happily send out information, but the office isn't set up for personal visits.

If you plan to stay for eight days or more in summer, ask the tourist office(s) about the Osttirol Card (€26.90).

The post office (Map 26, #17; Postamt 9900) is on Hauptplatz, virtually opposite the train station. Its opening hours are 7.30am to 7pm Monday to Friday and 8am to 11am Saturday; it exchanges foreign currency (cash only).

There's not yet an Internet cafe in Lienz, but you can surf and send emails for free at the library (Lienz Bücherei; Map 26, #5; ☎ 639 72), Muchargasse 4, open 9am to noon and 3pm to 6pm Monday to Friday (to 7pm Tuesday and Thursday).

Schloss Bruck

This well-preserved 13th-century castle overlooks the town from the west. It is the

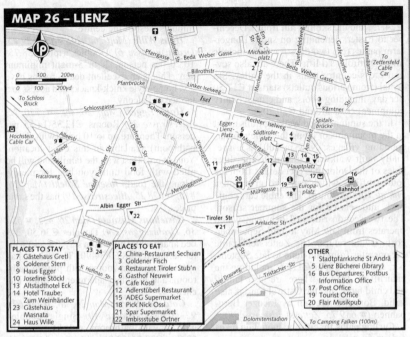

MAP 26 – LIENZ

0 100 200m
0 100 200yd

PLACES TO STAY
7 Gästehaus Gretl
8 Goldener Stern
9 Haus Egger
10 Josefine Stöckl
13 Altstadthotel Eck
14 Hotel Traube;
   Zum Weinhändler
23 Gästehaus
   Masnata
24 Haus Wille

PLACES TO EAT
2 China-Restaurant Sechuan
3 Goldener Fisch
4 Restaurant Tiroler Stub'n
6 Gasthof Neuwirt
11 Cafe Kostl
12 Adlerstüberl Restaurant
15 ADEG Supermarket
18 Pick Nick Ossi
21 Spar Supermarket
22 Imbissstube Ortner

OTHER
1 Stadtpfarrkirche St Andrä
5 Lienz Bücherei (library)
16 Bus Departures; Postbus
   Information Office
17 Post Office
19 Tourist Office
20 Flair Musikpub

former seat of the counts of Görtz and houses the **Heimatmuseum** (☎ 625 80, Schlossberg 1; €6.20/3.60 adult/student; open 10am-6pm daily Palm Sun-1 Nov), which exhibits local crafts and items connected with folklore. There's a 15th-century Romanesque chapel sporting colourful frescoes. The museum also displays 19th- and 20th-century art by East Tirolean artists. A whole gallery is devoted to Albin Egger-Lienz (1868–1926), who dwelt on themes of toil, conflict and death. Expunge his morose vision with the view from the castle tower.

Stadtpfarrkirche St Andrä
St Andrew's Church (Stadtpfarrkirche St Andrä; Map 26, #1; ☎ 621 60, Pfarrgasse 4, open daily daylight hours except during services) is north of the Isel River. This impressive Gothic building is noted for its murals (some dating from the 14th century), organ loft (1616) with winged organ and two 16th-century tombstones, sculpted in red Salzburg

marble. There's also a 'Schöne Madonna' (1430), displaying the classic 'S' stance of this style. Albin Egger-Lienz is buried in the memorial chapel in the graveyard. There's a good view of the Dolomites from the church area – visit in the early evening when the peaks catch the sun.

Activities
South of the Drau River is the Dolomitenstadion (Map 26), a **sports complex** comprising a stadium, swimming pool and tennis courts.

Downhill **skiing** takes place on the **Zettersfeld**, where runs are mostly medium to easy. The Zettersfeld cable car station is north of the Isel (signposted). The top section of the cable car is complemented by five ski lifts at elevations of between 1660 and 2278m. **Hochstein** (2057m) is another skiing area, with its cable car station (Map 26) west of the centre. A free bus runs from the train station to the two cable car valley stations in summer and winter high seasons. One-day ski passes for the two mountains cost €24.75, and the ski lifts run from 1 December to Easter, depending on snow. Longerterm passes (eg, two days for €48) include all of Osttirol's ski lifts. There are also several cross-country trails in the valley. Ski rental (from various outlets) starts at €17.50 per day, including boots, and cross-country equipment costs around €10.20.

In the summer, good **walking** trails await in the mountains or along the valley to surrounding villages. New in 2001 is a specially built walkway clinging to the sheer sides of the Dolomites (get details from the tourist office, which can also give you a *Hiking Tips* brochure). The cable cars come back into service for the summer season. The two-section ride to Hochstein, which operates from late May to mid-September, costs €7.30 return. The Zettersfeld cable car operates from mid-June to late September, and costs €8, or €11.65, including the chairlift to 2214m. There are also family and child fares, and the Osttirol Card is also valid. Both lifts are run by Lienzer Bergbahnen (☎ 639 75, Zettersfeldstrasse 38).

Cycling paths for city and mountain bikes radiate from Lienz.

Special Events

Dolomitenlauf is a famous cross-country skiing championship that takes place on the third Sunday in January. On the second weekend in August, Lienz hosts its annual Stadtfest, when it costs €4.40 to enter the town centre to view and partake in the celebrations. Summer also sees a series of events representing Tirolean culture, as well as free concerts on Hauptplatz and in other squares (at 8pm on Wednesday and Sunday).

Places to Stay

Budget *Camping Falken* (☎ 640 22, fax 640 22-6, e camping-falken@tirol.com Eichholz 7) Price per adult/site €4.90/8.80, plus €0.60 tax. Open mid Dec-late Oct. This camping ground is south of the Drau, and is convenient to various sporting facilities.

Lienz offers plenty of inexpensive private rooms and a single night's stay is often possible. Several good choices are a few minutes west of the centre.

Haus Wille (Map 26, #24; ☎/fax 629 25, Drahtzuggasse 6) Doubles/triples €8.75-10.20 per person, 2- or 3-night minimum stay. This is an excellent deal – rooms have TV, home-style knick-knacks and access to a terrace or balcony.

Haus Egger (Map 26, #9; ☎ 720 72, Alleestrasse 33) Rooms €12.35-14.55 per person. There are up to 10 beds (with shared bathroom) available in this quiet location. You eat breakfast with the family and will be plied with food until you beg for mercy. Along the road, *Josefine Stöckl* (Map 26, #10; ☎ 628 25, Alleestrasse 19) has the same prices.

Gästehaus Masnata (Map 26, #23; ☎ 655 36, Drahtzuggasse 4) Doubles €36.50, 2-3 bed apartments (minimum stay 1 week) winter/summer €38.60/34.90. This place has spacious, modern rooms with private bathroom, and excellent apartments with a kitchen.

Goldener Stern (Map 26, #8; ☎/fax 621 92, Schweizergasse 40) Singles/doubles with private bathroom and TV €29.10/53.80, €22.55/40.70 without; add €1.50 per person if only staying 1-2 nights. Closed mid Oct-early Dec & Easter-late May. Relax in white rooms with floral frieze, either in the old-fashioned, 600-year-old Gasthof (inn) or in the more modern garden annexe.

Mid-Range & Top End *Gästehaus Gretl* (Map 26, #7; ☎ 621 06, fax 621 06-4, Schweizergasse 32) Singles/doubles €24.75/46.70. Closed around March-May & Oct-pre Christmas. Run by the same family as the ceramics shop out front, this place has big, refurbished rooms with private bathroom and TV, a lift and courtyard parking.

Altstadthotel Eck (Map 26, #13; ☎ 647 85, fax 647 85-3, e altstadthotel.eck@utanet .at, Hauptplatz 20) Singles/doubles €32.70/65.70, larger doubles €72.70. A fine top-end choice, this place has an ideal location, creatively decorated corridors and historical ambience. Its rooms are large and have high ceilings, private bathroom, satellite TV, sofa and comfortable chairs. The hotel also has a restaurant.

Hotel Traube *(Map 26, #14; ☎ 644 44, fax 641 84, e hotel.traube@tirol.com, Hauptplatz 14)* Singles €52-80, doubles €104-160, depending on style & season. Ask about special package deals. This atmospheric, stylish hotel has a rooftop indoor swimming pool. Its large rooms have all the usual amenities, and public areas feature artworks acquired from an old church.

Places to Eat

Supermarkets include an **ADEG** (Map 26, #15) at Hauptplatz 12 and a **Spar** (Map 26, #21) at Tiroler Strasse 23.

Imbissstube Ortner *(Map 26, #22; ☎ 623 91, Albin Egger Strasse 5)* Meals €2.55-4.40. Open 10.30am-9pm daily, closed Jan-April. This simple place specialises in tasty rotisserie chicken, sprinkled with delicious spices; in fact, outside summertime that's usually all it does. The smell of the chickens sizzling on the spit outside is enough to make vegetarians join Meat-Eaters Anonymous. A half-chicken *(Hendl)* costs just €2.55.

Cafe Kostl *(Map 26, #11; ☎ 620 12, Kreuzgasse 4)* Meals €4-6.50. Open 7am-8pm Mon-Fri, 7am-noon Sat. This cafe-bar has tables inside and out. Food is cheap if limited, and it also does breakfasts.

China-Restaurant Sechuan *(Map 26, #2; ☎ 651 22, Beda Weber Gasse 13)* Lunch menus €4.05-4.75, evening meals €6-13. Open 11.30am-2.30pm & 5.30pm-midnight daily. Though prices are lower than average, the quality is just as good. The 15 weekday lunch menus are a particularly good deal.

Pick Nick Ossi *(Map 26, #18; ☎ 710 91, Europaplatz 2)* Meals €4.40-11.65. Open 11am-2am daily. Opposite the tourist office, the restaurant on the ground floor serves a range of cheap food (pizzas, grills, salads and snacks) – nearly all choices are under €7. There's a games room downstairs.

Adlerstüberl Restaurant *(Map 26, #12; ☎ 625 50, Andrä Kranz Gasse 5)* Meals €6-15.20. Open 8.30am-midnight daily. This is a good place to try Austrian and Tirolean specialities within old-style rooms.

Restaurant Tiroler Stub'n *(Map 26, #4; ☎ 636 63, Südtiroler Platz 2)* Meals €6.20-17.50. Open 11am-11pm daily. This place offers a wide range of food, including 'senior' meals, vegetarian daily specials and Austrian and Tirolean dishes. If you haven't eaten for a week, take on the filling *Tirolerstub'n Platte* (€34.90 for two). There are lots of outdoor tables, which overlook the square.

Gasthof Neuwirt *(Map 26, #6; ☎ 621 01, Schweizergasse 22)* Meals €6.50-12. Kitchen open 10am-10pm daily. This place has local, Austrian and other grilled dishes, as well as a daily vegetarian menu. There are many different rooms with various decor themes; on the walls of the *Fischerstube* (Fisherman's Room) is a rogue's gallery of stuffed fish that didn't quite make it onto the dinner plate. The fish that do, though, are very appetising: the *Forelle Neuwirt* (trout) swims under a sea of mushrooms and tomatoes, and costs €11.30.

Goldener Fisch *(Map 26, #3; ☎ 621 32, Kärntner Strasse 9)* Meals €6.50-16. Kitchen open 11am-10pm daily. This is another Gasthof with a good restaurant, several rooms and a garden.

Zum Weinhändler *(Map 26, #14; ☎ 644 44, Hauptplatz 14)* Meals €8.20-18.20. Kitchen open 11am-10pm daily. Located in the Hotel Traube, this is one of the best restaurants in town, offering creative versions of international and regional dishes. The same hotel also has a decent (and affordable) pizza restaurant.

Entertainment

Flair Musikpub *(Map 26, #20; mobile ☎ 0676-602 57 85, Ing Ägidius Pegger Strasse)* Open 5pm-1am daily. At the side of the Creativ Center, this sometimes smoky bar has live music once a week, which can be anything from rock to country (entry for concerts €5 to €10).

Pick Nick Ossi *(Map 26, #18; ☎ 710 91, Europaplatz 2)* The downstairs room of this restaurant has pool tables (€1.50 per game), table football, loud music and a (very) young clientele.

Getting There & Away

Regional transport in Tirol comes under the wing of the Verkehrsverbund Tirol (VVT). For information on VVT transport tickets, which are valid for travel between Tirol and East Tirol, see the Tirol chapter introduction.

Bus The bus departure point is in front of the train station. The Postbus information office (Map 26, #16; ☎ 649 44) is open 8am to noon and 2pm to 4pm Monday to Friday. There are bus connections to the East Tirol ski resorts of St Jakob, Sillian and Obertilliach, as well as northwards to the Hohe Tauern National Park (see the Grossglockner Road section for more details). Buses to Kitzbühel (€12.40, 110 minutes) are quicker and more direct than the train, but they only go one to three times a day. Buses to Kufstein are also quicker than the train.

Train Most train services to the rest of Austria go east via Spittal-Millstättersee, where you usually have to change trains. Trains to Salzburg take about three hours (€24.75). This is also one route to Innsbruck, changing at Schwarzach-St Veit. However, a quicker and easier route to Innsbruck is to go west via Sillian and Italy. Austrian rail passes are valid for the whole trip only on 'corridor' trains *(not* the one at 8.32am) – see the Innsbruck Getting There & Away section in the Tirol chapter for more details. Lienz train station has bike rental and currency exchange facilities.

Car & Motorcycle To head south, you must first divert west or east along Hwy 100, as the Dolomites act as impassable sentries. For details of road routes to the north, see the Getting Around section at the beginning of this chapter.

Tirol

The province of Tirol (often spelled Tyrol in English) is the engine that drives Austrian tourism: in 2000 it had 7.5 million visitors, nearly twice as many as its nearest rival, Salzburg province. The reason they all come is the Alps. This is classic Austrian scenery, with quaint wooden chalets amid the foothills of precipitous peaks.

Numerous highly developed resorts offer myriad sporting opportunities, particularly skiing. In summer, walking takes over, but winter remains the busiest season. The more sedentary visitor can simply enjoy the magnificent views and fresh alpine air.

The Tiroleans are a proud lot, as evidenced in the traditional saying: 'Bisch a Tiroler, bisch a Mensch' – 'If you're Tirolean, you're a (real) person'. The implied put-down of non-Tiroleans isn't really directed at foreigners, it's more a dig at their fellow Austrians, particularly the Viennese. They could easily adapt the saying: If you're in Tirol, you're somewhere.

For information on Lienz in East Tirol, see the Hohe Tauern National Park Region chapter.

History

Despite the difficult Alpine terrain, Tirol has experienced influxes of tribes and travellers since the Iron Age. In 1991, the 5500-year-old body of a man was discovered preserved in ice in the Ötztal Alps (see the boxed text 'Entombed in Ice' later in this chapter). The Brenner Pass (1374m) allowed the region to develop as a north-south trade route.

Emperor Maximilian's fondness for Innsbruck increased the region's status. Under his rule (1490–1519) the town became an administrative capital and an artistic and cultural centre. The duchy of Tirol was ruled from Vienna after the death of Archduke Sigmund Franz in 1665.

In 1703 the Bavarians attempted to capture the whole of Tirol, having contested control of parts of the north of the province for many centuries. In alliance with the

Highlights

- Ski all day and party all night in St Anton, one of Austria's top winter resorts
- Admire the Goldenes Dachl (Golden Roof) in Innsbruck against the spectacular backdrop of the Nordkette Mountains
- Stroll through the gardens and museum collections of Schloss Ambras in Innsbruck
- Visit the larger-than-life bronze statues in Innsbruck's Hofkirche
- Guzzle Gauderbier during the rural Gauderfest in Zell am Ziller
- Indulge in skiing and après-ski activities in chic Kitzbühel

French (during the War of the Spanish Succession), they reached as far as the Brenner Pass before being beaten back.

Another Franco-Bavarian alliance during the Napoleonic Wars saw Tirol incorporated into Bavaria. In 1809 Andreas Hofer led a successful fight for independence, only to have Vienna return Tirol to Bavaria under a treaty later that year. Hofer continued the struggle, and was shot by firing squad on Napoleon's orders on 20 February 1810.

A further blow was dealt by the Treaty of St Germain (1919): Prosperous South Tirol was ceded to Italy and East Tirol was isolated from the rest of the province.

East Tirol is ringed by mighty Alpine ranges to the north, south and west, and

TIROL

MAP 27 – TIROL

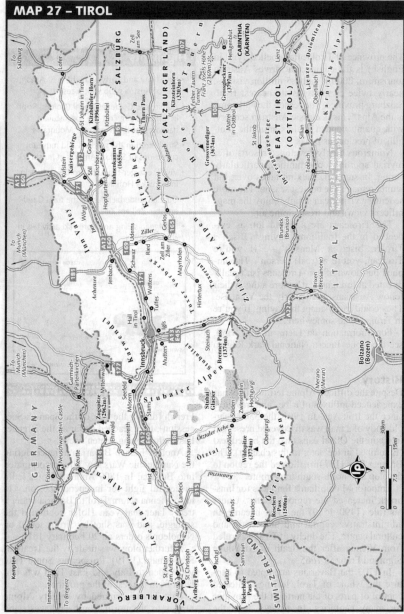

See Map 23: Hohe Tauern National Park Region p.227

though the Felber Tauern Tunnel (opened in 1967) in Salzburg has improved access to fellow Tiroleans, the region retains strong social and economic links with its eastern neighbour, Carinthia.

Orientation & Information

River valleys wind through the Alpine ranges that crowd the skyline. The most important is the Inn Valley, which provides the main east-west passage through Tirol.

Tirol is an ideal playground for skiers, walkers, mountaineers and anglers, and tourist offices release plenty of glossy material to promote these pursuits. The provincial tourist board, Tirol Werbung (Map 28, #30; ☎ 0512-72 72, fax 0512-72 72-7, e tirol .info@tirolwerbung.at), is at Maria Theresien Strasse 55, A-6010 Innsbruck. It's open 8am to 5pm Monday to Friday.

Useful free guides to Tirol in English distributed by the office include the *Tirol Guide*, a general overview; *Mountain Guide*, detailing walking itineraries, mountain huts and mountaineering schools; *Cultural Heritage Guide*, containing museum information; *Cycling Guide* and *Mountain Bike Guide* outline cycling routes. There's also *Signpost to the Snow*, which lists winter sports options; and *Snowboard Guide*, which grades snowboard possibilities.

The Web site w www.tiscover.com/tirol has lots of useful info; you should also check out w www.livingroom.tirol.com.

Tirolean Cuisine

Regional specialities include *Tiroler Knödel*, dumplings with diced bacon; *Tiroler Gerstlsuppe*, a barley soup; *Gebackene Schinkenfleckerl*, soufflé with square noodles and ham; *Schlutzkrapfen*, ravioli filled with spinach and cheese; *Tiroler Rindersaftbraten*, sliced braised beef with parmesan; *Tiroler Saftgulasch*, a goulash with diced bacon that is often served with polenta; and *Tiroler Kirchtagskrapfen*, fritters filled with dried pears, prunes and poppy seeds.

Getting Around

Regional transport comes under the wing of the Verkehrsverbund Tirol (VVT). Its head office (☎ 0512-56 16 16) is at Bodem Gasse 9, Innsbruck. The fare system is rather complicated, with at least two different types of ticket available for each journey. A brochure (unfortunately, in German only) explains the options. Prices cover journeys on city buses, trams, Bundesbuses and also ÖBB (Austrian Federal Railway) trains. VVT fares for journeys within Tirol are often lower than the 'normal' ÖBB train fare for long trips, but more expensive for shorter ones, so ticketing clerks need to check the rate under both systems (experienced ones will automatically offer the lowest fare). Fares quoted in this chapter are either ÖBB or VVT, depending on which is the lowest. Also, make sure you're getting the best ticket for your purposes: VVT zonal day passes are often much cheaper than buying separate tickets for individual journeys, and if you're staying in Innsbruck, it's generally worth paying extra to add city travel onto your regional tickets, instead of buying separate day passes.

Streckenkarten tickets are VVT tickets for specific routes priced according to distance. The minimum price (up to 3km) is €1.50 for a single or €2.95 for a day pass; the maximum for any trip in Tirol (including to/from East Tirol) is €13.10 each way. Additionally, Tirol is divided into 12 overlapping transport regions, each with its own system of passes (*Netzkarten*) for unlimited travel. However, Innsbruck is a special case, even though it apparently falls within three regions. A pass for any region (excluding travel within Innsbruck city) costs €12.40/22.60 per day/week, or €26.20/50.20 per day/week for all 12 regions. To add travel in Innsbruck to one of the three regional cards that cover the vicinity there's a small extra charge (€0.45 for one-way trips, or €1.60 for a day pass). Travel in small towns is usually covered under the regional passes, but if you *only* want to travel in a particular town get a city pass instead, costing €2.95 for a day or €6.40 for a week.

Monthly and yearly tickets are also available, and there are reductions for children, senior citizens and families.

Innsbruck

☎ 0512 ● pop 120,000 ● elev 575m

Innsbruck dates from 1180, when the small market settlement on the north bank of the Inn River expanded to the south bank. This was made possible by a bridge that had been built a few years previously and which gave the settlement its name, Ynsprugg.

In 1420 Innsbruck became the ducal seat of the Tirolean line of the Habsburgs. Emperor Maximilian I built many of the monuments that can be seen today; Archduke Ferdinand II and Empress Maria Theresa also played a part in shaping the city. More recently, the capital of Tirol has become an important winter sports centre – it staged the Winter Olympics in 1964 and 1976.

The diverse attractions of the city, coupled with beautiful scenery and top-class skiing, make Innsbruck a destination that offers something for everybody.

Orientation

Innsbruck is in the valley of the Inn River, scenically squeezed between the northern chain of the Alps (the Karwendel) and the Tuxer Vorberge (Tuxer mountains) to the south. Extensive mountain transport facilities radiate from the city and provide ample walking and skiing opportunities, particularly to the south and west. The town centre is very compact, with the Hauptbahnhof (main train station) just a 10 minute walk from the pedestrian-only old town centre (Altstadt). The main street in the Altstadt, Herzog Friedrich Strasse, connects with Maria Theresien Strasse. It's a major thoroughfare but is closed to private transport.

Innsbruck's exhibition centre is on Ingenieur Etzel Strasse, about 1km north of the Hauptbahnhof.

Information

Tourist Offices The main tourist office (Map 29, #30; ☎ 53 56, fax 53 56-43), Burggraben 3, is on the ground floor. It sells ski passes and public transport tickets and staff will book hotel rooms (€2.95 commission). It's open 8am to 6pm daily,

though hours usually extend to 7pm in summer.

There's a smaller branch in the Hauptbahnhof (Map 28; ☎ 58 37 66), open 9am to 9pm daily (8am to 10pm July to September). Further offices are at the city approach of the main highways: on the A12 autobahn to the east and west, and on the Brenner Pass road in the south. They are open 10am to 9pm daily between June and September and noon to 7pm Monday to Saturday between October and May. Another office is on Kranebitter Allee to the west, open mid-June to 30 September noon to 7pm daily (10am to 9pm in July and August).

Although all of these tourist offices are privately run, they provide plenty of free literature in English, including brochures detailing sightseeing opportunities, activities and practical information. They also supply simple city maps from the tear-off sheet for free, or there's a more detailed map costing €0.75, though note that this map is available free at many hotels.

The city-run tourist board (☎ 598 50, fax 598 50-7, e info@innsbruck.tvb.co.at), above the main tourist office, mostly fields telephone and email inquires, not private callers. It's open 8am to 6pm on weekdays, 8am to noon on Saturday.

'Club Innsbruck' is a guest card (*Gästekarte*) that's obtainable free from your accommodation; it gives various discounts on transportation and admission fees. It also entitles you to join free guided mountain walks, run from June to September; contact the main tourist office for details.

The Innsbruck Card, another tourist offering, gives one free admission to all of the main sights in and around Innsbruck, as well as travel on cable cars and free use of public transport for the duration. It's available from the main tourist office and costs €21.50/24/29.10 for 24/48/72 hours.

In the Hauptbahnhof, staff at the *Jugendwarteraum* (youth waiting room) can give useful tips on sights, entertainment and HI accommodation. It is closed from mid-July to mid-September; hours are otherwise 11am to 7pm Monday to Friday, 10am to 2pm Saturday.

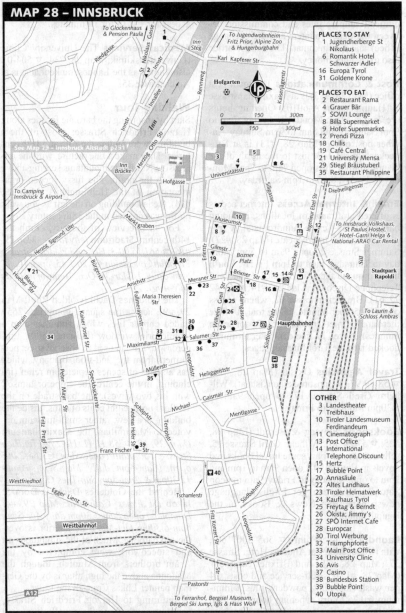

MAP 28 – INNSBRUCK

PLACES TO STAY
1 Jugendherberge St Nikolaus
6 Romantik Hotel Schwarzer Adler
16 Europa Tyrol
31 Goldene Krone

PLACES TO EAT
2 Restaurant Rama
4 Grauer Bär
5 SOWI Lounge
8 Billa Supermarket
9 Hofer Supermarket
12 Prendi Pizza
18 Chilis
19 Café Central
21 University Mensa
29 Stiegl Bräustuberl
35 Restaurant Philippine

OTHER
3 Landestheater
7 Treibhaus
10 Tiroler Landesmuseum Ferdinandeum
11 Cinematograph
13 Post Office
14 International Telephone Discount
15 Hertz
17 Bubble Point
20 Annasäule
22 Altes Landhaus
23 Tiroler Heimatwerk
24 Kaufhaus Tyrol
25 Freytag & Berndt
26 Ökista; Jimmy's
27 SPÖ Internet Cafe
28 Europcar
30 Tirol Werbung
32 Triumphpforte
33 Main Post Office
34 University Clinic
36 Avis
37 Casino
38 Bundesbus Station
39 Bubble Point
40 Utopia

TIROL

See Map 29 – Innsbruck Altstadt p251

To Glockenhaus & Pension Paula

To Jugendwohnheim Fritz Prior, Alpine Zoo & Hungerburgbahn

To Camping Innsbruck & Airport

To Innsbruck Volkshaus, St Paulus Hostel, Hotel-Garni Helga & National-ARAC Car Rental

To Laurin & Schloss Ambras

To Ferrarihof, Bergisel Museum, Bergisel Ski Jump, Igls & Haus Wolf

Hofgarten

Inn Steg

Inn Brücke

Hauptbahnhof

Stadtpark Rapoldi

Westbahnhof

Westfriedhof

0   150   300m
0   150   300yd

Money The Hauptbahnhof has exchange facilities (compare rates and commission between the ticket counters and the exchange office) and a Bankomat. The tourist office also exchanges money.

Post & Communications The main post office (Map 28, #33) is at Maximilianstrasse 2 (Hauptpostamt A-6010). Opening hours are 7am to 11pm Monday to Friday, 7am to 9pm Saturday and 8am to 9pm Sunday. Another post office (Map 28, #13) is at Brunecker Strasse 1–3, just to the north of the Hauptbahnhof. It is open 7am to 7pm Monday to Friday, 8am to 1pm Saturday.

Email & Internet Access Internet access is offered at a range of locations, including bars, hostels – even laundromats! A free place is the SPÖ Internet cafe (Map 28, #27), Salurner Strasse 2, open 9am to 5pm Monday to Thursday, 9am to 1pm Friday. You'll have to queue there, unlike at International Telephone Discount (Map 28, #14; ☎ 59 42 72 61), Bruneckerstrasse 12, where access costs €1.50 per minute. In the tourist office there are Internet terminals (€0.75 for seven minutes) as well as free computer terminals hooked into the Tirol Internet pages.

Travel Agencies Ökista (Map 28, #26; ☎ 58 89 97, e innsbruck@oekista.at), Wilhelm Greil Strasse 17, is open 9am to 5.30pm Monday to Friday.

Bookshops Freytag & Berndt (Map 28, #25; ☎ 57 24 30), Wilhelm Greil Strasse 15, sells many maps plus some travel books and novels in English. It's open 9am to 1pm and 2pm to 6pm Monday to Friday, 9am to noon Saturday. You can get English-language newspapers from News & Books in the Hauptbahnhof.

Laundry Bubble Point (☎ 565 0007 50), with two locations, at Andreas Hofer Strasse 37 (Map 28, #39) and Brixner Strasse 1 (Map 28, #17), is self-service and costs €4 per wash (including powder), plus a minimum €0.75 to dry. Opening hours are 7am to 10pm Monday to Friday, 7am to 8pm

Saturday and Sunday. They have Internet access for €0.75 for 10 minutes.

Medical Services The University Clinic (Universitätsklinik; Map 28, #34; ☎ 504-0), also known as the Landeskrankenhaus, is at Anichstrasse 35.

Walking Tour
Start by absorbing the baroque facades along Herzog Friedrich Strasse; most of these buildings were built in the 15th and 16th centuries. They make a fine picture, with the impressive Nordkette mountains soaring above them to the north. The fussy rococo ornamentation of the Helblinghaus (Map 29, #14), the last building on the left as you walk north, was created in the 18th century.

For an overview of the city, climb the 14th-century **Stadtturm** (city tower; Map 29, #16; ☎ 561 15 00-3, Herzog Friedrich Strasse 21; adult/concession €2.20/1.45; open 10am-5pm daily 1 Mar-31 Oct, 10am-6pm daily July-Aug).

The **Goldenes Dachl** (Golden Roof; Map 29, #9), across the square, comprises 2657 gilded copper tiles which shimmer atop a Gothic oriel window (built in 1500). Emperor Maximilian used to observe street performers from the 2nd-floor balcony, which has a series of scenes depicted in relief (including, in the centre, the emperor himself with his two wives). The balustrade on the 1st floor bears eight coats of arms. Inside the building is a new, rather small museum devoted to Maximilian, the **Maximilianeum** (Map 29, #9; ☎ 58 11 11, Herzog Freidrich Strasse 15; adult/concession €3.65/2.90; open 10am-6pm daily May-Sept, 10am-12.30pm & 2pm-5pm Sun-Tues Oct-Apr).

Behind the Goldenes Dachl is **Dom St Jakob** (St James' Cathedral; Map 29, #4; Domplatz; open 8am-7.30pm daily Apr-Sept, 8am-6.30pm Oct-Mar). Its interior is over-the-top baroque. Much of the sumptuous art and stuccowork were completed by the Asam brothers from Munich, though the Madonna above the high altar is by the German painter Lukas Cranach the Elder.

Returning to Herzog Friedrich Strasse, continue south along the equally imposing

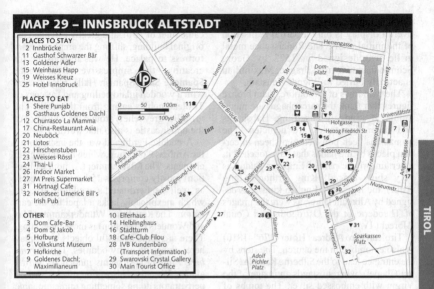

MAP 29 – INNSBRUCK ALTSTADT

PLACES TO STAY
2 Innbrücke
11 Gasthof Schwarzer Bär
13 Goldener Adler
15 Weinhaus Happ
19 Weisses Kreuz
25 Hotel Innsbruck

PLACES TO EAT
1 Shere Punjab
8 Gasthaus Goldenes Dachl
12 Churrasco La Mamma
17 China-Restaurant Asia
20 Neuböck
21 Lotos
22 Hirschenstuben
23 Weisses Rössl
24 Thai-Li
26 Indoor Market
27 M Preis Supermarket
31 Hörtnagl Cafe
32 Nordsee; Limerick Bill's Irish Pub

OTHER
3 Dom Cafe-Bar
4 Dom St Jakob
5 Hofburg
6 Volkskunst Museum
7 Hofkirche
9 Goldenes Dachl; Maximilianeum
10 Elferhaus
14 Helblinghaus
16 Stadtturm
18 Cafe-Club Filou
28 IVB Kundenbüro (Transport Information)
29 Swarovski Crystal Gallery
30 Main Tourist Office

Maria Theresien Strasse. The tall, slender **Annasäule** (St Anne's Column; Map 28, #20) was erected in 1706 to mark the repulsing of a Bavarian attack in 1703. A statue of the Virgin Mary stands at the top; St Anne is depicted at the base. After the next intersection is a fine baroque facade belonging to the **Altes Landhaus** (Map 28, #22), built in 1728 and now the seat of the provincial government. Another 200m south is the 1765 **Triumphpforte** (Triumphal Arch) which commemorates the marriage of the then emperor- to-be, Leopold II.

Hofburg

The Hofburg (*Imperial Palace; Map 29, #5; ☎ 58 71 86, Rennweg 1; adult/senior/student €5.10/3.65/3.30; open 9am-4.30pm daily*) dates from 1397, but has been rebuilt and extended several times since then. A major influence was Maria Theresa, who imposed her favourite baroque and rococo styles; the Hofburg pales into insignificance, however, when compared with her other home, Schloss Schönbrunn (see the Vienna chapter). The grand rooms of the Hofburg are decorated with numerous paintings of Maria Theresa and her family; the faces of her 16 children look strangely identical (particularly in the white room) – maybe the artist was intent on avoiding royal wrath arising from sibling rivalry in the beauty stakes. The impressive **Riesensaal** (Giant's Hall) is a 31m-long state room with ceiling frescoes and marble, gold and porcelain embellishment.

Tours are available, but they're usually conducted in German only; a booklet in English costs €1.85.

Hofkirche & Volkskunst Museum

Both sites share an entrance at Universitätstrasse 2 (☎ 58 43 02). Open 9am-5pm Mon-Sat, 9am-noon Sun. Combined entry adults/students €5.45/4.

The **Hofkirche** (*Imperial Church; Map 29, #7; adult/student €2.20/1.50, free Sun & holidays via separate church entrance*), opposite the Hofburg, contains the massive but empty sarcophagus of Maximilian I, decorated with scenes from his life. Most of the reliefs were created by Flemish sculptor Alexander Colin (1527–1612), who also produced the kneeling bronze figure of the emperor (1584). The tomb is considered the finest surviving example of

TIROL

German Renaissance sculpture, though the overall display is only a partial realisation of the initial plans. The Renaissance metal grille was designed in 1573 by Georg Schmiedhammer from Prague. Maximilian is actually buried in Wiener Neustadt.

The twin rows of 28 sombre, giant bronze figures that flank the sarcophagus are memorable, if strangely unsettling. Habsburgs and other dignitaries are depicted. The bronze has been polished to a sheen in certain places by the hands that have touched it; a certain private part of Emperor Rudolf is very shiny indeed! King Arthur (König Artur), the legendary English king, was designed by Albrecht Dürer, as were the images of Theoderic of the Ostrogoths and Count Albrecht IV.

Tirolean hero Andreas Hofer (1767–1810) is also entombed in the church. The steps by the entrance lead to the **Silberne Kapelle** (Silver Chapel), wherein stands an image of the Virgin with embossed silver. The tombs of Archduke Ferdinand II and his wife, a commoner, are also inside.

The **Volkskunst Museum** *(Folk Art Museum; Map 29, #6; adult/student €4.40/ 2.55)* includes utensils and musical instruments, though most space is devoted to a series of rooms from Tirolean dwellings.

Tiroler Landesmuseum Ferdinandeum

This museum *(Map 28, #10; ☎ 59 48 89, Museumstrasse 15)* houses a good collection of art and artefacts, including Gothic statues and altarpieces and a collection of Dutch and Flemish masters. The original reliefs from the Goldenes Dachl are to be found here, and there's a 1:20,000 scale relief map of Tirol in the basement. It will re-open in 2003 after extensive renovations.

Schloss Ambras

Schloss Ambras *(☎ 34 84 46, Schlossstrasse 20; adult/concession €7.20/5 Apr-Oct, €4.40/2.90 Nov-Mar; open 10am-5pm daily Apr-Oct, 2pm-5pm Wed-Mon Nov-Mar)*, south-east of the town centre, is a fine Renaissance castle and can easily occupy visitors for several hours. Archduke Ferdinand

II acquired the castle in 1564, the year he became ruler of Tirol, and greatly extended the original building, shifting the emphasis from fortress to palace. He was responsible for creating the impressive Renaissance **Spaniche Saal** (Spanish Hall), a long room with a wooden inlaid ceiling and frescoes of Tirolean nobles gazing from the walls. The grisaille (grey relief) around the courtyard of the upper castle is also noteworthy.

Archduke Ferdinand was the instigator of the Ambras Collection, which has three main elements. The **Rüstkammer** (Armour Collection) mostly comprises 15th-century pieces, as well as Ferdinand's wedding armour, which inexplicably lacks a lapel for the carnation. The **Kunst und Wunderkammer** (Art and Wonders Collection) is more interesting. There are some beautiful objects on display here, alongside many oddities. The *Nuremberg Plate* (1528) seems innocuous at first glance, but closer inspection reveals several perpetrators doing something unmentionable to a victim's posterior.

The **Portraitgalerie** contains room upon room of portraits of Habsburgs and other nobles. Portrait No 158 (Room 10) shows a whiskered Charles VIII masquerading as a peasant, wearing a hat masquerading as an armchair. Maria Anna of Spain (No 126, Room 22) wins the prize for the most ludicrous hairstyle. When portraits of Habsburgs begin to pall, you can unwind by strolling in the extensive castle gardens.

Guided tours are available and cost €2; they could be in English with advance reservation. Entry is cheaper in winter as some parts of the castle may be closed. To get there take tram No 6 or bus K; tram No 3 will also take you reasonably close. Another option is to take the special shuttle bus from the Altes Landhaus, which runs during castle opening times.

Bergisel

On the southern outskirts of Innsbruck, Bergisel was the site of the famous battle in 1809 at which Andreas Hofer defeated the Bavarians. The **Bergisel Museum** *(☎ 58 23 12, Bergisel 1; adult/student €2.55/1.10; open 9am-5pm daily 1 Apr-31 Oct)* contains memorials to Tirolean freedom fighters from this and other battles.

Alpine Zoo

The Alpenzoo (☎ 29 23 23, *Weiherburggasse 37; adult/concession €5.80/4; open 9am-6pm daily, 9am-5pm late Sept-late Mar)* is north of the Inn River, about 1.5km from the town centre. It features a comprehensive collection of alpine animals, including amorous bears and combative ibexes. To get there, walk up the hill from the northern end of Rennweg or take the Hungerburgbahn (the funicular to Hungerburg), which is free if you buy your zoo ticket at the bottom.

Next to the Hungerburgbahn lower station there's a circular building; inside is the **Rundgemälde** (☎ 58 44 34, *Rennweg 39; admission €2.35; open 9am-5pm daily 1 Apr-30 Oct)*, a 1000-square-metre panorama painting of the Battle of Bergisel. Included is an exhibition detailing epic overland trips by the Austrian travel writer Max Reisch (1912–85); though there's no English text, this is a surprising gem, and extremely evocative of the days before long-distance travel became so easy.

Skiing

There are five main ski areas around Innsbruck, and most have been used in Olympic competitions. All are connected by ski buses which are free to anyone with the 'Club Innsbruck' card (see the Tourist Offices section, earlier in this section). The closest ski region to the city is the Hungerburg area, to the north. The others are to the south or the west: Igls, Mutters, Tulfes and Axamer Lizum. Skiing is varied, with most runs geared to intermediates. At Bergisel there's a ski jump which, rather disconcertingly, overlooks a graveyard. A one-day ski pass costs up to €24.70 depending on the area, though the Glungezer lifts cost only €18.60 on weekdays.

You can ski year-round on the Stubai Glacier, which is a popular excursion from Innsbruck (see the Around Innsbruck section). The glacier and the five Innsbruck regions are included in the Glacier Ski Pass, which starts at €79 for three days. The Super Ski Pass additionally covers the Arlberg and Kitzbühel areas; it costs €120 for four days' skiing within six days. The regional passes are sold at the tourist office; buy passes for the individual areas at the ski lifts. Rental of skis, boots and poles starts at €13.20 per day for downhill and €6.60 for cross-country.

Walking

Above the Hungerburgbahn soars the two-section Nordkette cable car. This reaches the Hafelekar Belvedere at 2334m. This area is ideal for walking and offers spectacular views. Special services run to Seegrube (1905m, the mid-station on Nordkette) till 11.30pm on Friday evening so that the lights of Innsbruck can be enjoyed from above; call ☎ 29 33 44 for information.

Language Courses

The Innsbruck University conducts intensive German-language courses during July and August. For further details contact the Innsbrucker Hochschulkurse Deutsch (☎/fax 58 72 33, e ihd-univ-innsbruck@uibk.ac.at; during summer ☎ 507-4418), Universität Innsbruck, Innrain 52, A-6020 Innsbruck. A three-week course (60 hours) costs €400 and a six-week course (120 hours) costs €785. Other courses are listed on w www.ihd .uibk.ac.at. German-language courses are also available at Inlingua (☎ 56 20 30, e inlingua@tirol.com).

Organised Tours

Sightseeing bus tours of the city depart at noon daily (and also at 2pm from June to September) from outside the Hauptbahnhof. They last two hours and cost €11.70 (children €5.10, or free if under six years). Tourist offices and specified travel agents make tour bookings for this and other city tours.

Special Events

The best known annual event is the series of early music concerts (Festwochen der Alten Musik) conducted over most of July and August. This is dominated by baroque operas, and prices range from €19.65 to €87.25, with a 20% reduction for people aged under 27. The venues include Schloss Ambras, the

Landestheater and the Hofkirche – the latter two offer standing room for around €9. The main tourist office sells tickets and runs a Festwochen Hotline (☎ 561 561), or visit w www.altemusik.at.

From 26 November to 22 December, there's a Christmas market in the Altstadt.

Places to Stay – Budget

Camping *Camping Innsbruck Kranebitten (☎/fax 28 41 80, e campinnsbruck@hot mail.com, Kranebitter Allee 214)* Prices per adult/tent/car €5.45/2.95/2.95. Open Apr-Oct. This place is a few kilometres west of the town centre; there is a restaurant on site.

Private Rooms The tourist office has lists of private rooms in Innsbruck and Igls costing from €13.50 to €22 per person per night. Igls is a few kilometres south of town; get there by tram No 6 or bus J.

Haus Wolf (☎ 54 86 73, Dorfstrasse 48, Mutters) Rooms with one to three beds €13.50 per person. This friendly place is farther afield. It's surrounded by wonderful scenery and guests say that the effort of getting there is well worthwhile. All guests get a big free breakfast. Take the Stubaitalbahn (Stubai Valley railway) from Südtiroler Platz in front of the Hauptbahnhof (€2.20, or €5.25 for a day pass including Innsbruck city transport; 30 minutes), which departs every 50 minutes till 10.30pm. Get off at the Birchfeld stop.

Hostels *Jugendherberge St Nikolaus (Map 28, #1; ☎ 28 65 15, fax 28 65 15-14, e innsbruck@hostelnikolaus.at, Innstrasse 95)* Dorm beds €13.85, including sheets, singles/doubles/triples/quads 21.80/18.20/ 15.65/14.90 per person with shared shower. Doors locked 10am-5pm, check-in 5pm-11pm, night key available. This independent backpacker hostel is convenient for the centre, but gets mixed reports from travellers. There's a cellar bar, which can be noisy, and Internet access. The attached restaurant serves inexpensive Austrian food and is a good place for socialising. You can walk here from the Hauptbahnhof (about 2km), or take the half-hourly bus D from

outside the station. You can usually leave bags in the restaurant during weekdays up to 2pm.

Jugendherberge Innsbruck (☎ 34 61 79, fax 34 61 79-12, e yhibk@tirol.com, Reichenauerstrasse 147) Dorm beds first/ additional night €11.30/9.10, €0.55 reduction under 18. Doors locked 10am-5pm, check-in 5pm-10pm, curfew 11pm. This HI hostel has a kitchen and very slow washing machines (€3.30). Singles/doubles for €26.20/37.80 are available in July and August. Take bus O from Museumstrasse.

Volkshaus Innsbruck (☎ 39 58 82, mobile ☎ 0664-266 70 04, fax 34 10 86, Radetzkystrasse 47) Dorms (2, 4 or 6 beds) €13.80. Overlooking sports fields, this HI hostel is handy for its daytime check-in, 8am to 8pm, or later with notice, though the reception is often unstaffed so you may have to call the mobile number. Get there on bus R from the Hauptbahnhof.

In July and August there are a couple of extra hostels to try. *St Paulus (☎ 34 42 91, fax 34 42 91-20, Reichenauerstrasse 72)* and *Jugendwohnheim Fritz Prior (☎ 58 58 14, fax 58 58 14-4, Rennweg 17b)* have similar prices to the above hostels, with check-in from 5pm.

Student Rooms As in Vienna, student accommodation is pressed into service for tourists in the summer, from July to August or September.

Internationales Studenthaus (☎ 501, fax 501-15, Rechengasse 7) Singles/doubles with private facilities €31/55, or €24/42 with common shower. Reception is open 24 hours. This is the most convenient student residence. It's right by the university to the west of town and has 567 beds.

Hotels & Pensions *Glockenhaus Pension (☎ 28 65 15, fax 28 65 15-14, Weiherburggasse 3)* Singles/doubles/triples €29.10/ 43.60/65.40. Breakfast/reception at Jugendherberge St Nikolaus (see above). Rooms, all with private shower/toilet, are in a quiet location, and there's 24-hour access, but it can be a pain walking down the hill for breakfast.

Pension Paula (☎ 29 22 62, fax 29 30 17, e office@pensionpaula.at, Weiherburggasse 15). Singles/doubles with private shower & toilet €33.50/53.80, with shared facilities €28.50/43.60. Up the hill towards the zoo, this 26-bed pension is popular so book ahead. There's no convenient public transport but parking is no problem.

Innbrücke (Map 29, #2; ☎ 28 19 34, fax 27 84 10, e innbruecke@magnet.at, Innstrasse 1) Singles/doubles with shower & toilet €32.70/58.20, with shared facilities €25.50/ 43.60. Convenient for the Altstadt, these no-frills rooms are large but the side-street is surprisingly noisy.

Ferrarihof (☎/fax 57 88 98, Brenner-strasse 8) Singles/doubles with either private or shared shower €22/40. Reception in the bar downstairs, open 10am-midnight daily. This place is south of town, just off the main road. There is plenty of parking space, and it's 500m from tram No 1. The new owner is renovating rooms.

Laurin (☎/fax 34 11 04, Gumppstrasse 19) Singles/doubles with private shower €29.80/46.60, with shared facilities €26.20/ 39.30. This average-standard budget place has a cheap cafe-restaurant that's closed Wednesday. It's behind the station and near to the Gummpstrasse stop on tram No 3. There's a lift and parking spaces.

Gasthof Schwarzer Bär (Map 29, #11; ☎ 29 49 00, fax 29 49 00-4, Mariahilfstrasse 16) Singles/doubles €36.40/65.50. Convenient yet affordable, this guesthouse is in an old house with big, modern rooms, each with with shower, toilet and TV.

Places to Stay – Mid-Range & Top End

Binders Hotel (☎ 334 36-0, fax 334 39-99, e hotel@binders.at, Dr Glatz Strasse 20) Single/doubles €42.25/71.95 with private shower and toilet, €35.65/48 with shared facilities. This amenable place is behind the Hauptbahnhof, five minutes' walk along the route of tram No 3. The pricier rooms have individual colour schemes. All have cable TV and telephone.

Hotel-Garni Helga (☎ 26 11 37, fax 26 11 37-6, e hotel.helga@tirol.com, Brandlweg

3) Singles/doubles with shower, toilet, TV and telephone €47.30/61.80. Though it's 3km north-east of town, in an unappealing locality littered with car lots, this place is good value for its facilities (free sauna/whirlpool bath and indoor swimming pool). Buses O and No 4 run close by (stop: Grenobler Brücke).

Weisses Kreuz (Map 29, #19; ☎ 594 79, fax 594 79-90, e hotel.weisses.kreuz@eunet.at, Herzog Friedrich Strasse 31) Singles/doubles with private shower & toilet €59/90, with shared facilities €35/65, 'superior' doubles €102. This 500-year-old inn played host to a 13-year old Mozart, and it's probably the best three-star choice in the Altstadt. All of the rooms are spacious, neat and comfortable and the superior doubles are worth the extra cost. Prices drop slightly in winter.

Weinhaus Happ (Map 29, #15; ☎ 58 29 80, fax 58 29 80-11, Herzog Friedrich Strasse 14) Singles/doubles with shower, toilet and TV €50.90/87.30, €7.30 discount per room in April, Oct & Nov. This old house is almost as atmospheric as Weisses Kreuz, though room decor is pretty standard.

Goldene Krone (Map 28, #31; ☎ 58 61 60, fax 58 01 89-6, e r.pischl@tirol.com, Maria Theresien Strasse 46) Singles/doubles €65/ 100. This three-star hotel, near the Triumphpforte, is convenient for both the Altstadt and the Hauptbahnhof. It has smallish but well-equipped rooms with shower, toilet and TV. Prices are lower in winter, and there are also a few rooms using shared shower and toilet (€35/45).

Goldener Adler (Map 29, #13; ☎ 57 11 11, fax 58 44 09, e office@goldeneradler.com, Herzog Friedrich Strasse 6) Singles/doubles €86.50/128. This four-star place has welcomed many famous people through its portals in the past 600 years – see the plaque by the entrance. The public areas have an abundance of character, rather more, in fact, than the comfortably modern but somewhat sanitised rooms, which all have a shower, toilet and TV.

Hotel Innsbruck (Map 29, #25; ☎ 598 68-0, fax 572 280, e office@hotel innsbruck.com, Innrain 3) Singles/doubles

€65.50/109. This place is near the river in the Altstadt. Most rooms have antique-style furnishings, all have a bathroom and TV. Good on-site facilities include a sauna and swimming pool (free) and a garage (€13.10).

Romantik Hotel Schwarzer Adler *(Map 28, #6; ☎ 58 71 09, fax 56 16 97, e info@ dradler.com, Kaiserjägerstrasse 2).* Singles €91-134, doubles €132-189, suites for two people €233-407. Rather expensive but very stylish, the suites are a joy to behold, and even the standard rooms often have bathrooms that glitter with Swarovski crystals. All rooms have bathroom and TV.

Europa Tyrol *(Map 28, #16; ☎ 59 31, fax 58 78 00, e hotel@europatyrol.com, Südtiroler Platz 2)* Singles €102-160, doubles €148-255. This hotel, opposite the Hauptbahnhof, is the only five-star place in town. The rooms and lobby are as grand as you would expect, and it has a top-class restaurant. Breakfast is included, and suites are available.

Places to Eat

Some of the bars listed in the Entertainment section also serve food.

Self-Catering There is a large indoor food and flower *market* (Map 29, #26) by the river in Markthalle, Herzog Sigmund Ufer, open 7.30am to 6.30pm Monday to Friday, 7am to 1pm Saturday. Opposite, on Innrain, is a large *M Preis* supermarket (Map 29, #27), open 7.30am to 6.30pm Monday to Friday, 7.30am to 5pm Saturday. *Billa* (Map 28, #8) and *Hofer* (Map 28, #9) supermarkets are close together on Museumstrasse.

Self-Service & Budget Like other cities, Innsbruck has various snack stands providing cheap filling fodder such as sausages and chips. Some of these only come out at night to reel in the going-home-half-drunk trade.

Hörtnagl Cafe *(Map 29, #31; ☎ 597 29-40, Hörtnagl Passage, Burggasse)* Snacks/ meals €2.20-7.25. Open 6.30am-10pm Mon-Sat, 10am-10pm Sun. Attached to the Hörtnagl supermarket, this is a cheap and convenient snack stop in the centre; there's even a garden terrace.

Neuböck *(Map 29, #20; ☎ 58 10 13, Herzog Friedrich Strasse 30)* Meals €4-9.50. Open 7am-6pm or 7pm daily. This meat/deli shop serves simple sit-down meals.

Nordsee *(Map 29, #32; ☎ 57 28 81, Maria Theresien Strasse 11)* Sandwiches/meals €1.90-9.50. Open 9am-7pm Mon-Fri, 9am-3pm Sat. There are several branches of this fast-food fish joint around town; some are open until 5pm on Saturday.

University Mensa *(Map 28, #21; ☎ 507 89 01, 1st floor, Herzog Sigmund Ufer 15)* Lunch €3.50-6.65. Open 8am-6pm Mon-Thurs, 8am-2.30pm Fri. Choose between the larger self-service hall (closes at 2pm) or the slightly more expensive cafe with table service – either way you can get a three-course meal for a small outlay.

SOWI Lounge *(Map 28, #5; ☎ 216 06 68, Universitätsstrasse 15)* Two-course menu €4. Open 8am-5pm Mon-Thurs, 8am-3pm Fri, closed over Christmas. This Mensa for the business studies university has salad and vegetable buffets and outside tables on a grassy quadrangle. Incidentally, SOWI stands for Sozial-und Wirtschaftswissenschaftliche – now you know why they use an acronym!

China-Restaurant Asia *(Map 29, #17; ☎ 58 08 01, Angerzellgasse 10)* Meals €6.20-12, Three-course lunch specials Mon-Sat €5. Open 11.30am-2.30pm & 6pm-11pm daily. At this above-average restaurant, you get lots of food in the excellent lunches.

Lotos *(Map 29, #21; ☎ 57 86 63, Seilergasse 5)* Meals €6.90-14.90. Open noon-2.30pm & 6pm-11pm daily. This Chinese restaurant in the Altstadt has an all-you-can-eat buffet at lunchtime on weekdays for €6.20.

Thai-Li *(Map 29, #24; ☎ 56 28 13, Marktgraben 3)* Meals €9.10-14.90, Three-course lunch menu €7.15. Open 11.30am-2.30pm & 5.30pm-11pm daily. This top-quality Thai place has tasty yet reasonably-priced food.

Prendi Pizza *(Map 28, #12; ☎ 58 42 42, Viaduktbogen 5)* Pizzas €3.65-7.80. Open 11am-midnight daily. This eat-in or takeaway place offers a selection of over 30 pizzas – even the cheaper small pizzas are a decent size.

Churrasco La Mamma (Map 29, #12; ☎ 58 63 98, Innrain 2) Meals €6-15. Open 9am-midnight daily. This place has a range of Italian food, a salad buffet and outside tables by the river.

Restaurant Rama (Map 28, #2; ☎ 28 51 23, Innstrasse 81) Meals €4.40-9. Open 11.30am-2.30pm & 5.30pm-11.30pm Tues-Sun, 5.30pm-11.30pm Mon. Reservations advised. Also known as Shashi's, this small place has a jovial English-speaking host and excellent Indian food. Big pizzas start at €4.40, but the best option is one of the Indian curries for €7.20 – the price includes rice and *naan* bread.

Shere Punjab (Map 29, #1; ☎ 827 55, Innstrasse 19) Meals €6.20-9.50, three-course weekday lunches €5.45. Open noon-2.30pm & 5.30pm-11.30pm daily. This restaurant is also good for Indian food. Though the some of the dishes tend towards the bland, you can't complain about the prices. They also do pizzas.

Restaurant Philippine (Map 28, #35; ☎ 58 91 57, Müllerstrasse 9) Mains €6.90-12.75, small/large salad buffet plate €3.10/6.20. Kitchen open 11.30am-2pm & 6pm-10pm. This vegetarian restaurant is decked out in light colours. It has vege-only main dishes, two-course weekday lunches and a fine salad buffet. English-language menus are available.

Café Central (Map 28, #19; ☎ 5920 Gilmstrasse 5) Meals €5.55-12.80. Open 7.30am to 11pm daily. This Viennese-style coffee house offers English newspapers, Austrian dishes and piano music (8pm-10pm Sun).

Mid-Range & Top End *Stiegl Bräustuberl (Map 28, #29; ☎ 58 48 88, Wilhelm Greil Strasse 25)* Meals €5.90-14.60. Open 9am-midnight Mon-Sat. Tuck into competent Austrian and Viennese standards while seated at tables with check-pattern table-cloths and plastic flowers. Stiegl beer is €2.50 for 0.5L.

Grauer Bär (Map 28, #4; ☎ 59 24-0, Universitätsstrasse 5). Mains €5.90-16. Open 11.30am-2pm & 6pm-11pm daily. This hotel restaurant offers creative yet affordable cuisine in a comfortable, arcaded room. Most of the main courses are priced

above €10.50, though there are cheaper light meals.

Chilis (Map 28, #18; ☎ 56 73 30, Bozner Platz 6). Meals €7.05-18.25. Open 10am-midnight daily. Come here for colourful decor, Mexican food and steaks.

Most places in the Altstadt are a bit expensive, and generally serve a combination of Tirolean, Austrian and international food.

Gasthaus Goldenes Dachl (Map 29, #8; ☎ 58 93 70, Hofgasse 1) Meals €6.50-16.75. Open 7.30am-midnight daily. This place provides a civilised environment for tasting Tirolean specialities such as *Bauerngröstl*, a pork, bacon, potato and egg concoction served with salad (€9.30).

Weisses Rössl (Map 29, #23; ☎ 58 30 57, Kiebachgasse 8) Meals €5.90-14. Open 11am-2.30pm & 6pm-10pm Mon-Sat. Book ahead in the high season. This restaurant is good for regional food and set menus.

Hirschenstuben (Map 29, #22; ☎ 58 29 79, Kiebachgasse 5) Meals €6.60-18. Open 6pm-11pm Mon, 11am-2pm & 6pm-11pm Tues-Sat, closed 1-14 June. Located opposite Weisses Rössl, Hirschenstuben has vaulted rooms and a menu that encompasses both local and Italian dishes. Book ahead in the high season.

Goldener Adler (Map 29, #13; ☎ 57 11 11, fax 58 44 09, Herzog Friedrich Strasse 6) Mains €8.40-21, cover charge €1.50. Open (depending on demand) 11.30am-midnight daily. This hotel has three restaurants. The one on the 1st floor is the most elegant, but the cellar-style ground floor Goethe Stube in summer sometimes has the added attraction of a zither player.

Romantik Hotel Schwarzer Adler Restaurant (Map 28, #6; ☎ 58 71 09, Kaiserjägerstrasse 2). Meals €10.90-21.50, cover charge €1.50. Open 11.30am-2pm & 6pm-10.30pm Mon-Sat. This upmarket eatery provides all the trimmings – flowers and candles on the table, attentive service and top-notch Austrian and international food.

Entertainment

Ask at the tourist office about 'Tirolean evenings' (€16.75 for brass bands, folk dancing, yodelling and one drink). Innsbruck has its own symphony orchestra; it and other ensembles perform regularly in various venues. Schloss Ambras hosts a series of classical music concerts in summer. Between mid-May and late September medieval brass music is performed from the Goldenes Dachl balcony every Sunday at 11am.

The *Landestheater* (Map 28, #3; ☎ 520 74-4, **e** kassa@landestheater.at, Rennweg 2) stages year-round performances ranging from opera and ballet to drama and comedy. The ticket office is open 8.30am to 8.30pm Monday to Saturday, 5.30pm to 8.30pm Sunday and holidays.

Cinemas around town offer a special deal on Monday, when all seats are sold at the rate of the cheapest seasts (usually €5.10). *Cinematograph* (Map 28, #11; ☎ 57 85 00, Museumstrasse 31) shows independent films in their original language (all tickets €5.85). See their Web site at **w** www .cinematograph.at for more information.

Utopia (Map 28, #40; ☎ 58 08 70, Tschamlerstrasse 3) Open 6pm-1am Mon-Sat, 8pm-1am Sun. This cafe-bar (with Internet access) has fixtures from its former incarnation as a factory still in place. There's a celler bar that has live music or other events, usually at weekends (variable entry fee). At the time of research there was talk it might change its name, so check locally.

Treibhaus (Map 28, #7; ☎ 58 68 74, Angerzellgasse 8) Entry €7.30-18.50. Open 10am-1am Mon-Sat. This cafe has an attached venue where a range of events are held most nights, eg, parties, cabaret or diverse live music. Its Web site is at **w** www .treibhaus.at.

Elferhaus (Map 29, #10; ☎ 58 28 75, Herzog Friedrich Strasse 11) Meals €5.70-9.30. Open 10am-2am daily. This popular student hang out has a long, narrow bar and restaurant with live music on the 11th of the month (free entry). There is a huge selection of beer from Austria and elsewhere (starting at €2.20/2.95 for 0.3/0.5L). This place gets very busy and stuffy.

Cafe-Club Filou (Map 29, #18; ☎ 58 02 56, Stiftgasse 12) Open 7.30pm-4am daily. This chic cafe and disco is in an Altstadt backstreet. The downstairs bar and disco

(free DJ) opens around 10pm but doesn't get lively till midnight; most drinks are more expensive in this club section (eg, €3.50 for a small beer), though food is the same price as in the cafe.

Dom Cafe-Bar (Map 29, #3; ☎ 57 33 53, Pfarrgasse 3) Meals €4-7.20. Open 10.30am-2am daily. This busy drinking-oriented establishment in the Altstadt has good pasta and other dishes; there's a bar area and a cosier room at the back.

Limerick Bill's Irish Pub (Map 29, #32; ☎ 58 20 11, Maria Theresien Strasse 9) Guinness €4.10 a pint (0.58L). Open 4pm-1.45am daily. The Austrian craze for Irish bars has reached Innsbruck, and this pub has occasional live Irish music.

Jimmy's (Map 28, #26; ☎ 57 04 73, Wilhelm Greil Strasse 17) Open 11am-2am Mon-Sat. This place, near the Ökista travel agency, is popular with snowboarders.

You'll find a clutch of late-night bars and clubs nestled in the railway arches along Ingenieur Etzel Strasse. This district is called the Viaduktbögen; the busiest area is from 500m to 1200m north of the train station, where drinkers simply roll/stroll/stagger from bar to bar as the fancy takes them.

The Innsbruck *casino* (Map 28, #37; ☎ 58 70 40, Salurnerstrasse 15) is open daily from 3pm (slot machines from noon).

Shopping

Tirolean crafts include embroidered fabrics, wrought iron and glassware. There are many souvenir shops in the cobbled streets of the Altstadt offering loden hats, wood carvings, grotesque masks and other Tirolean products.

Tiroler Heimatwerk (Map 28, #23; ☎ 58 23 20, Meraner Strasse 2) Open 9am-1pm & 2pm-6pm Mon-Fri, 9am-noon Sat. This shop has good-quality, fairly pricey craft products.

Swarovski Crystal Gallery (Map 29, #29; ☎ 512 57 31 00, Herzog Friedrich Strasse 39) Open 8am-6.30pm Mon-Sat, 8am-6pm Sun Apr-Oct, 8am-6pm Mon-Fri, 8am-1pm Sat Nov-Mar. This is a gleaming showcase for the famous Swarovski crystals.

Kaufhaus Tyrol (Map 28, #24; ☎ 59 15-0, Maria Theresien Strasse 33) Open 9am-6.30pm Mon-Fri, 9am-5pm Sat. This large department store stocks a wide range of products.

A *flea market* appears on Saturday morning on Franziskanerplatz, the pedestrian section at the east end of Burggraben.

Getting There & Away

Air The small airport (☎ 225 25-0) is at Fürstenweg 180. Tyrolean Airways (☎ 05-05 55) is the main carrier and flies daily to Vienna, Amsterdam, Frankfurt and Zürich.

Bus The Bundesbus station (Map 28, #38) is by the Hauptbahnhof. The ticket office is near the Jugendwarteraum in the smaller of the Hauptbahnhof's two halls.

Train The Hauptbahnhof is the most convenient Innsbruck station, though some local trains also stop at the Westbahnhof (which is actually to the south) and at Hötting (to the west).

Fast trains depart every two hours for Bregenz (€23.30, three hours) and Salzburg (€27.65, two hours). From Innsbruck to the Arlberg, most of the best views are on the right-hand side of the train. Two-hourly express trains head north to Munich (€26 plus supplements, two hours, via Kufstein) and south to Verona (€24.30, four hours). Kitzbühel can be reached hourly (€11.65, one hour; direct service every second hour).

Four daily trains (three on Sunday) go to Lienz, passing through Italy. The 1.53pm train is an international train; it costs €22.25; if you're travelling on an Austrian rail pass you must pay €10.20 extra for the Italian section. The other trains are Austrian 'corridor' trains, and you can disembark in Italy; these only cost €13.10 (a VVT fare), and Austrian rail passes are valid for the whole trip.

For train information, call ☎ 05-1717, 24 hours.

Car & Motorcycle The A12 and the parallel Hwy 171 are the main roads heading west and east. Highway 177, to the west of Innsbruck, heads north to Germany and Munich. The A13 is a toll road (€8) running south through the Brenner Pass to Italy. En route

you'll cross the Europabrücke (Europe Bridge); it's 777m long and passes over the Sill River at a height of 190m, making it Europe's highest bridge. Toll-free Hwy 182 follows the same route, passing under the bridge.

Getting Around

To/From the Airport The airport is 4km to the west of the town centre. It's served by bus F, which leaves every 15 or 20 minutes from Maria Theresien Strasse (€1.60). Taxis charge about €8 for the same trip.

Public Transport Tickets on buses and trams cost €1.60 (from the driver; valid upon issue), or €4.85 for a block of four when bought in advance. Tickets bought in advance must be stamped in the machines at the outset of the journey. Advance purchase passes cost €3.20 for 24 hours and €10.10 for one week (Monday to Sunday). They're not valid for the Hungerburgbahn. The fine for riding without a ticket is €38. Advance tickets can be bought at Tabak shops, the tourist office and the IVB Kundenbüro (Map 29, #28; ☎ 53 07-240) at Stainerstrasse 2. The IVB office is open 7.30am to 6pm weekdays and can also issue VVT tickets (see the Getting Around section at the beginning of this chapter for contact details).

Parking on unmarked streets is not restricted. Most streets near the centre have a blue line; you can park on these for a maximum of 1½ or three hours during set times (approximately shop hours). The charge is €0.55/1.10/2.20 for 30/60/90 minutes; get tickets from the pavement dispensers. Parking garages (such as the one under the Altstadt) cost about €15 per day.

Taxis cost €3.80 (€4.15 after 10pm and on Sunday) for the first 1.3km, thereafter about €1.40 per kilometre. Numbers for radio taxis are ☎ 20 20 70 and 53 11.

Car Rental Local offices include:

Avis (Map 28, #36; ☎ 57 17 54) Salurner Strasse 15
Budget (☎ 58 84 68) Leopoldstrasse 54
Europcar (Map 28, #28; ☎ 58 20 60) Salurner Strasse 8

TIROL

Hertz (Map 28, #15; ☎ 58 09 01) Südtiroler Platz 1
National-ARAC (☎ 20 63 60) Haller Strasse 165

Bicycle Rental The office in the Hauptbahnhof is open 7am to 6.30pm (6pm on
Saturday) daily.

Around Innsbruck

If you're using Innsbruck as a base to visit
the area, remember that VVT tickets allow
you to add an Innsbruck pass to the ticket for
an extra cost of €1.60 (see the Getting
Around section at the beginning of this chapter for more information).

IGLS
☎ 0512 ● pop 2200 ● elev 900m
Igls (Map 27) is just a few kilometres south
of Innsbruck, at the terminus of tram No 6
(Innsbruck city tickets are valid). This charming and picturesque resort achieved world
recognition when it was a site for the 1976
Winter Olympics, for which a toboggan and
bobsleigh run was built. Igls is covered by the
Innsbruck ski pass. Staff at its tourist office
(☎ 0512-37 71 01, fax 0512-37 71 01-7,
e igls@inns bruck.tvb.co.at), Hilberstrasse
15, can help you find accommodation.

HALL IN TIROL
☎ 05223 ● pop 12,500 ● elev 574m
Hall lies 9km east of Innsbruck (Map 27),
and enjoyed past importance for its salt
mines. Staff at the tourist office (☎ 562 69,
fax 562 69-20, e hall.tirol@netway.at),
Wallpachgasse 5, will do their best to convince you that there's plenty to see in the present too. They're not wrong – Hall has an
attractive old town centre, and it's certainly
viable to pay a visit on the way to or from
Innsbruck. There are inexpensive places to
eat in the centre.

If you do stop off, explore the area around
Oberer Stadtplatz, the centre of the town.
The 15th-century **Rathaus** (☎ 58 45, Oberer
Stadtplatz) is distinctive and has a courtyard
with crenated edges and mosaic crests. Ascend the stairs and turn left to view an impressive wood-panelled room. Across the

square, the 13th-century **Pfarrkirche** (parish
church) has an off-centre chancel and is predominantly Gothic in style. Less than 200m
to the east is the **Damenstift**, a convent
founded in 1557 and graced by a baroque
tower.

A few minutes' walk south is **Burg Hasegg**
(☎ 442 45, Burg Hasegg 6, open 10am-noon
& 2pm-5pm daily, closed Fri-Sun Nov-Mar),
site of the tower that has become an emblem
of the town. This castle had a 300-year career
as a mint for silver coins (Thalers, the root
of the modern word 'dollar'), and you can
also mint your own coin here. On-site options include taking a brief interior tour
(€3.65), visiting the small, historical Stadtmuseum (€1.50), or ascending the tower and
taking the interior tour as part of a city tour
(€5.10). Book the city and interior tours via
the tourist office.

Getting There & Away
Highway 171 goes almost through the town
centre, unlike the A12/E45, which is over
the Inn River to the south. The train station
is about 1km south-west of the centre; it is on
the main Innsbruck-Wörgl train line, but
only regional trains stop there. Taking the
bus is easiest, as they stop at the town centre. From Innsbruck (€2.20, 10 minutes),
Bus No 4 leaves every 15 minutes.

WATTENS
The main reason to visit this small town is
for the **Crystal Worlds** (Swarovski Kristall-
welten; Kristallweltenstrasse 1; admission
€5.45, free for children up to age 12 or with
the Innsbruck Card; open 9am-6pm daily).
It's an inventive series of well-presented
light-and-sound displays featuring the famous Swarovski crystals – the crystal dome
is particularly disorientating. Also included
is the world's biggest crystal (62kg) and ambient music by Brian Eno. Spending over
€7.30 in the shop entitles you to a refund of
one third of the entry fee.

Getting There & Away
Wattens (Map 27) is only 20 minutes by
train from Innsbruck, but then you're faced
with a 20-minute walk (about 3.5km) to the

Crystal Worlds. Taking the bus (bay No 5 from outside Innsbruck's Hauptbahnhof, €3.05 each way, every 20 minutes) is better, because even though it takes 45 minutes, it stops right outside.

SCHWAZ
☎ 05242 ● pop 11,000 ● elev 535m

Schwaz (Map 27), 18km east of Hall, is another former mining town, except that silver and copper were the bounty sought (much of it finding its way to the Hall mint). During its heyday in the 15th and 16th centuries it was the second most populous town in Tirol after Innsbruck. Houses built during these prosperous years survive in and around the central Stadtplatz.

For information on the town and accommodation possibilities, contact the tourist office (☎ 632 40, fax 656 30, e schwaz -pi11@netway.at) at Franz Josef Strasse 2.

Things to See & Do
The large **Pfarrkirche,** dating from the 15th century, bears 15,000 copper tiles on its roof. Although the church has a Gothic structure, it has a baroque interior. A similar combination can be seen in the **Franziskanerkirche,** which has 15th-century wall paintings in the cloisters depicting Christ's Passion.

About 1.5km east of the town is **Schau Silberbergwerk** (☎ 723 72-0, Alte Landstrasse 3a; tour adult/senior/student €13.10/ 10.90/6.55; open 8.30am-5pm daily, 9.30am-4pm 1 Nov to 30 Apr, closed 16 Nov-25 Dec), a former silver mine which you can visit on a tour that includes a mini-train ride into the mountain; allow two hours.

Getting There & Away
The bus to Schwaz also passes through Hall and Wattens; by rail, only regional trains stop. The trip to/from Innsbruck takes 25 minutes and costs €4.25 each way.

STUBAI GLACIER
It's possible to ski year-round on this glacier, which is a popular excursion from Innsbruck. The pistes are varied enough to cater for most skiers. The summer skiing area is at an elevation of between 2900m and 3300m.

Walkers are attracted to the network of footpaths lower down in the valley. The Stubaital (Stubai Valley) branches off from the Brenner Pass route (A13/E45) a little south of the Europabrücke and runs south-west. The glacier itself is about 40km from Innsbruck.

Getting There & Away
The journey to the foot of the glacier takes 80 minutes by hourly 'STB' bus from Innsbruck's Bundesbus station; one-way tickets can be bought from the driver (€6.70), return tickets need to be purchased in advance (€12.40); the last bus back is usually at 5.30pm. Stubai Glacier ski passes cost €32 for one day or €21 for the afternoon. The Innsbruck tourist office offers a complete packages to the glacier, which compare favourably with going it alone. In summer it costs €44, including transport, passes and equipment rental. In winter, the STB bus is free with 'Club Innsbruck', and the price for the tourist office package reduces to €41.50.

SEEFELD
☎ 05212 ● pop 2800 ● elev 1180m

This prosperous, attractively situated resort (Map 27) hosted the Olympic Nordic skiing competitions in 1964 and 1976. Seefeld is popular year-round, but especially in winter. The resort is easily visited on a day trip from Innsbruck, though there are plenty of (pricey) places to stay. The centrally located tourist office (☎ 23 13, fax 33 55, e info @seefeld.tirol.at), Kloster Strasse 43, can outline the options. Telephone inquiries about accommodation are fielded from 8.30am to 8pm Monday to Saturday.

Things to See & Do
Pfarrkirche St Oswald This church in the village centre dates from the 15th century. Above the Gothic doorway is a decorative tympanum depicting the 14th-century martyrdom of St Oswald and the miracle of the host (an event which caused the church to become a pilgrimage site; see the boxed text, below). Other features include the winged Gothic altar, the wooden font and the fine ceiling vaulting in the chancel. Ascend the inside stairway to view the

Blutskapelle (Chapel of the Holy Blood), which houses some 18th-century stuccowork and paintings by Michael Huber.

Seefeld receives plenty of affluent, furclad tourists who take leisurely strolls round the streets and footpaths, opt for a horse-drawn carriage, or simply lounge around one of the six (!) five-star hotels. The walk south to the **Wildsee** (lake) is pleasant, or you could climb the small hill behind the church for good views of the resort, the lake and surrounding peaks.

Downhill **skiing** is mainly geared towards intermediates and beginners. The local ski pass costs €28 for one day. The two main areas are Gschwandtkopf (1500m) and Rosshütte (1800m); the latter connects to higher lifts and slopes on the Karwendel range. The resort's speciality is cross-country skiing, with 200km of trails (*Loipe*) across the valley. They go all the way to **Mösern**, 5km distant, where there are excellent views of the Inn River and peaks beyond it.

Places to Stay

The cheapest option is a room in one of the many private houses; as is the case with hotels and pensions, prices are highest in winter. Look for signs in windows, or ask at the tourist office.

Gruggerhof (☎/fax 32 54, Leutascher Strasse 64) Rooms €23.35 per person. This B&B pension is 500m west of Dorfplatz, and is perhaps the best, reasonably-central budget option. All rooms have balcony, sink and shared shower.

Landhaus Seeblick (☎ 23 89, fax 23 89-50, Innsbrucker Strasse 165) Rooms €27.65 per person. Overlooking the Wildsee, most rooms have wood balconies and a view of the lake; all come with shower and toilet.

Haus Hell (☎ 2660, fax 2660-16, Olympiastrasse 296) Rooms €36.40-45.80 per person. Though a very small place, it's big enough to have an indoor swimming pool. Its rooms have a shower, toilet and TV.

Hotel Garni Dorothea (☎ 25 27, fax 25 27-73, Kirchwald 391) Rooms €49.50-60 per person. This three star B&B hotel, on the hill above Gruggerhof, has a swimming pool, sauna and other facilities. Rooms all have shower, toilet and TV.

Places to Eat

The hub of the resort, Dorfplatz, has a couple of cheap *Imbiss* (snack) places, as well as a plethora of mid-price restaurants.

Putzi's (☎ 49 55, Bahnhofstrasse) Snacks/meals €2.20-11. This budget possibility has both a takeaway section and a sit-down cafe. The fare is simple – schnitzels, pizzas, burgers and the like.

Seefelder Stuben (☎ 22 58-90, Innsbrucker Strasse) Meals €5.90-16. Open 11am-11pm daily. Located opposite an *Albrecht* supermarket, this restaurant offers reasonable-value Austrian and Italian food.

Bahnhof Restaurant (☎ 24 43) Meals €6.50-14. Open 8am-9pm Mon-Sat &

The Miracle of the Host

These days, miracles are thin on the ground, but back in the Middle Ages miracles such as that commemorated on the tympanum of Pfarrkirche St Oswald in Seefeld could make the reputation of a town or village.

During the Easter communion of 1384, a local bigwig named Oswald Milser (no relation to the church's patron saint) decided he was too important to settle for an ordinary communion wafer; instead, he demanded a large clerical one. The timid priest obeyed, whereupon the floor of the church softened beneath Oswald's feet and began to swallow him up. The priest retrieved the wafer from the greedy citizen and the ground firmed up again, saving Oswald. He subsequently repented, and died penniless two years later. The wafer, once examined, was discovered to have been miraculously marked with blood, presumed to be that of Christ; hence the apartment in the church which held the miraculous wafer is called the Blutskapelle (Chapel of the Holy Blood).

9am-9pm Sun. This place (in the train station) is a bit rough-and-ready, attracting male drinkers and card players, but it also serves big platefuls of tasty Austrian food.

Restaurant Hocheder (*☎ 24 69, Kloster Strasse 121)* Meals €7-17. Open noon-2pm & 6.30pm-10pm daily. This hotel-restaurant is a decent choice for mid-price food, serving both Austrian and international dishes.

Wintergarten (*☎ 25 71, Münchner Strasse 215)* Meals €9-22. Kitchen open 11.30am-1pm & 6pm-10pm daily, closed between seasons. Diners come to this gourmet restaurant in Hotel Tümmlerhof for its light and creative cuisine.

Graham's Pub (*☎ 22 58 72, Münchner Strasse 136)* Open 2pm-2am daily. For après-ski drinking, try this place behind the Hotel Eden. It shows sports on satellite TV and has live music once a week.

Getting There & Away
Seefeld is 25km north-west of Innsbruck, just off the Germany-bound Hwy 177. The road follows the floor of the Inn Valley till it rises sharply (1:7 gradient) near Zirl. The train track starts climbing the north side of the valley much sooner after departing Innsbruck, providing spectacular views across the whole valley, especially if you sit on the left (€3.55, 30-40 minutes, hourly departures). Trains run hourly to Mittenwald (€3.65, 20 minutes) and Garmisch-Partenkirchen (€6.40, 50 minutes), both in Germany.

EHRWALD
Ehrwald's crowning glory is the **Zugspitze** (2962m), which marks the border between Austria and Germany and looms mightily over the village. A modern, fast cable car (€31 round-trip) sails to the top, where there's a restaurant and a magnificent panorama. All of the main Tirolean mountain ranges can be seen, as well as the Bavarian Alps and Mt Säntis in Switzerland. North of the Zugspitze is Garmisch-Partenkirchen, Germany's most popular ski resort, which also offers access to the mountain summit.

Ehrwald is linked with other resorts in Austria (including Seefeld) and Germany (including Garmisch-Partenkirchen) under

the Happy Ski Pass (adult/child €77/47 for minimum three days).

For information on accommodation and activities, you can contact the tourist office (☎ 05673-23 95, fax 05673-33 14, e ehr wald@zugspitze.tirol.at) in the town centre. Staff find rooms free of charge, or there's an accommodation board with free telephone.

Getting There & Away
To reach Ehrwald from Seefeld by train you have to pass through Germany, but Austrian rail tickets are valid for the whole trip (€8.20, 1½ hours, hourly).

Drivers can follow the rail route, or approach from the south via the Fern Pass (1216m); it's open all year and has a maximum gradient of 1:8. Bundesbuses allow you to get there from the west (eg, from Reutte, €3.95).

North-Eastern Tirol

This part of the Tirolean province is dominated by two east-west mountain chains, the Kitzbüheler Alpen and the Zillertaler Alpen. A road and rail route between Innsbruck and Salzburg diverts into Germany near Kufstein; the alternative route that dips south between the Kitzbüheler Alpen is slower but more scenic.

THE ZILLERTAL
The Zillertal (Ziller Valley) is well developed for summer and winter sports. It is one of the most densely populated valleys in the region and attracts plenty of tourists. The Zillertal runs south between the Tuxer Voralpen and the Kitzbüheler Alpen. Guarding the entrance to the valley is Jenbach (population 6000), which stands on the north bank of the Inn River. The narrow Ziller River meanders along the length of the broad valley. Small resorts provide all amenities, but attractive cow pastures, chalets and church spires are offset by unsightly lumber yards and electricity pylons. The farthest resort from Jenbach, at the head of the valley, is Mayrhofen.

All of the resorts have a tourist office, and there's also an office for the whole valley

(☎ 05288-871 87, fax 05288-871 87-1, e zillertal-werbung@netway.at, w www .zillertal.at). The magazine *Zillertaler Gästezeitung* (partially in English) covers the valley in great detail. It has lists of sights and events and provides a lot of practical information. There's also the smaller-sized *Zillertal Guide*.

There are five camping grounds within the valley. Uderns, about one-third of the way south into the valley, has a year-round *HI hostel (☎ 05288-620 10, fax 628 66, e finsingerhof@utanet.at, Finsingerhof, Finsing 73)* charging €13.85 for dorms. Accommodation prices at most places are usually slightly higher in the winter, which are the prices quoted here. Most beds are in chalet-style properties, whether pensions, private rooms, holiday apartments or farmhouses. Ask staff at the tourist offices for help in finding somewhere (they usually won't charge), as there are dozens of options in each resort. Wherever you stay, inquire about the resort's guest card (Gästekarte).

Note that many places close between seasons, usually early April to late June and early November to mid-December, this includes many of the hotels, restaurants and bars mentioned below.

Activities

The main **skiing** resort is Mayrhofen (see the Mayrhofen section later in this chapter), but there is downhill and cross-country skiing elsewhere. The Zillertaler Superskipass covers all 150-odd lifts in the valley; it starts at €98 (children €59) for the minimum four days, or €116 (€70) including the glacier ski lifts. Ski buses connect the resorts.

Walking is strongly emphasised in summer. A famous network of trails is the Zillertaler Höhenstrasse in the Tuxer Voralpen. Trails lead from the resorts of Ried, Kaltenbach, Aschau, Zell and Ramsau. Mountain huts at elevations of around 1800m provide overnight accommodation. Between early June and early October a Z-Ticket is available, covering the whole valley and valid for one use per day of cable cars, trains, buses and swimming pools; for

six/nine/12 days it costs €36/50/63 per adult, €18.50/25/31.50 per child.

Other sporting possibilities include rafting on the Ziller River, tennis, paragliding and cycling. The Ziller and its tributaries are also good for fishing, but permits are only valid for certain stretches.

Special Events

From late September to early October the cow herds are brought down from the high pastures, an event known as the Huamfahrerfest. The cows wear elaborate headdresses for the occasion, and the clanging of cow bells accompanies the efforts of amateur musicians. In Zell am Ziller they come down on the first Sunday in October, an event called Almabtrieb. In Mayrhofen the descent occurs on the first and second Saturdays in October, when the sprawling *Krämermarkt* takes over the village centre. Its wares include food, curios, crafts and cow bells.

Getting There & Away

All trains along the Inn Valley (including express IC and EC trains) stop at Jenbach. Destinations, reached hourly, include Innsbruck (€5.25, 30 minutes), Kufstein (€5.70, 30 minutes) and Kitzbühel (€7.85, one hour).

Getting Around

The Zillertal is serviced by a private railway line, the Zillertalbahn, which is based in Jenbach, the departure point for trains and buses up the valley and elsewhere. For information on this service, call ☎ 05244-606-0 or visit w www.zillertalbahn.at.

A steam train (*Dampfzug*) runs twice a day in summer, once a day in winter: it takes about 85 minutes to reach the last stop, Mayrhofen. If you just want to get from A to B, take the normal train (*Triebwagen*) as it costs about half the price. Departures from Jenbach are 22 minutes past the hour between 7.22am and 6.22pm. European rail passes are valid, and the Austrian Vorteilscard gets 50% off. The regional VVT ticket, costing €12.40/22.60 for one day/ week, is also valid.

Buses also run down the valley every hour or so; the first/last from Jenbach is at 6.05am/9.05pm and the first/last from Mayrhofen is at 5.35am/7.10pm.

ZELL AM ZILLER
☎ 05282 • pop 2000 • elev 580m

A former gold mining centre and now the main market town in the valley, Zell am Ziller (Map 27) retains its sense of fun, especially during the Gauderfest (see Special Events later in this section). It's usually marketed as Zell im Zillertal, as that includes the surrounding hamlets.

Orientation & Information

The tourist office (☎ 22 81, fax 22 81-80, e tourist.info.zell@netway.at) is at Dorfplatz 3a, near the train tracks: from the Zell am Ziller train station, turn right along Bahnhofstrasse and right again at the end, a five-minute walk. The office is open 8.30am to 12.30pm and 2.30pm to 6pm Monday to Friday; in the high season it also opens 9am to noon and 4pm to 6pm Saturday, and 4pm to 6pm Sunday. Outside (on the rail track side) is a useful computer info screen and free accommdation telephone.

At the other end of Dorfplatz is the post office, with bus stops at the rear.

Things to See & Do

Off Dorfplatz is the **Pfarrkirche**,which was built in 1782 in an unusual circular design, with side altars all the way around and interior wall scenes in pastel colours by Franz-Anton Zeiller (1716–93). Outside, most of the graves feature similar but distinctive black metal crosses with tracery surrounds.

The tourist office will provide copious information on all activities and organise free guided walks in summer. Ask about the **Abenteuer Goldbergbau** (☎ 48 20, w www.goldschaubergwerk.com, Hainzernberg 73, admission €9.45, children €4.75; open year-round), a two-hour tour of a nearby goldmine. Zell has a new Freizeitpark with adventure swimming pools, tennis courts and lots more.

Pizza-Air (☎ 22 89-0, mobile ☎ 0664-200 42 29, w www.zell.cc, Zellbergeben 4) is not some fancy new delivery service for Italian food; it offers piloted **paragliding** trips of three to 25 minutes' duration (€51 to €109). It is based in Pizza-Café Reiter, on the western side of the Ziller River. Several rival firms offer similar deals.

Special Events

Wafting around hot air currents (with or without the aid of a paraglider) is not recommended after a bellyful of Gauderbier, an incredibly strong beer (reputedly over 10% alcohol) brewed specially for the Gauderfest. This festival takes place on the first weekend in May (admission €5.90 Friday, €7.30 Saturday or Sunday), and participants show off long-established rural skills: playing music, dancing and drinking heavily. The lavish main procession (participants wear historic costumes) and wrestling take place on Sunday.

Places to Stay & Eat

Rooms in chalet-style homes are found everywhere in and around Zell.

Camping Hofer (☎ 22 48, fax 22 48-8, e office@campinghofer.at, Gerlosstrasse 33) Price in winter/summer per adult €5.45/4.95, site €6.90/5.45. This place is east of the train tracks, and has a restaurant and swimming pool.

Gasthof Waldheim (☎ 23 22, fax 23 22-4, Hainzenberg 2) Singles/doubles €30/55.50. Near the camping ground, this chalet with balconies has Tirolean music in the restaurant once a week. Rooms have a shower and toilet.

Frühstückspension Kerschdorfer (☎/fax 25 11, Unterdorf 18) Singles/doubles with bathroom €23.25/39.25. This chalet, 250m from Dorfplatz, has pleasant rooms, some with a balcony. To get here, head for the river and turn right. There's a TV room and a sunny first-floor terrace.

Hotel-Restaurant Rosengarten (☎ 24 43, fax 24 43-4, Rosengartenweg 14) Singles/doubles €25.50/51. Yet another chalet with balconies, this one has the advantage of a sauna, an inexpensive restaurant (Austrian food €5.50 to €16.75, 11am to 9pm daily) and great views to the south. The rooms are equipped with a shower, toilet and TV. It's a couple of minutes east of the rail tracks, and open in off season.

If you have more money to spend, look to the hotels on or near Dorfplatz.

Hotel Bräu (☎ 23 13, fax 23 13-17, e hotel-braeu@telecom.at, Dorfplatz 1) Singles/doubles €61/105. This place has well-equipped rooms, off-street parking and a sauna (free for guests). Its restaurant has wood panelling, old stoves and a mid-price menu, including Austrian and international dishes (€8.75 to €15); open 7.30am to midnight daily.

For self-caterers, there's a **Billa** supermarket on Bahnhofstrasse, open till 7pm or 7.30pm Monday to Friday, 5pm Saturday.

Pizza-Café Reiter (☎ 22 89-0, mobile ☎ 0664-200 42 29, Zellbergeben 4) Large pizzas €5.10-8.40. Open 11.30am-2pm & 7pm-midnight daily. This is a good après-ski place (parties 5pm to 7pm Monday, Tuesday and Thursday).

SB Restaurant (☎ 22 71, Unterdorf 11) Meals €3.65-6.55. Open 11am-9pm daily. This self-service annexe of the Zeller Stube is perhaps the best place for a cheap feed. It serves snacks, soups and salads plus simple meals.

Getting There & Away
The Triebwagen´ train costs €1.75 to Mayrhofen (13 minutes) and €3.95 to Jenbach (44 minutes). There are special reduced fares on the Gauderfest weekend. Zell am Ziller is the start of the Gerlos Pass route to the Krimml Falls. Postbuses run from mid June to early October, with departures at 8.52am and 4.12pm (€10, 80 minutes).

MAYRHOFEN
☎ 05285 ● pop 3600 ● elev 630m
A picturesque chalet village, Mayrhofen guards the approach to four Alpine valleys.

Orientation & Information
Am Marktplatz leads from the train station to Durster Strasse. The tourist office (☎ 67 60, fax 67 60-33, e mayrhofen@zillertal.tirol.at) is in Europahaus, a conference centre on Durster Strasse. It's open

8am to 6pm Monday to Friday, 9am to noon Saturday, 10am to noon Sunday. In high season it also opens 2pm to 6pm Saturday. Pick up the comprehensive brochure Mayrhofen from A-Z; it's free and written in English. Outside Europahaus is an electronic 24-hour accommodation board.

Things to See & Do
Mayrhofen offers legion **skiing** and **walking** opportunities. It's also home of the Zillertal mountaineering school (☎ 628 29, Hauptstrasse 458), run by the internationally-known mountaineer Peter Habeler. Its Web site is w www.habeler.com.

Inquire at the tourist office about guided walks (free with the Gästekarte). Return cable car fares on Ahorn and Penken are €10.90 in summer; the peaks and valleys all around provide fine vistas.

Mayrhofen's local ski pass, valid for ski lifts on Ahorn, Penken and Horberg (29 in total), costs €26.90 for one day. The resort also provides easy access to year-round skiing on the Hintertux Glacier, reaching an altitude of 3250m. In winter, a day pass costs €33 and free ski buses go there (a 20km, 45-minute trip). In summer, a day pass costs €27 but there are fewer lifts and Bundesbuses are the only transport (hourly, €6.20 return).

Erlebnisbad (☎ 625 59-0, Waldbadstrasse 539; three-hour pass for pools/sauna €10/90/8.75; open daily, hours vary according to season) is an enjoyable swimming pool complex that has indoor and outdoor pools, an aquaslide, whirlpools and saunas.

Keep an eye out for events staged in the Europahaus, such as Tirolean evenings.

Places to Stay
Campingplatz Kröll (☎/fax 625 80, fax 56, Laubichl 127) Price per adult/car/tent €4.45/2.05/2.05, singles/doubles with bathroom €21.10/39.25. Open all year. This camping ground and guesthouse is in the north of the village in the district known as Laubichl.

Duftner Rosa (☎ 637 08, Maidlergasse 547) Rooms €12 per person. These simple rooms with shared shower in a private house are the cheapest in the village centre.

Unfortunately, the owner is getting on a bit in years and will stop offering rooms if her health declines, so phone ahead.

Hotel-Garni Central (☎ *623 17, fax 623 17-33, Hauptstrasse 449*) Apartments €39.25 for one or two people, €62 for four; singles/doubles with shower, toilet, telephone, TV and balcony available in summer only €27.50/52.30. This place offers modern, comfortable apartments that are very good value. In summer, guests have the option of using apartments as singles/doubles and having breakfast included.

Landhaus Alpenrose (☎ *622 19, fax 630 29, Wiesl 463*) Apartments €59 for two people, up to €131 for seven. This place is near the ski lift and has parking places. The fully equipped apartments range in size and have luxuries like a dishwasher.

Places to Eat

Supermarkets include a *Billa* and a *Spar*, both on Brandberg Strasse.

China-Restaurant Singapore (☎ *639 12, Scheulingstrasse 371*) Meals €5.10-10.90. Open 11.30am-2.30pm & 5.30-11.30pm daily. The two-course set lunches Monday to Friday (€5.10 to €5.75) are good value. There are menus in English.

Restaurant Andreas Hofer (☎ *632 45, Schwendaustrasse 206*) Meals €6.55-18.60. Open 9am-1am daily in season, 4pm-1am Tues-Sun off-season. Given that this place is named after the Tirolean freedom fighter, it's not surprising that it concentrates on Austrian and Tirolean food. The garden has restaurant seating and a kids' play area.

Cafe Edelweiss (☎ *622 08, Brandberg Strasse 352*) Meals €5.85-20.75. Open 11am-midnight daily. This place does everything reasonably well, whether it's snacks, pizzas, Austrian food or grills.

The plush *Hotel Elisabeth* (☎ *67 67, Einfahrt Mitte 432*) offers several options. There's *Mamma Mia*, serving cheap Italian food (11am to 1am daily, open in off season), or *Wirtshaus zum Griena*, with midprice Tirolean fare (11am to 11pm, closed Monday and between seasons). At the top of the pile is *Die Gute Stube* (*The Good Room; kitchen open 6.30pm-9.30pm daily,*

late Dec to mid-March only). Main dishes €16.75-26.20. Though this is rather presumptuously named, it does tend to live up to its billing, and serves fine gourmet international dishes.

Entertainment

Mo's Eiscafe & Musicroom (☎ *634 35, Hauptstrasse 417*) Snacks/burgers/pizzas €2.85-7.65. Open 4pm-1am Sun & Mon, noon-1am Tues-Sat. This American-style bar offers free live music at 9pm from Tuesday to Saturday.

Scotland Yard (☎ *623 39, Scheulingstrasse 372*) Open 7pm nightly. This is a British-style pub. There are very few red phone boxes left in England, but there's one here!

Getting There & Away

By Triebwagen train, it's €4.55 each way to Jenbach (55 minutes).

ACHENSEE

Achensee (Lake Achen) is the largest lake in Tirol, about 9km long and 1km wide. But size isn't everything – its beautiful situation amid forested mountain peaks is what brings in the tourists during summer. The Achenseebahn, a private cogwheel steam train, makes the trip from Jenbach (€13.10 one way, €17.45 return; Eurail/Inter-Rail not valid). There are up to seven departures a day between early May and late October. Boat tours of the lake cost €10.90 and take nearly two hours, and the departure from Seespitz is coordinated with the arrival of the train from Jenbach. Several resorts around the lake offer water and winter sports.

KITZBÜHEL

☎ 05356 • pop 8200 • elev 762m

Kitzbühel (Map 30) was founded way back in the 9th century BC. It developed as a copper and mining centre, and is now a fashionable and prosperous winter resort. It's a place where you're assailed by plenty of glitz and glamour – not least in the tourist brochures.

Orientation & Information

Bahnhof Kitzbühel, the main train station (where you can hire bikes), is 1km north of

MAP 30 – KITZBÜHEL

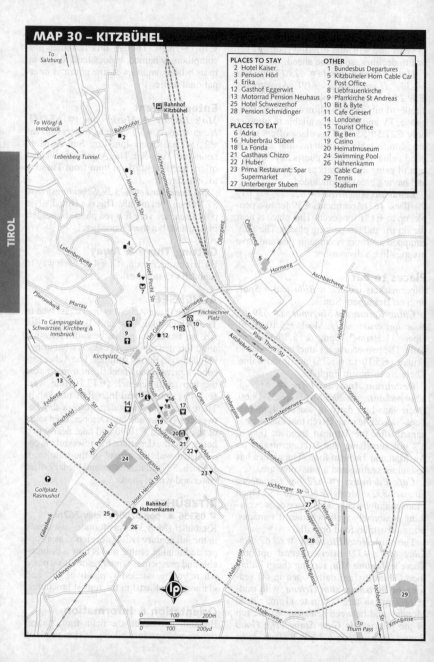

PLACES TO STAY
2 Hotel Kaiser
3 Pension Hörl
4 Erika
12 Gasthof Eggerwirt
13 Motorrad Pension Neuhaus
25 Hotel Schweizerhof
28 Pension Schmidinger

PLACES TO EAT
6 Adria
16 Huberbräu Stüberl
21 La Fonda
21 Gasthaus Chizzo
22 J Huber
23 Prima Restaurant; Spar Supermarket
27 Unterberger Stuben

OTHER
1 Bundesbus Departures
5 Kitzbüheler Horn Cable Car
7 Post Office
8 Liebfrauenkirche
9 Pfarrkirche St Andreas
10 Bit & Byte
11 Cafe Grieserl
14 Londoner
15 Tourist Office
17 Big Ben
19 Casino
20 Heimatmuseum
24 Swimming Pool
26 Hahnenkamm Cable Car
29 Tennis Stadium

the hub of the resort, Vorderstadt. The tourist office (Map 30, #15; ☎ 621 55-0, fax 623 07, e info@kitzbuehel.com), Hinterstadt 18, is in the pedestrian-only part of the town centre. It's open in low season 8.30am to noon and 2.30pm to 6pm Monday to Friday, 8.30am to noon Saturday. In high season, it's open from 8.30am to 6.30pm weekdays, 8.30am to noon and 4pm to 6pm Saturday, 10am to noon and 4pm to 6pm Sunday. There's lots of information in English; the pocket-sized *Portrait* will tell you everything you need to know about activities and events. Staff will find accommodation free of charge, or you can make use of the electronic accommodation board and free telephone outside. The Gästekarte offers various discounts to overnighters.

Various banks will change money; some have change machines accessible 24 hours daily.

The post office (Map 30, #7) (Postamt 6370) is on Josef Pirchl Strasse. Internet access (€0.15 per minute) is at Cafe Grieserl (Map 30, #11; ☎ 660 15; open daily in season), Im Gries 30, or Bit & Byte (Map 30, #10; ☎ 666 40; open shop hours), Im Gries 1a.

Things to See & Do

Picturesque gabled houses dominate the pedestrian centre – get that camera clicking! Kitzbühel has a couple of interesting churches just north of Vorderstadt. **Pfarrkirche St Andreas** *(Map 30, #9; ☎ 666 59, Pfarrauweg 2)* was built in the 15th century; Gothic features such as the nave remain despite the subsequent baroque face-lift. Some of the interior frescoes are by local artist Simon-Benedikt Faistenberger (1695–1759); he added to the work of his grandfather, who created the high altar. Faistenberger also had a hand in the adjoining **Liebfrauenkirche** (Map 30, #8), which has a sturdy square tower. Both churches are north of Kirchplatz, near the town centre.

Another cultural diversion is provided by a visit to the newly renovated **Heimatmuseum** *(Map 30, #20; ☎ 672 74, Hinterstadt 32; adult/children €2.20/0.40; open 10am-4.30pm Mon-Sat)*, which has sections on local history and winter sports.

Skiing

Kitzbühel runs are suitable for all ability levels. The ski area extends from 800m to 2000m and offers 160km of pistes accessed by 60 ski lifts. The Hahnenkamm (1655m), south-west of the town, was the first downhill piste to be opened in Austria in 1928. There's a huge network of runs and lifts on the ridge up and behind. A cable car (Map 30, #26) leaves from the south of Kitzbühel.

Across the valley to the north-east is Kitzbüheler Horn (1996m), which has mostly intermediate runs. This is a favoured mountain for snowboarders; it also has a cable car that leaves from Kitzbühel (Map 30, #5). The ski region includes the peaks around the nearby resort of Kirchberg (see that section later in this chapter), and extends as far as Thurn Pass in the south, the gateway to Salzburg province and the Felber Tauern Tunnel.

A one-day ski pass costs €32 in the high season (approximately Christmas, New Year and from February to early March) and €30 at other times. Use of ski buses is included. The two-day pass (€58.20) includes free entry to the swimming pool (Map 30, #24). Before 21 December and after mid-March, some pensions offer guests 'Skihit' reductions on ski passes – inquire in advance if they're part of the scheme. A day's equipment rental starts about €15 for downhill gear or €8 for cross-country skiing equipment.

The Kitzbüheler Alpen ski pass includes the whole region (260 lifts, 680km of runs) and costs €160 for six consecutive days.

Walking

Dozens of summer walking trails surround the town and provide a good opportunity to take in the scenery. The tourist office organises free guided walks for Gästekarte holders and supplies free walking maps. Get a head start to the heights with a cable car pass that also covers Bundesbus connections; they cost €32.70 for three days travel within seven days, or €43.25 for six days in 10. Individual ascent tickets cost €13.85 (€12.35 with Gästekarte; children half-price) on either Hahnenkamm or Kitzbüheler Horn, and the descent is free

TIROL

with the ascent ticket. Of the two peaks, vista vultures generally consider the view to be superior from Kitzbüheler Horn: The jagged Kaisergebirge range dominates to the north, and beyond the Kitzbüheler Alps the Grossglockner and Grossvenediger are visible in the south.

There is an **alpine flower garden** (☎ 628 57; free admission; open daily in summer) on the slopes of the Kitzbüheler Horn. You can drive up as far as the Alpenhaus: the road toll of €3.65/1.8.5 per car/motorcycle and €1.45 per person includes a reduction on prices in the restaurant there. The 120 different types of flower bloom at different times: most are in the spring (June), and summer (mid-July to mid-August), though some tardy species wait till autumn (September). Hahnenkamm also has a museum (☎ 6957, Hahnenkammbahn top station; free admission; open 10am to 4pm daily summer and winter) that exhibits skiing equipment collected over the last 100 years.

The scenic **Schwarzsee** lake, about 3km north-west of the town centre, is a fine location for summer swimming. There are two beach complexes, each costing about €3.30 per day.

Special Events
The Hahnenkamm professional downhill ski race takes place in January and is a spectacular event.

Late July sees tennis stars compete in the Austrian Open, which is held at the tennis stadium (Map 30, #29) just off Jochberger Strasse.

Places to Stay
A single night surcharge (€1.50 to €3) usually applies on top of published rates, but try to negotiate in the low season. Prices are higher at Christmas and in February, July and August; they are highest in the winter high season, which are the prices are quoted here.

Campingplatz Schwarzsee (☎ 628 06, fax 644 79-30, Reither Strasse 24) Price per person/site €7.20/8. Open year-round. This pricey camping ground is by the shores of the Schwarzee. Local trains stop at Schwarzsee, but then you have a 10- to

15-minute walk to the north-west side of the lake.

Many private homes have rooms available. They offer up to 10 beds apiece; around €18 per person is usual, though farther-flung farmhouses will be cheaper. Places are listed in the tourist office's hotel list.

Hotel Kaiser (Map 30, #2; ☎ 647 08, fax 662 13, **e** hotelkaiser@a-topmail.at, Bahnhofstrasse 2) Beds in four-bed rooms with bunks and shower/toilet €18.90-23.30 per person, singles/doubles 30.60/46.60. Phone ahead for availability. Conveniently close to the main station, this hotel courts youth groups and backpackers.

Pension Hörl (Map 30, #3; ☎/fax 631 44, Josef Pirchl Strasse 60) Singles/doubles with shower €23.30/43.60, with shared facilities €19.70/36.40. This place offers simple yet pleasant rooms, though some do suffer a bit of traffic noise.

Pension Schmidinger (Map 30, #28; ☎ 631 34, fax 719 94, Ehrenbachgasse 13) Rooms with shower/toilet €21.90 per person, with shared facilities €18.20. This good-value pension is unusual in that it is open year-round. Some rooms are old fashioned, though those with a bathroom are usually renovated, and sport cheerful colours. Prices can be fairly fluid.

Motorrad Pension Neuhaus (Map 30, #13; ☎/fax 622 00, **e** info@motorradpension.at, Franz Reisch Strasse 23) Singles/doubles with shower and toilet €27.70/55.30, with shared facilities €24.75/49.45. Prices drop in the low season and for longer stays. This central place offers wood-panelled rooms and special deals for motorcyclists in summer.

Gasthof Eggerwirt (Map 30, #12; ☎ 624 37, fax 624 37-22, **e** info@eggerwirt -kitzbuehel.at, Untere Gänsbachgasse 12) Singles/doubles with bathroom & TV €57/105. This atmospheric Gasthof, down the steps from the churches, has a painted facade and attractive rooms. Parking is available.

Hotel Schweizerhof (Map 30, #25; ☎ 627 35-0, fax 627 35-57, **e** schweizerhof@tirol .com, Hahnenkammstrasse 4) Singles €99-117, doubles €175-211. This four-star hotel with its well-equipped rooms is near the Hahnenkamm cable car station. Ask about reasonably priced packages that include sports or beauty treatments.

*Erika (Map 30, #4; ☎ 648 85, fax 646 74-13, **e** hotelerika@netway.at, Josef Pirchl Strasse 21)* Singles €102-164, doubles €183-287. This period building is set in its own gardens. It has excellent facilities such as an indoor swimming pool, sauna, steam bath, solarium and massage service. All rooms have bathroom and cable TV.

Places to Eat
There's a *Spar* supermarket (Map 30, #23) at Bichlstrasse 22.

J Huber (Map 30, #22; ☎ 624 80, Bichlstrasse 14) Meals €4.40-9.10. Open 8am-1.15pm & 3pm-6pm Mon-Fri, 8am-noon Sat. This deli/meat shop has a sit-down section serving inexpensive snacks and hot food.

Prima Restaurant (Map 30, #23; ☎ 638 85, Bichlstrasse 22) Meals €4.95-8.75, two-course set menu with drink €7.20. Open 9am-9pm daily high season, 9am-6.30pm Mon-Fri & 9am-2pm Sat summer & low season. This self-service chain restaurant offers average food but great prices. Look for cut-price offers an hour before closing. There's a first-floor sun terrace.

Huberbräu Stüberl (Map 30, #16; ☎ 656 77, Vorderstadt 18) Meals €5.40-16, three-course menu €6.55-9.45. Open 8am-midnight Mon-Sat, 9am-midnight Sun. A busy, sometimes friendly place, it serves good Austrian cooking at very reasonable prices. As the evening wears on, eating becomes less prevalent and drinkers become more voluble; beer costs €2.50 for 0.5L.

Adria (Map 30, #6; ☎ 627 29, Josef Pirchl Strasse 17) Meals €5.25-9.10. Open 10am-midnight daily, 9am-2pm & 5pm-11.30pm daily in off season. This place serves Italian dishes and is near the post office; it's less crowded than places in the centre, but just as good.

La Fonda (Map 30, #18; ☎ 736 73, Hinterstadt 13) Snacks/meals €3.35-10.70. Open 4pm-midnight daily. This Tex-Mex place serves up surprisingly cheap (most meals are under €6.60) if so-so food; there's a bar and an enjoyable, upbeat ambience.

Gasthaus Chizzo (Map 30, #21; ☎ 624 75, Josef Herold Strasse 2) Meals €6.90-17.80. Open 11am-11pm daily; closed Tues in low season. This is a good place to try Austrian food. Meals are served in a large room with lots of wood decor, or in the hedge-lined garden; there's an adjoining bar.

Gasthof Eggerwirt (Map 30, #12; ☎ 624 37, Untere Gänsbachgasse 12) Meals €7-19, three-course menu €11.75. Open 10am-10pm daily, closed off season. This place offers quality local cuisine in frescoed rooms. There are also terrace tables.

Unterberger Stuben (Map 30, #27; ☎ 661 27-0, Wehrgasse 2) Dishes €8-22, or €62 for multi-course menu. Kitchen open 6.30pm-9.30pm daily Dec-Mar & July & Aug, 6.30pm-9.30pm Wed-Mon Sept & Oct. Book ahead in the high season. This rustic but elegant restaurant has an extensive menu. Try some of the *Kohlroulade auf Trüffelkartoffel* (cabbage stuffed with veal, served with truffles and mashed potato) for €12.75.

Entertainment
Kitzbühel has many discos and pubs – there are several on Hinterstadt. You can meet other English-speakers at *Big Ben (Map 30, #17; ☎ 711 00, Vorderstadt 31, open 9am to 1am daily)* or at the *Londoner (Map 30, #14; ☎ 714 28, Franz Reisch Strasse 4, open noon to 3am daily in winter, 6pm to 2am daily in summer)*; the latter gets particularly crammed full with young drinkers. Both places are open in low season.

If you've more money than you need (unlikely in Kitzbühel), you can always lighten your pockets in the *casino (Map 30, #19; ☎ 623 00, Hinterstadt 24)*, open from 7pm nightly.

Getting There & Away
There are approximately hourly train departures from Bahnhof Kitzbühel to Innsbruck (€11.65, 1¼ hours) and Salzburg (€19.65, 2½ hours). Regional trains between Wörgl and Zell am See stop at Kitzbühel Hahnenkamm train station, which is closer to the town centre than Bahnhof Kitzbühel. To Kufstein (€6.70, one hour), change at Wörgl.

Getting to Lienz by train is awkward: two changes are required and it takes more than four hours. The bus is direct and takes only two hours leaving from outside Bahnhof Kitzbühel (€12.35; buy tickets from the driver or the Bahnhof); departures are 10.50am daily, 3pm (Saturday), 5.10pm (Monday to Friday) and 7.20pm (Sunday).

Heading south to Lienz, you pass through some marvellous scenery. Highway 108 (the Felber Tauern Tunnel) and Hwy 107 (the Grossglockner Road, which is closed in winter) both have toll sections; for details, see the Hohe Tauern National Park Region chapter.

KIRCHBERG
☎ 05357

This resort provides access to the same ski slopes as Kitzbühel and is a slightly cheaper base than its famous neighbour – as one skier described it, people wear Swatches not Rolexes. Many travellers looking for work in the ski season base themselves here.

The tourist office (☎ 23 09, fax 37 32, e info@kirchberg.at), at Hauptstrasse 8, is open 8.30am to 6pm Monday to Friday year round, with limited opening in high season on weekends; there's an accommodation board outside with a free telephone.

Places to Stay & Eat
Appartement-Pension Austria (☎ 44 23-0, fax 44 23-1, e hesse_peter@hotmail.com, Lendstrasse 26-28) Rooms or apartments with shower and toilet €25.50 per person, with breakfast. This is a good place for job seekers who arrive in autumn; the owner can give useful pointers, as well as providing lower rates in November (around €16/22 for singles/doubles, without breakfast).

Pension Groderer (☎/fax 22 45, Neugasse 12) Singles/doubles with shower and toilet €26.20 per person. This is a typical chalet with balconies; it overlooks the church graveyard so the neighbours are quiet!

For food, there are lots of possibilities in the centre, including two supermarkets on Dorfstrasse.

Ristorante Nabucco (☎ 350 99, Hauptstrasse 1). Meals €5.45-14.90. Open 11am-

midnight daily in season, closes 2pm-5pm off season. You'll find a good range of Italian food here, and you can enjoy it out on the sun terrace.

Although smaller than Kitzbühel, Kirchberg can be lively at night. English-speakers generally crowd into the *London Pub (39 93, Schlossergasse 13, open in season from 5pm to late nightly).*

Getting There & Away
Ski buses make the 6km trip from Kitzbühel every 10 or 15 minutes during the day. Bundesbuses (Map 30, #1) run during the summer. From the train station, turn left then bear right for Hauptstrasse (500m). Buses stop at various stops, including Hauptstrasse. Train departures to Kitzbühel (€1.55, 10 minutes) are hourly till 10.05pm.

ST JOHANN IN TIROL
☎ 05352 • pop 6500 • elev 660m

St Johann is 10km north of Kitzbühel. There are some attractive buildings to enjoy in the town centre, not least the baroque **Pfarrkirche** (1723–32), which contains paintings and stuccowork by Simon-Benedikt Faistenberger. **Skiing** here is suitable for all abilities, but especially intermediates; a day ski pass for the area costs €26.50 (children €13.50).

Places to Stay & Eat
Accommodation is available to suit a range of budgets. To find somewhere to stay, bear left from the train station to reach the tourist office (☎ 63 33 50, fax 652 00, e info@st.johann.tirol.at), Poststrasse 2; it has brochures, an accommodation board and a free phone accessible 24 hours in the foyer.

The Huberbräu brewery has been soothing parched throats in St Johann since 1727. The best place to imbibe is the *Huberbräu Bräustuberl (☎ 622 21, Brauweg 2. Open 10.30am-10pm daily),* above the brewery itself. The square-sided tower is 500m from the train station, and is clearly visible. Light or dark beer costs €2.40 for 0.5L, and there are inexpensive Austrian favourites on the menu. Enjoy the view over the town from tables inside or out.

Getting There & Away

St Johann is on the IC rail route between Zell am See and Innsbruck, and is the stop before Kitzbühel when travelling west. It is also at an important road junction, where the north-south Hwy 161 intersects with the east-west Hwy 312. Trains between St Johann and Kitzbühel are hourly (€1.55, eight minutes); there are also Bundesbuses.

KUFSTEIN

☎ 05372 ● pop 14,500 ● elev 503m

Tourists are drawn to Kufstein (Map 27), near the German border, by its lakes and medieval castle.

Orientation & Information

Kufstein is the northernmost Austrian town in the Inn Valley. The train station is on the west bank of the Inn River, a three-minute stroll from the core of the town, Stadtplatz, on the east bank. This is where you'll find the tourist office (☎ 622 07, fax 614 55, e kufstein@netway.at), Unterer Stadtplatz 8. Opening hours are 8.30am to 12.30pm and 2pm to 5pm Monday to Friday and, except in November and for a few weeks pre Easter, 9am to noon Saturday. Staff will hunt down accommodation without charging commission. If you decide to stay overnight, ask for the Gästekarte, which has different benefits in summer and winter.

Things to See & Do

Control of the town has been hotly contested by Tirol and Bavaria through the ages. The first recorded reference to the fortress, **Festung Kufstein** (☎ 602 350; admission €8/6.55 summer/winter; open 9am-5pm daily Easter-mid Nov, 10am-4pm daily mid Nov-Easter), was in 1205 when it was owned by Bavaria. Kufstein swapped hands twice before Maximilian I took the town for Tirol in 1504. The bulky **Kaiserturm** (Emperor's Tower) was added to the fortress in 1522. In 1703 the town was razed by fire during a siege by the Bavarians. The siege failed, but the Bavarians belatedly won the prize in 1809 during the Napoleonic Wars, only to have it returned to Austria five years later as a result of the Congress of Vienna.

Festung Kufstein dominates the town from its hill overlooking Stadtplatz. Inside is a wide-ranging but not over-large **Heimatmuseum** that includes temporary exhibits dealing with local culture and natural history. Displays are imaginatively presented and incorporate creative lighting and excerpts of suitable music. The lift up to the fortress/museum is included in the entrance fee.

Elsewhere in the fortress you can view the **Heldenorgel** (Heroes Organ), below the Kaiserturm. This massive instrument has 4307 pipes, 46 organ stops and a 100m gap between the keyboard and the tip of the pipes; the resultant delay in the sounding of the notes makes playing it a tricky business. Keep an ear out for recitals at noon and (in July and August) 5pm – the music can easily be heard from Stadtplatz and elsewhere, though there's also a special listening auditorium on Stadtplatz by the church (€0.75; included in fortress entrance fee).

When the fortress is closed in the evening you can walk up the path (in under 15 minutes) and roam around the castle walls and grounds free of charge. There are fine views of the valley below.

Running east of Kufstein is the **Kaisergebirge** range, a rugged landscape soaring to 2300m and extending as far as St Johann in Tirol. It exercises walkers, mountaineers and skiers alike. The Kaisergebirge is actually two ranges, split by the east-west Kaisertal (Kaiserbach Valley). The northern range is the Zahmer Kaiser (Tame Emperor) and the southern is the Wilder Kaiser (Wild Emperor) – no medals for guessing which has the smoother slopes. The cable chair up Wilder Kaiser from Kufstein costs €8 (€10.20 return; open May to October).

The lakes around Kufstein are an ideal destination for cyclists; you can rent bikes in the train station. Bundesbuses visit some of the lakes – get a timetable from the tourist office. The smaller, closer lakes are in the wooded area west of the Inn River, where there's a network of walking trails. Hechtsee, 3km to the north-west, and Stimmersee, 2.5km to the south-west, are both attractively situated, and both have swimming areas with entrance fees. Hechtsee is flanked by two other lakes,

Egelsee and Längsee. Larger lakes such as the Walchsee, Hintersteinersee and the Thiersee are farther afield, to the east. A free city bus goes to Hechtsee in summer during fine weather (ask at the tourist office).

Places to Stay

Camping Kufstein (☎ 622 29-55, fax 636 894, Salurner Strasse 36) Price per adult/tent/car €3.85/2.80/2.95. Open May to October. This shaded camping ground is by the river, 1km south of Stadtplatz.

Hotel Gisela (☎/fax 645 20, Bahnhofplatz 4) Singles/doubles with shower €18.20/36.40, optional breakfast €3.65 per person. This old, spacious building is opposite the train station. It's slightly run-down, but it is cheap and convenient, and is probably OK for a short stay.

A few blocks south-east of the fortress are a couple of decent places on residential Mitterndorfer Strasse.

Pension Striede (☎ 623 16, fax 623 16-33, Mitterndorfer Strasse 20) Singles/doubles €23/46. This place is attached to an orthopaedic centre – hospital-like rooms have a shower and toilet, and a balcony or access to the large garden. It's best to phone ahead outside clinic hours (which are 7am to noon Monday to Thursday, 7am to 11.30am Friday) as there may be nobody around.

Pension-Café Maier (☎ 622 60, no fax, Mitterndorfer Strasse 13) Singles/doubles €25.50/51. This old house has reasonable rooms with bathrooms and a grassy garden. Though the cafe is closed on weekends, you can check-in then if you phone ahead.

Hotel Gasthof Goldener Löwe (☎ 621 81-0, fax 621 81-8, e goldener.loewe@kufnet.at, Oberer Stadtplatz 14) Singles/doubles €41.50/71.50. If you want to stay in the centre of town, this hotel has an attractive facade, a restaurant and nearby garage parking. Rooms are variable, however: some could do with a renovation. All have a shower, toilet, TV and phone. Rates drop for over two nights.

Places to Eat

Less than 200m north of Oberer Stadtplatz, along Reischsstrasse, is the Inntal Center, with shops and a large supermarket.

Prima SB (☎ 638 96, Inntal Center, 1st floor) Meals €5.25-7.30, two-course lunch including drink €6.50. Open 8am-6.30pm Mon-Fri, 8am-5pm Sat. This self-service restaurant has a terrace. (Don't mistakenly go into the ground-floor cafe, Prima Gondola.) It has the usual choice of schnitzels, pasta and salad buffet offered by this chain, though after 2pm there are also pizzas for just €3.80.

For more ambience, the area to explore is Unterer Stadtplatz. A pleasant pedestrian area, it has several restaurants with outside tables, and the prices are very reasonable. There's even a **Spar** supermarket at No 27 for self-caterers: it's open 7.30am to 7pm Monday to Friday, 7.30am to 1pm Saturday.

Café Restaurant Auracher (☎ 627 26, Unterer Stadtplatz 11) Meals €4.75-12. Open 9am-midnight daily. A comfortable place, with outside tables and several interior sections, it serves good Austrian dishes at bargain prices. There are set menus (eg, three courses for just €5), daily specials and reduced-price seniors' or kids' meals.

Enricos Pizza Paradies (☎ 719 60, Untere Stadtplatz 11) Pizzas €4.40-7.30. Open 11am-2pm & 5pm-11pm daily. Around the corner from Auracher (though part of the same building) is this small, good-value pizza parlour.

Inncafe Hell (☎ 645 23, Unterer Stadtplatz 3) Snacks/meals €3.30-7.65. Open 9am-10pm daily in summer, 9am-8pm daily in winter. Though the small selection of meals is adequate, and the cakes and ice cream are tempting, the best thing about this place is the outside terrace overlooking the river.

Getting There & Away

The hourly train trip to Kitzbühel (€6.70, change at Wörgl) takes about an hour. The easiest road route is also via Wörgl.

Kufstein is on the main Innsbruck-Salzburg train route; trains to Salzburg (€21.80, 1¼ hours) only run every two hours, but those to Innsbruck (€10.50, 50 minutes) are hourly, as some trains funnel down from Germany (Munich), which is on a direct line a little over an hour away.

Postbuses leave from outside the train station; for information, call ☎ 623 85.

SÖLL
☎ 05333 ● pop 3000 ● elev 720m

Söll is a well-known ski resort 10km south of Kufstein (Map 27). In the 1980s it had a reputation for attracting boozy, boisterous visitors who were at least as interested in après-ski as *actuel-ski*. In the 1990s, however, the resort attempted (with some success) to re-brand itself as a family resort – not a bad idea because the night scene was never too diverse.

The highest skiing area overlooking the resort is Hohe Salve at 1827m, though Söll has also combined with neighbouring resorts Itter, Hopfgarten, Kelchsau, Westendorf and Brixen to form the huge Skiwelt area – 250km of pistes, with numerous blue (easy) runs.

The staff at the tourist office (☎ 52 16, fax 61 80, e info@soell.com) in the centre of the village will provide you with further information on activities and can help find you accommodation.

Getting There & Away
Söll is on Hwy 312 between Wörgl and St Johann in Tirol. It is not on a train line, but Bundesbuses run from Kufstein every couple of hours between 5.50am and 6.40pm (fewer on Sunday).

Western Tirol

The Inn River slices through mountain ranges from east to west until it reaches Landeck, at which point it twists south and goes into (or more accurately, flows out of) Switzerland. The Arlberg ski region, covered later in this chapter, traverses the provincial border between Tirol and Vorarlberg.

STAMS
☎ 05263

Stams (Map 27) is a small town visited primarily for its **Cistercian abbey** *(Zisterzienstift;* ☎ *62 42, Stiftshof 1),* founded in 1273 by Elizabeth of Bavaria, the mother

of Conradin, the last of the Hohenstaufens. The exterior is dominated by two sturdy baroque towers, added in the 17th century. The most impressive feature of the church interior is the high altar (1613): the intertwining branches of this version of the 'tree of life' support 84 saintly figures surrounding an image of the Virgin. Near the entrance is the **Rose Grille**, an exquisite iron screen made in 1716. Telephone ahead about guided tours.

The town's small tourist office (☎/fax 67 48), Bahnhofstrasse 1, is only open 8.30am to 11.30am on Monday, Tuesday, Thursday and Friday (daily in July and August).

Getting There & Away
Stams is in the upper Inn Valley, on the rail route between Innsbruck and Landeck, but only regional trains stop there (fare from Innsbruck €5.70). Both the A12/E60 and Hwy 171 pass near the abbey.

THE ÖTZTAL
The Ötztal (Ötz Valley) is the most densely populated of the three river valleys that run north from the **Ötztaler Alpen** (Ötztal Alps) until they drain into the Inn River. The Ötztaler Alpen guard the border to Italy and are home to numerous glaciers that shimmer between soaring peaks. The highest summit in the region is Wildspitze (3774m). Mountaineers, walkers and skiers can find plenty to occupy themselves. Contact the various tourist offices about accommodation; prices are 30% to 50% lower in summer.

The Ötztal is dotted with villages in picturesque locations along the banks of the Ötztaler Ache. From **Umhausen** an enjoyable 40-minute, signposted walk goes to the Stuibenfall waterfall. Umhausen also has the **Ötzi Dorf** *(☎ 05264-201 13; €4.40, open 10am-6pm daily May-Oct),* an archaelogical open-air park that re-creates the world of the ice man (see the 'Entombed in Ice' boxed text).

Sölden (1377m) is a ski resort that has a mountain annexe, Hochsölden (2090m). Some of the pistes are long and demanding and include glacier skiing. The Giggijoch cable car climbs up to a special snowboarding area above Hochsölden, and the Gaislachko-gel cable car rises to 3058m and provides sweeping views of the whole Ötztaler Alpen. The tourist office (☎ 05254-510-0, fax 05254-510-520, e oetztalarena@netway.at) is at Rettenbach 466.

Three kilometres south of Sölden is **Zwieselstein**, where the Venter Ache (Venter stream) branches to the south-west. Paths lead up to Wildspitze from the end of this valley.

Farther south is attractive **Obergurgl** (1930m), another well-known skiing resort that's popular with families. It's the highest parish in Austria. Pistes are mostly suitable for beginners and intermediates and continue right to the edge of the village. Hohe Mut (2659m) is a justly famous lookout, accessible by chair lift. Obergurgl is actually at the head of the valley, but the road doubles back on itself and rises to **Hochgurgl** (2150m). Here the pistes are a little steeper and the views equally impressive. One tourist office (☎ 05256-6466, fax 05256-6353, e info@obergurgl.com) and one ski pass (€33.50 per day) cover both resorts. A gondola allows easy transfers between Obergurgl's and Hochgurgl's pistes.

Just beyond Hochgurgl, where the road makes a sharp right-hand turn, is another viewing point, the **Windegg Belvedere** (2080m). The road continues into Italy where it joins the course of the Timmelsbach River.

Entombed in Ice

In September 1991 German hikers in the Ötztal Alps came across the body of a man preserved within the Similaun Glacier. Police and forensic scientists were summoned to the scene. They carelessly hacked the body out of the ice, not yet aware of the importance of the find. The body had been found some 90m within Italy, but was appropriated by the Austrians and taken to Innsbruck University to be studied.

Although a Swiss woman quickly identified the body as that of her father, who had disappeared on the glacier in the 1970s, experts initially decided it was about 500 years old: the ice man, nicknamed 'Ötzi' or 'Frozen Fritz', was thought to have been a soldier serving under Archduke Ferdinand. Carbon dating, however, revealed he was nearly 5500 years old, placing him in the late Stone Age.

Ötzi became big news. More so because the state of preservation was remarkable: even the pores of the skin were visible. In addition, Ötzi had been found with 70 artefacts, including a copper axe, bow and arrows, charcoal and clothing. Over the next six years he was thoroughly examined and analysed. Physiologically he was found to be no different from modern humans. His face was reconstructed, right down to his dark hair and blue eyes. X-rays showed he had suffered from arthritis and frostbite, and his ribs had been broken. He had died between late August and late September.

Despite these discoveries, the experts could not agree on what had brought Ötzi up 3000m into the Alps. Perhaps he had sheltered in a cave from a wintry squall, but had frozen to death. Or maybe he'd been a shaman, communing with spirits in the cave. A hunter, taking flight? A shepherd, returning with his herd to Italy from the summer pastures in Austria? And what had he been doing with a copper axe, when he predated the Bronze Age? Conflicting theories raged back and forth. The tussle over jurisdiction of the body was another issue. Innsbruck University reluctantly and permanently relinquished Ötzi to the Italians in 1998, when he became the centrepiece of a new museum in Bolzano. In 2000 Ötzi was unfrozen briefly to allow further tests, but no conclusive data was uncovered.

Not everybody was worried about the finer points of his background and heritage, however. Several Austrian and Italian women contacted the university shortly after the discovery and requested that they be impregnated with Ötzi's frozen sperm. The scientists could not oblige: although well-preserved in many respects, Ötzi no longer had a penis. 'We don't know if it's shrunk or has been eaten by an animal', one scientist explained. Alas, Ötzi would not become the oldest father in the world.

Getting There & Away

No trains enter the valley. Get off the train at Ötztal Bahnhof on the Innsbruck-Landeck IC route and pick up a Bundesbus from there. In the summer and winter high seasons buses depart approximately hourly (only every two hours in the low season) and go as far as Obergurgl (€7.60, 90 minutes). From approximately mid-July to mid-September two morning buses continue as far as Timmelsjoch, on the Italian border.

If you have your own transport, you should be able to get at least as far as Hochgurgl all year, but the road beyond into Italy (via the Timmelsjoch Pass) is generally blocked by snow in winter. It's also a toll road; the one-way cost is €7.65/6.55 for cars/motorcycles.

IMST

☎ 05412 • pop 7500 • elev 830m

Imst is beautifully situated and has a couple of interesting buildings in the old centre. It's mainly known for its **Shrovetide festival**, the Schemenlaufen (ghost dance), which takes place every four years, the next being in 2004

(usually early February). The centrepiece of this occasion is a colourful procession of 'ghosts', which the less credulous spectator will realise are actually locals wearing elaborate costumes and masks. Learn more about the festival in the Fasnachthaus (€3.50, open 4pm-6pm Tuesday, Thursday and Saturday), at the parish church on Streleweg.

The tourist office (☎ 69 10-0, fax 69 10-8, e info@imst.at) at Johannesplatz 4 can tell you about rafting on the River Inn, as well as the Fasnachthaus and the Shrovetide festival.

Getting There & Away

The town is slightly to the north of the main east-west roads (the A12 and Hwy 171), and is served by Bundesbuses and trains.

LANDECK

☎ 05442 • pop 7500 • elev 816m

Landeck is an important transport junction, guarding the routes to Vorarlberg, Switzerland and Italy. The town has been standing sentinel for centuries, as demonstrated by its hillside fortifications.

Fantasy Castles

Some of Germany's prime attractions are a short trip by car or bus from western Tirol, near the town of Füssen, and include the fantastic castles of Ludwig II (1845–86), last king of Bavaria and cousin of the Empress Elisabeth. Ludwig was found drowned in suspicious circumstances in Lake Starnberg. Perhaps it was as well that he died without heirs, for he was at least a couple of slices of Brot short of a Bavarian breakfast. The so-called 'mad monarch' had three obsessions in life: Richard Wagner, swans and building castles. The first two are clearly seen in the decorations of the third.

Ludwig's most famous creation is Neuschwanstein, a mishmash of architectural styles that inspired Walt Disney's Fantasyland castle. Visited by around one million tourists a year, it is beautifully situated on a pine-clad hill, with a backdrop of shimmering peaks and a deep blue lake. Images of swans are everywhere, including in light fittings, door handles and basin taps. A large painted image on the walls of Ludwig's study indicates that his musings were generally less than erudite: it shows Ludwig being intimately attended by near-naked nymphs. The setting for the scene is a grotto, which is exactly what Ludwig had built in the next room.

A little way down the hill is Hohenschwangau. This was not built by Ludwig but is where he lived as a child. Structurally it is not as eccentric as its neighbour, but it is still well worth a visit.

The castles are situated a few kilometres from Füssen and are accessible by guided tour (in English). Füssen is about 15km north of Reutte.

Farther east is Ludwig's Schloss Linderhof. This is visited mainly for its grounds, particularly the ludicrous Wagner-inspired golden conch boat. To get there from Reutte, take the minor road that skirts the northern shore of the Plansee.

Orientation & Information

The town centre of spread-out Landeck is east of the right-angle bend of the Inn River, where that river converges with the Sanna. The train station is 1.5km to the east: walk left on leaving the station and stay on the same side of the river (even though the main built-up area seems to be on the other side). Local buses also make the trip (€1.40 one-way, €2.50 return).

The main street in the centre is Malser-strasse, where you'll find the tourist office (☎ 623 44, fax 678 30, e tvblandeck@net way.at), open 8.30am to noon and 2pm to 6pm Monday to Friday, 8.30am to noon Saturday. There's an accommodation board outside the office.

Things to See & Do

The **Stadtpfarrkirche**, behind the tourist office, was built in 1493 and displays Gothic features such as network vaulting and a winged altar (16th century). On the hill above stands **Schloss Landeck,** which now contains a museum of local history (☎ 632 02, Schlossberg; adult/senior/student €3.65/ 2.95/1.85; open 10am-5pm daily late May-30 Sept, 2pm-5pm 1-26 Oct). Originally built in the 13th century, a fire destroyed it 500 years later and the subsequent rebuilding was not true to the original form. There is a fine view of the valley from the castle tower.

Like everywhere in Tirol, Landeck attracts the odd skier or two, though hikers in the summer are more numerous. The Venet cable car can transport visitors of either type to Krahberg at 2208m. See the Walking & Skiing special section for a description of a hike in the Kaunertal, which branches from the Inntal just south-west of Landeck.

Places to Stay

Sport Camp Tirol (☎ 646 36, fax 640 37, e sportcamptirol@msg.at, Mühlkanal 1) Tent sites or bungalows €13.10 per person. Open year-round. This camping ground on the north bank of the Sanna River also arranges white-knuckle activities.

Budget travellers could do worse than find a room in a private house: the most likely

hunting area is west of the Inn and south of the train line; there's a path leading uphill near the rail tracks (the road is less direct) – the following two places are along here.

Landhaus Zangerl (☎/fax 626 76, Herzog Friedrich Strasse 14) Double/triple rooms with bathroom €13.10 per person. Here you can find window flower boxes, a garden, and great value.

Pension Paula (☎ 633 71, Herzog Friedrich Strasse) Singles/doubles with shower and toilet €22.60/37.80. This chalet with balconies is back from the street, near Burschlweg.

Tourotel Post (☎ 69 11, fax 69 11-71, Malserstrasse 19) Singles/doubles €48/75. This central hotel has comfortable, renovated rooms with shower, toilet, TV and telephone; on site are a solarium, sauna and restaurant.

Places to Eat

There are various places to eat near the post office along Malserstrasse, including two supermarkets.

Prima (☎ 627 91, Malserstrasse 36) Meals €4.50-8.80. Open 7.30am-6pm Mon-Fri & 7.30am-5pm Sat. This self-service place has a varied menu, encompassing set meals, a salad buffet and pastries.

Wienerwald (☎ 69 11, Malserstrasse 19) Meals €5.50-9.50. Open 7am-midnight daily. This chain restaurant offers the usual chicken-oriented dishes.

Hotel Schrofenstein (☎ 623 95, Malser-strasse 31) Meals €6.60-21.40. Open 7am-midnight daily, closed late Oct-early Dec. The restaurant in this four-star hotel dishes out quality regional cuisine, including seasonal specialities.

Getting There & Away

Landeck is on the east-west IC express train route, 50 minutes from Innsbruck (€10.50, hourly) and one hour and 50 minutes from Bregenz (€16.60). Bundesbuses head in all directions, departing from outside the train station and/or from the bus station in the town centre.

The A12/E60 into Vorarlberg passes by Landeck, burrowing into a tunnel as it approaches the town. Highway 315, the Inn

Valley road, passes through the centre of town and stays on the east side of the river.

THE INN VALLEY

The Inn Valley (Inntal) extends for 230km within Tirol. Its initial stretch, south of Landeck, is the only section not shadowed by railway tracks. There's little of major interest in this region, though **Pfunds** is picturesque. Many homes here are similar in design to those found in the Engadine, a region in Graubünden, Switzerland, farther up the Inn Valley.

South of Pfunds, you have the choice of routes; either road offers a corniche section with fine views. If you continue along the Inn you'll end up in Switzerland (infrequent buses). Alternatively, if you turn left (south) to Nauders you'll soon reach South Tirol (Italy) by way of the Reschen Pass (1508m; open year-round). Various Bundesbuses run from Landeck to Nauders, where you can transfer to an Italian bus to Merano in Italy (four or five a day; total trip at least 3¾ hours).

THE PAZNAUNTAL

The Paznauntal (Paznaun Valley) runs parallel to the Inn Valley, but farther to the west. It's divided from its more famous neighbour by the Samnaun mountain chain. The main settlement in the valley is **Ischgl** (population 1350; altitude 1400m). This attractive resort is considered to be one of Austria's best ski areas, despite (or because of) its relative isolation. It shares its skiing pass (€29 for one day; reductions for seniors and children) with Samnaun, a duty-free area in Switzerland. The tourist office (☎ 05444-52 66-0, fax 05444-56 36, e info@ischgl.com) in the centre of Ischgl can tell you more.

Getting There & Away

Only a secondary road (188) runs along the valley, crossing into Vorarlberg at Bielerhöhe where there are good views. This pass (2036m) is closed in winter and to caravans at all times. There's a toll of €10.90 for cars and €10.20 for motorcycles. The road rejoins the main highway near Bludenz. Regular Bundesbuses travel along the valley as far as Galtür (10km beyond Ischgl); they originate in Landeck.

Arlberg Region

The Arlberg region, shared by Vorarlberg and Tirol, comprises several linked resorts and is considered to have some of the best skiing in Austria. St Anton (described below) is the largest and least elitist of these fashionable chalet resorts but, even here, budget travellers can kiss their savings goodbye. For the other Arlberg resorts, see Western Arlberg in the Vorarlberg chapter.

The winter season is long, with snow reliable till about mid-April. Summer is less busy (and cheaper), though still popular with walkers. Even so, some of the restaurants, bars and discos that swing during the ski season are closed. Most others will close between seasons, and open for summer from late June to October. Many guesthouses and some hotels do likewise.

Skiing

A single ski pass covers the whole region. It is valid for at least 80 ski lifts, giving access to 260km of prepared pistes and 180km of high Alpine deep-snow runs. Passes cost €37 for one day, €101 for three and €193 for seven. These are the prices for the high season, though there are various reductions near the beginning and end of the main season, eg, 'Firnwochen' weeks, that is, the weeks pre-Christmas and post mid-April, are about 15% to 20% cheaper. The first and last few days of the season (so-called 'Schneekristallwochen') are 50% cheaper. Most of January and early to mid-April are also about 10% cheaper. Various other tickets are available, such as hourly tickets, a points-system ticket, or passes for specific lifts. Children get reductions on all tickets, as do seniors (except for some hourly tickets). Just €10 buys a season ticket for kids aged under six and seniors over 75.

For one day's downhill equipment rental, expect to pay from €19 for skis and poles, and €6.60 for boots.

Getting There & Away

St Anton is the easiest access point to the region. It's on the rail route between Bregenz (€6.40, 1½ hours) and Innsbruck (€12.35, 1¼ hours), with fast trains every one or two hours. St Anton and St Christoph are close to the eastern entrance of the Arlberg Tunnel, the toll road connecting Vorarlberg and Tirol. The tunnel toll is €9.45 for cars and minibuses. You can avoid the toll by taking the B197, but no vehicles with trailers are allowed on this winding road.

Getting Around

Bundesbuses run between St Anton and Lech, stopping at St Christoph and Zürs en route. They are hourly (till about 6pm) in winter, reducing to four a day in summer; the full trip costs €3.35/6.70 one way/return (35 minutes), or pay €7.30 for a day pass. Taking a minibus taxi, which can be shared between up to eight people, is another option: the trip from St Anton to Lech costs €43.60. Some routes (for example from Zürs to Alpe Rauz, a ski area near St Christoph) are included with the ski pass.

ST ANTON AM ARLBERG
☎ 05446 ● pop 2400 ● elev 1304m

This is the Arlberg Region's largest resort, enjoying an easy-going atmosphere and vigorous nightlife. St Anton's main problem is its popularity: high season is very busy, and in low season there are weekend crowds.

The resort hosted the World Alpine Skiing Championships in February 2001, a prestiege event which heralded a flurry of new developments in town, including the shifting of the rail track and train station to the south. The course of the old track (just north of the pedestrian zone) is to be developed as a park, with curling and an ice rink.

Orientation

St Anton is strung out along the northern bank of the Rosanna River. The train station is near the centre (a pedestrian-only zone) and most of the ski lifts. Farther east and on the northern side of the railway tracks is the area called Nasserein. Farther east still is St Jakob, with just one convenient ski lift, a run ending at Nasserein.

Information

The tourist office (Map 31, #21; ☎ 226 90, fax 2532, e st.anton@netway.at) is in the Arlberg Haus, less than five minutes' walk from the train station and set back from the road. It's open daily in the high season and from Monday to Friday between seasons, with hours adjusting to demand. Outside is an accommodation board, hotel lists and a free telephone, so you can sort out somewhere to stay at any time.

The post office (Map 31, #16) (Postamt 6580) is near the Rosanna River, off the northern end of the pedestrian zone.

Mailbox (Map 31, #17), Fussgängerzone 49, has internet access for €0.20 per minute; it's open 9am to 9pm daily in high season, 11am to 7pm (perhaps closing one or two days a week) in low season.

To the west of the town on Rudi Matt Weg is St Anton's **museum** (Map 31, #25), devoted to skiing and local culture; entry is €1.50 (open 3pm to 10pm, closed Sunday).

Activities

St Anton went down in skiing history as the place where Hannes Schneider pioneered the Arlberg method in the early 20th century. The resort offers some of the best **skiing** in Austria for experts, with many difficult runs, both on and off-piste. In fact, St Anton is one of the best resorts in Austria for off-piste skiing on powder snow. Cable cars go all the way up to Valluga (2811m), from where experts can go off-piste all the way to Lech (with a ski guide only). Galzig (2185m) is along the way to Valluga. There are nursery slopes on Gampen (1850m) and Kapall (2330m), but generally the skiing is not suited to beginners.

Snowboarders share the same ski slopes, though there's also a snowboard 'fun park' on Rendl with a half pipe and different jumps. The Rendl area is on the southern side of the Rosanna River, where lifts go as high as Gampberg (2407m). There's also a 4km-long toboggan run (The Beleuchtete Rodelbahn), starting from Gampen,

MAP 31 – ST ANTON AM ARLBERG

PLACES TO STAY	29 Karl Schranz	14 Nah & Frisch	16 Post Office
3 Haus am Fang	Hotel; Jagdstube	Supermarket	17 Mailbox
4 Tiroler Frieden		20 Pomodoro	19 Funky Chicken
5 Enzian	**PLACES TO EAT**	26 Fahrnerstub'n	21 Tourist Office
8 Pirker	1 Alt St Anton	27 Floriani's	22 Krazy
10 Moostal	Restaurant		Kanguruh
11 Stockibach	2 Rodelhütte	**OTHER**	23 Sennhütte
18 Hotel Post;	Restaurant	7 Pfarrkirche	24 Mooserwirt
Piccadilly	9 Fuhrmann Stube	13 Kartouche	25 Museum
	12 Spar Supermarket	15 Underground	28 Bus Station

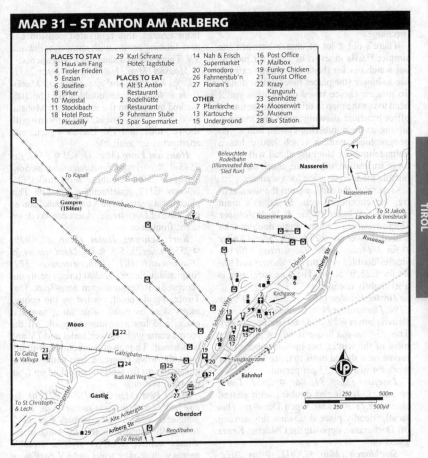

TIROL

then swinging by the Rodelhütte restaurant and ending near the Alt St Anton restaurant. Toboggan rental at sports shops costs about €5.90 per day.

Six kilometres to the west of St Anton is **St Christoph** (1800m), a much smaller place with only about six hotels, all expensive. It has lifts going to the Galzig area.

Though packs of partying youngsters dominate the winter scene, the age profile of summer visitors is somewhat older.

Other activities include indoor swimming, sauna, massage, ice skating, tennis and squash.

Places to Stay

There are nearly 200 B&Bs in and around St Anton, and a similar number of holiday apartments. Accommodation prices are significantly higher in winter. The prices quoted here are the prices for the winter high season. Many places have six different prices levels through the year – two in summer and four in winter, and summer prices can be as low as half the price of those in winter. In winter high season, you need to book ahead, and even then it's hard to get a place for just a couple of days (weekly stays, Saturday to Saturday, are usual). Shorter stays (only a few days) will usually incur a surcharge.

There's not a lot of choice between the simpler B&Bs in terms of value for money, but watch out for those that charge extra to use a shower (the places listed below don't). To make a choice based on location you'll need to use the map in this book or the tourist office brochure showing prices and map positions, as the numbering system follows no geographical pattern (each house has a unique number). Booking ahead will save a lot of frustration; otherwise, check the board outside the tourist office for vacancies.

Generally, the farther from the town centre, the cheaper it gets. St Jakob's main street has **Schuler** (*☎/fax 3108, St Jakober Dorf-strasse 33)*, where single/doubles with shared shower are €27.65/39.25, and **Sailer** *☎/fax 2814, St Jakober Dorfstrasse 120)* has singles/doubles with private shower and toilet for €25.50/50.90. The Nasserein area is also slightly cheaper.

Tiroler Frieden *(Map 31, #4; ☎ 2247, fax 2194, Dorfstrasse 149)*. Doubles/triples using shared shower €29.10/43.60 (summer price). This 75-year-old house is full of groups for most of the winter, but in November offers rooms on a shared basis to those looking for work for just €12.35 per person.

Josefine *(Map 31, #6; ☎ 2651, Dorfstrasse 334)* Singles/doubles with shared shower €23.30/43.60. Open Dec-Apr. This small, friendly place is down a tiny turning off Dorfstrasse, opposite the Goldenes Kreuz guesthouse.

Stockibach *(Map 31, #11; ☎/fax 2072, Kirchgasse 484)* Singles/doubles €30.60/61.10. Open in the off season; full with Swedish groups in February and March. Situated near the church, you get attractive rooms with wood fittings, and (in doubles) a balcony.

Enzian *(Map 31, #5; ☎/fax 2403, e haus.enzian@st-anton.at, Dorfstrasse 177)* Doubles €69.80. This 10-room pension is not far from the main pedestrian area, beyond the church. It offers pleasant modern-style rooms, each with private shower, toilet and TV.

Pirker *(Map 31, #8; ☎ 2310, fax 23 10-22, e haus.pirker@ski-arlberg.com,*

Dorfstrasse 241) Doubles €105. Just along from Enzian, this renovated pension has new-looking rooms with shower, toilet and TV. There's also a sauna and apartments.

Moostal *(Map 31, #10; ☎ 2831, fax 2831-30, e haus.moostal@st-anton.at, Marktstrasse 487)* Singles/doubles €54.60/105. Tucked away from the main street, Moostal gives you white, bright, clean rooms with shower, toilet and TV. There's a sauna and apartments are available.

Haus am Fang *(Map 31, #3; ☎ 3543, fax 3543-4, e christoph.battisti@utanet.at, Sonnenwiese 508)* Doubles with toilet/TV/balcony €112, apartments €100-230. This place has a genial hostess and a sauna, and as it's north of Dorfstrasse, skiers can ski down to the front door.

Karl Schranz Hotel *(Map 31, #29; ☎ 2555-0, fax 2555-5, e hotel.karl.schranz@st-anton.at, Alte Arlbergstrasse 372)* Singles/doubles €102/200 (credit cards not accepted). Reception open 8am-8pm. This Tirolean-style hotel, owned by the eponymous skier, is good value for a four-star place, and has a swimming pool. All the rooms come with shower, toilet and TV and half-board. Though it is about 1km uphill from the town centre, a free shuttle takes guests to and fro (call to be picked up from the train station).

Hotel Post *(Map 31, #18; ☎ 221 30, fax 2343, e hotel.post@st-anton.co.at, Fussgängerzone 55)* Singles/doubles €135/245. A friendly four-star hotel slap-bang in the village centre, it offers stylish, sizeable rooms with shower, toilet and TV. Staff wear traditonal Tirolean garb. There's a sauna, jacuzzi, steam bath and Internet access, all free for guests. Tea lovers will have a field day at the generous (free) breakfast, with numerous loose teas to choose from.

Places to Eat

Some of the bars mentioned in the Entertainment section also serve food. Restaurants and bars are described in *arlbergrevue*, a detailed free magazine in English available from the tourist office.

Self-caterers have a choice of supermarkets. There's a **Nah & Frisch** (Map 31, #14) in the *Fussgängerzone* (pedestrian zone). Nearby, the *Spar* supermarket *(Map 31, #12; Dorfstrasse 470)* is usually open 7am to 7pm Monday to Friday, 7am to 8pm Saturday, though the hours reduce on Sunday, holidays and off-season. Inside, the *Murr* deli counter *(☎ 2202-31)* serves hot takeaway lunches from Monday to Saturday (from €4 to €5.45); meals must be pre-ordered by 9.30am, and collected anytime after 11am; however, they're only kept hot until noon.

The only other cheap way to fuel up is to use the few takeaway stands or bakeries around the village, because most restaurants have few or no dishes below €7.30.

Pomodoro (Map 31, #20; ☎ 3333, Fussgängerzone 70) Pizza/pasta €6.35-8.60. Open 5pm-midnight daily Dec-Apr. English speakers favour this place near the tourist office, perhaps more for the atmosphere than the quality of the pizzas.

Floriani's (Map 31, #27; ☎ 2330, Alte Arlbergstrasse 92) Meals €6.40-9.45. Open 4pm or 5pm-midnight, closed Mon. Sample Italian or Austrian food served up in a wood-panelled room.

Fuhrmann Stube (Map 31, #9; ☎ 2921, Dorfstrasse 456) Dishes €6.50-13.50. Open 10am-midnight daily, hot food till 10pm; in low season closed till 4pm Tues & Thurs, in summer closed Tues all day. This family-friendly place, north of the pedestrian zone, has good-value Austrian food.

Fahrnerstub'n (Map 31, #26; ☎ 235 37, Alte Arlbergstrasse 93) Dishes €7.65-16.75. Kitchen open 5.30pm-9.30pm daily winter, closed Tues & Wed in low season. This small, comfortable place opposite Floriani's serves good Austrian and Tirolean food. It's closed in the summer.

Most of the top hotels in the resort have quality restaurants, which are also open for the summer season.

Jagdstube (Map 31, #29; ☎ 297 70, Alte Arlbergstrasse 372) Dishes €7.30-17.50. Open 3.30pm-midnight daily. This rustic hotel restaurant in the Karl Schranz Hotel serves good local fare.

Brunnenhof (☎ 2293, 47, St Jakober Dorfstrasse, St Jakob) Main courses €16.75-23.30. Reserve ahead: table reservations

accepted for 7pm-9pm, closed Wed & May-Nov. This restaurant outside of town has a deserved reputation as being one of the best in Arlberg. Expect Austrian food, but with gourmet flourishes.

Entertainment

If you come in summer, forget about nightlife, as all the following places (and almost all others in St Anton) are only open from December to April. Aside from those on the slopes, these are in the village centre.

On the lower ski slopes, lively après-ski bars (with dancing) include *Krazy Kanguruh (Map 31, #22)*, which does good burgers, and *Mooserwirt (Map 31, #24)*; *Sennhütte (Map 31, #23)* is more traditional.

Piccadilly (Map 31, #18; ☎ 2213-276, Fussgängerzone 55) Cover charge €4.40. Open 4pm-2am daily. This English-style pub has live music.

Underground (Map 31, #15; ☎ 2000, Im Gries 530) Open 4pm-2am daily, cover charge ranges from free to around €3.65. This friendly, busy venue has two parts, each with live music. There is a bar/disco downstairs and a ground-floor bistro with food.

Kartouche (Map 31, #13; ☎ 2244-0, Dorfstrasse 42) Open 10pm-4am daily, free entry. Owned by the Hotel Schwarzer Adler, this bar has English football on TV, and a DJ.

Funky Chicken (Map 31, #19; ☎ 2169, Fussgängerzone 70) Beer €2.55 per half litre, grilled half chicken €4.30. Open 6pm-2am Wed-Mon. Behind Pomodoro, this is the cheapest bar in the centre, popular with resort workers and young people.

Getting There & Away

For train information call ☎ 2402-385; also see Getting There & Away in the Arlberg Region introduction. Bundesbuses depart from stands (Map 31, #28) to the west of the tourist office.

Getting Around

Free local buses go to outlying parts of the resort (such as St Jakob). They only run till about 6.30pm, though in winter there's also an hourly night bus (€2.95). Most buses call just west of the tourist office.

Vorarlberg

The small state of Vorarlberg extends from the plains of Bodensee (Lake Constance) in the north to the Silvretta group of Alpine peaks in the south. It offers many outdoor activities as well as access to Liechtenstein, Switzerland and Germany. The provincial capital, Bregenz, hosts a spectacular annual music festival.

The local people speak an Alemannic dialect of German which is closer to Swiss-German (Schwyzertütsch) than to standard German. This is a lingering legacy of Germanic Alemanni tribes who raided southwards and had settled in eastern Switzerland and Vorarlberg by the 6th century. In the early 15th century, Vorarlberg suffered great damage during the Appenzell War with the Swiss Confederation. Relations with its neighbour improved later: in 1918 the state became independent of Tirol and sought union with Switzerland, a move blocked by the Allied powers in the postwar reorganisation of Europe.

Orientation

At 2600 sq km, Vorarlberg is the smallest Austrian province after Vienna, and is home to 332,000 people. The Arlberg skiing region is split between Vorarlberg and Tirol – see the Tirol chapter for coverage of St Anton.

Information

The provincial tourist board is Vorarlberg Tourismus (Map 33, #7; ☎ 05574-425 25-0, fax 05574-425 25-5, ℮ info@vbgtour.at, ⓦ www.vorarlberg-tourism.at), Postfach 302, A-6901 Bregenz. Prospective visitors with children should contact the office in advance for details of the many activities for kids available throughout the province during July and August. Also ask for the A3 size map of Vorarlberg, with sightseeing information (in English) on the reverse side.

Getting Around

Vorarlberg has six overlapping transport regions: there's the north-west (Rheintal),

Highlights

- Stroll around the quaint old town centre of Bregenz
- Lap up a musical production on a floating stage during the Bregenz Festival
- Immerse yourself in the watery attractions of Bodensee
- Consume chocolate and beer in Bludenz
- Hob-nob with jetsetter skiers in upmarket Lech

west (Oberland), south (Bludenz), south-west (Walgau), east (Arlberg) and north-east (Bregenzerwald). Kleinwalsertal in the east is not covered by these regions. A travel pass for a single region costs €7.30 (families €9.45) for one day or €14.55 for one week. A travel pass for all the regions costs €11.65 (families €14.55) per day or €21.80 for a week. Children, seniors and disabled people pay half-price. Passes are available for city transport in Bludenz, Bregenz, Dornbirn, Feldkirch, Götzis and Lech; day passes cost €2 (families €2.55) and one-week passes are €5.85.

For further transport information, contact the Verkehrsverbund Vorarlberg (☎ 05522-83577-3200, ℮ info@vvv.feldkirch.com), Herrengasse 12, Feldkirch.

BREGENZ

☎ 05574 ● pop 28,000 ● elev 398m

Bregenz is a compact provincial capital. It was the seat of the counts of Bregenz after

VORARLBERG

MAP 32 – VORARLBERG

Bodensee (Lake Constance)
Lindau
Pfänder Tunnel
Hard
Bregenz
Immenstadt
Sonthofen
GERMANY
Schwarzenberg
Lustenau
Dornbirn
Egg
Bregenzerwald
Hohenems
Oberstdorf
Ebnit
Dornbirner Ache
Riezlern
Götzis
Hirschegg
Mittelberg
Rankweil
Laterns
Kleinwalsertal
Feldkirch
Grosswalsertal
Warth
Lech
Zürs
Arlberg
Pass
Bludenz
Klostertal
Flexen Pass
Stuben
Arlberg
Pass
Vaduz
Brand
Arlberg Tunnel
St
Christoph
Schruns
St Anton
am Arlberg
Schesaplana
(2965m)
Lünersee
Montafon
Ischgl
Silvretta
Hochalpenstr
Bielerhöhe
Pass (2036m)
Silvretta
Stausee
SWITZERLAND
LIECHTENSTEIN
SWITZERLAND
Walgau
Brandnertal
Rhine
A14
516
201
Allgäuer Alpen
0   15   30km
0   9   18mi

the 8th century and was part of Bavaria during the Napoleonic Wars.

Bregenz's most compelling attraction is Bodensee, which provides the setting for the annual music festival that places the town firmly on the cultural map of Austria.

Orientation
Bregenz is on the eastern shore of Bodensee. The town centre is about 10 minutes' walk east of the train station. Local buses also make the trip (€1.05, or €2 for a day card); bus No 1 continues to the Pfänder cable car.

The newer part of town is near the boat landing stage; the older part, known as the Oberstadt, is inland.

Information
The tourist office (Map 33, #7; ☎ 4959-0, fax 4959-59, e tourismus@bregenz.at), Bahnhofstrasse 14, is open 9am to noon and 1pm to 5pm Monday to Friday, and 9am to noon Saturday. During the Bregenz Festival, its opening hours are 9am to 7pm Monday to Saturday and 4pm to 7pm Sunday. It provides good city maps and listings of accommodation, consulates and activities. It also sells permits (€5.85 per day) for fishing on the lake, and has a free, slower-than-paint-drying Internet terminal. The provincial tourist office (see Information earlier in this chapter) is upstairs in the same building, open 9am to noon and 1pm to 5pm Monday to Friday.

The post office (Map 33, #11; Postamt 6900), on Seestrasse, is open 8am to 7pm Monday to Friday, 9am to noon Saturday. S'Logo (Map 33, #28; ☎ 441 91), Kirchstrasse 47, is an Internet cafe charging €0.08 per minute, and is open 5pm to midnight daily.

Things to See & Do
The **Oberstadt** (old town) certainly merits a stroll; quaint homes with shutters and frescoes line cobbled streets, and some houses are built into the old city walls.

The centrepiece and town emblem is the bulbous, baroque **Martinsturm** *(St Martin's Tower; Map 33, #25; ☎ 466 32, Martinsgasse; admission €0.75; open 9am-dusk daily May-Sept & Easter, 2pm-5pm daily other times)*, built in 1599. It's topped by the largest onion dome in Central Europe. On the ground floor there's a church with 14th-century frescoes, and on the upper floors is a small military museum (Vorarlberger Militärmuseum), with the benefit of good views.

The half-timbered **Altes Rathaus** (old town hall; Map 33, #26) was designed by the baroque architect Michael Kuen and built in 1662. Further south, off Thalbachgasse, **Stadtpfarrkirche St Gallus** (parish church; Map 33, #29) has a plain exterior, but the baroque and rococo interior is surprisingly light and delicate.

Near the shore of Bodensee, the **Vorarlberger Landesmuseum** *(Map 33, #9; ☎ 460 50, Kornmarktplatz 1; adult/student €1.50/ 0.75; open 9am-noon & 2pm-5pm Tues-Sun, daily during Bregenz Festival)* outlines the region's history, culture and crafts, and has a collection of works by Swiss-born artist Angelika Kauffmann (1741–1807).

VORARLBERG

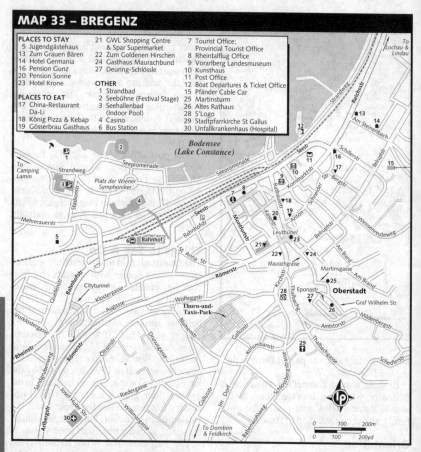

MAP 33 – BREGENZ

PLACES TO STAY
5 Jugendgästehaus
13 Zum Grauen Bären
14 Hotel Germania
16 Pension Gunz
20 Pension Sonne
23 Hotel Krone

PLACES TO EAT
17 China-Restaurant Da-Li
18 König Pizza & Kebap
19 Gösserbräu Gasthaus

21 GWL Shopping Centre & Spar Supermarket
22 Zum Goldenen Hirschen
24 Gasthaus Maurachbund
27 Deuring-Schlössle

OTHER
1 Strandbad
2 Seebühne (Festival Stage)
3 Seehallenbad (Indoor Pool)
4 Casino
6 Bus Station

7 Tourist Office; Provincial Tourist Office
8 Rheintalflug Office
9 Vorarlberg Landesmuseum
10 Kunsthaus
11 Post Office
12 Boat Departures & Ticket Office
15 Pfänder Cable Car
25 Martinsturm
26 Altes Rathaus
28 S'Logo
29 Stadtpfarrkirche St Gallus
30 Unfallkrankenhaus (Hospital)

Nearby, on Seestrasse, is the **Kunsthaus** *(art museum; Map 33, #10;* ☎ *485 94, Karl-Tzian-Platz; adult/concession €4.40/2.95; open 10am-6pm Tues-Sun, 10am-9pm Thur, closed Mon).* Built in 1997 to house changing exhibitions of modern art, the architecture (glass and steel exterior, concrete interior) of this cuboid creation is supposed to look like a lamp.

The **casino** *(Map 33, #4;* ☎ *451 27, Platz der Wiener Symphoniker 3; gaming tables open 3pm-4am Sun-Thurs, 3pm-4am Fri & Sat, slot machines noon-midnight Sun-Thurs, noon-1am Fri & Sat)* is behind the train station *(Bahnhof)*. Spend money, buy disappointment: there's no better place.

The peak of the **Pfänder** (1064m) offers an impressive view of the lake and beyond; to the east, the Allgäuer Alpen range can be seen. A cable car *(Map 33 #15;* ☎ *421 60-0, Steinbruchgasse 4; adult/senior/youth €5.45/4.95/4.40 one-way, €9.45/8.50/7.60 return)* operates year-round, except during November maintenance, from 9am to 7pm. Walk south through the woods from the top station to find a viewing table. At the top there is also a **Greifvogelflugschau** *(bird of prey show; mobile* ☎ *0663-053040, Pfänder 1; adult/*

Bodensee Excursions

Bodensee (Lake Constance) is a major summer holiday resort for Austrian, German and Swiss tourists. As well as many water sports, there are interesting sights around the lake which can easily be visited during a boat trip from Bregenz. There are plenty of youth hostels and cosy guesthouses if you want to stay overnight.

Considered in anticlockwise order (the direction the boats travel), the closest place to Bregenz is **Lindau** in Germany. Of interest in this island village are a Bavarian lion monument and an old Rathaus (town hall) with murals. **Friedrichshafen** is where Graf Zeppelin built his overgrown cigar-shaped balloons, an achievement commemorated in the town's Zeppelin museum. Picturesque **Meersburg** has many half-timbered houses built in the classical German style, and two castles overlooking the vineyard-patterned hills. **Überlingen** has the Cathedral of St Nicholas, with a four storey altar (dating from the 17th century) and a dozen side altars. **Konstanz** (Constance), the largest town on the lake and linked to Meersburg by car ferry, has a Gothic cathedral and a lively student population. The flower island of Mainau is close by.

Switzerland has fewer points of interest around the lake. **Kreuzlingen**, the Swiss annexe of Konstanz, contains nothing of great sightseeing importance. **Arbon** has a historical museum in a 16th-century castle, and some half-timbered houses. **Rorschach** has a museum containing old cars, motorcycles and vending machines. A short train ride south from Rorschach is **St Gallen**, with an excellent late-baroque cathedral and adjoining rococo library (these are a Unesco World Heritage site), plus many buildings with oriel windows in the old town.

The international Bodensee Festival takes place from early May to early June. Most events (concerts, cabaret, theatre etc) are on the German side of the lake, particularly around Friedrichshafen. The Bregenz tourist office has a comprehensive timetable of Bodensee boats, trains and buses.

child €3.50/1.85; open 11am-2.30pm daily May-Sept), where feathered performers show off aerial feats, and a no-fee animal park.

There is a bathing complex (☎ 442 42, Strandweg) just to the north-west of the train station. It includes the open-air **Strandbad** (Map 33, #1; adult/concession €2.95/2.20; open 9am-8pm daily mid May-1 Sept), with lakeside access, a couple of pools and a self-service restaurant; and the year-round **Seehallenbad** (indoor pool; Map 33, #3; adult/student/senior €3.50/2.55/2.80; open 9am-9pm Tues-Fri, 9am-7pm Sat, 10am-6pm Sun & holidays).

A range of **boat trips** and excursions out of Bregenz are offered from May to September by the Bodenseeschifffahrt ferry service of the Österreichischen Bundesbahnen (ÖBB; Austrian Federal Railways; Map 33, #12; ☎ 428 68, Seestrasse 4). Schedules are available from the boat station, train station or tourist office; see also the boxed text 'Bodensee Excursions' and the Getting There & Away section later in this chapter.

Sailing and **diving** are on offer at Lochau, 5km north of town.

Special Events

The Bregenz Festival takes place from late July to late August. Operas, orchestral works and theatrical productions with international performers, are performed on the Seebühne (Map 33, #2), a vast, open-air floating stage at edge of the lake, north of the train station. For information and tickets, contact the Ticket Center (☎ 407-6, fax 407-400, **w** www .bregenzerfestspiele.com), Postfach 311, A-6901 Bregenz, about nine months before the festival. Tickets cost anywhere between €40 and €130. The festival includes other locations (eg, the Kunsthaus), where events may be cheaper, or even free.

Places to Stay

Camping Lamm (☎ 717 01, fax 71745-4, Mehrerauerstrasse 51) Price per adult/tent/ car €3.30/3.30/2.55. Open 1 May to mid-October. Bregenz has four camping grounds near or on the lake. This one is the cheapest, yet also the closest to the train station (about 1km to the west).

Jugendgästehaus (Map 33, #5; ☎ 428 67, fax 428 67-88, e bregenz@jgh.at, Mehrerauerstrasse 3-5) Beds in 6-8 bed dorms €16.75. Reception open 7am-10pm daily. Housed in a former needle factory, the spacious dorms have high ceilings. Single, double or family occupancy is possible for a surcharge. This HI hostel also has a restaurant (open to all; lunch/dinner €5.60/6.20) and Internet access.

Rooms in private houses cost around €17 to €21 per person and are invariably good value; some are situated on the scenic lower slopes of the Pfänder. These rooms, and holiday apartments, appear on the tourist office's accommodation list. Stays of under three days may not be possible, or will incur a surcharge. Staff at the tourist office will book rooms for €2.20 commission, which is an especially useful service during the festival. Expect prices during the festival to be higher than those quoted here.

Pension Gunz (Map 33, #16; ☎/fax 436 57, Anton Schneider Strasse 38) Singles/doubles with private shower €26.90/48, 2 doubles with shared bathroom €42.20. Reception in downstairs cafe, open 8am-8pm, check in 11am-6pm, closed Tues & Mar. Good-value rooms have rustic-style floral paintings on bed-ends and wardrobes.

Pension Sonne (Map 33, #20; ☎/fax 425 72, e office@bbn.at, Kaiserstrasse 8) Singles/doubles with private bathroom €33.50/61.50, without €27/49.50. Closed Jan & Feb. This convenient, family-run pension has reasonably sized rooms which vary in outlook and decor (many have a homey touch).

Hotel Krone (Map 33, #23; ☎ 421 17, fax 421 17-4, Leutbühl 3) Singles/doubles with private bathroom €38.60/60.40, without €28.40/45.80; reductions outside summer. Right in the centre of town, this creaky old house offers rooms that are huge and well-kept.

Zum Grauen Bären (Map 33, #13; ☎ 428 23, fax 428 23-8, Reichsstrasse 8) Singles/doubles with private bathroom €43.60/65.50, without €30.60/43.60. Open Mar-Nov. This two-star place is near where the boat trips depart. Though perhaps on the expensive side, some rooms are very large; the TVs in the rooms only pick up Austrian channels.

Hotel Germania (Map 33, #14; ☎ 427 66-0, fax 427 66-4, e office@hotel-germania.at, Am Steinenbach 9) Singles €62-80, doubles €95-124. This four-star place particularly tries to attract cyclists, and rents bikes and organises bike tours. It also offers garage parking and a fitness room and sauna, which are all free for guests. Rooms have private bathroom, TV, phone and fast ISDN Internet connection, and there's a quality restaurant (the kitchen is open 4pm to 9pm daily).

Places to Eat

Some of the places mentioned under Places to Stay are also worth trying for food.

The *GWL* shopping centre, at Leutbühel 2, has a *Spar* supermarket (Map 33, #21), which is open 8am to 7pm Monday to Thursday, until 7.30pm Friday, until 5pm Saturday; attached is a self-service restaurant, open 8am to 6pm Monday to Friday, until 4pm Saturday. Meals cost from €4.40 to €8, and there's a salad buffet for €0.90 per 100g. The pricier restaurant on the 1st floor has serving staff and access to a terrace.

König Pizza & Kebap (Map 33, #18; ☎ 538 81, Rathausstrasse 6). Pizzas €4.15-6.20, doner kebabs €2.95-4.75. Open 10am-2am Mon-Sat, 4pm-2am Sun. This small cafe belies its fast-food ethos by providing warm decor and candles on the table. Pizzas are OK, but the kebabs are great.

China-Restaurant Da-Li (Map 33, #17; ☎ 534 14, Anton Schneider Strasse 34) Weekday lunch menu €4.75-6.20, including soup or spring roll, weekday lunch buffet €6.90, other meals €6.55-16. Open 11.30am-2.30pm & 5.30pm-11.30pm daily. Tuck into standard Chinese fare beneath a slightly tacky painted mirror ceiling.

Gösserbräu Gasthaus (Map 33, #19; ☎ 424 67, Anton Schneider Strasse 1) Austrian snacks & meals €4.95-12.25. Open 9am-1am daily. Once inside, turn left for the comfortable, cultured Gösserstuben; alternatively, head right for the rap-sac, where you can eat the same meals as in the Gösserstuben, though the emphasis is more on beer-compatible snacks. The rap-sac itself is a curious design hybrid: there is the modern, re-modelled, nightclub-esque room, or the traditional wood-panelled room.

Zum Goldenen Hirschen (Map 33, #22; ☎ 428 15, Kirchstrasse 8) Meals €5.85-17.80. Open 10am-midnight Wed-Mon. A haunt for locals, this restaurant serves good Austrian food in an eye-catching room with heraldic crests, antlers and lots of wood.

Gasthaus Maurachbund (Map 33, #24; ☎ 440 20, Maurachgasse 11) Mains €8-18.60. Open 11am-2pm & 5pm-midnight Tues-Sat, 11am-2pm Sun, closed Mon. This is also a good, albeit more expensive, place for Austrian food.

Deuring-Schlössle (Map 33, #27; ☎ 478 00, Ehregutaplatz 4). Meals €14.50-29. Kitchen open noon-2pm & 6pm-10pm, closed noon-2pm Mon. This elegant building in the old town houses the best restaurant in Bregenz and is the refined setting for gourmet dishes, including fish from the lake. You can opt to have a different, specially selected glass of wine with each course of a multi-course menu. Accommodation is also available.

Getting There & Away

For Rheintalflug flights, which fly to Altenrhein, Switzerland, see Air in the Getting Around chapter or visit the company's office at Bahnhofstrasse 10 (Map 33, #8; ☎ 488 00-0).

Bundesbuses to destinations in Vorarlberg (including Dornbirn; €2.05, 30 minutes) leave from outside the train station.

Trains to Munich (€34.55, 2½ hours, every two to three hours) go via Lindau; trains for Konstanz (€5.40, 1½ hours, every two hours) go via the Swiss shore of the lake. There are also regular departures to St Gallen and Zürich. Trains to Innsbruck (€21.85, 2¾ hours) depart every one to two hours, calling en route at Feldkirch (€4.25, 25 minutes) and Bludenz (€6, 45 minutes). Feldkirch and Bludenz can also be reached via slower regional trains (in 45 minutes and 70 minutes

respectively), departing every 30 minutes or so; for return trips to both places it's cheaper to buy a day pass instead. The train station has a train information office and an ATM Bankomat.

Boat services operate from early April to mid-October, with more frequent departures in summer. For information on this so-called *Weissen Flotte* (white fleet), call ☎ 428 68. From Bregenz to Konstanz by boat (€12; via Lindau) takes about 3¾ hours and there are up to seven departures per day.

A Bodensee Pass (€24.95 for 15 days) entitles the holder to half-price tickets on boats, trains and buses. Alternatively, buy transferable day passes (€18.35 per set of three) valid for free travel on boats. Inquire also about the Bodensee family card, which allows free travel for children.

BREGENZERWALD

This is the area around Bregenz. It is less wooded than the name implies (*'Wald'* means forest), being a combination of tree-lined hills, small villages and open pastures. Skiing (both downhill and cross-country) and walking are popular. The most dramatic natural feature is the **Rappenlochschlucht** (Rappenloch Gorge), through which the raging Dornbirner Ache flows.

Staff at the Bregenzerwald tourist office (☎ 05512-2365, fax 05512-3010, e info@bregenzerwald.at) at Postfach 29, Loco 613, Egg, can expound on the attractions of the region. To inquire about guided walks through the gorge, contact the Dornbirn tourist office (☎ 05572-22188), Rathausplatz 1.

In Schwarzenberg (east of Dornbirn), the **Schubertiade** summer music festival runs for two weeks in late June and two weeks in early September. This celebration of Schubert's work is very popular, so you need to inquire about tickets months in advance. Contact Schubertiade GmbH (☎ 05576-720 91, fax 05576-754 50, w www.schubertiade.at), Postfach 100, A-6845 Hohenems.

Getting There & Away

The easiest access point to the area is Dornbirn, at which frequent InterCity (IC) and regional trains stop on their way to/from Bregenz (eight to 16 minutes away). Thereafter, private transport, Bundesbus, bike or foot is the way to explore the region. The Dornbirn-Ebnit Bundesbus (every two hours, 6.39am to 5.39pm) will take you to the Rappenlochsbrücke stop for the gorge (€2.05, 22 minutes). Hourly Bundesbuses run between Dornbirn and Egg (€2.50, 30 minutes). In Dornbirn, call ☎ 05572-22631 for Bundesbus information.

FELDKIRCH
☎ 05522 • pop 29,900 • elev 450m
Feldkirch has a long history: its town charter was granted in 1218, and 'Feldkirichun' appeared in records as early as 842. It's also the gateway to Liechtenstein, a parcel-sized principality to the west famous for its postage stamps and wines.

Orientation & Information
The town centre is a few minutes' walk south of the train station (turn left upon exiting). The tourist office (☎ 734 67, fax 798 67, e tourismus@wtg.feldkirch.com), Herrengasse 12, is in the centre of town; Herrengasse leads off from Domplatz (Cathedral Square). Its opening hours are 9am to 6pm (closed noon to 1pm in winter) Monday to Friday, and (July and August) 9am to noon Saturday.

The post office (Postamt 6800) is opposite the train station.

Things to See & Do
The town retains an aura of its medieval past, with old patrician houses lining the squares in the centre, and a couple of towers surviving from the ancient fortifications. Both Neustadt and Marktplatz have arcaded walkways. **Domkirche St Nikolaus** (Cathedral St Nicholas) has Late Gothic features and vibrantly coloured stained glass. The painting on the side altar to the right of the main altar is by local boy Wolf Huber (1480–1539), a leading member of the Danube school.

The 12th-century **Schloss Schattenburg** dominates the town, and can be reached by stairs or road. This castle was the seat of the counts of Montfort until 1390. Extensive views can be enjoyed from the keep, and the museum (☎ 724 44, Burggasse 1; admission €1.85/0.75 adult/student; open 9am-noon & 1pm-5pm Tues-Sun, closed Nov) has displays of religious art and historical artefacts. The castle is also the setting for folklore evenings (details are available from the tourist office).

There's a **Wildpark** (animal park; admission free), in which 200 species roam, about 1km to the north-west of the town centre.

At **Laterns** there are ski slopes, with lifts up to 1785m. From Feldkirch it's about 30 minutes by car, but over an hour by Bundesbus (change at Rankweil). A one-day ski pass costs €23.70 (family cards available).

Special Events
Feldkirch showcases classical music in a two-week festival starting in late May; get details and tickets from the tourist office. Other festivals include a **wine festival** on the second weekend in July and a **jugglers' festival** on the first weekend in August. In winter there's a Christmas market.

Places to Stay
Waldcamping (☎/fax 743 08, Stadionstrasse, Gisingen) Site €13.70/11.05 per double summer/winter. This camping ground offers a quiet, forest-fringed location for year-round camping; take bus No 2 from the train station to the last stop (3.5km).

Jugendherberge (☎ 731 81, fax 793 99, Reichsstrasse 111) Bed in 8-bed dorm €10.80, bed in 2-bed room €14.50, heating surcharge in winter €2, reduction of €1.50 for own bedding. Reception open 7.30am-10pm, closed 10am-5pm Sun, closed for 2 weeks early Dec. Dinner €7.20. This HI hostel is 1.5km north of the train station (bus No 2 trundles past) in a historic building that formerly served as an infirmary. It has been completely modernised inside and has good facilities.

Private rooms are an economical option, but you'll find hotels and pensions surprisingly expensive – Switzerland may be nearby but that's no excuse to charge Swiss prices. The best deals are away from the town centre.

Gasthof Engel (☎/fax 720 56, Liechtensteiner Strasse 106) Singles/doubles €24.75/ 39.25. Closed Mon. Less than 2km south-west of the centre in Tisis (the Liechtenstein Bundesbus runs past), this Gasthof has a restaurant, garden, parking and old-fashioned rooms with shared bathroom and painted wardrobes.

Hotel Hochhaus (☎ 822 48, fax 82287, Reichsstrasse 177) Singles/doubles €43.60/ 72.70. If you like traffic noise, you'll love this place. For others, it represents an adequate resting-up point close to the train station. It's behind the post office, and has rooms with private bathroom and TV, and balconies overlooking a busy street.

Hotel Central Löwen (☎ 720 70-0, fax 720 70-5, **e** central.loewen@hotel.vol.at, Neustadt 17) Singles/doubles €48/75.60 The modern rooms of this centrally located hotel are a good size, and have TV and private bathroom. Guests can use the sauna and steam bath. At the time of writing, ownership was expected to change, so expect some renovations.

Places to Eat

There's a *Spar* supermarket (Neustadt 19) in the town centre. *Interspar (St Leonhards Platz)* is a larger supermarket and general store selling everything from washing machines to bicycles. It's open 8.30am to 7pm Monday to Thursday, 8.30am to 7.30pm Friday, and 8am to 5pm Saturday. It also has a cheap cafe with meals for around €4.40.

Johanniterhof (☎ 829 903, Marktgasse 1) Meals €6.40-15.65. Open 8am-midnight daily. For affordable Austrian food, including many vegetarian choices, look no further than Johanniterhof. There's a large room with wooden pillars, or make for the beer garden around the back.

Schlosswirtschaft Schattenburg (☎ 724 44, Burggasse 1) Meals €7.30-18.20. Open 10am-midnight Tues-Sun, closed Mon & Nov. This restaurant in the castle is another spot for good Austrian food without excessive prices.

Gasthof Lingg (☎ 720 62, Kreuzgasse 10) Meals €7.85-18.20. Open 10am-2pm & 6pm-midnight winter, 8am-midnight summer, closed Sun 2pm & Mon. With a good location overlooking Marktplatz from Kreuzgasse, this place is a good choice if you fancy dining on something slightly more upmarket.

Getting There & Away

Bundesbuses to destinations around Vorarlberg depart from outside Feldkirch's train station.

Two buses per hour (one per hour at weekends) depart for Liechtenstein from in front of the train station, calling at Katzentrum (behind the tourist office) en route. To reach Liechtenstein's capital, Vaduz (€2.35, 40 minutes), it's sometimes necessary to change buses in Schaans. Liechtenstein has a customs union with Switzerland, so you'll pass through Swiss customs before entering Liechtenstein. Trains to Buchs, on the Swiss border, pass through Schaans, but only a few stop there. Buchs has connections to major destinations in Switzerland, including Zürich and Chur.

Feldkirch is on the main road and rail route between Bregenz (€4.25, 25 to 45 minutes, every 30 minutes) and Tirol.

BLUDENZ

☎ 05552 • pop 14,500 • elev 588m

Bludenz is a pleasant, unassuming town, standing at the meeting point of five valleys: Klostertal, Montafon, Brandnertal, Grosswalsertal and Walgau.

Granted its town charter in 1274, Bludenz was the seat of the Habsburg governors from 1418 to 1806. The arrival of the railways in the late 19th century allowed the town, a former silver mining centre, to become an important commercial base. At the same time there was an influx of settlers from the Val Sugana, in northern Italy, resulting in today's Italianate ambience. Textiles, chocolate and beer are Bludenz's main industries.

Orientation & Information

The town centre is on the northern bank of the Ill River. The tourist office (Map 34, #5; ☎ 621 70, fax 675 97, **e** tourismus@bludenz.at), Werdenbergerstrasse 42, is five minutes' walk from the train station; just walk up Bahnhofstrasse and turn left at Werdenbergerstrasse. It's open 8am to noon Monday to Friday, and (July and August only) 9am to noon Saturday.

The post office (Map 34, #8; Postamt 6700), opposite the tourist office at Werdenbergerstrasse 37, changes cash and has a free Internet terminal. It's open 6.30am to 7pm (cash counters until 5pm) Monday to Friday, and 6.30am to noon Saturday.

East of the tourist office is a small pedestrian-only shopping area.

Things to See & Do

One of Bludenz's most enjoyable features can't even be seen. Almost anywhere you wander in the centre, the rich, enticing aroma of chocolate will fill your nostrils. The **Suchard chocolate factory** is right opposite the train station; there are no conducted tours but there is a shop (Map 34, #14) where you can buy the produce at decent prices (eg, 100g bar of Milka for €0.65). It's open from 9am to 11.30am and 1.30pm to 4.30pm Monday to Friday (4pm on Friday). Chocolate also plays an important part in the children's **Milka chocolate festival** in mid-July, when 1000kg of the stuff is up for grabs in prizes. See the Festivals of Austria boxed text in the Facts for the Visitor chapter for more information.

For other attractions, join one of the free **city tours** organised by the tourist office; they depart from the tourist office at 10am

MW

Monday between June and September. The most distinctive architectural feature in town is the parish church, **St Laurentiuskirche** (Church of St Lawrence; Map 34, #4). It was built in 1514 and has an unusual octagonal, onion-domed spire. Several covered staircases lead up to the church; one has a war memorial within. There's also a **Stadtmuseum** *(city museum; Map 34, #9; ☎ 636 21, Kirchgasse 9; admission €1.50; open 3pm-7pm Mon-Sat Jun-early Sept, closed holidays)*. This small, seven-room museum outlines the history of the old town.

Bludenz is a good base for exploring the surrounding valleys. There are 15 **skiing** areas within a 40km radius. Ski bus transport to/from Bludenz is sometimes included in the price of ski passes (eg, the €28.75 one-day pass for Sonnenkopf). Ski passes are obtained from the relevant resort; if you don't yet have your pass but are wearing ski clothes, you may not have to pay for the bus. A private train takes skiers to Schruns (€2.05, 20 minutes, hourly), a resort to the south-east. **Walking** and **cycling** are other popular activities.

A cable car *(☎ 627 52, Hinterplärsch; adult/senior €4.75/4 up, €3.65/ 2.95 down, €7.65/5.85 return; open 10am-5pm Nov-Apr, 9am-6pm May-Oct)* goes up to Muttersberg at 1384m. Catch the No 1 bus from in front of the train station to the cable car station, or walk 1km north of the town centre.

Places to Stay

Ask for the *Gästekarte* (guest card) if you stay overnight in town.

Camping Seeberger (Map 34, #1; ☎ 625 12, Obdorfweg 9) Site €16.35 per double. Open year-round. This camping ground is about 600m north-west of the centre.

Staff at the tourist office will reserve accommodation without charging any commission. Private rooms are the best value for budget travellers, even though a surcharge of €2.20 to €3.65 per day usually applies for stays under three days. Rooms in the suburbs give you more for your money but are less convenient.

Haus Feuerstein (☎ 320 32, Schillerstrasse 22) Single/doubles €18.90/33.50.

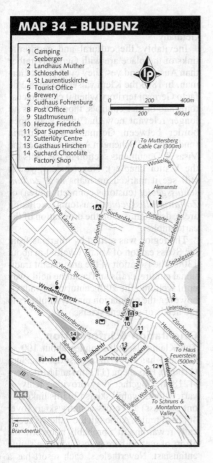

MAP 34 – BLUDENZ

1 Camping
　Seeberger
2 Landhaus Muther
3 Schlosshotel
4 St Laurentiuskirche
5 Tourist Office
6 Brewery
7 Sudhaus Fohrenburg
8 Post Office
9 Stadtmuseum
10 Herzog Friedrich
11 Spar Supermarket
12 Sutterlüty Centre
13 Gasthaus Hirschen
14 Suchard Chocolate
　Factory Shop

To Muttersberg
Cable Car (300m)

Alemannstr

Winkelweg

Stuttgarter

Suchardstr

Alte Landstr

Obdorfweg

Atmaulweg

Walserweg

Oberfeldweg

Spitalgasse

St Anna Str

Werdenbergerstr

Aulweg

Fohrenburgstr

Muttrstr

Untersteinstr

Herrengasse

Zürcherstr

Bahnhofstr

Sturnengasse

Wichnerstr

Werdenbergerstr

Bahnhof

To Haus
Feuerstein
(500m)

Salzweg

A14

Ill

Hermann-Ignaz-Wolf-Str

To Schruns &
Montafon
Valley

To
Brandnertal

The house is about 1km east of the pedestrian area, and offers just one single and two doubles.

Landhaus Muther *(Map 34, #2; ☎ 657 04, fax 657 11, Alemannstrasse 4)* Singles/doubles €25.50/50.90. This is a pleasant, small-scale guesthouse offering modern-looking rooms with private bathroom. Walking to the old town takes about 10 minutes.

Herzog Friedrich *(Map 34, #10; ☎ 627 03-0, fax 627 03-81, Mutterstrasse 6)* Singles/doubles €43/74. This place is centrally located, has a restaurant and sports

three stars; its exterior is fairly stark, but the interior is much less so. Each room has a private bathroom, TV and phone.

Places to Eat

In the pedestrian-only area in the town centre is the **Kronenhaus** department store, with a **Spar** supermarket *(Map 34, #11; Werdenbergerstrasse 34)*. But for sit-down eating, continue walking west for four minutes to the **Sutterlüty** centre *(Map 34, #12; Werdenbergerstrasse 5)*, which is open 8am to 7pm Monday to Friday, 8am to 5pm Saturday. Inside is a **Eurospar** supermarket and a cafe serving snacks and meals for €2 to €6.50.

Sudhaus Fohrenburg *(Map 34, #7; ☎ 633 44, fax 633 44-4, Werdenbergerstrasse 53)* Austrian meals €5.70-12.75. Open 11am-2am Mon-Thur, 11am-4am Fri & Sat, 10am-3am Sun. A major feature of this large place is the many varieties of local Fohrenburger beer (from €2.80 per 0.5L), which is hardly surprising as the brewery (Map 34, #6) is across the road. At night, Sudhaus is a lively meeting place for young people attracted by live music or other events several nights a week (and of course the beer!). There's also a large garden with outdoor tables.

Gasthaus Hirschen *(Map 34, #13; ☎ 686 80, Sturnengasse 19)* Meals €6.20-14.55, lunch menu with soup €6.90. Open 10am-2pm Mon, 10pm-midnight Wed-Sat, 10am-10pm Sun. This restaurant serves Austrian food in comfortable, rustic surroundings. It has a tree-lined beer garden across the street.

Schlosshotel *(Map 34, #3; ☎ 630 16-0, Schlossplatz 5)* Meals €9-20. Open 11am-1.45pm & 6pm-10pm daily. The restaurant in the town's only four-star hotel just happens to be one of the best in Bludenz, and serves Austrian fare plus a few international dishes.

Getting There & Away

Bludenz is on the east-west IC rail route, two hours from Innsbruck (€17.30, every two hours) and 45 minutes from Bregenz (€6, hourly). By regional train, Bregenz-Bludenz is 70 minutes (every 30 minutes).

VORARLBERG

The east-west A14 road passes just south of the Ill River and the town centre. The Silvretta Road, leading to Silvretta Stausee (reservoir) and the Bielerhöhe Pass (2036m) into Tirol, heads south-east from Bludenz along the Montafon Valley. To cross the pass, there's a toll for cars/motorcycles €10.90/10.20.

Bundesbuses run down all five valleys around Bludenz. For details of prices and timetables, call ☎ 05522-73973-3200.

BRANDNERTAL
☎ 05559

The Brandnertal (Brand Valley) runs southwest of Bludenz. About 12km from Bludenz is the resort of **Brand** (elevation 1037m). It offers accommodation and winter sports (€27.65 for a one-day ski pass; reductions for young people and seniors), and its ski school has received good reports. For more information, contact the tourist office (☎ 555-0, fax 555-20, e brand@brand.vol .at) in the Gemeindezentrum in the centre.

The road from Brand climbs to provide good views and ultimately leads to **Lünersee** (sounds like a mad name for a lake). To reach the lake, at 1907m, you have to make a 400m ascent by cable car (€ 4.10/6.85 one-way/ return, late May-mid Oct only). Lünersee has been dammed to produce hydroelectric power. Overlooking the lake is the Schesaplana peak (2965m), straddling the Swiss border, which can be climbed from the lake in about three hours.

Getting There & Away
There is a Bundesbus every one to two hours from Bludenz as far as Brand Innertal (€2.05, 33 minutes). The additional 7km bus trip (€1.60, 20 minutes) to the Lünerseebahn cable car station is run only in the summer, as the road (1:8 gradient) is often blocked by snow in winter.

KLEINWALSERTAL
This oddity of a place is more German than Germany. It's in the east of Vorarlberg, and most of it is surrounded by German territory. Furthermore, access from the south is precluded by the towering Allgäuer Alpen,

meaning the only way in or out is through Germany.

Inevitably, the cultural and economic links of the place are with Germany rather than Austria, and yes, they even speak German. In 1893 the Kleinwalsertal became de facto German territory when it came to customs and border controls, though this is no longer relevant now that there's an open border between Germany and Austria (under the EU Schengen Agreement; see the Visas & Documents section in the Facts for the Visitor chapter). Nevertheless, you'll still see it marked on maps as a *Zollanschlussgebiet* (customs connection area) or *Zollausschlussgebiet* (customs exclusion area), depending upon the orientation of the cartographer.

The region was settled by migrants from the Swiss canton of Valais (Wallis) in about 1300. The isolation of the area meant traditional culture, crafts and costume held sway until well into the 20th century. Nowadays, however, the population mainly ministers to the needs of affluent skiers.

Orientation & Information
The Kleinwalsertal occupies about 100 sq km, and has three main resorts: Riezlern (1100m), Hirschegg (1124m) and Mittelberg (1218m). Together they provide plenty of variety for downhill skiers (30 lifts linked by one ski pass) and cross-country skiers (over 40km of trails). Although the valley is scenically rewarding, it's probably not worth the effort of getting here unless you're a skiing enthusiast. Nevertheless, each resort has a tourist office that will try to convince you otherwise; the largest is in Hirschegg (☎ 0551-5114-0, e kwt_tourismus@vol.at).

Hotels and restaurants in the area are expensive; the only cheap accommodation is in the mountains above the resorts, in alpine huts and small inns away from the centre.

Getting There & Away
Kleinwalsertal is on Hwy 201, running north from Mittelberg to Oberstdorf and Sonthofen in Germany. A right turn at Sonthofen (Hwy 199) leads to Reutte, in Tirol. A few kilometres further north on the 201 is Immenstadt,

where Hwy 308 will allow you to re-enter Vorarlberg from the north. The nearest rail line terminates at Oberstdorf, close to the Austrian border, from where there are infrequent buses to Kleinwalsertal. Another option is the Bundesbus from Reutte.

WESTERN ARLBERG
☎ 05583

The Arlberg area is a prime skiing destination. Though it straddles Vorarlberg and Tirol, a general ski pass covers all of its resorts. Note that the resorts in western Arlberg don't have street names, and each business has a unique house number. For details of ski prices, seasons, transport options and the region's biggest resort (St Anton am Arlberg), see the Arlberg Region in the Tirol chapter.

The northernmost and largest village here is **Lech** (1450m). This upmarket resort is a favourite with royalty, film stars and anybody who likes to pretend to be such from behind dark glasses. Ski runs are mainly medium and easy, with some advanced off-piste possibilities. A cable car goes up Rüflikopf (2362m), but most of the lifts and runs are on the opposite side of the valley, on the Krigerhorn (2178m) and Zuger Hochlicht (2377m). The Lech ski school (☎ 2355, fax 3849-6, W www.skischule-lech.com) can arrange helicopter skiing (from €233 for four people). Lech's tourist office (☎ 2161-0, fax 3155, e lech-info@lech.at) is in the centre of the resort, on the main road. It's open daily in the high season.

Six kilometres to the south lies **Zürs** (1716m), a smaller resort but with its own tourist office (☎ 2245, fax 2982, e zuers info@zuers.at) on the main street. A cable car ascends to Trittkopf (2423m); across the valley the Zürsersee cable car climbs to 2206m, where there's a lake and a further lift to whisk you to 2450m.

One kilometre south of Zürs is the **Flexen Pass** (1773m), after which the road splits: the western fork leads to **Stuben** (1407m), the eastern one to St Christoph and Tirol.

Places to Stay
The cheapest accommodation options are in private rooms or holiday apartments, but it's

wise to book in advance. If you just arrive on spec, seek the help of the local tourist office; the Lech and Zürs offices each have an accommodation board and a free telephone that are always accessible.

Jugendheim (☎ 2419, fax 2419-4, No 244) Beds in 2, 4, 6 or 8-bed dorm €32.70 half-board. Closed May, Jun & mid Sept-mid Dec. Check in from 4pm. Despite its upmarket profile, Lech has a hostel, 2km to the north-east of the main resort in the village of Stubenbach. However, it's full with school groups for most of the winter, and doesn't accept backpackers in summer (only Vorarlberg families). Phone ahead and you might get lucky.

Pension Brunelle (☎ 2976, No 220) Rooms €25.50/16 per person winter/summer. This bargain place near the centre of Lech, on the road towards Stubenbach, has a small sun terrace and simple, variable rooms with shared bathroom.

Haus Nenning (☎ 2408, fax 30538, No 149) Singles/doubles €54.60/94.50 winter, €25.50/50.90 summer. This convenient three-star place is just north of the main street in the centre, near the Schlegelkopf lift. Its rooms are wood-panelled and have private bathroom and TV.

Places to Eat
Eating cheaply in Lech is all but impossible, unless you stock up at one of the two **supermarkets** (open daily in season) in the centre.

Hagen Metzgerei Snacks & meals €1.45-11.65. Open 9am-12.30pm & 3pm-6.30pm daily. This meat shop and deli is on the main street, east of the post office and by the bridge. It serves affordable hot and cold snacks and meals, including grilled chicken and Wiener schnitzel.

Ambrosius Stube (☎ 3365, No 229) Meals €6.40-14.40. Open 11.30-10.30pm daily. This surprisingly affordable place is in the centre of Lech, by the Rüflikopf lift. There's a sunny terrace where you can enjoy regional and Austrian food.

Charly Pizza (☎ 2339, No 261) Pizzas €6.90-21.10. Open 11am-2pm & 4pm-midnight daily, closed between seasons. This place is at the beginning of the road to

Stubenbach, and serves decent pizzas and other Italian food

If you're flush with funds, there are plenty of quaint places in Lech where you can eat very well – just follow your nose.

Getting There & Away

Lech can be reached by bus from St Anton (3.35/6.70 one-way/return, 35 minutes,

hourly in winter, four daily in summer), from where there are train connections to the rest of Austria. Buses go over the Flexen Pass (via Zürs), which is open year-round, but has been known to be blocked in winter. Lech can also be approached from the north, via the turning at Warth (1494m). Infrequent Bundesbuses travel this route in summer, terminating at Reutte.

Salzburg Province

Salzburg province (Salzburger Land) has something to appeal to everyone. The city of Salzburg draws visitors from near and far; it's a tourist magnet second only to Vienna. To the east of the city is a sublime landscape of mountains and lakes, the Salzkammergut (covered in the following chapter). To the south are found mightier mountain ranges, towering above ski villages, cascading waterfalls and spa resorts. Salzburg province also has the lion's share of the Hohe Tauern National Park, covered in an earlier chapter in this book.

History

Salzburg, the provincial capital, was the chief town in the region as far back as Roman times. In about 696 St Rupert established a bishopric there, which was subsequently elevated to an archbishopric with authority over the dioceses of Bavaria.

The archbishops increasingly became involved in temporal matters and in the 13th century were granted the titles of Princes of the Holy Roman Empire. Their powers extended to an area up to twice the size of present-day Salzburg province and included parts of Bavaria and Italy.

Economic strength was built on mining: there were some gold mines (now within Tirol and Carinthia) but salt, the so-called 'white gold', had been more important since Celtic times. This is acknowledged in various place names (salt being *Hall* in Celtic and *Salz* in German). See the Salzkammergut chapter for more on salt mining.

Wolf Dietrich von Raitenau (1587–1612) was one of Salzburg's most influential archbishops and instigated the baroque reconstruction of the city. However, an unsuccessful dispute with powerful Bavaria over the salt trade led to his imprisonment, during which he died.

Paris Lodron (1619–53) managed to keep the principality out of the Thirty Years' War. Salzburg was also neutral during the War of the Austrian Succession a century later, but

Highlights

- View Salzburg's baroque domes and spires from Festung Hohensalzburg or Mirabellgarten
- Soak up the atmosphere of Salzburg's magnificent old town
- Knock back a litre or two in the Augustiner Bräustübl
- Cool down on a hot day via a close encounter with the trick fountains at Schloss Hellbrunn
- Visit the hill-top fortress and spectacular ice caves at Werfen

about this time its power and prosperity began to diminish. During the Napoleonic Wars Salzburg was controlled by France and Bavaria, before becoming part of Austria in 1816.

Orientation

Salzburg province is roughly triangular and totals 7154 sq km. It's home to 482,000 people, and borders Germany and Italy.

The Salzach River rises in the south-west of the province, flows east, turns north at St Johann im Pongau, and marks the border with Germany north of Salzburg city.

Information

The provincial tourist board is Salzburger Land Tourismus (☎ 0662-66 88, fax 0662-66 88-66, **e** info@szgtour.co.at), Postfach 1,

A-5300 Hallwang bei Salzburg. This office deals with marketing and postal, email or telephone inquiries; Salzburg has an office for inquiries in person (see the Salzburg Information section).

Tourist offices sell the Salzburger Sommer Joker, a card which gives free entry to 180 attractions in Salzburger Land. It's available from around 10 May to 26 October and costs €40/20 for adults/children. Valid for 16 days, it's an excellent deal – it'll pay for itself after a few cable-car rides, and it even includes a 24-hour Salzburg Card (see the Salzburg Information section).

Salzburg

☎ 0662 ● pop 145,000 ● elev 425m

The city of Salzburg stands in a breathtaking setting and is rich with magnificent architectural treasures. The baroque church spires of the old town, with the Festung Hohensalzburg (fortress) rising in back of them, are an unforgettable sight. The old town itself (officially, Salzburg Historic Centre) is also one of Austria's six Unesco World Heritage sites.

The city's descent into poverty in the 18th century was a blessing in disguise: it

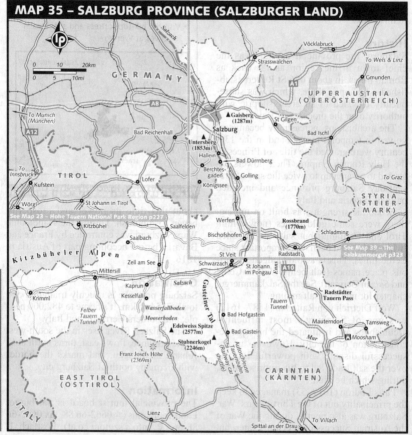

MAP 35 – SALZBURG PROVINCE (SALZBURGER LAND)

ensured that the historic buildings that are currently attracting high-spending tourists were repaired rather than replaced. Another fortuitous factor in Salzburg's tourist pre-eminence was the birth of Wolfgang Amadeus Mozart (1756). Ironically, the city that gave the composer scant encouragement during his lifetime now can't get enough of him (or the influx of well-heeled music lovers).

In Salzburg, the influence of Mozart is everywhere. There is Mozartplatz with its Mozart statue, the Mozarteum music academy, Mozart's birthplace and Mozart's resi-

dence. His music dominates grand festivals and the more humble outpourings of street musicians alike. Chocolate confections and liqueurs are even named after him. Devotees of a rather different musical genre are also drawn to the city in surprising numbers: in 1964 the city and nearby hills were alive with the making of the film *The Sound of Music*.

If your wallet is thin, don't worry: this town also offers plenty for budget travellers. It costs nothing to walk around and take it all in. Admiring the gorgeous views, entering churches, courtyards and gardens puts no demands on shallow pockets.

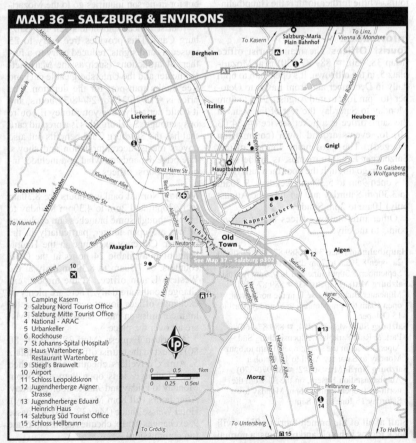

MAP 36 – SALZBURG & ENVIRONS

1 Camping Kasern
2 Salzburg Nord Tourist Office
3 Salzburg Mitte Tourist Office
4 National - ARAC
5 Urbankeller
6 Rockhouse
7 St Johanns-Spital (Hospital)
8 Haus Wartenberg;
  Restaurant Wartenberg
9 Stiegl's Brauwelt
10 Airport
11 Schloss Leopoldskron
12 Jugendherberge Aigner
  Strasse
13 Jugendherberge Eduard
  Heinrich Haus
14 Salzburg Süd Tourist Office
15 Schloss Hellbrunn

SALZBURG PROVINCE

Orientation

The city centre is split by the Salzach River. The compact old part of town, mostly pedestrian-only, is on the left bank (known as *linkes Salzachufer*), with the Festung Hohensalzburg dominant on the Mönchsberg. Most attractions are on this side of the river. The new town, the centre of business, is on the right bank *(rechtes Salzachufer)*, along with most of the cheaper hotels. You may also hear people talk of the old town as being on the south or west bank.

Mirabellplatz, on the right bank, is a hub for both local buses and city and country tours. A little further north is the Hauptbahnhof and the Bundesbus station.

Information

Tourist Offices The main tourist office (Map 38, #50; ☎ 889 87-330) is at Mozartplatz 5, in the old town. It's open 9am to 6pm daily in December and from Easter to October (to 7pm July to mid August), 9am to 6pm Monday to Saturday the rest of the year. In the same office is a ticket service (☎ 84 03 10) for events around town (commission charged). The provincial tourist office, Salzburger Land Tourismus, is in the same building; go through the door then turn right. It's open 9am to 5.30pm weekdays, 9.30am to 3.30pm Saturday and (in July and August only) 10am to 3pm Sunday.

Other information offices are at arrival points to the city:

Hauptbahnhof (Map 37; ☎ 889 87-340) Platform 2a; open 8.30am to 7pm daily (to 8pm May and September, 8.30pm June and July, 9pm August)
Salzburg Mitte (Map 36, #3; ☎ 889 87-350) Münchner Bundesstrasse 1, in the north-west; open 10am to 6pm Monday to Saturday April to 15 October
Salzburg Süd (Map 36, #14; ☎ 889 87-360) Park & Ride Parkplatz, Alpensiedlung Süd, Alpenstrasse, in the south; open 10am to 6pm Monday to Saturday April to 15 October
Salzburg Nord (Map 36, #2; ☎ 88 970-370) Autobahnstation Kasern, on the A1 from the north-east; open 10am to 6pm Monday to Saturday 15 June to 30 Sept

Staff at all of the branch tourist offices will book rooms in hotels and pensions; a normal commission is €2.20. They also sell a town map *(Stadtplan)* for €0.75, though you could just as easily make do with the free *Hotelplan*. The free *Salzburg Card* booklet details opening hours and entry fees for important sights.

Salzburg Information (☎ 889 87-0, fax 889 87-32, **e** tourist@salzburg info.at), at Auerspergstrasse 7, is the head tourism office for the region. Advance hotel reservations placed through this office (☎ 889 87-314, fax 889 87-32) are free. It also deals with marketing and congress inquiries and sends out tourist brochures (☎ 889 87-430, fax 889 87-435), but for in-person inquiries go to the Mozartplatz office.

Tourist offices and hotels sell the Salzburg Card. This provides free entry to 25 museums and sights, reduced entry to a further 24 attractions (such as the Marionettentheater and the Untersberg cable car) and free public transport for the duration. The price is €18/26/32 for 24/48/72 hours, and it could certainly save you money if you're busy enough. Salzburg Plus is a prepaid card that has the Salzburg Card benefits but also covers meals, accommodation and shows. The price depends on what you include; inquire at tourist offices.

Money Normal banking hours are 8.30am to 12.30pm and 2pm to 4.30pm Monday to Friday, though some branches and exchange offices are open longer, particularly in the summer. Currency exchange in the Hauptbahnhof is available 24 hours at the ÖBB counters, or 7.30am to 8.30pm daily at the Western Union office. At the airport, exchange booths are daily. There are plenty of exchange offices downtown, but beware of high commission rates. Bankomats (ATMs) are all over the place.

American Express (Map 38, #51; ☎ 80 80) is next to the tourist office at Mozartplatz 5. AmEx travellers cheques are encashed free of charge. It is open 9am to 5.30pm Monday to Friday and 9am to noon Saturday. After hours (till 8pm Monday to Saturday), Hotel Weisse Taube (Map 38, #53), Kaigasse 9, exchanges AmEx cheques at the same rate (no commission).

Post & Communications The post office (Map 37, #3; Bahnhofspostamt 5020) at the Hauptbahnhof, Südtiroler Platz 17, is open 6.30am to 9.30pm weekdays, 8am to 8pm Saturday and 1pm to 6pm Sunday and holidays, including for cash currency exchange. In the town centre, the main post office (Map 38, #55; Hauptpostamt 5010), Residenzplatz 9, is open 7am to 7pm Monday to Friday (currency exchange till 5pm), and 8am to 10am Saturday.

Email & Internet Access Piterfun (Map 37, #9; e office@piterfun.at), Ferdinand Porsche Strasse 7, is open 10am to 11pm daily, and access costs €1.85/2.95/5.10 for 15/30/60 minutes. International Telephone Discount (Map 37, #7; ☎ 88 31 94), Kaiserschützenstrasse 8, is €1.10 for 10 minutes, but does have cheap international telephone calls (9am to 11pm daily). There's also the expensive Internet Café at Mozartplatz 5 (Map 38, #49), which charges €0.15 per minute.

Travel Agencies The student and budget agency Ökista (Map 37, #5; ☎ 45 87 33), Fanny-von-Lehnert Strasse 1, is open 9am to 5.30pm Monday to Friday.

Bookshops Motzko (Map 37, #17; ☎ 88 33 11), Elisabethstrasse 1, stocks English-language books. Across the road, on Rainerstrasse, is its travel branch, Motzko Reise (Map 37, #20). By platform 2a in the Hauptbahnhof is News and Books, with international newspapers and magazines.

Medical Services & Emergency The Landeskrankenhaus (hospital), St Johanns-Spital (Map 36, #7; ☎ 44 82-0), is at Müllner Hauptstrasse 48, just north of the Mönchsberg; phone ☎ 141 for an ambulance. The police headquarters (☎ 63 83-0) are at Alpenstrasse 90.

Gay & Lesbian Travellers The Homosexuelle Initiative, HOSI (Map 37, #31; ☎ 43 59 27, fax 43 59 27-27, e office@hosi.or.at), has a branch at Müllner Hauptstrasse 11. It runs a bar at this address on Wednesday (from 7pm), Friday and Saturday evenings (both from 8pm till late).

Laundry Norge Exquisit (Map 38, #3; ☎ 87 63 81), Paris Lodron Strasse 16, offers self-service machines (€5.25 to wash, €1.85 to dry and €2.05 for soap), service washes and dry-cleaning. It's open 7.30am to 6pm weekdays and 8am to noon Saturday.

Walking Tour

Take time to wander around the many plazas, courtyards, fountains and churches in the baroque old town. Start by absorbing the bustle of Domplatz and the adjoining Kapitelplatz and Residenzplatz. The hub-bub from the market competes with the clip-clop of horses' hooves and the rhythms of classical and folk street-musicians. Portrait painters add to the scene. Residenzplatz also has a Glockenspiel (Map 38, #57) that chimes at 7am, 11am and 6pm.

The vast **Dom** (*Cathedral; Map 38, #83; Domplatz*) has three bronze doors symbolising – from left to right as you face them – faith, hope and charity. Constructed between 1614 and 1657, this was the first building north of the Alps to exhibit the Italian baroque style. Inside, admire the dark-edged stucco, the dome and the Romanesque font where Mozart was baptised. Ecclesiastical treasures and oddities are exhibited in the **Dommuseum** (*☎ 84 41 89; adult/senior €4.40/3.30; open 10am-5pm Mon-Sat, 1pm-6pm Sun & holidays early May–mid-Oct*).

From here, turn left at the first courtyard off Franziskanergasse for **Stiftskirche St Peter** (*Map 38, #84; St Peter Bezirk*) dating from 847. This abbey church is remarkable for its baroque ostentation. It's as if a dozen churches have been plundered to fit this one out: the walls are crammed with emotive paintings and swirling stucco, and there are 15 side altars. There's also a fine organ with a clock and statues. The graveyard contains **catacombs** (*Katakomben; Map 38, #85; ☎ 84 45 78-0; adult/student €0.90/0.60; open 10.30am-5pm Tues-Sun May-Sept; 10.30am-3.30pm Wed & Thur, 10.30am-4pm Fri-Sun Oct-Apr*).

SALZBURG PROVINCE

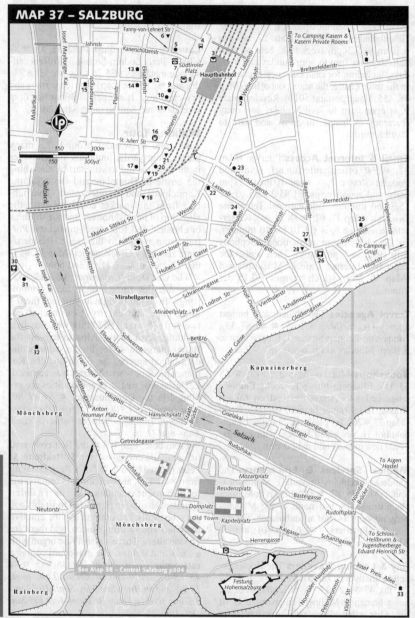

MAP 37 – SALZBURG

See Map 38 – Central Salzburg p304

MAP 37 – SALZBURG

PLACES TO STAY	PLACES TO EAT	7	International Telephone
1 Elizabeth Pension	6 Eurospar Supermarket &		Discount
2 Sandwirt	Restaurant	8	City & Bundesbus Depar-
13 Pension Adlerhof	11 Billa Supermarket		tures; Lokalbahn Station
14 Hotel Hohenstauffen	18 K+K StieglBräu Restaurant	9	Hertz; Piterfun (Internet Cafe)
15 Jugendherberge	19 Imbiss Wurst	10	Avis
(Haunspergstrasse)	21 China-Restaurant Fuky	12	Budget
22 Lasserhof	27 Restaurant Saloniki	16	Shell 24-Hour Garage
24 International Youth	28 Restaurant	17	Motzko
Hotel	Wegscheidstuben	20	Motzko Reise
25 Pension Bergland		23	Europcar
32 Schloss Mönchstein	OTHER	26	Die Weisse
& Paris Lodron	3 Post Office	29	Kongresshaus
Restaurant	4 Bundesbus Departures	30	Augustiner Bräustübl
33 Jugendgästehaus	5 Ökista	31	HOSI

Returning to Franziskanergasse you'll come to the **Franziskanerkirche** *(Franciscan Church; Map 38, #81; ☎ 84 36 29-0, Franziskanergasse 5; admission free; open daylight hours)*, revealing Romanesque, Gothic and baroque elements spanning the 13th to 18th centuries. The best feature is the baroque high altar, presumed to be by Johann Bernhard Fischer von Erlach, complementing the carved Madonna by Michael Pacher.

The western end of Franziskanergasse opens into Max Reinhardt Platz, where you'll see the back of Fischer von Erlach's **Kollegienkirche** *(Collegiate Church; Map 38, #68; Universitätsplatz; admission free; open daylight hours)*, also known as the Universitätskirche. This church is considered an outstanding example of the baroque, more for its overall structure than for the decor. The interior is bare and almost austere compared with the fussy ornamentation of Stiftskirche St Peter. The few embellishments don't overly impress: the cherubs and dusty clouds above the altar are a bit ridiculous and the shiny gold figures below lack subtlety.

Walk left on leaving the church to reach Herbert von Karajan Platz and the **Pferdeschwemme** (horse trough; Map 38, #74), a rather elaborate drinking spot for the archbishops' mounts. Created in 1700, this is a horse-lovers' delight, with rearing equine pin-ups surrounding Michael Bernhard Mandl's 'horse tamer' statue. (There are also impressive horsey fountains in Residenzplatz and Kapitelplatz.) From the horse trough, turn

right around the corner and join the bustling crowds along **Getreidegasse** (Map 38), where many shops have distinctive wrought-iron signs. Some interesting passageways and courtyards lead from this street. Turning right down Alter Markt will bring you back to Residenzplatz.

Festung Hohensalzburg

Festung Hohensalzburg *(Hohensalzburg Fortress; Map 38, #90; ☎ 84 24 30-11, Mönchsberg; admission to courtyards adult/family €3.60/8.75, to interior €3.60/8.75; open 9am-6pm daily)* is, in more ways than one, the high point of a visit to Salzburg. It takes about 15 minutes to walk up the hill from the old town, or you can use the **Festungsbahn** funicular *(Map 38, #86; ☎ 84 26 82, Festungsgasse 4; up/return €5.55/6.35 including entry to courtyards)*. The fortress was extended by the archbishops over many centuries. The greatest influence on its present structure was Leonhard von Keutschach, Archbishop of Salzburg from 1495 to 1519. His symbol was the turnip, and this peculiar motif appears 58 times around the castle, usually as a wall relief.

The outlook to the north over the city is simply stupendous. The view to the south is of Alpine peaks, including the Untersberg (1853m); in the foreground, the isolated house in the middle of the big field once belonged to the archbishop's groundskeeper, though tour-guide mythology insists it was the home of a shunned official executioner.

SALZBURG PROVINCE

MAP 38 – CENTRAL SALZBURG

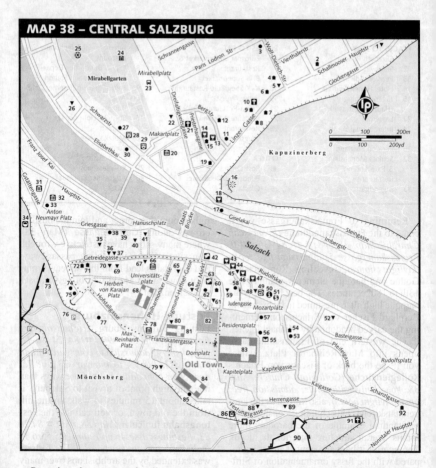

Roaming the courtyards allows you to enjoy the turnips, the views and to visit the terrace cafe, but it doesn't give access to the interior of the fortress. For this – and it's well worth seeing – you need to pay extra; an audio guide in English will help you find your way around. You'll encounter grisly torture chambers, the lookout tower and impressive state rooms (featuring a fine tiled stove, Gothic carvings and Leonhard's state-of-the-art en suite toilet). There are also two small museums (allow about 20 minutes for each) which cover history, arms, WWII photos and more tools of the torture trade.

Below the castle on the eastern side is **Stift Nonnberg** (Map 38, #91), the oldest convent in German-speaking lands, founded by St Rupert around 700. Its church is Late Gothic and you can often hear the choir singing.

Museums & Galleries

The **Haus der Natur** (*Museum of Natural History; Map 38, #31;* ☎ *84 26 53, Museumplatz 5; adult/student €4.40/2.55; open 9am-5pm daily*) is outstanding. You could spend hours wandering round its many diverse and well-presented exhibits. In addition to the usual flora, fauna and mineral displays, it

MAP 38 – CENTRAL SALZBURG

PLACES TO STAY
2 Hotel Restaurant Hofwirt
4 Wolf Dietrich
6 Amadeus
7 Junger Fuchs
8 Goldene Krone
9 Institut St Sebastian
15 Schwarzes Rössl
19 Hotel Gablerbräu
54 Hotel Wolf
60 Zur Goldenen Enten
71 Goldener Hirsch; Restaurant
    Goldener Hirsch; S'Herzl
72 Blaue Gans
73 Naturfreundehaus; Stadtalm
92 Hinterbrühl

PLACES TO EAT
1 Billa Supermarket
5 SKS Spicy Spices
22 Cafe San Marco
26 Vegy Vollwertimbiss
35 Sternbräu
36 Eduscho
37 McDonald's
39 Billa Supermarket
40 Wilder Mann
41 Zum Eulenspiegel
45 Zum Mohren
48 K+K Restaurants am
    Waagplatz
52 Mensa GesWi
59 An Bing

61 Café Konditorei Fürst
64 Café Tomaselli
65 Hotel Elefant
67 Nordsee
69 Fabrizi Espresso
70 Nordsee
79 St Peter's Stiftskeller
80 Mensa Toscana
88 Weisses Kreuz
89 St Paul's Stub'n

OTHER
3 Norge Exquisit (Laundrette)
10 Sebastianskirche; Mausoleum
    of Wolf Dietrich
11 Inlingua
13 Schnaitl Pub
14 Zum Fidelen Affen
16 Kapuzinerberg Viewpoint
17 Filmkulturzentrum
18 Shrimps Bar
20 Mozart-Wohnhaus
21 Dreifaltigkeitskirche
23 Albus Bus to Gaisberg
24 Schloss Mirabell
25 Dwarf's Garden
27 Mozarteum
28 Marionettentheater
29 Landestheater
30 Salzburger Landesreisebüro
31 Haus der Natur
32 Carolino Augusteum
    Museum
33 Szene

34 Mönchsberg Lift
38 Transport Information Office
42 US Consulate
43 Shamrock Irish Pub
44 O'Malleys
46 Vis-à-Vis Café-Bar
47 Stiegl Hell
49 Internet Café
50 City & Provincial Tourist
    Offices
51 American Express
53 Hotel Weisse Taube
55 Main Post Office
56 Salzburger Heimatwerk
57 Glockenspiel
58 Kopfberger (shop)
62 Josef Holzermayr
63 British (UK) Consulate
66 Mozarts Geburtshaus
68 Kollegienkirche
74 Pferdeschwemme
75 Festspiele Ticket Office
76 Altstadt Garage
77 Festspielhaus
78 Rupertinum
81 Franziskanerkirche
82 Residenz Gallery
83 Dom (Cathedral)
84 Stiftskirche St Peter
85 Catacombs
86 Festungsbahn
87 StieglKeller
90 Festung Hohensalzburg
91 Stift Nonnberg

has exhibits on physics and astronomy (unfortunately, all signs are in German) plus bizarre oddities such as a stomach-churning display of deformed animals on the 4th floor. There are also many tropical fish and an excellent reptile house with lizards, snakes and alligators. It even has an inexpensive terrace cafe with fixed-price lunch menus.

Overlooking Residenzplatz, the **Residenz** (*Map 38, #82; ☎ 80 42-26 90, Residenzplatz 1; adult/concession €7.30/5.55; open 10am-5pm daily*) was built between 1596 and 1619. This less-than-modest home allows you to see the baroque luxury the archbishops endured while they sweated over sermons about humility and charity. Johann Michael Rottmayr created some of the frescoes, which are well complemented by rich stucco-work and furnishings. A hand-held

audio guide in English will give you all the commentary you need while visiting these *Prunkräume* (state rooms). The admission price includes the **Residenz Gallery** (*☎ 80 04 51, Residenzplatz 1; open 10am-5pm daily Apr-Sept, 10am-5pm Thur-Tues Oct-Mar*), though this can also be visited separately (adult/concession €4.75/3.65). It displays European art from the 16th to 19th centuries and includes good Dutch and Flemish works.

In the **Rupertinum** (*Map 38, #78; ☎ 80 42-36, Wiener Philharmoniker Gasse 9; adult/concession €4.40/2.95; open 10am-6pm Thur-Tues, 10am-9pm Wed mid-July–31 Aug; 10am-5pm Tues, Thur-Sun, 10am-9pm Wed Sept–mid-July*), 20th-century art comprises its not particularly stunning permanent collection, but most space is devoted to

SALZBURG PROVINCE

temporary exhibitions. The building dates from the 17th century.

The **Carolino Augusteum Museum** *(Map 38, #32; ☎ 84 11 34-0, Museumplatz 1; adult/senior/student €2.95/2.20/1.10; open 9am-5pm Wed-Sun, 9am-8pm Tues; also 9am-5pm Mon July, Aug & Dec)* has an interesting collection covering local history with recourse to paintings by local artists, Roman mosaics, Gothic statues and utensils. There are some illuminating room interiors evoking historical periods and styles but no signs in English.

There are two Mozart museums; they're popular, pricey and cover similar ground. Both contain musical instruments, sheet music and other memorabilia of the great man.

Mozarts Geburtshaus *(Mozart's Birthplace; Map 38, #66; ☎ 84 43 13, Getreidegasse 9; adult/concession €5.10/4; open 9am-7pm daily July & Aug, 9am-6pm daily Sept-June)* is where he lived for the first 17 years of his life. Displays include the mini-violin that Wolfgang played as a toddler.

The **Mozart-Wohnhaus** *(Mozart's Residence; Map 38, #20; ☎ 87 42 27-40, Makartplatz 8; adult/concession €4.75/3.65, or combined with Geburtshaus €8/6.20; open 9am-7pm daily July & Aug, 9am-6pm daily Sept-June)* has more to offer if you only want to visit one Mozart museum. This is where he lived for seven years from 1773 and the building has been restored to its original structure (it was damaged in WWII). Commentary and musical excerpts are delivered via hand-held devices activated by infrared signals and there's a slide show that concentrates on Mozart's early years and extensive travels. (The later Vienna-based years are all but ignored. Why could that be?) Downstairs is the **Mozart Ton-und Filmmuseum** *(☎ 88 34 54, Makartplatz 8; admission free; open 9am-1pm Mon, Wed & Fri, 1pm-5pm Tues & Thur)*, an archive of celluloid homages to the maestro, mostly of interest to the ultra-enthusiast or research student.

Less aesthetic tastes are catered for in **Stiegl's Brauwelt** *(Map 36, #9; ☎ 83 87-14 92, Bräuhausstrasse 9; adult/senior €9.10/8.30; open 10am-5pm Wed-Sun)*, Austria's largest private brewery. The extensive museum takes you through the brewing process, shows you how to order a beer in 20 languages, and persuasively makes the case that beer is a very good thing indeed. It's pretty good value considering the entry price includes a small gift and a trip to the bar for two free beers and a free pretzel. Take bus No 1 or 2 to Bräuhausstrasse.

Schloss Mirabell

This palace (Map 38, #24) in Mirabellgarten was built by the worldly prince-archbishop Wolf Dietrich for his mistress, Salome Alt, in 1606. Salome bore the archbishop at least 10 children (sources disagree on the exact number – poor Wolf was presumably too distracted by spiritual matters to keep count himself). Johann Lukas von Hildebrandt gave the building a more baroque appearance in 1727. Its attractive gardens were featured in *The Sound of Music*, and this is a great place to relax. Since there are no interior tours, the gardens are also the main reason to visit. A most harmonious and often-photographed view can be obtained from the northern end. Because the interior of the palace houses government offices, the doors are open 8am to 4pm Monday to Friday – take a look inside at the marble staircase, adorned with baroque sculptures by George Raphael Donner. Concerts and other extravaganzas are held in the palace.

From the palace, cross Makartplatz and have a look from the entrance lobby at the interior of the **Dreifaltigkeitskirche** *(Holy Trinity Church; Map 38, #21; ☎ 87 74 95, Dreifaltigkeitsgasse; open daylight hours)*. It was created by Johann Bernhard Fischer von Erlach at the end of the 17th century; the dome fresco by Rottmayr depicts a congested celestial scene.

Mausoleum of Wolf Dietrich

This restored mausoleum, in the graveyard *(Map 38, #10; Linzer Gasse; open 7am-7pm Mon-Sun)* of the 16th-century Sebastianskirche (St Sebastian Church), has some interesting epitaphs. In a wonderful piece of arrogance, the aforementioned archbishop ordered the faithful to 'piously commemorate the founder of this chapel' (ie, himself) and 'his close relations', or expect 'God Almighty to be an avenging judge'. Mozart's father and widow are also buried in the graveyard.

Walks

Old town is squeezed between Kapuzinerberg and Mönchsberg hills, both of which have a good network of footpaths. There is a viewpoint (Map 38, #16) at the western end of the Kapuzinerberg, with ramparts built during the Thirty Years' War: the climb up from the stairs near the southern end of Linzer Gasse takes 10 minutes. On Mönchsberg, consider walking from Festung Hohensalzburg down to the Augustiner Bräustübl (see the Entertainment section, later).

Language Courses

German-language courses are offered at Inlingua (Map 38, #11; ☎ 87 11 01, fax 87 11 01-85, e inlinguasbg@fc.alpin.or.at), Linzer Gasse 17–19. Prices and courses on offer here are comparable to those mentioned in the Language Courses section in the Vienna chapter, though Salzburg Card holders will get a €21.80 discount.

Organised Tours

One-hour walking tours of the old city (€7.30) leave at 12.15pm daily (except Sunday during winter) from the main tourist office. Coach tours of the city and environs usually have free hotel pick-up. Some also leave from Mirabellplatz, including the renowned Sound of Music Tour, which is by far the most popular with English-speaking visitors (see the boxed text 'The Sound of Dollars').

These tours last from three to four hours and cost around €30. They take in major city sights featured in the movie and include a visit to the Salzkammergut region. Though the tours are enduringly popular, reports from travellers are mixed. A lot depends on the approach of the guide (make sure they don't deviate from the itinerary unless you want them to) and your fellow passengers. The tours can certainly be dull if people don't enter into the spirit of the occasion, but if you happen to go in a group

with the right mix of tongue-in-cheek enthusiasm it can be brilliant fun. For years, manic Julie Andrews impersonators have flounced over the fields, screeching 'the hills are alive' in voices to wake the dead, and elderly 'youths' have skipped across the benches in the summer house (gazebo), chanting 'I am 16 going on 17'. Sadly, the latter rite of homage is no longer possible:

The gazebo is now locked. No tourists can leap from bench to bench, as a result of an 85-year-old fan imitating Liesl and falling – breaking a hip.
J Smethurst

Coincidently, the actress who played Liesl also fell in the summer house during rehearsals for filming. She had to complete the scene with a heavily-strapped sprained ankle.

Other organised tours explore Bavaria, Salzbergwerk (Salt Mines), the Werfen ice caves, the city and the Salzkammergut. Tours are conducted by various agencies, the most prominent of which are Salzburg Panorama Tours (☎ 87 40 29, w www.panoramatours .com) and Salzburg Sightseeing Tours (☎ 88 16 16); both are on Mirabellplatz. The Sound of Music Tour booked through the Jugendgästehaus (see Hostels – Left Bank in the Places to Stay section) is the cheapest.

Special Events

The Salzburg Festival (Salzburger Festspiele) takes place from late July to the end of August and includes music ranging from Mozart (of course!) to contemporary. This is the high point in Salzburg's cultural calendar, and a time when the city takes on a new vitality; just beware of the crowds. Several events take place each day in different locations, with as many as 180 orchestral, operatic and theatrical events staged.

Prices vary from €3.65 to €335; the cheapest prices are for standing-room tickets, which can usually be prebooked. Most tickets sell out months in advance. Write for information as early as October to: Kartenbüro der Salzburger Festspiele, Postfach 140, A-5010 Salzburg, or visit w www .salzburgfestival.com. People under 26 years

The Sound of Dollars

The 1965 Hollywood musical *The Sound of Music* immortalised the story of the real-life von Trapp family. The movie adaptation of their lives paints a vivid picture of a devoted family whose high morals guide them towards a better life, but the events that lay ahead of the real von Trapp family followed a rather less harmonious course.

After climbing every mountain to escape Nazi-occupied Austria, the von Trapp family finally arrived in a tiny mountain village in Italy. Having left their home and fortune behind, the family suddenly had to work for a living and so turned to singing. The Trapp Family Singers were an immediate success and began touring Europe and eventually America. The now-famous family emigrated to America and in 1939 bought a farmhouse in the hills of Stowe, Vermont, and founded the Trapp Family Music Camp and Lodge.

In 1947 Captain von Trapp died, but the family continued performing until 1957, when the von Trapp children were free to lay down their lederhosen and concentrate on their own families and careers. Most of the children remained working together at the lodge, while Maria worked as a missionary in New Guinea with Father Wasner, the family priest who had fled Austria with them.

In 1980 the lodge burnt down, but the wealthy von Trapps were able to rebuild it as a 93-room hotel and cross-country ski centre with an additional 100 time-share apartments.

Maria von Trapp died in 1987 aged 82. Her death ignited a family feud which split the once-devoted von Trapp family in two. Wrangling family members fighting over shares of the Trapp Family Music Camp and Lodge, 2200 acres of land in Stowe and movie royalties saw a slew of court hearings and multimillion-dollar payouts. Despite the behind-the-scenes disputes, the Trapp Family Lodge remains a major attraction, with 150,000 visitors a year. The hills of Vermont are alive, no longer to the sound of music, more likely to the rustle of banknotes.

In contrast to the millionaire lifestyles of the real von Trapps, the seven child stars (actually, 16-year-old Liesl was played by a 21-year-old!) who portrayed the siblings in the movie fared less well. They received modest flat-rate fees for their performances. Though the Oscar-winning film went on to gross millions and pretty much bankrolled Twentieth Century Fox for the next decade, no subsequent bonuses or royalties were paid to them.

This international mega-success, upon its release in Austria, was pulled from cinemas after just three days. Many Austrians disliked the way that *The Sound of Music* portrayed them as subservient pawns of the Nazis. Nevertheless, the film has still generated a good deal of money in Salzburg over the years – the rustle of banknotes is indubitably alive and well here too!

Wendy Bashford & Mark Honan

old are eligible for reduced price deals for two or more events. Try checking closer to the event for cancellations – inquire at the ticket office (Map 38, #75; ☎ 84 45-579, fax 84 45-760, **e** info@salzburgfestival.at), Herbert von Karajan Platz 11. Its opening hours during the festival are 9.30am to 1pm and 2pm to 5pm daily.

Other important music festivals are at Easter (Osterfestspiele for one week) and the Whit Sunday weekend (Pfingstkonzerte). Mozart Week is held in late January. Salzburg is also known for its Christmas Market in December.

Places to Stay – Budget

Accommodation is at a premium during the Salzburger Festspiele, so book ahead (you may pay even higher prices than the summer prices quoted here). In the more expensive places, prices are usually lower in winter. The tourist office's *Hotelplan* lists accommodation options, including several camping grounds.

Camping *Camping Kasern (Map 36, #1; ☎/fax 45 05 76, **e** schwarzkopf@aon.at, Carl Zuckmayer Strasse 26)* Price per adult/tent/car €4.75/2.55/2.55. Open 1 Apr-31

Oct. This place is just north of the A1 Nord exit, within walking distance of Salzburg-Maria Plain train station.

Hostels – Right Bank *International Youth Hotel (YoHo; Map 37, #24; ☎ 87 96 49, fax 87 88 10, e office@yoho.at, Paracelsusstrasse 9)* Beds in 2-bed/4-bed/8-bed dorm €14.55/ 12.35/10.90, add €1.50 for 1st night, No lock-out, check-in/reception open 24 hours. If you're travelling to party, head for this popular hotel-cum-hostel – there's a bar with loud music and cheap beer (€2.20 for 0.5L), and no school groups. The staff are almost exclusively young, native English-speakers. Guests get some discounts on local sights. YoHo also organises outings and screens *The Sound of Music* daily. Phone reservations in busy times are accepted no earlier than one day before, though you can email reservations for any date. Showers cost €0.75, lockers an extra €0.75, while breakfast costs from €1.10 to €3.30, and dinner from €2.20 to €6.20.

Jugendherberge Haunspergstrasse (Map 37, #15; ☎ 87 50 30, fax 88 34 77, Haunspergstrasse 27) Beds in 2-bed/4-bed dorm €18.20/13.85, breakfast €2.20. Open July & Aug, reception/check-in open 7am-2pm & 5pm-midnight. A student residence for the rest of the year, this summer HI hostel is west of the Hauptbahnhof.

Institut St Sebastian (Map 38, #9; ☎ 87 13 86, fax 87 13 86-85, Linzer Gasse 41) Dorm beds €14.55, sheets (if required) €2.20. Singles/doubles €26.20/43.60, with bathroom €30.55/52.35. This place is attached to Sebastianskirche, literally and administratively (the church bells are loud in some rooms). It doubles as a student residence and has a roof terrace and kitchens. Prices are marginally lower in winter and you can check in during the day (ring the bell if reception is unstaffed).

Jugendherberge Aigner Strasse (Map 36, #12; ☎ 62 32 48, fax 62 32 48-4, e hostel.aigen@salzburg.co.at, Aigner Strasse 34) Beds in 2-/4-/6-bed dorm €17.90/15.70/ 13.55, breakfast €2.20. Open year-round, check-in from 5pm. This HI hostel, south of the Kapuzinerberg in Aigen, is slightly inconveniently located, though you can walk to the old town in 20 minutes (or take bus No 49).

Hostels – Left Bank *Naturfreundehaus (Map 38, #73; ☎ 84 17 29, Mönchsberg 19)* Dorm beds €9.85, showers €0.75, breakfast €2.55-3.50. Open 1 May-15 Sept, check-in 9am-9pm, curfew 1am. Also known as Stadtalm, this place with marvellous views is clearly visible high on the hill west of the fortress. Take the stairway up from near Max Reinhardt Platz, or the Mönchsberg lift (Map 38, # 34; €1.50/2.40 up/return, operates 9am to 9pm or 11pm) from A Neumayr Platz. It's sometimes too cold to open the dorms (no heating), so phone ahead and check availability. As well as breakfast, the restaurant provides hot meals (see Places to Eat).

Jugendgästehaus (Map 37, #33; ☎ 84 26 70-0, fax 84 11 01, e jgh.salzburg@jgh.at, Josef Preis Allee 18) Beds in 2-/4-/8-bed rooms €20/15.30/11.65, add €2.20 for 1st night if staying only 1-2 nights. Reception open 7am-12.30am, check-in from 1pm. This large, modern and busy HI hostel has a good location, free showers and lockers, and bike rental for €7 per day. The daily Sound of Music tours are the cheapest in town at €25.45, starting at 8.45am or 1.30pm. The film is also screened daily.

Jugendherberge Eduard Heinrich Haus (Map 36, #13; ☎ 62 59 76, fax 62 79 80, e hostel.eduard-heinrich@salzburg.co.at, Eduard Heinrich Strasse 2) Beds in 2-/ 4-/6-bed dorm €15.30/ 13.10/10.90, breakfast €2.20. Open year-round, check in from 5pm. This HI place is south of town; bus No 51 or 95 will get you within 400m (stop: Polizeidirektion).

Private Rooms Salzburg's private rooms aren't quite the bargain they are elsewhere in Austria: they cost a minimum of €19 per person anywhere near the city centre. Ask for the tourist office's list of private rooms and apartments.

If you're prepared to travel, Kasern, just north of the city, offers better value and a choice of several places. They're all within 10 minutes' walk of the local train station,

Salzburg-Maria Plain (Map 36; €1.45 from the Hauptbahnhof) – some places will even pick you up from there if you call ahead. The terminus of bus No 15 would also get you within walking distance.

From the train station, walk up the hill along Bergstrasse to find a couple of private rooms, including **Seigmann** (☎ 45 00 01, Bergstrasse 66), where the singles/doubles/triples with shared facilities cost €18.20/29.10/41.50.

At the crossroads, turn left to find places on Panoramaweg. **Christine** (☎/fax 45 67 73, Panoramaweg 3) and **Lindner** (☎/fax 45 66 81, Panoramaweg 5) offer rooms of up to four beds with shared facilities for €12.35 to €14.55. Solo travellers will have to share. Both places are operated together (the hostesses are sisters) and they're fine choices, providing good breakfasts and a family atmosphere. Guests can use Lindner's kitchen.

Hotels & Pensions *Sandwirt (Map 37, #2; ☎/fax 87 43 51, Lastenstrasse 6a)* Singles/doubles with shared shower €21.80/34.90, doubles/triples/quads with private shower & TV €42.20/52.40/64. This good-value place is behind the Hauptbahnhof (cross the tracks via the footpath bridge) and set back from the street. The rooms are clean, reasonably large and quiet, and staff are helpful. There's courtyard parking.

Elizabeth Pension *(Map 37, #1; ☎/fax 87 16 64, e info@pension-elisabeth.at, Vogelweiderstrasse 52)* Singles/doubles €22/34, with shower €25.50/39.50, with bathroom & TV €42.20/75.60. The standard rooms here are smallish but nicely renovated, and the hosts are friendly. The rooms with toilet and TV are larger, and were newly built in 2000 on the top-floor extension. The cheaper singles are not available July to August. It's close to the Breitenfelderstrasse stop of bus No 15, which heads for the town centre every 15 or 30 minutes.

Junger Fuchs *(Map 38, #7; ☎ 87 54 96, Linzer Gasse 54)* Singles/doubles/triples €23.30/30.60/40.70. The rooms are simple but fair-sized, and better than the cramped corridors would suggest. They have shared showers. The good location for the price

makes it one of Salzburg's better budget deals. Room rates are the same year-round; breakfast is not included.

Schwarzes Rössl *(Map 38, #15; ☎ 87 44 26, fax 87 44 26-7, Priesterhausgasse 6)* Singles/doubles €31.25/50.90. This student residence welcomes tourists from July to September and offers predicably simple (though clean and sizeable) rooms with shared shower.

Hinterbrühl *(Map 38, #92; ☎ 84 67 98, fax 84 18 59, Schanzlgasse 12)* Singles/doubles/triples €34.20/41.50/47.25, doubles & triples with bathroom €72.70, breakfast per person €4.40. Reception (in downstairs restaurant) open 8am-midnight daily. Though expensive for a budget place, prices are merited by its location in the old town. Rooms are generally basic, but variable; room No 14 is large, with a balcony and lounge area.

Places to Stay – Mid-Range

Right Bank *Pension Bergland (Map 37, #25; ☎ 87 23 18, fax 87 23 18-8, e pkuhn@ berglandhotel.at, Rupertgasse 15)* Singles/doubles €45.10/74.20. The owner painted many of the pictures that hang in this friendly, family-run place. No smoking is allowed in the light, pristine rooms, which all have bathroom and cable TV. Bikes are available for hire at €5.45 per day, and Internet access is €1.50 for 10 minutes. Though a little way east of the centre, it's still reasonably convenient.

Pension Adlerhof *(Map 37, #13; ☎ 87 52 36, fax 87 36 636, Elisabethstrasse 25)* Singles/doubles with bathroom & TV €50.20/80, doubles with shared facilities €58.20; reductions in low season. This place is near the Hauptbahnhof. Some rooms are modern with pine fittings, others have old-style painted furniture, and there's a baroque-style breakfast room. Parking is limited.

Goldene Krone *(Map 38, #8; ☎ 87 23 00, fax 87 23 00-66, Linzer Gasse 48)* Singles/doubles €29.10/58.20, with bathroom €43.60/72.70. Some of the rooms here have church-like groined ceilings, which add a bit of character.

Amadeus *(Map 38, #6; ☎ 87 14 01, fax 87 14 01-7, e salzburg@hotelamadeus.at,*

Linzer Gasse 43-45) Singles €53-68, doubles €87-130. This place, across the road from Goldene Krone, offers similar room quality, but with bathroom and cable TV. It has a dazzling blue and white breakfast room.

Trumer Stube *(Map 38, #12;* ☎ *84 47 76, fax 87 43 26,* **e** *hotel.trumer-stube@eunet .at, Bergstrasse 6)* Doubles with bathroom & cable TV €89-103, single occupancy €56-89 (not always available in summer). This family-run hotel is close to the old town, and provides clean and pleasant rooms in floral 'Laura Ashley' style.

Hotel Restaurant Hofwirt *(Map 38, #2;* ☎ *87 21 72-0, fax 88 14 84-99,* **e** *hotelhof wirt@abnet.at, Schallmooser Hauptstrasse 1)* Singles/doubles €62/102. This convenient three-star hotel has free private parking and standard businesslike rooms with bathroom and cable TV, perhaps a little lacking in warmth.

Left Bank *Haus Wartenberg (Map 36, #8;* ☎ *84 42 84, fax 84 84 00-5, Riedenburger Strasse 2)* Singles €32.70-47.25, doubles €62-102. Haus Wartenberg offers variable rooms, most with bathroom, in a characterful building dating back 400 years. The manager is something of a maverick, so expect the unexpected from your stay. It's within walking distance of the old town, and many bus routes run along nearby Neutorstrasse.

The following places are in the old town; the convenience means you pay more for what you get. Parking can be limited, though many places have an arrangement for reduced prices at parking garages.

Blaue Gans *(Map 38, #72;* ☎ *84 13 17, fax 84 13 17-9,* **e** *office@blauegans.at, Getreidegasse 43)* Singles/doubles €62/91. An old house, which was substantially remodelled in 1998, this offers modern, stylish rooms with private facilities.

Hotel Wolf *(Map 38, #54;* ☎ *84 34 53-0, fax 84 24 23-4, Kaigasse 9)* Singles €57-80, doubles €80-128. This three-star hotel has appealing rooms kitted out in modern or rustic style, with bathroom and cable TV.

Zur Goldenen Ente *(Map 38, #60;* ☎ *84 56 22, fax 84 56 22-9,* **e** *ente@eunet.at, Goldgasse 10)* Singles/doubles €57/86. This

700-year-old house retains some original features, and no room is quite like any other. All have private facilities and TV. See Places to Eat for details of its restaurant.

Places to Stay – Top End

All places mentioned here provide rooms with private bath or shower, toilet, TV and telephone.

Lasserhof *(Map 37, #22;* ☎ *87 33 88, fax 87 33 88-6,* **e** *hotellasserhof@magnet .at, Lasserstrasse 47)* Singles/doubles around €65/94. Prices are negotiable depending on how busy the place is. Sizeable rooms, some in rustic style, have eye-catching features, such as the hand-made Venetian chandeliers, and some have balconies. There's free parking on the street.

Wolf Dietrich *(Map 38, #4;* ☎ *87 12 75, fax 88 23 20,* **e** *office@salzburg-hotel.at, Wolf Dietrich Strasse 7)* Singles €65-72, doubles €107-136. This hotel has excellent facilities including an indoor pool, sauna, solarium, bar and a good organic restaurant (Restaurant Ährlich). The decor aims for homely elegance, with some success. Garage parking costs €10.

Hotel Gablerbräu *(Map 38, #19;* ☎ *889 65, fax 889 65-55, Linzer Gasse 9)* Singles/ doubles €72/116. A hotel for nearly 575 years, this convenient place has rooms of varying sizes and a lobby area on each floor.

Hotel Hohenstauffen *(Map 37, #14;* ☎ *87 21 93, fax 87 21 93-51,* **e** *hohenstauffen @aon.at, Elisabethstrasse 19)* Singles €58-94, doubles €94-144. This hotel is convenient for the Hauptbahnhof and parking (€7.30) is no problem. The stylish rooms are all different – some even have a four-poster bed.

Goldener Hirsch *(Map 38, #71;* ☎ *80 84-0, fax 84 33 49,* **e** *welcome@goldenerhirsch .com, Getreidegasse 37)* Singles €192-531, doubles €262-575, excluding breakfast. This classy, central five-star hotel has 70 rooms in three houses; they vary in size and colour scheme but all are in a rustic style. The valet parking service costs €25.50 per day.

Schloss Mönchstein *(Map 37, #32;* ☎ *84 85 55-0, fax 84 85 59,* **e** *salzburg@monch stein.at, Mönchsberg Park 26)* Singles €248, doubles €248-335. This ivy-clad place is as palatial as the name suggests. Its pastoral, isolated setting favours those with their own transport, and it has a tiny chapel that's popular for weddings.

Places to Eat

Salzburg need not be expensive for food. Quick, hot snacks or meals can be had at various deli shops and outdoor food stands, including in the old town. While sightseeing, nip into *Eduscho (Map 38, #36; Getreidegasse 34 & other locations around town)*, where a small, strong cup of coffee costs only €1.05; you'll have to stand.

To experience the best of Salzburg's coffeehouse culture, go to Alter Markt. *Café Tomaselli (Map 38, #64; ☎ 84 44 88, Alter Markt 9)* is the city's most famous cafe, while *Café Konditorei Fürst (Map 38, #61; ☎ 84 37 59, Brodgasse 13)* opposite is also worth a visit. Both are open approximately 8am to 9pm daily and have lots of cakes and outside tables, though only Tomaselli has English-language newspapers.

Note that you can also eat at some of the places mentioned in the later Entertainment section.

Self-Catering & Fast Food On Universitätsplatz and Kapitelplatz there are *market stalls* and *food stands*. Also in the old town, there's a small *Billa* supermarket *(Map 38, #39; Griesgasse 19)*. On the right bank, there are several supermarkets on Schallmooser Hauptstrasse, including another *Billa (Map 38, #1)*. *Eurospar (Map 37, #6)* is opposite the Hauptbahnhof. *Shell* garage *(Map 37, #16; St Julien Strasse 33)* has a shop open 24 hours, with snacks, provisions and alcohol. A *fruit and vegetable market* occupies some of Mirabellplatz on Thursday morning.

The Hauptbahnhof has several fast-food places, including a burger and schnitzel joint, *Eurosnack*, open 10am to 9pm daily. *Imbiss Wurst (Map 37, #19; Rainerstrasse 24)* is a deli shop serving half-chickens for €2.85 (open 7.30am to 6pm Monday to Friday). There's a *McDonald's (Map 38, #37; Getreidegasse 26)* and the fast fish chain *Nordsee (Map 38, #67 & 70; Getreidegasse 11 & 27)*.

Self-Service Restaurants The best budget deals are in the university Mensas on the left bank. The courtyard *Mensa Toscana (Map 38, #80; ☎ 8044-6909, Sigmund Haffner Gasse 11)* is the most convenient place, and is open year-round. The *Mensa GesWi (Map 38, #52; ☎ 8044-6905, Rudolfskai 42)* is closed in July and August. They offer a set two-course lunch from 11.30am to 2pm Monday to Friday, which costs €2.95 for students (with ISIC card) and €3.45 for others. Don't go too late as the daily specials run out. They're also open for drinks and snacks 8.30am to 6pm (Monday to Thursday) or to 3pm (Friday).

Eurospar (Map 37, #6; ☎ 45 84 66 826, Südtiroler Platz 11) Meals €3.65-5.85. Open 8am-7pm Mon-Fri, 7.30am-5pm Sat. Within the Forum shopping centre, this has a supermarket on the ground floor, and a self-service restaurant on the 1st floor where from 6pm to 7pm on weekdays all meals are half-price.

Budget Restaurants – Right Bank *Cafe San Marco (Map 38, #22; ☎ 87 84 52, Dreifaltigkeitsgasse 13)* Meals €4.40-5.90. Open 9am-10pm Mon-Sat. This small cafe has cheap pizza and pasta, and tempting Italian ice cream.

Restaurant Wegscheidstuben (Map 37, #28; ☎ 87 46 18, Lasserstrasse 1) Meals €5.70-12.50. Open 10am-midnight Mon-Fri, 10am-3pm Sun. This restaurant caters for locals and has all the usual Austrian standards, as well as a good-value set meal available lunchtime and evening.

Restaurant Saloniki (Map 37, #27; ☎ 87 87 85, Lasserstrasse 2) Meals €8-15.65. Open 11.30am-2.30pm & 5.30pm-midnight Mon-Sat. This is the place for all things Greek: lots of pillars, statues and Greek flags, piles of meat skewers, and live music (free) on the last Friday of the month.

SKS Spicy Spices (Map 38, #5; ☎ 87 07 12, Wolf Dietrich Strasse 1) Meals & snacks €1.60-6.20. Open 10.30am-10pm Mon-Sat, noon-9pm Sun. This is the best of the few vegetarian places in town. It offers Indian food at low prices, soothing ambient music, a range of *ayurvedic* teas, and tables inside and out.

Vegy Vollwertimbiss (Map 38, #26; ☎ *87 57 46, Schwarzstrasse 21)* Salad buffet €3.05-4.75, lunch menu €7.15. Open 11am-5pm Mon-Fri. Both a shop and small restaurant, Vegy is an option for your veggie fix.

China-Restaurant Fuky (Map 37, #21; ☎ *87 33 96, Rainerstrasse 24)* Meals €4.75-10.90. Open 11.30am-10pm daily. This unfortunately named place offers several very cheap set menus for lunch and dinner.

Budget Restaurants – Left Bank Chinese restaurants are scattered around Salzburg. Some, like *An Bing (Map 38, #59;* ☎ *84 64 18, Goldgasse 13),* have inexpensive weekday lunch menus.

St Paul's Stub'n (Map 38, #89; ☎ *84 32 20, Herrengasse 16)* Meals €5.70-9.90. Open 5pm-1am Mon-Thur, 5pm-2am Fri & Sat. This informal bar, on the 1st floor with an outside terrace, has good-value meals and snacks, such as a huge plate of *Ripperl* (ribs) for €7.20.

Fabrizi Espresso (Map 38, #69; ☎ *84 59 14, Getreidegasse 21)* Meals €6-8.60. Open 7.30am-7pm Mon-Sat, 10am-6pm Sun & holidays. This calm retreat of a cafe is hidden away in a small, pretty courtyard. It serves cakes, snacks and a few hot meals.

Wilder Mann (Map 38, #40; ☎ *84 17 87, Getreidegasse 20)* Meals €6.20-12.75. Open 9am-11pm Mon-Sat. With surprisingly low prices considering its location in the old town, this place dishes up typical Austrian fare in an old-fashioned hunting-lodge-style interior.

Stadtalm (Map 38, #73; ☎ *84 17 29, Mönchsberg 19)* Meals €3.85-8.50. Open 10am-10pm daily mid-May–mid-Sept, 11am-6pm daily mid-Sept–mid-May. Stadtalm, up on Mönchsberg, is worth visiting for the view, though the food's good value too.

Mid-Range Restaurants *K+K StieglBräu Restaurant (Map 37, #18;* ☎ *87 76 94, Rainerstrasse 14)* Meals €6-15.50. Open 11am-midnight daily. This large beer-hall style restaurant serves Austrian food and has a salad bar. It has several large rooms, flowers on the table, cheap weekday lunches, four choices of Stiegl draught beer and a garden.

Sternbräu (Map 38, #35; ☎ *84 07 17, Griesgasse 23)* Meals €6.20-15. Open 9am-midnight daily. Tucked away in a courtyard between Getreidegasse and Griesgasse, Sternbräu is an enjoyable place with garden seating and many dining rooms. It serves good Austrian food, including fish specials.

The same courtyard where you find Sternbräu contains *La Stella* with stylish Italian food and *Pavillon* with self-service snacks.

Weisses Kreuz (Map 38, #88; ☎ *84 56 41, Bierjodlgasse 6)* Meals €5.85-17.50. Kitchen open 11.30am-3pm & 5pm-11pm Wed-Mon. This place offers Austrian food, but a better choice is its menu of Balkan specialities. *Djuvec* (rice, succulent pork, capsicum and paprika) for €6.50 is excellent, or try the Balkan Plate (a selection of five dishes) for €10.10.

Hotel Elefant (Map 38, #65; ☎ *84 33 97, Sigmund Haffner Gasse 4)* Meals €8-12.50. Open 10am-midnight Wed-Mon. This hotel restaurant offers traditional Austrian fare, either on the ground floor or in the cellar restaurant.

St Peter's Stiftskeller (Map 38, #79; ☎ *84 12 68-0, St Peter's Bezirk 1/4)* Meals €9.30-21.50. Kitchen open 11am-10.30pm daily. This historic restaurant is in a courtyard by Stiftskirche St Peter. Though firmly tourist territory, it's a fine place to relax on a sunny summer's day to the accompaniment of live music. There are also many evocative dining rooms.

Zur Goldenen Ente (Map 38, #60; ☎ *84 56 22, Goldgasse 10)* Meals €7.20-17. Open 11.30am-9pm Mon-Fri. This atmospheric, rustic restaurant offers tempting meat and fish dishes, including duck and king prawns.

Zum Mohren (Map 38, #45; ☎ *484 23 87, Judengasse 9)* Mains €7.50-17.80. Open 11am-10.30pm Mon-Sat. This cellar restaurant has some eye-catching decorative features. Meat dishes are usually above €10, while some vegetarian or salad-based meals are cheaper.

Restaurant Wartenberg (Map 36, #8; ☎ *84 84 00, Riedenburger Strasse 2)* Meals €8.60-15.90. Open noon-2pm & 6pm-10pm Mon-Sat. This restaurant inside Haus

Wartenberg, west of Mönchsberg, has an informal atmosphere and decor ranging from the plain to the baroque. The frills are mostly reserved for the food, which is basically Austrian but with subtle and tasty innovations.

Top-End Restaurants *K+K Restaurants am Waagplatz (Map 38, #48;* ☎ *84 21 56, Waagplatz 2)* Meals €10.50-19, cover charge €1.50. Open 11am-2pm & 6pm-10.30pm daily. For quality Austrian and international fare, head upstairs to *Die Stuben*, where the ambience is elegant and restrained. On the ground floor there's the less formal *S'Gwölb*, where the kitchen is open all day for inexpensive meals and there's no cover charge.

Zum Eulenspiegel (Map 38, #41; ☎ *84 31 80, Hagenauerplatz 2)* Meals €12.30-19.60, cover charge €1.60. Open 11am-2pm & 6pm-10.30pm Mon-Sat. By Mozarts Geburtshaus, this rickety old place occupying several floors has cosy surroundings and good food (though the cartoon menus suggest downmarket leanings, contrary to its upmarket reality).

Restaurant Goldener Hirsch (Map 38, #71; ☎ *80 84-0, Getreidegasse 37)* Meals €22.50-25.50. Open noon-2.30pm & 6.30pm-9.30pm daily; closed Sun in winter. This gourmet restaurant in the hotel of the same name offers fabulous food.

S'Herzl (Map 38, #71; ☎ *84 84-889, Getreidegasse 37)* Meals €10.50-17.50. Open 11.30am-9.30pm daily. The Goldener Hirsch hotel contains this rustic restaurant as well as its gourmet sibling, Restaurant Goldener Hirsch. Some of the dishes are similar, and they come from the same kitchen, but here you can fill your belly without blowing your budget.

Paris Lodron (Map 37, #32; ☎ *84 85 55-0, Mönchsberg Park 26)* Meals €23.25-24, cover charge €2.95. Open 11am-2pm & 6pm-10pm daily. At the top of the range is this restaurant in Schloss Mönchstein. Enjoy lavishly prepared food in an opulent setting, all shining silverware and soft classical music. Dishes are presented with pride and panache. Reserve in advance.

Entertainment
Music, Film & Theatre *Marionettentheater (Map 38, #28;* ☎ *87 24 06-0, Schwarzstrasse 24; tickets €18-35; open May-Sept, Christmas, Easter & Mozart Week in Jan)* This theatre has been delighting visitors for 80 years. These ingenious puppets sing and dance to recordings of famous operas and ballets.

Mozarteum (Map 38, #27; ☎ *87 31 54, Schwarzstrasse 26-28; tickets €11-51)* Less frivolous musical events are staged here, next door to the Marionettentheater.

Special *Mozart concerts* (aimed at tourists) are performed at various locations around town, sometimes in historical costumes or with dinner included. Inevitably, there's also a *Sound of Music* show *(☎ 82 66 17; tickets from €27)*, performed from May to October.

Landestheater (Map 38, #29; ☎ *87 15 12-0, Schwarzstrasse 22; tickets €5.10-56)* Musicals and ballets are sometimes performed here, as well as plays.

Festspielhaus (Map 38, #77; ☎ *84 45-579, Hofstallgasse 1)* This is the main venue for operas and operettas and is built into the sheer sides of the Mönchsberg.

Filmkulturzentrum (Map 38, #17; ☎ *87 31 00, Giselakai 11)* Hollywood as well as non-mainstream films are screened here in the original language (€6.90).

Szene (Map 38, #33; ☎ *84 34 48, Anton Neumayr Platz 2)* Szene stages avant-garde productions encompassing dance, theatre and music, and also hosts parties and DJs. There's even a relaxed cafe.

Urbankeller (Map 36, #5; ☎ *87 08 94, Schallmooser Hauptstrasse 50)* Admission around €8.75. Open 5pm-midnight Mon-Sat. This place incorporates a Jazzclub, which hosts live jazz every second Friday from around September to April.

Rockhouse (Map 36, #6; ☎ *88 49 14, Schallmooser Hauptstrasse 46)* Admission €8-25. This is Salzburg's main venue for rock and pop bands – check the local press for details. There's also a tunnel-shaped bar, open 6pm to 2am Monday to Saturday, that has DJs (usually free) or bands (admission from €8).

Bars & Clubs The liveliest area for bars, clubs and discos is the area near the Radisson Hotel on Rudolfskai. Claustrophobes should beware – these places get packed. Particularly crowded are the two bar-filled passages at Rudolfskai 22 and 26. One such bar, *Stiegl Hell (Map 38, #47)*, in the Rudolfskai 26 passage, is aptly named for those who don't enjoy being crushed shoulder to shoulder with semidrunk youths, suffering bruised ears through overloud music and ingesting half a packet of cigarettes with each breath. For those who enjoy such things, it's ideal! It's open 5pm or 7pm to 2am Monday to Saturday.

Vis-à-Vis café-bar *(Map 38, #46; ☎ 84 12 90, Rudolfskai 24)* Open 8pm-5am daily. This neon-lit cellar bar is less frantic and more sophisticated than many other places nearby.

O'Malleys (Map 38, #44; ☎ 84 92 58, Rudolfskai 16) Open 6pm-2am Sun-Thur, 6pm-4am Fri & Sat. This Irish pub has Guinness and occasional live music.

Shamrock Irish Pub (Map 38, #43; ☎ 84 16 10, Rudolfskai 10) Open 3pm-2am Sun & Mon, 3pm-3am Tues & Wed, 3pm-4am Thur-Sat. Offering much the same formula as O'Malleys, this pub is equally popular.

Bars on the right bank are generally less crowded and more relaxed than the sardine sweat-holes of Rudolfskai.

Schnaitl Pub (Map 38, #13; ☎ 87 56 68, Bergstrasse 5) Open 7pm-2am Mon-Sat. This place has a studenty, slightly grungy feel, and is quite a good place to chill out. There are videos and table football.

Zum Fidelen Affen (Map 38, #14; ☎ 87 73 61, Priesterhausgasse 8) Meals €5-10.50. Open 5pm-midnight Mon-Sat. This is a popular, old-style drinking venue with decent food and tables inside or on the pavement.

In the vicinity of the Mönchsberg lift there are some late-night bars.

There are also a couple on Steingasse, including the *Shrimps Bar (Map 38, #18; Steingasse 5)*, a busy yet laid-back place where the food is worth a taste. It's open from 5pm to midnight daily.

Augustiner Bräustübl (Map 37, #30; ☎ 43 12 46, Augustinergasse 4-6) Open 3pm-11pm Mon-Fri, 2.30pm-11pm Sat, Sun & holidays. This place proves that monks can make beer as well as anybody: the quaffing clerics have been running this huge beer hall for years. It's atmospheric and Germanic, even though it's often filled with tourists. Beer is dispensed from the self-service counter, either in 1L (€4.40) or 0.5L (€2.20) mugs; beer via the waiters costs €5/2.50. Meat, bread and salad ingredients (reasonably priced) are available from the shops in the foyer. Eat inside or in the enormous, shady beer garden.

StieglKeller (Map 38, #87; ☎ 84 26 81, Festungsgasse 10) Meals €6.20-10.90. Open 10am-11pm daily May-Sept. This beer hall has an enjoyable garden overlooking the town. Beer is cheapest from the self-service taps by the garden (€2.35 for 0.5L).

Die Weisse (Map 37, #26; ☎ 87 22 46, Rupertgasse 10) Meals & snacks €2.35-9.30. Open 10.30am-midnight Mon-Sat, 4.30pm-midnight Sun & hols. This is the Gasthof of the Salzburger Weissbierbrauerei, a small brewery which creates its own very palatable dark and cloudy brew. The beer is the main attraction (€2.35/2.85 for 0.3/0.5L), which can be imbibed inside or in the shaded garden, though the food is also good value.

Shopping

Not many people leave Salzburg without sampling some of the Mozart confectionery. *Mozartkugeln* (Mozart balls) are chocolate-coated combinations of nougat and marzipan; they cost around €0.40 per piece (cheaper in supermarkets) and are available individually or in souvenir packs. These are sold throughout Austria but it's only in Salzburg that you'll find whole window displays devoted to Mozart merchandise, the chocolate joining forces with liqueurs, mugs and much else.

Josef Holzermayr (Map 38, #62; ☎ 84 23 65, Alter Markt 7) Try this shop for homemade variations on the standard Mozart balls.

Aside from Mozart-related items, Salzburg offers many chances to buy world-class goods, including clothing, both traditional and international. Getreidegasse is the main street for shopping and souvenirs. Elsewhere, try *Kopfberger (Map 38, #58; ☎ 84*

56 36, *Judengasse 14*) for woodcarvings and ***Salzburger Heimatwerk*** *(Map 38, #56; ☎ 84 41 19, Residenzplatz 9)* for glassware, CDs, books, china and fabrics relating to the province.

Getting There & Away

Air Salzburg airport (Map 36, #10; ☎ 85 80-251) has regular scheduled flights to Amsterdam, Berlin, Brussels, Frankfurt, London, Paris, Zürich and elsewhere, including main Austrian cities. For Austrian Airlines, Lauda Air or Tyrolean Airlines call ☎ 85 45 11.

Bus Bundesbuses depart (Map 37, #4) from outside the Hauptbahnhof on Südtiroler Platz, where timetables are displayed. There's Bahnbus information counters in the train information office in the Hauptbahnhof; for Postbus information call ☎ 46 60 330.

Hourly buses leave for the Salzkammergut between 6.30am and 8pm – destinations include Bad Ischl (€7.30, 1¾ hours), Mondsee (€4.40, 50 minutes), St Gilgen (€4.40, 50 minutes) and St Wolfgang (€6.55, 1¾ hours). Including Salzburg city transport with these tickets costs an extra €0.75 (see the ticket machines at the departure bays).

Train Salzburg is well served by IC and EC services. For train information call ☎ 05-1717 (8am to 8pm daily), or visit the office in the Hauptbahnhof. Tickets (no commission) and train information are also available from Salzburger Landesreisebüro (Map 38, #30; ☎ 88 28 21-16), Schwarzstrasse 11.

Fast trains leave hourly for Vienna's Westbahnhof (€33.45, 3¼ hours), travelling via Linz (€16.60, 1¼ hours). The two-hourly express service to Klagenfurt (€26.20, three hours) runs via Villach.

The quickest way to Innsbruck is by the 'corridor' train through Germany; trains depart at least every two hours (€27.65, two hours) and stop at Kufstein. Trains to Munich take about two hours and run every 30 to 60 minutes (€25.30, but ask about special weekend deals at counter No 1 or 2); some of these continue to Karlsruhe via Stuttgart.

Car & Motorcycle Three autobahns converge on Salzburg and form a loop around the city: the A1 from Linz, Vienna and the east, the A8/E52 from Munich and the west, and the A10/E55 from Villach and the south. The quickest way to Tirol is to take the road to Bad Reichenhall in Germany and continue to Lofer (Hwy 312) and St Johann in Tirol.

Hitching Getting a lift from Salzburg to Munich is notoriously difficult. Consider taking the bus or train across the border before you waste too much time on the autobahn slip road.

Getting Around

To/From the Airport Salzburg airport is less than 4km west of the city centre at Innsbrucker Bundesstrasse 95. Bus No 77 leaves from outside and terminates at the Hauptbahnhof. This bus runs from around 6am to 11pm and doesn't go via the old town (though it intersects with bus No 29, which will take you there). A taxi to the airport from the centre costs about €9.

Bus Bus drivers sell single bus tickets for €1.60. Other tickets must be bought from Tabak shops or tourist offices; day passes (valid for a calendar day) are €2.95 and single tickets (€1.35 each) are sold in units of five. Prices are 50% less for children aged six to 15 years; those under six years travel free.

The transport information office (Map 38, #38; ☎ 44 80-62 62) is at Griesgasse 21. Bus routes are shown on city and hotel maps; bus Nos 1, 2, 6 and 51 start from the Hauptbahnhof and skirt the pedestrian-only old town.

Bus Taxi 'Bus taxis' operate nightly from 11.30pm to 1.30am (3am on weekends) for a cost of €2.55. Hanuschplatz is the departure point for suburban routes on the left bank, and Theatergasse for routes to the right bank.

Taxi Taxis cost €2.40 (€3.15 from 10pm to 6am) plus around €0.90 per kilometre. To book a radio taxi (€0.75 surcharge), call ☎ 81 11 or ☎ 17 15.

Car & Motorcycle Driving in the city centre is hardly worth the effort. Parking places are limited and much of the old town is only accessible by foot. The largest car park near the centre is the Altstadt Garage (Map 38, #76) under the Mönchsberg. Attended car parks cost around €1.85 per hour. Rates are lower on streets with automatic ticket machines (blue zones); a three-hour maximum applies (€3.05, or €0.55 for 30 minutes) 9am to 7pm on weekdays and perhaps also on Saturday (it'll say on the machine).

Car rental offices include:

Avis (Map 37, #10; ☎ 87 72 78) Ferdinand Porsche Strasse 7
Budget (Map 37, #12; ☎ 87 34 52) Elisabethstrasse 8a
Europcar (Map 37, #23; ☎ 87 42 74) Gabelsbergerstrasse 3
Hertz (Map 37, #9; ☎ 87 66 74) Ferdinand Porsche Strasse 7
National-ARAC (Map 36, #4; ☎ 87 16 16) Vogelweiderstrasse 69

Bicycle The bike-rental office in the Hauptbahnhof is open 7am to midnight daily from April to September, and charges standard rates. The bikes for rent at the stand in Residenzplatz in summer are more expensive, though there are 'economy' bikes at €29.10 for one week.

Fiacre Rates for a fiacre (horse-drawn carriage) for up to four people are €30.60/60 for 25/50 minutes. The drivers line up on Residenzplatz.

Around Salzburg

Hellbrunn, Gaisberg and Untersberg are best visited as an excursion from Salzburg. Hallein and Werfen can also be visited as a day trip or explored in a more leisurely fashion en route to sights farther south.

HELLBRUNN

Four kilometres south of the centre of Salzburg's old town is the popular **Schloss Hellbrunn** (Map 36, #15; ☎ 0662-82 03 72-0, Fürstenweg 37), built in the 17th century by bishop Marcus Sitticus, Wolf Dietrich's nephew. You can tour the interior of this baroque Schloss (admission €2.95), but the biggest draw is the **Wasserspiele** section in the grounds (adult/student €5.85/4.40). This contains many ingenious trick fountains and water-powered figures. They were installed by the bishop and are activated by the tour guides, who all seem to share the bishop's infantile sense of humour. Expect to get wet! Tours run every 30 minutes 9am to 5.30pm daily May to September, 9am to 4.30pm daily April to October, with hourly evening tours to 10pm in July and August.

There is no charge to stroll round the attractive Schloss gardens; these are open year-round till dusk. On the hill overlooking the grounds is the small **Volkskunde-museum** (Folklore Museum; ☎ 0662-82 03 72-21; admission €1.50; open 9am-5pm daily mid-Apr–mid-Oct).

Also in the grounds is **Tiergarten Hellbrunn** (☎ 0662-82 01 76; adult/student €5.10/3.65; open from 8.30am daily, last entry 6.30pm May–mid-Sept, 5.30pm Mar, Apr, mid-end Sept, 4pm Nov-Feb (Fri & Sat till 9.30pm mid-June–mid-Sept). This zoo is naturalistic and open-plan in summer; the more docile animals are barely confined.

Getting There & Away

Bus No 55 stops directly outside the Schloss every half-hour (€1.50, city passes valid). Pick it up from Salzburg's Hauptbahnhof or Rudolfskai in the old town.

GAISBERG

The peak of Gaisberg (Map 35; 1287m) is east of Salzburg old town, at the edge of the city limits. A lookout point provides an excellent panorama of the town and the Salzkammergut.

Unless you have your own transport, the only way up is to take the Albus Bus (Map 38, #23; ☎ 0662-42 40 00) from the northern end of the Aicher Passage on Mirabellplatz (€2.20 one way, 30 minutes). Check schedules as they are very infrequent, especially on weekends. From November to March the bus only goes as far as Zistelalpe, about 1.5km short of the summit.

SALZBURG PROVINCE

UNTERSBERG

This is the peak to the south of the town (Map 35), reaching to a height of 1853m. The panorama of the Tirolean and Salzburg Alpine ranges is more spectacular than from Gaisberg. The summit is accessible by cable car (€9.85 up, €8.75 down, or €16.35 return) which runs year-round except for about two weeks in April and six weeks from 1 November. Get to the valley station by city bus No 55 to St Leonhardt.

HALLEIN

☎ 06245 • pop 20,000 • elev 461m

The main reason to visit Hallein (Map 35) is the Salzbergwerk (salt mine) at Bad Dürrnberg (Map 35), on the hill above the town. The town was once settled by Celts, who provided its name.

Orientation & Information

The train station is east of the Salzach River: walk ahead, bear left and then turn right to cross the river for the town centre (five minutes). En route you pass near the tourist office (☎ 853 94, fax 853 94-14, e office@ hallein-tourism.at), Mauttorpromenade, on the narrow Pernerinsel island adjoining the Stadtbrücke. It is open 9am to 5pm Monday to Friday. In summer it's usually open part of the weekend too. The post office (Postamt 5400) is opposite the train station.

Things to See & Do

The sale of salt from the Bad Dürrnberg mine (☎ 852 85-15, Ramsaustrasse 3; open 9am-5pm daily Apr-Oct, 11am-3pm daily Nov-Mar) filled Salzburg's coffers with much revenue during its days as an ecclesiastical principality. It is believed inhabitants were mining salt as long as 4500 years ago, but production has now been replaced by guided tours (adult/student €14.60/13.10). At this mine there's the bonus of a brief raft trip on the salt lake. Overalls are supplied for the tour.

If you don't have a car, the easiest way to reach Bad Dürrnberg is to take the cable car (☎ 807 37, Zatloukalstrasse 3), about a 10-minute walk from Hallein's train station. The adult/student return fare is €9.60/8.50,

or including entry to the mine €20.35/18.20, and it operates 8.50am to 5.50pm daily May to early October. A cheaper option is the 5km, 11-minute bus ride (€1.50) from outside the station, but departures are infrequent at weekends. You could also walk to the mine, but it's a steep 40-minute climb; from the centre, walk up to the church with the bare concrete tower, turn left along Ferchl Strasse, and follow the 'Knappensteig' sign pointing to the right after the yellow Volksschule building.

Hallein has some elegant 17th- and 18th-century houses in Salzach style, as well as the Keltenmuseum (Celtic Museum; ☎ 807 83, Pflegerplatz 5; adult/concession €4/2.55; open 9am-5pm daily Apr-Oct). The museum displays interesting Celtic artefacts and details the history of salt extraction in the region (English notes available).

Special Events

The Halleiner Stadtfestwoche comprises 10 days of diverse events in late June, including live music (from classical to world music), street theatre, clowns and processions. Some of these events are free.

Places to Stay & Eat

Jugendherberge (☎ 803 97, fax 803 97-3, Schloss Wispach, Wiespachstrasse 7) Dorm beds €12.35, if fewer than three nights €14.55. Reception open 7am-noon & 5pm-8pm daily (later arrivals by prior arrangement) mid-Apr–mid-Oct. Hallein's HI hostel is in a former stately home 1.4km north of both the station (route is signposted) and the town centre. There's a bathroom on every floor and good breakfasts. Staying there allows you to pay just €1.25 to swim in the Freibad next door (€3.65 normally).

Anna Rieger (☎ 752 54, Gamperstrasse 28) Doubles/triples with shared shower €29.10/34.90. Though there are just five beds, these private rooms are cheap and near the cable-car station.

Pension Mikl (☎ 802 29, Ederstrasse 2) Singles/doubles €22.55/39.25, with bathroom €25.50/43.60. Reception (in cafe) open 6am-9pm Mon-Sat. This eight-bed place is in the town centre.

Hotel Hafnerwirt (☎ 803 19, fax 803 19-45, Salzachtal Bundesstrasse Süd 3) Singles/doubles with bathroom & TV €40/72. Though the rooms are average for a three-star place, this is conveniently located between the train station and the centre. The background traffic hum is but a minor irritation.

China-Restaurant Sun-Ly (☎ 832 47, Ederstrasse 6) Meals €4.40-10.10. Situated in the town centre, the best deals here are the weekday lunches.

Stadtkrug (☎ 830 85, Thunstrasse) Meals €6.55-10.80. Open 11am-2pm & 5pm-midnight Mon-Fri, 5pm-midnight Sun. A bargain for weekday lunches, the food served here is Austrian: eat all you like at the buffet for €6.70.

Gästehaus Unterholzerbräu (☎ 812 03, Oberhofgasse 4) Meals €5.85-13.85. Open 9am-midnight Tues-Sat, 9am-2.30pm Sun. Also known as Gasthaus Röck, this place serves Austrian food, fish and grills. To find it, head west to the edge of the pedestrian zone and turn left.

For self-caterers, there's a *Billa* supermarket *(Mauttorpromenade 1)* situated on Pernerinsel.

Getting There & Away
Hallein is 30 minutes or less south of Salzburg by bus or train (both €2.95), with departures every 30 to 60 minutes. Hallein train station rents bikes.

BERCHTESGADEN
Although this town (Map 35) is in Germany, it is easy to visit from Salzburg. It achieved fame (or perhaps notoriety) for the Eagle's Nest, a retreat built by Adolf Hitler on the Kehlstein summit. The Salzbergwerk north of town proves the Germans are also able to turn salt into money – proceeds from Berchtesgaden have long contributed to Bavaria's power and wealth. Popular tours follow a similar schedule to those in Hallein and the Salzkammergut, except that they're cheaper here.

Five kilometres south of Berchtesgaden is **Königssee** (Map 35), an attractive lake providing boat tours and a scenic setting for

walks. This area is a national park, and some people consider that it offers the best walking in Germany.

For more information on the above, contact the town tourist office (☎ 08652-9670, fax 96 74 00, e info@bertesgaden.de), opposite the train station in Königsseer Strasse, or refer to LP's *Germany* guidebook.

Getting There & Away
Berchtesgaden is 30km south of Salzburg on Hwy 160. Direct buses and trains run hourly from the city (€6.40, one hour). Salzburg's tour operators offer a five-hour tour to the Eagle's Nest (€42.90).

WERFEN
☎ 06468 ● pop 3500 ● elev 525m
Picturesque Werfen (Map 35) provides access to a top attraction, the Eisriesenwelt ice caves.

Orientation & Information
The town stands on the northern side of the Salzach River, five minutes' walk from the train station: cross the river and head towards the castle. The tourist office (☎ 5388, fax 7562, e info@werfen.at) is at Markt 24, in the centre of the town. It is open 9am to 5pm Monday to Friday (sometimes closing from noon to 2pm), except from mid-July to mid-August when it's open till 7pm weekdays and from 5pm to 7pm Saturday. Tourist office staff will book accommodation for no commission.

Eisriesenwelt Höhle
These caves *(☎ 6468; open 9am-4.30pm daily Jul & Aug, 9am-3.30pm daily May, June, Sept-26 Oct)* in the mountains are the largest accessible ice caves in the world. They contain 30,000 sq m of ice and about 42km of passages have been explored. During a 75-minute tour (€7.30) you visit several immense caverns, containing some beautiful and elaborate ice shapes. Unfortunately, the powerful illumination provided by a series of magnesium flares is all too brief. The tour (in German; perhaps also in English in high season) visits about one-fiftieth of the caves.

The caves were first entered in 1879 but it was Alexander von Mörk who pioneered the most extensive exploration, and his ashes lie in the 'cathedral' cave.

Take warm clothes because it can get cold inside the caves, and you need to be fairly fit (some people may find the stairs a bit difficult).

Getting to the caves is a bit of an effort, though the trip offers fantastic views. A minibus service (€5.10 return) operates from the train station along the steep (up to 23 degrees) 6km road to the car park, which is as far as cars can go. A 15-minute walk brings you to the cable car (€8.70 return); from the top station it is a steep 15-minute walk to the caves. Allow at least four hours for the return trip from the train station (including tour), or three hours from the car park (peak-season queues may add an hour). The whole route can be walked, but it's a hard four-hour ascent, rising 1100m above the village.

You can also explore the Dachstein ice caves, which are near Obertraun; in the Salzkammergut.

Burg Hohenwerfen

Burg Hohenwerfen (☎ 7603; adult/student/family €9.10/7.60/20; open 9am-6pm daily Jul & Aug; 9am-5pm daily May, June, Sept; 9am-4.30pm daily Apr, Oct & Nov) stands on the hill above the village, in an extremely photogenic location. It was originally built in 1077 for an archbishop of Salzburg, but the present fortress dates from the 16th century. The entry fee includes a temporary exhibition, a permanent falconry museum, and a guided tour of the interior (in German, but ask for the audio handset in English); this covers the chapel, dungeons, arsenal and belfry. A highlight is a dramatic 20-minute falconry show in the grounds, with a wonderful backdrop of the Tennengebirge mountain range. The walk up from the village takes 20 minutes.

Both the fortress and the ice caves can be fitted into a day trip from Salzburg if you start early; visit the caves first, and be at the fortress by 3pm for the last falconry show (the other show is at 11am).

Places to Stay & Eat

Werfen is a small village with only a few hotels (usually with a restaurant). Private rooms are an option, such as *Rudolf Färbinger* (☎ 5615, Hirschenhöhstrasse 2) offering doubles without/with bathroom for €36.40/40; it's behind Restaurant-Hotel Obaurer.

Goldener Hirsch (☎ 5342, Markt 28) Doubles with shower €40.60. Not the most helpful of owners, but the price is right.

Kärntnerhof (☎ 5214, fax 7175, Markt 31) Singles/doubles €22.90/44.35. Over half of the biggish rooms in this place have a balcony, all have bathroom and TV, and there's a large dining area (including a terrace at the back) serving affordable Austrian food.

Several restaurants, including a pizzeria, await on Markt, the main street, as well as an *ADEG* supermarket (Markt 28).

Zur Stiege (☎ 5256, fax 5256-4, Markt 10) Doubles with bathroom & TV €52.50. This place has a few rooms but the main business is its restaurant, which has a good reputation. Meals cost €14.20 to €21.50 (reserve first).

Restaurant-Hotel Obauer (☎ 5212, fax 5212-12, Markt 46) Singles €80-99, doubles €120-144. In the culinary stakes, this place is tops – the restaurant is acclaimed as one of the finest in the whole of Austria. Creative mains (mostly Austrian in origin, but with French and Italian influences) cost €21.50 to €29.10. You have to make reservations, especially as rest days vary. The stylish rooms have all the comforts expected of a four-star place – the radios in the bathrooms are a nice touch – and the staff pamper guests and diners with equal diligence.

Getting There & Away

Werfen can be reached from Salzburg by Hwy 10. Trains from Salzburg (€5.85) run approximately hourly and take 50 minutes.

Southern Salzburg Province

The main attractions in the south are covered in the Hohe Tauern National Park Region chapter, but the following are worth a look if you're passing through the south-east of the province. Tamsweg and Mauterndorf are both in the Lungau region; staff at the Lungau tourist office (☎ 06477-8988, fax 8988-20, e info@lungau.net, w www.lungau.co.at), Postfach 19, A-5582, Lungau, can tell you about ski passes and accommodation.

TAMSWEG
☎ 06474 • pop 5000 • elev 1024m

Tamsweg (Map 35) is the main town in the Lungau. You may want to stop off to look at **St Leonhardkirche** (☎ *06474-6870*), a 15th-century Gothic church on a hill outside the town. It has some impressive stained-glass windows, particularly the Goldfenster (gold window) to the right of the chancel. After a statuette of St Leonardwas found, an event depicted in the Goldfenster, the church became a well-known pilgrimage site.

In the centre of town, the attractive **Marktplatz** is lined with rustic-style inns as well as the 16th-century Rathaus, a rather grander, turreted edifice.

Tamsweg is known for its Samsonumzug (Samson Procession) which takes place on two days in late July and on a couple of other variable dates in summer. The biblical character and other famous figures are depicted in giant size and paraded through the streets.

Getting There & Away
Tamsweg is a 10km detour from Hwy 99, which connects Radstadt and Spittal an der Drau. It's at the terminus of a private rail line that branches off from the Vienna-Klagenfurt main line at Unzmarkt. See the Murau section in the Styria chapter for details.

MAUTERNDORF
☎ 06472 • pop 1600 • 1122m

Both a summer and winter resort, Mauterndorf (Map 35) has the added attraction of a **castle** (☎ *7426; adult/family €7.50/19; open 10am-5pm daily May-21 Oct)*. This was built by the archbishops of Salzburg in the 13th century on the site of a Roman fort. In 1339 the castle chapel (with Gothic frescoes) was added and in 1452 a winged altar was installed. The castle houses a regional museum, and is the venue for various

cultural events. It is believed that in the Middle Ages the main road passed directly through the castle courtyard. This facilitated the collecting of tolls from road users, but presumably also entailed a defence risk. The locals were lucky not to encounter a Trojan horse trundling along the road.

Getting There & Away
Mauterndorf is on Hwy 99. Bundesbuses go along this route, but it's not on a rail line.

RADSTADT
☎ 06452 • pop 4000 • elev 856m

Radstadt (Map 35) retains much of its medieval fortifications – the walled centre of town, with three round turrets, is an impressive sight. There's also a **Stadtpfarrkirche** (parish church) that combines Gothic and Romanesque elements and has an interesting graveyard.

Despite these delights, most visitors flock to Radstadt and the surrounding resorts to participate in winter skiing. Together, the resorts form the huge **Sportwelt Amadé** skiing area; 120 lifts give access to 320km of pistes, mostly suitable for intermediate and beginner skiers. For information, contact the Salzburger Sportwelt Amadé (☎ 06457-29 29, fax 27 09 29, e info@sportwelt-amade.co.at, w www.sportwelt-amade.com).

The same mountains attract walkers in summer. Overlooking Radstadt to the north is **Rossbrand** (Map 35; 1770m). If you wear rose-tinted spectacles as you make the ascent, you might believe the claim made by an over-enthusiastic tourist office that this is the most famous viewpoint in the eastern Alps.

Getting There & Away
Radstadt is on the route of two-hourly IC trains running between Innsbruck and Graz – both are about three hours away. Zell am See (€9.45, 70 minutes) and Bruck an der Mur (€20.35, 2¼ hours) are also on this route.

From Radstadt, Hwy 99 runs into Carinthia, then climbs to the Radstädter Tauern Pass (1739m): caravans not recommended. Just to the west is a busier north-south route, the A10/E55, which avoids the high parts by going through a 6km tunnel.

The Salzkammergut

This 'earthly paradise', as described by Franz Josef I, is a popular holiday region to the east of Salzburg. The lure of the many lakes makes summer the main season in this area, but winter has its attractions too. You can simply relax and take in the scenery, or get involved in the numerous sports and activities on offer. In summer, walking and water sports are favoured; in winter, some walking paths stay open but downhill and cross-country skiing are more popular. Some pensions and private rooms close for the winter.

If you plan to fish, be sure to check with the local tourist office about permits, permitted seasons and other regulations – these may include rules about permitted times and equipment.

Orientation

The Salzkammergut is split between three provinces. Upper Austria takes the lion's share including the largest lake, Attersee, its two neighbours, Mondsee and Traunsee, and the ever popular Hallstätter See in the south. Bad Ischl, also in Upper Austria, is the geographical and administrative centre of the Salzkammergut. East of Hallstätter See is a small region within Styria, comprising Bad Aussee and its lakes. Salzburg province has most of Wolfgangsee, and some less important lakes to the west and north-west. In this region of mountains and lakes, most taller mountains are in the south and most larger lakes in the north.

Information

In addition to the local tourist offices – there is one in almost every resort – the provincial tourist offices can be helpful, though they usually only hold resort brochures for their own region within the Salzkammergut. See the Salzburg, Upper Austria and Styria chapters for addresses and opening times of these offices. The provincial tourist offices in Salzburg city and Linz (Upper Austria) have a good supply of brochures. In Styria, infor-

Highlights

- Savour the varied attractions of Hallstatt – from stunning views to decorated human skulls
- Explore the wondrous Dachstein ice caves at Obertraun
- Discover the antique ceramics and lakeside castles of Gmunden
- Admire Pacher's magnificent altar in the pilgrimage church of St Wolfgang
- Take in the captivating panorama of lakes and mountains from the Schafberg

mation is held in the main Graz tourist office (for personal callers) and the provincial office (for information by post), also in Graz.

The Salzkammergut has its own tourist board, known as the Ferienregion Salzkammergut (☎ 06132-269 09-0, fax 06132-269 09-14, e info.salzkammergut@upper austria.or.at, w www.salzkammergut.at), Wirerstrasse 10, Postfach 130, A-4820 Bad Ischl. It mostly has general information, however, and isn't geared to receive personal callers. For region-wide information you're probably better off contacting the Salzkammergut Info-Center (see the Bad Ischl section, following).

The Salzkammergut is dotted with hostels and affordable hotels, but the best deals are probably rooms in private homes or farmhouses – despite the prevalence of single-night surcharges (about €2.20). Tourist

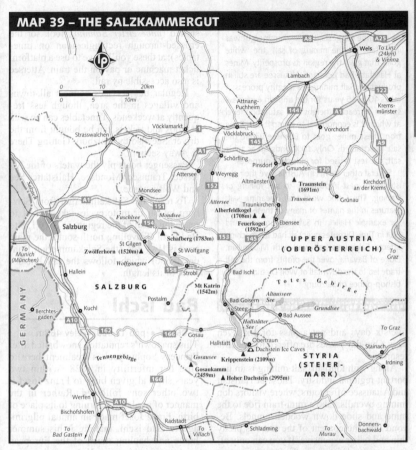

MAP 39 – THE SALZKAMMERGUT

offices can supply lists of private rooms, as well as details of Alpine huts at higher elevations. Most resorts have a *Gästekarte* (guest card) which offers a variety of discounts. Make sure you ask for a card if it is not offered spontaneously. It must be stamped by the place you're staying in (even at camping grounds) to be valid. Show it before paying for bus tickets, as some journeys may be free.

The Salzkammergut Card, available from tourist offices and hotels, costs €4.75. It is valid between 1 May and 31 October for the duration of your holiday in the region.

Cardholders are entitled to a 25% discount on about 110 attractions – sights, ferries, cable cars and some Bundesbus routes. It's not transferable.

A winter ski pass is available from ski lift stations for the Salzkammergut-Lammertal region, which includes 80 cable cars and ski lifts serving 145km of ski runs. It costs €112.50 (children €65.50) for five days, €129.50 (€74) for six days, €143.50 (€82) for seven days and €205 (€121) for 10 days. It is also valid for a number of free ski buses. Look for low-season offers in January and after early March, when you can pay for

Salt Mines

As its name suggests, the Salzkammergut was important for the mining of salt, the 'white gold' that gave the region its prosperity. Mines at Hallstatt, Bad Ischl and Altaussee are still in production. Salt mining is a lengthy process: it takes 10 to 15 years for the brine in each new section to reach a height and saturation level at which it is economical to pump it out. Brine from these mines goes to Ebensee where the salt is extracted. Only 10% ends up as table salt; the rest is used for industrial purposes.

Several other towns in Austria owe their existence or past importance to salt mining or trading. The Celtic word *Hall*, meaning salt, features in the names of many of these towns, for example Hallein in Salzburg province and Hall in Tirol. Disputes over salt had far-reaching effects: Salzburg's 'salt war' with Maximilian, Duke of Bavaria, over the profits from the salt trade led to the downfall of Wolf Dietrich, archbishop-prince of Salzburg.

---

five/six days and get a pass for six/seven days. One-day passes are offered for specific resorts.

Along with tourism, salt mining is an important regional industry. Those at Hallstatt and Altaussee offer tours, where visitors don mining overalls, take a mini-train ride to the mine and slide down wooden tunnels. Beyond this, the content of the tours is pretty thin and rather expensive. If you can only afford one guided tour in the mountains, opt for the ice caves at Obertraun instead. Details of all tours are provided in the relevant sections for each of these towns.

Getting Around

The main rail routes pass either side of the Salzkammergut, but the area can be crossed by regional trains on a north-south route. You can get on this route from Attnang-Puchheim on the Salzburg-Linz line, or from Stainach-Irdning on the Bischofshofen-Graz line. The rail line linking these two access points is 108km long, and hourly trains take 2½ hours to complete the journey (and they're often

late). Smaller stations on this route are unstaffed (*unbesetzter Bahnhof*; look for the crossed-through rectangle icon on timetables); at these you'll have to use a platform ticket machine or pay on the train. Attersee is also accessible by rail.

Regular bus services connect all towns and villages in the area, though less frequently at weekends. Timetables can be seen at stops and tickets can be bought from the driver. See also the Salzburg Getting There & Away section.

Passenger boats ply the waters of the Attersee, Traunsee, Mondsee, Hallstätter See and Wolfgangsee.

To reach the Salzkammergut from Salzburg by car or motorcycle, take the A1 to reach the north of the region, or Hwy 158 to Bad Ischl. Travelling north-south, the main road is Hwy 145 (the Salzkammergut Bundesstrasse) which follows the rail line for most of its length.

Bad Ischl

☎ 06132 • pop 13,000 • elev 468m

This spa town's reputation snowballed after Princess Sophie took a treatment here to cure her infertility in 1828. Within two years she had given birth to Franz Josef I; two other sons followed. Rather in the manner of a salmon returning to its place of birth, Franz Josef made an annual pilgrimage to Bad Ischl, making it his summer home and hauling much of the European aristocracy in his wake. However, deviating from salmon behaviour, Franz Josef returned to his spiritual home to make not love but war – usually on deer, but ultimately on the whole world.

Orientation & Information

Bad Ischl's town centre is compactly contained within a bend of the Traun River.

The tourist office or *Kurdirektion* (Map 40, #11; ☎ 277 57-0, fax 277 57-77, e office@kd-badischl.or.at) is west of the train station at Bahnhofstrasse 6. It is open 8am to 6pm Monday to Friday, 9am to 3pm Saturday, 10am to 1pm Sunday and holidays.

NC

Franz Josef, a regular at Bad Ischl, became
emperor when just 18 years old

The Salzkammergut Info-Center (Map 40,
#7; ☎ 240 00-0, **e** office@salzkammergut
.co.at) at Götzstrasse 12, is open from 9am to
8pm daily (to 10pm in summer). It is a helpful private agency, and can provide region-
wide information and hotel bookings (no
commission). It also has bike rental (€7.30
for 24 hours) and Internet access (€1.10 for
10 minutes).

The post office (Map 40, #12; Postamt
4820) is on Bahnhofstrasse (standard opening hours). There are moneychanging facilities at the post office and train station.

Things to See & Do

Stroll around town, admiring the plentiful
Biedermeier-style buildings; if you walk
along the Esplanade you'll reach the **Stadtmuseum** *(city museum; Map 40, #22; ☎ 254
76, Esplanade 10; admission €4; open
10am-5pm Thur-Tues, 2pm-7pm Wed July-
Aug; 10am-5pm Thur-Sun & Tues, 2pm-7pm
Wed Apr-June & Sept-Oct; 10am-5pm Fri-
Sun Jan-Mar; closed Nov)*. It deals with
local history and culture. Across the river is
the **Lehárvilla** *(Map 40, #15; ☎ 269 92,
Lehárkai 8; adult/student €4.40/1.85; open
9am-noon & 2pm-5pm daily May-Sept)*, former home of the operetta composer Franz
Lehár. For longer walks, see the tourist office's suggestions on the reverse of the city

map. Also ask about the free guided city
walks in summer.

Franz Josef's summer residence was the
Kaiservilla *(Map 40, #2; ☎ 232 41, Jainzen
38; admission €9.50; open 9am-11.45am &
1pm-4.45pm daily 1 May–mid-Oct, 9am-
11.45am & 1pm-4.45pm Sat & Sun Easter
& Apr)*. He stayed in this villa for 60 years,
from 1854 to 1914, and it was here that he
signed the declaration of war on Serbia that
started WWI. The emperor had the habit of
getting up for his daily bath as early as
3.30am – somebody should have told him
that holidays are meant for relaxation. The
villa was his hunting lodge (though rather
grand for that purpose) and contains an ob-
scene number of hunting trophies; most of
his victims are now no more than antlers on
the wall, but the 2000th (!) chamois he shot
is presented in its stuffed entirety.

The villa can be visited only by guided
tour, which is usually given only in German,
but there are written English translations.
The tour takes 40 minutes and includes entry
to the Kaiserpark grounds (which costs
€2.90 separately).

The small **Photomuseum** *(Map 40, #1;
☎ 244 22; adult/student €1.10/0.75; open
9.30am-5pm daily 1 Apr-31 Oct)*, in the
Marmorschlössl building in the park, has
some interesting old photographs and cameras on display.

Bad Ischl's local peak is **Mt Katrin**
(1542m) which provides views and walking
trails (see the Walking & Skiing special section). In summer, the cable car costs €11.65
return. In winter, there is downhill skiing
(€18 for a day pass) on the mountain. The
area also has some cross-country skiing
trails.

The **Fahrzeugmuseum** *(Transport Museum; ☎ 266 58, Sulzbach 178; admission
€5.10; open 9am-6pm daily 1 Apr-31 Oct)*
displays a varied collection of motorised
transport, such as airplanes, helicopters, motorcycles, cars and army vehicles. It's about
4km south of the town centre; Bad Goisern/
Hallstatt Bundesbuses stop 200m away.

The tourist office has details on health
treatments such as those on offer at the
Kaiser Therme *(Map 40, #8; ☎ 233 24-0,*

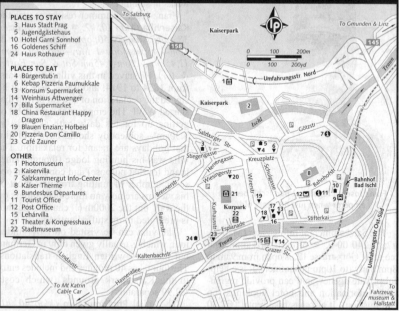

MAP 40 – BAD ISCHL

PLACES TO STAY
3 Haus Stadt Prag
5 Jugendgästehaus
10 Hotel Garni Sonnhof
16 Goldenes Schiff
24 Haus Rothauer

PLACES TO EAT
4 Bürgerstub'n
6 Kebap Pizzeria Paumukkale
13 Konsum Supermarket
14 Weinhaus Attwenger
17 Billa Supermarket
18 China Restaurant Happy Dragon
19 Blauen Enzian; Hofbeisl
20 Pizzeria Don Camillo
23 Café Zauner

OTHER
1 Photomuseum
2 Kaiservilla
7 Salzkammergut Info-Center
8 Kaiser Therme
9 Bundesbus Departures
11 Tourist Office
12 Post Office
15 Lehárvilla
21 Theater & Kongresshaus
22 Stadtmuseum

w www.kaisertherme.co.at) at Bahnhofstrasse 1. If you're interested, you can down a mug-full of the mineral-rich waters here (€1.50).

Special Events

Free *Kurkonzerte* (spa concerts) are performed once or twice a day (except Tuesday) during summer; ask the tourist office for venues and times. An operetta festival takes place in July and August; for details and reservations contact Büro der Operetten Festspiele (☎ 238 39, fax 238 39-39, **w** www.operette.badischl.at), Kurhausstrasse 8, A-4820. The Bad Ischler Stadtfest in late August features two days of diverse music from disco to choir (entry into the town centre €6 per day).

Places to Stay

Staff at the tourist office will help find rooms free of charge, or you can use the 24-hour accommodation board in the foyer.

Jugendgästehaus (Map 40, #5; ☎ 265 77, fax 265 77-75, **e** jgh.badischl@oejhv.or.at, *Am Rechensteg 5)* Dorm bed €13.75, singles/doubles with private shower €25.50/36.50. Reception open 8am to 1pm and 5pm to 7pm. Closed 6–21 Jan & 7–27 Dec. This nondescript HI hostel is in the town centre behind Kreuzplatz. Dinner costs €5.50.

Haus Rothauer (Map 40, #24; ☎ 236 28, *Kaltenbachstrasse 12)* Singles/doubles €19.65/36.40. This pleasant private house offers renovated rooms with shower, toilet and TV, modest prices and a convenient location. Phone ahead to check availability and make sure someone is there when you intend to arrive.

Haus Stadt Prag (Map 40, #3; ☎/fax 236 16, *Eglmoosgasse 9)* Singles/doubles €27/51. Closed Nov. This old-fashioned place offers large rooms, all with a shower and toilet, kitted out in a range of styles.

Hotel Garni Sonnhof (Map 40, #10; ☎ 230 78, fax 230 78-5, *Bahnhofstrasse 4)* Singles

€48-70, doubles €59-104. This place, in a pastoral garden setting, is ideal for the train station and has private parking. All rooms have shower, toilet and TV.

Goldenes Schiff (Map 40, #16; ☎ *242 41, fax 242 41-58,* e *office@goldenes-schiff.at, Adalbert Stifterkai 3)* Singles €48-72, doubles €79-128. Overlooking the river, this four-star hotel has a solarium, sauna, a good restaurant and parking places. Room prices depend on size, season and aspect – a river view with balcony in summer puts you in the highest price category. All have shower, toilet and TV.

Places to Eat

Supermarkets include *Billa* (Map 40, #17) on Pfarrgasse and *Konsum* (Map 40, #13) on Auböckplatz.

China Restaurant Happy Dragon (Map 40, #18; ☎ *234 32, Pfarrgasse 2)* Lunch menus €4.65-6.20 Mon-Sat, not on holidays, main dishes €6.50-10.90. Open 11.30am-2.30pm & 6pm-11pm daily. Located by the Schröpferplatz bridge, there are outside tables overlooking the river. The food encompasses Indian meals and is above average.

Pizzeria Don Camillo (Map 40, #20; ☎ *277 35, Wiesingerstrasse 5)* Pizza/spaghetti €4.30-8, salads €2.60-5.50. Open 11am-2pm & 5pm-11pm daily. This enjoyable Italian restaurant has outside tables overlooking the Kurpark. *Kebap Pizzeria Pamukkale (Map 40, #6; Kreuzplatz 12)* also serves cheap pizzas (and kebabs).

Bürgerstub'n (Map 40, #4; ☎ *235 68, Kreuzplatz 7)* Meals €6.90-14.50, salad buffet €3.30-4.75. Kitchen open 11.30am-3pm & 6pm-9pm Mon-Sat. Back from the street in a courtyard, this relaxing place has lots of plants and good Austrian food. Sometimes, it's even open on Sundays.

Blauen Enzian (Map 40, #19; ☎ *289 92, Wirerstrasse 4)* Meals €6.50-12.50. Open 11am-2pm & 6pm-midnight Mon-Sat. This informal place, back from the main street with a courtyard, offers pasta, regional and national food and salads. Almost next door is the popular *Hofbeisl* (Map 40, #19) an atmospheric place for a drink with baroque decor, loud music (open 9am to 4am daily).

Café Zauner (Map 40, #23; ☎ *237 22, Esplanade)* Meals €7.65-13.50, cakes €2.15-5.85. Open 10am-9pm daily 1 May-30 Sept. Sample imperial elegance at this upmarket cafe.

Weinhaus Attwenger (Map 40, #14; ☎ *233 27, Lehárkai 12)* Dishes €7.65-12.75. Open 11.30am-2pm & 6pm-11pm Tues-Sun. This quaint chalet with a relaxing garden proffers prime quality Austrian cuisine.

Getting There & Away

Bundesbuses depart (Map 40, #9) from outside the train station. There are hourly buses to Salzburg (€7.30, 85 minutes) between 5am and 7.20pm (6.20pm on weekends), via St Gilgen. To St Wolfgang (€2.95), you often have to change at Strobl (the bus will be waiting and the same ticket is valid). Buses run to Hallstatt every couple of hours (€3.80, 50 minutes), with some continuing to Obertraun.

Trains depart hourly (see Getting Around earlier in this chapter). It costs €2.95 to Hallstatt but, unlike the bus, you must add the cost of the boat from Halstatt station (see the following Hallstatt Getting There & Away section). There are hourly trains to Gmunden (€5.20, 45 minutes); and to Salzburg via Attnang-Puchheim (€15.55, around two hours, hourly).

Most major roads in the Salzkammergut go to or near Bad Ischl; Hwy 158 from Salzburg and the north-south Hwy 145 intersect just north of the town centre.

Southern Salzkammergut

The Dachstein mountain range provides a stunning 3000m backdrop to the lakes in the south. Transport routes go round rather than over these jagged peaks.

HALLSTÄTTER SEE

The big draw in the south is this lake (Map 39), at 508m. Hallstatt is the most famous resort and gets hordes of day-trippers. Just 5km round the lake lies Obertraun, the closest resort to the Dachstein ice caves. Either place would make a suitable base from which to explore the locality. The Hallstatt-Dachstein region became a Unesco World Cultural Heritage site in 1997.

Circular excursion round the lake are offered by Hemetsberger (☎ 6134-8228, Am Hof 126; 75 minute trip €8; operates July–mid-Sept weather depending). There are three boats a day from Hallstatt; disembarkation is possible.

HALLSTATT
☎ 06134

Nowadays Hallstatt (Map 39) is prized mainly for its picturesque location, though its history spans 4500 years. The Hallstatt Period (800 to 400 BC) refers to the early Iron Age in Europe and was named after the settlers who worked the salt mine; near the mine entrance, 2000 flat graves were discovered dating from 1000 to 500 BC. In AD 50, the Romans were also attracted by the rich salt deposits.

Orientation & Information
Seestrasse is the main street; some other streets are mere pedestrian paths. Turn left from the ferry to reach the tourist office (☎ 8208, fax 8352, e hallstatt-info@ eunet.at) at Seestrasse 169. It's open 9am to noon and 2pm to 5pm Monday to Friday; in summer it may open weekend mornings, depending on demand. The office sells an English-language walking guide (€5.85).

The post office (Postamt 4830) is around the corner from the tourist office and changes money.

Things to See & Do
Hallstatt is set in idyllic, picture-postcard scenery, wedged in a narrow space between steep mountains and the placid lake. The setting alone is enough to justify a visit. The tour buses that roll in stay only a few hours and then the village returns to a calmer state. Join everyone else strolling down the quaint streets, snapping up souvenirs and photographs in equal measure.

The 15th-century Catholic Pfarrkirche (parish church; ☎ 8279, Kirchenweg 40) has

Gothic frescoes and three winged altars: arguably the best one, on the right, dates from 1510 and shows saints Barbara and Katharina, with Mary in the middle. You shouldn't miss the macabre Beinhaus (Bone House; ☎ 8279, Kirchenweg 40; admission €0.75; open 10am-6pm daily) behind the church; it contains rows of neatly stacked skulls, upon which have been painted flowery designs and the names of their former owners. These human remains have been exhumed from the too-small graveyard since 1600.

The village has a newly rebuilt and revamped two-part museum (☎ 8206, W www .museum-hallstatt.at, Seestrasse 56; combined entry adult/child €6/3; open 10am-4pm daily Apr & Oct, 10am-6pm May-Sept). It covers the region's early history, crafts and fauna. Some Celtic and Roman excavations can be seen in Dachsteinsport Janu (☎ 8298, Seestrasse 50; admission free; closed Sun Nov-Apr), a shop opposite the tourist office.

Above the village on the Salzberg (salt mountain) is the Salzbergwerk (salt mine; ☎ 8400; adult/child €10.20/5.10; open 9.30am daily late Apr-late Oct). Tours (usually in German, plus a short English film) dwell on the fate of a 3000-year-old miner, found preserved in the salt in 1735. The last tour is at 4.30pm from late May to mid-September; at other times it's at 3pm. A funicular costing €4.75/7.65 one-way/return will take you to Rudolfsturm (Rudolf's Tower), 15 minutes' walk from the mine. Alternatively, either of two scenic walking trails will get you from Hallstatt to the tower in 45 minutes. There's an excellent view from the public terrace of Rudolfsturm. Other walking suggestions are given in the Walking & Skiing special section.

Gasthof Hallberg is the base for Hallstatt's scuba diving school, and the ski school is at the Gasthof Zauner; see the following Places to Stay and Places to Eat sections.

Hallstatt has an unusual Corpus Christi procession: the shoreline is so crowded that some participants take to the water in boats.

Places to Stay
Some private rooms in the village are only available in summer; others require at least

a three night stay. Prices are around €15 per person. Your best bet is to elicit the help of the tourist office, which will willingly ring round for you without charge. There's an accommodation board with free phone in Lahn (the southern part of the village). Lahn has the cheapest private rooms.

Campingplatz Höll (☎ 8329, fax 8329-1, **e** camping.klausner@magnet.at, Lahnstrasse 7) Price per adult/tent/car €4.90/ 3.30/2.60. Open 15 Apr-15 Oct. This camp ground is conveniently located, south of the centre.

Jugendherberge (☎ 8212, fax 200 15, Salzbergstrasse 50) Dorm beds €8, sheets €2.50. Check-in approx 5pm-6pm. Open 1 May-30 Sept, depending on the weather. Some dorms have lots of beds and are cramped. Phone ahead as reception hours are irregular; it's usually full with groups in July and August. Breakfast costs €3.30.

TVN Naturfreunde Herberge (☎/fax 8318, **e** toeroe.f@magnet.at, Kirchenweg 36) Beds in 20-bed dorm €9/10, 4–8-bed room €10, breakfast €3, sheets free/€3 if staying over/under three nights. Check-in 11am-2pm & 4pm-10pm Wed-Mon, 5pm-10pm Tues. This place is just below the road tunnel, by the waterfall. The smaller rooms are OK, but the dorms have beds crammed into every spare space. It's run by the *Zur Mühle Gasthaus*, which shares the building.

Bräu Gasthof (☎ 200 12, Seestrasse 120) Singles/doubles €38/66. Rooms are available year-round, and most have a balcony and antique furniture; all have a bathroom and TV.

Gasthof Hallberg (☎ 8286, fax 8286-5, **e** scuba@ping.at, Seestrasse 113) Singles/ doubles €36.50/65.50. Interesting artefacts rescued from the lake by the diving school surround the stairway leading to the homey rooms, which all have a bathroom and TV.

Gasthof Zauner (☎ 8246, fax 8246-8, **e** zauner@hallstatt.at, Marktplatz 51) Singles €41.50-49.50, doubles €75.60-91.60; add €16 per person for half-board. Meals €8.20-19. Closed mid-Nov–mid-Dec. This family-run place has old-style, pine embellished rooms – some with a balcony and view of the lake, all with shower, toilet, TV and telephone. The **restaurant** is renowned for its good food (especially fish) and wines.

Places to Eat

Zur Mühle (☎ 8318, Kirchenweg 36) Meals €5.40-10.60. Open 11am-2pm & 5pm-9pm Wed-Mon. This restaurant has good prices for Austrian and Italian food.

Bräu Gasthof Restaurant (☎ 200 12, Seestrasse 120) Meals €7.25-14.50. Open 10am-9pm daily late April–mid-Oct. This restaurant dishes out well-prepared Austrian food; eat in vaulted rooms or outside by the lake. Along the road is a summer-only *open-air bar* with limited cheap food.

Kongress Stuberl (☎ 83 11 59, Seestrasse 169) Meals €6.20-14.50. Open 11am-10pm daily, closed Tues Oct-Apr. This small restaurant by the tourist office is another good place to eat.

Pferdestall (☎ 200 00, Seestrasse 156) Meals €4.10-18. Once a stable (tables are built the old horse stalls), this small place turns out cheap pizza/pasta and pricier meat dishes. A *Konsum* supermarket is nearby.

Getting There & Away

There are around six buses a day to/from Obertraun and Bad Ischl, but none after about 5pm. Get off the Bundesbus at the Parkterrasse stop for the centre and the tourist office, or at Lahn (at the southern end of the road tunnel) for the Jugendherberge hostel.

Hallstatt train station is across the lake. The boat service from there to the village (€1.85) coincides with train arrivals (at least 10 a day from Bad Ischl; total trip 45 minutes). Though trains run later, the last ferry connection leaves Hallstatt train station at 6.44pm. Car access into the village is restricted from early May to late October: electronic gates are activated during the day. Staying overnight in town gives free parking and a pass to open the gates.

OBERTRAUN
☎ 06131

This spread-out village (Map 39) appears to be totally enclosed within a crater of mountains; it's a pleasing trick of perspective.

Orientation & Information

Obertraun is on the northern bank of the Traun River, at the start of the narrow and steep-sided valley leading east to Bad Aussee. The tourist office (☎ 351, fax 342-22, e tourismus@obertraun.or.at) is in the Gemeindeamt, open 8am to noon and 2pm to 5pm Monday to Friday. In July and August it's open 8am to 6pm weekdays and 9am to noon Saturday. The Dachstein ice caves are south of the river, a pleasant 20-minute walk through the woods (take path No 7; signposted).

The resort Gästekarte entitles you to a variety of useful discounts.

Dachstein Caves

The best of these caves (Map 39) are the **Rieseneishöhle** (Giant Ice Caves); ask at the caves' ticket office about tours in English. The caves are millions of years old and extend for nearly 80km in places. The ice itself is no more than 500 years old but is increasing in thickness every year – the 'ice mountain' is 8m high, twice as high as when the caves were first explored in 1910. There are some unusual and beautiful formations, such as the 'ice chapel'.

The **Mammuthöhle** (Mammoth Caves) are basically more of the same except without the ice formations. They are worth seeing, if only for the atmospheric slide show projected within a far cavern, accompanied by swelling music mingling with the sound of ceaselessly dripping water. The tour is in German only.

Both sets of **caves** (☎ 8400-1830; each cave/combined ticket €7.30/10.09; open early May-late Oct) are 10 minutes' walk from the first stage of the Dachstein cable car (station Schönbergalm) at 1350m; near the station is the ticket office for the caves. The cable car operates every 20 minutes; a return ticket costs €12.35. Each tour takes nearly an hour; be at the ticket office at the latest by 3pm in summer and 2pm in autumn to have time to do both tours.

The **Koppenbrüllerhöhle** (☎ 8400-1830; guided tour €6.55; open mid-Apr–30 Sept) are water-filled caves, and all part of the same Dachstein cave system. They're down the valley towards Bad Aussee.

Other Attractions

The Dachstein cable car has three stages, the highest being **Krippenstein** (Map 39) at 2109m; various viewpoints and walking trails await, providing excellent vistas of the Dachstein range to the south and Hallstätter See to the north. In winter this is also a ski region (€25.50 for a one day pass). Uniquely, you can indulge in nude cross-country skiing up here (inquire at the tourist office).

Obertraun has a grassy **beach** area (admission free) with changing huts, a small waterslide, a children's play area and boat rental.

Places to Stay & Eat

Look for the many private rooms (from €12) and holiday apartments in the village.

Campingplatz Hinterer (☎ 265, fax 8368, Winkl 77) Price per adult/tent/car €5.25/4.75/2.20. Open May-Oct. This informal grassy camp ground is by the lake, south of the river.

Jugendherberge (☎ 360, fax 360-4, e obertraun@jutel.at, Winkl 26) Dorm bed adult/under 19 €15.70/14.20, additional €1.50 for single night. Doors locked during the day; check-in 5pm-8pm. This HI hostel is a 15 minutes' walk from the train station: cross the river and take the first street on the left. Lunch and dinner cost €5.85 each.

Obertrauner Hof (☎ 456-0, fax 456-78, e obertraunerhof@eunet.at, Hauptstrasse 90) Singles €29.10-36.40, doubles €50.90-65.40. Closed mid-Nov–mid-Dec, and Thur except in July & Aug. This Gasthof has big modern rooms with a toilet and shower, and a range of prices, depending upon the length of stay and season. The restaurant serves decent Austrian food (€6.20 to €10.20).

Gasthof Höllwirt (☎ 394, fax 394-4, Hauptstrasse 29) Meals €5.70-10.20. Open 11am-9pm daily, closed Wed Sept-June. This is a good family restaurant with seating inside and out. It also has a few double rooms (€42.20 with shared shower, €58.20 with bathroom and TV).

Restaurant Pizzeria Kegelbahnen (☎ 335, Obertraun 178) Meals €4.75-10.60. Open 3pm-midnight Tue-Fri, 10am-midnight Sat & Sun. This place is near the beach and boat landing point. The pizzas are not expensive, and there's also a skittles alley to keep you occupied.

By the tourist office is a *Konsum* supermarket that's open 7.30am to noon and 3pm to 6pm Monday to Friday, 7am to noon Saturday.

Getting There & Away

Bus connections between Hallstatt and Obertraun are patchy, with only five or fewer running per day, but it's possible to hitch, or the walk takes 50 minutes. Four or five boats per day run between Obertraun and Hallstatt in summer (€3.60, 25 minutes).

You can rent bicycles from Obertraun-Dachsteinhöhlen, the train station for the village. Obertraun-Koppenbrüllerhöhle is the station for the water cave (€1.45, four minutes); trains only stop here in summer when the caves are open. There are trains to Bad Ischl (€3.85, 30 minutes, hourly).

BAD AUSSEE

☎ 03622 • pop 5100 • elev 650m

Bad Aussee is the chief Styrian town in the Salzkammergut. It provides access to two lakes, as well as being a health resort. The sound of rushing water, emanating from the swiftly flowing Traun, is everywhere in town.

Orientation & Information

The tourist office (Map 41, #15; ☎ 523 23, fax 523 23-4, e info@badaussee.at) is in the town centre, at Oppauer Platz. The office is open 8am to noon and 2pm to 6pm Monday to Friday; except during winter it's also usually open a few hours on weekend mornings. Close by is Kurpark, which is apparently the geographical point (*geografischer Mittelpunkt;* Map 41, #13) on which the whole country would pivot – no doubt an untested theory. Across the street is the post office (Map 41, #16; Postamt 8990), with a bus information counter. The train station is 2km south of the town centre.

Things to See & Do

Bad Aussee has a couple of Gothic churches, and the **Kammerhof Museum** *(Map 41, #3; ☎ 525 11-21, Chlumeckyplatz 1; admission €2.95; open 10am-noon & 3pm-6pm daily June-Sept; 3.30pm-6pm Tues, 9.30pm-noon Fri & 10am-noon Sun Oct-May)*, covering local history and salt production, housed in the 17th-century Kammerhof.

Vital Bad Aussee (Map 41, #2; ☎ 553 00-0, w www.VitalBad-Aussee.co.at, Chlumeckyplatz 361) offers a **sauna** (admission €10.20, open 2pm-8pm Wed, Thur, Sat, Sun; 2pm-10pm Mon, Tues, Fri), **swimming pool** (admission € 6.90, open 9am-8pm Mon-Sat, 11am-8pm Sun & holidays) and various health treatments.

Four kilometres north of Bad Aussee is **Altausseer See** (Map 39), a small lake with the village of Altaussee on its western side. From the village you can access the **Altaussee Salzbergwerk** *(☎ 06134-8400; tours €10.90; hourly tours 10am-4pm daily 30 Apr-30 Sept; 10am, noon & 2pm early Apr-29 Apr & Oct; 2.30pm Thur Nov-early Apr)*, where art treasures were secreted during WWII. A scenic road, the Panoramastrasse, climbs most of the way up Loser (1838m), the main peak overlooking the lake. The toll for the return trip is €2.95 for cars plus €3.65 per person, and €3.65 for motorbikes. You'll need snow chains if you wish to travel the road during the winter.

Grundlsee (Map 39), 5km north-east of Bad Aussee, is a longer, thinner lake, with

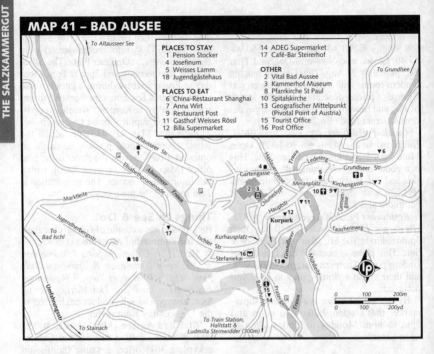

MAP 41 – BAD AUSEE

To Altausseer See

To Grundlsee

PLACES TO STAY
1 Pension Stocker
4 Josefinum
5 Weisses Lamm
18 Jugendgästehaus

PLACES TO EAT
6 China-Restaurant Shanghai
7 Anna Wirt
9 Restaurant Post
11 Gasthof Weisses Rössl
12 Billa Supermarket

14 ADEG Supermarket
17 Café-Bar Steirerhof

OTHER
2 Vital Bad Aussee
3 Kammerhof Museum
8 Pfarrkirche St Paul
10 Spitalskirche
13 Geografischer Mittelpunkt
   (Pivotal Point of Austria)
15 Tourist Office
16 Post Office

Altausseer Str
Elisabethpromenade
Altausseer Traun
Marktleite
Jugendherbergsstr
To Bad Ischl
Gartengasse
Chlumeckyplatz
Hauptstr
Meranplatz
Kirchengasse
Grundlseer Str
Gemsengasse
Hadalargasse
Ledeteeg
Traun
Kurpark
Ischler Str
Kurhausplatz
Stefaniekai
Grundlseer Traun
Tauscherweg
Mühlleite
Bahnhofstr
Praterstr
Traun

To Stainach

To Train Station,
Hallstatt &
Ludmilla Steinwidder (300m)

0   100   200m
0   100   200yd

---

a good viewpoint at its western end as well as walking trails and water sports (including a sailing school). Extending from the eastern tip of the lake are two smaller lakes, **Toplitzsee** (where the Nazis tested weapons and dumped counterfeit currency) and **Kammersee**. Boats tour all three lakes from May to October (€11.30 for the full tour). Call ☎ 8613 for information.

Special Events
Ascension Day, usually in late May/early June, sees the start of the Narzissenfest, lasting three or four days, with processions, music, and animals made of flowers. Entry costs from €7.30 to €10.90 per day.

Places to Stay
Staff at the tourist office will help to find accommodation free of charge, or there is a 24-hour information touch-screen outside nearby. Many homes around Altausseer See and Grundlsee offer cheap private rooms;

which are listed along with pensions and camp grounds in the Bad Aussee brochure available from the tourist office.

HI *Jugendgästehaus (Map 41, #18; ☎ 522 38, fax 522 38-88, e jgh.badaussee@jgh.at, Jugendherbergsstrasse 148)* Beds in 1- to 4-bed rooms with shower €16.75. Reception open all day July-Aug, closed 1pm to 5pm Sept-June. Hostel closed 1 Nov-24 Dec. This modern building is on the town's hill. It's 15 minutes' walk by road, but there are shorter (unlit) footpaths.

Ludmilla Steinwidder (☎ 551 24, e alexandra.steinwidder@cmk.at, Bahnhofstrasse 293) Singles/doubles with private shower €16/32, with shared shower €13.85/27.70. This private house, opposite the Kegelbahn, is 500m towards the train station from town. The elderly hostess is friendly but doesn't speak English.

Josefinum (Map 41, #4; ☎/fax 521 24, Gartengasse 13) Singles/doubles with shower/toilet €18/32, with shared facilities

€16/30. Additional €1.50 for single night stay. This peaceful retreat has 13 singles and three doubles. It's run by nuns so be on your best behaviour (no smoking in bedrooms). Telephone ahead for evening arrival.

Pension Stocker (Map 41, #1; ☎ *524 84, fax 524 83, Altausseer Strasse 245)* Rooms €21.10-23.25 per person. Located 500m north-west of Kurhausplatz, this pension has been extensively renovated and has pristine rooms with shower, toilet and TV and (limited) off-street parking. The large garden overlooks tennis courts.

Weisses Lamm (Map 41, #5; ☎ *524 04, fax 524 04-4, Meranplatz 36)* Singles/doubles €29.10/51. Run by the Strenberger sisters, this friendly place has modern, welcoming rooms with shower, toilet and cable TV.

Places to Eat

China-Restaurant Shanghai (Map 41, #6; ☎ *523 92, Grundlseer Strasse 236)* Meals €4.75-12.50. Open 11.30am-2.30pm & 5.30pm-11pm daily. Come here for inexpensive weekday lunches.

Anna Wirt (Map 41, #7; ☎ *536 86, Kirchengasse 28)* Meals priced by weight. Open 5pm-1am Mon-Sat. This inexpensive Heurigen has good hot and cold buffets – look out for the smoked trout.

Gasthof Weisses Rössl (Map 41, #11; ☎ *521 77, Hauptstrasse 156)* Meals €6.50-14. Open 9am-midnight Fri-Wed. A family-friendly restaurant, this place serves national fare, including fish meals.

Restaurant Post (Map 41, #9; ☎ *535 55, Kirchengasse 162)* Meals €7.20-18. Open 4pm-10pm Tues-Fri, 11am-10pm Sat & Sun. Looking for a traditional restaurant with a wide choice of Austrian food, a garden, and occasional live music? You've found it.

Café-Bar Steirerhof (Map 41, #17; mobile ☎ *0676-799 7979, Ischler Strasse 81)* Pizzas €6.20. Open 8pm-3am daily. Though mostly a drinking venue, this place offers some pretty good pizzas too.

There's an *ADEG* supermarket (Map 41, #14) on Bahnhofstrasse, by the tourist office, and a *Billa* (Map 41, #12) on Hauptstrasse.

Getting There & Away

Bad Aussee is on the rail route from Bad Ischl to Stainach-Irdning, with trains running hourly in both directions.

Buses run every one or two hours from the train station to both lakes (around 15 minutes), calling at Bad Aussee en route; the fare to either lake or to Bad Aussee is €1.50.

GOSAUSEE
☎ 06136 • elev 923m

This small lake (Map 39) is flanked by the impressively precipitous peaks of the Gosaukamm range (2459m). The view is good from the shores (it takes a little over an hour to walk around the lake). The Gosaukammbahn cable car goes up to 1475m (€9.85 return), where there are further views and walking trails. Before reaching the lake you pass through the village of **Gosau** (Map 39), which has its own tourist office (☎ 8295, fax 8255, e tourismus@gosau .gv.at), with an accommodation board situated outside.

Getting There & Away

Gosau is at the junction of the only road to the lake and can be reached by Hwy 166 from Hallstätter See. Bundesbus services run to the lake from Bad Ischl (€4.95, 65 minutes, every one to two hours), via Steeg.

Northern Salzkammergut

The areas two most popular lakes are Traunsee – with the three resorts of Gmunden, Traunkirchen and Ebensee – and Wolfgangsee, which is home to the resorts of St Wolfgang and St Gilgen, and which also provides access to the Schafberg peak (1783m).

TRAUNSEE

The eastern flank of this lake (the deepest in Austria at 192m; Map 39) is dominated by rocky crags, particularly Traunstein (1691m). The resorts are strung along the western shore and are connected by rail. Infrequent Bundesbuses run between them, sometimes

THE SALZKAMMERGUT

continuing to Bad Ischl. Boats operated by Traunsee Schiffahrt (☎ 07612-667 00, W www.traunseeschiffahrt.at, Traungasse 12a, Gmunden) tour the shoreline, from Gmunden to Ebensee, between late April and late October; frequencies peak in July and August. The full one-way trip costs €6.55 (children €5.10). For several journeys, investigate the Punktekarte: €18.20 worth of travel for €15.30. The famous paddle steamer Gisela, once boarded by Franz Josef, takes to the waves on weekends and holidays in July and August (a €1.50 surcharge applies).

GMUNDEN
☎ 07612 • pop 14,000 • elev 440m

Gmunden is known for its castles and ceramics. It was established in 909 and received a town charter in 1278. Gmunden was a former administration centre for both the Habsburgs and the salt trade.

Orientation & Information

The town centre is on the western bank of the Traun River and has the Rathausplatz at its heart. Just to the west is the tourist office (Map 42, #8; ☎ 643 05, fax 714 10, e info .gmunden@upperaustria.or.at), Am Graben

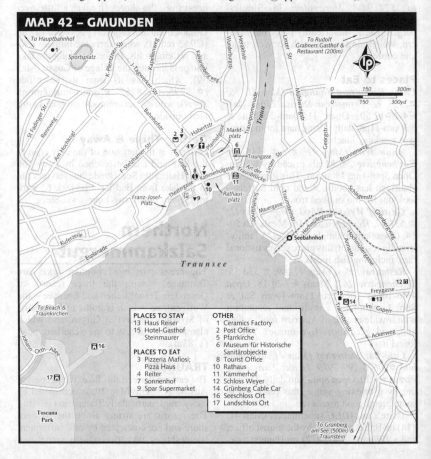

MAP 42 – GMUNDEN

Traunsee

Toscana Park

To Grünberg am See (500m) & Traunstein

PLACES TO STAY	OTHER
13 Haus Reiser	1 Ceramics Factory
15 Hotel-Gasthof Steinmaurer	2 Post Office
	5 Pfarrkirche
PLACES TO EAT	6 Museum für Historische Sanitäräbjeckte
3 Pizzeria Mafiosi; Pizza Haus	8 Tourist Office
4 Reiter	10 Rathaus
7 Sonnenhof	11 Kammerhof
9 Spar Supermarket	12 Schloss Weyer
	14 Grünberg Cable Car
	16 Seeschloss Ort
	17 Landschloss Ort

2, open 8am to noon and 1pm to 6pm weekdays (till 5pm on Friday). In summer there's no lunch break, Friday hours extend to 7pm, and weekend hours are 9am to noon and 4pm to 7pm Saturday, 10am to noon Sunday. Staff at the office will find rooms free of charge.

The post office (Map 42, #2; Postamt 4810) is 200m up the hill on Bahnhofstrasse.

Things to See & Do

Start explorations in the Rathausplatz, which contains the Rathaus, complete with a ceramic glockenspiel that chimes tunes at 10am, noon, 2pm, 4pm and 7pm. More ceramics can be seen in the **Kammerhof** *(Map 42, #11; ☎ 794-244, Kammerhofgasse 8; adult/child €3.05/0.80; open 10am-noon & 2pm-5pm Mon-Sat, 10am-noon Sun and holidays May-Oct)* just to the east. It covers antique Gmunden ceramics and local history and has an art gallery on the top floor.

Porcelain and other valuable artefacts can be seen in the elegant environment of **Schloss Weyer** *(Map 42, #12; ☎ 650 18, Freygasse 27; admission €4.80; open 10am-noon & 2pm-5.30pm Tues-Fri, 10am-1pm Sat May-Sept)*, east of the Traun. For ceramics as it applies to toiletry matters, flush out the **Museum für Historische Sanitärobjeckte** *(Sanitary Objects Museum; Map 42, #6; ☎ 796-294, Traungasse 4; adult/child €3.05/0.80; open 10am-noon & 2pm-5pm Tues-Sat, 10am-2pm Sun & holidays)*. To uncover yet more ceramic secrets, ask the tourist office about tours of local ceramic factories.

North of the Rathausplatz is the **Pfarrkirche** *(parish church; Map 42, #5; ☎ 642 17, Kirchplatz)*, a Gothic building later remodelled as baroque and noted for an altar (dating from 1678) by Thomas Schwanthaler.

Walks along the Esplanade are enjoyable. Head south for 1.5km to reach **Toscana Park** (Map 42), a protected nature area on a peninsula, which contains a castle (Landschloss Ort (Map 42, #17); now a forestry school). Connected by a causeway is another castle, **Seeschloss Ort** *(Map 42, #16; ☎ 654 99, Ort 1; admission free; open 24 hours)*. The 17th-century edifice, jutting into the lake, is clearly visible from the Esplanade and forms a fine picture. The castle has achieved recent

fame through being portrayed as a hotel in a German-language TV series, *Schlosshotel Orth* – fans of the series often ask to stay here, though there are no bedrooms! It has an attractive arcaded courtyard, wherein resides a cafe/restaurant, and a small chapel.

The town has schools for sailing, waterskiing and windsurfing and a **beach** *(adult/concession €4.75/3.20 per day)* just south of Toscana Park.

Gmunden provides access to the **Grünberg** lookout (984m). A cable car (Map 42, #14; €9.60 return) ascends from the east side of the lake, or it's easy to walk up.

Places to Stay

Private rooms are the best deal for budget travellers. Prices start around €15 per person – ask the tourist office for help in tracking them down.

Haus Reiser *(Map 42, #13; ☎/fax 724 25, Freygasse 20)* Singles/doubles €21.80/36.50, €25.50/43.60 if less than three nights. This attractive private home is near Schloss Weyer and has a TV room and garden. There are seven bright, fresh rooms; all but two have bathrooms.

Rudolf Grabners Gasthof *(☎ 641 69, fax 641 69-2100, e rgs.rest@gmx.at, Scharnsteiner Strasse 15)* Singles/doubles €30.60/50.90. Rooms (with shower and toilet) are reasonable value here, and there's plenty of parking spaces.

Hotel-Gasthof Steinmaurer *(Map 42, #15; ☎ 704 88, fax 704 88-31, e steinmaurer@aon.at, Traunsteinstrasse 23)* Singles €44-51, doubles €77-84. This place is by the Grünberg cable car and across the road from a public beach. The variable-sized rooms, with shower, toilet, cable TV, telephone and balcony, have neutral furnishings. The busy restaurant has outside seating.

Grünberg am See *(☎ 777 00, fax 777 00-33, e gruenberg@vpn.at)* Singles €51-60, doubles €95-105. If you have a car (or Traunsee ferries stop close by), this lakeside hotel to the south is a good option. Rooms are large and modern with shower, toilet and TV. The hotel has a small stretch of private beach.

Places to Eat

A large *Spar* supermarket (Map 42, #9) awaits at Kursaalgasse 5, off Franz Josef Platz; it's open 8am to 6.30pm Monday to Thursday, 7.30am to 7.30pm Friday, 7.30am to 5pm Saturday.

Reiter (Map 42, #4; ☎ 642 96, Rinnholz Platz 6) Snacks/meals €1.10-5.50. Open 8am-1pm & 3pm-6pm Mon, Tues, Thur, Fri, 8am-1pm Wed, 7am-noon Sat. This meat store has cheap hot and cold meals and a couple of tables. There are also a few snack stands on the Esplanade.

Pizzeria Mafiosi (Map 42, #3; ☎ 666 02, J-Tagwerker-Strasse 1) Pizza/pasta €3.30-6.60. Open 9am-10pm daily. This small, eat-in or take-away place offers great prices and reasonable quality. Next door is the almost identical *Pizza Haus* (Map 42, #3).

Sonnenhof (Map 42, #7; ☎ 636 39, Theatergasse 4) Mon-Fri set lunch menu €4.75-5.85, mains €5.85-8.75. Open 11.30am-2.30pm & 5.30pm-11.30pm daily. This Chinese restaurant is in a courtyard opposite Rathausplatz.

Grünberg am See (see Places to Stay, earlier) Meals €6.60-16.80. Open 9am-midnight daily. This lakeside hotel restaurant has terrace seating and great fish meals.

Rudolf Grabners Restaurant (see under Places to Stay, earlier) Meals €15-20. Open 10am-2pm & 6pm-midnight Wed-Sun. This place looks deceptively plain from the outside, but it's gourmet quality; reserve ahead.

Getting There & Away

Three rail lines converge on Gmunden. Two loop down from Lambach on the Linz-Salzburg route and terminate at Gmunden Seebahnhof, the closest station to the town centre. However, Lambach is bypassed by express trains, one of these lines is for goods trains only and the other is a slow private line which requires a change at Vorchdorf-Eggenberg. This means that the Gmunden Hauptbahnhof, on the Salzkammergut Attnang–Puchheim to Stainach-Irdning line, is the easiest to get to. The Bad Ischl–Gmunden train fare (€5.20, 45 minutes, hourly) includes the tram ride to the centre.

Getting Around

The Hauptbahnhof is 2km north-west of the town centre: tram G regularly departs from outside it to Franz Josef Platz, including after every train arrival. Single tickets cost €1.35, but a *Tagesnetzkarte* (day card; €1.75) is also valid for the two local bus lines. A family day card costs €2.65.

TRAUNKIRCHEN

☎ 07617 • pop 1500

The attractive hamlet of Traunkirchen (Map 39) sits on a spit of land about halfway along the western shore of the Traunsee.

Information

The small but helpful tourist office in the town centre, the Tourismusbüro (☎ 2234, fax 3340, e traunkirchen@traunsee.com), is part of the Gemeindeamt building at Ortsplatz 1. Staff can provide room listings, information on sights in English and a useful walking map with English text. It's usually open 8am to noon and 1pm to 5pm Monday to Friday, though in July and August hours extend to 8am to 6pm weekdays, 9am to noon and 2pm to 6pm Saturday.

Things to See & Do

The main point of interest in the village is the wooden Fischerkanzel *(Fisherman's Pulpit; ☎ 2234, Klosterplatz 1, open 8am to 5pm or 6pm daily)* in the Pfarrkirche (parish church). It was carved in 1753 and depicts the miracle of the fishes, with the apostles standing in a tub-shaped boat and hauling in fish-laden nets. The composition, colours (mostly silver and gold) and detail (even down to wriggling, bug-eyed fish) create a vivid impression. The church has some fine baroque altars and portraits of the apostles (Judas is notable by his absence). The church was built by the Jesuits before their suppression in 1773.

The spire on the hill belongs to the Johannesbergkapelle, a chapel built in the 14th century or earlier. On the southern side of the hill (the opposite side to the parish church) is a war memorial.

Festival processions take place on 5 January and Corpus Christi.

Mozart chocolates

Looking down into Residenzplatz across to the Dom, Salzburg

Figures from *The Magic Flute* in the gardens of Schloss Hellbrunn, Salzburg

Salzburg at dusk

Horses and carriages in the Residenzplatz, Salzburg

Paracelsus monument

Getridegasse, Salzburg

Edelweiss

Cheerful flower boxes on brightly painted walls are a tradition

Places to Stay & Eat

Ask the staff at the tourist office to help you find accommodation (they don't charge commission).

Strand-Camping (☎/fax 2281, Uferstrasse 46) Price per adult/tent/car €5/3.65/1.10. Open 1 May-30 Sept. This camping ground is by the lake at Viechtau, north of the resort.

Seepension Zimmermann (☎ 2371, fax 2360, Am See 1) Doubles €37-51, plus €3.65 for a single night stay. Open Easter-1 Oct. This place is central and right by the lake, with a superb grassy garden and beach area. Each room is different: all have a shower, most have a toilet.

Gasthof Goldener Hirsch (☎/fax 2260, Ortsplatz 8) Singles/doubles with shower/toilet €25/46. Meals €4.95-8.50. Open 8am-midnight daily May-Sept. This inn is on the main street, 60m from the tourist office. The characterless but adequate rooms often have a balcony. The restaurant has good Austrian food, including fish specialities.

Next to the tourist office there's a *Konsum* supermarket, open 7.30am to noon and 3pm to 6pm Monday to Friday, 7am to noon Saturday.

Getting There & Away

Traunkirchen Ort is on the north-south train line, 12km from Gmunden (€2.95, 12 minutes, hourly). It's a four-minute walk to the centre from this unstaffed train station; take the path that passes under the tracks. The main Traunkirchen station is farther from the resort.

EBENSEE

☎ 06133 • pop 8700 • elev 425m

Ebensee (Map 39) is on the southern shore of the Traunsee. There is little to see in the town itself.

Take the cable car (€11.65/9.85/15.30 up/down/return, hourly) that climbs up to **Feuerkogel** (1592m), where there are walking trails leading across a flattish plateau. Within an hour's walk is Alberfeldkogel (1708m) with an excellent view over the two Langbath lakes. Feuerkogel also provides access to winter **skiing** (€22 for a day pass; easy to medium slopes).

For details of water sports and accommodation, contact the local tourist office (☎ 8016, fax 4655, e info.ebensee@upper austria.or.at), Hauptstrasse 34, by the Landungsplatz train station.

Places to Stay & Eat

The HI *Jugendherberge (☎ 6698, fax 6698-85, e ebensee@jutel.at, Rindbachstrasse 15)* Dorm beds adult/over 19 years €11.65/10.20. Additional €1.50 for a single-night stay. Open Apr-Oct. This renovated hostel is 15 minutes' walk anticlockwise round the lake; each dorm has a bathroom.

Gasthof Auerhahn (☎/fax 5320, Bahnhofstrasse 55) Singles/doubles €24.75/45.10. Meals €5-12. Open 8am-midnight daily. This place by Ebensee train station has bright rooms with a bathroom and cable TV, good Austrian food and a garden. On the 15-minute walk north to the lake (along Bahnhofstrasse and Hauptstrasse) you'll find several affordable restaurants and supermarkets.

Getting There & Away

The train station for the centre and the boat landing stage is Ebensee-Landungsplatz, rather than the larger Ebensee station. The town is 17km north of Bad Ischl (€2.95 by train, 20 minutes, hourly) and the same distance south of Gmunden.

GRÜNAU

If you want to get off the beaten track, consider going to Grünau (Map 39), east of Traunsee. Trains run there from Wels (€6, one hour, two-hourly) and (less convenient) buses run from Gmunden (€5, 45 minutes, every one or two hours).

Tree House Backpacker Hotel (☎ 07616-84 99, fax 85 99, e treehousehotel@hot mail.com, Grünau 525) Bed in 1- to 6-bed room with shower & toilet €15-18 per person. This fine hostel offers a sauna, tennis court, Internet access, two bars, dinners, adventure excursions and adjacent skiing.

ATTERSEE

The largest lake in the Salzkammergut (Map 39) is flanked mostly by hills, with mountains in the south. Resorts cling to the shoreline, offering the usual water leisure activities. The main resort is **Attersee**, which has a museum and a couple of churches. Its tourist office (☎ 07666-7719, fax 07666-7719-19, e info.attersee@netway.at) is in the centre at Nussdorferstrasse 15; staff will help you to find accommodation.

Attersee-Schifffahrt boats make two circuits of the lake: one covering the north (€5.85, 75 minutes) from mid-April to late October, the other circling the south (€10.20, 2½ hours) from late April to mid-September. Both tours stop at Attersee town.

Getting There & Away
Two lakeside towns, Attersee and Schörfling, are connected to the rail network, each by a line branching from the main Linz-Salzburg route (though only regional trains stop): for Kammer-Schörfling change at Vöcklabruck and for Attersee town change at Vöcklamarkt.

WOLFGANGSEE
This lake (Map 39) plays host to hordes of summer and weekend visitors escaping the city and is easily accessible from Salzburg. In addition to the two main resorts, St Wolfgang and St Gilgen, it has **Strobl** on the eastern shore (population 2750), a pleasant but unremarkable place. It's at the start of a scenic toll road (€2.95 per car and per person) to Postalm (1400m). Wherever you stay, ask about the local Gästekarte.

A ferry service operates from Strobl to St Gilgen, stopping at various points en route. Services are from early May to late October, but more frequent during the high season from early June to early September. The journey from St Wolfgang to St Gilgen (€4.25) takes 40 minutes and boats sail approximately hourly from 8.45am to 5.45pm (half-hourly till 6.45pm in the high season). In the other direction, the first departure from St Gilgen is at 9.15am. Holders of the Austrian Vorteilscard get a 15% fare reduction.

A historic path, the pilgrim's way, connects St Gilgen and St Wolfgang via the western shore. It's a half-day walk.

Schafberg
Wolfgangsee is dominated by the 1783m Schafberg mountain (Map 39) on its northern shore. At the summit you'll find a hotel, a restaurant and phenomenal views over mountains and lakes (especially Mondsee, Attersee and, of course, Wolfgangsee). If you don't fancy the three to four hour walk from St Wolfgang, ascend by the cogwheel railway which runs from early May to late October. Departures are approximately hourly between 8.25am and 5.40pm but the trip is so popular that you probably won't be able to get on the next train to leave: queue early, purchase a ticket for a specified train and then go for a wander along the lake or around St Wolfgang until your train departs.

It takes 40 minutes to reach the top station, which is only a few metres short of the hotel and viewing point. The fare is €10.90 up or €18.20 return; holders of the Austrian Vorteilscard get a 15% fare reduction.

ST WOLFGANG
☎ 06138 • pop 2800 • elev 549m
St Wolfgang (Map 39) was founded in 976 by the Bishop of Regensburg, Germany (who was later canonised) and has achieved renown as a place of pilgrimage.

Orientation & Information
The main streets of Pilgerstrasse and Michael Pacher Strasse join at the pilgrimage church. A road tunnel bypasses the village centre, and there are carparks at either end.

The tourist office (☎ 2239-0, fax 2239-81, e info@stwolfgang.at), Au 140, is at the eastern tunnel entrance. Opening days and hours vary through the year; in peak summer it's open daily, in winter it's closed afternoons on Wednesday and Saturday and all day Sunday.

Things to See & Do
The major sight is the incredible **pilgrimage church** *(Wallfahrtskirche, ☎ 2321; open 9am-6pm daily)*, built in the 14th and 15th centuries. It's virtually a gallery of religious art, with several altars (from Gothic to baroque), a showy pulpit, a fine organ and many statues and paintings. The best piece is

the winged high altar built by Michael Pacher between 1471 and 1481, which has astonishing detail on the carved figures and Gothic designs. The church wardens were once so protective that the wings were kept closed except for important festivals. Now they are always open, except for eight weeks before Easter.

The baroque double altar by Thomas Schwanthaler is also worth a look. It was commissioned in 1675, reputedly to replace Pacher's effort which was considered old-fashioned and thus slated for destruction. According to an apocryphal story, it was Schwanthaler himself who persuaded the then abbot to retain Pacher's high altar.

Beside the church is a bronze **fountain** from 1515. A lengthy inscription includes rather condescending advice to poor pilgrims: if they can't afford wine, they should 'make merry' with the fountain's waters.

A tourist office booklet (free) details the many **water sports** on offer. A few minutes' walk anticlockwise round the lake is the start of the Schafberg railway.

Pacher's Religious Art

Michael Pacher was the dominant figure in Austrian religious art in the 15th century. He was born in Bruneck (South Tirol, now in Italy) in 1435 and died in Salzburg in 1498. His work was rooted in traditional Bruneck art but he also absorbed Dutch and, in particular, northern Italian influences. Pacher was a master of perspective and colouring and gave an impression of fluidity and movement to his statue groups. This is seen in his altar in the pilgrimage church in St Wolfgang. In creating this altar, as in several others, Pacher was aided by his brother Friedrich.

Pacher's style was much imitated – an example is the impressive altar in Kefermarkt, Upper Austria. His paintings and carvings are found in many museums, such as the Landesmuseum Ferdinandeum in Innsbruck (where Friedrich Pacher's work is also featured) and the Orangery of the Unteres Belvedere in Vienna.

Places to Stay

Camping Appesbach (☎ 2206, fax 2206-33, Au 99) Price per adult/tent/car €4.50/1.85/3. Open Easter-1 Oct. This camp ground is on the lakeside, 1km from St Wolfgang in the direction of Strobl.

St Wolfgang has some good *private rooms* (€12-22 per person), either in village homes or in farmhouses on the surrounding hills. Lists are available from the staff at the tourist office who will phone places on your behalf.

Haus am See (☎ 2224, Michael Pacher Strasse 98) Singles €15-25.50, doubles €18.20-46.50. Open May-Oct. Opposite the tourist office and by the lake, this pension has some bargain rooms available.

Gästehaus Raudaschl (☎ 2329, fax 23 29-6, e raudaschl-158@interaktive.com, Pilgerstrasse 4) Singles/doubles €25/46. Reception open 9am-6pm year-round. This central place offers convenient, homey, reasonably comfortable rooms with shower and toilet.

Im Weissen Rössl (☎ 2306-0, fax 2306-41, e office@weissesroessl.at, Im Stöckl 74) Singles €98-118, doubles €140-200. This is St Wolfgang's most famous hotel which, as the White Horse Inn, was the setting for Ralph Benatzky's operetta of the same name. It has rustic or modern-style rooms with all amenities. Service is good and the restaurant is highly regarded.

Places to Eat

Buy picnic materials at several supermarkets along the main street or at the larger **Konsum** supermarket 200m from the Schafberg cogwheel railway ticket office.

The main street has plenty of eating options ranging from cheap snack joints to quaint touristy restaurants. The centre is compact enough to explore before making a choice, so just follow your nose.

Pizzeria Mirabella (☎ 2353, Pilgerstrasse 152) Pizza €5.45-9.45. Open 11.30am-2.30pm & 5.30pm-10.30pm daily. This place has 1st floor tables overlooking the street.

Im Weissen Rössl (☎ 2306-0, Im Stöckl 74) This famous inn has two choices: the highly regarded Romantik Restaurant upstairs (mains €15.90-22.90, kitchen 6.30pm

THE SALZKAMMERGUT

to 9.30pm nightly) or the more egalitarian Seestüberl, right on the lakeside (€10-16.40, open 11.30am to 10pm daily).

Getting There & Away

The only road to St Wolfgang approaches from the east from Strobl. The Bundesbus service from St Wolfgang to St Gilgen (€2.95) and Salzburg (€6.55) goes via Strobl, where you usually have to change buses. Wolfgangsee ferries stop at the village centre (stop: Markt) and at the Schafberg railway.

ST GILGEN

☎ 06227 • pop 3000 • elev 550m

The ease of access to St Gilgen (Map 39), 29km from Salzburg, has boosted its popularity. Apart from the very scenic setting, there's not too much to see in the town.

Information

The local tourist office (☎ 2348, fax 726 79, e stgilgen@ping.at) is in the Rathaus at Mozartplatz 1. It's open daily from June to mid-September, Monday through Friday and Saturday morning for the rest of the year.

Things to See & Do

Near the Rathaus at Ischler Strasse 15 is the house where Mozart's mother was born, which now contains a few memorials to the musician (€0.75, open mid-June–mid-Sept except Monday). The **Muzikinstumente-Museum der Völker** *(folk music instrument museum;* ☎ *8235, Sonnenburggasse 1; admission €3.30; open 9am-11am & 3pm-7pm Tues-Sun 1 June-15 Oct; 9am-11am & 3pm-6pm Mon-Fri 16 Oct-6 Jan; 9am-11am & 3pm-6pm Mon-Thur, 9am-11am Fri & 3pm-6pm Sun 7 Jan-31 May)* has two rooms filled with obscure musical instruments from around the world, plus (summer only) a 25-minute film on Mozart.

Like all lakeside resorts, St Gilgen offers **water sports** such as windsurfing, water-skiing and sailing. The Erlebnisbad *(☎ 7147, Mondseer Strasse 12)* just to the north of the boat station, has a Strandbad (beach, admission €2.95, open 9am-8pm daily early June-31 Aug, 2pm-8pm Tues-Sun 1 Sept-late Oct)

and a Hallenbad (indoor swimming pool, admission €5.85; open same hours as the Strandbad, plus varying hours for most of the rest of the year). A little further, beyond the yacht club, is a small, free beach with a grassy area.

The mountain rising over the resort is **Zwölferhorn** (Map 39; 1520m); a cable car (€10.90/ 16 one-way/return) will whisk you to the top where there are good views and walks. Skiers ascend in winter.

Places to Stay & Eat

Jugendgästehaus Schafbergblick (☎ 2365, fax 2365-75, e *jgh.stgilgen@oejhv.or.at, Mondseestrasse 7)* Singles €21.90, bed in 10-bed dorm €11. Check-in noon-1pm & 5pm-7pm, night-time access key provided. Closed two weeks early Jan and (usually) one week before Christmas. This HI hostel is almost like a hotel in its facilities and attitude, though it does receive the usual school groups. All rooms/dorms have shower; some have private toilet and lake view. Two- and four-bed dorms are also available. Breakfast is an extensive buffet. Staying here also gives free entry to the swimming pool.

Staff at the tourist office will help you to find somewhere to stay, or there's an accommodation board, accessible 24 hours every day, opposite the bus station. The cheaper places (private rooms etc) are mostly away from the centre.

Gasthof Rosam (☎ 2591, e *rosam@aon .at, Frontfestgasse 2)* Singles €24.75-49.50, doubles €39.25-49.50. Open Easter–late Oct. Just two minutes from the St Gilgen boat station, this family-run place has fresh, new-looking rooms with shower, toilet and TV. The small restaurant area serves large portions of good Austrian food for €5.85 to €9.90. The kitchen is open 11am to 2pm and 5pm to 9pm, closed on Wednesday in April and May.

San Giorgio (☎ 203 50, Ischler Strasse 18) Meals €5.40-9.10. Open 5pm-11pm Mon, Tues & Thur-Sat, 11am-2pm Sun & holidays, closed Wed. This Italian restaurant by the lake has eat-in (inside or in the garden) or take-away food. The interior is supposed to evoke the outdoors, complete with tree murals, street lamps and a gravel floor. Pizza is the meal of choice here. There's also a bar/disco downstairs, open from 9pm. The owners claim it's the oldest disco in Austria – at 60 years old, that's maybe three times the age of most of the clientele.

Zur Chinesischen Mauer (☎ 7029, Schwarzenbrunner Strasse 3) Meals €5.75-10. Open 11.30am-3pm & 5.30pm-11.30pm daily. This Chinese restaurant is just off Mozartplatz, and offers the usual weekday lunch menus for around €5.75.

Gasthof Zur Post (☎ 2157, fax 2157-600, e office@gasthofzurpost.at, Mozartplatz 8) Singles €30-33, doubles €57-80; add €3.65 per person for stays under three nights. Meals €6.55-13.85. Closed Thur to 5pm and Wed except from June-early Sept. This rustic-style chalet has a pictorial scene painted on the facade. Inside, it's like two hotels. The first floor has the quaint, old-fashioned rooms you'd expect, though the upper floors have been completely modernised (quite tastefully too). All rooms have a shower, toilet and cable TV. The owners plan to put in a lift. The Austrian and regional food is also pretty good.

Getting There & Away
St Gilgen is 50 minutes from Salzburg by Bundesbus (€4.40), with hourly departures until early evening; some buses continue on to Stobl and Bad Ischl. The bus station is near the base station of the cable car. Highway 154 provides a scenic route north to Mondsee. For details on the ferry service to/from St Wolfgang, see the Wolfgangsee section earlier in this chapter.

MONDSEE
☎ 06232 • pop 3000 • elev 493m
This lake (Map 39) is noted for its warm water; coupled with its closeness to Salzburg (30km away), this factor makes it a popular lake for swimming and other water sports. The village of Mondsee is on the northern tip of the crescent-shaped lake. The tourist office (☎ 2270, fax 4470, e info@mondsee .org) is at Dr Franz Müller Strasse 3, between the church and the lake. It's open daily in summer and weekdays the rest of the year.

Segelschule Mondsee (☎ 3548-200, fax 3548-232, w www.segelschule-mondsee.at), Robert Baum Promenade 3, is the largest **sailing school** in Austria. It offers sailing and windsurfing courses, plus boat/board rental costing from €9.45/7.30 per hour.

The main cultural interest in the village is the 15th-century **parish church**. The baroque facade was added in 1740. This large church achieved brief fame when featured in the wedding scenes of *The Sound of Music* movie, but it's worth visiting in any case for its many altars and statues.

Next door, in part of the former abbey, is a **museum**, the Museum Mondseeland und Pfahlbaumuseum *(Wrede Platz; adult/student €2.95/1.50; open 10am-5pm or 6pm Tues-Sun 1 May-early Oct, 10am-5pm Sat-Sun and holidays mid-late Oct)* devoted to local history and crafts, including archaeological finds from the Mondsee Culture of the late Stone Age and early Bronze Age.

Places to Stay & Eat
For lists of hotels and restaurants, ask at the tourist office.

Jugendgästehaus (☎ 2418, fax 2418-75, e jgh.mondsee@oejhv.or.at, Krankenhausstrasse 9) Singles/doubles with shower & toilet €25.50/36.50, beds in 4-bed dorms €12.35-16. Open 1 Feb–mid-Dec, reception open 8am-1pm & 5pm-7pm Mon-Fri, 5pm-7pm Sat-Sun & holidays. This HI hostel has 70 beds.

Gasthof Grüner Baum (☎ 2314, fax 7602, Herzog Odilo Strasse 39) Singles/doubles €36.50/50 (€40/57 if less than three nights). Completely renovated in 1999, the large rooms are clean, modern and have shower, toilet and TV.

Gasthof Blaue Traube (☎ 2237, fax 2237-7, e blaue.traube@magnet.at, Marktplatz 1) Singles/doubles with shower & toilet €36/57. Reach the cheerful, comfortable rooms via a sumptuous swirling staircase – which you'll have to use as there's no lift. The restaurant serves Austrian food for €6 to €14.60.

There's a *Spar* supermarket on Rainerstrasse 5. On Marktplatz are several places with good atmosphere and food.

Imbissstube (☎ 3512, M Guggenbichler Strasse 5) Snacks/meals €1.85-9.45. Open 8am-10pm Mon-Sat. Behind the post office, this simple place serves sausage snacks and Austrian meals; it has stand-up and sit-down sections, as well as outside seating.

Seestern-Fische (☎ 6009, Herzog Odilo Strasse 25) Meals €6.40-16.35. Open 11.30am-2pm Tues-Wed, 11.30am-2pm &

6pm-midnight Thurs-Sat. This restaurant is known for its good seafood.

Getting There & Away

Plenty of Bundesbus routes run to/from Mondsee, including an hourly service from Salzburg (€4.40) that takes 40 to 55 minutes. However, there are only three buses a day to St Gilgen (€4.40, 20 minutes).

Upper Austria

Upper Austria (Oberösterreich) occupies almost 12,000 sq km and is home to more than 1.3 million people. The province's most important holiday area contains the lakes and mountains of the south-west (see the Salzkammergut chapter). Elsewhere, Upper Austria offers abbeys, quaint and attractive towns in the north and east and a disturbing reminder of Nazi occupation, the Mauthausen concentration camp. Adolf Hitler was born in the province, in Braunau am Inn. His favourite city was Linz, for which he had great (unrealised) plans, including making it the architectural jewel of the Danube.

Orientation & Information

Upper Austria is mostly flat, with the Danube running roughly west to east. The river is an important trade artery, though it is less scenic than the stretch in Lower Austria.

The provincial capital is Linz, also the location of the provincial tourist office, Oberösterreich Tourismus (Map 44, #44; ☎ 0732-77 12 64, fax 0732-60 02 20, e info@upperaustria.at, w www.tiscover.com/upperaustria), Schillerstrasse 50, A-4010 Linz.

Getting Around

Regional transport in Upper Austria is linked under Oberösterreichischer Verkehrsverbund tickets. Prices depend on the number of zones you travel in, and you can buy single tickets as well as daily, weekly, monthly or yearly passes. If you have a city pass for Linz, Wels or Steyr, you get a one-zone discount for regional travel. For information, call ☎ 0732-61 76 17 or check w www.ooevv.at.

Linz

☎ 0732 • pop 207,500 • elev 266m

Though Linz is an industrial town and a busy Danube port, you'll find a surprisingly

charming and picturesque old town centre. Unfortuantely, the southern suburbs show a depressing skyline of belching smokestacks due to Linz's important industries: iron, steel and chemicals.

In Roman times Linz was a fortified camp called Lentia which soon achieved importance for its position on trade routes. Linz was granted the status of regional capital in 1490 by Friedrich III, who was then a resident of the town.

Orientation

Linz lies on both sides of the Danube, with the old town and most attractions on the south bank. Hauptplatz, an elongated, spacious square, is the hub; it is mostly car-free and abuts Landstrasse, a shopping street with a pedestrian-only section. The Hauptbahnhof is about 1km to the south and has a range of facilities, including shops and places to eat.

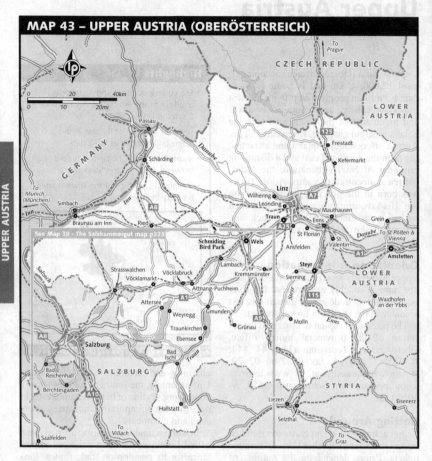

MAP 43 – UPPER AUSTRIA (OBERÖSTERREICH)

CZECH REPUBLIC

To Prague

LOWER AUSTRIA

GERMANY

To Munich (München)

Passau

Schärding

Danube

Freistadt

Kefermarkt

125

Simbach

Inn

Braunau am Inn

Ried

Inn

A8

Wilhering

Linz

Leonding

Traun

A7

Mauthausen

Enns

Grein

To St Pölten & Vienna

Danube

A25

St Florian

St Valentin

A1

Amstetten

Ansfelden

See Map 39 - The Salzkammergut map p323

Schmiding Bird Park

Wels

Lambach

Kremsmünster

Sierning

Steyr

LOWER AUSTRIA

Strasswalchen

Vöcklamarkt

Vöcklabruck

Attnang-Puchheim

A1

115

Waidhofen an der Ybbs

Salzach

Attersee

Weyregg

Gmunden

A9

Molln

Enns

Steyr

Traunkirchen

Grünau

Ebensee

A8

Salzburg

Bad Ischl

Traun

STYRIA

Bad Reichenhall

Berchtesgaden

A10

SALZBURG

Liezen

Eisenerz

Hallstatt

Selzthal

To Villach

Saalfelden

To Graz

0 20 40km
0 10 20mi

Information

Tourist Offices The tourist office (Map 44, #17; ☎ 7070-1777, fax 77 28 73, e tourist .info@linz.at), Hauptplatz 1, is open 8am to 7pm Monday to Friday, 9am to 7pm Saturday, and 10am to 7pm Sunday and holidays. From 1 November to 30 April it closes an hour earlier. Staff will search out accommodation free of charge.

The Sparda Bank in the Hauptbahnhof has a free telephone line to the tourist office. It's open 8am to 6pm Monday to Friday, 8am to 2pm Saturday, and there's a computer touch screen outside with tourist information.

Personal callers are welcome at the provincial tourist office (Map 44, #44; see the Orientation & Information section at the start of this chapter), which is open 8.30am to noon and 1pm to 4.30pm Monday to Thursday, 8.30am to noon Friday.

The tourist office and hotels sell the Linz City Ticket (€20), which will probably save you money. It provides a restaurant voucher worth €10, a free city tour and free admission to a few attractions, including the Ars Electronica Center. The Junior version for children aged 6 to 15 years costs €8 (no meal voucher). You could instead (or as well) acquire the Linzer Museumskarte, giving entry to Linz's 10 museums for just €7.30.

Post & Communications The main post office (Map 44, #54; Postamt 4020), opposite and to the west of the Hauptbahnhof, is open 7am to 10pm on Monday to Friday and 9am to 6pm on Saturday. There's another post office (Map 44, #20; Postamt 4010) on Domgasse.

Email & Internet Access There's the Bignet internet.cafe (Map 44, #28) at Promenade 3, which is open 10am to midnight daily, but a much cheaper place is Chat.net (Map 44, #2) in the Lentia 2000 shopping centre, Blutenstrasse 13. It's open 9.30am to 9.30pm Monday to Friday, 9.30am to 6.30pm Saturday, and charges €1.45 for 50 minutes. You can also log on at the Ars Electronica Center (see the Things to See & Do section).

Travel Agencies American Express (Map 44, #45; ☎ 66 90 13), Bürgerstrasse 14, is open 9am to 5.30pm Monday to Friday, 9am to noon Saturday. It has financial and travel agency services and charges no commission for cashing AmEx travellers cheques.

Ökista (Map 44, #30; ☎ 77 58 93) is at Herrenstrasse 7; it's open 9am to 5.30pm Monday to Friday.

Medical Services The Krankenhaus (hospital; Map 44, #38; ☎ 78 06-0) is 1km east of the town centre at Krankenhausstrasse 9. If offers emergency treatment, as does the Unfallkrankenhaus (Map 44, #52; ☎ 69 20-0), Blumauerplatz 1.

South Bank

Consider following the walking tour of the town centre outlined in the *Linz treasure trail* pamphlet, available from the tourist office (in English).

The large Hauptplatz is surrounded by baroque buildings, including the **Altes Rathaus** (Map 44, #17), which retains some earlier Renaissance elements. The Altes Rathaus also houses **Linz-Genesis** *(Map 44, #18; ☎ 7070-1920, Rathausgasse 8, free*

entry; open 9am-1pm & 2pm-6pm Mon-Fri), a museum detailing the town's history; the displays activate themselves as you approach. A focal point of the square is the **Dreifaltigkeitssäule** (trinity column; Map 44, #15) sculpted in Salzburg marble in 1723. This 20m-high baroque pillar commemorates deliverance from war, fire and plague. Hauptplatz hosts a **farmers' market** from 9am to 2pm on Tuesday and Friday.

Just west of Hauptplatz is the **Landhaus** (Map 44, #25) on Klosterstrasse, the seat of the provincial government. It was constructed between 1564 and 1571. Wander into the arcaded courtyard to see the **Planet Fountain** (1582), which predated the arrival of the great German astronomer Johann Kepler, who taught for 14 years in a college once sited here.

Up the hill to the west of Hauptplatz is **Schloss Linz** (Map 44, #12). This castle has been periodically rebuilt since 799 and provides a good view of the many church spires in the centre. Friedrich III once resided here. It also houses the **Schlossmuseum** *(☎ 77 44 19, Tummelplatz 10; admission €3.65; open 9am-6pm Tues-Fri, 10am-4pm Sat, Sun & holidays)*. Displays cover art, artefacts and weapons, starting with the Bronze Age, passing through Roman times and winding up in the 19th century. Temporary exhibitions may cost extra.

The enormous, graceless, neo-Gothic **Neuer Dom** *(New Cathedral; Map 44, #40; ☎ 77 78 85, Herrenstrasse 26; open approx 7am-8pm daily)*, built in 1855, features exceptional stained glass, including a window depicting the history of the town. At 131m high, its spire is the second-highest in Austria after Stephansdom in Vienna. The **Alter Dom** *(Old Cathedral; Map 44, #22; ☎ 770 866-29, Domgasse 3; open 7am-noon & 3pm-7pm daily)* is where Anton Bruckner served as church organist. The style is 17th-century baroque, with the usual stucco and marble decor.

Other churches of interest include the **Minoritenkirche** *(Minorite Church; Map 44, #26; ☎ 7720-1175, Klosterstrasse 7; open 8am-11am daily)* featuring paintings on the side altars by Johann Schmidt of Krems, and

UPPER AUSTRIA

UPPER AUSTRIA

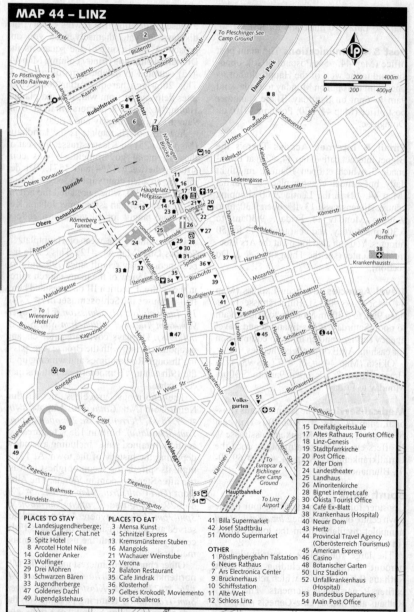

MAP 44 – LINZ

15 Dreifaltigkeitssäule
17 Altes Rathaus; Tourist Office
18 Linz-Genesis
19 Stadtpfarrkirche
20 Post Office
22 Alter Dom
24 Landestheater
25 Landhaus
26 Minoritenkirche
28 Bignet internet cafe
30 Ökista Tourist Office
34 Café Ex-Blatt
38 Krankenhaus (Hospital)
40 Neuer Dom
43 Hertz
44 Provincial Travel Agency
   (Oberösterreich Tourismus)
45 American Express
46 Casino
48 Botanischer Garten
50 Linz Stadion
52 Unfallkrankenhaus
   (Hospital)
53 Bundesbus Departures
54 Main Post Office

PLACES TO STAY
2 Landesjugendherberge;
  Neue Gallery; Chat.net
5 Spitz Hotel
8 Arcotel Hotel Nike
14 Goldener Anker
23 Wolfinger
29 Drei Mohren
31 Schwarzen Bären
33 Jugendherberge
47 Goldenes Dachl
49 Jugendgästehaus

PLACES TO EAT
3 Mensa Kunst
4 Schnitzel Express
13 Kremsmünsterer Stuben
16 Mangolds
21 Wachauer Weinstube
27 Verona
32 Balaton Restaurant
35 Cafe Jindrak
36 Klosterhof
37 Gelbes Krokodil; Moviemento
39 Los Caballeros
41 Billa Supermarket
42 Josef Stadtbräu
51 Mondo Supermarket

OTHER
1 Pöstlingbergbahn Talstation
6 Neues Rathaus
7 Ars Electronica Center
9 Brucknerhaus
10 Schiffsstation
11 Alte Welt
12 Schloss Linz

the **Stadtpfarrkirche** *(parish church; Map 44, #19;* ☎ *77 61 20; Pfarrplatz, open daylight hours)* with a tomb containing the heart of Friedrich III.

Linz has its share of greenery. **Danube Park** trails alongside the river and boasts unusual metal sculptures. The **Botanischer Garten** *(botanical garden; Map 44, #48;* ☎ *7070-1880, Roseggerstrasse 20; adult/child €0.75/free; open 8am-5pm daily Nov-Feb, 8am-6pm Mar & Oct, 8am-7pm Apr & Sept, 7.30am-7.30pm May-Aug)* flaunts a plethora of cacti and orchids.

North Bank

Clearly visible from the old town is the **Pöstlingberg** (537m) on the north bank, providing fine views. At the summit is a twin-spired baroque church dating from the 18th century. The walk up is gentle, or you can take the Pöstlingbergbahn that runs every 20 or 30 minutes till 8pm. It costs €3.20 return (or €5.10 including unlimited rides on tram No 3 – get this ticket from the tourist office). Tram No 3 goes from the Hauptbahnhof, via the town centre to the lower station (Pöstlingbergbahn Talstation; Map 44, #1). At the top is a **grotto railway** *(*☎ *7801-7506, Am Pöstlingberg 16; adult/child €4/2.05; open 10am-5pm daily Sat before Easter-2 Nov, 10am-6pm May-Aug)*. This includes a short trundle past scenes from fairy stories, followed by a walk along a mini fairy-tale street.

At the northern side of the Nibelungen Brücke (bridge) is the **Ars Electronica Center** *(Map 44, #7;* ☎ *7272-0, Hauptstrasse 2; adult/concession €6.20/3.30; open 10am-6pm Wed-Sun)*, exhibiting interactive computer wizardry and giving free Internet access. There are lots of computer simulations at this self-proclaimed 'Museum of the Future', with numerous staff on hand to explain what's going on. An impressive exhibit is the Cave of Virtual Reality, which allows you to take a 3D trip though space and time (explore the universe, visit a Renaissance city). There's also a virtual reality flying machine that will whisk you around the museum and over virtual landscapes (expect to queue).

Opposite, a **flea market** springs forth in front of the Neues Rathaus *(Map 44, #6)* from 6am to 2pm on Saturday.

The **Neue Gallery** *(Map 44, #2;* ☎ *7070-3601, Blütenstrasse 15; adult/concession €4.40/2.20, depending on exhibitions; open 10am-6pm Fri-Wed, 10am-10pm Thur Oct-June, 10am-6pm Mon-Wed & Fri, 10am-10pm Thur, 10am-1pm Sat late June-31 Aug)* exhibits a moderate collection of German and Austrian art from the 19th and 20th centuries. At the end of 2002 the collection will shift to a new building across the river near the Brucknerhaus, re-christening itself Lentos Kunstmuseum in the process.

Special Events

The famous Bruckner Festival (Brucknerfest; ☎ 77 52 30, fax 7612-201, **e** kassa@liva.co.at) is held during September. Concerts (seats €15 to €88, standing-room €3.65 or €7.30) are held primarily at the city's premier music venue, Brucknerhaus (Map 44, #9; ☎ 7612-0, **w** www.brucknerhaus.at), Untere Donaulände 7. It's preceded by the Ars Electronica Festival (a technology exhibition), which takes place in early September. Both festivals coincide with Klangwolke (cloud of sound) concerts in Danube Park, when there's free music and lasers sear the night sky.

The Linz city festival, starting in late May or early June and running for three or four weeks, brings free rock, jazz and folk to the central district. In late July there's a street artists' festival.

Places to Stay – Budget

Camping *Pleschinger See (*☎ *24 78 70)* Price per adult/tent €3.30/3.30, showers €0.75. Open May-Sept. This site is in a protected area (no motor vehicles) about 5km north-east of the Nibelungen Brücke. It's on the north bank by the lake and the Danube cycle track.

Pichlinger See (☎ *30 53 14, fax 30 53 14-4, Wiener Bundesstrasse 937)* Price per adult/tent €3.85/3.65. Open Mar-Nov. This site is about 16km south-east of town; infrequent Bundesbuses run there from the Hauptbahnhof. It has a restaurant.

Hostels There are three HI hostels in Linz.

The *Landesjugendherberge (Map 44, #2;* ☎ *73 70 78, fax 73 70 78-15,* **e** *ljh-linz .post@ooe.gv.at, Blütenstrasse 19-23)* Bed in two- to five-bed rooms €9.45/7.65 over/ under 19 years, additional €1.85 in winter. Breakfast €1.50. Check in 7am-7pm Mon-Fri, 7am-9am & 5pm-7pm Sat & Sun. Reception may stay open till 10pm if it's busy, so phone ahead. This hostel is in a tower block on the north bank – take the lift up within the multistorey car park. It's intended for groups but individuals can stay. Rooms have private shower and toilet.

The *Jugendherberge (Map 44, #33;* ☎ *78 27 20, fax 78 17 894,* **e** *zentrale@jutel.at, Kapuzinerstrasse 14)* Bed in room with private shower & toilet €12/9.85 over/under 19 years, breakfast €2.20. No curfew. Check-in 6pm-8pm, or later by arrangement. Usually closed Oct-Feb, but phone to check. This hostel is small, central and more personal. There's a washing machine and a common room.

The *Jugendgästehaus (Map 44, #49;* ☎ *66 44 34, fax 66 44 34-75,* **e** *jgh.linz@ oejhv.or.at, Stanglhofweg 3)* Singles/doubles €26.75/40, four-bed dorms €14.40 per person. Check-in 9am-4pm & 6pm-9pm Mon-Fri, 6pm-9pm Sat & Sun. Closed 22 Dec-7 Jan. This hostel is housed in a modern building near Linz Stadion. Both the rooms and the dorms have private shower and toilet.

Hotels & Pensions There aren't many budget places in town.

Goldenes Dachl (Map 44, #47; ☎*/fax 758 97, Hafnerstrasse 27)* Singles €18.90, doubles €33.50-37.80, breakfast €2.20-3.65 per person. Reception open 10.30am-2pm & 5pm-11pm Mon-Fri, 5pm-11pm Sat, and at other times with advance notice. This small Gasthof is one block south of the Neuer Dom. The newish-looking rooms are good value but have a shared shower.

Wienerwald Hotel (☎ *77 78 81, fax 77 78 81-30, Freinbergstrasse 18)* Singles/doubles €21.10/35.60. This hotel-restaurant is next to the western terminus of bus No 26 (last one leaves town at 7.46pm!), 1.5km from the town centre. It has a restaurant serving the usual chicken dishes. The rooms, all with shared shower, are reasonably large and decent value, and once re-building has finished there'll be some with private shower and toilet. Credit cards are accepted and there's ample parking. Reserve ahead.

Places to Stay – Mid-Range & Top End

Goldener Anker (Map 44, #14; ☎*/fax 77 10 88, Hofgasse 5)* Singles/doubles with private shower and toilet €36/59, without €23/43. Breakfast €5.45 per person. This place off Hauptplatz is attractively priced considering its central location, on a lively street with cafes and bars. Rooms are plain but pleasant, and have TV.

Schwarzen Bären (Map 44, #31; ☎ *77 24 77, fax 77 24 77-47, Herrenstrasse 9-11)* Singles €57-66, doubles €72-95. This mid-range hotel provides comfortable rooms in a convenient location. The higher prices are for re-modelled rooms with designer open-plan bathrooms. All rooms have private shower, toilet and satellite TV. Garage parking costs €5.85 per night.

Wolfinger (Map 44, #23; ☎ *77 32 91, fax 77 32 91-55,* **e** *wolfinger@austria-classic -hotels.at, Hauptplatz 19)* Singles €62-77, doubles €95-110. This stylish hotel is in the pedestrian zone. The historical ambience is accentuated by archways, stuccowork and period furniture. Rooms have a shower, toilet and TV. The best rates are at weekends.

Arcotel Hotel Nike (Map 44, #8; ☎ *76 26-0, fax 76 26-2,* **e** *nike@arcotel.co.at, Untere Donaulände 9)* Singles €66-117, doubles €73-160. This hotel in tower block next to the Brucknerhaus offers good views, rooms with shower, toilet and TV, and an indoor swimming pool.

Spitz Hotel (Map 44, #5; ☎ *73 64 41-0, fax 73 08 41, Fiedlerstrasse 6)* Singles/doubles €72/120. A Best Western hotel with a modern ambience, all rooms have, of course, a bathroom and TV.

Drei Mohren (Map 44, #29; ☎ *77 26 26-0, fax 77 26 26-6,* **e** *hotel.drei.mohr en@aon.at, Promenade 17)*. Singles €73-88, doubles €102-120. Small-scale and with personal service, this place is central and has free parking. All rooms have a shower, toilet and TV.

Places to Eat

Linz is the home of a tempting almond pastry and raspberry cake, the Linzer torte. A good place to sample it is *Cafe Jindrak* *(Map 44, #35;* ☎ *77 92 58, Herrenstrasse 22)*, open 8am to 6pm Monday to Saturday.

Self-caterers can shop at supermarkets, including a *Mondo* (Map 44, #51) at Blumauerplatz and a *Billa* (Map 44, #41) on Landstrasse. There are plenty of cheap Würstel (sausage) stands lining the Volksgarten on Landstrasse. You'll also have no trouble finding a Chinese restaurant with the usual bargain-price weekday lunches.

Mensa Kunst (Map 44, #3; ☎ *78 98-316, Sonnensteinstrasse 11)* Meals €3-4.25. Open 8am-6pm Mon-Thur, 8am-2pm Fri. This university cafe over the bridge is the best place in town for a low-cost feed.

Schnitzel Express (Map 44, #4; ☎ *70 03 66, Rudolfstrasse 1)* Meals €3.60-6.50. Open 11am-10pm daily. Just north of Nibelungen Brücke, this very cheap self-service place has a range of schnitzels.

Mangolds (Map 44, #16; ☎ *78 56 88, Hauptplatz 3)* Hot/cold buffet €1.15 per 100g. Open 11am-8pm Mon-Fri, 11am-5pm Sat, closed holidays. This self-service vegetarian restaurant exudes freshness.

Gelbes Krokodil (Map 44, #37; ☎ *78 41 82, Dametzstrasse 30)* Meals €5.90-9. Open 11am-1am Mon-Fri, 5pm-1am Sat, Sun & holidays. This restaurant has a shaded terrace and lots of veggie choices.

Verona (Map 44, #27; ☎ *78 31 00, Landstrasse 13)* Meals €4.75-14.20. Open 11am-2.30pm & 5pm-11.30pm daily. An Italian restaurant in a courtyard off Landstrasse, it has keen prices and 47 pizza varieties.

Josef Stadtbräu (Map 44, #42; ☎ *77 31 65, Landstrasse 49)* Meals €5.25-11. Open 10am-4am daily. This is an excellent choice for decent beer (they make their own) and food in a buzzing environment. There's a big beer garden and live music from 5pm on Sunday (April to October). From 11am to 3pm Monday to Friday they serve an all-you-can-eat brunch for €6.40.

Los Caballeros (Map 44, #39; ☎ *77 89 70, Landstrasse 32)* Meals €7.15-21.65. Open 11am-2pm daily. This Mexican restaurant offers a special deal at weekday lunchtimes: €6.40 buys you an all-you-can-eat meal.

Wachauer Weinstube (Map 44, #21; ☎ *77 46 18, Pfarrgasse 20)* Meals €5.85-8.75. Open 11am-midnight Mon-Fri, closed holidays. Come here for for a limited range of inexpensive Austrian food in a quiet wine tavern.

Balaton Restaurant (Map 44, #32; ☎ *77 90 28, Klammstrasse 7)* Meals €7.20-17.30. Open 11.30am-2pm & 6pm-midnight Tues-Sun. This is a great spot for inexpensive Hungarian cuisine served in a comfortable environment.

Klosterhof (Map 44, #36; ☎ *77 33 73, Landstrasse 30)* Meals €6.40-17.50. Open 9am-midnight daily. This large and popular eatery occupies a 17th-century building. Each dining room has a different ambience and there's a huge beer garden.

Kremsmünsterer Stuben (Map 44, #13; ☎ *78 21 11, Altstadt 10)* Meals €15-24. Open noon-3pm & 6pm-midnight Tues-Fri, 6pm-midnight Mon & Sat. This expensive, typical Austrian place is the choice for gourmets; dishes have been adapted to suit more refined tastes.

Entertainment

Café Ex-Blatt (Map 44, #34; ☎ *70 77 93 19, Waltherstrasse 15)* Open 10am-2am Mon-Fri, 6pm-2am Sat & Sun. More of a bar than a cafe, this place attracts a crowd mainly in their 20s to 40s, including many students. It has candles on the tables, walls crammed with pictures, pizza for €6.50 and beer for €3.05 (0.5L).

Alte Welt (Map 44, #11; ☎ *77 00 53, Hauptplatz 4)* Open 11.30am-2.30pm & 5pm-1am Mon-Fri, 5pm-1am Sat. This place has music and cultural events twice a week (rarely in summer), as well as creative Austrian food (€6.50-11.60).

Posthof (☎ *77 05 48-0,* **W** *www.posthof .at, Posthofstrasse 43)* This place east of downtown is a centre for contemporary music, dance and theatre, particularly avant-garde events. The opening times depend on the event, as does the admission price (free to €30).

Landestheater *(Map 44, #24; ☎ 76 11-0,* **w** *www.landestheater-linz.at, Promenade 39)* Seats €5.85-37.80, standing-room €1.45-4.40. Programs here are generally more traditional.

Moviemento *(Map 44, #37; ☎ 78 40 90,* **w** *www.moviemento.at, Dametzstrasse 30)* Admission €6.20. Showtimes vary. This movie house shows original-language, non-mainstream films.

There is a ***casino*** *(Map 44, #46; ☎ 69 50-0, Rainerstrasse 2-4, open 3pm-3am daily)* in the Hotel Schillerpark. ***Linz Stadion*** *(Map 44, #50; ☎ 573 11, Roseggerstrasse 41)* stages sports events and major pop concerts.

Getting There & Away

Air Linz airport mostly handles national and charter flights. For information call the airport direct on ☎ 07721-600-0. Austrian Airlines (☎ 05-1789) is at Schubertstrasse 1; from Landstrasse, walk east down Bismarckstrasse for three blocks.

Bus Bundesbuses depart from stands (Map 44, #53) near the Hauptbahnhof, beyond the small park to the west. There's a bus information counter (☎ 61 71 81) open 8.20am to 11.30am and noon to 3.30pm Monday to Friday.

Train Linz is on the main rail route between Vienna and Salzburg, with express trains hourly in both directions. Slower trains also service this and other routes. At least three trains depart daily for Prague (€27.35 each way, €42.45 for a weekend return; six hours, change at Summerau). For train information call ☎ 05-17 17.

Car & Motorcycle The city has good road connections. The east-west A1/E60 passes the south of the city; the A7 branches north from there and skirts the old city centre.

Boat The Schiffsstation (literally, ship station; Map 44, #10) is at Untere Donaulände 1, on the south bank just east of Nibelungen Brücke. Wurm + Köck (☎ 78 36 07,

w www.donauschiffahrt.de) sends boats westwards to Passau from mid April to late October (€20.70/23.70 one-way/round-trip; one daily, takes six to seven hours). There's also one boat weekly to Vienna (€54/60 one-way/round-trip, 11½ to 15½ hours). The longer times are for journeys heading upstream (westwards).

Getting Around

Linz airport is 12km south-west of the town. A taxi would cost at least €22, so it's just as well there's a direct airport bus that starts in Urfahr Jahrmarktgelände, on the north bank, and calls at the Hauptbahnhof (€1.90, 40 minutes, every two hours).

Public transport includes trams (such as the No 3 between the Hauptbahnhof and Hauptplatz) and buses, but by early evening some services stop or become infrequent. Get single tickets (€1.50; correct change required) from pavement dispensers, which also supply day passes (€2.95) and weekly passes (€9.50, valid from first use), as do Tabak shops. Drivers don't sell tickets – buy and validate your tickets before you board.

Linz has offices for all the major car hire firms, including Avis (☎ 66 28 81), Europaplatz 7; Europcar (☎ 60 00 91), Wiener Strasse 91; and Hertz (Map 44, #43; ☎ 78 48 41), Bürgerstrasse 19. There's free car parking at Urfahrmarkt.

You can hire bikes at the Hauptbahnhof from 9am to 8pm daily (see the Getting Around chapter for rates).

Around Linz

The following places can be visited on day trips from Linz, but to fully experience the character of these towns, you should plan to stay overnight. If you enjoy rococo interiors, consider also visiting the church of the **Cistercian abbey** *(☎ 07226-2311-12, Linzerstrasse 4; free; open daylight hours)* at Wilhering, 9km west of Linz, on the south bank of the Danube. It is breathtaking for its extremely elaborate but delicate ornamentation.

MAUTHAUSEN

☎ 07238 • pop 4500

Nowadays Mauthausen (Map 43) is a pleasant small town on the north bank of the Danube east of Linz, but its status as a quarrying centre prompted the Nazis to site a concentration camp *(Konzentrationslager)* here. Prisoners were forced into slave labour in the granite quarry and many died on the so-called *Todesstiege* (Stairway of Death) leading from the quarry to the camp. In all, some 100,000 prisoners died or were executed in the camp between 1938 and 1945.

The city's **museum** *(☎ 2269, Erinnerungsstrasse 1; adult/concession €1.85/0.75; open 8am-4pm daily 1 Feb-15 Dec, 8am-6pm Apr-Sept)* tells the story of this and other camps (such as those at Ebensee and Melk) using German text, charts, artefacts and many harrowing photos. Visitors can see the living quarters (each designed for 200, but housing up to 500) and the gas chambers. In the camp and on the approach to the quarry there are numerous poignant memorials to the deceased. Some people feel that charging to see such horrors is inappropriate; in other countries, camps such as Auschwitz and Dachau have free entry.

Despite its past, today Mauthausen contains more than just memories of Nazis; pause for awhile in the centre. On the side of the house at Heindlkai 31, by the main road, there's a scene in relief showing a sadistic dentist at work. Round the corner, facing the Danube, is Chalet Wedl, with a colourful facade, relief paintings, and distinctive features such as the giant spider's web on the metal gate. West along Heindlkai are places to stay and eat, as well as the tourist office (☎ 2243), Heindlkai 13, which is open 1pm (11am July and August) to 7pm daily from 1 May to 31 September. In winter, information is available next door at Gasthof Zur Traube (☎ 2023-0). Single/double rooms here go for €35/54 with shower and TV.

Getting There & Away

Mauthausen train station is about 1.5km east of the town centre and can be reached hourly from Linz in about 30 to 50 minutes (€5.85 one-way, €8.75 day return),

depending upon connections in St Valentin. You can rent a bike from the station, which eases the 5km journey to the camp (signposted KZ Mauthausen). If you want to walk, you can do it in 45 minutes: walk through the town (15 minutes) and then take the signposted footpath *(Fussweg)* to the right after the Freizeitzentrum (bikes can take this route too).

The bus from Linz takes 55 minutes and gets you about 3km closer to the camp than the train. Another option is to take the Wurm + Köck boat from the Schiffsstation in Linz (€7.30/8.75 one-way/round-trip, 1¼ hours) leaving at 9am Saturday and returning at 8.45pm Sunday.

ST FLORIAN

☎ 07224 • pop 5600 • elev 300m

This town (Map 43) has one of the best abbeys in Upper Austria, if not the whole country, and is easily accessible from Linz. St Florian was a Roman who converted to Christianity and was drowned in the Enns River (in 304) for his pains. In many Austrian churches he is represented wearing Roman military uniform and dousing flames with a bucket of water.

Orientation & Information

St Florian is a market town 15km south-east of Linz. The centre of town is Marktplatz, where there's a small tourist office (☎/fax 56 90, e info.stflorian@netway.at) at No 2, open 9am to 1pm Monday to Friday (closed December and January). The post office (Postamt 4490) is also here.

Augustinian Abbey

The baroque spires of the Augustiner Chorherrenstift *(Augustinian abbey; ☎ 89 02, w www.stift-st-florian.at, Stiftstrasse 1; abbey tours adult/student €5.05/4.40; tours 10am, 11am, 2pm, 3pm & 4pm daily Easter-31 Oct)* are visible from anywhere in town. The abbey dates from at least 819 and has been occupied by the Augustinians since 1071. The baroque appearance was created between 1688 and 1751 by Carlo Carlone and Jakob Prandtauer. The main entrance, framed by statues, is especially impressive, particularly when bathed in the afternoon sunlight.

The abbey features lavish apartments, resplendent with rich stucco and emotive frescoes. They include 16 emperor's rooms (once occupied by visiting popes and royalty) and a library housing 125,000 volumes. The Marble Hall is dedicated to Prince Eugene of Savoy, a Frenchman who led the Habsburg army to victory over the Turks in many battles. Prince Eugene's Room contains an amusing bed featuring carved Turks.

The high point of the interior is the **Altdorfer Gallery**, displaying 14 paintings by Albrecht Altdorfer (1480–1538) of the Danube school. There are eight scenes of Christ and four of St Sebastian – all vivid and dramatic with an innovative use of light and dark. Altdorfer cleverly tapped into contemporary issues to depict his biblical scenes (for example, one of Christ's tormentors is clearly a Turk).

The **Stiftskirche** *(abbey church; open approx 7am-10pm daily)* is almost overpowering in its extensive use of stucco and frescoes. The altar is made from 700 tonnes of Salzburg marble, and the huge organ (1774) was the largest in Europe at the time it was built. Anton Bruckner was a choir boy in St Florian and was church organist from 1850 to 1855; he is buried in the crypt below his beloved organ. Also in the crypt are the remains of 6000 people, their bones and skulls stacked in neat rows.

The abbey interior is accessible by a one-hour guided tour, usually in German (notes in English), though phone ☎ 89 02-10 to see if you can join an English tour. The Stiftskirche can be visited without joining a tour.

Attached to the abbey is the **Historisches Feuerwehrzeughaus** *(Fire Brigade Museum; ☎ 42 19, Stiftstrasse 2; adult/student €2.20/ 1.85; open 9am-noon & 2pm-4pm Tues-Sun 1 May-31 Oct)*. It displays historic fire engines, hoses, buckets and other firefighting paraphernalia.

Schloss Hohenbrunn
Less than 2km west of town is Schloss Hohenbrunn, built between 1722 and 1732 in the baroque style; the architect was Jakob Prandtauer. This stately home houses the fairly interesting (though unusual) **Jagd Museum** *(hunting museum; ☎ 89 33, Hohenbrunn 1; adult/student €2.20/1.85; open 10am-noon & 1pm-5pm Tues-Sun 1 Apr-31 Oct, closed public holidays)*. Blood sports are celebrated everywhere here: in art, ornaments, implements, weapons and even the castle stuccowork.

Places to Stay & Eat
St Florian has about eight small-scale places to stay, and a *Spar* supermarket the Lagerhaus bus stop.

Zum Goldenen Pflug *(☎ 42 26, Speiserberg 3)* Singles/doubles with shower €21.80/36.40, doubles with shower and toilet €43.60. This is your basic no-frills accommdation near the abbey gates. Phone ahead to guarantee a room.

Gasthof Erzherzog Franz Ferdinand *(☎ 42 45-0, fax 42 45-9, Marktplatz 13)* Singles/doubles €40/66. This is the largest (71 beds) and fanciest (three stars) place in St Florence. The rooms all have a shower, toilet, TV and telephone. It also has a restaurant.

Gasthaus Goldener Löwe *(☎ 89 30, Speiserberg 9)* Meals €6.20-8.80. Open 11am-midnight Thur-Tues. This Gasthaus by the abbey gates serves Austrian dishes and has a courtyard and garden. Main meals are served at midday – after 2pm there are only snacks and drinks.

Gasthof Zur Traube *(☎ 42 23, Speiserberg 1)* Meals €5-12.30. Open 10am-2pm & 5pm-midnight Fri-Wed. This is a traditional, comfortable place to enjoy Austrian food. Two-course weekday lunches (€5.25 and €6) are a good deal.

Getting There & Away
St Florian is not accessible by train. Buses depart from opposite Linz Hauptbahnhof and take 25 minutes to reach St Florian (€1.85, 30 minutes). Frequent buses do the trip, but they don't all have St Florian marked on the front. Buses to Sierning and Molln call at Hohenbrunn after St Florian (€1.80 from Linz).

STEYR
☎ 07252 • pop 43,000 • elev 310m

Like Linz, Steyr (Map 45) has an attractive town centre despite its heavy industries; it was also the first town in Europe to have electric street lighting (1884). The iron industry has been the backbone of its prosperity since the Middle Ages. Steyr made armaments in WWI and WWII and, in 1944, was bombed for its trouble. During the Allied occupation it was a frontier town between the US and Soviet zones.

Orientation & Information
The picturesque town centre is contained within the converging branches of the Enns and Steyr rivers. The Hauptbahnhof (Map 45, #10), on the eastern bank of the Enns, is about eight minutes' walk from the pivotal Stadtplatz. The tourist office (Map 45, #13; ☎ 532 29-0, fax 532 29-15, e info@tourism-steyr.at) is in the Rathaus, at Stadtplatz 27; it's open 8.30am to 6pm Monday to Friday, 9am to noon Saturday. At Christmas time, Saturday hours extend to 4pm and it's also open 10am to 3pm Sunday. (Steyr is busy then because nearby Christkindl has a post office issuing special Christmas postmarks.)

To the west of the Hauptbahnhof is the main post office (Map 45, #12; Hauptpostamt 4400), open 7.30am to 7pm Monday to Friday and 8am to 11pm Saturday. Cash can be exchanged during these hours, but not travellers cheques. Another post office is at Grünmarkt 1, near Stadtplatz, where there are several Bankomat machines.

Things to See & Do
Steyr's main points of interest are clustered on or around Stadtplatz. A 17th-century fountain is at the centre of the long, narrow square. One of the most noteworthy buildings is the 18th-century **Rathaus** (Map 45, #13), with a church-like belfry and a rococo facade. Opposite, at No 32, is the **Bummerlhaus** (Map 45, #15), a 13th-century symbol of the town with its Gothic appearance and steep gable. Other buildings round the square have distinctive arcades and courtyards – some house modern businesses: wander into the bank at No 9 and the Kleiderbauer

clothes shop at No 14. You can admire the fine facade of **Stadtplatz No 12** (Map 45, #7), with its angels and crests, and see where Franz Schubert lived at No 16.

Two highly visible buildings at the northern end of the Stadtplatz area are **Schloss Lamberg** (Map 45, #5), which was restored in baroque style in 1727 after a fire damaged the town centre, and **Michaelerkirche** (Map 45, #2), just across the Steyr River where it meets the Enns, which has a large gable fresco.

At the southern end of Stadtplatz is **Marienkirche** (St Mary's Church; Map 45, #18; ☎ 531 29, Grünmarkt 1; open daylight hours), a mix of Gothic and baroque styles, with an extremely ornate high altar and pulpit. The alcoves for the side altars are rich in stucco; the one to the left of the entrance contains a statue of St Florian.

Up the hill to the west is the **Stadtpfarrkirche** (Map 45, #20; Brucknerplatz 4), a Gothic creation from the 15th century. It shares some features with Stephansdom in Vienna, just as it shared the same architect, Hans Puchsbaum, but it's a cruder work. Down the steps to the south is the **Heimatmuseum** (Municipal Museum; Map 45, #22; ☎ 575 548, Grünmarkt 26; free admission; open 10am-4pm Tues-Sun, closed Tues Nov-Mar, open 10am-4pm daily Dec). Housed in the 17th-century granary Innerberger Stadel, it has displays of history, culture and folklore, including mechanical puppets.

Places to Stay
Campingplatz Forelle (☎/fax 780 08, e for ellesteyr@gmx.at, Kermatmüllerstrasse 1a, Münichholz) Price per adult/tent or car €4.25/5.10. Open Apr-Oct. This place is about 2km north of town on the eastern bank of the Enns (take bus No 1 from the centre).

Jugendherberge (Map 45, #23; ☎/fax 455 80, Hafner Strasse 14) Beds in dorm per person over/under 19 years €6.05/5.55. Reception open 3pm-10pm Mon-Fri & 5pm-10pm Sat, Sun & holidays, closed 23 Dec-8 Jan. This HI hostel is behind and to the south of the Hauptbahnhof: to get there, pass under the tracks via Damberggasse, take the second street on the right after the

UPPER AUSTRIA

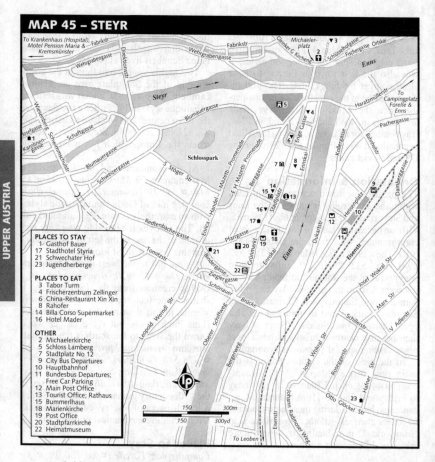

MAP 45 – STEYR

To Krankenhaus (Hospital),
Motel Pension Maria &
Kremsmünster

Michaeler-
platz

Enns

To
Campingplatz
Forelle &
Enns

Steyr

Schlosspark

PLACES TO STAY
1 Gasthof Bauer
17 Stadthotel Styria
21 Schwechater Hof
23 Jugendherberge

PLACES TO EAT
3 Tabor Turm
4 Frischerzentrum Zellinger
6 China-Restaurant Xin Xin
8 Rahofer
14 Billa Corso Supermarket
16 Hotel Mader

OTHER
2 Michaelerkirche
5 Schloss Lamberg
7 Stadtplatz No 12
9 City Bus Departures
10 Hauptbahnhof
11 Bundesbus Departures;
   Free Car Parking
12 Main Post Office
13 Tourist Office; Rathaus
15 Bummerlhaus
18 Marienkirche
19 Post Office
20 Stadtpfarrkirche
22 Heimatmuseum

0   150   300m
0   150   300yd

To Leoben

---

overpass bridge and then bear right onto
Viktor Adlerstrasse.

Other than these options, budget travellers will have a problem in Steyr. The
few cheap choices (including private
rooms) are inconveniently far from the
centre.

Motel Pension Maria (☎ 710 62, fax
710 62-66, Reindlgutstrasse 25) Singles/
doubles €25.50/43.60. Restaurant closed
Sat & Sun; check-in possible on these days
with advance notice. This peaceful place is
2km west of the town centre, a short walk
beyond the hospital *(Krankenhaus)*, where

bus No 2B stops. Rooms have a bathroom
and cable TV.

Gasthof Bauer (Map 45, #1; ☎ 544 41,
Josefgasse 7) Singles/doubles €29.80/55.
Restaurant open Wed-Mon. This small place
is about 10 minutes' walk from the town centre. The renovated rooms (with shower and
toilet) are good value, as is the inexpensive
restaurant. Check-in is difficult to arrange on
Tuesday even if you call ahead.

Schwechater Hof (Map 45, #21; ☎ 530 67,
fax 477 054, **e** schwechaterhof.steyr@aon.at.
Leopold Werndl Strasse 1) Singles/doubles
€47/70. Located behind the Stadtpfarrkirche,

this hotel-restaurant offers standard mid-range accommdation with shower, toilet, cable TV and telephone.

Stadthotel Styria (Map 45, #17; ☎ 515 51, fax 515 51-51, **e** info@styriahotel.at, Stadtplatz 40) Singles/doubles €72/101. This place is in the next category up, with well-furnished rooms that have a bathroom, cable TV and telephone. The sauna and solarium cost extra.

Places to Eat

Stadtplatz hosts an **open-air market** on Thursday and Saturday mornings. It also has snack stands, as well as a **Billa Corso** supermarket (Map 45, #14; Stadtplatz 30).

Frischerzentrum Zellinger (Map 45, #4; ☎ 524 71, Enge Gasse 13) Meals €3.60-7.20. Open 8am-6pm Mon-Fri and 7am-noon Sat. This deli shop has a self-service cafe at the rear. The salad buffet costs €0.75 per 100gr.

China-Restaurant Xin Xin (Map 45, #6; ☎ 470 34, Enge Gasse 20) Meals €4.50-11.70. Open 11am-3pm & 5pm-11.30pm Tues-Sun, 11am-3pm Mon. The best deal here are the two-course lunch menus offered Monday to Saturday (€4.50 to €6), though there are also cut-price evening deals too.

Schwechater Hof (Map 45, #21; ☎ 530 67, Leopold Werndl Strasse 1) Meals €6-14. This rustic hotel restaurant serves up a range of Austrian food, either inside or in the shaded garden.

Hotel Mader (Map 45, #16; ☎ 533 58, Stadtplatz 36) Dishes €6.60-16.80. Kitchen open 11am-11pm Mon-Sat. This hotel provides reliable Austrian cuisine. You can chose your environment – wine cellar, bar, winter garden – though the menu is the same in each section.

Rahofer (Map 45, #8; Stadtplatz 9) Meals €7-19. Open 9am-midnight Tues-Sat. A covered passage off Stadtplatz leads to an attractive courtyard, where you'll find this good-quality Italian restaurant.

Tabor Turm (Map 45, #3; ☎ 729 49, Taborweg 7). Meals €8-17. Open 9am-11pm Wed-Sat, 9am-5pm Sun & Mon. This restaurant dishes out competent Austrian fare, but

its best feature is the terrace with a fine view over Steyr. Climb up via the stairs on the east side of Michaelerkirche.

Getting There & Away

Trains from Linz (€7.30, 40 minutes) are direct every two hours, or require a change at St Valentin. Trains continue south into Styria. Steyr Hauptbahnhof has a restaurant and a travel information office.

Bundesbuses leave from a new station (Map 45, #11) above the Hauptbahnhof (where there's also free car parking). Four buses a day go to St Florian (€4.40, 50 minutes). Buses run to Linz (€7.30, 70 minutes) approximately hourly. City buses leave from outside the Hauptbahnhof to the north. Steyr is on Hwy 115, the road branching from the A1/E60 and running south to Leoben.

WELS

☎ 07242 • pop 62,000 • elev 317m

Wels (Map 43) is an agricultural hub with a historic and appealing centre. Most of the countryside comes to town for the agricultural fair and Volksfest carnival, which together take over Wels in early September.

The tourist office (☎ 434 95, fax 479 04, **e** office@tourism-wels.at) is at Kaiser Josef Platz 22.

Things to See & Do

The focal point of the town is the long **Stadtplatz**, lined with historic buildings and eye-catching facades. Branching off are several attractive courtyards (for example, at Stadtplatz 34). Audio guides (€3.30) or written notes (free) to central sights are available from the tourist office. At the western end of Stadtplatz, in the former leather workers' district, is a tower, the **Ledererturm** (1618), and at the eastern end is the **Stadtpfarrkirche,** with a fine Romanesque porch and Gothic stained glass. Opposite the church, Stadtplatz 24 bears paintwork from 1570 and was occupied by Salome Alt, the mistress of Salzburg's prince-archbishop Wolf Dietrich.

Behind Stadtplatz 14 is the stately **Kulturzentrum Burg** where Maximilian I breathed his last in 1519. It now houses a museum (☎ 235 735, Burggasse 13; adult/concession

€3.65/1.50; open 10am-5pm Tues-Fri, 2pm-5pm Sat, 10am-noon & 2pm-4pm Sun & holidays); among the exhibits are two room interiors (rustic and Biedermeier), and some ingenious small puppets activated from underneath. North of the tourist office, is the **Stadtmuseum** (☎ 235 694, Pollheimer Strasse 17; admission free; open 10am-noon & 2pm-5pm Tues-Fri, 10am-4pm Sun & holidays), which contains Roman finds such as the Venus of Wels, a small, beautiful bronze statue.

Places to Stay & Eat

Staff at the tourist office can help you find somewhere to stay. The town also has many places to eat in the centre for a range of budgets, including a surprising number of Chinese restaurants – just explore Stadtplatz and Franz Josef Platz.

Jugendherberge (☎ 235-757, fax 235-756, e jugendherberge@wels.at, Dragonerstrasse 22) Dorm beds €9.20, doubles with shower and toilet €20.10. Check in 5pm-7pm, 5pm-9.30pm in Jul & Aug. Open year-round. This HI hostel is just five minutes' walk north-west of Stadtplatz, and has spacious rooms.

Pfeffermühle (☎ 455 97, Gärtnerstrasse 7) Singles/doubles with private shower cubicle €25.50/47. Meals €4.75-8.65. This combination place-to-stay–Chinese-restaurant is on the northern side of the train station (not the side with the bus station). It has a garden, cheap lunch menus, off-street parking and sizeable, renovated rooms.

SB Am Eck (☎ 757, Bahnhofstrasse 13) Meals €4.40-6.70. Open 9am-4pm Mon-Fri. This simple self-service restaurant has bargain deals: main courses from €4.40, with soup and dessert only an extra €0.60 each.

There's a *Spar* supermarket just beyond the Ledererturm.

Getting There & Away

The train station is 1.25km north of Stadtplatz. The bus station is in front of the train station. The town is on the express (IC and EC) rail route between Linz and Salzburg, just 16 minutes south-west of Linz (€3.85,

several per hour). There's also a line running to Passau on the German border.

Bundesbuses run to numerous destinations, including Ebensee, Gmunden, Bad Ischl, Lambach and Linz.

LAMBACH
☎ 07245

The small town of Lambach (Map 43) is 10km south-west of Wels. Its **Benedictine abbey** (Benediktinerstift; ☎ 217 10, Klosterplatz 1; tours €4.40, 2pm daily Easter-31 Oct) was founded in 1056, though much of the present edifice dates from the 17th century when the church was rebuilt in baroque style. The abbey has a theatre (the only one of its kind in Austria), but more striking are the Romanesque frescoes from the 11th century. They are extremely well preserved and betray the influence of the styles of south-eastern Europe, unusual in Austria. They can only be accessed by guided tour.

Getting There & Away

Lambach is on the Linz-Salzburg rail route but, unlike Wels, IC and EC express trains don't stop here. Local trains to/from Wels (€2.95) take 11 minutes.

SCHMIDING BIRD PARK

The Zoologischer Garten Vogelpark Schmiding (Map 43; ☎ 462 72, Schmiding 19; adult/senior/student/child €9.45/8/ 6.20/ 4.40; open 9am-5pm daily mid Mar-mid Nov) is Austria's largest bird park, home to 350 bird species. It also has giraffes, antelopes, monkeys, a children's area and an interesting ethnological museum. Last entry is at 5pm, though you can stay in the park till 7pm.

The park is about 7km north-west of Wels, in Krenglbach. Buses go from Wels every two to three hours (€1.90, 45 minutes; less frequent at weekends). Alternatively, Haiding train station on the Wels-Passau route is about 2km north of the park.

KREMSMÜNSTER
☎ 07583

There is another **Benedictine abbey** (☎ 52 75, w www.kremsmuenster.at, Stift 1; adult/ family €4.75/11.65; tours 10am, 11am, 2pm

& *4pm daily Easter-31 Oct)* at Kremsmünster (Map 43), overlooking the Krems Valley. Although it was established in 777, it too owes much to baroque remodelling in the early 18th century. Stuccowork and frescoes are much in evidence in the church, library and **Kaisersaal** (Emperor's Hall). The most acclaimed piece in the treasury is the *Tassilo Chalice*, made of gilded copper and donated to the monks by the Duke of Bavaria in about 780. These sights can be visited only on a one-hour guided tour. The **Sternwarte** *(observatory tower; adult/family €5.10/12.35; tour 10am & 2pm daily 1 May-31 Oct)* houses a wide-ranging museum collection, and can be visited on a separate guided tour. Also of interest are the five fish ponds from the late 17th century, sporting statues and arcades (€0.75 entry).

About 1.5km east of Kremsmünster is a **music instrument museum** *(musikinstrumenten museum; ☎ 52 47, Schloss Kremsegg; adult/family €5.10/10.90; open 9am-5pm daily 1 Apr-31 Oct)*. Staff at the Kremsmünster tourist office (☎ 72 12, e tourismus@kremsmuenster.at), Rathausplatz 1, will tell you more.

Getting There & Away
Kremsmünster is on the IC rail route between Linz and Graz via Selzthal (direct trains every two hours). Kremsmünster Markt station is 30 minutes from Linz (€5.85, every one or two hours). Buses from Wels (€2.95, 30 minutes) run regularly Monday to Friday, less so at weekends.

FREISTADT
☎ 07942 • pop 7500 • elev 560m
This medieval fortified town (Map 43) is one of the main sights in the Mühlviertel region. Freistadt was important for its position on the salt route to Bohemia.

Orientation & Information
The compact town centre is within the old city walls. Right in the centre is Hauptplatz, with a small tourist office, the Mühlviertler Kernland (☎ 757 00, fax 757 00-20, e info .kernland@netway.at) at No 14. It is open 9am to 5pm Monday to Friday; from May to

September it stays open till 7pm, and also opens 9am to noon Saturday.

Immediately to the west of the city wall is the main north-south route, Hwy 125; known as Linzer Strasse in the south of the town, Promenade where it abuts the old centre and Prager Strasse in the north. There's a post office (Postamt 4240) at Promenade 11.

Things to See & Do
The city walls, with several gates and turrets, are mostly intact and surrounded by a grassy fringe. The **Hauptplatz** has some interesting old buildings with ornate facades. On the southern side of the square is the 14th-century parish church, which is Gothic with a baroque tower. Waaggasse, just west of the Hauptplatz, is lined with striking architecture, including some with sgraffito designs.

Just beyond the north-eastern corner of Hauptplatz is a **Schloss** (castle), dating from 1390, with a square tower topped by a tapering red-tiled roof. Inside is the Schlossmuseum *(☎ 722 74, Schlosshof 2; adult/senior €2.40/1.60; open for tours 9am, 10.30am, 2pm & 3.30pm Tues-Fri, 10.30am & 2pm Sat, 2pm Sun May-Oct)*. It contains the usual historical and cultural displays as well as a collection of 600 works of engraved and painted glass (*verre églomisé*).

Places to Stay & Eat
Camping Ground (☎ 725 70, fax 725 70-4, e ffc@magnet.at, Eglsee 12) Price per adult/tent €3.30/1.85. You can pitch your tent here, just outside the old centre, to the west of the Feldaist River by the Tenniscenter.

Jugendherberge (☎ 743 65, e jugend herberge.frei@aon.at, Schlosshof 3) Dorm beds €7.30. Open June-Sept. Reception is open 5pm to 8pm, but phone ahead as the owner is not always around. This small HI hostel is in front of the Schloss.

Pension Pirklbauer (☎ 724 40, fax 724 40-5, Höllgasse 2-4) Singles/doubles €18.20/32. Rooms are excellent for the price: theyr'e large, comfortable and have a shower, toilet, satellite TV and pine fittings; there's also a garden. It's in the south-western corner of the old centre.

Beer For All

Freistadt's brewery makes several varieties of Freistädter Bier, and has been in operation since 1777. The relationship between the town and its brewery is unlike that of any of the other 65-odd breweries in Austria: this is a *Braucommune*, owned jointly by the 149 households located within the town walls. A share in the brewery is conferred by owning one of these houses – people who sell lose their stake to the purchaser, so don't expect to find too many of these homes on the market! Realistically, the brewery cannot be taken over by any competitor, as the business would have to buy the whole town in order to take control.

In the old days, the owners of the brewery would get their share of the profits in liquid form, which would be distributed in *Eimer Bier* containers holding 56L. Each owner might get up to 130 containers! Nowadays, for better or worse, owners instead get a cash payment of equivalent value.

All of the guesthouses and inns in the town serve the local brew, and each outlet is entitled to send its regulars on a free tour of the brewery once a year (usually on a Tuesday). The tour guide will tell you that the brewery makes an average of 120,000L of beer a week, and that the bottling plant can handle up to 14,000 bottles per hour. The tour concludes with a free sampling of the produce. You might be lucky enough to get to go along if you are friendly with an inn owner at the right time of year. Alternatively, telephone the brewery office (☎ 757 77) during office hours to ask if you can join a tour.

Früstückspension Hubertus (☎ 723 54, fax 723 54-7, e office@cafe-pension-hubertus.at, Höllplatz 3) Singles/doubles €18.20/32. Close to Pirklbauer, this pension is another good choice, providing rooms with a shower, toilet and cable TV, a cafe, parking places and helpful staff.

Hotel Zum Goldenen Adler (☎ 721 12, fax 721 12-44, e goldener.adler@hotels-freistadt.at, Salzgasse 1) Singles/doubles €41/67. Meals €4.80-14.50. Open 7am-midnight daily. Located in the historic centre, this hotel offers variable rooms with shower, toilet, telephone and cable TV, and good facilities, including a tiny outdoor pool, sun terrace, sauna and solarium. The elegant restaurant serves reasonably-priced Austrian food, including a couple of veggie dishes.

Haider Imbiss (☎ 722 37, Eisengasse 18) Snacks/meals €1.85-5.60. Open 6am-6pm Mon-Thur, 7.30am-6pm Fri, 7.30am-12.30pm Sat. This deli shop serves hot snacks and meals and also has a few sit-down tables. Along the road there's a *Billa* supermarket (Eisengasse 13).

Ratscherrnstube (☎ 726 68, Hauptplatz 1) Meals €5-11.30. Open 8am-midnight Tues-Sat, 8am-4pm Sun. This restaurant primarily caters for locals by serving tasty and filling Austrian standards.

Hotel-Gasthof Deim (☎ 722 58, Böhmergasse 8-10) Meals €6.90-16. Open 11.30am-midnight daily. This atmospheric place has some Gothic and rustic features that serve as a nice backdrop to the tasty regional specialities that are served here.

Getting There & Away

Freistadt is on a direct rail route from Linz (€5.85, 70 minutes, two hourly). This line then wriggles its way north to Prague; Czech rail fares are lower than those in Austria, so you can save money if you're travelling north by waiting and buying (in Czech currency) your onward tickets once you've crossed the border.

Freistadt train station is 3km south-west of the centre – it's a long walk, and buses to the centre run only at 8.25am and 11.25pm. A better option from Linz is to take the bus, as these stop in the centre (€5.85, 70 minutes, hourly Monday to Friday, infrequent at weekends).

Highway 125, the main route to and from Linz, passes adjacent to the walled centre and then continues its way northward towards Prague.

KEFERMARKT
☎ 07947

There's one particular reason to visit Kefermarkt (Map 43): the **Pfarrkirche St Wolfgang** *(☎ 62 03, Oberer Markt 1; open approx 7am-8pm daily)*, also known as the Wallfahrtskirche. Although this is not as famous as the pilgrimage church in the village of St Wolfgang in Salzkammergut, its Gothic altar (the Flügelaltar) is of comparable beauty and similar design. The identity of the 15th-century sculptor is not known. The altarpiece of limewood is 13.5m high, with latticework fronds rising towards the ceiling. At the centre are three expressive figures, carved with great skill (left to right as you face them): St Peter, St Wolfgang and St Christopher. The wings of the altar bear religious scenes in low relief. The rest of the decorations in the church are baroque.

If you want to stay, there are a couple of adjacent places down the hill from the church.

Gasthof Zehethofer 'Zur Goldenen Sense' (☎ 62 77, Oberer Markt 11) Singles/doubles shared shower €19/38. Open 7am-midnight Tues-Sun. Meals €4.40-7.65. Rooms are ageing and plain, but the food is good value.

Gasthof Horner (☎ 62 20, fax 66 77, Oberer Markt 13) Singles/doubles with shower, toilet & TV €26/44. Meals €5.70-8. Open 7am-midnight Wed-Mon. Rooms are

clean and fresh, but no arrivals are accepted on Tuesday when the restaurant is shut.

Kefermarkt is 10km south of Freistadt (€1.55 by train) and the church is about 1km north of the train station.

BRAUNAU AM INN
☎ 07722 • pop 17,500 • elev 352m

Geographically isolated from the rest of the province, Braunau (Map 43) has achieved unwanted attention as the birthplace of Hitler (see the boxed text 'Hitler's Home Town'). It would prefer to be described as *die gotische Stadt* (the Gothic city).

Braunau's sights could occupy you for a couple of hours. **Stadtplatz** is a long square lined with elegant homes in pastel shades, with a 13th-century gate tower at the southern end. The spire of the parish church, **Stadtpfarrkirche St Stephan**, is one of the tallest in Austria, at almost 100m. Close by is the former church, St Martin's, containing a war memorial.

The tourist office (☎ 626 44, fax 843 95, e tourismusverband.braunau@netway.at) is at Stadtplatz 9.

Places to Stay & Eat

Options include a *camp site (☎ 873 57, fax 842 68-140, Quellenweg)* and a *youth hostel (☎/fax 816 38, Osternbergerstrasse 57, Osternberg)*, though both are closed in winter.

Hotel Gann (☎/fax 632 06, Stadtplatz 23) Singles/doubles with shower €25.50/42.50,

---

Hitler's Home Town

Hitler was born here in 1889 with the unprepossessing moniker of Adolf Schicklgruber. The nonedescript Geburtshaus (birth house) still stands at Salzburger Vorstadt 15, just south of Stadtplatz. His family remained here for two years after he was born before moving to Linz. In 1938, when Hitler stormed through Braunau at the head of his troops and tanks, he did not stop at his old house.

Braunau tries to play down its Hitler connection. The *Führer* is ignored in most tourist literature. No plaque marks his birthplace. In 1989 a belated, oblique acknowledgment came with the placing of a lump of stone from Mauthausen (where there was a Nazi concentration camp) on the pavement outside the house. Even this fails to mention Hitler: Its inscription simply reads

Für Frieden Freiheit und Demokratie   For peace, freedom and democracy
nie wieder Faschismus   Never again fascism
millionen Tote Mahnen.   Millions of dead admonish.

with shower, toilet & TV €29.50/44. This small-scale, cosy hotel is ideally situated and has a cellar bar.

Stadtplatz has a range of places to eat, including snack joints, a supermarket, a pizzeria and a Chinese restaurant.

***Bogner** (☎ 683 43, Stadtplatz 47)* Meals €5-12. Open 8.30am-1am Mon-Sat, 2pm-10pm Sun. This place has outside tables and serves Austrian food. It calls itself 'Austria's smallest brewery' and has several home-brewed beers to try.

Getting There & Away

Braunau is the terminus of the regional train service from Steindorf bei Strasswalchen (€5.85, 45 minutes). Steindorf is on the Linz-Salzburg IC rail route. Braunau also has rail connections to Wels and to Munich. If you're going to Munich by car, take Hwy 12 (the E552).

Braunau receives plenty of touring cyclists because it lies on two bike routes: the Innsbruck-Passau Inntal Radweg and the Salzburg River track to Salzburg.

Lower Austria

Lower Austria (Niederösterreich) is rather overshadowed by Vienna, which it surrounds. Although the city is a separate province, all things, it seems, revolve around the national capital. All the tourist literature markets the province as 'The Land Round Vienna'.

Efforts to forge a separate identity were not helped by Vienna's former status as Lower Austria's provincial capital, while also the federal capital and having its own provincial government. In 1986 St Pölten became the capital of Lower Austria and the task of exploiting the province's accessibility from Vienna, while at the same time trying not to be overwhelmed by the city, began in earnest.

It's not a futile endeavour. Lower Austria has plenty to offer in its own right: the Danube (Donau) Valley is justly praised for its wines, castles and abbeys, the Wienerwald attracts walkers and spa seekers, and Semmering is a famous holiday region in the south.

Orientation & Information

Lower Austria is the country's largest province, covering 17,174 sq km, and has the largest population (1.5 million) of any region except Vienna. Geographically, it is dominated by the Danube Valley, which is also the focus of tourism. The land is relatively flat and fertile (it has the highest percentage of land under cultivation in Austria) though mountains reach 2000m high in the south.

St Pölten has absorbed the administrative functions of the province, but the tourist information office is still in Vienna; contact Niederösterreich-Information (☎ 01-536 10-6200, fax 01-536 10-6060, **e** tourismus@noe.co.at, **w** www.niederoesterreich.at), A-1010 Wien, Postfach 10.000. It can give information about the 'Welcome Ticket' scheme, which entitles you to B&B with private shower/toilet for €16.75 per person. The city tourist office in St Pölten holds only localised information on the province.

St Pölten

☎ 02742 • pop 50,000 • elev 267m

Nearly 2000 years ago St Pölten was known as Aelium Cetium, but the town all but disappeared with the departure of the Romans. The arrival of the Augustinians in the 8th century saw it regain importance, and the country's newest provincial capital has the oldest municipal charter, granted in 1159. It also has a smattering of baroque buildings: baroque master Jakob Prandtauer was once a resident.

Orientation & Information

The town centre is a compact, mostly pedestrian-only area to the west of the Traisen River. The tourist office (Map 47, #18; ☎ 353 354, fax 333-2819, **e** tourismus@st-poelten.gv.at), inside the Rathaus

MAP 46 – LOWER AUSTRIA (NIEDERÖSTERREICH)

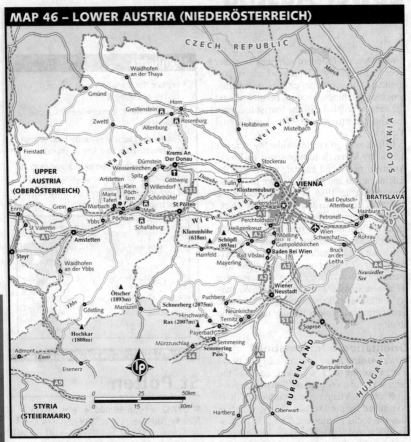

on Rathausplatz, is a 500m walk from the Hauptbahnhof. Opening hours are 8am to 5pm Monday to Friday, November to March. From April to October hours are 8am to 6pm weekdays, 9am to 5pm Saturday, and 10am to 5pm Sunday. Ask for the *St Pölten Gästeservice* booklet (in German, but with useful listings) and the city map *(Stadtplan)*. Next door is a travel agency; outside is an accommodation map and a telephone you can use to make free calls to hotels and guesthouses.

The Hauptbahnhof has a similar accommodation search facility outside (Map 47,

#3); it also has money-exchange counters, open daily, and a Bankomat.

The post office (Map 47, #2; Postamt 3100) is near the Hauptbahnhof. Its opening hours are 7am to 8pm Monday to Friday, 7am to 1pm Saturday.

Log on at Mail Boxes Etc (Map 47, #22; ☎ 799 04), Schillerplatz 1, for €3.65 per hour. It's open 7.15am to 6pm weekdays, 7.15am to 12.30pm Saturday.

Things to See & Do

Follow the walking tour of the town centre (outlined in English in the tourist office's

Your City Guide leaflet), or hire a copy of the office's taped walking tour for €1.50. The architecture is not exclusively baroque – Kremser Gasse 41 has an Art Nouveau facade *(Map 47, #6)* by Josef Olbrich, the creator of the Secession building in Vienna.

Rathausplatz is the hub of the town and has at its centre a **Dreifaltigkeitssäule** *(Trinity Column; Map 47, #12)*, constructed in 1782. Several eye-catching buildings line the square, including the rococo **Franziskanerkirche** *(Franciscan Church; Map 47, #11; ☎ 353 220-0, Rathausplatz 12; open daylight hours)*, completed in 1770. This

has side altar paintings by Kremser Schmidt.

Close to Rathausplatz are several places of interest, including the **Institut der Englischen Fräulein** *(Map 47, #20; ☎ 352 188-0, Linzer Strasse 11; admission free; open daylight hours)*, a convent founded in 1706, which has a classic baroque facade, and several frescoes by Paul Troger in the chapel. The tiny **Museum im Hof** *(Map 47, #14; ☎ 353 477, Hess Strasse 4; admission free; open 9am-noon Wed, Fri & Sat)* dwells on recent history, particularly from a worker's viewpoint.

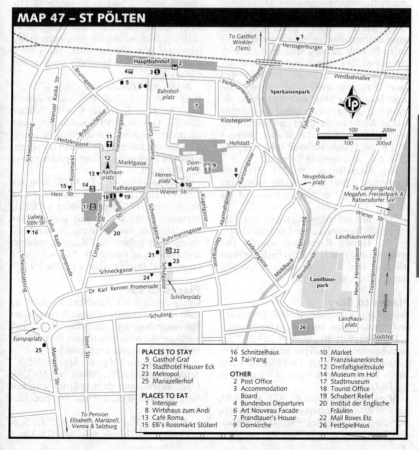

MAP 47 – ST PÖLTEN

LOWER AUSTRIA

PLACES TO STAY
5 Gasthof Graf
21 Stadthotel Hauser Eck
23 Metropol
25 Mariazellerhof

PLACES TO EAT
1 Interspar
8 Wirtshaus zum Andi
13 Café Roma
15 Elli's Rossmarkt Stüberl

16 Schnitzelhaus
24 Tai-Yang

OTHER
2 Post Office
3 Accommodation Board
4 Bundesbus Departures
6 Art Nouveau Facade
7 Prandtauer's House
9 Domkirche

10 Market
11 Franziskanerkirche
12 Dreifaltigkeitssäule
14 Museum im Hof
17 Stadtmuseum
18 Tourist Office
19 Schubert Relief
20 Institut der Englische Fräulein
22 Mail Boxes Etc
26 FestSpielHaus

Across the road is the **Stadtmuseum** *(Map 47, #17; ☎ 333-26 43, Prandtauerstrasse 2; adult/student €1.50/0.75; open 10am-5pm Tues Sat)*, which covers history from Roman times to the mid-19th century. The house at Rathausgasse 2 *(Map 47, #19)* has a baroque facade, complete with a relief of Schubert (the composer was a frequent visitor).

Herrenplatz has a small morning **market** *(Map 47, #10; daily except Sunday)* which expands into the adjoining Domplatz on Thursday and Saturday. Domplatz was the heart of the ancient Roman town. The 13th-century **Domkirche** *(cathedral; Map 47, #9; ☎ 353 402-0, Domplatz 1; open daylight hours)* has a 77m-high tower and much baroque ornamentation, which was added in the early 18th century. The interior, with lashings of fake marble and gold, was designed by Jakob Prandtauer. Note the painted figure that seems about to fall on you if you stand before the altar, and the hole in the organ that captures the stained glass image behind. Many of the paintings here are by Daniel Gran, who lived at Wiener Strasse 8 for a while. Prandtauer lived at Klostergasse 1 *(Map 47, #7)*, north of Domplatz.

The **Freizeitpark** *(☎ 251 510, Am Ratzerdorfer See)* is a lakeside sports and leisure complex to the north-east of the town.

Cultural (and administrative) activities are mostly centred in the Landhausviertel, by the Traisen River between the two bridges. Here you'll find the **FestSpielHaus** *(theatre; Map 47, #26)*, exhibition centre, shops, offices and a lot more.

Places to Stay

Budget options are very limited. There are a few private rooms, but none in the centre.

Campingplatz Megafun (☎ 251 510, Am Ratzerdorfer See) Sites per adult/tent €3.65/2.20. Open year-round. This lakeside camp site is 3km to the north-east of the centre in the Freizeitpark.

Mariazellerhof (Map 47, #25; ☎ 769 95, fax 769 95-8, Mariazeller Strasse 6) Singles €26.20-33.50, doubles €46.60-48. Reception 7am-11am & 4pm-9pm. Renovated in 2001, many of its rooms have kitchen facilities, and all have shower, toilet, cable TV and telephone.

Pension Elisabeth (☎ 727 14, fax 727 14-8, Mariazeller Strasse 164) Singles €26.20-33.50, doubles €46.60-48. Reception 7am-11am & 4pm-9pm. This pension, 1.5km south of Mariazellerhof, is owned by the same family. Most rooms are marginally cheaper but there are no kitchens; rooms do have shower, toilet, cable TV and telephone.

Gasthof Graf (Map 47, #5; ☎ 352 757, fax 352 757-40, e hotel.graf@aon.at, Bahnhofplatz 7) Singles/doubles with private shower/ toilet & TV €40/64, without toilet €29/46. The rooms with shower/toilet in this pension-restaurant have been nicely renovated; the cheaper ones with only a shower cubicle are generally smaller and slightly drab.

Stadthotel Hauser Eck (Map 47, #21; ☎ 733 360, fax 783 86, e m.hauser@eunet .at, Schulgasse 2) Singles €38-48, doubles €60-73. This small Art Nouveau hotel near the pedestrian zone, has comfortable rooms with shower, toilet, cable TV and telephone, a lift and a restaurant. Nearby parking costs €7.30 a night.

Metropol (Map 47, #23; ☎ 707 00-0, fax 707 00-133, e metropol@austria-trend.at, Schillerplatz 1) Singles/doubles €85/121. Metropol is the town's only central four-star hotel. It has modern, standardised rooms with bathroom, TV and telephone, and a sauna and steambath. All rooms have (expensive) Internet access via the TV.

Places to Eat

Cheap eating is not a problem. North of the train line, on Herzogenburger Strasse, is an *Interspar* shopping centre *(Map 47, #1)* with a self-service restaurant (dishes from €4.10) on the 1st floor, and a supermarket.

Schnitzelhaus (Map 47, #16; ☎ 765 95, Schiessstattring 27) Meals €3.60-7.95. Open 10am-10pm daily. Fill up with fast food, schnitzel-style, at this self-service chain restaurant.

Tai-Yang (Map 47, #24; ☎ 731 39, Schneckgasse 12) Meals €4.75-13.75. Open

11am-2.30pm & 5pm-11pm daily. This Chinese restaurant offers weekday set lunches of the usual stir-fried fare.

Café Roma (Map 47, #13; ☎ 356 383, Rathausplatz 5) Meals €1.35-1.60. Open 9am-1am daily. A versatile cafe offering cakes, ice cream and cut-price deals on late-night alcoholic drinks. At lunch (11am to 2pm) on weekdays it has an unbelievable deal – spaghetti bolognaise for €1.35 and spaghetti carbonara for €1.60.

Wirtshaus zum Andi (Map 47, #8; ☎ 218 14, Ranzonigasse 3) Meals €4-8.50. Open 9am-midnight Thurs-Mon, 9am-2pm Tues. This is the place for inexpensive Austrian food in a simple, sometimes smoky interior or a pleasant courtyard garden.

Elli's Rossmarkt Stüberl (Map 47, #15; ☎ 354 269, Rossmarkt 5) Meals €5.10-13.60. Open 8am-11pm Mon-Fri, 8.30am-2pm Sat. This place serves Austrian food, including several vegetarian options.

Gasthof Winkler (☎ 364 944, Mühlweg 64) Meals €7-18. Open 9.30am-2.30pm & 5.30pm-midnight Tues-Fri, 10.30am-2pm Sun. This upmarket restaurant is about 1km north of the Hauptbahnhof and offers good regional and seasonal dishes. On Sunday lunchtime there's an extensive buffet for €12.

Getting There & Away

St Pölten is 60km west of Vienna, on the hourly express train route running from Vienna's Westbahnhof (€9.05, 35 minutes) to Linz (€16.60, 1¼ hours) and beyond. From St Pölten, trains run north to Krems (€4.55, 40 minutes, hourly) and south to Mariazell €10.90, 2½ hours, two-hourly).

St Pölten has equally good road connections: the east-west A1/E60 passes a few kilometres south of the city and the S33 branches north from there, bypassing St Pölten to the east, and continuing to Krems. The east-west Hwy 1 passes through the city centre, from which Hwy 20 branches south to Mariazell.

Bundesbuses (eg, to Klosterneuburg, €10.20, 1½ hours, four each weekday) and taxis depart from outside the Hauptbahnhof (Map 47, #4).

The Danube Valley

The historical importance of the Danube Valley as a corridor between east and west ensured that control of this area was hotly contested. Consequently there are hundreds of fortresses in Lower and Upper Austria, including many monasteries and abbeys with defences to match conventional castles. The Wachau section of the Danube, between Krems and Melk, is the most scenic, with wine-producing villages, forested slopes, vineyards and imposing fortresses at nearly every bend.

The *Gästekarte* for the Wachau and Nibelungengau region offers a host of benefits for anyone staying in the region (approximately between Ybbs and Krems). If you stay in one resort you can get the benefits for *all* resorts, such as free entry to Melk's open-air swimming pool in the summer. Cards are provided with your accommodation and are funded by the nightly resort tax of around €0.80 per adult per night, which is usually included in the price of your room. The Wachau-Nibelungengau regional office (Map 48, #20; ☎ 02732-856 20, fax 874 71, e wachau@netway.at) is on the 1st floor at Undstrasse 6, A-3504 Krems, and is open 9am to 4.30pm weekdays.

This section covers the main Danube Valley attractions in order from west to east.

Getting Around

A popular way of exploring the Wachau region is by boat. G Glaser (Map 6, #8; ☎ 01-08 201, e g.glaser@xpoint.at, w www.user .xpoint.at/g.glaser/shipping.htm), 02, Handelskai 265, Vienna, is a helpful sales agent that sells tickets for all boat services, including on a paddle steamer going from Tulln to Melk on weekends from May to September (€10.95/17.45 one-way/return).

DDSG Blue Danube (☎ 01-588 80-0, fax 01-588 80-440, e info@ddsg-blue -danube.at, w www.ddsg-blue-danube.at), 01, Friedrichstrasse 7, Vienna, operates steamers between Melk and Krems from late March to late October, with three departures daily (only one in the first and last few weeks

LOWER AUSTRIA

of the season). The full trip takes 1 hour 40 minutes going downstream and an hour longer going upstream (ie, Krems to Melk); the fare is €14.55/19.65 one-way/return. From either town to Spitz costs €8/10.90 one-way/return. Boats also stop at Dürnstein. A commentary en route (in English) highlights points of interest. You get a discount of 20% off DDSG's Wachau fares if you have Inter-Rail, Eurail or Austrian Domino rail passes. Bicycles can be taken on board free.

The stretch east of the Wachau and on to Vienna is less interesting, so DDSG runs boats from Dürnstein to Vienna only once in each direction on Sunday, early May to 30 September (€14.55, 4¼ to 5¾ hours). See Linz in the Upper Austria chapter for information on the limited Linz-Vienna services.

Brandner (☎ 07433-25 90-21, e schiffahrt@brandner.at) has two boats daily on the Krems-Melk stretch, sailing from late April to mid-October. Melk-Krems is €15.50/20.50 one-way/return, or it's €9/12 from either town as far as Spitz. Bicycle transport is also free.

Ardagger (☎ 07479-64 64-0, e dsa@pgv.at) does two-hour tours of the Strudengau area, which includes Grien and Ybbs (€12), most Sundays and holidays between Easter and 26 October.

The route by road is also scenic and cycling is extremely popular in summer. There is a bicycle track along the south bank from Vienna to Krems, and along both sides of the river from Krems to Linz. East of Vienna, a bicycle track runs north of the river to Hainburg. Most tourist offices in the region can provide useful cycling information. If you're driving, Hwy 3 links Vienna and Linz and stays close to the north bank of the Danube for much of the way.

The rail track that runs along the north bank of the Danube takes slow local trains (2nd class only). It makes 31 stops on the 120km, three hour trip between Krems and St Valentin, including at Dürnstein, Weissenkirchen, Spitz, Emmersdorf, Klein Pöchlarn, Grein and Mauthausen. But only one train a day completes the full route (four in summer): most trains only run between Krems and Emmersdorf and between Grein

and St Valentin. Some of the small stations are unstaffed; you must buy a ticket from ticket machines or on the train.

WEST OF MELK

Amstetten is south of the Danube, on the main road/rail route between Linz and Melk. It has little of tourist interest, though it does stand at the junction where road, river and rail routes head south. If you're travelling this way into Styria, be sure to stop off at **Waidhofen an der Ybbs**, a stunningly attractive riverside town, with historic gabled houses, arcaded courtyards and dramatic onion domes.

North-east of Amstetten, on the Danube, is Ybbs. The stretch of the river from Ybbs to Melk is known as the Nibelungengau, after the medieval epic poem, the *Nibelungenlied*, which was mostly set in these parts (see Literature in Facts About Austria). After Ybbs, the next boat stop is at Marbach. Three kilometres along a road that wriggles northwards from here is the pilgrimage church of **Maria Taferl** (☎ *07413-278, Maria Taferl 1; open 7am-7pm daily*). This baroque creation with two onion domes was the work of Jakob Prandtauer, who also worked on the abbey at Melk.

About 5km north-east of Maria Taferl, taking minor roads, is **Artstetten**, notable for an onion-domed castle that has been much modified in the last 700 years. It was formerly owned and occupied by Archduke Franz Ferdinand, to whom a **museum** (☎ *07413-83 02, Artstetten 1; adult/senior/student €5.85/5.10/4.40; open 9am-5.30pm daily 1 Apr-2 Nov)* is devoted. The assassination of the archduke and his wife sparked WWI. The tomb of the unlucky pair is in the church. Artstetten is 3km north of Klein Pöchlarn, which is across the river from its larger cousin, Pöchlarn. There's no bridge, but these places are linked by ferry. Danube steamers stop at the Pöchlarn side.

MELK

☎ 02752 • pop 6500 • elev 228m

Lying in the lee of its imposing monastery-fortress, Melk is an essential stop on the Danube trail.

Historically, the site of Melk was of great importance to both the Romans and the Babenbergs. In 1089 the Babenberg margrave Leopold II donated the castle to Benedictine monks, who converted it into a fortified abbey. Fire destroyed the original edifice, which was completely rebuilt between 1702 and 1738 according to plans by Jakob Prandtauer and his follower, Josef Munggenast. Extensive restorations were completed in 1995.

Orientation & Information

The train station is 300m from the town centre. Walk 50m down Bahnhofstrasse to reach the post office (Postamt 3390), open 8am to noon and 2pm to 6pm Monday to Friday, 8am to 10am Saturday. Turn right for the Jugndherberge or carry straight on, taking Bahngasse for the central Rathausplatz.

Turn right at Rathausplatz for the tourist office (☎ 523 07-410, fax 523 07-490, e melk@smaragd.at) at Babenbergerstrasse 1. It's closed from November to March (unless staff happen to be there); otherwise it's open 9am to noon and 2pm to 6pm weekdays, 10am to 2pm Saturday, and (May to September) 10am to 2pm Sunday. In July and August, Monday to Saturday hours stretch to 9am to 7pm. Staff at the office will make room reservations.

Bicycles can be rented at the train station.

Stift Melk

This Benedictine abbey (☎ 555-232, w www.stiftmelk.at, Abt Berthold Dietmayr Strasse 1; adult/senior/student €5.10/4.75/ 2.55, guided tour €1.50, family €13.10/ 10.20 with/without guided tour; open 9am-5pm daily late Mar-early Nov, until 6pm May-Sept) dominates the town from its commanding hill site, and provides an excellent view from the terrace. Monks have resided here for over 900 years. Visitors are permitted to roam the abbey buildings unaccompanied, but regular guided tours highlight interesting details and are well worth the small extra charge.

The huge **monastery church** is enclosed by the buildings, but still dominates the complex with its twin spires and high octagonal dome. The inside is baroque gone mad, with endless prancing angels and gold twirls, but is still extremely impressive. The theatrical high altar scene, depicting St Peter and St Paul (the two patron saints of the church), is by Peter Widerin. Johann Michael Rottmayr did most of the ceiling paintings, including those in the dome.

Other high points are the library and the mirror room: both have painted tiers on the ceiling (by Paul Troger) to give the illusion of greater height. The ceilings are slightly curved to aid the effect. Imperial rooms, where various dignitaries stayed (including Napoleon), contain museum exhibits.

During winter, the monastery can be visited by guided tour only. Even in summer, phone ahead to ensure you get on an English-language tour. If you also want to visit Schloss Schallaburg (see that section later in this chapter), get a combined ticket.

Old Town Centre

Other interesting buildings around town date mostly from the 16th and 17th centuries. Try the walking tour outlined in the tourist office map, particularly along the pedestrian-only Hauptstrasse and Sterngasse. Don't miss the excellent facade of the Altes Posthaus at Linzer Strasse 3–5.

Special Events

The Melker Sommerspiele (mid-July to mid-August) features open-air theatre. Whitsuntide baroque concerts are held in Stift Melk during May.

Places to Stay & Eat

Camping Melk (☎ 532 91, Kolomaniau 3) Sites per adult/tent/car €3.35/2.55/1.85. Reception/restaurant open 8am-10pm daily Mar-Oct. Meals €5.45-10.50. Based at the Melker Fährhaus Jensch, this camping ground is 1km out of town, to the west of the canal where it joins the Danube. The restaurant has two-course weekday lunches for €5.45.

Jugendherberge (☎ 526 81, fax 542 57, Abt Karl Strasse 42) Bed in 4-bed dorm with shower under 19/adult €9.10/11.70. Check-in 5pm-9pm. Open 31 Mar–mid-Oct. This

HI hostel is 10 minutes' walk from the station. Doors are locked during the day. There are sports and games facilities and parking spaces. Add a one-time €1.85 surcharge if staying under three nights.

The tourist office accommodation leaflet lists inexpensive private rooms. Most are away from the centre of town; an exception is *Hammer* (☎ 528 23, Bahnhofstrasse 7), charging €16 per person.

Gasthof Goldener Stern (☎ 522 14, fax 522 14-4, Sterngasse 17) Singles €20-24, doubles €34-40. Reception/restaurant closed Fri & Sat in winter, Tues & Wed in summer. This place offers good prices for the centre and rooms (all with shared shower) are non-standardised and sizeable. The restaurant serves affordable Austrian and vegetarian food.

Gasthof Weisses Lamm (☎ 540 85, Linzer Strasse 7) Singles/doubles €26/40. The eight old-style rooms with bathrooms on offer are good value.

Gasthof zum Goldenen Hirschen (☎/fax 522 57, Rathausplatz 13) Singles/doubles with private shower €31/47, with shared shower €29/43. Meals €5.85-10.20. Open 7am-11pm daily. This 16th-century house has pleasant if compact rooms. Its *Rathauskeller* restaurant has Austrian food, including fixed-price two-course menus.

Stadt Melk (☎ 525 47, fax 525 47-19, e hotel.stadtmelk@netway.at, Hauptplatz 1) Singles €48-55, doubles €60-80. Meals €14.20-23.30. Kitchen open noon-2.30pm & 6pm-9.30pm daily. This three-star place has stylish, modern-style rooms with shower, toilet and TV. The restaurant is gourmet quality, and the proprietor maintains an extensive wine cellar – the wine menu is as thick as a book!

Self-caterers can stock up at the *Spar* supermarket, in the town centre at Rathausplatz 9. It's open 7am to 6pm weekdays, 7am to noon Saturday.

Pizzeria Venezia (☎ 512 24, Linzer Strasse 7) Meals €4.75-10.50. Open 11am-2.30pm & 5pm-11pm daily. Sharing a building with Gasthof Weisses Lamm, this restaurant offers tasty pizzas, plus pasta and Greek dishes. There are outside tables.

China Restaurant Krone (☎ 536 70, Linzer Strasse 7) Meals €6.40-8.55. Open 11am-2.30pm & 5.30pm-11pm Tues-Sun. This restaurant has the usual cheap lunches Monday to Friday.

Getting There & Away

Boats leave from the canal by Pionierstrasse, 400m to the north of the abbey. Trains to Melk depart from Vienna's Westbahnhof (€12.10, hourly, 1¼ hours), sometimes changing at St Pölten.

SCHLOSS SCHALLABURG

This splendid Renaissance castle-cum-palace (☎ 02754-6317, W www.schallaburg .at, Schallaburg 1; complex and exhibition adult/senior/student/family €6.55/5.10/2.95/ 13.10; open 9am-5pm Mon-Fri, 9am-6pm Sat, Sun & holidays late Apr-late Oct), 5km south of Melk, is a rewarding excursion. The architectural centrepiece is a two-storey arcaded Renaissance courtyard with magnificent terracotta arches. The rich red-brown carvings set against whitewashed walls cry out to be photographed. There are some 400 terracotta images, completed between 1572 and 1573. The largest figures support the upper storey arches – note the court jester sniggering in the corner. Below these are pictorial scenes and a series of mythological figures and masks. A recorded commentary (€0.75) explains the significance of some of the images. Annually the castle hosts a prestigious exhibition – in past years Tibet, magic and the Habsburgs have been covered. Combined tickets with nearby attractions (eg, Stift Melk, €9.85) are usually on offer.

There's an excellent mid-range *restaurant* in the castle.

Getting There & Away

There are only four Bundesbuses a day from Melk to Schallaburg (€2.20, 10 minutes). Hiring a bike from Melk train station gives more flexibility.

MELK TO DÜRNSTEIN

In addition to the many vineyards, look for peaches and apricots that are grown on this

Sunny day for street life in Mondsee, near Salzburg

Intricate carvings at St Florian Abbey in Upper Austria

St Florian Abbey, Upper Austria

The peak of Feuerkogel towers above a village in the Salzkammergut

MARK HONAN

The magnificent Benedictine Abbey in Melk

DIANA MAYFIELD

Lanner/Strauss monument in Kurpark, Baden

DIANA MAYFIELD

Visiting musicians in Krems, on the Danube

DIANA MAYFIELD

An early-morning moment in Josefplatz, Baden

DIANA MAYFIELD

Cyclists in the Rathausplatz, Melk

The Venus of Willendorf

The 25,000-year-old Venus of Willendorf is one of the most famous prehistoric sculptures of the human form. Discovered by archaeologist Josef Szombathy in 1908, it has since become an icon of the original 'Earth Mother'. There is much debate about what clues the 5cm-tall sandstone figure can reveal about life in 23,000 BC. Some believe the sculpture shows the esteemed role of women in prehistoric society and that mankind worshipped a female deity or Earth Mother.

Others reject Venus' status as goddess, arguing that the attention to detail, from her plaited hair to her dimpled arms, suggests that the artist used a living model, although a lack of face and feet would seem to refute this. If, however, the figure was modelled on that of a real woman, her generous body reveals clues about that woman's status. In a hunter-gatherer society, such a body would equate with an unusually sedate lifestyle, implying a special social status.

The tiny figurine may have served as a good-luck charm, carried on hunting missions to ensure a fruitful catch. The red ochre staining could represent blood spilt while foraging, or menstrual blood, indicating that Venus was a symbol used to promote fertility.

Whatever the Venus of Willendorf signified in prehistoric times, today her great age and voluptuous form make her a symbol of fertility, procreativity and nurturing, as well as a modern-day commodity in reproduction art. The statue is on show in the Naturhistorisches Museum (Natural History Museum) in Vienna.

MH

Lisa Ball

30km-long passage of the Danube. Even the steepest hills are terraced and cultivated.

Shortly after departing Melk you pass the 12th-century **Schloss Schönbühel**, standing high on a rock on the south bank, which officially marks the beginning of the Wachau Region. There's also a Servite monastery (the Servites were a mendicant order of friars) dating from the 17th century. Immediately afterwards, on the same side, are the ruins of **Burg Aggstein**, a 12th-century castle complex built by the Kuenringer family. These so-called 'robber barons' are said to have imprisoned their enemies on a ledge of rock (the Rosengärtlein), where the hapless captives faced starvation, unless they opted for a quicker demise by throwing themselves into the abyss below.

On the opposite bank **Willendorf** soon appears, where a 25,000-year-old sandstone statuette of Venus was discovered (see the boxed text 'The Venus of Willendorf').

A further 5km brings **Spitz** into view, a peaceful village with attractive houses. The parish church (☎ 02713-2231, Kirchenplatz; open 8am-6pm daily) is unusual for its chancel, which is out of line with the main body of the church. Other noteworthy features are the 15th-century statues of the 12 apostles lining the organ loft; most wear an enigmatic expression, as if being tempted by an unseen spirit to overindulge in the communion wine. It's a Gothic church with crisscross ceiling vaulting, yet has baroque altars. The fountain in front and the vine-covered hills rising behind make a pretty picture. One hill, the Tausendeimerberg, is so-named for its reputed ability to yield a thousand buckets of wine per season. The tourist office (☎ 02713-23 63, e info.spitz@ wvnet.at) in the village centre can give information about accommodation.

Six kilometres farther along the north bank is **Weissenkirchen**. Its centrepiece is a hill-top fortified parish church (☎ 02715-2203, Weissenkirchen 3; open 8am-7pm daily Easter-1 Nov, 8am-5pm Sat & Sun 2 Nov-Easter). This Gothic church was built in the 15th century and has a baroque altar. The garden terrace, if open, provides good views of the Danube. Below the church is the charming Teisenhoferhof arcaded courtyard, with a covered gallery and lashings of flowers and dried corn. The **Wachau Museum** (☎ 02715-2268, Weissenkirchen 177; adult/student €2.20/1.10; open 10am-5pm Tues-Sun 1 Apr-31 Oct) is here, containing work by artists of the Danube school. The tourist office (☎ 02715-26 00, **e** weissenkirchen@ utanet.at) is in the village centre.

After Weissenkirchen the river sweeps to the right and yields a fine perspective of Dürnstein.

Getting There & Away

All scheduled boats stop at Spitz, but only the westward Brandner boats call at Weissenkirchen. The Wachau railway runs along the north bank, connecting all of the villages on that side. Krems to Spitz costs €3.20 (25 minutes, hourly); you can hire bikes at Spitz train station. Drivers wishing to stay close to the river can choose a road on either bank.

DÜRNSTEIN

☎ 02711 • pop 1000 • elev 209m

One of the prime destinations in the Wachau, Dürnstein achieved notoriety in the 12th century when King Richard I (the Lionheart) of England was imprisoned here.

Orientation & Information

From the train station, walk ahead and then right for the village walls (about five minutes). En route you pass the tourist office (☎ 200), in a little hut in the corner of the eastern car park. It's only open from April to October: 1pm to 7pm Monday, Thursday and Friday, 11am to 7pm Saturday and Sunday. You can get information from the Rathaus (☎ 219, fax 442, **e** duernstein@ netway.at) on Hauptstrasse, the main street 7.30am to noon and 1pm to 4pm weekdays all year.

The boat landing stage is below the dominating feature of the village centre, the blue and white parish church.

Things to See & Do

High on the hill, commanding a marvellous view of the curve of the Danube, stand the ruins of **Kuenringerburg**, the castle where Richard was incarcerated from 1192 to 1193. His crime was to have insulted Leopold V; his misfortune was to be recognised despite his disguise when journeying through Austria on his way home from the Holy Lands; his liberty was achieved only upon the payment of a huge ransom of 35,000kg of silver (which partly funded the building of Wiener Neustadt). It was here that the singing minstrel Blondel attempted to rescue his sovereign. The walk up from the village takes about 15 to 20 minutes.

In the village, Hauptstrasse is a cobbled street with picturesque 16th-century houses, wrought-iron signs and floral displays. Views are also good where the road descends at the western end of the village.

The meticulously restored **Chorherrenstift** (abbey church; ☎ 375 or 227, Stift 1; adult/student €2.20/1.50; open 9am-6pm daily 1 Apr-31 Oct) is all that remains of the former Augustinian monastery. Founded in 1410 and now functioning as the parish church, it received its baroque facelift in the 18th century (overseen by Josef Munggenast, among others). The exterior has plenty of saints and angels adopting pious poses on and around the pristine blue and white steeple; the interior effectively combines white stucco and dark wood balconies. Kremser Schmidt did many of the ceiling and altar paintings. Entry includes access to the porch overlooking the Danube and an exhibition on the Augustinian monks who once ruled the roost here (up until the monastery was dissolved by Joseph II in 1788).

Places to Stay & Eat

Private rooms are cheapest; for example, **Hermine Wagner** (☎ 265, Hauptstrasse 29) has four beds from €14.55 per person.

Pension Böhmer (☎/fax 239, Hauptstrasse 22) Singles €31, doubles €38-62. This place doubles as a wine shop and has rooms that are on the small side with shower, toilet and TV.

Pension Altes Rathaus (☎/fax 252, Hauptstrasse 26) Singles/doubles €37/51. Closed Dec-Feb. This pension with quiet and largish rooms with bathrooms is reached through an attractive courtyard.

Gasthof Sänger Blondel (☎ 253, fax 253-7, Klosterplatz) Singles €57, doubles €80-99. Meals €6.90-13.90. Kitchen open 11am-9pm Tues-Sat, 9am-4pm Sun. Relax in the comfortable bedrooms, which have shower, toilet, TV and traditional-style furnishings, then enjoy a meal in the shaded garden.

Gartenhotel Weinhof (☎ 206, fax 206-8, **e** *gartenhotel.duernstein@netway.at, Dürnstein 122)* Singles €54-70, doubles €68-110. This cosy hotel is about 1km west of the centre, with a range of rooms in either the main building or the annexe. Guests enjoy numerous facilities including a sauna, outdoor swimming pool, garden and restaurant. Rooms have shower, toilet and TV.

Goldener Strauss (☎ 267, Hauptstrasse 18) Meals €6.20-10. Open 10am-9pm Wed-Mon. This old Gasthaus turns out inexpensive regional food and has a small garden.

Alter Klosterkeller (☎ 292, Anzuggasse) Cold snacks/meals €1.90/4.75. Open 3pm-10pm Mon, Wed-Fri, 2pm-10pm Sat & Sun. This *Buschenschank* (wine tavern) is just outside the village walls on the eastern side) and overlooking the vineyards. Wine is €1.60 a *Viertel* (0.25L). For other wine taverns, get the calendar of opening times from the tourist office.

Restaurant Loibnerhof (☎ 828 90, Unterloiben 7) Meals €8.90-20.50. Kitchen open 11.30am-9.30pm Wed-Sun. This lakeside restaurant is 1.5km east of Dürnstein; it's highly regarded and reasonably priced.

Getting There & Away

Krems and Weissenkirchen are both about 20 minutes away by Brandner boat (€5.50). By hourly train, the fare is €1.90 to either. Dürnstein's train station is called Dürnstein-Oberloiben.

KREMS AN DER DONAU

☎ 02732 • pop 23,000 • elev 202m

Krems lies on the north bank of the Danube, surrounded by terraced vineyards. It was first mentioned in documents in 995, and has been a centre of the wine trade for most of its history.

Orientation & Information

Krems comprises three linked parts: Krems to the east, the smaller settlement of Stein (formerly a separate town) to the west, and the connecting suburb of Und. Hence the local witticism: *Krems und Stein sind drei Städte* (Krems and Stein are three towns).

The centre of Krems stretches along a pedestrian-only street, Obere and Untere Landstrasse. The tourist office (Map 48, #20; ☎ 826 76, fax 700 11, **e** austropa.krems@netway.at) is between Krems and Stein at Undstrasse 6, in the Kloster Und building. It's part of the Austropa travel agency, and sells packages to Austrian attractions. It's open 9am to 7pm weekdays and 10am to noon and 1pm to 7pm weekends. Between 1 November and 30 April hours are 9am to 6pm weekdays and 10am to noon. Room reservations are made free of charge, and there's a free phone and accommodation board outside.

The main post office (Map 48, #19; Postamt 3500) is at Brandströmstrasse 4–6. There's Internet access (€0.10 per minute) at www.net-cafe (Map 48, #5), Untere Landstrasse 3, open 8am to 10pm Monday to Saturday, 10am to 10pm Sunday and holidays.

The boat station (Map 48, #23) is on Donaustrasse, about 2km west of the train station.

Things to See & Do

There are several Renaissance and baroque houses lining Untere and Obere Landstrasse in Krems, and Steiner Landstrasse in Stein; a peaceful stroll along these cobbled streets is rewarding. Quaint courtyards hide behind some of the old facades, and the odd remnant of the city walls remains. The distinctive **Steinertor** *(Map 48, #14)* on Obere Landstrasse dates from the 15th century; this triple-towered gate is the town's emblem. Near the **Linzertor,** in Stein, is the house occupied from 1756 by the artist Martin Johann Schmidt, often known as Kremser Schmidt.

Krems has several churches with interiors worth investigating. **Pfarrkirche St Veit**

MAP 48 – KREMS AN DER DONAU

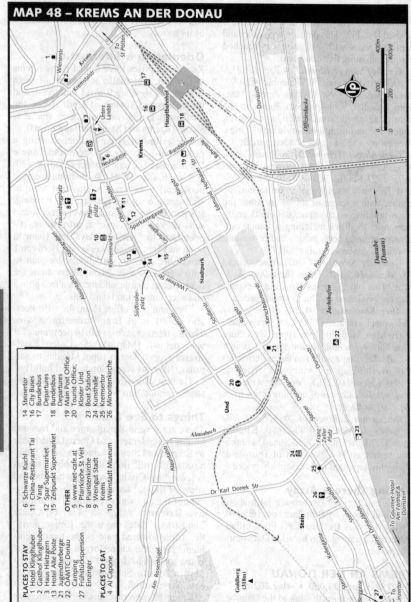

LOWER AUSTRIA

PLACES TO STAY
1 Hotel Klinghuber
2 Gasthof Klinghuber
3 Haus Hietzgern
21 Hotel Alte Poste
22 ÖAMTC Donau Camping
27 Frühstückspension Einzinger

PLACES TO EAT
4 Al Capone

6 Schwarze Kuchl
11 China-Restaurant Tai Yang
12 Spar Supermarket
15 Zielpunkt Supermarket

OTHER
5 www.net-cafe.at
7 Pfarrkirche St Veit
8 Piaristenkirche
9 Weingut Stadt Krems
10 Weinstadt Museum

14 Steinertor
16 City Buses
17 Bundesbus Departures
18 Bundesbus Departures
19 Main Post Office
20 Tourist Office; Kloster Und
23 Boat Station
24 Kunsthalle
25 Kremsertor
26 Minoritenkirche

(Map 48, #7; ☎ 832 85, Pfarrplatz 5; open approx 7am-7.30pm daily), is fitted out in baroque style, though it had earlier Gothic and Romanesque incarnations. The ceiling frescoes are by Kremser Schmidt. The 15th-century **Piaristenkirche** *(Piarist Church; Map 48, #8; ☎ 820 92, Frauenbergplatz; open approx 7am-6pm daily)*, behind Pfarrkirche St Veit, has Gothic vaulting, huge windows and baroque altars.

The **Weinstadt Museum** *(Map 48, #10; ☎ 801-567, Körnermarkt 14; adult/concession €3.65/2.55; open 1pm-6pm Wed-Sun, 9am-6pm Tues Mar-Nov)* is housed in the atmospheric confines of a former Dominican monastery (the Dominikanerkirche). As you might expect, the museum gives an exposition of wine-making, though there are also displays of early archaeological finds, as well as some of Kremser Schmidt's paintings.

Close to the Kremsertor is an arts centre, the **Kunsthalle** *(Map 48, #24; ☎ 826 69, fax 826 69-16, e office@kunsthalle.at, w www.kunsthalle.at; Franz Zeller Platz 3, admission €3.65-7; open 10am-6pm daily, closed Mon Oct-mid-May)*. Temporary displays organised by the centre are sometimes held in the **Minoritenkirche** *(Map 48, #26)* in Stein.

The free street plan from the tourist office details other points of interest. Wine buffs can enjoy tasting 100 different wines in the **Kloster Und** *(Map 48, #20; ☎ 826 76, Undstrasse 6; admission €13.10; open 1pm-7pm Wed-Sun, 1pm-7pm daily May-Sept, closed Jan & Feb)*, home of a wine college. **Weingut der Stadt Krems** *(Map 48, #9; ☎ 801 440, Stadtgraben 11; open 8am-noon & 1pm-5pm Mon-Sat)* also has wine tasting (€0.75 per glass).

Special Events

In August, Krems hosts its Niederösterreichische Landesmesse, a folklore festival staged every second year (next in 2002). The annual Donau festival of the arts, with some events held in Krems, runs from mid-June to early July.

Places to Stay

Many places charge a surcharge of €1.50 to €2.50 for a single-night stay. As ever, private rooms are a good deal, and details of these are in the tourist office's accommodation brochure.

ÖAMTC Donau Camping *(Map 48, #22; ☎ 844 55, Wiedengasse 7)* Site per adult/tent/car €4.40/2.20/2.95. Open Easter–mid-Oct. This lakeside camp site is just east of the boat station.

Jugendherberge *(Map 48, #21; ☎ 834 52, fax 834 52-4, e oejhv.noe.krems@aon.at, Ringstrasse 77)* Bed in 4–6-bed dorm €12.20, additional €2.20 surcharge per night for stays of one or two nights. Closed 9am-5pm, check-in 5pm-8pm. Open 1 Apr-30 Oct. This HI hostel has excellent facilities for cyclists, such as a garage and an on-site repair service.

Haus Hietzgern *(Map 48, #3; ☎/fax 761 84, Untere Landstrasse 53)* Doubles/triples with shower/toilet €22 per person. Open 1 June-31 Aug. This home has four guest rooms; it has an ideal central location and a baroque facade.

Frühstückspension Einzinger *(Map 48, #27; ☎ 823 16, fax 823 16-6, Steiner Landstrasser 82)* Singles €36, doubles €24-27. This pension in Stein offers elegant, old-style rooms with shower, toilet and TV arranged around an attractive courtyard.

Hotel Alte Poste *(Map 48, #13; ☎ 822 76, fax 843 96, Obere Landstrasse 32)* Singles/doubles with private shower & TV €39/60, without €27/48. Doubles with shower/toilet & TV €34. Open March–mid-Dec. This 500-year-old house provides good rooms and an enchanting courtyard.

Gasthof Klinglhuber *(Map 48, #2; ☎ 869 60, fax 869 60-50, e klinglhuber@netway.at, Wienerstrasse 2)* Singles €44-58, doubles €70-88. Overlooking the river, this Gasthof offers renovated or slightly older rooms, but either way furnished to a good standard with polished wooden floors and with shower, toilet, TV and telephone.

Gourmet-Hotel Am Förthof *(☎ 833 45, fax 833 45-40, e hotel.foerthof@netway.at, Förthofer Donaulände 8)* Singles €44-73, doubles €88-124. Open 15 Mar-15 Jan. About 500m west of Stein, this small hotel has a romantic ambience, a garden and an outdoor swimming pool. Rooms all have bath or shower, toilet and TV. Prices vary depending on the room size and season.

Hotel Klinglhuber (Map 48, #1; ☎ 821 43, fax 821 43-50, e klinglhuber@net way.at, Wienerstrasse 12) Singles €63-72, doubles €99-118. This is the recently built (garnering an architectural award along the way), modern-style companion to the original Gasthof. Four-star rooms have all facilities (bathroom, TV, telephone), and plenty of light from big windows.

Places to Eat
Supermarkets include *Spar (Map 48, #12)* on Obere Landstrasse and *Zeilpunkt (Map 48, #15)* in the shopping centre by the Steinertor.

Near where Untere and Obere Landstrasse join there are several snack bars and take-away bars.

Schwarze Kuchl (Map 48, #6; ☎ 831 28, Untere Landstrasse 8) Meals €4.75-7.50. Open 8am-7.30pm Mon-Fri & 8am-5pm Sat. This is a small, simple, inexpensive cafe. The kitchen is open until 6.30pm.

China-Restaurant Tai Yang (Map 48, #11; Obere Landstrasse 5) Meals €4.40-11. Open 11.30am-2.30pm & 5.30pm-11.30pm daily. This restaurant is back from the street and has courtyard seating; weekday lunch menus are a good deal.

Al Capone (Map 48, #4; ☎ 754 44, Untere Landstrasse 30-32) Meals €4.60-11.70. Open 11.30am-2.30pm & 5pm-midnight daily. Come here for inexpensive Italian and Greek food and gangster-themed decor.

Gasthof Klinglhuber (Map 48, #2; ☎ 821 43, Wienerstrasse 2) Meals 6.50-13.50. Open 7am-11pm daily. This restaurant has terrace seating overlooking the Krems River and serves tasty Austrian food. Most meals are above €8.75, though a few cheaper, light meals are also served.

Hotel Alte Poste (Map 48, #13; ☎ 822 76, Obere Landstrasse 32) Meals €6.50-18. Open 7am-10pm Thur-Mon, 7am-2pm Tues March–mid-Dec. This old-fashioned place has a pleasant restaurant, with tables inside or in a courtyard. Local wine costs from €2 per Viertel.

Gourmet-Hotel Am Förthof (☎ 833 45, Förthofer Donaulände 8) Meals €6.90-

21.80. Open 7am-midnight Tues-Sun 15 Mar-15 Jan, 7am-midnight daily Apr-Oct. As its name implies, this is a good place to eat, particularly for regional specialities. The kitchen is open until 10pm.

Don't omit a visit to a *Heurigen* (wine tavern); most are out of the centre and provide an authentic experience in eating and drinking. They're only open for two- or three-week bursts during the year: get the timetable from the tourist office.

Getting There & Away
Four or five daily Bundesbuses (two or three at weekends) depart for Melk from outside the train station (€5.85, 65 minutes). Local buses also go between Krems and Stein (€1.50, every 30 minutes). There are trains every hour to Franz Josefs Bahnhof in Vienna (€12.10, one hour).

Bikes can be rented at the train station, Camping Donau and some hotels. Cyclists are very welcome in Krems; some hotels have bike garages and repair facilities.

AROUND KREMS
Stift Göttweig
This abbey *(☎ 02732-85581-231, w www .stiftgoettweig.at, Furth bei Göttweig; adult/ student €4.40/2.20, guided tour €1.50; open 10am-5pm daily 21 Mar-15 Nov)* was founded in 1083 and given to the Benedictine order 11 years later. Six kilometres south of Krems, the abbey's position on a hill makes its towers and onion domes clearly visible from afar (and you can view to afar from the garden terrace or the restaurant in the abbey grounds). What remains today is mostly the baroque work begun in 1719 following a devastating fire. The plans for rebuilding were never fully realised, resulting in an asymmetric but impressive complex. The abbey church has ceiling frescoes (dating from 1739) by Paul Troger; Kremser Schmidt also contributed to the church and to the imperial apartments, which are part of the abbey.

Getting There & Away Only two or three daily buses leave from outside Krems train station (€2.20, 15 minutes), and none on

Sunday. Going via train (to Klein Wien, on the St Pölten line) is another possibility.

WALDVIERTEL

North and west of Krems is the Waldviertel, a less-visited forested region, which is ideal for off-the-beaten-track walking and outdoor sports. You'll also find affordable accommodation, ambience that is typical of rural Austria, and a smattering of historical buildings. English is not so widely spoken in these parts. For more information on local attractions, including Stift Zwettl, contact the Tourismusregion Waldviertel (☎ 02822-541 09-0, fax 02822-541 09-36, e touris mus@wvnet.at), Hauptplatz 4, A-3910 Zwettl.

An important site in the region is the Benedictine **Stift Altenburg** (☎ 02982-3451-21, w www.stift-altenburg.at, Stift 1; adult/ senior/student/family €7/6/3/14, plus €1.50 for guided tour; open 10am-5pm daily 1 Apr-1 Nov, to 6pm 14 June-2 Sept; tours 11am, 2pm & 3pm Sat & Sun 1 Apr-1 Nov), founded in 1144. In the ensuing centuries it was all but destroyed by plundering hordes, until extensive baroque rebuilding began in 1650. The abbey library (with ceiling frescoes by Paul Troger) and the crypt (featuring frescoes by Troger's pupils) are among the most impressive examples of their kind in Austria. The abbey church was created by Josef Munggenast between 1730 and 1733. The church contains some of Troger's best frescoes (in the central dome, and above the high and side altars). The gilded organ dates from 1773. You can visit the church without taking a tour.

A few kilometres south of Altenburg is **Schloss Rosenburg** (☎ 02982-2911, Rosenburg am Kamp; tours adult/concession/family €7.35/5.85/16.10, or €9.45/ 8.05/ 21.95 including falconry and pageantry; open 9am-5pm daily 1 Apr-1 Nov). This multi-turreted edifice was built between the 14th and 17th centuries. Falconry shows are between 11am and 3pm. A similar distance west of Altenburg is the 16th-century **Schloss Greillenstein** (☎ 02989-8080-21, Greillenstein 1, interior tours €5; open 9.30am-5pm daily 1 Apr-31 Oct, to 6pm July & Aug).

Getting There & Away

Rosenburg is on a rail line that runs north from Krems (€3.05, 55 minutes, every two hours). For the other destinations you'll have to rely on Bundesbuses if you don't have your own transport; call ☎ 01-71101 for bus information.

Zwettl is on a rail line but it's a very circuitous route from Krems, involving two changes, whereas the Bundesbus is direct (€8.40, three or four buses daily, one to 1½ hours).

TULLN

☎ 02272 • pop 12,300 • elev 180m

Formerly a Roman camp called Comagena, and named as a town settlement in 791, Tulln calls itself the 'Birthplace of Austria' and was in effect the nation's first capital.

Orientation & Information

Tulln is 29km west of Vienna, on the south bank of the Danube River. The centre of town is the pedestrian-only Hauptplatz. The tourist office (☎ 658 36, fax 658 38, e tull ner.donauraum@aon.at) is one block north at Minoritenplatz 2. It's open 9am to 6pm Monday to Friday, and 1pm to 6pm weekends and holidays. From 1 October to 30 April hours are only 9am to noon weekdays. Staff reserve rooms without charging commission.

Tulln train station is 15 minutes' walk south-east of Hauptplatz; from the station, turn right into Bahnweg, right at Brückenstrasse, and left onto Wiener Strasse. Tulln Stadt is an S-Bahn station (for suburban trains from Vienna), just five minutes' walk south of Hauptplatz along Bahnhofstrasse.

Café Lime, Hauptplatz 5, offers daily Internet access for €0.10 per minute.

Things to See & Do

Next to the tourist office, in the Minoritenkloster, is a complex of museums, the **Tullner Museen** (☎ 619 15, Minoritenplatz 1; adult/concession €2.20/1.45; open 3pm-6pm Wed-Fri, 2pm-6pm Sat and 10am-6pm Sun & holidays). Collections cover the city's history, both ancient and modern (including geology and Roman finds); one section deals with fire-fighting.

On the riverside is the **Egon Schiele Museum** (☎ 645 70, Donaulände 28; adult/concession €2.95/2.20; open 9am-noon & 2pm-6pm Tues-Sun). The exhibition vividly presents the story of the life of the Tulln-born artist – ask for the extensive English notes. Schiele is famous for his provocative nudes; he was briefly imprisoned in 1912 following the seizure of 125 erotic drawings (some were of pubescent girls, and Schiele was also in trouble for allowing children to see his explicit works). The premises are a former jail and contain a mock-up of his cell, though Schiele was actually jailed in Neulengbach. There are 100 of his works on display (plus copies), mostly sketches and early paintings.

Pfarrkirche St Stephan (☎ 623 38-0, Wiener Strasse 20; open daylight hours) is a Romanesque church, with alterations in Gothic and baroque style. Behind is a 13th-century polygonal funerary chapel, where frescoes depict some less than evil-looking devils. The crypt below has stacks of ex-humed bones – if you want a look, ask for the key in the Paulussaal at the other end of the church.

The town offers a variety of sports near the boat station, to the east of the centre, including a swimming pool complex (☎ 624 80, Karl Metz Gasse 1; entry €3.30; open 2pm-9pm Tues-Fri, 9am-9pm Sat, 9am-7pm Sun). The tourist office has plenty of information for cyclists.

Places to Stay & Eat

Donaupark Camping (☎ 652 00, fax 652 01, e campingtulln@oeamtc.at, Hafenstrasse 4) Price per adult/tent/car €5.85/4.40/4.40. Open Easter-early Oct. This camp site is east of the centre, near the harbour and sports facilities. You can rent a tent for €5.10.

Alpenvereins Herberge (☎ 626 92, Donaulände 1) Dorm beds €11.85, mattress on floor (own sleeping bag required) €9.65. Open 1 May-31 Oct. This place is beside the river, 300m west of the centre, and is reached by a pedestrian/cycling path. There's also an inexpensive restaurant.

Familien und Jugendgasstehaus Tulln (☎ 651 65, fax 651 65-4, e oejhw-wien -noe@telecom.at, Marc Aurel Park 5) Bed in 4–6-bed rooms with shower & toilet €11.70, plus €1.85 for stays of under three nights. Check-in 5pm-9pm. Open 1 Apr-31 Oct. North of St Stephan's, this HI hostel opened in 2001.

Private rooms are also a good option. Central choices are **Haus Elisabeth** (☎ 642 27, Nussallee 5), with a garden and doubles for €40.70 with shower/toilet or €28.35 without; and **Elisabeth Keindl** (☎ 633 37, Wilhelmstrasse 16), charging €36.40 for doubles with shower, toilet and TV.

Hotel-Restaurant Zur Rossmühle (☎ 624 11-0, fax 624 11-33, e rossmuehle@ tulln.com, Hauptplatz 13) Singles €51-73, doubles €65-103. Meals €11-18.50. Kitchen open 11.30-2pm & 6pm-10pm Tues-Sun. This place has an imperial aura and a veritable jungle of plants in the lobby, complete with tweeting birds. The rooms have high ceilings and a bathroom and TV. The restaurant is good quality, with interesting presentations of national dishes.

China Restaurant Pagode (☎ 624 64, Brudergasse 5) Meals €4.30-14.20. Open 11.30am-3pm & 5.30pm-11pm daily. Located off Hauptplatz, this restaurant offers cheap Chinese meals, especially at lunchtime Monday to Saturday. There's also an affordable sushi bar.

Albrechtsstuben (☎ 646 50, Albrechtsgasse 24) Meals €4.75-11.50. Open 8.30am-11pm Tues-Sat, 8.30am-3pm Sun. This restaurant is frequented by locals. It has good Austrian cooking, including fish and vegetarian choices, and a garden.

There's a **Zielpunkt** supermarket on Hauptplatz.

Getting There & Away

Tulln is reached hourly by train or S-Bahn (line 40) from Vienna's Franz Josefs Bahnhof (€4.60). The train is quicker (25 minutes), but only stops at the main Tulln station, while the S40 stops at Tulln Stadt. Heading west, trains go to Krems (€6.10, 40 minutes, hourly) or St Pölten (€6.70, one hour, hourly). The road to/from Vienna is Hwy 14, via Klosterneuburg.

KLOSTERNEUBURG
☎ 02243 • pop 33,000 • elev 192m

Overlooking the river at Klosterneuburg is a large Augustinian abbey, **Stift Klosterneuburg** (☎ *411-212,* **w** *www.stift-kloster neuburg.at, Stiftplatz 1; tour adult/concession €6.20/2.55; open 9am-5pm daily),* founded in 1114. The abbey buildings are mostly baroque and can be visited daily on a 45-minute guided tour (in English possible with advance notice). The abbey church is also baroque, despite its neo-Gothic spires. An annexe to the church contains St Leopold's Chapel. This houses the **Verdun Altar**, which is covered with 51 enamelled panels showing biblical scenes. It was constructed in 1181 by Nicholas of Verdun and is an unsurpassed example of medieval enamelwork.

Klosterneuberg is an easy excursion from Vienna, or you can ask the tourist office (☎ 343 96, **e** tourismus@klosterneuburg .com) about the accommodation options, which include a camp site and a youth hostel.

Getting There & Away
Klosterneuburg is on the S-Bahn route from Vienna to Tulln. Klosterneuburg-Kierling is the station closest to the abbey (€1.55 from Franz Josefs Bahnhof). Alternatively, walk there from Kahlenberg (at the end of bus No 38A from Vienna).

PETRONELL
☎ 02163 • pop 1250 • elev 190m

The village of Petronell lies close to the Danube, 38km east of Vienna. In Roman times it was the site of Carnuntum, a regional capital believed to have had 50,000 inhabitants. Ruins of that town extend to Bad Deutsch-Altenburg, 4km to the east.

Orientation & Information
Petronell train station is 1km south of the main street, Hauptstrasse. At the entrance to the archaeological park, at Hauptstrasse 296, is an office containing the March-Donauland tourist office (☎ 335 55-10, fax 335 55-12, **e** md-online@netway.at), open 8am to 5pm Monday to Friday, as well as the archaeological park information office

(☎ 3377-0, fax 3377-5, **e** info@carn untum.co.at), open 9am to 5pm Monday to Sunday.

Bad Deutsch-Altenburg's tourist office (☎ 02165-624 59, **e** baddeutsch-alten burg@netway.at) is at Erhardgasse 2.

Things to See & Do
The relics of Carnuntum's former glories are not particularly stunning, but added together they do make a reasonably diverting day – a combined ticket for the three priced attractions below costs €7.65 (concession €6.20).

Petronell's archaeological park (☎ *3377-0, Hauptstrasse 296; adult/concession €3.65/2.95; open 9am-5pm daily late Mar-early Nov)* lies on the site of the old civilian town. This park includes ruins of the public baths, a reconstructed temple, and tours and activities for children. The **Heidentor** (Heathen Gate; free) was once the southwest entrance to the city and now stands as an isolated anachronism amid fields of corn.

Along the road to Bad Altenburg is a grass-covered amphitheatre that formerly seated 15,000 (☎ *3377-0, Wienerstrasse 52; adult/concession €2.20/1.45; open 9am-5pm daily late Mar-early Nov).*

Bad Deutsch-Altenburg has a museum (☎ *02165-624 80, Badgasse 40-46; adult/concession €4.40/2.95; open 10am-5pm Tues-Sun late Mar-early Nov, 10am-5pm Sat & Sun early Nov–mid-Dec & mid-Jan–late Mar)* devoted to the Carnuntum era. This town also has a health spa, with iodine sulphur springs (28°C).

Hainburg, 3km farther east, is a possible additional excursion. It has further ancient relics, in the form of sturdy city gates and hilltop ruins.

Places to Stay & Eat
Gasthof Zum Heidentor (☎*/fax 2201, Hauptstrasse 129)* Singles/doubles with shower/toilet & TV €23.30/39.30. Meals €4.40-9.10. Rooms are renovated, and the restaurant has a beer garden, cheap lunch menus and children's play area. There's a **Denk** supermarket nearby on Hauptstrasse.

LOWER AUSTRIA

Hotel Marc Aurel (☎ *2285, fax 2285-60,* e *hotel.marc-aurel@contact.at, Hauptstrasse 173)* Singles/doubles €40-43, doubles €51-58. Meals €7.20-11.20; kitchen open 11.30am-2pm & 6pm-9.30pm. This is a small step up in quality – the pricier bedrooms are larger and newer, with shower, toilet, TV & telephone. The restaurant serves reliable Austrian and international dishes.

Bad Deutsch-Altenburg has a wider range of places to stay and eat – a good street to explore is the central Badgasse.

Pension Mittermayer (☎ *02165-628 74, Badgasse 20)* Singles/doubles €19/35. This small pension has simple, pleasant rooms with shared shower.

Pension Riedmüller (☎ *02165-624 73, fax 02165-624 73-32,* e *pension-riedmueller@ netway.at, Badgasse 28)* Singles/doubles €24/40. This place has decent rooms with private shower/toilet & TV and a cafe.

Stephanstub'n (☎ *02165-647 11, Badgasse 34)* Meals €6.60-14.20. Open 10am-10pm Tues-Sun. This hotel restaurant has affordable Austrian food, including a selection of veggie options.

Getting There & Away

From Vienna, S7 train (direction: Wolfsthal) departs Wien Nord hourly, calling via Wien Mitte. The 70-minute journey to Petronell costs €6.05, or €4.65 if you already have a Vienna city travel pass. To get to Bad Deutsch-Altenburg or Hainburg costs an extra €1.55.

The cycle path from Vienna goes along the north bank of the Danube, crosses to the south at Bad Deutsch-Altenburg, and continues into Slovakia.

NATIONAL PARK DONAU-AUEN

This national park, established in 1996, runs in a thin strip on both sides of the Danube, extending from the edge of Vienna to the Slovakian border. It was created to try to protect an environment that was threatened by the building of a hydroelectric power station in Hainburg. You'll find plentiful flora and fauna, including 700 species of fern and flowering plants, and a high density of

kingfishers (feeding off the 50 species of fish). There are guided tours by foot or boat. For more information contact Nationalpark Donau-Auen (☎ 02212-3450, fax 02212-3450-17, e nationalpark@donauau en.at, w www. donauauen.at).

Wienerwald

The Wienerwald (Vienna Woods) is a place to get off the beaten track and enjoy nature. **Walking** is popular, with numerous trails meandering through the trees. Schöpfl (893m) is the highest point, and has a panoramic lookout (with an Alpine hut open year-round). The signposted walk to Schöpfl lookout takes about two hours, starting from the car park off the Hainfeld-Laaben road, near the Klammhöhe Pass. Walking and cycling trails are shown on the *Wienerwald Wander und Radkarte*, available free from regional tourist offices.

Attractive settlements speckle the Wienerwald, such as the wine-growing centres of Perchtoldsdorf, Mödling and Gumpoldskirchen. Inquire at the respective tourist offices about accommodation. The tourist board for the Wienerwald (☎ 02231-621 76, fax 655 10, e wienerwald@netway.at) is at Hauptplatz 11, A-3200 Purkersdorf, just west of Vienna.

Mödling (population 20,500) was once favoured by the artistic elite escaping from Vienna: Beethoven's itchy feet took him to Hauptstrasse 79 from 1818 to 1820, and Schönberg stayed at Bernhardgasse 6 from 1918 to 1925. Mödling tourist office (☎ 02236-267 27, fax 02236-267 27-10) is at Elisabethstrasse 2, behind the Rathaus.

Mayerling has little to show now, but the bloody event that occurred there (see the boxed text 'Mystery at Mayerling') still draws people to the site. The Carmelite convent (☎ *02258-8703-2275, Mayerling 1; admission €1.50; open 9am-noon & 2pm-6pm daily)* can be visited, but all you see is a chapel and a couple of rooms of mementoes. Six kilometres to the northeast is **Heiligenkreuz**, where there's a 12th-century Cistercian abbey (☎ *02258-8703,*

Mystery at Mayerling

It's the stuff of lurid pulp fiction: the heir to the throne found dead in a hunting lodge with his teenage mistress. It became fact in Mayerling on 30 January 1889, yet for years the details of the case were shrouded in secrecy and denial. Even now a definitive picture has yet to be established – the 100th anniversary of the tragedy saw a flurry of books on the subject, and Empress Zita claimed publicly that the heir had actually been murdered.

The heir was Archduke Rudolf, 30-year-old son of Emperor Franz Josef, husband of Stephanie of Coburg, and something of a libertine who was fond of drinking and womanising. Rudolf's marriage was little more than a public facade by the time he met the 17-year-old Baroness Maria Vetsera in the autumn of 1888. The attraction was immediate, but it wasn't until 13 January of the following year that the affair was consummated, an event commemorated by an inscribed cigarette case, a gift from Maria to Rudolf.

On 28 January, Rudolf secretly took Maria with him on a shooting trip to his hunting lodge in Mayerling. His other guests arrived a day later; Maria's presence, however, remained unknown to them. On the night of the 29th, the valet, Loschek, heard the couple talking until the early hours, and at about 5.30am a fully dressed Rudolf appeared and instructed him to get a horse and carriage ready. As he was doing his master's bidding, two gun shots resounded through the still air. He raced back to discover Rudolf lifeless on his bed, with a revolver by his side. Maria was on her bed, also fully clothed, also dead. Just two days earlier Rudolf had discussed a suicide pact with a former mistress. Apparently he hadn't been joking.

Almost immediately the cover-up began. Count Hoyos, a guest at the lodge, told Maria's mother that it was Maria who killed both herself and the archduke with the aid of poison. The official line was proffered by Empress Elisabeth, who claimed Rudolf died of heart failure. There was no hint of suicide or a mistress. The newspapers swallowed the heart failure story, though a few speculated about a hunting accident. It was only much later that Rudolf's suicide letter to his wife was published in her memoirs, in which he talked of going calmly to his death.

Throughout the lies and misinformation, the real victim remains Maria. How much of a willing party she was to the suicide will never be known. What has become clear is that Maria, after her death, represented not a tragically curtailed young life but an embarrassing scandal that had to be discreetly disposed of. Her body was left untouched for 38 hours, after which it was loaded into a carriage in such a manner as to imply that it was a living person being aided rather than a corpse beyond help. Her subsequent burial was a rude, secretive affair, during which she was consigned to the ground in an unmarked grave (her body was later moved to Heiligenkreuz). Today the hunting lodge is no more – a Carmelite nunnery stands in its place.

LOWER AUSTRIA

Heiligenkreuz 1, W *www.stift-heiligenkreuz .at; tours €4.95, tours 10am Mon-Sat, 11am, 2pm, 3pm & 4pm daily)* The chapter house is the final resting place of most of the Babenberg dynasty, which ruled Austria until 1246. Maria Vetsera's grave is also here, and can be seen without joining the tour. The church and the cloister both combine Romanesque and Gothic styles. The abbey museum contains 150 clay models by Giovanni Giuliani (1663–1744), a Venetian sculptor who also created the Trinity column in the courtyard. Heiligen-

kreuz's tourist office (☎ 02258-8720, e heigem@aon.at) is near the abbey.

Between Mödling and Heiligenkreuz, boat tours can be taken on Europe's largest underground lake, **Seegrotte Hinterbrühl** *(☎/fax 02236-263 64,* W *tourist-net.co.at /seegr1.htm, Grutschgasse 2a; tour per adult/child €4.75/ 2.95; open 8.30am-noon & 1pm-5pm daily Apr-Oct, 9am-noon & 1pm-3pm Nov-Mar).* This former mine flooded with 20 million litres of water in 1912 and consequently shut down. It reopened to tourists as a display mine in 1932. The site was used by the German army to build aircraft during WWII. The 45-minute tours may be in English if you phone ahead.

Getting There & Away

To explore this region, it's best if you have your own transport. Trains skirt either side of the woods and the bus service is patchy. The Baden to Alland Bundesbus stops at Heiligenkreuz (€1.55, 20 minutes) and at Mayerling Altes Jagdschloss (€3.05, 45 minutes), but it's fairly infrequent, especially on Sunday. From Mödling (reached on the Vienna Südbahnhof-Baden train

route), there are frequent buses going to Hinterbrühl (bus Nos 364 and 365; €1.55, 17 minutes) that sometimes continue to Heiligenkreuz and Mayerling.

The main road through the area is the A21 that loops down from Vienna, passes by Heiligenkreuz, then curves north to join the A1 just east of Altlengbach.

BADEN BEI WIEN

☎ 02252 • pop 23,500 • elev 230m

On the eastern edge of the Wienerwald, the spa town of Baden has a long history. The Romans were prone to wallow in its

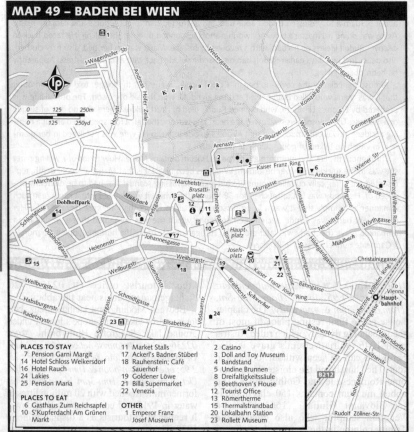

MAP 49 – BADEN BEI WIEN

PLACES TO STAY
7 Pension Garni Margit
14 Hotel Schloss Weikersdorf
16 Hotel Rauch
24 Lakies
25 Pension Maria

PLACES TO EAT
6 Gasthaus Zum Reichsapfel
10 S'Kupferdachl Am Grünen Markt

11 Market Stalls
17 Ackerl's Badner Stüberl
18 Rauhenstein; Café Sauerhof
19 Goldener Löwe
21 Billa Supermarket
22 Venezia

OTHER
1 Emperor Franz Josef Museum

2 Casino
3 Doll and Toy Museum
4 Bandstand
5 Undine Brunnen
8 Dreifaltigkeitssäule
9 Beethoven's House
12 Tourist Office
13 Römertherme
15 Thermalstrandbad
20 Lokalbahn Station
23 Rollett Museum

LOWER AUSTRIA

medicinal springs. Beethoven came here many times in hope of a cure for his deafness. The town flourished in the early 19th century when it was adopted by the Habsburgs as their favourite summer retreat. Baden mostly closes down in winter.

Orientation & Information

The centre of town is the pedestrian-only Hauptplatz; the train station is 500m southeast. A couple of minutes' walk west of Hauptplatz is the tourist office (Map 49, #12; ☎ 226 00-600, fax 807 33, e touristinfo .baden@netway.at) at Brusattiplatz 3, open 9am to 6pm Monday to Saturday, 9am to noon Sunday and holidays. From November to Easter, hours are 9am to 5pm weekdays only.

The VIP Card (free if you stay three nights or more in any type of accommodation) gives very useful benefits, such as discounts on entry prices and free walking tours.

Things to See & Do

Baden exudes health and 19th-century affluence, an impression endorsed by the many Biedermeier-style houses. The **Dreifaltigkeitssäule** *(Map 49, #8)* on Hauptplatz dates from 1714.

The town attracts plenty of promenading Viennese at the weekends. All and sundry make for the **Kurpark**, a magnificent setting for a stroll. Rows of white benches are neatly positioned under manicured trees in front of the bandstand *(Map 49, #4)*, where free spa concerts *(Kurkonzerte)* are performed from May to September, usually at 4.30pm daily except Monday. Elaborate flower beds complement monuments to famous artists (Mozart, Beethoven, Strauss, Grillparzer etc). The **Undine Brunnen** *(fountain; Map 49, #5)* is a fine amalgam of human and fish images.

The **casino** *(Map 49, #2; ☎ 444 96, Kaiser Franz Ring 1)* has gaming tables (open 3pm-3am; dress code) and slot machines (open 1pm-3am; no dress code). ID is required for entry.

The **Emperor Franz Josef Museum** *(Map 49, #1; ☎ 411 00, Hochstrasse 51; adult/ senior/student €2.20/1.50/0.75; open 2pm-6pm Tues-Sun Apr-Oct)*, north of the centre, displays local folklore.

The **Rollett Museum** *(Map 49, #23; ☎ 482 55, Weikersdorfer Platz 1; adult/ concession €2.20/ 0.75; open 3pm-6pm Wed-Mon)*, south-west of the centre, covers aspects of the town's history (like the bomb damage in WWII). The most unusual exhibit is the collection of skulls, busts and death masks amassed by the founder of phrenology, Josef Gall (1752–1828). This apparently cranky science, which held that criminal characteristics could be inferred from the shape of a person's skull, disturbingly brings to mind modern claims of the discovery of a 'criminal gene'.

Beethoven's former house *(Map 49, #9; ☎ 86 800-230, Rathausgasse 10; adult/concession €2.55/1.10; open 4pm-6pm Tues-Fri, 9am-11am & 4pm-6pm Sat, Sun & holidays)* is now a museum, but there's not much to see. There's also a **doll and toy museum** *(Map 49, #3; ☎ 410 20, Erzherzog Rainer Ring 23; adult/concession €2.55/1.10; open 4pm-6pm Tues-Fri, 9am-11am & 4pm-6pm Sat, Sun & holidays)*.

Baden's reputation as a health spa rests firmly on the existence of its 14 **hot springs**, with a daily flow of 6.5 million litres. The waters emerge at a temperature of 36°C and are enriched with sulphur, chlorine and sulphates. The town has various indoor and outdoor pool complexes, for medicinal or frivolous purposes. In the latter category is the **Thermalstrandbad** *(Map 49, #15; ☎ 486 70, Helenenstrasse 19-21; all day entry €5.50 Mon-Fri, €6.50 Sat & Sun; open 1 May-30 Sept)* with sulphur and normal pools, plus imported sand. Other bathing options include the **Römertherme** *(Roman baths; Map 49, #13; ☎ 450 30, Brusattiplatz 4; entry €8-18.50; open noon-10pm Mon, 10am-10pm Tues-Sun)* by the tourist office.

Special Events

In June, a rose festival is held in the Rosarium gardens in the Doblhoffpark and an operetta festival begins. June to August is the season for trotting races *(Traberen*; entry around €3), held at the track 1.5km to the east of the town centre.

Places to Stay

Unfortunately, the few private rooms are the only option for those on a tight budget; get a list from the tourist office.

Lakies (Map 49, #24; ☎ 229 38, *Vöslauerstrasse 11*) Singles/doubles with shower €13.50/27. This house is 250m south of Josefsplatz, and has a kitchen. Phone well ahead as it's often full.

Pension Garni Margit (Map 49, #7; ☎ 897 18, fax 226 27, *Mühlgasse 15-17*) Singles/doubles with no access to a shower €26/45, with shower/toilet €35/53. This pension is 500m east of Hauptplatz; it has a homey ambience and a garden.

Pension Maria (Map 49, #25; ☎ 430 33, fax 430 33-32, *Elisabethstrasse 11*) Singles/doubles with shower/toilet €33/54. Sporting three stars, this place has a garden swimming pool (summer only) and off-street parking.

Hotel Rauch (Map 49, #16; ☎ 445 61, *Pelzgasse 3*) Singles €32-36, doubles €54-59. This hotel is next to the Doblhoffpark, in a typical Baden building with high ceilings and mini bath tubs. Rates depend on room size and the season.

Hotel Schloss Weikersdorf (Map 49, #14; ☎ 483 01-0, fax 483 01-150, *Schlossgasse 9–11*) Singles €73-98, doubles €131-160. Stay here to experience a genuine castle ambience and appearance, which is usually reflected in room furnishings. All rooms have shower, toilet and cable TV. The hotel adjoins the park. There are cheaper rooms in the annexe (€51-60 and €80-88), which houses the sauna and indoor swimming pool (both free for guests).

Places to Eat

There's a *Billa* supermarket (Map 49, #21) at Wassergasse 14, but the best places for compiling hot or cold snacks are the market stalls you'll find on Brusattiplatz (Map 49, #11).

S'Kupferdachl Am Grünen Markt (Map 49, #10; ☎ 416 17, Brusattiplatz 2) Meals €5.70-9.50. This small place by the market stalls offers a more comfortable environment for consuming Austrian meals and snacks.

Goldener Löwe (Map 49, #19; ☎ 484 69, Braitnerstrasse 1) Meals €4.50-11. Open 11.30am-3pm & 5.30pm-11.30pm daily. One of several Chinese restaurants in town, it offers a variety of cheap lunch menus Monday to Saturday, and outside tables overlook the Schwechat River.

Gasthaus Zum Reichsapfel (Map 49, #6; ☎ 482 05, Spiegelgasse 2) Meals €5.60-10.90. Open 5pm-11.30pm Mon & Wed-Fri, 11am-2pm & 5pm-11pm Sat & Sun. This place can't decide if it's a beer hall or a wine tavern, the advantage is that it offers several varieties of ale on tap as well as a selection of open wines. It also serves inexpensive meals and snacks, including various vegetarian choices.

Venezia (Map 49, #22; ☎ 443 20, Wassergasse 16) Meals €4.75-12.75. Open 11.30-2.30pm & 5.30pm-11pm Mon-Thur, 11.30-11pm Fri-Sun. This Italian restaurant has bigger-than-the-plate pizzas and off-street outside tables.

Ackerl's Badner Stüberl (Map 49, #17; ☎ 412 32, Gutenbrunnerstrasse 19) Meals €7.70-16. Open 11am-2.30pm & 6pm-10pm Wed-Mon. This family-friendly Austrian inn has good mid-price food.

Café Sauerhof (Map 49, #18; ☎ 412 51-6, Weilburgstrasse 11–13) Meals €9.50-13.50. Open 7am-6pm daily. In the plush Hotel Sauerhof, this cafe is worth visiting for the extensive Sunday brunch (€28.40, Sept-June); on the first Sunday in the month there's live jazz (€3.50 extra).

Rauhenstein (Map 49, #18; ☎ 412 51-6, Weilburgstrasse 11–13) Meals €15-22. Open 6pm-11pm daily. Hotel Sauerhof also houses this gourmet restaurant serving international dishes.

Baden is not known for its nightlife, but to combine wine and dining, ask the tourist office for the opening schedule of the various Heurigen.

Getting There & Away

Two to four trains an hour run to Wiener Neustadt (€3.05, 20 minutes) and Vienna's Südbahnhof (€4.45, or €3.05 with a Vienna city pass; 20 to 30 minutes). For the same price from Vienna, you could take the Lokalbahn tram that goes from Kärntner Ring (opposite Hotel Bristol) to Josefsplatz in Baden (every 15 minutes, one hour). Hourly buses (€5.85, 40 minutes) do the same route.

The north-south road routes, Hwy 17 and the A2, pass a few kilometres to the east of the town.

Southern Lower Austria

This region includes the edge of the Alps, the highest and best known peak being Schneeberg at 2075m. In the south-east are several mountains approaching 2000m, such as Hochkar and Ötscher (both have chair lifts).

WIENER NEUSTADT
☎ 02622 • pop 40,000 • elev 265m

First known simply as Neustadt (New City) or Nova Civitas, this city was built by the Babenbergs in 1194. It became a Habsburg residence in the 15th century, during the reign of Friedrich III. His son, Maximilian I, was born in the town. Wiener Neustadt was severely damaged in WWII and only 18 homes were unscathed. Historic buildings that were damaged have been restored.

Orientation & Information
The centre of town is the large Hauptplatz, where you'll find the tourist office (Map 50, #14; ☎ 373-468, fax 373-498) at No 3, in the Rathaus complex. It's open 8am to 5pm Monday to Friday, 8am to noon Saturday. Unfortunately, the tourist office doesn't have a great deal of information in English, but it does at least have a free booklet, *Cultural Promenade*, which describes the central sights and gives their locations on a map. There's also the *Young Generation Guide*, written by local students, detailing youth-oriented bars and cafes. Most of the streets leading off Hauptplatz are for pedestrians only.

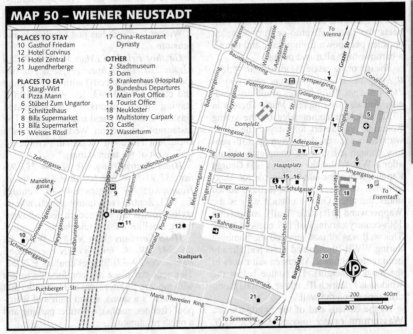

MAP 50 – WIENER NEUSTADT

PLACES TO STAY
10 Gasthof Friedam
12 Hotel Corvinus
16 Hotel Zentral
21 Jugendherberge

PLACES TO EAT
1 Stargl-Wirt
4 Pizza Mann
6 Stüberl Zum Ungartor
7 Schnitzelhaus
8 Billa Supermarket
13 Billa Supermarket
15 Weisses Rössl

17 China-Restaurant Dynasty

OTHER
2 Stadtmuseum
3 Dom
5 Krankenhaus (Hospital)
9 Bundesbus Departures
14 Main Post Office
14 Tourist Office
18 Neukloster
19 Multistorey Carpark
20 Castle
22 Wasserturm

LOWER AUSTRIA

The train station is less than 1km to the south-west. It has bike rental, a travel agency and a Bankomat. Next door is the main post office (Map 50, #11; Postamt 2700), open 7am to 6pm Monday to Friday, 7.30am to 12.30pm Saturday.

Things to See & Do

Spacious **Hauptplatz** is lined with elegant buildings, not least the three parts of the Rathaus (first mentioned in 1401), featuring an arcade and colourful crests. An outdoor market fills the square daily except Sunday, though the busiest days are Wednesday and Saturday. East of Hauptplatz is **Neukloster** *(Map 50, #18)*, a 14th-century Gothic church with striking baroque fittings (closed for renovation till some time in 2002).

The Romanesque **Dom** *(cathedral; Map 50, #3; ☎ 373-440, Domplatz; open daylight hours)*, erected in 1279 but subsequently much rebuilt, has a rather bare and grey exterior, and two severe-looking square towers. The interior has an unbalanced look, caused by the chancel being out of line with the nave, and the asymmetric arch that connects the two. Fifteenth-century wooden apostles peer down from pillars, and there's a baroque high altar and pulpit.

The imposing **castle** *(Map 50, #20; ☎ 381-0, Burgplatz 1; admission free; visits only at 10am & 2pm daily)* houses a military academy, founded by Empress Maria Theresa in 1752, and later commanded by the young Rommel, pre 'desert fox' days. The castle with its four towers dates from the 13th century, though it had to be completely rebuilt after WWII. Within the complex is **St Georgs Kapelle**, with a fine late-Gothic interior. Maximilian I, who was born in the castle, is buried under the altar. On the outside wall is the Wappenwand (Heraldic Wall) comprising 15th-century carvings of 107 coats of arms. This wall was all that survived the bombing during WWII (the stained glass had already been removed to the Altaussee salt mines in the Salzkammergut). The statue below the window is Friedrich III, whose AEIOU motto also appears on the wall.

At the eastern end of the Stadtpark is a **Wasserturm** *(water tower; Map 15, #22)*,

built between 1909 and 1910. Its shape intentionally apes the gilded goblet *(Becher)* donated to the townsfolk by King Matthias Corvinus of Hungary after he took the town in 1487. A copy of this chalice can be seen in the **Stadtmuseum** *(Map 50, #2; ☎ 373-440, Petergasse 2a; adult/concession 2.20/ 1.10; open 10am-5pm Tues & Wed, 10am-8pm Thur, 10am-4pm Sun & holidays)*; the original is housed in the Rathaus.

Wiener Neustadt is a convenient base for those wishing to undertake an excursion to Schneeberg (see that section later in this chapter).

Places to Stay

Jugendherberge *(Map 50, #21; ☎/fax 296 95, e oejhv-noe@oejhv.or.at, Promenade 1)* Bed in 4-bed dorm with shower/toilet €11.65, singles/doubles €15.30/30.60. Breakfast €2.60, kitchen available. Check-in 5pm-8pm, 1st floor. This HI hostel is the pale house in the Stadtpark, near the water tower. Phone ahead as it's run by a family, and they may not always be around; the place is often full anyway.

Wiener Neustadt has just five hotels and pensions.

Gasthof Friedam *(Map 50, #10; ☎ 230 81, fax 230 81-4, Schneeberggasse 16)* Singles/doubles (twin beds) with shower/toilet and cable TV €32/43, less €2.20/2.95 if staying three nights. This renovated Gasthof is the only real budget choice. The restaurant (closed on Wednesday) has a cheap lunch menu. It's less than 10 minutes' walk west of the train station.

Hotel Zentral *(Map 50, #16; ☎ 237 93, fax 237 93-5, e hotel-zentral@innosys.at, Hauptplatz 27)* Singles €40-46, doubles €57-73. Zentral is certainly central, and its stylish rooms have a modern feel, shower/ toilet, satellite TV and telephone.

Hotel Corvinus *(Map 50, #12; ☎ 241 34, fax 241 39, e hotel@hotel-corvinus.at, Bahngasse 29–33)* Singles/doubles €72/55. This four-star place has comfortable rooms with modern furniture and shower, toilet and TV. There's a sauna, steam bath and whirlpool (free for guests), off-street parking and a plush restaurant.

Places to Eat

There are **Billa** supermarkets on Bahngasse *(Map 50, #13)* and Hauptplatz *(Map 50, #8)*. Hauptplatz also has several *Würstel* stands.

Schnitzelhaus (Map 50, #7; ☎ 252 73, Grazer Strasse 76) Meals €3.60-7.95 Open 10am-10pm daily. Come here for fast, cheap schnitzels.

Pizza Mann (Map 50, #4; ☎ 207 44, Grazer Strasse 44) Meals €3.40-7.60. Open 11am-midnight daily. This pizza chain restaurant is reasonable value for eat-in or takeaway pizzas.

China-Restaurant Dynasty (Map 50, #17; ☎ 244 70, Kesslergasse 5) Meals €4.10-13.10. Open 11.30am-2.30pm & 5.30pm-11pm daily. One of several Chinese restaurants in town, this has cheap lunches and a range of other special deals.

Weisses Rössl (Map 50, #15; ☎ 233 04, Hauptplatz 3) Meals €5.10-9.50. Open 7am-9pm Mon-Fri, 7am-5pm Sat. Quaint, and with outside tables, this Gasthaus serves inexpensive Austrian food.

Stargl-Wirt (Map 50, #1; ☎ 223 26, Grazer Strasse 54) Meals €5.50-9.90. Open 8am-10pm Mon-Fri, 11am-2pm Sat & Sun. This enjoyable place prides itself on its schnitzels (13 variations, €7.65 each) and beer (four brews on tap). There's also a fine beer garden.

Stüberl Zum Ungartor (Map 50, #6; ☎ 234 55, Ungargasse 21) Meals €4.95-14.40. Open 9am-10pm Tues-Fri, 9am-3pm Sat & Sun. This place has tasty Hungarian food and a comfortable, vaulted interior.

Getting There & Away

The 30 to 45 minute train journey from Vienna's Südbahnhof to Wiener Neustadt costs €7.50 (two to four departures per hour). Trains also run almost hourly to the Hungarian shopping town of Sopron (€4.60, 45 minutes). Bundesbuses depart from the northern end of Wiener Neustadt train station, where there's a bus information office *(Map 50, #9; ☎ 373-426)*.

The city has excellent road links: a few of the options to/from Vienna are the A2 or Hwy 17.

SEMMERING

☎ 02664 • pop 1100 • elev 1000m

This spread-out mountain resort, which became a favourite with moneyed tourists at the turn of the century, is famed for its clean air. Semmering also has skiing facilities.

Orientation & Information

Semmering sits on a south-facing slope above the Semmering Pass. There's no real centre to the resort: it's mostly ranged along Hochstrasse which forms an arc above the train station. Parking is not a problem.

Outside the unstaffed train station there's a map. Go left and follow the paths to 'Passhöhe'. In 20 minutes you reach the Kurverwaltung tourist office (☎ 200 25, fax 200 29, **e** semmeringtourismus@aon.at). It's at the Raiffeisen bank where Hochstrasse branches from Hwy 306, and is open 9am to noon and 1pm to 4pm Monday to Friday (8.30am to 4.30pm Monday to Friday in winter). The Tourismusregion Südalpin regional tourist office (☎ 2539-1, fax 2335, **e** noesued.rumpler@gmx.at) is in the same building (enter round the back) and is open 8am to 4pm Monday to Friday and (in winter) 8am to noon Saturday.

Things to See & Do

Outdoor activities are the resort's main draw, including **walking**. The tourist office can sell you the *Wanderkarte* map (text in German) or give you brochures outlining scenic walks. Overlooking Semmering to the south is the **Hirschenkogel** (1340m), where a new cable car (with a space-age style glass oval lower terminal) whisks walkers (€6.55/9.85 one-way/return) or skiers (€24 for a day pass) up to the top. A day pass for all three local ski regions costs €27.

The resort has two ski schools (☎ 2471 or ☎ 8538), a golf course (☎ 2471), mini-golf and tennis courts. The swimming pool, sauna complex and fitness room in the four-star Hotel Panhaus (☎ 8181, **w** www.panhaus.at) can be used by non-guests (admission €8.75 weekdays, €13.25 weekends).

An excursion can be made to the north along the scenic **Höllental** (Hell's Valley), a deep, narrow gorge created by the Schwarza

River. Along the route from Semmering (by winding, local roads) you pass the Raxblick viewpoint. A little farther on is Hirschwang, where in 1926 Austria's first cable car was built. You can ascend via the Raxseilbahn to 1547m (€8.30/14.40 one-way/return) for a 360° panorama. Hirschwang is where you join the Höllental.

Places to Stay & Eat

Most places close during the off season (approximately Easter to June, November to mid-December). Semmering has few options for budget travellers, other than a couple of small-scale private houses. Unless stated otherwise, all of the places below are on Hochstrasse, near the two tourist offices. The higher end of Hochstrasse is where the more expensive hotels reside. Also on this street is a *Billa* supermarket, open standard hours.

Haus Mayer (℡ 2251, fax 14, e *mayer .reisen@netway.at, Hochstrasse 257)* Rooms €23 per person. This house has good-value rooms with shower and balcony, but they only rent to nonsmokers. It also doubles as a travel agency.

Haus Tonn (℡ 2264, Hochstrasse 108) Doubles with bathroom €43.60, single without €17.50. Phone ahead. Though the house itself is architecturally uninspiring, the same can't be said for the sweeping views from some rooms.

Gasthof Edelweiss (℡ 2284, fax 228 55, e *edelweiss@lion.cc, Hochstrasse 57)* Singles €28-32, doubles €56-64. Meals €5.85-13.50. This quaint wooden chalet has decent rooms with shower, toilet and satellite TV, a popular restaurant and a lovely secluded garden.

Gasthof Berghof (℡ 2320, fax 2320-4, e *gasthof.berghof@utanet.at, Hochstrasse 271)* Singles/doubles €30/60. Meals €4.75-10.80. This place is round the corner from the tourist offices. It has homey, non-standardised rooms with shower, toilet and TV; doubles also have a balcony. The restaurant serves decent Austrian food.

Pension-Restaurant Löffler (℡ 2304, fax 2304-8, e *michael.loeffler@aon.at, Hochstrasse 174)* Singles/doubles €33/59. Meals €5.75-16. This place has fresh, modern, slightly pricey rooms with shower, toilet and satellite TV. The Austrian meals are good and inexpensive, and there are outside tables.

Hotel-Restaurant Belvedere (℡ 2270, fax 226 742, e *hotel.belveder@telecom.at, Hochstrasse 60)* Singles/doubles €33/66-52/102. Meals €5.70-18.20. This family-managed hotel has excellent facilities for a three-star place: use of the swimming pool and sauna are all included in the room price, and there's a large garden and patio area. The rooms all have shower, toilet, TV and balcony. The restaurant has regional dishes, including fish and seasonal specialities.

Getting There & Away

From Semmering, the rail route to the northeast passes through some impressive scenery of precipitous cliffs and forested hills (make sure you sit on the right). The route, incorporating many bridges and tunnels, was Europe's first Alpine railway and was completed in 1854 by Karl Ritter von Ghega, and has now been granted Unesco World Heritage status. The most scenic section is the 30 minute stretch between Semmering and Payerbach (€4.25). There's a direct service from Semmering to Vienna's Südbahnhof (€14.85, 1¾ hours, usually hourly). Travelling south-west to Graz (€12.35, 2¼ hours, every one or two hours), you must first take a regional train to Mürzzuschlag.

By road (Hwy 306), the Semmering Pass (985m) marks the border between Lower Austria and Styria. Excursions along the Höllental are easiest if you have your own transport. Bundesbuses do run to Hirschwang and Raxblick, but departures are infrequent.

SCHNEEBERG

The popular ascent up Schneeberg by cogwheel steam train is a full day excursion, providing excellent views and good walks. The top station, Hochschneeberg, is at 1795m. Nearby is a *hotel* and *restaurant*, and a viewing terrace by a small chapel dedicated to the Empress Elisabeth (wife of Franz Josef). From the station, a path leads to Klosterwappen and Fischerhütte; these are each about a 70-minute walk from the station, and 20 minutes from each other.

The path to both is initially the same. After 30 minutes it splits: the steeper left-hand path goes to **Klosterwappen** (2075m), identifiable by the radar and cross on the ridge. This fork provides the best view of the Raxalpe range and the upper reaches of the Höllental, with the ribbon-like road winding its way on the far side of the valley. A path goes down into the valley, while a flattish walk along the ridge will bring you to *Fischerhütte (☎ 2313, Hochschneeberg 9)*, offering food and lodging. Up the hill behind Fischerhütte is the Kaiserstein viewpoint (2061m), with a beehive-shaped monument to Emperor Franz I. The most impressive part of the view from here is the Breite Ries, a bowl-shaped area of erosion with stark grey and red cliffs.

Getting There & Away

There are trains from Wiener Neustadt to Puchberg am Schneeberg (€4.55, 46 minutes, hourly), which is where you board the Schneeberg cogwheel train. A leaflet giving times of the Schneeberg train is available at many Austrian train stations, or you can call ☎ 02636-3661-20 or log on to the **w** www .schneebergbahn.at. Trains operate from late April to early November, and the full ascent from Puchberg to Hochschneeberg takes about 85 minutes (€13.10/€21.80 one-way/return). Trains depart frequently according to demand (which is usually high). There's always a guaranteed ascent/descent at 9.45am/2.05pm; in July and August further guaranteed trains ascend at 8.30am, 9.45am and 11.45pm, and descend at 2.25pm and 4.20pm.

Puchberg itself has places to stay and eat – ask the tourist office (☎ 02636-2256, **e** tourismusbuero@puchberg.at).

To walk from Puchberg up to Hochschneeberg takes three hours or more. Klosterwappen is on the long-distance path, the Nordalpenweg, which runs from Bodensee (in Vorarlberg) to the Wienerwald.

Language

This German language guide contains pronunciation guidelines and basic vocabulary to help you get around Austria. For background information on Austria's language milieu see the Language section at the end of the Facts about Austria chapter.

It may be a surprise to know that German is, in fact, a close relative of English; English, German and Dutch are all known as West Germanic languages. The High German that is used today comes from a regional Saxon dialect. The fact that many German words survive in the English vocabulary today makes things a lot easier for native English speakers. While that's good news, the bad news is that, unlike English, German has retained clear formal distinctions in gender and case.

The polite form of address in German involves using the third person plural with verb forms, eg *Haben Sie ...?*, as against *Hast du ...?* (Do you have ...?). In this guide the polite form is used unless otherwise indicated. If in doubt it's always best to use the polite form. Note that in German all nouns are written with a capital letter.

If you want a more comprehensive guide to the language get hold of Lonely Planet's *German phrasebook*. In it you'll find everything you need to know about German grammar along with a vast array of useful phrases divided into chapters such as Meeting People, Going Out, Social Issues, Shopping and Activities; there's also a special section on varieties of German (such as that spoken in Austria).

Pronunciation

Unlike English or French, German has no real silent letters: you pronounce the k at the start of the word *Knie* (knee), the p at the start of *Psychologie* (psychology), and the e at the end of *ich habe* (I have).

Vowels

As in English, German vowels can be pronounced long, as the 'o' in 'pope', or short, as in 'pop'. As a rule, vowels are long before one consonant and short before two consonants: the o is long in the word *Dom*, 'cathedral', but short in the word *doch*, 'after all'.

a	short, as the 'u' in 'cut' or long, as in 'father'
au	as the 'ow' in 'vow'
ä	short, as in 'cat' or long, as in 'care'
äu	as the 'oy' in 'boy'
e	short, as in 'bet' or long, as in 'obey'
ei	as the 'ai' in 'aisle'
eu	as the 'oy' in 'boy'
i	short, as in 'it' or long, as the 'ee' in 'see'
ie	as the 'ee' in 'see'
o	short, as in 'not' or long, as in 'note'
ö	as the 'er' in 'fern'
u	as in 'pull'
ü	similar to the 'u' in 'pull' but with lips stretched back

Consonants

Most German consonants sound similar to their English counterparts. One important difference is that b, d and g sound like 'p', 't' and 'k', respectively when word-final.

b	as in 'be'; as 'p' when word-final
ch	as in Scottish *loch*
d	as in 'do'; as 't' when word-final
g	as in 'go'; as 'k' when word-final (except after i, when it's as 'ch' in Scottish *loch*)
j	as the 'y' in 'yet'
qu	as 'k' plus 'v'
r	can be trilled or guttural, depending on the region
s	as in 'sun'; as the 'z' in 'zoo' when followed by a vowel
sch	as the 'sh' in 'ship'
sp, st	as 'shp' and 'sht' when word-initial
tion	the 't' is pronounced as the 'ts' in 'its'
v	as the 'f' in 'fan'
w	as the 'v' in 'van'
z	as the 'ts' in 'its'

Basics

Good day.	*Grüss Gott.* (pol)
Hello.	*Servus/Grüss Dich/*
	Griassdi. (inf)
Goodbye.	*Auf Wiedersehen.*
	Pfiati/Ciao (inf)
Yes.	*Ja.*
No.	*Nein.*
Please.	*Bitte.*
Thank you.	*Danke.*
That's fine/	*Bitte sehr.*
You're welcome.	
Sorry. (excuse me,	*Entschuldigung.*
forgive me)	
Do you speak	*Sprechen Sie*
English?	*Englisch?*
How much is it?	*Wieviel kostet es?*
What's your name?	*Wie heissen Sie?*
My name is ...	*Ich heisse ...*

Getting Around

What time does the ... leave?	*Wann fährt ... ab?*
What time does the ... arrive?	*Wann kommt ... an?*
boat	*das Boot*
bus (city)	*der Bus*
bus (intercity)	*der (Überland-)Bus*
plane	*das Flugzeug*
tram	*die Strassenbahn*
train	*der Zug*
What time is the next boat?	*Wann fährt das nächste Boot?*
I'd like to hire a car/bicycle.	*Ich möchte ein Auto/ Fahrrad mieten.*
I'd like a ...	*Ich möchte eine ...*
one-way ticket	*Einzelkarte*
return ticket	*Rückfahrkarte*
1st class	*erste Klasse*
2nd class	*zweite Klasse*
left luggage lockers	*Schliessfächer*
timetable	*Fahrplan*
Where is the bus stop?	*Wo ist die Bushaltestelle?*
Where is the tram stop?	*Wo ist die Strassen- bahnhaltestelle?*
Where is the train station?	*Wo ist der Bahnhof (Bf)?*

Signs

Eingang	**Entrance**
Ausgang	**Exit**
Voll/Besetzt	**Full/No Vacancies**
Auskunft	**Information**
Offen	**Open**
Geschlossen	**Closed**
Polizeiwache	**Police Station**
Zimmer Frei	**Rooms Available**
Toiletten (WC)	**Toilets**
Herren	**Men**
Damen	**Women**

Where is the ferry terminal?	*Wo ist der Fährhafen?*
Can you show me (on the map)?	*Können Sie mir (auf der Karte) zeigen?*
I'm looking for ...	*Ich suche ...*
Go straight ahead.	*Gehen Sie geradeaus.*
Turn left.	*Biegen Sie links ab.*
Turn right.	*Biegen Sie rechts ab.*
near	*nahe*
far	*weit*

Around Town

a bank	*eine Bank*
the city centre	*die Innenstadt*
doctor	*der Arzt*
the ... embassy	*die ... Botschaft*
my hotel	*mein Hotel*
hospital	*das Krankenhaus*
library	*die Bibliothek*
the market	*der Markt*
the newsagency	*der Zeitungshändler*
the pharmacy	*die Apotheke*
the police	*die Polizei*
the post office	*das Postamt*
a public toilet	*eine öffentliche Toilette*
the telephone centre	*die Telefonzentrale*
the tourist office	*das Fremden- verkersbüro*
bridge	*Brücke*
castle	*Schloss/Burg*
cathedral	*Dom*
church	*Kirche*
island	*Insel*
lake	*See*
main square	*Hauptplatz*
monastery/convent	*Kloster*

mosque	*Moschee*
mountain	*Berg*
old city	*Altstadt*
ruins	*Ruinen*
square	*Platz*
tower	*Turm*

What time does it open/close?	*Um wieviel Uhr macht es auf/zu?*

Accommodation

Where is a cheap hotel?	*Wo ist ein billiges Hotel?*
What is the address?	*Was ist die Adresse?*
Could you write the address, please?	*Könnten Sie bitte die Adresse auf- schreiben?*

hotel	*Hotel*
guesthouse	*Pension, Gästehaus*
youth hostel	*Jugendherberge*
camping ground	*Campingplatz*

Do you have any rooms available?	*Haben Sie noch freie Zimmer?*

I'd like ...	*Ich möchte ...*
a single room	*ein Einzelzimmer*
a double room	*ein Doppelzimmer*
a room with a bath	*ein Zimmer mit Bad*
to share a dorm	*einen Schlafsaal teilen*
a bed	*ein Bett*

for one/two nights	*eine Nacht/zwei Nächte*

How much is it per night/person?	*Wieviel kostet es pro Nacht/Person?*
Is breakfast included?	*Ist Frühstück inbegriffen?*
Where is the bath/shower?	*Wo ist das Bad/die Dusche?*

Food

grocery	*Lebensmittelgeschäft*
delicatessen	*Delikatessengeschäft*
restaurant	*Restaurant/Gaststätte*
breakfast	*Frühstück*
lunch	*Mittagessen*
dinner	*Abendessen*

I'd like the set lunch, please.	*Ich hätte gern das Tagesmenü, bitte.*
Is service included in the bill?	*Ist die Bedienung inbegriffen?*
I'm a vegetarian.	*Ich bin Vegetarier (m) Vegetarierin. (f)*

Time & Days

What time is it?	*Wie spät ist es?*
today	*heute*
tomorrow	*morgen*
yesterday	*gestern*
in the morning	*morgens*
in the afternoon	*nachmittags*

Monday	*Montag*
Tuesday	*Dienstag*
Wednesday	*Mittwoch*
Thursday	*Donnerstag*
Friday	*Freitag*
Saturday	*Samstag, Sonnabend*
Sunday	*Sonntag*

Health

antiseptic	*Antiseptikum*
aspirin	*Aspirin*
condoms	*Kondome*
constipation	*Verstopfung*
contraceptive	*Verhütungsmittel*
diarrhoea	*Durchfall*
medicine	*Medizin*
nausea	*Übelkeit*
sunblock cream	*Sonnencreme*
tampons	*Tampons*

I'm allergic ...	*Ich bin gegen ... allergisch.*
to antibiotics	*Antibiotika*
to penicillin	*Penizillin*

Emergencies

Help!	*Hilfe!*
Call a doctor!	*Holen Sie einen Arzt!*
Call the police!	*Rufen Sie die Polizei!*
I'm lost.	*Ich habe mich verirrt.*

I'm ...	Ich bin ...
diabetic	*Diabetikerin* (f)
	Diabetiker (m)
epileptic	*Epileptikerin* (f)
	Epileptiker (m)
asthmatic	*Asthmatikerin* (f)
	Asthmatiker (m)

Numbers

0	*null*
1	*eins*
2	*zwei*
3	*drei*
4	*vier*
5	*fünf*
6	*sechs*
7	*sieben*
8	*acht*
9	*neun*
10	*zehn*
11	*elf*
12	*zwölf*
13	*dreizehn*
14	*vierzehn*
15	*fünfzehn*
16	*sechzehn*
17	*siebzehn*
18	*achtzehn*
19	*neunzehn*
20	*zwanzig*
21	*einundzwanzig*
22	*zweiundzwanzig*
23	*dreiundzwanzig*
24	*vierundzwanzig*
25	*fünfundzwanzig*
30	*dreissig*
40	*vierzig*
50	*fünfzig*
60	*sechzig*
70	*siebzig*
80	*achtzig*
90	*neunzig*
100	*hundert*
1000	*tausend*

one million	*eine Million*

Austrian Words

Though the grammar is the same as standard German, there are also many words and expressions that are used only by Austrians. Some words will be used throughout the country, others are only in use in particular regions, although they will probably be generally understood. Most would not automatically be understood by non-Austrian German speakers. On the other hand, the 'normal' German equivalent would be understood by Austrians.

Most of the greetings and farewells that we've included in the list of useful phrases are common only to Austria. *Servus* is an informal greeting, and can also be used when taking your leave. The word has been adopted as a motto by the Austrian national tourist office. *Grüss dich* or *Griassdi* (literally 'greet you') is also a familiar, informal greeting. It's especially used by people who don't want to bring God into the conversation (rather than *Grüss Gott* – 'greet God'). For 'goodbye', *Auf Wiederschauen* is the standard phrase (in Germany also); *Baba*, *Pfiati* or *Ciao* is less formal.

It's quite possible you may want to tell people that you've been drinking. If you're tipsy you can say *Ich bin beschwipst* or *Ich habe einen Schwips*. If you're definitely the worse for wear, the Viennese dialect expression is *I'hob an dulliö*. If you're very drunk, you could say *Ich bin zu*, though everyone will probably have figured that out already.

Some useful Austrian words are: *Blunzen* (black pudding); *Erdäpfel* (potato); *Faschiertes* (minced meat); *Gerstl* (money); *Karfiol* (cauliflower); *Maroni* (roasted chestnut); *Maut* (toll charge); *Müch* (milk); *Obers* (cream); *Paradeiser* (tomatoes); *Scherzl* (crust of bread); and *Stamperl* (glass for Schnapps). See the Food section in the Facts for the Visitor chapter for more useful food-related words. To request the bill in a restaurant, simply say 'Zahlen, bitte' (pay, please).

Words that are more specifically Viennese include:

Beisl	small tavern for food and drink
Bim	tram
Haberer	friend
Stiftl	glass (for wine)
Verdrahn	to sell

Glossary

Abfahrt – departure (trains)
Achterl – glass holding 0.125L
Ankunft – arrival (trains)
ANTO – Austrian National Tourist Office
ATM – see *Bankomat*
Ausgang – exit
Autobahn – motorway
Autoreisezug – motorail train

Bad – bath (spa resort)
Bahnhof – train station
Bahnsteig – train station platform
Bankomat – automated teller machine (ATM), cashpoint
Bauernhof – farmhouse
Beisl – small tavern or restaurant
Berg – hill or mountain
Besetzt – occupied, full
Bezirk – (town or city) district
Biedermeier period – 19th-century art movement in Germany and Austria
Bierkeller – beer cellar
Brauerei – brewery
Bundesbus – state bus, run by the railway (Bahnhbus) or the post office (Postbus)
Bundesländer/Länder – federal provinces
Bundesrat – Federal Council (upper house – government)
Burg – castle/fortress
Buschenschank/Buschenschenken – wine tavern(s)

Dirndl – women's traditional dress
Dorf – village
D Zug – medium-fast train

EC – EuroCity, express train
EEA – European Economic Area, comprising European Union states plus Iceland, Liechtenstein and Norway
Einbahnstrasse – one-way street
Eingang, Eintritt – entry
Elektroboot – motorboat
EN – EuroNight, international and domestic night train
E Zug – fast train
EU – European Union

Fahrplan – timetable
Feiertag – public holiday
Ferienwohnungen – self-catering holiday apartments
Festung – fortress
Fiacre – small horse-drawn carriage
Flohmarkt – flea market
Flughafen – airport
Flugpost – air mail
Föhn – hot, dry wind which sweeps down from the mountains, mainly in early spring and autumn
FPÖ – Freedom Party (politics)
Freizeitzentrum – sports and leisure centre
Friedhof – cemetery

Gästehaus – guesthouse, perhaps with a restaurant
Gasthaus – inn or restaurant, without accommodation
Gasthof – inn or restaurant, usually with accommodation
Gästekarte – guest card; issued by hostels and resorts and used to obtain discounts
Gemeindeamt – local authority office
Gemütlichkeit – 'cosiness'; a quality much valued by Austrians
Gendarmerie – police
Glockenturm – clock tower
Gondelbahn – gondola

Hafen – harbour, port
Haltestelle – Bus or tram stop
Hauptbahnhof – main train station
Hauptpost – main post office
Heurigen – wine tavern(s)
Heuriger – 'new' Heurigen wine
IC – InterCity, express train
Imbiss – snack bar

Kaffeehaus/Café Konditorei – coffee house
Kärnten – Carinthia (Austrian province)
Konsulat – consulate
Krügerl – glass holding 0.5L
Kurzparkzone – short-term parking zone

Land/Länder – province(s)
Landesmuseum – provincial museum
Landtag – provincial assembly (governmental term)
Langersamstag – 'long' Saturday, the first Saturday of the month; shops open to 5pm
Langlauf – cross-country skiing
Lieder – lyrical song
Luftseilbahn – cable car

Mahlzeit – Austrian salutation at the commencement of a meal
Maut – toll (or indicating a toll booth)
Mehrwertsteuer (MWST) – value-added tax
Mensa – university restaurant
Mitfahrzentrale – hitching organisation

Nationalrat – National Council (lower house – government)
Not(ruf) – emergency (call)

ÖAMTC – national motoring organisation
ÖAV – Austrian Alpine Club
ÖBB – Austrian federal railway
Österreich – Austria
ÖVP – Austrian People's Party (politics)

Parkschein – parking voucher
Pfarrkirche/Stadtpfarrkirche – parish church
Pfiff – glass containing 0.125L
Platz – town or village square
Polizei – police
Postamt – post office
Postlagernde Briefe – poste restante

Radler – mixture of beer and lemonade
Radverleih – bicycle rental
Rathaus – town hall
Ruderboot – rowing boat
Ruhetag – 'rest day', on which a restaurant is closed

S-Bahn – suburban train system
SC – SuperCity, express train
Schlepplift – ski lift
Schrammelmusik – popular Viennese music for violins, guitar and accordion

Secession movement – early 20th-century movement in Vienna seeking to establish a more functional style in architecture; led by Otto Wagner (1841–1918)
Selbstbedienung (SB) – self-service (restaurants, laundries etc)
Sesselbahn – chair lift
sgraffito – mural or decoration in which the top layer is scratched off to reveal the original colour/medium underneath
SPÖ – Social Democrats (politics)
Stadtmuseum – city museum
Standseilbahn – funicular
Steiermark – Styria (Austrian province)
Stift – abbey
Strandbad – designated bathing area on a lake or river, usually with an entry fee
Studentenheime – student residences

Tabak – tobacconist
Tagesteller/Tagesmenü – the set dish or meal of the day in a restaurant; sometimes abbrev as 'Menü'
Tal – valley
Telefon-Wertkarte – phonecard
Tierpark – zoo
Tor – gate
Tretboot – paddleboat (pedalo)
Triebwagen – the name for the normal (vs steam) train in Tirol

U-Bahn – urban underground rail system
Urlaub – holiday

Vienna Circle (Wiener Kreis) – group of philosophers centred on Vienna University in the 1920s and 1930s
Vienna Group (Wiener Gruppe) – avant-garde art/literary movement formed in the 1950s
Viertel – 0.25L (drinks); also a geographical district

Wäscherei – laundry
Wien – Vienna
Würstel Stand – sausage stand

Zimmer frei/Privat Zimmer – private rooms (accommodation)

LONELY PLANET

You already know that Lonely Planet produces more than this one guidebook, but you might not be aware of the other products we have on this region. Here is a selection of titles that you may want to check out as well:

Vienna
ISBN 1 86450 195 2
US$14.99 • UK£8.99

Central Europe phrasebook
ISBN 1 86450 226 6
US$7.99 • UK£4.50

Central Europe
ISBN 1 86450 204 5
US$24.99 • UK£14.99

Western Europe
ISBN 1 86450 163 4
US$27.99 • UK£15.99

German phrasebook
ISBN 0 86442 451 5
US$5.95 • UK£3.99

Europe on a shoestring
ISBN 1 86450 150 2
US$24.99 • UK£14.99

Read This First: Europe
ISBN 1 86450 136 7
US$14.99 • UK£8.99

Europe phrasebook
ISBN 1 86450 224 X
US$8.99 • UK£4.99

Available wherever books are sold

LONELY PLANET

ON THE ROAD

Travel Guides explore cities, regions and countries, and supply information on transport, restaurants and accommodation, covering all budgets. They come with reliable, easy-to-use maps, practical advice, cultural and historical facts and a rundown on attractions both on and off the beaten track. There are over 200 titles in this classic series, covering nearly every country in the world.

 Lonely Planet Upgrades extend the shelf life of existing travel guides by detailing any changes that may affect travel in a region since a book has been published. Upgrades can be downloaded for free from **www.lonelyplanet.com/upgrades**

For travellers with more time than money, **Shoestring** guides offer dependable, first-hand information with hundreds of detailed maps, plus insider tips for stretching money as far as possible. Covering entire continents in most cases, the six-volume shoestring guides are known around the world as 'backpackers bibles'.

For the discerning short-term visitor, **Condensed** guides highlight the best a destination has to offer in a full-colour, pocket-sized format designed for quick access. They include everything from top sights and walking tours to opinionated reviews of where to eat, stay, shop and have fun.

CitySync lets travellers use their Palm™ or Visor™ hand-held computers to guide them through a city with handy tips on transport, history, cultural life, major sights, and shopping and entertainment options. It can also quickly search and sort hundreds of reviews of hotels, restaurants and attractions, and pinpoint their location on scrollable street maps. CitySync can be downloaded from **www.citysync.com**

MAPS & ATLASES

Lonely Planet's **City Maps** feature downtown and metropolitan maps, as well as transit routes and walking tours. The maps come complete with an index of streets, a listing of sights and a plastic coat for extra durability.

Road Atlases are an essential navigation tool for serious travellers. Cross-referenced with the guidebooks, they also feature distance and climate charts and a complete site index.

Lonely Planet Guides by Region

Lonely Planet is known worldwide for publishing practical, reliable and no-nonsense travel information in our guides and on our Web site. The Lonely Planet list covers just about every accessible part of the world. Currently there are 16 series: Travel guides, Shoestring guides, Condensed guides, Phrasebooks, Read This First, Healthy Travel, Walking guides, Cycling guides, Watching Wildlife guides, Pisces Diving & Snorkeling guides, City Maps, Road Atlases, Out to Eat, World Food, Journeys travel literature and Pictorials.

AFRICA Africa on a shoestring • Botswana • Cairo • Cairo City Map • Cape Town • Cape Town City Map • East Africa • Egypt • Egyptian Arabic phrasebook • Ethiopia, Eritrea & Djibouti • Ethiopian Amharic phrasebook • The Gambia & Senegal • Healthy Travel Africa • Kenya • Malawi • Morocco • Moroccan Arabic phrasebook • Mozambique • Namibia • Read This First: Africa • South Africa, Lesotho & Swaziland • Southern Africa • Southern Africa Road Atlas • Swahili phrasebook • Tanzania, Zanzibar & Pemba • Trekking in East Africa • Tunisia • Watching Wildlife East Africa • Watching Wildlife Southern Africa • West Africa • World Food Morocco • Zambia • Zimbabwe, Botswana & Namibia
Travel Literature: Mali Blues: Traveling to an African Beat • The Rainbird: A Central African Journey • Songs to an African Sunset: A Zimbabwean Story

AUSTRALIA & THE PACIFIC Aboriginal Australia & the Torres Strait Islands •Auckland • Australia • Australian phrasebook • Australia Road Atlas • Cycling Australia • Cycling New Zealand • Fiji • Fijian phrasebook • Healthy Travel Australia, NZ & the Pacific • Islands of Australia's Great Barrier Reef • Melbourne • Melbourne City Map • Micronesia • New Caledonia • New South Wales • New Zealand • Northern Territory • Outback Australia • Out to Eat – Melbourne • Out to Eat – Sydney • Papua New Guinea • Pidgin phrasebook • Queensland • Rarotonga & the Cook Islands • Samoa • Solomon Islands • South Australia • South Pacific • South Pacific phrasebook • Sydney • Sydney City Map • Sydney Condensed • Tahiti & French Polynesia • Tasmania • Tonga • Tramping in New Zealand • Vanuatu • Victoria • Walking in Australia • Watching Wildlife Australia • Western Australia
Travel Literature: Islands in the Clouds: Travels in the Highlands of New Guinea • Kiwi Tracks: A New Zealand Journey • Sean & David's Long Drive

CENTRAL AMERICA & THE CARIBBEAN Bahamas, Turks & Caicos • Baja California • Belize, Guatemala & Yucatán • Bermuda • Central America on a shoestring • Costa Rica • Costa Rica Spanish phrasebook • Cuba • Cycling Cuba • Dominican Republic & Haiti • Eastern Caribbean • Guatemala • Havana • Healthy Travel Central & South America • Jamaica • Mexico • Mexico City • Panama • Puerto Rico • Read This First: Central & South America • Virgin Islands • World Food Caribbean • World Food Mexico • Yucatán
Travel Literature: Green Dreams: Travels in Central America

EUROPE Amsterdam • Amsterdam City Map • Amsterdam Condensed • Andalucía • Athens • Austria • Baltic States phrasebook • Barcelona • Barcelona City Map • Belgium & Luxembourg • Berlin • Berlin City Map • Britain • British phrasebook • Brussels, Bruges & Antwerp • Brussels City Map • Budapest • Budapest City Map • Canary Islands • Catalunya & the Costa Brava • Central Europe • Central Europe phrasebook • Copenhagen • Corfu & the Ionians • Corsica • Crete • Crete Condensed • Croatia • Cycling Britain • Cycling France • Cyprus • Czech & Slovak Republics • Czech phrasebook • Denmark • Dublin • Dublin City Map • Dublin Condensed • Eastern Europe • Eastern Europe phrasebook • Edinburgh • Edinburgh City Map • England • Estonia, Latvia & Lithuania • Europe on a shoestring • Europe phrasebook • Finland • Florence • Florence City Map • France • Frankfurt City Map • Frankfurt Condensed • French phrasebook • Georgia, Armenia & Azerbaijan • Germany • German phrasebook • Greece • Greek Islands • Greek phrasebook • Hungary • Iceland, Greenland & the Faroe Islands • Ireland • Italian phrasebook • Italy • Kraków • Lisbon • The Loire • London • London City Map • London Condensed • Madrid • Madrid City Map • Malta • Mediterranean Europe • Milan, Turin & Genoa • Moscow • Munich • Netherlands • Normandy • Norway • Out to Eat – London • Out to Eat – Paris • Paris • Paris City Map • Paris Condensed • Poland • Polish phrasebook • Portugal • Portuguese phrasebook • Prague • Prague City Map • Provence & the Côte d'Azur • Read This First: Europe • Rhodes & the Dodecanese • Romania & Moldova • Rome • Rome City Map • Rome Condensed • Russia, Ukraine & Belarus • Russian phrasebook • Scandinavian & Baltic Europe • Scandinavian phrasebook • Scotland • Sicily • Slovenia • South-West France • Spain • Spanish phrasebook • Stockholm • St Petersburg • St Petersburg City Map • Sweden • Switzerland • Tuscany • Ukrainian phrasebook • Venice • Vienna • Wales • Walking in Britain • Walking in France • Walking in Ireland • Walking in Italy • Walking in Scotland • Walking in Spain • Walking in Switzerland • Western Europe • World Food France • World Food Greece • World Food Ireland • World Food Italy • World Food Spain **Travel Literature:** After Yugoslavia • Love and War in the Apennines • The Olive Grove: Travels in Greece • On the Shores of the Mediterranean • Round Ireland in Low Gear • A Small Place in Italy

Lonely Planet Mail Order

onely Planet products are distributed worldwide. They are also available by mail order from Lonely Planet, so if you have difficulty finding a title please write to us. North and South American residents should write to 150 Linden St, Oakland, CA 94607, USA; European and African residents should write to 10a Spring Place, London NW5 3BH, UK; and residents of other countries to Locked Bag 1, Footscray, Victoria 3011, Australia.

INDIAN SUBCONTINENT & THE INDIAN OCEAN Bangladesh • Bengali phrasebook • Bhutan • Delhi • Goa • Healthy Travel Asia & India • Hindi & Urdu phrasebook • India • India & Bangladesh City Map • Indian Himalaya • Karakoram Highway • Kathmandu City Map • Kerala • Madagascar • Maldives • Mauritius, Réunion & Seychelles • Mumbai (Bombay) • Nepal • Nepali phrasebook • North India • Pakistan • Rajasthan • Read This First: Asia & India • South India • Sri Lanka • Sri Lanka phrasebook • Tibet • Tibetan phrasebook • Trekking in the Indian Himalaya • Trekking in the Karakoram & Hindukush • Trekking in the Nepal Himalaya • World Food India **Travel Literature:** The Age of Kali: Indian Travels and Encounters • Hello Goodnight: A Life of Goa • In Rajasthan • Maverick in Madagascar • A Season in Heaven: True Tales from the Road to Kathmandu • Shopping for Buddhas • A Short Walk in the Hindu Kush • Slowly Down the Ganges

MIDDLE EAST & CENTRAL ASIA Bahrain, Kuwait & Qatar • Central Asia • Central Asia phrasebook • Dubai • Farsi (Persian) phrasebook • Hebrew phrasebook • Iran • Israel & the Palestinian Territories • Istanbul • Istanbul City Map • Istanbul to Cairo • Istanbul to Kathmandu • Jerusalem • Jerusalem City Map • Jordan • Lebanon • Middle East • Oman and the United Arab Emirates • Syria • Turkey • Turkish phrasebook • World Food Turkey • Yemen **Travel Literature:** Black on Black: Iran Revisited • Breaking Ranks: Turbulent Travels in the Promised Land • The Gates of Damascus • Kingdom of the Film Stars: Journey into Jordan

NORTH AMERICA Alaska • Boston • Boston City Map • Boston Condensed • British Columbia • California & Nevada • California Condensed • Canada • Chicago • Chicago City Map • Chicago Condensed • Florida • Georgia & the Carolinas • Great Lakes • Hawaii • Hiking in Alaska • Hiking in the USA • Honolulu & Oahu City Map • Las Vegas • Los Angeles • Los Angeles City Map • Louisiana & the Deep South • Miami • Miami City Map • Montreal • New England • New Orleans • New Orleans City Map • New York City • New York City City Map • New York City Condensed • New York, New Jersey & Pennsylvania • Oahu • Out to Eat – San Francisco • Pacific Northwest • Rocky Mountains • San Diego & Tijuana • San Francisco • San Francisco City Map • Seattle • Seattle City Map • Southwest • Texas • Toronto • USA • USA phrasebook • Vancouver • Vancouver City Map • Virginia & the Capital Region • Washington, DC • Washington, DC City Map • World Food New Orleans **Travel Literature:** Caught Inside: A Surfer's Year on the California Coast • Drive Thru America

NORTH-EAST ASIA Beijing • Beijing City Map • Cantonese phrasebook • China • Hiking in Japan • Hong Kong & Macau • Hong Kong City Map • Hong Kong Condensed • Japan • Japanese phrasebook • Korea • Korean phrasebook • Kyoto • Mandarin phrasebook • Mongolia • Mongolian phrasebook • Seoul • Shanghai • South-West China • Taiwan • Tokyo • Tokyo Condensed • World Food Hong Kong • World Food Japan **Travel Literature:** In Xanadu: A Quest • Lost Japan

SOUTH AMERICA Argentina, Uruguay & Paraguay • Bolivia • Brazil • Brazilian phrasebook • Buenos Aires • Buenos Aires City Map • Chile & Easter Island • Colombia • Ecuador & the Galapagos Islands • Healthy Travel Central & South America • Latin American Spanish phrasebook • Peru • Quechua phrasebook • Read This First: Central & South America • Rio de Janeiro • Rio de Janeiro City Map • Santiago de Chile • South America on a shoestring • Trekking in the Patagonian Andes • Venezuela **Travel Literature:** Full Circle: A South American Journey

SOUTH-EAST ASIA Bali & Lombok • Bangkok • Bangkok City Map • Burmese phrasebook • Cambodia • Cycling Vietnam, Laos & Cambodia • East Timor phrasebook • Hanoi • Healthy Travel Asia & India • Hill Tribes phrasebook • Ho Chi Minh City (Saigon) • Indonesia • Indonesian phrasebook • Indonesia's Eastern Islands • Java • Lao phrasebook • Laos • Malay phrasebook • Malaysia, Singapore & Brunei • Myanmar (Burma) • Philippines • Pilipino (Tagalog) phrasebook • Read This First: Asia & India • Singapore • Singapore City Map • South-East Asia on a shoestring • South-East Asia phrasebook • Thailand • Thailand's Islands & Beaches • Thailand, Vietnam, Laos & Cambodia Road Atlas • Thai phrasebook • Vietnam • Vietnamese phrasebook • World Food Indonesia • World Food Thailand • World Food Vietnam

ALSO AVAILABLE: Antarctica • The Arctic • The Blue Man: Tales of Travel, Love and Coffee • Brief Encounters: Stories of Love, Sex & Travel • Buddhist Stupas in Asia: The Shape of Perfection • Chasing Rickshaws • The Last Grain Race • Lonely Planet ... On the Edge: Adventurous Escapades from Around the World • Lonely Planet Unpacked • Lonely Planet Unpacked Again • Not the Only Planet: Science Fiction Travel Stories • Ports of Call: A Journey by Sea • Sacred India • Travel Photography: A Guide to Taking Better Pictures • Travel with Children • Tuvalu: Portrait of an Island Nation

LONELY PLANET

ESSENTIALS

Read This First books help new travellers to hit the road with confidence. These invaluable predeparture guides give step-by-step advice on preparing for a trip, budgeting, arranging a visa, planning an itinerary and staying safe while still getting off the beaten track.

Healthy Travel pocket guides offer a regional rundown on disease hot spots and practical advice on predeparture health measures, staying well on the road and what to do in emergencies. The guides come with a user-friendly design and helpful diagrams and tables.

Lonely Planet's **Phrasebooks** cover the essential words and phrases travellers need when they're strangers in a strange land. They come in a pocket-sized format with colour tabs for quick reference, extensive vocabulary lists, easy-to-follow pronunciation keys and two-way dictionaries.

Miffed by blurry photos of the Taj Mahal? Tired of the classic 'top of the head cut off' shot? **Travel Photography: A Guide to Taking Better Pictures** will help you turn ordinary holiday snaps into striking images and give you the know-how to capture every scene, from frenetic festivals to peaceful beach sunrises.

Lonely Planet's **Travel Journal** is a lightweight but sturdy travel diary for jotting down all those on-the-road observations and significant travel moments. It comes with a handy time-zone wheel, a world map and useful travel information.

Lonely Planet's eKno is an all-in-one communication service developed especially for travellers. It offers low-cost international calls and free email and voicemail so that you can keep in touch while on the road. Check it out on **www.ekno.lonelyplanet.com**

FOOD & RESTAURANT GUIDES

Lonely Planet's **Out to Eat** guides recommend the brightest and best places to eat and drink in top international cities. These gourmet companions are arranged by neighbourhood, packed with dependable maps, garnished with scene-setting photos and served with quirky features.

For people who live to eat, drink and travel, **World Food** guides explore the culinary culture of each country. Entertaining and adventurous, each guide is packed with detail on staples and specialities, regional cuisine and local markets, as well as sumptuous recipes, comprehensive culinary dictionaries and lavish photos good enough to eat.

Index

Text

A

abbeys & monasteries
  Admont 199
  Altenburg 375
  Dürnstein 370
  Friesach 216
  Göttweig 374-5
  Heiligenkreuz 378-9
  Klosterneuburg 377
  Kremsmünster 356-7
  Lambach 356
  Melk 367
  Millstatt 224
  Nonnberg 304
  St Florian 351-2
  Stams 275
  Wilhering 350
accommodation 62, 74-7
Achensee 267
Actionism 133
activities 59-60, see also
  individual entries
Admont 199
aerial sports 59-60
air travel 83-8
  airlines 83
  airports 83, 164
  to/from Austria 85-8
  travellers with special
    needs 85
  within Austria 95
Allgäuer Alpen 286, 294
alpine huts 64
alpine railway 386
alpine reservoirs 230
Altausseer See 331
Amstetten 366
animals, see fauna
Apetlon 174
architecture 33-5
Art Nouveau 35
arts 24-36, see also individual
  entries
Artstetten 366
Attersee 337-8
Austrian National Tourist Office
  (ANTO) 41, 100

Austrian Open-Air Museum
  190
Austrian People's Party (ÖVP)
  18, 21
avalanches 58, 71
Axamer Lizum 252

B

Babenbergs 12, 105, 367
Bad Aussee 331-3, **332**
Bad Blumau 200
Bad Deutsch-Altenburg 377-8
Bad Dürrnberg 318
Bad Gastein 237-40, **237**
Bad Hofgastein 240
Bad Ischl 324-7, **326**
Bad Kleinkirchheim 224
Baden bei Wien 380-3, **380**
bargaining 46
Bärnbach 191-3
beer 81
Beethoven, Ludwig van 28-9
Berchtesgaden (Germany) 319
Berg, Alban 31
Bergisel 252-3
bicycle travel, see cycling
Biedermeier period 33, 35
Bielerhöhe 69
Bielerhöhe Pass 294
birds 67, 171, 174, 356
Bludenz 291-4, **293**
boat travel
  to/from Austria 93
  within Austria 103
Böckstein 240
Bodensee 287
books 49-51, see also literature
Brahms, Johannes 30
Brand 294
Brand Valley, see Brandnertal
Brandnertal 294
Braunau am Inn 359-60
Bregenz 284-9, **286**
  accommodation 287-8
  attractions 285-7
  Bodensee boat trips 287
  Bregenz Festival 287
  food 288-9
  getting there & away 289
Bregenzerwald 289-90

brewing (Freistadt) 358
Bruck an der Mur 196-7, **197**
Bruckner, Anton 30
burg, see also castles & palaces
Burg Forchtenstein 171
Burg Hochosterwitz 219-20
Burgenland 167-75, **168**
Bürgeralpe 194
Burgruine Landskron 215
bus travel
  local buses 103-4
  regional bus passes 88
  to/from Austria 88
  within Austria 95
business hours 59

C

camper vans, see car travel
camping 74
car travel 90-2, 98-102
  driving distances 99
  driving licence 42
  fuel 92
  motoring organisations 100-1
  parking 100
  rental 101-2
  road rules 99-100
  to/from Austria 90-2
  tolls & taxes 100
  vehicle insurance 91
  within Austria 98-102
Carinthia 202-25, **203**
  central 210-15, **210**
  eastern 215-21
  western 221-5
Carinthian Open-Air Museum,
  see Kärntnian Freilichtmuseum
Carnuntum 377
casinos 82
castles & palaces 277
  Aggstein, Burg 369
  Alt Kainach castle 192
  Alte, Burg (Gmünd) 221
  Ambras, Schloss 252
  Belvedere, Schloss 34, 134-5
  Bruck, Schloss 240-1
  Burgruine Landskron 215
  Eggenberg, Schloss 182
  Esterházy, Schloss 168-9
  Forchtenstein, Burg 171

Bold indicates maps.

Greillenstein 375
Hasegg, Burg 260
Hellbrunn, Schloss 317
Hochosterwitz, Burg
    219-20
Hofberg (Innsbruck) 251
Hofberg (Vienna) 119-20
Hohenbrunn, Schloss 352
Hohensalzburg, Festung 303-4
Hohenschwangau
    (Germany) 277
Hohenwerfen, Burg 320
Kuenringerburg 370
Kufstein, Festung 273
Lamberg, Schloss 353
Landsberg, Burg 189
Landskron, Schloss 196
Linderhof, Schloss 277
Linz, Schloss 345
Mirabell, Schloss 306
Neuschwanstein
    (Germany) 277
Obermurau, Schloss 200
Ort, Landschloss 335
Ort, Seeschloss 335
Porcia, Schloss 222-3
Riegersburg, Schloss 200
Rosenburg, Schloss 375
Schallaburg, Schloss 34, 368
Schattenburg, Schloss 290
Schönbrunn, Schloss 35,
    130-2
Schönbühel, Schloss 369
Weyer, Schloss 335
cathedrals, see individual entries
chamois 20
Charlemagne 12
children, travel with 57
Christmas markets 140, 141
churches, see individual
    entries
cinema 36
climate 18-19
coffee 80, 153
conduct, see cultural
    considerations
consulates 42-3
convents, see abbeys &
    monasteries
costs 46
courses 60
    language 138, 253, 307
credit cards 45
cross-country skiing 71
cultural considerations
    36-7, 40
currency, see money

customs regulations 43-4
cycling 92, 102

D

Dachstein ice caves 330
Dachstein range 330
Danube River 343
Danube Valley 361, 365-78
design 35-6
Deutschlandsberg 189
disabled travellers 56-7
Dobratsch 215
Doderer, Heimito von 32
dom, see individual entries
Donau, see Danube River
Donau-Auen National Park 378
Doppler, Christian Johann 23
Dornbirn 289
drinks 80-1
Dürnstein 370-1

E

Eagle's Nest (Germany) 319
Ebensee 337
ecology, see environmental
    issues
economy 22
edelweiss 20
Edelweiss Spitze 234
education 22-3
Egelsee 274
Egg 290
Ehrenhausen 189-90
Ehrwald 263
Eisenerz 198-9
Eisenstadt 167-71, **169**
    accommodation 170
    attractions 168-9
    food 170
    getting there & away 170-1
    special events 169-70
Eisriesenwelt Höhle 319-20
electricity 52
email services 49
embassies 42-3
emergencies 58, 65
entertainment 81-2, 154-61
environmental issues 19-20,
    40, 65-7
Erlaufsee 195
Erzberg 198
etiquette, see cultural
    considerations
Europa Sports Region 228
Europabrücke 259
Europapark 205-6, **206**

European Union (EU) 17-18, 22
exchange rates 44

F

Faaker See 215
fauna 20
fax services 48
Felber Tauern Road 226
Feldkirch 290-1
Fern Pass 263
festivals 61-2, see also special
    events
Festung Hohensalzburg 303
Feuerkogel 337
fiacres 166, 317
films 36
Flexen Pass 295
flora 20
food 77-80
Franz Josef 16, 325
Franz Josefs Höhe 234
Frauenalpe 200
Freedom Party (FPÖ) 18
Freistadt 357-8
    brewery 358
Freud, Sigmund 23-4, 32, 133
Friesach 216-18
Fuschertörl 234

G

Gaisberg 317
Gamlitz 67
Garmisch-Partenkirchen
    (Germany) 263
Gasteiner Tal 237-40
Gauderbier festival 265
gay travellers 56, 118-19,
    156, 301
Gemeindealpe 194
Gerlitzen 215
geography 18
geology 18
Gerlos Pass 233-4
Giant Chocolate festival 62, 292
glaciers 235
glassblowing 192
Gluck, Christoph Willibald von 26
Gmünd 221
Gmunden 334-6, **334**
gold mining 240, 265, 297
Goldeck 223
Goldenes Dachl 34, 250
Gosau 333
Gosausee 333
government 18, 20-1
Graukogel 238

Graz 177-88, **178**, **180**
  accommodation 183-4
  attractions 179-83
  entertainment 186-7
  food 184-6
  getting around 188-9
  getting there & away 187-8
  Landeszeughaus 181
  shopping 187
  special events 183
  tourist offices 179
Grillparzer, Franz 24
Grossglockner 226
Grossglockner Road
  226, 234-6
Grossvenediger 226, 228
Grünau 337
Grundlsee 331-2
Grünersee 196
Gurk 218
Gurk Dom 34, 218
Guttal 234

H

Habsburgs 13-16, 105, 252
Hafelekar Belvedere 253
Hahnenkamm 269-70
Haider, Jörg 21
Hainburg 377
Hall in Tirol 260
Hallein 318-19
Hallstatt 69, 328-9
Hallstätter See 327-8
Handke, Peter 32
hang-gliding 59-60
Haus der Natur 304
Haydn, Josef 26-7, 168-9
  Haydnhaus 169
health 52-5
  medical services 52-3
health spas, see spa towns
Hechtsee 273
Heiligenblut 236
Heiligenkreuz 378-9
Hellbrunn 317
Hermagor 67-8
heurigen (wine taverns)
  156-7
hiking, see walking
Hinterglemm 72, 229
Hintersteinersee 274
Hintertux Glacier 266
Hirschegg 294

Hirschenkogel 385
history 12-18
hitching 92-3, 102
Hitler, Adolf 16, 155,
  319, 359
Hochgurgl 276
Hochosterwitz 219-20
Hochsölden 275
Hochstein 241
Hochtor 234
Hofburg (Innsbruck) 251
Hofburg (Vienna)
  119-20
Hofkirche 251-2
Hohe Salve 275
Hohe Tauern National Park
  Region 226-44, **227**
Höllental 385-6
hostels 74-5
hotels 75-6
Hundertwasser, Friedensreich
  131, 200
Hungary 167
Hungerburg 253

I

ibex 20
ice caves 330
Ice Man, the 276
Igls 260
Illmitz 174
Imst 277
Inn Valley 279
Innsbruck 68, 72, 248-60,
  249, **251**
  accommodation 254-5
  activities 253
  attractions 251-3
  entertainment 257-8
  food 256-7
  getting around 259-60
  getting there & away 259
  Hofburg 251
  Hofkirche 251-2
  Schloss Ambras 252
  shopping 258-9
  special events 253-4
  tourist offices 248
  walking tour 250-1
insurance
  health 71
  travel 42
  vehicle 91
Internet
  access 49
  resources 49

Ischgl 72, 279
itineraries 38

J

Jenbach 263, 267
Josephinum 132-3
Jugendstil (Art Nouveau) 35

K

Kaisergebirge 273
Kaisertal 273
Kammersee 332
Kaprun 72, 228-30
Karlskirche 34, 133-4
Kärnten, see Carinthia
Kärntner Freilichtmuseum 220
Katrin 69
Kefermarkt 359
Kirchberg 72, 272
Kitzbühel 70, 72, 267-72, **268**
Kitzsteinhorn 229
Klagenfurt 202-10, **204**
  accommodation 207
  attractions 205-7
  entertainment 209
  food 208-9
  getting around 209-10
  getting there & away 209
  special events 207
Klamm reservoir 230
Kleinwalsertal 294-5
Klimt, Gustav 33, 134
Klosterneuburg 377
Klosterwappen 387
Knappenstube 234
Köflach 191
Kollegienkirche 34, 303
Königssee (Germany) 319
Koppenbrüllerhöhle 330
Kreischberg 200
Krems an der Donau 371-4, **372**
Kremsmünster 356-7
Krimml Falls 232-3
Krippenstein 330
Krumpendorf 210
Kufstein 273-5
Kunsthistorisches Museum 126-8

L

Lake Achen, see Achensee
Lake Constance, see Bodensee
Lake Neusiedl, see Neusiedler See
Lake Wörth, see Wörthersee
Lambach 356
Landeck 277-9

Bold indicates maps.

Landeszeughaus 181
Längsee 274
language 37, 388-91
   courses 138, 253, 307
Laterns 290
Lauda, Niki 81, 86
laundry 52
Lech 295
legal matters 58-9
Lehár, Franz 31
Leoben 198
lesbian travellers 56, 118-19,
   156, 301
Lienz 240-4, **241**
   accommodation 242
   activities 241-2
   attractions 240-1
   entertainment 243
   food 243
   getting there & away 244
Linz 343-50, **346**
   accommodation 347-8
   attractions 345-7
   entertainment 349-50
   food 349
   getting there & around 350
   special events 347
   tourist offices 344-5
Lipizzaner stallions 130, 191
literature 24, 32, see
   also books
local transport 103-4
Lower Austria 361-87, **362**
   southern 383-7
Lünersee 294
Lurgrotte 190-1

M

magazines 51
Magdalensberg 220
Mahler, Gustav 30
Maier, Hermann 81
Mammuthöhle 330
maps 38
Maria Saal 220-1
Maria Taferl 366
Maria Theresa 14-15
Maria Wörth 211
Mariazell 193-6, **194**
marmot 20, 21
Matrei 68
Mauterndorf 321
Mauthausen 351
Mayerling 378
maypoles 217
Mayrhofen 266-7

measures, see weights &
   measures
Melk 366-8
Metternich, Klemens von 15-16
Millstatt 224-5
Milser, Oswald 262
Mittelberg 294
Mödling 378
monasteries, see abbeys &
   monasteries
Mondsee 341-2
money 44-7
   bargaining 46
   costs 46
   credit cards 45
   euro 45
   exchanging money 44
   taxes 46-7
   tipping 46
   travellers cheques 44-5
Mooserboden reservoir 230
Mörbisch 173
Mösern 262
motorcycle travel 90-2, 98-102
   driving distances 99
   driving licence 42
   fuel 92
   motoring organisations 100-1
   parking 100
   road rules 99-100
   to/from Austria 90-2
   tolls & taxes 100
   touring 92
   within Austria 98-102
Mt Katrin 69
mountain safety 65
mountain transport 103
mountaineering 236
Mozart, Wolfgang Amadeus
   27-8, 299, 306
Murau 200
music 25-31
museums, see individual entries
Musil, Robert 32
Muster, Thomas 81
Mutters 253
Muttersberg 292

N

Napoleon 15, 16
Naschmarkt 162
national parks
   Hohe Tauern National
      Park 226-44
   Donau-Auen National
      Park 378

Neusiedl am See 171-2
Neusiedler See 20, 67, 171-5
newspapers 51
Niederösterreich, see Lower
   Austria
Nordalpenweg 387
Nordkette 68, 250, 253

O

Obergurgl 276
Oberösterreich, see Upper
   Austria
Obertraun 329-31
organised tours, see tours
Ossiacher See 215
Ötztal, The 68, 275-7

P

Pacher, Michael 35, 339
painting 32-3
paragliding 59-60, 265
Pasterze Glacier 234
Paznauntal 279
Peggau 190
pensions 75-6
people 22
Petronell 377-80
Pfunds 279
philosophy 23-4
photography & video 51-2
Piber 191
   Lipizzaner stud farm 191
Podersdorf 174-5
politics 18, 20-1
Popper, Karl 23
population 22
Pörtschach 210-11
postal services 47
Pöstlingberg 347
Prandtauer, Jakob 34, 351, 366
public holidays 59
Pyramidenkogel 211

R

radio 51
Radstadt 321
rafting 230
rail passes, see train travel
Rappenlochschlucht 289
'Red Vienna' period 105
religion 37
Reschen Pass 279
Reutte 277, 294
Riegersburg 200-1
Rieseneishöhle 330

Riezlern 294
Roman ruins 33, 126, 132
Rosanna River 280
Rosegg Wildpark 211
Rossbrand 321
Rudolf, Archduke 379
Rust 172-3

S

safe travel 57-8
St Andrä 215
St Anton am Arlberg 73,
    280-3, **281**
St Barbara Kirche 192-3
St Christoph 281
St Florian 351-2
St Gilgen 340-1
St Johann in Tirol 272-3
St Pölten 361-5, **363**
    accommodation 364
    attractions 362-4
    food 364-5
    getting there & away 365
St Veit an der Glan 218-19
St Wolfgang 338-40
salt mines 260, 297, 310, 316,
    324, 318, 328, 384
Salzach River 297
Salzburg 298-317, **299**,
    302, 304
    accommodation 308-10
    attractions 301-7
    entertainment 314-15
    Festung Hohensalzburg 303-4
    food 312-14
    getting around 316-17
    getting there & away 316
    museums & galleries 304-6
    shopping 315-16
    special events 307-8
    tourist offices 300
    tours 307
    walking tour 301-3
Salzburg province
    297-321, **298**
Salzkammergut, The 322-42,
    323
Samnaun (Switzerland) 72, 279
sausage stands 78
Schafberg 338
Schesaplana 294
Schiele, Egon 376
Schladming 82

schloss, see also castles &
    palaces
Schloss Ambras 252
Schloss Belvedere 34, 134-5
Schloss Eggenberg 182
Schloss Esterházy 168-9
Schloss Hellbrunn 317
Schloss Mirabell 306
Schloss Riegersburg 200-1
Schloss Schönbrunn 35, 130-2
Schmiding Bird Park 356
Schmittenhöhe 228-9
Schneeberg 386-7
Schöpfl 376
Schönberg, Arnold 31
Schörfling 338
Schubert, Franz 29-30
Schwarzsee 270
Schwaz 261
science 23-4
sculpture 35-6
Secession movement 35
Seefeld 261-3
Seegrotte Hinterbrühl 379-80
Seewinkel 173-4
Semmering 385-6
Semmering alpine railway 386
senior travellers 57
sgraffito 34
shopping 82
Sigmund Freud museum 133
silver mining 261, 291
skiing 59, 70-3, 194, 200, 215,
    224, 228, 266, 275-6, 295,
    321, 337, 340
    alpine huts 64
    Arlberg 279-80, 295
    avalanche warning 58
    Bludenz 69, 292
    costs 70
    dangers 71
    Hohe Tauern National Park
        236, 238
    Innsbruck 72, 253
    Ischgl 72
    Kaprun 72
    Kirchberg 72
    Kitzbühel 72, 269
    Lech 73
    Lienz 241-2
    Mayrhofen 264, 266-7
    passes 70
    Saalbach-Hinterglemm 72
    St Anton am Arlberg 73, 280
    Salzkammergut-Lammertal
        323-4
    schools 71

seasons 70-1
Seefeld 262
Söll 275
Stubai Glacier 261
Zell am See 229
Zillertal 264
snowboarding 71, 280-1
Social Democrats (SPÖ) 18, 21
Sölden 275-6
Söll 275
Sound of Music, The 51, 69,
    299, 308
spa towns 76, 224
    Bad Deutsch-Altenburg 377-8
    Bad Gastein 238
    Bad Hofgastein 240
    Bad Ischl 324-7
    Bad Kleinkirchheim 224
    Baden 380-3
    Böckstein 240
    Warmbach Villach 214-15
Spanish Riding School (Spanis-
    che Reitschule) 160-1
special events 59, 61-2
    Bodensee festival 287
    Bregenz festival 287
    Brucknerfest 347
    Christmas markets 140, 141
    Dolomitenlauf 242
    Festwochen der Alten Musik
        253-4
    Gauderfest 265
    Giant Chocolate festival 62,
        292
    Halleiner Stadtfestwoche
        318-19
    Haydntage 170
    Huamfahrerfest 264
    Ischler Stadtfest 326
    Klagenfurter Stadtfest 207
    Lederhosen Meeting 62
    Linz City festival 347
    Melker Sommerspiele 367
    Murenschalk 196
    Narzissenfest 332
    Niederösterreichische
        Landesmesse 373
    Perchten Festival 238
    Perchtenlaufen 62
    Rauchkuchldumpling
        Festival 62
    Salamanca Festival 223
    Salzburger Festspiele 307
    Samsonumzug 321
    Schemenlaufer 277
    Schubertiade 289-90
    Shrovetide festival 277

Bold indicates maps.

Spectaculum 216
Steirischer Herbst 183
Styriarte 183
Summer of Music 139-40
Vienna festival 139
Vienna Opera Film
   festival 140
Viennale Film Festival 61
Wien Modern festival 140
special sections
Austria & Music 25-31
Vienna Walking Tour 121-5
Walking & Skiing in
   Austria 63-73
spectator sports 81, 82
Spittal an der Drau 221-4, **222**
Spitz 369
Sportgastein 240
Stams 275
Steiermark, see Styria
Stephansdom 34, 119
Steyr 353-5, **354**
stift, see abbeys & monasteries
Stift Melk 34, 367
Stimmersee 273
storks 172
Strauss, Johan the Elder 30
Strauss, Johan the Younger 30
Strauss, Richard 31
Strobl 338
Stubai Glacier 261
Stubaital 68
Stuben 295
Stübing 190
Stubnerkogel 238
student cards 42
Stuibenfall 275
Styria 176-201, **177**
Styrian Wine Routes 67, 188-9
Styrian Iron Road 198
Süleyman the Magnificent 13-14

T

Tamsweg 321
taxis 104
telephone services 47-9
television 51
Tennengebirge 69
theatre 36
Thiersee 274
Third Man, The 51, 140
time 52
tipping 46
Tirol 245-83, **246**
   north-eastern 263-75
   western 275-9

toilets 52
Toplitzsee 332
tourist offices 40-1
tours 93-4, 104
traditional culture 36
train travel 96-8, **95**
   Austrian rail passes 91, 97
   European rail passes 90-1
   to/from Austria 89-92
   within Austria 97
Traunkirchen 336-7
travellers cheques 44-5
Traunsee 333-7
Tulfes 253
Tulln 375-6
Turks 13-14
Tyrol, see Tirol

U

Uderns 264
Umhausen 275-7
Unesco World Heritage Sites 39
   Graz historic centre 179-82
   Hallstatt-Dachstein
      region 327
   Salzburg historic centre 301-7
   Schönbrunn palace &
      gardens 130-2
   Semmering alpine
      railway 386
   Wachau region 366-75
Untersberg 318
Upper Austria 343-60, **344**

V

van Beethoven, Ludwig, see
   Beethoven, Ludwig van
Velden 211
Venus of Willendorf 369
Verdun Altar 375
video, see photography & video
video systems 51
Vienna 105-66, **108-9**, **110-
   11**, **112-15**, **116**
   accommodation 140-8
   activities 137-8
   attractions 119-20
   bars & clubs 154-6
   cemeteries 135-6
   churches 119, 132-4
   entertainment 154-61
   food 148-54
   getting around 164-6,
   getting there & away 162-4
   history 105-6
   Hofburg 119-20

Heurigen 156-8
Innere Stadt 119-20
Kunsthistorisches
   Museum 126-8
museums 126-9, 132-3, 137
Schloss Belvedere 134-5
Schloss Schönbrunn 130-2
shopping 161-2
Spanische Reitschule (Span-
   ish Riding School) 160-1
special events 139
Stephansdom 119, 122
tourist offices 107
tours 139
Vienna Boys' Choir 159
walking tour 121-5, **123**
Vienna Boys' Choir 31, 159
Vienna Circle 23
Vienna Group 32, 33
Vienna Philharmonic
   Orchestra 31
Vienna Secessionists 32
Vienna Woods, see Wienerwald
Vienna Workshops 35-6
Villach 212-14, **212**
visas 41-2
von Doderer, Heimito, see
   Doderer, Heimito von
von Gluck, Christoph Willibald,
   see Gluck, Christoph
   Willibald von
von Metternich, Klemens, see
   Metternich, Klemens von
von Trapp family 308
von Webern, Anton, see
   Webern, Anton von
Vorarlberg 284-96, **285**
Vorteilscard 97

W

Wachau region 366-75
Wagner, Otto 129
Waidhofen an der Ybbs 366
Waldviertel region 375
walking 59, 63-9, 102-3, 200,
   262, 266, 337, 385, 386-7
   alpine huts 64
   Bielerhöhe 69
   Gamlitz 67
   Hallstatt 69
   Hermagor 67-8
   Hohe Tauern National Park
      227-8, 229-30, 233, 238
   Innsbruck 68, 253
   Katrin 69
   Kitzbühel 269-72

Lienz 242
Matrei 68
mountain safety 65
Neusiedler See 67
Ötztaler Alpen 68
responsible walking 65-7
Stubaier Alpen 68
Tennengebirge 69
Vienna 138
Wienerwald 378
Zillertal 264
Warmbad Villach 214-15
water sports 60-2, 171, 172, 174, 195, 210, 224, 230, 339, 340, 341
Wattens 260-1
Webern, Anton von 31
weights & measures 52

Weissenkirchen 369-70
Wels 355-6
Werfen 319-21
western Arlberg 295-6
Wiener Neustadt 383-5, **383**
Wienerwald 378-83
wild flowers, see flora
Wildpark Ferleiten 234
Wildsee 262
Wildspitze 275
Willendorf 369
Windegg Belvedere 276
windsurfing, see water sports
wine 80-1, 156-7, 172
wine taverns 31
Wittgenstein, Ludwig 23
Wolf, Hugo 30
Wolfgangsee 338-41

women travellers 55-6
work 60-2
Wörther See 205-6, 210-12
Würstel stands 78

Y
youth cards 42

Z
Zell am See 228-32, **229**
Zell am Ziller 265-6
Zettersfeld 241
Zillertal 263-75
Zugspitze 263
Zürs 295
Zwieselstein 276
Zwölferhorn 340

Boxed Text

Air Travel Glossary 84
Alpine Reservoirs 230
And Now for Something Completely Different... 62
Art through Action 33
Avalanche Warning 58
Beer For All 358
Bodensee Excursions 287
Buying Opera & Theatre Tickets 159
Coffee Concoctions 80
Corpse Disposal, Viennese Style 138
Dachstein or Werfen? 330
DIY Wiener Schnitzel 79
Entombed in Ice 276
Euro Note 45
European Rail Passes 90-1
Fantasy Castles 277

Festivals of Austria 61
Glacier Watching 235
Glassblowing in Bärnbach 192
Gustav Klimt 134
Highlights 39
Hitler's Home Town 359
Hitler's Vienna 155
Hot Wine and Cold Snow: Vienna's Christmas Markets 142
Lauda Air Takes Off, Hits Turbulence 86
Marmot Society 21
Maypole Madness 217
Meat Treat 78
Miracle of the Host, The 262
Mother Theresa 15
Municipal Museums 137
Museumsquartier 133

Mystery at Mayerling 379
Otto Wagner 129
Pacher's Religious Art 339
Peace Empire & a Hundred Waters 131
Road Distances 99
Salt Mines 324
Sigmund Freud 24
Sound of Dollars, The 308
Spa Resorts 76
Sporting Feats 81
Telephone Numbers Explained 49
Third Man, The 140
Top Trips 103
Turks & Vienna, The 14
Venus of Willendorf, The 369
Winning Ways With Wine 157

MAP LEGEND

CITY ROUTES

Freeway —— Freeway	⊏ ⊐ ⊐ ⊐ Unsealed Road
Highway —— Primary Road	One Way Street
Road —— Secondary Road	Pedestrian Street
Street —— Street	⊓⊓⊓⊓⊓⊓ Stepped Street
Lane —— Lane	)— — — Tunnel
On/Off Ramp	Footbridge

REGIONAL ROUTES

Tollway, Freeway	
Primary Road	
Secondary Road	
Minor Road	

BOUNDARIES

—■—■— International	
—■—■— State	
— — — Disputed	
Fortified Wall	

HYDROGRAPHY

River, Creek	Dry Lake; Salt Lake
Canal	Spring; Rapids
Lake	Waterfalls

TRANSPORT ROUTES & STATIONS

——◯—— Train	⊩——⊩—🚠 Cable Car, Funicular
Disused Railway	—⊣▢ Ferry
——Ⓤ—— U-Bahn	— — — — Walking Trail
Underground Train	· · · · · · · Walking Tour
——▢·· Tramway	Path

AREA FEATURES

Building	Market	Beach
Park, Gardens	Sports Ground	Cemetery
		Campus
		Plaza

POPULATION SYMBOLS

✪ **CAPITAL** National Capital	● **CITY** City	● Village Village
◉ **CAPITAL** State Capital	● Town Town	Urban Area

MAP SYMBOLS

■ Place to Stay	▼ Place to Eat	● Point of Interest
✕ Airport	Cinema	☀ Lookout	▣ Shopping Centre
⊖ Bank	⬤ Cycling	▲ Monument	Stately Home
Bus Stop	Embassy, Consulate	Museum	Swimming Pool
Bus Terminal	Fountain	Parking	Theatre
Camping	✛ Hospital	Police Station	Tourist Information
Castle, Chateau	Internet Cafe	Post Office	Winery, Vineyard
Cathedral, Church	Lighthouse	Pub or Bar	Zoo

Note: not all symbols displayed above appear in this book

LONELY PLANET OFFICES

Australia
Locked Bag 1, Footscray, Victoria 3011
☎ 03 8379 8000 fax 03 8379 8111
email: talk2us@lonelyplanet.com.au

UK
10a Spring Place, London NW5 3BH
☎ 020 7428 4800 fax 020 7428 4828
email: go@lonelyplanet.co.uk

USA
150 Linden St, Oakland, CA 94607
☎ 510 893 8555 TOLL FREE: 800 275 5555
fax 510 893 8572
email: info@lonelyplanet.com

France
1 rue du Dahomey, 75011 Paris
☎ 01 55 25 33 00 fax 01 55 25 33 01
email: bip@lonelyplanet.fr
www.lonelyplanet.fr

World Wide Web: www.lonelyplanet.com *or* AOL keyword: lp
Lonely Planet Images: lpi@lonelyplanet.com.au

SHADOW OVER THE FENS

A gripping crime thriller full of suspense

JOY ELLIS

JOFFE
BOOKS

Published 2016 by Joffe Books, London.

www.joffebooks.com

© Joy Ellis

Originally published as "Shadowbreaker" by Robert Hale.

ISBN- 978-1-911021-63-6

For Rosemary Keywood and Rachel Appleby.

CHAPTER ONE

As Detective Inspector Nikki Galena locked the door of her Fenland home, a shiver of anticipation coursed through her. She gazed across the wide expanse of remote marsh, took a deep savouring breath of the fresh salty air and smiled. It felt good to be back where she belonged.

Across Cloud Fen she could see the mist clearing, and a green gold morning slowly waking up the salt marsh with its bright clear light. She stepped into the garden and wondered what this new dawn would bring with it, apart from the arrival of her new sergeant. Her smile widened. She had been waiting for this moment for a while and it was something she both welcomed and dreaded.

Detective Sergeant Joseph Easter was joining her CID team. It was also his first day back after being injured on duty. She had no illusions that his new position would be a breeze, because it wouldn't be. It would be a testing time for both of them.

She just hoped that he was as match fit as he claimed to be.

Nikki crunched her away across the gravel drive to her car and muttered a small prayer of thanks that for once the nick was unusually quiet. At least she wouldn't be throwing the poor sod straight in at the deep end.

'At last! Nikki! I was beginning to think I'd never see you again!'

A tall, craggy faced man, wearing tracksuit bottoms, a bright red rugby shirt and a black rucksack, brought his bike to a halt, hurriedly climbed off and grinned warmly at her.

'Martin! How have you been?' Nikki welcomed the friendly hug, then pushed him back and stared at him. 'Hey, you look good!' She had known him for more years than she cared to remember. He was her closest neighbour, even though he lived some quarter of a mile away down a narrow track that led onto the marsh.

The man beamed at her. 'I'm fine, but all the better for hearing your news. I've seen the workmen out here for a few weeks now. They told me that you were planning on moving back.'

'It was time to come home, Martin.' As Nikki spoke those words, she knew it was true. She'd been gone too long. Stuck in the town; spending every waking hour hunting down drug dealers. She had driven herself on until she could barely remember what life was like before her drug-crushing crusade had eaten into every part of her existence.

'Glad to hear it.' Martin Durham brushed a swathe of wavy iron-grey hair from his eyes and looked up appreciatively at her old farmhouse. Fresh paint glistened in the morning sunlight. 'Nice job! The weather out here takes no prisoners. I was beginning to wonder if the east wind was going to claim it before you!'

'It was in a bit of a state, wasn't it?' She suddenly felt horribly guilty for neglecting her old family home for so long. 'But this winter, I promise you'll see smoke rising from the chimney again.' She glanced at her watch. 'Oh Lord! I'm sorry to dash off, but the Fenland Constabulary calls. Why don't you come round for a coffee at the weekend? We can catch up.'

'Thanks, I'll do that. Actually I've got a little bit of interesting news for you, but it can wait until then. Oh, and . . .' he looked at her weather-beaten front gate, '. . . I see your workmen didn't get as far as this. I was going to give my fences a coat of wood preserver tomorrow, I'll do this at the same time, if it helps?'

'Great. If it's no trouble?' Nikki clicked the central locking on her car. 'But be sure to let me know what I owe you, that stuff costs a fortune.'

'I don't think one gate will break the bank! Consider it a welcome home present.' With a wave, he climbed back on his bike, hauled his rucksack up over his shoulder, and pedalled off in the direction of his cottage.

Nikki slid into her car, leaned back, and allowed herself a long sigh of relief.

It had not been an easy decision to return home, but then her last case had changed a lot of things in her life. Now, having had some time to reflect, she knew it had thrown her a life-line. Her vigilante-style, one-woman mission to clean Greenborough of drugs had nearly cost her her career, and was beginning to turn her into the most blinkered and disliked officer in the area. And that was not the kind of woman she wanted to be. Just meeting Martin again made her realise just how thoughtful people could be. Maybe the whole world was not populated by evil shits after all.

As the tall figure in the scarlet shirt slowly disappeared from view, she felt a kind of peace wash over her. It was really good to be back. She belonged here in this strange and remote water-world, with its great stretches of marshland, teeming with wild life, and with a big, big sky hanging over everything.

With one final glance up at the old house, she turned the key in the ignition and pulled out onto the lane. At last, she was ready and willing to take on whatever

3

Greenborough nick decided to chuck at her. It was going to be a good day.

* * *

As Nikki began her drive from Cloud Fen, Joseph Easter touched his fingertips on the turquoise tiled wall of the pool and burst through the surface of the sparkling water.

Fifty lengths. Nowhere near the distance he used to do, but he was getting there. He stood for a moment getting his breath back. Every day showed improvement. He could now do a pretty impressive ten miles on the hardest programme on the exercise bike without too much pain. He lay on his back and floated for a while. And it wasn't even pain any more, well nothing like what he had suffered just after the operation.

He glanced at the clock. He didn't want to be late on his first day at his new station. He swam easily back to the steps and pulled himself reluctantly from the warm pool. Until today he had spent almost two hours every morning in the club gym and the small pool, doing all he could to get strong enough to pass the medical that would let him return to work.

Joseph padded into the changing room, collected his towel and toilet bag from his locker, and went for a shower. The FMO had grudgingly allowed him back, with a few reservations about what duties he should avoid for a while, but all in all it had been a pretty good outcome. His only worry was that although his body was recovering, he had no way of knowing how his mind would react to an unexpected situation. And he wouldn't know that until the next time the shit hit the fan. He could test his muscles and his physical endurance, but as far as he knew, there was no simple test for his mental state. Which meant there was little point in worrying about it. He was finally free to join DI Galena's team, so he'd better just get on with it.

He grinned to himself as the soapy water cascaded down his back. Into the lion's den.

As he rubbed shampoo into his mop of light brown hair, he remembered his first meeting with his new boss. Instead of welcoming him to his temporary assignment, she had been acid-tongued, short-tempered and bloody rude. Joseph laughed aloud, then stuck his head under the stream of hot water. Because despite all of that, he had liked her. Well, maybe 'like' was not quite the right word, but he *had* recognised a dedicated, honest copper beneath the hard-as-nails exterior. He could not have been more delighted when she asked him to leave his old nick and work with her permanently at Greenborough.

He towelled himself down and dressed. Somewhere during that last case that they had worked together, they had forged some sort of unspoken bond. He had felt it, and he was pretty sure that she had too. Why else would she have requested that he transfer from Fenchester?

Joseph dried his hair and stared at himself in the mirror. He didn't look different, but he knew that deep down he had changed. He looked at his reflection. In his eyes he saw the same old intensity, although maybe there was something else there now? He forced a grin to banish the gloomy mood that was threatening to wash over him. Maybe it was just that the locker-room mirror needed cleaning.

Joseph gathered up his kit, pushed it in his gym bag and walked down the corridor to the foyer, thinking as he went about his new position. He wasn't daft enough to believe that working with DI Galena would be easy. As individuals, they were complete opposites, but somehow their varied approaches brought them, by different avenues, to the same conclusions. And *that* would catch them villains.

As the automatic doors sighed back, he smiled to himself. They had all the right ingredients to make a damned good team. His expression darkened. Just as long

5

as they both allowed the past to stay where it belonged and not creep into the present.

Sunshine warmed Joseph's face as he stepped outside, and his smile returned. This was not the time for raking up old garbage. Today was all about fresh starts, and if he didn't get a wriggle on, his first words from his new guv'nor would be a rollicking for being late.

He loped across the car park, unlocked his boot and threw his bag inside. As he closed it again, he noticed someone give him a friendly wave. He lifted his hand automatically, then walked around and got into the driver's seat.

The other early morning swimmer was a dark-haired woman who he had seen briefly a few times before. She was thin, but not in a skinny way. She looked lean and core fit like an athlete. He paused and watched her make her way towards the club entrance. Her stride was confident, and her limbs moved with a graceful fluidity. Joseph found himself staring unashamedly through the windscreen at her, and for a man who had always believed that looks were not the only thing that mattered, it came as something of a shock. There was definitely something very attractive about the woman's appearance.

Joseph shook himself. He'd never been late for work in his entire life, and he didn't intend to start today. With an annoyed snort, he started the engine, released the handbrake and sped noisily from the car park, but not before one last glance in his mirror to watch the dark-haired woman disappear into the building.

* * *

He had not been sure what to expect from the team, but Joseph's entrance into the CID room was accompanied by a rowdy chorus of cheers and an assortment of handshakes and back-slapping.

'Great to see you again, Sarge!' DC Cat Cullen's grin almost sliced her face in two.

'Love the hair!' Joseph stared wide-eyed at the short blond spikes and the emerald green Mohican-style strip that ran from her forehead to the nape of her neck.

'Yeah, cool, isn't it? The guv'nor's had me getting down and dirty with some of Greenborough's youth. On a covert surveillance case, you understand.'

'I'm never quite sure with you, Cat. Your disguises suit you a bit too well!'

'Sarge! How are you?' The big form of Dave Harris muscled in and grasped his hand, pumping it up and down with ferocious delight.

'Doing well, my friend. And happy to be here, I can tell you. There are only so many old movies you want to watch!'

'So, you really have decided to join us at last, Detective Sergeant.' Nikki Galena's voice instantly quelled the chit-chat.

Joseph had not even noticed her come in. 'Yes, ma'am. But only on the condition that our next case is considerably less injurious than the last one.'

A pained look passed swiftly across her face, then the Inspector shrugged her shoulders. 'There are no guarantees in this line of work, Joseph. Let's just hope that lightning doesn't strike twice, shall we?' She threw him a rare smile and held out her hand. 'Welcome to the team. We are glad to have you on board.'

The room rippled with comments of agreement, and as Joseph gripped her hand in his, he felt a lump form in his throat. He'd worked with this small group of people for such a short time on his assignment, but there were already his trusted comrades. That was what that kind of case did to you, brought you close together and tied you with the tightest bonds.

With difficulty, he tried to formulate a reply, but the words would not come.

'Okay, you lot!' The guv'nor saved him. 'Fun and games over! Bugger off and catch me some criminals!' She studied him carefully and he wondered what she was thinking. 'Coffee and a chat in my office sounds good to me. You're buying.'

DI Galena turned and marched out of the CID room, and Joseph smiled to himself. He'd heard that she had mellowed, and wondered how such a metamorphosis could have been achieved. Now he knew. It was subtle. She still yelled at everyone, but there was just the hint of a twinkle in her eye now. The Ice Maiden was still very much in charge, but there was the slightest melting, a softening around the edges, and it suited her.

As he scurried obediently off to the coffee machine, the smile remained on his face.

* * *

Behind the closed doors of her office, Nikki allowed the façade to fall away. 'Good to have you back, Joseph. There were a few moments back there, when I wondered . . .' The rest went unsaid.

'You and me both, ma'am.' Joseph took a deep breath and held it for a while. Then he slowly exhaled and said, 'But here we are again.'

'And this time as a fully paid up member of the team.' Nikki sipped her coffee. 'Are you going to move into the town?'

'Not sure yet, ma'am. I want to get it right, not just grab the first thing that comes along.' He pushed his hand through his hair and leaned back in his chair. 'I feel kind of different since I came out of hospital. I think I'll stick it out at the B & B for a while. My room's not too bad, and I'm actually getting sort of attached to Mrs Blakely's 1960s retro-style of decoration.'

Nikki nodded. 'Probably a wise move not to rush things.'

'Yes. I think I'll get my flat in Fenchester on the market, then when it sells, sit on the money until I'm ready to make a move.'

'Well, if you get stuck, you can store whatever you want out at Cloud Cottage Farm. Apart from the house itself, I've got some pretty useful outbuildings, and they're all dry and secure.'

'Thanks, ma'am. I may take you up on that.' He looked at her hopefully, 'So, anything interesting going down in CID?'

'Before I fill you in on our work status, I need to say one thing.' She leant forward. 'I'll bring this subject up only once, then it's going to be business as usual, okay?' She didn't give him chance to reply, but hurried on. 'If anything bothers you, or if anything is too strenuous, I want you to be perfectly honest with me, and we'll find a way around it. I want no big hero stuff, and no being a martyr either, got it?'

Joseph nodded reluctantly. 'Loud and clear, guv. But honestly, I've not spent weeks in physio and the gym getting myself fit to go and mess it all up in my first week back.' He flashed those infuriatingly sincere eyes at her, and Nikki was forced to believe him.

'Right. Lecture over. Any questions?'

'Can't think of any, although I'm delighted to see Dave Harris is with CID now.'

'He sailed through the interview board, I'm glad to say. His experience and local knowledge are a great asset.'

Joseph nodded. 'Plus he's a really good bloke. So, what are we working on at present, ma'am?'

'Nothing heavy, unless you count the mountain of paperwork that the last month generated.' She grimaced, then pulled a thin file across the desk. 'Frankly we're about as quiet as I can remember.' She opened the folder. 'A spate of small fires. Most likely arson.'

'Kids?'

'We thought so, but now we're not so sure. The last one took out a lock-up at the back of the big garage on Monk Street. It was lucky that Trumpton got there smartish, or there could have been a major incident, what with dozens of motors and the petrol reservoirs.'

Joseph frowned. 'What makes you say it's not kids?'

'The fire investigation officer said an accelerant had been used, but he swears it wasn't just bored yobs. He said there was a 'professional' feel to it.'

'A serious fire-starter does not bode well, ma'am.'

Nikki nodded. 'I know. But that was two weeks ago, three fires in as many nights, and now it's gone quiet. I don't know whether to be relieved or worried.' She closed the folder. 'Other than that, Cat and Dave are working on a cannabis farm investigation, but they are pretty close to a conclusion, then we have all the usual suspects; car ringing, break-ins, the ever-present drug trafficking, a bit of fraud, but nothing worthy of mention.'

'So basically it's same old, same old, other than the fires,' Joseph stretched. 'And which one of those tasty delights have you got lined up for me, ma'am?'

'Actually it's none of them,' she sighed. 'Well, not just yet anyway. You're with me for a few days.'

'What kind of investigation?'

'There isn't one.' She exhaled, and wondered how to explain her latest problem.

'The super wants us to help him. The auditors are in, and apart from drowning in a sea of paperwork, some faceless civilian in a comfy office has decided that our area is way over and above the national average for sudden deaths.' She leant forward and rested her elbows on the desk. 'They're scared shitless that the media will get hold of the statistics and have a field day with them. The super wants them checked, and fast.'

Joseph looked perplexed. 'But what's that got to do with us? It's a medical issue, surely?'

'I thought that to start with, but as I looked deeper I realised that it's not just 'sudden' deaths, where the doctor signs the certificate and that's that. There's an awful lot of occasions where we've classed them as 'suspicious' deaths and involved forensics.'

'To what outcome?'

'Shown up as suicides mainly, and although it's nowhere near the levels seen a while ago in Wales, it's still unsettling.'

'I thought the suicide rates were falling in the UK?'

'That's what the Government Statistics Office says. In fact, a few years back, the east of England was reported to have one of the lowest rates in England and Wales. I think that maybe why *our* figures stood out like a bloody beacon.'

Joseph frowned. 'Is there any particular age group or gender involved in these figures?'

Nikki shook her head slowly. 'No. And I'm at a loss to find any kind of common denominator amongst them.' She finished her coffee, then said, 'Sorry, I know this is not CID work, but Superintendent Bainbridge really needs us to help his find some answers for his little bureaucrat.'

Joseph shrugged. 'Then let's do it.

'It's not too depressing for you, is it? All things considered?'

He smiled warmly at her, and she understood why there were so many cow-eyed women dribbling their way around the station today.

'I'm fine with it, ma'am. In fact, I'm so glad to be alive, it's actually a pretty good assignment for me. If I were depressed, then maybe not, but . . .'

Her phone rang and interrupted Joseph. It was a harassed Rick Bainbridge. She listened to what he had to say, murmured her assent and hung up.

'Gotta go. The super wants an update on my findings so far.' She gave him a rueful smile. 'Such as they are. Oh, and he sends his regards and his apologies for not getting down to see you, but I suspect that the auditor may have nailed him to his desk.' She handed Joseph a sheaf of papers 'Copies of everything I've managed to dig up. See what you think and we'll toss some ideas around when I get back.'

* * *

Joseph trawled through the articles for over an hour, and as he did his upbeat mood began to disappear. He'd been in some pretty dark places in his life, maybe a lot more than most, but he had never considered taking his own life. Now, as he read reports from a myriad of agencies and help organisations, he was sickened to realise just how many people actually did.

The figures seemed staggering. One suicide in the UK every eighty-two minutes? Surely that couldn't be right? He placed the paper down and stared at it. And why should the Greenborough area be worse than any other? He frowned. Maybe it wasn't. Figures could be manipulated to fit any given situation, and although stats were not his favourite pastime, he was quite good with them. So, in the absence of any proper police work, perhaps he should spend some time hunting out anomalies, or grey areas that had been engineered to represent something other than what they really were.

With a small sigh, Joseph opened a second folder and removed the sheets of statistics. Suddenly those old movies that he had become so fed up with recently, were actually starting to look really good.

CHAPTER TWO

Charles Cavendish-Small pointed upwards dramatically. 'And this ladies, gentlemen, and children, is the high-spot of our tour.' He paused, hoping that for once someone would understand the pun. They rarely did, and he wondered why he bothered. 'The tower. It was built in three stages, beginning with Early English and ending in Perpendicular. Historically, each stage represented the growing wealth of our town, and from the viewing platform you will get a most rewarding and magnificent view across Greenborough, the river, the surrounding Fens, and out to the Wash.'

The guide stepped lightly across the stone floor, careful to avoid walking on the memorial stones, and indicated towards an archway. 'If you would like to climb the steps, please follow me, but be warned, they are steep, and they are the only route up to the tower. There are small side recesses to wait in should others be using the steps to descend.' He glanced around at his small party. They all looked pretty healthy, although two of the old dears from the History Group would be soaking their knees in Radox for a few days afterwards. Nothing too awful had ever happened on his tours, but his fellow guide,

Arthur, had had to cope with two panic attacks and a severely twisted ankle in just one weekend last summer.

'If anyone is in any doubt about their ability to climb, or has blood pressure or heart problems, please wait here, or feel free to go to the church café for a drink. We should be approximately half an hour. Thank you.'

With a slightly theatrical flourish, he swept his charges towards the screened archway. 'Follow me, and take great care. We don't want any accidents.'

There had been the usual gasps of amazement when the group stepped into the viewing area and looked out across the great tapestry of the flatlands. And today the visibility was particularly good. Clear bright blue sky, white fluffy clouds and a golden sun.

Charles sometimes looked at his visitors with less than delight, but he loved his beautiful parish church, and he loved this magical view across the county. On days like today, you could see as far as the north Norfolk coast.

He did a quick head count, assured himself that no one had been left gasping on the stairs, and began to identify various landmarks.

'Please? What is that?' asked a foreign tourist with a heavy Germanic accent.

Charles followed the pointing finger and smiled. 'That is the ruin of the Fenland Abbey of St Cecelia. Little is left except that wonderful high arch and the remains of the chapel.'

'And is that the docks?' asked one of a small party of school children, pointing to a series of cranes.

'Absolutely, young man. This end for the fishing boats and the new part is the Port of Greenborough. And, oh yes! If you look towards the estuary you can just see the masts of a cargo ship making her way towards the Wayland River.'

People pointed, took photographs and generally chatted amongst themselves, all agreeing it was certainly worth the climb. Charles let them enjoy the view for a while, then began to organise their descent.

'Right, if we are all ready. I'll . . .' he paused at the top of the stone stairwell and looked down pensively. It should be clear. There were no more tours today. He listened again, but someone was definitely on their way up, and pretty quickly at that.

'Sorry, folks. Can you all stand back for a moment, there's someone . . .' Before he could finish, he was elbowed firmly in the solar plexus, and found himself doubled over on the floor, gasping for breath.

'Hey! You can't . . . !'

A face, contorted beyond anything that Charles had ever seen, hung over him.

The man had burst through the opening from the stairs, and scattered the little group like nine pins. Now he was suspended over Charles like a hideous gargoyle from the ancient architecture that had somehow come to life and was bent on devouring him.

Pure, mind-numbing fear kept Charles a prisoner, then a terrified scream from one of the youngsters broke the spell.

This had to be a panic attack. But if it was, it had to be the very worst kind, and if he didn't calm the man, and damned quickly, someone was going to get hurt. The last thing Charles needed was a frenzied dash for the stairs.

'Keep calm everyone! It's okay! Really,' he gasped. 'Let me help you.' He held out his hand to the man. 'Please! Sit down here with me. Come on, you can do it.'

For one second, Charles thought he had got through. Then with a strangled scream, a sound that Charles would hear every night for years to come, the man turned and ran to the high stone balustrade, climbed up onto the ledge, and without a moment's hesitation, threw himself over.

Silence engulfed them all, then one the children began to whimper and Charles scrambled to his feet and rushed to look over the wall. A couple of the group appeared at his shoulder, while others took the children and tried to calm them. All Charles could do was stare down at the broken figure below them.

The man had fallen the equivalent of nine floors, before hitting the wall that flanked the waterway. To Charles's horror, as they looked on helplessly, the lifeless body slid slowly from the wall, and dropped, like a sack of unwanted rubbish, into the sluggish tidal waters of the Wayland River.

CHAPTER THREE

'Ma'am!'

Nikki closed the superintendent's door, and looked up to see Joseph hurrying down the corridor towards her.

'Sergeant Conway's just asked me to tell you that there's been an incident. I'm afraid we have a jumper.'

Nikki's heart sank. 'Not the multi-storey car park again?'

Joseph shook his head. 'St Saviour's Tower.'

'Hell-fire! When did this happen?'

'Uniform have only just had the shout, guv. The duty sergeant said if you wanted to attend, he wouldn't deploy another senior officer.'

'Tell him we are on our way, then meet me in the yard. I'll go pick up my keys from the office.'

* * *

A blue-and-white cordon had been put across the entrance to the church grounds, and Nikki could see uniformed officers posted at the entrances and footpaths. A cluster of people were gathered by the main church door, some sat on the steps and others paced nervously up and down the path. A WPC was talking with them and had her arm tightly around a child of about eight or nine.

Three more youngsters sat huddled close together on a low wall close to where the policewoman stood. Nikki took in the pale faces, slack mouths and wide, frightened eyes, and to her distress, realised that the children must have witnessed the fall.

'Over here, ma'am.' Joseph indicated towards a small group of figures leaning over the river wall. 'The doctor's there, and it looks like Yvonne and Niall must have been first on scene.'

Nikki felt relief to see WPC Yvonne Collins and PC Niall Farrow in attendance. They were a crew that she had something of a liking for. They had worked with her on several occasions and she thought that the older woman and the younger man made a good combination.

'What have we got here?' she asked.

'White male, ma'am. Jumped from the viewing platform.' Niall stared up at the tower almost disbelievingly.

'Into the river?'

'No, Inspector.' The doctor, a usually jovial man, who carried a little too much weight around his girth than was healthy for him, turned and approached them. 'Hit the wall first, I'm afraid. Snapped his back like a dry twig. You can tell by the way he's lying.'

'He's out of the water then?' asked Joseph.

The doctor nodded. 'Sort of. It's a bit difficult to see him from here. He went in, but immediately drifted into the mud around a submerged derelict boat. The tides on its way out, so he'll be going nowhere.'

'Have you been down there, Doctor?'

'Yes, close enough to check everything that I needed to, but you'll need a few strong backs to get him out, I can tell you!' He brushed mud from his trouser legs. 'And yes, before you ask, he is most certainly dead.'

'Well, we'd better take a look, Sergeant.' Nikki walked towards the wall.

'Ma'am?' Yvonne Collins followed her. 'Forgive me for sticking my oar in, but will forensics be taking some photos before they get him brought up?'

Nikki frowned. 'It's the usual procedure. What's bothering you, Constable?'

'I don't know, ma'am, but I'm sure this isn't straightforward. Yes, he jumped. There are fifteen witnesses to testify to that, but . . .' She paused, then looked directly at Nikki. 'They all say he was either scared to death of something or someone, or he was completely off his head.'

'Sane rational people don't often throw themselves from high buildings, Yvonne.'

'But the children, ma'am. I keep thinking about the children.' Yvonne held her stare. 'Determined suicides, those who plan to jump, are usually very deliberate and very organised. They would never pick a time when the platform was full of tourists and little kids, now would they?'

Nikki groaned inwardly to think of children witnessing such a horrible thing. 'Then he *had* to be high on something. Oh hell, poor choice of words, but he must have been wasted to do a thing like that.'

'Probably was. But when you talk to the witnesses I think you'll agree that there is a very odd feel about this, ma'am.'

'Okay, I hear what you say and I trust your intuition, but before I do anything I need to go see this poor sod for myself.'

'Niall will help you down, ma'am. There's some slippery steps, and believe me, they're lethal. Then you have to hang over a narrow ledge, an old walkway of some kind. Our man is in the mud that's dredged into the bottom of that old boat.'

It took a few minutes to get down to the water level, and Niall steadied her as she leaned around the slimy brickwork of the ledge.

'I can see hi . . .' Nikki's words froze in her throat, and her mouth dried to chaff.

Lying in the reddish-brown river mud, his body impossibly twisted, and his face half submerged in a brackish puddle of water, was a man she knew.

Her mind flashed up a picture from earlier that day. A man in a scarlet rugger shirt and dark jog pants. A man waving happily as he rode off home. The man who had just offered to paint her gate. 'Martin?' Her voice crackled with emotion. 'Oh no!'

'You know him?' Joseph moved to her side, his hand on her shoulder. 'Guv?'

Nikki shrank back away from the water, but the sight of the filthy scarlet shirt stayed with her. 'He's my neighbour. He was coming for coffee at the weekend.' She knew the words sounded crass, but it was all she could think of. They were going to catch up. That's what she'd said.

Joseph exhaled loudly, and when she turned to him, his expression was full of concern.

'It's okay, it's okay.' Nikki gathered herself. This was a seemingly impossible thing to happen. Martin had seemed so . . . she tried to find the right word, so *normal*.

'Who is he, ma'am?' asked Niall softly.

Nikki straightened up, and took a deep breath. She might be a hardened police officer, but a shock was still a shock. It was just that she knew how to deal with her emotions quicker than others. 'Martin Durham, of Knot Cottage, Buckledyke Lane, Cloud Fen. He lives alone on the edge of the marsh. As far as I know there is only his sister to notify. Both his parents are dead and he was unmarried. The sister's name is Elizabeth. She lives with her partner somewhere in Old Bolingbroke.' She turned to the police constable. 'And I want to be the one to go out to his cottage. Sergeant Easter and I will go directly after we've finished here.'

'Yes, ma'am, I'll radio it in straightaway.' Niall Farrow scrambled back up the wet steps to where his crewmate waited.

Nikki stared from the greenish waters of the River Wayland, up to where WPC Yvonne Collins was leaning over the wall, her hand outstretched to Niall. Yvonne's keen policeman's nose had been right. Maybe something terrible in Martin's life had driven him to kill himself, but he would *never* have done it in such a manner to cause suffering to others, especially children. She might not know him intimately, but she knew him better than most.

'Right, well, we'd better get a SOCO down here, then let uniform to sort out recovery.' She looked intently at Joseph. 'I am going to be *so* interested in what the post-mortem shows, especially the toxicology report.'

CHAPTER FOUR

As Nikki drove the familiar marsh lanes towards Cloud Fen, she knew that something had changed forever. Knot Cottage had always been simply 'Martin's place.' That was what the local villagers called it. Half of them would be hard-pressed to tell you its postal address.

'So what was this guy like?' asked Joseph.

'Dependable. Help anyone. Loved the marshes.' Nikki saw a picture in her mind of her peeling and weather-beaten garden gate, and wasn't sure if she'd ever have the heart to get it painted again.

'But still a bit of a loner?'

She frowned. 'Not really. Yes, he lived alone and he didn't talk about himself much, but he joined in with village stuff. And he was a regular at the Wild Goose.'

'Forgive me for saying, but where exactly is this 'village' you keep mentioning?'

Nikki smiled and slowed down as a long-eared hare bounded out into lane ahead of her. 'Ah, well, Cloud Fen Village is kind of scattered, and there's not much of it anyway. It's like so many of these outlying communities, the cottages are few and far between, the post office that doubled for the corner shop, was closed years ago, and all that's left is the chapel, with a service every third Sunday in the month, and the Wild Goose.' She watched as the hare dashed off into one of the great potato fields that edged the road. 'Frankly, we are lucky to still have the pub, the way things are going.'

'It is kind of yokel-ish, isn't it?'

'Careful, Town-Boy! You're talking about the place where I was born!'

'Sorry.' Joseph hung his head in mock shame. 'Do we go past your place?'

'Cloud Cottage Farm? No, we turn off just before it. But you can see it from Martin's. It's only a short way back across the marsh.'

'I wonder what will happen to the cottage?'

Nikki wondered too, but before she could answer her radio call sign blared out.

'A silver Suzuki Grand Vitara 4x4 registered to Martin Durham has been found abandoned not far from the church, ma'am.'

'Abandoned?'

'Seems that way, ma'am. We've had reports of the same car being driven erratically a few minutes prior to Durham entering the church. One witness says it looked as though he were having some kind of seizure, contorted face and all that.'

Nikki slowed to negotiate a corner, then said 'Okay, just get the car to the pound and secure it. I may need a SOCO to check it out for me. Thanks. Over and out.' Nikki relayed what had been said to Joseph and for the next five minutes they drove in silence, until she pulled the car into Buckledyke Lane

'Wow! What a place to live!' exclaimed Joseph. Then added quickly, 'And I mean that in a good, if somewhat remote, sort of way.' He stared across the vast expanse of marshland, to the distant horizon that shimmered and sparkled like a strip of silver foil.

'You should see it at sunrise,' said Nikki softly. 'My childhood bedroom looked in this direction, and my father told me I was truly blessed to wake to this sight every day. I never really appreciated it when I was five, but now I know he was right.'

'The cottage looks very neat, guv. Are we going to have to force an entry?'

Nikki threw him a withering look. 'This is a Cloud Fen, two up, two down cottage, Sergeant. We turn the handle and open the door. And if he's actually locked it for some reason, the key will be under the door mat.'

'You don't lock your doors?' asked Joseph in amazement.

She began to walk slowly up the path to the front door. 'I do these days. But then a farmhouse may be considered fair game for rich pickings. Not that there are any, but the thieves wouldn't know that until they got in. I think it's being a copper, I feel it my duty to think about security.'

'And the flak would be pretty heavy if your colleagues knew you went out and left the place wide open.'

'There is that, of course.' She arrived at the door, then veered off right along a narrow path and went around to the back. 'No one uses front doors out here.' She smiled. 'If you're going to tread mud in, do it in the kitchen, not the best room.'

She moved slowly across the backyard, then paused. She'd been in here so many times that she knew exactly what she would find even before she opened the door.

'Shall I?' asked Joseph. 'This can't be very pleasant for you.'

'No, I'm fine. It just seems so odd, I'm having trouble getting my head around it.'

'Maybe he will have left a note. That may explain things better.'

Nikki shrugged. Somehow she knew there would be no note. Just a mystery, and even if it never became a police matter, it would be one she would have to solve.

The door was unlocked.

'Surely, if you were going to go out, never to come back, you'd lock the door?' mused Joseph, half to himself.

'Would it matter? If things meant so little, and you wanted to die, would you care?'

They stepped onto the quarry-tiled floor of the kitchen, and a feeling of warmth greeted them. Partly because the place was a little time warp of old country living, clean, fresh and welcoming, and partly because a heavy iron pot was simmering gently on the solid fuel stove.

Joseph looked at Nikki and bit his lip. 'I don't think we are going to reason our way out of that one, do you, guv?'

She didn't answer. Something had happened to Martin Durham, between the time that he had spoken to her, and his fateful trip to St Saviour's Tower. Something devastating. 'You take the ground floor, Joseph. I'll check upstairs.'

'Are you looking for anything in particular, guv?'

'Just a good reason for a sane, happy man to top himself.'

'Oh, simple then.'

Nikki climbed the stairs. She had only been to the upper floor once before. It must have been many years ago, because her daughter Hannah was still coming home on the school bus, and she'd been keeping an eye open for the familiar blue-and-white coach that stopped at the end of Buckledyke Lane. Martin had picked up some kind of bug, but had been too proud to ask for help. She had had a bad feeling that all was not well, and called in. Lucky she had. An hour later an ambulance was tearing towards Greenborough General with a blue light flashing.

The main bedroom was like the rest of the cottage. Well cared for, and although a little basic, with old wood floors and heavy, plain wooden furniture, it was clear that the man loved his tiny home. There was just one photograph on his bedside table. Two smiling women, arms around each other's shoulders, one very much like him, and the other considerably younger, with a cheeky grin. Elizabeth and Janna.

Nikki picked it up, and shook her head. She'd better look for his address book and get Elizabeth's number. Even if uniform had already traced her, Nikki knew her well enough to want to offer her condolences. She replaced the frame exactly where it had sat, and stared at the woman's face. I have a feeling that you aren't going to know any more about this than I do, she thought. This death was not planned.

'Guv,' Joseph called up the stairs. 'There are an awful lot of prescription drugs in a cabinet down here. I think you should take a look at them.'

'On my way.' Nikki slid open the drawer in the bedside table. Neat lines of tablet boxes filled the space. 'Oh shit!' She closed the drawer and went to see what Joseph had found.

'I'd say this guy was very ill, wouldn't you, ma'am?' Joseph was standing in a small shower room that Martin had obviously had built onto the back of the cottage, and was pointing to the interior of a large glass-fronted cabinet. Without even looking closely, Nikki knew that the stacks of boxes were from a pharmaceutical company.

'Are they all legitimately his?'

'The labels are all marked up Martin Durham.'

'Then you're right. He must have been very poorly. But he never said a thing.'

'Which could explain a lot. Maybe he went into town for a hospital appointment, and got really bad news. News that he just couldn't handle.'

Why couldn't she believe that? It was a perfectly logical suggestion. 'Check it out, Joseph. And go out to the car and get some evidence bags. We'll need these.' She pointed to the boxes. 'Do any of the drugs mean anything to you?'

'There are a lot of antibiotics, ma'am. Penicillin, Amoxicillin, but I'm afraid the others mean nothing.' Joseph knelt down and studied them. 'This man was clearly reliant on medication big-style.'

'We'll have to talk to his GP, and get his hospital notes released.'

Nikki watched Joseph go out, and looked around the familiar old sitting room. In the past, they'd sat around the open fire, drunk hot chocolate and played Scrabble, Martin, Hannah and herself. Hannah had always liked him. She would be very sad if she knew what had happened, but Nikki would not be telling her. Her precious daughter was in a coma, and when Nikki talked to her, she told her only happy things.

'Shall I bag them all, or one of each kind, ma'am?' Joseph broke her reverie.

'Bag them all. And there are more upstairs beside the bed, get them too. Was there any post, by the way?'

'Nothing recent. A bit of junk mail and a bill or two.'

'Bank statement?'

'No, and his writing desk, unlike the door, *is* locked, and I couldn't find a key.'

Nikki looked around. Had she ever seen Martin at the desk? Maybe. Where would he hide a key? Nikki looked inside a vase, moved a few books, then shook her head. 'His sister may know, if not, I'm afraid we'll have to force it open. Meanwhile, and until I've spoken to Elizabeth, I'm going to secure the cottage. We may have to get a team in to check it out, but your serious illness theory may close this case without further investigation.'

Joseph nodded, but unenthusiastically. 'You're not convinced are you?'

Nikki puffed out her cheeks and shook her head. 'It may have a bearing on it, but no matter how bad the news that he received was . . .' Like Yvonne, she was thinking about the children. '. . .he simply could not have done it in the way that he did.'

'But he *did* do it, ma'am.'

'Yes, he did, Joseph, and *we* have to find out why.'

CHAPTER FIVE

'Sorry, but it all looks pretty straightforward to me, Nikki.' Superintendent Rick Bainbridge leant back in his chair and stared at her. 'He must have been so doped up that he didn't realise there were people already up on the viewing platform. If he were out of his head he may not have even seen them.'

'He saw them alright, sir. WPC Collins has given me the statements that she collected. Everyone said he appeared terrified of something, and one little lad said that Martin "was afraid of *them,* especially the tour guide, when he held his hand out to him to help him."'

The superintendent shrugged. 'Well, I don't know what to deduce from that comment, if anything. The poor little kid was probably traumatised. And it must have happened so quickly, it's a wonder anyone had time to take note of anything.'

'Actually the witnesses were unusually consistent in their statements, sir,' said Nikki testily. 'And I would not disregard what the boy said. Children can be very perceptive.'

Rick Bainbridge threw her a worried look. 'I think maybe you're a bit too close to this, Inspector. *If* it needs investigation, and I hope for our budget's sake that it doesn't; I'll give it to one of the other teams.'

'I'm fine, honestly, Super.' Nikki tried to keep her voice neutral, even though she was anxious not to lose the investigation. 'And there's little we can do until the tox screen comes back. I'll just check out the usual avenues while we wait. There may have been money worries, or some personal issues that, along with the heavy medication, just triggered something. The coroner is going to want everything we can get together for the inquest.'

'Okay. Stick with it for now, but don't forget, people aren't always what they seem. He may have been a good neighbour, but just how well did you really know him? Don't forget, you'd been living in the town for almost a year before you went back to Cloud Fen. Things change. People change.'

Nikki nodded. 'You're right, sir. And don't worry, I'll check everything as I would any other suspicious death, I won't get phobic over it.' She threw him what she hoped was a sincere smile and said. 'Maybe I'm just sensitive to this because of those statistics you've got me working on.'

It was the super's turn agree. 'Ah, yes. At best they don't make easy reading, then this happens to a friend. It's understandable. Just don't look for things that aren't there.'

'Of course not, sir. So, if that's all?'

'Yes, yes, go. I have to get back to the damned auditor anyway. Just keep me up to speed, Inspector.'

Outside the door, Nikki heaved a sigh of relief. She would have to tread warily and endeavour to hold her tongue a little more. Her gut instinct screamed that something was horribly wrong about Martin Durham's death. Something so wrong, that she couldn't even bring herself to say the word suicide. Whatever, she would get to the bottom of it, and the easiest route was to keep the investigation closely under her control.

* * *

Joseph looked up as the boss came back into the CID room. 'How did it go, guv?'

The DI raised her eyebrows. 'In professional terms, Sergeant, I nearly screwed up.' She flopped into a chair. 'He reckons I'm too close. I only just managed to convince him to leave it with me, but I'm going to play things closer to my chest in future.'

Joseph nodded. 'Well, you've just had a call from Elizabeth Durham. She is devastated, but she wants to talk to you. I said we'd call on her first thing tomorrow morning, if that's okay?'

'Absolutely. Did you get the full address?'

Joseph glanced at his notebook. 'Yes, ma'am. Monk's Lodge. I've got directions.'

'Good. We'll go immediately after the morning briefing.'

'So what can I do now?' asked Joseph.

'I've got some paperwork that won't wait another day, so perhaps you would ring Martin's GP and go have a word with her? I'm pretty sure he saw Dr Helen Latimer. Her practice covers most of Cloud Fen. Her surgery is in Church Gate. The number is in the book.'

'I'm on to it, ma'am.'

* * *

Helen Latimer confirmed that she was Martin's doctor and she reluctantly consented to see him before her four p.m. surgery began, as long as he could get there in time. He checked his watch, quickly calculated how long their earlier trip to Cloud Fen had taken, and decided it should give him at least twenty minutes with the GP. Just enough time if he got a move on. As he grabbed his jacket and car keys and hurried from the office, Joseph felt a surge of what he could only call happiness. The case might be a sad one, but it felt *so* good to back at work again.

The traffic out of the town was sluggish, although Joseph knew that once he reached the roads that led to the marshes the congestion would disappear.

But right now, he was stationary. Not something that his tight timetable had allowed for. As he tapped his fingers impatiently on the steering wheel and waited for his lane to start moving again, he caught sight of a group of men running along the curb. From their clothes, he thought they might be land workers, and they were trying to cross the busy road by dodging in and out of the slow moving vehicles. Several of them were laughing and shouting in an Eastern European language. Suddenly one of them ran around his car, then leaned across and slapped his palm loudly against the windscreen, then stared through it.

Joseph automatically recoiled at seeing a man's eyes only inches away from his own. Then he almost leapt backwards in his seat, his heart hammering in his chest.

He released his belt, swung around and tried to see where the man had gone, but he was already on the far pavement and hurrying away.

Joseph threw open the door of the car, stood up and stared after the retreating figure, but in seconds the man had disappeared.

A horn sounded loudly behind him, and he flopped back behind the wheel and put the car into gear. As he moved forward he decided that he *had* to have been mistaken. Apparently everyone has a double, and he'd just had the misfortune to see one.

As the lights changed and the road opened up again, he decided he had totally overreacted. The man had been running around with a pack of foreigners, ergo he was also a foreigner. So that settled it. How stupid could you get?

He indicated off the main road and headed for the marshes. A long straight drove-road extended out ahead of him for as far as the eye could see. He put his foot down, and as the car surged forward, he felt as if he had taken back control of himself. He even managed a small laugh at his own stupidity. What on earth would a man who he had last seen in another continent twelve years ago, be doing playing chicken in Greenborough High Road? It was unthinkable, and plain idiotic. He slowed the car as he approached a hump-back bridge over a water way, and tried to get his mind back to the late Martin Durham.

The boss was convinced there was something not right about the manner of Durham's death, and even though he had unearthed that cache of prescription drugs in Knot Cottage, Joseph was starting to believe that she might be right.

When he finally arrived at the small converted bungalow that served as a surgery, Joseph had forgotten about his earlier case of mistaken identity, and his focus was fully back on the job in hand.

If Dr Helen Latimer had sounded brusque on the phone, her manner softened considerably when she met Joseph in person.

'I'm so sorry, Sergeant. The news came as something of a shock. I'm afraid I may have sounded rather short. It wasn't intentional.' She smiled at him apologetically. 'Can I get you a coffee, or a tea?'

Joseph accepted the offer, and looked around the consulting room as Latimer went to organise the drinks. It was like being in someone's sitting room. No modern medical equipment, nothing other than a desk, a computer, two chairs and an examination couch. There were no nasty posters either; the ones that show reddish-brown muscles stretched over skeletons, or eyeballs protruding from bony skulls. Dr Latimer seemed to prefer watercolours of the Cornish coast, and studies of black Labradors.

On that basis alone, Joseph decided that he'd quite like her to be his GP.

The doctor passed him a mug of coffee and sat down. He decided she must be in her late thirties, early forties, but was a strikingly good-looking woman, with shoulder-length, wavy chestnut hair and deep brown eyes. Her skin had a rich olive tint that made him think she may have some Mediterranean origins.

He took his time and carefully explained everything they knew about the incident, and when he had finished, Helen Latimer shook her head emphatically and said, 'No way! Absolutely no way in a million years! I *know* Martin, and yes he did have medical problems, but his illness was managed and his drug regime well maintained.' She held out her hands, palms up, and said, 'I don't understand.'

'You seem to be the third woman involved in this that categorically refuses to believe Martin Durham was capable of doing what he did,' said Joseph.

'Who else are we talking about, Sergeant?'

'My boss, DI Galena, and the WPC who was first on scene.'

Helen Latimer gave him a strange enigmatic smile. 'Nikki Galena is your boss?'

'This is my first day as a permanent member of her team, Doctor, although I *have* worked with her before.' He returned the smile, with what he hoped to be an equally cryptic quality.

'Mm.' She nodded. 'And as I remember, she and Martin were close, but she moved to the town, didn't she?'

'The DI recently moved back to Cloud Fen.' Joseph grew serious. 'She spoke with Martin this morning. She said he was on really good form.'

'Then what in heaven's name happened?' mused the doctor.

'We rather hoped that you may be able to help us there.'

Helen Latimer shook her head. 'Sorry, but all I can do is release his medical records to you. The coroner's going to need them anyway.'

'Why did Martin need so many drugs?'

'His immune system was damaged by illness and cancer treatment that he suffered in his early twenties.'

'What sort of cancer?' asked Joseph.

'Cancer of the spleen.'

'Was there a chance that it had returned?'

'Definitely not. They performed a splenectomy, and he had yearly re-assessments. I have always been kept well informed by the oncology clinic.' She sat back and gave Joseph a rather sad smile. 'Regarding his immune deficiency problems, I have only been his doctor for just over a year, so frankly I was maintaining an already carefully planned drug regime. It's actually quite ironic, but we had been discussing a complete review. New drugs are being developed all the time, and I was anxious that he have the most efficient medication for his needs.'

'And was he happy about that?'

The doctor frowned. 'Not initially, I have to admit. He seemed very reticent to alter anything, but last week he turned up for an appointment, all chirpy and bright, and said he'd like to go ahead.'

'And did you?'

'Heavens, no! I needed to do a lot of research into his past history and prior medication before I'd even consider making changes, Sergeant.' She gave Joseph a mildly reproachful look. 'I would have needed to run all my suggestions past his consultant. This is complex, and not a thing that I would undertake lightly. I hadn't even begun the process.'

'I see. And there was nothing else that you felt may be bothering him?' asked Joseph.

She shook her head. 'As your boss said, the last time I saw Martin Durham, he was in fine form. In fact, he seemed so well I wondered if I should be even considering changing his medication.'

'If it ain't broke, don't fix it?'

'Exactly. But this time it was Martin who said we should explore new therapies. He was really enthusiastic. Considering his earlier reluctance, I was quite surprised.'

'Mm, I wonder what prompted the change of heart?'

'I guess we'll never know now, Sergeant, and I'm afraid you will have to excuse me, I have patients waiting, and I still need to organise those medical records for you.'

Joseph stood up and held out his hand. 'I appreciate your time, Doctor Latimer.'

'You're welcome. And do ring me if you need anything else.' She paused, 'Or if you discover anything that you think I should know about.'

'I will, thank you.' Joseph turned to leave.

'Oh, and good luck working with DI Galena, Sergeant Easter.' There was a slight chill to the words.

As Joseph approached the reception desk, he wondered what the history was between Helen Latimer and his boss, because the undercurrent was practically pulling his feet from under him.

Half an hour later, Joseph left, with a large sheaf of notes in a thick brown envelope under his arm. He was sure it would mean very little to him, but it would certainly be of great use to the pathologist.

As he climbed into the driving seat and did up his safety belt, he was suddenly shocked by a vivid flashback to the face in the windscreen. Just for a second, it was there again. Rough, coarse skinned, uneven teeth, ice-blue eyes and unwashed, dull blond hair. My God, it was so like him, it was scary.

Joseph shook his head free of the unwanted vision, and jammed his key into the ignition. He didn't want to admit it, but he was obviously still a bit shaky. The hospital had said it would take time, so maybe he was not quite as fit as he had first thought. Or maybe it was just first-day nerves. A friend of your boss, turning up dead on your debut morning was not exactly what you would choose.

With a sigh, he drove away, with even more questions swirling around in his head, than when he arrived.

CHAPTER SIX

As evening settled over the fen, lights came on in the scattered assortment of houses and cottages. Nikki looked from her upstairs window, across the shadowy marsh lanes and fields, and felt a deep sadness that Knot Cottage remained in darkness.

She sat down heavily on her bed and wondered about the super's words. Maybe you really didn't know the people around you, even the ones you felt quite close to. She had known Martin for some fifteen years, and had never had an inkling about his illness.

She let out a long, audible sigh. Everyone had secrets. There were certainly things about her that Martin would never have known. In fact, there were things about her that only a very small handful of people knew.

And then there was Joseph. His past was a closed door. A locked room. Bolted and secured as tightly as a Bank of England vault.

She stood up and went downstairs. She needed a drink.

The kitchen still had a faint smell of paint, not unpleasant, just fresh and clean. She had been surprised how well the old place had scrubbed up, and even although today's dreadful events had placed a heavy blanket of melancholy over everything, she was still glad to be back home on Cloud Fen. And she was glad that Joseph had decided to join the team.

She splashed wine into a glass, sipped it slowly, then placing the glass on the old scrubbed pine table, the one she had sat at to eat her eggy soldiers as a small girl, she thought about Joseph. Maybe she should have spared him the grim task of suicide statistics on his first day. He had seemed really subdued when he returned from his trip to see Helen Latimer. Nikki gave a little snort. But then who wouldn't? Dear Helen could be a caustic cow sometimes.

She took another sip of the Merlot and tried to decide what to eat. Food was never high on her list of priorities, and it was ten to one that it would be yet another omelette. Unlike Martin. He had always prepared and cooked delicious meals for himself. She saw again the pot simmering on the old stove. She had looked in it, and noted the fresh vegetables and thick meaty stock. Martin took great care of his diet. Something she rarely seemed to find time for.

Taking eggs from a chicken-shaped pottery container, she broke three into a glass bowl, added salt, pepper, a few herbs and a splash of milk, then whisked it together thoughtfully. Helen Latimer might be a bitch, but she would surely have been as charmed as every other woman in the county by Joseph Easter's sexy good looks. Surely even Helen wouldn't have upset him on first meeting. So why did he seem so distracted, so troubled? She should have asked him, but he seemed keen to get away, and she couldn't blame him. It had been a pretty depressing day, all in all.

Nikki removed a fork from the cutlery drawer, then served up her meagre supper on one of her mother's best plates. There was something enormously reassuring about having familiar old things about her again. Her rented flat in Greenborough had been basic, minimalist, Spartan. She smiled to herself. Who was she kidding? Depressingly austere was closer to the truth. Still smiling ruefully, she switched on the radio and tuned it in to Radio 4 Extra. She badly needed something to lift her spirits, and a hammy old wireless show might do the trick.

She ate the eggs, and half-heartedly began to listen to a classic episode of *Hancock*, but after a while she switched it off. It seemed somehow disrespectful, knowing what had happened earlier that day, and as she washed up, she found herself hoping that Joseph had not returned to work too soon.

The tinkling sound of a windchime from the floor above, distracted her from her worrying thoughts. She glanced at the clock. The tide had turned, and was bringing in a strong blow off the sea. She had better go up and latch the windows, just in case there was a summer squall.

In her bedroom, she paused to once again look in the direction of Martin's place — and found herself rooted to the spot.

A tiny point of light was moving around inside Knot Cottage.

Nikki blinked a few times and refocussed her eyes. There was no doubt, someone was in Martin's cottage, and whoever it was had no sodding right to be there!

With a muffled curse, Nikki raced down the stairs, grabbed a flashlight and her mobile phone and raced from the farmhouse.

There was no way she could take the car, whoever was there would hear her coming and leg it. She had no choice but to go on foot and she covered the quarter of a mile in record time.

At the gate she sunk down for a moment into the deep shadows and caught her breath. Keeping perfectly still, she watched the darkened cottage carefully. Whoever was in there might not be alone. Her ears strained to make out sounds, but there was little other than the whisper of the wind across the marsh and the eerie call of a night owl.

With great care, she crept towards the side of the cottage, and made her way round to the back door. It was open just a crack. No doubt to facilitate a speedy exit if required.

Rustling sounds were coming from inside. As if someone were leafing swiftly through a newspaper, trying to find a particular article. Nikki stood behind the door, and tried to see exactly where the intruder was.

He was still in the sitting room, so whatever he was looking for was obviously proving more difficult to find than he had expected. She stared in, but could only make out a black shape behind the fine light point of the torch, and he was hunched over Martin's dining table.

Nikki tried to think. It seemed to her that she had two choices. Rush in and challenge him, or keep low and follow him when he came out. Sadly, although following him could mean catching whoever it was red-handed, it could also mean she could lose him completely, especially if he had a vehicle concealed nearby.

Which left little choice. Nikki swung a hefty kick at the door, reached inside and with a loud shout, flicked on the light switch.

It had been a pretty good idea, and it would have worked, if the intruder had not tripped the fuses on the electric meter when he broke in.

By the time she realised what had happened and switched on her flashlight, the man was upon her.

Nikki fought back. She had never backed off from a fight and rarely came off second best in a tussle, but circumstances were not in her favour. Her assailant caught her a crushing blow in the ribs, one that totally winded her, and by the time she had regained her breath, he was gone. She staggered out after him, but heard the sound of a powerful motorcycle engine roar into the night, and realised that there would be no chasing him.

Cursing and swearing her way to the meter, Nikki flipped up the switches, and squinted as the light came on.

'Shit! Shit!' she shouted out loud.

The sitting room was wrecked. Martin's precious belongings lay broken and shattered in untidy piles across the carpet.

She looked around in both dismay and anger, and found herself fighting back tears. 'I just hope you never found whatever it was you were after, you bastard scumbag!' She tried to wipe the salty water from her cheeks with the sleeve of her blouse. 'Bastard!'

Still cursing, Nikki pulled her mobile from her pocket, breathed a sigh of relief that it was still working, and quickly punched the speed dial number for the police station.

CHAPTER SEVEN

The main car park of the Greenborough Fitness Club and pool was deserted. Joseph parked close to the door and pulled his gym bag from the seat beside him. He had taken to getting there just before six thirty when the club opened. He liked the calm of the place in the early morning, and plunging into an empty pool had a decadence that he secretly enjoyed. He'd always tried to find time for a swim, mainly early like this to prep him for the day ahead, but sometimes he'd go in the evening, to wash away the stresses of a gruelling shift. Greenborough club had quite limited facilities but as he was somewhat limited himself, that suited him perfectly.

He cruised steadily up and down in the warm water and tried to forget that he'd had a sincerely crap night. His sleep had been interrupted by disturbing dreams that had left him feeling uneasy and edgy. Martin Durham's peculiar death had not helped, and neither had that weird incident with the man in the High Road.

He switched from breast-stroke to crawl, and tried to concentrate entirely on his breathing. It didn't work, so he flipped over, stared at the ceiling to keep in lane, and propelled himself backwards for a few lengths. Part of him wanted to see that jaywalker again, to see him properly, note the differences, then laugh at himself for being such a prat. And another part of him was loathe to meet the doppelgänger of such a brute of a man.

Joseph turned in the water and ducked under. The rushing in his ears whisked away the unwanted thoughts, and holding his breath, he swam underwater until he touched the wall.

He had another fifteen minutes before he had to hit the shower room. He hauled himself out of the pool, rinsed himself off under one of the poolside showers, and walked along the wet tiled floor to the steam room.

A thick steamy cloud made it impossible to see if he were alone in the small room, but a movement on the top seating ledge told him he wasn't.

'Mind if I join you?' he asked his unseen companion.

'Be my guest. I'm practically expiring! I'm sure they rent this out at night to a lobster boiling company!' A tall figure leaned forward, then slipped down to the lower ledge.

A tiny shiver rippled through him, as her leg lightly brushed his shoulder as climbed down.

'I swear they've turned the temperature up this morning.'

Noting it was the woman from the car park, Joseph silently agreed that it was becoming extremely hot indeed in the tiny enclosed space.

'Bryony.' The woman held out a well-manicured hand. 'I've seen you here before.'

He took her hand, and was surprised by the firmness of her grip. 'Joseph. Pleased to meet you.'

The woman stood up. 'Sorry, Joseph, I hate to be rude, but I've got a busy morning lined up. See you again, no doubt?'

Joseph flashed her his brightest smile. 'I hope so.'

After the glass door had closed, he let out a long, low whistle. He really would need a cold shower today, and the steam had nothing to do with it.

* * *

'Well, you look a damn sight happier than you did when you left last night,' murmured Nikki as he entered her office.

Joseph raised his eyebrows. 'And you look like you've had a run in with the riot squad!' He stared at the purple shadow that was staining one cheekbone, and did not miss the fact that she was protecting her rib cage. 'What happened, ma'am?'

She stood up and winced. 'Come with me to the super's office. He wants the gruesome details too and I don't know if I have the energy to say it all twice.'

He walked beside her along the corridor to the lifts.

'Some bastard broke into Martin's cottage last night.' Her voice was low, and full of contempt.

'You're joking!'

'Do I look like I'm joking, Sergeant?' she growled.

'Sorry. It was only an expression of incredulity. I wasn't questioning you.' He shook his head in disbelief. 'Are you okay?'

'I'll live.' She pressed the button for the lift. 'But I cannot tell you how much I'd like to meet that intruder again.'

'Preferably in the custody suite.'

'I'm not too worried where it is, Sergeant. I just want the opportunity to even the score.'

Joseph couldn't ignore the dark shade of the old Nikki Galena in those words, but chose to hold his tongue.

The lift sighed to a halt, and they made their way to Rick Bainbridge's office where Nikki filled them in on what had occurred.

'Sounds like an opportunist to me,' speculated the super. 'Bad news travels fast. Maybe someone got to hear of Durham's death, knew the place would be empty and ransacked it.'

'Sorry, sir, but whoever that was, was looking for something specific.'

'And what the devil would that be?'

'Initially, a key, sir.' Nikki bit the inside of her cheek. 'Joseph and I looked for it earlier, only we *replaced* the vases and the ornaments that we searched, we didn't smash them to pieces.'

'A key to what?' asked the super.

'Martin's desk. It was locked when we were there.' Her expression hardened. 'It's matchwood now.'

The super's brow knitted into a wrinkled frown. 'But what was he looking for?'

Nikki shrugged. 'I've no idea.'

'Whatever it was, it was very important to him,' added Joseph. 'After all, you called out that you were the police, and he still thought it was worth knocking seven bales out of you.'

'Thank you for reminding me of that, Sergeant,' said Nikki nursing her side. 'And another thing, it wasn't a lucky wallop either. The intruder knew exactly where to hit me to incapacitate me.'

'So what are you saying, Nikki? That Durham was involved in something dodgy?'

'I don't know what the hell I'm saying!' Her face was a mask of confusion. 'I just know that a kind and generous man, someone I thought I knew, has committed a terrible act, and I have the horrible feeling that nothing is quite as it seems at Knot Cottage.'

The super allowed her outburst to abate, then said, 'Have you had your injuries checked out?'

She nodded. 'The FMO was treating a prisoner when I came here last night. It's only bruising. It'll pass.'

'So where do you want to go from here?'

Joseph threw her a warning glance. She needed to cool down, or the super would give the case to another team. He saw her close her eyes for a moment, and he knew that she had understood his meaning.

'We'll just continue gathering evidence for the inquest, sir.' Her voice was calmer. 'And as soon the sergeant and I have spoken to Martin Durham's sister, we'll make a careful search of Knot Cottage.' She took a deep breath. 'I know that I disturbed him, and I'm still not entirely sure that he found what he was looking for.'

The super nodded. 'Then you'd better get a man out there to keep an eye on the place. And we *should* watch your home too, but finances probably won't stretch.'

'There's been an officer at Martin's since last night, and I can take care of myself, thank you, sir,' said Nikki, then she gave him a half grin. 'It may have been pitch black but the intruder didn't get away scot-free. In the scuffle I managed to grab a few strands of his hair. It's gone to the lab for DNA testing.'

Joseph smiled broadly. 'Good on you, ma'am! If he's on the database, we've got him.'

'And even if he isn't, if we get a suspect, we can place him at the scene of the crime. Good work.' The super stood up and pulled a face. 'Now, I've got an appointment with the auditor from hell, so if that's all?'

'Right, sir, we'll get out to Old Bolingbroke.'

'Just remember to report in later, Inspector.'

'Wilco, sir.'

* * *

'I'll drive, ma'am,' said Joseph tactfully. 'Help me to get a feel for the area.'

Nikki agreed, knowing full well that he was thinking only of her, which was great because her side was killing her.

'We take the main road north, out of Greenborough, and pick up the A16. I'll direct you in as we get closer.'

Joseph pulled out of the station yard, and slipped easily into the light traffic flow. 'So, you know Elizabeth Durham?'

'Not well. I've met her a few times. She came over as being a very genuine, friendly person. She and Martin were close. He told me they were inseparable during their college days.'

Joseph slowed down at a pedestrian crossing and waved a small group of children across. 'Students together? What did they study?'

'I'm not sure really, although Elizabeth is some sort of tree person,' said Nikki, trying to remember the full title of her chosen profession. 'Well respected, apparently.'

'I guess you're not talking about a lumberjack or a tree hugger?'

Nikki smiled. 'I'm not sure about her personal habits, but she is, let me get this right, an arboriculturist. Martin called her a landscape architect.'

'Funny that. There aren't too many trees here on the Fens.'

'There are where we are going. It may only be a twenty minute drive but you'll notice a big difference in the countryside. It's less agricultural closer to the Wolds. Lots more trees.'

'And you say she lives with her partner. What does he do?'

'*She*. Her partner is Janna Hepburn-Lowe.'

Joseph threw her a swift glance, then returned his eyes to the road. 'From *the* Hepburn-Lowe family?'

'Yup. They've been together for years.' Nikki groaned and tried to ease herself into a more comfortable position. 'Do try to avoid bloody manhole covers, Joseph. My ribs feel like they've been kicked by a horse!'

'Sorry. Go on.'

'Janna's another nature lover. She owns a massive garden centre quite close to where they live.' She tilted her head to one side. 'And it wasn't Daddy's millions that provided it either. Janna actually worked there as a kid, Saturday job or something. Loved it so much she finished up buying it when the original owners retired.'

'Good for her,' said Joseph, then his face clouded over. 'But I guess that rules out financial worries on Martin's part. If he *was* in debt and his sister loved him, she'd hardly let him get suicidal over money troubles. Not when your partner is loaded.'

'Exactly.' She pointed to a large sign. 'Get in the right hand lane, right at the roundabout, and you're on the road to the A16, okay?'

'Roger, ma'am.'

Nikki shifted again, trying to keep the seatbelt away from her bruised side. 'You know, I have a really bad feeling about all this, Joseph, and it is nothing to do with knowing Martin.' She stared out of the car window. 'That man who trashed Knot Cottage? He was a pro, I'm sure of it.'

'Then it's good that we have uniform watching the place until we get there. It shouldn't be too difficult to spot your man's modus operandi for his search, even if he tried to make it look like the super's opportunist burglar.'

'Did he get what he was after, I wonder?' sighed Nikki.

'And what could be *that* important?' countered Joseph.

Nikki sat back, and felt a steely determination creep over her. 'I don't know yet, Joseph. But I'm damn sure that I won't rest until find out what the hell's going on.'

Joseph nodded emphatically. 'I don't doubt you for one minute, ma'am. And for what it's worth, I'm with you all the way.'

* * *

Elizabeth Durham opened the door to them herself, and although it was a very long time since they'd last met, Nikki recognised her immediately.

On the surface, the woman covered her grief well, but the dark-rimmed eyes, the slight tremors of the hands, and the occasional lapses in concentration, gave her sorrow away as clearly as if she were wearing widow's weeds.

She invited them into the lounge, a large, airy, high-ceilinged room that opened into a splendid, well-stocked garden room. 'I still can't believe it,' she said, after the introductions had been made. 'And I don't understand.'

'No one does,' said Nikki simply. 'We are all at a loss to know what could have caused him to do such a thing. And Elizabeth, I am so very sorry. Martin was such a good friend and neighbour.'

She wordlessly shrugged her acceptance of the condolences, then suddenly looked exhausted and lowered herself down onto the deep cushions of the sofa. With a flourish of one hand, she indicated for them to do the same, and she watched them as they chose two chairs opposite her. 'Can I get you some refreshments?'

Nikki and Joseph both declined. It seemed almost too much to ask. As if that one small act of boiling a kettle might cause the floodgates to break.

'When will I be able to have him back? To organise his funeral?'

Nikki swallowed. 'I'm afraid that depends on the coroner, Elizabeth. The inquest opens the day after tomorrow, but it will be adjourned, awaiting all the reports.' She gave her an apologetic smile. 'It's a complicated case, with both witness statements and a lot of forensic reports. It will take time to prepare, and there will be a lot for him to consider.'

'So it may be held up for some time?'

Nikki chose her words carefully. 'Maybe, or he may allow you to bury him.'

'But my brother wanted to be cremated. Oh, it will be a cremation, definitely.'

This was not going well. Elizabeth was a highly intelligent woman, but shock had blurred her normally sharp mind.

'The thing is . . .' Joseph's soft voice had taken over. 'The thing is, Ms Durham, that we are all *very* worried about Martin's sudden decision to end his life. We need to explore every avenue to understand what happened, and until we are satisfied with our findings and a satisfactory explanation has been reached, we cannot allow Martin's body to be cremated.' He paused. 'For your sake, and for your brother, we need to provide you with answers.'

'The coroner may feel that you need some sort of closure,' added Nikki gently. 'So he could grant you permission for a burial, then later, when a verdict has been reached, Martin's wishes could be followed.'

Elizabeth's eyes filled with tears. 'Dig him up?'

'I know it sounds awful, but it's done very discreetly, with the utmost care and compassion,' added Joseph. 'And please don't concern yourself. It may never come to that.'

'Where is Janna?' asked Nikki, concerned that Elizabeth was alone.

A small smile spread across her face. 'She's slipped over to the garden centre while you are here with me. She needs to tie up a few things with her manager. She's taking some time off so that I don't have to deal with this alone.'

'That's good.'

'She's a good person,' said Elizabeth. 'And she's worried sick over me.'

'Would it be too soon to ask a few questions?' Nikki did not want to cause any more distress, but she still needed to tell Elizabeth about the break-in at Knot Cottage.

'No, I'll do all I can to help.' She visibly rallied. 'And I'm sorry about just now, I don't know what came over me.' She looked at them in turn, then abruptly stood up.

'First, some coffee. Why don't you both go down to the garden room? There's a lovely view over the gardens, and you can just see Janna's pride and joy in the distance. I'll fetch the drinks, and then I'll do my best to answer your questions.'

Nikki followed Joseph down three shallow steps, and into the big conservatory. The scent of jasmine and some other sweet, oriental flower hit her immediately. 'This is beautiful!' she whispered.

'This is expensive!' returned Joseph. 'Very, very expensive.' He pointed to a panel on the wall. 'State-of-the-art automated blinds, automatic humidity and temperature control. Very nice indeed.'

And the exterior of the property was like manicured parkland. 'How the other half live,' she breathed. 'And I guess that is the fabled garden centre.'

At the bottom of the rolling lawns, and on the far side of a long pasture, sunlight was glinting off a massive glass structure.

'This lodge was the gatehouse for the original estate.' Elizabeth stood at the top of the steps. 'We added the garden room, plants being a passion for us both, and we've drawn up plans to build a Victorian-style orangery.'

'That would be some project to undertake,' said Joseph.

'If we ever find the time. But excuse me, the coffee will be ready.'

Nikki glanced impatiently at her watch. She wanted to talk to Elizabeth, but she needed to get back to the cottage to try to find out what had been stolen.

'Black or white?' Elizabeth placed a tray on a decorated rattan table, picked up the cafetière, and poured the coffee.

Nikki decided that there was no time left for procrastination. She took her drink, sat in big cane chair by the window, and said, 'When did you last see your brother?'

'About a week ago. He came for supper a couple of times a month.'

'And how did he seem?'

'Top form.' She sipped her drink tentatively. 'That's what makes it all so hard to understand. We both commented on how, oh, how *happy*, he seemed.'

'More than usual?'

'Maybe. Or perhaps he was just pleased because a paper he'd written was coming up for publication shortly.'

'Oh really? On what subject?' asked Joseph with interest.

'Salt marsh ecology, management and restoration.' She gave them a weak smile. 'Sounds pretty heavy, doesn't it? When Martin was younger he wanted to be a forensic botanist, but his illness put paid to that. When he recovered, he did continue to study biology and botany, and the marshes provided him with constant interest.'

'I knew that he was pretty interested in the local plant life, but I had no idea he was *that* knowledgeable.' Nikki was starting to wonder if she actually knew anything about Martin Durham. 'Did he have any money worries?'

'My brother was not rich, but he was financially secure, and the cottage was his, no mortgage. He had no debts either. So no, that was not the problem.'

'And there is nothing that you can think of that may have been bothering him?'

'I've gone over and over this, since the moment I heard he was dead, but there's nothing, absolutely nothing.'

'Did he mention anything to you about changing his medication?' asked Joseph abruptly.

Elizabeth's hand trembled for a moment, then her jaw clenched. 'What do you mean?'

Nikki stared at her. Why should that question bother her?

Joseph gave her an innocent look. 'Sorry, but we understand that he was keen for his GP to revise his regime?'

'Oh, that! Yes, I believe she had suggested new drugs were available. I'm not sure if he'd decided to go ahead though.'

'And I hate to ask this,' added Joseph, 'but did he ever take any recreational drugs?'

Elizabeth Durham suddenly laughed out loud. 'Martin? That's a joke! He was phobic about his medication! He took nothing that could upset the balance. Not even a herbal remedy. Ask anyone at the Wild Goose, he'd gone there for years, and I guarantee you, he never took one sip of alcohol in all that time, so drugs? No, Sergeant. He wouldn't have dared!'

'I'm sorry, but I had to ask,' said Joseph quietly. 'Because he was not acting rationally when he went to St Saviours Church.'

'I should say not. He killed himself, didn't he?' said Elizabeth icily.

'There is another problem, Elizabeth,' interjected Nikki. 'Knot Cottage was broken into last night. I accosted the intruder, but sadly he got the better of me.' She indicated to her bruised face.

'Oh!' Elizabeth's hands flew up to her mouth. 'How could they? Some thugs, I suppose? Looking for money for drugs! It's always that these days, isn't it? Oh, poor Martin, he was so particular about his home.'

Please! Don't worry about me! thought Nikki, but said. 'I believe the intruder was after something in particular. Would you have any idea what that could be?'

Elizabeth's eyes narrowed slightly. 'No. He had nothing of great value.'

'What about his papers, maybe the one about the salt marsh? Would it have any monetary significance?'

She shook her head. 'No. Years of work, yes, but it's not about making money.'

Nikki felt a mild sense of discomfort surrounding Martin's sister, but pressed on. 'So there would have been nothing of importance inside his locked desk, then?'

'Nothing that I know of,' replied Elizabeth shortly.

'Well, thank you for your help,' Nikki stood up. 'I'm sorry if we distressed you.'

'Will you keep me notified of any developments?'

Nikki nodded. 'Of course, and we may need to speak to you again. Right now, we are going back to Knot Cottage.'

'You know Martin thought a lot of you and Hannah,' Elizabeth said suddenly. 'He was very upset when Robert left you, although he never liked the man, I'm afraid.'

'No one in their right mind liked my ex-husband, Elizabeth,' said Nikki with a grimace. 'The only good thing about him was his daughter.'

'And how is Hannah now?'

'No change, although they are talking about sending her to a clinic in Belgium, in Liege.' Nikki didn't want to talk about Hannah, and stepped a little closer to the door. 'They offer no promises, but they understand her problem better than most.'

Elizabeth seemed to sense her discomfort, nodded sadly and changed the subject.

'When do you think I will I be able to go over and clean up? I'd like to go soon. Martin would hate it to be in a mess.'

Nikki understood what she meant. His place was always immaculate. Too immaculate, she wondered? 'We'll ring you.' She took a card from her bag and handed it to Elizabeth. 'My mobile number and direct line is on that. If you think of anything, no matter how insignificant, contact me, okay?'

* * *

Joseph drove carefully through the gate, making sure to avoid a large uneven manhole, and onto the main road. 'What was that all about?'

'Pass. She was fine, although naturally distraught about her brother, until you mentioned the drugs, then she nearly disappeared up her own bottom. But why?'

'Not sure, but I got the distinct impression that she knew exactly what was in that locked desk.'

'Which is more than we bloody do,' muttered Nikki. 'And I've been wondering about his obsession for cleanliness, he's always been that way and I never really thought much about it. Now I'm wondering if he was scared of infections. What with having to take all those tablets to keep healthy.'

'Probably was,' Joseph nodded. 'I'm sure I would be.'

Nikki clutched at her waist as they approached a level-crossing. 'Shit! That's tender!'

'Then I suggest we find somewhere to grab a hot drink, a sandwich, and you take some very strong painkillers before we go on to Knot Cottage.'

'I agree, and I know where we can get all that for free,' she grimaced through the pain. 'My kitchen.'

CHAPTER EIGHT

Knot Cottage had thrown up nothing of interest. The only papers left, in a small stationery drawer in the broken desk, were some diet sheets and lists of vitamin and mineral supplements.

Only one thing had claimed Nikki attention, and that was an old photograph. One of Martin, Hannah and herself, collecting samphire out on the marsh. Wind rippled their hair into ringlets, and tugged at their clothes. She remembered the day, and the buckets of the fleshy-leaved plant that her aunt wanted for pickling, but she couldn't for the life of her recall who had taken the picture. It had made her feel both nostalgic and mildly confused as to why Martin had kept it.

Now the photo sat on her desk. She rather liked it, and it would mean nothing to anyone else, so for now at least, it would stay with her.

Joseph was sorting the paperwork they had brought back, and she was re-reading the witness statements, when he phone rang.

'Mr Cavendish-Small, what can I do for you?'

The man sounded on edge, which Nikki thought to be quite understandable considering what he'd been through.

'I just keep feeling that it was all my fault, Inspector, but I was terrified that my sightseer's may rush for the stairs, you see. And that would have been a terrible disaster, and there were children to consider.'

'How could it possibly have been your fault?'

'Because I reached out to him. And he recoiled, as if I were the devil incarnate.' The man paused, then said, 'One of the kiddies said the man was afraid of me, and I believe the boy was right, but what could I have done to scare him so badly that he . . .'

'Listen to me, Mr Cavendish-Small. It was absolutely nothing to do with you. We don't know what upset the balance of his mind, but I assure you, it happened to him long before he ever got near that viewing platform.'

'Common sense says that you are right, Inspector Galena, but you didn't see his eyes! I'll never forget them. They looked like the sort of thing you see in horror films, not in your own parish church.'

Nikki felt desperately sorry but could not console him. How could she? It must have been quite horrific. 'All I can say is that it wasn't your fault, sir. That poor man was just very sick. Beyond anyone's help. The most important thing is that no one else was hurt, and that was down to you. You did very well under dreadful circumstances, sir.'

The man's voice seemed to lack all power, and he said, 'Thank you, Inspector, it's kind of you to say that, but I still believe I may have been to blame.'

Before Nikki could reply, she realised that Charles Cavendish-Small had hung up. She replaced her phone, stared at the old photograph propped up against her monitor screen and thought, Oh Martin, what have you done?

* * *

Joseph was having trouble concentrating. For some reason, every time he found himself with a few moments to himself, his mind wandered to the woman from the pool. Bryony, she had called herself. He didn't think he'd ever met anyone with that name before. He wondered what she did for a living, and he also wondered if she were married. Because that would be where his fantasy ended. He didn't do married. In fact it had been years since he did anything that involved a relationship of any kind. He had one failed marriage of his own, and one difficult daughter living in another country. And it still hurt, so . . .

He picked up his mobile phone from the desk and went to find the boss. He needed some work to keep his mind from straying.

In the corridor he was practically leapt on by Cat Cullen and Dave Harris. He knew from their beaming faces that they had just had a really good result.

'Wacky baccy farm all sorted?' he asked.

'Not just one! Three of them, Sarge!' Cat's eyes sparkled.

'*And* we got all but one of the little scrotes who were running them,' added Dave.

'Drinks are on us tonight, Sarge, over in the Hammer at seven. Can you make it?'

'I'll be there, and good work. The guv'nor will be well pleased.'

'We'll just need to get the paperwork done, and we are free to help you out, Sarge.' Dave gave him a shrewd look. 'I hear not everything in the garden is blooming?'

'And that the guv took a beating?' added Cat in little more than a whisper.

Joseph nodded. 'There's a bad feeling about this enquiry all right. Even I'm unsettled by it, and I never knew the poor guy who topped himself.'

'Well, as from tomorrow we are all yours. Maybe four heads will be better than two.' Cat skipped off like a little kid going to a party. 'Don't forget! Seven o'clock at the Hammer!'

'Is the guv'nor okay, Sarge?' Dave had real concern in his voice.

'Very sore, in more ways than one. The bruises she can handle, but she's far from happy that the assailant decked her.'

Dave smiled. 'Ah yes, that would smart. But as long as she's not badly hurt.' He moved off down the corridor. 'See you later, Sarge.'

The DI wasn't in her office, and Joseph really didn't feel like going back to the suspicious death reports, so he headed for the vending machine outside the mess room. The guv'nor's sandwich had worked at the time, but he felt a strong desire for a chocolate boost.

As he strolled along the window-lined corridor, he thought about her home on the fen. It was the kind of house he would have loved to have brought up lots of kids in; and at least three dogs and a cat. She'd always referred to it as a cottage, but it was a proper family farmhouse, and it seemed all wrong for her to live there alone.

He pushed some coins into the machine, pressed a button and waited. At least it would be better bet than the slum of a town flat she'd rented, in order to be closer to the drug dealers. Cloud Cottage Farm was a lovely old place, and he sincerely hoped she'd be happy back there. If he were honest, he'd never really felt comfortable on the wide open flatlands, but seeing Cloud Fen today, he had to admit that there was an airy kind of magic to it, and it was slowly winning him over.

He picked up his Snickers, peeled off the wrapper and balled it up. The bin was a little further along the corridor, and he aimed, threw, and missed. With a snort of disgust he picked it up and placed it inside, glancing out of the big picture window as he did. There was not much to see. Just a narrow lane that ran along the side of the station and down towards the river. It was fairly regularly used, but right now there was only a dog walker and a couple of old men, deep in conversation.

He bit into the chocolate, and thought about Bryony. Maybe he should ask her to go for a drink with him. It couldn't hurt, and if she said no, well at least he'd tried.

Joseph sighed, and watched as the dog walker disappeared, and a woman with a shopping trolley took his place.

With something of a shock, he suddenly realised that he didn't want Bryony to say no. Since his last case his priorities had changed. He thought of the Nikki Galena, all alone in that big house, and he knew that he didn't want to be like that. He wanted someone to share his life with. He didn't want to just exist and work, he wanted to live.

He straightened up, and smiled to himself. He'd go to the pool tomorrow and he'd sound her out. Then if she happened to be unattached, well, just a drink, no one could take offence at that, now could they?

The thought had barely had time to compute though his brain, when everything froze. He was no longer aware of anything going on around him. He heard nothing, and saw nothing, other than the man who was standing down in the lane, staring up at him, his right hand touching his forehead in a smart salute.

Joseph almost gagged on the chocolate.

It was him. Not a double, not a figment of his imagination. It was Billy Sweet.

* * *

'Joseph? You okay?' Nikki stood just metres away from him, but he didn't seem to notice her. For a moment she thought he was ill, then she saw his expression. She tried to read what she saw, but it was difficult. Confusion, disbelief, and what looked like fear, all clouded his handsome face.

'I . . . I thought . . .' He turned to the window and stared anxiously out.

'What, Joseph? What's wrong?'

'There was man in the, uh, lane.' His speech was stilted. 'Someone I once knew.'

Nikki raised her eyebrows. 'And presumably someone you didn't like very much?'

Joseph's expression hardened. 'I hated him.' He suddenly leant back against the wall and shook his head. 'That's a word I never wanted to hear myself say again. I thought I'd learnt all about forgiveness. But then I never thought I'd see *him* again.'

'Who is he?' asked Nikki.

'A bad man,' answered Joseph slowly. 'A very bad man.'

Nikki walked over to the window and looked down into the empty lane. 'And you are sure it was him?'

'It was him.'

'Where was he?'

'Directly below us. Staring up here. At me.' His face screwed up. 'But how would he know I was here?'

Nikki frowned. 'With all this glass, if he kept watch on the station for a while he'd spot you sooner or later. Let's check out the CCTV. What's his name, by the way?'

For a moment Nikki thought that Joseph was not going to be able to speak. He was certainly having trouble naming the devil.

'Billy Sweet,' he murmured. 'But don't be fooled by the name. He's pure evil.'

'Come on. Let's go to the control room. See if we can find him.' Nikki led the way, and having told the civilian in charge what area they wanted to trace, sat down in front of the computer screens and waited.

'Two old gits having a barney, and some old biddy with a shopper, now where is our man?' She stared at the monitors. 'Ah, there, is that . . . ? No, it's a bloke and a dog.'

'Where did you say he stood?' asked the CCTV operator. Nikki looked at Joseph, who explained again.

'Then he must have got into the blind spot, Sergeant. There's one area where the cameras aren't aligned properly. I've been asking maintenance to sort it for weeks.'

'But surely we'd see him walking into the lane?' asked Nikki.

'Not if he came up Hour Glass Alley. It converges into the area with no coverage.'

'Fat lot of bloody good that is!' growled Nikki. 'These really are sodding useless! When you need one, they are either vandalised or there's no one available to watch them.' She turned to Joseph. 'Sorry, Sergeant. But your man got lucky.'

Joseph exhaled. 'Maybe. Or . . .'

Nikki observed him carefully. Whatever this Sweet character had done in the past, it was having one hell of an impact right now, and she didn't like it. She had never seen him so rattled, and the last thing Joseph needed was some creepy blast from the past ruining the life he was just getting back together.

She stood up and walked to the door. 'Coffee, in my office. We need to talk.'

In the short time that Nikki had known Joseph Easter, he had demonstrated incredible self-control. Being an impatient person herself, there had been times when his laid-back approach had made her want to tear his head off his shoulders. And he never talked about himself. The tiny pieces of his life that she was acquainted with had not been shared without considerable pain. The one thing she did know was that he had once been a soldier, a special forces operative. And she had the distinct idea that Billy Sweet came from that area of his past.

She stirred her coffee thoughtfully and contemplated the word *eggshells*. 'Right. Before you tell me to butt out, my friend, I'm going to play devil's advocate here. What I say may not be my true opinion, but hear me out.'

Joseph looked at her over the top of his coffee mug, and nodded silently.

'Clearly you haven't seen this person for years. Could you possibly be mistaken?'

'He looked exactly the same as I remember him, and his face is etched on my memory for reasons that I'd prefer not to discuss, ma'am,' said Joseph stonily.

'Well, that's odd for starters. He should have aged.'

'Maybe he had. I didn't see him for more than a second or two.'

Nikki decided not to press the point that if he'd only seen him fleetingly, he could well have been wrong. 'Moving on. Is it probable that this man should turn up in Greenborough?'

'No. Highly improbable.' Joseph ran a hand through his hair and shook his head slowly. 'I thought about that the last time I saw him and . . .'

'You've seen him before?' she exclaimed. 'You never said!'

'It was when I was driving out to see Dr Latimer.'

'I *knew* you were troubled by something when you came back! I thought Helen had upset you.'

Joseph told her about his encounter, then sat back and shrugged. 'I'd convinced myself that it was just some guy that reminded me of Billy Sweet. But now, I'm sure it was him, ma'am. Dead certain.'

'Does he have some sort of unfinished business with you, Joseph?'

Joseph's eyes narrowed. 'I don't know. Maybe he knew that I suspected him of some terrible things, maybe not. The other men he served with didn't want him near them either. He was fearless, but he was a psycho, ma'am. And a loose cannon like that could cost you your life, or that of your comrades. But no, the last I heard he had shipped out and joined a private security force, by that time I was in Civvy Street. End of story, or so I thought.'

'You once told me you had a bad mission, was he part of it?'

Joseph closed his eyes. 'I can't go there right now, ma'am.'

Nikki knew the answer. 'Okay. So what do we do next?'

'I don't know.' He scratched his head. 'Why on earth would he be here?'

'I suggest we ask him.'

His eyes widened. 'And how are we going to do that? He's like a will-o'-the-wisp. Here one moment and gone the next.'

'Well, did you notice his clothes?'

Joseph thought for a minute. 'Dark zipper jacket, thin nylon material, black jeans and a T-shirt. Pale, dirty white or grey, maybe. Shoes were some kind of suede trainers, really grubby.'

Nikki nodded. 'Good. Excellent, in fact. Let's go back to the control room and get them to track him. Hopefully there's more than one camera in this town that is actually working, so they should have a good chance of spotting him. Especially if he decided to play chicken in the middle of the Greenborough High Road yesterday, don't you think?'

'Good point, ma'am. And I appreciate your concern, but this is hardly a police matter. We've got a lot of work to do on Martin's case.'

'Naturally the investigation comes first, but I don't want some creepy shit freaking out my detectives! So we deal with him, then get on with our own work, okay?'

Joseph stood up, looking slightly less harassed. 'Let's do it.'

* * *

'What do you mean, inconclusive?' Nikki felt her temperature begin to rise.

'Sorry ma'am, we found the incident that Sergeant Easter described, but the footage is too grainy to identify anyone specific. It's certainly not clear enough to lift an image.'

'Oh great! Okay, let me have a tape of it anyway. Thanks for trying.'

The woman left and Nikki sank down in her chair. If they had managed to get a mugshot of the man, she could circulate it and get him brought in. Joseph could then have looked at him close up, and that would have been that. Either a simple case of mistaken identity or Joseph would have to take an unwanted trip down memory lane.

She gnawed on the inside of her cheek. Just say Joseph was correct and this Billy Sweet really was rampaging down a Lincolnshire High Street. What the hell did he want? It had to be something to do with Joseph. She wondered what Billy Sweet had done. If the whole unit despised him, it had to be something pretty grim.

'Ma'am? You wanted me?' Cat Cullen leant around the door. Her recently emerald green striped hairstyle was now reduced to just white blond spikes.

Nikki grinned at her. 'Very good work with the cannabis farms, Detective. An excellent result.'

'Ta, guv. Dave and me are pretty chuffed with ourselves.'

'You have every right to be.' Nikki jabbed her thumb in the direction of a chair.

'I want you to do me a little favour before we discuss your next investigation. You've spent a lot of time on the streets recently, would this man mean anything to you?' She handed Cat, Joseph's written description of Billy Sweet.

'Phew, that could be half the guys that I've been hanging out with, but it really doesn't sound like anyone I could name. Want me to make enquiries, guv?'

Nikki nodded, then looked up as the CCTV operator appeared in the doorway and handed her a CD.

'Stick this in the machine, Cat. It may help, although I'm told the quality is crap.'

Cat took the CD and switched on the viewer. After a few moments they were watching three lanes of painfully slow moving traffic.

'This will never make the Cannes Film Festival, ma'am. When does the action start?'

'About now I should think. There's Joseph's Ford, at a standstill in the middle lane.'

'And what are those yobs doing?'

'They are the ones that we are interested in. Watch Joseph's vehicle. One of those men apparently hammered on his windscreen, then ran away.'

'Wow!' said Cat. 'If that's their idea of fun, they really need to get out more.'

As Joseph had described, the group of men ran in and out of the traffic, dodging and weaving as the vehicles moved forward or stopped. Then one of them broke away and dived in front of Joseph's Ford.

'The quality *is* crap. You're right.' Cat leaned in closer. 'What's he doing?'

'Looks like he's slapping the windscreen. Now he's leaning over the bonnet and staring inside.'

'What an arsehole,' Cat frowned. 'And now he's off.'

Nikki stared at the screen. No question, the man was unidentifiable. But now she looked at Joseph. He had jumped out of his car and was staring around anxiously, trying to see where the man had gone.

'The sarge overreacted a bit, didn't he, guv?' asked Cat. 'It was only some prat, doing what prats do.'

Nikki didn't answer. She'd been thinking exactly the same thing, and whether the man was Billy Sweet or Lord Lucan, Joseph clearly believed he had seen a ghost.

'Go out for the afternoon, Cat. Ask around. See if this description rings any bells with anyone, and concentrate on the West Street Quarter, those other men were apparently foreign.'

'Sure. No problem. And if I find him?'

'Ring me, and steer well clear. Understand? No contact with him. He maybe an innocent party, but just as easily, he may be very unpleasant.'

As Cat stood up to leave, Nikki added, 'And keep this just between us for the present, okay?'

Cat tapped the side of her nose. 'Got it, ma'am. I'll be silent as the grave.'

As the young detective closed the door, Nikki looked back to the photograph of Martin Durham. She was getting sidetracked by Joseph's problems, but Martin was dead, and Joseph was alive and troubled.

Somehow she'd find time for both.

CHAPTER NINE

The Hammer and Anvil pub was packed with celebrating police officers and civilians.

'They don't need much encouragement, do they?' yelled Dave, above the ear-splitting noise of voices and music.

Joseph forced a grin. He had not wanted to come, but he was part of the team now and he didn't want to let Cat or Dave down. 'What are you having, mate?' he asked.

'I'm fine, Sarge. I've got a pint and that'll do me.' He pointed towards the bar. 'The first drink goes on the DI's slate. And as that doesn't happen too often, I'd have a large one if I were you!'

Joseph eased between the packed tables, and found that the bar was least crowded right at the far end. As he shouldered his way into the queue he decided that this kind of gathering really wasn't his thing. He'd do the rounds, smile, speak to everyone he knew then quietly disappear.

'As I stand *no* chance of ever reaching the bar, would you be kind enough to get me a G & T while you're there, Joseph?'

He spun around and saw Bryony standing behind him.

'My pleasure! Although I could be some time by the look of this lot!'

'I'll be over by the door to the restaurant. It's quieter there. Do you need a ball of string to find your way back to me?' she asked with a smile.

'Don't worry. I came first in orienteering.' He returned the smile, then added, 'although I was only twelve at the time.'

She melted into the crowd, and when Joseph had recovered from the surprise at seeing her, he wondered if she were alone, or maybe waiting for someone. Did women go to rowdy pubs alone these days? Maybe they did. He was pretty out of touch with the social scene.

Finally, with their drinks firmly grasped in both hands, he found her.

'What on earth is going on?'

'The Old Bill are celebrating slinging a few more villains in the slammer.'

Her brow wrinkled, and he thought it made her look even more attractive. 'What?'

'Arrests. We've made some good arrests today.'

'Ah, so you are a policeman.'

Joseph smiled sheepishly and hoped that she wouldn't throw up her hands and run screaming from the pub. ''Fraid so.'

'Ah, I wondered what you did for a living.'

Relief swept over him. So she'd been thinking about him too.

'Actually, we've met before. Before the fitness club, I mean, but I don't think you'd remember me. You were pretty poorly.'

It was Joseph's turn to frown. 'I must have been half dead not to remember you.'

Bryony laughed. 'You probably were! It was at the hospital a few months ago. I was visiting my brother. It was Curlew Ward, wasn't it?'

He nodded. 'But I'm really sorry. You see I don't remember much about the first few days there. I was pretty out of it.'

'It's all right. Are you fully recovered?' She laughed again. 'Silly question! You'd hardly be 'slinging villains in the slammer' if you were still incapacitated, now would you?'

'Probably not, although I am very passionate about my job.'

'I like passion.' Bryony grinned broadly, picked up her drink and raised it in salute. 'Cheers, Joseph.'

'Indeed.' He clinked his glass against hers. 'This is too weird. You know I'd fully intended to accost you at the pool tomorrow, and ask you if you'd like to go for a drink, and voila! Here we are!'

'Funny that. I had the same plan. Although I was going to give you one chance to get in first, for the sake of your male pride.'

Joseph felt his stomach give a little lurch. 'So I assume you would have said yes?'

'Assume nothing, Joseph. It doesn't pay.' She looked him full in the eyes, 'Except on this occasion.'

'I'm glad to hear that, Bryony. So, how come you're here tonight?'

'Don't ask!' She gave him a mock frown. 'Today has been a catalogue of disasters. Although this seems to be making up for it somewhat.' She sipped her drink. 'For my sins, my boss has organised myself and a work colleague to arrange a charity event. We are supposed to be scouting out suitable pubs for a scavenger hunt.'

'My boss never gives me jobs like that! Some might say that was a very enjoyable task.'

'And it might have been, if we hadn't picked one that was evacuated because a fire alarm went off, another that was full of hairy bikers, and in the one before this; my friend had a pint of lager tipped all over her and went home in a huff! This was the last one, so I thought I'd check it out and get it over with, and found all this going on!' She pulled a face. 'I was just on my way out, when I saw you.'

'Detective Sergeant Joseph Easter to the rescue, madam!' He held out his hand.

'Bryony Barton, ex-damsel in distress. Thank you!' She took his hand and bowed her head, then laughed out loud. 'Can we go somewhere quieter? Or is it obligatory to stay until you're rat-arsed?'

'Not in the slightest. But tradition demands that I must just congratulate the arresting officers, then I'm all yours.' He stood up. 'Excuse me, I'll be back in five.'

* * *

Niall leant on the bar and dug Yvonne sharply in the ribs, 'Gossip Alert! Gossip Alert!'

'For God's sake, Niall, mind my drink! You know, for a trendy young geezer, you are the biggest old woman on the force!'

'Shut up and look! The Sarge is chatting up that super-cool bird in the blue dress!'

'Are you sure she's not chatting him up? He *is* probably the best-looking bloke in Greenborough.'

Niall snorted. 'I'm devastated! I thought you loved me, Vonnie!'

'Of course, I do! In a motherly kind of way.' Yvonne placed her glass on the bar and tried not to stare across to where Joseph Easter sat talking animatedly to the striking-looking woman. Good luck to you, she thought. After all you've been through, you deserve a bit of fun.

Niall was still talking. 'Well, I don't know what the DI will make of that! Dear me! Whatever is he thinking of?'

Yvonne threw him a puzzled look. 'What are you rambling on about? Half a shandy and you're practically incoherent! You can't be suggesting that Holy Joe and Old Nik are an item, are you? Are you quite mad?'

'Oh Vonnie! Don't be naïve! There are meant for each other!'

'Huh? The sergeant and the DI! I've never heard anything so barmy!'

'Five squid says she's going to be pissed off as hell when she finds out about this!'

'You're on, honey-child! Although I'm going to hate to take your pocket money quite so easily.'

'Where is DI Galena anyway?'

Yvonne took a big gulp of her wine. 'I saw her going into the super's office just before we left, but she'll be along soon.' She glanced back and raised her eyebrows. 'Uh-oh, looks like the good sergeant has tired of our company already. And who could blame him! That woman has one heck of a good figure!'

'I'll second that!' whispered Niall.

'Put your eyeballs back in, Niall, and try to stop drooling.'

'Sorry, Mother. Fancy another?'

'My turn.' Yvonne took her purse from her bag, and watched with a smile as the sergeant escorted the woman to the door and they both disappeared into the street.

* * *

Joseph took Bryony to a small Italian restaurant, where they shared a carafe of house red, and ate a chef's special of four cheese ravioli and a salad. At around ten she said she had an early start the next day, so Joseph walked her down to the taxi rank.

'Will you be at the pool tomorrow?' he asked hopefully.

'Not tomorrow, I have to go to Gainsborough for a meeting, but I'll be there on Friday.'

'I'll see you there then.' For a moment he felt like a tongue-tied kid, scared to say the wrong thing, but

72

desperate to get the girl to see him again. 'And when I do, perhaps you would accept an invitation to dinner on Saturday evening?'

'Ask me on Friday, Joseph. And thank you for being my saving grace tonight.'

'Anytime.'

A taxi moved slowly up the rank towards them. 'My number.' He handed her a card, and gave her a brief peck on the cheek. He wanted to kiss her, really kiss her, but . . . then it was too late. Bryony was leaning towards the driver's window and telling him an address on the far side of town, one that Joseph immediately made a mental note of. He opened the door for her and watched her get in.

As he closed the door, he glanced across the road to the railway station buildings, and saw a man standing in the shadows, watching them intently. He was hardly visible, but Joseph caught sight of a dull gleam of pale hair in the orange glow of a street lamp

'What's wrong, Joseph?' asked Bryony. There was a tinge of concern in her voice. 'You're as white as a sheet.'

'A man. Over there.' He pointed.

'Where?' She cast her eyes this way and that.

'He's gone. You didn't see him?' Joseph tried to get the panic out of his voice.

'Sorry, no. Who is he?'

'No one.' He covered his anxiety with a smile. 'No one at all. See you Friday. Take care, and thank you for tonight.'

Bryony looked at him for a long while, then smiled back. 'Goodnight, Joseph.'

As the car pulled away, she called from the open window, 'Got a good memory? Remember this!' Then she called out her telephone number, and the window closed and she was gone.

Joseph grabbed a pen from his pocket, wrote the number on his hand, and watched the car until it turned on the High Street. Then he sprinted across the road. He paced up and down the railway approach, looked in every hiding place, and tried doors to see if any were open, but the station was deserted.

This time he really wasn't sure about what he'd seen. The shadows had concealed the figure. All he knew was that *someone* had been there, and he had slipped out of sight quickly enough for Bryony not to see him.

After one last look around, Joseph gave up and walked back towards the taxi rank. As he got close, he decided that he could not face being shut inside a cab. It was a fair distance, but he'd walk. He had so much on his mind, he could do with the time alone to try to make sense of things.

He pushed his hands deep into his pockets and strode off in the direction of his lodgings. As he walked into the night, all he wanted to think about was Bryony. But try as he might, every time he remembered the outline of her face, it was overpowered by the ugly, uneven features of Billy Sweet.

CHAPTER TEN

'Good morning, Sergeant.' Nikki's voice echoed across the CID room. 'My office, please.' Joseph felt distinctly as if he'd been summoned for a caning by the head mistress.

He closed the door and looked at her speculatively. 'Ma'am?'

'A friendly word to the wise, my friend. Next time you plan an assignation, try to arrange it in a different pub to one that contains half the Fenland Constabulary! I've heard nothing else since I got in!'

'But . . . !' Joseph spluttered, 'But I never . . . it wasn't an assignation, ma'am! She was there by chance, and I know her from the fitness club. Like me, she swims most mornings. That's all.'

'Oh really? But you'd left before I even made it as far as the pub front door, and together, I hear. Or has the grapevine got it wrong?'

'Well, yes, I mean, no.' Joseph felt like a total idiot. For some reason, he hadn't thought about what his colleagues would say the next day, and clearly, they were saying a lot. He looked up miserably, and saw his boss grinning at him.

'Well done! At least that may quell some of the other things they say about you! Those mess room gossips won't have a leg to stand on now, when they call you Holy Joe or Mr Goody Two-Shoes.'

'Thanks for reminding me, ma'am. But I thought they'd already given up on that.'

'They probably have. I wouldn't know. I don't pay the slightest attention to them anyway.' She smiled up at him. 'Why should I? While they are sniping at you, they are leaving me alone. I just couldn't resist having a little dig myself. Frankly, I'm pig sick that I missed seeing her. Quite a looker, I hear.'

Joseph groaned and sank down into a chair. 'I'm beginning to wish I'd given last night a miss.'

'No, you're not, and you know it,' she leant forward. 'What's she like, Joseph?'

A small smile spread across his face. 'She's gorgeous.'

'More. I need details.'

'Well, her name is Bryony Barton, she's thirty, and she works for the Public Analyst, here in Greenborough. Funnily enough, she saw me first when I was in the hospital. Her brother was in the same ward.'

'And she has a good sense of humour, likes the theatre, dogs, and walking barefoot in the sand at sunset?'

Joseph tried to look aggrieved, but it was so rare that DI Galena openly enjoyed something so much, he didn't have the heart to stop her.

'Well, we did talk, and we seem to have quite a lot in common, but . . .' Joseph stopped as Cat Cullen appeared in the doorway.

'Ma'am. Sorry to interrupt, but . . .'

Joseph had expected Cat to take the mickey out of him more than anyone, but to his surprise, her expression was serious and her tone unusually grave.

'. . . some kids have found a body.'

The boss sighed. 'Great. As if I hadn't got enough on my plate with Martin's death. What do we know, Cat?'

'A male, guv. Found in some wasteland off Beale Street. Throat cut.' She threw a sideways glance to Joseph, and he didn't like the look on her face. 'Thing is, and obviously I haven't seen him yet, but he fits the description of the man that Sergeant Easter is looking for.'

Joseph felt a spasm grip his gut. Sweet? Dead?

He closed his eyes. When he'd left the army, he'd spent a lot of time trying to make his life right again. Trying to understand things on a deeper level. And he'd succeeded. Not through religion, although a lot of his fellow officers thought that was the case, but with a more spiritual approach to life.

He opened his eyes again. So why did he feel such delight in hoping that another human being was dead? It went against everything he believed in.

'Joseph?' The DI was staring at him. 'I said, I think you need to see this.'

'Yes, of course, ma'am.' He stood up. The answer to his own question was clear. Billy Sweet wasn't a human being. To be classed as that, you needed belong or relate to the nature of mankind, and there was nothing kind about Sweet. He took a deep breath. 'Let's go.'

* * *

The body was still in situ, although an awning had been hastily erected around it to protect the scene and block it from view.

Joseph, the DI, and Cat carefully picked their way over stones and rubbish to the covered area.

'Ah, the good detective inspector! And my old Fenchester friend, Joseph! How are you, dear boy?' Without waiting for an answer, the tall, beanpole of a man pushed his wire-rimmed glasses further up onto the bridge of his hawk nose, and beamed benignly at Cat. 'And we must not forget you, lovely lady, although we haven't yet been introduced.' He peered at the DI.

'Cat Cullen meet Professor Rory Wilkinson. Home Office pathologist. Forensic science wizard, and the possessor of the darkest sense of humour imaginable. And another ex-pat from Fenchester.' She gave him a grim smile.

'You forgot your usual slanderous comment about allegedly being a raging queen,' he added, sounding slightly put out at the omission.

'Sorry, and that. So what have you got for us?'

'An interesting one to be sure. But not pleasant.'

'Murder can be pleasant?'

'Murder can be many things, Inspector,' said the pathologist enigmatically. 'But this is not some crime of passion, or a fight that got out of hand. This is an execution. Now, if you'd all like to follow me?'

Joseph didn't want to follow him anywhere. Joseph wanted to turn his back and walk away. The word execution had sent a ripple of horror down his spine. He had seen too many executions, and he still saw them, when sleep would not come or when a nightmare took possession of his slumbers.

Rory Wilkinson moved beneath the cordon, lifted the canvas flap to the awning, and invited them inside as cordially as if it were a garden party. 'Mind yourselves, the ground is somewhat uneven, and the copious quantity of blood doesn't help either.'

Joseph breathed in, held his breath, and moved reluctantly into the temporary shelter.

No one spoke immediately. Even the garrulous pathologist seemed somewhat in awe of his newest acquisition.

The man lay on his side, his knees bent, ankles tightly tied with some kind of thin rope, and his hands tied in the same manner behind his back. He had been made to kneel for his last moments on this earth. His throat had been sliced from ear to ear, and he had fallen sideways, allowing his lifeblood to ooze into the weeds and the detritus of the waste ground.

Bile rose in Joseph's throat. This was something that belonged in his past. Something he had prayed that he would never see again.

He swallowed, and steeled himself to look at the body.

A black nylon bomber jacket, old jeans, a T-shirt, though the blood had made its original colour impossible to see, and scuffed and worn trainers.

Unsteadily, he took a few steps backwards, then ducked out under the canvas to drag in some gulps of fresh air.

The dead man was ugly, had a rough cut thatch of corn-coloured hair, uneven features and pale blue eyes, but he wasn't Billy Sweet.

* * *

Nikki sat in the car and stared across at him. 'You are sure?'

'Absolutely. I've never seen that man before.' Joseph looked pale and gaunt. 'Although there is a resemblance.'

'Could it have been the man that you think has been following you?'

'No, ma'am. The man I saw was Billy Sweet.' His lips drew tighter. 'But thinking about it, the dead guy may have been the man I saw hanging around the station buildings last night. Beale Street is only a few minutes from there.' He rubbed hard at his temple. 'If only there had been some kind of identification on him,' muttered Joseph. 'It would have given us somewhere to start.'

Nikki shrugged. 'No such luck. We'll just have to wait for the fingerprint check, a photo image identification, and failing all that, DNA tests.' She took a deep breath.

'And you have to consider that this may have nothing whatsoever to do with you, or this guy who has been watching you.'

'Billy killed him.' Joseph's voice was little more than a monotone. 'I've seen his work before.'

'You mean this Billy Sweet has already killed in this manner?' asked Nikki incredulously.

'Oh yes.' Joseph gave a small humourless laugh. 'It was a kind of hobby of his.'

'You're making me feel sick,' said Nikki through gritted teeth.

'So now you know why I'm half out of my mind at the thought of him being here in Greenborough, amongst people I care about.'

'And the only connection that we know about, to Billy Sweet and Greenborough, is you, Joseph.' Nikki bit on the side of her thumb nail. 'I think it's time to take this back to the station. We'll set up the murder room, then go over everything that we know so far. And Joseph . . . ?' She looked at him with real concern in her eyes. And although she did not want to compound his problems, she knew that she had to ask some questions that he would find hard to cope with. 'You do know that we are going to have to go over some pretty unpleasant stuff, don't you? About your past.'

Joseph slumped back into his seat, as if all his energy had sapped away and left only a limp shell. 'Then we're going to need a very large bottle of Scotch and a tape recorder, because if I do manage to talk to you, the story will be told once and only once, okay?'

'I'll buy the whisky,' said Nikki flatly. 'And for your sake, I think this part will be best dealt with away from the station, don't you?' She gave him an enquiring look. 'So, your place or mine?'

'Have you *seen* my place, ma'am?' he answered, showing a hint of the old Joseph.

'Then Cloud Fen it is. After we've done the preliminaries back at the nick. Seven o'clock, and bring a toothbrush. You won't be driving afterwards.'

CHAPTER ELEVEN

Nikki left the others preparing the murder room, went to her office and closed the door. She needed some time alone to try to get her head around what was happening.

Martin Durham's unexplained suicide still haunted her. Over and over she saw him, riding off down the lane on his bicycle, waving to her. He'd said he had something to tell her, "a little bit of interesting news." His face had been alive, bright. Then apparently he had prepared a stew for lunch, jumped into his car and driven to Greenborough, where a few hours later he lay dead in the stinking mud of the Wayland River.

Nikki gave a shaky little sigh. She'd read somewhere that suicide was a permanent solution to a temporary problem. Could something *that* terrible have happened between the hours of 7.30 a.m. and midday? Something awful enough to make Martin Durham kill himself?

She reached across and picked up the old picture that was still propped against her monitor. She felt sad now that she had seen him so infrequently while she was staying in the town. He had been a great support to both her and Hannah when her ex-husband Robert left home. Not pushy, not intrusive, just there. And now he'd gone, and she owed it to him to put the record straight. She didn't want him written off as some flaky saddo, because he was far from that, and maybe she were the only one who would have the incentive and the wherewithal to bring the truth to light.

'Hang on in there, Martin,' she whispered. 'Things have gone a little mad here right now, but I'll find out what happened, I promise.'

'First sign of madness, Nikki, talking to yourself.'

She had been so engrossed in her own thoughts that she hadn't even heard Rick Bainbridge enter her office. She grinned ruefully, 'And what is the second sign, Super? Because I'm sure to be displaying it.'

'I'm not sure. Something about looking for hairs on your palms, I think.' He stared at the picture that was still in her hand. 'Who's in the photo?'

She passed it across for the superintendent to see. 'My old neighbour, Martin Durham, Hannah and I.'

'I never realised that you were that close.' He scrutinised the snap, then handed it back to her.

'We were just good neighbours, sir. Kind of there for each other. Cloud Fen is a small, outlying community; it's what you do.'

'Then no doubt his loss will hit hard.'

Nikki nodded. 'He was a good man, he will be missed.' She stared up at the superintendent and was pretty sure it was not Martin that he wanted to talk about.

As if on cue, he sat down and said, 'But that's not why I'm here. I want your honest opinion on Sergeant Easter.'

Nikki was somewhat taken back. She had sure it would be a request for a report on the dead man, but Joseph? 'Why? What's wrong?'

The super's brow wrinkled into furrows. 'I'm concerned that he's come back too soon, Nikki. I saw him yesterday and I didn't like the look on his face. He seemed totally distracted by something.'

Nikki thought quickly. If Joseph's possible involvement with the dead man came to light too soon, the superintendent would have them off the case before she could draw breath. 'Ah, I see the grapevine hasn't stretched its sticky little tendrils in your direction yet, sir.' She mustered a broad smile, 'Our Joseph has got a new flame. And if the rest of the station is right, he has every right to look preoccupied, sir. Apparently she's a stunner.'

'Joseph?'

'The one and the same.'

'Good Lord!'

'My sentiments precisely. But don't worry about him, sir, he's still on the ball regarding his work. He's been nose to the grindstone ever since he started.' She lost the smile. 'And we *are* busy, sir, what with Martin, and now the death in Beale Street.'

'Mm. That was my next question. Is this execution-style murder true, or have the rookies hyped it up?'

'It's true, sir.' Nikki decided to keep her information to the minimum for the time being. 'I've never seen anything like it before. Professor Wilkinson has said he will prioritise the post-mortem, so we should get his preliminary report pretty quickly.'

'And we have no idea of the man's identity?'

'None, but hopefully we'll get some answers soon. Everyone is geared up for the investigation, and the murder room should be ready by now.' She looked at him seriously. 'I'd better get back out there, sir. I'll keep you updated of everything as we go along.'

'Good. And let me know if you need more detectives. Some of the enquiries being dealt with at present can afford to go on the back burner.'

'Thanks, Super. I'll ascertain where this is going, and let you know.' She looked at him hopefully. 'Do you think Sergeant Conway could spare me a couple of bodies for some leg work? Yvonne and Niall would be a great help if they were free?'

The super shook his head, then gave her an exasperated half-smile. 'Oh, alright, I'll do my best, but no promises, Nikki. You know that CID should work closely with uniform, not just commandeer their staff, as and when.'

'I'd really appreciate it, sir.'

'As I said, no promises.' He walked to the door, then turned back, a disbelieving smile playing across his face. 'A real stunner, you say?'

'Absolutely, sir. Haven't seen her myself, but the words that are being bandied around are pretty descriptive. 'Stunning' was the mildest of several very colourful, and graphic adjectives.'

'Oh, I can imagine exactly what kind of words the mess room have come up with, and most of them quite unrepeatable, I should think.' He shook his head again. 'Poor old Joseph!'

Nikki raised her eyebrows. 'Hardly! If what I hear is right, it's lucky old Joseph!'

* * *

'Ma'am?' Joseph looked at her, a puzzled expression on his face. 'What's with the super? I could swear he winked at me?'

'Oh dear, you may have me to thank for that.'

'Thank you for what?'

'Just think about it, Sergeant. What have half the station been talking about, until we had a murder land on our patch, that is? Just believe me, what I told the super is all for the best.'

Joseph shook his head, and remained totally bemused.

Nikki turned to Dave. 'Are we all set up?'

'Yes, ma'am. And you've just received a note from Professor Wilkinson.' He handed her an envelope.

'Okay, get everyone together, and we'll take a look at what we've got so far.' She tore open the envelope and looked at the copperplate script that was Rory Wilkinson's everyday handwriting.

My Dear Inspector. As you were tactful enough not to demand an immediate answer to that age old question, "Can you give me a time of death?", I have made it my business to provide you with a little gift, my closest 'guesstimate,' pre-post-mortem findings, of course. I believe our man was executed, and there is no doubt that is what happened, between ten and eleven o'clock last night. It was quite warm last evening, and although the rigor mortis was advanced, it had not reached the point of full body rigidity. Our insect friends were naturally enjoying themselves enormously, but the eggs had not hatched into maggots, so we are looking at the fact that he had been dead for less than twelve hours when he and I were introduced.

I can also confirm, even without detailed examination that your killer is right-handed. The incised wound was made by the killer standing behind the victim, and the cut extends from high up close to the ear, sweeps downwards across the throat, then back up again. The cut is left to right, indicating a right-handed assailant. It was a clean, efficient, and highly effective move, so alas, I suspect this is not the first time that this person has used this particular procedure.

See! It pays not to hassle your friendly pathologist at the scene of the crime!

My opinion and prelim report, will be on your desk tomorrow, God willing.

And now back to my cold cadaver,

Felicitations

Rory. MD, BCh, MRCP, FRCPath, Life-time Member of the Judy Garland Fan Club, etc. etc.

Nikki smiled to herself. Professor Wilkinson had a reputation for stalling if pressed over the elusive time of death, although it hadn't been easy, she had purposely refused to ask him his opinion. She now had her answer and more.

She looked up and smiled smugly, as the door opened and Yvonne Collins and Niall Farrow walked in. Things were progressing exactly as planned.

'Okay, guys, find a seat and we'll recap on what we know.' She walked to the front of the room. 'And until we get the forensic reports back, we'll stick to the facts. We can throw ideas around when we know more.'

Nikki drew in a deep breath. Joseph's involvement would stay in the background for now, with one small exception, his jaywalker. 'Right, last night between the hours of ten and eleven p.m. . . .' She clearly described everything they had found on the filthy wasteground in Beale Street, and when she paused to gather herself, a low murmur of disbelief greeted her.

'Dear God,' muttered Niall. 'Sounds like something from Vietnam, not Greenborough.'

Nikki silently agreed, then continued. 'He had no identification on him, but his description is approx.. five foot ten, naturally blond hair, blue eyes and no distinguishing features other than a small scar on his wrist. No visible tattoos or birthmarks, although the full examination may show something. We have him as about thirty-five, maybe younger.' She listed his clothes, and watched as they all scribbled down what she said. 'Now,' she looked at her team. 'We are already running a fingerprint check and his picture will be circulated, but I don't need to tell you that we need to get on top of this really quickly. Whoever killed him is a highly dangerous individual, and we have no idea if this is just a one-off, a personal vendetta, or the start of a killing spree. Whatever, we don't want what appears to be a professional hitman on our streets for long.'

A murmur of agreement ran around the room.

'So, we need CCTV checks for that whole area, including the station. Officers out asking questions of local residents and workers, not that there are many as that spot is pretty low density housing, and we need a real push on identifying the dead man.'

'I was in the vicinity of the station last night, ma'am,' said Joseph slowly. 'I saw a man loitering in the shadows and went to investigate, but he had disappeared. I'm not saying it was the same person, and the street lights drained everything of colour, but I think he had blondish-fair hair.'

Nikki nodded. 'Hopefully there may be some working cameras that will show him up.' She was glad Joseph had mentioned the fact that he was there *before* the CCTV check began. 'A completely separate incident occurred the day before, again involving Sergeant Easter. Some men were messing around on the High Road, dashing in between cars. One of them hammered on the sergeant's windscreen as he was going out to Cloud Fen to conduct an interview. We've got them on camera, but it's very poor quality. The thing is, the man was of the same build and description, and wore similar clothes. May be coincidence, may not.'

She looked up and saw Joseph looking at her apprehensively, but she had no intention of telling anyone about the man he had seen in the alley, or of his fears about knowing the identity of an evil man in their midst. All in good time. She wanted to hear the history of Billy Sweet, and get Joseph's involvement with him clear in her head long before she discussed it with the team.

'Okay, sort out who does what between yourselves. I know we are pretty well stuck until we get some reports and some answers back, but do what you can, and try to get some sleep tonight. We could be pretty busy until we catch this killer.'

She turned to Joseph. 'Come with me. There are a few details I need to discuss while the others organise themselves.'

In her office, she told him about the super noticing that he wasn't himself.

'He must have seen you after you spotted your mystery man in the lane. He thought you'd come back too soon, and I have to say that you did look like shit.'

'I probably did.' Joseph sighed. 'Ah right, so you told him I was love-struck?'

'It was the first thing that came into my mind, and it worked. So, if he winks at you again, don't worry, he's not a friend of Dorothy. Just run with it, I need you here with me, not being sent on extended R & R again.' She scratched her head thoughtfully. 'By the way, did your new woman, what's her name . . . ?'

'Bryony.'

'Oh, yes, Bryony. Did *she* see this shadowy figure?'

'No. He disappeared as soon as I pointed towards him.'

'Shame, it would have helped to have another pair of eyes see him.'

'Tell me about it,' he grumbled. 'But she was in the cab by that time, and the station buildings were not in her line of vision.'

'When are you seeing her again?' The words were out of her mouth before she could stop them. 'Sorry, Joseph, it's none of my damned business what you do. Hell, I must have sounded just like your mother!'

'Believe me, you are nothing like my mother.' Joseph gave her a rueful smile. 'And to be honest, I'd planned on seeing her at the pool tomorrow, work permitting. And I was going to ask her out for dinner on Saturday evening, but now I'm not sure if I should be planning anything, with Billy Sweet out there.'

She looked at him for a while, then gave a little shrug. 'I'm not sure what I'd do. But as I said, it's none of my business and I shouldn't have asked.'

For some reason that she couldn't explain, not even to herself, she really didn't want to know about Bryony. 'Now, I'd really better chase up these fingerprints.'

He stood up to go.

'Do you like pasta?' she asked suddenly.

'My favourite. Why?'

'Tonight. My cooking skills are hardly legendary, but my pasta is reasonably edible. And if it is rubbish, hopefully enough Scotch should make it seem passable.'

'I'm sure it will be great,' said Joseph. 'Did you mean it about the toothbrush?'

'Oh yes. No way are you leaving Cloud Fen tonight, Sergeant. And I haven't just spent a fortune doing up the guest room to have no one stay in it!'

Joseph didn't answer immediately, but just nodded as he went out, then turned and said. 'Thanks, I do appreciate it. This won't be easy.'

Nikki felt a pang of sadness. She'd been in some seriously bad places herself in the past. 'I know, Joseph, and if there was any other way, but . . .'

'If people are going to die, I have no choice, do I?'

'I'm afraid you don't.' She touched his arm lightly. 'But that doesn't make it any easier, does it?'

'No one in their right mind would want to walk back into a nightmare. Let's just hope it turns out to be a cathartic experience, shall we?'

Nikki watched him leave and shivered, because she knew that whatever kind of experience Joseph was going to have, it was going to be far from cathartic.

CHAPTER TWELVE

Joseph crunched the gears, and uncharacteristically swore out loud. He should take more care on these lethal marsh lanes. They concealed insidious little bends that sneaked out of nowhere and with the tall, reedy marsh grass on the boggy verges, and the deep ditches either side . . . ? He shivered. If you finished up in a ditch, you could be there for a week before someone found you.

With an effort, he pulled himself together and tried to relax. Pretend it's just supper with a good friend. A few drinks, then a few more, and let the alcohol loosen the tongue. Share some deep secrets, have another drink, and crash out. Simple.

He laughed bitterly. He hadn't done that for many a year, not since . . . he abruptly brought his thoughts to a halt. It was far too soon to be going there.

Joseph slowed down and made himself take in the view over this weird water-world. It certainly was a strange place, and he wasn't sure if he loved it or hated it. For one thing, it was rare to find a place that completely wrecked your sense of perspective. You could go up on the sea bank, and if the east wind would allow you to stand upright and see clearly, you could stare into infinity. Or so the long, straight paths that disappeared into the horizon would have you believe. The marshes, the rivers, the great endless fields, and the ever-present 360 degrees of sky, could reflect and magnify your moods like no other place he had ever been, and he had travelled more than most. If you were sad, the remoteness echoed your misery, but if you were happy, the sheer magnitude of the sky above, the clouds forming new landscapes every moment, could lift you to unimaginable heights.

With every trip he made, he felt more confused about it. He smiled to himself. One thing was certain, DI Galena loved it. She was a different person when she was out here. She belonged, and Joseph could *feel* her closeness to the place.

He dropped a gear and eased around one of those long, and incredibly deceiving bends, before continuing his train of thought.

The boss and Cloud Fen. It was quite strange. Nikki Galena was a tough, independent woman, and a bloody good copper. She might have tempered down her tunnel-visioned obsession for ridding the streets of drug dealers, but she was still steely and driven. Someone who you would place in a city, or at very least a town like Greenborough, not out here in these misty groves of solitude. Maybe she needed them, to rid her mind of the grim happenings that her job insisted she deal with on a daily basis. Maybe this was her security blanket. Perhaps she wrapped herself in the sea-frets to free herself from the dreadful things that man did to man. A place of escape.

Joseph smiled and sighed. In the distance he could see the outline of Cloud Cottage Farm, and he felt both relieved that he'd survived the marsh lanes, and apprehensive about what the night may bring.

The farmhouse looked welcoming. Evening sunlight glinted off the windows, and he thought that it would be good to arrive home each night, and find something like this waiting for you. Good, but not perfect, because after years of being alone, he was coming to realise that *alone* wasn't what he wanted. It suited the boss, and until recently, it would have suited him. He turned onto the lane that led to her home, and wondered why his change of heart? It had to be his brush with the Grim Reaper.

Joseph slowed down and saw the gates were wide open for him. It was time to let the melancholy stuff go. Time to paint on another face.

He swung in and parked around the back of the property, next to a big old red brick barn. He jumped out, took a deep breath of the ozone-laden air, then went round and retrieved a bulging plastic bag and a small overnighter from the boot. At least he had the first part of the evening planned, even though he knew it was purely a diversionary tactic. He would salvage the meal. If the boss was such a pants cook, she would relish his help, and he loved to cook. Chopping and dicing, blending and sautéing was *his* way to unwind, to escape.

He walked around to the back door, recalling what she had told him about no one using the front, and vaguely wondered why he had bothered to lock the car. As he waited for her to answer his knock, he decided that some therapeutic cooking would definitely serve him well, because if there were ever a time when he needed to relax, it was now.

* * *

'Okay, so where did you learn to do all that?' asked the boss, clearly impressed. 'And so quickly! I'd still be reading the instructions on the pasta packet.'

Joseph glanced down at the old pine table, now colourful with bowls of steaming pasta and sauce, green salad, tomatoes and olives, and richly aromatic garlic and herb bread.

'College. I'd seen some of my fellow student's pasty faces and pimples, and decided that I was going to pass out with diplomas and degrees, not malnutrition and scurvy.' He picked up a bottle of Merlot that had been left to breathe while he cooked. 'Red okay for you, ma'am?'

'Red, pink, white, all okay for me, thank you.' The boss sighed happily and took two glasses down from a Welsh dresser. 'And we're off duty tonight, Joseph. So on this occasion, Nikki is fine.'

He poured the wine into the glasses, and held his up to hers. 'Cheers, Nikki.'

'To you, Joseph.' The crystal made a small ringing sound. 'You have no idea how much better this meal is than the one I had planned.'

'I doubt it, ma . . . Nikki. I'm sure you are a perfectly good cook, it's just not your thing, that's all.'

'Not quite what my daughter used to tell me, but hey! Let's eat!'

Half way through the meal, Joseph lay down his napkin. 'I just wanted to say thank you for not making me fess up to my past in front of the team.' He sipped his wine. 'Frankly, I don't think I could have done it.'

'That would have been incredibly insensitive,' said Nikki. 'I may be a hard-arsed cow at times and I want to catch the killer, but not at the expense of my sergeant.'

Joseph nodded. There was something about the atmosphere in the old kitchen. They were sitting talking, as dozens of others must have done over several generations, and it felt warm and intimate. 'You do know that you are probably the only person I could share this with, don't you?'

Nikki looked at him across the top of her glass. 'Well, I guess we've been through a couple of pretty emotive situations in the short time we've known each other.' She smiled at him. 'And you were the one to accompany me 'down where it's twisted and dark' when I needed to offload. So I guess it's just a reversal of roles this time.'

Joseph decided that he felt very comfortable in this old room with the pine furniture, the Butler sink, the pottery chickens and the ancestral memories. He poured some more wine, and they finished their supper.

'Does cognac keep?' she asked, as he stacked plates into the dishwasher.

'Not in my house. But that's just due to my propensity for fine brandy. Why?'

'When the builders were clearing the attic to work on the wiring and the insulation, they found some old boxes belonging to my father. I brought them down to sort out and found an unopened bottle of cognac.' She raised an eyebrow at him. 'Worth a try, do you think?'

'Is it ever! What's on the label?'

'Several layers of dust, I should think.' She opened the larder and removed a tall straight bottle with two rather scuffed and faded off-white labels on the front.

Joseph carefully took it from her and his eyes widened. 'We can't drink this!'

'Oh, gone off has it? Then we'll revert back to the whisky and I'll pour that down the sink.'

'No!' Joseph almost choked at the threat of tipping the spirit away. 'This is a Croizet 1961! It's rare, Nikki, and would probably cost you over £300 to buy!'

'God, my father is a sneaky old devil! What on earth was he squirreling that away for?' She stared at the bottle in disbelief, then grinned and said, 'Oh well, at least its drinkable. I'll get a couple of balloon glasses, then we can do it properly.'

Joseph touched the bottle with something like reverence, then laughed out loud at his boss's total disregard for the heritage of such a fine spirit. But who was he to complain? He'd tasted some fine brandy before, but this would be a first.

Nikki returned from the lounge, glasses in hand. 'You do the honours, Joseph. The way I look at it is this; I never even knew it was there. My poor father doesn't know what year it is any more, sadly he doesn't even know his only daughter, so he won't be objecting. And if I'd never returned to live here, then that bottle would either have been left in the attic for some other bugger to lift, or taken to the dump, so . . . ?'

'Let's say the house is welcoming you home, shall we?'

'I like that. Want to go through to the sitting room, or would you rather stay here?'

'Stay here.' He replied without even thinking. 'I love the feel to this room.'

'That's what my mother always said. She said it felt safe, and even if she was on her own, she felt as if the family were around her.'

As Joseph carefully unsealed the bottle, he knew exactly what the perceptive woman had meant. 'Okay, here goes nothing!' He poured the amber liquid into the brandy balloons and gently sniffed one of them. 'Oh my! That is something else. Let's hope its anaesthetic properties are as good as its bouquet.'

Nikki took hers from him and sipped it tentatively. 'No way would I pay three hundred quid for it, but it is very nice. Thank you, Daddy.'

Joseph was lost for words. He just sat there smiling inanely and wishing he had been born to an indecently wealthy French family.

The silence that engulfed them was as comfy as a pair of old slippers, and Joseph suddenly knew that he had run out of excuses. There was nothing left to come between him and the horrors of his past.

'You said that when you go through a difficult time with someone, you feel very close to them afterwards, or words to that effect.' He stared into the glinting crystal goblet. 'So I think you'll understand when I say that it was like that with my army comrades. They say you're brothers in arms, but that doesn't even get close. Those men are everything to you. You love them in a way that . . .' he paused looking for the right words, but not truly finding them. 'You've got to have been part of something like that to know just how much your mates mean to you.'

He took another sip of the cognac and looked across at his boss. He had the feeling that she was a going to be a good listener. It took a very special person just to listen, and not butt in, criticize or compare your story to something from their own past.

'It was never my intended career, but I loved being a soldier, Nikki, and I was a good one.' A sigh slipped from between his lips. 'A natural.'

'I can believe that,' said Nikki softly. 'I've seen how you react under pressure.'

He nodded, and wondered how long he could make one sip of that rare cognac last.

'You already knew that I was with UK special forces. But I was actually part of an elite team that dealt with very delicate special ops. And I thrived on it, Nikki, until Billy Sweet poisoned everything.'

He gripped his glass tightly, and his next drink was more of a slug than a sip. He knew that Nikki's company, his relaxed surroundings and the brandy were making the telling of this story as easy as it would ever be, but he still wanted to run away before he had to fully enter that dreadful pit of memory.

Nikki seemed to sense his difficulty, and reached across to refill his glass. 'You had a bad mission, didn't you? Where were you?'

'Africa,' he whispered.

There was no turning back. Joseph set his jaw firmly forward. 'I know it's Sweet that you are interested in, but to appreciate what happened, you have to know a bit about what we were doing.' He took a deep breath. 'Four of us were sent out to the Democratic Republic of Congo to look for a small unit of men who had disappeared without trace.' He swallowed hard, as the filthy smells and the stinking heat rushed back at him. 'The country was a living nightmare. Hell on earth. Massacres, child soldiers, systematic rape, and a refugee crisis that helped to destabilize the whole of the eastern Congo. It was worse than anything I'd ever seen, and I'd been in some shit-holes before.' He swirled the cognac around and around in the glass, and tried to lose himself in the topaz vortex. 'No matter what I say, Nikki, it could never convey how terrible it was, but try to imagine this. In the area where we were deployed, three quarters of all the children had disappeared. Three quarters!' He closed his eyes and tried not to hear the heart-rending wails of the women.

'So why were the first group out there?' prompted Nikki, trying to keep her voice steady.

'It was to do with precious metals and minerals. The whole place is a great big geological treasure chest, but greed and the conflict have just left it like one blasted, shameful battlefield. The group had been sent to a village called Zutu. There was a mine there, one that was being overseen by European scientists and engineers. It had rich seams of valuable minerals. Not just gold, copper or diamonds, even though they were common enough, they were mining minerals like niobium, pyrochlore, coltan, and germanium. All needed by hi-tech industries, like for nuclear reactors or space technology.' Joseph shivered a little, even though the kitchen was still warm. 'We knew that one of the scientists had been murdered, and two engineers were missing, that's why the first group went out. To get the remaining staff to safety, and find and bring home the missing men.'

'But they disappeared too?'

'They accomplished their mission, retrieved the hostages and got the rest of the staff extracted by helicopter, but they went back to Zutu.'

Nikki frowned, but said nothing.

'They contacted HQ with their coordinates saying that they had discovered something else, something that intelligence had not briefed them about.' Joseph shifted uncomfortably in his chair. 'After that, they sent just one communication, regarding a neighbouring village called Ituga. A terrifying report about women and children being taken as slaves and forced to opencast mine minerals, sometimes with their bare hands, and give everything they found to their rebel captors. These women were also expected to prostitute themselves, and if they refused you can guess what happened to them. The unit's plan was to recon the other mine, assess the potential for an evacuation, and either request assistance or deal with it immediately. It was a covert mission, and imperative that the identity of the sponsor was concealed. It couldn't be known that the British government was involved, not in that hotbed of political shit.' He drank more brandy. 'My team was Kilo Charlie Zero. We were a four man patrol, and we shipped out as soon as communication with Ituga broke down.'

Joseph stood up and walked slowly around the kitchen, touching ordinary homely objects, as if trying to ground himself in the present. 'We found the unit in a cave close to the mine. Three of them had been butchered, and the fourth was sitting there with the bodies, too traumatised to speak.' He ran his hand across the cold surface of a marble chopping block. 'I'd served with one of them before, Terry Bourne, he was a fine soldier, and an extraordinary human being.' A picture of the tousle-haired man with a boxer's nose and a big smile came unbidden into his thoughts. Rough and tough on the outside, but inside, a rare gentleman. 'We radioed our findings in, got the bodies to a place of safety ready to be brought home, and took the remaining soldier with us. We requested a helicopter evacuation for him and our dead, but there was heavy rebel fighting close by and they couldn't comply. My commanding officer made the decision that we go in and finish the job ourselves.'

'Find out what was going on at the Ituga mine?'

'Yeah, and send back full intelligence,' Joseph sighed, 'And that's where it all went pear-shaped.' He flopped back down into his chair. 'I'm not sure if any of us really knew what happened, but we got a radio message telling us that a group of rebels had been seen bringing in a new batch of women and children. According to our information, they were being held in a large hut prior to selection for duties, and the rebels were regrouping ready for their next sortie in a cave close to the perimeter of the mine.'

Joseph licked his lips and steeled himself to speak. 'Our intel was wrong. It was the women who were in the cave that we attacked. Somehow in the bedlam that followed, we managed to get only two of the woman out, most of them died.' He glanced across at Nikki's face. It was set as if in stone, and he had no idea what she was thinking.

'And the children?' She finally asked.

'There were no children this time.'

Nikki's face softened. 'Thank God for small mercies. And Billy Sweet? Where does he fit in?'

Joseph took another gulp of his drink. This was the worse bit. The bit he had relegated to the deepest, darkest part of his memory. The accidental killing of the women had been devastating, life-destroying. But what had come next was the stuff of nightmares. He rubbed his hand across his mouth.

'We were hopelessly outnumbered, and we'd lost the element of surprise. We fell back, taking the two women and the silent soldier.' He stood up again, and began to pace. 'As night fell, we found a deserted building, an old shelter, a store of some kind. It was way outside the perimeter and well hidden.' Joseph saw it in his mind's eye, saw the sun-bleached wood and the corrugated metal sheets that served as a roof, and suddenly he was there, back in Africa.

'All clear!' he called out, as he checked the last part of the deserted shack. He relaxed a little, but kept his rifle at the ready. 'Get the women inside; it'll get cold pretty quickly.' He stood back as his comrades entered the building.

'It's going to be a long night, Bunny.' His friend, Cameron McBride, hitched up a rag of material that was hung at the glass-less window and tried to decide how best to keep guard until morning. 'The terrain sucks. Too many dead spots for snipers to hide in. Two hour watches, two men awake at all times, I reckon.'

'Yeah.' They called him Bunny because of his surname. He was the Easter Bunny.

'I'll take the first watch.'

'Me too,' added Teddy Churchill, wiping grime and other unspeakable substances from his boots.

'I'll sort out some rations, get the women and this lad fed.' Kenny Williams' dirty face crinkled up in frustration. 'Daren't risk a fire though, its cold grub or nothing.'

Joseph's stomach was in no fit state for food, hot or cold, and he was grateful to get outside into the night. The bloodbath in the mine was still playing itself out in his head. How could everything have gone so wrong?

He was still hearing the screams echoing around in his mind, when Teddy sidled up to him and whispered.

'There's movement down on the track, 500 metres south.'

They moved together into the darkness and watched the narrow road.

Joseph flipped down his night-vision sights, and saw figures huddled in the scrubby trees that flanked the track. 'Go get Cam and Kenny.'

Moments later, the four soldiers eased themselves further down the incline, to get a better look at their ghostly intruders.

They watched for a while, then Cam tapped his arm and gestured towards the shadows. 'They are women! Thank God! Some of them must have escaped!'

'Are they alone?' whispered Kenny.

'Can't see.'

'Bait,' murmured Teddy grimly. 'It's a trap.'

Joseph suddenly froze. 'Or a lure. To get us away from the shack.'

Cam inhaled sharply, then said, 'No, the squaddie's with them, the girls will be alright. He's a mess, but he's still a soldier.' His confidence faded. 'Surely they wouldn't . . . ?'

'I'm going back.' Joseph knew something was terribly wrong. 'One of you come with me.'

As he began to climb back up towards the shack, he felt Cam move in behind him. 'Bad vibes, man.'

Joseph didn't answer.

Like wraiths in the night, they drifted up to the door, and slipped inside.

The coppery, metallic smell hit them instantly, and it was something they were both horribly familiar with. Then they heard the sound. A weird, sing-song keening; like nothing Joseph had ever heard either before or since.

'Oh God, oh God,' whispered Cam.

The women were dead. They had been hogtied and their throats neatly slit. And sitting on his haunches in front of them rocking backwards and forwards, was the young soldier. When he realised that he was no longer alone, the horrible noise that was issuing from his throat ceased, and for the first time since they arrived in Ituga, he spoke.

Actually he screamed. 'They made me watch! The bastards made me watch!'

Joseph stared at him.

'They were waiting! They came in! They came in as soon as you'd gone!'

'And you let them do this!' Cam's voice was even louder.

'I couldn't do anything,' blubbered the young man.

'And they left you alone, did they? I don't fucking think so!' Cam sneered at the soldier. 'You ran away, didn't you? You shitty little coward! You left these women to be slaughtered, and you hid!'

Until then Joseph had said nothing, then he asked, 'What's your name, soldier?'

'Sweet, sir. Billy Sweet. And I didn't run. They held me and made me watch, I swear. Then something scared them. They pushed me to the floor and ran off.'

Joseph's powerful flashlight lit up the man's eyes, and he shivered. It might have been the trauma he had suffered, or it might have been the light, Joseph was never sure, but the soldier had the unblinking pale eyes of a fish. Cold, dead eyes.

Suddenly Joseph was back in the kitchen, his breathing laboured, and Nikki was beside him, pressing the glass into his shaking hands.

'Take a sip, Joseph, go on. It's okay. *You're* okay, honestly.'

He took a long shuddery breath. 'Yes, I am aren't I?'

'Are you up to finishing the story, or . . . ?'

'I've come this far, let's get it done with.' He fought to control the shaking. 'When it was light, I searched for signs of intruders. There were none. I looked for a knife, but the terrain was too difficult. You see, the others believed he was a coward. I believed he was a murderer.' He stretched, trying to unknot his cramped muscles. 'A week later, I went back to that area to help mop up the rebels, and I heard talk. Talk about a baby-faced white soldier who had killed his own comrades.' Joseph looked at Nikki. 'I knew then I'd been right about Billy Sweet.'

'*He* butchered his friends?' Nikki's voice rose several octaves. 'And the women?'

'I believe so. But no witnesses came forward, and there was no proof. He was sent for psychological evaluation, given a long holiday somewhere nice, and allowed back on active duty two months later.'

'My God! How come they didn't see through him?'

'Psychopaths are brilliant and convincing liars.' Joseph shrugged. 'Ironic, isn't it? It was me that finished up on the scrapheap. I couldn't cope with what had happened at the mine. Those poor women died, and we killed them. They were supposed to be the rebels.' He gave one last sigh. 'Billy Sweet marched back to war, and I threw my rifle into a river and went home.'

'You never saw him again?'

'Just once. A week or so before I got my honourable discharge. I was helping out at a training camp in the Brecon Beacons, and I heard a group of soldiers complaining about one of the men. I heard them mention the name, and I *had* to go take a look at him. That's how come I know his face. He'd changed, of course. I don't think he was ever as young as he seemed. He'd got older, got tougher, and uglier. But his eyes were just the same.'

'Did he see you, and did he recognise you?'

'Oh yes. From the derisory smile on his evil face, I'd say, most definitely.'

Nikki looked across at him, her face drawn and sombre. 'And you believe that that was the man who jumped in front of your car in the Greenborough High Road?'

When he answered, the words were slow and deliberate. 'Yes. The man I saw was Billy Sweet.'

* * *

They talked on until one in the morning. They talked about families, about his soul-searching journey after he left the army, about the police force, and of living on the fen. She talked about Martin, and she even managed to let Joseph talk about Bryony, although she still felt that inexplicable feeling of discomfort deep inside when he mentioned the other woman.

Whatever, it was good to have him there. She had told the super that she could take care of herself, and she had never been frightened to be alone, but like it or not, Cloud Fen was a remote spot when there was a violent thug on the loose, and Joseph's presence was a distinct comfort.

She had given him the guest room, the room that had been hers as a child, and told him to try to catch the sunrise. The dawn over the marsh was as beautiful as anywhere in the world.

As she slipped into her own bed, she thought about Joseph, lying just a few feet away from her, and sighed. She hoped he would see the sun come up, sending dazzling flame fingers across the oily dark waters of the marsh. He could do with some bright light to warm the sadness that lived inside him.

CHAPTER THIRTEEN

Joseph had certainly seen the sunrise, as he had seen every other hour of the night. It had nothing to do not being tired. He had been exhausted, totally drained by everything that he had dredged up from the mud of his past. He was simply scared to sleep. He knew only too well the nightmares that were lurking in his head, waiting to crawl and slither into his dream sleep.

So he had got to see the dawn. And as Nikki had said, it had been spectacular. For a moment or two he had been able to lose himself in it, as the deep, blood-red orb that was the sun broke free of the dark horizon. He wished he could stay there, basking in its breathtaking beauty, but there was a killer close by, and the time for relaxing would only come when Sweet was behind bars, or beneath the ground.

Joseph had showered and gone downstairs to find Nikki, already dressed, and trying to prise a hunk of burnt toast from the toaster with a knife. He had declined the offer of a cooked breakfast and settled for coffee and a cold croissant, then after thanking her for both her hospitality and the incredibly good brandy, drove away from Cloud Fen and headed towards the swimming pool.

He had time for a half an hour's swim before he started work and it might help to wash away the shadows that still clung to him.

He had just completed his twentieth length, when the changing room door opened and Bryony walked in. She waved brightly and went to one of the poolside showers, allowing him time to take in the sight of her.

She was wearing a black sports swimsuit with a scarlet flash down the sides, and looked every inch the athlete. He ducked under the water for a moment and tried to understand why he felt such an idiotic delight in her being there.

'Hi, you!' she said as she broke the water inches from his face.

'Glad you made it,' he said, pushing his wet hair back from his face.

'As if I'd miss the chance of seeing you.' She grinned at him, then rolled over on her back and glided effortless up the half empty pool. 'Keep up, slowcoach!'

He pushed off and took a few powerful strokes, but he was still not even close to her. Bryony was completely at home in the water and moved through it with both grace and ease. He was not a bad swimmer, although nothing like he had been, even so he was not rubbish, but right now he felt like a lumbering whale next to a dolphin.

It took him about ten minutes to find a stroke that enabled him to keep up with her, and even then he was sure that she was slowing down to let him catch her.

The water felt good, and he didn't want to leave, but the big clock at the end of the pool was telling him otherwise. 'I've got to go.'

'So soon?' Water glistened on her smooth skin, and Joseph silently cursed the fact that he had to work.

'We've got a lot on, I'm afraid.'

'Big case, Mr Detective Sergeant?'

Joseph bit his lip and thought, yeah, big as they come and the timing stinks. 'Something like that.' He swam on his side towards the steps. 'So how about Saturday? Are we on for dinner?'

Bryony swam towards him and planted a light kiss on his cheek before plunging down beneath the bright blue water and swimming off.

'Take that as a "yes", shall I?' He called after her, then realised that he was not supposed to know where she lived. 'Where shall I pick you up?'

'I'll meet you at seven, outside that dreadful pub of yours,' she shouted.

He waved to her and pushed open the changing room door. That was just fine, but this time he'd make sure it was not heaving with policemen.

* * *

'We've got a match, Joseph.'

Nikki was already in the murder room, and sifting through a pile of fresh reports.

'On?' He threw his jacket over the back of his chair and moved to her side.

'Our execution victim. His name is Chris Forbes. His fingerprints turned up on the police computer. Nothing heavy, just some trouble over taking a car without the owner's consent.'

'Was he a local, ma'am?' asked Joseph.

'Yes, he's from the Carborough Estate. Bit of a rough family, but other than that one incident, he seems to have been clean.' She paused, then added, 'So why did he finish up dead?'

'I would think wrong place, wrong time. He simply had the misfortune to bump into something nasty in the night.' Joseph's eyes narrowed. 'None of Billy's other victims had done anything wrong either.'

'Maybe. The family has been informed and there's a liaison officer with them. Dave was in early so he went straight over, we'll talk to them later.' Nikki looked at him pensively. 'And Joseph, I suggest we keep everything that we discussed last night, just between us for the time being. And you need to try to keep your emotions under tight control, even if you see this man again.' She shook her head. 'Otherwise everything will have to come out in the open, and I don't want you to have to face all that, not officially, unless there is absolutely no other way.'

Joseph nodded. 'If we catch him it will be a different ball game, but until then I'll do my best to keep a lid on my reactions.' He gave her a relieved smile. 'I really appreciate that, thank you.'

'No problem. Now grab a pile of these reports and help me check them, and a very strong coffee may help.' She held out a sheaf of paperwork.

Joseph took them and grinned. 'Can you believe that brandy?

'I can't believe we drank half a bottle of the stuff, that's for sure!' She grimaced, 'Or maybe I can.' She flopped into a chair and looked up at him with a pained expression. 'You didn't actually go swimming earlier, did you?'

'Yup.' He felt a thrill run through him as he recalled those soft lips touch his cheek, 'And I'm glad I did.'

'Ah, Bryony.'

Joseph smiled and nodded, although he wondered if he had imagined a slight hint of disapproval.

'Then just keep your wits about you, Sergeant. Don't get too distracted.' Her old tone was back, so he just grinned and went to get the coffee.

As he placed the cups under the dispenser and waited, he glanced through the reports. Nothing leapt out, other than a memo from the SOCO who had checked Knot Cottage.

He returned to the murder room and put the drinks on the desk. 'You were right about whoever turned over Martin Durham's drum. The SOCO says it was a pro.'

'I said he was!' His boss frowned angrily. 'Your average blagger would never have disabled me that easily.'

She scanned the memo and made a snorting noise. 'No trace evidence found at scene. No fingerprints, footprints, stray hairs, no bloody nothing.'

'Are we surprised?'

'No, not at all. I just half hoped that we wouldn't have to wait for the DNA on that hair that I managed to yank from his scalp.'

'Makes it even more important that you did.'

'I suppose. I just wish things happened as fast as they do in *CSI* or *NCIS*.'

'I don't think the Fenland Constabulary's budget could run to a dedicated state-of-the-art forensics lab like Abby Sciuto's. We are lucky to have *cars*, even if half of them are clapped out! Sadly this is the real world.'

'And it's a psych ward run by the inmates.' Nikki threw up her hands. 'We've got this fabulous building, cost a fortune, and we have to sign in triplicate and wait for three weeks if we need a new stapler!' With a disgusted grunt she picked up the telephone that had shrieked out from the desk in front of her.

'Yes, DI Galena here. Oh, hello Rory.' She listened for a moment, then holding the receiver between her chin and her shoulder began sorting through the remaining reports. 'Got it! Yes, hang on.' She opened the thin envelope and began to read. After a second or two she said, 'But I don't understand.'

Joseph looked at her. Her voice had dropped to little more than a sigh.

'That seems impossible, Professor.' After a while she thanked him and hung up. 'The tox report on Martin. His bloodstream was flowing with doxepin hydrochloride, in the form of a drug called Sinepin. The professor thought he should draw my attention to it prior to delivering his full opinion.'

Joseph frowned. 'I don't remember seeing any drugs of that name at Knot Cottage.'

'There weren't any. I have a list of all the medication that he was legitimately taking, and all bar one were present in the report, and Rory is very concerned.'

'What kind of drug is this Sinepin?' he asked.

'No idea. The professor is bringing his preliminary findings over at lunchtime and he'll give us the details then.' Nikki picked up her coffee cup and stared into it. 'They couldn't have been recreational. Martin *never* took drugs. Hell, I've spent half my life with drug users, I'd have spotted signs.'

'They sound like prescription drugs,' said Joseph. 'So how did he get hold of them?'

The boss shrugged. 'This is getting more shitty by the hour.' She looked worried. 'And we should be getting our heads around Chris Forbes' murder.'

'I've been thinking about that. The type of rope that was used may be of help to us.' He sucked in air, then lowered his voice so that only she could hear him. 'Soldiers always have string or twine in their kit. I'll be interested to hear what kind it is.'

The boss said nothing, but just nodded.

'And the knots the killer used. I should have been more attentive, but the shock of seeing the body in that position, I just . . . I just had to get out of there.'

'Don't be too hard on yourself, Joseph. It's hardly surprising, is it?' There was compassion in her voice. 'But if you can, check the photographs as soon as we have them, I'm sure the report will pick up on the way the victim was bound.'

'I'll certainly be able to tell you if it was a military-style attack.'

'Let's just wait and see, shall we? Part of me is still hoping that this is nothing to do with you.' The boss gave him a un-enthusiastic look. 'Although the other part is pretty sure that's not the case.' She closed a file with a snap. 'But let's not jump the gun. Hard evidence is what we require.'

Joseph nodded, then looked up as the door opened and Dave Harris walked in. His face was drawn and his eyes deep and sad. 'That's one side of police work that I hate.'

'Don't we all,' said Nikki. 'So, anything helpful from the parents?'

Dave sat down heavily and shook his head. 'All but useless, guv. Chris Forbes lived at home, he was thirty-four, but he was not bright, if you catch my drift?'

'Learning difficulties?' asked Joseph.

Dave nodded. 'Not severe, but his younger brother said that the lift never went up to the top floor. Chris was happy in his own little fantasy world, and sadly the family were happy to let him live there.'

'Something they are no doubt regretting,' murmured Nikki.

'He didn't work, and spent most of his time in pool halls with his drop-out mates. To be honest, I don't think he was bad, just highly impressionable and very trusting.'

'And no one took him too seriously, I suppose?'

'That's the point, Sarge. Who listens for long to a Walter Mitty? His brothers admitted that he'd been going on about some "brilliant bloke" who bought him drinks, but as none of them had actually met him, and as they didn't give a toss who Chris was drinking with, we have no description.'

'Where did he drink? Or play pool? Maybe we can track this new friend that way?' said Nikki.

'The Plough on River Street was his local, guv. Cat's checked it out already. He *was* there with a stranger recently, but no one took any notice of him. The description was hazy, just kind of ordinary, non-descript, and he always wore a knitted beanie hat.' Dave pulled a face. 'The only thing that did come up was that Chris called this new friend by a nickname.'

'And that was?'

'He called him Snaz, ma'am.'

Joseph fought to stifle an involuntary gasp, and when he glanced up he saw Nikki staring at him.

'Well, that's a start, Dave. Go grab yourself some breakfast, okay?'

As the door closed, she raised her eyebrows enquiringly. 'Right, Joseph, what spooked you?'

Fighting to keep his voice level, he said, 'The Russian special forces soldiers are called *Spetsnaz*, ma'am. Billy Sweet held them in pretty high regard, and he always referred to them as the Snaz.' He looked at her enquiringly. 'Now where do you sit on the subject of coincidences?'

* * *

An hour later, Cat knocked lightly on Nikki's door and stuck her head around. 'Got a minute, ma'am?'

'Only if you've got me something on Chris Forbes' friend Snaz?'

'I went back to the Plough, ma'am, to see one of Chris's old friends. This bloke Liam mentioned seeing Chris with a stranger outside a dodgy pool parlour down by the docks. A dirty dive called the Paper Wall.'

'Want me to check it out, ma'am?' asked Joseph.

'No offence, Sergeant, but I think we'll leave it to Cat. She has the knack of blending in rather well in dubious joints, don't you, detective?' She smiled at Joseph. 'Sorry, but she'll get more than you from their kind of clientele. You look a tad too wholesome for the Paper Wall.'

'You make it sound as if I should be selling *War Cry*,' said Joseph huffily.

'If the cap fits, mate!' laughed Cat. 'You leave this one to me. I have a rare talent for disguise when undercover.'

'I know, I've seen you in action, remember?' Joseph closed the report he'd been reading.

'So, what am I trying to find out, while I'm stamping on the cockroaches?'

'If anyone can give us an ID on a man with the tag, Snaz.'

'You do know they won't have CCTV, and their security consists of a eighteen stone, tattooed woman who looks harder than Desperate Dan?'

'You mean Gloria,' Nikki smiled. 'Yeah, start with her. As long as she wasn't already juiced up by the time Chris and his new friend got there, she would have clocked them alright. Get round there as soon as they open, okay?'

'Can't wait.'

'Well, if that's the case, why don't you rope in Yvonne and Niall and go around *all* the local pool halls and pubs to try to find someone who can finger this mystery man that Chris had been spending time with. We need a face, Cat.'

'No problem, ma'am.' Cat gathered up her jacket and headed for the door. 'Time for a swift change of clothes, and then show us committed.'

Nikki glanced up at the clock. Professor Wilkinson should be with them shortly with the preliminary reports on Martin's death, and it was a report that was worrying the life out of her. Strangely, even the execution of Chris Forbes couldn't rid her of the constant nagging anxiety about her old neighbour and his horrible death.

'More coffee, ma'am?' asked Joseph.

'Make that three. Rory has his black, no sugar.'

A few moments later Rory Wilkinson stuck his head round the door, and waved a large white paper bag. 'I come bearing gifts! And I don't mean gruesome goodies from the path lab either.'

No matter how grim her thoughts had been, this unorthodox forensic genius always managed to bring a smile to her face. 'Then welcome, Professor. Grab a seat. Joseph is already getting refreshments.'

'Which should go nicely with these.' He tore open the bag and revealed three enormous chocolate éclairs. 'Called in at the *boulangerie* en route. *C'est manifique, n'est ce pas?*'

'Oh Lord! I should say so! If Joseph doesn't get a move on he'll be unlucky.'

As if on cue, Joseph shouldered the door open and entered carrying three large mugs of coffee. 'Haven't missed anything, have I?'

'Nearly, but not quite,' said Nikki, looking longingly at the thick chocolate covering the cream-filled choux pastry. 'Right, so are these to help sweeten the mood, knowing about your other gift, the one in the giant brown manila folder?'

'Ah, so astute! Every inch the detective, ma'am.' He grinned. 'But no, actually I missed breakfast and I'm starving.' His face became a little more serious. 'Although I have to say, the tidings that I bring are by no means straightforward.'

'As if I thought they would be,' sighed Nikki, taking a bite out of her éclair. 'So, whenever you are ready?'

The pathologist put down his coffee mug, dabbed at the corners of his mouth with a white handkerchief, and sat back. 'Well, Mr Durham died as the result of his fall from the church tower, this we know. His injuries were a little different to those normally expected from a fall from such a great height, because of the fact that he hit the wall and not a flat hard surface. He shattered his spinal column at the areas of the second, third and fourth lumbar vertebrae, severing the spinal cord and shearing through the arteries.' Rory pointed to the folder. 'There's much more, of course. It's all in there. Crushed ribs, massive head injury and inter-cranial bleeds, caused as his head was swung down against the wall when his back broke. Liver damaged, et al., but this is to be expected, wholly understandable, and it's none of this that worries me.'

Nikki was feeling a mild nausea sweep over her. This was an old friend that Rory was describing, and it didn't make pleasant listening. She tried not to think of broken, splintered bones and quickly said, 'It's the toxicology report, isn't it?'

Rory nibbled delicately on his éclair and nodded, 'Mm, exactly.' He removed a thick batch of papers from his file, skimmed through them, then laid them on the desk and looked up. 'I'll try to simplify this for you. And please don't think that I'm insulting your intelligence, dear hearts, but forensic toxicology is complex, and it's still one of the most difficult tasks to prove death by poisoning.'

'He was poisoned?' asked Joseph, almost choking on his coffee.

'Oh no, well, not in the way that you mean, but, there again, one *could* say that . . .'

'Rory?' Nikki bit her lip. 'Come to the point.'

'Sorry. What I mean is this; Martin Durham killed himself by leaping from the tower. Fact. He did this because he was under the effect of a powerful hallucinogen. Fact. But did he purposefully take the drug himself, or was it administered to him by person or persons unknown? Unproven.'

'Tell us about the drugs,' said Joseph. 'He had a real cache of them at his home.'

'And thereby hangs another mystery,' replied Rory. 'But let's take this step at a time, shall we? We took samples from his blood, urine, stomach contents, liver, what was left of it, and his vitreous humour. You see, you are not just looking for the toxins, you are looking for their effects, in the form of metabolites. So, using a combination of mass spectrometry and gas spectrometry we isolated and identified samples of all his prescription drugs, bar one. *Plus* another substance, the one that turned out to be doxepin hydrochloride.'

Nikki stared across the desk at Rory. 'You just said, "bar one". Why would he take all his meds and leave one out? Is it something that he didn't need to take regularly?'

'Oh no, it's part of his daily regime.'

'And the other one? The hallucinogen? What would that be taken for?'

'It's used, quite legitimately, as an anti-anxiety drug, an antidepressant. It's similar to Amitriptyline. But, as with a lot of chemicals, it's not the drug itself, it's the quantity that is taken. And this was a dose large enough to trigger an acid trip in an elephant.'

'But Martin never used recreational drugs. He didn't smoke and he didn't drink.'

'Then that could have made its effect on him even more severe.'

Joseph placed his mug on the desk and stared at it. 'There were no pharmaceutical company boxes or bottles in Martin's home that were antidepressants, of that I am sure. And as his GP never mentioned them, how did he get hold of them, and why take it anyway? By accident?'

'That's possible, of course,' said Rory. 'But frankly, I doubt it. It's the missing tablet that has me foxed.' He pushed his glasses further up onto the bridge of his nose and peered at Nikki. 'From what I understand, Martin Durham was a meticulous man, and very careful with his medication. You knew him, so am I right?'

'Bear in mind I never knew he took medication, but otherwise, most certainly. His house was spotless. He cooked wholesome food and exercised regularly.'

'I deduced that much from the state of his body and the contents of his stomach.' He puffed out his cheeks and made a low, whistling sound. 'So why miss one tablet? Anyone who takes pills regularly has a specific routine, and if those tablets are life sustaining, you are very particular indeed.'

'Common sense would dictate that somehow he took the Sinepin accidentally, believing it to be his other tablet,' said Joseph thoughtfully. 'Do they look alike, Professor?'

'Not at all. The antidepressant is a brightly coloured gelatine capsule, the colour varying as to the strength of the dose, and his own drug was a small yellow tablet. No way would he have confused them.'

'Then he was deliberately given it, by someone else,' muttered Nikki. 'Maybe the man who ransacked his cottage?'

'This is ludicrous!' exclaimed Joseph. 'We are talking about an ordinary man. Someone who lives in a small village, in a time-warp cottage, with a love for the marshes, and not a scrap of scandal to his name. Why on earth should he be targeted, maybe even killed, by some shady professional hitman? I just doesn't make sense.'

'We need to find out more about Martin's past,' said Nikki flatly. 'How much do we really know about the people around us? Not much, I'm willing to wager.'

Rory nodded. 'For what it's worth, I really think that's where you *should* start. If he were given that drug intentionally, then you *have* to find out who is behind it. This time just one man died, but he could have taken any one of those poor souls up on the viewing platform with him. And there were children there, weren't there?'

Nikki nodded dumbly. She knew a bit about hallucinations. She'd seen enough junkies on bad trips. Kids whose senses were telling them lies, making them believe all manner of nightmares. A string of questions flooded into her mind. What on earth had Martin become involved in? What could be so awful that he should be sent to such a terrible death? Or was she just being paranoid? There were most likely other far more common-or-garden reasons for what happened, and maybe the break-in was just that, and the intruder really did just land her with a lucky punch. Maybe.

'And then there is my other little mystery regarding his medication.' Rory adjusted his glasses again. 'I did a little ferreting of my own, because I was puzzled to see that most of his tablets were issued by Dr Latimer of Cloud Fen, and two others came in plain white boxes with the tablet name and dosage on the side, but no maker's name. They most certainly did not come from any of the suppliers that I know.'

'Internet?' enquired Joseph. 'Isn't that where people self-medicate themselves these days?'

'Ah-ha! Two minds! But no, dear Joseph. Sadly my mini-investigation has proved us wrong. I've no idea where these drugs come from.'

Nikki looked towards Joseph. 'Time for you to take another trip to Dr Latimer's surgery, I think.'

The pathologist smiled, 'I have my doubts that she will know any more than we do, but I'd be interested to see her expression when you tell about this little conundrum. And I have to leave this with you now.' Rory pushed the file across the desk to her. 'Don't read it after dark.' He took another, thinner file from his bag. 'Now we come to the unfortunate Mr Christopher Forbes. And this is much more straightforward. A deliberate and ruthless murder, carried out with minimum fuss and scarily skilfully executed.'

'A professional?' asked Nikki, before Joseph could speak.

'Most definitely. Knew exactly the right amount of pressure to use, and the correct angle of the blade for a clean and fatal cut.'

'A contract killer, then?'

Rory took a deep breath. 'I'd say this man had more of a military background. Hitmen prefer guns. It's impersonal. A gun distances the killer from the victim. You have to be very sure of yourself, and very cool, to use a knife. Not many people have the nerve to get *that* up close with their prey.'

Nikki looked at Joseph, but his face was set in stone. She knew he'd just had the confirmation he'd been waiting for.

'And there was very little trace evidence on the body. Probably nothing, after we've eliminated the few odd hairs on his clothing. Frankly I'm not expecting much at all.' Rory stretched. 'The only thing that we have with a connection to the murderer is the rope that he used to tie the man, and sadly it's pretty common stuff. The kind you

118

can pick up in any marine chandlers or outdoor pursuit store.'

Nikki heard Joseph murmur the word 'damn' under his breath.

'So apart from a positive gallery of photographs, that is all I have for you at present, and I need to get back. So, it's over to you, my friends.' Rory stood up. 'And *do* let me know what you discover about that mysterious missing pill. It's the sort of accursed thing that bugs your every waking moment, and then robs you of your sleep.'

'Isn't it just,' said Nikki vehemently. 'But I'll get to the bottom of it, Professor. I promise you that.'

'Oh, I'm sure you will, Inspector dearest, just don't take too long. I shall be positively haggard with worry! And you've no idea just how much I value my beauty sleep!'

With a curt bow and a flourish of his hand, he was gone, and Nikki and Joseph were left in the silent office. Rory's exit had taken with it every ounce of humour and life from the room.

Suddenly Joseph stood up. 'I should go and see Dr Latimer.'

Nikki frowned at him. 'In a moment, but don't you have anything to say about Chris Forbes' death?'

'What's to say, ma'am? He was killed by a military-trained operative. I knew that.'

'We'll find him, Joseph. Someone at the Paper Wall will give us an ID, then we can look for him in earnest.'

'*I* can give you an ID, ma'am, but if he doesn't want us to find him, we won't find him. End of.'

'This isn't the jungle, Sergeant, it's a market town in the Fens! You can't sneeze here without half the town offering you a hankie.' She looked at him long and hard. 'And we still have no absolute proof that it is Billy Sweet. This could be some nasty scam. Have you considered that there may be someone out there who wants to get at you for putting their nearest and dearest in the Scrubs or somewhere equally as salubrious? An old case? Someone who has decided it's payback time? It does happen, Joseph.'

Joseph didn't answer, but just stared down at his feet.

'We have to be objective, you know that,' Nikki reasoned. 'It's like Martin's death. I *knew* him, and my gut tells me that someone engineered his demise deliberately, but I have to consider that it may have just been a terrible accident. Maybe some half-brain in the Wild Goose thought he looked a bit down, and stuck a little helper in his orange juice, who knows? Maybe something went wrong in the pharmaceutical factory, perhaps a rogue tablet got mixed in with others, and he'd taken it before he realised. I don't want to, Joseph, but I have to look down all the avenues.'

'I guess you're right.' His voice was low and almost husky. 'I'm sorry, ma'am, but it's hard to think about any other scenario when it all seems so clear, so vividly clear.'

'I know.' Nikki did know, but right now it wasn't helping. 'Look, maybe you should concentrate on Martin for a bit, and I head up the hunt for our assassin. I don't mean permanently, just until we've gathered a bit more information. Keep each other up to date with everything, and back each other up as and when required. How does that sound?'

'Sure.' He gave her a weak smile. 'Maybe it's for the best.'

'Okay, so bugger off to dear Helen Latimer, and the best of British.'

'What *is* it with you two?' asked Joseph, a hint of his usual humour creeping back into his voice.

'Old history, Joseph, very old history. Probably neither of us can honestly remember why we finished up as such eye-gouging adversaries, but . . .' she gave a little laugh, 'we are so used to bitching about each other that it comes as second nature.'

'Mm,' Joseph looked at her shrewdly. 'I'm willing to bet the good doctor knows *exactly* why you two don't get on. Maybe I should ask her about it.'

'Do that, sonny-boy, and you'll be back in Fenchester before you can blink!'

'Ha!' His grin widened, 'Caught you there! But when these two cases are over, I want to know *all* the sordid gossip, okay?'

'Sort this mess, and I'll be glad to sit down with the rest of that brandy, and bare my very soul! Sordid bits and all! Now, sod off, Sergeant, and find me some answers, some I can believe in.'

CHAPTER FOURTEEN

As Joseph drove towards Cloud Fen, Nikki delivered a diluted version of her report to the superintendent. She had decided not to dwell on the suggestion that Martin Durham may have met with his maker by design. It would not take much for Rick Bainbridge to remove her from the case, and any suggestion by her of foul play could be misconstrued as 'being emotionally too close.' So as far as she could, she concentrated on the death of Chris Forbes.

'Sir, we have a well-liked, although highly impressionable man, not retarded, but certainly not the brightest light on the Christmas tree, murdered by a trained killer. And we have unearthed nothing so far to indicate a motive for the killing.'

The super thought about it for a moment, then said, 'Well, it seems that he frequented public houses and pool halls, maybe he overheard something he shouldn't and the killer didn't trust him not to shoot his mouth off.'

'Possibly, sir. We'll know more when we get an ID on this man who had been hanging around with him. If the mystery man was the murderer, then it sounds as if Chris was being groomed, although for what, I can't imagine.'

'A clinical killing like this is very rare, Nikki. It's the sort of thing you hear about in war zones, not Greenborough.' His face screwed up into a leathery mask of concern. 'As a matter of interest, what did Joseph make of it?'

Nikki used one of Joseph's own blank expressions, and said 'Much the same as you, sir. Why?'

'Just wondered.'

Joseph's past was not common knowledge, and although the superintendent knew about his background, he was unaware that Nikki also knew, and right now, she wanted it to stay that way.

'And where are we with your suicide case, Martin Durham?' continued the super.

'There is some concern over the drugs in his system brought up by the tox report. Joseph has driven out to speak to his GP about it. And nothing's shown up from the break-in at Knot Cottage.'

'Oh well, keep me up to speed on that.' He sighed and shook his head. 'And thinking about suicides, all this has rather put paid to the work that you were doing for me, hasn't it? The statistics on un-natural deaths?' His face darkened. 'You wouldn't believe it, we have an execution-style murder on our patch, and still I'm being asked for bloody useless figures and sodding reports. It's crazy.'

'We've not given up on it, sir. We'll do our best to get something together for you.' Nikki suddenly felt sorry for him. Rick had been a great copper, but slowly he had come to hate everything that promotion had brought with it. There were times when she knew that he would rather be back on the beat, than organising flow charts and initiatives, and juggling budgets. 'Don't worry, sir. Joseph is a wizard with figures, if there is an anomaly there, I'm sure he'll spot it.'

'The murder comes first, Nikki. I know that. But if you can sneak an hour or two on them sometime, I'd be grateful.'

Nikki left his office and wandered down to the canteen in search of a snack and a hot drink. Her head was a mess. Joseph was worrying her senseless and she had no one to talk to about it.

She took her lunch back to her office and half-heartedly unwrapped an unappetizing-looking sandwich. Unless there was something that Joseph wasn't telling her about this Billy Sweet, she could not fathom why some psycho should suddenly leap back from the past and start stalking him.

She chewed slowly and wondered if she should try to get some kind of trace on Sweet. Not that she had a clue where to begin. Joseph had mentioned that he had gone to work for a private security force, which sounded very much like the man was now a mercenary soldier and that meant his movements would be very hard to track. Probably impossible.

She sipped her drink. She really didn't believe that Joseph had held anything back. He honestly seemed as confused about what was happening as she did. And if he was right, and it was Sweet, why kill a vulnerable man like Chris Forbes? She picked up a pen and scribbled answers on piece of paper.

1) The super's idea. CF was silenced for knowing something.
2) The killer's a psycho, he doesn't need a reason.
3) Practice. CF was not his primary target.
4) Mistaken identity.
5) CF could have been anyone, he was killed purely to get Joseph's attention.

Nikki ringed number 5. Then added, *To freak Joseph out.* She underlined it in heavy strokes. No matter how much she hated the thought, Joseph did seem to be the key. And if that were the case, how much longer could she keep this under wraps?

She finished her mouthful, threw the rest in the bin and stood up. She needed a recognisable face to that new 'friend' of Chris Forbes, and she needed it before the shit hit the fan for Joseph.

* * *

Joseph pulled the Ford off the main road, and headed back on himself along a narrow lane that led to a small wetlands nature reserve. He knew that he should be getting back to the station, but he felt overwhelmed by the sudden need to get away from the furore of the murder enquiry. He wanted a few minutes alone, to think. And as he had driven away from Cloud Fen, he remembered what Nikki Galena had once told him about going to the sea bank 'to get her head together.'

After half a mile he pulled into a sheltered parking area almost completely surrounded by trees and bushes. A weather-beaten painted sign told him that parking was free, although cars were left at the owner's risk. Too right, he thought. Secluded and miles from anywhere. The perfect spot for a bit of vehicle vandalism.

He locked his car and offered a small prayer that it would remain as he left it, complete with CD player, and hopefully all its wheels, then followed the path through the trees and up to the high river bank.

To his left were the lagoons, shallow watery pools frequented by waterfowl and waders, and to his right, the river bank ran for miles out into the marshes, and finally on to the estuary. It wasn't Nikki's famous sea bank, but it was the next best thing.

He looked both ways, then chose the lagoons, and seeing no one else around, wandered along the track to one of the dilapidated bird-hides.

The steps up were rickety, and the door was little better. It swung open with a creak loud enough to scare every bird on the east coast. Inside there was a weird smell of salt-damp wood and a mustiness that was less than pleasant. He opened the observation flap, hooked it up and sat on the wooden bench to look out.

At first he saw only sedge grass, reeds and the oily dark waters of the lagoons, but after a while he realised that there was movement all around him. Tiny warblers clung to the reeds, their harsh repetitive song echoing across the pools. A heron stood seemingly motionless in the shallow water, and above him a skylark's song rose and fell continuously.

He knew he didn't have long, but this was what he needed right now. A place of solitude; somewhere to put his thoughts in order. He took a deep breath, held it, then allowed his mind to go over what had just occurred at the Cloud Fen Surgery.

Predictably, Dr Latimer had been furious. She had never prescribed any form of antidepressants for Martin Durham, and flatly denied any knowledge of the other two types of tablets that he had been taking. She had stared at the photo of the plain white boxes in complete amazement, and demanded to know where he had got them from. She had then proceeded to blame Joseph and his team for not comparing Martin's medical notes with the drugs they had found at the house. It had taken a while to placate her, and even then, Joseph had finally left feeling ill at ease. Either Martin had been seeing two doctors, or he had been obtaining drugs illegally, and that just didn't gel with the kind of person that his sister and the DI had described. He had made a mental note to ring the oncology clinic that conducted Martin's yearly follow-up, maybe they could throw some light on his mixture of medication.

He stretched his aching back and watched as a curlew probed its long down-curved beak into the edge of the water searching for food. And Martin Durham was not the only problem. There was the other matter, the one he could hardly bear to think about. The fact that poor, trusting Chris Forbes might have died because of him.

He chewed on a rough nail, and tried to relax the turmoil in his head. He cursed softly. It really wasn't fair. Until the moment when he had seen that horrible face peering through his windscreen, things had been good. Really good. He had come to terms with himself. Accepted that he couldn't change the horrors of his past, but that he must not let them ruin the present or his future. He had let the bitterness of his divorce go, and made inroads to some kind of peace with his daughter. He had taken a new job with a boss that he had learnt to respect, and he'd survived an attack. Yes, things were good. Until Billy Sweet's ugly face had appeared and tainted everything.

Joseph looked down, and saw deep indentations in the palms of his hands. He had clenched his fists so tightly that his nails had almost broken the skin.

How could things swing around so quickly? How . . . ?

His mobile broke the silence, and for a second, made his heart race. He flipped it open expecting to see the guv'nor's name, but to his surprise, it was Bryony.

He stared at it, but didn't answer it. Apart from his job, she was the only happy thing in his life at present, and he was scared to get involved with her. If Sweet was after him, there would be no better way to get to him, than through a girlfriend. So for her sake he should keep his distance.

The tinny ringtone seemed to go on for ever, but finally it stopped, and the quiet in the small hut became almost deafening. Sweet was even souring his hopes and dreams.

He pushed the phone back into his pocket, then closed down the hatch. He should get back.

Remarkably the car was still there, and in one piece. 'Thank you,' he murmured to his unseen angels, and unlocked it. As he did, he heard his phone bleep, telling him that he had a text message.

"Am having a seriously shitty day. A drink would help. Would your BIG CASE allow it? Ring me. Bry"

Joseph stared at the message, his finger hovering over the reply button. If he didn't contact her, she wouldn't wait for ever. And what if he was wrong about everything? Maybe some villain from his past *had* decided to set him up for a fall. It would appear that he was still pretty shaky after his recent trauma, so perhaps he was letting his imagination get things out of proportion. By letting Bryony go, he could be ruining a chance for some happiness in his life.

He stared at his mobile phone, and felt like Don Camillo talking to JC, weighing up his worldly options against his moral conscience. With a sigh, he closed his phone and pushed his key into the ignition. JC wins. The risk was too great.

* * *

The murder room was now alive with CID officers. A series of photographs, dates, times, places and names were spread over the big glass case board. Most of it he could handle easily, but the picture of Chris Forbes clinical assassination made him shudder every time he looked at it.

Dave Harris acknowledged him with a wave.

'Anything new, Dave?' he asked, sliding behind his desk

'Not yet, Sarge. Cat's just rung me and said they were having no luck at all. Reckoned she'd never heard the words 'average,' 'nondescript,' and 'ordinary' used so often.'

'And I suppose he always wore a hat or a hoody?'

'Exactly. Making it almost impossible to give a description.'

'Is the boss in, Dave?'

'Fuming quietly in her office. I think she'd hoped that we would have been able to circulate at least an e-fit by now.' He pulled a face. 'I hope you've got some good news for her if you're planning on going in there unarmed.'

'Thankfully I've got a few phone calls to make first.' He logged in to his computer and searched the file on Martin Durham until he found the name of the oncology clinic that he had attended. He scribbled down the number and lifted the phone.

'Oncology suite. Good afternoon. How may I help you?'

The voice sounded too young to be anything other than a Brownie, but he explained who he was and asked to be put through to whoever was in charge. After a while he was passed on to a fully-fledged Girl Guide. He swiftly explained the situation, then gave her the police station number and asked her to ring them direct to confirm his authenticity.

It took only five minutes for his desk phone to ring.

'I'd be glad to assist, Detective Sergeant Easter, but I'm afraid we do not have a patient of that name.'

'But I have copies of reports sent to a Dr Helen Latimer in Cloud Fen. Now I can understand that you would prefer not to discuss this over the phone, but . . .'

'Sorry, Sergeant, it's not that. I've checked our database thoroughly. We have never treated anyone of that name. And before you ask, I have cross-checked the spelling.'

Joseph thanked her and slowly replaced the phone. What had Helen Latimer said to him, when he first spoke to her? "I've had regular updates from his oncology clinic."'

With a frown he picked the phone back up and dialled the doctor's number. 'Yes, it *is* important.' His tone held no room for negotiation, and soon he heard Dr Latimer's voice. The woman was clearly unhappy at having her work interrupted.

'Sorry but this is urgent,' he snapped. 'I need to know if you ever recall ringing Martin Durham's oncology clinic personally.'

The woman went silent for a while, then in a considerably softer voice said, 'Now you come to mention it, there was never any need to. They always contacted me, either by phone, or by mail.' She paused. 'What's this all about, Sergeant Easter?'

'I wish I knew, Doctor. Really I do.' He thanked her and hung up. Bad mood or not, it was time to see the DI.

* * *

'Never heard of him! There has to be some mistake.'

'The administrator was adamant. I think we really need to find out a lot more about your neighbour, don't you?' said Joseph.

Nikki felt the muscles in her neck tense. It seemed as if her fears about Martin were about to be realised.

For a while she said nothing, as thoughts madly careered about in her head, then she looked down at the heap of paperwork on her desk. 'This isn't going to help either.' She tapped her finger on the files. 'The sudden death statistics that we were working on?' She gave Joseph a wry smile. 'It's all right, I'm not skiving off the murder investigation. It's just that the super is still being hounded for bloody figures, and I needed something to occupy my mind while I was waiting for Cat and her crew to get back.' She sorted out two reports and handed them across to Joseph. 'I was getting them into some form of order, and I saw a name I recognised. When I looked further, I started to feel twitchy. Look at these and tell me what you think.'

She sat back and observed him while he studied the papers. This was not the Joseph who had first come to Greenborough. That man had been calm, quietly sure of himself and completely in control. The Joseph who sat opposite her now looked drawn and preoccupied. He seemed as if his mind was in constant debate over something, and if she didn't know him better she would have said he was frightened.

After a while he looked up. 'I see what you mean, ma'am. But two other cases of suicide in very stable, apparently happy people, doesn't mean much, does it?'

Nikki shrugged. 'These are just basic summaries, no autopsies, or any other reports. I think we should check them out. Both caused something of a stir at the time, I do remember that.' She rubbed her eyes. 'I'd hate to think we missed something, and that bad things were happening to good people.'

She took the paper from him, stared at it, then dredged what she could remember from her memory. 'Amelia Reed. Age fifty-one. Bit of a local hero, in as much as she rescued and cared for stray and ill-treated animals. She drowned in her bath. No history of mental illness. There were questions as to whether it was suicide or accidental death. There were some other questions too, but I can't recall what they were. I do know an open verdict was returned.'

Joseph nodded thoughtfully. 'And the other one?'

'Paul Cousins, age fifty-two. Seen running towards the railway lines as if all the hounds of hell were pursuing him, only it wasn't hounds that caught up with him, it was the 9.45 from Peterborough. The day before he'd become a grandfather for the first time.'

'Running as if pursued,' said Joseph thoughtfully, 'Surely that's a similar scenario to Martin? And are these recent cases?'

'Within the last twelve months.'

'Maybe I should get someone to pull the full reports just in case there are any more factors that could connect them?' Joseph rubbed hard on his chin. 'Although frankly I think we may be wasting precious time.'

'Maybe, but this still has to be done.' She jabbed her finger at the statistics, 'I've no intentions of leaving the super in the brown and sticky stuff.' Nikki exhaled loudly.

'And I *know* *we* have a violent killer out there, and he *has* to be caught. But there is something very wrong with Martin's death too, and if someone is inducing innocent people to kill themselves, then this other assassin is just as bad and equally as deadly.'

'Maybe we should hand it over to another team,' said Joseph dubiously

'And which case would you hand over, Joseph?' Nikki looked at him steadily. 'One seems to be connected to you, and the other to me.'

Joseph looked directly into her eyes but did not answer.

'Not easy is it? And although no way would I expect you to explain everything about your past to another team, I feel that I owe Martin to find out who did this to him.' She abruptly stood up and began to pace the office. 'You see I think I may have done him a disservice, unintentionally, that is.'

'Maybe I shouldn't ask this . . . ?' Joseph turned his head slightly to one side. 'And I know he was practically old enough to be your father, but was there more to your relationship than just being neighbours?'

A while ago, Nikki would have thought nothing of throwing him out of the office, but now she just shook her head, and handed him the photo of Martin, Hannah and herself. 'No never. But I think maybe I missed the signs.'

He stared at the picture. 'That he cared for you?'

'Mm. I think I was so wrapped up in my own life, my own problems, that I never saw it. That, and as you so delicately mentioned, he was such a lot older than me. I never even considered the possibility.'

'And are you basing that supposition purely on this,' Joseph passed the photo back.

'No. There's something else.' She drew in a long breath and stared at the picture. 'You know how long my daughter's been in hospital, don't you? Well, someone has been sending her a small bunch of freesias. Same day, every week, without fail. This is the first time for over a year when there have been no flowers.'

'And you think Martin sent them?'

'Who else? It certainly wasn't her father,' she said bitterly. 'That bastard visited once, then rang me and said it was all too traumatic and flew back to the States. We haven't seen him since.'

'You've tried to find out who sent them?'

'Oh yes. But they used a town florist and paid cash, via an envelope through the door. No name and no card attached.'

'It's certainly odd, but it sounds like something that will never be explained.'

'Probably not. I certainly can't ask him now, can I?'

'So what do we do about the two investigations?'

'We juggle them. The super has provided a lot of back up to help with Chris Forbes' murder enquiry, so I suggest you and I delegate as much of the leg work that we possibly can, and meantime we keep digging up all we can about Martin, and these other suspect suicides. *And* we need to see Martin's sister again. I'm damn sure she knows something that she wasn't prepared to tell us last time.'

Joseph nodded, and Nikki could see a flicker of relief in his eyes. Not that she believed it would last for long. Even if their killer was not Sweet, he seemed to be doing a good job in remaining unidentified, which kept Joseph in a permanent state of agitation. And that helped no one.

'If it helps, I'll stay on tonight and try to crunch some numbers for the super. Before all this blew up, I'd thought of a way to get a better overall view, cross forces. See what criteria they use, and how they arrive at their figures.'

Nikki hated to say 'yes' when Joseph looked so exhausted, but she had the feeling that he wouldn't rest even if he did go home. There was far too much on his mind. 'If you could, just a couple of hours would be great.' She flopped back down in her chair. 'I'll stay too, and I'll send out for a Chinese, if you like?'

'Suits me, ma'am. Mrs Blakely has threatened a corned beef hash tonight and I'm not too sure I could stomach it.'

'Mm, doesn't sound quite your thing, Joseph.'

He threw her a small smile. 'Oh I'm fine with hash generally, but I happened to see the sell-by date on the tin of corned beef. That's what's worrying me.'

'Ah, right. Chinese it is then.'

CHAPTER FIFTEEN

Cat Cullen and the others arrived back just after six. There was little to report, and nothing that would help their identification of Snaz.

'I can't believe how sodding thick some people are!' she grumbled. 'No one could give us hair colour, no distinguishing marks or tattoos, no label wear or designer clothing, and no name, other than some of them heard Chris call him Snaz.'

'And since the murder he has conveniently disappeared,' added Niall, unbuckling his heavy equipment belt.

Nikki remained impassive, she had expected little else. 'Okay, well you guys get home, grab some sleep and be back early.' She looked across at the big figure of Dave Harris, who still sat hunched over his computer, doggedly thumping on the keyboard. 'And that includes you, Dave.'

'Right you are, ma'am. I'm pretty well finished here.' He double clicked the mouse and a printer whirred into life. 'Everything I can find on Amelia Reed and Paul Cousins.' He raised his eyebrows. 'And there's quite a bit.'

Nikki took the information from him and went to her office. She had already tried to get hold of Elizabeth

Durham, and been greeted by an answerphone. She had left a message asking her to get in touch as a matter of some urgency.

Now, as Joseph was flicking through reams of figures on the computer screen, there was little left for her to do but to tackle Dave's reports.

She sat back and began to thumb through them. Dave had been his usual thorough self, and even printed off local newspaper articles on the deaths. As she began to read, the stories flooded back to her.

Two deaths that had shocked their nearest and dearest to the core.

Paul Cousins' horrific method of dying had left several pasty-faced officers searching the railway line for missing internal organs, and his wife requiring long-term psychiatric treatment. Like Martin, he had no money worries, but Paul was surrounded by a close family, and the coming of the first grandchild had apparently been a total joy.

Nikki skimmed down the press cuttings, and words like disbelief, impossible, and bombshell kept reoccurring. The same words that she could use in relation to Martin.

There were similar descriptions regarding Amelia Reed, although the circumstances regarding her death were far more obscure. Did she black-out? Was she held under? Or did she drown herself? Every aspect was hacked around for weeks in the papers. As a woman, she seemed full of fire and had a real passion for helping animals. She was someone who had been known to take on gangs of badger baiters, and on one occasion, before the fox-hunting ban, a full complement of scarlet-coated huntsmen. She had climbed over walls, fences and barbed wire to rescue ill-treated dogs and various forms of livestock, and was thanked by receiving several broken bones and a criminal record.

Not exactly a scaredy-cat, were you, Amelia? thought Nikki.

She turned to another account, read it, then frowned and read it again. A neighbour had reported hearing Amelia remonstrate loudly with someone about an hour before she died, but on investigation there was no indication of anyone else ever being in the house. This was backed up by the fact that one of her dogs, a faithful and possessive Jack Russell, never barked at all during what had seemed like a heated argument.

Nikki quickly checked against the police statements, and found the name of the neighbour. She ran her finger down the details and stopped at the telephone number. This had happened a year ago, but there was a good chance that the person still lived there.

She picked up the phone and dialled.

'Mr Matthews? Excellent! Now I'm sorry to ring like this, but I was wondering . . .' Nikki explained that they were reviewing the case and needed his help. They talked for a while, then she thanked him and hung up. She could be wrong, but her gut feeling said otherwise. She grabbed the rest of the notes and hunted through for the PM results.

'Damn!' she swore out loud. Then she went over it again. There was a considerable amount of medication in her blood, but no mention of any abnormally high doses of an hallucinogen. She stared at the list of drugs, but apart from a water tablet, they meant nothing to her. She cursed again.

From Mr Matthew's description of what he had heard, Nikki could have sworn that Amelia was not arguing, but having a bad trip, shouting at demons. That would have answered the problem of no one else having been seen, and the dog not barking. But why didn't the drug show up in her blood? Maybe it was a Rohypnol type? One that did not stay in the system for long. She pushed the file to one side. That could be it, but she needed Professor Rory Wilkinson to confirm it.

Nikki's hand hung over the phone, then she stopped. Best to check out the PM on Paul Cousins first.

She scanned the report, but could find nothing from toxicology. With a small snort of irritation, she went through it again. Everything else was there, except the tox screen. 'Shit!' The one report she really needed had vanished into the wonderful never-never land of Gone Missing.

'Food's here, ma'am.' Joseph's voice calmed her somewhat. 'Shall I bring it in?'

Nikki stood up. 'No, I'll come out there. I'm just about to start dusting the ceiling with these old reports.'

'Sorry about that. I'm not doing too badly actually.' He set out several foil food trays on his desk and pulled the lids off. 'Smells good.' He passed her a fork. 'I don't think the super has too much to worry about with these statistics, you know. Whoever compiled them in the first place should be shot. On closer examination, they've omitted to take into consideration a lot of regional variables and I suspect that part of it is compiled by estimates based on out of date trends, so to be honest I . . .'

'Joseph. Speak English. And pass the soy sauce, please.' She took the sachet from him and tore it open. 'What you are saying is that the survey is crap, is that right?'

'You do have a remarkable way with words, ma'am. But in a nutshell, yes.'

'And you can prove that statement?'

'I should be able to. In fact, given a little longer I can probably produce some pretty convincing data.'

'Just enough to get the superintendent off the hook will do nicely.' Nikki eased her fork into some Singapore noodles and transferred them to her plate. 'You know what is really scary about this?'

'What the noodles?'

Nikki threw him a hopeless look. 'No, wally, the stats. If we hadn't been asked to look at them, we'd never have seen these other suspect cases.'

'And are they suspect?' asked Joseph, taking a bite out of a spring roll.

'I'd stake my pension on the fact that there's more to both of them than met the eye of the coroner.'

'That *is* scary.'

'And if we're right, will we find more?' said Nikki quietly.

'Let's sort these first, shall we?'

Before Nikki could answer, Joseph's phone rang. He flipped it open, stared at it for a while, then closed it again. As he did, his brighter mood seemed to fade.

'Bryony?' she asked tentatively.

'Bryony.' He pushed some food around his plate, but didn't eat anything.

'You think you might be putting her in danger, don't you?'

Joseph laid his fork down. 'I need proof about Billy Sweet. Without it, I'm in limbo. Damned if I do, damned if I don't.'

'It wouldn't hurt to talk to her, would it?' Nikki wondered why she was encouraging him.

'I suppose I should. I hate to keep ignoring her calls. After all, I did give her my number.'

Nikki felt a hint of something she didn't understand; something that she certainly wasn't going to start analysing right now. 'Yes. You're a lot of things, Joseph Easter, but you're not rude. So ring back and apologise.'

'Okay, I'll do it when we've eaten.'

'Do it now.'

'I need to eat.'

'Then microwave it later. Go phone Bryony.'

* * *

She watched him as she ate, and although she couldn't hear the conversation, his body language spoke volumes. Whoever Bryony was, he enjoyed her company, and from the expression on his face, she understood that the woman had forgiven his uncharacteristic bad manners.

Nikki threw away the empty cartons and her paper plate, returned to her office and wondered where that relationship was going to go.

She walked around her desk and sat down. Whatever, it wasn't her business, but this case was. And she needed to move it forward. She left a message on Rory Wilkinson's voicemail, and wondered what to do next. Elizabeth Durham was the obvious next stop, but she'd have to wait until the woman rang her.

She looked through the window in her office door and saw Joseph back at his desk, typing with one hand, and eating cooling sweet-and-sour with the other. She smiled. She should be glad for him, pleased that he had found someone. And she was. Of course she was.

With a small shake of her head, Nikki turned back to the reports and began to read.

* * *

It was almost an hour later when Joseph knocked on her door.

'I'm going to make a move, ma'am, if that's alright? I've set up a regional fact sheet. It'll take a bit longer to collate all the relevant figures, but I've got a lot of information to hand from various agencies.' He grinned at her. 'We could get a gold star from the super, *if* I get it right.'

'That's great. Good work, Joseph. Now go meet your lady.'

She wasn't sure if it was the light, but she thought she saw a reddish hue creep up his neck.

'It's just a drink. Give me a chance to explain how difficult it is when there's an enquiry running.' He looked a little like a teenager trying to explain himself. 'I'm going to try to put things on hold until . . .' he shrugged.

'I know. Until you have that proof that you are looking for.' She really did feel like his mother, and she didn't like that feeling. 'Now shut up and bugger off. I've got work to do.'

* * *

Bryony had suggested a small bar down by the river, and as it was not a regular hang-out place for policemen, he readily agreed.

She had looked hauntingly beautiful when he saw her, and he had felt a strange sadness sweep over him, because he knew that his job could prevent this relationship from ever coming to anything.

They had talked for a couple of hours, and finally Joseph confessed that he was involved in the murder enquiry that was on the whole town's lips, and that he may have to take a rain check until it was over. And then he told her that even if they did see each other, it was no picnic dating a copper. He would make arrangements, then have to cancel at the last minute. He would not get to ring her when he promised to, and sometimes he may have to work long into the night and not see her at all.

And she had simply smiled and said surely that was par for the course. If she wanted nine to five, she'd date a banker.

The only thing he didn't tell her was that he feared for her safety.

Around eleven, he called a cab and waited in the bar with her until it arrived.

'Sort your case out quickly, Joseph,' she slipped her arm through his. 'I've got plans for us.'

'I like the sound of that,' he whispered. 'And I may have one or two of my own.'

'Good. I like variety.' She laughed softly, then looked up as taxi cab drew up outside. 'Looks like this is me. Can I drop you off?'

'No, thanks. I like to walk, and it's in the opposite direction.'

'Are you sure you wouldn't like to squeeze into the back with me?'

Joseph would have loved nothing better, but knew it was far too dangerous, for several different reasons, and all he could lamely say was, 'Soon, I promise.'

This time he kissed her. And for a moment, everything was fine in his world. As fine as it got, until he opened his eyes, and on the far side of the street he saw Billy Sweet.

'Joseph? What . . . ? Oh God, not again!' Bryony pulled herself away from him and spun around. 'Where?' she asked urgently.

'He's . . . he was right there.' He pointed towards the wall that ran along the river bank. 'Right there.'

'Then come on!'

To his horror, Bryony sprinted away from him and ran across the road. 'No!' He roared. 'Leave him!'

Bryony faltered, then turned and looked back at him appealingly. 'We can't let him get away with this Joseph, whoever he is, he can't keeping stalking you.'

'No, Bryony! He could be dangerous!' He ran across to where she stood, and put his arms tightly around her. 'At least you saw him this time.'

There was a short pause, then she said, 'Of course I did, just fleetingly. I think he went over the wall and along that towpath that runs under the bridge.'

'Did you see his face?'

'No. It's too dark.'

'And he was wearing a blasted hoody,' he whispered.

'Look, lady, do you want to go home or not? The clock's still ticking you know.'

Joseph waved to the taxi driver. 'She's just coming.' He turned back to Bryony. 'Text or ring me when you get home, okay? Just to let me know you're safe.'

She pulled her jacket around her. 'I was just going to say the same thing to you.' Her lovely face screwed up into an expression of deep concern. 'Is he something to do with your case?'

'I have no idea, Bry, but I pray he isn't.'

'Please come in the cab with me,' she urged.

Joseph walked her across the road. 'Best not. If he is watching me, I don't want to lead him to your place.'

'Then take care, Joseph. Take great care.' She kissed him again, and opened the rear door of the cab. 'Call me,' she mouthed through the closed window.

He nodded and the taxi pulled away.

Joseph walked across the road and leaned on the river wall. A little way below him the narrow towpath snaked off and under the bridge, where it disappeared into darkness. It was too late to follow him now. He might have caught him earlier, but certainly not with Bryony to worry about.

Bryony. He pushed his hands deep in his pockets and set off for home. Had he said too much? Or too little? He hadn't wanted to scare her, but then it would appear that she wasn't easily scared. Without a second thought, she had taken off like a shot from a gun. He smiled in the darkness, and she wasn't fazed by his line of work either. So maybe, when the dust settled . . . A frisson of fear snaked between his shoulder blades. He was getting ahead of himself, and there was one nasty glaring fact that he seemed to be trying to avoid. Sweet had seen Bryony. In fact, he'd seen her twice.

The shiver intensified. He'd been a fool. He should never have agreed to meet her. If anything happened to her . . . he couldn't bear to think about that possibility. Now he was desperate for her call. How long would it take? Fifteen minutes max. He bit his lip, and increased his pace. He just wanted to be back at his digs.

He strode along the river road then branched off towards Salmon Park Gardens. That was the quickest route, and now he was beginning to worry about his landlady as well. What if Sweet got in? He'd think nothing of topping an elderly woman. For her sake, he'd better stay at the nick. He was sure that the boss would make allowances for him under the circumstances. He'd pack a bag as soon as he got home, and then . . . Joseph froze in his tracks, and involuntarily clamped his hands over his ears.

Dear God! Please no! He slowly took his hands away, but still he heard it.

The empty avenue in front of him echoed with a strange, eerie wail. It was high pitched, unearthly, and horribly familiar. He'd only heard it once before, but he would never forget it. It was the terrible keening that Billy Sweet's throat had produced as he sat in front of those slaughtered women back in the Congo.

He spun around, trying to pin point where it was coming from, but then it abruptly stopped.

Joseph tensed, straining to make out any other sounds, then suddenly he smelt the stench of death, felt the humid jungle heat on his skin and heard the cries of the dying. He was back on patrol, using every sense to locate the enemy. He dropped low to the ground and crouched in the shadows, waiting.

Hearing nothing, he silently moved forward, then he caught the faintest breath of a sigh brought to him on the breeze, and it was coming from the edge of the park.

He narrowed his eyes and took careful note of the terrain, checking instinctively for obstacles and hazards. There was a jumble of shrubbery, waiting for the gardeners to prune it back, and a dense cluster of small trees forming a dark canopy. Not good, he thought to himself. Too many places to hide.

On the far side of the park, he could hear laughter. Kids yelling out obscenities to each other, then laughing again. Just stay there, he murmured, keep out of this.

He straightened up and inched further forward, looking this way and that, and feeling naked without his M-16 assault rifle.

'Oh Bunny? Bunny, where are you?'

The sing-song voice took him by surprise and bile surged up into his throat. He swung round to the direction that it came from. He'd wanted proof. Now he had it. 'Show yourself, you murdering scumbag!' he hissed.

'Over here, Bunny dear,' sang the voice, but this time it sounded more distant.

Joseph broke cover and ran towards the spot where the deranged sound had originated, but before he could reach it, he pitched forward and crashed to the ground. Something had been thrown across the path, directly beneath his feet.

He cursed, rolled over and peered around him. Then he realised that he was covered in something sticky. Something sticky, warm and reeking of copper. Or was it iron? He had never quite worked that one out. Did it matter right now? No, it didn't.

Joseph eased himself up and away from the man's body, and with a quick appraisal to check that the killer was not about to launch himself on his unprotected back, took a Maglite from his pocket and shone it down.

Corn-coloured hair, pale eyes, a grey hooded jacket, faded jeans and a throat slit from ear to ear.

There was no point in checking for signs of life. From the strange tilted angle of the head, Joseph could see into the severed windpipe. He sighed, switched off the torch, and slowly sank back so that he was sitting on his heels.

It wasn't Billy Sweet that lay on the blood-red ground, but it did look a bit like him. As Joseph pulled his mobile from his pocket and called for help, he wondered how he would feel if it *had* been the renegade soldier, the psychotic killer of women and comrades alike?

The answer was he didn't know, but however he may have felt, it had to be better than this.

He gave his location, a brief account of what had occurred, closed his phone, and sat in the purple shadows of Salmon Park Gardens and cried.

CHAPTER SIXTEEN

'Nikki? Where are you?'

She carefully negotiated a blind bend then pressed the button on her radio. 'A mile from home, Super. Approaching Cloud Fen.'

'I need you at the hospital, immediately.'

Nikki slammed on the brakes, reversed the car at speed into a farm track, then whipped it back onto the road. 'On my way, sir.'

She knew better than to ask what was occurring. Rick Bainbridge would have said if he could, but the tone of his voice had told her that it was serious, and that was enough for her.

Her headlights scored piercing darts of light across the lonely fen, and in minutes, she was screaming back down the dual-carriageway towards Greenborough.

The car park was almost empty when she got there. She left the car as close to the A & E department as she could, locked it and ran across the ambulance bay to the front entrance. She had no idea what had happened, but something nagged at her gut, telling her that it concerned Joseph. She just prayed that he had not been injured again.

She had barely set foot through the automatic doors, when the superintendent appeared from a side room and beckoned to her.

She followed him into the tiny office and closed the door. The room, a place where the triage nurse usually assessed the urgency of attention to the walking wounded, seemed crowded by the large frame of Rick Bainbridge and herself.

'Is it Joseph, sir?' That was all she really wanted to know.

'Indirectly.' The big man leaned against a trolley and folded his arms. 'It's okay, he's not injured, but he's badly shaken.' The harsh light did little for his pallor. 'There's been another murder.'

'Oh hell. Another, so soon?' She had not expected that. 'When and where, sir?'

'Just over half an hour ago, in Salmon Park Gardens.' He ran a beefy hand through his iron-grey hair. 'A white male, throat cut and no ID, as before, and Joseph had the bad luck to find him.'

Nikki closed her eyes and let the information wash over her. Joseph really did not need this right now. She thought fast. She needed to see her sergeant before the super started asking tricky questions. 'Can I see him, sir? After all he's been through he's going to need a friend with him.'

'Shortly.'

Actually, now would be good, she thought.

'I need to talk to you, Nikki.' He pointed to an uncomfortable-looking plastic chair. 'Sit down.'

It was a definite command, and reluctantly, she obeyed.

'I'm afraid, we have a problem.'

Her heart sank. This did not sound good. 'And that is?' she asked, trying to keep the anxiety from her voice.

'I asked you if you thought that Joseph had returned to work too soon, didn't I?'

Nikki nodded. 'And I categorically stated that I believed that he was fine.' She gave the man a defiant stare and said, 'And I still stand by that opinion.'

'Well, I'm afraid that I'm not so sure.' He returned her stare. 'When uniform reached the scene tonight, Joseph was in a very bad way.'

'So what! Forgive me, but two bodies and a jumper in your first days back after getting injured on duty is not what I'd call easy street, sir.'

'I agree, but when I said a *bad way*, I meant it. He seemed far more traumatised than I would have expected, Nikki.' He paused, seeming to weigh something up, then said. 'There are things about Joseph's past that you are not privy to, and let me just say that given his history, he should not have reacted in the way that he did.'

Nikki wanted to scream, but gritted her teeth and said, 'I *know* that he was a soldier, I know he was special forces, but he's still a human being, a caring and compassionate one. There's only just so much a body can take, sir. *Anybody!*'

Rick Bainbridge raised one eyebrow. 'It was my belief that I was the only one on the station to know.'

'You are, apart from me, and that's how he wants it to stay.' She gave a loud sigh. 'I'm sorry, sir, but we went through a lot together on that last case. We both shared a few secrets when it got really shitty.'

Bainbridge softened. 'I suppose you did. But I'm really worried about him, Nikki. And I'm sure you'll understand that he has to go back on sick leave for a while, and we'll need to get him re-evaluated as to be properly fit for work.'

'But that'll take forever, sir! Can't we just play it by ear, and ask Joseph how he feels about it?'

'He's on sick leave, Inspector. No buts.'

She opened her mouth to protest, then shut it again. She was going to get nowhere tonight, so she may just as well save her breath. 'Whatever you say, sir. Now can I go and see him?'

∗ ∗ ∗

Joseph lay on a trolley and stared at them. To Nikki, his eyes seemed unnaturally dilated and his speech was slightly slurred. 'Can I go home? I want to get out of here.'

'The paramedics gave you a sedative to calm you down.' The superintendent patted his arm. 'You've had one hell of a shock, Sergeant. They won't let you leave until the doctors are happy that you're safe to be on your own.'

'I'm okay, sir. I just feel a bit woozy, that's all.'

'He can come back to my place, sir. I can keep an eye on him,' said Nikki, trying to keep her tone as matter of fact as possible.

'If it's not too much trouble, ma'am,' Joseph gnawed on his bottom lip, then looked across to the super. 'Would you ask the doctor for me, sir? Understandably I don't have the best memories of hospitals, and I really need to get out.'

Rick Bainbridge nodded, said 'I'll do what I can,' then pulled back the curtain and walked across to the central nursing station.

The moment he was out of earshot, Joseph leant forward, grabbed Nikki's hand and pulled her close. 'It was him, ma'am. No question.' His voice was little more than a whisper.

'Billy Sweet? You actually saw him at the crime scene?' gasped Nikki.

'I heard him.'

Nikki saw a shudder run through Joseph, then he said, 'Please, get me discharged. I *have* to talk to you.'

'Okay, but it'll take a while, and you need fresh clothes. Give me your key, I'll go see your landlady, tell her you're not too well, and we'll pack you a bag. You can tell me everything when we're back on Cloud Fen.'

Joseph nodded, then shivered again. 'I keep hearing him.'

'He actually spoke to you?' asked Nikki.

'He called me Bunny.' He shook his head. 'No one other than my army mates ever called me that.'

'Oh Jesus, this is a mess.'

'Tell me about it.' He leant back into the pillow and closed his eyes. After a moment he opened them and said, 'Would you do me a favour, guv? I know it's cheek, but . . .'

'Don't tell me. Ring Bryony?' Nikki asked.

'They took my clothes and my mobile for forensics. I was supposed to ring her, ma'am. She'll be worried sick, especially if she gets to hear about this new murder.'

'You know her number?' Nikki took out her own mobile and listed a new contact.

'I think so.' He murmured a few numbers to himself, then thought again and finally got it right.

Nikki punched it in. 'What do you want me to tell her?'

'Just that I'm safe, and I'll talk to her soon.' He looked up at Nikki. 'There's one good thing though.' He gave her a weak smile. 'Billy was watching us from the river walk, and this time Bryony saw him too.'

'Really? But that's fantastic!' Her hopes rose. 'Could she identify him?'

'Too dark, but she saw him, and that's what counts.'

She saw *someone*, thought Nikki, fighting back the disappointment, and that's not nearly good enough.

'Uh-oh, the super's coming back,' muttered Joseph. 'Any joy, sir?'

'Half an hour, maybe.' The super eased himself into the only chair in the cubicle.

'Great.' Nikki picked up her bag from the floor. 'He needs clothes, sir. If you are going to be here, I'll dive out and get them.'

* * *

151

It was almost two in the morning when they arrived at Cloud Cottage Farm, and after half three when she finally closed the door on the guest bedroom.

Nikki hadn't expected to have her visitor back quite so soon, but if she were honest, and disregarded the terrible circumstances that surrounded his second visit, it was a relief to have him there.

After Joseph had settled down to sleep off the sedative, Nikki walked out into the garden. A whole skyful of stars glittered and shone in the indigo heavens, and she sat on a wooden bench that her grandfather had made, and stared up at them. Sometimes the vastness of the skies over the marshes almost scared her. They made her feel so small, that she wondered if she, or any of her petty problems, really existed. But tonight they were her friends; they simply helped her to think.

Two men had died. Executed. Two men who bore a resemblance to someone from Joseph's past. A killer from Joseph's past to be exact.

And there her thoughts came to a halt. Stars or no stars, she could see no further.

Joseph had said that he heard Billy call out to him, but had he? Someone could have been calling their dog for all she knew.

She had met the paramedics at the hospital, and they had said that Joseph had been weeping uncontrollably when they found him, saying it was all his fault. Luckily, they had no reason to think he meant anything other than he hadn't been quick enough to save the man. Not that anyone could have saved him. He had been professionally dispatched, exactly like Chris Forbes. And making such a gruesome discovery, well, falling over it to be precise, would have hardly helped Joseph's war-torn mind. He could have imagined anything, anything at all. She sighed out loud. And *she* was the one having a go at the super for suggesting that Joseph's mental state was shaky!

Nikki drew her jacket closer around her. It was a beautiful night, but there was a chill breeze coming in from the sea. She should get some sleep herself. Joseph was probably as safe with her as anywhere, and if he had to take more leave, he would be comfortable here.

With one last look up to the stars, she shivered then hurried back inside, taking more care than usual to lock and bolt the door.

* * *

As the door closed and the light in the kitchen went out, a dark figure slid silently from his hiding place. He had been so close, so close that he could smell her perfume. Although it wasn't perfume, was it? It was a combination of shower gel, shampoo and deodorant. And then there had been coffee, and the hint of aromatic food that clung to her clothes.

The mouth smiled, but the eyes stayed as they always did. The police ate such rubbish food, it was no wonder that they rarely got to enjoy retirement.

He sighed. If he had just reached out his hand, he could have touched her. And he would like to have done that. Liked it very much. But not now. There was a schedule to stick to. An operation to see through. And that was what he was good at.

Seeing things through to the end.

CHAPTER SEVENTEEN

The morning briefing had been a hurried affair. Nikki had laid out the facts for her officers, bare bones with no embellishment, then split them into teams and put them to work.

Back in her office, she was suddenly overwhelmed by a feeling of loss; which for a dyed-in-the-wool loner was something of a new experience. She had spent most of the last two years *trying* to go solo, doing everything she could to avoid having a permanent sergeant at her side, and now her wish had been granted, she hated it.

She had spent the last part of the night unable to sleep, tossing and turning and unusually edgy. Several times she had got up and stared down into the shadowy garden, unaware of why she was doing it, but somehow just trying to calm the feeling of foreboding. But that never happened, and when it was time to get up, she still felt jittery. She had taken Joseph some breakfast on a tray, and offered him the freedom of her DVD and CD collection, not that for one moment she believed that he would be relaxed enough to enjoy anything like that. And then the realisation dawned on her that he would be marooned on Cloud Fen with no transport. Which considering the things that had happened was not a smart move, so she had promised that as soon as she was able, she'd get his car out to him. Luckily, he had left it in the staff car park when he had left to meet his girlfriend.

Nikki pursed her lips. She had spoken to Bryony as directed, and had been strangely unsettled by the conversation. Not that either of them had made anything other than extremely polite comments. Although clearly upset by Joseph's experience, the woman reacted in a sensible way, not snivelling or throwing a girly wobbler. She had expressed her concern in an intelligent manner, and for some unfathomable reason, even that had managed to irritate Nikki.

She shook her head, and decided that Joseph's love life should be very low on her priority list right now. Two murders and a suicide definitely ticked more boxes for attention than beautiful Bryony-bloody-Barton.

'Ma'am?' Dave Harris looked enquiringly at her. 'Have you got a moment?'

Nikki threw him a knowing look. 'Okay, detective, what's worrying you?'

'The Sarge, ma'am.' He took the only other chair in the office, and pulled it a little closer to her desk. 'I was reading between the lines at this morning's meeting, and I'm concerned that he's not at work today. Is he alright, ma'am?'

Nikki took a deep breath. Right now she needed an ally. And as Dave was one of the few officers on the station that she would trust with her life, maybe she was being a fool to keep the whole situation to herself. She didn't want to betray Joseph in any way, but another perspective could make all the difference.

'Because I happen to think that you are the most dependable and honest copper I know . . .' she looked at him shrewdly, 'I'm going to ask for your help, Dave. But what I'm going to tell you stays right here, with you and me, okay?'

He nodded slowly. 'Absolutely, ma'am.'

'Right, well, you asked about Sergeant Easter . . .'

It didn't take long to explain a watered-down version of the situation, one that did not involve any mention of what happened in the Congo, and at the end, Dave simply said, 'It doesn't surprise me to hear about his old career, ma'am. I'd often thought that may be the case from the way he conducted himself, but he's too much of a gentleman to be a disillusioned squaddie.' He smiled. 'I like Sergeant Easter, I have a lot of time for him, ma'am, so just tell me how I can help, and I'll do it.'

'I want you to trace Billy Sweet. Start with army records. We know his original unit, and an approximate time when he left to go to this private security force, but from there on it's going to be tricky. And Dave, not a word to anyone, not even the super. If he starts asking questions, refer him to me.'

'No problem, ma'am. But the murder room is hardly the place for a discreet enquiry, is it?'

'Work from here. Use my computer and my phone. You shouldn't be disturbed.' She scribbled down the few facts that she knew about Sweet and handed them to Dave. 'I'm going to be out for about an hour. I don't like the thought of Joseph being stranded on the marsh with no vehicle, and as uniform are stretched the limits, I'll take his Ford myself and he can drop me back. He's not an invalid, and I've got some paperwork he can do from home.' She noted Dave's surprised look and said, 'It's not this case, don't worry. And I'm not being a slave-driver, he needs something to keep him occupied. If the super hadn't pulled rank on him, he'd be here right now.'

'I'm sure he would, ma'am. Give him my best, won't you?'

Nikki picked up the pile of folders that contained the statistics that Joseph had been working on and the info that Dave had pulled up on the suicides, and pushed them under her arm. 'Of course. And Dave, try to get us a photo of Sweet. Doesn't matter if it's old, we can always get Cat to get her techie mates to age enhance it for us.' She paused at the door. 'Thanks for this. I owe you.'

'Thanks for what, ma'am?' Dave gave her an angelic look and logged in to her computer.

* * *

'Naturally I gave him the sanitised version, I just don't want you to think I've grassed you up in any way.' Nikki looked at Joseph hopefully.

'I'd never think that.' He heaved a sigh. 'Dave is a good old boy. If I had to tell anyone, it would be him. Besides, with me in dry dock, you need someone to trust.'

Nikki opened the key box on the kitchen wall, removed a spare front-door key and handed it to Joseph. 'Keep it. It's always good to have someone else hold a house key. Martin always had one when . . .' she let the rest of the sentence fade away.

'And what on earth are we going to do about *that*?' asked Joseph fretfully. 'It was going to be tough enough with two of us, but now?' He threw up his hands in frustration, 'Why the devil did the super have to do this? I'm perfectly fit to work!'

'Then work from here. Uninterrupted, and with all the free tea and coffee you can drink.' She pointed to the folders that lay on the kitchen table. 'Drop me back to the nick, then get back here and get your head into these.'

Joseph stared at them, then gave her a grudging smile. 'Ah . . . the stats. So you mean I won't be watching twenty back episodes of *The Bill* after all?'

'The stats are only there if you have the heart to look at them, but those suicides really could do with some attention.' Her face darkened. 'I'd wager a pound to a penny that you'll find something wrong if you look hard enough.' She handed him his car keys. 'The computer is all set up in the study, along with some reference books and directories that may prove useful. *The Bill* can wait, I think.

Now, if you'd be kind enough to put on your chauffeur's cap, I need to get back before I'm missed.'

As they walked the door, Joseph gently touched her arm. 'I do appreciate you letting me stay here, ma'am. I'm not sure what I would have done otherwise.'

Nikki gave him a long, searching look, then said, 'It's okay. After all, you're not just my sergeant, you're my friend. And *please* ditch all that 'ma'am' stuff while you are under my roof, it makes me feel like some aged crone!'

'I don't think so!' He gave her arm the slightest of squeezes before letting go. 'But I guess we'd better crack on. Time is hardly on our side, and we *both* have work to do now.' He picked up his wallet from the table and held the door open for her. 'Your carriage awaits.'

* * *

Joseph dropped his boss off close to the gates of the nick, then retraced his journey back to Cloud Fen. The more times he did the trip the less the winding and dangerously narrow lanes seemed to bother him, and as he reached the bottom of Buckledyke Lane, he slowed down and stared across to Knot Cottage.

Martin Durham had certainly lived in an idyllic location, as long as you could cope with solitude.

He wound the window down, turned off the engine and sat looking at the tiny cottage. He tried to imagine Martin coming home, lighting the fire, and preparing his dinner. Now that was something he could relate to. The preparation of food was almost a spiritual thing to him. And it would appear that Martin had been a fellow connoisseur of vegetable slicing and the careful filleting of sea-fresh fish.

Before he had even made a conscious decision to go back into the cottage, he found himself out of the car and walking down the lane.

The door was closed, but the blue-and-white police cordoning tape had gone. Forensics had finished and the restricted access had been lifted. He tried the door, and to his surprise, it swung open. 'Naughty! Naughty!' he murmured, and thought that someone should have their wrists slapped for that.

He stepped inside, and was shocked to see the place almost as tidy as it had been on his first visit. SOCOs and big-foot coppers did not leave the scene in this condition, that was for sure. He moved into the kitchen, glanced out of the window, and that was when he saw the bright red MG parked around the back. A car he had seen before, in Old Bolingbroke when they had gone to interview Martin's sister, Elizabeth.

Without delay, he quietly retraced his footsteps, through the lounge and back to the front door, where he proceeded to ring the bell.

'Yes?' An upstairs window had opened and a face looked out.

He held up his warrant card for the woman to see. 'DS Joseph Easter' He squinted in the sunlight. 'Would I be right in thinking that you are Janna Hepburn-Lowe?'

The window closed with a slam, and he heard footsteps coming down the stairs.

'May I come in?' He didn't wait for an answer, but strode past her into the lounge. 'My! You've not wasted time getting the place tidied, have you?'

The woman must have been in her forties, but her white-blonde hair, cut in a short messy style made her look years younger. She wore jeans and a bright green T-shirt with the logo 'I Support Tree Love' emblazoned across the front, and much as he would have loved to make a comment, he diplomatically decided against it.

'Martin would have *hated* his cottage being left in that state. Sorry, but I thought you lot had finished?'

'*Us* lot have, miss. It was *me* that wanted another look.'

'Ms, actually, and don't let me stop you. I'm nearly finished anyway.' She threw him an accusatory look. 'This was somebody's home you know, it was left in an appalling state. And that was apart from what the burglar did.'

'It was the intruder who trashed the place, *Ms* Hepburn-Lowe. I saw what he did.' He raised an eyebrow. 'Any idea what he was looking for?'

'What do you mean?' The woman stiffened. 'It was just some thug seeing what he could find after he'd heard that Martin was dead, wasn't it?'

'Was it?' asked Joseph. 'I certainly don't think so, and nor do you. Where is Elizabeth Durham?'

'She's gone to the tip, if you must know. Taken Martin's broken and damaged belongings.' She returned his stare with a look that reflected both hostility and fear. 'And I wouldn't bother to wait for her, she'll be ages. There was rather a lot of stuff ruined.'

'So, did you find what you were looking for?' he asked amiably.

'I think you'd better go,' she said grittily.

'And I think you'd better start telling me the truth. Or maybe your Elizabeth will get a call saying that you're down at the police station helping us with our enquiries. We take a dim view of people who waste police time.'

The woman blanched, and Joseph hated himself for being so hard, but he knew that something was amiss, and pussy-footing around would get him nowhere.

Janna suddenly lost all her aggression, and she sounded exhausted when she said. 'We found nothing.'

Joseph also softened his tone. 'Was it something very important? Something that could help us discover why he died like that?'

'Whoever broke in must have thought that, that's for sure.' Janna pointed to a seat. 'Come and sit down.' She followed him in and flopped into a high-backed armchair. 'I don't know much, I'm afraid. You'll really have to speak to Elizabeth.' She leaned forward, and stared at him earnestly. 'All I can say is that we think they were looking for paperwork regarding something that happened a very long time ago. Long before he came to live here.'

'What was he involved in, do you know?'

Janna shook her head. 'Martin wasn't *involved* in anything, Detective Sergeant. He was a good man. I just know something happened, but neither Elizabeth or Martin would ever say what it was.' She looked at him earnestly. 'I'm not even sure if Elizabeth knows much. I suspect Martin never told her everything, but she may know more than I do. And that's all I can honestly tell you.'

'Well, I do appreciate that, but I'll have to see Elizabeth. Will she really be ages?' He smiled at her.

''Fraid so. That was actually the truth. I said I'd meet her back at home. She was going on somewhere after the dump.'

'When you see her, would you get her to ring my boss straightaway please?' He gave her the number for the station.

Janna took the card and nodded. 'Elizabeth's already had one message to ring the DI, but we needed to get out here and see for ourselves first. Sorry about that.' She walked him to the door, then said, 'He was killed, wasn't he? I don't know how they did it, but he *was* killed.'

Joseph decided not to lie. 'Unofficially, I believe his death is suspicious, and we have to get to the bottom of it.' He gave her his most sincere look. 'We really do need your help.'

'Then I'll make sure Elizabeth phones you.'

He thanked her and walked back up the lane to his car. As he walked he rang the guv'nor on his mobile and quickly filled her in on what he'd discovered. Just before he signed off he said. 'You're right, ma'am. You really do get more done by working from home.'

* * *

Nikki may have liked the thought of Joseph calling Cloud Fen 'home' but she didn't like the look on the Cat Cullen's face as she approached her. 'Okay, what's the matter?'

Cat seemed reticent to speak, but finally said, 'I'm a bit concerned, guv, about these murder victims? I'm supposing that you've noticed that they are both dead ringers, pun not intended, for the bloke you asked me to find. The bloke who was hassling the sarge?'

'Not the sort of thing that's easy to miss, actually.' Nikki wondered how long it would be before she had to let *all* of her staff in on the full story. 'Have we got a name for the latest victim?'

'We think he's David Ryan, also from the Carborough Estate, ma'am. His wife reported him missing this morning. He fits the description, so we've sent a car to collect her. Poor cow, she's got two little kids.' Cat jammed her hands into her jeans pockets, then looked up directly at Nikki. 'Is the sarge involved in this in some way?'

'He may be, Cat,' said Nikki carefully. 'But until we're certain, I can't say.'

'An old case come back to haunt him?'

'Could be.'

'Then I'd like to help, ma'am. If there's anything I can do, you know me, I'd rather slit my wrists than betray a confidence.'

Nikki did know that, and hated keeping those closest to her in the dark, but she had Joseph to consider.

Cat was still speaking. 'Sergeant Easter is a pretty cool guy in my book, ma'am, and I wouldn't like to think that he was in deep shit and I'd not helped to dig him out, so to speak.'

'Then keep trying to find the man that Chris Forbes had been hanging around. Find me Snaz.' She stopped. 'But Cat, if you do, don't you dare try to apprehend him, understand? He could be the most dangerous man you'll ever meet.'

Cat pulled on her denim jacket. 'Wilco, guv. I'm onto it, and this time I'll find something.' With a determined expression, she turned and left the room.

Nikki walked back to her office, and found Dave studying a computer printout.

'Great timing, guv. We've got a picture coming through. It's about ten years old, but it's something.'

Nikki nodded. She was desperate to see what Billy Sweet really looked like. 'Is it from his old regiment?'

'No, it's an unofficial one that I sourced from an Internet site set up by ex-military personnel. An old mate of mine used it to find an old para comrade.'

'I can't think that anyone sane would want to tie up with this creep. What's he doing on a site like that?'

'He's not listed as a contact, guv. I was checking out his old unit, and he's in the background of a group shot that someone posted. There's a list of names beneath it and the computer search homed in on it.'

'Good work, Dave. Anything from official channels?'

'Plenty, I'm working through it now, but as you said, the trail goes decidedly chilly when he got himself discharged and went private. Oh, and before I forget, the super rang down a few minutes ago. Wants to see you.' A whirring sound interrupted him. 'Ah, here's the photo now. It's been cropped and enhanced to isolate your man.' He took the sheet from the printer tray, looked at it, then passed it to her.

In one fleeting glance, Nikki believed everything Joseph had ever told her about Billy Sweet.

He looked to be in his mid-twenties, with a deeply tanned face and close-cut blond hair. He was holding what Nikki thought maybe a grenade launcher, and was wearing camouflage fatigues. He was smiling at the camera, but when Nikki looked closer, his eyes made her shudder. It was as if the flash had deadened them somehow, made them look cold and lifeless. But somehow she knew that if she ever had the misfortune to meet this man, this was exactly what she would see.

'That's good enough, Dave. Skip the age enhancement.'

Dave took it back and stared at it. 'Fair gives you the willies, doesn't it? He's holding that weapon like anyone else would hold a baby, like he loves it.'

'But his eyes are not exactly loving, are they?'

'Straight from the freezer, ma'am.' Dave gave a theatrical shudder. 'There's definitely something missing from that young man.'

'The human part, I think. Print off a load of these, Dave, but only give them to the team. Much as I'd like to swamp the streets with them, I need a bit more proof before I go public.' She pulled out her phone. 'And Cat will definitely need one.'

Cat let out a little whoop of delight into her mobile. 'Great! That will certainly help. On my way back up, ma'am.'

'I've got to see the super, pick it up from Dave. And for the time being this is just between us. Good hunting.' She closed her phone and turned to Dave. 'Did the super say what he wanted?'

'No, ma'am. But he sounded pretty harassed.'

'Wonderful. I'd better get up there.'

'Guv, how much does Cat actually know?'

'Not nearly as much as you, although I can't leave her in dark for much longer.'

'Don't worry, I won't be gossiping. I'm too damned busy.'

* * *

When Nikki reached the super's office, he was not alone. Standing by the window, with a sheaf of papers in his hand was Chief Superintendent Ian Walker. Not a man who had ever endeared himself to Nikki, in fact she disliked him intensely, and the feeling was probably mutual.

'Sorry. I'll come back later.' She made to leave, but to her annoyance the super called her back.

'We both need to talk to you, Nikki. Have a seat.'

She looked from one to the other, and felt a sinking feeling in her gut. Just like the old days! 'Something wrong, sir?'

'We don't know. We have some serious concerns, and would like your opinion.'

The chief placed the papers on the desk, perched on it, just a few feet from her face, and stared directly at her. 'DS Joseph Easter. I understand he's on sick leave?'

Nikki nodded uneasily. 'That's correct, sir. Superintendent Bainbridge thought he might be stressed by his recent discovery of the body in Salmon Park Gardens.'

'And what do *you* think about him, Inspector?' The man's eyes glittered like a hawk spotting a juicy plump pigeon.

'I think he's had a rough few days, but all things considered, I believe he is handling everything exceptionally well.'

'So you don't think that he may have returned to active duty too soon?'

'Not at all. He's functioning perfectly well. In fact, as we speak he is working from home on some statistics for the superintendent, voluntarily, of course.' She smiled benignly.

'Mm.' To Nikki's relief, he stood up and returned to his eerie by the window.

'Sir?' Nikki turned to Rick Bainbridge. 'What's happened? Why the third degree?'

The super shook his head. 'It's nothing like that, Nikki. We are just worried about him. About his mental state.'

'Look at this from our point of view,' chipped in the human bird of prey. 'A man who has suffered serious trauma recently returns to work, and in three days is confronted by a broken body in the river, an execution-style slaying, and then falls over a recently butchered man in the park. Do you blame us for asking his senior officer as to whether he's holding up or not?'

Nikki gritted her teeth so tightly that her jaw ached. 'Of course not, sir, I'm just not sure that you are listening to my opinion.'

'There is another thing,' said the chief, completely ignoring her comment. 'And I'm referring to last night's murder. I have spoken personally to both the scene-of-crime officers and the pathologist, and other than blood evidence belonging to the victim, DS Easter's prints are the only others there. There is nothing to be found on the body, and the scene is free from any other contamination or evidence.'

Nikki's eyes narrowed. 'And what exactly does that mean?'

'Think about it, Inspector. But before you do, is it true that the sergeant was upset by some man leaping in front of his stationary vehicle the other day?'

'What on earth has that got to do with the murders?'

'The man in question looked very much like the two dead men, didn't he?'

Nikki heard the sound of blood rushing in her ears. She had no idea how the chief had got hold of his information, but she really didn't like where the conversation was going. 'There was a vague resemblance, I suppose.'

'I put it to you, Inspector, that there was a marked similarity! I find it very worrying to have two men murdered in this town, who both resemble a man who has upset one of my officers.' Walker slowly blinked his hooded eyelids.

'Surely you can't think that Joseph has anything to do with these deaths?'

'The killings were carried out by a military-trained assassin. Sergeant Easter, as I believe you already know, has a military background. And thinking about it, he was also in the vicinity of the first murder, in fact he is the only person identified on the railway station's CCTV around the time of death.'

'*You*, sir, are accusing Joseph of double murder?'

'No, I'm not, but I'm going to have to suspend him pending further enquiries.'

'What!' She jumped up.

'Nikki, please.' The super stood up, his eyes begging Nikki to calm down. 'Just hear us out.'

She flopped backward like a rag doll, and stared up at Rick Bainbridge. This wasn't happening. 'Suspension?' was all she could say.

He looked sadly at her. 'For his own sake, until we are satisfied that Joseph is in no way involved in all this, he must be relieved of his duties.'

'Involved?' Nikki's voice was husky.

'Joseph has to undergo a psychiatric evaluation. We have to rule out that he has not suffered more trauma than we suspected.'

'Sir, I know I'm no shrink, but Joseph is not capable of something like that, and he is perfectly well-balanced.' Her temper was rising again, and it was getting hard to hold it back. 'God! Just because he cried after he'd fallen headlong over a horribly mutilated man, you all seem to think he's a fruitcake! I'm telling you, anyone would have cried, I would and you would! It was a natural reaction. There's nothing wrong with Joseph's brain.'

'It's not his brain we are talking about, Nikki. It's his mind. And you know that.'

She did. And she knew an awful lot more than the super or the bloody chief, but for the time being, she needed to keep that very close to her chest.

A heavy silence descended over them, then the super said, 'He's still staying with you, isn't he?'

'Yes, sir,' she muttered. 'For as long as he wants.'

'Then I'll come over and see him this evening. I'll explain everything, and we are all just going to have to work doubly hard to sort this out.'

'This will devastate him, sir. After all he's been through, he's a bloody hero, and this is what happens. Great force we work for, I don't think!'

The tall, bird-like man at the window coughed loudly. 'I am still here, Inspector. And I suggest you save your vitriolic comments for the mess room.' He held her gaze fixedly. 'Or the sergeant may not be the only one in hot water.'

Nikki bit her tongue and decided that if anyone ever wanted to murder the chief, she'd probably go find them a suitable weapon. But then again, she didn't want to get thrown off the case, for Joseph's sake she had to find the killer. Which meant it was time for humble pie, no matter how sick it made her feel.

'I'm sorry, sir. It's just the shock. Sergeant Easter is a damned good officer, and all this seems surreal, but I shouldn't have lost my temper, I realise that.'

'Apology accepted.' Then he added, in a pompous tone, 'On this occasion.'

'Thank you, sir.' She looked down, trying hard not to follow it up with "You self-opinionated, arrogant git." 'May I go, sir? I need to get my head round this.'

The super nodded. 'I'll see you tonight. Around seven,' he paused, 'and Nikki, I'd appreciate it if you left it to me to break the news to Joseph. Correct procedure and all that?'

'Oh, you're welcome, sir.'

* * *

Having spoken to Janna Hepburn-Lowe and finally getting something positive out of her, Joseph felt better about his enforced sick leave. Maybe he really could put the time to good use, and perhaps it was safer for everyone else if he kept a low profile until someone got a handle on Billy Sweet.

He made himself a coffee, and as he stirred in a spoonful of sugar, admitted to himself that he was having difficulty even thinking about what had happened the night before in Salmon Park Gardens.

He took his coffee to the study, placed it on the desk and pulled a music album from Nikki's CD rack. As the melodic strains of Coldplay wafted around the small room, he tried to fathom what had caused his ridiculously over-emotional reaction to what had happened. Sure it had been a shock, but he'd seen far worse on the battlefield and not turned into a blubbering bag of jelly.

In his mind he saw again the carnage caused by a roadside bomb, then he saw his friend Gerry get ripped in two by a pressure mine. Terrible things, but things a career soldier learned to cope with. But last night had been too weird to explain, and so had his behaviour afterwards. In truth, there were parts he didn't remember too well, but the medics had given him a sedative, so perhaps that would explain the blank bits.

He flopped down at Nikki's desk, and pulled the files towards him. Maybe he shouldn't even try to analyse his actions. Stress did funny things, and he'd sure been stressed of late.

He opened one of the statistics files, and turned to the computer. As he had uninterrupted time to kill, he'd get the stats put to bed first. That would keep the super happy, and then he would be able to throw all his energies into working on the Martin Durham case. He allowed himself a small smile, but he'd do all that, *after* he'd phoned Bryony.

He tapped her number into the desk phone and waited. Maybe it was his imagination, but he was certain that his heart rate had risen. After half a dozen rings, she answered, and her relief at hearing him for herself flooded down the phone.

'Joseph! I was worried sick! I didn't know what to think.'

'I'm so sorry. I would have contacted you if I could, you do know that, don't you?'

'Of course, that's why I was so frightened. I knew that you were not the type to just ignore me. I knew something must have happened. And thank your boss for me, would you? Her call was much appreciated, although she didn't tell me much other than you were okay and would contact me when you could.'

'I'm not surprised, Bry. She couldn't have said more, there had been another murder, and I was the one to find the body.'

He heard a soft gasp from the other end.

'I'm fine though, honestly,' he lied.

'Was it anything to do with your stalker?' Her voice was low, as if she didn't want to be overheard.

'It may have been, Bry. I think he killed the man that I found, but I have no proof. Still, at least you saw him. Up until now it's just been me, but you being there last night will make all the difference. Now I know that I'm not going mad!' He passed the receiver to the other hand and leaned back in the chair. 'The thing is, I want to see you, really I do, but until I've found out what this is about, I dare not. Do you understand what I'm saying?'

'Sadly I do.' She gave a little humourless laugh. 'Just my luck! I meet the most gorgeous bloke, and for once he's not gay or married, he doesn't work on an oil rig, and he doesn't suffer from halitosis or Saint Vitus Dance, but he's still about as inaccessible as a nun's knickers!'

Joseph laughed. And it felt good. 'Sorry. But I will make it up to you, I promise.'

'You'd better. Now, are you sure we couldn't meet somewhere? Somewhere where no one knows either of us? Just for a coffee, maybe?'

Every inch of him yearned to say yes, but there was no way he would risk Bryony crossing paths with Billy Sweet again. He shivered. 'Absolutely not.'

'Oh well, worth a try. But I can ring you, can't I?'

Joseph hadn't told her where he was, or that his blood-covered mobile was sitting in a laboratory in a sealed bag. 'Best I ring you for a day or so, Bry. My phone got damaged and I haven't had time to organise a new one. I'll ring you on a landline, until I'm up and running again.'

'Then I guess that will have to do, but if you don't ring, I may have to get myself arrested, just to get to see you.'

'I'll ring. I promise. Bryony, I can't wait to see you again. You're very special, you know.'

'So are you, Joseph. Ring me tonight?'

'Try to stop me.'

It had been hard to hang up. And he had been right about his heart rate, because his pulse was racing. With a shaky laugh at himself, he finished his coffee, and returned to the super's statistics with renewed vigour.

* * *

As the end of the day approached, Nikki was strung out like a high wire. There was no news from Cat, Dave was embroiled in his hunt for Sweet and with no Joseph to bounce ideas off, she felt completely exasperated. And she dreaded going home.

As the hours ticked by, she had felt more and more aggrieved by the fact that they were going to suspend Joseph, but at around four thirty when Dave went for a break, she sat alone in her office with a large sheet of white paper and a marker pen, and brainstormed everything she knew. After ten minutes, the paper was covered by scribbled words, and Nikki was beginning to feel decidedly uncomfortable. She may hate what the chief superintendent was doing, but she could see where he was coming from. He had to be very careful, and he was covering both his own and the Fenland Constabulary's back.

Nikki stared at the paper, and suddenly one word stood out. The name Bryony. She had *seen* the man who Joseph believed to be Billy. And Nikki needed to know exactly what kind of witness she would be.

She pulled out her phone and clicked on Contacts.

The phone answered almost immediately, and Nikki apologised if she was interrupting anything important.

'Only a coffee break, although with my workload at present, a break is like gold dust. How can I help you?'

Bryony sounded pleasant and relaxed. Far more so than the night before.

'Joseph tells me that you saw a man watching him, by the river wall at 11.10 last night, is that correct?'

The woman hesitated, before saying. 'You know that Joseph is terrified of him?'

'I do, but could you answer the question, please? What did he look like?'

Again there was a pause, and Nikki began to get both irritated and concerned.

'It was very dark, I hardly saw anything, although I think he had a hoody.'

'How tall, what build?'

'I'm not sure. I . . . well, oh damn it! No, Inspector, I never actually saw him.'

'But you told Joseph that you did!'

'Oh, I know I shouldn't have, but he was *so* distressed because he was the only one to ever spot him, that . . .' Bryony didn't sound so relaxed now. 'I'm sorry, I just couldn't bear to tell him that I hadn't seen the man for the second time.'

'You really saw no one at all?' asked Nikki, carefully enunciating every syllable.

'There was no one to see, Inspector. I turned around and the path by the river wall was empty. Even if he had jumped over and dropped down onto the towpath, I'm sure I would have seen him,' she sighed loudly. 'I'm sorry if I did wrong, but I really like Joseph, and I hated to see him so disturbed.'

'We *all* really like Joseph, Miss Barton, but lying won't help him one bit.' She knew her tone was frosty, but Bryony had just dashed her one hope of keeping Joseph out of trouble. She stared at her paper sheet, and put a thick cross through the name Bryony, her only witness to the fact that Billy Sweet even existed.

After she hung up, she stared again at the paper. One section said, *Chris Forbes, Railway station. Beale Street. No witnesses. No CCTV. Only one to see a stranger in the shadows, Joseph.*

The next section said, *Man in lane by nick. No CCTV footage. Seen only by Joseph. And she had been there then, and she saw no one other than the people on the CCTV.*

Man seen at river wall, only by Joseph.

Salmon Park Gardens. No witnesses. Only Joseph present.

Nikki's mouth had dried to a degree where it was almost impossible to swallow.

She thought hard about what she knew about him.

Joseph Easter, ex-Special Ops, suffered PTSD after a bodged operation in Africa, went on a journey of personal discovery before joining the police force. Admirable officer, makes detective sergeant then loses his DI at Fenchester and gets a temporary transfer, to a division where a bad case leaves him hospitalised.

Nikki's mind raced. Okay, so he'd had a tough life, but he had been fine until that man had appeared in the road in front of him.

That was the pivotal point. Everything that had happened, happened after that.

With a snort of disgust she grabbed the pen and looked at all the sections again.

Fact, she scribbled, *the CCTV at the nick is crap. Known black-spots, and they were exactly where Billy had stood. Fact. Joseph **could** have seen him.*

*The station. Poorly lit and poor security. Cab was not in the same line of vision. Fact. Joseph **could** have seen a man in the shadows.*

The river. Bryony was obviously totally wrapped up in the gorgeous Joseph's arms. The man could have shown himself to Joseph, then before she could stop dribbling over the sergeant and turn around, he could have vaulted the wall and run away. Not exactly fact, but possible.

And the second murder. The assassin could have been dressed in protective gear to make his kill. There was no CCTV in that part of the gardens. Fact. Joseph could have been set up.

She pushed her chair back and let out a long shuddery sigh. It didn't look good, and all right, she now understood why Walker was shitting hot bricks, but it was by no means cut and dried. And if Billy Sweet was the jungle guerrilla that Joseph said he was, then he would be easily clever enough to avoid cameras and witnesses. He'd survived war zones, Greenborough would be kid's stuff.

'Sorry, ma'am. Can I get on, or is it inconvenient?'

She had been so involved in her thoughts that she hadn't heard Dave enter. 'Come on in.' She folder up the paper, pushed it into her drawer and stood up. 'All yours.'

'Oh, before I start, the Salmon Park Gardens victim has been positively identified as David Ryan. His wife has also confirmed that he's been spending some time with some new mate, a guy who seemed to just show up one day when her husband was tinkering with his car. Dead helpful, apparently, but the wife never actually saw him.'

'Name?' asked Nikki, already knowing what she would hear.

'Just called him Snaz, guv. No name, no description. Ryan just told her that he was a wizard with engines.' Dave eased behind her desk, clicked on the emails and began printing them off. 'Ah, reams more info, I see.'

'I'll leave you to it, but don't work too late, will you? Your lovely wife needs you even more than me.' She walked towards the door, then heard a groan behind her.

'Hold up, ma'am. I think you'll want to see this.' Dave's voice was sombre. 'It's the copy of a death certificate. Billy Sweet is dead. Has been for four years.'

* * *

It had taken Nikki sometime to assimilate the bombshell that Dave had delivered, and the first thing she wanted was confirmation that the certificate was kosher.

'There's little doubt, ma'am.' Dave produced several other documents. 'He was involved in something on the Colombia/Ecuador border in South America. Containing marauding paramilitary groups, it says, and fighting with a small private force. A report states that Sweet died along with three others. Their Land Rover was ambushed.' He shrugged. 'No survivors.'

'Was he flown home for burial?'

'Doesn't look like it, guv. He was estranged from his family, and not being in the army anymore, I can't see anyone forking out a fortune to get him back, can you?'

'Probably not.' Nikki's head was still spinning. 'Who identified the body?'

Dave thumbed through several sheets of paper. 'Another ex-British army, turned soldier of fortune, by the look of it. Ah, and it says here that his personal effects were returned to England, where they were collected some while later by a relative. His body was interred in Colombia. There's a note of the location, some unpronounceable place outside Bogotá.'

'No chance of mistaken identity, then?'

'I'll dig deeper, ma'am. But there's an awful lot of official paperwork here, and it all looks pretty authentic.'

'Try to trace the man who identified the body, Dave. Several years have passed, maybe he's back here now. Get all the details you can, okay?'

'No problem, ma'am But would tomorrow be alright? I really need to get home.'

Nikki nodded. 'Of course. And thanks for what you've done today.'

'Not quite what we wanted to hear, though, ma'am.'

'You can say that again.' Nikki's brow furrowed. 'Where do we go from here?'

Dave tidied the paperwork into neat piles. 'Are you going to tell Joseph?'

'Good question, but I think not. Well, not just yet, he's got enough on his plate right now. So, Dave, keep this quiet for a bit longer, okay?'

Dave gave her a reassuring smile, and tapped the side of his nose. 'Mum's the word, guv. Give him my best.'

Alone in her office, Nikki stared at the death certificate. This changed everything. The last thing in the world that she wanted was for Chief Superintendent Walker to be right about Joseph's state of mind. If she were honest, she'd hate him to be right about anything at all. Sadly though, most of the aces that she thought she had up her sleeve were proving to be jokers, and Walker's case was becoming stronger by the minute. Nikki leaned back in her chair, and let out a long, audible sigh. She had rarely felt so confused, but no matter how bad she felt she needed to get home to Cloud Fen, and get there before the super. The least she could do was warn Joseph of what was to come. And procedure could go to hell.

CHAPTER EIGHTEEN

If she had felt bad before, now she felt like a complete shit.

Joseph had opened the door, a satisfied grin on his face, and presented her with a completed set of revised statistics for the superintendent. *And* she could smell something aromatic emanating from her kitchen.

'It's not much, hope you don't mind but I raided your frugal freezer and Spartan store cupboard and threw something together for supper.'

'Of course I don't mind. But surely nothing from my larder could smell that good?'

'Well, I did stop at that little farm shop just off the marsh lane, and picked up some fresh vegetables to bolster it up a bit.' He walked back to the kitchen and checked the stove. 'I thought we'd eat just after seven, if that's okay?'

Nikki's heart sank. At seven they would be receiving an uninvited guest. 'There's something I have to tell you, Joseph.'

'Shall we talk over a glass of wine?' He stood in front of her, a bottle of white in one hand, and a red in the other. 'You choose.'

'Whatever, just make it a large one.' There was no easy way to tell him. 'Joseph, Chief Superintendent Walker collared me this afternoon.'

'Haven't met him yet. Isn't that the guy who looks like a carrion crow wearing gold braid?'

'You got it, and he's after blood, Joseph. Yours.'

'Mine?' He handed her a glass of sparkly white wine, then stepped back and stared at her. 'Why?'

Nikki looked at him miserably. 'It seems top brass, in their infinite wisdom, are concerned about your health.' She took a slug of wine and shook her head in disgust. 'The super is coming here tonight to talk to you, and I want you to be prepared for the worst. He said they may be suspending you for a while.'

Joseph turned back to the hob, picked up a spoon and stirred whatever was in the iron pan. After a while, he said. 'I had a feeling this was going to happen.'

'Well, I didn't!' exploded Nikki. 'And I damn well told them so!'

Joseph gave a humourless chuckle, but kept his back to her. 'I'm sure you did. And I'm sure you got a bollocking for your trouble.'

'Sort of,' she muttered. 'Well, yes I did, and then I had to grovel to that beady-eyed, beak-nosed prig in order to stay on the case.'

'But it worked, didn't it?' Joseph turned quickly and she saw deep concern in his eyes. 'You are still on it?'

'Yeah, it worked. And I'm still leading. Just.' She took a slower sip of wine this time. 'And don't worry, Joseph. I promise to get to the bottom of this.'

'To be honest, everyone maybe safer with me out of the way for a while.' His voice lacked power and had a wistful tremor to it.

'I'm not sure I agree with that, but I'm going to get every available officer onto this. I want it cleared up fast. I want my sergeant back.'

He looked at her over the rim of his glass. 'Me too.'

'Do me one favour?'

'Of course.'

'Don't tell the super I warned you. You know, protocol, procedures and all that crap?'

'No problem. But how should I react? Shocked? Because I'm not. Angry? I'm disappointed, but not angry.' He shrugged. 'I don't know how I feel actually.'

'Then tell him that. Be honest.' She sat down at the kitchen table and looked up at him. 'And we need to be honest with each other too, Joseph. These killings have to stop, and you and I are going to have to explore the mind that is carrying them out. I *have* to find out what his endgame is, and stop him before he gets that far.'

'I'm not sure how you will achieve that, Nikki, but I'll help you all I can.'

'Thank you, Joseph.' Nikki gave him a long look. She had just said about being honest, and she was being far from that. If he knew that Billy Sweet was long dead, what would it do to him? Well, she wasn't about to find out. She needed a lot of answers to a lot of questions before she hit him with that little rocket.

'Do you think the super will want supper? I seem to have cooked enough for the whole team.'

'Probably not. I doubt he'll have much appetite after practising what to say to you.'

'He's got no choice, has he? If the order comes from higher up, he's just the mouthpiece, and I respect Superintendent Bainbridge.' He gave her a half-hearted smile. 'I won't give him a hard time.'

'I'll disappear when he gets here. Give you some privacy.'

'No. Stay. Please?'

'Who could resist such a plaintive plea?' Nikki smiled back. 'Sure I'll stay. I respect Rick Bainbridge too, and I like him, but I still think he deserves a bit of stick, don't you?'

'Okay, but nothing too harsh.' He sat down opposite her. 'You may need to keep him on our side.' He drew in a breath. 'At least I've done his figures, and I think he'll like the results. Now I can concentrate on Martin Durham.'

'You want to continue?' asked Nikki, trying to keep the surprise out of her voice.

'It'll have to be in an unofficial capacity, but I can follow up the other suicides using public sector info, can't I?'

'If you're okay with that, I'll get you everything you need. Well, as much as I can without dropping us both in the mire. At least it's a way to keep all our balls in the air, so to speak.'

'You nail Billy for me, Nikki, and I'll find you some answers about Martin. Deal?'

Nikki felt a shiver pass across her shoulders. Someone had already nailed Billy. So who was she chasing now? 'Deal,' she said with as much enthusiasm as she could muster, 'and the sooner the better. Now, what exactly is in that pan on the stove?'

* * *

Rick Bainbridge did eat with them, then left at around nine, with Joseph's warrant card safely in his inside pocket.

Joseph had pulled out all the stops to make the task easier for the super, too many for Nikki's liking, but then it wasn't her being suspended. Joseph had to deal with it he saw fit.

After they had cleared up the supper dishes, Nikki poured them both a snifter of her father's cognac and they talked for another hour before she turned in. As she pulled her bedroom curtains she reflected on what a world-class shitty day it had been. She had had such high hopes for her new team, and in just a few days everything, in the immortal words of Dave Harris, had gone to rat-shit. Somehow she needed to get her finger out and find Joseph's murdering stalker.

With a sigh she sunk into her bed and pulled the duvet around her. And now thanks to her beloved chief, she was without her sergeant. 'Great, fucking great,' she whispered as she closed her eyes.

* * *

Joseph stood at the window and looked down into the shadowy garden below. A few hours back he had come a hair's breadth from going out to meet Bryony. He had phoned her as promised, and they had talked for over half an hour and although the whole thing had a teenage dream feel to it, he liked it and it relaxed him.

Now it was after one in the morning, and he was far from relaxed. Not that he should be too worried about the late hour, he had no work to get up for. The plain fact was the news of his suspension had floored him. He had done his best to cover his true feelings, but he was devastated. Going right back to his school years, he had been conscientious and hardworking, and he'd never been 'removed' from anything in his life. And now, with his movements severely restricted, he was going to have to find a way to get to Billy through Nikki.

For a while he paced the room, but the old floorboards creaked and he didn't want to disturb whatever sleep she may be lucky enough to get, so he pulled on a sweater and quietly slipped out.

Making sure that he had his door key in his pocket, Joseph left Cloud Cottage Farm and walked down the moonlit lane to the marsh. He needed to think what his next move would be.

More to the point, he needed to think what Billy's next move would be. And he needed to think fast, before someone else died.

Joseph was not the only one who could not sleep. Nikki's mind had no intentions of letting her switch off, and highest on her list of insomnia-inducing problems was

Joseph and his conviction that a dead soldier was going around killing the residents of Greenborough.

She tossed around trying to get comfortable, but only succeeded in losing the duvet. She dragged it back from the floor and then pummelled her pillow angrily before flopping back into it. No matter how bad it looked, and Jesus, right now it looked sodding dreadful, she could not bring herself to believe that Joseph was in anyway other than an involuntary one, involved. There was obviously a connection, but what it was she could not begin to understand, and the dead of night was not the best time to be logical.

Nikki squeezed her eyes tight shut and decided it was time for the word game. She needed to slip her brain into a different gear, and the game usually worked. Take a letter of the alphabet and name all the film titles you could. She shifted to her side. Last time it was *F* so . . .

Genevieve, Gigi, The Great Escape, The Great Gatsby.

What if Joseph really were still suffering from the aftermath of his attack? What if the man who pulled a face at him through his windscreen reminded him of other horrors, African horrors?

Concentrate, Nikki. *Gallipoli, Gremlins, Guess Who's Coming to Dinner?*

And what if all that trauma came bubbling back to the surface? What if . . . ?

She yawned. *The Green Mile, Ghost, Gone With the Wind.*

First thing in the morning she'd talk it through with Dave. And maybe Cat. Dave had experience and age on his side, but Cat had intuition and an almost feral streetwise instinct about her. She had the feeling that she would be needing them both.

Gothika. Get Carter. Ghostbusters.

As sleep began to gently dull her senses, she vaguely heard footsteps on the stairs, but told herself that it was no wonder Joseph was awake. All evening he'd seemed so in control, but she was sure that deep down he was hurting.

She wondered if she should go down and keep him company, but before she could make a decision, she drifted unresisting, into the arms of Morpheus.

CHAPTER NINETEEN

Her waking moment was a far less peaceful affair, with her alarm shrieking in one ear, the phone blaring in the other.

'DI Galena,' she mumbled, still trying to silence her clock with her other hand.

'Nikki, can you get in, pronto?' The superintendent sounded out of breath.

'Yeah, of course.' She scrambled from her bed, still holding the phone. 'What's happening?'

'I'll tell you when you get here. Quick as you can.' The phone clicked, then hummed softly. Damn! She flung the receiver back in its cradle then hastily pulled her duvet up in a poor semblance of tidiness. A shower would have to wait. As would breakfast. She pulled clothes swiftly from drawers and cupboards, then hoping she didn't look too much of a rag-bag, hunted for some shoes.

As she moved along the landing she saw that Joseph's door was still closed, but hearing the soft, sonorous sound of his breathing, she ran down the stairs, scribbled him a note, and dashed to her car. The super had left her in no doubt regarding urgency, but she just wished he'd told her why. Guessing, these days, was a pretty unnerving pastime, and her imagination was already on high alert.

As she swung past the lane to Knot Cottage, she felt a pang of sorrow tug at her heart. Martin was being put on the back burner again and that was not how she wanted it to be. Luckily Joseph was still game to keep delving, which was something, but it wasn't her, and she still felt horribly guilty about her promise to her old friend.

And this melancholia was getting her precisely nowhere.

With a grunt of irritation at herself, she pulled up onto the main road, and jammed her foot down. Something had happened, and she needed to know what the hell it was, and she wouldn't do that by dawdling along like a bloody tourist.

She didn't quite beat her PB for speed from Cloud Fen to the nick, but it had been an impressive ride, and most effective in concentrating her wandering thoughts. As she strode through the foyer, she had left the weak, sensitive woman wandering somewhere on the marsh, and she was now one hundred per cent tenacious detective again.

'The super?' she barked to the desk sergeant.

'Murder room, ma'am. With the chief.'

She raised a hand in acknowledgement, and cursed under her breath. Walker was rarely seen at this hour, and his presence didn't bode well.

'Nikki.' The super looked grey, and she guessed that he'd had about as much sleep as she had. 'Sorry to drag you from your bed but there's been another incident.' He glanced across to the chief, who looked irritatingly immaculate and very well rested, and said, 'Shall we take this into my office?'

After the door closed, he said, 'There was an attempted abduction in the early hours of the morning. Another young man with similar facial features and hair colour to the two dead men. But this time he survived.'

'So what went wrong?' asked Nikki urgently. 'If it was our ultra-efficient assassin, how come his victim escaped?'

'Pure luck, by the sound of it,' said the chief.

'Yes, chance,' added the super. 'One of our uniformed crews made an unofficial stop at the bakery on West Lee Road, at just before three in the morning.'

'Unofficial? That bakery practically relies on us for their doughnut sales! Our lads are there all hours of the day and night!'

'Maybe, but last night one of the baker's wanted to show off his new Kawasaki motorcycle. He took our two men out to the back car park, and that was when they disturbed something.'

'They saw him?'

'No. The footpath along the back has no street lights, and by the time our officers got there, the attacker had done a vanishing act through the back alleys.'

'And the victim? Did he see anything?'

'Too busy trying to avoid being murdered, Inspector,' said the chief sourly. 'But he did get a glimpse of what the man was wearing.'

'And?' asked Nikki.

The chief picked up a statement and read, 'Desert boots and camouflage pants.'

'Military?'

'You can buy any of that on the market or from a surplus store.'

'And is the victim badly injured?'

The super stretched. 'Thankfully not, other than a bruised neck and being scared half to death.'

'What was he doing there, sir?' asked Nikki.

'We think he was sneaking back home after an assignation with his mate's wife. His version varies slightly from that, but I don't think it's too important. It's the other man we want, and this time let's just hope that we get lucky with some DNA from the intended mark.' He leaned forward and in a confidential tone, said, 'This does make something a little easier though. Joseph wasn't involved this time,' he smiled at her, his relief plain to see, 'because he was with you, miles away on Cloud Fen.'

'And no doubt you will confirm that, Nikki?' The chief blinked his hooded eyes.

She threw him a withering look. 'Absolutely. There when I went to bed, there when I got up, and I heard him pacing the floor for half the night.' She gave him her best attempt at a smile and added, 'So can he come back to work, sir?'

'No, Inspector. His mental state is still in question. I want a full evaluation and medical report before that can happen.'

Yes, you would, wouldn't you, she thought, but just nodded and said, 'Of course.'

'We've got the man who was attacked downstairs, Nikki,' said the superintendent. 'He's been checked over at the hospital and given the all clear, so I expect you'd like a word with him.'

Nikki nodded. 'I'll brief my team, then I'll go speak to him, sir.'

'Right, well I have a meeting.' The chief picked up his hat from the table and walked to the door. 'Keep me up to date, Superintendent.'

Nikki followed him out and saw the retreating figure of Walker heading towards the lifts. She had sworn to him that Joseph had been in her home from dusk to dawn, but had he?

As she made her way along the corridor, all she could hear were footfalls on the stairs of Cloud Cottage Farm, and maybe the sound of a door closing? She'd rather stick pins her eyes than tell the chief, but in truth, she had no idea where Joseph had been at three that morning.

* * *

Dave and Cat arrived early, both carrying paper bags and polystyrene beakers. By that time Nikki had put together a pretty concise overview of the whole murder case, and after instructing them to bring their breakfast into her office, she closed the door and proceeded to tell them everything she knew. She left nothing out, except the details of the massacre in the Congo and Joseph's unfortunate involvement. She did tell them however that Billy Sweet had been suspected of killing both his own mates and innocent women.

'And Joseph believes this lunatic is here in Greenborough?' asked Cat incredulously.

'He's certain of it.' Nikki drummed her fingers on the desk. 'But as Dave will explain, this can't be true.'

Dave detached the death certificate from a sheaf of papers and handed it to Cat.

'Oh dear. So *who* is running around town trying to eradicate corn-dolly haircuts and pale blue eyes?' Cat nibbled on her lip. 'And we mustn't forget that all the victims are Billy Sweet lookalikes.' She scratched her head. 'I don't get it.'

'Well, I've been up half the night thinking about it, and this is my only conclusion.' Dave stared at his Danish as if he hoped that it would give him inspiration. 'It's got to be an old case, something from Fenchester. We have to get him to think about anyone who has threatened him or bears him a serious grudge.'

'But where does Billy Sweet come into it?' asked Cat.

'Hate is a powerful emotion. It can make a man very patient.' Dave took a small bite of his pastry. 'Someone has taken a lot of time to go back into the past, and they found a nasty rotten apple called Sweet. The very reason that Joseph threw up his glowing career in the army.'

'But we've established that Sweet is dead,' added Nikki impatiently.

'But Joseph doesn't know that, does he?' said Dave patiently. 'So you find someone who looks like him, then you make sure that Joseph believes it *is* him.'

'Mm, that's possible,' said Cat hopefully. 'And what a perfect time to hassle the sarge. When he's just returned from sick leave and is still pretty shaky.'

'Sorry . . .' Nikki rubbed her forehead. 'Surely you're missing something. Why would this Pseudo-Sweet kill people? Why not just haunt Joseph, and send him quietly batty?'

'Because,' said Dave. 'The real Sweet was a killer. It's part of the package if he's to convince Joseph.'

Nikki considered his point. 'Okay, I'll run with that, but where does all this finish? What is his endgame?'

'To ruin the sarge, I'd reckon,' muttered Dave grimly.

'And it looks like it's working, wouldn't you say, ma'am?' added Cat. 'He's already been relegated to knitting socks and watching *Loose Women*.'

'He's not quite that bad yet,' said Nikki ruefully. 'But I get your point.'

'Let's just hope it's not going to go one step further,' said Dave ominously. 'And the sarge becomes the final victim.'

'Oh shit,' whispered Cat. 'The assassin is clearly being paid very well by someone, so that could be the logical finale for total revenge. Put the frighteners on him, then kill him.'

At that, the office fell silent, and several things ran through Nikki's brain simultaneously. If that were the case, then Joseph was not safe out on the fen. He was actually very vulnerable. And something Cat had just said jarred off an even worse scenario. One that she didn't even dare to voice out loud.

Cat had mentioned Joseph's recent trauma. So what if there was no revenge plot? What if there was no Billy Sweet? Real or otherwise. What if the face in the windscreen had just been some brainless yob, one who closely resembled the worst person Joseph had ever met? And it had sent his mind into freefall. Could Joseph be hunting this mythical being down and killing men who were unfortunate enough to look like Sweet?

Nikki physically shook her head to rid herself of those terrible thoughts. Of course he wasn't a killer! He was her sergeant and her friend! He was living under her roof, and she cared about him. A lot, actually. The idea that she had just considered belonged to people like Walker, or the gutter press, not to Nikki Galena. 'Okay, any other thoughts?' she snapped.

'I think I'm with Dave, ma'am,' said Cat, 'But, if you don't mind me saying, Joseph is only a sergeant. I can understand him being threatened with a damn good thumping, or getting his car vandalised, but surely death threats are more the suited to the higher ranks, the ones who actually head up the investigations. Joseph is a worker, not a big cheese. If some villain got slammed up forever, wouldn't he or his loved ones, go for someone like you, or the super, maybe?'

'You can still piss someone off, no matter what your rank, Cat. And who's to say we are dealing with someone sane?'

'That's right,' Dave nodded vigorously. 'If you're short on your quota of marbles, rational thinking doesn't apply.'

'So we check his old cases?' asked Cat.

Nikki nodded. 'I'll ring him and ask him to get us a list of 'possibles' together. And until then, you Dave, follow up those enquiries on Sweet, and Cat, keep busy until I've made my call, then come with me and we'll talk to the one that got away.'

'Ah yes, the third lookalike? Will do.' Cat stood up, and gave a small laugh. 'Shame they're not all still alive, we could start a Billy Sweet tribute band.'

As Cat left, a civilian messenger knocked on the door. 'Sorry to interrupt, ma'am, but there's someone to see you downstairs.'

'A name would be helpful.'

'Sorry.' The woman glanced at a memo held firmly in her hand. 'Bryony Barton, ma'am.'

Nikki felt her lips purse together, then she forcibly relaxed them and said, 'I'll be right down.'

'Ah,' said Dave knowingly, and then shut up as she lobbed a few imaginary daggers in his direction.

'Ah nothing.'

'Whatever you say, guv.' Dave grinned. 'But I was only going to offer to see her for you, as you're so busy?'

'Drooling is not gentlemanly, Dave. Please slip a bromide in your tea and get on with your work. I can manage, thank you.'

Nikki hurried down the corridor, and silently cursed the super for interrupting her morning ablutions. Her outfit didn't even qualify as bag-lady chic. It was more like she had dressed herself entirely from Help the Aged, and now she was to meet Joseph's stunning new girlfriend. O deep joy!

Nikki stared at her surreptitiously from the office behind the front desk, and felt her heart sink.

Joseph had been right. Bryony was beautiful. But not in a glamorous way, she was not fashion magazine, size zero and brainlessly sort of gorgeous, she had more the beauty of the panther. She was one of those incredibly lucky people who seemed to be perfectly proportioned, and knew exactly how to dress to make the best of everything.

And she looked intelligent, which made Nikki definitely wish she had allowed Dave to take her place.

A low babble of voices pulled her from her reverie, and she realised that breathing was becoming difficult due to the office rapidly filling up with testosterone. At least ten male officers had magically appeared from nowhere and were collectively staring towards the waiting area.

'For goodness sake! Haven't you lot got something better to do?' she exclaimed. The expected chorus of 'No!' followed her as she left.

'Bryony?' She stretched out a hand. 'Nikki Galena. You wanted to see me?'

The handshake was surprisingly firm. 'Thank you. I'm sorry to bother you. I'll only take a few moments of your time.'

Nikki glanced across to the sergeant. 'Is there a free interview room, Jack?'

'Number three, ma'am. All yours.'

'This way.' Nikki made herself walk confidently, but still felt like one of the ugly sisters escorting Cinderella.

She held back the door and indicated towards a chair. 'Sorry it's not more comfortable, but most of our guests aren't here for the fine facilities.' She managed to install a smile for the occasion. 'What can I do for you, Bryony?'

The woman looked up at her, her expression concerned and intense. 'Joseph rang me last night, Inspector. He told me that he'd been suspended. Is that true?'

'Joseph's not in the habit of lying.' She kept her own gaze impassive. 'It's true.'

'Oh no.' The woman seemed to visibly crumple. 'This is my fault, isn't it?'

Nikki felt confused, but didn't show it.

'You suspended him because of what I told you, didn't you? But the thing is, I don't think I put it very well, Inspector.'

Nikki sat down opposite her. 'First, *I* did not suspend him, and second, your failing to identify the mystery man had no bearing on why Joseph was asked to rest up for a while.' She was not known for her tact, but she thought that sounded fairly acceptable.

'But I still let him down.'

'You finally told the truth, and believe me, that's a far better bet than lying.' She stared at the fine-boned face and porcelain skin, and said. 'Have you told Joseph that you didn't actually see anyone?'

Bryony shifted around in the uncomfortable chair, and stared at the table in front of her. 'Not yet. I've been going over and over it. Now I honestly don't know if someone was there or not. It was dark, and I admit, my attention was rather more on Joseph than what was happening on the other side of the road.' She hung her head. 'All I know is, Joseph truly thought someone was watching us. His face changed from a smiling, relaxed man, to some kind of awful mask. He was terrified, Inspector. And when I made to run over to the river path, he *screamed* at me to let the man go.'

Nikki watched the other woman carefully. Bryony was not finding this easy, and it was obvious to Nikki that she really did care about Joseph, which was not exactly what she wanted to know right now.

'I know that you won't be able to tell me where he is, Inspector, but is he all right? I feel dreadful that I can't see him, but he says it's too dangerous.'

'He's only thinking of you, Bryony. And I know you wouldn't want to add to his present worries, he has a lot to deal with right now,' she paused, 'but yes, he's taken everything very well, all things considered.'

'Well, that's something. I'll just have to be satisfied with his calls until this is all over.' She straightened her skirt, even though it didn't need it, and looked almost coyly at Nikki. 'I've never met a man like Joseph before. He's so . . .'

Special? Different? Caring? Honest? Nikki automatically filled in the gap.

'. . . so selfless, and gentlemanly. And that's rare in a good-looking man.'

Nikki nodded. Yes, that was two pretty good adjectives, but at this point in time Joseph's love life was not what she wanted to be talking about. 'I'm sorry, I have to get on. I hope I've put your mind at rest?' She stood up.

'You have, and thank you for your time.' Bryony said, picking up her handbag. 'And, Inspector, if you see him or speak to him, please don't tell him I was here, or what I said to you. I think it's down to me to explain to him, don't you?'

'I think you *should* explain things.'

'I will. I promise. And maybe I should come clean about a few other things as well.'

Nikki tensed. 'Like what?'

Bryony gave a small conspiratorial laugh. 'It's okay. It's nothing serious, and nothing to do with what is going on, but I've liked him for ages. I saw him months ago at Greenborough Hospital, and I tried to find out about him.' She halted as she approached the door. 'I thought a gorgeous man like that would be bound to have either a wife or a significant other, so I kind of engineered an 'accidental' meeting.'

'The fitness club?' asked Nikki, trying to keep the surprise out of her voice.

'Mm. I do swim and I do exercise, but I'm a strong swimmer, so I've always used the big pool out at Carness. I was dropping off a friend at the Greenborough club one day, and couldn't believe that he was there, in the pool! I immediately bought a membership, and the rest is history.'

'And the meeting in the Hammer?'

'Oh God! You make me sound like a stalker. No, that was for real. My boss truly was organising a charity scavenger hunt.'

'You really like him, don't you?' said Nikki almost sadly.

Bryony looked at her for a minute, apparently weighing something up, then said, 'I've had some seriously shitty experiences in the past, Inspector. My opinion regarding men is not high, but Joseph is different. Very different.'

'Then I strongly urge you to tell him everything. Policemen don't like being lied to, Bryony, no matter how well-meaning your intentions. We get lies every day from the bad guys, so we don't expect it from the good ones.'

'I've been a complete fool, haven't I?' Bryony drew in a breath. 'But I do hear what you say, and thanks.'

Nikki escorted her back to the foyer, and as she turned to leave, Bryony said. 'Take care of him for me, Inspector. I think he's very lucky to have you for a friend.'

Nikki moved closer to her and spoke in a soft but urgent voice. 'I'll do my best. Just don't be tempted to see him, Bryony. Considering how you feel, it could be very dangerous, for both of you, understand?'

Bryony nodded slowly, then moved towards the automatic doors. 'I understand.'

Nikki listened to the whoosh of the doors, and made her way thoughtfully back to her office.

* * *

As Bryony Barton crossed the street, and walked down the narrow side road to where her car was parked, a man watched her with great interest.

He did not attract attention to himself. He realised a long while ago that Good Ordinary People preferred to avert their eyes from his kind. And he had a lot of things about him that those Good Ordinary People would rather not associate with. He was dirty for one thing. His clothes told of neglect and abuse, ergo, he would smell. GOP's didn't like bad smells at all. He had strange eyes, which probably meant drugs, and oh my! How GOP's hated drugs! And he was pretty big, which meant don't pick on him. A fight would definitely see a GOP coming second. Oh yes, and he was begging. Which was the only risky thing in his beautifully practised repertoire for blending in perfectly with the pavements, the trodden-in chewing gum and the dog shit. The paper cup with Please Give scribbled on it could be the weak link, because some of the GOPs were actually Do-Gooders, and DGs looked upon beggars as a large part of their insurance to travel on the road to heaven. Beggars were to be fed, nurtured and cosseted, at arm's length of course, but that could be dangerous.

Today however he was having an invisible day, which suited him perfectly.

That meant that no one saw him stand up, slip catlike across the road, and as Bryony opened her car-door, he was behind her. Breathing in her perfume.

Escada. Magnetism.

My God, the woman had good taste.

But sadly there wasn't time right now to extol her virtues, because there was work to be done and an exacting schedule to keep to.

In less than a minute, the car had pulled away, and the side road was once again empty, with no trace of either Bryony Barton, or her invisible follower.

CHAPTER TWENTY

Joseph looked up from the computer screen and rubbed his eyes. He could hardly believe that it was after one o'clock and somehow he had finally calmed down enough to concentrate on Martin Durham.

Nikki had called earlier and told him that Sweet had attempted to kill again. The news had almost sent him to the wire, but somehow he'd managed to drag himself back. Deep down he knew that the only way he was going to come through this with his sanity intact was to throw his whole self into working. Which sounded great, but without his warrant card he was stuffed! Even with the Durham case, he had taken his search about as far as it could go without using official channels. He needed Nikki to get him some more information, but with the world going crazy at Greenborough nick, he didn't have the heart to bother her. Then on the other hand, perhaps he should, because there were things about those two odd deaths, Amelia Reed and Paul Cousins, that were starting to bug him.

He pushed his chair back and stretched his cramped legs. On the desk in front of him was a rough list of known villains who might carry a grudge against him.

Nikki had wanted him to think about old cases, but although there were a lot of them, and some where vague threats had been made, no one stood out as being flaky enough to want to destroy him. He pushed the list to one side. It was a total waste of time. No crook he had ever banged up would organise a vendetta like this. And right now he needed a break. He wanted to think objectively about Reed and Cousins and everything else was getting in the way. Maybe he should go out for a while. Go get some food in. Some proper food, not makeshift junk. Something he could use as therapy to help him think.

He stretched again, stood up and tried to remember what was the most labour intensive dish he had ever cooked. And what would Nikki like? Frankly, she seemed to enjoy anything that was put in front of her. He smiled. It was nice to cook for someone else. And that made him think about Bryony, and he couldn't wait to prepare a meal for her. He was sure she'd appreciate it. Not that Nikki didn't, but it would be different cooking for a . . .

He stopped himself. A what? What would Bry become? A lover? A partner? He wasn't sure, and dreaded to let himself get too far ahead. And where exactly did he intend to do this fancy cooking? His digs had very limited facilities and certainly didn't include a *Master Chef* kitchen.

Again his mind wandered. He had said he'd sit on the money from his Fenchester home after he'd sold it, but maybe he should be looking for somewhere in or around Greenborough.

And maybe he should damn well keep his mind firmly on his work. He had no right to make plans for anything or anybody until Billy Sweet had been caught. Even thinking of that name made him angry. Sweet had no right to walk back into his life and bring his whole world crashing down around his feet.

With a muttered curse, Joseph picked up the phone, dialled Nikki's landline and asked her if there was any new developments.

'Nothing yet, Joseph.'

The boss sounded preoccupied, and why shouldn't she? 'I was wondering if you'd heard from Elizabeth Durham?' he asked.

'She rang earlier, but with all of this going on, I can't get out to see her.'

'Could I go, ma'am? I'm well and truly stuck here. There are things I need to know about Martin and I'm sure she could help.'

There had been a long wait, then in a low voice, she said, 'I'd rather you didn't, Joseph. I don't want the chief on my back. But then again, it has nothing to do with the main murder enquiry and I'm not your jailer, so if you did take upon yourself to go out for an afternoon ride, I would know nothing about it, would I? Just don't breathe a word about your suspension to anyone. We could both finish up down the Job Centre.'

'I have to go out anyway, unless you want us to starve. I thought I'd try the big supermarket on the Old Bolingbroke Road?'

'How convenient. But Joseph?'

'Yes, ma'am?'

'Take care, won't you? We haven't caught this killer yet, and I'm really not sure that it's wise for you to be trailing round the countryside alone.'

* * *

He had rung Elizabeth before he set out, and she had seemed pleased that he was able to see her. When he arrived, the door was opened by Janna.

'I'm surprised that you could spare the time, with these awful murders to investigate.' Her comment was not sarcastic, just a genuine observation, then she led him through to the garden room and flopped into one of the deep comfortable chairs. 'Have a seat, Sergeant.'

'Thanks. It's true we're busy, but the boss doesn't want you to feel that we are doing nothing about Martin's death.'

'Elizabeth will be grateful for that. She's starting to get very jumpy about everything, especially the break-in.'

'Wouldn't anyone feel jumpy?' Elizabeth had just done one of her famous silent entrances.

'I think you have every right,' said Joseph seriously and took out his notebook and a pen. 'Now I wonder if you would help me out with the answers to some questions?'

Elizabeth sat down. 'Anything I can tell you, I will.'

'Janna mentioned that something happened to your brother, a very long time ago. What was it?'

'Sadly, he never told me much, but it concerned his health and some treatment that he received. He was very poorly, he nearly died, but when he recovered, he had changed.'

'How so?'

'It's hard to say, but he was different.' A perplexed expression clouded her features. 'Maybe these will help you to understand.' She leant down and picked up a box that sat on the floor beside her chair. 'You are welcome to take them as long as I get them back.'

Joseph took the box and opened it. Inside were two large envelopes, one marked BEFORE, and the other, AFTER. Inside were press cuttings and dozens of photographs. Some coloured, others black-and-white. Most had names, dates and locations carefully written on the back.

'I couldn't remember all the names or places. But you'll see when you look through, he has gone from being outgoing and gregarious, to becoming a loner.'

'Oh, he was not that bad,' chipped in Janna. 'He just liked the marshes and his work. Everyone on Cloud Fen loved him, he was hardly some Fenland Howard Hughes, now was he?'

'You never knew him before, sweetheart.'

'A brush with death does alter people,' said Joseph gravely.

'I'm sure. But there were other things. We'd always been so close, but he just stopped confiding in me, Sergeant. He had been practically penniless, then he came home and he had money in his pocket, and he would never say where it came from.'

Joseph thought quickly. It sounded like a bungled operation, or some medical blunder that had ended up in an out-of-court payout. 'Where was he treated?'

'The Gordon Peace Memorial Hospital. It closed when they built Greenborough General.'

'I recall hearing the name somewhere.' Joseph racked his brain for a connection, but nothing materialised. 'I'll try to look into that, but the length of time that had passed won't make it easy, neither will the fact that all their notes will have been transferred, maybe even destroyed, years ago.'

'Martin was adamant that there had been no blunders, if that's what you're thinking. He said they had done all they could, and he was indebted to them.'

Maybe he was, but maybe he had accepted a hefty bung, and was happy with his lot. Joseph scribbled a few notes, then asked. 'About his medication? Am I right in thinking that you were upset when we asked about them before?'

Elizabeth Durham sighed. 'I'm sorry. It was all rather too much to handle at the time.' She sat back. 'His ongoing medication had been something of a *bête noire* for me. They gave him some quite awful side effects, and no matter what I told him about medical advances, he refused to have them reviewed. He said that the clinic who looked after him knew exactly what they were doing and that I wasn't to interfere.'

'It was the only thing they ever argued about,' added Janna.

'Would that be the oncology clinic?'

'I think so.' Elizabeth frowned. 'It must have been. He didn't go anywhere else.'

'Did you ever go with him?'

She gave a cheerless shake of her head. 'Never. He never allowed me to.'

Now, there's a surprise, thought Joseph. 'So, when you two decided to turn sleuth, you were checking Knot Cottage for anything that could relate to his time in hospital?'

They both nodded glumly. 'Sorry about that, Sergeant. We weren't trying to hamper your investigation, we just thought we might recognise something that would mean little or nothing to you.'

'But there was nothing at all.'

'Nothing. Either the intruder took them, or they were never there.'

'One last question, Ms Durham. Did Martin ever mention, or do you know of Paul Cousins, or Amelia Reed?'

'Amelia! We all knew her, Sergeant. St Francis was a positive philistine compared to Amelia! She was an animal angel, poor soul, until that terrible accident.'

'Or was it suicide?' added Janna quietly. 'They never gave a verdict, remember?' She stared at Joseph. 'You surely don't think there's a connection, do you?'

'No, I'm just trying to make comparisons, and as they were both local, I wondered if you or your brother may have known them.'

'The name Cousins means nothing, but Amelia was an institution around here. We went to the same school, were quite friendly at one point, although that seems a very long time ago.' Elizabeth Durham pointed to the box of photographs. 'I think there's a snap of all of us in there.'

'Sergeant?' Janna leaned forward. 'When I saw you last you indicated a possibility of foul play? Do you still feel that way?'

'I can't comment officially,' said Joseph cautiously. 'But I am very disturbed by the whole scenario, it just doesn't ring true, and there are too many unanswered questions regarding his medication.'

'Like what?' asked Janna.

'He received tablets from his GP, a controlled regime that she was hoping to revise in the near future, but he also had other medication, in plain white boxes.'

'They would be the ones that he received direct from the clinic,' responded Elizabeth. 'They were sent either by courier, or Martin would collect them from the post office in the next village.'

A prickle of discomfort jabbed away in Joseph's head. Clever, considering the clinic said they had never heard of Martin Durham. Still, now was not the time to share this knowledge. 'And that was a long-term thing, was it?'

'Oh yes, for years.'

'I think I'd better go see this clinic,' said Joseph, almost to himself.

'Then perhaps you would you be kind enough to notify them of my brother's death, and tell them to stop sending the medication?'

'Of course. Happy to.' Best that way, mused Joseph. We don't want too many people getting involved in that place. Not until we've found out why they are denying all knowledge of Martin. 'Now I should be getting back. But thank you for your assistance.'

'Any time, Sergeant Easter. And if I find anything else that may be helpful to you, I'll ring the station, shall I?'

'Ring DI Galena direct. I'm out and about rather a lot at present. She'll pass anything on, I can assure you.'

* * *

It took Joseph two hours to shop and find his way back to Nikki's place. And when he finally arrived on the fen, ominous dark clouds were moving in from the east, and the marsh was beginning to lose its magic. In fact, to the town-boy even the air seemed charged and threatening.

'Too much sky,' he muttered as he pulled bulging bags of shopping from the boot.

Once inside he felt better, especially when he entered the kitchen. He had thought it before, but there was such a good feel to that particular room that if he had lived there permanently, it would have been the hub of his universe.

He unpacked the provisions and put them away, then pulled out a sealed package from the last of the bags and unwrapped a new pay-as-you-go mobile phone. He had felt naked without any form of contact while driving, and this would suffice until he got his own all-singing, all-dancing version back from the lab.

He inserted the SIM card, set it up and activated it. As he waited for it to charge, he rang Bryony on the landline. After a while he hung up. She would probably be busy. Maybe he shouldn't phone her at work anyway, a lot of companies didn't appreciate their staff taking personal calls. Still, it was strange that her voicemail didn't pick up.

Not to worry, he told himself, they'd have a long talk later that night, right now it was time for his therapeutic hobby.

Joseph chopped, sliced and diced for half an hour, then with a contented sigh, covered all his preparations with cling-film and stored them in the fridge. He then cleaned the table down, and went to get the Durham family picture archive and all his previous notes, photos and files on Reed and Cousins.

He looked at the photos first, laying them out over the table, and quietly scanning them. It didn't take long to understand what Elizabeth had meant. His early pictures showed a true live wire, a Jack the Lad, surrounded by friends, grinning, pulling faces and acting the fool. The later ones were far more subdued, and generally they featured only Martin, although one or two were taken with Elizabeth. A close brush with death? Joseph shivered, then replaced the recent ones in their sleeve, and concentrated on the early years. If he were to find something, he was sure it came from a long time ago.

He then looked at the notes and files pertaining to Amelia, Paul and Martin, scribbling down anything that might be relevant, then cross-checking them. Dates of birth, addresses, schools, religion, hobbies, early jobs, family history. Nothing particularly linked them, except the fact that Martin's sister had gone to school with Amelia, and that wasn't enough.

Joseph returned to the photographs, but after thirty minutes still had found nothing. With a grunt of disapproval, he got up to stretch his legs, but as he did so he clipped the folder on Amelia Reed with his elbow, and sent pictures and reports flying across the quarry tiles.

Grabbing them back up, and trying to replace them in some semblance of order, he was struck by something he hadn't noticed before. A forensic photograph of Amelia's body. But it wasn't the pale corpse that drew his eye, like iron-filings to a magnet. To one side of her, on a shelf close to the bath, was a tablet box. A plain white tablet box.

Joseph raced through to the study and scanned the picture. As soon as he had it on the screen, he zoomed in on the packet, and let out a low whistle. The enhanced picture showed a box of the same dimensions as the ones found at Knot Cottage, and the only thing on it was a small rectangular label. It was exactly the same as Martin's.

He printed off the picture and picked up the phone. 'Ma'am, I need a favour.'

Nikki had sounded horribly distracted, but scribbled down his request. 'I'll get Yvonne or Niall to go down and see what they can find, but it'll take a while, you know what the evidence store is like.'

'At least the store is on the premises. At Fenchester our store was twenty miles away in a secure unit.'

'And you realise there may be nothing there. It's not as if Paul Cousin's death was considered a murder.'

'I know that, ma'am. But it's on record that there was such a furore when it happened that a lot of questions were asked, and serious enquiries were made, to cover ourselves I guess, but his medication was definitely sent for analysis.'

'Okay, well, I'll ring you if they find anything.' He heard her yawn, then she said, 'Is everything alright there?'

'Apart from looking like Armageddon outside.' He glanced at the window and saw diagonal splashes of rain across the glass. 'I think we're in for a summer storm.'

'They can be quite spectacular out on the marsh. I'd batten down the hatches if I were you.'

'Will do. Any idea what time you'll be back? I have a small banquet planned, and a nice Sancerre chilling in the fridge.'

'I can't say, Joseph, and I'm not sure I'm that hungry, so please don't go to a lot of trouble.'

He frowned down the phone. Generally, when you mentioned food or wine, Nikki showed considerable enthusiasm. 'Hey! It's no trouble,' he said sincerely. 'You are being good enough to put me up, the least I can do is look after you, and maybe even rekindle your culinary spirit?'

'*Re*-kindle?' she asked. 'I don't think that spark ever got ignited in the first place.'

There was at least a slight hint of amusement. 'I'll try to get back by seven, okay?'

'Then go careful on the roads. This is the first rain we've had for weeks, so it could be slippery.'

'Thank you, Grandmother. I'll be sure to heed your sage advice.' She hung up abruptly and left him wondering what was going on at the nick, and whether anyone would find what he was looking for in the evidence store.

He walked slowly back to the kitchen and began to gather up the pictures. Elizabeth had said that there was one of Amelia. From the press cuttings she had appeared tall and willowy, with a wiry strength, strong jutting jaw-line and piercing intelligent eyes. He wondered what she had looked like as a young woman. He skimmed through the names on the back, then saw *Martin, Barry, Mel, Lewis and me. Home after second term at uni.* Mel? Amelia? He looked closer.

The picture showed five friends fooling around beside a rust-bucket of a Ford Anglia. Elizabeth was easy to spot, so as Amelia was the only other girl, he quickly identified her, and even back then her appearance was striking. Joseph stared at the photograph and memories of his own uni days washed over him. This was considerably earlier of course, Martin had been fifty when he died, almost fifteen years older than him, but the dynamic of the group looked very similar.

He wondered where they were, but as he was not a local, he wasn't sure. Then he made out a lot of other cars in the background, and saw part of a large sign, in particular the word, *Gordon.* Maybe the Gordon Peace Memorial Hospital? Joseph stared again. Funny place for kids to hang out.

Suddenly his thoughts started to crank up again. He'd seen mention of this hospital somewhere in Paul Cousin's notes. That was why it had rung a bell when Elizabeth had mentioned it earlier! That, and something else. But to his annoyance, the something else was still lying dormant in some closed compartment of his brain.

Whatever, it actually linked all three. Not that he should get too hopeful. The hospital served a wide area, and Martin, Paul and Amelia were locals, it stood to reason they would have attended at some point in their lives.

He turned the photo over again. There was no date on it, but that could easily be checked with Elizabeth. He sat back and smiled at the table full of old pictures. It all starts here. I'm certain of it. And if the evidence store came up trumps too, we've finally got a lead.

At four p.m. the phone rang.

'You are one jammy sod, Joseph Easter! Yvonne has located a box marked Cousins in the evidence store. And guess what's in it?'

'Medication?'

'Too right. And one lot of tablets is in a very familiar plain white box.'

'Yes!' Joseph punched the air. 'That's it! Now we've got a place to start!'

CHAPTER TWENTY-ONE

Nikki arrived home just as the storm hit. Winds gusted straight in from the North Sea and battered against the old house, and it was all she could do to keep upright as she fought her way from the car.

She practically fell inside and slammed the door behind her, then was greeted by the most delicious smell of cooking.

'I thought I said no trouble!' she said, pulling off her soaking wet jacket.

'Eat what you want, and the rest will freeze.' Joseph grinned at her. 'It's the Easter version of a bloody good takeaway!'

'You can cook Indian?' said Nikki, half believing that if it didn't come from the Taj takeaway, it didn't exist.

'Very relaxing, preparing Eastern food, all those lovely spices to grind and blend.'

'You're something else, you know that? Most people do a crossword, or play Sudoku to unwind; you grind spices and chop chillies.' Nikki shook her head in amazement, and stepped out of her sodden shoes. 'It's certainly wild out there tonight, but it should subside when the tide turns.'

'I've taken the liberty of running you a bath. I thought you'd probably get drenched.' He turned back to the stove. 'When you're through, this should be just about ready.'

Nikki went upstairs and took off her wet clothes then slipped on her dressing gown. She pulled some casual slacks and a soft fleecy top from her wardrobe and went to the bathroom.

As he had said, her bath was run, and a glass of wine stood close to the taps. Standing against it was a note. It just said, 'Relax.'

Nikki eased herself down into the silky hot water and found herself fighting back tears. She couldn't recall anyone ever doing this for her before. Robert, her ex-husband could be called a lot of things, but thoughtful wasn't one of them, and her few other fleeting affairs had been just that, fleeting. No time for niceties.

For a moment she hated herself for ever even dreaming that this attentive and gentle man could be so psychologically damaged that he could systematically hunt down and kill people.

She sipped the chilled wine, savoured it, and decided that Bryony was a lucky woman, a very lucky woman. She would miss Joseph when he left, and not just for his culinary skills. The old place felt like a home while he was there.

She soaked for a while, going over what the day had produced, which wasn't much, then she allowed herself to think about Martin Durham. She couldn't believe that Joseph had made such headway. She just wished that she could do the same with the Greenborough assassin.

Nikki stood up and wrapped herself in a thick fluffy towel before stepping out of the bath.

'Five minutes!' echoed up from downstairs.

'Coming,' she called back. She pulled on her clothes and carefully holding her wine, ran downstairs.

* * *

'For a woman with no appetite, there's precious left for the freezer,' commented Joseph. 'I'd hate to see you when you are really hungry!'

'Not a pretty sight, believe me. But that was too good to leave, thank you.' She paused. 'Tell me what else you've found out about our suspicious deaths.'

'Very little, I'm afraid, apart from a tenuous connection to the Gordon Peace Memorial Hospital, but even the Internet doesn't give much info on it.'

'There was uproar when they built the Greenborough General and forced its closure. Protest marches and everything.'

'I keep thinking that I know something else about it, but it escapes me.'

Nikki took a mouthful of wine. 'Can't help you there, I'm afraid. I never needed to go there as a child, and I've kind of grown up with Greenborough General.'

'It'll come to me, no doubt. So? Was it really as bad as it sounded at work today? You seemed hairspring taut, when I spoke to you.'

Nikki sat back and held out her glass for a top-up. 'It was about as shitty as it gets. Victim number three was so freaked out about what had nearly happened that he was all but useless. He'd spent time with sodding Snaz, but his description was rubbish. Then he begged us to let him stay in the cells, just in case his attacker was waiting to finish him off.'

'I bet the custody sergeant liked that.'

'We found an out of town relative that was prepared to take him, until it's safe to go home.'

'And I wonder when that will be?' muttered Joseph morosely.

For a moment Nikki felt angry, then sadness took over. For all his brave front, his fancy cooking, and his commitment to finding out what had happened to Martin, Joseph was hurting. Hurting and scared about what was going to happen next.

'I'm doing my best, honestly, Joseph.'

'I know. And don't think I don't appreciate it,' he said miserably. He ran his hand through his hair. 'It's just that I've never felt so frustrated, so totally helpless.' He gave her a dark look. 'Well, actually I have, just once, and that was all to do with Billy Sweet. He really does have a knack for screwing up my life.'

Nikki didn't like his sombre mood and decided to change the subject. 'Have you spoken to Bryony today?'

'Not yet.' He drank his wine and stared into the glass. 'I tried earlier but her phone was switched off. Busy at work I guess. I'll ring her later.'

Nikki hoped that Bryony would do as she'd said and tell Joseph that she hadn't seen his stalker. She frowned to herself when she considered how Joseph would take that news. He was hanging onto Bryony's status as an eyewitness to keep himself sane. She sipped her drink and thought it best not to predict his reaction but just to deal with it when it happened. 'So, I guess it's time to discuss where we go next with Martin Durham.' She looked across at Joseph and raised her glass. 'Well done, by the way. That was astute of you to spot that medication box in the forensic photo of Amelia.' 'Thanks. Oh, but you must look at this.' Joseph got up and left the room, returning a few moments later with a photograph.

Nikki stared at it, then smiled when she saw a grinning and happy young Martin Durham. 'Just look at you, not a care in the world,' she whispered.

Joseph leaned over her shoulder and pointed to the sign. 'And this *has* to be what links them, Nikki. The hospital. Those tablets must have originated from there.'

'But the hospital has long gone, so who is sending them out now?'

'That is going to be my next line of enquiry. There has to be a paper chain, and if I can trace it back, I'll find the source.' Joseph bit his lip anxiously. 'As long as my recently imposed civilian capacity allows me to.'

Nikki stared at him. 'So what if I allocated you some help? In the form of either Niall or Yvonne?'

Joseph straightened up. 'Would you? That would be great!'

'Well, let's face it, if we weren't hunting down our killer, Martin's case would be active. It would have a whole team of officers asking questions, not just one constable.' She smiled at him. 'Yes, I'll sort that. We just have to keep shtum over precisely what they are doing, okay?'

Joseph grinned. 'Well, I'd be the last one to argue with that.' His face grew serious. 'But please don't put your neck too far onto the block for me, Nikki. I know how close to the wind you're sailing by even letting me proceed with this investigation, no matter how covertly.'

'Oh, don't worry too much on that score. I'll be discreet, but with my reputation, it's pretty well expected of me!' She leaned back in her chair and stared at the photograph. 'Are there any more like this?'

Joseph shrugged. 'I'll get the box. Some of them may mean more to you than me.'

For half an hour they sorted through the old pictures. Some of the ones taken on Cloud Fen made Nikki feel quite nostalgic.

'Look at this.' Joseph brought her back to the present. 'Tell me what you see.'

Nikki stared at the dog-eared picture. Once again the five friends hung around the old car, and initially Nikki thought they were consecutive shots, then she noticed subtle differences.

'There are fewer leaves on that tree, and the girls have light jackets on. This was taken at the same spot, close the hospital, but at a different time of year.'

'So they met there, or drove there on a regular basis.' Joseph frowned. 'But why?'

'A sick friend?' Nikki ventured. 'When Hannah was first ill, I practically lived at the hospital.'

'Maybe.' Joseph didn't look convinced. 'Would you have any objections if I gave Martin's sister a ring?'

'None at all. She's bound to recall what they were doing.'

While Joseph was in the study, Nikki piled up the plates and began to load the dishwasher. Thunder was rumbling ominously over the marsh, and the lights suddenly flickered a few times.

'Oh great,' she muttered, and began to rummage around in the cupboard beneath the sink. Power cuts were not unusual on the fen and she always kept a couple of battery-powered storm lanterns at the ready. 'The perfect end to a sodding awful day.'

Nikki checked the lanterns were working, then went through to the study to close the computer down. Joseph sat at her desk, staring thoughtfully at the photo. 'Any joy?'

'Oh, I think so,' said Joseph softly. 'In fact we may have just stumbled on a real lead.' He looked up at her. 'Elizabeth said that as students they were all feeling the pinch financially.'

'Nothing new there then.'

Joseph raised his eyebrows. 'Just remember the timescale. We are talking about the early seventies. To get some extra cash, Martin, Elizabeth and their friends signed up with a clinic run by the hospital.'

'What sort of clinic?'

'Common cold cure trials and sleep studies, apparently.'

Nikki let out a low whistle.

'And *that* is why the Gordon Peace Memorial rang bells. Do you ever recall reading about the Porton Down experiments?'

Nikki frowned and tried to think. All she could recall was that Porton Down had been, and probably still was, a government and military research centre testing biological and chemical weapons. 'Nerve gas, wasn't it? Sarin and CS gas were developed there, weren't they?'

'They certainly were, but I was thinking about the allegations made about unethical human experimentation.' Joseph's voice had taken on a very different timbre, and it was one that Nikki recognised from when they first met. He sounded enthusiastic and eager to get to the truth. 'The thing was, Porton Down worked loosely in collaboration with a CCU that was located at Harvard Hospital to the west of Salisbury. But they weren't the only ones experimenting. There was another centre in the east of England. Here to be precise, at the Gordon Peace Common Cold Unit!' He looked at her intently. 'That's why the name rang a bell! They were investigated way back in the 50s, but whatever went wrong was overshadowed by the more documented one about Porton Down and the national servicemen who had been conned into taking part in something that they didn't understand. You remember? They were given extra pay and extra days leave if they volunteered for testing drugs for the common cold, except some of them were tested with nerve agents.'

'And one died, didn't he?' Vague memories were returning to Nikki. Her face screwed up in confusion. 'But surely you're not suggesting that those kids were caught up in some dreadful experiment right here in Greenborough? This was years later.'

'The trials didn't stop. Elizabeth Durham has just told me that lots of the students went through them in the 70s, but some, Martin and Amelia included, volunteered for several, and whatever tests they were, they had nothing to do with colds.'

'And she didn't?'

'No, she said that some of her friends felt quite strongly about doing their bit for medical science, but she wasn't comfortable in the role of a guinea-pig.'

'Did she say what the other trials were about?'

'She has no idea. Apparently Martin and Amelia were really cagey about what it involved. Then her brother was diagnosed with cancer and they forgot all about the trials.'

Nikki took a long shaky breath. 'I don't like where this is going.'

'Nor do I if we find ourselves up against the MOD.' Joseph set his jaw. 'We just have to hope there's no connection to the military and whatever was going on in that unit was a privately funded trial.'

An ominous rumble of thunder added gravity to his words, and Nikki shivered. Martin Durham, Amelia Reed, Paul Cousins, and who else? Three known deaths, all fairly recent, and connected by sinister medication and an experiment that took place decades ago. She struggled to get her head around it. 'We need to know everything we can about those trials. We should go see Elizabeth Durham.' Nikki regarded Joseph seriously. 'Tonight.'

'In this?' Joseph's eyes were wide. 'We'll be lucky to get as far as the main road without calling the coastguard!'

Lightning flickered around the room and a deafening crack of thunder made Nikki jump. 'Jesus! It's right overhead.' She leaned across the desk and pulled one of the storm lanterns closer. 'If this keeps up, ten to one we lose the bloody power.' She thumped her fist down and cursed. 'Damn it! I really need to talk to Martin's sister. She's our only link to what happened to him.'

'Talk to her on the phone.' Joseph lifted the handset and offered it to her. 'Ask her to dig out everything she can about the CCU, and I'll go out there first thing in the morning and see her.'

'I suppose.' Nikki sighed and took the phone from him. She tapped the button a couple of times, then rolled her eyes and slammed it back in its cradle. 'Great! Now the lines are down.'

'Mobile?'

Nikki shook her head. 'And get a signal out here in the middle of a bloody storm? I don't think so.'

'How long do these summer storms last?' asked Joseph.

Nikki glanced at the clock. 'It should move away when the tide turns, which is in about an hour, or it could rumble around all night long.'

'Well, if you are really worried, I'll wait until it subsides a bit then I'll drive up to Old Bolingbroke and talk to her tonight.'

'I'll come with you.'

'No.' Joseph stared at her. Concern played across his face. 'You need some rest. You've got a murder enquiry hanging over you, and Billy Sweet is still out there somewhere.' He leaned across and squeezed her shoulder gently. 'Listen, I know Martin Durham is important to you, but catching Billy is important to me, and to anyone else who accidentally crosses his murdering path, and there's sod all I can do about him right now. It's all down to you and the team, Nikki.' He let his arm fall but still looked her full in the face. 'I'll do this for you, if you keep focussed on catching that murdering bastard for me.'

Nikki swallowed. Billy Sweet was dead, but how could she tell Joseph? And even if his name was not Sweet, there still a killer wandering the streets of Greenborough.

'Okay. But go careful, these lanes are treacherous at the best of times.'

'I'll be back before you know it.' He paused just long enough to pick up the two old photos and push them into his pocket. 'Just get some sleep. And don't you dare wait up. You look shattered. I'll fill you in on everything tomorrow.'

Maybe it was the wine, or the weight of so many deaths draped around her shoulders, but Nikki suddenly felt mind-numbingly tired. Exhaustion swept over her, and she felt herself nodding. 'Okay, okay. I get the message. Just watch those bloody roads, you hear?'

'Loud and clear, ma'am.'

As Nikki forced herself to stand, she heard him pulling a waterproof jacket from the coat cupboard, and then the front door clicked shut. She yawned. He hadn't even waited for the rain to ease. For a moment she felt guilty. Elizabeth may know nothing more than she'd already told him, and frankly, whatever she did know could have waited until the morning. Hell, he was going to have one awful drive, and maybe a fruitless one, but for some reason Martin seemed to be calling out to her, and she had no wish to ignore him. They were onto something; she felt that in her heart. And because of everything else she had on her plate right now, it would have to be down to Joseph to prove it.

CHAPTER TWENTY-TWO

As Joseph drove away from the coast, the rain slackened. He could still hear the thunder rumbling in the distance but he could tell from the condition of the roads that the worst of the storm had been confined to the marshes. By the time he reached Elizabeth's home he could see clear dark skies and twinkling stars.

The downstairs lights in the big lodge house were still on and he felt a rush of relief that the two women had not turned in for the night.

Janna opened the door and beckoned him inside. She smiled wanly at him. 'We had a feeling we might see you tonight. It's about the clinical trials, isn't it? You think Martin's death is connected?' She suddenly gathered herself. 'I'm sorry. Look at you, you're soaked! Let me take your jacket.'

Joseph took off his wet coat and handed it to her. 'I should have phoned ahead, but the storm on the coast took out the phone lines. I hope this isn't an imposition?'

'Not at all. Go on down to the garden room. Elizabeth is there. I'll go make us all hot drinks.'

Elizabeth Durham was standing staring out of the great picture window into the night. On hearing him enter she turned, and he thought that she might have been crying.

'Am I intruding, Ms Durham?' he asked softly.

'Ah, Detective Sergeant Easter. No, of course not. Please, have a seat, I was just being silly and selfish, and feeling horribly sorry for myself.' She gave him a rueful look. '*And* I was wondering how much I really knew about my beloved brother.'

'When something like this happens, I think we are made very much aware of just how much we humans hold back from sharing what is going on deep inside. Even from those closest to us.'

'I need to know what happened, Sergeant. If I don't, it'll eat and eat away and drive me mad.'

Joseph nodded. He thought about Billy Sweet and knew exactly how she felt. 'We'll find your answers, I promise.' He took the two photos from his pocket, stood up and walked across to Elizabeth. 'I know it was a very long while ago but I really need you to tell me everything you can remember about those trials and the people in the pictures.'

Elizabeth stared at each photo in turn. 'From the moment we spoke, I've thought about nothing else.' She blinked slowly. 'I'm just not sure what I can tell.'

'Did you know who actually ran the Common Cold Unit?'

'Not at the time. We believed it was just a research side to the hospital itself, but then rumour had it that it may be a government run organisation.'

Joseph's heart sank. That was not the kind of thing he wanted to hear.

'But later still Martin told me that it was privately funded by a pharmaceutical organisation.'

His spirit lifted. 'Did he mention a name?'

Elizabeth shook her head. 'He just said it was massive, based abroad and encompassed a lot of smaller companies. I don't think he knew any more than that.'

'So you and your friends in those photos all took part in the same studies?'

'Initially, yes. It was Martin, Amelia, Barry Smith, John Goring and myself, we were part of a larger group that was split in two. The procedure was nasal drops of cold virus, then half the group given placebos and the other half cold cures.'

'Were you ill afterwards?'

'Not really. A few developed assorted cold-like symptoms. Just coughs, sneezes, raised temperatures. One girl I remember was rather poorly, but nothing major.'

Joseph frowned. 'And this Barry Smith and John Goring? Are you still in touch with them?'

'Barry died young. Killed in a car smash not long after he left university, and I lost contact with John. He went abroad to work years ago.'

Janna appeared with a tray of hot drinks and placed them on a low table. As she handed them around, she paused and took the picture from her partner. 'I've been wondering something, Liz? If your little group of the famous five were all grinning happily here, who took the photograph?'

It was Elizabeth's turn to frown. 'I can't remember.'

'And the second one was taken at a different time of the year,' added Joseph, 'but it's still the five of you. Maybe the same person took that one too?'

Elizabeth rubbed her temples as if trying to coax back an old memory. 'I can see him, just vaguely. A friend of Martin's. He had long wavy untidy hair and shabby clothes. But what the hell was his name?'

'Was he in your group?'

'No. He was one of the few kids who did the sleep studies. He was with us because Martin used to give him a lift into the hospital from the village. Davey! That's it! Davey Kowalski! Lord, I haven't thought about him in years.'

Joseph checked the spelling and wrote the name in his notebook. He'd get a check run on both Goring and Kowalski first thing in the morning. He drew in a long breath. 'I hate to ask this, but did you ever think the trials and Martin's illness might have been connected?'

'No, never.' She shook her head emphatically. 'He assured me that he had the medical team at the trials to thank for his life. He would have died had they not made the diagnosis and acted so swiftly in getting him the right treatment. I know it *sounds* like a medical disaster. You do hear of terrible cases where clinical trials go badly wrong, but I'm certain that wasn't it. My brother wasn't a very good actor, and he really wouldn't have a word said against the team of researchers. If something had gone wrong, I think I'd have known, Detective Easter, really I do.'

'But he did change, didn't he? You said he lost his spark.'

'Maybe I read too much into that. Cancer changes people, and Martin was a vibrant young man. A young man forced to spend the rest of his life on a crushing drug regime and following a much restricted lifestyle to the one he probably had seen for himself. Surely anyone would change?'

'Of course, you're right,' said Joseph softly, but inside he felt that Martin's sister's beliefs were a long way from correct.

The little group fell silent, then Janna suddenly stood up. 'Liz? Did you say Kowalski?'

The other woman nodded, then watched as Janna retrieved a briefcase from behind one of the chairs and began to strew its contents across the marble-tiled floor.

'It's here somewhere, damn it.' Janna rummaged impatiently through reams of paperwork.

'What on earth are you looking for?' asked Elizabeth.

'This!' Janna jumped up triumphantly. 'It has to be the same man!' She waved a typed sheet at him. 'Listen to this, it's a letter of resignation from one of my staff. Linda

Kowalski.' She scanned the sheet quickly then read out the relevant part. '*Really sorry*, etc, etc, *been so happy in my job*, blah, blah, but, yes, this is it! *But due to my brother David's illness and I have decided to give up work to look after him. Please God he recovers and is allowed home.*' She handed him the letter and said, 'So how many David Kowalskis do you know?'

'It could be the same man,' said Joseph. 'If his age corresponds?'

'Linda is in her fifties. She told me they are true yellowbellies, born and bred here in the Fens. The name comes via their grandfather who was a Polish immigrant.'

'Well, the age may fit.' He looked across to Elizabeth. 'Did Martin's friend Davey have a sister?'

'Two, I think.' She nodded slowly. 'And another thing, I'm pretty sure he was on the last trial with Martin.'

Joseph drew in a long breath. Then that was the man he needed to speak to, and the sooner the better. He turned to Janna. 'Do you know why David is so ill?'

'No idea, but I know he's in intensive care at Greenborough General.'

Joseph's mind raced. A failed suicide maybe? He needed to get onto the hospital. 'Could I borrow your phone book, please?'

'Use the phone in the kitchen, Sergeant,' said Janna. 'Greenborough General's number is on the chalk board. It's listed between the doctor and the vet.'

He returned to the garden room a few minutes later. 'I need to go see them, but it could well be the same man.' He quickly drained his coffee cup. 'Thank you both for all this and I promise to keep you updated in what we uncover.'

Outside in the car Joseph checked the time. Almost midnight, and without his warrant card it was useless going to the hospital. There was nothing left but to go home. He pulled his new phone from his pocket and smiled in the darkness, *after* he'd phoned Bryony.

He began to punch in her number, then closed the phone again. Was this fair? They were not even what you might call an item. Yes, they were on the brink of an affair, there was no denying that, but did he have the right to start ringing her at any godforsaken hour just because it suited him?

He slumped back in his seat and wondered what to do. Bryony had given him every indication that she wanted to take their relationship further. She would probably appreciate a call, knowing how scary everything had been of late. Joseph took a deep breath and re-dialled her number. After a moment or two he heard the voicemail cut in. Well, that settled that.

'Eh, hello Bry, it's me, Joseph. Um, well, it's really late I know, but I just wanted you to know that I'm fine and I'm looking forward to catching up with you. I'll ring you in the morning before you go to work.' He paused. 'I miss you, Bry, and I can't wait to get all this sorted out so that we will have some time to get to know each other better. You take care. Speak soon. Bye.'

He closed the phone and sighed. He had hoped that she would have picked up his call. She was the one bright star in all this mess right now. The one sane and solid thing for him to hold on to.

Joseph turned the key in the ignition and prayed that Nikki Galena would find a way to stop Billy Sweet, before he destroyed everything beautiful in his life.

CHAPTER TWENTY-THREE

Nikki must have left very early, because when Joseph emerged at around six thirty, he found a short note propped against the toaster. It simply said that she hadn't forgotten that she had promised to send him some help. He could expect someone as soon as she could arrange it, hopefully just after nine o'clock.

He showered and dressed, then unenthusiastically ate a couple of slices of toast and marmalade. Beside his plate sat an A4 writing pad. If he were to have some help, he couldn't afford to waste time. He should sort out his enquiries into those that could be tackled by a civilian, in this case himself, and those that needed an official warrant card to obtain answers.

He sipped at his mug of tea and began to get his thoughts into some sort of order. And that wasn't easy when all he could think about was a dark-haired, elfin-faced woman; a woman who wasn't answering her phone.

Joseph rinsed his plate and wished vehemently that he had not stopped Bryony from ringing him. It really would do no harm for her to have his new mobile number. She was hardly likely to plague him with calls. Yes, he'd leave it on her voicemail, that would stop him worrying himself sick every time she left her phone switched off. Joseph quickly recorded his second message, then opened his notebook and began to write.

David Kowalski was top of his list. First and foremost they must ascertain that he was the same man who had been a friend of Martin. And if he was, then why was he in hospital, and would he be in any state to talk to them.

Next he wrote: Cold Cure Unit. Somehow they had to find out if it had been originally run by a pharmaceutical company, then see if it was still operational.

Under that he scribbled oncology unit. Now that was really bugging him. Joseph placed the pen carefully on the pad, and hoping someone would be in early, went to find their number.

The manager had not arrived, but the receptionist seemed eager to help. 'There is only one other possibility, Sergeant.' The accent was heavily Geordie. 'Some private referrals aren't always listed in our records. Dr Muller's patients for example, his secretary kept a separate appointment diary.'

Joseph felt a glimmer of hope. 'Could I speak to Dr Muller or his secretary?'

'I'm sorry, Dr Muller left six months ago. Went back to Europe, I believe, although I have no idea where.'

The glimmer faded and went out. Joseph thanked him and hung up; he knew a dead end when he was down one.

He sighed and found his concentration wandering from the all-important work sheet to the phone that lay on the table tantalisingly close to his right hand. He'd have thought that Bryony would have checked her mail by now, and part of him had been expecting a call. He hoped that there was nothing wrong. Maybe his dangerous situation had scared her off. It was an awful lot to ask of anyone, yet alone a new girlfriend. She didn't seem like the type to get cold feet, but having a murderer stalking your date could send the toughest Amazon heading for the hills.

He stared at the clock. If he hadn't promised Nikki that he would do all he could to find out what had happened to Martin, he would have driven over to Bryony's home, and spoken to her before she left for work. As it was, the best he could do was to ring her office. He was probably being stupid and over protective, but with Billy Sweet still out there, Bryony's lack of communication was giving him the jitters. All he wanted was a few words to say that she was safe.

As if on cue, his phone burst into a loud, tinny discordant tune, and he grabbed at it, his heart thumping in his throat.

'Joseph? You sound weird? Something wrong?'

His heart sank. 'Nikki, eh, no nothing's wrong. I just need to change the ringtone on this new phone, it scares the pants off you when it rings.'

'Oh, right. Well, just to say that Niall Farrow is on his way to you. Yvonne was my first choice, she's more experienced, but she's also cleverer at fending off questions as to where her crewmate is, so you have Niall, okay?'

'Great. We'll get stuck in as soon as he arrives. How are things there?'

'About as busy as Christmas Eve in Tesco's car park. It's bedlam. Anything more from Elizabeth last night?'

'Maybe. I'll check them out and report my findings, but I was just wondering . . .'

'I'm not sure I like the tone of your voice, Joseph. Don't tell me you want more help?'

'Not help exactly, just a small favour.'

'And that is?'

'It's Bryony. I haven't been able to get an answer on her phone. We agreed to talk last night but she never answered. Same thing this morning.'

There was a silence, and Joseph wondered what Nikki was going to say. When she did finally speak he noted concern in her voice. 'And what are you thinking exactly?'

'I'm not sure. I may be panicking unnecessarily, but he did see her. Billy Sweet saw her. Down at the river walk. And he knows that she saw him too, which could put her in grave danger, couldn't it?'

Another silence. This time longer.

'Joseph.' Nikki sounded tense.

'What?' He frowned at the phone. 'Nikki, has something happened?'

'Not what you're thinking, Joseph, so don't jump to conclusions, but there may be a good reason why Bryony hasn't answered your calls.'

His discomfort increased. 'And?'

'Oh shit! I'm not sure I should tell you this, but hell, you need to know. Just don't bite my head off, okay?'

Joseph began to feel a heady mix of concern and anger fill his mind. 'For God's sake, just tell me!'

'I spoke to Bryony yesterday, Joseph. I needed her to give me something more of a description of your stalker.'

Confusion blunted the growing anger. 'But I told you, she said that she only saw a shadowy figure jump over the wall and down onto the towpath.'

'I needed to hear her account, not yours, do you understand?'

Joseph swallowed. 'Yes, I suppose, but what did she say?'

'That she never saw anything, or anybody.'

'No! No, that's wrong!' His voice rose to almost a shout. 'She said . . .'

'I *know* what she said to you, but she saw how upset you were, and she wanted to give you some sort of support. She lied, Joseph. For your sake. She thought she was helping you.'

'And you knew this? So why the hell didn't you tell me last night?' He knew he should never speak to Nikki in that way, but the anger made his headache with its burning intensity.

'Because she wanted to tell you herself. She made me promise not to mention it. And I thought that was only right.' Nikki's voice had softened. 'And I believed she would, Joseph. She cares about you, I'm sure of that, and I thought that she deserved the chance to explain.'

'Well, she's obviously thought better of it,' he muttered. 'Probably thought better of the whole damn thing and she's dumped me. She just hasn't found the courage to actually tell me yet.'

'Don't get ahead of yourself, Sergeant!' barked Nikki, her voice now back to normal. 'We know nothing for sure, and I only told you that because I thought it would help you. Think about it! If she didn't see your killer, then he didn't see her either. So the chances of him going after her are negligible, yes?'

Joseph's head was spinning. 'I suppose, but . . .'

'Look, give me her address. I'll get someone to knock on her door. What time does she leave for work?'

Joseph checked his watch. 'In about fifteen minutes.'

'Damn it! Oh, if it makes you happy, I'll go myself, it'll be quicker than trying to organise someone else.'

He heard her chair squeak as she jumped up. He rattled off the address, then said, 'Thank you.'

'Yeah, and you really owe me, Joseph Easter. I'll ring you when I get there.'

Joseph stared at the phone. His hopes had been dashed. Once again, he was the only witness. No one else had ever seen that murdering bastard Sweet, unless they were being killed by him, and then they would have had the dubious pleasure of seeing those dead eyes staring through them. He shivered. The thought of Billy Sweet being the last thing you ever saw was terrifying.

He placed the phone back on the table, then almost yelped with shock as it rang again. He grabbed it, but saw it was a message rather than a call.

Joseph. Sorry 2 miss your calls. Mobile on the blink. Will sort it and ring tonight. Miss you 2. CU soon. Bryony xx

His breath caught in his throat. Thank God! He saved the message then pushed the button for dial. Shit! He'd just sent Nikki flying off on a wild goose chase! He punched in her name, and heard it ring only once before she answered it.

'This had better be good!'

'Ma'am! It's me! Cancel my last! I've just heard from her!'

'You are *so* lucky that I'd only got as far as the car! Is she okay?'

'I had a text, said her phone was malfunctioning. She sounds fine.'

'Are you happy with that?'

'Yeah, I'm sure it's kosher,' he sighed with relief. 'Thanks anyway, Nikki. I still owe you.'

'You're so right, sunshine! Now go get your fuzzy little head around Martin Durham's death, okay?'

'Roger! Over and out.'

* * *

Niall arrived ten minutes later, placed his car keys inside his hat and laid it on the kitchen table.

'Before we get to work, Sarge, the team asked me to tell you how sorry we all are, and that we are all right behind you. The chief must need his head read to be standing you down like this.' Niall flopped into one of the old pine chairs and gave Joseph a boyish grin. 'So, whatever I can do to help, bring it on.'

Joseph made more tea, and as he did, he carefully filled the young officer in on everything he knew about Martin Durham and the suspect 'suicides.'

'Phew.' Niall let out a low whistle. 'This all has a very bad feel to it, doesn't it?' He scratched his head. 'One thing I can tell you is that forensics say there is no more to be gleaned from Knot Cottage. It was the work of a highly trained pro, and no evidence was obtained that would help to identify the intruder. And sorry, but the guv'nor asked me to mention that the DNA that she extracted from him during their fight came up with no match on our database.'

'Damn it! We were kind of relying on that.'

'That's approximately what the DI said, only her version was more colourful.'

Joseph shrugged. 'Okay, so let's adjourn to the study and see what we can find out about David Kowalski. You ring the hospital, and I'll try to contact his sister.'

Linda Kowalski sounded nervous on answering the phone. 'Every time it rings I dread bad news,' she explained.

Joseph carefully told her why he was ringing, then waited for the woman to say that she had no idea what he was talking about. Instead, after a short pause, she simply said. 'We need to talk, Sergeant, and the sooner the better.'

Joseph took a sharp breath. 'When and where?'

'I'll be leaving for the hospital soon, but we need to talk privately. Do you know the playing field next the hospital? I'll be in a red Ford Ka. I'll meet you in the car park.'

Joseph lowered the phone, and looked across at Niall. 'What have you got?'

'David is critical. No chance of talking to him,' he pulled a face. 'Doesn't sound good, I'm afraid.'

'Then everything depends on his sister.' He stood up. 'We want the park next to the hospital, and separate cars may be sensible. I'll follow you.'

* * *

Linda Kowalski had grey hair and the look of a woman who had spent most of her years exposed to the elements. She smiled wanly at Joseph and he prayed that Niall's uniform and the fact that they were sitting in a Fenland Constabulary squad car would deter her from asking to see his warrant card. 'Why is David in hospital?' he asked gently.

'He had an allergic reaction to his medication.' She stared at him almost angrily. 'Although why? He's been on the same drugs for years.'

Joseph exhaled sharply. 'And were they as a result of clinical trials in his youth?'

Linda nodded grimly. 'I was on them too; all young and fired up to do our bit. But I opted out early, and Davey, passionate to this day, continued for years.'

'I hate to tell you this, but we have reason to believe that your brother's medication was tampered with.'

Linda suddenly grasped his wrist. 'So do I!'

'How much do you know about what went on?' asked Joseph urgently.

'Pretty well everything. And although David swore never to speak, I didn't.'

Joseph swung round to face Niall. 'You have to take Miss Kowalski to the station. Directly to DI Galena, understand?'

'Not before I've seen my brother,' she added firmly.

'You could be in serious danger, Linda. I need to get you to a place of safety.'

'Fine. After I've seen David.'

'I'll call for another crew, Sarge,' interjected Niall. 'We'll stick with Miss Kowalski, then they can keep watch on her brother while I take her back to the nick.'

'Yes, do it.'

As Niall radioed in, Joseph looked carefully at Linda Kowalski, 'What was the last trial about? It wasn't cold cures, was it?'

'Very few of the trials were,' she snorted distastefully. 'Mainly they were for rheumatoid treatments, testing with gold, or sulphasalazine. The last one however . . .' her voice dropped to a whisper, '. . . was for drugs that were being used to interrogate prisoners, well, foreign spies and traitors, more like. We are talking the Cold War, Sergeant.'

'So this *is* MOD stuff?'

'No, I don't think so. It was a big pharmaceutical corporation. We were told it was British and we truly believed that we were helping our country, now I'm not so sure.'

'And what was this drug? A truth serum?'

'No, a special kind of hallucinogen. It didn't make the user tell the truth, it altered their perceptions of reality, so things that normally would have been of paramount importance meant absolutely nothing.'

Joseph shivered. 'And did David know what he was being tested with?'

'Oh yes, they all did. The group was totally committed to the trials. They believed they were pioneers.'

Joseph thought about Martin, Amelia and Paul, and the terrible deception made him feel nauseous. 'So what happened?'

'They signed waivers. They were well paid, and when the drug proved to be a devastating mistake, they were offered a very large one-off payment and private medical care for the rest of their lives. Then they willingly signed more legal disclaimers that bound them from ever talking about the tests and everything and everyone involved. And why not? They believed the doctors were the good guys.'

'And *were* they looked after?'

'Absolutely. And with great care. Medication, regular check-ups and even highly qualified personal liaison managers to help with any problems.'

'Can you get hold of one of them for me?' asked Joseph quickly.

The woman's face darkened. 'Funny that. Their numbers are suddenly unobtainable.'

Joseph cursed silently, then murmured, 'So what's gone wrong?'

Linda shook her head. 'I really don't know. After all these years of support, why abandon them now?'

Not abandonment, thought Joseph, this is termination.

'There is one thing.' Linda stared at him. 'About a year ago a woman came sniffing round asking questions. David was sure that she was a reporter. He told her nothing and reported it to his liaison officer. He was pretty certain that he was the only member of the trials group that she'd managed to trace, but it was just after that that Amelia died.' She shrugged. 'Maybe nothing to do with the journalist, but . . . ?'

Joseph's mind raced. A reporter onto something? Can't kill the reporter, too high profile, so damage limitation? Quietly dispose of the 'loyal pioneers' so that there was nothing left to uncover.

'The other crew is pulling in, Sarge. We'll take it from here.' Niall pulled on his hat. 'You'll be safe with me. I'll escort you all the way, Miss Kowalski.'

'Take great care of her, Constable.' Joseph turned to Linda. 'And humour me here, will you? Please don't eat or drink anything until you are safe at the police station. Nothing at all, is that clear?'

Linda nodded, and as Joseph stepped from the car he knew that she totally understood the implications of his request. He watched the two vehicles pull away, then raced back to his Ford and rang Nikki.

'Then it's almost a given thing that they were murdered, isn't it, Joseph?' There was a tremor in his boss's voice. 'I really do have to thank you for that, and Martin would thank you too.'

'It's nothing, Nikki, but I suggest it's going to get even more difficult from here on in, finding those responsible. If we ever do,' he sighed. 'But still, if you can do as much for me with Billy Sweet, I'd be eternally grateful.'

'I will get you answers, Joseph. I will take this killer off the streets, I promise you.'

'I know you will. And no matter how painful this is for me, Nikki, you have to do whatever it takes, you know that, don't you?'

He hardly heard her reply. It was little more than an under breath. 'Whatever it takes, Joseph, I'll do it.'

As he drove back towards Cloud Fen, he prayed that she meant it.

CHAPTER TWENTY-FOUR

Nikki picked up the photograph of Martin, Hannah and herself and gave it a light kiss. 'I never believed for one moment that you could have voluntarily jumped from that tower, my friend, and certainly not in front of those little kids.'

She felt a surge of optimism. As Joseph had said, it wouldn't be easy, but they were on their way to clearing the stigma from her old friend's name.

Then she thought about Joseph. As she had replaced the handset, she felt his frustration pouring out across the ether. She'd come very close to being suspended herself on more than one occasion. She'd sailed too close to the wind and ruffled an awful lot of gold braid as she did, but somehow she had always managed to hang on to her position. Which made it all the tougher on Joseph. If they'd thrown the book at her, she would have deserved it. In the past she had crossed lines, cheated, bullied and flaunted the rulebook to get the drug dealers sent down. Joseph on the other hand had been an exemplary officer, honest, full of integrity and moral fibre, and it was *his* warrant card that was sitting in the super's filing cabinet along with a half bottle of malt whisky.

Nikki shook her head. It wasn't fair, but at least his enforced absence had brought them closer to unravelling the sinister cover-up and ruthless killing of innocent people.

She took a long look at the old picture, then placed it back on her desk. As she did, she noticed the scrap of paper on which she had written Bryony Barton's address. She picked it up and stared at it. Joseph had seemed quite happy at receiving the text, but had Bryony actually sent it? It had come from her number, but anyone could have tapped it in. She stared at her own cell phone. How many times had she left it unattended on the desk?

Allowing herself to forget Martin Durham for the first time in days, she looked again at the address. If she had been Joseph, knowing there was a killer on the loose, she wouldn't have been content with a text message. No way. And Bryony had been out of contact for quite a while now. Perhaps too long for comfort.

Nikki pushed back her chair and looked around her small office. Something wasn't right. With a determined snort, she pulled a contact file from her drawer. Joseph had told her that Bryony worked at the Public Analysts Laboratory, and that number would be listed. She ran a finger down the page, then stopped and grunted with satisfaction.

Nikki dialled the number and waited.

'I'm sorry but Miss Barton called in sick today. If it's regarding a sample for analysis, I can put you through to the technician who is covering her workload?'

Nikki paused, then said, 'No, it's nothing like that. I am DI Galena, Greenborough CID, and I need to speak to whoever is in charge.'

'I'll put you through to the lab manager.'

There was a period filled with clicking sounds and a melee of tinny music, then a deep voice said, 'Simon Lewis, how can I help you?'

Nikki introduced herself and told him that she needed to contact Bryony Barton on a matter of some importance. The man was naturally hesitant, so Nikki gave him the station number and after a few moments, he was back on the line.

'I understand her mobile is down so I need to check her home address with you, if that's okay?' Nikki quoted the street number that she had, and Lewis confirmed that it was correct.

'I'm not sure about her mobile being down though. I'm sure it was her number that showed up on the display when she rang in sick,' the man paused then added, '. . . even though it was her friend that spoke to me.'

Nikki felt a hard jolt of concern. 'Friend?'

'Yes, a man. But I didn't like to pry. I know very little about her private life so I rather assumed it was a partner.'

Nikki's mouth felt dry as she asked. 'How long has Bryony worked for you?'

'Around eighteen months now, I suppose.'

'And is she popular?'

'Very. She's an asset to our little team.' Lewis gave a short chuckle. 'Although I'm sure she won't be here long term. She is far too highly qualified to waste her life doing lab checks on dodgy kebabs.'

'Qualified in what way?' asked Nikki suspiciously.

'She is a biomedical scientist, Inspector. She specialised in pharmokinetics.'

'Is that as complex as it sounds?'

'Complicated is correct, and Bryony is top-notch.'

'So what's she doing with you?'

'It's nothing unusual, Inspector. When kids with PhD's are stacking supermarket shelves, this could be classed as a good job to have. And she's very happy here.'

Nikki thanked the man, but before she hung up she added. 'Sorry to ask, but is she helping you to arrange a charity event of some kind?'

'The scavenger hunt? Oh yes, it's for the Butterfly Hospice. Can we put you down for a donation?' he asked hopefully.

An image of her ailing father flashed across her mind. 'Sure. Put me down for twenty quid.'

Something was terribly wrong. She knew it as clearly as when a musician hit a bum note. It jangled like a cacophony of lies in her head. Nikki had a built-in warning system. A heightened sense of wrongness.

And right now it was smothering her. She was pretty certain that there was more to Bryony than Joseph knew about, but whatever that was, she may be in terrible danger.

She jumped up and opened her office door. 'Yvonne! Quickly, take a couple more uniforms and get yourself around to 176 Blackfen Road. Ring me directly you're on scene and let me know whether Bryony Barton is there and safe, okay?'

* * *

The answer was back in ten minutes.

'There's no response, ma'am. The next door neighbour says she hasn't seen her since early yesterday morning.' Yvonne sounded worried. 'Shall we force an entry?'

Nikki thought about the fall-out if she happened to be wrong. 'Yes. Do it now.'

A few seconds later she heard the sound of several crashes, then hurried footsteps.

'Place is clear, ma'am,' said Yvonne. 'There's no sign of a struggle, but we'll do a thorough check and report back in a few minutes.' The line went dead and Nikki was forced to wait for what seemed like an eternity before Yvonne got back to her.

'There's nothing to indicate that she was planning on doing a runner, ma'am. Her laptop is still on standby, Sky+ is set to record an OU lecture, and there's fresh milk and food in the fridge. And importantly, her clothes are still hanging in the wardrobe.'

'Is there a diary or a calendar? We need to know if she had any meetings planned.'

'Nothing, ma'am. I'd thought of that.'

Nikki thanked her and asked her to hurry back to the station, and bring the computer with her. It sounded to her like Bryony had had every intention of returning home but something or someone had prevented her.

'You look like you could do with this, guv.' Cat Cullen placed a mug of coffee in front of her.

'You are so right.' Nikki rubbed her forehead.

Cat perched on the edge of her desk. 'What's worrying you?'

'Bryony Barton,' murmured Nikki. 'She should be at work. She isn't. Work thinks she is at home sick. She isn't. No one has been able to contact her to actually talk to her since yesterday. All her belongings are untouched. Ergo, she isn't on her toes. Plus . . .' she stared at Cat uncomfortably, 'an unknown male rang her office this morning using *her* cell phone. And that makes me feel very uneasy indeed.'

'So where the hell is she?'

'I wish I knew, and weirdly it seems that I may have been the last one to see her.'

'You're worried about her connection with Joseph, and *his* connection with the psycho-assassin, aren't you?'

'That woman has been out of touch for around twenty-four hours,' Nikki shivered, 'that's far too long.'

'Does Joseph know?'

'No. He had a reassuring text from her, but I'm not so sure that *she* sent it.'

'Shouldn't we tell him?' asked Cat.

'Joseph's in a very dark place right now, Cat. He'll have to be told of course, but I have no way of even guessing how he will react. Not only that . . .'

Before she could continue, her desk phone rang.

'Ma'am? Sergeant Conway here. A couple of my officers have just attended a shout at 3 Granary Close, off Fishguard Avenue. We were called regarding a suspected break-in, but they've found the body of an IC1 male.'

Nikki stiffened. Not now. 'Please don't tell me he has blond hair and blue eyes?'

''Fraid so, ma'am. Forensics have been notified and are already on their way, but will you attend?'

'Damn right I will!' Nikki threw down the phone. 'Cat! With me!'

* * *

'Oh dear God,' whispered Cat, zipping up her protective suit. 'I had no idea there were so many men in Greenborough with blond thatches and blue eyes.'

The dead man looked like a wicked parody of Chris Forbes, although this man's life blood soaked into plush cream carpet, not weeds and filthy rubble. His hands were tied carefully behind him and the wide gaping wound across his throat was beginning to look horribly familiar. Nikki looked across at Professor Rory Wilkinson. 'Don't have to ask if it's the same MO, do I?'

'It seems that way, although this one must have put up a fight. His face is badly bruised, and . . .' Rory's expression was uncharacteristically serious. 'I don't know, I've only been here a few minutes, but . . .'

'You have reservations?' She looked at the dead man's corn-blond hair. 'Why?'

He stood up and stared down at the body. 'Not reservations exactly.' He gave her a tired smile. 'I've learnt never to assume anything until my investigations are complete.'

Nikki nodded slowly. That was fair comment, but she had the distinct feeling that the professor was not comfortable. 'One of my men says we have ID this time.'

'You do. And maybe that's what is odd.' He nodded towards an expensive-looking solid wood table. 'Over there, credit cards and a valid security pass card, although I have no idea to what it gives access. Your man says there is a pocket diary too. Something I'm sure you will be happy to ferret through.'

'Makes a change, that's for certain,' said Nikki. 'Which makes me wonder if he was disturbed and left in a hurry. The others had been carefully stripped of all ID.'

'That or he actually wants us to know who this victim is,' added Cat thoughtfully.

'Maybe.' She looked around. 'Or perhaps he's losing his touch. His last attack was thwarted, now this victim has been left with clear identification with him. Seems as if he's either getting careless or distracted.' She looked back to the pathologist. 'No other obvious evidence?'

'One thing. This man is clean and his clothes are well cared for, but your officers found a pile of filthy, and I mean absolutely rancid, clothes in the bathroom.' He rolled his eyes at her. 'But other than that, nothing yet, and probably won't be. Our poor SOCOs are tearing their hair out at lack of physical or biological evidence. They are sure it's the same professional clean-up job.' He looked around, 'And this flat was no slum to begin with, was it?' He pointed towards a painting that hung over a modern futuristic-looking stainless steel fireplace. 'I keep looking at that landscape and trying to tell myself it's a print, that it can't in a million years be a genuine Milton Avery.' His eyes widened. 'No way would an Avery be hanging, unprotected, in a classy little flat in Greenborough. But hell, I still keep looking at it.'

'Milton Avery?' asked Cat staring suspiciously at the strange painting.

'My dear girl, he was called the American Matisse, and one passed through Christie's in New York not so long ago for the princely sum of over nine hundred thousand dollars.'

'Then it's a print,' said Nikki flatly. 'This guy was clearly no Rockefeller.'

'Well, naturally they don't all fetch that kind of money. Maybe it's a family heirloom, or an investment.'

'And maybe it came from eBay for 99p with free postage, but this is not exactly helping our enquiry.' Being careful not to touch anything, Nikki walked over to the table and looked down at the security badge. 'Kurt Michael Carson. You really are a dead ringer for William Sweet, deceased, aren't you?' she whispered. From the inch square photo, there was no doubt that it belonged to the murdered man. 'I'll bag the diary and take it, then we'll let you get on doing your usual admirable job, Rory.'

'Be my guest. And I'll get my preliminary report to you in my normal speedy and efficient manner.'

'I'd expect nothing less.' Nikki threw him an almost affectionate smile as she turned to leave. 'And if I find that weird picture hanging on the mortuary wall next week, remember, I know where it came from.'

* * *

Cat yawned and stretched. 'I think I've just about exhausted all avenues, ma'am.'

'So recap for me.' Nikki also stretched her aching back.

'Kurt Michael Carson. British born, Dutch mother, English father. Age thirty-seven. Single. Works abroad and his company owns the property in which he was killed, the flat in Granary Close. Seems to have a healthy bank balance and no outstanding debts. He worked for an exporter called Carel Flora Bloemenexport. They export exotic flowers and plants from Holland. I rang them and spoke to his boss. The man was obviously shocked but asked if he could be kept informed as he would travel over to represent the firm at the funeral.'

'I hope you told him that could be some time yet?'

'I did. Oh, and Carson's worked for that company for four years. He's some kind of top rep, I think.'

'And how long has he been at that flat?' asked Nikki.

'I haven't been able to confirm that yet. The owners of the upstairs apartment said they have rarely seen him. He goes away for long periods and they've never been in conversation other than a casual greeting.' Cat yawned again. 'Looks like his only problem in life was that he closely resembled Billy Sweet.'

'Okay, well, tomorrow we will need to get out there and find someone who knew him. What's the betting that he magically developed a new best friend in the last few weeks?' She looked at Cat and saw dark lines under her eyes. 'And now, home. Get some sleep.'

'But what about Bryony Barton, guv? We still don't know where the devil she is.'

'Look, there's still a chance I'm overreacting. She may have another man in tow. She's a stunning-looking woman, and she could be shacked up somewhere drinking champagne and being drooled over by some handsome stud, while we run round like headless chickens searching for her.'

'You believe that?'

Nikki shrugged. 'No. But I'm not sure what I believe any more. None of us know much about her, do we?' She took a deep breath. 'Although strangely I do think she cares for Joseph. I'm going to get someone to check out the local CCTV footage. See where she went when she left here yesterday, then I'm going to check on Linda Kowalski, and *you*, detective, are going to do as I say and throw in the towel for today. You look knackered, and I need you daisy-fresh, okay?'

Cat raised her hands in surrender. 'Thanks, boss. But I'll be back in early, I promise.'

Nikki watched the woman leave, then picked up the phone and rang Joseph. She had no intention of telling him about her concerns for Bryony, and she wasn't too sure about letting on about the latest killing either. Maybe she'd just give him her ETA, then tell him everything over a glass of wine when she got home later.

CHAPTER TWENTY-FIVE

'I've got her.'

Joseph froze, as the pale, expressionless eyes of Billy Sweet swam into his head.

'And before you say anything, Bunny dear, I want you to listen *very* carefully. The gorgeous Miss Barton's life depends on your silence and your full attention.'

Joseph struggled not to scream obscenities down the phone, but the thought of Bryony being held by that animal kept his mouth obediently shut.

'Naturally you will want proof that she's still alive . . .' there was a small giggle in his voice, 'knowing my past record. And in a moment, I'll let her speak, but right now, soldier, just listen and follow orders. You will be at the rendezvous in exactly half an hour. You will tell no one, especially your piggy friends. If I suspect anything at all, pretty Bryony will be executed. Assuming you still have a modicum of sense, you will arrive alone at Knot Cottage in thirty minutes. Now, listen to this . . .'

There were some scraping sounds, a muffled groan, then Joseph heard her voice. It crackled with fear, but he had no doubt it was Bryony. 'Joseph! Help me! Please!'

There was a tiny break in her voice, then she whispered, 'He's insane. He *will* kill me.'

'Hold on, Bryony, I'll do anything he wants. I promise. Just hold on.'

There was a muffled cry, then he heard, 'Thirty minutes, Bunny-boy, and alone.' A hissing noise replaced the ugly voice, and then there was silence.

Joseph stared at the receiver, his face set in an expression of revulsion and fear.

Very slowly he put the phone down and took a long ragged breath. His first thought was to call Nikki. He was a police officer for God's sake, and not one to be intimidated by threats. Then he saw Bryony's face, and heard again the words, "He's insane. He will kill me." He of all people knew that she was right on both counts, and thoughts of talking to Nikki faded. He had to go to Knot Cottage, and he had to go alone.

* * *

Nikki sat alone in her office. Nothing was making sense any more, and the terrible feeling of wrongness was blocking cohesive thought and cramping her stomach. Bits of conversation filtered slowly into the word soup that used to be her brain, and she dropped forward, elbows on her desk and head in hands. What *was* it that was really tearing her up?

The thought came to her as clearly as a Fenland church bell ringing over the fields on a cloudless day. It was Bryony.

She pushed back her chair and almost ran out into the murder room. 'Dave! Yvonne! I need you! Now!'

As she turned back into her office, Dave was right with her and Yvonne only a step behind.

'Bryony Barton. I want to know everything you can dig up on her, and I mean everything.' She looked at them urgently. 'This is all I know to date, take it from there, and grab all the help you can.'

She rattled off the few facts that she knew about the woman and sat back.

'Why is this so important?' asked Dave anxiously.

Nikki frowned. 'I don't know, but trust me, it is. All I keep thinking is that Bryony arrived out of nowhere and has been Joseph's shadow ever since, and so has someone else, someone very dangerous.'

'Someone who kills people,' added Yvonne darkly.

'Exactly. There is something about Bryony that doesn't ring true, and now she's missing.' Her brow knit even tighter. 'Maybe she's not after Joseph at all. Maybe she's after the man we are calling Billy Sweet.'

'The killer?' asked Yvonne incredulously 'To stop him, or to help him?'

'I don't like the sound of either of those options,' muttered Dave. 'And there's another scenario, isn't there? What if the killer has snatched Bryony? We agreed that he is probably trying to get at Joseph, so who better to abduct than someone he really cares about?' Dave ran a hand through his hair and swallowed hard. 'We'd better get to work. Come on, Vonnie. You make a start; I'll grab a few more bodies and let's see what we can find.'

'I'll ring Joseph back,' said Nikki grabbing the phone. 'I'm really not happy with him being stuck out on the marsh alone.'

Joseph picked up almost immediately, and listened carefully to everything she said. After a moment or two he said, 'I'm okay, Nikki. I can take care of myself.'

'And I think you should come here directly, Joseph. Get off the fen.' She hadn't wanted to tell him, but hell, he'd hear soon enough. 'There's been another execution. Another Billy Sweet lookalike. You are not safe alone, Joseph. I want you where I can see you, so get yourself here, and fast. That's an order!'

'Okay. But there's something I must do before . . .' His words came out slowly and were edged with concern.

'Believe me, there is nothing more important than getting off Cloud Fen! And if you don't, I'll send a squad car to pick you up. Do you understand, Sergeant?'

'Don't do that, Nikki. I'll get there as soon as I can. I promise.'

'Be careful, Joseph. If anything happens out there, you are miles from help.' She lowered the phone back into its cradle but felt far from relieved by the call. Joseph had sounded strained and what on earth did he have to do that was so damned important? Nikki bit her lip. She had no idea what it was, but she was damned sure that for once it wasn't chopping bloody chilli peppers.

It took only fifteen minutes to get a basic profile of Bryony Barton.

'You're sure she has no siblings?' Nikki demanded of Yvonne.

'Absolutely. Only child of Dr Aaron James Barton, deceased, and Denise Clover Barton, née Bridgewater, of Kendal. Went to school in Carnforth, university at Lancaster, Bio-science degrees, honours, etc.'

'She said that she had a brother who was in the same ward in Greenborough Hospital as Joseph. And she told Joseph the same thing, said it was where she first saw him.'

'Well, that may be correct, but she wasn't visiting a brother, that's for certain. Mm . . .' said Yvonne thoughtfully, '. . . but she may have been visiting *someone* on that ward! I'll see if the hospital can open up Medical Records for me and get a list of patients treated over the same time as the sarge.'

As Yvonne disappeared, Dave placed a sheet of paper in front of her. 'Her whereabouts since she left Lancaster, according to the CV that she gave to her present employer.' He stabbed a finger onto the page. 'These were all verified by the PA lab manager. Some pretty technical posts, all with impressive titles that are Greek to me. Then six years ago she went to Germany for an interview, and from that point, things get fuzzy. She seems to have spent four and a half years chasing in and out of the country. One of our lads has identified her as a frequent flier with several major airlines, and all business class. Then bang, she takes a poorly paid job with the Public Analyst, buys a bijou property, and becomes Miss Perfectly Ordinary. Weird, or what?'

'Has anyone accessed her finances yet?' asked Nikki.

'Someone is onto that right now, guv. I'll go chase it up.'

Dave left and Nikki tried to calm the turmoil that was churning her guts into a tight knot. She played out an old conversation that Joseph had had with her about Bryony. Bit of a home-lover, he'd said. Didn't travel much except for the occasional winter sunshine top-up and her older brother was something of a tearaway. All lies. But why?

She rubbed at her sore eyes, then saw Yvonne approaching the door.

'We're in luck, guv! Just listen to this! One of the patients on Curlew Ward, who overlapped the sarge by one day, was Kurt Michael Carson. Bryony had to have been visiting the man who has just become the latest victim of Billy Sweet!'

'So they are all connected in some way!' Nikki banged her fist up and down on her desk. 'But hell's teeth, how?' She closed her eyes and tried to think. 'What was Carson in hospital for?'

'RTC with a drunk driver apparently, fractured cheek bone and some other minor injuries. The reason he was on the sarge's ward was they suspected abdominal bleeding. They did an exploratory op, sorted him out and he was discharged.'

'I think it's time to double-check that our dead guy is the same man.' Nikki picked up her phone and punched in the number for Professor Wilkinson.

Rory sounded exhausted. 'Yes, dear lady. I can confirm that our fresh cadaver has all those attributes, recently healed fracture of the zygomatic arch and a small surgical scar in the upper abdo, amongst numerous old injuries. He's one and the same, Nikki.'

'Thanks, Rory. Sorry to hold you up, I know how busy you are.'

'Mm, I'd be quite grateful if you could catch this public executioner. I've always loved variety, and I'm getting rather bored with identical methods of dispatch, not to mention the crow's feet that are multiplying around my eyes as we speak!'

'I'm working on it, believe me! Oh, Rory, by the way, what are pharmokinetics?'

'Ah, planning a change of career, are we? Well, it's the study of how drugs are absorbed into, distributed, then broken down and eliminated by the human body. Your scientist would work closely with each individual patient to make sure that they got the very best from a prescribed drug regime. It's a very personal, patient-focused thing.' He paused. 'I assume you are referring to your friend Martin Durham? It's the sort of thing that he would have benefited from.'

'No, it's nothing to do with Martin,' said Nikki slowly. 'We have a missing person, and that is her apparent occupation.'

'Complex stuff, Nikki. She must be a bright woman.'

'I'm sure she is,' mused Nikki. 'Thank you, Rory.'

* * *

Joseph slipped the key from the lock of Cloud Cottage Farm and walked soundlessly down the path. There was little to show of the recent storm. A few puddles in sheltered spots, but the lane had dried out, and air was still and warm. It would have been a beautiful evening, had his mind not been full.

He had a knife with him. It was carefully concealed in a small cash pocket in the waistband of his chinos. But even so, he felt naked, unprotected.

Knot Cottage seemed deserted, but it would. Sweet was a pro. There would be nothing on view to attract unwanted visitors. Vaguely Joseph wondered why Billy should even know about Martin Durham's home, but then Sweet would have been watching Joseph's every move, and the lonely little cottage was the perfect place for their reunion.

He wished with all his heart that he could be meeting Billy Sweet alone. To know that Bryony was close by was a distraction. She would be his Achilles' heel, his weak point. And Sweet would know that. In a military operation Joseph knew that he would have been steely cool, in total command of his responses, his actions and his reactions, but with a woman that you cared about in mortal danger, he had no idea how he would cope. Nothing like this had ever happened before. He slowed down. Except once. With Nikki.

Joseph gazed upwards into the dark sky, and murmured a small prayer. 'Keep us safe, keep us from harm, keep us from evil.'

The lane gave way to the track down to the cottage. Joseph braced himself. He had kept his side of the bargain. He had come alone. Now would Billy Sweet show some sort of respect for his action and spare Bryony?

He swallowed and involuntarily gave a soft humourless laugh. Who was he kidding? Sweet was a psycho, he wouldn't recognise morality if he tripped over it. No, if Bryony was to survive, it meant that he must dispatch Billy first, before he killed again.

Joseph shivered and reached out for the door handle. He wouldn't be entering in military style. No throwing back the door and charging in all guns blazing. He had nothing in his favour. He could do no more than walk into the spider's web and keep praying.

The door swung back silently. He took a step inside, half expecting a trip-wire and a flash of explosive, then when that didn't happen, he stood in the quiet and listened.

He knew he was not alone. His senses, still highly tuned to his surroundings told him that. The sound of a breath? The hint of a stirring of the air? A tiny movement in your peripheral vision?

Somewhere there was a light source. It was very dim, like a candle or a night-light. And in the shadows, Joseph knew that a figure was sitting in a high wing-backed armchair. It was angled away from him, but he saw the legs from the knees down, and the feet casually stretched out in front. He saw desert boots and the cuffs of army fatigues.

He wanted to leap on Sweet. Take him from behind and crush his windpipe. But he knew that he would never get close enough to even touch him.

'I came alone.' His voice sounded odd, even to his own ears.

The figure moved slightly, and Joseph saw the dull glint of metal in Sweet's lap. The muzzle of a gun was pointing to the only other chair in the sitting room. 'I knew you would. Sit down, Joseph.'

Whatever he had imagined, it was not this.

The light came from a tiny battery-powered storm lantern that stood in the hearth, and in its feeble glow, Joseph saw Bryony.

'Bry? My God! You're safe!' There was elation in his voice, and he wanted to rush forward, to grab her, hold her . . . but something stopped him. A trap? He steeled himself, then scanned the dark corners of the room. 'Where is he? Where's Sweet?'

Her voice was little more than a whisper. 'He's not here, Joseph.'

Confusion flooded his brain, and in the absence of a better idea, he moved numbly towards the other chair and sank slowly into it. 'Bry? The phone call? I don't understand.'

'My poor sweet Joseph, of course you don't understand, and why should you?' There was something like compassion in her voice. 'This is all such a mess, such a terrible mess.'

He stared at her, trying to make out the woman he cared so much about, but she was little more than a wraith in the darkness of the armchair. And he had been wrong about the camouflage trousers and boots. Maybe that was what he had expected to see. Actually she was wearing a dark long-sleeved T-shirt, khaki cargo pants and casual suede short boots. It was the gun that really couldn't get his head around.

'Do you love me, Joseph?'

He swallowed. It was not what he had expected her to ask him. And not at gunpoint. His mind twisted itself into knots. What was expected of him? What should he say? He took a few deep breaths and calmed himself. The truth had always worked in past 'I was beginning to think that way, yes.'

She eased forward in the chair and the light from the tiny lantern caught her eyes. For a minute he thought he saw hope in them, along with the traces of recent tears.

'Then we need to talk, Joseph. Because a lot depends on it.'

CHAPTER TWENTY-SIX

Dave placed a sheaf of papers on her desk and stepped back. 'I don't get it. Bryony is loaded! Accounts everywhere, both here and abroad, and they are just the ones we've managed to identify. Heaven knows what other offshore ones she has.'

Nikki jutted her jaw forward. 'God! We need to know more about her. Especially what she was doing from Germany onwards.'

'Sorry, but I'm stuck there, ma'am,' said Dave. 'She had no regular wage, but very large amounts of money were being paid in, and all untraceable.' Dave gave an exasperated sigh. 'I reckon she's one of those spooks. A spy.'

Nikki stared at him and a picture of Bryony swam into her mind. Strong, athletic, by her own admission a very strong swimmer, and highly intelligent, even if she made out otherwise. A highly qualified scientist.

Dave raised his eyebrows. 'I *was* joking, guv.'

'Maybe you're not so wrong,' breathed Nikki. 'I think I need the super to make some delicate enquiries to see if any other departments or agencies have interests her.'

Five minutes later the superintendent appeared in her office doorway. 'There have been some very hot secure lines active on your behalf, Nikki, but I'm sorry to say that she is not one of ours, and as far I can ascertain, not military or government either.' He looked anxiously at her. 'And as I wasn't warned off by anyone, I'm pretty confident that she's not in deep cover either.'

Nikki felt a rush of foreboding.

'Be careful, Nikki,' the super turned to leave. 'There are other agencies out there. Powerful ones that we have no connections to, so tread warily, okay?'

She nodded and watched him go. As the door closed, she lifted the receiver and dialled her own number. 'Come on, come on!' The phone rang on until the answerphone cut in. She banged it down and rang Joseph's mobile, praying he was on the road to the nick. 'Damn you! Why switch your bloody phone off at a time like this?'

She threw the phone down, then grabbed it back up as it rang again.

'Joseph?'

'Sorry, dear heart, it's me, Rory. Just something I thought I needed to mention regarding the late Mr Kurt Carson. I said he had old injuries, and although this may mean nothing, at least two of them were gunshot wounds.'

'What?'

'Doesn't quite tie in with pretty Dutch flowers and plants, does it? I'm sure it's a cut-throat business, but one does not generally shoot the competition, does one?'

Nikki replaced the receiver, and stood up. Something told her that Kurt Carson was the odd man out regarding the killer's executed victims. If he'd been shot sometime in the past, maybe he had also been a soldier or a mercenary. She needed to get Joseph to look at the body. There was a chance he would recognise him and fathom out what the hell was going on. She pulled on her jacket. It was an outside chance, but if nothing else, it was a damned good excuse to go find Joseph and drag him back to Greenborough.

'Dave! Keep me posted on any developments. I'll keep the radio open.'

* * *

Joseph's eyes were becoming accustomed to the gloom in the tiny cottage, but he wanted to see Bryony's face as she spoke to him.

'Can we have some more light in here? I don't like talking to a shadow. I want to look at you.'

'No. It's better as it is. The things I'm going to tell you belong in the darkness.' There was a shaky sigh. 'I just don't know where to start.'

Joseph could think of a hundred places, but all he could do was stare at her helplessly. 'What's going on, Bryony?'

'Your boss told me you hated lies, and I'm afraid I've had to tell you some, but that was before I realised how I felt about you. I don't want to lie anymore. But you may not like the truth, Joseph.'

'Try me.'

'I am in trouble, Joseph. Big trouble.'

His shoulders stiffened almost to the point of spasm. 'Please, Bryony, don't tell me this concerns Billy Sweet?'

Bryony laid the gun on the hearth, then reached across and took his hands in hers. 'I'm afraid it does. And I'm out of my depth and I'm scared.'

Her fingers were cold despite the warm evening, and he felt them tremble in his grip. 'How could *you* know that freak, that animal . . . that . . . ?' Words failed him, then a feeling of unease crept up his spine. 'Where is he, Bryony?'

'I don't know,' she shivered. 'All I know is that I've been playing a dangerous game, and I don't think I'm winning anymore.'

'Then you'd better tell me everything, lies and all.' Joseph mustered a smile and looked into those deep brown eyes. Such sadness. 'Maybe I can help you.'

Still clasping his hands, she blinked a few times then said, 'You know that I work for the PA laboratory, well, that's not my only job. I'm a doctor, Joseph. A scientist. I'm employed by a medical foundation. I used to work with a large team, now there are just two of us. We look after, well *looked* after, the welfare of a group of very special patients.'

Suddenly Joseph heard Linda Kowalski's voice. *They even have highly qualified liaison managers to help with problems.* Awareness flooded through him in a great wave. 'My God! *You* were looking *after* the clinical trials' victims?'

'Yes, and very well, until Billy Sweet arrived here.' She almost spat the name out, and Joseph recognised the venom as almost equalling his own. Bryony let go of his hands and flopped back in the chair. 'The foundation was closing down, relocating abroad. There were so few patients left from those old trials, that we offered them the chance of relocating with us and having continued care, or taking a very substantial final settlement. The choice was theirs.'

Joseph thought about Martin and his friends, now all dead, bar one that he knew off. 'How many were there, Bryony?'

'Forty years ago there were over two hundred. Now just a handful.'

Joseph frowned. He had had no idea there had been that many. Then he remembered Nikki saying that Martin had a bit of interesting news to tell her. Had that been it? 'And Martin Durham? Did he take your final settlement by any chance?'

'No, Joseph, he was one of the few who decided to go with us to Germany.'

Joseph screwed his eyes up tight and massaged the bridge of his nose. 'So . . . what happened to him?'

'Billy Sweet happened,' muttered Bryony tightly.

'What the hell has that psycho got to do with a medical foundation? Or with you for that matter?' His voice was little more than a growl. 'And who is it you work with?'

'I knew this wasn't going to be easy.' Bryony shook her head miserably. 'Well, my colleague is a lovely man called Kurt Carson. He is an ex-army medic, although his cover job is working for a flower wholesaler.' She bit her lip. 'And he was due to meet me here earlier but he hasn't turned up. I'm worried about him, Joseph. His phone is turned off, and we never do that.'

Pictures of Billy swam across Joseph's mind. He didn't know this Carson guy, but he certainly hoped that he hadn't run into Billy on his trip to the marsh. 'And Sweet's somehow connected to your organisation?'

'He had nothing at all to do with us. He was employed abroad mainly, as a troubleshooter. We needed to speed up the closure process and he was sent to help Kurt and I tie up loose ends, only his methods were not what we were expecting.' She moved in her seat. 'And then things got even worse. His past caught up with him. He saw you, Joseph, and he flipped.'

'But why?' whispered Joseph.

'He was scared of you. He said you were the only one who ever saw through him. Most people distrusted or feared him, but Joseph Easter understood him.'

'I could *never* understand that monster!' Joseph felt bile rising in his throat. 'But why kill those poor men who resembled him? Why not just kill me?'

'You are wonderfully naïve, Joseph.' Bryony sighed. 'Killing you was his endgame. But before that, he wanted to see you on the other side of the fence for once. To be suspected and accused of murder. You must have realised that he engineered it so that only you ever saw him.'

The individual notes were suddenly playing a tune in Joseph's head. That was where it was all heading. He had already been suspended. He was clearly suffering from stress and was always conveniently in the vicinity of the killings, the military-style killings. And who was the sick copper blaming? An imaginary soldier from his past. Very clever! Let's hear it for Billy Sweet! Joseph tensed as a thought crossed him mind. 'So what's this dangerous game you said you were playing?'

Silence spread through the cottage, then the harsh call of a night bird over the marsh broke the quiet and Bryony softly said, 'I pretended to help him. He asked me to watch you, get to know you.'

'That's why you came out with me?' croaked Joseph.

'Initially, yes. I needed to know what we were dealing with. I went along with him for a while in order to keep a close eye on him.' She looked at him unblinkingly. 'When I realised the danger you were in, and what a madman he was, Kurt and I decided to pull the plug on him. We made a phone call. Billy Sweet should have been removed by now, but . . . ?' She gave another little shrug of her shoulders, then moved closer to him. 'The thing is, everything has gone wrong. The foundation is spiriting me away. I will be out of the country by tonight, Joseph.' She slipped from the chair, knelt in front of him, and placed her head in his lap. 'Please, come with me.'

* * *

Nikki was about a mile from the town when she heard Dave's voice.

'Ma'am, I've just had some news from the pathologist. He says to tell you that Kurt Carson was not killed by the same person. There are subtle differences in the angle that the throat was cut, something that tells him Carson's killer was at least four inches shorter than the original murderer.'

'Oh shit.' Nikki put pressure on the accelerator. 'Anything else?'

'Plenty, guv. But I have to tell you that our enquiries about both Kurt Carson and Bryony Barton are going to rat-shit, if you'll pardon the expression. Everything seems to be shutting down on us.'

'How exactly?'

'Like when Yvonne rang Carson's company back, the number is unobtainable. Then she checked them out with the registry of Dutch exporters. They don't exist.'

'And Bryony?'

'Her accounts are closing down, ma'am. Funds are being electronically moved out and transferred, but we can't find the path they are taking. IT says an automated fail-safe system has been set in motion. One click on a computer or a single phone call could have activated it.'

She's closing up shop, thought Nikki . . . Whoever she is, she's on the move.

'And that's not all, ma'am. I've saved the best till last.' Dave spoke animatedly for a few minutes, then hung up. Nikki took a moment to assimilate the information, then floored the accelerator pedal and headed for the marsh. The farmhouse was in darkness when she arrived, and the door was locked.

Joseph's car was still around the back, and Nikki felt a frisson of fear snake across her shoulder blades. She pulled out her own keys and slipped in through the backdoor.

She stood still and listened. She knew the house was empty, but she checked anyway, running from room to room calling Joseph's name out loud. A few moments later she was back in the kitchen. Either he had been taken by force, and there was no evidence to support that, or he went off with someone he knew, or . . . Nikki paused . . . or he went out on foot.

Nikki ran back outside and stared over the oily black waters of the marsh. There really was only one place that you could walk to, unless you were in training for a marathon, and that was Martin's place. As soon as she thought it, she knew she was right. Joseph had said he had something to do, and that something, or someone, was waiting at Knot Cottage. Quickly checking that she had her phone safely in her pocket, she began to run down the lane towards the marsh edge and Martin's old home.

* * *

Joseph ran his hand gently though her hair, then lifted the beautiful face up, and kissed her. For a moment he remembered his dream of cooking for her, of getting a little place where they could be together, of getting to know each other better. But now he knew that would never happen.

'I'm good at my job, Joseph. My organisation will look after us, and I have money, a lot of money. And contacts. We could start again, Joseph. Another life in another country, somewhere far away from the shadows of the past. Be honest, what is there here for you in this crummy backwater town?'

Joseph methodically listed them in his head:

Friends that I care about. A job I love. Colleagues that would walk on hot coals for me. And I have a beautiful daughter that I want to get to know one day. A daughter who has high ideals and believes that good will always triumph over evil. One that would turn her back on a fugitive father for ever. Oh yes, for all the good it has done me this time, at least I now know that I have the capability to love again.

'Say something,' whispered Bryony.

Joseph wished he could. He wished he could have said, "Yes. Let's go!", but the alarm bells in his head were drowning out everything. He wanted to believe her. He could have easily convinced himself to do just that. It wouldn't have taken much, but instead he heard himself say, 'The telephone call from Sweet. The one that got me here. How did that work?'

'I got him to record it the other day. I told him we could use it as a lure, to get you to walk into a trap. I would play it at a given time, and he would be waiting for you.'

'So why use it tonight?' Joseph asked quietly. 'I would have come simply because you asked me, without the theatricals. You know that.'

'Because I had to be sure you'd come alone, Joseph. I couldn't risk you telling anyone that you were meeting me, not if we are to get away together. No, the tape ensured that you'd say nothing.' She looked up at him pleadingly, 'We need to go soon. It's all set up. My people . . .'

'And who are your people, Bry?'

'Just believe that they are taking medical science forward for the greater good. Every single person who works for them, no matter what their role, is deeply committed. But we really don't have time for this, Joseph. I'll explain everything later I promise you.' She sank back on her haunches and looked up at him imploringly. 'Come with me, please! First, because I love you, and second, because the alternatives are not good.'

He looked at her, pain etched all over his face, and knew that she realised he was going to refuse her.

At that point, the dynamics in the room suddenly changed. For the first time since he entered the cottage, he felt threatened. He straightened and felt a rush of adrenalin course through him. He knew what was wrong.

Bryony's hand was moving imperceptibly towards the hearth, and the gun.

Joseph acted instinctively, lunging forward, grabbing the gun, then rolling away. In a fraction of a second he had pulled her to her feet and was behind her, with the muzzle pressed to her temple. 'Tell me about those alternatives?' he enquired coldly.

'Oh, Joseph, you've made a terrible mistake.' Her voice had changed, lost the softness. 'And don't fool yourself. You couldn't do it.' Bryony slowly and deliberately turned her head to look him in the eyes. 'Sorry, but it's just not in you to hurt me, yet alone kill me.'

'Don't underestimate me, Bryony.' Joseph stepped back, gripping the gun with both hands and keeping it trained on her head. 'I was a soldier too, remember? Killing people is on the curriculum.'

She smiled at him. 'But not like this.'

He knew that she was right. He had been a good soldier, not a homicidal lunatic like Billy. But then he was also a good copper, and his instincts were screaming at him to recognise Bryony, not as the woman he had fallen for, but as a treacherous liar.

'Bryony, I'm sorry, really I am. But there are questions that need to be answered.' He stared at her down the barrel of the gun, and fought back tears of his own. Why did it have to be like this? 'You've lied to me, haven't you? All along the line.'

'Oh, I've lied, Joseph, about practically everything.' A brief look of pain passed across the beautiful face. 'Although not about my feelings.' She took a deep breath. 'But you've made your choice. Now I'm walking out of here, and you, my love, are going to let me.'

'Oh, I don't think so.'

The voice made both Joseph and Bryony spin round in surprise.

Nikki moved away from the doorway, and Joseph vaguely saw a set of bar cuffs in her hand. 'It's all over, Bryony. Time to go.' She began to step towards the woman.

'No, guv! Keep back. Switch on the lights.'

Nikki stopped mid-stride, then eased back to the door and flipped down the switch.

Nothing happened.

'Just stay away from her, ma'am. I believe she's dangerous.'

'Oh I know she is, Joseph . . . I've recently met Mr Kurt Carson, or should I say Billy Sweet, posthumously, that is. I've seen Bryony's work first-hand.'

Joseph felt a horrible coldness seep through him, but he never let his eyes, or the muzzle of the gun, leave Bryony. 'What are you saying, Nikki?'

'She killed your nemesis, Joseph. Amongst others.'

'Well done, Detective Inspector.' Bryony slowly and deliberately clapped her hands together. 'Excellent work.'

'We need support, ma'am.' Joseph tried to keep his voice steady, but inside he was boiling with rage and hurt.

'Already on their way. Let's just keep everything calm,' said Nikki.

'I couldn't be calmer, Inspector,' said Bryony sardonically. 'It's you who looks a trifle agitated. But then I suppose you must be *so* relieved that your little puppy dog here is still breathing.' Her eyes glittered in the pale light of the lantern. 'I know it's happened to you before, but it must be terrible to see him bleed!'

Before Joseph knew what had happened, a burning pain seared through his left hand. The nerves and muscles went into spasm, his finger involuntarily jerked on the hair trigger and the gun exploded upwards and away from his grasp.

'Keep totally still!'

Joseph's ears still rang with the report from the gun, and he realised that he had made a potentially fatal mistake. In the poor light he had not seen the wicked looking blade that Bryony had strapped to the inside of her wrist. With a groan of pain, he grasped his injured hand, pressed it to his body and tried to staunch the bleeding.

Nikki remained by the door, her mouth slightly open in shock, and hatred burning in her eyes.

And once again, Bryony held the gun. 'Make no mistake. I am leaving now, and I will kill you if you try to stop me.'

'No, you're not.' Nikki's voice was husky, but the words were slow and determined. 'You are a cold-blooded killer and you've assaulted my colleague. I can't let you.'

'Do as she says,' gasped Joseph. 'Please, Nikki.'

'Ooh, please Nikki!' Bryony imitated Joseph's appeal. 'How touching. But also practical, Inspector. I'd listen to Joseph, if you value your life.'

'Ah, but there's the problem,' returned Nikki, her voice as cold as an Arctic night. 'I don't.' And without hesitation Nikki threw herself forward.

Joseph's scream mingled with the roar of the second shot, and the two figures crashed to the floor in front of him. Before he could even move, something hit his foot. He swung down, pain like acid flaring through his hand, but somehow he managed to grab the gun.

By the time he had straightened up, one of the two woman was on her feet and running towards the door.

'Stop, or I fire,' he yelled.

Bryony halted and turned around. The knife was still in her hand. 'Oh Joseph, I told you before, you're a lovely man, but you're no killer.'

When the blast from the third shot died had away, he whispered, 'And I told you not to underestimate me, my love.'

EPILOGUE

Joseph pushed open the door to her room with his shoulder. One hand was strapped firmly across his chest and held there by a padded sling, and the other hand grasped a large bunch of candy pink roses and silver-grey eucalyptus. 'I've just seen Linda Kowalski. Her brother is out of ITU and doing well. Now, how goes it with you?'

'I'm glad to hear about David, and I'm easier today.' Nikki eased herself up the bed and grimaced. 'Well, a bit easier. For a flesh wound, it damn well hurts! And you?'

'Extremely inconvenient, especially getting dressed and anything else that requires pulling up your trousers.' He grinned at her. 'Other than that, pretty good. The surgeon reckons I should get most of the movement back, as long as I keep up the physio.'

'I bet you and the therapists are on first name terms by now?'

'Yes, there is a certain amount of déjà vu to my visits.' He smiled and laid the flowers on the bottom of the bed. 'For you.'

'They're lovely, Joseph. Are you going to arrange them for me?'

'Probably not. It was difficult enough just carrying them into the lift and pressing the button. I'll leave it to the nurses.' He sat in the chair next to her bed and looked at her searchingly. 'How are you really?'

Nikki dropped the smile. 'If you must know, I'm still pretty shaky.'

'Me too.' He stared down at the floor. 'I can't get my head around the fact that she was so *ruthless*. You know, I really thought . . .' his voice trailed off into silence.

'That she cared? Well, for what it's worth, I think she did, until you rejected her, then the *woman-scorned* bit came into play. Don't beat yourself up, Joseph, she had me fooled, and I was actively looking for things to distrust. You, sunshine, had no hope.' She picked up a thin folder from her locker and passed it to him. 'The super gave me this. It's for our eyes only. He thought it may help.'

'A dossier on Bryony?'

'Just a précis of what they've already compiled.'

'I don't think I want to see it right now,' said Joseph, placing it unopened on the locker.

'I've read it,' Nikki shrugged. 'You should too, when you're up to it. The main thing to know is that she alone was designated to bring 'closure' to the Gordon Peace guinea pigs, and that included Martin. She was no carer, Joseph. She killer the carer, she was the fixer.'

'I thought as much,' said Joseph with a sigh. 'When Dave told me about her expertise with drugs and their effects, it all fell into place. It was her organisation that provided the white boxes of medication, wasn't it?'

'In the guise of caring and generous healthcare professionals, they provided everything for their precious guinea pigs. The big financial payouts, the close follow-up treatment and ongoing medical care, which included their medication.' Nikki moved uncomfortably. 'The super reckons that eighteen months ago there must have been a leak, forcing them to wrap up their British operations, but they decided to do it slowly and insidiously so it wouldn't lead back to the old trials.'

'And who would notice the odd suicide or accidental death, when they were months apart?'

'Exactly. Bryony was sent in to doctor their drugs and send them to their death. And she was doing fine until the organisation wanted everything speeded up and Billy Sweet was seconded to help out.' She looked at him painfully. 'You did hear that Sweet was headhunted for his dubious talents by Bryony's organisation? That they 'killed him off' in South America, then gave him a new identity, as Kurt Carson?'

Joseph nodded, then asked, 'Did you know immediately that the last killing was Sweet himself?'

'No, I only found out as I drove out to find you. His face was pretty battered, intentionally of course, Bryony didn't want us to recognise him too quickly. And we didn't, but Dave had given a photo of Billy to Rory. In it he was holding a weapon of some kind and it showed a badly deformed finger, and Kurt Carson had an identical injury. Rory then used the picture and a computer-generated version of Kurt's skull, and hey presto. One and the same.'

'If you believe in Karma, one would consider that a fitting end for such an evil man.' Joseph gave a little shiver. 'Bryony's organisation may be powerful but they made a mistake recruiting Billy Sweet. Although I'm sure he was very effective until he finished up in hospital, saw me, and went on that killing spree. One thing though, I'm surprised that Bryony managed to get the better of him so easily.'

'Simple. She did what she did best. She drugged him. That was something else Dave informed me of on my trip to Cloud Fen. Rory picked up on tell-tale signs and later found that Sweet had been immobilized before his throat was cut.'

'Dear Lord, and to think that I . . .' Joseph shook his head, then swiftly changed the subject. 'And Bryony's organisation? Do we have any leads?'

'We're out of our depth there. With the Kowalskis' statements the super knew that we were on to something, but guess what? He's been ordered not to pursue it.'

Joseph gritted his teeth, 'And the shadows close ranks and block us out.'

Nikki nodded, and for a moment they sat in silence with their own thoughts. 'So when did it dawn on you that you were being spun a yarn?' she finally asked.

Joseph gently massaged his injured hand. 'Several things didn't ring true, but the main one was when she told me that Martin was going abroad. It took a second or two, but I remembered all you'd told me about him, about his love for the marsh, how fond he was of his sister, and his precious Knot Cottage. He wouldn't have upped and buggered off, just for the sake of some medical care.'

'You're right. Linda Kowalski told me that they were all promised a big final settlement, then their care would be down to their respective GPs, but in truth, the organisation could never have risked it. Their death sentences had already been signed.'

'And the executioner dispatched,' Joseph added painfully. 'But let's forget all that for a moment.' He turned to her and she allowed those dark, earnest eyes to bore into hers. 'There is still one question I have to ask.'

Nikki had known this moment would come, but said nothing.

'Did you really mean that you didn't value your life? I've played those last few moments over and over, and I'm still not sure why you did what you did.'

Nikki stared down at the pale green counterpane. What could she tell him? The truth was that there was no way she could have risked his life again. Not for a second time. She had to stop Bryony somehow, and her method may have been a tad gung-ho, but that was Nikki Galena for you. 'I guess I saw the red mist, that's all. I thought if I could distract her, you might finally get your finger out and actually do something!'

'Right. I see,' Joseph pulled a face. 'Okay, so you're not going to tell me.'

'Not yet. Maybe I'm not sure of the answer myself.' She smiled at him, 'Now my turn for a question. When you shot Bryony . . . ?'

'Did I mean to kill her?' He shook his head. 'No, she was right about that. I couldn't have done it. That would have made me no better than Billy Sweet.'

'I'm glad, Joseph. Because for Martin's sake, I want her to stand trial.'

Joseph drew in a breath. 'Don't get your hopes up. If her dark and shadowy employers are as powerful as I believe, she'll never she get near a courtroom.'

Before Nikki could answer, the door opened and two women stood beaming at them.

'Elizabeth! Janna! Come in.' Nikki patted her bed for Janna to sit, and Joseph stood up and gave Elizabeth his chair.

'To cheer you up,' said Elizabeth brightly, and placed a large, colourful plant on her locker.

Nikki stared at it. It had a mass of dark green heart-shaped leaves and huge waxy red flowers, each with a thick, fleshy cream spike rising from them. 'My! That's, uh, exotic! Thank you.'

'Latin name, Anthurium Andreanum,' said Elizabeth knowledgably.

'Common name, Willy Lily!' laughed Janna.

It was agony to laugh, but suddenly Nikki felt great. She could afford to laugh again. The nightmare was over.

'And this is to cheer *you* up, Sergeant.' Janna handed Joseph a fob with two keys hanging from it. 'We have no problem at all with your suggestion, and Martin would most certainly have approved.'

Nikki threw an enquiring glance at Joseph.

'I'm renting Knot Cottage.' He looked at her earnestly.

'Really?' Nikki's mouth dropped.

'Are you quite sure that you won't be haunted by everything that happened there?' Janna asked.

'I'm absolutely certain,' Joseph nodded determinedly. 'I know what happened was terrible, but in a funny kind of way it finally gave me closure from Billy Sweet.' He turned to Nikki, 'From the moment I set foot in Martin's home I knew it was a very special and well-loved place. And of course I'd be closer to you, if you don't mind having a new neighbour?'

Nikki felt a warmth suffuse through her. So there would be smoke rising from the chimney, and the lights would burn in the evening again, and like before, they would have been lit by someone she cared for. 'No objections at all. When are you planning on moving in?'

'As soon as my new landlords here have replaced the sitting-room carpet. It's in a shocking state!'

Nikki placed a hand tentatively over the large dressing around her waist. 'Eh, sorry about that.'

'Oh, don't feel too bad,' said Joseph. 'Professor Wilkinson took great delight in telling me that there are actually three different blood groups splattered between the hearth and the front door. Something of a record in his book.'

Janna groaned theatrically. 'I was warned about police humour.' She stood up and smiled across at Elizabeth. 'And we should go. Let Nikki rest.'

'Yes, we only came to say thank you. Without you both; Martin's murder would never have come to light. His death would have always been thought of as a callous drug-fuelled act of madness. His memory would have been tainted for ever.' Her voice caught, and Janna continued for her.

'But now we can grieve properly. And so can the friends and families of Paul Cousins, Amelia Reed and the other poor souls who died.'

Joseph nodded, then smiled to lighten the mood. 'Yes, it's lucky that there are still few tenacious old bulldogs left on the force.' He tilted his head towards Nikki, 'Or should I have said, stubborn, fool-hardy, pig-headed, persistent, obstinate . . .'

'Let's stick with tenacious, shall we, Sergeant? Or do you actually have a hankering to go back to traffic for the next ten years or so?'

* * *

After the two women had left, Joseph sat back down and grinned wickedly at Nikki.

'So, there is just one thing left. One mystery that has yet to be solved.'

Nikki looked at him suspiciously. 'And that is?'

Joseph leaned closer. 'Dr Helen Latimer. Martin's GP at Cloud Fen? You said that when the case was over you'd dish the dirt regarding your mysterious feud.'

A knowing smile spread over Nikki's face. 'I'm sorry, Joseph, you must be mistaken. I have absolutely no idea what you're talking about.'

Section of article in *The Times*, 14 August

GREENBOROUGH POISONER DIES

The body of Bryony Barton, the woman accused of engineering the 'suicide' deaths of more than ten people in the last eighteen months, was found yesterday. The manner of her death remains a mystery, as she was in the process of being transported to court. On arrival she was found dead on the floor of the police transportation vehicle. The Fenland Constabulary are asking for information regarding one of the escorting officers who has since disappeared.

Full story on pages 4 and 5

THE END

Thank you for reading this book. If you enjoyed it please leave feedback on Amazon, and if there is anything we missed or you have a question about then please get in touch. The author and publishing team appreciate your feedback and time reading this book.

Our email is office@joffebooks.com

www.joffebooks.com

ALSO BY JOY ELLIS

CRIME ON THE FENS
SHADOW OVER THE FENS

Made in the USA
Middletown, DE
13 February 2018